ACHI 2016

The Ninth International Conference on Advances in Computer-Human Interactions

April 24 - 28, 2016

Venice, Italy

ACHI 2016 Editors

Alma Leora Culén , University of Oslo, Norway
Leslie Miller, Iowa State University - Ames, USA
Irini Giannopulu, UPMC, France
Birgit Gersbeck-Schierholz, Leibniz Universität Hannover, Germany

Printed from e-media with permission by:

Curran Associates, Inc.
57 Morehouse Lane
Red Hook, NY 12571

Some format issues inherent in the e-media version may also appear in this print version.

Printed by Curran Associates, Inc. (2016)

International Academy, Research, and Industry Association (IARIA)
412 Derby Way
Wilmington, DE 19810

Phone: (408) 893-6407
Fax: (408) 527-6351

petre@iaria.org

Additional copies of this publication are available from:

Curran Associates, Inc.
57 Morehouse Lane
Red Hook, NY 12571 USA
Phone: 845-758-0400
Fax: 845-758-2633
Email: curran@proceedings.com
Web: www.proceedings.com

TABLE OF CONTENTS

ACHI 1: USABILITY AND UNIVERSAL ACCESSIBILITY I

ACHI 2: SOCIAL ASPECTS OF HUMAN-COMPUTER INTERACTION I

ACHI 3: SOCIAL ASPECTS OF HUMAN-COMPUTER INTERACTION II

ACHI 4: INTERACTION DEVICES

ACHI 5: HUMAN-COMPUTER INTERACTION IN EDUCATION AND TRAINING I

ACHI 6: HUMAN-COMPUER INTERACTION IN EDUCATION AND TRAINING II

ACHI 7: USABILITY AND UNIVERSAL ACCESSIBILITY II

ACHI 8: DESIGN AND EVALUATION I

ACHI 9: DESIGN AND EVALUATION II

ACHI 10: DESIGN AND EVALUATION III

ACHI 11: DESIGN AND EVALUATION IV

ACHI 12: USER MODELING AND USER FOCUS I

ACHI 13: HUMAN-ROBOT INTERACTION I

ACHI 14: OTHER DOMAINS APPLICATIONS

ACHI 15: USER MODELING AND USER FOCUS II

ACHI 16: HUMAN-ROBOT INTERACTION II

ACHI 2016

Forward

The Ninth International Conference on Advances in Computer-Human Interactions (ACHI 2016), held between April 24 and April 28, 2016 in Venice, Italy, continued a series of events targeting traditional and advanced paradigms for computer-human interaction in multi-technology environments. The conference also covered fundamentals on interfaces and models, and highlighted new challenging industrial applications and research topics.

ACHI was initially proposed as a result of a paradigm shift in the most recent achievements and future trends in human interactions with increasingly complex systems. Adaptive and knowledge-based user interfaces, universal accessibility, human-robot interaction, agent-driven human computer interaction, and sharable mobile devices are a few of these trends. ACHI 2016 also brought a suite of specific domain applications, such as gaming, e-learning, social, medicine, teleconferencing and engineering.

The event was very competitive in its selection process and very well perceived by the international scientific and industrial communities. As such, it has attracted excellent contributions and active participation from all over the world. We were very pleased to receive a large amount of top quality contributions.

The conference had the following tracks:

- Usability and universal accessibility
- Social aspects of human-computer interaction
- Interaction devices
- Human-computer interaction in education and training
- Design & evaluation
- User modeling and user focus
- Other domain applications
- User modeling and user focus
- Human-robot interaction
- Interactive systems
- Principles, theories, and models
- Interfaces

We take here the opportunity to warmly thank all the members of the ACHI 2016 technical program committee, as well as the numerous reviewers. The creation of such a high quality conference program would not have been possible without their involvement. We also kindly thank all the authors that dedicated much of their time and effort to contribute to ACHI 2016. We truly believe that, thanks to all these efforts, the final conference program consisted of top quality contributions.

Also, this event could not have been a reality without the support of many individuals, organizations and sponsors. We also gratefully thank the members of the ACHI 2016 organizing committee for their help in handling the logistics and for their work that made this professional meeting a success.

We hope ACHI 2016 was a successful international forum for the exchange of ideas and results between academia and industry and to promote further progress in the field of computer-human interaction. We also hope that Venice, Italy, provided a pleasant environment during the conference and everyone saved some time to enjoy the unique charm of the city.

ACHI Advisory Committee

Leslie Miller, Iowa State University - Ames, USA
Alma Leora Culén , University of Oslo, Norway
Hermann Kaindl, Vienna University of Technology, Austria

ACHI 2016

Committee

ACHI Advisory Committee

Leslie Miller, Iowa State University - Ames, USA
Alma Leora Culén , University of Oslo, Norway
Hermann Kaindl, Vienna University of Technology, Austria

ACHI 2016 Technical Program Committee

Andrea Abate, University of Salerno, Italy
Eugenio Aguirre Molina, University of Granada, Spain
Andrea Alessandro Gasparini, University of Oslo, Norway
Majed Alshamari, King Faisal University, Saudi Arabia
Florian Alt, University of Munich, Germany
Margherita Antona, Foundation for Research and Technology - Hellas (FORTH) - Heraklion, Greece
Leena Arhippainen, University of Oulu, Finland
Mukesh Barange, École Nationale d'Ingénieurs de Brest, France
Wieslaw Bartkowski, University of social sciences and humanities - School of form, Warsaw, Poland
Michael Bauer , Heilbronn University, Germany
Marios Belk, University of Cyprus, Cyprus
Peter Berkelman, University of Hawaii-Manoa, USA
Karsten Berns, University of Kaiserslautern, Germany
Jane Billestrup, Institute of Computer Science - Aalborg University, Denmark
Mark Billinghurst, University of Canterbury, New Zealand
Karlheinz Blankenbach, Pforzheim University, Germany
Gunnar Bolmsjö, University West, Sweden
Clodis Boscarioli, Western Paraná State University (Unioeste), Brazil
Mohamed Bouri, EPFL, Switzerland
Christian Bourret, Université Paris-Est Marne-la-Vallée (UPEM), France
Lourdes Brasil, University of Brasília at Gama, Brazil
Gerd Bruder, University of Hamburg, Germany
Marcin Butlewski, Poznan University of Technology, Poland
Luis Carriço, University of Lisbon, Portugal
Silvio Cesar Cazella, Federal University of Health Sciences of Porto Alegre (UFCSPA), Brazil
Jessie Y.C. Chen, U.S. Army Research Laboratory - Human Research & Engineering Directorate, USA
Jacek Chmielewski, Poznań University of Economics, Poland

Ryszard S. Choras, University of Technology & Life Sciences - Bydgoszcz, Poland
Thomas Christy, School of Computer Science at Bangor University, UK
Sharon Lynn Chu, Virginia Tech, USA
José Coelho, University of Lisbon, Portugal
Cesar Alberto Collazos O., University of Cauca - Popayán, Colombia
André Constantino da Silva, Instituto Federal de São Paulo, Brazil
Sandra Costa, University of Minho, Portugal
Lynne Coventry, Northumbria University, UK
Manuel Cruz, Immersion Corp., Canada
Leonardo Cunha de Miranda, Federal University of Rio Grande do Norte (UFRN), Brazil
Urska Cvek, Louisiana State University Shreveport, USA
Dragos Datcu, Netherlands Defence Academy, The Netherlands
Lucio Tommaso De Paolis, Salento University - Lecce, Italy
Nancy Diniz, Rensellaer Polytechnic Institute, USA
John M. Dolan, Carnegie Mellon University, USA
Rolf Drechsler, DFKI - Bremen, Germany
Carlos Duarte, University of Lisbon, Portugal
Ismael Duque, University of Hertfordshire, UK
Martin Ebner, Graz University of Technology, Austria
Anastasios A. Economides University of Macedonia - Thessaloniki, Hellas
Larbi Esmahi, Athabasca University, Canada
Sascha Fagel, Zoobe GmbH, Germany
Michael Farrugia, University College Dublin, Ireland
Peter Forbrig, University of Rostock, Germany
Karim Fraoua, Université Paris-Est- Conservatoire des arts et métiers, France
Somchart Fugkeaw, Mahidol University - Nakhonpathom, Thailand
Mathias Funk, Eindhoven University of Technology, The Netherland
Miguel Garcia, University of Valencia, Spain
Matjaz Gams, Josef Stefan Institute- Ljubljana, Slovenia
Marta Gatius, Universitat Politècnica de Catalunya, Spain
Cristina Gena, Università di Torino, Italy
Panagiotis Germanakos, University of Cyprus, Cyprus
Irini Giannopulu, Pierre & Marie Curie University - Paris VI, France
Denis Gillet, Swiss Federal Institute of Technology (EPFL), Switzerland
Mehmet Göktürk, Gebze Institute of Technology, Turkey
Luis Gomes, Universidade Nova de Lisboa / UNINOVA-CTS - Monte de Caparica, Portugal
Pascual Gonzalez, University of Castilla-La Mancha, Spain
Bernard Grabot, LGP-ENIT, France
Andrina Granic, University of Split, Croatia
Toni Granollers, University of Lleida, Spain
Vic Grout, Glyndwr University - Wrexham,UK
Jaume Gual Orti, Universitat Jaume I – Castellón, Spain
Celmar Guimarães da Silva, University of Campinas, Brazil
Maki K. Habib, The American University in Cairo, Egypt

Till Halbach, Norwegian Computing Center / Norsk Regnesentral (NR), Norway
Lynne Hall, University of Sunderland, UK
Kristian J. Hammond, Northwestern University - Evanston, USA
Riad Hammoud, BAE Systems, USA
Sung H. Han, POSTECH, South Korea
Lane Harrison, Tufts University, USA
Christoph Hintermüller, Guger Technologies OG – Schiedlberg, Austria
Richard Hoadley, Anglia Ruskin University, UK
Thomas Holz, University College Dublin, Ireland
Olivier Hugues, MINES ParisTech, PSL - Research University - Center for Robotics, Paris, France
Ilias Iliadis, IBM Research - Zurich, Switzerland
Jamshed Iqbal, National University of Computer and Emerging Sciences (FAST-NUCES), Islamabad, Pakistan
Ryo Ishii, NTT Communication Science Laboratories - NTT Corporation, Japan
Dragan Ivetic, University of Novi Sad, Serbia
Jari Due Jessen, Technical University of Denmark, Denmark
Ran Jiao, Beihang University - Beijing, China
Gareth Jones, Dublin City University, Ireland
Suhas Govind Joshi, University of Oslo, Norway
Hanmin Jung, Korea Institute of Science & Technology Information, Korea
Janusz Kacprzyk, Polish Academy of Sciences - Warsaw / IEEE Fellow, Poland
Katarzyna Kaczmarek, Systems Research Institute - Polish Academy of Sciences, Warsaw, Poland
Hermann Kaindl, Vienna University of Technology, Austria
Ahmed Kamel, Concordia College - Moorhead, USA
Athanasios Kapoutsis, Centre for Research and Technology Hellas | Information Technologies Institute, Greece
Koji Kashihara, Tokushima University, Japan
Hamed Ketabdar, Deutsche Telekom Laboratories - TU Berlin, Germany
Jonghwa Kim, University of Augsburg, Germany
Youngmin Kim, Korea Electronics Technology Institute (KETI), South Korea
Michael Kipp, University of Applied Sciences Augsburg, Germany
Frank Klawonn, Ostfalia University of Applied Sciences - Wolfenbuettel, Germany
Jesuk Ko, Gwangju University, South Korea
Uttam Kokil, Kennesaw State University, USA
Anita Komlodi, University of Maryland - Baltimore County, USA
Heidi Krömker, Technische Universität Ilmenau, Germany
Satoshi Kurihara, Osaka University, Japan
Andrew Kusiak, The University of Iowa, USA
Wen-Hsing Lai, National Kaohsiung First University of Science and Technology, Taiwan
Vidas Lauruska, Siauliai University, Lithuania
Soo-Young Lee, KAIST and RIKEN BSI, Korea
Dagmawi Lemma, Addis Ababa University, Ethiopia
Alma Leora Culén , University of Oslo, Norway
Cynthia Y. Lester, Tuskegee University, USA

Tsai-Yen Li, National Chengchi University - Taipei, Taiwan
Yangmin Li, University of Macau - Taipa, Macao
Chin-Teng (CT) Lin, National Chiao-Tung University, Taiwan
Wei-Kai Liou, National Taiwan Normal University, Taiwan
Flaminia Luccio, University Ca' Foscari of Venice, Italy
Jean-Luc Lugrin, Universität Würzburg, Germany
Sergio Luján Mora, University of Alicante, Spain
Ameersing Luximon, Hong Kong Polytechnic University, Hong Kong
Francisco Madera, Universidad Autonoma de Yucatan - Merida, Mexico
Jacek Mandziuk, Warsaw University of Technology, Poland
Antonio Maria Rinaldi, Università di Napoli Federico II, Italy
Célia Martinie, IRIT | University Toulouse 3, France
Andrea Mason, University of Wisconsin-Madison, USA
Christoph Mayer, Technische Universität München, Germany
Daniele Mazzei, FACE Team | Research Center "E.Piaggio" - University of Pisa, Italy
Troy McDaniel, Arizona State University, USA
Daniel R. Mestre, Aix-Marseille University, France
Harald Milchrahm, Technical University Graz, Austria
Leslie Miller, Iowa State University - Ames, USA
Peyman Moghadam, CSIRO, Australia
Yasser F. O. Mohammad, Assiut University, Egypt
Vincenzo Moscato, University of Naples, Italy
Jaime Muñoz-Arteaga, Universidad Autónoma de Aguascalientes, México
Fazel Naghdy, University of Wollongong, Australia
Toru Nakata, National Institute of Advanced Science and Technology (AIST), Japan
Deok Hee Nam, Wilberforce University, USA
Claudia Nass, Fraunhofer Institute for Experimental Software Engineering, Germany
Andreas C. Nearchou, University of Patras, Greece
Roger Ng, Hong Kong Polytechnic University, Hong Kong
Grace Ngai, Hong Kong Polytechnic University, Hong Kong
Gregory O'Hare, University College Dublin (UCD), Ireland
Zahen Malla Osman, Centre d'Etude et de Recherche en Informatique et Communications (CEDRIC), France
Yushan Pan, University of Oslo & Aalesund University College, Norway
Evangelos Papadopoulos, National Technical University of Athens, Greece
Igor Paromtchik, INRIA - Saint Ismier, France
Alexandru Patriciu. McMaster University - Hamilton, Canada
Diana Peppoloni, University for Foreigners of Siena, Italy
Estelle Perrin, CReSTIC | Reims University – Charleville-Mezieres, France
Antonio Picariello, DIETI - Università di Napoli "Federico II", Italy
Jose Pinto, Universidade do Porto, Portugal
Marina Puyuelo Cazorla, Universitat Politècnica de València (UPV), Spain
Didier Puzenat, Université des Antilles et de la Guyane - Pointe-à-Pitre, Guadeloupe
Rafael Radkowski, Iowa State University, USA

Nitendra Rajput, IBM Research - New Delhi, India
Marco Antonio Ramos Corchado, Universidad Autónoma del Estado de México, Mexico
Xiangshi Ren, Kochi University of Technology, Japan
Arcadio Reyes Lecuona, University of Málaga, Spain
Andreas Riener, University Linz - Linz/Donau, Austria
Antonio Maria Rinaldi, Università di Napoli Federico II, Italy
Joel Rodrigues, Intituto de Telecomunicações / University of Beira Interior, Portugal
Andrzej Romanowski, Lodz University of Technology, Poland
Agostinho Rosa, Lasseb-ISR-IST / Technical University of Lisbon, Portugal
Paul Rosenthal, Technische Universität Chemnitz, Germany
José Rouillard, Université des Sciences et Technologies de Lille, France
Rebekah Rousi, University of Jyväskylä, Finland
Juha Röning, University of Oulu, Finland
Sandra Sánchez Gordón, Escuela Politécnica Nacional, Ecuador
Antonio José Sánchez Salmerón, Universidad Politécnica de Valencia, Spain
Corina Sas, Lancaster University, UK
Munehiko Sasajima, Osaka University, Japan
Dominique Scapin, INRIA - Le Chesnay, France
Trenton Schulz, Norwegian Computing Center, Norway
Shunji Shimizu, Tokyo University of Science, Suwa, Japan
Maria Augusta Silveira Netto Nunes, Universidade Federal de Sergipe (UFS), Brazil
Johanna Silvennoinen, University of Jyväskylä, Finland
Berglind Smaradottir, University of Agder, Norway
Ross Smith, University of South Australia, Australia
Jaka Sodnik, University of Ljubljana, Slovenia
Dimitris Spiliotopoulos, University of Peloponnese, Greece
Emilija Stojmenova, University of Ljubljana, Slovenia
Weilian Su, Naval Postgraduate School - Monterey, USA
Tsutomu Terada, Kobe University, Japan
Daniel Thalmann, VRlab/EPFL - Lausanne, Switzerland
Robert J. Teather, McMaster University, Canada
Edgar Thomas, Federal University of Pernambuco | Brazil's Government, Brazil
Hiroaki Tobita, Sony CSL Paris, France
Godfried T. Toussaint, New York University Abu Dhabi, United Arab Emirates
Nikolaos Tsagarakis, Istituto Italiano di Tecnologia (IIT-Genova), Italy
Lazaros Tsochatzidis, Democritus University of Thrace, Greece
M. Sarosh Umar, Aligarh Muslim University, India
Connie (J.I.L.) Veugen, VU University Amsterdam, Netherlands
Michael L. Walters, University of Hertfordshire, UK
Ina Wechsung, Technische Universität Berlin, Germany
Charlotte Wiberg Umeå University, Sweden
Hanna Wirman, Hong Kong Polytechnic University, Hong Kong
Yingcai Xiao, University of Akron, USA
Fan Yang, Nuance Communications, Inc., USA

Jie Yin, CSIRO ICT Centre, Australia
Claudia Zapata del Rio, Pontifica Universidad Católica del Peru - Lima , Peru
Leyla Zhuhadar, Western Kentucky University, USA
Alcínia Zita Sampaio, Technical University of Lisbon, Portugal

Copyright Information

Do More Pictures Mean More Effort?

Investigating the Effects of Monocular Depth on Target Detection in a 3D WIMP Pictures Folder

Markos Kyritsis
Computer and Information Science Dept.
Higher Colleges of Technology
Sharjah, UAE
mkyritsis@hct.ac.ae

Stephen Gulliver[1], Eva Feredoes[2] & Winai Nadee[1]
[1]Henley Business School, Dept. of Business Informatics
[2]School of Psychology & Clinical Language Sciences
University of Reading
Reading, UK
s.r.gulliver@henley.ac.uk

Abstract— **The limited commercial success of 3D WIMP interfaces, despite ongoing efforts, leads us to question whether depth itself is detrimental to task performance due to, e.g., an increase in the amount of clutter, or if the lack of any success can be mostly attributed to unsuitable interactivity with input devices made for 2D interfaces. In this study, we evaluate a common interactive task -browsing a pictures folder- and argue that despite an increase in the number of nontarget distractors available on the screen when introducing monocular depth, there is no decrease in target detection times, nor are there any changes in cognitive load (as measured through pupillometric data). Interestingly, eye tracking data indicates that this is not due to a lack of fixations, as participants tend to spend proportionally less time fixating on pictures in front of them as more items become available in the background. Finally, our participants made significantly more target identification errors when there were only two picture-layers of visible depth, when compared to four picture-layers. We therefore suggest adding monocular depth cues to 3D WIMP photo gallery or desktop pictures folder applications.**

Keywords- Interaction & Interface Evaluation, 3D WIMP; Visual Search; Eye Tracking

I. Introduction

The WIMP interface is undoubtedly the most essential and common method of interaction for the everyday user when it comes to human-computer interaction. Bundled with all the major operating systems, this type of interface is the first thing a newcomer would be expected to use in order to complete everyday computing tasks. Even though there exist variations across the wide range of platforms that host WIMP desktop interfaces, the actual design has remained relatively unchanged for the past 40 years, despite periodic predictions from various research teams of shifts towards alternative methods of interaction [3][4][8]. However, this is not due to a lack of interest from academia or industry, as is evident by theoretical upgrades, the most popular of which is arguably the addition of monocular depth [1][5][10][14][15][17]. Nevertheless, any attempts to include depth have been met with either commercial failure (e.g., project looking glass developed by LG3D) or have not really seen much of a success, such as the fairly recent acquisition of the Bumptop desktop (www.bumptop.com) by Google.

A. *Finding a target picture: a visual search task*

When consider the task of finding a picture in a folder, we are, in essence, conducting a visual search task, a common paradigm used for studying selective attention in the areas of cognitive psychology and neuroscience. In these types of paradigms we are interested in how long it takes for a participant to detect a target amongst nontargets in environments of varying size, as well as how many target identification errors occur. The efficiency of the task is affected by both exogenous bottom-up orientation cues such as colour, size, movement and other features, as well as top-down endogenous orientation cues guided by e.g., working memory [18]. As described thoroughly by the Feature Integration Theory (FIT) [16] concerning exogenous orientation, when the target is surrounded by homogenous nontargets, then the search is considered efficient, preattentive, and not influenced by increases in set size, instead causing a 'pop-out' effect allowing for parallel search. On the other hand, heterogenous nontargets (i.e., the target differs to some nontargets in one feature, but is similar in others) leads to a conjunction search, requiring the binding of features and hence increases in attentional resources and an inefficient serial search.

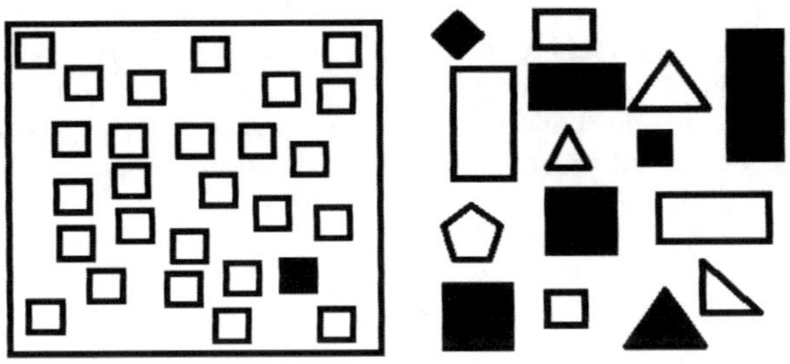

Figure 1. Left - Feature search, finding the black box is effortless and not susceptible to changes in set size; Right - Conjunction Search, the heterogeneous distractors lead to higher attentional resource requirements, making this type of search more inefficient and more susceptible to changes in set size

For complex picture targets and nontargets, as one would expect from pictures in a folder, we can assume that the search will be inefficient, and heavy on attentional resources, and one may therefore be tempted to simply infer that by adding more items in depth we would essentially be increasing the set size and making the search task even less efficient. On the other hand, past studies have shown that depth itself can be considered a bottom-up feature, as well as a guidance property during a visual search task [11][13]. For this reason, target detection may not suffer, as stimuli in depth could efficiently be ignored during the task through the use of a sub-nesting strategy. These strategies have been routinely observed when participants are asked to e.g., find a red 'k' amongst red and blue letters, which will lead to blue letters being ignored, although particularly salient stimuli (e.g., a mostly yellow picture amongst otherwise blueish pictures) may still capture attention, as shown by [9]. Regardless, there is, to the best of our knowledge, no compelling evidence to describe how this would affect target detection.

B. *Including Monocular Depth*

Studies have had mixed opinions on whether the addition of depth holds any real advantages in terms of interaction quality. There is evidence, from qualitative data, that suggests a positive attitude by users towards a desktop that includes both depth and physics [1], as well as some limited evidence that supports an increase in performance during certain tasks when depth is included in the system [15]. On the other hand, studies have found a decrease in performance in certain user tasks (such as finding a file in a folder) [6][7][9]. In all of these studies there are several merits as well as pitfalls. The study by [1], being more oriented towards the engineering of a physics-based desktop and less focused on the human cognitive limitations, essentially does not provide evidence as to whether such an interface would be indeed beneficial in terms of usability.

The studies by [6][7] and [9] compared 2D and 2.5D, to a 3D interface, not accounting for the changes in the interaction styles, and whether the 2D input device is unsuitable for this type of interaction (even if the y-axis was constrained to make interaction more simple). In other words, when looking for a target picture in a folder, by not systematically increasing the layers of visible depth, the researchers did not consider whether the increased amount of nontarget distractors was the reason it takes users longer to find the target in these environments, or whether it has more to do with interaction using a 2D mouse in 3D space.

Therefore, rather than a holistic approach (3D WIMP vs 2D WIMP), we instead argue the need to investigate the benefits of including monocular depth to each user-based task independently. As shown in [9], there was no benefit to adding depth in a folder populated with text files, however, when target stimuli were perceptually salient, target detection times decreased significantly in a pictures folder. Therefore, for the scope of this study we only considered the potential benefits of a 3D interface in browsing the pictures folder for a target picture.

II. Current Study

In this paper, we investigate the impact of depth on target detection times and errors by developing a 3D WIMP pictures folder, and systematically increasing the number of visible layers of images from two to four. Since we were interested in seeing whether increases in visible depth, and hence set size, would lead to more items being attended during the trial as one would expect from a serial search, or whether participants effectively ignored the increased visible layers as a form of a sub-nesting strategy, we used an eye tracker to explore whether there is a relationship between depth and the number of fixations on each layer of visible depth, as well as measure any changes in pupil size, which has been shown to be a good reflection of mental effort [2].

III. Method

A. *Participants*

Having received ethical approval from the University of Reading School of Psychology and Clinical Language Sciences, we recruited 18 participants (15 women, 3 men, age range: 21 - 27, mean age: 24.23), to take part in our experiment. All participants had normal or corrected to normal vision, while none claimed to suffer from colour blindness or any other disorders that would impact the selective attention task. The participants were asked to sign consent forms, asked to read the information sheets, and were debriefed at the end of the experiment.

B. *Materials and Design*

The 3D pictures folder (Figs. 2 & 3) was built using Javascript and the three.js library (a popular retained mode library for 3D development) and was optimized to run well on the Google Chrome web browser. The folder was then populated with 304 pictures of 190x190 pixel resolution made up of people, groups of people, animals, and various objects. Each visible layer was made up of 16 pictures, while the groups themselves were of equal size and placed in the environment following a random uniform distribution.

Figure 2. The 3D WIMP pictures folder with four visible layers

The space between each picture on the horizontal axis was set to be $1/10^{th}$ of the total screen width (which was 192 pixels when the layer was as "close" to the screen as possible), while the space between each picture on the vertical axis was set to $1/20^{th}$ of the total screen height (which was 60 pixels when the layer was as "close" to the screen as possible). The distance between the layers was set to ten default arbitrary units in 3D "depth" as set by the three.js library.

Figure 3. The 3D WIMP pictures folder with two visible layers

Since the target was selected randomly for each trial, differences in low-level (bottom-up) feature complexity and semantic differences with nontargets was not controlled, however, we expect that the random sampling of pictures from multiple categories, as well as the random selection of the target in each trial leads to a decreased likelihood of our results being affected from large differences in salience between target and neighbouring nontargets.

Figure 4. A ray-casting algorithm was used to measure the number of fixations on each layer

The mouse interaction purposely resembled the classic 2D WIMP interface, even though movement occurred along the z axis (in and out of the environment) using the mouse scroll wheel. This movement was essentially a translation of image on the z-axis, and no transition animations were used. Rotations along the x or y axis were not implemented, in order to decrease the overall complexity of interacting in a 3D environment using a 2D input device [12]. Rotations on the z axis were implemented, however this feature was disabled during the experimental stage in order to facilitate the overlay of eye tracking data to the environment.

An Eyelink 1000 eye-tracker (SR Research, Montreal) was used to record fixations. The chin rest was placed 70cm away from a large 28" monitor (16:10 aspect ratio), with a screen resolution of 1920x1200 pixels, while the sampling rate for the eye tracker was set to 500 samples every second. Calibration was kept at < 0.50 of error, (~ less than half the width of a human thumb at arm's length).

Our software recorded the number of intersections between eye fixations and pictures, as well as pupil size, with iterations occurring asynchronously every millisecond, with ~30ms maximum delay. The fixation measurement was implemented using a ray casting algorithm that would measure a fixation in the same way a mouse click would work when selecting a picture (Fig. 4). The target detection times were extracted from the eye tracking data once a fixation had occurred on the target that subsequently led to its selection using the mouse. Target identification errors were measured by the amount of clicks on a nontarget during each trial. The whole process has been summarised in Fig 6.

C. *Procedure*

After a small automated tutorial on the user interface, participants were presented with a random target in the beginning of each trial. Once they felt they were ready to begin, participants were instructed through text on the screen to press the spacebar and start the trial (Fig. 5).

Figure 5. A random target would appear before the beginning of every trial. Participants were expected to maintain the target in working memory during the visual search task

Upon target detection, the participants would click on the target and proceed to the next trial, if they made an error and clicked on a nontarget, that picture would be coloured red to provide feedback to the participant that they had made a recognition error. Furthermore, if the participant felt they were unable to find the target image they could choose to skip the trial (this was logged as a failed trial). At the end of either 64 trials or one hour, the experiment would end. Furthermore, participants were allowed to take short breaks every 10 minutes, hence, the eye tracker was calibrated and validated before each block of trials. Only seven participants managed to finish all the trials, while the range overall was from 32 to 60 (mean = 54.33, σ = 11.31).

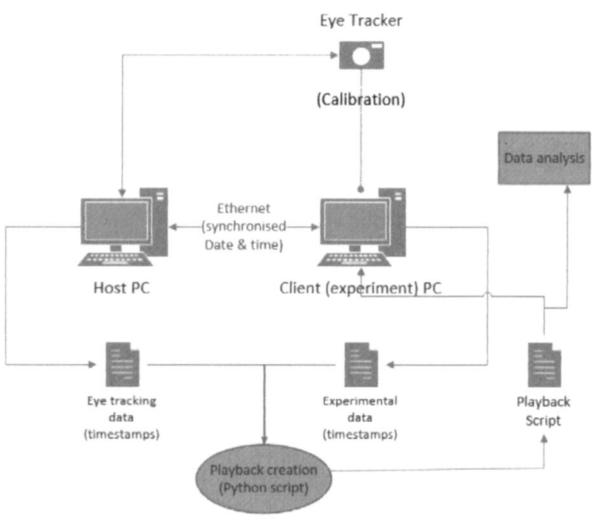

Figure 6. System Architecture illustrating the connections between the eye tracking and experimental machine, as well as the process of extracting playback information and data for the analysis

IV. RESULTS

The target detection time (RT) data did not follow the normal distribution, therefore, the non-parametric Kruskal-Wallis test was used in place of a one-way ANOVA, with visible depth as the independent categorical variable with three levels (two - four layers of visible depth), and RT as the dependent continuous variable. We failed to find any evidence to support that increasing the layers of visible depth lead to an increase in RT, since our results were not significant. However, using Kruskal-Wallis to investigate whether there was a significant main effect of depth on target identification errors; we found a significant result ($H = 6.8$, $p = 0.03$), while pairwise comparisons using Dunnett's procedure (with two layers of visible depth as the control), revealed that trials with four layers of depth produced significantly fewer errors than trials with two layers of depth ($p = 0.05$). This was not the case when comparing trials of two layers with trials of three layers of depth.

To investigate the results further, we took the ratio of fixations from our eye tracking data between the first layer of depth and all other layers. Formally this can be expressed as: $\forall_i \in \{0,\ldots,n\}$. $R_i = F_i / (F_i + O_i)$ where R is the vector of fixation ratios, F is a vector populated with number of intersections on the first layer, and O is a vector populated with number of intersections on other layers. Even though the fixation ratio data did not fit the normal distribution, we successfully transformed the data to satisfy the normality assumption by simply raising all the values to the power of two. This was then confirmed subjectively using QQplots and objectively using Shapiro-Wilk ($p > 0.05$), allowing us to use a one-way ANOVA for the analysis. The test revealed that the layers of visible depth had a significant effect on fixation ratio ($F(2, 132) = 11.63$, $p < 0.001$), while multiple comparisons using the Tukey test reported significantly lower ratio of first layer to other-layers fixations when there were three visible layers of depth compared to two visible layers of depth ($M_{diff} = -0.07$, 95% CI, [-0.13, -0.01], $p = 0.02$), as well as when there were four visible layers of depth compared to two layers of depth ($M_{diff} = -0.12$, 95% CI, [-0.18, -0.06], $p < 0.001$). We did not, however, find a significant difference in fixation ratio when comparing three and four layers (Fig. 7). Finally, average pupil size was also extracted for each level of depth and compared using Kruskal-Wallis (since the data, again, did not fit the normal distribution), however, the results were not significant, indicating no changes in pupil size as a result of increased visible depth. Finally, it is worth mentioning that we did not find an increase in target detection times and errors in relation to trial number (i.e., there was no measurable performance decrease due to fatigue).

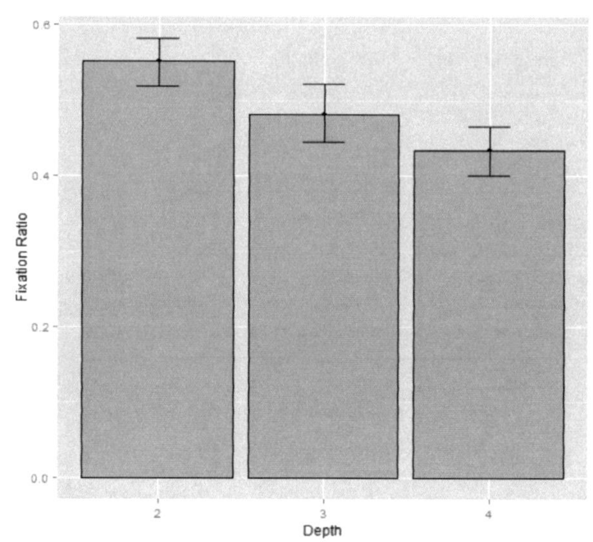

Figure 7. Ratio of fixations between the first layer of depth and all other layers, as visible leayers of depth increase. (Error bars are 95% CI)

V. DISCUSSION

The result of our study supports that increases in the item set size (in this case, pictures) caused by adding more layers of visible depth does not impact overall target detection times. One may be tempted to assume that this is due to a top-down sub-nesting strategy, where pictures in depth are effectively ignored in order to support the very serial and inefficient search that one would expect from complex pictorial stimuli. This is not entirely true, however, as our eye tracking data revealed that by making more layers of visible depth available to participants, fixations on the first layer decreased significantly (at least when comparing three or four layers with two layers of depth).

We hypothesise that the decreased ratio of fixations on the first layer compared to other layers is either the result of (a) randomly occurring (due to the random distribution of items) highly perceptual feature contrasts in depth that capture attention (bottom-up), or (b) nontargets with features that resemble the target stimulus that may be harder to differentiate when unattended in depth (possibly because of the smaller picture size), capturing attention due to feature similarity to the target in memory (top-down). To further explore this, we conducted an exploratory meta-analysis of the data in order to see if increased depth also led to increased selection of items in depth. Much to our surprise it did not, illustrating that the relationship is very complex and warrants further investigation. Finally, increased layers of visible depth lead to decreased numbers of target identification error, but only when comparing two layers to four layers of depth.

In conclusion, contrary to previous studies, which found depth to decrease performance in a 3D WIMP, our results are more optimistic, and suggest that adding depth does not impact target detection for this particular type of user action (find a picture in a folder). However, there is undoubtedly strong evidence to support that 3D WIMP interfaces do not work well (as can be seen by a plethora of previous studies), probably due to the lack of a suitable input device that can facilitate interaction in three-dimensions. Our results do not contradict past studies, per se, but rather indicate that if a more suitable 3D input device was manufactured, then 3D WIMP picture folders and photo galleries would not lead to a degradation of performance in the task of target detection. This supports the need for further research into novel devices that can perhaps replace the 2D mouse, although past attempts have failed in this regard (e.g., the 3D mouse is hard to use long-term since it leads to fatigue). Finally, we present these results with caution, as our study focused exclusively on usability and performance, rather than user experience. Therefore, we cannot argue that users would find a 3D picture folder compelling, even if it does not lead to performance degradation. In this regard, further research using qualitative methods would be appropriate, as well as a suitable next step for this research topic.

REFERENCES

[1] A. Agarawala and R. Balakrishnan. "Keepin'it real: pushing the desktop metaphor with physics, piles and the pen." Proc. ACM conference on Human Factors in computing systems (SIGCHI 06), Apr. 2006, pp. 1283-1292.

[2] D. Alnaes, M.H. Sneve, T. Espeseth, T. Endestad, S.H. van de Pavert, and B. Laeng. "Pupil size signals mental effort deployed during multiple object tracking and predicts brain activity in the dorsal attention network and the locus coeruleus." Journal of vision, vol 14, Apr. 2014, pp. 1-1.

[3] J. Biström, A. Cogliati, and K. Rouhiainen. "Post-wimp user interface model for 3d web applications." Helsinki University of Technology Telecommunications Software and Multimedia Laboratory, Dec. 2005

[4] D.A. Bowman, E. Kruijff, J.J. LaViola, and I. Poupyrev. "An introduction to 3-D user interface design." Presence: Teleoperators and virtual environments, vol 10, Feb. 2001 pp. 96-108.

[5] J. Boyle, S. Leishman, and P.M. Gray. "From WIMPS to 3D: The development of AMAZE." Journal of Visual Languages & Computing, vol 7, Sep 1996, pp. 291-319.

[6] A. Cockburn and B. McKenzie. "Evaluating the effectiveness of spatial memory in 2D and 3D physical and virtual environments." Proc. ACM conference on Human factors in computing systems (SIGCHI 02), Apr 2002, pp. 203-210.

[7] A. Cockburn A. "Revisiting 2D vs 3D implications on spatial memory." Proc. of the fifth Australian Computer Society conference on Australasian user interfaces, vol 28, Jan 2004, pp. 25-31.

[8] R.J. Jacob, A. Girouard, L.M. Hirshfield, M.S. Horn, O. Shaer, E.T. Solovey and J. Zigelbaum. "Reality-based interaction: a framework for post-WIMP interfaces." Proc. of the ACM conference on Human factors in computing systems (SIGCHI 08), Apr. 2008, pp. 201-210.

[9] M. Kyritsis, S.R. Gulliver, S. Morar and R. Stevens. "Issues and benefits of using 3D interfaces: visual and verbal tasks." Proc. Fifth ACM International Conference on Management of Emergent Digital EcoSystems (MEDES 13), Oct 2013, pp. 241-245.

[10] A. Leal, C.A. Wingrave and J.J. LaViola Jr. "Initial explorations into the user experience of 3D file browsing." Proc. 23rd British Computer Society HCI Group Annual Conference on People and Computers: Celebrating People and Technology, Sep 2009, pp. 339-344.

[11] E. McSorley and J.M. Findlay. "Visual search in depth." Vision Research, vol 41, Dec. 2001, pp. 3487-96.

[12] J.D. Mulder. "Menu Selection in Desktop Virtual Reality." Proc. Central European Multimedia and Virtual Reality Conference, 2005, pp. 121–128.

[13] K. Nakayama and G.H. Silverman. "Serial and parallel processing of visual feature conjunctions." Nature, vol 320, pp. 264-265.

[14] K. Nirmal and N. Mishra. "3D WIMP put into action for 3D GUI." International Journal of Emerging Technology and Advanced Engineering, vol 3, Apr. 2013, pp. 598-605.

[15] G. Robertson, M. Czerwinski, K. Larson, D.C. Robbins, D. Thiel and M. Van Dantzich. "Data mountain: using spatial memory for document management." Proc. 11th annual ACM symposium on User interface software and technology, Nov. 1998, pp. 153-162.

[16] A.M. Treisman and G. Gelade. "A feature-integration theory of attention.' Cognitive psychology, vol 12, Jan. 1980, pp. 97-136.

[17] H. Wenjun. "The Three-Dimensional User Interface." INTECH Open Access Publisher, 2008, doi: 10.5772/5910.

[18] J.M. Wolfe. "Guided search 2.0 a revised model of visual search." Psychonomic bulletin & review, vol 1, Jun. 1994, pp. 202-38.

Towards a Service-based Architecture for Web Accessibility Federated Evaluation

José R. Hilera, Salvador Otón, Carlos I. Martín-Amor
Dept. Computer Science
University of Alcalá
Alcalá de Henares, Spain
e-mail: jose.hilera@uah.es, salvador.oton@uah.es,
carlosivan.martin@edu.uah.es

Cristian F. Timbi-Sisalima
Grupo de Investigación en IA y Tecnologías de Asistencia
Universidad Politécnica Salesiana
Cuenca, Ecuador
e-mail: ctimbi@ups.edu.ec

***Abstract*— This paper presents a work in progress aimed to develop a universal architecture based on Web services and semantic Web technologies, for evaluating Web accessibility by using a federation of multiple evaluation tools, and compounding a unique result report combining semantically the reports obtained by each tool. The definition of a standard interface for evaluation services is proposed, and its implementation using RESTful Web API (Application Programming Interface) is described. Services for automatic semantic composition of reports are described using W3C (World Wide Web Consortium) standards as RDF(S) (Resource Description Framework Schema), OWL (Web Ontology Language), SPARQL (Sparql Protocol and RDF Query Language) and EARL (Evaluation and Report Language).**

Keywords-Web accessibility; a11y; Web service; federated evaluation; semantic Web; Web api; metatool.

I. Introduction

The accessibility of a Web site is essential to make it understandable, usable and practical for all users, including disabled people. To help determine the accessibility of a Web site, the World Wide Web Consortium has published the Web Content Accessibility Guidelines (WCAG) [1] that have been adopted as an international ISO (International Organization for Standardization) standard [2]. This standard establishes the minimum requirements for a Website to be accessible, overcoming barriers of access to any type of user. Other organizations have published their own Web accessibility requirements, such as Section 508, by the United States government; BITV (Barrierefreie Informations Technik Verordnung) by the Germany Government; or Stanca Act, by Italy Government. In general all these have much in common with WCAG that defines 61 accessibility success criteria to be satisfied by Web applications or Websites. To quantify the accessibility of a Website, the standard has created three levels of compliance: level A is reached by a Web site that accomplishes 25 specific success criteria, AA level requires meeting other 13 criteria, and AAA level is obtained when all criteria (61) are satisfied.

Developers and testers of Websites can verify the success criteria using accessibility evaluation tools. The W3C maintains a Web page with the list of the most important tools [3], including online tools. In general, an online evaluation tool is a Web application that allows the user to enter the URL (Uniform Resource Locator) of the Website to be tested obtaining an assessment report, which includes the accessibility requirements verified, those non-verified (requiring manual assessment), errors found and warnings. However, not all the tools have the same efficiency making essential the execution of different tools to complement the results. This procedure is tedious, as each tool uses a different user interface with different options and various formats for the results. To solve this problem, this paper presents a work in progress aimed to develop a universal architecture for evaluating Web accessibility using a federation of multiple evaluation tools, and compounding a unique results report combining semantically the reports obtained by each tool.

The following section describes the proposed architecture. In Section III, the definition of a standard interface for the accessibility evaluation services included in the architecture is presented. Section IV describes the basic services proposed for semantic composition of results reports. In the final section, some conclusions and other related works are presented.

II. Service-based Architecture

The proposal architecture is for any accessibility evaluation meta-tool system, which uses other evaluation tools in a federated way, receiving an evaluation request from a user, launching calls to a pool of federated tools, and finally compounding a single assessment report for the user, based on the results of each of the remote tools invoked. To implement this system, a service-based architecture with three layers is proposed (Figure 1). The choice of an architecture based on Web services is mainly given by the independence of the implementation details of each of the assessment tools available online. Each tool is independent from the rest, establishing its own decisions, and acting under its own autonomy. The levels proposed are as follows:

Layer 3. It represents the user (person or software) who wants to perform a simultaneous evaluation of the accessibility of a Website using multiple assessment tools. To do this, the user must provide the URL, or HTML (Hyper Text Markup Language) code, of the page to analyze, the accessibility evaluation standard to apply (WCAG 2.0, Section 508, etc.), and data about the federation of tools (at least, the selection of tools to participate in the federated evaluation).

Layer 2. At this level there are the services that manage user interface (*Front-end management*), and process the user data (*Back-end management*). From these data, a federation service module is responsible for determining how to connect with the final assessment tools provided by the user. Then, launches the requests for evaluation to those involved, and receives reports with the results. At this level, there are other support services, explained in Section IV, for filtering and adapting the format of reports, and the semantic composition of a single overall evaluation report.

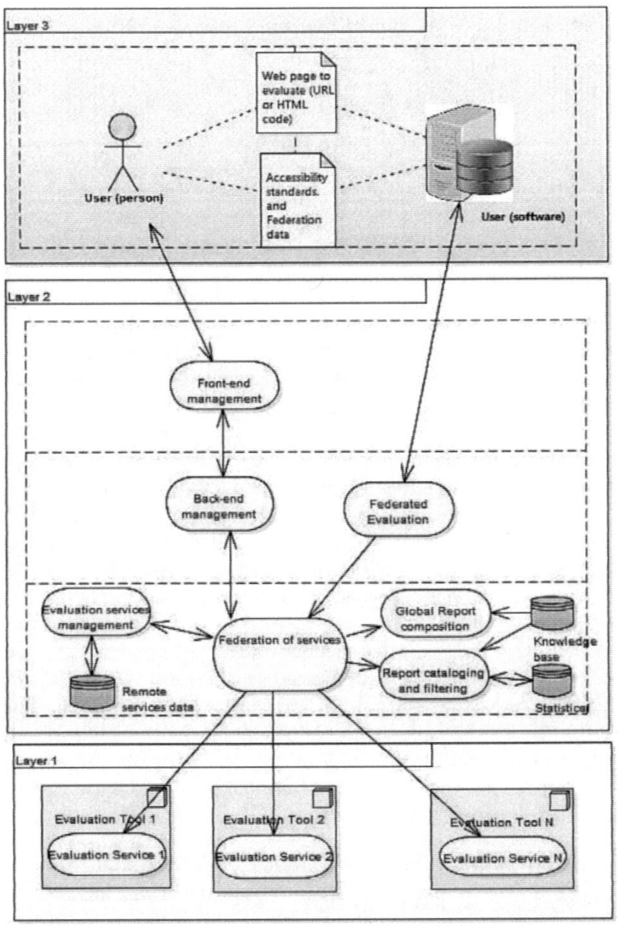

Figure 1. Service based architecture for accessibility evaluation.

Layer 1. It includes remote tools that perform the evaluation of the accessibility of Web sites, and should expose its functionality as a Web service *(Evaluation Service)* with a standard interface, as it is explained in the following Section.

III. STANDARD INTERFACE FOR EVALUATION SERVICES

There is a growing number of online Web accessibility evaluation tools. And some of them expose their functionality through Web services using RESTful Web API technology [4]. This is the case of the following free use tools: AChecker [5], OWA [6], Tenon [7] and WAVE [8].

Surely, the tendency to offer functionality through Web services will be extended to other existing online tools, which are now Web applications with user interface to be used with a Web browser. The problem is that every tool creates its own services, and its own input and output parameters, being different in all cases. As an example, Table I shows the input parameters of the evaluation service exposed by the four cited tools. It can be seen that, in general, at least the address of the Website to evaluate and a user ID or password are required. But there are tools offering other optional parameters, such as the evaluation standard to be applied. This is the case of AChecker with an optional "*guide*" parameter, whose default value is "WCAG2-AA", but that can refer to other standards such as the American "Section 508", the Italian "Stanca-act" or the German "BITV1". The other tools do not offer this possibility, because they only evaluate according to the WCAG standard.

TABLE I. API REQUEST PARAMETERS OF EVALUATION TOOLS

AChecker	Required: uri, id. Optional: guide, output, offset.
OWA	Required: format, url, key. Optional: level, resolution.
Tenon	Required: key, url (or src). Optional: appID, certainty, waitFor, fragment, importance, level, priority, ref, store, projectID, uaString, viewPortHeight, viewPortWidth.
WAVE	Required: key, url. Optional: format, reporttype.

Also, the information that the tools include in response to the request made after the evaluation of accessibility is different in each case. Table II shows the data in response.

TABLE II. API VALIDATION RESPONSE OF EVALUATION TOOLS

AChecker	**resultset**, **summary**, **status**, **sessionID**, **NumOfErrors**, **NumOfLikelyProblems**, **NumOfPotentialProblems**, **guidelines** (guideline, results (result (resultType, lineNum, columnNum, errorMsg, errorSurceCode, repair, sequenceID, decisionPass, decisionFail, decisionMade, decisionMadeDate))), **errors** (totalCount, error (message)).
OWA	**Date, message, result** (elements (forms, iframes, images, links, linksImages, tables, total), image, level, principles, resolution, summary, url).
Tenon	**status**, **message**, **documentSize**, **responseExecTime**, **responseTime**, **sourceHash**, **request** (appID, certainty, docID, importance, key, level, priority, priorityWeightissueLocation, ref, responseID, projectID, uaString, url, viewport, fragment, store), **clientScriptErrors** (message, stacktrace), **globalStats** (allDensity, errorDensity, warningDensity), **resultSummary** (density, issues, issuesByLevel, tests), **resultSet** (bpID, certainty, priority, errorDescription, errorSnippet, errorTitle, position, ref, resultTitle, signature, standards, tID, xpat), **apiErrors** (line, message, sourceId, tID).
WAVE	**status** (error (code, description)), **categories** (description, count, items (count, id, description)), **statistics** (creditsremaining, pageurl, pagetitle, waveurl, time, allitemcount, totalelements).

Another problem is the format of the result. AChecker, OWA and Tenon allow to optionally specify the format as an input parameter: HTML, XML (eXtensible Markup Language), JSON (JavaScript Object Notation); while Tenon always returns the information in JSON format.

In short, it can be seen that it is difficult to combine all the results and unify the input parameters, so it would be necessary to create a standard interface to be met by tools interested in participating in the federation of their services. Authors of this paper are working on creating a universal interface proposal, covering all possible input data, and producing a result with self-descriptive structure, based on the standard language EARL [9].

TABLE III. EXTRACT OF AN EVALUATION REPORT USING OWA API

```
@prefix earl: <http://www.w3.org/nss/earl#> .
@prefix ptr: <http://www.w3.org/2009/pointers#>.
@prefix doap: <http://usefulinc.com/ns/doap#> .
@prefix a11y: <http://example.org/a11yResources.owl#> .
@prefix wcag2: <http://www.AccessibleOntology.com/WCAG2.owl#>.

ex:assertion_OWA a earl:Assertion ;
earl:assertedBy a11y:OWA_API ;
earl:subject <http://www.example.org/page.html> ;
earl:test wcag2:SuccessCriterion_111;
earl:result ex:OWAResult .

wcag2:SuccessCriterion_111 a earl:TestRequirement .

a11y:OWA_API a earl:Software;
  doap:name "OWA Web Service API";
  doap:homepage <http://observatorioWeb.ups.edu.ec/oaw/apirest.jsf> .

ex:OWAResult a earl:TestResult;
  earl:outcome earl:failed;
  earl:pointer ex:ptr1_OWAResult .

ex:ptr1_OWAResult a earl:Pointer, ptr:LineCharPointer;
ptr:lineNumber "37";
ptr:charNumber "8" .
```

Tables III and IV show EARL extracts of reports to be used in Section IV. In both cases, for simplicity, the reports are represented using the Turtle RDF serialization syntax [10], although they could be obtained in other formats such as RDF/XML or JSON-LD (JSON for Linked Data). The reports consist of a list of triplets *"subject predicate object"* to describe the results. For example, the report in Table III indicates that a fail has been found, because of the noncompliance with the success criteria 1.1.1 of WCAG 2.0 on line 37 in the Web page www.example.org/page.html, using as evaluation tool the API provided by OWA.

IV. SERVICES FOR SEMANTIC COMPOSITION OF REPORTS

A problem to be solved when trying to do a joint or federated evaluation of the same Website, is how to combine the results obtained by each tool. It may be the case shown in Figure 2, in which a user wants to use two tools, and to evaluate the Web page according to the rule Section 508 existing in the US. In this case, only the AChecker tool can evaluate Section 508. However, the other can make an evaluation according to a similar standard as is WCAG 2.0.

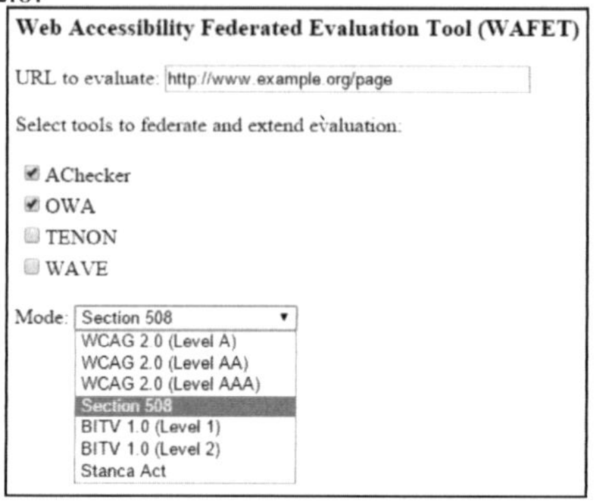

Figure 2. Basic user interface of a federation based meta-tool.

The solution proposed here is to include in the architecture a service and a knowledge base, both based on semantic technologies such as ontologies, able to help determine the equivalence between both standards. In this context, semantic technologies refers to technologies that facilitate the description of the meaning of information, so that this information can be compared or combined with other information with similar meaning without the need of the intervention of a person, using for that a specific software, such as intelligent agents.

Ontologies are implemented using semantic Web techniques, such as OWL, RDF (S) and SPARQL [11]. And they are compatible with the EARL language to describe individual reports returned by each tool. There are ontologies to model the WCAG standard, as the one referenced in Table III, but new ontologies must be created to conceptualize other standards, as Section 508, and apply techniques for mapping ontologies to align all involved. The authors of this paper are collaborating in the creation of ontologies about accessibility to model standards (section508.owl in Table IV), but also to model and classify evaluation tools (a11yResources.owl in Table IV).

TABLE IV. EXTRACT OF AN EVALUATION REPORT USING ACHECKER API

```
@prefix s508: <http://example.org/section508.owl#> .

ex:assertion_AChecker a earl:Assertion ;
earl:assertedBy a11y:AChecker_API ;
earl:subject <http://www.example.org/page.html> ;
earl:test s508:req_1194_22_a;
earl:result ex:ACheckerResult .

s508:req_1194_22_a a earl:TestRequirement .

a11y:AChecker_API a earl:Software;
  doap:name "AChecker Web Service API";
  doap:homepage <http://achecker.ca/checkacc.php> .

ex:ACheckerResult a earl:TestResult;
  earl:outcome earl:failed;
  earl:pointer ex:ptr1_ACheckerResult .

ex:ptr1_ACheckerResult a earl:Pointer, ptr:LineCharPointer;
ptr:lineNumber "25";
ptr:charNumber "10" .
```

Table V shows Turtle RDF code for declaring in the knowledge base that the success criterion 1.1.1 of WCAG 2.0 is semantically equivalent to the requirement 1194.22 (a) of Section 508. Both standards require that in an accessible Web page, a text equivalent for every non-text element shall be provided. Thus, a combined report can be composed using SPARQL [12] and a software reasoner that can make inferences from rules in ontologies. The authors are using for this Jena, an open source Java framework that allows programming SPARQL queries and has integrated reasoning, but also it allows us embed external reasoners as Pellet, or FaCT Racer [13].

As an example, Table VI shows a possible query and Table VII the result. It can be seen that through the mechanism of reasoning in the knowledge base, it has been inferred that the requirement 1.1.1 detected by OWA is equivalent to 1194.22 (a) of Section 508, and appears as such in the report, since the user had indicated (Figure 2) that he/she wanted to evaluate accessibility according to Section 508.

TABLE V. EXTRACT OF THE KNOWLEDGE BASE

```
@prefix owl: <http://www.w3.org/2002/07/owl#> .
@prefix s508: <http://example.org/section508.owl#> .
@prefix wcag2: <http://www.AccessibleOntology.com/WCAG2.owl#> .

s508:req_1194_22_a  a s508:Requirement;
s508:hasDescription "1194.22(a) A text equivalent for every non-text element shall be provided"@en .

s508:req_1194_22_a owl:sameAs wcag2:SuccessCriterion_111 .

wcag2: SuccessCriterion_111 a wcag2:SuccessCriterion;
wcag2:hasDescription "Non-text Content: All non-text content that is presented to the user has a text alternative that serves the equivalent purpose, except for the situations listed below."^^xsd:string .

wcag2:SuccessCriterion_111 owl:sameAs s508:req_1194_22_a .
```

TABLE VI. SPARQL SENTENCE TO OBTAIN A COMBINED REPORT

```
prefix earl: <http://www.w3.org/nss/earl#>
prefix ptr: <http://www.w3.org/2009/pointers#>
prefix doap: <http://usefulinc.com/ns/doap#>
prefix s508: <http://example.org/section508.owl#>
SELECT ?tool ?desc ?line ?char
WHERE { ?a a earl:Assertion .
        ?a earl:assertedBy ?tool .
        ?a earl:test ?req .
        ?req a s508:Requirement .
        ?req s508:hasDescription ?desc .
        ?a earl:result ?res .
        ?res earl:outcome earl:failed .
        ?res earl:pointer ?pt .
        ?pt ptr:lineNumber ?line .
        ?pt ptr:charNumber ?char . }
```

TABLE VII. RESULT OF THE SPARQL QUERY

tool	desc	line	char
AChecker_API	"1194.22(a) A text equivalent . . ."	25	10
OWA_API	"1194.22(a) A text equivalent . . ."	37	8

Another problem that arises by combining results is the possibility of inconsistencies between the results of different tools for the same accessibility requirement. For example, a tool can determine that the success criterion 1.1.1 is satisfied because all images have an alternative text, whereas another more advanced tool could determine that the goal was not met because it has detected as alternative text images the filename of the image archive, which is not suitable to describe an image. The proposed architecture includes a filtering service to help resolve these cases. This service must also manage preferences expressed by the user on how to resolve conflicts, but can also access the knowledge base and a database with statistical results of previous assessments that help determine the reliability of each tool for each requirement. This is in line with what other experts proposed [14].

V. CONCLUSIONS

This is a work in progress that provides a solution to the problem of interoperability between tools for evaluating Web accessibility, and allows automatic composition of evaluation reports from different sources. No other proposals have been found to solve this problem. There are studies that address part of the problem, as is the case of [15], which also proposed an architecture and use of EARL format to compare results from different tools, but neither combining results nor using Web services. There are also tools that reuse open source available from other evaluation tools, is the case of QuickCheck [16], reusing specific functionality of the tools Chrome Developer Tool, Axe Engine and HTML Code Sniffer, but without the possibility of combining the results or federation, as it is not based on Web services.

The main contributions of this work are mainly two: first, a new standard API for online accessibility evaluation tools that serves as a single and common interface through which it can access all the functionality offered by any of the current tools, and flexible enough to support new functionality to appear in the future. A second contribution is a new mechanism based on this interface that, using federation of services and semantic technologies, allows combining the results of evaluations of the same Website by different tools, applying different criteria or preferences established by the user.

The idea of federating services and sematic combination has been proposed and applied previously by the authors of this paper, having implemented similar architectures in other application areas, such as the federation of search results in distributed learning objects repositories [17]. This previous experience is now been applied to implement the proposed architecture for the case of Web accessibility evaluation.

We are currently working on implementing a first version of a prototype that meets the architecture and basic functional requirements that reflect the main ideas described in this paper. The goal is that it can be useful especially for evaluators who know standards such as WCAG or Section 508. In the future, additional requirements will be considered, such as those relating to the usability of the tool and ease of interpretation of the evaluation results, so that it can be used even by people who do not have a thorough understanding of Web accessibility standards.

ACKNOWLEDGMENT

Thanks to ESVI-AL EU project, and "Master on Software Engineering for the Web" of the University of Alcalá.

REFERENCES

[1] Web content accessibility guidelines (WCAG) 2.0. World Wide Web Consortium, 2008.

[2] ISO/IEC 40500:2012, information technology -- W3C Web content accessibility guidelines (WCAG) 2.0. International Organization for Standardization, 2012.

[3] Web Accessibility Evaluation Tools List. Wide Web Consortium, 2014. http://www.w3.org/WAI/ER/tools/. [retrieved: 03, 2016]

[4] L. Richardson and M. Amundsen, RESTful Web APIs, O'Reilly Media, 2013.

[5] AChecker Web Service API. Inclusive Design Research Centre, 2011. http://achecker.ca/documentation/web_service_api.php. [retrieved: 03, 2016]

[6] Observatorio de Accesibilidad Web (OWA). Universidad Politécnica Salesiana, 2016. http://observatorioweb.ups.edu.ec/oaw/apirest.jsf. [retrieved: 03, 2016]

[7] Tenon API Documentation. Tenon, 2015. http://www.tenon.io/documentation/. [retrieved: 03, 2016]

[8] WAVE API. WebAIM, 2015. http://wave.webaim.org/api/. [retrieved: 03, 2016]

[9] Evaluation and Report Language (EARL) 1.0. World Wide Web Consortium, 2011.

[10] RDF 1.1 Turtle. World Wide Web Consortium, 2014.

[11] Semantic Web. World Wide Web Consortium, 2015. http://www.w3.org/standards/semanticWeb/. [retrieved: 03, 2016]

[12] SPARQL 1.1 Query Language. World Wide Web Consortium, 2011.

[13] Reasoners and rule engines: Jena inference support. Apache Software Foundation, 2015. https://jena.apache.org/documentation/inference/. [retrieved: 03, 2016]

[14] Automated WCAG Monitoring Community Group. World Wide Web Consortium, 2015. https://www.w3.org/community/auto-wcag/. [retrieved: 03, 2016]

[15] N. Fernandes, R. Lopes, and L. Carriço, "Architecture for Multiple Web Accessibility Evaluation Environments". 6th Int. Conf. UAHCI 2011, July 2011, pp 206-214, ISBN: 978-3-642-21671-8.

[16] P. Nawaz. QuickCheck, 2015. https://github.com/mpnkhan/quickcheck/. [retrieved: 03, 2016]

[17] S. Otón et al. Service oriented architecture for the implementation of distributed repositories of learning objects. Int. Journal of Innovative Computing, Information and Control. Vol. 6(3A), 2010, pp. 843-854.

Enhancing User Experience of Users with Disabilities

Application to Open Educational Resources Websites

Rosa Navarrete
Departamento de Informática y Computación
Escuela Politécnica Nacional
Quito, Ecuador
rosa.navarrete@epn.edu.ec

Sergio Luján-Mora
Department of Software and Computing System
University of Alicante
Alicante, Spain
sergio.lujan@ua.es

Myriam Peñafiel
Departamento de Informática y Computación
Escuela Politécnica Nacional
Quito, Ecuador
myriam.penafiel@epn.edu.ec

Abstract— **At present, User Experience (UX) is a recognized concept that appraises the quality of user interaction on websites. Despite the fact that users with disabilities face obstacles that hinder their experience in Web interaction, the UX concept has not been extended to include their specific requirements. This work proposes an empirical review of the aspects that impact on UX of users with disabilities, including not only the Usability and Information Architecture but also Accessibility issues. The context of the application is related to Open Educational Resources (OER) websites due to their importance for opening learning opportunities to all people around the world. Although the UNESCO Paris Declaration on OER (2012) recognized that "everyone has the right to education," people with disabilities are still excluded from full participation in OER-based learning because of design issues on OER websites. Further, we have considered the standards and best practices that should be applied to these aspects to recognize the problems that need to be addressed to improve the quality of the UX of users with disabilities, particularly in OER websites. The results of this work contribute to a better comprehension of UX from the perspective of users with disabilities in order to support the inclusive vision of the OER Initiative.**

Keywords— Open Educational Resources; OER; User Experience; UX; Web accessibility; Web usability; Information Architecture.

I. Introduction

The statistics presented by the World Health Organization in the World Report on Disability (2011) [1] states that one billion people, about 15% of the world's population, live with some form of disability. Further, according to the United Nations [2], the population of older adults will increase from 841 million (11.7%) in 2013 to 2 billion (21.1%) in 2050. These data show the importance of this vulnerable group of population which, according to the United Nations, is still excluded from equitable access to educations, health, employment and social protection.

Concerning the Web, users with visual and hearing impairments, restricted movement of the upper limbs, cognitive issues, and problems related to aging, face barriers when interacting on the websites [3]. These issues are related to the lack of accessibility considerations in Web design.

On the other hand, at present, one of the bases for a quality Web design is the User Experience (UX). This is a broadly defined term that involves all the aspects that influence the interaction of a user with a website, including attainment of goals, and subjective aspects such as the satisfaction of non-instrumental (or hedonic) needs, and acquisition of positive feeling and well-being [4]. However, this concept has not spread to address the particular requirements of users with disabilities.

In this work, we propose an empirical review of the supporting aspects that influence the quality of UX, such as Web usability and Information Architecture, and, considering the particular needs of users with disabilities, we include Web accessibility as an essential aspect of UX.

In a complementary way, we propose standards and best practices for each aspect in order to define recommendations for improving UX quality of users with disabilities. This proposal does not consider a specific disability, but it presents recommendations related to some of the common disabilities.

Furthermore, the UNESCO Paris Open Educational Resource Declaration (OER) (2012) [5] recognized the worldwide impact of OER usage and the need for inclusion of all society groups, in particular, people with disabilities. The term OER was coined by UNESCO (2002) [6] to refer to digital contents that support education and has been released under open license to be used and re-purposed by others. These digital contents are stored in repositories available through websites at a global level [7] and include full courses, course materials, textbooks, and any other tool used to support access to knowledge [8].

Some OER websites do not consider essential aspects of UX, such as Web accessibility [9][10], and supporting aspects, such as Web usability and Information Architecture [11]. Since users with disabilities need to interact with OER websites, it is relevant to review how these aspects affect their UX.

Due to the importance of education as a fundamental right for all people, including people with disabilities, we have tackled the UX of users with disabilities in OER websites, because, the quality of UX for these users could encourage their inclusion in OER-based learning opportunities. As a demonstrative context of the aspects of

UX that need improvement, we are referring to a large-scale OER website.

The structure of the paper is as follows. Section II describes the concept of UX and the main aspects of UX to be addressed. Each of these aspects is presented in the next sections. Section III discusses the Web accessibility concept and the accessibility guidelines; Section IV presents Web usability issues and their impact on users with disabilities, Section V presents the basis of Information Architecture. Finally, Section VI presents the Conclusion and Future work.

II. User Experience

User Experience (UX) focuses on having a deep understanding of users, their needs and their limitations. This is a paramount consideration in relation to users with disabilities because they use the Web in a different way than other people.

According to the results of a survey that considers the point of view of researchers and practitioners, there is an agreement that UX is dependent on the context of the website and the individual interaction on the website. It means that UX is particular for a user and his own goals on a website [12]. This agreement matches with the definition of UX in the standard ISO 9241-210:2010 Ergonomics of Human-System Interaction [13]: "A person's perceptions and responses resulting from the use and/or anticipated use of a product, system or service".

The different definitions of UX emphasize different aspects. For example, one of the precursors of this term states that UX implies all aspects of the users' interactions within the website, considering their expectations about the attainment of their goals [14].

Other authors complemented this definition pointing out that the concept of UX embraces efficiency, effectiveness, and task accomplishment satisfaction [15]. While other authors [4] proposed, a holistic approach of UX that includes subjective aspects, such as the feeling of control, the appreciation of the pleasant look of the website, and positive aspects such as happiness or engagement. Thereby, UX can be conceptualized in a holistic approach aiming for a balance between pragmatic aspects related to task fulfillment and other non-task related aspects (hedonic and aesthetic, enjoyment).

There is not a shared understanding of the fields pertaining to UX. Different approaches from academics and practitioners highlight some different elements and aspects. The most common aspects are usability and Information Architecture.

Garret [14] considers elements of UX, such as user needs, the functional specifications and content requirements, the interaction design, and Information Architecture that provide the basis for navigation design.

In a similar way, Fenn and Hobbs [16] prioritize the importance of Information Architecture for UX. Roto [17] emphasizes the role of usability in three blocks that configure UX, the context, the system and the user.

Nevertheless, the specific case of users with disabilities is not mentioned. Hobbs, Fenn, and Resmini [18], and Tokkonen and Saariluoma [19] agree in considering usability and the Information Architecture as the aspects implied in UX, in addition to other aspects, such as user, product and company, for a corporative vision of UX.

Other authors [20] [21] use the concept of UX to guide the software development process. They also include considerations about usability and Information Architecture as part of the requirements definition.

In the literature review we have not found a reference of Web accessibility as an aspect involved in UX. Hence, in this work, we propose to add Web accessibility as a key aspect of UX from the perspective of users with disabilities. For this reason, the improvement of the three aspects: Web accessibility, Web usability and Information Architecture enables enhancing the UX for all users including user with disabilities.

III. Web Accessibility

Web accessibility is an inclusive practice and hence an essential aspect that needs to be addressed to ensure access and interaction with the website by people with disabilities. Web accessibility aims to remove barriers that prevent people with disabilities in participating equitably in Web activities [3].

The Web Content Accessibility Guidelines (WCAG) 2.0 [22], recognized as an International Organization for Standardization (ISO) standard (ISO/IEC 4500) [23] in 2012, is the most spread reference standard that guides the accessible Web design.

This standard is structured under four principles with guidelines associated to each one.

1. Perceivable. Enable users to perceive the information being presented.
2. Operable. Enable users to operate the interface.
3. Understandable. Enable users to understand the information as well as the operation of the user interface.
4. Robust. Enable to maintain access with technologies advance.

Each guideline has a set of verifiable success criteria that are not technology-specific. Each criterion is associated with a conformance level A, AA, AAA, which indicates its impact on accessibility. To ensure minimal conditions for accessibility the AA level of compliance is required.

Web accessibility cannot be reliably ensured because it depends on the user and his context; i.e. the kind and degree of disability of the user and his expertise level in using assistive technology [24].

However, accessibility can be improved if the website meets an accessibility standard. In this work, we propose the use of the method called "conformance review" to verify if an OER website meets WCAG 2.0 requirements. This method can identify a larger range of diverse accessibility problems than other methods [25].

Further, it can be supported by the use of automated tools that reduce the time and effort of the compliance evaluation [26]. These tools are software applications or online services that check the success criteria that are machine-testable.

Nevertheless, not all success criteria can be tested automatically, and some require the expert human judgment.

Further, these tools can produce false or misleading results, such as false-positives or failures in identifying issues [27].

By way of illustration, we show the evaluation of OER Commons, a prestigious large-scale OER website, with two accessibility evaluation tools. The evaluation for both tools is configured to WCAG 2.0 level AA. Figure 1 displays a fragment of the screenshot that highlights the accessibility review results with AChecker [28]. These results show zero (0) for Known Problems, Likely Problems, and Potential Problems.

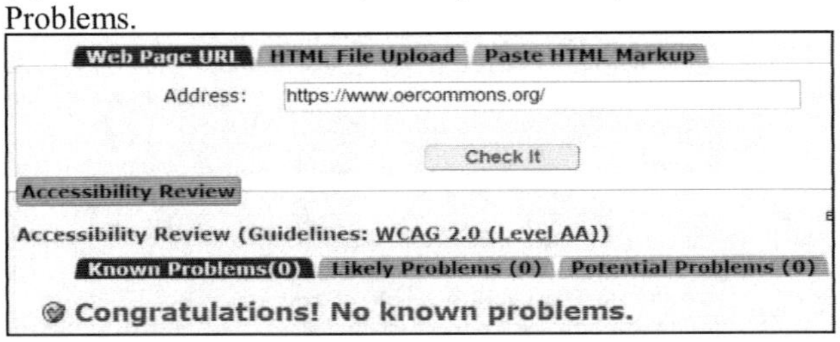

Figure 1. OER Commons Accessibility evaluation with AChecker.

On the contrary, Figure 2 displays a fragment of the screenshot that highlights the accessibility review results with TAW [29]. These results show 47 problems and 396 warnings. The failures identified in this accessibility conformance review need to be solved to improve website accessibility. It is advisable to review the techniques that provide guidance to Web content authors on meeting the success criteria of WCAG 2.0 [30].

Figure 2. OER Commons Accessibility evaluation with TAW.

These are not necessarily contradictory results because each tool performs the accessibility review with different coverage, completeness, and correctness. Therefore, it is recommendable to use more than one tool to complement and compare the evaluation results, improving their accuracy. There is a wide availability of these evaluation tools [31], but not all of them can verify the compliance with WCAG 2.0.

IV. WEB USABILITY

According to the standard ISO 9241-11: 1998 Guidance on Usability [32] usability is "The extent to which a product can be used by specified users to achieve specified goals with effectiveness, efficiency and satisfaction in a specified context of use". Therefore, Web usability refers to the ease of use of the website, besides, the effectiveness, efficiency and satisfaction of goal achievement [15]. Effectiveness means the reliability and completeness in the goal achievement. Efficiency represents the effort and the resources expended by the user in the goal achievement. Satisfaction refers to the extent to which the expectations of the user are met.

Further, Web usability is closely related to Web accessibility; both have similar goals, and some guidelines overlap significantly [33]. Best practices of Web usability contribute to better UX of users with disabilities and without disabilities. Some general usability practices are also included in accessibility guidelines because they can be barriers for people with disabilities. For example, a good practice for usability is the operation of the interface without a mouse, and it is also an accessibility guideline that states that all functionality must be available from a keyboard. This condition is helpful for users with mobility impairment or blind who experience difficulties to operate a mouse.

The standard, ISO 9241-151:2008 Ergonomics of human-system interaction -- Part 151: Guidance on World Wide Web user'interfaces [32] provides a set of guidelines for usability. It is important to verify if the website is compliant with these guidelines in its design to improve usability. Due to the lack of space, we only present a description of the main topics covered in each category and how these guidelines could affect the UX of users with disabilities in OER websites.

The categories are presented as main and secondary according to the topics that they address and their impact on OER websites. Table I shows the main categories that impact the achievement of primary tasks, i.e. searching and retrieving of resources, and Table II presents secondary categories that are complementary to the achievement of the primary tasks.

By way of example, we review the usability on OER Commons website. On this website, we found a menu for adjusting preferences that improve usability and hence the UX. Figure 3 highlights a design resource that allows the modification of visual presentation of the interface with these characteristics: Text and Display (text size, text style, line spacing, and color & contrast); Layout and Navigation (table of contents); Links (larger, bold, and underlined); and, Inputs (larger for buttons, drop-down menus, text fields).

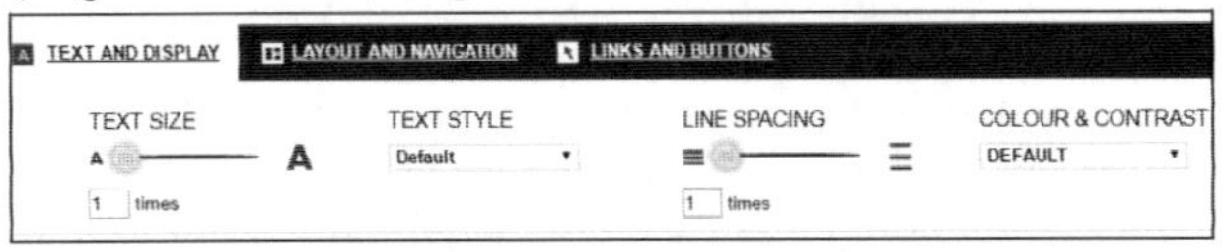

Figure 3. OER Commons Learner Options to enhance usability.

Another good practice of usability enables the user to know how many results were retrieved and customize the number of results per page, as we can see in Figure 4.

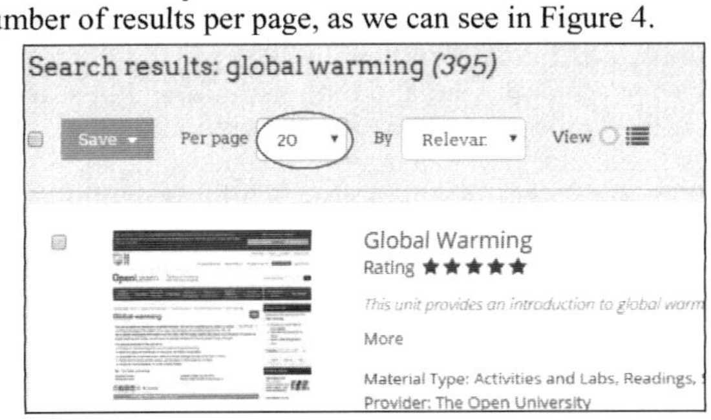

Figure 4. OER Commons display search results per page.

TABLE I ISO 9241-11 MAIN CATEGORIES OF USABILITY

Category (ISO 9241-151:2008)	Users' disability	Impact on users with disabilities
Home Page The content of the home page is focusing on users' tasks; the major options are explicitly represented through navigation menus that are organized in a logic order in a task-oriented manner. All the core tasks are reachable from this page.	Blindness	Options to guide the main tasks (search or browse the resources) on the home page simplifies the amount of information that users who use a screen reader need to listen before to take a decision.
	Cognitive	The clarity and pertinence of the information encourage the comprehension by users with cognitive disabilities.
Task Orientation The number of screens for task completion has been minimized; there are minimal requirements of scrolling and clicking for task completion; the key tasks are easy to carry out; the metaphors and icons are understandable by users; the interface is easy to learn for novice users.	Blindness	These guidelines are valuable for blind users because it reduces the amount of information that they need to listen for task achievement.
	Low vision	Users with low vision who use screen magnifiers do not lose the vision of all context because of the scrolling requirements. For example, a list of resources that need vertical scroll.
	Cognitive	The use of common icons and metaphors and a simple interface encourage the comprehension by users with cognitive disabilities.
Navigation The navigation is predictable and convenient to users' goals; the navigation includes global and local navigation, wizard navigation, breadcrumbs, site map; the information that users are most likely to need is easy to reach from most pages; navigation tabs are located at the top of the page; the navigation system is broad and shallow (many items on a menu) rather than deep (many menu levels). The use of the keyboard is enabled to operate the navigation.	Blindness	A blind user needs to identify the structure of a menu. Many levels on a menu affect its comprehension. For example, the categorization of the resources should be available through a different mechanism than a menu. Also, breadcrumbs help blind users to know where they are and where they come from.
	Upper limbs impairment	The use of the keyboard to operate navigation instead of the mouse is the alternative for users with movement restriction on upper limbs.
	Cognitive	The simplest and logical presentation of menus enables better comprehension of the choices to users with cognitive disabilities.
Information Architecture The categorization of content is visible and useful to users; the category labels accurately describe the information in the category; the content organization allows the grouping, filtering, and sorting of resources.	All	The categorization of the resources is a critical aspect of improving usability in OER websites. It implies a logical grouping of resources that facilitate their searching and retrieving.
Search The search box and advanced search are clearly distinguishable on the home page; the search results page is helpful to the user, it shows how many results were retrieved, ranked by distinct parameters, and allows the user to configure the number of results per page. The advanced search allows the searching refinement based on simultaneous parameters; the search results page displays useful meta-information that include accessibility characteristics and format of the resource, the creator or provenance of the resource, the educational level, and creation date.	All	The primary goal in OER Websites is the search and retrieve of the resources, indeed the searching facilities support the effectiveness and efficiency in this objective. For example, if the search and search advanced features are located in the home page, the users can execute this tasks immediately. The searching refinement on simultaneous parameters enables the accuracy of the searching of the resources.
Forms and Data entry The forms are designed so users can complete simple tasks by entering only essential information; the pull-down menus, radio buttons and check boxes are used in preference to text entry fields; the fields on forms contain default values when appropriate; the fields contain example or model answers to make the expected input evident; there is a clear distinction between required and optional fields; the forms allow users to navigate with keyboard and distinguish the field with focus; the labels are close to the data entry field and meaningful.	Blindness	The simplification in form entry helps to blind users to avoid errors. For example, the labels of the fields, and default values or example values, also the identification of optional or required.
	Low vision	Because of the use of screen magnifier, the users with low vision need to distinguish the field with focus, and the labels of the fields.
	Upper limbs impairment	The forms need to be operated with the keyboard instead of the mouse.
	Cognitive	The context help in forms, such as default values or model answer as well as the labels for fields encourage the comprehension by people with cognitive disabilities.

Nevertheless, on the same website, we found a usability failure in search results display.

Figure 5 shows that, at the bottom of the search results display, only the option "Load more" appears; it is proven to be inefficient for several hundreds of results.

The lack of pagination to display a list of resources is a usability failure because users cannot navigate inside the subsets of search results (pages) to select what they need. The list of hundreds of resources becomes a very long vertical scroll. This also impact on the comprehension of the results, because they are presented out of the context of the option to refine the search.

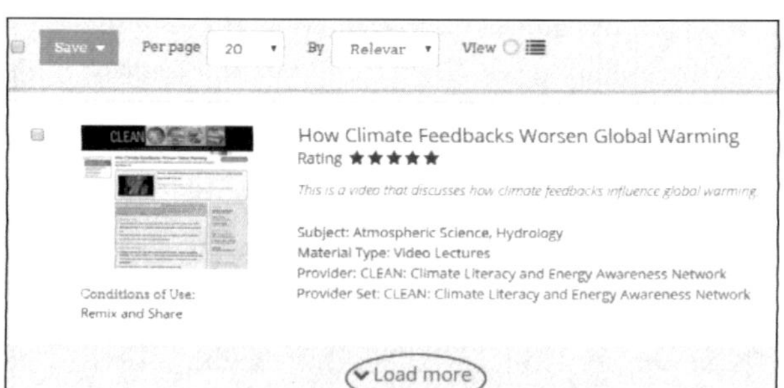

Figure 5. OER Commons usability failure..

TABLE II ISO 9241-11 SECONDARY CATEGORIES OF USABILITY

Category (ISO 9241-151:2008)	Users' disability	Impact on users with disabilities
Trust and Credibility The content of the website denotes to be up-to-date and reliable; each page follows the pattern design of the website; there are no grammatical, spelling or typographic errors	All Blindness Cognitive	The absence of writing errors encourages the comprehension of users with cognitive disabilities and allows an accurate recognition of the word by the screen reader.
Writing & Content quality The text is concise; the information is organized hierarchically; headings and subheadings are straightforward and descriptive; each page is clearly labelled with a meaningful title that makes sense to users; the links have descriptive titles and match the title of destination pages.	All Blindness Cognitive	The structure of the information helps to users who use screen reader and users with cognitive disabilities to understand the content. The precise description of the links is helpful to users to take the decision about where they can go on the website.
Page layout & Visual design Each page has a layout consistent with the website style; the page does not need horizontal scrolling; the fonts are readable; the most frequently used topics, features and functions are placed in a highlighted position on all pages; the website has an attractive appearance.	All Low vision	Users with low vision who use screen magnifiers can lose the context vision if there is horizontal scrolling on the page. Also, they require readable fonts. All users with disabilities require that the most frequently used topics, such as search or browse of the resources are located in highlighted position on all pages.
Help, Feedback & Error tolerance The website provides context-sensitive help and feedback about errors; the website uses appropriate selection methods (e.g., pull-down menus) as an alternative to typing; pages load in five seconds or less; error messages are explicit about the nature of error and the next action; the user is warned about slow-loading pages.	All	The context-sensitive help is a usability characteristic that facilitate the interaction of all users including users with disabilities.

V. INFORMATION ARCHITECTURE

The Information Architecture in the context of Web environments is related to data storage and its structure [16]. In this work, we have adopted the concept of Information Architecture by Morville & Rosenfeld [34] that defines it as the relationships between the website content and its functionality. Information Architecture involves the underlying organization, labeling, search, and navigation system within the website.

In OER Websites, Information Architecture enables a comprehensive and integrated structure of information available about resources for their searching and retrieval. This is achieved through the use of classifications, taxonomies, and metadata that enables the classification and description of each resource.

A key aspect of Information Architecture in OER websites is the metadata standards used to describe and categorize the resources. Some OER websites use a non-standardized way to label the resources instead of the metadata standard

This issue affects the ability to find resources; without a common system of identification, users cannot easily search the resources [11]. Indeed, users often cite this issue as a major stumbling block hindering their more widespread use of the resources [35].

The most important metadata standards that include accessibility and educational field descriptor are Institute of Electrical and Electronics Engineers (IEEE) Learning Object Metadata (LOM) [36], and Learning Resource Metadata Initiative (LRMI) [37]. Not all metadata standards include these descriptors, therefore, they fail to identify resources for users with disabilities [38].

Furthermore, there is a lack of agreement about metadata usage; while the main OER websites use a metadata standard, others describe resources using their own methods such as XML-based schemas or heterogeneous taxonomies [39].

The main recommendation about Information Architecture to improve UX is the adoption of a metadata standard that enable meaningful categorization and classification of the resources in OER websites.

This enables better navigation system and search system on these websites.

VI. CONCLUSION AND FUTURE WORK

Although the concept of UX has a broad view that implies subjective aspects inherent to users, in this work, we have focused on the aspects that are controlled by Web designers to improve the UX of users with disabilities.

The context of the analysis has been the OER websites considering the searching and retrieving of resources as the primary users' goals. We have reviewed the extent of the application of standards and best practices related to Web accessibility, Web usability, and Information Architecture that positively impacts on UX of users with disabilities, but this benefit is also extended to all users.

The outcomes of this review contribute to a better understanding of the challenges and barriers that users with disabilities face and that hinder them from taking advantage of this educational opportunity. Further, these outcomes can be used by Web designers and Web masters of the OER websites to make the corrective actions towards enhancing the UX for all users, including users with disabilities.

In our future work, we are planning to address the UX depending on assistive technology and the type of disability. It is important to clarify that cognitive disabilities need a particular approach to the UX because of each user condition and require a joint effort with other areas such as medicine or psychology.

Finally, in this research, we have reviewed the UX on OER websites, but we have not explicitly included the UX of resources themselves, which require a more broad study that includes aspects related to pedagogical and didactic of the resource to be suitable for users with disabilities.

ACKNOWLEDGMENT

This work has been supported by the PII-DICC-005-2015.

REFERENCES

[1] World Health Organization, "World Report on Disability," 2011. [Online]. Available: http://goo.gl/q88CuW. [retrieved: March, 2016].

[2] United Nations, "World Population Ageing," 2013. [Online]. Available: http://goo.gl/g3tU7U. [retrieved: March, 2016].

[3] W3C, "Introduction to Web Accessibility," 2005. [Online]. Available: http://goo.gl/013Vgd. [retrieved: March, 2016].

[4] M. Hasssenzahl and N. Tractinsky, "User experience - a research agenda," in Behaviour & Information Technology, vol. 25, Taylor & Francis, 2006, pp. 91-97.

[5] UNESCO, "World Open Educational Resources (OER) Congress," 2012.

[6] UNESCO, "Forum on the Impact of Open Courseware for Higher Education in Developing Countries: Final report," Paris, France, 2002.

[7] D. Atkins, J. Seely Brown, and A. L. Hammond, "A review of the Open Educational Resources (OER) Movement: Achievements, Challenges and New Opportunities," February 2007. [Online]. Available: http://goo.gl/GlJ3GQ. [retrieved: March, 2016].

[8] T. Caswell, S. Henson, M. Jensen, and D. Wiley, "Open Educational Resources: Enabling Universal Education," The International Review of Research in Open and Distance Learning, vol. 9, no. 1, 2008, pp.1-11.

[9] R. Navarrete and S. Luján-Mora, "Accessibility considerations in Learning Objects and Open Educational Resources," Proc. 6th International Conference of Education, Research and Innovation (ICERI 2013), Nov. 2013, pp.521-530.

[10] R. Navarrete and S. Luján-Mora, "Evaluating accessibility of Open Educational Resource website with a heuristic method," Proc. 9th International Technology, Education and Development Conference (INTED 2015), Mar. 2015, pp.6402-6412.

[11] R. Navarrete and S. Luján-Mora, "Evaluating findability of Open Educational Resources from the perspective of users with disabilities: A preliminary approach," Proc. Second International Conference on eDemocracy & eGovernment (ICEDEG 2015), Apr. 2015, pp. 112-119.

[12] E. L.-C. Law, V. Roto, M. Hassenzahl, A. P. Vermeeren, and J. Kort, "Understanding, scoping and defining user experience: a survey approach," Proc. Conference on Human Factors in Computing Systems (CHI 2009), 2009, pp. 719-728, doi: 10.1145/1518701.1518813.

[13] ISO, "ISO 9241-210:2010 Ergonomics of Human-System Interaction Part 210: Human-Centred Design for Interactive Systems," 2010.

[14] J. J. Garrett, The elements of User experience – User centered design for the Web, New Riders, 2002.

[15] H. Petrie and N. Bevan, "The evaluation of accessibility, usability and user experience," The Universal Access Handbook, CRC Press, 2009, doi: 10.1201/9781420064995-c20.

[16] T. Fenn and J. Hobbs, "The Information Architecture of Meaning Making," Reframing Information Architecture, Human-Computer Interaction Series, Springer , 2014, pp. 11-30, doi: 10.1007/978-3-319-064925_2.

[17] V. Roto, "User Experience Building Blocks," The 2nd COST294-MAUSE International Open Workshop, 2006, pp. 124-128.

[18] J. Hobbs, T. Fenn, and A. Resmini, "Maturing a Practice," Journal of Information Architecture, vol. 2, no. 1, 2010, pp. 37-54.

[19] H. Tokkonen and P. Saariluoma, "How User Experience is Understood?," Proc. Science and Information Conference (SAI), Oct. 2013, pp. 791-795.

[20] A. Gasparini, "A Holistic Approach to User Experience in the Context of an Academic Library Interactive System," Proc. 4th International Conference (DUXU 2015), Aug. 2015, pp.173-184.

[21] M. Wincker, C. Bach and R. Bernhaupt, "Identifying User eXperiencing factors along the development process: A case study," Proc. IW on the Interplay between User Experience Evaluation and Software Development (I-UxSED 2012), Oct. 2012, pp.37-42.

[22] W3C, "Web Content Accessibility Guidelines (WCAG) 2.0," 2012. [Online]. Available: http://goo.gl/uS7DEZ. [retrieved: March, 2016].

[23] ISO, "ISO/IEC 40500:2012," [Online]. Available: http://goo.gl/Dhk6IW. [retrieved: March, 2016].

[24] G. Brajnik, "Beyond Conformance: The Role of Accessibility Evaluation Methods," in 2nd International Workshop on Web Usability and Accessibility, IWWUA08, Auckland - New Zealand, 2008.

[25] G. Brajnik, "A comparative test of web accessibility evaluation method," Proc. 10th Int. ACM SIGACCESS Conference on Computers and Accessibility, ASSETS, 2008, pp. 113-120, doi: 10.1145/1414471.1414494.

[26] W3C, "Web Accessibility Evaluation Tools List," 2014. [Online]. Available: http://www.w3.org/WAI/ER/tools/. [retrieved: March, 2016].

[27] M. Vigo, J. Brown, and V. Conway, "Benchmarking web accessibility evaluation tools: measuring the harm of sole reliance on automated tests," in Proceedings of the 10th International Cross-Disciplinary Conference on Web Accessibility, New York, USA, 2013.

[28] AChecker, "Web Accessibility Checker," 2014. [Online]. Available: http://achecker.ca/checker/index.php/. [retrieved: March, 2016].

[29] TAW, "TAW3 Online," 2014. [Online]. Available: http://www.tawdis.net/ingles.html?lang=en/. [retrieved: March, 2016].

[30] W3C, "Techniques for WCAG 2.0," [Online]. Available: https://goo.gl/IpnCal. [retrieved: March, 2016].

[31] W3C, "Web Accessibility Evaluation Tools List," 2014. [Online]. Available: http://www.w3.org/WAI/ER/tools/. [retrieved: March, 2016].

[32] ISO, "ISO 9241-151:2008, Ergonomics of human-system interaction -- Part 151: Guidance on World Wide Web user interfaces," 15 05 2008. [Online]. Available: http://goo.gl/uLD3Fc. [retrieved: March, 2016].

[33] W3C, "Web Accessibility and Usability Working Together," 2010. [Online]. Available: https://www.w3.org/WAI/intro/usable. [retrieved: March, 2016].

[34] P. Morville and L. Rosenfeld, Information Architecture for the World Wide Web, 3rd Edition ed., O'Reilly, 2006.

[35] The William and Flora Hewlett Foundation, "Open Educational Resources: Breaking the Lockbox on Education," 2013. [Online]. Available: http://goo.gl/W8AovD. [retrieved: March, 2016]

[36] IEEE, "IEEE Standard for Learning Object Metadata," 2009. [Online]. Available: https://goo.gl/V9kgUE. [retrieved: March, 2016]

[37] LRMI, "Learning Resource Metadata Initiative," 2014. [Online]. Available: http://dublincore.org/dcx/lrmi-terms/1.1/. [retrieved: March, 2016]

[38] R. Navarrete and S. Luján-Mora, "Metadata in Open Educational Resources websites: a review from the perspective of disabled users' requirements," Proc. 6th International Conference on Education and New Learning Technologies (EDULEARN 2014) , Jul. 2014, pp.111-120

[39] S. Dietze, S. Sanchez-Alonso, H. Ebner, H. Qing Yu , D. Giordano, I. Marenzi, and B. Pereira Nunes, "Interlinking educational resources and the web of data: A survey of challenges and approaches," Emerald Program: electronic library and information systems, vol. 47, no. 1, 2013, pp. 60-91, doi: 10.1108/00330331211296312.

Interactive Gesture Chair

Muhammad Muhaiminul Islam, Shamsul Arefin, Hasan Mahmud, Md. Kamrul Hasan
Systems and Software Lab (SSL), Department of Computer Science and Engineering
Islamic University of Technology (IUT)
Dhaka, Bangladesh
e-mail:{foysol16, sajib312, hasan, hasank}@iut-dhaka.edu

Abstract— **Nowadays, computer operators and office workers have a sedentary lifestyle. Technology is continuously improving, but our actions become more mechanic. Office employees have to stay in front of the PC almost all the day long and this sedentary behavior is not good for their health. As a consequence, people of all ages suffer through health problems which are related to ergonomic factors. Doctors always suggest to take breaks and move during work hours to decrease the probability of a chronic disease. We are proposing a system to interact with the PC using a chair. By equipping a chair with motion sensing, the movement gesture of a user can be detected which can be used as input device for the PC. We have applied a machine learning algorithm to calculate the threshold for detecting three types of gestures (tilt backward, rotate right, rotate left) to control Windows Photo Viewer. The user evaluation shows that more than 80% of the users found it interesting and they achieved around 92% accuracy while controlling the application.**

Keywords—sedentariness, gesture chair, Ergonomic factors, HCI, MPU-6050

I. INTRODUCTION

During everyday office work, we generally control our computers with keyboard and mouse sitting in front of them. When we work in our office in front of computer, we spend most of our work time in a sedentary way. We remain seated when we are on our way to the office by car, during meetings, during lunch, etc. This sedentary behavior is considered as an important ergonomic factor which may lead to a variety of chronic diseases for people of all ages [23]. Due to prolonged seating, people may suffer from back pain, neck pain, etc. Therefore, many proposals have emerged to keep people moving during their work day. However, for most of the office workers, it is difficult to achieve a considerable reduction of the time spent seated within the office environment. To promote physical activity even in such sedentary situations, this work explores the possibilities of using an interactive office chair to smoothly integrate physical activity into the daily working routine. By equipping a flexible chair with a motion sensor, the movements of a person sitting on the chair can be tracked and transformed into input events that trigger various actions on a computer. Besides, interacting with computers for a long period of time is tiresome also, so there is a need of an alternate way to do the tasks other than regular mouse and keyboard operations. This way, the "Interactive Gesture Chair" becomes an input device that is ubiquitously embedded into the working environment and provides an office worker with the possibility to use the movements of his body for rotating, tilting or bouncing a chair to intuitively control operations on desk computers. . Considering health issues, in our proposed architecture, the user has to move his body which is at least better than staying a long period of time in the same position. Recently, Massachusetts Institute of Technology (MIT) have started working on chair gesture [11][14][15]. Utilizing these chair gestures into a frequently used application is challenging. The success of this 'interactive gesture chair' depends on proper integration of the gestures with a frequently used desktop application. We can see that 'Windows Photo Viewer' is an application which is frequently used to view photos by the people of all ages and professions such as teachers, students, researchers, office workers etc. We have integrated our 'Interactive Gesture Chair' with a customized Windows Photo Viewer to watch pictures considering the ergonomic issues, which will reduce the probability of developing chronic disease.

We have collected data from sensors attached with the chair and labelled them with gesture names (tilt backward, rotate right, rotate left). We applied decision tree algorithm to automatically calculate threshold values to determine gestures. Afterwards, these gestures are mapped with windows commands to control the photo viewer application.

The rest of the paper is structured as follows. In Section II, we present the related work. In Section III, we describe our system design. Section IV discusses the implementation and Section V presents the evaluation of our proposal. We conclude in Section VI.

II. RELATED WORKS

Nowadays people are trying to design some natural ways to interact with computers instead of mouse and keyboard. To follow that, people are equipping sensors with frequently used things to establish communication with a PC. A chair is one of the frequently used pieces of furniture to be equipped with sensors to use as input device of computer. In the previous works of Media Interaction Lab [14][21] they have used Gyroscope and Accelerometer to detect movement of the chair and controlled multimedia player by some defined gestures. Another chair based gesture detection [15] uses Lumia smartphone for getting sensors data which performs both music player control and Web browsing. The Unadorned Desk [22] is an example for this kind of interaction. It uses physical space around a desktop computer for mouse input. Internet Chair [6] was used for performing tilting, rotating gestures for browsing and navigation through Web pages. ChairIO [1] introduced chair based gaming control like joystick. The ChairMouse [3] translated natural chair rotation into cursor movement for effective navigation through large displays.

In all existing works, thresholding approach is applied to detect gestures. Thresholding does not work properly because the threshold was empirically determined which has some problems in case of gesture variation produced by various users of different weight and height. Thresholding does not give a universal threshold value that will work for every user. We have collected data of the people of different regions of the world such as Africa, Middle East and Asia and then we applied a decision tree algorithm. The decision tree would give better result than a threshold.

III. System Design

To detect the movements of the chair we need to equip the chair with accelerometer and gyroscope. For that we need a Magnetic Pickup Unit (MPU), MPU-6050 sensor. MPU-6050 is an Inertia Measurement Unit (IMU) sensor. Among many IMU sensors, we found that MPU 6050 to be the most reliable and accurate IMU sensor. Apart from being significantly cheaper than the other sensors, the MPU 6050 performs much better too. The MPU 6050 is a 6 DOF (Degrees of Freedom) or a six axis IMU sensor, which means that it gives six values as output: three values from the accelerometer and three from the gyroscope. The MPU 6050 is a sensor based on MEMS (Micro Electro Mechanical Systems) technology. Both the accelerometer and the gyroscope are embedded inside a single chip. This chip uses I2C (Inter Integrated Circuit) protocol for communication [23].

The MPU 6050 communicates with the Arduino through the I2C protocol. Arduino [24] is an open source framework, a mega board to read inputs from sensor such as MPU 6050. The MPU 6050 is connected to Arduino as shown in Figure 1.

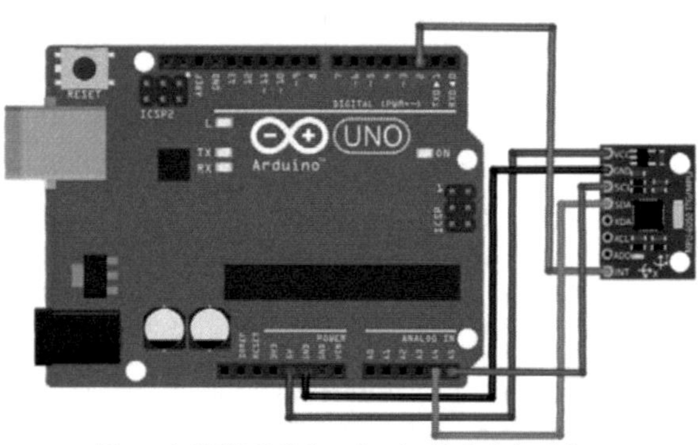

Figure 1. MPU 6050 interfaced with Arduino Mega

IV. Implementation

Our proposed system is shown in Figure 4. It is a portable system because we can move the chair anywhere while the sensors are accoutered at the back side of the chair. We have collected the data from the accelerometer and gyroscope for the people of different weights and ages for rotating right, rotating left and tilting back. Values have been passed through a Bluetooth device to PC from Arduino to analyze. We have used a machine learning algorithm which is a decision tree to find out the threshold value for 3 gestures (tilt backward, rotate right, rotate left). To apply a decision tree on our collected data we had to label our data by left, right, back and steady (no gesture). Before labeling our data we have discarded the first 200 data points from every gesture instance to remove noise. The main functionality of a machine learning algorithm is to classify the input data into a class. If an input data cannot be classified into any class then that input data is classified into no class. As 'no class' we have used 'steady' to define that the current input data cannot be classified into rotate left, rotate right or tilt back. After labeling the data, we made a file that includes only labeled data. We used that file as an input file for Weka [25] to run the decision tree on that labeled data. After running the decision tree on the labeled data, it generates a threshold value for every gesture as shown in Figure 3. We used that threshold values to define gestures. Using these defined three gestures, we have controlled Windows Photo Viewer. Rotate Right gesture is used to view next photo, rotate left gesture is used to view previous photo and Tilt Back Gesture is used to turn ON/OFF the slide show, as shown in Figure 2. The tabular representation of gesture mapping is shown in Table 1.

Figure 2. Definition of gestures

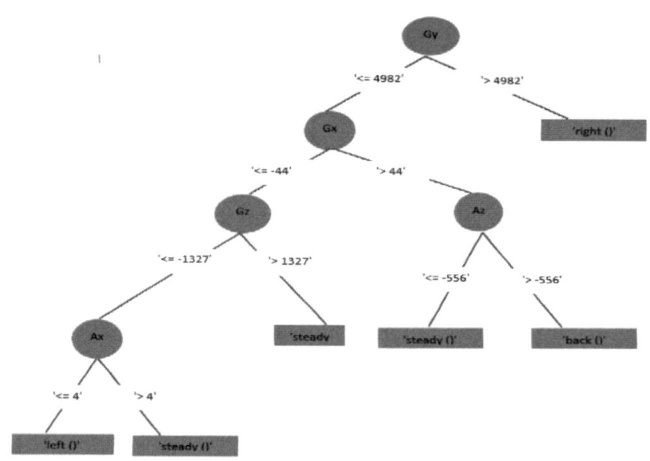

Figure 3. Result of decision tree

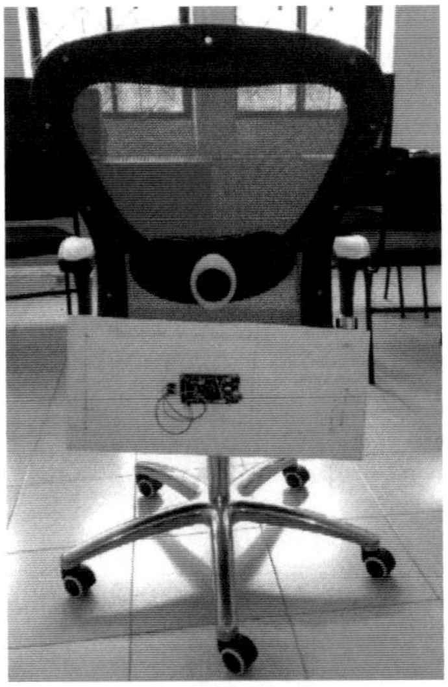

Figure 4. Back View of Chair

TABLE 1: TABULAR REPRESENTATION OF GESTURE MAPPING

Rotate left	To view previous photo
Rotate right	To view next photo
Tilt backward	To ON/OFF slide show

V. EVALUATION

The primary purpose of our evaluation was to evaluate the current system by end users to facilitate future change. We chose 10 users as participants to evaluate our system to different extent. They were selected based on their weight and height. Their weight was 46 to 146kg and height was 60 inch to 80 inch. Our experiment also shows that threshold depends on height and weight. That is why height and weight are important factors in gesture recognition. Participants were randomly assigned to perform some gestures from the set of defined gestures. We have defined so far rotate left, rotate right and tilt back gestures. For now we experimented with Windows Photo Viewer of Microsoft Windows 7. Some photos were selected and kept into a folder for this evaluation purpose. One of these photos was opened by Windows Photo Viewer. Then Windows Photo Viewer was controlled by the gestures, such as ON/OFF slide show, view next photo, view previous photo. Users performed various gestures in random order. Each of them performed different gestures for a specific duration of 300 seconds. During this time, the number of gestures detected for each user was slightly different. For example, one performed 70 gestures but another performed 56 gestures in 300 seconds. Also, we counted correct and incorrect detection of gestures. The error rate was around 5 per 60 gestures. There was another challenging issue of detecting tilt back gestures, people having more weight felt easy to perform the tilt back gesture. Users had to fill out a small questionnaire with various aspects of the experiment. We found almost 70-80% had found it interesting, 10-15% found it somehow cumbersome. Questionaries' also include some open ended questions about improving our system. Some said, it would be better if the program would have good graphical user interface. Some pointed out that, unintentional movement sometimes triggers meaningless gesture events. Participants seemed to be concerned about accidentally triggering actions on the computer through naturally occurring movements (e.g., fidgeting, stretching). Indeed, since users are constantly moving while seated on chair, a major challenge for chair-based interaction is how to effectively distinguish chair gestures from natural body movement that may occur unconsciously during regular work. An easy approach to avoid such unintentional input is to let the user decide when gesture input started by providing mechanisms to toggle gesture start or stop dynamically when they need. Some more manual mode-switching (e.g., pressing button on UI or maybe some voice controls) will be part of our future research. Moreover, some participants had bitter comments regarding the chair gestures as they became annoyed or tired when performing over a longer period of time. Since moving the whole body to perform gestures with an active chair involves more muscles than standard mouse or keyboard use, a certain level of fatigue may occur with frequently giving gesture input. However, we still can consider potential positive sides (i.e., breaking up the monotony, relaxing) over negative effects (i.e., fatigue, distraction) of the proposed gestural chair interaction.

VI. CONCLUSION AND FUTURE WORK

We designed a system considering the chair gestures as optional input modality so that people can use these gestures occasionally when they prefer to interact with computers. To do that a chair is accoutered with accelerometer and gyroscope sensors. These sensors data provides us the opportunity for real-time interaction with various types of computer applications. We applied decision tree to find a universal threshold on the sensor data to define gestures and we found a universal threshold for every gesture. For that we faced some challenges. One of the challenges was to detect tilt back gestures, people having more weight felt easy to perform the tilt back gesture but the people having less weight faced some difficulties to perform tilt back gesture. We have overcome this challenge by using decision tree algorithm. Another challenge was to distinguish chair gestures from natural body movement that may occur unconsciously during regular work. Therefore, in the future, we will attach an indicator which will tell the system when to apply gestures. Another challenge was to remove noise from sensor data. In the future, we will approach some other machine learning algorithms for improving detections of such gestures.

REFERENCES

[1] S. Beckhaus, K. Blom and M. Haringer , "ChairIO –The Chair-Based Interface. In Concepts and Technologies for Pervasive Games." 2007, 231–264.

[2] M. Van Beurden, W. Ijsselsteijn and Y. De Kort. , "User Experience of Gesture Based Interfaces: A Comparison with Traditional Interaction Methods on Pragmatic and Hedonic Qualities." GW 2011.

[3] A. Endert , P. Fiaux , H. Chung, M. Stewart, C. Andrews , C. North , "ChairMouse: Leveraging Natural Chair Rotation for Cursor Movement on Large, High-Resolution Displays". ACM alt.CHI, 2011.

[4] T. Springer , "The Future of Ergonomic Office Seating." Knoll WorkplaceResearch,2010. [https://www.knoll.com/media/477/936/wp_future_ergonomic_seating.pdf]

[5] M. Karam and M. C. schraefel. . , "A taxonomy of gestures in human computer interactions." Technical report ECSTR-IAM05-009, Electronics and Computer Science, University of Southampton, 2005.

[6] M. Cohen, "The Internet Chair." International Journal of Human Computer Interaction 15, 2 (2003).

[7] I. Daian, A. M. Van Ruiten, A. Visser and S. Zubić , "Sensitive Chair: A Force Sensing Chair with Multimodal Real Time Feedback via Agent." In Proc. ECCE '07, ACM Press (2007).

[8] N. Owen, A. Bauman, and W. Brown , "Too much sitting: a novel and important predictor of chronic disease risk?" In British Journal of Sports Medicine 43, 2 (2009), 81–83.

[9] J. Forlizzi, C. DiSalvo, J. Zimmerman, B. Mutlu and A. Hurst, "The SenseChair: The lounge chair as an intelligent assistive device for elders." In Proc. DUX '05, AIGA (2005), 31.

[10] R. J. K. Jacob, "Eye Movement-Based Human-Computer Interaction Techniques: Toward Non-Command Interfaces." In Advances in Human-Computer Interaction (1993), 151–190.

[11] K. Probst, J. Leitner, F. Perteneder, M. Haller, A. Schrempf, and J. Glöckl, "Active Office: Towards an Activity-Promoting Office Workplace Design." In Proc. CHI EA '12, ACM Press (2012), 2165–2170

[12] D. Saffer, "Designing Gestural Interfaces." O'Reilly Media, 2008.

[13] H. Pohland R. Murray-Smith , "Focused and Casual Interactions: Allowing Users to Vary Their Level of Engagement." CHI 2013, 2223–2232.

[14] K. Probst, D. Lindlbauer, P. Greindl, M. Trapp, M. Haller , B. Schwartz, and A. Schrempf, "Rotating, Tilting, Bouncing: Using an Interactive Chair to Promote Activity in Office Environments." CHI EA 2013, 79–84

[15] K. Probst, D. Lindlbauer, M. Haller, B. Schwartz, and A. Schrempf, "A Chair as Ubiquitous Input Device: Exploring Semaphoric Chair Gestures for Focused and Peripheral Interaction." CHI 2014.

[16] T. Baudeland M. Beaudouin-Lafon, "Charade: Remote Control of Objects Using Free-hand Gestures." InCommunications of the ACM 36, 7 (1993).

[17] T. Vanhala, V. Surakka, and J. Anttonen, "Measuring Bodily Responses to Virtual Faces with a Pressure Sensitive Chair." In Proc. NordiCHI '08, ACM Press (2008), 555–559.

[18] S. Nanayakkara, L. Wyse, and E. A. Taylor, "Effectiveness of the haptic chair in speech training." In Proc. ASSETS '12, ACM Press (2012).

[19] B. MacKay, D. Dearman, K. Inkpen, and C. Watters, "Walk'n Scroll: A Comparison of Software-based Navigation Techniques for Different Levels of Mobility." In Proc. MobileHCI '05, ACM Press (2005), 183–190.

[20] K. Probst, D. Lindlbauer, M. Haller, B. Schwartz, A. Schrempf, 2014. , "Exploring the Potential of Peripheral Interaction through Smart Furniture", in Peripheral Interaction: Shaping the Research and Design Space, Workshop at CHI 2014.

[21] D. Hausen, S. Boring, and S. Greenberg, "The Unadorned Desk: Exploiting the Physical Space around a Display as an Input Canvas." INTERACT 2013, 140–158

[22] W. F. Booth, Ph.D., K. C. Roberts, Ph.D. and J. M. Laye, Ph.D. , "Lack of exercise is a major cause of chronic diseases." Compr Physiol. 2012 April ; 2(2): 1143–1211.

[23] Inter Integrated Circuit (I2C) protocol: http://i2c.info/

[24] Arduino introduction: https://www.arduino.cc/en/Guide/Introduction

[25] Weka 3: Data Mining Software in Java: http://www.cs.waikato.ac.nz/~ml/weka/index.html

Is Aging the New Disease?

Anita Woll
Department of Informatics
University of Oslo
Oslo, Norway
email: anitwo@ifi.uio.no

***Abstract*—In this paper, we discuss the phenomenon of aging in relation to Hofmann's three perspectives on disease including disease, illness and sickness role. We further discuss how the introduction of technology supported elderly care changes our perspectives on aging into becoming more disease focused. Especially, in user situations where technology supported care is introduced in order to prevent and reduce individual risks of prospective elders at risk of becoming wanderers, or who need support in order to avoid- or reduce outcomes of falls. Thus, even if early introduction of technology supported care is recommended in order to realize assistive technology to its potential benefits, we raise critical concerns in how this also can change our view of aging from being a natural process of life into a disease focused phenomenon.**

Keywords-aging; disease perspective; assistive technology; social implications of technology use.

I. INTRODUCTION

What classifies a condition to be defined as a disease? Moreover, is aging a disease? Depending on whom we are addressing these questions to, we can expect different answers according to Hofmann [1]. There are well established international classification systems such as the International Classification of Diseases (ICD) that define and classify diseases on the basis on a minimum set of criteria [2]. However, even the ICD system changes over time as new diseases constantly are introduced, and some diseases are reclassified as rather being natural phenomenon as new knowledge is gained. Hofmann [1] debates that the classification systems and the criteria that define diseases are fluctuating over culture – historical time, and that these changes are based on our worldview, or gained knowledge and science. For example, homosexuality was formerly classified as a disease in Norway until the year of 1977 [1]. Homosexuality was viewed as a deviation from normality, and one of the primary reasons for classifying homosexuality as a disease was to avoid the homosexuals in feeling stigmatized [1]. Moreover, those who were gay were not able to sexual reproduce humankind. However, as new technology, knowledge and science were developed, homosexuality was over time viewed as a normal sexual orientation, and human reproduction is achievable as new technology can treat many of those who are infertile.

The classification of a condition can be made from different perspectives on disease by the characteristics to whom that are represented: the medical health professionals (*disease*), the person who is being ill (*illness*) and the society (*sickness role*) [1], see table 1 below. The different terms presented in table 1 can have different departures of how we view the phenomenon of aging, and these perspectives are important to understand initially in order to discuss if we could classify aging as a disease or rather as a natural process of life. The term *illness* is associated with the person who is experiencing the negative subjective illness [1]. This negative experience of being ill can be present by the subjective experience of pain and suffering, or symptoms or a collection of symptoms (syndrome) [1]. The term *disease* is reserved to the medical professionals who based on objective signs and markers are able to classify a condition according to the established classification systems of diseases and related health problems (e.g., ICD [2]) [1]. For example, a person can experience to be ill, without necessary the health professionals approval of the illness as being a disease. Moreover, the term *sickness* role is associated with a certain social behavior that is colored by phenomena such as social status and privileges. Thus, the sickness role is defined by norms and values based on inter-subjective relationships within the society [1].

TABLE I. THE THREE CENTRAL PERSPECTIVES ON DISEASE ACCORDING TO HOFMANN [1]. COPYRIGHT: HOFMANN [1, P.134]

Term	Meaning	Characteristics
Illness, To be ill	(Negative) subjective experience of the person who is being ill.	Pain/Suffering, Symptoms, Syndromes (collection of symptoms).
Disease, To have a disease	Signs and classifications observed and identified by health personnel.	Signs, Marker.
Sickness, Sickness role.	To be perceived as having a sickness role in a society.	Social behavior.

However, why all this eager to define a specific condition as a disease? The main reason is that a disease diagnosis gives an ill person welfare benefits including the rights for cure (if existing) or treatment (to regain health, reduce pain, reduce risks, prolong life/ life-sustaining treatments etc.), as well as a pause from duties and financial benefits, such as paid sick leave [1]. Moreover, the society represented by the government influences the redistribution of tax money including making socioeconomics decisions. For example, the government decides which diagnoses are the most valuable to treat according to the Diagnosis-Related Group (DRG) system [5] or which diagnosis that qualifies for retirement. The government also decides indirectly which diseases should gain more research finances in order to obtain new knowledge for improved treatment.

The health care system can also have an interest in treating those who are most valuable treating according to performance-based financing of health care services as defined by the DRG system. Furthermore, the health care system is influenced professionally by the pressure from the society and is forced to keep focus on diseases that are valued as important research areas / grant areas. These few examples illustrate the complexity of defining a specific condition as a disease or not, and show that there are several stakeholders involved, and that defining a condition as a new disease has, among others, individual-, socio-economical and medical consequences. Thus, the relationship between the different perspectives on *disease*, *illness* and *sickness* is highly intertwined as they all influence and rely on each other.

A growing elderly population demands us to design new ways of delivering health care in order to develop a sustainable elderly care systems based on cost – efficient use of scarce health care resources and shortage of health care professionals. Several initiatives have been explored in order to provide care services to more care takers by less use of resources [3]. Thus, the introduction of assistive technology is valued as an essential instrument in future elderly care; but then we have to succeed in incorporate ICT – supported elderly care in the overall elderly care trajectory – and not just in specific acute phases, e.g., as a follow-up intervention after hospital admission [4]. There are a number of ethical dilemmas by the introduction of technology supported elderly care. Prior studies that have touched on these dilemmas are concerned about concepts such as intrusion of the privacy, stigma of assistive technology use, or (false) trust in the safety of technology use.

In many studies, the conclusion is that the ethical implications need to be balanced with the personal gain of assistive technology use, e.g., the mastery of living as an independent individual. This paper adds to the existing HCI literature by expanding the knowledge on how technology use within elderly care can have personal, medical and social impacts on our view of aging. Thus, this paper aims to make a contribution by widening the debate on ethical aspects concerning assistive technology use among elders. We are doing so by discussing aging in the light of the following research questions (RQ):

RQ1: Is aging a disease according to Hofmann's three perspectives on disease?

RQ2: Are the three perspectives on disease and aging changed when assistive technology is introduced to support the aging population?

The paper is organized as follows: Section 1 introduces the research objective of this paper. Section 2 presents the background. Section 3 summarizes the related work. Section 4 discusses how the different perspectives on disease and aging are changed when technology is introduced into the caring for elders. Section 5 presents summary of this paper.

II. BACKGROUND

In this section, we present and discuss the three perspectives on disease in relation to the phenomenon of aging.

A. The disease perspective

Medical professions define diseases after well-established international medical classification systems such as ICD (specialist health care), the International Classification of Primary Care (ICPC) (primary care) and Diagnostic and Statistical Manual of Mental Disorders (DSM) (psychiatry) [1]. These classification systems hold a number of criteria that could coincide with the subjective experience of aging including physical dysfunction, progressive impairment, various treatment and preventive efforts, changes in social structure and deviations in social behavior [1]. Therefore, several of these classification criteria could diagnose age-related symptoms and signs of aging into various diseases. However, a sum or combinations of various criteria gathered from the classification system are not sufficient or necessary in order to define something as a disease. Nevertheless, aging is defined as decline in organs and functions; as a result of normal arts and age-related biological processes, thus these processes cannot be said to be disease related nor a deviation from normality in the aging population [1]. It is also important to note that most elderly persons actually live a more or less active life. Statistics Norway [6] reports that as many as 74 % of the elderly Norwegian population (above 67 years of age) are non-users of municipal health care services. Therefore, aging is not a disease viewed as an isolated phenomenon. However, the reminding 26 % of elderly persons that are health care receivers have additional diseases [7]. These numbers display that it is important to separate aging and diseases / age-related diseases.

In the Global Burden of Disease Study 2013 (GBD 2013) [8], there is no death cause referred to as old age. However, old age could be indirectly the cause of death, but the death cause is always disease specific. The eight most frequent death causes in Norway 2013 are listed below, in addition to the number of deaths in parentheses [9]:

1. Myocardial infarction and other ischemic heart disease (7290)
2. Alzheimer's disease (4126)
3. Stroke (4020)
4. Lung cancer (2283)
5. COPD (2176)

6. Pneumonia (2083)
7. Colon cancer (1999)
8. Fall (incl. hip fractures and other injuries) (1193)

Alzheimer's diseases are the second most frequent cause of death in Norway in 2013. Alzheimer's diseases are according to the Alzheimer's organization *"not a normal part of aging"*[10], however the most dominant risk factor for Alzheimer's is aging, as the majority of persons who are suffering from these diseases are from 65 years of age [10]. However, there are exceptions as early onset of these diseases can appear in younger years and the Alzheimer's Association [10] says that almost 5 % of these incidents are present already from the age of 40 – 50 years.

Aging increases the risk of diseases and death [11], thus for some health professionals, e.g., the geneticists, increased risk for diseases and death are enough to define the cause as a disease. Hence, preventive efforts are made in order to avoid development of diseases, e.g. surgical treatment can be done in order to reverse or reduce the risks for hereditary breast-ovarian cancer syndrome by undergoing mastectomies and/or remove the ovaries in cases where the geneticists have identified abnormal BRCA1 gene [12]. However, as discussed above; aging and diseases are not objectively concurrent. Aging is rather a natural biological process, and currently there is no cure that can stop the process of aging, even if some treatments give promises of slowing down the process of aging [13] [14]. Thus, in order to stop aging you have to die young, which is not normality in the western world where the life expectancy is set to be approx. 82 year as average for both genders [15].

Nevertheless, the outcome of relatively harmless diseases such as the seasonal flu have much worse prognosis for elderly people above 65 years of age as their human immune defenses weaken with aging [16]. Similar can other minor diseases cause major health consequences for elderly people, e.g., urinary tract infection and constipation can lead to acute delirium [17]. Other examples are; the mortality caused by hip fracture for elderly Norwegian is as high as 25 % of 10 000 registered incidents per year. The mortality percentage is not directly linked to the fracture itself, but the strains of the fracture are worsening their general health and sickness [18]. Hence, the elderly people's vulnerability and mortality after falls including hip fractures is present as the eight most frequent death cause in Norway in 2013 [9].

No general practitioner (GP) or specialist health care doctor would give a sick leave to a working person of 60 years solely based on observed signs and markers of aging. There has to be an additional disease present. Thus, based on the disease perspective; aging is not a disease.

B. *The illness perspective*

Albert, Munson and Resnik [19] state that a *"...disease is best understood as a departure from normal functioning"* [19, p. 160]. What is the characteristic of normal functioning for aging people are probably a subjective perspective, as well as depending on the context and individual's experiences of what is normal functioning. An active younger person that exercises three times a week is more likely to keep on exercising at older age, but at reduced and adjusted pace. However, even if the normal functioning is subjective experienced as being abnormal compare to younger years of life, the abnormality is still a normal process within the aging population. The onset of the biological aging starts already at 20 years of age, where aging is characterized by a gradual reduction of the body's organs and functions, which is said to be 50 % reduced at 70 years of age [7]. However, this reduction of organs and functions is not classified as a disease from the disease perspective of medical professionals, however persons of old age have increased vulnerability for diseases, mortality and stress [7]. Additionally there is also present a mental and social aging process that onset later in life. Mental aging refers to reduced memory capacity, and the subjective experience of everything going slower than it did before. Social aging is associated with a decrease in social contact. The reduction in social life is especially present after retirement. The energy level of elderly persons decreases, and even if wanting to participate in social activity, elderly persons are often cutting down on social networking, which can make them vulnerably for loneliness and isolation [7].

The *senior report* of Oslo municipality [20] has brought attention to active aging. In doing so, the health government in Oslo has emphasized that each elderly person has a responsibility for self- caring to the extent it is possible, and that families should increase their involvement in the caring for their elderly relatives. This is comparable to the global health movement of developing strategies for successful aging, whereas the concept embraces aging as something positive, and refers to physical, mental and social well-being in older age [21][22]. However, prior studies have displayed findings that the elderly people's subjective experiences of quality of life are weighted higher than the absence of diseases [21] [23].

The notion of successful aging aims to develop strategies to increased adaption of aging well. These strategies vary over time as new knowledge is gathered. However, lifestyles strategies such as diets, physical exercising, non - substance use, social activities, prevention or treatment of depression, in addition to positive attitude and reduction of stress are some examples [22], [24], [25]. The notion of successful or active aging can also have an opposite effect for those elderly people who are not mastery aging well. Especially, can this be the case for those elderly persons who have additional diseases. Pushed to the extreme; the society can blame those elderly who have not lived their life according to the successful aging strategies. We know that factors such as socio – economics can have impacts of life expectancy [26] and for some elderly people the society's expectations of active aging and increased self – care activities cannot be fulfilled. Subjective life quality for some elderly persons can also be that aging is experienced as illness as decline in general health, limited capabilities and/or functional abilities make them struggle with daily life activities, and we know that the transition from work life to pension life can be experienced as brutal for some [25] [27]. The experiences from someone's younger life are also likely to affect the subjective experience of older age.

The poet and philosopher Ralph Waldo Emerson (1803–1882) is famously quoted for "*All diseases run into one, old age*" that has origin from the Emerson's essay Circle (1841). Emerson's somehow extreme description of old age can be interpreted as old age leads to the only "disease" that none human are able to escape, as death is the only fixed and known outcome of life. Other translations could be that the author argues for the fact that it is the sum of diseases or lived life that is the most essential factor of our final experience of old age.

The illness perspective is a subjective perspective, thus people of old age may define aging as an illness if they experiencing aging as painful and negative. However, most elderly people (74 %) do not have a need for public health care services according to Statistics Norway [6], so the majority of elderly Norwegians are likely to think of aging as a natural process of life.

C. *The sickness perspective*

One understanding of the perspective of sickness is that it is a social constructed phenomenon as the notion of age has different meanings and values within cultures and nations [27]. Thus, there is a belief that Eastern and Asian culture value and honor the wisdom of their elderly people to a greater extent than the industrialized Western countries – however there are scarce literatures supporting this hypothesis according to Löckenhoff and co - authors [27]. Moreover, the western world has been criticized for their youth focused societies, where cultural traditions have outdated elderly persons as they retire from work life [27].

The aging population has in past decades been stigmatized by the view of elderly people being a burden for the society, especially has this been the case in several Western countries [27]. This negative value of the aging population can also be reinforced by the mass media's focuses and stressing about how to cope with the growing proportion of elderly people in the society in conjunction with scarce health care resources and shortage of health care professionals. Moreover, there have been tendencies that research studies have focused on the negative aspects of aging where elderly people have been viewed as more care needy in opposite to resourceful human beings. Several contributors have in resent time claimed that aging is in fact a disease, and should therefore be treated [28] [29]. Consequently, Caplan [28] requires the society to put in extensive resources to do research on how to cure aging so we can live longer under the assumption that the cure of aging also includes maintenance of the younger people's health and quality of life. However, this standpoint brings up ethically dilemmas that conflicts with the earth's sustainability, and is sensitive as many people on the earth struggles to survive their 60 years. One of the Caplan's argument for curing aging is that premature born babies get treatment, which Caplan argues are conflicting with the evolution theory and survival of the fittest – thus he questions why not elderly people should be saved from dying [28]. However, there is a different between premature babies that have a potential for life and human reproduction versus elderly persons who have lived a life and are done with reproduction. It is also a question of prioritization of scarce health care resources, and curing aging should not be on the top list of health care issues that need to be resolved.

The sickness perspective is based on norms from the inter-subjective relationships within the society. The society may define aging as a sickness when they still are young, or are experiencing signs of aging – or making effort in slowing down the aging processes with various measures. However, the society's sickness perspective of aging is rather linked to additional diseases such as Alzheimer's diseases and other age-related diseases, so per definition aging as an isolated phenomenon is not classified as a sickness itself. Thus, aging is not sickness from the sickness role perspective.

In the previous sections, we have discussed how aging can be classified according to the various perspectives on disease, illness or sickness role. We argue that none of the three perspectives is defining aging as a disease. However, we understand that from a subjective experience; elderly persons can have own experience of aging as being an illness. Further in this paper, we want to discuss if the introduction of assistive technology influence our discussion of aging being a natural process of life.

III. RELATED WORK

There are no other HCI studies that have explored upon the different perspectives of diseases in regard to the phenomenon of aging and technology use. However, several studies from interdisciplinary research communities have examined various ethical aspects of assistive technology use, often in the context of people with dementia and Alzheimer's diseases. These research contributions are focused on concepts and issues in regard to the following: autonomy [30] [31] [32] [33] [34] [35] [36] [37], privacy issues [38] [39] [40], stigma of assistive technology use [41] [42] [43], affordance [44] [45] and safety [46] [47] [48].

However, Greenhalgh and co-authors [30] discuss illness and frailty in the living body by use of phenomenology. They are doing so in order to develop a phenomenologically and socio-materially informed theoretical model of assistive technology adoption and use by older people. However, they do not discuss aging in the light of the different perspectives on diseases, but rather how the experienced body influences the technology use and appropriation. The authors [30] argue that providers of assistive living technologies are not supporting the users in coping with their illness in everyday life activities. Moreover, the authors [30] state that introduction of technologies in order to support for independent living require for solutions that support the users in "*think with things*" [p. 86] to increase usability and user experiences.

IV. APPLYING THE DIFFERENT PERSPECTIVES ON DISEASE ON TECHNOLOGY – SUPPORTED ELDERLY CARE

The classification of a disease often comes along with the fact that "*something can be done*" [1, p. 24]. Hofmann [1] refers to infertility and the innovation of assisted reproduction as one of the driven forces of redefining infertility as being a disease. This, according to Hofmann [1], indicates that in situations where something can be done in order to "*control or intervene*" [p. 24] we are willing to include these into our disease perspective [1].

Technical solutions that aim to support elderly persons with Alzheimer's diseases or technology to prevent falls for those having fall tendency are important interventions in order to reduce the risk of mortality. Hence, these types of technologies could fit into the prescription of having the function to control or intervene in order to reduce the risk for accidents with severe outcome. Especially considering that Alzheimer's diseases are the second most frequent cause of death among elderly people, and falls are reported as the eight frequent cause of death. But then again, Alzheimer's diseases are not a natural part of aging. However, in order to succeed in incorporating assistive technology into the overall ICT- supported elderly care system it is considered beneficial to introduce technology at early onset of old age, e.g. before the elderly person is diagnosed with Alzheimer's diseases. However, the person has to be at risk for Alzheimer's diseases if defending a formal consent of installing door controller or other technical solutions such as Global Positioning System (GPS) to either use technology for diagnostic purposes, or to control and prevent accidents if the person has a social behavior that make the family concerned.

A. *From the disease perspective: Introduction of assistive technology to support the aging population*

Delegation of health care services to technology in the caring for elderly persons brings up a number of ethical dilemmas, especially in relation to protecting the elderly people's right to privacy. It is also important to emphasize that use of assistive technology is not merely affecting the elderly persons, but also bring the elderly peoples' families and public health care staff within its scope. For example, technologies that alert in a pre-defined situation require an infrastructure where "someone" responds to the alert or acts when the collected information requires some action. That "someone" could be health care staff and/or family, which means that they also need to familiarize themselves with the introduced technology. And the housing – oriented care system has a motivation for including the family to a greater extent in the care network – as past institutionalization of care services has resulted in the family being less involved in practical matter or in the caring for their relatives [49]. The phenomenon of aging has advanced into becoming increasingly disease focused from the perspective of disease in user cases where the GP and municipal health care service make a formal decision of introducing assistive technology for the purpose of reducing the risks of potential accidents and/or diseases.

B. *From the illness perspective: Introduction of assistive technology to support the aging population*

A home is perceived as a private sphere and should be protected against the health authorities intruding with mandatory sensors for monitoring purposes. Thus, it is a danger that introduction of assistive technology within the home will do something about the elderly residents' perceptions of the home.

The purpose and gain of the elderly person using assistive technology should be weighed against the intrusion of the elderly person's private sphere. In a Norwegian Official Report [3], it is argued that use of technology within welfare services can give the elderly possibilities to extend their time living as self-reliant in their private homes. Thus, technology that controls or intervenes in order to prevent diseases and mortality can slow down age related diseases and prevent risks for accidents. However, elderly persons may also experience the introduction of assistive technology as an intrusion to the home, as well as they may fear that technology is replacing social contact. This is especially true in user cases where technology is introduced in a top-down approach from the public health care system.

Moreover, the elderly persons could have increased negative subjective experience of being ill, or get the impression of being vulnerable for diseases and accidents as all these interventions must have a purpose. Thus, from the illness perspective of aging, aging has an increased illness-focus by the preventive efforts being made in the homes of elderly persons in order to reduce the risks for additional diseases and/or accidents.

C. *From the sickness perspective: Introduction of assistive technology to support the aging population*

In this scenario, it is essential to address the question: assistive technology for whom? As in the long run who are the benefiters of the increased ICT supported elderly care. Is it the community, health care system, patient / user or their families? It could also appear that there might be potential conflicts of interest between these stakeholders. The society will benefit from a more efficient use of scarce health resources, and use of technology in the elderly care will generate a need for additional manpower, which again will reduce the work load on health care staff. The Health governance is forced to develop a more cost efficient elderly care system as increased safety efforts in the home can reduce repeated hospital admissions and decrease the need for long term stay in nursing homes.

The future plan of having a health watch call center for more efficient treatment and safety system will require access to shared patient health record systems within all levels of the health care services. Thus, all these preventive efforts are turning elderly persons who may not have any health care needs into potential users or patients of a health watch call center.

The families of elderly persons can use public technology for remote visits and then feel less guilty of not going on a home visits to their loved ones. Thus, from the sickness - role perspective of aging, aging has got an increased sickness-focus by the preventive efforts being made in the homes of elderly persons in order to reduce the risks for additional diseases – and the society's need of prolonging the time elderly persons can live in their ordinary homes.

It is also a dilemma to use the society's scarce health resources on elderly persons who are considered as non-users of health care services for preventive purposes.

The resources used on preventive measures can pay off in the long run if the elderly persons have reduced need for complex health care services in the future. However, there is a lack of research that explores upon the health economics gains of implementing assistive technology into the overall elderly care.

The perspectives on disease and the relationship between disease, illness and sickness role are changed when assistive technology is introduced as an incorporated part of the ICT-supported elderly care for preventive efforts when no other diseases are identified, see figure 1 (as Appendix). The reason is because assistive technology is also introduced into the homes of elderly person who have no health care needs – but who are at risk of diseases or accidents that can have fatal outcome. Thus, preventive measures made to control or intervene in the private homes of elderly persons give an increase disease focus on aging.

However, this has to be separated from user cases where assistive technology is introduced in order to support elderly person with additional diseases such as known Alzheimer's diseases – the technology is then a treatment measures in order to support additional disease and not aging. Thus, it is important to recognize that it is a difference between aging and assistive technology usage for preventive measures supporting "healthy" elderly persons, and aging and assistive technology usage in user situation where the elderly person has additional diseases that need to be controlled or intervene for safety reasons or treatment purposes.

V. SUMMARY

In this paper, we have discussed aging in relation to the three perspectives on disease including disease, illness and sickness role by addressing two research questions:

RQ1: Is aging a disease according to Hofmann's three perspectives on disease?

RQ2: Are the three perspectives on disease and aging changed when assistive technology is introduced to support the aging population?

Thus, we argue that the phenomenon of aging is not a disease according to Hofmann's three perspectives of disease when looking at aging as an isolated phenomenon. Thus, aging is acknowledged as a natural process of life in regard to RQ1. It is also emphasized that aging and ordinary diseases / age–related diseases need to be separated as the majority of elderly persons in Norway (74%) are non-users of public health care services. Moreover, we recognize that even if aging increases the risks for diseases and death; diseases like Alzheimer's diseases are still not a normal part of aging.

We have also discussed further how the introduction of assistive technology affects our perspectives on aging as being a natural process of life in order to address RQ2. Especially, in user situations where the technology is introduced to prevent and reduce individual risks, such as technical efforts made to support potential wanderers, or persons with fall tendencies. We argue that the phenomenon of aging gets an increased disease focus when applying all the different perspectives of disease. Especially, in cases where assistive technology is introduced to "healthy" elderly persons who have no ordinary diseases or age – related diseases, but who are at risk of getting diseases.

Prior research studies have brought attention to other aspects of assistive technology use, such as privacy, stigma and safety. We recognize use of Hofmann's disease perspectives as highly informative in order to bring the ethical debate further and by this highlight other aspects of assistive technology use within the elderly care.

Future research needs to be aware of how the move of assistive technology into the homes of elderly people can challenge our perspectives of aging as being a disease. Thus, if assistive technology for preventive purposes is scaled to a larger proportion of elderly persons, we need to re-debate if turning aging into a disease is actually beneficial for us as a society.

"*Since life itself is a universally fatal sexually transmitted disease, living it to the full demands a balance between reasonable and unreasonable risk*" [50, p. 44].

ACKNOWLEDGMENT

The author wants to acknowledge the Norwegian Research Council for the grant 222011 titled "*Developing new Smart house Technology to support and assist elderly in private and public spaces at Care + housing.*"

REFERENCES

[1] B. Hofmann, What is diease? 2nd ed., Oslo: Gyldendal Akademisk, 2014.

[2] International Classification of Diseases (ICD), World Health Organization, version 2016, retrieved October 2015. Access from: http://apps.who.int/classifications/icd10/browse/2016/en

[3] Ministry of Education and Research, NOU 2011:11 – Innovation in care, Ministry of Health and Care Services, Oslo, 2011.

[4] A.Woll and T. E. Bratteteig, Design of an elderly care trajectory for increased accessibility and user support of housing oriented care services. Unpublished.

[5] The Directorate of Health, Retrived: November 2015 https://helsedirektoratet.no/finansieringsordninger/innsatsstyrt-finansiering-isf-og-drg-systemet/drg-systemet

[6] Statistic Norway, Elders use of health care services. Retrived: November 2015, Oslo: Statisics Norway.

[7] The Norwegian Medical Association (NMA), "Knowledge about elders and their dieases", retrieved: October 2015 Access from:

http://legeforeningen.no/Emner/Andre-emner/Publikasjoner/Statusrapporter/statusrapport-om-situasjonen-i-helsetjenesten-nar-du-blir-gammel-og-ingen-vil-ha-deg/kapittel-2-kunnskap-om-eldre-og-eldres-sykdommer/

[8] GBD 2013, Global, regional, and national age–sex specific all-cause and cause-specific mortality for 240 causes of death, 1990–2013: a systematic analysis for the Global Burden of Disease. Study 2013, retrieved: October 2015. Access from: http://www.thelancet.com/pdfs/journals/lancet/PIIS0140-6736(14)61682-2.pdf

[9] The Norwegain Institute of Public Health, These are the death cause in Norway and the rest of the world - Findings from the international burden of disease project, retrieved: October 2015, Access from: http://www.fhi.no/eway/default.aspx?pid=239&trg=Area_7064&Main_6157=6261:0:25,9086&MainContent_6261=7064:0:25,9086&Area_7064=6178:113361::0:7065:1:::0:0

[10] Alzheimer's Association, "What Is Alzheimer's?" Retrived: October 2015. Access from: http://www.alz.org/alzheimers_disease_what_is_alzheimers.asp

[11] D. Harman, "The Aging Process: Major Risk Factor for Disease and Death" Proc. of the National Academy of Sciences of the United States of America, vol. 88, No. 12 (Jun. 15, 1991), 1991, pp. 5360-5363

[12] T. B. Bevers et al, "Breast Cancer Risk Reduction", version 2.2015 clinical practice guidelines in oncology clinical practice guidelines in oncology. Journal of National Comprehensive Cancer Network, 13, 2015, pp.880-915

[13] D. Gems, "What is anti-aging treatment", Experimental Gerontology, vol. 58, 2014, pp.14–18.

[14] National Institute on Aging, "Can We Prevent Aging?", U.S. department of health and human services, 2012.

[15] UN data, Life expectancy Norway 2015, retrieved: October 2015. Access from http://www.globalis.no/Statistikk/Levealder

[16] Center for diseases control and prevention (CDC), retrived: October 2015. Access from: http://www.cdc.gov/flu/about/disease/65over.htm

[17] Oslo University Hospital (OUS), Method book for specialists in internal medicine: Delirium, acute confusional, retrived: October 2015, Access from http://www.helsebiblioteket.no/retningslinjer/metodebok/geriatri/delirium-akutt-forvirring

[18] NRK, Thousands elders die after a hip fracture. Retrieved 18. October 2015. Access from: http://www.nrk.no/livsstil/tusenvis-dor-etter-hoftebrudd-1.12176988

[19] D. A. Albert, R. Munson, M. D. Resnik, Reasoning in medicine. Baltimore, 1988, MD: Johns Hopkins University Press.

[20] Senior report, Oslo Municipality, retrived: october 2014, Access from:http://www.sak.oslo.kommune.no/dok/Vedlegg%5C2014_05%5C1049733_1_1.PDF

[21] J. W. Rowe and R. L. Kahn (1997), "Successful aging", The Gerontologist, vol. 37 (4), 1997, pp 433-440.

[22] S. Katz, (2013) "Active and Successful Aging. Lifestyle as a Gerontological Idea." Recherches sociologiques et anthropologiques vol. 44(1), 2013, pp.33-49.

[23] J. F. Fries, "Reducing Disability in Older Age." JAMA, vol. 288 (24): 2002, pp. 3164–6. doi:10.1001/jama.288.24.3164. PMID 12495399

[24] D. V. Jeste, M. Ardelt, D. Blazer, H. C. Kraemer, G. Vaillant, T. W. Meeks, (2010). Expert Consensus on Characteristics of Wisdom: A Delphi Method Study. The Gerontologist, Vol. 50(5) 2010, pp. 668–80. doi:10.1093/geront/gnq022. PMC 2937249. PMID 20233730.

[25] K.A. Hamblin, "Changes to Policies for Work and Retirement in EU15 Nations (1995- 2005): An Exploration of Policy Packages for the 50-plus Cohort", International Journal of Ageing and Later Life, vol. 5(1): 2010, pp. 13-43.

[26] S. S. Bassuk, L. F. Berkman, B. C. Amick (2002) "Socioeconomic status and mortality among the elderly: findings from four US communities", Am J Epidemiology, vol. 155(6), 2002, pp. 520-33.

[27] C. Lökenhoff, D. S. Lee, K. M. L. Buckener, R. O. Moreira, S. J. Martinez, M. Q. Sun , "Cross-Cultural Differences in Attitudes about aging: Moving beyond the East – West dichotomy." S.T. Cheng et al (eds.) *Successful aging*, 2015, DOI 10.1007/978-94-017-9331-5_19.

[28] A.L. Caplan (2005). "Death as an unnatural process", Science and Society, Vol. 6(1), 2005, pp. 72–75. doi: 10.1038/sj.embor.7400435 PMCID: PMC1369280

[29] T. Greenhalgh, J. Wherton, P. Sugarhood, S. Hinder, R. N. Procter, R. Stones. "What matters to older people with assisted living needs? A phenomenological analysis of the use and non-use of telehealth and telecare". Social Science & Medicine, vol. 93, 2013, pp. 86–94.

[30] M. Tosato,V. Zamboni, A. Ferrini, M. Cesaru, "The aging process and potential interventions to extend life expectancy".Clinical interventions in aging, vol. 2(3) 2007, pp. 401 – 412.

[31] C. Satchell and P. Dourish,"Beyond the user: use and non-use in HCI.", Proc. Annual Conference of the Australian Computer–Human Interaction Special Interest Group: Design: Open, vol. 411, 2009, pp. 9 – 16 ACM, Melbourne,

[32] K. Shankar, "Pervasive computing and an aging populace: methodological challenges for understanding privacy implications" Journal of Information, Communication and Ethics in Society, vol. 8 (3), 2010, pp.236 - 248.

[33] M. Skubic, G. Alexander, M. Popescu, M. Rantz, J. A. Keller,"A smart home application to eldercare: current status and lessons learned". Technology and Health Care, vol. 17(3), 2009, 183-201. doi: 10.3233/THC-2009-0551.

[34] S. Bjorneby et al. (2004). "Ethical considerations in the ENABLE project". Dementia, vol. 3(3), 2004, pp. 297-312.

[35] R. Landau, S. Werner, G. K Auslander, N. Shoval, J. Heinik, 2010; "What do cognitively intact older people think about the use of electronic tracking devices for people with dementia? A preliminary analysis." International Psychogeriatrics vol. 22 (8), December 2010, pp 1301-1309

[36] A. Sharkey and N. Sharkey, "Granny and the robots: ethical issues in robot care for the elderly", Ethics Inf Technol, vol. 14, 2012, pp. 27–40.

[37] Sparrow R, Sparrow L (2006) In the hands of machines? The future of aged care. Minds Mach 16:141–161

[38] H. Remmers, "Environments for ageing, assistive technology and self-determination: ethical perspectives." Informatics for Health and Social Care, vol. 35(4), 2010, pp. 200-210

[39] A. J. Bharucha,V. Anand, J. Forlizzi, M. A Dew,C. F. Reynolds, S. Stevens, H. Wactlar, "Intelligent assistive technology applications to dementia care: current capabilities, limitations, and future challenges" The American Journal of Geriatric Psychiatry: Official Journal of the American Association for Geriatric Psychiatry, vol. 17, 2009, pp. 88–104.

[40] G. Demiris, M. Rantz, M. Aud, K. Marek, H. Tyrer, M. Skubic, A. Hassam, (2004). «Older adults' attitudes towards and perceptions of ''smart home'' technologies: A pilot study." Medical Informatics and the Internet in Medicine, vol. 29, 2004, pp. 87–94.

[41] B. K. Hensel, G.Demiris, K.L. Courtney, "Defining obtrusiveness in home telehealth technologies: A conceptual framework." Journal of the American Medical Informatics Association, vol. 13, 2006, pp. 428–431.

[42] V. Faucounau, Y. H. Wu, M. Boulay, M. Maestrutti, A. S. Rigaud, "Caregivers' requirements for in-home robotic agent for supporting community-living elderly subjects with cognitive impairment" Technology and Health Care: Official Journal of the European Society for Engineering and Medicine, vol. 17, 2009, pp. 33–40.

[43] L. Magnusson, E.J. Hanson, M. Nolan, "The impact of information and communication technology on family carers of older people and professionals in Sweden." Ageing and Society, vol. 25 (05) September 2005, pp 693-713.

[44] J. Coughlin, L.A. D'Ambrosio, B. Reimer, M. R. Pratt, "Older adult perceptions of smart home technologies: implications for research, policy and market innovations in healthcare". Proc. IEEE Engineering in Medicine and Biology Society, 2007, pp. 1810–1815.

[45] B. Penhale and J. Manthorpe, "Using electronic aids to assist people with dementia",. Nursing and Residential Care, vol. 3, 2001, pp. 586–589.

[46] C.M.P.M. Hertogh (2004). "Between autonomy and security: Ethical questions in the care of elderly persons with dementia in nursing homes" In G.M.M. Jones & B.M.L. Miesen (Eds.), Care-giving in Dementia, 2004, pp. 375–390, East Sussex: Brunner-Routledge.

[47] A. Melander-Wikman, Y. Faltholm, G. Gard, "Safety vs. privacy: Elderly persons' experiences of a mobile safety alarm" Health and Social Care in the Community, vol. 16, 2008, pp. 337–346.

[48] R. Landau, G. K. Auslander, S. Werner, N. Shoval, J. Heinik, "Families' and professional caregivers' views of using advanced technology to track people with dementia." Qualitative Health Research, 20, 2010, pp. 409–419.

[49] S. O. Daatland and B. Otnes, Housing oriented elderly care: Development trends, Report, vol. 16, 2014, Oslo: NOVA

[50] P. Skrabanek and J. McCormick, Follies and fallacies in medicine. 1990, Glasgow: Tarragon Press.

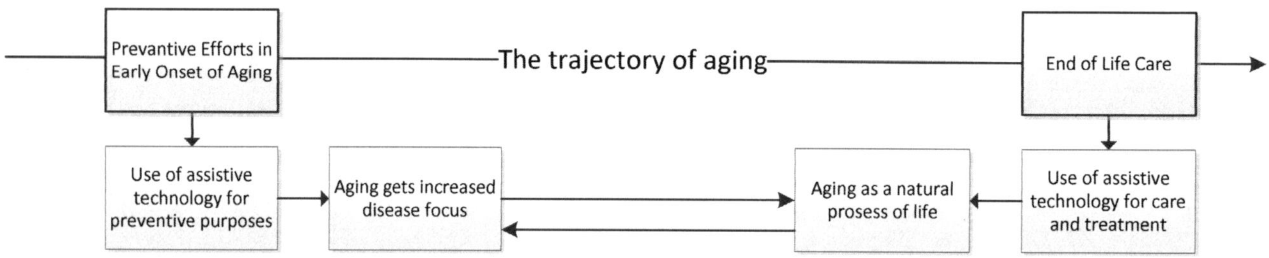

Figure 1. A simple model illustrating how the phenomenon of aging gets increased disease focus when technology is introduced as part of preventive efforts to prospective elders at risks, as well as later introduction of technology is viewed as efforts that are done in order to support aging as a natural process of life.

Probing Privacy in Practice

Privacy regulation and instant sharing of video in social media when running

Joakim Karlsen and Susanne Koch Stigberg
Department of Computer Science
Østfold University College
1757 Halden, Norway
{joakim.karlsen, susanne.k.stigberg}@hiof.no

Jo Herstad
Department of Informatics
University of Oslo
0372 Oslo, Norway
johe@ifi.uio.no

Abstract— **This paper examines privacy as something people do, seeing privacy as a constant negotiation of technical and social aspects of technology use. To be able to examine privacy aspects of live video sharing on social media, we have designed and deployed a technology probe in amateur running events. The findings suggest that audio wouldn't be shared a lot in this context, since it captures audible signs of fatigue. Further, it seems that sharing of performance indicators are problematic, so it is more likely that the probe would be used to mediate the general experience of taking part in a running event. Lastly it seems that very few would be comfortable with immediate sharing and would like to have the option of removing recordings and control its recipients. Overall, we find that when confronted with new mediating information technologies, people are quickly able to re-negotiate their privacy boundaries, using earlier experience with similar technologies.**

Keywords- privacy; instant sharing, social media; video; mobile interaction.

I. Introduction

Privacy involves a broad range of concerns within legislative practices, social practices, cultural differences and digital and urban/domestic architecture. The activities of regulating our personal space, closing and opening doors, avoiding and seeking others, are privacy performed in practice. As our everyday life is performed with electronic networked services, this is increasingly a concern both for the HCI research community and the public at large [1]. Bellotti and Sellen [2] identified a set of challenges pertaining to privacy in digital pervasive environments as a result of separating the users activity and the site of its effects in digital media spaces. Agre [3] has written extensively on privacy concerns and digital technologies, in particular advocating privacy as an issue not simply of individual needs, but something that arises from social roles and relationships. In this perspective, privacy is a culturally embedded and changing practice of everyday living. However, there is limited empirical research on "doing" privacy as an on-going negotiation of technical and social aspects in everyday situations, with some exceptions [4].

To get a deeper understanding of the privacy aspects of one particular context, sharing live video on social media while running, we have conducted two explorative field studies using what Hutchinson et al. [5] has coined a "technology probe". Our technology probe enabled participants in two running events to capture and share video on Facebook by opening and closing their hand. To be able to analyze and discuss the results of probing this context, we have revisited Palen and Dourish [6] work on privacy and information technology. In their perspective, the user's choice of sharing or not sharing his / her first-person feed with a larger group, can be framed as a constant negotiation of his / her privacy boundaries, a "process where people optimize their accessibility along a spectrum of "openness" and "closedness" depending on context." [6]. According to them a "genre of disclosure" is a stable and recurrent social practice where representations enabled by technology use are met with certain expectations. When these are broken privacy concerns are raised. Technology has the ability "to disrupt or destabilize the regulation of boundaries" [6].

Our technology probe, a video recording and live streaming device for use in a public setting, have challenged our users to negotiate their privacy boundaries in this context. The aim of this study has then been to investigate *how users participating in running events negotiate their disclosure, identity and temporal privacy boundaries when using a technology probe for instant sharing of video on Facebook and to examine how this is a re-negotiation of previously experienced genres of disclosure.*

After a brief summary of related work, we will explicate the framework of "genres of disclosure" in Section 2, before describing in Section 3, how we have probed the running and sharing context by making a fully working technological probe and deploying it in a real world setting. We will continue with a summary of our findings in Section 4, and in Section 5, we will discuss several patterns in how the privacy boundaries has been negotiated by our users. Lastly we will discuss how these patterns can be seen as re-negotiations of boundaries set up by earlier experiences with similar technologies.

A. Related work

The technology probe developed in this study has similarities with both sports-tracking and life-logging technologies, and researchers interested in these fields have to some extent discussed privacy concerns with these technologies. The use of tracking devices for training and fitness purposes is common, but mostly for private purposes. But when these applications are networked and become more similar and/or integrated with other social media platforms people may experience expectations of joining and sharing

[7][8]. Ojala and Saarela [8] categorize the motivation for joining and sharing into:

- get feedback and guidance
- get content of others
- reputation and status
- comparing results

Other studies have pointed out the importance of social support and accountability, as strong motivational factors to share exercising data [9][10]. Deborah Lupton has identified self-improvement as the main motivational factor for self-tracking [11], and has developed five "modes of tracking", that include a private mode, but also pushed, communal, imposed and exploited modes [11]. The exploited mode raises privacy concerns and "refer to the ways in which individuals' personal data (whether collected purely for their own purposes or as part of pushed, communal or imposed self-tracking) are repurposed for the (often commercial) benefit of others.

Privacy concerns have been raised by wearable computing and life-logging pioneer Steve Mann [12]. Data from logging your own life, can according to him, be misused by other people, government and media. He problematizes that history becomes a "freezer not a dustbin", something that can have negative social consequences. Two recent studies have investigated privacy aspects of life logging using wearable cameras, from the life-loggers perspective [13] and from the bystander perspective [14]. From the life-logger perspective, people preferred to manage privacy in situ, as a result of the perceived sensitivity of the context. Most of the users in the reported study were concerned about the privacy of bystanders [13]. From the bystander perspective, people reported indifferent or negative responses to being recorded by a wearable camera. Many users expressed interest in being asked for permission and in devices for blocking the recording [14].

Generally, users are aware of privacy issues with sharing information on social media [8][9], and tend to prefer a friends-only social media profiles [15]. When digital media sharing crosses boundaries into public domains, both intentionally and unintentionally, users are less able to control their identity [16].

II. PRIVACY

In 1890, Warran and Brandeis [17] published their seminal article "the right to privacy" where they write:

> Instantaneous photographs and newspaper enterprise have invaded the sacred precincts of private and domestic life; and numerous mechanical devices threaten to make good the prediction that 'what is whispered in the closet shall be proclaimed from the housetops' (ibid).

From these early discussions on the conditions for protecting privacy and ways of regulating privacy by law, there is an increasing focus on privacy as our everyday lives are partly performed online. The list of mechanical devices could today be extended to electronic devices that capture, store and potentially distribute dynamic information from the peoples context, such as audio, video, location and biometric data. Palen and Dourish [6] have proposed a framework for a nuanced understanding of privacy in a networked world. Their framework builds on the seminal work of Altman [18][19], and identifies three boundaries that are central to the negotiation of more or less openness and closedness.

The first and most basic boundary is the *disclosure boundary*, that is, what information to reveal or keep from others. For example, should I share this picture of my new bulldog on the net, or should I keep it for myself?

Secondly, the *identity boundary* is defined by the role taken on by the user. A user can for example represent an organization, such as the member of the dogs rights organizations, or represent herself personally.

Finally, the *temporal boundary* is about the effects of persisted information. Unintended recipients can interpret the information left behind in a networked system at a later time, and there is little or no way of controlling the interpretation of information, or the context in which it is interpreted. For example, the article about dogs right in your local newspaper or social network you shared in 2007, discussing a city plan, can be read and interpreted in 2016 in a very different discussion about the housing of dogs.

One of the most important insights from Altman's work is that privacy is not a static set of rules, but rather a dynamic process, a constant negotiation depending on the situation. In other words, privacy is something that is actively negotiated and performed. Grudin [20] puts this in the context of situated action, which is what allows the constant negotiation just described:

> Why then the uneasiness, the widespread attention to privacy? It may reflect an awareness at some level of something more fundamental than privacy that is being challenged: The steady erosion of clearly situated action. We are loosing control and knowledge of the consequences of our actions, because if what we do is represented digitally, it can appear anywhere and at any time in the future. We no longer control access to anything we disclose [20].

Indeed, where are the boundaries of situated action when the information about the situation is broadcasted with networked technologies? With viewing privacy through the framework proposed by Palen and Dourish [6] as an activity, something that users "do" and negotiate instead of "have a right to", there is a possibility of gaining insights into ways that this is practiced.

III. PROBING

Technology probes as defined by Hutchinson et al. [5] are simple, flexible, adaptable technologies deployed to find out about the unknown. Probes are not prototypes and should be used in the early stages of projects to investigate new perspectives that can constrain and open future designs [21]. Technology probes support playful interactions with new technology in new contexts and provoke participants' reactions [22].

Hutchinson et al. designed technology probes with three goals in mind:

- understanding the needs and desires of users in real-world setting
- field-testing the technology
- inspiring participants and researchers to think about future technology and its use

Studies have deployed technology probes, focusing on only one or several of these three research goals. In [23], simple step counters are used as ready-made technology probes to study teenagers' motivation for exercising and to find out important lessons for the design of future devices. In [24], technology probes are applied to measure and assess texting and updating functionality of situated displays. In [25], a mobile technology probe is designed to better understand if and when intimate couples desire to hold hands when apart.

Similar to [25], we have designed a mobile technology probe. Our research goal is to understand privacy with instant video sharing on social media while running. We have tried to create a realistic situation for users to experience instant video sharing in practice. To make sure that we were able to probe for privacy concerns in our research design, we have strived to design the probe to be simple, wearable and robust, something that is especially important for intimate, mobile context [25].

A. Hardware and Software

Our technology probe in Figure 2, consists of two parts: a mobile phone for recording and sharing videos to Facebook and a sport glove that functions as a remote control for the mobile phone. We fitted the glove with a flex-sensor and a wearable Arduino mini-processor called LilyPad. Flex-sensors are a form of resistors that change their resistance depending how hard they are bent. The LilyPad can detect these changes and transform the analogue resistance values to integer values. In the probe, these values are sent via Bluetooth to a mobile phone. The application on the phone maps the values to specific functions. Single or multiple fingers can be fitted with sensors, and this setup can support detection of many different hand gestures. In our study, we needed two functions, on and off, mapped to recording and sharing video on Facebook, so we only fitted one sensor to the middle finger on the glove. All technical components were hidden inside the glove. A red recording led was the only visible part and the glove appeared as a normal sport glove from a distance.

B. Design

"Probes are meant to collect usage data, but if users are deterred from using them because of their appearance, design should become a priority" [25]. Studies have shown that the wearability of the smart phone is not optimal for interactions on the move, for example running and walking [26][27]. To improve wearability of the phone we made careful design choices regarding placement of the phone, how the users should interact with the phone and the mapping between these interactions and the phones functions for recording and sharing video.

1) Placement: The first set of design choices concerned the placement of the phone while running. Gemperle et al. [28] recommend placing larger and heavier devices on non-moving parts of the body throughout the movement. To be able to capture video in a first person perspective, the phone needs to be positioned on the front of the body directed forward. We solved these requirements by mounting the phone in a neoprene hip belt with a see through pocket facing forward.

2) Interactions: Secondly we addressed the problems with touchscreen interactions while running. These interactions are in effect not possible in this situation, without disturbing the running experience. Users often have to stop to look at the screen and press a button [27]. We aimed to design a more unobtrusive input mode using a sports glove with movement sensors.

3) Mapping: The last design choices concerned the mapping of gestures to functionality. Rico and Brewster [29] recommend using gestures that are familiar in feeling or appearance. For our technology probe the start and stop recording functions need to be mapped to suitable hand gestures. They should be simple enough to perform while running and they should not have other predefined meanings. Simple hand gestures that we observed during the design process were making a fist, tapping fingers together, open hand, spread fingers, waving right/left. We ended up tying distinct hand gestures metaphorically to the mapped functions;

- hand open (record and share)
- hand closed (stop recording and sharing)

C. Deployment

We deployed the probe in two running events taking place in Strömstad, Sweden on November the 8th and Wolfen, Germany on December the 28th, 2014. The three main criteria for choosing the events were that they had good 3G coverage, they were accessible to the researchers and that they were semi-professional with medium distance tracks (5 and 10 km). We recruited three participants for the first field trial and three for the second, from local sports clubs and directly at the events. We paid their registration fee and they received a 10€ flower present card for participating. In Table 1, we have listed the participants with age, gender and experience with sports tracking and social media.

TABLE 1. PARTICIPANTS

#	Event	Age	Gender	Sports Tracking	Social media
#1-1	Strömstad	30s	Male	Yes	Moderate
#1-2	Strömstad	30s	Female	Yes	Active
#1-3	Strömstad	40s	Female	Yes	Moderate
#2-1	Wolfen	20s	Male	Yes	Moderate
#2-2	Wolfen	20s	Male	Yes	Moderate
#2-3	Wolfen	20s	Female	Yes	Moderate

In Strömstad, the researchers met up one hour before the start time at 12 pm. The first half hour we registered the informants for the 5km track and checked the probes. Until

Figure 1. Starting any minute

the start at 1 pm we fitted the technology to the individual participants and gave them brief explanations of how they could use it. They tried out the gestures, and at the same time we calibrated the on / off thresholds to their hand movements. We explained how the video they were going to record was shared on Facebook. The informants used from 24 to 34 minutes to complete the track and from 1:45 pm we conducted semi-structured interviews with each of them. We had prepared a set of guiding questions focusing on the participants' experience of instant video sharing using the probe in regard to negotiating their privacy boundaries.

In Wolfen, we followed the same procedure as in Strömstad, with some small differences. The race started earlier at 10 am, and one of the participants chose to run the 10km track.

We used open coding to analyze the collected data independently from each other, followed by a collaborative session, were we resolved small differences and agreed on the main findings.

IV. FINDINGS

All six participants, in the two separate field studies, expressed that the events were well organized and as they expected. It seemed that they felt at home in what they saw as small and friendly happenings. Figure 1 shows runners in Strömstad just before the start. The participants were more or less competitive or serious about the races, but all six said they enjoyed the experience. It didn't seem that participating in the study by using the technological probe, took away from their participation in the events themselves. In the following we denote the participants using two digits, the first for the event and the second for participant (#event-participant).

When it came to placement of the probe as shown in Figure 2, the most competitive of the three in the first field study #1-1, thought that the extra weight of the smartphone and belt on the chest was bothersome. He said the belt wasn't tight enough so it moved enough to irritate him. In the second field study one participant mentioned that it is important that the belt was positioned right. For him the belt was strapped on too low and he had to move it up while running. The other four participants in the two field studies did not report that they were bothered at all, and said they forgot about the placement of the mobile phone after a short while.

Figure 2. The equipment

All six participants said that the hand gestures were easy to perform and appropriate for controlling the video stream.

> It is very natural to extend the hand. [...] so to turn it on with that is better than using a closed hand. #1-1

> There is no middle way. Either you open or you close your hand. This simple. #2-1

None of the participants proposed an alternative hand gesture that could have worked better for this purpose. All of them said they "forgot" the interface after a while, but they all kept on using it and continued recording video throughout the races.

A. *Privacy Boundaries*

The participants had few reflections on how "being a camera" in public can be problematic to others.

> No I did not think about them [*other people*]. Do I need to think about them? #2-3

They recorded a lot when they had people nearby, in the starting area especially, and also when they were running almost alone.

1) Disclosure boundary: Their attention was on when the camera should be turned on, the framing of the image and what sounds were recorded. Three of the participants had a competitive focus during the races and turned on the camera when they improved their position.

> ...I thought it was funny when I ran down the hill, because I am really fast at running downhill, then I usually overtake many of the other runners. So I turned on the camera on top of the hill, then let go... and thought this was really fun. #1-1

Participants #1-2, #1-3 and #2-3 were concerned about the framing of the image. The first said that she was worried because she is short, and that she filmed only the road and nothing else. The second said she tried to keep a dangling headphone-wire away from the camera. The third was worried about her hands swinging in front of the camera. Figure 3 shows two screenshots from the captured video.

Most of the participants were acutely aware of the sound captured when recording. Participant #1-1 gave comments intended for a listener. Participant #1-3 said she was really worried about recording heavy breathing and other audible signs of fatigue. Participant #1-2 turned the camera off because she needed to say something she didn't want anyone to hear. She felt that the sound was more important than the image.

> ...one thinks about, yes, first and foremost what one says, for what one sees can't be influenced. But what one says, I thought about that a lot. #1-2

Participant #2-3 hadn't been aware of the audio and was embarrassed afterwards because she talked a lot with other people while recording.

2) Identity boundary: All participants expressed that sharing video from participating in a sports event on social media could be positive for their image.

> It wouldn't matter if some of this were published, because then people would see that I am active and... yes, I have to admit that this appeals to me, it lowered the threshold for... the social. #1-1

Participants #1-1, #1-3, #2-1, #2-2 were skeptical though, and related that they rarely exposed themselves in this way. Participant #1-1 and #1-3 said that sharing from sports activities could be seen as bragging, and they would be careful of coming across as betters on social media. They both expressed irritation with other people sharing their training activities on Facebook.

> ...when people share training logs, I have cycled 70km for example, deserving beer and taco, then I think this is bragging. #1-1

But both these informants were more positive to sharing if the content were without tracking information.

> I think, yes - sharing a film, that's nice, but sharing how far you have run, how fast and all that, that is for me, not others. Film is fun of course, that could be amusing. #1-3

In contrast to the skeptical participants, informant #1-2 and *#2-3* said they loved to share from activities they participate in, including sports, and that they saw no problems with using the probe to do this.

> Yes, I share a lot, also from sports activities. I love running so this is nothing strange. #1-2

> It was cool. It is a new way to communicate with friends. Facebook is made to share things. *#2-3*

Figure 3. Screenshots from captured video

3) Temporality boundary: When it came to what the participants wanted to happen with the shared videos from the event, they answered differently. Participant #1-1 said that he wanted control of the videos. He would have preferred to have them sent to his private inbox for editing before they were published. The most likely thing he would make is a "best of" edit from the competition. But when the videos were already published he was not certain what to do.

> ...to me it is unpleasant that the videos are out there, then I can just ask for them to be deleted. Except when I cross the goal line or something. I'll see about that. #1-1

Both participants #2-1 and #2-2 wanted to keep the videos on their computers. Participant #2-1 didn't mind having them online since he is in good shape. In contrary to this, participant #2-2 wanted them removed or shared with selected friends only. Participant #1-2 didn't see any problems with the videos being published. She expressed no desire to erase them and hadn't really thought of this as a problem. She said that maybe someone would look at them, maybe not. Participant #1-3 was more skeptical, but was also comforted by the videos limited appeal. She was more worried about the audio of her huffing and puffing.

> ...if it is interesting to others then it can be out there, but I don't know if that is the case. I don't know that [laughs]. If it is a video, where I reveal myself, for example with breathing and puffing in the background, then I think I would have removed it. #1-3

Participant *#2-3* said she would keep the videos that are fun and remove videos less interesting to others.

> It depends, how they look. So if there is anything funny, for example when Lars passes me, if this was good, when I would keep it online and write a comment under. *#2-3*

V. Discussion

When it came to running the events the participants had different agendas, but they participated according to what was expected of them. They followed the logic of the event, the instructions from the organizers, ran the designated track and put effort into the running according to physical capabilities. They related to their time and rank in the race and happily received their prizes. None of them did anything that could be conceived as "outside" the social obligations of the events themselves. None of their actions were "out of place" [30]. The wearing of and interaction with the technological probe seemed to be unobtrusive to the participation in the event and the participants quickly understood the function of the technology and the mapping between gestures, actions and feedback.

A. Negotiating openness / closedness

When using the three privacy boundaries to understand the results of this study it is evident that the participants negotiated these boundaries differently. There are findings from the trials that point towards openness, and some that point towards closedness. It is important to note that the privacy boundaries are negotiated together. It is difficult to consider one boundary without taking the other two into account.

The first, and maybe the most interesting pattern we see, mostly concerning the disclosure boundary, is related to sensing. None of the participants thought that the first-person image was problematic, but several of them were more concerned with the audio. Both talking and audible signs of exhaustion were mentioned as problematic to share with others. It seems that the first person view, where the participant was not visible in the image, was conceived as less private than the audio. The users understanding of the video image recorded by the probe facilitated more openness and their understanding of the nature of the audio triggered privacy concerns and more closedness. An interesting follow-up study would be to repeat the experiment with the camera mounted so that the runner could be part of the image.

The second pattern, mostly related to the disclosure and identity boundary, is about what the participants chose to record and their explanations of why they did so. We see two main stories told, with emphasis on the competition and with emphasis on the experience. Three of the participants recorded when something interesting happened in the competition, for instance overtaking other runners in the race. The other three didn't care much about this aspect, but recorded what they thought was interesting like nice scenery or social interactions. This pattern seems to point towards openness, all participants recorded a lot and with some narrative intentions. The interviews seem to indicate that the reason for this was that the probe didn't record and share any performance indicators, like pulse and speed. The recordings were not revealing their standing in the race or other precise measures of performance. This seemed to be important to the participants independent of how well they performed in the race. It seems that quantitative measures of their performance would have triggered more privacy concerns and lead towards more closedness.

The third pattern, mostly related to the temporality boundary, is the participants' wish to have control of the recordings. The decision they had, of turning the recording on and off, was not enough. All the participants except one wanted to be able to delete unfavorable or boring recordings before or after they were published to Facebook. Most of the participants wanted to share the recordings with a selected group of people if they could, controlling not only what they shared but also with whom. These findings seem to indicate that the participants were uneasy about the immediate and indiscriminate sharing done by the probe, pointing towards more closedness. But at the same time many of the participants were intrigued by the experience with the technological probe. It seems that they were open to experimenting with the format as long as they could have the option of removing recordings afterwards and have more control of their recipients. This is relatively easy to do on a social media platform like Facebook and this finding points in the direction of openness. Maybe the participants would be inclined to share more easily as a result of more experience with the probe.

B. Re-negotiation of privacy boundaries

The concept of "privacy genre" is mainly a descriptive term, since genres are historically situated as social practice. In our study we have developed a probe that gave our informants experience with new technology, exploring what could be called a proto-genre, but not a genre. The sharing of live video on Facebook while running is not exceptionally new or outlandish, but still not something that many people do as part of their everyday activities. So what we have been probing is mainly how people are able to negotiate privacy boundaries when using new and not commonly used information technologies. In this perspective, we have found that people rely heavily on previous experience with similar technologies when negotiating privacy boundaries "fresh". They rely on earlier and established genres of disclosure related to, in our case combinations of sports tracking, photography and social media. In this study, we were surprised by how quickly and consciously this process was undertaken by our informants, and how efficiently new boundaries where negotiated building on old. At the same time, we found that unfamiliar aspects of the proto-genre articulated by the probe, triggered the most intense and partly unresolved negotiations of privacy boundaries; the clearest example being the recording and live sharing of "first-person" sound.

These findings attest to the usefulness of the concept of genre of disclosure both as an analytical tool but also as a perspective useful when designing and exploring mediating technologies. People's practical everyday experience with negotiating privacy, framed and understood as a social situated dynamic, can give good guidance of what will trigger privacy concerns and what will not. This study is an initial exploration of designing and deploying technology probes to investigate privacy concerns with mediating technologies. Our results indicate that technology probes can be designed to disrupt or destabilize existing genres of disclosure, giving researchers the opportunity to study these closer, mining the interstices between them.

VI. CONCLUSION

In this study, we have explored privacy concerns with instant sharing of video in social media. To understand the co-dependent technical and social aspects of instant sharing and privacy, as framed by the concept of "genres of disclosure" [6], we have developed a technological probe and conducted two field studies at running events in Sweden and Germany. In each field study three participants were fitted with a working probe sharing video instantly to Facebook by opening and closing the hand. The probe performed according to the intentions of the research design, opening up for investigating privacy in practice.

The findings suggest that audio wouldn't be shared a lot in this context, since it captures audible signs of fatigue. Further, it seems that sharing of performance indicators are problematic, so it is more likely that the probe would be used to mediate the general experience of taking part in a running event. Lastly it seems that very few would be comfortable with immediate sharing and would like to have the option of removing recordings and control its recipients. Overall, it seems that people, when using new mediating technologies, rely heavily on earlier experience with similar technologies when negotiating the privacy boundaries, emphasizing the historically situated nature of privacy in practice.

We believe that probing wearable technology in the field has been important for this study, and see how our findings open up for further studies with similar mediating technologies, in other mobile contexts.

REFERENCES

[1] P. Dourish and K. Anderson, "Collective Information Practice: Emploring Privacy and Security As Social and Cultural Phenomena," Hum-Comput Interact, vol. 21, no. 3, Sep. 2006, pp. 319–342.

[2] V. Bellotti and A. Sellen, "Design for Privacy in Ubiquitous Computing Environments," in Proceedings of the Third European Conference on Computer-Supported Cooperative Work 13–17 September 1993, Milan, Italy ECSCW '93, G. de Michelis, C. Simone, and K. Schmidt, Eds. Springer Netherlands, 1993, pp. 77–92.

[3] P. E. Agre and M. Rotenberg, Technology and Privacy: The New Landscape. MIT Press, 1998.

[4] P. Kumar and S. Schoenebeck, "The Modern Day Baby Book: Enacting Good Mothering and Stewarding Privacy on Facebook," in Proceedings of the 18th ACM Conference on Computer Supported Cooperative Work & Social Computing, New York, NY, USA, 2015, pp. 1302–1312.

[5] H. Hutchinson et al., "Technology Probes: Inspiring Design for and with Families," in Proceedings of the SIGCHI Conference on Human Factors in Computing Systems, New York, NY, USA, 2003, pp. 17–24.

[6] L. Palen and P. Dourish, "Unpacking 'Privacy' for a Networked World," in Proceedings of the SIGCHI Conference on Human Factors in Computing Systems, New York, NY, USA, 2003, pp. 129–136.

[7] R. Ling, "From ubicomp to ubiex(pectations)," Telemat. Inform., vol. 31, no. 2, May 2014, pp. 173–183.

[8] J. Ojala and J. Saarela, "Understanding Social Needs and Motivations to Share Data in Online Sports Communities," in Proceedings of the 14th International Academic MindTrek Conference: Envisioning Future Media Environments, New York, NY, USA, 2010, pp. 95–102.

[9] S. A. Munson, E. Krupka, C. Richardson, and P. Resnick, "Effects of Public Commitments and Accountability in a Technology-Supported Physical Activity Intervention," in Proceedings of the 33rd Annual ACM Conference on Human Factors in Computing Systems, New York, NY, USA, 2015, pp. 1135–1144.

[10] R. Teodoro and M. Naaman, "Fitter with Twitter: Understanding Personal Health and Fitness Activity in Social Media." in ICWSM, 2013.

[11] D. Lupton, "Self-Tracking Modes: Reflexive Self-Monitoring and Data Practices," Social Science Research Network, Rochester, NY, SSRN Scholarly Paper ID 2483549, Aug. 2014.

[12] S. Mann, "Wearable computing: a first step toward personal imaging," Computer, vol. 30, no. 2, Feb. 1997, pp. 25–32.

[13] R. Hoyle et al., "Privacy Behaviors of Lifeloggers Using Wearable Cameras," in Proceedings of the 2014 ACM International Joint Conference on Pervasive and Ubiquitous Computing, New York, NY, USA, 2014, pp. 571–582.

[14] T. Denning, Z. Dehlawi, and T. Kohno, "In Situ with Bystanders of Augmented Reality Glasses: Perspectives on Recording and Privacy-mediating Technologies," in Proceedings of the 32Nd Annual ACM Conference on Human Factors in Computing Systems, New York, NY, USA, 2014, pp. 2377–2386.

[15] F. Stutzman and J. Kramer-Duffield, "Friends Only: Examining a Privacy-enhancing Behavior in Facebook," in Proceedings of the SIGCHI Conference on Human Factors in Computing Systems, New York, NY, USA, 2010, pp. 1553–1562.

[16] S. Lindtner, J. Chen, G. R. Hayes, and P. Dourish, "Towards a Framework of Publics: Re-encountering Media Sharing and Its User," ACM Trans Comput-Hum Interact, vol. 18, no. 2, Jul. 2011, pp. 5:1–5:23.

[17] S. D. Warren and L. D. Brandeis, "The Right to Privacy," Harv. Law Rev., vol. 4, no. 5, 1890, pp. 193–220.

[18] I. Altman, "The Environment and Social Behavior: Privacy, Personal Space, Territory, and Crowding.," Brooks / Cole Monterey, CA, 1975.

[19] I. Altman, "Privacy Regulation: Culturally Universal or Culturally Specific?" J. Soc. Issues, vol. 33, no. 3, Jul. 1977, pp. 66–84.

[20] J. Grudin, "Desituating Action: Digital Representation of Context," Hum-Comput Interact, vol. 16, no. 2, Dec. 2001, pp. 269–286.

[21] W. W. Gaver, A. Boucher, S. Pennington, and B. Walker, "Cultural Probes and the Value of Uncertainty," interactions, vol. 11, no. 5, Sep. 2004, pp. 53–56.

[22] C. Graham and M. Rouncefield, "Probes and Participation," in Proceedings of the Tenth Anniversary Conference on Participatory Design 2008, Indianapolis, IN, USA, 2008, pp. 194–197.

[23] H. M. Edwards, S. McDonald, and T. Zhao, "Exploring Teenagers' Motivation to Exercise Through Technology Probes," in Proceedings of the 25th BCS Conference on Human-Computer Interaction, Swinton, UK, 2011, pp. 104–113.

[24] D. Fitton, K. Cheverst, M. Rouncefield, and A. Dix, "Probing technology with technology probes," in In Equator Workshop on Record and Replay Technologies, 2004.

[25] S. O'Brien and F. "Floyd" Mueller, "Holding Hands over a Distance: Technology Probes in an Intimate, Mobile Context," in Proceedings of the 18th Australia Conference on Computer-Human Interaction: Design: Activities, Artefacts and Environments, New York, NY, USA, 2006, pp. 293–296.

[26] J. Bergstrom-Lehtovirta, A. Oulasvirta, and S. Brewster, "The Effects of Walking Speed on Target Acquisition on a Touchscreen Interface," in Proceedings of the 13th International Conference on Human Computer Interaction with Mobile Devices and Services, New York, NY, USA, 2011, pp. 143–146.

[27] J. Marshall and P. Tennent, "Mobile Interaction Does Not Exist," in CHI '13 Extended Abstracts on Human Factors in Computing Systems, New York, NY, USA, 2013, pp. 2069–2078.

[28] F. Gemperle, C. Kasabach, J. Stivoric, M. Bauer, and R. Martin, "Design for wearability," in Second International Symposium on Wearable Computers, 1998. Digest of Papers, 1998, pp. 116–122.

[29] J. Rico and S. Brewster, "Gestures All Around Us: User Differences in Social Acceptability Perceptions of Gesture Based Interfaces," in Proceedings of the 11th International Conference on Human-Computer Interaction with Mobile Devices and Services, New York, NY, USA, 2009, pp. 64:1–64:2.

[30] S. Harrison and P. Dourish, "Re-place-ing Space: The Roles of Place and Space in Collaborative Systems," in Proceedings of the 1996 ACM Conference on Computer Supported Cooperative Work, New York, NY, USA, 1996, pp. 67–76.

"Personality-Friendly" Objects: A New Paradigm For Human-Machine Interaction.

Niccolò Rosini*, Lorenzo Cominelli†, Michael Pieroni†, Filippo Chiarello‡, Daniele Mazzei † and Gualtiero Fantoni*
*Dep. of Industrial and Civil Engineering, University of Pisa, Italy
Email: nicco.rosini@gmail.com, g.fantoni@ing.unipi.it
†Research Center E. Piaggio, University of Pisa, Italy
Email: daniele.mazzei@centropiaggio.unipi.it
‡Dep. of Energy, Systems, Territory and Construction Eng., University of Pisa, Italy

Abstract—**This work introduces the concept of "personality-friendly" objects. Its goal is to investigate the relationship that can exist between specific interactive products and the users' personalities. Nowadays, it seems that every object being advertised and put on the market has its own personality. This creates a strong and immediate connection between the customer and the object but often it does not go beyond the aesthetic level or the dialectic of the advertisement. For this reason, a methodology for the categorisation of interactive products has been developed. With this classication, we intend to measure the compatibility between the human way of thinking and the use of products. A set of experiments have been done and their results are reported in this work.**

Keywords*–*Usability; Personality-Friendly; Human-Machine Interaction; Human-Computer Interaction; Myers-Briggs (MBTI).

I. Introduction

In recent years, everyday life devices like smart-phones, smart-watches, etc., evolved considerably at both structural level (e.g., novel interfaces) and functional level (e.g., novel services). In addition, the split between hardware and software, that guarantees regular firmware updates, allows to fully exploit the potential of the devices hardware adapting their functionalities to the user's needs.

The continuous interaction with these devices is changing our life modifying our habits and attitudes. For instance, recent studies report that a typical smart-phone user interacts with their phone about 150x per day [1].

The emerging phenomenon of the Internet of Things (IoT) [2], [3] is bringing us to become part of the technology-based immersive scenarios (i.e., smart-homes, smart-offices, etc.) where a heterogeneous set of *smart devices* or *objects* is interconnected through the network providing the users with added functionalities and services.

The conversion of our daily-life spaces and routines in smart ecosystems brings our smart devices to become a sort of appendix of our body and, more importantly, of our brain. Indeed, while interacting with smart devices and technology, humans tend to adapt their behavior to the communication skills of the machines they are using, exactly as a farmer does with their animals.

The grand challenge in designing innovative smart objects is the inversion of this paradigm. Designers need to figure out how to build machines that are able to communicate with users in a natural way so as to adapt their communication skills to the level of their users.

In addition, humans have a natural attitude to humanize technology and to associate personality to it [4]. For this reason, the judgment about devices personality is guided by several factors. Most of these factors are directly related with the device like the shape [5], the associated advertisement and the object functionalities and behaviour. On the other hand, the user personality affects the judgment and acceptance of the device.

In 2015, Pieroni et al. [6] proposed a novel framework for the personality-driven design of IoT smart devices called Affective Internet of Things (AIoT). In this paper, the authors tried to endow smart objects with affective capabilities to be used within the network and to enhance the level of communication while introducing affective interactions. The AIoT objects can endow different human-inspired personalities having also humanized reaction to somatic (i.e., sensors) and social (i.e., object-object interaction) stimuli.

While the link between associated personality and device behaviours and shapes have been already investigated, a comprehensive analysis which also includes other factors (i.e., advertisement, functionalities and human personality) doesn't exist yet. This analysis is essential to enable the development of interfaces that fully exploit the potential communication capabilities of these emerging devices.

Our aim is to investigate how the humans perceive the currently available technologies in terms of personality. In this particular work, a model that can be used for the classification of interactive products is developed and tested. The paradigm is based on the assumption that the user personality is a key factor driving the approach of the human to the machine. Indeed, any message or feedback sent by the machines is interpreted differently by humans according to their specific personality. We started by analyzing the distinctive features of the different human personalities and the interaction flow between users and objects. The analysis allowed to establish what factors determine the compatibility between the approach of the machine and the one of the user. The products are then classified according to which psychological type best fits them, in terms of the minor cognitive effort required to establish the interaction. The paradigm of *Personality-Friendly* Objects is based on this concept of compatibility and if included in the AIoT is expected to raise the level of communication and regulate the modalities of the human-machine dialogue on the basis of the traits that characterise the user's personality.

In summary, this work proposes and tests a methodology that allows to determine which are the user personalities that are the most suitable to use a specific interactive object. For the method assessment, we selected five well-known interactive objects according to their relevance with different levels of interaction and engagement. The rest of the paper is organized as follows: SectionII introduces objectives, possible applications and requirements related to the paradigm of personality-friendly objects; SectionIII describes the model used for the classification of products and services; the experimental protocol is discussed in SectionIV while the experiments and the results in SectionV; the conclusion and future research directions are given in SectionVI.

II. PERSONALITY-FRIENDLY OBJECTS

In this section, we propose the paradigm of *personality-friendly* objects in which any interactive system can be classified as compatible with certain types of human personalities on the basis of how it usually leads the human-machine interaction. The idea relies on the evidence that humans exploit their own mental process and resources when using interactive devices, therefore personal attitude in perception and action can make some devices more suitable for a particular subject but rather difficult for another person. In other words, a personality-friendly object owns those features in terms of appearance, affordances, functions, behavior and advertisement that allow subjects with a specific personality to interact with the object by using familiar mental processes. Such a classification is fundamental to guide the design of new products or the redesign of existing ones as well as to prevent many of the difficulties encountered by users in using objects. In order to achieve this goal, a dedicated classification instrument needs to be developed taking into account the many different situations of human-machine interaction.

A. Applications

The personality-friendly objects paradigm could have a large pool of applications and implications on the devices development and design. Firstly, adapting technology to user's psychological type might offer many advantages in terms of usability and user experience and, hence the name, make it possible to overcome the current concept of *user-friendly*. The possibility to associate an interactive object to a predetermined category of users leads to numerous and immediate practical repercussions in both the design of products and their commercialization and positioning on the market. For example, a product could be redesigned to make it more compatible with people who currently experience difficulties in the interaction. Another example is related to a product that now addresses a market niche and could be developed in multiple versions in order to attract different types of customers.

Secondly, assuming to know the personality of a user, in the development of a smart object a designer could include some functionalities and communication modalities that make the interaction with the device more immediate and easily understandable for that specific person. In addition, products may adjust their behavior, e.g., by modifying timing and frequency of dialogue in order to be not too intrusive (or conversely, to constantly keep company) and to meet user preferences. For example, considering a smart-watch, for an extroverted person it could act accordingly so as to continuously provide sound and light stimuli; while for an introverted person it could minimize the incentives to those strictly necessary in order to avoid disturbing the user. Analyzing the state-of-the-art for smart-watches, they seem designed to meet mainly extroverted people. This simple example shows how this tool could guide and improve the design of human-machine interaction for a single product.

Finally, considering the future smart environment scenarios (e.g., smart-home, smart-office, and the AIoT [6]) it is immediate to think about new applications that could benefit of the proposed paradigm. This would mean building an intelligent, personalized room that is harmonic in the way it reacts to events and custom-tailored to easily interface with the personality of people who live there. Furthermore, knowing the personality and the mood of the user makes possible to program the affective objects in the room in order to try to re-establish a positive mood within the domain (and therefore also in the user) when the negative emotional state of the person disturbs the environment.

B. Requirements

In order to implement a method for the classification of interactive objects and evaluate its possible benefits, it has been necessary to define several requirements:

1) What can be classified: the methodology to be developed and tested should allow to classify both real products and services. In fact, each service in which the interaction with the client (also through a human operator) is subject to procedures can be included in the classification. Following this we claim that what is true for products also applies to this type of services. On the contrary, if there was not any specific procedure, each call would be an interaction that differs from all the others and every interaction should be classified separately.

2) Limits of the classification: many multi-purpose devices have a large pool of functionalities that can be used by the user to accomplish several possible goals. This could lead to a misleading classification. Therefore, in cases where the product has several features or can be used for different purposes, it is recommended to consider only a single function and a single goal separately. The results obtained by decomposing a single product can then be integrated in a manner which is the most appropriate following a case-by-case approach.

3) Classification Process: the object classification occurs through a survey by submitting a questionnaire to the users. Preferably, the person performing the classification should have the chance to interact with the product for a period of time adequate to personally test all possible aspects of the interaction with that object. If, for practical reasons, this is not possible the person should thoroughly analyze the product on written description attempting to answer to the preliminary questions which are intended to guide the analysis.

On one hand, in literature we found several psychology studies aimed at modelling cognitive mechanism and estimating human performance in performing certain task (e.g., *Model Human Processor* (MHP) [7]). This data have been extensively used in the design of interactive objects in order to meet the human needs and resources.

On the other hand, these studies do not provide information about the dynamics that generate different behaviors in different people under identical conditions and that is more related to subject personality. For this reason we have developed the model of personality-friendly objects in order to consider the effect of different human personalities in the context of human-machine interaction.

III. The Objects Classification Model

This Sectionsummarizes the pillars of the proposed classification model.

A. Outline of Human-Machine Interaction

The simplest way to represent interaction between a system and a user is represented by the *feedback loop*. According to the scheme shown in Figure 1) the interaction occurs as follows: the user in the attempt to accomplish his goal gives one or more inputs to the system, which receives and replays according to its own behavior and communication modalities. At this point the user analyzes the responses of the system, then he/she interprets and compares them with the one expected. The outcome of this comparison determines what should be the next user action. Each new user action towards the machine triggers a new cycle of action and response.

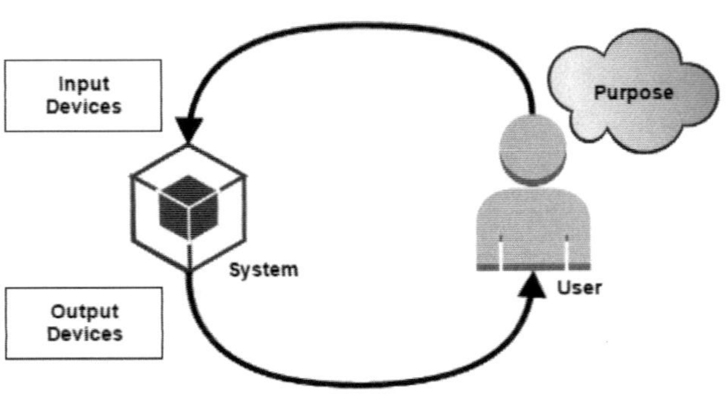

Figure 1. The Human-Machine interaction model based on *feedback loop*.

In this work we refer to the feedback loop model for describing the human-machine interaction. The necessary change done to the model consists in observing the interaction from the user perspective. From this point of view the human-object interaction is a situation in which the person is engaged alternately in two activities: to gather information about the object (and the context if necessary) through the five senses; to process the responses towards the object or to judge the situation that are both based on the data which have been previously acquired.

For example, in a common interaction with an ATM the user needs to acquire data by seeing (or by listening to) the information shown on the monitor (or transmitted from the speaker); then he/she uses this information to process the answers by pushing a button or by judging their own economic situation on the basis of the balance that has been just communicated.

Referring to the model of Norman [8] it is possible to identify the moments of the interaction in which the user may have difficulties in achieving the desired goal through the system. The problems arise when the subject is within two *gulfs*:

- **gulf of execution**, when on the basis of collected data the user has to switch from the intention to the action towards the system;
- **gulf of evaluation**, when on the basis of collected information the user has to assess the results of their actions.

The aim of our work is to classify any interactive system according to its compatibility with the different human personalities. Compatibility is measured from the point of view of the user and it is defined with the degree of naturalness with which a person interacts with the system. This is determined by (i) the effort necessary to obtain useful information, and (ii) the possibility for the user to respond (or judge) in the right way (in order to achieve the purpose of the interaction) without altering their own usual way of thinking.

In other words, the lower the cognitive effort required to overcome the two gulfs of execution and evaluation, the more the product is compatible with a certain personality.

B. Psychological Background

Regarding the personality, many theories have been proposed over the years [9], but a common vision at the academic level has not been reached yet. We analysed the available theories [10] and, for the purpose of this work, we selected the Jung's theory of personality types [11] and in particular the work of Briggs Myers and her mother, who developed the Myers-Briggs Type Indicator (MBTI) in the field of work psychology [12]. The essence of the theory is that the much seemingly random variation in the behavior is actually quite orderly and consistent, being due to basic differences in the ways individuals prefer to use their perception and judgment [13]. The indicator identifies sixteen psychological types, meaning sixteen different ways that people have to perceive reality, evaluate and act accordingly. The types, commonly called personalities, differ from each other in terms of how a person is located compared with four dichotomies.

The aim of this study is to understand how people approach the human-machine interaction. For this reason, to outline the personality traits that influence this process it is necessary to take into account only the process of information acquisition and the process of elaboration of answers or judgments. These two mental processes are defined in accordance with the psychological theories of reference: *perceiving* and *judging*. What is important for our work is the fact that according to the vision of Jung and Myers [13] a person may obtain information (*perceiving*) through two different ways:

Sensing (S) - acquiring data through the five senses in order to perceive information that are relevant in the environment;

Intuition (I) - collecting information by perceiving the possibility beyond the facts, focusing on the relationships between the facts and linking them together to build a model that justifies the changes of events over the time.

Also according to the same vision [13] a person can organize information and reach conclusions (*judging*) through two different ways:

Thinking (T) - making decisions impersonally through logical processes, assessing the consequences of choices or actions.

Feeling (F) - making decisions with respect to their deepest convictions and basing on subjective considerations.

Each person uses every day all of these four mental functions. However, each human being has a personal attitude in using one particular feature for perceiving and one for judging. Every person tends to follow their innate tendency and, even if unconsciously, to behave in a certain way. Having the possibility to use their preferred way of perceiving, or judging, in their own mental processes is extremely helpful for persons in order to feel more competent, secure and natural [13]. Behaving according to these preferences generates a sense of well-being, energy and satisfaction. Therefore there is a strong link between usability (especially one of its component, i.e., satisfaction) and user's personality. We used both to define the degree of naturalness of an interaction.

C. *The Proposed Questionnaire*

The framework described above outlines the link between the human personality and the way in which the user dialogues with a system. Here we describe a methodology that can be used to analyze objects and to determine their compatibility with different individual preferences and therefore human personalities. In particular the proposed questionnaire consists of two parts: the first part is dedicated to investigate how the product is delivering information to the user and the second part is about examining what kind of responses are required by the system in order to achieve the user's purpose. These two parts are intended to investigate the two phases in which we have previously outlined the interaction according to the requirements reported in SectionIV.

The first phase, the acquisition of information by the user, is associated with the two ways in which a person can deal with the mental process of *perceiving* (i.e., *sensing* or *intuition*). This first phase consists of seven closed questions conceived for analysing the stimuli sent from the product to the user during the interaction. The user filling out the questionnaire, in light of him/her experience with the object, has to declare how much the description reported in the questionnaire is adequate for illustrating the stimuli that are sent from the object. Selecting among multiple answers, the users shows their agreement with the description of the product and implicitly expresses whether this acquisition of information is easier through the use of *sensing* or *intuition*. On this basis it is possible to classify a product as *sensing-friendly*, if it facilitates this type of approach, *intuition-friendly* (vice versa) or *neutral*, if the stimuli are acquired equally through both the approaches.

The second phase, the processing of responses by the user towards the object (or elaboration of judgments on the current situation) is associated with the two ways in which a person can deal with the mental process of *judging*. Each of the seven questions investigates what are the types of judgements and responses required by the system from the user. The person who fills out the questionnaire declares how much the features that are reported in the questionnaire are adequate or not to describe the opinions and responses required. In practice this part of the questionnaire exploits the same methodology of the previous one but is aimed at classifying the object under study as *thinking-friendly*, *feeling-friendly* or *neutral* if it requests both kind of responses.

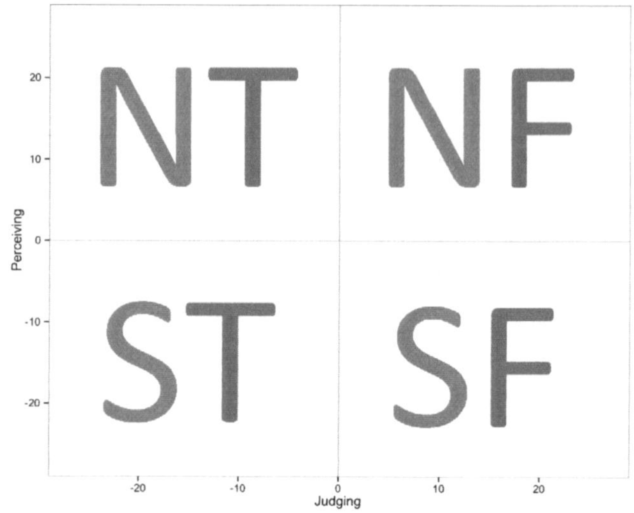

Figure 2. The space in which we represent the results of classifications, the *J-P plane*. The plane is divided in four quarters. In blue we highlighted the functions of *perceiving*, in gray those concerning *judging*.

D. *The J-P Coordinate System*

While the user fills out the questionnaire he/she expresses the level of agreement (through a scale of five values) with the statements. The answers are analyzed assigning points to each value. The two outer values lead to the attribution of four points to an approach (e.g., *sensing*) and zero points to the opposite approach (in this case *intuition*). The two inner values assign in one case three points to an approach (e.g., *thinking*) and one point to the opposite approach (*feeling* in this case). The central value assigns two points to both approaches. The maximum difference that you can get for the score of one approach against its opposite is twenty-eight points.

The results of classification can be represented in the *J-P plan* which is a Cartesian coordinate system where the x-axis represents J the *axis of judging* and the y-axis is P the *the axis of perceiving*. The goal is to identify a point in the plan which is the result of each classification. The J axis measures the difference between the score of *feeling* and the score of *thinking*. In this way a single value describes the user phase of *judging*: positive if the product is *feeling-friendly*, negative if it is *thinking-friendly*. The same for the P axis. In this case the single value measures the phase of *perceiving*: positive if the product is *intuition-friendly*, negative if it is *sensing-friendly*. Figure 2 shows an example of a J-P plane used to plot the results of our analysis.

IV. Experimental Protocol

This section shows the experiments we carried out in order to assess the consistency of the classification methodology and the model behind it. The experiments are oriented to evaluate (i) the comprehensibility of the questionnaire by people; (ii) whether the opinion of most people regarding the same interactive object might be agreed. In the case when most of people describes the same product, through the questionnaire, in a similar manner, it could be argued that the human-machine interaction can be categorised according to a particular subset of parameters. Since these parameters were created on the basis of trends (and recurring behaviors) that the psychological theory associated to individual preferences, it would be possible to support the principle that products could be classified according to the personality and then according to the paradigm of personality-friendly.

The experimental protocol has been built around the following pillars:

- people involved in the test did not have previous experience with the questionnaire or with its theoretical basis; participants have been informed that it was based on psychological basis only afterwards;
- the sample of participants was represented by 82 master students in Management Engineering of the University of Pisa;
- a real usage experience with the objects analyzed by the questionnaire was not possible for logistical reasons. To overcome such a limitation, each student was asked to read a pre-compiled description;
- all the object descriptions had the same structure and focused on how the user's interaction takes place with that particular interacting system;
- thanks to the descriptions, there was no information asymmetry between the participants. Descriptions contained images and videos, and have drawn from encyclopedias, press releases, reviews of industry experts and user manuals in order to avoid any authors' opinion or authors' influence.

In this first analysis, we classified five distinctive interactive systems requiring a different level of engagement to both gather information and reach a conclusion. The first system is the Tamagotchi which is a handheld electronic game created in 1996[1]. The aim is to ensure that the protagonist of the game lives as long as possible and grows politely. For people it is, like all games, a form of interactive entertainment. The second system is the Furby (1998)[2], a little and furry puppy available in various colors. It can be roughly considered an evolution of the Tamagotchi with more interacting functions. The third system is a video cassette recorder (VCR), an electronic device used for home entertainment. The fourth interacting system is a service, the Black Jack that consists in a gambling card game taking place between the dealer and the players. The last interacting system is a design installation that has as main subject the one who benefits from it entering in it. Everything must be built to change, or solicit, the viewer's perception, which becomes part of the work. Without the viewer, the design installation does not make any sense.

Before starting with the analysis, a 'warm-up exercise' was performed to introduce the students to the tool. After reading the description about the functioning and interaction with each object, fifty-nine students have been asked to complete the questionnaire related to these objects.

V. Results and Discussion

We did not record particular problems regarding the comprehensibility of the questionnaire. In order to establish if the students who analyzed the same case studies were aligned on the same conclusions, we analyzed their answers. This is important because through the closed answers they described the interaction that a user plays with the product to achieve a certain purpose in a particular context. If these descriptions were consistent, we can say that the questionnaire is versatile, meaning that it can be applied to very different interactive objects, but also that it is possible to categorise products according to the degree of compatibility with human personalities.

The overall classification result is reported in Figure 3 and shows that every considered product is characterised by a different degree of compatibility with human personalities. Each product has its own way to provide information and to react to the users actions. Therefore, the system leads the person to use only a subset of cognitive processes. For instance, the design installation is in the top right quarter of the J-P plane. This means that the object sends stimuli in a manner consistent with intuition users and requires mental processes which are usual for feeling users. The centroid of the point cloud has coordinates $J = 13$ and $P = 8.1$. The data demonstrate that the interaction between a user and an installation should be done in an empathic way, it requires an approach that consists in harmonizing with the environment (feeling) while understanding rationally its every single parts is quite useless. In addition, the installation requires the ability to abstract the meaning of what the user sees, to understand how the different parts are combined and communicate together. Such results are consistent with an intuition-friendly user. Instead, the Blackjack is easier for people who usually interact with the world in a logical and intuitive way.

Although the results are similar each participant has classified the objects in a slightly different way. As reported in Table I, the variance is smaller when people describe how a product sends stimuli (e.g., the mean value of the variance is about 64 for the SN dichotomy) than when they have to imagine the results of their actions with the system (e.g., the same value is about 90 for the TF dichotomy). Such behavior can be explained by the evidence that second exercise has much more solutions than the first one.

The video recorder has rather low values of the variance because this device is almost in every house and during the test everybody remembers how it works. Conversely, understanding how to interact with Tamagotchi and Furby through their descriptions is not easy for a student who has never interacted with them thus implying the high level of variance for the TF dichotomy. However the provided descriptions of both Tamagotchi and Furby are able to clarify efficaciously how these toys send stimuli (i.e., low values in the SN dichotomy).

The variances of variances are 116 for the TF dichotomy and 113 for the SN dichotomy. The values of the variance fluctuate a bit probably because some products are well known by the students while others are barely new, e.g., everyone had a notion of a VCR, few have already played Blackjack, many have seen Tamagotchi or Furby but no one has ever been into the described design installation.

The interacting systems were chosen in order to have a different level of interaction and engagement with the humans, then we can consider how the path of the consumer electronics has been evolved over the last decades. Figure 3

[1]https://en.wikipedia.org/wiki/Tamagotchi

[2]https://en.wikipedia.org/wiki/Furby

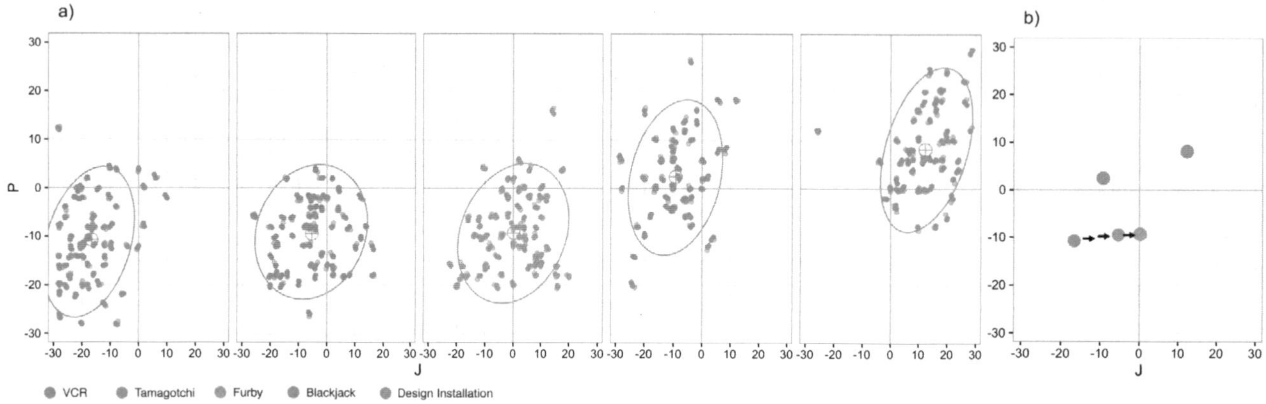

Figure 3. a) Personality-friendly object classification of five interacting systems: Tamagotchi, Furby, Video Cassette Recorder, Black Jack and Design Installation. Each centroid of the point clouds is represented though a crossed circle and the ellipse reports the 95% interval of confidence
b) Position of the five interactive systems (Tamagotchi, Furby, Video Cassette Recorder, Black Jack and Design Installation) within the J-P plane. The arrows report the evolution of the consumer electronics.

TABLE I. AVERAGE AND VARIANCE TABLE

VCR		Tamagotchi		Furby		Black Jack		Design installation	
Avg.FT	Avg.SN	Avg.TF	Avg.SN	Avg.FT	Avg.SN	Avg.FT	Avg.SN	Avg.FT	Avg.SN
-16,65	-10,71	-5,35	-9,45	0,16	-9,24	-9,24	2,45	12,37	8,14
Var.TF	Var.SN	Var.TF	Var.SN	Var.TF	Var.SN	Var.TF	Var.SN	Var.TF	Var.SN
78,29	69,62	102,66	46,34	102,57	57,16	80,25	74,63	84,4	71,98

shows the centroids related to the five case studies highlighting with arrows the evolutionary path made by the electronic devices for entertainment. According to the students answers $(J = -16,6; P = -10,7)$ it is evident that VCR is characterised by a remarkable compatibility with the mental function named thinking. The interaction between a traditional electronic device (e.g., video recorder) and the user is led by an algorithm, which works only in a logical and objective way. Probably this is the cause of this kind of compatibility. Tamagotchi works through a similar algorithm but this fact is not explicit because each stimulus sent by the device and each answer of the user are about the needs of a puppy. The participants seem to perceive such a difference, in their opinion $(J = -5,4; P = -9,4)$ it is possible to interact with Tamagotchi not only through the logic but also via an emotional way (i.e., mental function named feeling). For a person who prefers reaching conclusions through an emotional way a Tamagotchi is more natural to use than a video recorder. Tamagotchi was the first electronic product equipped with this feature and probably this was one of the reason of its enormous commercial success. This idea is supported by the analysis of Furby, which can be considered the evolution of Tamagotchi. It results equally compatible with both thinking and feeling people $(J = 0,2; P = -9,2)$. In our opinion, the designers of the Furby have improved the compatibility with the people who prefer the feeling function in order to reach a trade-off and to create a product suitable for a larger audience.

VI. CONCLUSION

In this paper, the new paradigm of personality-friendly products is presented. Its scope is to clarify the influence of the personality of people during their interaction in the context of human-machine interaction. To achieve this goal we proposed and tested a questionnaire for the classification of interactive objects. This tool is based on a model for describing the human-device interaction and a model for human personalities (i.e., Jung's theory of personality types) that allows to categorize products on the basis of certain characteristics that may occur or not in the human-machine interaction. The approach we propose here derives from MBTI and it was demonstrated to be useful in mapping the ability of an inanimate object to be friendly with respect to different types of users on the basis of their personalities. The experimental results showed how different objects are designed to better fit with particular sets of users than with others. This paradigm looks at the interaction with objects from the point of view of different users so as to be able to highlight different features of the object itself. Future studies will be oriented to refine the classification tool in terms of number of questions and level of details. In addition, we will test the model in the design of the interaction between people and humanoid robots, and in the field of smart object affordances. In long term vision, this methodology will help the designer to customize the human-device interaction taking into account the differences between the personality of potential users by using both questionnaires and real interactions with the products.

VII. ACKNOWLEDGEMENTS

This work was partially funded by the European Commission under the 7th Framework Program project EASEL, Expressive Agents for Symbiotic Education and Learning, under Grant 611971-FP7- ICT-2013-10.

References

[1] M. Meeker and L. Wu, "D11 internet trends," http://www.kpcb.com/file/kpcb-internet-trends-2013/, 2013, kPCB - Kleiner, Perkins, Caufield & Byers.

[2] L. Atzori, A. Iera, and G. Morabito, "The internet of things: A survey," Computer networks, vol. 54, no. 15, 2010, pp. 2787–2805.

[3] D. Mazzei, G. Montelisciani, G. Fantoni, and G. Baldi, "Internet of things for designing smart objects," in Internet of Things (WF-IoT), 2014 IEEE World Forum on. IEEE, 2014, pp. 293–297.

[4] B. Reeves and C. Nass, How people treat computers, television, and new media like real people and places. CSLI Publications and Cambridge university press, 1996.

[5] P. Prieto, G. Fantoni, and R. Campolmi, "On products shapes and personalities," Proceedings of the International Conference on Engineering Design, ICED, vol. 7 DS75-07, 2013, pp. 217–226.

[6] M. Pieroni et al., "Affective internet of things: Mimicking human-like personality in designing smart-objects," in Internet of Things (WF-IoT), 2015 IEEE 2nd World Forum on. IEEE, 2015, pp. 400–405.

[7] S. K. Card, A. Newell, and T. P. Moran, "The psychology of human-computer interaction," 1983.

[8] D. A. Norman, The psychology of everyday things. Basic books, 1988.

[9] D. Schultz and S. Schultz, Theories of personality. Cengage Learning, 2012.

[10] Y. Yan and P. Childs, "Creativity tool selection for design engineers in idea generation." in DS 80-8 Proceedings of the 20th International Conference on Engineering Design (ICED 15) Vol 8, Milan, Italy, 27-30.07. 15, 2015, pp. 359–370.

[11] C. G. Jung, Psychological types. Routledge, 2014.

[12] I. Myers and P. Myers, Gifts differing: Understanding personality type. Nicholas Brealey Publishing, 2010.

[13] I. B. Myers, M. H. McCaulley, N. L. Quenk, and A. L. Hammer, MBTI manual: A guide to the development and use of the Myers-Briggs Type Indicator. Consulting Psychologists Press Palo Alto, CA, 1998, vol. 3.

Young and Creative - a Designerly Approach to Enhance Interventions in the Public Space

Andrea Alessandro Gasparini
Department of Informatics and University of Oslo Library
University of Oslo
Oslo, Norway
E-mail: a.a.gasparini@ub.uio.no

Abstract— **The public space is often offset for young people, where bold and complex routines usually may result in more or less functional solutions, sometimes even in unpleasant design. More than ever the future depends on the engagement of youth in the public arena, and as a counterweight to unpleasant design, youth creativity may have in some case an extremely powerful effect in urban environments. On the other hand, it is questionable how their surroundings are prepared and willing to learn and absorb their inputs. The concept of divergent and convergent thinking is used as a viable framework to address and understand youth creativity in public spaces. Using data gathered over several years from a group of skaters, the paper gives new insight in how they learn, create and share new knowledge and how they envision the possibility to design and change their surroundings. Finally, this paper argues for using a designerly supported framework to enhance youth's creativity and design in public spaces, based on collaboration and co-creation across technology, space and grounded on their creative mindset.**

Keywords-creativity; design thinking; divergent thinking; convergent thinking; public space.

I. INTRODUCTION

Why does youth interact with their surroundings in unpredictable ways? How can all the stakeholders who belong to the public space ecology be prepared and willing to learn and absorb their inputs? Skateboard, snowboard, punk milieu are some examples of youth searching for expression outside normal social boundaries. Their dialogue and narrative is often strong and visual (see Fig. 1), in some occasions addressing inequity in the society, problems with environment, urbanism and sustainability [1], but also pointing out new ways of defining and creating the way they want to live in the modern society. Their actions sometimes evolves and becomes fine art, where Banksy is a well known example of interventions in the public space [2]. The need of interventions and redesign in public space can also be argued as a reaction to unpleasant design, where the *blue light* in public toilets or public bench where it is impossible to lay down (also named anti-homeless) are some examples [3]. Even though youth's explorative efforts sometimes may be perceived as provocations, using a designerly perspective when understanding the way they wish to communicate in public urban space, may give new insight. On the other side of the provocative scale, for some group of less explorative western youth, Social Media (SoMe) has given them the possibility to meet, discuss and share in a digital space, in ways unthinkable a decade ago. Their discourses are often hidden from the public space or, at least they believe that, and therefore giving them the possibility to bring their voice to an arena more visible in the public space [4], may help who among them is not already engaged with creative activity in the public space. Defining youth require an adequate correctness difficult to achieve in this paper, therefore we choose to loosely address them as more or less provocative. Another reason to use a simplified scale is argued by the fact that using qualities to define youth ranging from kindness and rule-following attitudes, to risky behavior and disobedience [5], often accommodate only the adult world. How youth perceive themselves is often unclear and different for those outside, making it more difficult to *develop* solutions that may help them. This paper argues for a designerly based framework to enhance youth's creativity and design in public spaces, based on collaboration and co-creation across technology, space and grounded on their creative mindset.

Figure 1. Intervention in the public space. Photo by Gasparini.

The structure of the article is as follows: Section II presents a framework of creative thinking in the light of convergent and divergent thinking. Section III uses a designerly approach when the core of creativity is addressed. Section IV contains the results of observations and interviews conducted with a group of skaters. Section V presents an enhanced framework, Section VI contains an analysis of the findings and argues for the use of a framework to enhance youth's creativity and design in public spaces, while Section VII concludes the paper.

II. A FRAMEWORK FOR CREATIVE THINKING

Several different theoretical approaches are possible in order to understand the human act of creativity. This pluralism of theories includes ten different main approaches [6], ranging from developmental and cognitive to problem finding and problem solving. Creativity as an act must be self-discovered and self-disciplined [7], while how a person is more or less "*sensitive to problems*" [8] is a critical factor when a problem needs to be found and solved. As a viable framework to address and understand youth's creativity in public spaces, the use of the concept of *divergent* and *convergent* thinking is interesting. In fact, both types of thinking are required if creativity shall be obtainable [9]. Table I shows attributes needed for divergent thinking [9], while Table II for convergent thinking.

TABLE I. DIVERGENT THINKING

	Divergent thinking
1	Being unconventional
2	Seeing the known in a new light
3	Combining the disparate *information*
4	Producing multiple answers
5	Shifting perspective
6	Transforming the known
7	Seeing new possibilities
8	Taking risks
9	Retrieving a broad range of existing knowledge
10	Associating ideas from remote fields

Overall, the ten attributes in Table I describes the thinking phases needed for a person to think outside their safe boundaries in life and thus change their perspective. This willingness to open to a broader understanding of the problem area and get more insight is crucial to produce unexpected combinations of the known. Table II shows the needs that are required to complete a creativity process, where the act of converging into a narrowed path and constrains are mandatory and help toward a viable solution of a problem or innovative result.

Creativity in groups also needs to be addressed when analyzing all the attributes in Tables I and II. For example, *social loafing* in creatives groups is a common problem [10], and in addition another undesired effect can emerge as risky and creative ideas tend to not be shared as they can be misunderstood [10]. This tension may result in conventional and polite exchange of ideas, often resulting in incremental changes only.

TABLE II. CONVERGENT THINKING

	Convergent thinking
1	Recognizing the familiar
2	Combining what "belongs" together
3	Being logical
4	Homing in on the single best answer
5	Reapplying set techniques
6	Preserving the already known
7	Achieving accuracy and correctness
8	Playing it safe
9	Sticking to a narrow range of obviously relevant information
10	Making associations from adjacent fields only

III. DESIGNERLY PERSPECTIVES ON CREATIVITY

A framework able to *enhance* youth's creativity and design in public spaces needs to address divergent and convergent thinking. Design Thinking (DT) [11], [12] may help find a suitable framework since both divergent and convergent thinking are two of the main factors in a DT process. The power of DT as an approach is the use of design methods to define more precisely the problem and, at the same time solve it. The elaborative forces present in a DT process are rapid prototyping, abductive thinking and empathy for the user perspectives. The result of an abductive thinking process is the problem-solving process aforementioned, which is based on an educated guess. In the DT process one uses actively the divergent thinking to bring inside the creative process as much insight as possible. This is especially necessary when one is creative in the rapid prototyping phase. This type of thinking is interesting in regards to the attributes in Table I row 6, 9 and 10, where knowledge is an important factor. One could derive from this designerly perspective that youth may gain substantial support if a new framework may give them access to more tailored knowledge. In a DT process, an emphatic relation to the users perspective is mandatory [13], even in Tables I and II this perspective is not explicitly defined. In regards to youth a further analysis on their emphatic behavior could gain better insight and define its role properly. During the DT process, numerous prototypes are produced, and the best one is chosen, based on an educated guess. This process can be explained as follow: the definition of the problem emerges simultaneously with the solution. In the convergent thinking process this fits with row 4 in Table II, "Homing in on the single best answer". Findings in [14] supports this view when youth is interacting with their surroundings, are framing questions and producing answers and solutions: "Comparisons indicated that the adolescents generated significantly more responses to the discovered problems than the presented problems.". This is in line with a DT approach and may give a stronger support for a designerly perspective on how divergent and convergent thinking are tightly linked with DT, and why perspectives from young people in this context may be relevant to look into.

IV. CASE STUDY

Skaters as a group are interesting as they interact with their context in various ways, always looking for new arenas to use and explore and a willingness to the recuperation of existing material [15] to construct skateboarding locations. The data used to analyze the framework was gathered in short periods of observation in vivo, throughout several years, using informal discussions and interviews of a group of five skaters living outside a large city in Scandinavia. The group of skaters in this case study was only male, a very typical composition of groups in the skating milieu. The boys also had a quite normal distribution of character, ordinary and polite youth from middle-class families. The observation of this group started in 2010 just at the beginning of their interest in the skate milieu. All five were around twelve years old, and had other sports activities beside the practice of skating. Their interest bloomed fast and after a short period, they were often visiting skateboard parks in their living area. They also used the skateboard as a means of transportation to the nearby school, which they attended. After a while, the municipality and a local sports organization built a large skate ramp outside the school. The group also used to make their own smaller ramps and used part of streets, sidewalk, and small stairs to train in the art of skating. As a reason for choosing the path into the world of the skaters, coolness [16] was the most prevalent. The parks in the surrounding area were of different type and build. One was of concrete inside an old plastic storage hall, turned communal, without any adult supervision, while others were more bureaucratically organized. The latter type of skateboard park was, of course, larger and had several demanding ramps, usually made of woods. The storage hall skating park, not far from their home, consisting of concrete ramps and obstacles both outside and inside the hall, was the preferred one by this group of youth, and when visiting, sharing ideas and tricks with other skaters were common. Skating to the nearby grocery store and eating together did not require great effort; neither did asking for tips and tricks, and the other skaters always replied positively. The social context and the feeling of being part of the milieu were as well important.

Inventing or reinventing unusual types of games was also part of the skate life they adhered to, an example was "The skate", where one skater of the group made a trick and the rest had to copy. The peculiar part was the type of tricks, it could be new ones, or just invented there and then. Another interesting point they mentioned was the dynamics inside the group, as they used it as a platform to socialize between them. A revealing observation for the author was the act of buying skateboards. The effort and engagement in the discussion about the quality of wheel, the form and quality of the wood board and the colorful design underneath, was crucial of being part of the group and a strong socialization force and a symbol of group expression. The skating interest also affected their preference regarding the type of games on the game console everyone had at home, and what kind of movie to watch on television and online on the YouTube platform. Observations revealed other interesting aspects of how they had built up a social context around their living. Driven by the success of international skaters, their plans for the future were also affected, and making "*a world of their own*", they could interact with the surroundings based on its own terms and, as they pointed out, it allowed them to combine ideas and meaning from the group in a fruitful way.

After some years, one by one, stopped being part of the skate group although they hung together in other contexts, like sport or online gaming. As a reason for dropping out, they explained, that after a longer period of skating, some of them had difficulty to catch up with the most endowed among them. As this article is being written also the last one has partially given up being a professional skater. The last discussion with members of the group was performed this year, and dealt with their participation in the skate milieu, how they first became interested and how, in retrospect, the knowledge about tricks and movement was learned among them.

The focus was changed now, more in the direction of how they perceived what happened, what was the dynamic, and what they learned from their skating period. What they remembered and praised now was the positive socializations they had and the willingness to share competence and cooperate when working with new tricks and ideas. One trick question the author managed to ask them was what adults could learn from the skating milieu and how to implement this insight in real life. They explained the necessity of sharing the nice experiences one finds when being part of a group so including as the one they were part of. Values like openness and belonging were the ones mostly rewarded. In regards to implementing their wishes of a more inclusive community and public space, they had some adequate plans. Building places for youth to meet and share their common interest, make it easier for youth to participate in sporting activities and bring more people on to the street to make the urban space less frightening, were good ideas of intervention and redesign in public space.

V. AN ENHANCED FRAMEWORK

Using observations and data presented in the case study and additional insight from several studies of youth made by the author in the context of school when adapting new technologies and their response to coolness in the learning context [16]–[18], an enhanced framework for divergent and convergent thinking is presented. The framework defines *possible* behaviors for both the provocative and the less provocative youth in Tables III and IV. Each attribute may give relevant knowledge about what we can learn from both the more or less provocative youth, how to support them, and eventually how to transfer this creative mindset to youth not already engaged in creativity and design efforts in public spaces. Row one (*Being unconventional*) in Table III fits well when addressing youth acting outside their boundaries, and seeing the known in new light, from row two, was present in the group of skaters in the case study, as they always were out searching and hunting for new experiences and finally elaborating them into novel skating competence.

TABLE III. DIVERGENT THINKING IN YOUTH

Divergent thinking		Tendency for behavior among provocative youth	Tendency for behavior among less provocative youth
1	Being unconventional	Often in place	Difficult
2	Seeing the known in a new light	Often in place	Difficult
3	Combining the disparate *information*	Difficult	Often in place
4	Producing multiple answers	Possible	Possible
5	Shifting perspective	Often in place	Difficult
6	Transforming the known	Possible	Possible
7	Seeing new possibilities	Possible	Difficult
8	Taking risks	Often in place	Difficult
9	Retrieving a broad range of existing knowledge	Difficult	Possible
10	Associating ideas from remote fields	Difficult	Possible

For the provocative youth, row 3, 9 and 10 in Table III have in common a need for retrieving enough and relevant knowledge to accomplish a creative task and a possible indication that they may have problems in achieving that goal. Although observations from the case study show that the youth in the skate group often used several digital channels, peers and older participants of the milieu they belong to, to get information, the question is whether this effort is adequate. The area of interest, in this case skating, may be niche based and the attribute "*Associating ideas from remote fields*" (row 10) seems to require additional perspectives outside their range.

For the less provocative youth, the attributes in row 3, 9 and 10 may be more often in place, and a timely question could be if a cooperation between the less and more provocative youth could help the latter achieve their goal. Table IV, presenting attributes contributing to convergent thinking [9], is also interesting as the attributes seems to be more difficult for provocative youth to achieve, as the thinking phases are more close to a mature mindset. In fact, the final goal in schools is the concretization of the learning process in tests and exams, requiring primarily convergent thinking [19], and this paper addresses also the necessity to find out how youth manages to perform this form of thinking, as it is mandatory to accomplish creativity [9].

Rows 6, 9 and 10 in Table IV can be related to how the knowledge and the competence of a person need to converge and to be closely related to the problem area. Therefore this tension between the different tendencies the more or less provocative youth has, may have a specific effect especially in rows 6, 9 and 10, as it seems that a cooperation between them has fruitful results.

Finally, the attribute in row 8, (*Playing it safe*), is the only one with an obvious opposite value between the two different types of youth behavior, and have the inverse value in Table III (*Taking risk*). This attribute is quite interesting as it has an enormous impact, and implies that collaboration between youth with different behavior has to occur for creativity to take place.

TABLE IV. CONVERGENT THINKING IN YOUTH

Convergent thinking		Tendency for behavior among provocative youth	Tendency for behavior among less provocative youth
1	Recognizing the familiar	Often in place	Often in place
2	Combining what "belongs" together	Often in place	Often in place
3	Being logical	Possible	Possible
4	Homing in on the single best answer	Often in place	Often in place
5	Reapplying set techniques	Often in place	Often in place
6	Preserving the already known	Difficult	Often in place
7	Achieving accuracy and correctness	Possible	Possible
8	Playing it safe	Difficult	Possible
9	Sticking to a narrow range of obviously relevant information	Difficult	Possible
10	Making associations from adjacent fields only	Difficult	Possible

In fact, collaboration and co-invention between youth with opposite provocative behavior has some testimonial stories in company start-ups like Apple, Google, and Facebook. Even today, innovative companies seems to be governed by a mindset rather than management rules.

VI. DISCUSSION

The introduction of the paper has pointed out several examples of motivation to support and enhance youth's creativity and design in public spaces. As mentioned youth often interact with their surroundings in unpredictable ways, while today's society is not prepared or willing to learn and absorb their inputs. One can observe youth staying and hanging out on the outside of stores or inside malls, or skate communities using concrete, wood and more to construct new infrastructure and reshaping the public space as a way to comment and address more or less functional solutions in urban life. Artists have also used the urban and public space as an arena to communicate their narrative and understandings of today's living in visual ways (Fig. 2) [20].

One relevant question to ask is, if the urban living of today is the one we need and wish for? Allowing interventions and creativity in the public space to be an accepted form of communication and not a counterculture, seems not so easy. A current example is how easily even Banksy interventions in the public space have gotten censored when addressing the unpleasant reality of the European refugee politics (see Fig. 3) [21].

Figure 2. Companie Willi Dorner, Bodies in Urban Spaces [1][**20**].

Exclusion is also a form of censoring, with countless of examples and reducing the possibility young people have to intervene in the public urban space, represented by an example from a restriction of skaters in the Metro stations in Oslo (see figure 4). A final example of negative intervention in the public space is the attempt by a cultural institution in the Italian city of Bologna to dismantle different graffiti artwork and move them into an exhibition, often without permissions [22].

Figure 3. Banksy urban intervention being censored in London [**21**]. Photo from a news report by the Norwegian Broadcasting Corporation [**23**].

The group of skaters in the case study lived and perceived the public and social space from a creative stand. For them, the environment was linked to the attributes of divergent and convergent thinking as part of a creative effort, where the Design Thinking approach gives a sound understanding. One of the tension between the interventions of the skaters and creativity in the public space is the temporal use of the space, while this volatile attribute is difficult to monitor the effects of [15]. Addressing the different elaborative forces in Design Thinking may have good perspectives to give youth a framework consisting of a platform to cooperate on and enhance creativity, bringing together the physical and digital world where youth act in, and finally to take advantages of their willingness to make changes in a creative way. This way of interaction can also resolve the issue with the temporal use of space.

A platform for digital interventions may be consisting of a group of services included in the SoMe sphere to allow them to meet, discuss and share, after all, the majority of youth has smartphones, and using those services in the public space should be quite normal. The platform should also support a bridge between the physical and digital space based on the Internet of Things (IoT) where light, sound, smell and the narrative of living in form of pictures, text and drawing, could act as a catalyst for interventions. In regards to technology, every day new tools, gadget and services are entering the SoMe and IoT market, and youth often tries to redesign them in unpredictable ways, and in unthinkable areas, for instance like libraries [24]. The Internet of Things has already opened new frontiers in regards to interaction in the public area, from controllable street lights in the aim of the sustainable city, to city art, as in the use of light drones in Austria [25].

Figure 4. Restrictions in the Oslo Metro stations. Photo by Gasparini

A holistic approach to both SoMe and the IoT using Design Thinking gives a deeper understanding of how divergent and convergent thinking can be fully enhanced to support creativity among youth wishing to be engaged in civic matters. The case study shows their interest in contributing, whilst they did not have an easy platform to use.

However some new trend seems promising. Geo tags, Google street presents the public space with an augmented reality [26], and in this context the users has already allowed their own privacy be more open. The trend represents a willingness to share their locations. The use of Tinder, Facebook and others applications are examples of urban living connect with the digital word, and can be seen also as a digital layer that can be modelled and designed, and therefore promising for new solutions and possibility.

The elaborative forces of Design Thinking, for instance rapid prototyping, may take advantages of the tension in the creativity act when performed by the more or less provocative youth. Tables III and IV show they both need mentoring as it seems necessary in regards to knowledge acquisition, and knowledge transfer between them as the approach to gathering the correct insight is quite different. A platform to help them cooperate and enhance creativity should support a service where youth could get access to knowledge in an easy way. Using the possibility the Internet of Things and SoMe gives, the solution could function by using libraries, youth clubs, sports groups, schools, malls and more as an intersection between youth and access to knowledge, based on their creative mindset.

VII. CONCLUSION AND FUTURE WORKS

The paper proposed the use of a designerly based framework to *enhance* youth's creativity and design in public spaces, based on collaboration and co-creation across technology, space and grounded on their creative mindset. A platform where youth can share their interests and willingness in defining the way they want to live in the modern society should address how their divergent and convergent thinking functions. How skaters share information among them and their vision of the public space is an example of how young people are willing to share their insight and change their surroundings while the public space has a lack of platforms to engage them. Their willingness to make changes should be taken seriously and finally take the advantages of the impact they may have.

ACKNOWLEDGMENT

The author is grateful to the skaters and their parents to allow observations and interviews and to Ivan Gasparini for fruitful comments.

REFERENCES

[1] R. Klanten and M. Hübner, Urban interventions : personal projects in public spaces. Gestalten, 2010.

[2] W. Ellsworth-Jones, Banksy : The man behind the wall. London, 2012.

[3] G. Savičić and S. Savić, Unpleasant Design. Belgrade: G.L.O.R.I.A, 2012.

[4] X. Lin, J. Hu, and M. Rauterberg, "Review on Interaction Design for Social Context in Public Spaces," in Cross-Cultural Design Methods, Practice and Impact, P. L. P. Rau, Ed. Springer International Publishing, 2015, pp. 328–338.

[5] P. C. Rodkin, T. W. Farmer, R. Pearl, and R. V. Acker, "They're Cool: Social Status and Peer Group Supports for Aggressive Boys and Girls," Soc. Dev., vol. 15, no. 2, May 2006, pp. 175–204.

[6] A. Kozbelt, R. A. Beghetto, and M. A. Runco, "Theories of Creativity," in The Cambridge Handbook of Creativity, 2010, pp. 20–47.

[7] M. F. Shaughnessy, "An Interview with E. Paul Torrance: About Creativity," Educ. Psychol. Rev., vol. 10, no. 4, 1998, pp. 441–452.

[8] P. J. Guilford, "Creativity," Am. Psychol., vol. 5, no. 9, 1950, pp. 444–454.

[9] A. Cropley, "In Praise of Convergent Thinking," Creat. Res. J., vol. 18, no. 3, 2006, pp. 391–404.

[10] M. A. Runco, "Divergent thinking, Creativity, and Ideation," in The Cambridge Handbook of Creativity, Cambridge University Press, 2010.

[11] T. Brown, Change by design: how design thinking transforms organizations and inspires innovation. New York: Harper Business, 2009.

[12] T. Brown, "Design Thinking," Harward Bus. Rev., vol. 86, no. 6, 2008.

[13] A. Gasparini, "Perspective and Use of Empathy in Design Thinking," presented at the ACHI 2015, The Eighth International Conference on Advances in Computer-Human Interactions, 2015, pp. 49–54.

[14] M. A. Runco and S. M. Okuda, "Problem discovery, divergent thinking, and the creative process," J. Youth Adolesc., vol. 17, no. 3, 1988, pp. 211–220.

[15] G. M. Gutiérrez, "IDENSITAT: A Hybrid Anthropology of Identity, Creativity, and Intervention in Public Spaces," Am. Anthropol., vol. 115, no. 2, 2013, pp. 313–316.

[16] A. Culén and A. A. Gasparini, "Situated Techno-Cools: factors that contribute to making technology cool in a given context of use," PsychNology J., vol. 10, no. 2, 2012, pp. 117–139.

[17] A. L. Culen and A. Gasparini, "iPad: a new classroom technology? A report from two pilot studies," in Information Sciences and e-Society, 2011, pp. 199–208.

[18] A. Gasparini and A. L. Culen, "The iPad in a Classroom: A Cool Personal Item or Simply an Educational Tool?," in The Sixth International Conference on Advances in Computer-Human Interactions, Nice, France, 2013, pp. 204–209.

[19] M. A. Runco, "Creativity," Annu. Rev. Psychol., vol. 55, no. 1, 2004, pp. 657–687.

[20] "Cie.W.Dorner - Studio 70." [Online]. Available: http://www.ciewdorner.at/index.php?page=start. [Accessed: 27-Jan-2016].

[21] H. Ellis-Petersen, "Banksy's new artwork criticises use of teargas in Calais refugee camp," The Guardian, 24-Jan-2016.

[22] M. Smargassi, "Bologna, Blu cancella tutti i suoi murales: 'No alla street art privatizzata,'" Repubblica.it, 12-Mar-2016. [Online]. Available: http://bologna.repubblica.it/cronaca/2016/03/12/news/bologna_graffiti-135303806/. [Accessed: 17-Mar-2016].

[23] "NRK.no – Norwegian Broadcasting Corporation," NRK. [Online]. Available: http://www.nrk.no/. [Accessed: 27-Jan-2016].

[24] W. Evans, Building Library 3.0: Issues in Creating a Culture of Participation. Elsevier, 2009.

[25] "Spaxels | The Ars Electronica Quadcopter Swarm." .

[26] P. Oswalt, Urban catalyst : the power of temporary use. DOM Publ, 2013.

'Pop-up' Maker-spaces: Catalysts for Creative Participatory Culture

Sumit Pandey
Design of Information Systems, Department of Informatics
University of Oslo
Oslo, Norway
sumitp@ifi.uio.no

Swati Srivastava
Design of Information Systems, Department of Informatics
University of Oslo
Oslo, Norway
swatisr@ifi.uio.no

***Abstract*—The changing technology landscape has reshaped the relationship between producers and consumers and has signaled a shift towards more collaborative and social cultural forms. These changing cultural practices are referred to as 'Participatory Culture'. While the Internet offers an always on and readily accessible mode of engagement and involvement within participatory culture, these platforms need to be complemented with collaborative and creative participation in physical spaces for sustained engagement in real world cultural activities. Recent research on maker cultures and the growth of maker-spaces offers very relevant lessons in this regard. Using this research as a point of departure, we propose a decentralized and semi-organized form of maker-spaces called 'pop-up' maker-spaces that could act as triggers to create engagement within communities towards creative and collaborative production and informal knowledge sharing. Further, we describe three workshops that were setup as 'pop-up' maker-space environments as a part of a case study to discuss our findings and insights. While all the workshops had a pre-defined thematic area, the final outcomes were very different and represented differing conceptual and material explorations conducted by the participants.**

Keywords- Participatory Culture; Collaborative Spaces; Creative Engagement; Co-operation; Awareness; Motivation; Digital Engagement.

I. INTRODUCTION

The changing technology landscape has reshaped the relationship between producers and consumers and has signaled a shift towards more collaborative and social cultural forms. These cultures re-consider the passive role of consumers as mere users of content from controlled and established channels to a much more active social and collaborative role - one where they actively access content through ever increasing number of dispersed channels, discuss, re-appropriate and share it. Media scholars and the Human Computer Interaction (HCI) community refer to these changing cultural practices as "participatory culture" [1] - a culture of creation, re-appropriation, sharing and collaboration. Literature points to the importance of participatory culture in today's society including collaborative learning, an informed attitude towards intellectual property, better civic engagement and a more empowered concept of citizenship [1]. While the most common and current examples of participatory culture do seem to come from Internet based services and platforms, the history of participatory cultures predates these technologies and has always existed as a form of de-centralized expression particularly amongst the youth [2].

While the Internet offers an always on and readily accessible mode of engagement and involvement within participatory culture [3], research suggests that such platforms are not always successful in sustained engagement in real world civic and cultural activities [4][5]. Papert [6] also stressed on the importance of face to face interaction, with a diverse mix of skill levels, from complete beginners to experts, for informal learning in a social setting. While participatory culture is discussed exclusively as a form of Internet based media production and sharing [7]–[9] there is growing interest in the HCI community on a different but, in our opinion, closely related phenomenon of 'maker cultures' [10]. Maker cultures refer to alternative practices of material and technology ownership and use with a focus on Do It Yourself (DIY) repairs, craft, hacking, digital fabrication and electronic tinkering [10][11]. Research has also highlighted [11]–[13] the role of collaborative co-creation spaces called 'maker-spaces' [14] and 'fablabs' [15] in catalyzing maker cultures. These spaces aim to create accessible co-production platforms for physical products and promote collaborative and social problem solving [14][16], which is in-line with Jenkins' [1] description of participatory culture. Hence, we propose that platforms like maker-spaces should be seen as the physical counterparts of online content production and sharing platforms and have the potential to configure participatory cultures within communities by aiding creative production and discussion. However, while maker-spaces and maker culture in general have an openness, democratization and empowerment driven intent [10][12][14], critical research has also pointed out the gaps between the ideal nature of their intent and the realities of practice [17][18]. The highly technological nature of the material and culture in maker-spaces tends to also make them exclusive and limited to a 'techno-savvy' audience [13]. In light of such critiques, we suggest that maker-spaces need to take a more decentralized and semi-organized form with permanent spaces being complemented by 'maker' community run temporary or 'pop-up' maker-spaces that could serve to engage larger communities in the means of creative and collaborative production and informal knowledge sharing. We argue that the temporal nature of these pop-up maker-spaces could serve to create interest in otherwise disengaged communities and help translate the open and democratic intent of the maker culture without requiring the large scale investments needed for a traditional maker-space. Moreover, the advent of 'maker' oriented portable kit based technology platforms like littleBits [19], SAM [20] and Printrbot [21] allows these spaces to take a mobile and decentralized shape and does not limit them to fixed areas with expensive hardware on site. Hence, we suggest these 'pop-up' maker-spaces could act as bridges for grassroots participation by virtue of being accessible and offering a low barrier to entry.

In this paper, we use one such platform, littleBits [19], and examine the role it can play in conjunction with specific spatial arrangements and low-fidelity materials in configuring a 'pop-up' maker-space setup intended to provoke creative engagement within different communities. We describe three workshops that were setup as 'pop-up' maker-space environments as a part of a case study to discuss our findings and insights. While all the workshops had a pre-defined thematic area, the final outcomes were very different and represented differing conceptual and material explorations conducted by the participants.

The paper is structured as follows: The conceptual considerations and the technological platform that we build on to develop the construct of pop-up maker spaces is introduced in Section II. In Section III, we present our case study using three workshops that used the pop-up maker space construct in real world scenarios and highlight our approach with participants from different age groups and professional areas of practice. Finally, we discuss our findings in Section IV followed by a conclusion in Section V.

II. Conceptual and Technological Considerations

In this section, we briefly outline the theoretical considerations that helped frame the approach and design of the elements of decentralized and mobile "pop-up maker-spaces".

A. *Participatory Cultures*

Jenkins et al. [1], in their seminal work, defined participatory culture as

"a culture with relatively low barriers to artistic expression and civic engagement, strong support for creating and sharing creations, and some type of informal mentorship whereby experienced participants pass along knowledge to novices."

They also argue that a participatory culture also allows its members to believe in their contributions and feel "some degree of social connection" [1] with others and their opinions about their creations. In general, participatory cultures reward participation but do not force it. This idea stems from the advancements in technology that has allowed people to shift from their roles of passive consumers to active creators of content and more recently products using self-fabrication techniques [22][23]. Further, Delwiche and Handerson [24] discuss three broad classifications within participatory culture, depending on the nature of participation. Their work suggests that the nature of participatory culture is largely defined by real world factors like space, participants and their level of engagement with the community and the media being generated.

1) Consensus cultures

This is an "agreement based" culture that is typically work or productivity oriented, usually with specific goals that need to be met or problems that need to be addressed. A special form of this kind of participatory culture can be seen in "expert cultures" where people with "specialized knowledge" come together like in think tanks.

2) Creative cultures

This is a culture which encourages its participants to create, re-purpose, remix, share and comment within a safe and supportive environment. Participants are often very passionate about their areas of interest and creativity and are willing to share and build on their knowledge and creations. This kind of participatory culture is known to foster sustained engagement. The maker, remix and art cultures are examples of this type of culture. Work within this thesis would primarily explore participatory culture in this context.

3) Discussion cultures

This is a culture that fosters participation around specific topics of personal and professional interest rather than specific objects and outcomes. Engagement in this kind of culture is varied with participant's interests changing over time. Since the objective of this kind of culture is discussion and debate, the nature of participant exchange may vary from support to heated disagreement, often in real time. News sites and fan forums are examples of this type of culture. The discussion outlined in this paper primarily concentrates on creative cultures, with its focus on collaborative exchange, sustained engagement and creative production.

B. *Maker Culture*

Maker culture refers to practices related to DIY, craft, electronic tinkering and technology repair leading to the development of alternate notions of material ownership and use within 'maker communities' [12]. Lately, maker cultures have been given a lot of interest within HCI with empirical studies on maker identities and values [12], analysis of the modes of material engagement [25][26] and larger investigations into the democratizing effects of maker culture on technology and technological practices. Maker culture is also turning into a popular phenomenon rather than a fringe activity for specialized communities largely propelled by the rise of maker-spaces, hacker-spaces or fab labs across the world [10]. While discussions on maker cultures tend to take a largely technology centric stand point as opposed to the media centric outlook of participatory cultures, we argue that there is a natural overlap between them with a focus on practices of community building, knowledge sharing and democratized expression and material access. Further, we suggest that maker spaces provide the spatial setting and cultural framework for sustained engagement with diverse means of creative production.

C. *LittleBits*

LittleBits [19] is a technological platform for aiding rapid prototyping and electronic tinkering aimed at people with little to no prior experience with electronics. The platform is designed to be modular and plug and play in nature with little to no configuration needed. It consists of an assorted set of color coded magnetic 'bits' that encapsulate a specific function like temperature sensing, light sensing, USB power, Direct Current (DC) powered motors, servo motors, Light Emitting Diode (LED) lights and so on. Based on the nature of the bits, they are divided into four categories – power (blue), input (pink), output (green) and wire (orange). These functions can be arranged in linear sequences that can then be triggered using programmatic, cloud connected or sensor driven bits. The color coding of the functions allows for ease in identification and configuration aided by their magnetic nature that only allows the bits to be connected in their correct orientation (since the bits repel each other in an incorrect orientation). The bits by themselves are intended to act as alternatives to bare bones electronics components and allow ease of use while prototyping the interactive functions of a concept. Therefore, they are intended to be used along with other lo and hi-fidelity materials that would create the external form and tangible interfaces for the concept being prototyped. LittleBits [19] were chosen as the technological material for the purposes of our workshops because of their ease of use and configurability due to the limited time available to the participants in a pop-up maker-space scenario.

III. Case Studies

As stated in the introduction, our goal was to explore the portable kit-based platform littleBits [19] as a material in a workshop setting to explore the construct of a 'pop-up' maker-space for configuring creative participatory cultures. These workshops were conducted as a part of larger project, which aims to investigate technology centric design interventions as a means of configuring public engagement and participatory culture. In this paper we describe and discuss the outcomes from three workshops conducted with different user groups: (i) Children from the age group of 7 to 12 years, (ii) Design researchers, (iii) Professional graphic designers. These groups highlight a broad spectrum of creatively inclined individuals with differences in age, nature of practice and access to technology. While all three groups identified engaged with creative production, with children regularly engaging in creative activities at school and in their home environment, design researchers using various prototyping methods in their design projects and graphic designers primarily engaging with creative production in a professional setting, all groups had limited to no experience with the use of tangible technological materials in practice.

We organized pop-up maker spaces in a workshop setting with each group of participants separately. Due to the differences in the nature of each group, the approach used to engage with them in the workshop was different. However, the physical space in each case was temporarily converted into a maker space like setting, with free and easy access to prototyping materials like colored paper, card sheets, foam boards, paints, scissors, brushes, ice-cream sticks, rubber bands, cups, assorted lego bricks and play-doh (Figure 1). Multiple littleBits [19] workshop kits were used as the primary technological material for provoking electronic tinkering. The quantity of each material differed based on the themes of each workshop. This also helped us evaluate the role and impact of supportive materials on the nature and form of engagement when used in conjunction with littleBits [19].

Figure 1. The spatial setup (top) and the materials used (bottom) in the pop-up maker-space.

As the workshops were conducted in the form of open pop-up maker spaces, the format of participation was either open (walk-in) or sign-up (pre-registation) based. While the sign-up based workshops began with an informal introduction to the littleBits [19] platform and a loosely defined theme for the day and ended with a presentation and feedback, in the open workshop setting, the introduction was interspersed between the activities. Previous experience with littleBits [19] or any other technological tools was not required for any of the workshops.

The sub-sections below describe each workshop in greater detail. Photo-documentation was the main analytical tool used for the purposes of this research. Therefore, a large number of photographs were collected during the workshops, both of the final outcome as well as the interim explorations by the participants. These photographs were then analyzed to identify differences in the mode of engagement and processes undertaken by each group of participants to arrive at their respective outcomes.

A. *The First Workshop with Children*

The first workshop was conducted as an open (walk-in) exploratory pop-up maker space with children. It was conducted as a four hours long workshop, with 23 participating children. There were three moderators in the workshop. All moderators were well versed with littleBits [19] and were practicing designer researchers and 'makers'. The theme of this workshop was "Sound and Motion". This workshop was setup as a part of a larger maker event, open for children from the age group of 7-12 years. An enclosed hall was taken up for the workshop adjacent to a library's open lounge area. The materials for the workshop included the littleBits [19] kits and craft materials described earlier. As there was no planned introductory session, artifacts such as a bend sensor controlled wind mill and a simple draw-bot were made and displayed on the tables in the workshop area along with the littleBits [19] and the craft materials to give a visual explanation of the bits' potential and to provoke interest. Multiple copies of the littleBits [19] 'getting started' guide containing simple projects were also placed on the tables. The tables were arranged linearly with chairs for working. The bits themselves were grouped by color and kept on a central table along with other materials.

The workshop started with children observing the demonstrative interactive artifacts. The moderators gave a quick demo of the different ways of connecting the bits to the children in small groups by connecting and making a small circuit with sound and light. The participants explored the bits on their own for half an hour in the workshop. The interaction between the participants and moderators was more intense during this exploratory phase when the children were trying to identify different possibilities of using the bits. However, after the first half an hour, children started working on their own projects. Some of them who knew each other beforehand worked in groups of two while rest engaged with them individually. While most of the projects started with creating a sound or light driven artifact, slowly they progressed towards creating a button driven car, a drawing car and interactive music boxes that worked through different sensors (Figure 2).

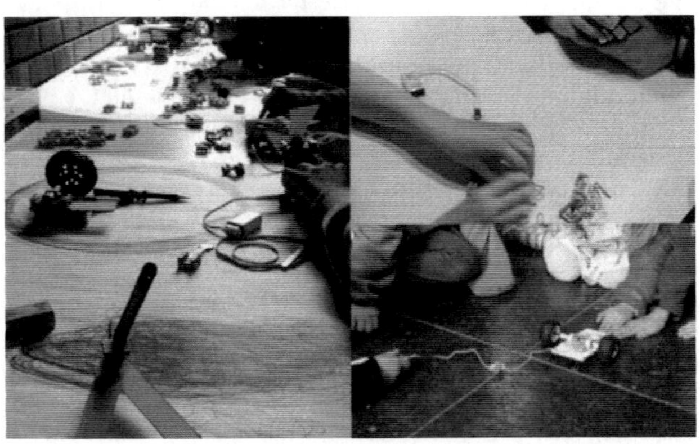

Figure 2. Some outcomes from the first workshop.

Looking at the artifacts made by the participants, littleBits [19] in conjunction with the available craft materials and the open spatial configuration where all the participants engaged in similar activities played a pivotal role in triggering creative engagement. Further, the ease of connecting littleBits [19] lowered the barrier to entry tremendously and a quick demo was effective and sufficient for the children to get started with making things. Finally, successfully being able to build feedback in the system developed confidence in them leading to greater engagement and attempts at creating more complex artifacts.

B. The Second Workshop With Design Researchers

This workshop was conducted in a design lab with similar materials as the first case at a university with eight participating design researchers. Amongst them, four were PhD fellows and the remaining participants were professors in design research. Participation in this workshop was based on pre-registration and it was conducted over a duration of three hours. The theme of the workshop was light and motion. The participants in this workshop had no previous experience with using littleBits [19].

This workshop started with a formal presentation on littleBits [19], which introduced the participants to the platform and its basic functions and interactions. Possibilities of using the platform as a prototyping tool in design projects were also explained briefly to closely relate the materials with the participant's practice. After the introduction, the participants used the littleBits [19] manual do some initial exploration followed by a round of brief ideation. They moved organically from very roughly thought out ideas to trying to make interactive prototypes of their concepts, highlighting the really low barrier to entry to the prototyping process. One wireless remote based car was made by one group of three participants while other participants made by a 'head banging' light device that blinks with neck motion, a drawing machine and Arduino [27] connected lights (Figure 3).

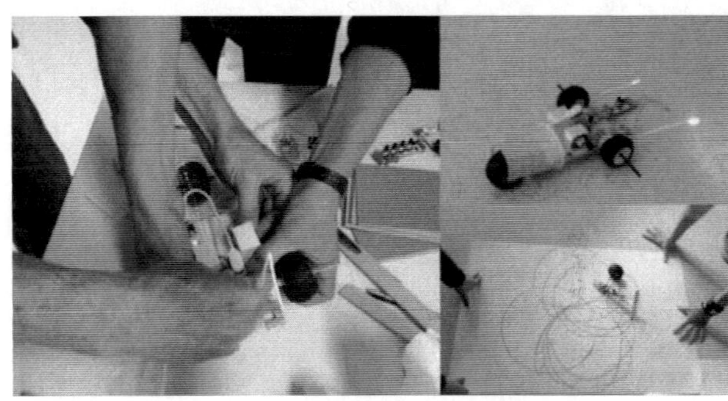

Figure 3. Light following bot and drawing bot created by participants in workshop 2.

We observed all the participants completely engaged in looking for extra materials on their own in their environment to complete their prototypes. Although all the participants felt that they lacked a very clear intent of a project to make something more complex and just littleBits [19] were not enough invoke more advanced projects ideas. However, most of them indicated that they wanted to come back to this space to prototype their own design ideas.

C. The Third Workshop with Graphic Designers

The third workshop was carried out in the context of a design school. There were twelve participating graphic design professionals and students in this workshop. An open foyer in the design school was identified as the space for setting up the pop-up maker-space. A similar set of materials was arranged for the participants in this workshop as well with a higher quantity of sketching and painting tools like brushes, different kinds of paints, crayons and markers due to the workshop theme - 'printing/drawing machines'. It was a full day workshop conducted over a duration of five hours. Like the previous workshop, the first activity in this workshop was a formal presentation on littleBits [19]. It was introduced as platform for quick prototyping and sketching in hardware and a tool that can be easily incorporated by graphic designers with no experience with technological prototyping as a means for creative expression. When the making session started, it was conducted as a round table activity. The participants formally introduced themselves and their backgrounds to each other. The initial plan was to do a similar exploration exercise with the bits followed by jumping into projects afterwards in groups. However, being practicing designers, the participants started to work with the platform while ideating concepts simultaneously. While two participants who were classmates made a group, others embarked on individual conceptualization and rapidly making ideas.

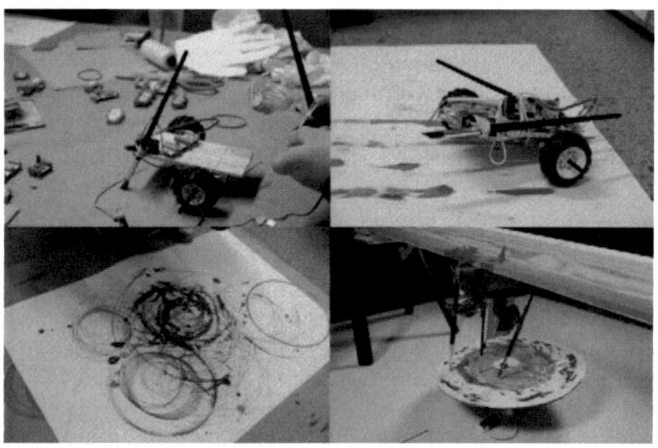

Figure 4. Drawing machines and artwork created in workshop 3.

This time we observed the participants did not spend time exploring littleBits [19] in isolation. Each one of them took time to plan their project outcomes and prepared materials for it. Their final projects were more finished in comparison to the previous workshops as well in addition to having very different interactions despite all of them being drawing machines (Figure 4).

IV. Discussion

We analyzed our first hand observations and documentation for insights with a keen focus on uncovering the role of modularized and easy to use technological platforms like littleBits [19] in shaping the physical spaces into cultures that foster creative engagement and lead to an organic sharing of knowledge and ideas.

Firstly, a clearly designated physical space with an open and exploration friendly configuration helped create a context for the exploration and use of the technological material (littleBits [19]) specifically and engaging with electronic tinkering in general. For example, in the first workshop with children, even before children could get a hands on 'maker' experience, the set up of the space with demonstrative artifacts, freely kept materials and bits, and various manuals combined with free seating arrangements conveyed the nature of the space. The crafts materials on display also contributed to the maker space environment. While the library's open lounge required greater efforts to convert it into a space for creative activity, the design studio for the second workshop and graphic design school foyer in the third workshop lent itself naturally to the nature of the activity.

Secondly, the technological material combined with quick access to seasoned makers in itself played a pivotal role in driving the creative focus and confidence in exploring ideas which previously seemed out of reach by the participants. For instance, during the first workshop children were fascinated by the interactive windmill on display but displayed hesitance in lifting and examining the artifact itself. However, when moderators helped them in making similar interactions on their own, it led to a realization of the ease of getting started with electronic tinkering and the fact that they could also create something similar to the artifact on display on their own. This led to the children being less in awe with what they were seeing but more engaged with what they could accomplish on their own by using the bits. Although one of the downsides of such a setup was that many children started making projects very similar to what was already on display. A similar but slightly different response was observed in the other two workshops, an introduction to the platform and a small session with the bits sufficed in breaking the fear of working with technological materials and participants then started focusing on their ideas and concepts rather than trying to learn the technology itself. We could see modularized easy to use platforms like littleBits [19] as an encouraging platform that seemed to get out of the way and instead let the participants have conversations and engage with making things without having to go through a prolonged learning processes. We argue that such quick access platforms are pivotal in creating initial interest in creative maker cultures at 'pop-up' or temporary spaces where there is limited time to engage with the materials at hand.

Thirdly, we observed that while the bits themselves largely formed the internal components of most ideas, they were the primary drivers of conversations and the exchange of knowledge. As discussed in Section II, this technological platform in itself consists of a large number of bits that encapsulate a single function that compound exponentially into a huge number of potentially complex interactions when configured into different kinds of arrangements. Therefore, it can be difficult and quite monotonous for one individual to sit and learn all of these functional characteristics and configurations. However, engaging in the act of making and in an organic and exploratory manner coupled with exchanges with other participants, the participants inadvertently get exposed to most of the different components through the process of helping and watching other people engage with them. This was observed more prominently in both the second and third workshop, where individuals working on their idea kept to themselves during the making process but constantly engaged in listening and contributing to the discussions around the function and use of a new bit along with inquiring about bits that they stumbled into or saw lying around.

Finally, craft materials were used to construct the physical form of the ideas conceptualized by the participants and remained pivotal in all the three workshops. The bits made complex concepts feasible and quicker to configure than with traditional electronic toolkits like the Arduino [27] but the craft materials allowed for the interactive functions to have an engaging and usable form. For instance, in one of the projects in the third workshop made by a two graphic design students, the function of a large scale drawing machine was prototyped using the bits but the concept could not have been complete without the rotating plates and the scaffolding for the paint bucket. Finally, the use of external camera lights added an element of drama to the art installation and made it even more engaging. Therefore, we argue that a technological platform like littleBits [19] needs to be situated within a larger ecosystem for exploratory and creative engagement. Specifically, in the case of a 'pop-up maker space' having a diverse set of electronic and non electronic reconfigurable tangible materials is critical to engage and fully involve participants and help them in physically realizing their ideas to their fullest potential. The temporal nature these pop-up arenas leave little space for isolated struggles with the tools themselves which can hamper the drive to work with the ideas in the limited timeframe.

V. CONCLUSION

The paper illustrates the use of 'pop-up' maker-spaces as a construct to configure creative culture based engagement and participation, using modular and easy to use technological platform in conjunction with craft based materials and an open spatial setup for fostering creativity in participating communities. Three workshops were organized, in the form of pop-up maker events. The first featured children from the age group of seven to twelve years, while the remaining two were focused on design researchers and graphic designers. The main tool for engaging the workshop participants in process of tangible construction and representation of their ideas was littleBits [19]. The process was photo documented and analysed.

First, we remark that using the modular technological platform, littleBits [19] for DIY prototyping proved effective for the workshop participants. While the intent of participating in the pop-up maker-spaces differed for all three categories of participants in the three workshops, the ease of access and understanding of littleBits [19] played a pivotal role in engaging the users. We witnessed that the participants engaged extensively with the bits and the other craft material provided to make their ideas in all the workshops.

Our key finding was that a hands on popup maker-space environment engaged participants in collaborative exchanges around an easy to use technological platform led to creative outcomes even though all the participants were completely new to electronic tinkering. The spatial configuration and access to technical and craft based materials helped catalyze the engagement and explorations. Moreover, they also served as triggers for exchange of knowledge and informal conversations among the participants who suggested alternative bits and techniques to each other based on their limited experience to aid the construction of each other's artifacts.

The insights and early results from these pop-up maker-spaces can serve as a foundation for further research on the role of technological toolkits and materials on sustained engagement and creative expression. Our future work would involve identifying design patterns for configuring pop-up maker-spaces along with exploring other technological toolkits, materials and diverse spatial configurations for exploratory and creative DIY engagements amongst participants.

VI. ACKNOWLEDGEMENTS

The authors are indebted to all the workshop participants for their participation and the Gemini UX Lab at the University of Oslo for supporting the project with the littleBits [19] platform. In addition, we would like to acknowledge Creative Europe for providing partial financial support through the People's Smart Sculpture project.

REFERENCES

[1] H. Jenkins, Confronting the Challenges of Participatory Culture: Media Education for the 21st Century. MIT Press, 2009.

[2] TEDxNYED - Henry Jenkins - 03/06/10. 2010.

[3] R. A. Hart, Children's Participation: The Theory and Practice of Involving Young Citizens in Community Development and Environmental Care, First Printing edition. New York: Routledge, 1997.

[4] "Our Space: Online Civic Engagement Tools for Youth." [Online]. Available: http://www.issuelab.org/resource/our_space_online_civic_engagement_tools_for_youth. [Accessed: 17-Mar-2016].

[5] "Can Games Motivate Urban Youth for Civic Engagement?" [Online]. Available: https://www.academia.edu/11321757/Can_Games_Motivate_Urban_Youth_for_Civic_Engagement. [Accessed: 17-Mar-2016].

[6] S. A. Papert, "Some Poetic and Social Criteria for Education Design," Jun. 1976.

[7] J. Hamilton, "OurPlace: The Convergence of Locative Media and Online Participatory Culture," in *Proceedings of the 21st Annual Conference of the Australian Computer-Human Interaction Special Interest Group: Design: Open 24/7*, New York, NY, USA, 2009, pp. 393–396.

[8] R. R. Johnson, M. J. Salvo and M. W. Zoetewey, "User-Centered Technology in Participatory Culture: Two Decades #x201C;Beyond a Narrow Conception of Usability Testing #x201D;," IEEE Transactions on Professional Communication, vol. 50, no. 4, Dec. 2007, pp. 320–332.

[9] D. Rotman, et al., "From Slacktivism to Activism: Participatory Culture in the Age of Social Media," in *CHI '11 Extended Abstracts on Human Factors in Computing Systems*, New York, NY, USA, 2011, pp. 819–822.

[10] M. G. Ames, J. Bardzell, S. Bardzell, S. Lindtner, D. A. Mellis and D. K. Rosner, "Making Cultures: Empowerment, Participation, and Democracy - or Not?," in *CHI '14 Extended Abstracts on Human Factors in Computing Systems*, New York, NY, USA, 2014, pp. 1087–1092.

[11] D. K. Rosner, S. Lindtner, I. Erickson, L. Forlano, S. J. Jackson and B. Kolko, "Making cultures: building things & building communities," 2014, pp. 113–116.

[12] A. Toombs, S. Bardzell and J. Bardzell, "Becoming Makers: Hackerspace Member Habits, Values, and Identities," Journal of Peer Production, 2014.

[13] D. Slatter and Z. Howard, "A place to make, hack, and learn: makerspaces in Australian public libraries," The Australian Library Journal, vol. 62, no. 4, Nov. 2013, pp. 272–284.

[14] A. Smith, S. Hielscher, S. Dickel, J. Soderberg and E. van Oost, "Grassroots digital fabrication and makerspaces: Reconfiguring, relocating and recalibrating innovation?," Sep-2013. [Online]. Available: http://www.sussex.ac.uk/spru/research/swps. [Accessed: 17-Mar-2016].

[15] "Fab Foundation – About Fab Foundation." [Online]. Available: http://www.fabfoundation.org/about-us/. [Accessed: 17-Mar-2016].

[16] L. Britton, "A Fabulous Labaratory: The Makerspace at Fayetteville Free Library," *Public Libraries Online*. .

[17] G. Hertz, Critical Making. Telharmonium, 2012.

[18] M. Ratto, "Critical making: Conceptual and material studies in technology and social life," The Information Society, vol. 27, no. 4, 2011, pp. 252–260.

[19] "littleBits: DIY Electronics For Prototyping and Learning." [Online]. Available: http://littlebits.cc/. [Accessed: 17-Mar-2016].

[20] "SAM Labs." [Online]. Available: https://samlabs.me/. [Accessed: 29-Feb-2016].

[21] "Printrbot | Affordable high resolution 3D printers." [Online]. Available: http://printrbot.com/. [Accessed: 29-Feb-2016].

[22] G. Ritzer and N. Jurgenson, "Production, Consumption, Prosumption The nature of capitalism in the age of the digital 'prosumer,'" Journal of Consumer Culture, vol. 10, no. 1, Mar. 2010, pp. 13–36.

[23] J. J. Burke, Makerspaces: A Practical Guide for Librarians. Lanham: Rowman & Littlefield Publishers, 2014.

[24] A. Delwiche and J. J. Henderson, The Participatory Cultures Handbook. Routledge, 2012.

[25] D. Rosner and J. Bean, "Learning from IKEA hacking: i'm not one to decoupage a tabletop and call it a day.," presented at the Proceedings of the SIGCHI Conference on Human Factors in Computing Systems, 2009, pp. 419–422.

[26] J. G. Tanenbaum, A. M. Williams, A. Desjardins and K. Tanenbaum, "Democratizing technology: pleasure, utility and expressiveness in DIY and maker practice," 2013, p. 2603.

[27] "Arduino - Home." [Online]. Available: https://www.arduino.cc/. [Accessed: 24-Jan-2016].

Visualizing Quantified Self Data Using Avatars

Isabella Nake, Aris Alissandrakis, and Janosch Zbick

Department of Media Technology
Faculty of Technology
Linnaeus University
Växjö, Sweden
Email: isabella.nake@gmail.com, {aris.alissandrakis, janosch.zbick}@lnu.se

Abstract—**In recent years, it is becoming more common for people to use applications or devices that keep track of their activities, such as fitness activities, places they visited, the music they listen to, and pictures they took. These data are used by the services for various purposes, but usually there are limitations for the users to explore or interact with them. Our project investigates a new approach of visualizing such Quantified Self data, in a meaningful and enjoyable way that gives the users insights into their data. The paper discusses the feasibility of creating a service that allows users to connect the activity tracking applications they already use, analyse the amount of activities, and then presents them the resulting information. The visualization of the information is proposed as an avatar that maps the different activities the user is engaged with, along with the activity levels, as graphical features. Within the scope of this work, several user studies were conducted and a system prototype was implemented to explore how to build, using web technologies, such a system that aggregates and analyses personal activity data, and also to determine what kind of data should and can be collected, to provide meaningful information to the users. Furthermore, it was investigated how a possible design for the avatar could look like, to be clearly understood by the users.**

Keywords–Quantified Self; Avatars; Data Visualization.

I. Introduction

Making active use of most entertainment, productivity, lifestyle, health and fitness, etc. applications and services can produce a large amount of personal data. There is a growing interest in collecting data generated from users' everyday lives, indicated by the increasing emergence of technologies and applications available to track users' activities. One of the commercial purposes for doing this is recommendation. An application used to listen to music does not only keep record of the songs that were played, but can also give recommendations to further songs and artists a user might like, based on the information of what other users are listening to. This is done, e.g., by Spotify [1]. A similar approach is used by Amazon, who provides recommendations for products based on what a customer bought in the past, what they have in their virtual shopping cart, their ratings and likes, as well as the behaviour of other customers who viewed or bought similar items [2]. There can also be other purposes, such as for maintaining personal records. A user might use an application in combination with her fitness activities to get detailed information on, e.g., how long and how fast she was running. But although many of the applications and services keep track of activity data, they do not necessarily provide detailed feedback to the users. Users are also not always aware of how often they are actually making use of some applications, e.g., how often they use an application that allows them to take pictures to share with their friends.

The concept of the Internet of Things (IoT) is rapidly growing, connecting more and more real-world physical objects, like household appliances, buildings and human bodies, as well as items like food or clothing, to the Internet [3]. Many devices are now available that, besides communicating with each other, can sense and collect a variety of data from users' behaviour. These include ubiquitous mobile phones and smart wearable devices. These substantial and heterogeneous data are used by the different services, but are not necessarily shared with the users, and usually there are limited ways to analyse and process the information.

Recently, interest has been growing in collecting data about health, sports, sleep and other activities within our everyday lives [4]. Although people worry about sharing too much information about themselves via social media platforms and being tracked by ad networks, the interest in generating more personal data is increasing [5], and this movement is called *Quantified Self*. As Swan [6] describes, "The quantified self (QS) is any individual engaged in the self-tracking of any kind of biological, physical, behavioural, or environmental information." To track the data, either applications or devices are used. The QS website (http://quantifiedself.com/guide/) lists more than 500 tools, which can be used for the data collection. Examples for tracked data are "weight, energy level, mood, time usage, sleep quality, health, cognitive performance, athletics, and learning strategies" [6]. One main aim of collecting QS data is to examine ones life [5]. Though some people might just be interested in storing information about themselves to remember it later on, others want to get a deeper meaning out of their data [7]. Those want to discover patterns to gain self-knowledge and self-awareness of their behaviour and thus have the possibility to change and improve their lives.

Large amounts of data are generated by and collected (usually by the different service providers) from users' everyday activities, as well as from making use of smart devices, wearables and of course mobile phones. The difficulty lies, as usually noted in the "big data" domain discussions, in interpreting the data into useful information (cf. [8]). Numerous applications exist which can visualize the data, but further research is necessary to offer easily-understandable information visualization, especially to cross-reference different types of data [9]. Although these "big data" are used by the applications and services for a variety of purposes, they remain mostly unavailable to the users, with limited ways to interact, explore and maybe get insights based of their own information. The work presented in this paper attempts to address this and explore ways to reclaim the ownership of these "big data" for more personal uses.

Our project investigates in particular how to build a system, using web technologies, to aggregate and analyse personal activity data (related to QS) in order to provide meaningful information to the user. The focus lies on identifying social media (and other) services that can be considered as sources of data, what kind of data can be collected from each of these services, how the data could be collected and aggregated into this system, as well as how often the collected data should be updated. Another equally important aspect of this project is to determine a possible (graphical) design for the visualization of the information so it is meaningful to, and understood by, the users. Based on previous work, it was assumed that a suitable visualization for such a system could consist of an "avatar" that would map the different activities the user is engaged with, along with the levels of those activities, as different graphical features.

The remaining of the paper is structured as following: Section 2 presents related work. The methodology is described in Section 3. An overview of the system prototype, which was developed in the context of this project, can be found in Section 4. Results and analysis of the study are shown in Section 5. Finally, Section 6 summarizes and concludes the study.

II. Related Work

Chang [10][11][12] wrote a three-part series about QS and *Gamification*, which can be defined as "the use of game design elements in non-game contexts" [13].He emphasizes the importance of making the data collection, and thus the sensors, ubiquitous and hidden, since people are not likely to change their usual behaviour just for getting some numbers, e.g., by having to enter all their activities manually in an application. Furthermore, he suggests to give scores and rewards for activities, based on predefined rules which are known by the users, rather than presenting numbers and graphs.

Within the scope of our project, a new approach of visualizing QS data is explored. The users should not have to start using a new tracking application for collecting their data, but having the data gathered from existing services they already use. After analysing the collected data, these would be visualized as an avatar. The avatar should show the users how active they are using certain services; this is something which they may not be aware of, or it could not directly correspond to their personal impression. It could also make them aware of the extent that the different services collect personal data from them. Such avatars could also be shared with friends, for example via social media platforms (posts, status updates, or even profile pictures). This sharing could allow for comparisons, or competing for which avatar shows the most or least activity for a certain service, which brings elements of Gamification into the QS domain.

A. Data Collection and Visualization

Research has been conducted to design personal visualizations and personal data presentations. Choe et al. [14] investigated how a visualization system should be designed to support Quantified Selfers, who might not be visualization experts or data scientists, with getting insights to their own data. The following four areas were proposed for the development of personal visualization systems: self-reflection as a personal insight, gaining valid personal insights, communicating personal insights and visual annotation for highlighting insights. Wang et al. [15] presented users different personal visualization designs to identify important elements in personal visualizations. Results showed that through abstract visualizations the users are more encouraged to explore their data and thus, those visualizations give them more insights.

To track QS data, usually either an app like *Moves*, or devices like *Fitbit* or *Nike+* can be used. Those services usually offer a website or a mobile application where the users can see values and related graphs for their activities.

An application that gives immediate feedback to the user in a more *playful* way is *FitCat*. FitCat is an application for the *Pebble* smartwatch, which tracks the fitness activities of the user. With the FitCat application, the watch shows a cat which behaves in the same way as the user: if the user is walking, the cat is walking; if the user is relaxing, the cat is relaxing. The more active the users are, the more virtual money they get within this application, which they can then use to make the cat happy.

A tool which allows the users to track any kind of data and tries to visualize them in meaningful and easy understandable graphs is *Loggr*. Similar to this tool is *mem:o*, which main focus lies on the design of the visualization using colourful circles. Although both tools give a nice visualization on the tracked data, the disadvantage of those two applications is that the user has to enter all the data manually. Since already a lot of applications exist which help the user to track different kinds of data, automatically aggregating the data in order to get a visualization would be preferable to manual data entry.

B. Avatar Creation

Related to the chosen visualization, the avatar, is the Musical Avatar [16], a personal avatar generated based on the users music preferences. Favorite music tracks, provided by the users, are analyzed and tagged with semantic descriptors. Those descriptors are then used to create a user profile which is then represented as a cartoonish avatar. This visualization only shows music preferences, and is not further updated based on current user activity.

Research has been conducted on using an avatar as motivational or biobehavioral feedback. Murray et al. [17] proposes an avatar as a digital representation of a user for mobile health applications. Their work presents a theoretical description on how the appearance and behaviour of an avatar can trigger changes of the user's health-related behaviour. Feedback via avatars was found to be easier to understand for the users, since they are human-like and we are interacting with other humans in our everyday lives, whereas interpreting graphs is not done so often and needs to be learned first. Scott et al. [18] investigated how avatars should be designed to be expressive and communicate feedback.

A lot of research has been conducted regarding personalized avatars for virtual environments (cf. [19][20][21][22]). The user's body structure as well as kinematic properties should be reflected in the avatar. One possible purpose of building an avatar based on the user's body is to create a personalized shopping avatar; the user can then put clothes

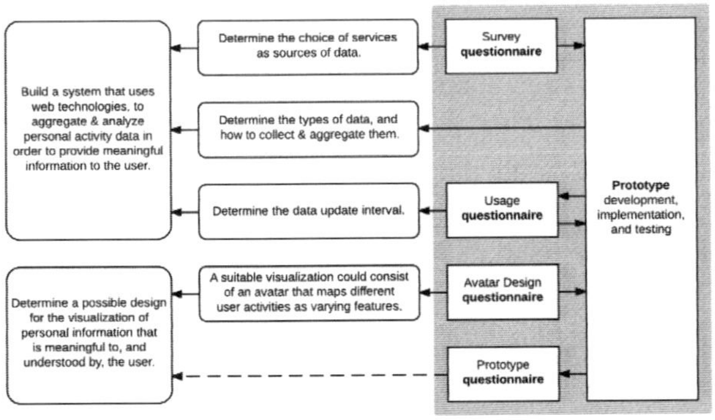

Figure 1. How the online questionnaires and the prototype development informed the research.

on the avatar "to preview the appearance of the items on the user" [23]. All those studies are building avatars based on the appearance of the user, but do not take the user's behaviour into account.

III. Methodology

Within the scope of this project, a series of online questionnaires were designed and a prototype was implemented. Figure 1 illustrates how the different questionnaires and the development of the prototype informed the research.

A. Online Questionnaires

Over the course of this project, three questionnaires were designed. An additional questionnaire, for the participants that allowed to have some of their activities monitored over a period of weeks, was also designed.

1) Survey Questionnaire: The aim of this initial questionnaire was to find out the popularity of different social network services and smart/wearable devices among potential users of the proposed system. By knowing which services and devices are familiar and actively used, an informed initial decision could be made regarding which services and devices the system prototype should support. Furthermore, the reasons why people started using those services/devices, the reasons why they keep using them, and how they share their activities, were investigated.

2) Avatar Design Questionnaire: This questionnaire was created to explore options and validate the graphical design of the avatar, in particular regarding the different graphical features that were intended to correspond to categories of activities, as identified by the previous Survey Questionnaire (and also considered feasible to support by the prototype). The aim of this questionnaire was to investigate if the participants could recognize, and interpret the meaning of, these features. Furthermore, it aimed to investigate if the way of indicating the different levels of those activities (by variations of the graphical features) was clear.

3) Usage Questionnaire: The final questionnaire was designed to investigate potential users' preferences regarding to how an avatar should be updated according to usage patterns, identified based on data that were collected using the prototype, as well as whether it should include date information.

B. Prototype Development

To investigate the feasibility of the proposed system, a prototype was developed. For testing purposes, ten participants were asked to register with the system, allowing to collect activity-related data from them over a period of a month. The purpose for collecting these data was to get a better understanding and identify patterns and levels of usage in the behaviour of users, regarding their activities. Those patterns were also used as the basis of the Usage Questionnaire.

1) Prototype Questionnaire: Additionally, as a thanking gesture for their assistance, once the collection period was over, the data from each participant were analysed and a personalized avatar was generated, corresponding to their activities during the testing period. But before their personal avatar was presented to them, to be shared on social media or used as a profile picture, they were shown the list of all the generated avatars and were asked to pick the one they thought represented them.

IV. System Prototype

A. Functionalities

The implemented system is a tool that allows users to connect their own accounts from other applications. The tool then aggregates the usage data and, based on analysis of how actively those applications were used, it can generate a graphical avatar which represents each user and (the level of) their activities.

1) Website: Part of the prototype is a website which includes a User Management System. Users can register and afterwards, they can connect their accounts from other applications/services. Since several services exist which support the same activities (e.g., *Instagram* and *Flickr* both let users upload and share their photos), the services are categorized. At the current stage, *Human API* ("fitness"), *Last.fm* ("music"), *Instagram* ("photos"), and *Twitter* ("social networks") are supported (see Survey Questionnaire results and Table II). After a period of collecting some initial data, the users are able to see their personalized avatar. This avatar can be exported (saved as an image) and then, e.g., be upload as the user's profile picture on Twitter or Facebook.

2) Data Collection and Aggregation: Based on the results of the Usage Questionnaire, once a day the data from all the services of each user are requested, analysed, and the level of each activity is saved into the database.

The same type of activities are collected from each service within a certain category. For example, for "fitness" the distance and duration of the sport or physical activities can be considered, for "music" the number of songs the user listened to, for "photos" the number of pictures the user uploaded or liked, and for "social networks" the number of posts the user wrote, commented, shared or liked. For each of these categories, the different dimensions (e.g., walking, running and biking for fitness, or posting, commenting, sharing, and liking for social networks) need to be combined into one value to be represented on the avatar. This is done in a very simplistic way and based on subjective impressions of the researchers based on the results of the data collection.

The activity value A for each category is calculated as follows. For *fitness*, the (sum of) the distance for each type

TABLE I. ACTIVITY LEVELS AS DEFINED IN THE PROTOTYPE, BASED ON PARTICIPANTS' DATA COLLECTION OBSERVATIONS.

		activity level	
category	**low**	**medium**	**high**
fitness	x< 10,000	10,000 ≤x< 100,000	100,000 ≤x
music	x< 100	100 ≤x< 1,000	1,000 ≤x
photos	x< 5	5 ≤x< 10	10 ≤x
social networks	x< 5	5 ≤x< 10	10 ≤x

provided by Human API was considered:

$$A_{fitness} = d_{walk} + 2 \times d_{run} + 3 \times d_{cycle} + d_{unknown} \quad (1)$$

weighted based on average speed assumptions. A way to correspond distance and duration for different types of sports was investigated, but nothing practical was found. One practical way would be to consider the calories that were burned, but only some wearable fitness devices can provide such information. For the "unknown" type, we simply assume it to be equivalent to "walking", especially if no different physical activities are combined.

For *music*, the number of songs provided by Last.fm was considered:

$$A_{music} = n_{songs} \quad (2)$$

For *photography* the number of pictures uploaded on Instagram was considered:

$$A_{photography} = n_{uploads} \quad (3)$$

For *social networks*, tweets, retweets and favourites were considered:

$$A_{socialnetworks} = n_{tweets} + \frac{n_{retweets}}{2} + \frac{n_{favourites}}{4} \quad (4)$$

Posting new content should be considered more active than responding or liking existing content.

3) Avatar creation: The level of activities can correspond into one of the following: *not connected*, *connected* (but no activity), *low activity*, *medium activity*, *high activity*. For each category, two limits were defined: any value lower than the first limit would indicate *low activity*, a value between those two limits would result in a *medium activity* and everything above the second limit would be considered as *high activity*. Table I shows the levels per category. Based on the category of those activities, features and feature variations can be added onto the base avatar figure and generate the most recent version for each user.

The overall design was intended to be monochrome (black and white) and minimalistic in an abstract, "cartoon", style (cf. the "Big Triangle" in [24]). The base avatar is a simple outlined figure, as shown in Figure 2a. To indicate that the user has connected a service, an additional feature is added to the avatar, as shown in Figure 2b. These are: a headband for fitness, earphones for music, a Polaroid camera for photos, and a smartphone for social networks. To indicate the levels of activity in each of them, three levels of variation are added: drops of sweat from the headband, music notes coming out of the earphones, photos dropping out of the camera, and birds (implying activity on Twitter) flying out of the smartphone, as seen in Figure 3. Each of the features and its variations was meant to occupy a separate and distinct part of the avatar, with no overlapping. Figure 4 shows different avatar examples.

(a) Base.

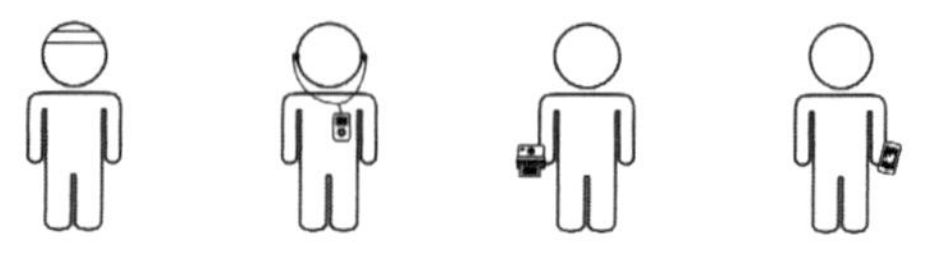

(b) Left to right: fitness, music, photo, social networks.

Figure 2. The avatar along with the features that indicate the different services.

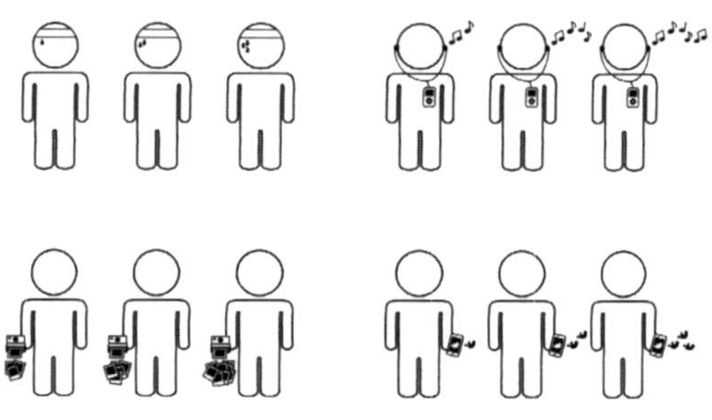

Figure 3. For each of the avatar features, variations that indicate increasing (left to right) levels of activity.

Figure 4. Different avatar examples.

B. System Architecture

The implemented system is distributed over three components (see Figure 5). The three components share one common database, but work independently from each other. The *User Interaction Server* is the only one that the user interacts with. This server hosts the website where the users can register and login, respectively, and where they can view their avatars. Using this server, they also connect external services (at the current stage *Human API*, *Last.fm*, *Instagram*, and *Twitter*) to be used for data gathering. During this connection process, the server obtains the users authentication credentials for each service and stores them in the database. Once the user is registered and has services connected, the *Data Collection Server* will request the user's data from each service, once a day. After the data is collected, it is analysed and the amount of activities are written into the database. The actual data, which were collected from the service, are not stored. The *Avatar Creation Server* queries the amount of activities for each user from the database on a regular basis and generates the avatar accordingly. The created avatar is then stored in the database.

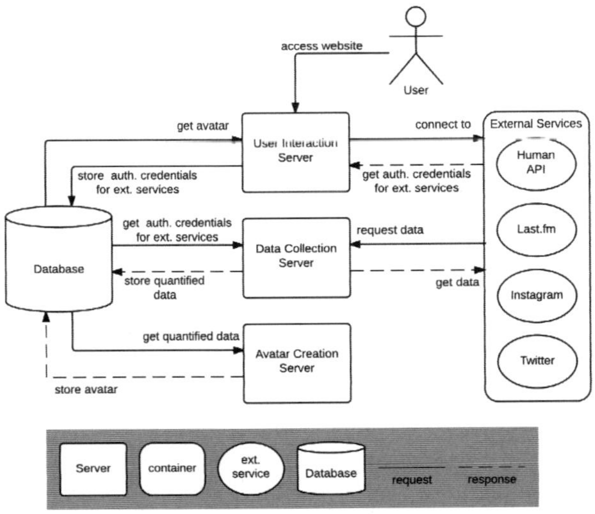

Figure 5. System architecture overview.

The system prototype architecture aims to provide maintainability, scalability and extensibility. Application Programming Interfaces (APIs) can change over time, services that do not have an API yet could offer one and also new services can come up in the future. To be able to cope with those changes and integrate new APIs without much effort, the system needs to be maintainable as well as extensible. Scalability helps not only to deal with more and more data, which is requested daily for each user, but also to handle a possibly increasing number of users.

Splitting the three functionalities of the system – user interaction, data collection and avatar creation – to three servers instead of having all functions on one server supports maintainability, scalability and extensibility. The system is "maintainable" due to being able to have two parts function properly even if an error occurs in the third part. Furthermore, the error cause can be searched within a limited environment, i.e., on the particular server that showed unusual behaviour, instead of the whole system. The "scalability" of the system is given, since not one single server has to handle all the requests from the users and the ones to the external services. While one server is responsible for managing the user requests and retrieving the authentication credentials, another server gathers the actual data from those services. Further scalability could be achieved by having two separate databases, one for storing the amount of activities and the other one for storing the avatar images. The separation of the three different functionalities makes it easier to add new functions to the system and makes is easily "extensible". Possible extensions are adding a new category or a new service in an already existing category, having more levels of activity for each category, and so on. In addition, the possibility of adding another server with new functionalities, which makes use of the data in the database(s), is given.

C. *Technological Background*

The development of the prototype application was intended to use currently emerging technologies. An important aspect was to build a maintainable, scalable and extensible system. To achieve this, not only a proper architecture is needed, but also the use of technologies that should support these characteristics. In this section, the tools and technologies that were used for the implementation are described.

1) HTML5, CSS3, and JavaScript: The client-side of the prototype application is built with *HTML5* in combination with *CSS3*. Additionally, *JavaScript* and its library *jQuery* is used.

2) Node.js, Express, and Jade: The server-side is based on *Node.js*. This platform allows to build fast and scalable network applications [25]. It makes use of a single-threaded and event-driven programming style together with a non-blocking, asynchronous I/O model [25][26][27].

Traditionally, when a process wanted to do some I/O operations, the process had to wait until the I/O operations were done and could only then continue running. To avoid those waiting times and having the possibility of several users at the same time, multi-threading was introduced. Each process can use different threads; within one process, all threads share the same memory. Using this model, another thread can use the CPU, as long as one thread is waiting for I/O operations to finish. If several CPUs are available, various threads can run at the same time. The disadvantage of this model is that programmers do not know which thread will be executed at which time, and need to take care of concurrent access to the shared resources. It is not unusual that bugs appear randomly, which can be hard to debug. Event-driven programming is an alternative to multi-threading, and used by Node.js. It is based on an event loop, i.e., one process contains only one thread. It basically runs two functions, event detection and event handler triggering, continuously. Every time the event loop detects that an event happened, it triggers the corresponding event handler, which is usually registered as a callback function. When I/O operations are performed, the process is not blocked and thus, several I/O operations can be executed in parallel.

In 2003, Kegel described first the C10K problem: how can one server support ten thousand concurrent clients [28][29]. Multi-threading allows serving multiple clients at the same time, but the number of threads is limited since only a certain amount of memory and processing power is available. Thus, multi-threading does not support a high capacity. In contrast, event-driven programming is more (resource) efficient. Using events as light-weight constructs and its non-blocking I/O model, Node.js is able to handle high capacity and thus, not facing the C10K problem.

Furthermore, the programming language used for Node.js is JavaScript. Its closures and first-class functions make it useful for event-driven programming. In addition, JavaScript is widely used in (client-side) HTML-based web applications. With Node.js, developers use JavaScript also on the server-side and therefore, only one programming language is needed. Another benefit of using JavaScript on both sides, is the *JSON* format, which is native to JavaScript and useful for any data exchange between the server and the client.

For the prototype, together with the Node.js platform, the *Express* framework is used to handle the middleware and *Jade* as template engine for HTML templates.

3) MongoDB: As data storage, the document-oriented, non-relational database *MongoDB* is used [30]. Non-relational – also called Not Only SQL (NOSQL) – databases like

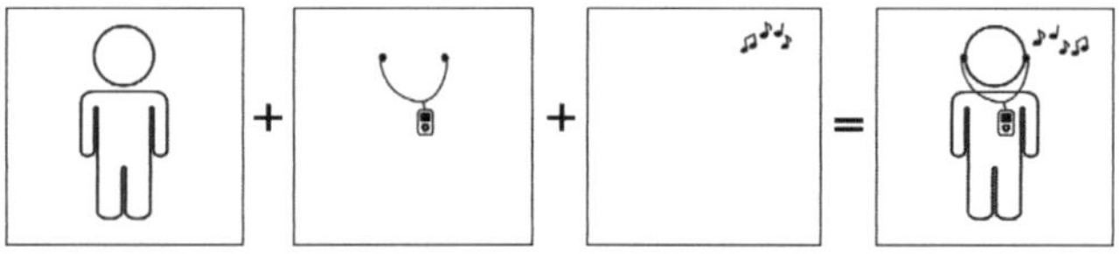

Figure 6. Composition of different images (base, feature, variation) to create each avatar.

MongoDB support scalability through *scaling out* (balancing data and load across multiple servers) which allows them to be used for a high amount of data [30][31][32]. In contrast, relational databases support only *scaling up* (getting a new and bigger machine), which makes them inefficient to be used for such a use case. In addition to effective scalability, MongoDB offers a good query performance even for a massive amount of data, which makes it very suitable for "big data" applications.

Since MongoDB uses "JSON-like" documents, it is easy to use together with the JavaScript code on the server-side through the Node.js platform [30]. Those documents can contain a complex hierarchical structure, which might correspond more to how object-oriented programmers think about their data than the, in traditional rational databases used, "rows". Furthermore, no definitions for those structures exist. Keys and values do not have a fixed type or size. It is easy, to add or remove fields within a document. This means, that the structure of the data can be easily changed if necessary. On the other hand, developers need to be careful to not end up in a complete mass of data.

4) ImageMagick: To generate the avatar based on the users activities, several images – up to two for each category (one for the feature and one for the variation) plus the base avatar – need to be composed dynamically on the web server (cf. Figure 6). For this purpose, the tool *ImageMagick* is used, which is a command line tool to create, edit, compose or convert bitmap images. The library *GraphicsMagick* allows to use the tool on a Node.js server.

5) Integrating APIs: The purpose of the system is to analyse each user's activities, via their use of various applications, and to then visualise the result as an avatar. Apart from determining popularity and usage from different services, to see which of those are reasonable to include in such a system, it was investigated which services offer a suitable API that would allow to gather the appropriate data.

One limitation can be the lack of access to an API, e.g., Nike+ has an API, but the company only gives access to specific partners and therefore, it could not be used for the current prototype.

On the other hand, there exist some APIs that already connect multiple services and allow developers to just integrate one API, while still be able to get data from all those sources. The users can then choose which of those service(s) they want to connect. The advantage of integrating only one combining API instead of separate ones for each service is not only less programming effort, but also guarantees that the data structure is the same, no matter from which application they are retrieved.

Developers integrating other services via their APIs need to be aware that those might change over time. Some changes only add new functionalities and do not affect currently running applications that already make use of this API. However, other changes require developers to integrate them in their applications, which can involve a lot of effort and time. For example, after the last change of the Facebook API, several applications needed to shut down because they were using functionalities which were not available any more (see http://techcrunch.com/2015/04/28/facebook-api-shut-down/).

Furthermore, some services do not allow to make use of any features that might not correspond to their core features and functionalities. For example, Facebook shuts down applications that would notify the users if someone unfriended them, because this would violate the Terms of Service (see Facebook Policy section 4.4, and Facebook Legal Terms section 3.2). Two examples were "Unfriend Finder" in 2013, and "Who Deleted Me" in 2015.

TABLE II. PARTIAL RESULTS REGARDING POPULARITY OF VARIOUS SOCIAL NETWORK SERVICES AND WEARABLES.

service or wearable	used often or sometimes	never used or not familiar
Facebook	74	4
Google Drive	59	19
Spotify	50	28
IMDB	50	28
Google+	43	35
Twitter	42	36
Instagram	39	39
LinkedIn	36	42
Wordpress	29	49
Flickr	28	50
Nike+	13	65
Fitbit	3	75

V. Results and Analysis

A. Survey Questionnaire

1) Demographics: Two identical versions of this initial questionnaire were created, one that was deployed in Sweden, and the other one in Austria. Note that many of the participants in Sweden were connected to Linnaeus University, and had an international background. There were no big differences detected in the results between the two groups, so in this section combined numbers are shown.

The questionnaire was filled out by 78 participants aged between 18 and 32 (average 24.8, standard deviation 3), whereof 40 were male and 38 female. 51 of the participants were located in Sweden, the rest in Austria.

2) Results: The initial questions presented two lists of social networks and wearables, respectively, and asked the participants to indicate which of those they are familiar with, and if so, how often they use them. Partial results are shown in Table II. Unsurprisingly, most participants used *Facebook*. In contrast, the majority of the participants were unfamiliar with smart devices and wearables (very few used *Nike+* or *Fitbit*).

The next questions investigated the reasons why the participants started to use social network services and/or wearables and why they are still using them. Most (around half) of the participants started to use different social network services to keep track of their activities, and that remains the reason that they still use them. But overall, it appears that most participants did not consider that they keep using the services for the same initial intentions.

A distinct difference between sharing behaviours was also noted: in Sweden, more participants shared on social media platforms, and in Austria more participants shared with their friends offline.

According to the results of the questionnaire, participants are interested in keeping track of their activities and how much time they spend on them. Furthermore, there is a higher percentage of people who start using an application with the intention to share their activities with others, than users who engage in actual sharing. Although the investigation of the reasons for this behaviour are beyond the scope of this paper, proposing a tool which creates a visualization (e.g., an avatar) based analysis of the activities, might help to increase the number of people who are actually sharing their activities (via this visualization). In addition, it would not only allow others to see "how active" users are, but also the users themselves to see their own activity levels, something that might differ from their personal impression.

However, the main outcome of this questionnaire was the initial selection of services which were integrated and supported by the developed prototype. Informed by the results, different categories of potential activities could be defined: *social networks* (Facebook, Twitter, Google+), *work related* (Google Drive, LinkedIn, Wordpress), *music* (Spotify), *films* (IMDB), *photography* (Instagram, Flickr), and *fitness* (Nike+, Fitbit). The following subsections consider these possible identified categories, and discuss which APIs were finally supported. Based on the previously presented architectural decisions, the prototype can be extended with more APIs per category or more categories without much effort.

Social Networks: The most actively used social media platform is Facebook. However, Facebook changed its API recently and requires an elaborate and long-winded review process which was considered as out of scope for this project and thus it was not included in the prototype. Google+ and Twitter were considered similarly popular. Due to development time constrains, the choice between them was based on the fact that it is more complicated to change (via API) the user profile picture on Google+ than it is on Twitter. Therefore, Twitter is initially supported as it fits easier with the envisioned overall system workflow.

Work Related: None of the services identified in this category offers a suitable API. *LinkedIn* has a restricted API that gives access only to personal data (no possibility to get another user's activities) for open use, and only official partners are allowed to have more access (see https://developer.linkedin.com/ and http://mashable.com/2015/02/12/linkedin-closed-api/). *Google Drive* and *Wordpress* did not provide any useful data about the users' activities and were therefore also not included in the prototype.

Music: Considering music, the API of *Last.fm* can be used. Users can listen to music directly on Last.fm, or they can connect this service with various other music services and applications, among others Spotify. Those connected applications then send the information about what songs the user is listening to Last.fm (Last.fm calls this "scrobbling"), which can then suggest songs to the user which are similar to the ones she listens to.

Films: *IMDB* has no official API and therefore was not supported by the prototype.

Photography: To keep track on how active the user is regarding photography, the *Instagram* API is used. Flickr also provides a suitable API but since more people stated to be using Instagram, for development time constrains, only the latter one was supported.

Fitness: As a variety of fitness applications can be used, similar with the music category, the decision was made to take advantage of the integration of the *Human API*, which combines many of them in one single API.

B. Avatar Design Questionnaire

1) Demographics: In contrast to the previous questionnaire, only one version was distributed, with an additional question in the end, stating if the participants were living in Sweden or abroad.

This questionnaire was filled out by 56 participants aged between 19 and 54 (average 27.5, standard deviation 7), whereof 29 were male, 25 female, one trans* and one who preferred not to disclose. 33 of the participants were located in Sweden.

2) Results: Based on the Survey Questionnaire and the technical feasibility, four categories of activities were identified and therefore considered as potential features of the avatar: *fitness* (via HumanAPI), *music* (Spotify, etc. via Last.fm), *photography* (Instagram) and *social networks* (Twitter). For each category for which the user has a service connected to gather data, a graphic feature could be added to the basic avatar. The levels of activity for each of these could be signified by variations of these features.

For the initial group of questions, the participants were presented different avatars and asked what they thought the avatar was doing. Most of the participants' interpretations corresponded to the design intentions: e.g., they associated headphones or earphones to listening to music, taking photographs with the Polaroid camera, and the smart phone with being active in social networks. But some designs were not so clear. In the avatar with the headband, 32% participants interpreted the "drops" as *blood* (and not as *sweat*), and therefore that the avatar was injured; however, 49% participants interpreted the same avatar design as being physically active.

The next group of questions showed different avatars and asked if the participants agreed that the avatar is doing a specific activity. Similar to the previous questions, most participants confirmed the intended design. But (in line with previous impressions), a few participants insisted that the "physically active" avatar was injured. Some additional comments were made (mainly by participants that did not agree) that the avatars were perceived as being too "passive", and not really "active".

The next group of questions examined the perception of the activity level variations. Two avatars were presented at the same time, having the same feature (headband, music player and earphones, Polaroid camera, or smart phone) but with additional variations (sweat drops, music notes, Polaroid photos, or birds). Encouragingly, very few participants misidentified the compared activity levels. Some offered alternative interpretations: e.g., some participants did not agree that being "more active" can be represented by an increased number of, e.g., photos or music notes; the user is simply taking more photos (which is not the same as having interest in photography) or listens to "louder" music.

The next group of questions presented avatars with a combination of features, and asked the participants to identify the activities, which the majority did correctly.

The final group of questions presented pairs of avatars with different activities and levels of activities, and asked the participants to compare them. Again, the majority of the participants did so correctly.

Overall, the results showed that the design was understandable by the participants, and that they seemed to understand what the different features where designed to represent.

The suggested feature for physical fitness, as well as the use of feature variations (amount) to symbolize different levels of activity, were not entirely clear to all participants. Many participants interpreted the drops as blood and thus did not see the avatar as physically active, but rather as injured. To overcome this issue, the use of colours might be taken into account. For example, *blue* drops might rather be associated with sweat than with blood. Another possible way to indicate activity levels would be to adjust the transparency and not the amount of, e.g., the music notes. This method could also potentially allow for more activity levels than the current "one plus three".

C. Usage Patterns

Ten participants (friends and colleagues from Linnaeus University, Sweden) were invited to register with the prototype system and let their data be collected over the period of a month. The aim of this data collection was to identify patterns in the behaviour of the users regarding their activities.

The first identified pattern is having low activity during most days, with a *peak* of a lot of activity for a, usually single, day. A typical example for this pattern was a user who took long bike tours once a week, which were tracked by a fitness application, but who did not track any other fitness activities. The second identified pattern is almost the inverse: having typically a lot of activity, and a sudden *drop* for one or two days. This behaviour was exemplified, e.g., by users who listened to a lot of music while they are working during the weekdays, but who hardly listened to their music during the weekends. The third identified pattern is of having more or less *consistent* activity. A user who was using a wearable device to keep track of all their steps during each day typically showed this type of pattern.

D. Prototype Questionnaire

After the collection period, an avatar was created for each participant according to their (overall) behaviour. Before these were revealed to them, the participants were given a list of all of the created avatars and they had to choose the one they think that represents them. Out of ten people, four selected the correct avatar, and another two selected an avatar that matches all the features of their avatar but that had different variations for at least one item. From the remaining participants, two selected an avatar that was similar, but that had one feature more or less than their actual avatar and a diverse number of features for at least one item. Only two users selected an avatar that was very dissimilar to their actual one.

E. Usage Questionnaire

1) Demographics: This final online questionnaire was filled out by 29 participants aged between 19 and 57 (average 27, standard deviation 7), whereof 14 were male, 13 female and two trans*. No location information was asked.

2) Results: This questionnaire was designed to investigate potential users' preferences regarding to how the generated avatar should be updated according to usage patterns, as well as whether it should include date information.

Interestingly, only slightly more than half considered that having some date information displayed with the avatar would be useful. Those that did also showed a strong preference for this information to be displayed below the avatar, mostly in a "name of month, date of month, year" format (e.g., May 15, 2015).

Based on observations regarding the identified activity patterns, two issues were investigated: how often should the avatar be updated (based on the activity information), and whether any peaks or drops of activity should persist over the subsequent days.

The participants were presented with three different stories (each corresponding to an activity pattern) and for each of those stories a series of figures with ways that the avatar could be updated. To keep things simple, each of the stories mentioned only a single category of activities – photos (Instagram), social networks (Twitter), and music – and the options were a (not explicitly stated) mix of update options (every day, every second day, every week) and persistence (peak or drop indicated on only according to the events of the story or smoothed over more days).

More frequent (every day or every other day) updates were shown to be the, not very surprising but consistent throughout, preference. What was not so expected was the preference for no persistence "smoothing" over time. These findings, together with the inclusion of date information, further informed the development of the system and the avatar design.

VI. Summary and Conclusion

It is hoped that the work presented in this paper can be further extended in terms of supported services and functionalities, any graphical design issues improved, and potential system users provided with a way to, at the same time, be entertained, as well as gain some insight by the visualization of their personal activities, reclaiming in a meaningful way the data that are collected from their personal activities.

A series of user studies (using online questionnaires) were conducted, and a system prototype was implemented within the scope of this research. This paper presents the development and the architecture of a proposed system, that can aggregate and analyse personal activity data in order to provide meaningful information to a user.

Based on the results of the Survey Questionnaire, a selection of most used social networks and wearable devices was identified and categorized. Not all of these could be currently supported; the implemented four categories (and the APIs) are *social networks* (Twitter), *music* (Last.fm), *photography* (Instagram), and *fitness* (Human API). Due to the extensibility of the proposed architecture, further services can be relatively easily added and supported in the future.

Not every service can be integrated in such a system, depending on the availability and suitability (restrictions, not relevant activity data) of an API. In some cases, there exist APIs that already combine different services and thus multiple services can be integrated with less implementation effort.

A selection of the available data were chosen to be analysed and visualized (in our context). For fitness, the distance of the sport/physical activities; for music, the number of songs the user listened to; for photography, the number of pictures the user uploaded; and for social media, the number of tweets, retweets and favourites. Every time the data are requested and analysed, only the category activity levels are afterwards stored in the system database, and not the collected data.

Based on the results of the Usage Questionnaire, the potential users would prefer to get updates frequently (every day or every other day), and the visualization not to consider any persistence ("smoothing" over time). Therefore, the data are requested and aggregated as well as analysed once a day, generating an updated (depending on the activities) avatar.

As a possible visualization of users' activities, the graphical representation as an avatar was chosen and further investigated and validated by the Avatar Design Questionnaire. For each category for which the user has a service connected, the base figure of the avatar gets an added feature (a headband to indicate fitness activities, earphones for music, a Polaroid camera for photography, or a smartphone for social networks). The representation of the levels of activity is done by adding some feature variations to the avatar: drops of sweat from the headband, music notes coming out of the earphones, photos coming out of the Polaroid, and birds (related to the Twitter logo) flying out of the smartphone. Although the overall graphic design was well received and understood by the participants, there is always further room for improvements (e.g., the feature and variations for the fitness category should be redesigned).

A. *Limitations*

During the development phase, as well as during the test run of the prototype, some aspects were identified which developers need to take special care of, and some which require further considerations and improvement.

When a "mashup" (an application that combines data requested from various other applications) is created, it is important to be aware of that this application will depend on those integrated services. One point of this dependency is the availability of those services. For example, on the day when the trial of the prototype was started, the Instagram API was (temporarily) not available and thus, the invited users who registered could not at that time connect their Instagram accounts. Luckily, a few days later, Instagram fixed that particular issue, and these users could then connect their accounts. Furthermore, only certain data can be requested via an API that the services provide. For instance, the Instagram API does not provide an easy way to get comments that a user wrote. Thus, only the uploaded pictures as well as the "likes" could be used.

Additionally, some services allow to specify a date for which the data are requested. This is very useful for the prototype, since the data is gathered once a day, for events that took place the previous day only. But some services do not provide this option. A few services (e.g., the Twitter API) allow to request all data after a specific id. This gives the possibility to get all new data since the previous request was made, but it is not certain that all those events happened on the specific day. However, it is hard to obtain some data on the first time the prototype requests them, especially if the user was already using this service for a long time. For example, again with Instagram, this caused a bug regarding the number of "likes", and therefore this data were not considered for the photography activity. Instead, only the number of photos is currently used. Further development could address and fix this issue.

Another aspect regarding the use of external services which needs to be taken into account, is that some services have a limited amount of requests which are accepted within a certain time frame. This is especially important if the mashup is used by a large number of users. For the trial of the current prototype, the API use stayed within those limits.

Another limitation of the proposed system is the rather simple analysis of the gathered data. Further investigations and user studies are necessary on how to combine the different dimensions per category into a composite value (e.g., walking, running and biking for fitness; posting, commenting, sharing and liking for social media or photography). The generation of avatars for the participants who registered for the system was determined on subjective impressions of the researcher based on the results of the data collection (to determine the activity levels). For further work on this project, a more general solution needs to be found.

Using an avatar as visualization of the activities, also has some limitations, since for example only certain levels of activities can be differentiated before the design gets too complex and incomprehensible for the users. The current system uses four different levels for each category (just connected, low activity, medium activity, high activity). Gathering data from more users could determine if this segmentation is enough or if more differentiation would be required.

B. *Future Work*

As mentioned in previous sections, the avatar design was kept simple, and this project has several possibilities to be enhanced by future work, further investigating the preferences of the users regarding a perhaps more complex design.

One interesting aspect would be to integrate more services in the existing categories, or even more different categories, to address more users.

An open issue is the analysis of the gathered data, especially when it comes to the combination of the different data dimensions of one service into one composite value. For example, fitness and health applications can report a variety of heterogeneous data (distance, time, heart rate, etc.); social networks as well. These could be represented as multiple sub-features on the avatar, or convert them to a common unit of measure (e.g., for fitness this could be the burning of calories).

The presented avatar generation used global values to define the activity levels for each category, meaning these values were the same for all users, independent on their individual behaviour. Another possibility would be to have personalized limits, depending on a user's behaviour – e.g., if she is usually very active, she needs to be "even more" active to have her avatar showing a "high" amount of activity, whereas other users who are usually inactive just need "some" activity to have their activity shown as high on the avatar. Another approach would be to compare the activity to the activity of the previous day(s) or even week(s). If the user is more active than she was during the previous timespan, the avatar shows high activity, if the user is approximately as active as during the previous timespan, the avatar shows medium activity and if the user is less active than during the previous timespan, the avatar shows low activity.

Since it was not clear for all participants that the higher amount of properties is connected to more activity, other ways of showing the different levels for each category could be investigated. As already mentioned before, one possibility would be to work with transparency. Another one might be to work with different colours for different levels. The use of colour could also disambiguate some features (e.g., clarifying that a physical active avatar is not injured and bleeding, by making the sweat drops, coming from the headband, blue).

REFERENCES

[1] M. Van Rijmenam, "How Big Data Enabled Spotify To Change The Music Industry," 2013, https://datafloq.com/read/big-data-enabled-spotify-change-music-industry/391 [retrieved: March 2016].

[2] J. Mangalindan, "Amazon's recommendation secret," 2012, http://fortune.com/2012/07/30/amazons-recommendation-secret/ [retrieved: March 2016].

[3] M. Swan, "Sensor mania! the internet of things, wearable computing, objective metrics, and the quantified self 2.0," Journal of Sensor and Actuator Networks, vol. 1, no. 3, 2012, pp. 217–253.

[4] C. Gurrin, A. F. Smeaton, and A. R. Doherty, "Lifelogging: Personal big data," Found. Trends Inf. Retr., vol. 8, no. 1, 2014, pp. 1–125.

[5] P. McFedries, "Tracking the quantified self [technically speaking]," Spectrum, IEEE, vol. 50, no. 8, 2013, pp. 24–24.

[6] M. Swan, "The quantified self: Fundamental disruption in big data science and biological discovery," Big Data, vol. 1, no. 2, 2013, pp. 85–99.

[7] D. Lupton, "Self-Tracking Modes: Reflexive Self-Monitoring and Data Practices," SSRN Electronic Journal, 2014.

[8] d. boyd and K. Crawford, "Critical questions for big data," Information, Communication & Society, vol. 15, no. 5, 2012, pp. 662–679.

[9] E. K. Choe, N. B. Lee, B. Lee, W. Pratt, and J. A. Kientz, "Understanding quantified-selfers' practices in collecting and exploring personal data," in Proceedings of the SIGCHI Conference on Human Factors in Computing Systems, ser. CHI '14. New York, NY, USA: ACM, 2014, pp. 1143–1152.

[10] T. Chang, "All the world's a game," 2012, http://techcrunch.com/2012/03/24/worlds-a-game/ [retrieved: March 2016].

[11] ——, "The 'so what' of the quantified self," 2012, http://techcrunch.com/2012/03/31/quantified-self-so-what/ [retrieved: March 2016].

[12] ——, "We are our scores: The aspirational self," 2012, http://techcrunch.com/2012/04/14/we-are-our-scores-the-aspirational-self/ [retrieved: March 2016].

[13] S. Deterding, D. Dixon, R. Khaled, and L. Nacke, "From game design elements to gamefulness: Defining "gamification"," in Proceedings of the 15th International Academic MindTrek Conference: Envisioning Future Media Environments, ser. MindTrek '11. New York, NY, USA: ACM, 2011, pp. 9–15.

[14] E. K. Choe, B. Lee, and m. c. schraefel, "Characterizing Visualization Insights from Quantified Selfers' Personal Data Presentations," IEEE computer graphics and applications, vol. 35, no. 4, may 2015, pp. 28–37.

[15] S. Wang, Y. Tanahashi, N. Leaf, and K.-L. Ma, "Design and Effects of Personal Visualizations," IEEE Computer Graphics and Applications, vol. 35, no. 4, jul 2015, pp. 82–93.

[16] D. Bogdanov, M. Haro, F. Fuhrmann, A. Xambó, E. Gómez, and P. Herrera, "Semantic audio content-based music recommendation and visualization based on user preference examples," Information Processing & Management, vol. 49, no. 1, 2013.

[17] T. Murray, D. Hardy, D. Spruijt-Metz, E. Hekler, and A. Raij, "Avatar interfaces for biobehavioral feedback," in Design, User Experience, and Usability. Health, Learning, Playing, Cultural, and Cross-Cultural User Experience, ser. Lecture Notes in Computer Science, A. Marcus, Ed. Springer Berlin Heidelberg, 2013, vol. 8013, pp. 424–434.

[18] M. Scott, L. Pereira, and I. Oakley, "Show me or tell me: Designing avatars for feedback," Interacting with Computers, 2014.

[19] N. Ahmed, E. de Aguiar, C. Theobalt, M. Magnor, and H.-P. Seidel, "Automatic generation of personalized human avatars from multi-view video," in Proceedings of the ACM Symposium on Virtual Reality Software and Technology, ser. VRST '05. New York, NY, USA: ACM, 2005, pp. 257–260.

[20] S. Piotr and K. Bozena, "Personalized avatar animation for virtual reality," in Information Technology, 2008. IT 2008. 1st International Conference on, 2008, pp. 1–4.

[21] M. Zollhöfer, M. Martinek, G. Greiner, M. Stamminger, and J. Süß muth, "Automatic reconstruction of personalized avatars from 3d face scans," Computer Animation and Virtual Worlds, vol. 22, no. 2-3, 2011, pp. 195–202.

[22] Y. Chen and Z.-Q. Cheng, "Personalized avatar capture using two kinects in a moment," in SIGGRAPH Asia 2012 Posters, ser. SA '12. New York, NY, USA: ACM, 2012, pp. 3:1–3:1.

[23] C. Lawrence, V. Tiscareno, and S. Ng, "Personalized shopping avatar," US Patent 8,818,883, August 2014.

[24] S. McCloud, Understanding Comics: The Invisible Art, 1993.

[25] M. Cantelon, M. Harter, T. Holowaychuk, and N. Rajlich, Node.js in Action. Manning, 2014.

[26] S. Tilkov and S. Vinoski, "Node.js: Using javascript to build high-performance network programs," IEEE Internet Computing, no. 6, 2010, pp. 80–83.

[27] P. Teixeira, Professional Node.js: Building Javascript Based Scalable Software. John Wiley & Sons, 2012.

[28] D. Kegel, "The c10k problem," 2006, http://www.kegel.com/c10k.html [retrieved: March 2016].

[29] L. Griffin, P. Elger, and E. de Leastar, "Project zeppelin: A modern web application development framework," in Formal Methods for Components and Objects, ser. Lecture Notes in Computer Science. Springer Berlin Heidelberg, 2013, vol. 7542, pp. 184–198.

[30] K. Chodorow, MongoDB: The Definitive Guide. O'Reilly Media, Inc., 2013.

[31] J. Pokorny, "Nosql databases: A step to database scalability in web environment," International Journal of Web Information Systems, vol. 9, no. 1, 2013, pp. 69–82.

[32] C. J. Tauro, S. Aravindh, and A. Shreeharsha, "Comparative study of the new generation, agile, scalable, high performance nosql databases," International Journal of Computer Applications, vol. 48, no. 20, 2012, pp. 1–4.

Human Activity Recognition using Smartphone Sensors with Context Filtering

Shah Md. Shihab Hasan, Mohshi Masnad, Md. Mohiuddin Khan, Hasan Mahmud, Md. Kamrul Hasan
Systems and Software Lab (SSL), Department of Computer Science and Engineering
Islamic University of Technology (IUT), Dhaka, Bangladesh.
email: shihab11@iut-dhaka.edu, aurkoiut@gmail.com, {mohiuddin, hasan, hasank}@iut-dhaka.edu

Abstract—**In recent times, application of Ambient Intelligent services, e.g. smart home, remote monitoring and assisted healthcare, the use of smart phones for the recognition of human activities has become a topic of high interest. Simple activities like sitting, running, walking can be recognized easily but semi-complex activities like ascending and descending stairs, slow running, jogging, fast running etc. are often difficult to recognize accurately. We aim to reduce the error rate of recognizing these kinds of activities by applying Dynamic Time Warping (DTW) algorithm and introducing context filtering. We used heart rate data and barometric pressure sensor data as elements of context filtering. We used a steady state as template and matched every activity with this steady state. To get optimum threshold values, we applied K Nearest Neighbor (KNN) algorithm on the score of DTW. After primarily classifying activities, we used the context filtering approach to further recognize activities by removing confusions. After completion of our study, we have seen that accuracy level has increased significantly for differentiating similar kinds of activities. Overall, our novel approach of applying DTW algorithm and applying context filtering shows considerable performance improvements at a low cost.**

Keywords-Human Activity Recognition (HAR), context filtering, DTW.

I. INTRODUCTION

In recent years, Human Activity Recognition (HAR) through smart phones became a well known field of research. As we have entered the era of intelligent environment, the automated detection of Activity has become a point of high interest. Intelligent environments generally exploit information gathered from users and their environments in order to produce an appropriate action [16]. In this regard, different studies have been conducted in this field. Based on these studies, we observed that basic locomotion activities like Walking, Running, Sitting, Lying on bed can be detected with good accuracy rate [15].However, similar activities, such as Going upstairs or downstairs, Slow running (Jogging), Fast Walking can not be detected perfectly [15]. It is important to detect these activities for development of systems that promote the improvement of people's Quality of Life (QoL) through the *recognition of human activities*. Especially, our focus is on differentiating and detecting similar kinds of activities: slow walking, fast running, going upstairs and going downstairs. We use DTW algorithm to recognize these activities from the inertial sensors available in smart phones. Moreover, we equipped the users with heart rate sensors and took the barometric pressure sensor data. These two factors are used to further improve the activity of the recognition. The latter factors are termed "context filters".

From the start of 21st century, HAR became a point of very high interest. In the beginning, it was confined to only surveillance using video camera but now it is incrementally used for different areas of study directly related to HAR. Ambient Intelligence (AMI) and Ambient Assisted Living (AAL) are two areas of study that are directly related to HAR.AMI is a system mainly focusing on environments that behave intelligently based on the actions of users associated with the system. These systems are unique in many ways, e.g. systems that intelligently anticipate the user needs based on information (e.g. activity patterns, past events and their solutions). These environments need seamless interaction between user and system. Smart Homes and Smart Cities are examples and concepts of such systems. Another important field is Ambient Assisted Living. This is accomplished by incorporating different systems together into a health monitoring system for elder people. Due to enormous advancement in Medical Science, people are living longer. One study based in Europe showed that by 2060 the elderly (namely people over 65 years) will be near 30% of the entire population as opposed to a 17% by 2010 [18]. In addition to the elderly, about 15% of the total population has some kind of disability (WHO 2011) [19]. So, there is a large area where AAL can bring numerous benefits. These AMI and AAL systems need continuous information from the user and from the environment. Detection of human activity can work as input to these kinds of systems. We aim to detect these activities unobtrusively by exploiting the use of smart phones as input to these kinds of systems.

The rest of this paper is organized as follows. Section 2 gives an overview of different approaches for the activity recognition problem. It also describes the reasons of choosing DTW algorithm as the classifier to classify and recognize activity. Section 3 proposes a solution to recognize human activity with further accuracy. Section 4 includes description of the implementation of the proposed methods and also contains the evaluation of proposed methodology. Section 5 presents our result analysis and comparison with different studies. Finally, Section 6 concludes the paper.

II. BACKGROUND STUDY

In HAR, different types of studies have been conducted so far:

A. External or Environmental Sensors

From the very beginning of activity recognition research, video cameras were the first choice. Video cameras were employed in Poppe [13] for marker-less vision-based human motion analysis. Apart from video cameras, Bian et al. [14] used microphones for sound source localization in a home environment for communication activity inference. Taka et al. [3] used a Microsoft Kinect's depth sensor as an ambient sensor for position and orientation tracking for an indoor monitoring system for Parkinson's disease (PD) patients. These kinds of systems require a static infrastructure which limits their range of operation to a constrained space. So for a static environment, such as in a room it gives satisfactory performance but for dynamic environments it is less useful.

B. Wearable Sensors

Wearable sensors are commonly attached to different body parts such as the waist, wrist , chest, legs and head, as shown in Figure 1.

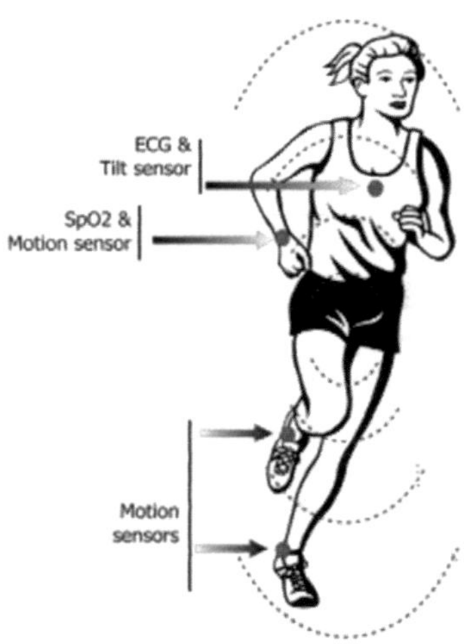

Figure 1. Wearable sensors

Skin temperature, heart rate, conductivity, Global Positioning System (GPS) location and body motion are some examples of variables that can be measured with current wearable sensor technologies [4]. All of the systems in this class are obtrusive and always conducted in a controlled environment. It is also relatively harder to synchronize the components of the system.

C. Smartphone as Wearable Sensor

Today's smart phones incorporate an array of diversified sensors within, e.g. inertial sensors (Accelerometer, Gyroscope), barometer, proximity sensor etc. and it also remains unobtrusive to users. As a result, it is now one of the main tools to recognize human activity automatically. Kwapisz et al. [5] used labeled accelerometer data from Android phones whereas Yang [6] used Nokia N95 phone. Miluzzo et al. developed CenceMe [7] using off-the-shelf, sensor-enabled mobile phones (Nokia N95) and exploited various sensors (such as a microphone, accelerometer, GPS, and camera) that are available for activity recognition. Different studies have been conducted using accelerometer embedded cell phones to detect physical activities with varying phone locations [8].

While basic activities can be recognized almost perfectly with smart phone sensors, semi–complex activities like ascending and descending stairs can be complex to recognize and differentiate between them [15].

D. Combining Different Sensors

This class of techniques involves including smart phone sensors along with other external sensors. Subramanya et al. in [9] built a model using data from a tri-axial accelerometer, two microphones, phototransistors, temperature and barometric pressure sensors, and GPS. Choudhury in [10] used multiple sensor devices consisting of seven different types of sensors to recognize activities. Cho et al. used a single tri-axial accelerometer, along with an embedded image sensor worn at the user's waist to identify nine activities [11]. Györbıróet al. [12] used "Motion Bands" attached to the dominant wrist, hip, and ankle of each subject to distinguish between six different motion patterns. Kawser et al. [1] used phone's accelerometer and another plantar pressure sensor attached in shoe to recognize activity. They mainly focused on combining data from different sensors and getting the final result based on these combined data.

As for the choice of classifier, one can use either temporal classifiers or non-temporal ones. In case of non-temporal classifiers like Decision Tree, Artificial Neural Network, k-Nearest Neighbor, K-Mean etc, one cannot provide the raw data as input directly to the classifier. First, one needs to extract some features from the raw data and then pass these features to the classifier. So there is a pre-processing on the raw data before sending it to classifier. In this case, the features that are mostly used are the following:

- Arithmetic Mean
- Standard Deviation
- Max, Min
- Median Absolute Deviation
- Frequency Signal Weighted Average

In case of temporal classifiers like AR and DTW, etc., there is no need for feature extraction. These algorithms take input of data as a time series. Moreover, one can easily plot the accelerometer and gyroscope data acquired from the smart phone into a time series. Hence, a temporal classifier is a better choice for classifying activities using the data acquired from smart phone sensors. As DTW works best on time series data, this makes DTW a good fit for our purpose.

A summarization of various HAR systems is provided in Table 1 below.

TABLE I. SUMMARY OF HAR SYSTEMS

HAR System	Sensors	Machine Learning Algorithm	Accuracy
1. Ferdaus, Sheikh, Richard (2015)	Accelerometer, Gyroscope, Planter Pressure Sensor	Decision Tree	94.37 - 99.53%
2. Davide, Alessandro, Luca, Xavier, Jorge (2012)	Accelerometer Gyroscope	Support Vector Machine	89.3%
3. Wu et al. (2012)	Accelerometer, Gyroscope	k-NN	90.2%
4. Jennifer, Gary, Samuel (2010)	Accelerometer, Gyroscope	Decision Tree, Logistic Regression, Multilayer N	91.7%
5.Maninni, Sabatini (2010)	2D-Accelerometer (Wearable)	NB, DT, kNN, ANN, GMM, cHMM	92.2 - 98.5%

From Table I, we can observe that, to obtain higher accuracy rate for recognizing Human Activities, Multimodal systems are more efficient than others.

III. OUR APPROACH

From the literature review, it is clearly observed that simpler locomotion activities can be detected easily but similar kinds of activities are difficult to differentiate. We are particularly interested in differentiating these similar activities correctly. As DTW algorithm has never been used before in HAR studies but it seems particularly suited for the purpose, we propose to apply DTW algorithm for classification purpose. We also introduce context filtering methods in HAR to filter the data for achieving a more precise result. Explanation of the context filtering is provided below.

We construct a multi-modal system that takes user's smart phone accelerometer and gyroscope value as input. It also concurrently records the change of altitude of the smart phone using its barometer sensor and the user's heart rate using a heart rate monitor during the period. Accelerometer and gyroscope values are used by the classifier to classify the data. The altitude and heart rate observation is then used as a context filter. So when classifier generates a result, it is passed through context filter and the output from the context filter is the final result.

From background study, we have shown that it is difficult for classifiers to classify similar activities like going upstairs and going downstairs, fast walking and slow running etc. The highest accuracy for detecting ascending and descending stairs is around 55-60%. The idea of context filter is particularly applicable here and it will be able to differentiate these similar activities using the observance on altitude and heart rate values and produce a more accurate result. It is often difficult to differentiate between these similar activities by only using accelerometer and gyroscope. But if we use barometer sensor here, this may improve the result. From the barometer sensor, we get the altitude. So while walking if the altitude of the person is increasing then we can assume that the person is going upstairs. If it is decreasing, then we can say the person is going downstairs. And if the altitude is stable, then we can assume the person is just walking. So, by normalizing the barometer and heart rate sensor values and then setting up rules corresponding with those, we can setup the Context Filter.

Context filter may not create an impact on the classified results instantly because the heart rate and the altitude values do not increase or decrease instantaneously. For example, when somebody starts running, his heart rate stays normal in the beginning but after a period of time, it starts increasing gradually. So our context filter will always be observing the altitude and heart rate values of the near past and will try to find a window containing noticeable fluctuation. When it will find it, it will again filter the results. This time it will filter with the new window for better optimization of the result. Figure 2 explains this scenario.

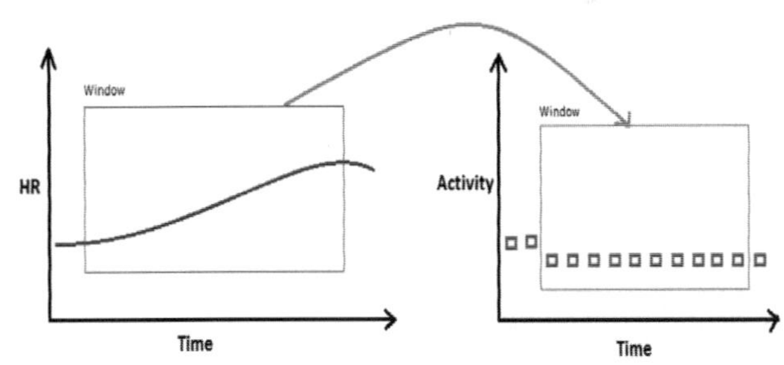

Figure 2. Context filtering Methodology

From the above figure we can see that rate of change of heart rate is gradually increasing.

IV. METHODOLOGY

Data from the Heart rate monitor and inertial sensor's data from Smartphone have been collected by an Android app. After collecting data in the Android app, it is sent to server through Wi-Fi. On the server side, all the data is processed by an offline data processing system. The classification of the data is done in the server. Figure 3 depicts the system architecture for our system.

For our study, we needed a smart phone which incorporates tri-axial Accelerometer, Gyroscope, and Barometric sensor. It must be ANT+ supported as we use Garmin Heart Rate Monitor as our sensor for obtaining heart rate data. A Samsung Galaxy S4 (I9505) smart phone was used in our experiment as it meets all the requirements.

Around 25 persons of different ages were chosen randomly for our data collection process. They were also different in physical built, height and weight.

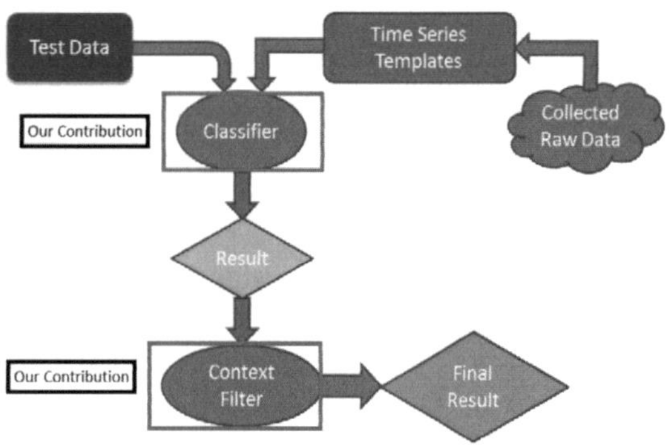

Figure 3. System Architecture

For developing the system, we built the Android app. This smart phone app was built using Android Development Tools (ADT) bundle which integrates a collection of the following programs:

- Eclipse: an integrated environment for the development of software projects with multi-language support.
- ADT plug-in: the toolset for Eclipse designed to allow the development of Android Apps.
- Android Software Development Kit (SDK): provides the API libraries and developer tools required to build apps for Android.
- ANT + SDK: provides the API libraries to use the ANT+ sensors.

From the Android App All data is passed to server via wireless medium. Then, on the server side all calculation is done. We take samples at a rate of 50 samples/second. The length of each activity sample is 8 seconds. We also calculate warp path by applying DTW algorithm. Warp path is calculated of every test data by taking the distance from the steady state. DTW works in only one dimension, but both the accelerometer and the gyroscope have three dimensions of data. So, we calculated the distance for each dimension and combined them to a single value which is our warp path using (1) and (2).

$$D_a = \sqrt{DTW(Xa)^2 + DTW(Ya)^2 + DTW(Za)^2} \quad (1)$$

$$D_g = \sqrt{DTW(Xg)^2 + DTW(Yg)^2 + DTW(Zg)^2} \quad (2)$$

Here D_a and D_g is the warp path for accelerometer and gyroscope, respectively.

For each template, each test data produced a warp distance indicating the difference from the steady state. Different kinds of activities produce different kinds of distances. So using this distance we can train a classifier which will take the warp path distance as input and then classify it to a class of activity.

D_a or D_g = DTW (Test Data)
Output = Classifier (D_a or D_g)

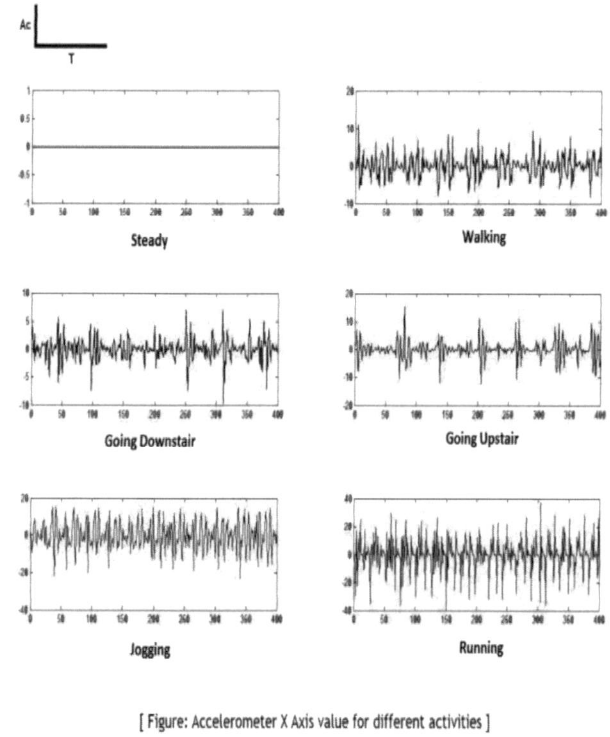

Figure 4. Accelerometer X axis value for different activities

If we observe the accelerometer x-axis values for different activities from Figure 4, then we will see that each of the activities has a specific pattern of acceleration amplitude levels during the activity. For example, in case of walking it is between 10 to -10, for jogging it is 20 to -20 and for running it is 40 to -40. However, the range is quite the same for walking, going upstairs and downstairs. All these characteristics remain consistent for the other accelerometer axis also. So if we compare these time series of the different activities with respect to a steady state then the output will be quite similar for walking, going downstairs and going upstairs but different for jogging and running.

There are three axis in accelerometer and DTW can be applied to only one time series at a time. So the warp path distance for each axis with respect to steady state has to be measured separately and then combined to get a single value. So we have calculated the DTW warp path distance for each axis and combined them to a single value using the approach illustrated in Figure 5.

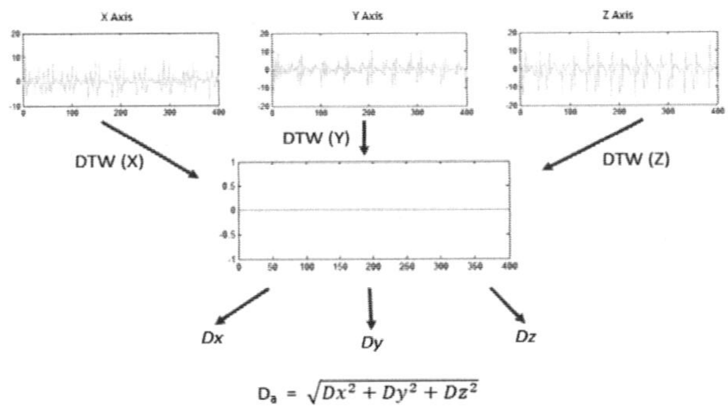

Figure 5. Applying DTW with respect to Steady State

We have already seen that the amplitude of acceleration differs for different kinds of activities. But, for walking, going downstairs and upstairs, the values are quite similar. That is why the total warp path distance (D_a) measured using DTW algorithm with respect to the Steady State is quite the same for these activities but different for jogging and running. Figure 6 shows the various warp path distance values for five different activities.

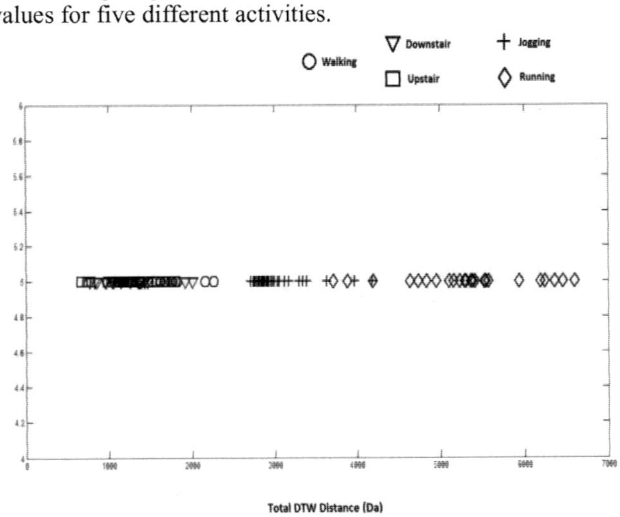

Figure 6. Total DTW distance in amplitude

It is clear from the figure that jogging and running has its separate zone but walking, going downstairs and going downstairs are in the same zone. So if we consider walking, going downstairs and going upstairs as a single class (Combined Class) then using the total warp path distance of an activity with a classifier, we can differentiate between the combined class, jogging and running. Using this characteristic, we have trained a k-NN classifier which takes the total warp path distance (D_a) of an activity as input and classifies into the combined class or jogging and running Though the basic classification can be accomplished by the aforementioned method, still the confusion remains as we do not know the true class of an activity when it is classified to the Combined Class. So here we are applying our context filtering approach which uses barometer sensor values to differentiate them. When a data is classified as Combined Class, we are again filtering the decision using Context Filtering.

If we take the differences of the altitude of the smart phone from starting to ending point of combined class activities, i.e.

$$dA = \textit{Altitude of ending point} - \textit{Altitude of starting point}$$

and plot them on a graph, it will look as depicted in Figure 7.

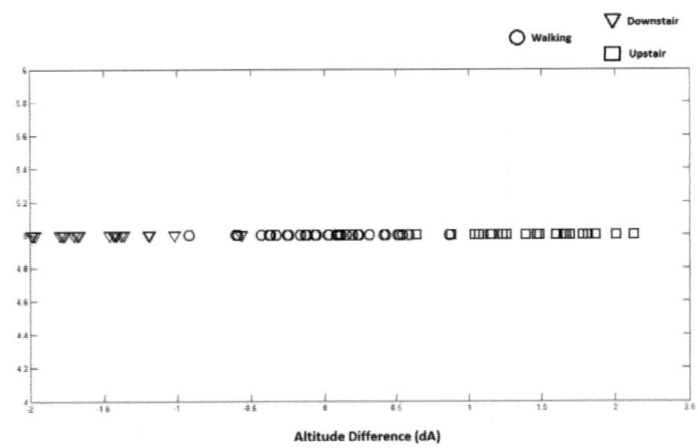

Figure 7. Altitude difference after applying KNN algorithm to find optimal threshold

So if we use ***dA*** of a combined class activity, we can easily differentiate them as each of walking, going downstairs and going upstairs has their own separate area and it is easily classifiable. We have used another k-NN classifier here which uses dA of a combined class activity to identify the true class. This is how an activity can be classified into one of the five classes by reducing the confusions.

V. RESULTS

Figures 8, 9 and 10 show the accuracy of detecting the five activities, respectively, using only accelerometer, only gyroscope and a combination of both sensors. On the basis of the different accuracy level of the different cases, it is clear that using only accelerometer in DTW produces better result in our approach. The computational complexity is also decreased as only the accelerometer is enough to detect the basic activity.

More importantly, the accuracy level for detecting similar activities like going downstairs and going upstairs has also been increased with respect to previous studies. For these two particular cases, we obtained accuracy of 92.85% and 100% respectively whereas in previous studies [5], the accuracy was 59.3% and 55.5%.

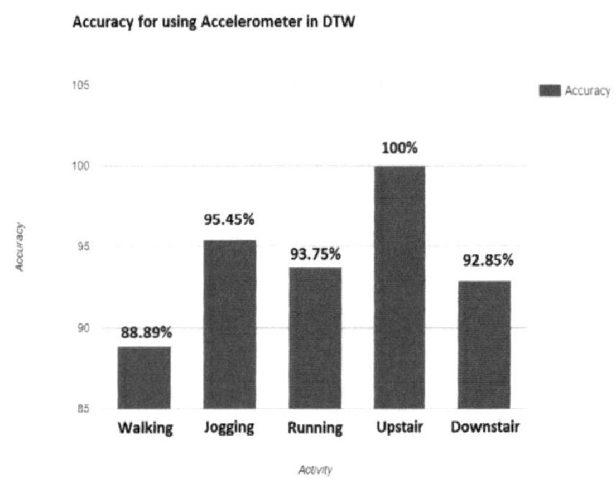

Figure 8. Accuracy using only Accelerometer

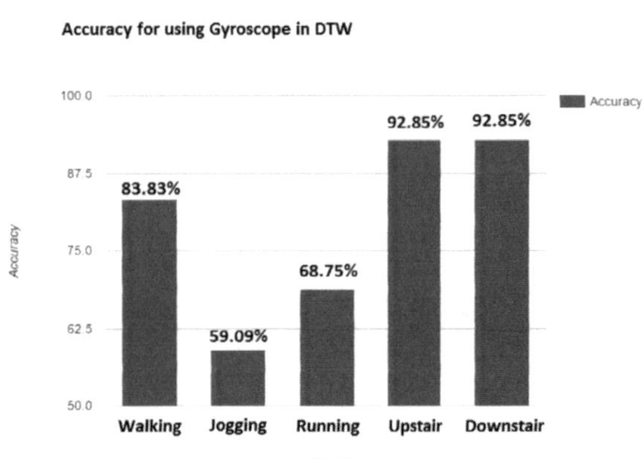

Figure 9. Accuracy for Using Only Gyroscope Value

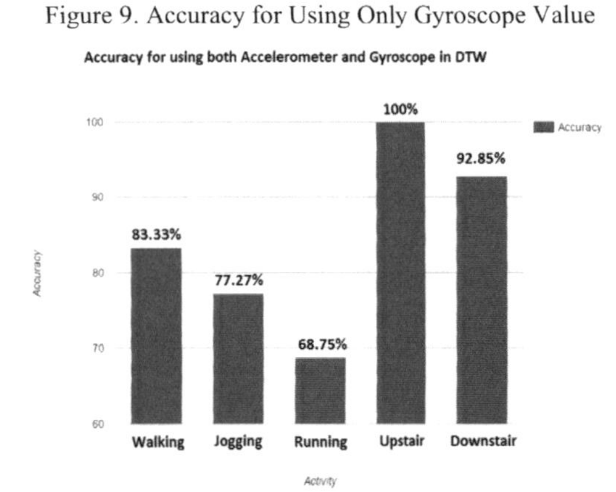

Figure 10. Accuracy for using Accelerometer & Gyroscope in DTW

Activity recognition success rate can again be increased for people of different category if we use only the data of that category as training samples. As people of different categories were chosen for our data collection process, the result we have acquired is quite for a general case.

VI. CONCLUSIONS

In this paper, we address some critical challenges of Activity Recognition with Mobile phones. DTW is an expensive algorithm with respect to time. May be this is the reason why this algorithm has not yet been used in this research field before, thinking that it may not be suitable for real time recognition. But rather using DTW for traditional template matching with respect to standard templates of each kind of activity, we are using it only once with respect to the steady state, reducing the sample number. We have also differentiated between similar activities like going upstairs and going downstairs. We all know that mobile phones have limited power capacity. So we have run our activity recognition classifier on our server instead on mobile phones to reduce the use of mobile battery. In the previous studies of human activity recognition, we have seen that the orientation and location of the smart phone was fixed to a certain part of a human body, mostly the waist. But we have placed the phone in the right pocket of the pant. So, it is more user friendly than the previous ones.

We also collected heart rate data during an activity. However, heart rate is mostly person dependent. Each person has a specific pattern of heart rate characteristic during an activity. So it is quite difficult to extract a universal feature from the heart rate values of a group of people. That is why we could not use the heart rate data to improve the classification result. However, as heart rate is person dependent, in case of user dependent classification, it may have some impact. This would be our future study to use heart rate for user dependent activity recognition learning. Recognition of semi-complex and complex activities like cooking, dancing, and travelling in bus etc. still remains a challenge. So along with locomotion activities, we will also try to recognize these complex and semi complex activities combining smart phone sensors and the knowledge we gain from our current work.

REFERENCES

[1] F. Kawsar, S. Ahamed, and R. Love, "Remote Monitoring Using Smartphone Based Plantar Pressure Sensors: Unimodal and Multimodal Activity Detection". In *Smart Homes and Health Telematics* (pp. 138-146). Springer International Publishing 2015.

[2] Jorge Luis Reyes Ortiz, "*Smartphone-based human activity recognition*". Springer, 2015.

[3] Boris Takač, "Position and orientation tracking in a ubiquitous monitoring system for parkinson disease patients with freezing of gait symptom." *JMIR mHealth and uHealth* 1.2 (2013)

[4] Yang, Guang-Zhong, and MagdiYacoub, "Body sensor networks." (2006): 500.

[5] Kwapisz,R. Jennifer, M. Gary Weiss, and A. Samuel Moore., "Activity recognition using cell phone accelerometers." *ACM SigKDD Explorations Newsletter* 12.2 (2011): 74-82.

[6] Yang and Jun, "Toward physical activity diary: motion recognition using simple acceleration features with mobile phones." *Proceedings of the 1st international workshop on Interactive multimedia for consumer electronics*. ACM, 2009.

[7] Miluzzo and Emiliano, "Sensing meets mobile social networks: the design, implementation and evaluation of the cenceme application." *Proceedings of the 6th ACM conference on Embedded network sensor systems*. ACM, 2008.

[8] Sun and Lin, "Activity recognition on an accelerometer embedded mobile phone with varying positions and orientations." *Ubiquitous intelligence and computing*. Springer Berlin Heidelberg, 2010. 548-562.

[9] Subramanya and Amarnag,"Recognizing activities and spatial context using wearable sensors." *arXiv preprint arXiv:1206.6869* (2012).

[10] Choudhury, Tonmoy, Sunny Consolvo, Brent Harrison, Jeffrey Hightower, Antonio Lamarca, Louis LeGrand, AzarRahimi et al. "The mobile sensing platform: An embedded activity recognition system." *Pervasive Computing, IEEE* 7, no. 2 (2008): 32-41.

[11] Cho and Yongwon, "SmartBuckle: human activity recognition using a 3-axis accelerometer and a wearable camera." *Proceedings of the 2nd International Workshop on Systems and Networking Support for Health Care and Assisted Living Environments*. ACM, 2008.

[12] Győrbíró, Norbert, ÁkosFábián, and GergelyHományi, "An activity recognition system for mobile phones." *Mobile Networks and Applications*14.1 (2009): 82-91

[13] Poppe and Ronald, "Vision-based human motion analysis: An overview."Computer vision and image understanding 108.1 (2007): 4-18.

[14] Bian, Xuehai, D. Gregory Abowd, and M. James Rehg, "Using sound source localization in a home environment." *Pervasive Computing*. Springer Berlin Heidelberg, 2005. 19-36.

[15] Incel, Ozlem Durmaz, Mustafa Kose, and CemErsoy, "A review and taxonomy of activity recognition on mobile phones." *BioNanoScience* 3.2 (2013): 145-171.

[16] Campbell and T. Andrew, "The rise of people-centric sensing." *Internet Computing, IEEE* 12.4 (2008): 12-21.

[17] Salvador, Stan, and Philip Chan, "FastDTW: Toward accurate dynamic time warping in linear time and space." *KDD workshop on mining temporal and sequential data*. 2004.

[18] European Commission. Directorate-General for Economic and Financial Affairs. *The 2012 Ageing Report: Underlying Assumptions and Projection Methodologies*. Office for Official Publications of the European Communities, 2011.

[19] WHO, *World Report on Disability: Summary*. Technical report, (UN World Health Organization, 2011)

Text Input System Using Hand Shape Recognition

Ahn,Yang-Keun
Realistic Media Platform Research Center
Korea Electronics Technology Institute
Seoul, Republic of Korea
e-mail: ykahn@keti.re.kr

Jung,Kwang-Mo
Realistic Media Platform Research Center
Korea Electronics Technology Institute
Seoul, Republic of Korea
e-mail: jungkm@keti.re.kr

Abstract— **This paper presents a method to recognize Korean language input using hand information extracted from 3D information taken from a single camera in a smart device environment. The presented method uses the shape information of an image of the hand as input for Korean mobile phone keyboards. Depth information is used to extract the region of the hand in real time. Through preprocessing, noise is removed from the extracted region, and the hand image is normalized with respect to its size and movement. The normalized image of the hand is projected using the rotation invariant Zernike basis function to ascertain its moment. These moment values of the hand's shape are compared to values saved in a database, and the character that has the closest moment value is input. The proposed method, which is designed to overcome the obstacle that people have unique hand shapes, makes use of a system that can easily become familiarized with an individual's hand shape information.**

Keywords-Hand Gesture; Gesture Recognition; Text Input System; Hand Shape; Shape Recognition.

I. INTRODUCTION

Electronic devices have become a staple of everyday modern life. While such devices have been growing smaller, their performance, an indicator of the progress made by the electronics industry, has been improving continuously. However, input methods for electronics are still restricted to traditional methods such as the mouse and keyboard. Recent advances have introduced the advent of touch control methods, but it is still difficult to control devices from a distance. Remote controls have offered some solutions to the issue of long-distance control, but even this method has the disadvantage of requiring hardware to be carried by the user.

In efforts to solve these types of issues, human computer interaction (HCI) research has been steadily progressing [1]. Within the field of HCI, hand movements that can simply and conveniently express a wide range of information are most commonly used [2]. Such hand movements are capable of controlling electronic devices, and may be applied to the fields of user interfaces (UI) and user experience (UX).

The Shape Key Input Interface (KII) presented in this paper is a system that recognizes the shape of the hand, associating it to a character in Korean to be used as input. Key factors in object recognition such as scale, translation, and rotation are normalized to achieve permanence in scale and translation.

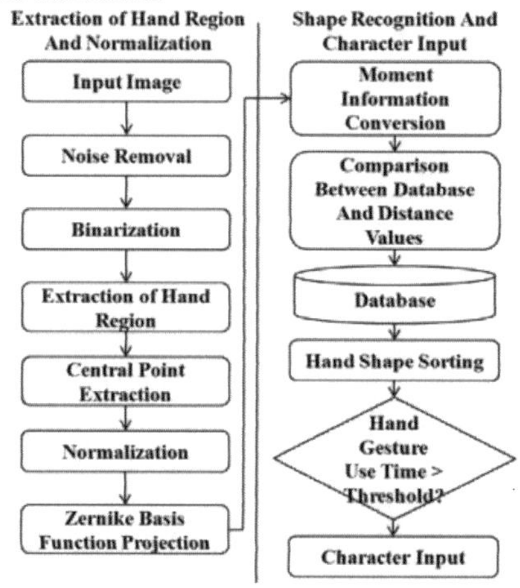

Figure 1. System Control Algorithm

Permanence in rotation is reached through application of a Zernike Shape Descriptor [4]. Rather than touching a designated space within a 3-dimensional space, recognizing the hand shape that corresponds to a keypad button makes input simpler. Additionally, a relatively small number of hand shapes are used, consequently allowing users to provide input without having to look at a keypad. To overcome the issue of different users having unique hand shapes, a system that can easily familiarize itself with users' hands and be customized according to users' tastes was implemented.

The system proposed in this paper is composed largely of two parts, a region extraction and normalization part and a shape recognition and character input part. The algorithm of this system is shown in Figure 1.

II. ZERNIKE MOMENT

Zernike moment is defined as a complex othogonal moment with an absolute value that is rotation invariant. The Zernike moment can be considered as a projection of the basis function, and the basis function of the n-th order at its m-th repetition is defined as follow:

$$V_{nm}(x,y) = V_{nm}(\rho,\theta) = R_{nm}(\rho)\exp(jm\theta) \quad (1)$$

V_{nm} is a set of equations that are normal to a unit circle in polar coordinates. Hence, there is no repetition of information. n is 0 or a positive integer, and m is a number that is even when $n-|m|$, and a non-negative integer when $|m| \leq n$. ρ is the distance from the origin to the point (x,y), and has a domain of $0 \leq \rho \leq 1$. θ is the angle that the point (x,y) creates with the x axis and has a domain of $0 \leq \theta \leq 2\pi$.

$R_{nm}(\rho)$ is a radial polynomial of the Zernike moment, and is expressed as given in equation (2).

$$R_{nm}(\rho) = \sum_{s=0}^{(n-|m|)/2} (-1)^s \frac{(n-s)!}{s!\left(\frac{n+|m|}{2}-s\right)!\left(\frac{n-|m|}{2}-s\right)!} \rho^{n-2s} \quad (2)$$

A Zernike moment of order n and repetition m Z_{nm} is expressed as in equation (3).

$$Z_{nm} = \frac{n+1}{\pi} \iint_{x^2+y^2 \leq 1} f(x,y) V_{nm}^*(x,y)\,dxdy \quad (3)$$

where V* represents the complex conjugate. To solve the Zernike moment for a discrete image, (3) can be approximated as shown in (4).

$$Z_{nm} = \frac{n+1}{\pi} \sum_x \sum_y f(x,y) V^*(x,y), x^2+y^2 \leq 1 \quad (4)$$

A. *Rotation invariant properties of Zernike moment*

The rotation invariant properties of the Zernike moment can be derived as follows. When an image $f(x,y)$ is converted into polar coordinates $f(\rho,\theta)$, an image rotated by an amount α is defined as given in equation (5).

$$f^r(\rho,\theta) = f(\rho,\theta+\alpha) \quad (5)$$

Applying equation (5) to equation (3) results in equation (6).

$$Z_{nm}^r = Z_{nm} \exp(jm\alpha) \quad (6)$$

Equation (6), shown above, is valid, and as such, it can be deduced that a rotated image affects only the topological values. Expressing this results in equation (7).

$$|Z_{nm}^r| = |Z_{nm}| \quad (7)$$

Hence, using the Zernike moment's absolute value as a feature value reveals its rotation invariant nature [5].

III. HAND SHAPE RECOGNITION INPUT METHODOLOGY

This section deals with using the Zernike moment to carry out hand shape recognition, and then translating information of the hand shapes to character input.

A. *Hand separation method*

As shown in Figure 2(a), the closest objects in the depth image are selected as potential candidates that may be the hand. This step resolves the issue of blindly selecting the closest object as the hand. Once the candidates are selected, the image is binarized (see Figure 2(b), and then labeling is performed to detect blobs, as seen in Figure 2(c). Once the blobs are found, the largest blob is selected as the hand Figure 2(d). Figure 2 illustrates the above process.

After hand area recognition, in order to perform Zernike basis function projection, the size and movement must be normalized. To normalize the hand region into even sizes, the hand's center of mass must be determined. To determine the center of mass, a distance transform is used. This changes the image such that the brightest pixel becomes the center of mass Figure 3(a). Once the center of mass is found, using it as a center, an inscribed circle is drawn. The inscribed circle can be found by taking the image of the hand region and transforming it into a contour image Figure 3(b), after which the minimum and maximum distances from the contours to the center of mass are calculated. The minimum distance is used to find the inscribed circle, and all pixel information below the edge of the circle is deleted as a means of removing the wrist area, leaving only an image of the hand Figure 3(c). Conversely, using the maximum distance, a circumscribed circle around the hand can be drawn, and then the maximum distance value is normalized to a predefined size in order to ensure invariance in size and movement Figure 3(d).

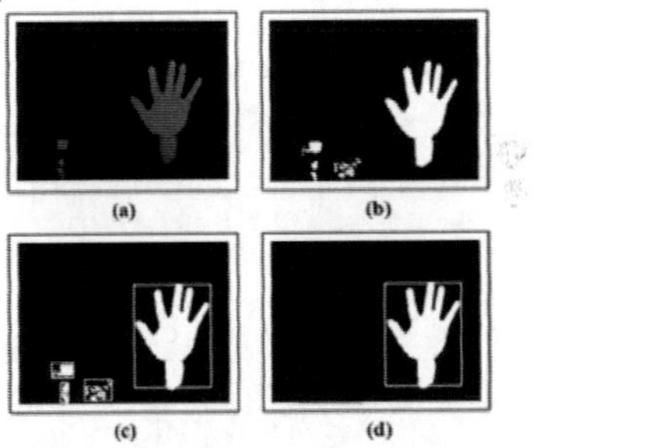

Figure 2. Hand separation process (a) Depth image (b) Binarization (c) Labeling (d) Largest blob detection

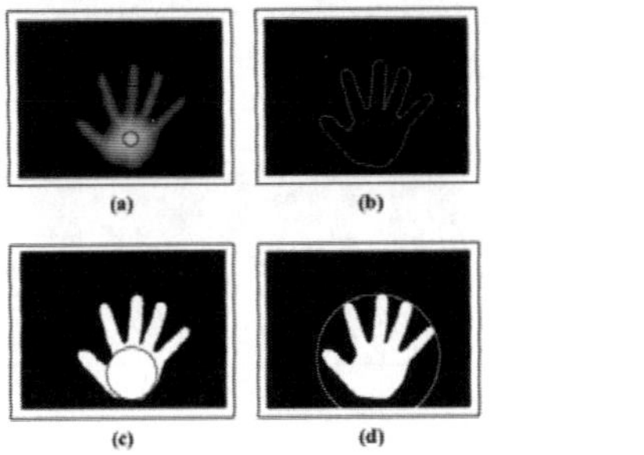

Figure 3. Normalization (a) Distance conversion (b) Contour image (c) Inscribed circle (d) Circumscribed circle

B. Hand image feature value extraction

The absolute value of the Zernike shape descriptor is rotation invariant, making strong recognition of the size, movement, and rotation of the hand images Figure 4(a) possible. In the previous section, the Zernike basis function, combined with the normalized image Figure 4(b) was projected to find the moment value Figure 4(c), leading to the determination of the image's feature values. To further describe the process, Figure 4 is provided below.

C. Recognition enhancement through labeling

Using only the numerical moment values calculated in the previous section, it is possible to proceed with matching and still retain a high recognition rate. However, during the comparison stage when the distance values are compared, outliers may lead to similar or completely different images being detected. This is especially true when there are numerous class variables, which is also when sorting performance is at its lowest. To offset such issues, a labeling technique is used to detect the number of fingers in the image. This particular metric is chosen as the number of fingers on a hand excellently reflects the geometric properties of the hand. However, the discernible types of shape information are limited, and only a maximum of five may be detected.

Comparable classes are largely divided into 5 groups and matched in order to minimize the possibility of error. The use of labeling to detect the number of fingers is shown below in Figure 5. Using labeling to find the number of fingers is simple. All pixel data within a circle with a certain radius extending from the center of mass are deleted. Figure 5(a) is the original image, and Figure 5(b) is the image of the circle used for blob detection. The number of blobs indicate the number of fingers, which in Figure 5(c) is 5.

Images with only one finger detected can the compared with other images with the same number of fingers to improve recognition rates and lower the number of match attempts required to sort images.

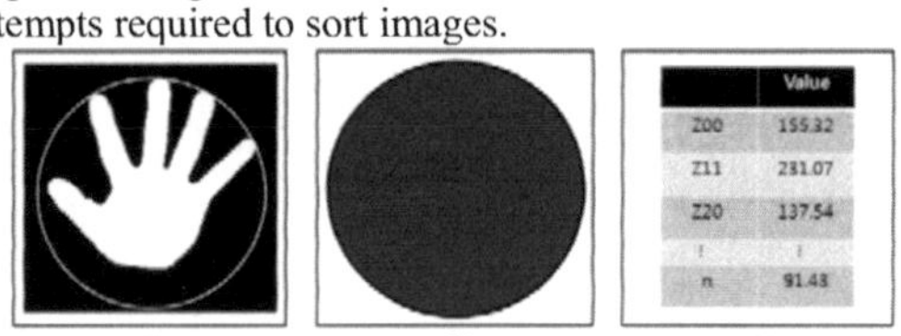

Figure 4. Feature value extraction process (a) Normalized image (b) Zernike basis function (c) Moment values

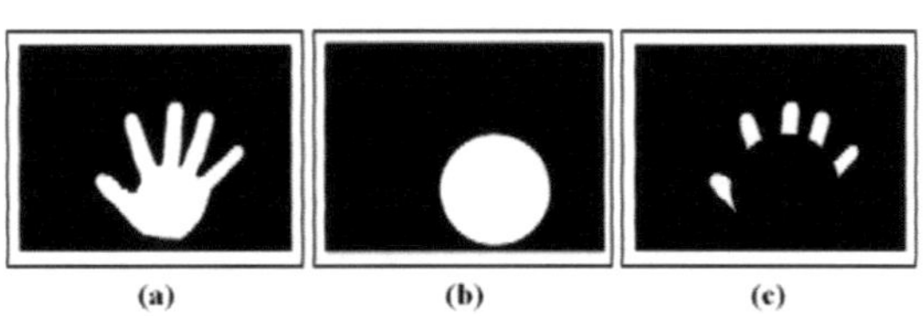

Figure 5. Labeling process (a) Original image (b) Circle image (c) Resultant image

D. User database creation

Identical hand shapes may actually turn out to have differing shape images or different Zernike moment values. Hence, this paper suggests the creation of a user independent and user independent database.

The user independent database is filled with hand shape information of numerous different people. The user dependent database saves all the moment values of each user's hand shapes.

The reason for creating two separate databases is to ensure a high rate of correct hand recognition even for first time users, and to lay groundwork for creating a personalized database to reach near-100% recognition rates.

E. Character input using hand recognition

To perform character input using images of hand shapes, a keypad, as shown in Figure 6, is used. The keypad differs from normal keypads in that each key corresponds to a certain hand shape. Users may imitate the shapes using their hands to type Korean characters. Figure 7 lists the 15 hand shapes and the numerical values they are linked to.

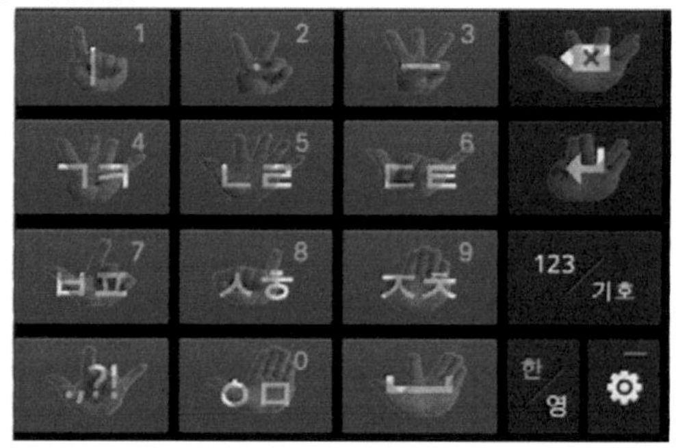

Figure 6. ShapeKII keypad

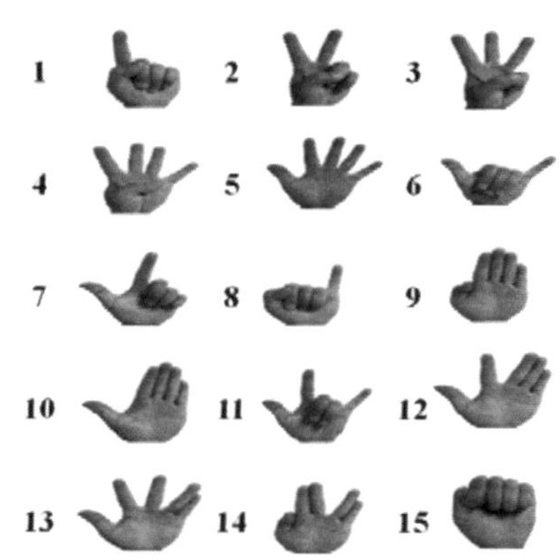

Figure 7. Hand shapes and their associated number values

IV. EXPERIMENT RESULTS AND APPLICATIONS

Tests were performed using a computer with an Intel Core i7-2600K 3.4GHz processor and 8GB of memory, along with a depth camera DS325 [6] linked at 60FPS. Software processing times are listed in [Table 1] below. Most of the time was used in creating the depth image. Considering the time required to compute the Zernike moment and the load required to run the process in real-time above 30FPS, it was decided that a 15-th order Zernike moment would be used. The q-recursive method introduced in [7] was applied to the Zernike moment to reduce the calculation time.

To conduct a validation, for the user independent database, 5 moment class values each of 15 hand shapes were saved – a total of 750 moment values. In the case of the user dependent database, 10 moment values were assigned to a hand shape – a total of 150 moment values. The sentence used to test the system was a Korean pangram, "키스의고유조건은입술끼리만나야하고특별한기술은필요치않다" that required 125 separate input characters, of which the input speed Figure 8 was measured. Additionally, all hand shapes from number 1 to 15 were repeated 10 times at random to test for accuracy.

The obtained results Figure 8 indicate that the mean time required to type one character is 0.79 seconds. When the user pre-registered his hand shapes, and then attempted to type while looking at the instruction screen, recognition reached over 98%, but the amount of time required between input increased. To increase the typing speed, the user memorized each shape and typed without referring to instructions. Although this method increased typing speed, typo probability increased. Figure 9 and Figure 10 present the recognition rates for 10 users who made each hand shape from number 1 to 15 randomly 10 times each for both the user independent and user dependent cases. The user independent case showed a 96.06% rate, which is acceptable. The user dependent case, on the other hand, although requiring an extra registration process, yielded a higher recognition rate of 98.06%.

TABLE I. PROCESSING TIME

Order(n)	Zernike	Depth Image	Total
0	1 msec	16 msec	17 msec
5	2 msec	16 msec	18 msec
10	7 msec	16 msec	23 msec
15	13 msec	16 msec	29 msec
20	25 msec	16 msec	41 msec

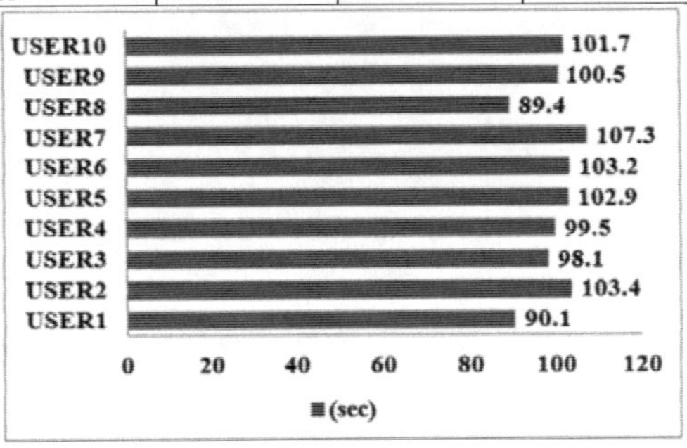

Figure 8. Pangram input time measurement

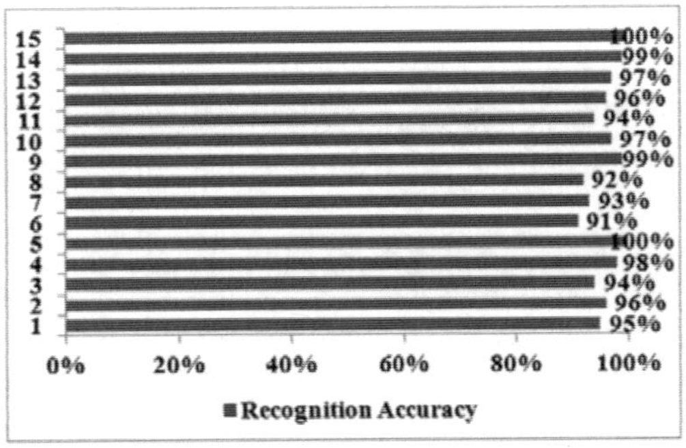

Figure 9. Independent user hand shape recognition accuracy

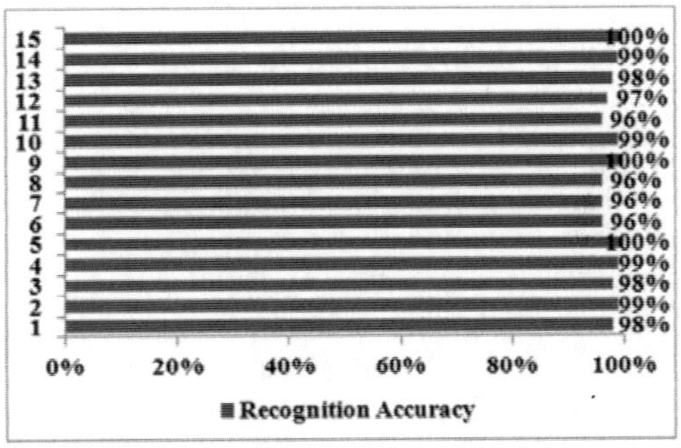

Figure 10. Dependent user hand shape recognition accuracy

A. Application

Taking into consideration the findings discussed in this paper, a program named ShapeKII was created. Figure 11 is the hardware setup used. A smart TV using a DS325 camera was installed in the top right. A gesture analysis was performed through a computer connected to the television by HDMI cable. Figure 12 illustrates an example of how ShapeKII is to be used.

Figure 11. System hardware configuration

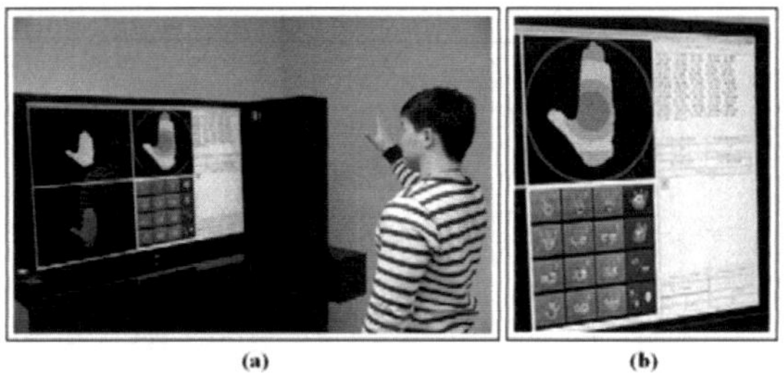

Figure 12. ShapeKII system (a) Character typing using hand shapes (b) Close-up of results screen

V. CONCLUSION

This paper proposed a Korean input system that uses a single depth camera to extract 3D information of a user's hand. The methodology presented worked regardless of the hand's location, using only the information of the hand's shape to type Korean. A user dependent database was employed so users could register their personal hand shapes, thereby increasing user friendliness. The presented method is currently limited to a short-range detection system, but it will be extended to longer-range detection in future work and will also be operable on smart devices.

REFERENCES

[1] R. Watson, "A survey of Gesture Recognition Techniques," Technical Report, TCD-CS-1993-11, 1993, pp. 1-31.

[2] P. Garg, N. Aggarwal, and S. Sofat, "Vision Based Hand Gesture Recognition," Proceedings of World Academy of Science, Engineering and Technology, vol.49, Jan 2009, pp. 972-977.

[3] M. Tosas, and B. Li, "Virtual Touch Screen for Mixed Reality", Proc. European Conference on Computer Vision, Lecture Notes in Computer Science, Prague, Czech Republic, vol 3058, May 2004, pp. 48-59.

[4] C. H. Teh and R T. Chin, "On Image Analysis by the Methods Of Moments" IEEE Transactions on Pattern Analysis and Machine Intelligence, vol, 10, no.4, 1988, pp. 496-513.

[5] A. Khotanzad and Y. H. Hong, "Invariant image recognition by zernike moments," IEEE Transactions on Pattern Analysis and Machine Intelligence, vol, 12, no.5, 1990, pp. 489-497.

[6] http://www.softkinetic.com

[7] C. W. Chong, and P. Raveendran, and R. Mukundan, "A comparative analysis of algorithms for fast computation of Zernike moments," The Journal of the Pattern Recognition Society, 2003, pp.731-742.

A Passive Stewart Platform Based Joystick to Control Spatially Moving Objects

Ibrahim Yildiz
Department of Mechatronics Engineering
Necmettin Erbakan University
Konya / TURKEY
e-mail: iyildiz@konya.edu.tr

Abstract— **Most of the spatially moving vehicles and game controllers use 2-3 degrees of freedom joysticks to manipulate objects position. However, most of the spatially moving vehicles have more than 3 degrees of freedom, such as helicopters, quadrotors, and planes. Therefore, additional equipment like pedals or buttons is required during the manipulation. In this study, a passive Stewart platform based six degrees of freedom joystick was developed to control spatially moving objects. The Stewart platform mechanism is a six-degrees of freedom parallel mechanism, which has been used for simulators. The main challenge of using a parallel mechanism to manipulate objects is the computational burden of its forward kinematics. Therefore, an artificial neural network was used for the forward kinematic solution of the Stewart platform mechanism to obtain the fastest response. Linear potentiometers were used for the Stewart platform legs. A mathematical model of a quadrotor was used to test the capability of the joystick. The developed spatial joystick successfully manipulated the virtual quadrotor model.**

Keywords- Spatial joystick; Stewart platform.

I. INTRODUCTION

The purpose of this study is to emphasize the difficulty of traditional manipulation techniques, which are using a multi-point control such as a lever, pedals, and collective lever. This multi-tasking event is obviously difficult considering learning, teaching and application procedure. Therefore, the main objective of this study is gathering control tools of any Spatially Moving Vehicles (SMV) into one hand. The advantages of one-handed manipulation are investigated with several scenarios, including reflection of external forces to SMV to the user's hand and force feedback control of the manipulation mechanism. In this research, a linear potentiometer based Stewart platform (SP) as a man-machine interface is proposed as a means of mechatronic design, kinematic analysis, and simulation environment to manipulate SMVs. Through the paper, first, the analysis of SP mechanism for kinematics and design of the system is investigated. Then, a "Quadrotor" is modeled using the Newton-Euler approach, a Proportional Integral Derivative (PID) controller is applied to the derived model and a user interface is constructed for operating both the Quadrotor model and Stewart Platform Mechanism (SPM) simultaneously. Lastly, the virtual Quadrotor model is manipulated with a real Stewart Platform Joystick.

Stewart-Gough Platform is a parallel mechanism which was first used as an universal tire test machine and a flight simulator by V. E. Gough (1956) and D. Stewart (1965), connecting a stationary lower and a mobile upper platform to the two ends of six actuators in parallel and obtaining three translational and three rotational Degrees of Freedom (DOF) in space [1][2].

Many methods were studied for the solution of the kinematics of the Stewart Platform Mechanism (SPM). A major piece of work on solving the forward kinematics of SPM was using the Bezout method [3]. This method allows deriving the kinematics from a 16-th degree equation with one unknown variable. The fact that one needs a numerical solution to obtain the final equation is one of the disadvantages of the method. Obtaining the answer from 16 solutions is one of the disadvantages of this method. Another solution method uses Newton-Rhapson algorithm and this was presented for solving the forward kinematics, iteratively [4]. This method usually converges to the solution. However, if one of the encoder data is not clear or wrong, the solution is not able to converge. A nonlinear observer was designed for predicting the 3 rotational and 3 translational displacements of the SPM by using the state variables of the mechanism, [5]. Artificial Neural Networks are also used for solving the forward kinematics of the SPM [6][7]. This method is the best suitable solution for real-time mechanisms.

Human and robot interaction introduces new control requirements over time [21]. One of them is the force control. Investigations and comparisons were made on many force control methods ranging from the simplest to the most complex [8]. An active stiffness control, which is one of the force control methods, was applied with the help of a program for controlling 3 translational and 3 rotational axes [9]. A pneumatically actuated 6x6 SPM was developed for endoscopic surgery. The relationship between the endoscope and the surface was provided by a force control algorithm [10]. Force control and tactile control methods, which are very important in terms of human-machine interaction, are frequently used in rehabilitation systems. 6x6 SPM was designed for the rehabilitation of the ankle with a user interface [11]. A 3-axis parallel robot was developed for the rehabilitation of the wrist and system performance was investigated including the therapist effect [12][13]. A 3x3 Stewart platform manipulator has been proposed to manipulate spatially moving vehicles with force feedback [18]. This mechanism has six linear actuators and a force/torque sensor to sense the applied force and it successfully manipulated spatially moving vehicles.

However, despite its small size, it is still too heavy for practical applications.

Unmanned Air Vehicles (UAV) have become the center of attraction due to their contributions to the military, rescue and aerospace technologies. An important part of research and development activities is the 4-rotor aircraft quadrotor, which has 4 DOF and motion capability at 6 axes. The Newton-Euler method has been used in many studies for obtaining the mathematical model of the quadrotor [14][15]. Traditional and robust control algorithms were also applied to a quadrotor [15][16][17]. A simplified deterministic model of a quadrotor was presented for investigating the problem of planning/re-planning [20]. In general, quadrotors and other aerial vehicles have multiple manipulation points. The main disadvantage of the developed manipulation mechanism is that the user must carry out multiple tasks at the same time in a standard multi-point manipulation. Briefly, the contribution of this work is that the designed mechanism allows the user to control all tasks from a single point. Section 2-A describes the mechatronic design of the passive Stewart platform mechanism. Section 2-B presents the forward kinematic solution of the mechanism. Section 2-C describes the user interface of the software and the specifications of the mathematical model of the quadrotor. Section 3 consists of the experimental results and discussions. Section 4 is the conclusion section and addresses future works.

II. Materials and Methods

A. Mechatronic Design and specifications

The legs of the SP consist of six linear potentiometers. The resistance of these potentiometers varies from 0 to 5 kΩ with the range of 0 to 100 mm. The diameter of the upper ring (mobile ring) of the SP is 100 mm. The diameter of the lower ring (stationary ring) is 140 mm.

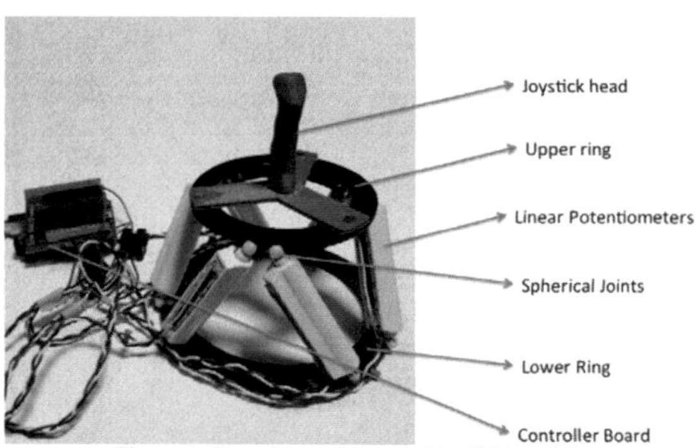

Figure 1. Experimental setup of the SP joystick.

Potentiometers were connected both to the upper and lower part of the SP with spherical joints. Analog input ports of an Atmega powered Arduino Uno board were used both to obtain voltage values from potentiometers and to send position and orientation values of the SP to the computer, which are obtained from forward kinematics. The experimental setup of the SP joystick can be seen in Fig. 1.

B. Forward Kinematics

Obtaining position and orientation of the mobile ring of the SP mechanism from the leg lengths can be called forward kinematics solution. Iterative solutions and optimized solutions to solve the forward kinematics of the SP mechanism have been proposed. However, iterative solutions are not suitable for real-time applications because of time delay. In this study, Artificial Neural Networks (ANN) are used to solve the forward kinematics of the SP, which is suitable for real-time applications because of fast response. First of all, the workspace of the SP mechanism is scanned with inverse kinematics to obtain training data, which are the leg lengths for inputs and position/orientation values for targets of ANN. Lawenberg & Marquard feed forward back propagation algorithm is used to train ANN. The architecture of the network can be seen in Fig. 2. Weight and bias values of the network are embedded in the controller board after training of the network. 20 neurons are used inside the hidden layer. The leg lengths of the SP, which are obtained from the potentiometer data, are the inputs to the network (1).

$$L = [L_1 \quad L_2 \quad L_3 \quad L_4 \quad L_5 \quad L_6] \qquad (1)$$

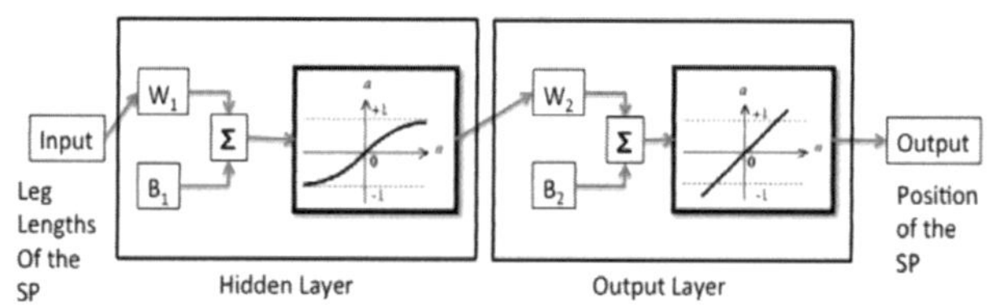

Figure 2. Artificial neural network architecture of the forward kinematics of the SP

The output of the hidden layer can be expressed using (2), where "L" is the leg length vector from (1), "W" and "B" are the weight and bias vectors obtained from the trained network, respectively. The weight value is the gain of an input of a neuron. This value changes over the training period of the neuron considering the importance of the input. As an example, if the effect of an input is important for the output, the value of the weight of the neuron should be bigger. The bias value is the minimum stimulation level of the neuron. The sensitivity of the neuron is inversely proportional to the bias value. Mentioned ANN coefficients are decided during the learning process. The output of a neuron could be a linear or nonlinear function of input values. In the present study, tangent sigmoid function (a special case of logistic function) is used for the neurons in the hidden layer and linear function is used for the neurons in the output layer.

$$Out_1 = 2/1 + \left(e^{-2(L.W_1+B_1)}\right) \qquad (2)$$

The output of the complete ANN gives the position and orientation vector of the SP as in (3).

$$Output = \left(2/1 + \left(e^{-2(L.W_1+B_1)}\right)\right).W_2 + B_2 \qquad (3)$$

C. Computer interface

The communication between the SP joystick and the computer was provided with an rs232 communication protocol [22]. A test program was written which includes the dynamic model of a quadrotor. The controller board of the SP joystick sends the position and orientation data to the computer. These outputs of the SP joystick are the reference inputs of the quadrotor model. A quadrotor mechanism has 6 degrees of freedom where two of them are dependent on angular motion around its x and y-axes. That means, if a quadrotor needs to move along x or y-axes, it must rotate itself around these axes.

Dynamic model and control strategies of a quadrotor have been investigated by many of researchers. In this study, the dynamic model of the quadrotor is constructed by using the Newton-Euler approach [14][15]. A schematic representation of a quadrotor can be shown in Fig. 3. $\mathbf{F}_{1-4}$ represents the thrust generated by the propellers, ℓ is the distance of the motors to the center of mass of the quadrotor, capital X, Y, Z is the translational displacement of the quadrotor, ϕ^q, θ^q, ψ^q are the rotational displacements of the quadrotor along the x, y, z-axes, M_t is the mass of the quadrotor, g is the acceleration due to gravity.

A quadrotor contains 4 dc motor actuated propellers, which are mounted on the body. Each propeller generates reverse torques onto the body of the quadrotor. The rotation directions of propellers are selected to eliminate this effect.

Spatially moving vehicles are exposed to various physical effects like aerodynamics, inertia, gravity, gyroscopic forces and friction. Some of the assumptions listed below were used for modeling.

- Ground effect is neglected.
- Propeller blades are not flexible.
- Construction of mechanism is rigid and symmetric.
- Thrust and drag forces are proportional to the square of propeller velocities.
- Air drag friction is included.

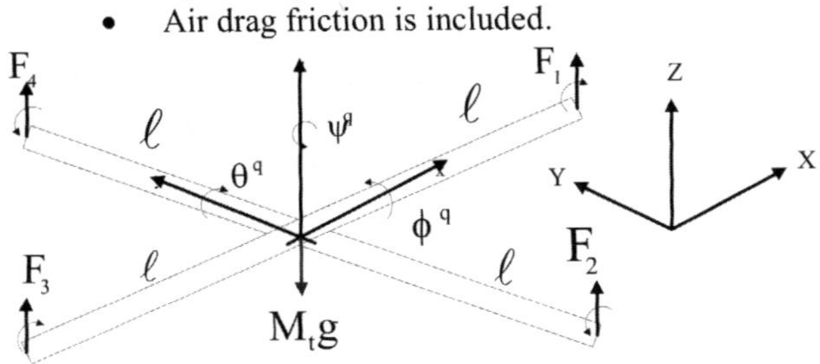

Figure 3. Schematic representation of a quadrotor

Proportional integral derivative (PID) control was used to control the 4-degree of freedom of the quadrotor, which can be seen in Fig. 4. The reference values of the controller were obtained from the output of the forward kinematics of the SP joystick. The position feedback of the quadrotor was obtained from the dynamic equations of the quadrotor. The PID coefficients of the controllers were decided after a series of simulation considering the settling time, overshoot and steady state error values.

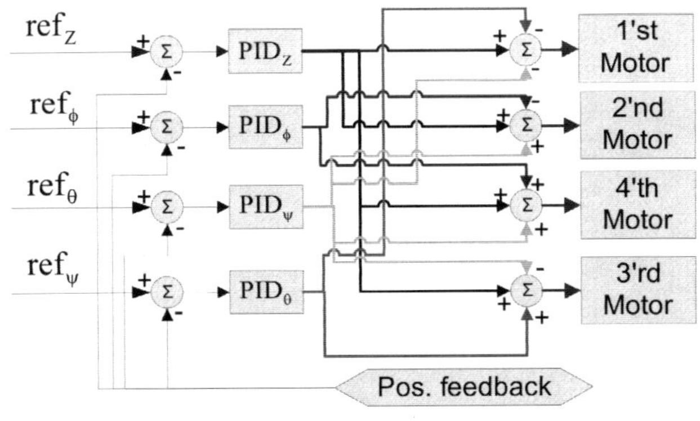

Figure 4. Control schematic of the quadrotor model.

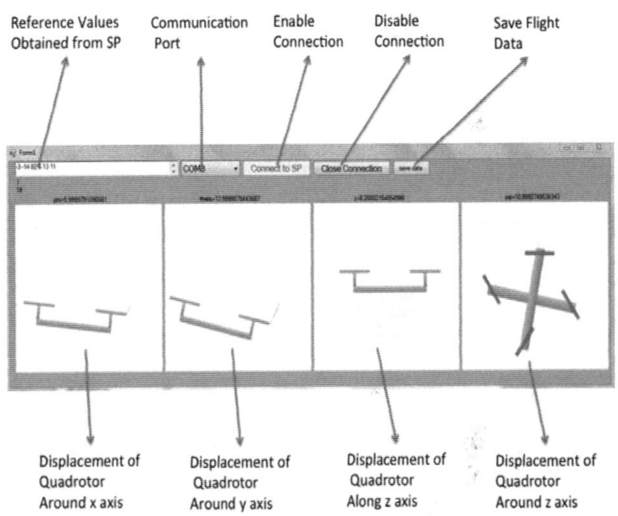

Figure 5. User interface of the test program

The developed user interface of the test program can be seen in Fig. 5. The user interface allows the user to observe both the incoming data from the SP and the action of the quadrotor model considering the reference data coming from the SP joystick.

III. RESULTS AND DISCUSSIONS

The dynamic model and the control of the quadrotor were tested with the developed interface. Reference values of 10 m for displacement along the z-axis, 45 degrees for displacement around the z-axis, 15 degrees for displacement around the x-axis, -15 degrees for displacement around the y-axis were used. The response of the controller is shown in Fig. 6. The dynamic model of the quadrotor successfully reaches the reference values.

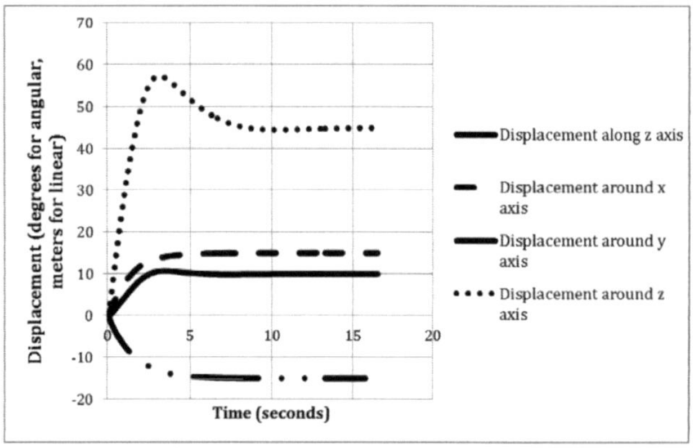

Figure 6. Response of the PID controllers

Manipulation of the dynamic quadrotor model was also tested with SP joystick. The reference values of the angular displacements of the quadrotor model are the displacement of the SP around the x, y and z-axes. The reference value of the linear displacement of the quadrotor along the z-axis was the multiplication of displacement of the SP along the z-axis with a coefficient. The test was performed by one inexperienced user. Moving the quadrotor model separately around the x, y, z-axis and along the z-axis was requested from the user.

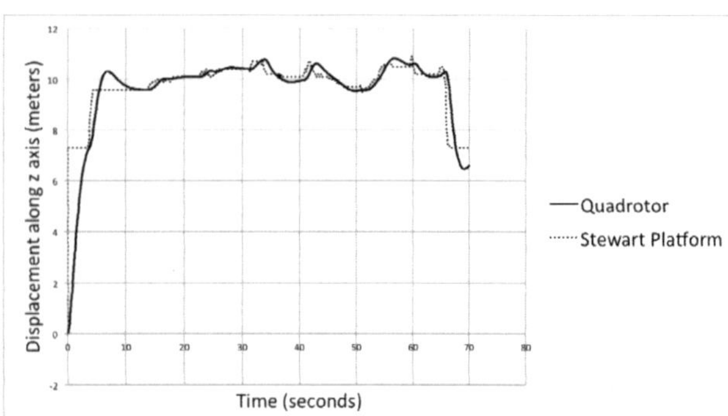

Figure 7. Displacement of the Quadrotor model and the SP joystick along the z-axis.

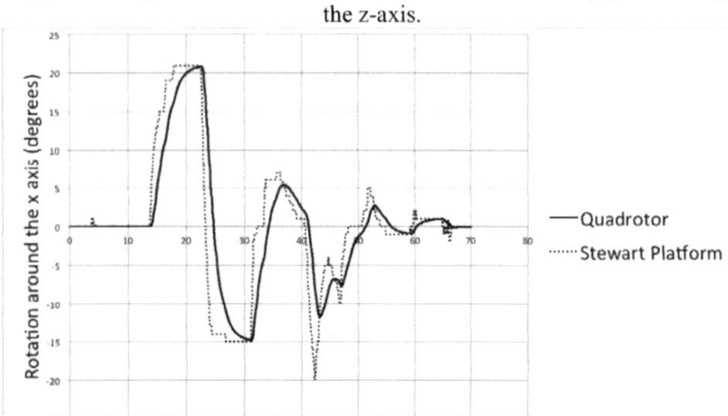

Figure 8. The angular displacement of the quadrotor and the SP joystick around the x-axis.

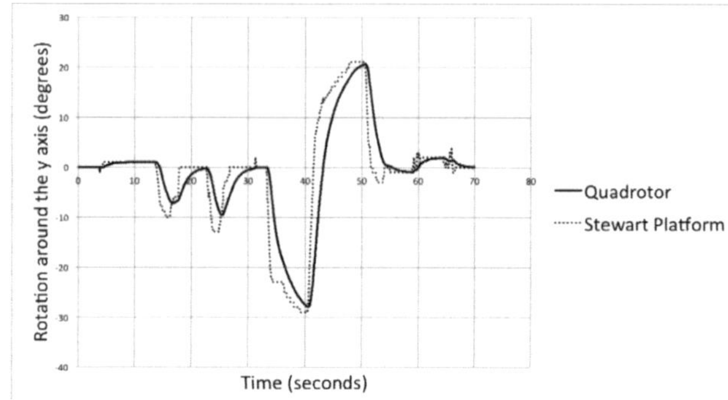

Figure 9. The angular displacement of the quadrotor and the SP joystick around the y-axis.

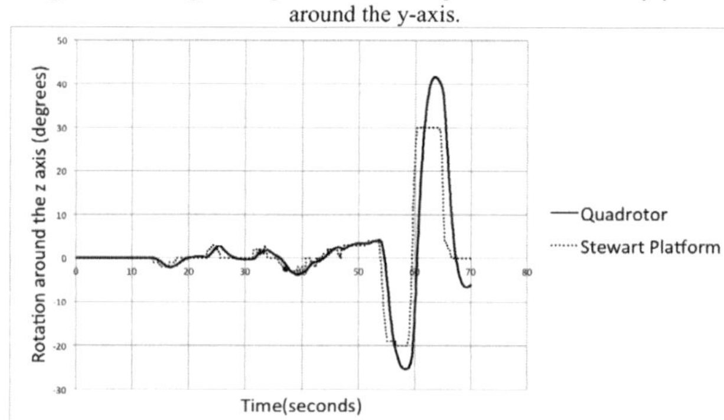

Figure 10. The angular displacement of the quadrotor and the SP joystick around the z-axis.

The quadrotor successfully reaches the incoming reference values from the SP. Fig. 7, 8, 9, 10 depict the displacement of both the quadrotor model and the SP joystick. The dynamics of the quadrotor and the PID controller cause a time delay between the reference values and the position of the quadrotor. This settling time of the quadrotor can be clearly seen in the mentioned figures.

IV. CONCLUSIONS

Manipulation of the spatially moving objects is important considering both the cost of the aerial vehicles and safety of passengers. Multiple manipulations might distract the user. The reason for many accidents is the distraction of the pilot or the user. Therefore, a passive 6 DOF Stewart platform based joystick was designed for single point manipulation. Classical iterative solutions of the forward kinematics of the SP cause time delays and errors considering real-time applications. Therefore, ANN was used for forward kinematics solution of the SP. A dynamic model of a quadrotor was derived for testing the manipulation of the SP joystick. PID controllers were used to control the axes of the quadrotor. A user interface was built containing the dynamic model of the quadrotor. Finally, the quadrotor model was successfully manipulated from a single point with the SP joystick.

It is very probable that the development of one point manipulation will become the center of attraction for most disciplines, including simulation or game development. The developed low-cost Stewart platform joystick solution promises to open a new era for man-machine interface. Haptic feedback with linear actuators instead of potentiometers should be provided for the user to sense both the inertial and other external forces is considered in future works.

REFERENCES

[1] D. Stewart, A Platform with Six Degrees of Freedom, UK Institution of Mechanical Engineers Proceedings, 180,1-15, 1965.

[2] V. E. Gough, Contribution to discussion to papers on research in automobile stability and control in tyre performance, by Cornell staff, Proc. AutoDiv. Inst. Mech. Eng., 392–395, 1956.

[3] P. Nanua , K.J.Waldron and V. Murthy, Direct Kinematic Solution Of A Stewart Platform, IEEE Transactions on Robotics and Automation, 6 ,438-444.B, 1990.

[4] K. Harib and K. Srinivasan, Kinematic and Dynamic Analysis of Stewart Platform Based Machine Tool Structures, Robotica, 21:541-554.

[5] S-H. Chen, C-I. Huang and L-C. Fu, Applying a Nonlinear Observer to Solve Forward Kinematics of a Stewart Platform, IEEE International Conference on Control Applications, 1183-1188, 2008.

[6] C.S. Yee and K. Lim, Forward kinematics solution of Stewart platform using neural networks, Neurocomputing, 16, 333-349, 1997.

[7] S.N. Yurt, E. Anlı and I. Ozkol, Forward kinematics analysis of the 6-3 SPM by using neural networks, Meccanica, 42,187–196, 2007.

[8] G. Zeng and A. Hemami, An overview of robot force control, Robotica ,15, 473–482, 1997.

[9] K.J. Salisbury, Active Stiffness Control of a Manipulator in Cartesian Coordinates, The 19th IEEE Conf. on Decision and Control, Albuquerque , 95-100, 1980.

[10] A.Benalli, P. Richard and P. Bidaud,Design, control and evaluation of a six DOF force fee,dback interface for virtual reality applications, Proceedings of the IEEE International Workshop on Robot and Human Interaction, 338-343, 1999.

[11] M. Girone, G. Burdea, M. Bouzit and V. Popescu, A Stewart Platform-Based System for Ankle Telerehabilitation, Autonomous Robots 10,203–212, 2001.

[12] A.Gupta, M.K. O'Malley, V. Patoğlu and C. Burgar, Design, Control andPerformance of RiceWrist: A Force FeedbackWrist Exoskeleton for Rehabilitation and Training, The International Journal of Robotics Research, 27(2) ,233–251, 2008.

[13] A.C. Satıcı, A. Erdoğan and V. Patoğlu, Design of a Reconfigurable Ankle Rehabilitation Robot and Its Use for the Estimation of the Ankle Impedance ,IEEE 11th International Conference on Rehabilitation Robotics, 257-264, 2009.

[14] T. Bresciani, Modelling, Identification and Control of a Quadrotor Helicopter, Department of Automatic Control, Lund University, Master Thesis ,2008.

[15] T. Hamel, R. Mahony, R. Lozano and J. P. Ostrowski, Dynamic modelling and configuration stabilization for a X4-flyer, IFAC 15th World Congress on Automatic Control, Barcelona, Spain, 1.2:3, 2002.

[16] S. Bouabdallah and R. Siegwart, Backstepping and Sliding-mode Techniques Applied to an Indoor Micro Quadrotor, proceedings of the IEEE, International Conference on Robotics and Automation, Barcelona, Spain, p. 2247-2252, 2005.

[17] S. Bouabdallah, A. Noth and R. Siegwart, PID vs LQ control techniques applied to an indoor micro quadrotor, Intelligent Robots and Systems, 3,2451-2456, 2004.

[18] V.E. Ömürlü and I. Yildiz, Self-Tuning Fuzzy PD - based Stiffness Controller of a 3x3 Stewart Platform as a Man-Machine Interface , Turkish Journal of Electrical Engineering and Computer Sciences, doi:10.3906/elk-1007-581 ,2010.

[19] N. Hogan, Impedance Control, An Approach to Manipulation: Part I, II, Int. J. of Robotics Res. 107,1-24, 1985.

[20] A. Chamseddine, Z. Youmin, C.A. Rabbath, C. Join and D. Theilliol, Flatness-Based Trajectory Planning/Replanning for a Quadrotor Unmanned Aerial Vehicle, IEEE Transactions on Aerospace and Electronic Systems, Vol:48, Issue:4,2832-2848, 2012.

[21] K.Salisbury, Issues in Human/Computer Control of Dexterous Remote Hands, IEEE Transactions on Aerospace and Electronic Systems, Vol:24, 591-596, 1988

[22] Electronics Industries Association, et al. EIA Standard RS-232-C Interface Between Data Terminal Equipment and Data Communication Equipment Employing Serial Data Interchange. International Organization for Standardization, Geneva, Switzerland, 1969.

Results of a 3 Year Study of a BCI-Based Communicator for Patients with Severe Disabilities

Pasquale Fedele, Myriam Gioia
Liquidweb s.r.l.
Siena,Italy
e-mail: {p.fedele, m.gioia}@liquidweb.it

Fabio Giannini, Alessandra Rufa
University of Siena
Siena,Italy
e-mail: {fabio.giannini, rufa}@unisi.it

***Abstract*— The Brain-Computer Interface (BCI) technology can convert brain electrical signals into commands able to control external devices without the need of any voluntary movement. This can be an innovative solution that allows interaction, especially for patients with pathologies such as Amyotrophic Lateral Sclerosis, Multiple Sclerosis, Muscular Dystrophy or ischemic/traumatic injuries, unable to use standard Augmentative Alternative Communication (AAC) devices because of the loss of limbs movements, gaze control or ophthalmological disorders. Among different approaches of signal analysis, a recent BCI device, Braincontrol Basic Communicator, based on event related desynchronization (ERD) produced by motor imagery (MI), has been recently developed by Liquidweb s.r.l. and used in the current study to overcome physical issues of these patients. The aim of this study was to verify the efficacy of the Braincontrol as an AAC device and to validate the training methodology with regards to patients in locked-in state (LIS). The study was conducted, from 2012 to 2015, on two groups: 42 patients with communication and motility disorder (of these 13 were in LIS and 10 in condition similar to the complete locked-in state, with no feedback and unknown cognitive status) and 63 healthy users. The results of this observation confirm that the device, after the first phase training, is efficient and robust for patients. Trainings have been completed successfully for all the healthy users and patients in initial and severe stage of the disease, only 2 out 42 patients failed the training. In particular, the 2 patients were in the condition similar to the complete locked-in state (CLIS). After this study, 17 locked-in patients have continued to use the system as a unique tool for communication.**

Keyword-Brain-Computer Interface (BCI); Augmentative and Alternative Communication (AAC); Assistive Technologies; Amyotrophic Lateral Sclerosis (ALS).

I. INTRODUCTION

Motor neuron diseases and degenerative neuromuscular disorders are characterized by a gradual loss of muscular function while usually retaining complete cognitive functions.

The progressive neurodegeneration induces progressive loss of upper and lower motor neurons, causing a progressive complete destruction of the peripheral and central motor system. The resulting condition is called Completely Locked-in State (CLIS).

If rudimentary control of at least one muscle is present, we speak of Locked-in State (LIS). The principal assistive technologies for LIS patients include residual movement controlled systems [16]-[17], voice-controlled systems, eye-tracking and brain computer interface (BCI). Brain-computer interface technology interprets electrical signals corresponding to a specific brain activity and allows the control of a computer or other external devices [1]-[13][18] (See Figure 1).

The interaction methods of BCI are classified on the identification and collection of the signal: there are Invasive, Partially Invasive and Noninvasive BCI.

The invasive category needs a neurosurgical implant of the sensors on the cerebral cortex, the partially invasive one requires the application of the sensors on the epidural or subdural space to record Electrocorticographic (ECoG) signal, while the noninvasive category uses external surface sensors in contact with the scalp permitting to record different kinds of signals, like Electroencephalography (EEG), Magnetoencephalography (MEG) and functional Magnetic Resonance Imaging (fMRI).

A different signal analysis, approaching to the EEG-BCI, includes Event-Related (P300) Potentials, Slow Cortical Potentials, Steady State Visual Evoked Potentials (SSVEP), Sensorimotor Rhythms (SMRs), and the Event Related Desynchronization or Synchronization (ERD/ERS) produced by Motor Imagery (MI).

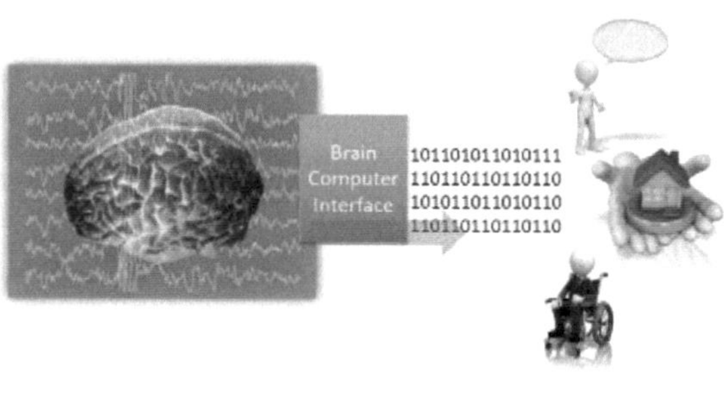

Figure 1. BCI Technology

Most of projects detects P300 Potentials or Visual Evoked Potentials but due to the need of sight in order to concentrate on the desired object, there are many patients who cannot use this technology. Furthermore, the weak electrical signal created by P300 requires gel-based EEG sensors, which means more time and hassle to prepare before use and clean after use.

Braincontrol system, instead, based on Motor Imagery, was developed by Liquidweb s.r.l. around the needs of CLIS and can also be used by blind people.

The first prototype, able to recognize 6 imagined movements, pull/push, top/bottom, left/right, was released in the fall of 2010 [14]. It has been continuously implemented between 2010 and 2012 and tested in the same period with more than 30 healthy volunteers providing excellent results and encouraging the development. The first version, Braincontrol "Basic Communicator", was completed in the middle of 2013. It fills a technological void for CLIS patients who cannot use eye-tracking systems or other assistive technologies.

Future versions of BrainControl, which are currently under development, will include advanced communication and entertainment (virtual keyboard, text-to-speech, social networks, email,), home automation (lights, temperature, etc.), control of a wheelchair and robotics (See Figure 2).

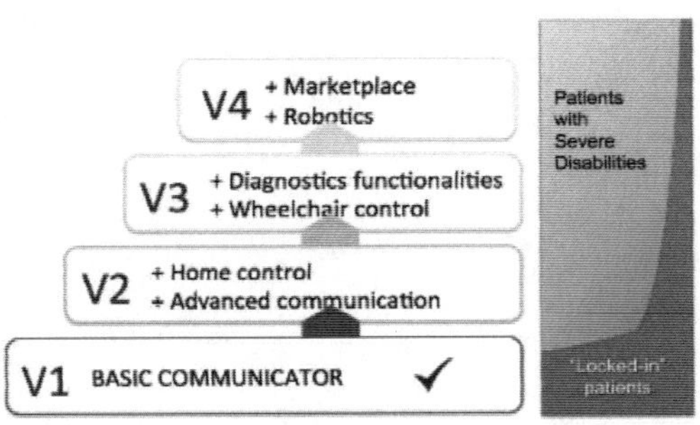

Figure 2. Roadmap

Working prototypes of all these functionalities have been developed and one of these, in robotic field, is BrainHuRo, a research project that applies BCI to humanoid robots [15].

The rest of the paper is structured as follows. Section II explains the aims of this study and the research protocol with Braincontrol. Section III reports the results of the study, concerning the percentage of success, while Section IV draws conclusions about the results.

II. Aim and Method

The first aim of this study was to verify the efficacy of Braincontrol as an effective AAC communicator in patients with communicative and motility disorder. This aim will be evaluated on performing specific tasks described below. The secondary aim was to validate the trainings methodology in terms of targets roadmap, sessions timing and number of sessions, with regards to patients in locked-in state, in particular using feedbacks and advices from the healthy control group. The interaction system used is a sensorimotor rhythm (SMR) based BCI on top of a neurological process known as Event-Related Desynchronization (ERD). The ERD is detectable as a decrease in power in the β-frequency band on corresponding motor cortices. It has to be adapted to person-specific by the use of machine learning techniques. The heart of Braincontrol is a proprietary classifier of EEG patterns based on neural network technology and combined with an adaptive Bayesian algorithm for customizing different needs in different patients. The EEG headset, by Emotiv Inc. [19], detects and transfers the signals to the computer through wireless technology. The electrodes simply need to be dampened using a saline solution, instead of a special gel required from other headsets. It works like a mental joystick, detecting 6 types of imagined movements (IM), allowing a computer or other external devices to be controlled (See Figure 3).

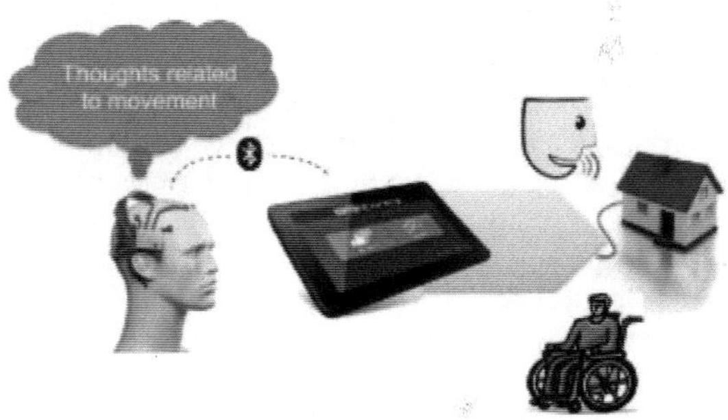

Figure 3. BraincontrolArchitecture

The device used for the study includes a "Yes/No/Don't know" Selector (See Figure 4) and a "Sentence Finder" (See Figure 5). The user interface uses a scanning mode to move between available options and utilizes just one movement-related thought to select the desired choice.

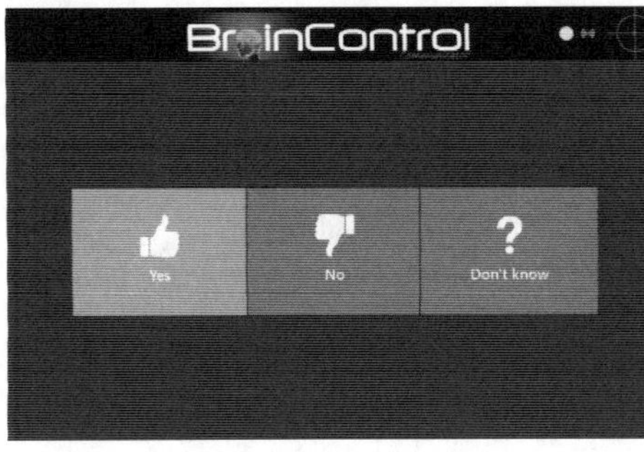

Figure 4. Yes/No/Don't Know Selector

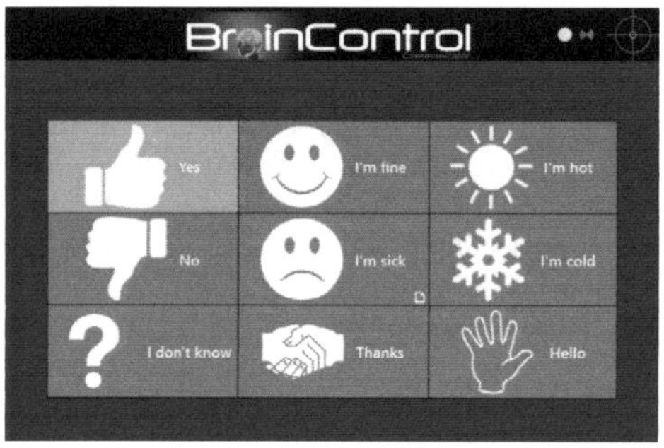

Figure 5. Sentence Finder

The trainings have been carried out in four remote sessions (video conference with remote desktop control) of one hour each, planned in one month period for each user, from August 2012 to June 2015, with two groups of users:

I. 63 healthy volunteers

II. 42 patients with communicative and motility impairment.

The sample of healthy users was considered as a control group, to improve the quality of trainings through advices and to verify eventual differences on the roadmap.

During the first training, the trainer explains to the patient how the system works, its functionalities and the training purpose, then he starts with multiple iterative sessions of calibration and testing. During the calibration phase (See Figure 6), the software records the EEG data from the user which was asked to stay focused for a few seconds on the movement-related thought that will be used for controlling the system.

The test phases consist of asking the patients to select predefined sequences of choices.

This iterative session is conducted for 30-40 minutes and is replicated in the followings 3 sessions during the first month. If the user selects at least 4 predefined choices without errors during the test phase, the training is considered successful.

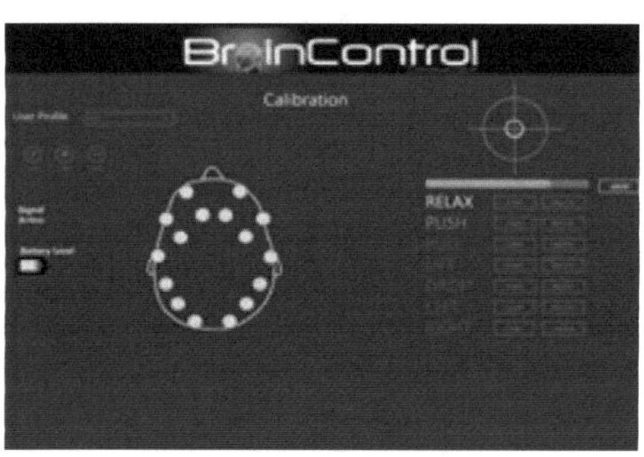

Figure 6. Calibration

After this first training phase the work is focused on the improvement of performances, by increasing the scanning speed and reducing the time of selection, in order to have a fast and efficient interaction.

III. RESULTS

In the period of August 2012 – June 2015 we carried out sessions of training with two groups of users:

I. 63 healthy volunteers

II. 42 patients with communicative and motility impairment

A. 19 in initial or severe stage of the disease

B. 23 locked-in (10 of these are in a condition similar to the complete locked-in state, with no possibility to give feedback).

The group of healthy volunteers, as the group IIA (19 initial and severe patients), completed successfully the training phase representing the 100% of the efficacy of the device.

Also in the LIS group (IIB) 21 out of 23 patients overcame the training phase (with a percent of 91% of success). The two, in particular, were in similar CLIS, in which cognitive abilities were unknown, and no kind of feedbacks was possible.

These results were stable over time, after the first phase of training. In patients who achieved the objectives it was possible to continue with the training and make them keen and able to use the device independently as a communicator.

IV. CONCLUSION

The aim of this study was to verify the efficacy and the effectiveness of Braincontrol as an AAC, improving training methodology with regards to patients in locked-in state. The study was conducted from 2012 to 2015, on a group of 63 healthy users and on 42 patients with communication or mobility impairment, planning four trainings in a one month period. The results of this observation confirm that the device, after the first phase training, is efficient and robust. Trainings have been completed successfully for all the healthy users and for patients in initial and severe stage of the disease. Only 2 out of 42 patients located in the locked-in group failed the training. In particular, these patients were in similar CLIS, in which cognitive status information where unknown. Seventeen locked-in patients, who really need this technology, are presently using the system as a communicator.

ACKNOWLEDGMENT

BrainHuro project has been realized between 2013 and 2015, partially funded by the Italian region of Tuscany (POR-CREO Fesr 2007-2013 – Le ali alle tue idee) and involved the University of Siena, Liquidweb s.r.l., Humanot s.r.l., Massimi Sistemi s.r.l. and Micromec s.r.l.

Declaration of Interest Statement

The authors disclose they have the following financial or other interests in objects or entities mentioned in this paper:

- Pasquale Fedele is founder and CEO of Liquidweb s.r.l., the company producer of the BrainControl;
- Myriam Gioia is a speech therapist, employee in Liquidweb s.r.l. with trainer role.

References

[1] T. Carlson, G. Monnard, and J. del R. Millán, "Vision-Based Shared Control for a BCI Wheelchair," International Journal of Bioelectromagnetism, vol. 13, no. 1, 2011, pp. 20-21.

[2] J. Carmena et al., "Learning to control a brain-machine interface for reaching and grasping by primates," PLoS Biology, Vol. 1, 2003, E42.

[3] N. Birbaumer et al., "A spelling device for the paralysed," Nature, 1999, pp. 297-298, 398.

[4] A. Buttfield, P. W. Ferrez, and J. del R. Millán, "Towards a robust BCI: error potentials and online learning," IEEE Trans Neural Sys Rehab, 2006; vol.14, pp. 164–168.

[5] N. Birbaumer, "Breaking the silence: Brain-computer interfaces (BCI) for communication and motor control," Psychophysiology, vol. 43, 2006, pp. 517-532.

[6] M. A. Lebedev and M. L. Nicolelis, "Brain-machine interfaces: past, present and future," Trends in Neurosciences, vol. 29, no 9, 2006, pp. 536–546.

[7] R. Sitaram, A. Caria and N. Birbaumer, "Hemodynamic brain–computer interfaces for communication and rehabilitation", Neural Networks, 2009.

[8] B. Z. Allison, E. W. Wolpaw and J. R. Wolpaw, "Brain-computer interface systems: progress and prospects", Expert Review of Medical Devices, vol. 4, no. 4, , 2007, pp. 463-474

[9] G. Dornhege, J. del R. Millán, T. Hinterberger and K. R. Müller, "Toward Brain-Computer Interfacing", MIT Press, 2007.

[10] M. Van Gerven et al., "The brain–computer interface cycle", J. Neural Eng., vol. 6, 2009.

[11] G. Pfurtscheller et al., "The Hybrid BCI", Frontiers in Neuroprosthetics, vol. 2-3, 2010.

[12] T. O. Zander and C. Kothe, "Towards passive brain–computer interfaces: applying brain-computer interface technology to human–machine systems in general", Journal of Neural Engineering, vol. 8, 2011.

[13] L. George and A. Lécuyer, "An overview of research on "passive" brain-computer interfaces for implicit human-computer interaction", International Conference on Applied Bionics and Biomechanics (ICABB), 2010.

[14] P. Fedele and M. Tavanti, "Braincontrol project" poster and demo, Mind Force conference, Centre for the Study of Complex Systems, University of Siena, 2010.

[15] A. Casals, P. Fedele, T. Marek, R. Molfino, G. G. Muscolo, C. T. Recchiuto, "A robotic suit controlled by the human brain for people suffering from quadriplegia," TAROS 2013. 14th Towards Autonomous Robotic, vol. Springer Lecture Notes in Artificial Intelligence.

[16] T. Carlson and Y. Demiris, "Human-wheelchair collaboration through prediction of intention and adaptive assistance," IEEE International Conference on Robotics and Automation, 2008, pp. 3926-3931.

[17] T. Carlson, G. Monnard, R. Leeb and J del R. Millán, "Evaluation of Proportional and Discrete Shared Control Paradigms for Low Resolution User Inputs," IEEE Intl. Conf. on Systems, Man, and Cybernetics, 2011, pp. 1044-1049.

[18] L. Tonin, T. Carlson, R. Leeb, J del R. Millán, "Brain-Controlled Telepresence Robot by Motor-Disabled People," 33rd Annual International Conference of the IEEE Engineering in Medicine and Biology Society, 2011, pp. 4227-4230.

[19] Emotiv Inc. website: www.emotiv.com [accessed March 2016]

JoGuide: A Mobile Augmented Reality Application for Locating and Describing Surrounding Sites

Fadi Wedyan

Department of Software Engineering
Hashemite University
Zarqa, 13315 Jordan
Email: fadi.wedyan@hu.edu.jo

Ibrahim Aloqily

Department of Computer Science and Its Applications
Hashemite University
Zarqa, 13315 Jordan
Email: izaloqily@hu.edu.jo

Reema Freihat

Department of Software Engineering
Hashemite University
Zarqa, 13315 Jordan
Email: reema.freihat@gmail.com

Suzan Wedyan

Department of Computer Science
Amman Arab University
Amman, Jordan
Email: susanwedyan@gamil.com

***Abstract*—Augmented Reality is a variation of virtual reality that allows users to view the real world augmented with virtual objects. Therefore, it can be used to produce systems that provide users with rich information about the scanned area. In this paper, we present an application that locates and provides the users with information about the local surrounding sites. The application, which we call *JoGuide*, is designed to help users in urban areas or tourism destinations to locate places of interest near them by moving the camera of the device in all possible directions to overlay information of places around them. Places captured by the camera are located by adding bins displaying the place name as defined by Foursquare.com database. *JoGuide* is developed with Android and is set to run on smartphones and tablets with different screen sizes, computational and memory capabilities.**

Keywords-Augmented reality; Mobile Computing; Mobile devices; Text in scene images; Android.

I. INTRODUCTION

Augmented Reality (AR) creates an environment in which real world and virtual world objects are presented together within a single display [1]. The core idea behind AR is overlaying computer generated graphics on top of the real world scenes to create a seamless spatially-registered environment [2]. The main goal of AR is providing applications and programs to the users that brings virtual information to their immediate surroundings and also to any indirect view of the real-world environment (e.g., live-video stream) [3].

Since the first appearance of AR concepts in the 1950's in the cinema industry, AR has immensely grown. Currently, AR applications can be found in many domains including medical visualization, entertainment, advertising, maintenance and repair, annotation, robot path planning, geographical information systems, and education [4] [3] [5].

The use of AR applications on mobile devices (e.g., tablets, smartphones, digital cameras) is gaining more attention due to the increasing power and decreasing prices of mobile devices. Moreover, mobile devices come with various input means (sensors, cameras, location) that facilitate the development of a wide range AR mobile applications. Mobile Augmented Reality (MAR) expands the set of services that AR offers to include a wide range of scenarios in the rich diversity of the mobile environments [6] [7]. AR can be used in many types of applications including entertainment and gaming, tourism, and navigation. A key feature of a MAR application is that it provides the user with context-related information in real time. This information can support various context-dependent applications. For example, information about surrounding places, products, events, or moving objects (e.g., transportation means) [8].

In this paper, we present a MAR application, called *JoGuide* (stands for Jordan Guide), for locating and providing information about surrounding sites, building, offices, or any buildings of interest. The application aims to facilitate the process of searching for sites surrounding the user. The application can be very useful especially for the user who goes to places never visited before (e.g., tourists). The application provides information about surrounding sites including landmarks, or small objects (e.g., shops, offices, restaurants, etc.) by moving the camera in the direction of the desired site. The information is displayed on the screen without blocking the view.

JoGuide is designed and implemented keeping in mind the importance of achieving the following attributes: reliability, usability, extensibility, and robustness. *JoGuide* is deployed to run on Android platform version 4.1 or later and is developed to work on devices with different screen sizes and computational capabilities. *JoGuide* uses Global Positioning System (GPS) sensor, phone network and Internet connection to determine current location. The application uses a global maps website called *Foursquare* [9] to get information about the sites of interest. The application uses the phone camera to catch the scene, sends it to the site and locates sites of interest. *JoGuide* allows users to learn more information about venues and places surrounded them.

The rest of the paper is organized as follows. Section II presents related work. Section III describes the design and implementation of the presented application. Section IV presents a demonstration of the application and discusses usage issues. Finally, conclusions and future work are discussed in Section V.

II. Related Work

In this section, we provide a summary of work in mobile augmented reality that aims at developing tourism and navigation applications. Please refer to [10], [11] for a complete survey on mobile augmented reality.

Dahne et al. [12] presented a software that runs on Laptops called *Archeoguide* to provide tourists with interactive personalized information about historical sites. The application was tested on the site of ancient Olympia in Greece. Using *Archeoguide*, users can view a virtual reconstructions of the ancient site. Images and videos are all loaded with the application (i.e., no real time communication is required).

Fockler et al. [13] developed an enhanced museum guidance application, called *PhoneGuide*, to introduce exhibitions. *PhoneGuide* runs on mobile phones and displays information on the phone when visitors targeted their mobile phone cameras at exhibits. *PhoneGuide* runs a perception neuronal network to recognize exhibits in images taken by the phone camera.

Elmqvist et al. [14] presented a mixed Reality platform for navigation assistance in indoor environments. The platform, which is called *3DVN*, provides a multi-modal user interface for navigating in existing physical buildings. *3DVN* supports both path finding and highlighting of local features.

Another museum guide was presented by Bruns et al. [15]. The guide uses widespread camera-equipped mobile phones for on-device object recognition in combination with pervasive tracking. It also provides location- and object-aware multimedia content to museum visitors.

Tokusho and Feiner [16] developed an application called *AR street view* which provided an intuitive way to obtain surrounding geographic information for navigation. When users walk on a street, street name, virtual paths and current location were overlaid on real world to give users a quick overview of environment around them.

Marimon et al. [17] developed an Android service platform called *MobiAR* for tourist information based on AR. *MobiAR* allows users to browse information and multimedia content about a city through their mobile phones. The platform handles location-based information, user preferences and determines the tourist resource the user is interested in.

Bihler et al. [18] developed a prototypical context-aware museum guide that uses ultrasonic signals, sent by a cheap, stand-alone emitter. The smartphone is able to recognize the exhibits by receiving a modulated ultrasonic signal, but in any museum an adaptation of the used frequencies is necessary.

Armanno et al. [19] developed an application called *SkyLineDroid* for virtual Heritage where Augmented Reality is used on mobile phones to support visitors of outdoor cultural heritage sites. Virtual and real world are overlaid on the device screen, according to device position and orientation, in order to immerse users in the 3D historical reconstruction of ancient buildings.

Rubino et al. [20] presented a general framework for the development of multimedia interactive guides for mobile devices called *MusA*. The framework has a vision-based indoor positioning system that allows the provision of several LBS, from way-finding to the contextualized communication of cultural contents, aimed at providing a meaningful exploration of exhibits according to visitors' personal interest and curiosity.

Chianese et al. [21] developed a location-based application that aims at exploiting several location-based services and technologies in order to realize a smart multimedia guide system. The system is able to detect the closest artworks to the user, make these artworks able to tweet and talk during users visit and capable of automatically telling their stories using multimedia facilities. The system was tested at a sculptures art exhibition within the Maschio Angioino castle, in Naples, Italy.

Murino et al. [22] presented an Android touristic application called *i-Street* whose aim is to detect, identify and read the street plates in a video flow and then to estimate relative pose in order to accurately augment them with virtual overlays. The application was tested in the historical centre of Grenoble, France, proving to be robust to outdoor illumination conditions and to device pose variance. The average identification rate in realistic laboratory tests was about 82%.

Jain et al. [23] adopted a top-down approach cutting across smartphone sensing, computer vision, cloud offloading, and linear optimization in order to develop location-free geometric representation of the environment and using this geometry to prune down the visual search space. They developed a system called *OverLay*, which is currently deployed in the engineering building and open for use to regular public.

III. Application Design and Implementation

We followed the Incremental Methodology in developing our application. We choose this approach because it has features that are suitable to our application. Mainly, it generates a working software early during the software life cycle, easier to test and debug during a smaller iteration, and easier to manage risks [24]. At a glance, incremental development slices the system functionality into increments where in each increment, a slice of functionality is delivered through cross-discipline work, from the requirements to the deployment. The unified process groups increments/iterations into the phases of: inception, elaboration, construction,and transition [24].

We show the package diagram of the proposed application in Figure 1. As the figure shows, the application consists of three main components, these are:

1) Graphical User Interface (GUI). The component contains the classes necessary for creating the GUIs. The classes contained in the package are shown in Figure 2. The component displays the following screens: (1) Splash Layout, which includes the start and the welcome screens. (2)ArActivity Layout: the main application screen, it combines two layouts, Camera Preview layout, which is a simple wrapper around a camera and a surface view that renders a centered preview of the camera to the surface to resize preview aspect ratio suitable for the screen of the device, and AR Overlay layout, which shows pins and venues names as text. (3) the output layout which show the view after calculating angle between user location and nearby venues.
   Venue information is updated every 50 ms by a request sent to Foursquare (using the communication package).
2) Location. Contains classes for managing location information. The contents of the component are shown in Figure 3.The location component is used by the GUI to get and update the user location. Location is detected every 30 seconds. That is, every 30 second the application sends a request to the GPS or network provider to get current user location.
3) Communication. Provides services to the other two components including: communicating with Foursquare, communicating with the GPS or the network provider to get location information, and checking Internet availability. Classes participating in the communication package are shown in Figure 4.

We choose to refresh the location every 30 seconds as a default value experimentally. The users can decrease this value when they are moving fast (e.g., driving on a highway) or increase it when they use the application while walking. Updating the scenes with information is performed every 50 ms to give the users a real-time experience and avoid losing important sites information.

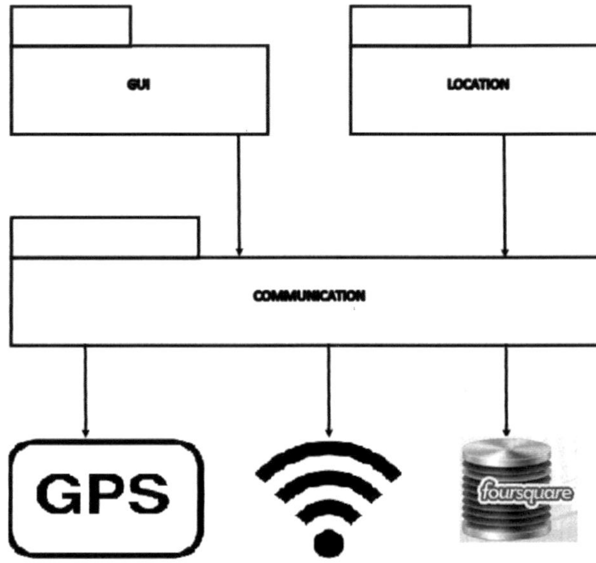

Figure 1. Package Diagram of *JoGuide*

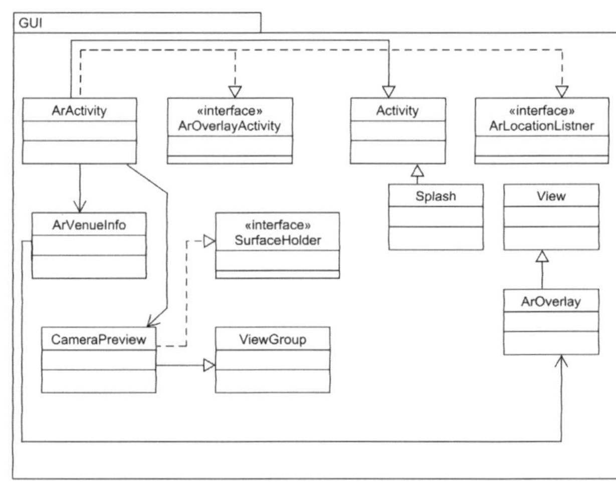

Figure 2. GUI Package

The location information from the GPS is sent to FourSquare to get information about the nearby venues. This information is used by the application to compute the angles between the user current location and the nearby venues. In addition, the application computes the rotation and orientation of the camera, using the smartphone sensor.

Using the internal measurement unit of the smartphone and the angles between current location and venues, we map the venues locations to their locations that appear on the

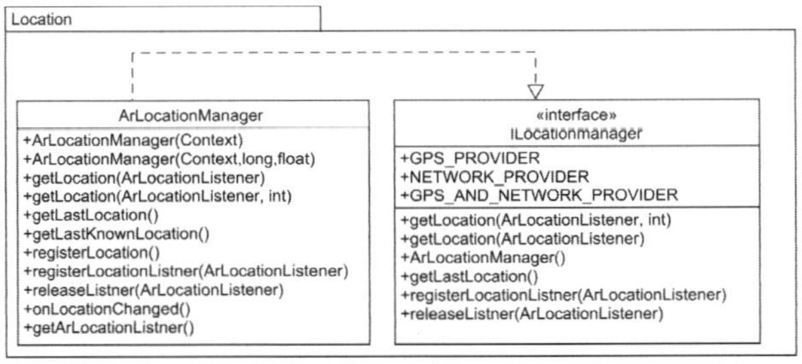

Figure 3. Location Package

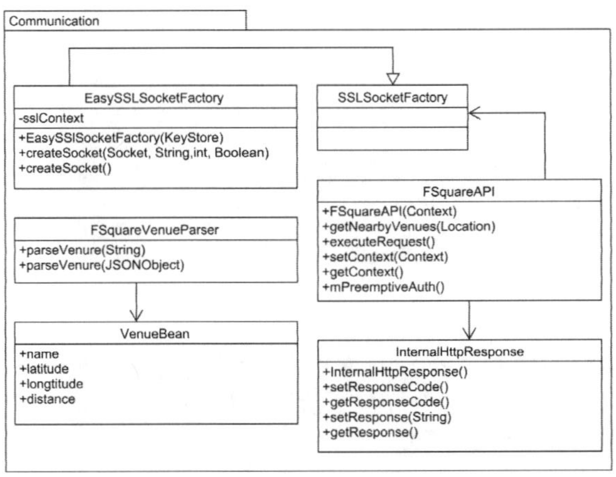

Figure 4. Communication Package

screen by drawing an icon on each venue found.

The prototype version of the application is implemented with Android. The following tools and software are used to implement *JoGuide*:

- Eclipse Indigo [25] with android plug-in.
- Microsoft Visio 2013 [26], for preparing the design documents. We used UML [27] to describe the system architecture.
- Adobe Photoshop CS5 [28], for designing icons and images.

IV. Demonstration

In this section, we demonstrate how *JoGuide* can be used to obtain information about surrounding sites and places. Figure 5 shows the first screen displayed when a user starts the application. When the application is loaded, it checks if the GPS is activated, and if an Internet connection is available. A message is displayed to the user to indicate whether any of these resources are not available. Otherwise, the start button becomes active and the user can start spotting.

Figure 6 shows the screen displayed as the user presses the start application button and *JoGuide* working by initializing camera and loading places. The application accordingly sends a request to Foursquare and the GPS. This might take some time depending on the Internet speed.

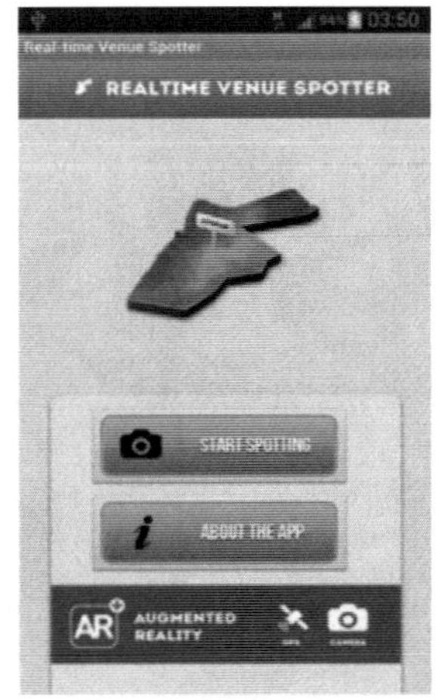

Figure 5. Start Screen of *JoGuide*

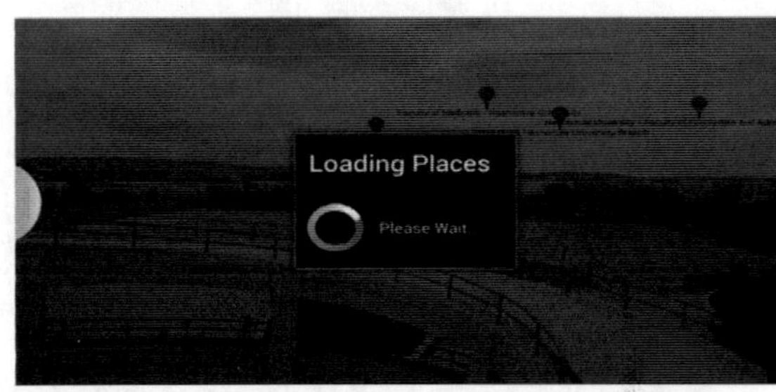

Figure 6. loading *JoGuide*

We tested the application in different urban sites, including the downtown of the city of Amman, Jordan, the city of Zarqa, Jordan, and the historical site of Petra, Jordan. In all our experiments, *JoGuide* shows to be an easy to use application, reliable, and provided the needed information about the sites and shops surrounding the user. In Figure 7, we show a camera shot with site information. We choose to display the sites pins in dark blue and the sites names in red in order to: (1) eliminate potential overlapping with objects that appear on the screen, and (2) allow the information to appear when the application is used in the dark. This is shown in Figure 8 which shows a screenshot of the application while used in the night. The icons are visible for the user and the red color can alert the user attention for the required site while the blue color is bright and easy to find on a dark background.

It is though important to emphasize that the accuracy of the displayed information depend on the information provided by FourSquare maps (which in turn depend on the information the municipality or the local government can

Figure 7. Camera shot augmented with sites information (taken at Hashemite University Campus)

Figure 8. A night screenshot of *JoGuide* (taken at the downtown of Amman, Jordan)

provide for public use).

In order to keep the application light, we only store the information retrieved from FourSquare obtained the current session (i.e., the currently spotted sites while the application is turned on). Users have the option of saving the augmented images in a special folder on the device or share them via email or Google Drive.

V. Conclusions and Future Work

In this paper, we presented an augmented reality based mobile application named *JoGuide*. The prototype version of the application is developed with Android, and requests data about available sites from maps service site. The application aims at easing the exploration of surrounding sites and helping people like tourists to identify nearby places of interest. In developing *JoGuide*, our target was to provide a lightweight application with few memory and computational requirements. We achieved our goal by minimizing the amount of data stored in memory, and by retrofiring the information via web services, and therefore, performing part of the computations on the server side. We tested the application in two major cities in Jordan and in one historical site. The application has shown to be easy to use, lightweight, and robust.

The presented work can be further extended in many directions including:

- Enabling the retrieval of more information about venues in order to give detailed and more accurate results about the venues and locations.
- Providing the option of saving the visited sites (i.e., trip tracker). This option will require saving information in a light local database.
- Providing a vocal guidance option for users with disabilities.
- Developing versions of the application that work on different platforms (e.g., iOS for iPhones, Windows phones).

ACKNOWLEDGMENT

The authors would like to thank the students who helped in implementing the presented work, namely: Shadi Ayman, Reham Bawaneh, and Nedaa Rahmeh. This work was supported in part by the Hashemite University under grant number 2013/19 to F. Wedyan.

REFERENCES

[1] P. Milgram, H. Takemura, A. Utsumi, and F. Kishino, "Augmented reality: A class of displays on the reality-virtuality continuum," in Photonics for industrial applications. International Society for Optics and Photonics, 1995, pp. 282–292.

[2] O. Bimber, B. Fröhlich, D. Schmalstieg, and L. M. Encarnação, "The virtual showcase," IEEE Computer Graphics and Applications, no. 6, 2001, pp. 48–55.

[3] J. Carmigniani, B. Furht, M. Anisetti, P. Ceravolo, E. Damiani, and M. Ivkovic, "Augmented reality technologies, systems and applications," Multimedia Tools and Applications, vol. 51, no. 1, 2011, pp. 341–377.

[4] R. T. Azuma, "A survey of augmented reality," Presence, Teleoperators and Virtual Environments, vol. 6, no. 4, August 1997, pp. 355–385.

[5] H.-K. Wu, S. W.-Y. Lee, H.-Y. Chang, and J.-C. Liang, "Current status, opportunities and challenges of augmented reality in education," Computers & Education, vol. 62, 2013, pp. 41–49.

[6] D. Wagner and D. Schmalstieg, "Making augmented reality practical on mobile phones, part 1," Computer Graphics and Applications, IEEE, vol. 29, no. 3, 2009, pp. 12–15.

[7] ——, "Making augmented reality practical on mobile phones, part 2," Computer Graphics and Applications, IEEE, vol. 29, no. 4, 2009, pp. 6–9.

[8] T. Olsson, T. Kärkkäinen, E. Lagerstam, and L. Ventä-Olkkonen, "User evaluation of mobile augmented reality scenarios," Journal of Ambient Intelligence and Smart Environments, vol. 4, no. 1, 2012, pp. 29–47.

[9] "FourSquare," URL: http://www.foursquare.com [retrieved: February, 2016].

[10] Z. Huang, P. Hui, C. Peylo, and D. Chatzopoulos, "Mobile augmented reality survey: A bottom-up approach," HKUST, Hong Kong University of Science and Technology, Tech. Rep., 2013.

[11] C. Arth, R. Grasset, L. Gruber, T. Langlotz, A. Mulloni, and D. Wagner, "The history of mobile augmented reality," Inst. for Computer Graphics and Vision, Graz University of Technology, Austria, Tech. Rep., 2015.

[12] P. Dähne and J. N. Karigiannis, "Archeoguide: System architecture of a mobile outdoor augmented reality system," in Proceedings of the first IEEE/ACM International Symposium on Mixed and Augmented Reality (ISMAR02), 2002, pp. 263–264.

[13] P. Föckler, T. Zeidler, B. Brombach, E. Bruns, and O. Bimber, "Phoneguide: museum guidance supported by on-device object recognition on mobile phones," in Proceedings of the 4th international conference on Mobile and ubiquitous multimedia. ACM, 2005, pp. 3–10.

[14] N. Elmqvist, M. Fjeld, D. Axblom, J. Claesson, J. Hagberg, D. Segerdahl, Y. Tai So, A. Svensson, M. Thorén, and M. Wiklander, "3dvn: A mixed reality platform for mobile navigation assistance," in ACM CHI2007 Workshop on Mobile Spatial Interaction, 2007, pp. 1–4.

[15] E. Bruns, B. Brombach, T. Zeidler, and O. Bimber, "Enabling mobile phones to support large-scale museum guidance," IEEE multimedia, no. 2, 2007, pp. 16–25.

[16] Y. Tokusho and S. Feiner, "Prototyping an outdoor mobile augmented reality street application," in Proceedings of the 8th IEEE Symposium on Mixed and Augmented Reality, October 2009, pp. 3–5.

[17] D. Marimon, C. Sarasua, P. Carrasco, R. Álvarez, J. Montesa, T. Adamek, I. Romero, M. Ortega, and P. Gascó, "Mobiar: tourist experiences through mobile augmented reality," Telefonica Research and Development, Barcelona, Spain, 2010.

[18] P. Bihler, P. Imhoff, and A. B. Cremers, "Smartguide–a smartphone museum guide with ultrasound control," Procedia Computer Science, vol. 5, 2011, pp. 586–592.

[19] G. Armanno, A. Bottino, and A. Martina, "Skylinedroid: An outdoor mobile augmented reality application for virtual heritage," in Proceedings of the International Conference on Cultural Heritage and Tourism (CUHT12), Cambridge, England, 2012, pp. 25–27.

[20] I. Rubino, J. Xhembulla, A. Martina, A. Bottino, and G. Malnati, "Musa: Using indoor positioning and navigation to enhance cultural experiences in a museum," Sensors, vol. 13, no. 12, 2013, pp. 17 445–17 471.

[21] A. Chianese, V. Moscato, F. Piccialli, and I. Valente, "A location-based smart application applied to cultural heritage environments," in Proceedings of the 22nd Italian Symposium on Advanced Database Systems,Sorrento Coast, Italy, June 2014, pp. 335–344.

[22] S. Messelodi, C. Modena, L. Porzi, and P. Chippendale, "i-street: Detection, identification, augmentation of street plates in a touristic mobile application," in Image Analysis and Processing ICIAP 2015, ser. Lecture Notes in Computer Science, V. Murino and E. Puppo, Eds. Springer International Publishing, 2015, vol. 9280, pp. 194–204.

[23] P. Jain, J. Manweiler, and R. Roy Choudhury, "Overlay: Practical mobile augmented reality," in Proceedings of the 13th Annual International Conference on Mobile Systems, Applications, and Services, ser. MobiSys '15, 2015, pp. 331–344.

[24] C. Larman and V. R. Basili, "iterative and incremental development: A brief history," Computer, vol. 36, no. 6, 2003, pp. 47–56.

[25] Eclipse Indigo, https://eclipse.org/, [retrieved: February, 2016].

[26] Microsoft Visio, http://office.microsoft.com/en-001/visio/, [retrieved: February, 2016].

[27] Object Management Group, "Unified modeling language," http://www.uml.org/, [retrieved: February, 2016].

[28] Adobe Photoshop CS5, http://www.adobe.com/products/photoshop.html, [retrieved: February, 2016].

A New Definition of Competence Developing Games

- and a framework to assess them –

Johannes Alexander König
Lab. for IT Organization & Management
FH Aachen University of Applied Sciences
Aachen, Germany
email: koenig@fh-aachen.de

Martin R. Wolf
Lab. for IT Organization & Management
FH Aachen University of Applied Sciences
Aachen, Germany
email: m.wolf@fh-aachen.de

Abstract—**There are different types of games that try to make use of the motivation of a gaming situation in learning contexts. This paper introduces the new terminology 'Competence Developing Game' (CDG) as an umbrella term for all games with this intention. Based on this new terminology, an assessment framework has been developed and validated in scope of an empirical study. Now, all different types of CDGs can be evaluated according to a defined and uniform set of assessment criteria and, thus, are comparable according to their characteristics and effectiveness.**

Keywords-Serious Games; Gamification; Business Simulations; Assessment.

I. INTRODUCTION

Using gaming concepts for teaching approaches provides the advantage of transferring the motivation of a gaming situation into a learning situation [1]. In addition, games provide a safe room which gives players the possibility to explore new behaviors or strategies without taking any risks on their health or their (business) environment [2]. There are three major kinds of games which are used in teaching context: Serious Games, Business Simulations/Games and the approach of Gamification. According to current research, there is no framework or tool that stipulates the capability to assess Serious Games, Business Simulation/Games and gamified applications in a structured and comparable way. One reason for this is the lack of an aligned terminology for such games. In Section II and Section III, a terminology suggestion will be further motivated and defined. Section IV describes a framework needed to handle the new terminology. Section V offers an overview about future work and further use.

II. MOTIVATING COMPETENCE DEVELOPING GAMES

A variety of publications defines the terms Serious Games, Business Simulations/Games or Gamification, e.g., [3][4][5]. Furthermore, there is a number of definitions for game concepts that are close to Serious Games (e.g., Game-based Learning). By now, some authors argue that these kind of game concepts are more or less equal to Serious Games [6]. Other authors try to elaborate differences between these concepts [7]. However, there is the conviction that characteristics, pedagogies and the way of game design are too different and that it is impossible to handle all three concepts within one approach.

In order to develop an umbrella term that combines the three concepts mentioned within one approach, similarities and differences had to be identified: All different kinds of game concepts try to teach someone something, by using different teaching approaches. There are very simple designed games that teach only pure information without any pedagogical concept or significant Game Design, Game Mechanics, e. g., a vocabulary trainer. Such applications are not inside the scope of the umbrella term because they are not real games. If you extend the vocabulary trainer with ranking systems or with a dynamic vocabulary in simulated conversations, you get a gamified application that starts touching the target field of the assessment framework. A vocabulary trainer teaching the vocabulary inside a 3D-world while telling a discoverable story (independent of the pedagogical nature of such a game) is – by definition – a Serious Game and, thus, inside the target field. Games in scope of the umbrella term CDG have one characteristic in common: They do not transfer information only, they also teach how to use them.

III. DEFINE COMPETENCE DEVELOPING GAMES

The European Parliament published a recommendation for the definition of the term 'competence' based on the work of the European Universities Continuing Education Network (EUCEN). They are defining 'competence' as follows: "'competence' means the proven ability to use knowledge, skills and personal, social and/or methodological abilities, in work or study situations and in professional and personal development…" [8]. This definition of competence describes the idea behind transporting knowledge -and how to use it- in a sophisticated way. Games have the ability to teach knowledge, skills, methodological abilities and how to use them. If needed, they can even teach attitudes (Examples: [3]). So CDG seems to be a suitable umbrella term. The following definition of CDG is based on the above-mentioned definition of 'Competence':

A Competence Developing Game (CDG), is a game that has the primary purpose to teach knowledge, skills and personal, social and/or methodological abilities, in work or study situations and in professional and personal development of the game player, by retaining the motivation of a gaming situation.

IV. PYRAMID ASSESSMENT FRAMEWORK FOR 'COMPETENCE DEVELOPING GAMES'

The "Pyramid Assessment Framework for 'Competence Developing Games'" (short PACDG-Framework) provides the possibility to assess any CDG in a systematic way. Assessment results are comparable even if CDG are different in their nature.

A. *Framework layers and steps*

With the PACDG-Framework CDGs are evaluated from a "Designer" and a "Player" perspective in seven separated steps that build up on each other (hierarchical structure).

The basic idea of having a designated "Designer"-Layer is to evaluate the game's potential by investigating the integral game components and the game's goals. To support this, the Designer-Layer includes the Pyramid-steps "Problem", "Learning Goal", "Story & Pedagogy" and "Game Design & Aesthetics".

The main goal of the "Player"-Layer is to investigate the effect on the players during and after playing the game. In scope of that, the game experience and the desired learning effect on the player are investigated. The basis for that are the Design-Layer results. However, the PACDG-Framework provides three pyramid-steps inside the Player-Layer: "Experience", "Aftereffect" and "Impact". Figure 1 illustrates the framework and described the framework steps.

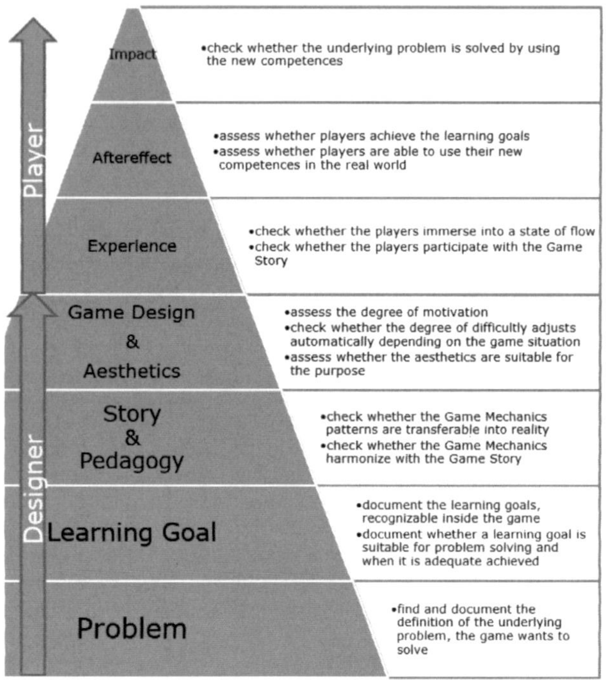

Figure 1. The PACDG-Framework

Using the framework means to execute the illustrated steps from bottom to top. Each layer focuses on another game part. Because of the hierarchical structure causes for failures or unwanted effects can be found in each underlying step. Every step requires different assessment operations. These operations are described on the right hand site of every step.

B. *Framework derivation and evaluation*

Game types summarized under the CDG umbrella entail a variety of frameworks, assessment tools, etc. The PACDG-Framework combines these established approaches that can be found e.g., in [9]. It represents a universal solution for all game types summarized under the CDG umbrella. Thus, in scope of its development, the most relevant and acknowledged game focusing concepts as well as their underlying measurement tools have been considered. Furthermore "Bloom's taxonomy of the Cognitive Domain" was taken into account as a common measurement tool for learning outcomes [10]. Table 1 shows which PACDG-Framework element has been mainly extracted from or is inspired by which approach. In order to establish an integrating concept by utilizing these different approaches the major work had to be done by adjusting the concepts among each other. That means, the PACDG-Framework combines these concepts avoiding the identified weaknesses. By this, it expanded the framework range. The original approaches presented in Table 1 support either Serious Games or Business Simulations. The PACG-Framework supports both and Gamification-Application beyond.

TABLE I. DERIVATION OF THE PACDG-FRAMEWORK

Base Approach	**PACDG-Framework Step**
Bloom's Taxonomy [11][12]	Impact
Annetta's Framework [13]	Experience Game Design
DPE Framework [14]	Game Design & Aesthetics Story & Pedagogy
SDGA Framework [15]	Learning goals
Eight fields instrument [2]	Aftereffect Problem

An empirical study with 39 education experts was conducted to validate the hierarchical PACDG-Framework structure. The results show that the framework structure is valid. First practical experiences using the framework show a very suitable way to assess all kinds of CDGs. In addition, the assessment results facilitate the description of game problems and the identification of the associated causes in a systematic way. The theoretical assumptions (game design & learning) on which the framework is constructed are based on many established and used approaches. That ensures a sophisticated level of validity for the theoretical aspects, too. By this, in short, the PACDG-framework validity is shown.

V. CONCLUSION AND FUTURE WORK

Further explanation about the empirical study and practical tests will follow in a longer version of this paper. In addition, more detailed assessment criteria underlying the assessment operations of each step are being worked on. They will contribute a better level of comparability between assessments. Next, the framework will be used to assess games developed for Cyber-Security trainings. By this, critical success criteria for this kind of games should be defined and used for developing an exemplary serious game within this scope.

REFERENCES

[1] E. Sanchez, "Key criteria for Game Desing," France, 2011. [Online]. Available from: http://archives.reseaucerta.org/meet/Key_criteria_for_Game_Design_v2.pdf [retrieved: 03, 2016].

[2] J. W. M. Kessels, P. Keursten and C. A. Smit, "The eight field instrument: analysis framework for training effects," Kessels & Smit, The Learning Company, 1996.

[3] D. Michael and S. Chen, "Serious Games: Games That Educate, Train, and Inform," Thomson Course Technology PTR, 2005.

[4] U. Blötz, „Planspiele und Serious Games in der beruflichen Bildung," Bertelsmann, 2015.

[5] M. Schulten, "Gamification in der Unternehmenspraxis: Status quo und Perspektiven," Dialogmarketing Perspektiven 2013/2014, Wiesbaden, Springer, 2014.

[6] K. Corti, "Gamesbased Learning a serious business application," PIXELearning Limited, 2006.

[7] C. Lampert, C. Schwinge and D. Tolks, "Der gespielte Ernst des Lebens - Bestandsaufnahme und Potenziale von Serious Games (for Health)," MedienPädagogik. 2009.

[8] EUCEN, "European Universities Continuing Education Network," 2009. [Online]. Available: http://www.eucen.eu/EQFpro/GeneralDocs/FilesFeb09/GLOSSARY.pdf [retrieved: 03, 2016].

[9] F. Hauser, A. Leich and K. Schiffer, „Facing the Challenge: Evaluation of Serious Games,"i-com Journal of Interactive Media, 2013, pp. 32-38.

[10] W. Sitte and H. Wohlschlägl, Eds., „Beiträge zur Didaktik des „Geographie und Wirtschaftskunde"-Unterrichts," 4th edition, Vienna: Department of Geography and Regional Research, University of Vienna, 2001.

[11] Forehand, M., "Bloom's Taxonomy: From Emerging Perspectives on Learning, Teaching and Technology;" Georgia: University of Georgia, 2012.

[12] Krathwohl, D. R, "A Revision of Bloom's Taxonomy: An Overview. In Theory Into Practice (Vol. 41)," College of Education, The Ohio State University, 2002.

[13] Annetta, L. A., "The "I's" have it: A framework for serious educational game design," In A. Gerianne, Review of General Psychology, Special Issue: Video Games: Old Fears and New Directions (Vols. 14, Nr. 2), 2010, pp. 105-112.

[14] Winn, B. M., "The Design, Play, and Experience Framework;" In R. E. Ferdig, Handbook of Research on Effective Electronic Gaming in Education. 3 edition, USA: Information Science Reference, 2009, pp. 1010-1024.

[15] Mitgutsch, K., & Alvarado, N., "Purposeful by design?: a serious game design assessment framework," Proceedings of the International Conference on the Foundations of Digital Games. Raleigh, North Carolina, 2012, pp. 121-128.

Moodle as a Support Tool in Higher Education

Academic Authorities Opinion

Myriam Peñafiel
Rosa Navarrete
Departamento de Informática y Computación
Escuela Politécnica Nacional
Quito, Ecuador
myriam.penafiel@epn.edu.ec
rosa.navarrete@epn.edu.ec

Stefanie Vásquez
Escuela de Formacion de Tecnólogos
Escuela Politécnica Nacional
Quito, Ecuador
maria.vasquez@epn.edu.ec

Sergio Luján-Mora
Department of Software and Computing Systems
University of Alicante
Alicante, Spain
sergio.lujan@ua.es

***Abstract*—The aim of this paper is to determine the intention of supporting the use of a Learning Management System (LMS) under Modular Object-Oriented Dynamic Learning Environment (Moodle), in the creation of virtual classrooms as support tools for on-campus work in higher education. We used as a case study the points of view of academic authorities from the National Polytechnic School. The opinion of this group was considered as they are responsible for policies in educational institutions: they lead and make decisions at the university. To prove this objective we considered perceived usefulness and easy usage. The Technology Acceptance Model (TAM) was applied; this helped to confirm that the hypothesis of virtual classrooms used as support tools in on-campus study is backed by academic authorities, and is in concordance with global, regional and local trends. The results of the research show that age influences the acceptance of new technologies. It is interesting to know that the perception of quality backed by technology is high and that, based on the TAM model, the ease of use and obtained benefits were determining variables in accepting Moodle as an on-campus support tool. This is important because they prove the current state of the use of Information and Communication Technologies (ICTs) at the university.**

Keywords-Moodle; virtual classroom; higher education; authorities.

I. INTRODUCTION

The use of Information and Communication Technologies (ICTs) in education is a coveted trend if we are to expand access, eliminate exclusion and increase the quality in education [1]. In general, ICTs are a set of different technological tools and resources, used to communicate, develop, spread, save and manage information. Within the educational context, ICTs promote digital literacy by generating essential skills and abilities for life [1].

Considering its transcendence and linkage with the teaching-learning process, ICT and education are two elements that must merge, in order for ICTs to be immersed in the teaching-learning process through a curriculum; complement, so as to provide dynamics and motivation necessary in the traditional teaching-learning process; and feed off, in order to mutually grow based on updating, renewal and innovation.

This investigation's objective is to determine the intention of using Moodle to develop virtual classrooms as support for on-campus learning. We used the views of the academic authorities of a University in Quito - Ecuador as a case study, a higher public education institution renowned for its engineering programs.

Regarding the authorities, the information desired is their perception of quality, ease of use and perceived usefulness of ICTs in the teaching-learning process, specifically in the use of virtual classrooms.

To achieve this goal, the paper is organized as follows. In Section II, we show the importance of using ICTs through Moodle as support tools for teaching-learning in higher education institutions. In Section III, we analyze the use of Moodle as an example of an ICT tool in education. Then, the used materials and methods are presented in Section IV. In Section V, the main results of the surveys answered by the academic authorities are presented. Finally, the main conclusions and future work are discussed.

II. USING ICTS IN EDUCATION AT GLOBAL, REGIONAL AND LOCAL LEVELS

A. Global and Regional Context

The inclusion of world policies supporting ICTs in education has been desired and expected for quite some time. The first policy referring to the integration of ICTs was declared explicitly in the Millennium Development Goals (MDG), described in goal 8F: "In cooperation with the public sector, provide access to benefits in new technologies, especially information and communication" [2].

In 2000 at the World Education Summit held in Dakar, Senegal, governments of 164 countries established eight objectives and twelve strategies in order to achieve Education for All (EFA) with a 2015 deadline. According to UNESCO´s follow-up report for EFA [3], the objective has not been reached but the number of children and teenagers without educations has decreased. A lot has been achieved in gender parity and government care for quality education, although financial support has not been available in the use of ICTs [1].

A tool to accomplish this is mentioned in strategy number 10: "Harness New Information to Help Achieve EFA goals" [3], but these policies have yet to be developed with regard to ICTs in education. However, the World Bank and UNESCO have supported the realization of global annual symposia on ICTs, and UNESCO has supported initiatives [4] that are a guide of ICT goals to achieve better results in education.

The World Summit on the Information Society (WSIS), held in 2003 and 2005, established a serious commitment between governments in pursuit of an inclusive information society. In the latest meeting in 2015, WSIS mentions two guidelines related to education in which Latin America and Caribbean sectors have to be included in their action plan. The inclusion of the ICTs is explicitly mentioned to reach this primary objective [5].

Meanwhile, in Latin America and the Caribbean, governments have circumscribed in their agendas the inclusion of ICTs in education as a priority theme, although, in real life, it does not have the same priority, mainly due to economic index factors that show obvious inequalities [5].

eLAC is an action plan for Latin America and Caribbean Information Society which states ICTs as tools designed to promote economic development and social inclusion [6][7]. Therefore, the Action Plan regarding Information and Knowledge Society of Latin America, sets the following policies regarding education:

"Develop and implement information technologies and communications for inclusive education," taking advantage of ICTs in the teaching-learning process with active participation of those involved.

"Universalize access and expand the use of information technology and communication for education" through broadband connection, ICT teacher training, using teacher learning networks, and regional educational portals [5].

B. Local Context

Within local context, the regulatory framework that promotes the inclusion of ICT in Ecuador's educational system is mentioned in the Academic Regulations Regime issued on November 21, 2013. It is the mandatory instrument for all the Higher Education Institutions, public and private, issued by the Council on Higher Education (CES). CES functions include planning, regulating and coordinating the Higher Education system which mentions the inclusion of ICTs in the curriculum, learning activities, learning modalities, digital literacy transversely into higher education, etc., as mandatory, in articles 15,26,27,28,37,38,42,43,45 [8].

C. Institutional Context

The National Polytechnic School (Escuela Politécnica Nacional EPN) where this study was carried out is considered the nation's top public institution by virtue of being a High Education Institution (HEI) benchmarked for its technical engineering, with an A institutional accreditation level [9].

According to the Regulation of Academic Regime (RAR), the University is aligned with current regulations and in light of these new state regulations, internal regulations have been updated considering government policies and following local, regional and global trends to support the use of ICTs.

This research wanted to consider the opinion of University academics responsible for this case study of using virtual classrooms that use ICTs in the teaching-learning process.

This information is relevant since the academic authorities are responsible for making decisions inside HEIs, and they also must answer global development and ICT trends. There are numerous investigations regarding the opinion of the students [10]-[14] and teachers [15]-[20], but not of university academics authorities [21]-[24].

III. Use of Moodle in Education

As we have seen, using ICTs in the teaching-learning process is one of the requirements made at all Higher Education Institutions at global and local level. They are valued and recognized as being an indicator of quality in higher education [25] so as to promote student intellectual qualities of higher order thinking, problem solving, communication skills and a profound knowledge of the teaching and learning tools [16].

From this perspective, promoting the imminent use of ICTs in the classroom using support tools such as blogs, wikis, virtual classrooms, etc. needs to strengthen students' digital skills [15][26]. It also requires teachers to develop their skills in using ICTs as 21st century competencies to face the challenges in changing scenarios and teaching methodologies [15][27][28].

The 2015 NMC Horizon Report for Higher Education [26], researches new technologies that will support the teaching-learning process in higher education. Among these technologies, we mention: mobile applications, cloud computing, open content, collaborative environments, adaptive environments, semantic applications, augmented reality, blended-learning, massive open online courses (MOOCs), game-based learning, etc.

Many of these technologies use educational platforms based on e-learning as support mainly at educational institutions that need organization in learning. They consider essential educational foundations in the teaching-learning process mediated by LMS in order to foster relevant learning, encourage critical thinking, collaborative and cooperative work [15][17][19][18][29][30][31].

A major change with the use of virtual classrooms through Moodle is where the learning environment changes and evolves the roles of the participants in the teaching-learning process. In this change the teacher ceases being the center of the process, giving prominence to the student, who becomes an active participant in his own learning process under the guidance of the teacher as facilitator in the cycle [7].

Another transformation is evidenced when the work space becomes a timeless space, thereby adapting to all the settings of teaching-learning in an open and accessible structure, according to the needs of the digital age in which we live.

Virtual spaces expand the boundaries between formal and informal education, producing effective learning in which teachers, experts and students contribute.

A. Educational Trends of Virtual Spaces in Higher Education.

Among the current trends in higher education we cite: new pedagogical models for teaching-learning; virtual learning tools to promote intelligent education, i.e. with the maximum potential; online universities for formal and non-formal learning saving time, space and money. In addition, we can mention e-learning support centers for universities, teacher training, as well as providing infrastructure and methodology; globalizing e-learning in order to include all regions by certifying qualifications; Open Educational Resources (OER), given their accessibility, efficiency and quality; and finally MOOCs, which encompasses all the advantages of e-learning and is massively supported by the best educational institutions in the world [31]. According these world trends, this research supports e-learning in the EPN; therefore, the investigation as previously mentioned, uncovers the support of the University´s authorities in using virtual classrooms under Moodle to support teaching-learning.

B. Moodle as Tool to Support the Teaching-learning Process.

There are many tools to support learning using ICTs, one being the virtual classroom. The virtual classroom is used both for full online learning (e-learning) and as support for on-campus or hybrid learning (b-learning).

The use of virtual classrooms is widespread today, but it is important to determine what their true function and use is in education.

This will allow us to determine what resources are used in the classroom, means of communication used by the participants, the types of materials used, etc. It will be considered that, while the tool plays a fundamental role as a vehicle in the educational process, it is not an end, and for this educational component, it is essential. [32].

There are numerous platforms for online course management, but EPN chose Moodle for its recognized advantages such as: being a General Public License (GNU) open source system, its fundamental teaching bases in social constructivism and a great learning community [33]. These make it a unique LMS. The ease of use for online course management and the availability of a variety of continuously updated resources and activities (such as mobile devices) make it the required worldwide platform. EPN has used several versions and currently it uses version 2.6 in graduate courses.

IV. MATERIALS AND METHODS

This investigation was carried out considering as a case study the EPN, a public institution referenced nationwide. An online survey was sent to the academic authorities and professors of the university who are responsible for making decisions within their academic units. Out of 383 teachers, only 77 (20%) answered as being authorities of the institution.

The survey was conducted with nineteen questions using the Likert scale [34]. The first part consisted of informative questions and the second part was concerned with previous experiences of virtual classrooms. Finally, we discovered the acceptance variables in the use of the tool. Only the relevant questions will be considered for the investigation; the questions used can be seen in Table 1.

TABLE I. QUESTIONS IN THE SURVEY

	Description	
Q.1	Select your gender	Female Male
Q.2	Your age	20-30 30-40 40-50 >50
Q.7	Have you ever taken online classes?	Yes NO
Q.8	How many classes have you taken?	No answer 1-3 4-6 >6
Q.9	What is your general perception about the quality of online classes?	Excellent Very good Good No good no bad Bad No answer
Q.10	What percentage of teachers at the University do you believe include the ICTs in their teaching practice?	>76% 51-75% 26-50% <25%
Q.11	Do you think University has to include online education in its study modes?	Yes No
Q.12	Which learning mode you consider more relevant in addition to the classroom in order to use it for a subject?	B-learning e-Learning no answer
Q.14	Do you think virtual classrooms will allow optimization of teacher's time and efforts?	Yes No
Q.16	Rate the usability of Moodle used at the University in order to implement it in virtual classrooms.	5 very easy 1 very difficult
Q.17	Indicate why you use the following Moodle communication tools?	
Q.18	Indicate what you use Moodle for?	
Q.19	Do you consider virtual classrooms under Moodle to be an accurate decision in order to be incorporated as support tool in the learning process?	Yes No

Prepared by the authors.

A. Metothodology

This study used as methodology the Davis [35] Technology Accept Model (TAM), used for a lot of investigations [15][18][36]-[41] in order to determine the acceptance of the technology now applied to conclude about the acceptance of LMS within Moodle used at the University.

The TAM model is based on the perceived ease of use and the perceived usefulness [15].

The perceived usefulness can be conceptualized as the belief of teachers that this tool will help them perform their duties, which can be seen in the learning outcomes in the curriculum [15].

Many studies on the acceptance of ICTs revealed that perceived usefulness and ease are key for their intended usage [15][19][36][42].

This paper will focus on the degree of acceptance by the academic authorities of ICTs in the classroom, specifically the level of acceptance of virtual classrooms under Moodle as tools to support classroom learning.

The ease of use and perceived usefulness by teachers are the most important factors that will allow us to predict the intention of using virtual classrooms [15]. Benefits such as improvement in performance are expected when these technologies are used.

V. RESULTS

The results obtained are as follows:

Question 1 Your gender? 31% of the authorities are women and 69% are men, which is approximately the promoted gender equality worldwide and is supported at the state level, and therefore the University.

Question 2. Your age? 34% were between 20 and 30 years old; 29% were between 31 and 40 years of age, 11% between 41 and 50 years and lastly, 26% were older than 50 years; this reflects young teachers' participation in the University decision-making process.

This generational change is due to new government policies, and it is important that they are open to the use of new tools such as Moodle.

Question 7. Have you ever taken online classes Question 8? And *how many classes have you taken*?

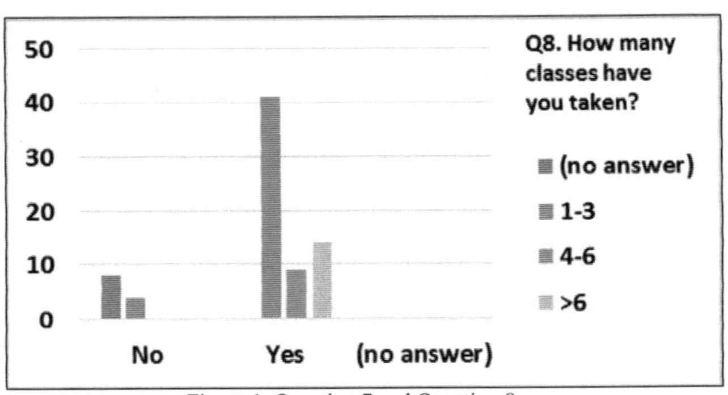

Figure 1. Question 7 and Question 8.

As it can be seen in Figure 1, 84% have taken an online class; the number of classes taken was not representative because they had taken only between one and three online classes. This shows us the reality of this university.

Question 9. What is your general perception about quality of online classes? 80% believed that quality of classes is good or excellent and 20% believed the quality was average or bad.

Question 9. *What is your general perception about quality of online classes?* and Question 8. *How many classes have you taken*?

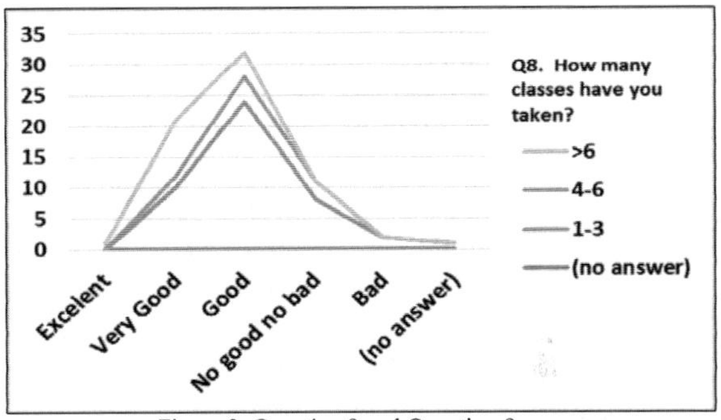

Figure 2. Question 8 and Question 9.

In this case, in Figure 2, a combination is done with the information questions. The results were: the more experience a professor has with the online education, the better the opinion about its quality.

Question 10. Do you think teachers at the University include ICTs in their practice and in what percentage? 49% of those surveyed believed that 25% of the University professors used ICTs; 39% of the authorities believed ICTs are used in 50% in classrooms. This is relevant because we can observe awareness of an existing problem.

Question 11. Do you think the University should include online education within its study modes? and *Question 12. Which learning mode you consider more relevant in addition to the classroom?*

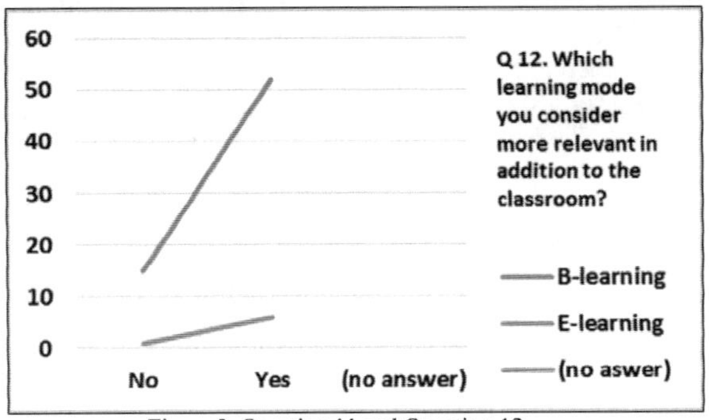

Figure 3. Question 11 and Question 12.

In these questions in Figure 3, 77% believe that virtual education has to be included in institutions, and more specifically 91% consider b-learning as the best option to support classroom work.

Question 14. Do you think virtual classrooms will allow optimization of teacher's time and effords? 74% answered affirmatively.

Question 16. Rate usability of Moodle to be used in virtual classrooms? Usability is the effectiveness perceived and the possibility of taking advantage of all its potential (1 very difficult- 5 very easy), 75% rated it as having an intermediate level of usability.

Question 17. Indicate why you use the following Moodle communication tools? Table 2 determines why you use the following communication Moodle tools in the classroom from the point view of the authorities: To increase communication frequency, the most used is chat (31%), Solving Doubts (34%), Present Case Studies (34%), Feedback (36%), Promoting knowledge construction (54%), Generate discussion (68) and Encourage participation (43) .They used the forum as a major communication tool in the classroom. For Case studies, the blog was the most used, with 31%. Finally, for Feedback, the mail was the most used with 22%, as seen in Table 2.

TABLE II. WHY YOU USE THE FOLLOWING MOODLE COMMUNICATION TOOLS

	Increase communication	Solve Doubts	Present Case Studies	Feedback	Promoting knowledge	Generate discusion	Encourage participation
Blog	5	11	31	18	24	9	15
Chat	31	23	3	11	5	12	22
Mail	22	18	8	22	0	0	5
Forum	23	34	34	36	54	68	43
Conference	19	14	19	11	9	7	12
No answer	0	1	5	3	7	4	3

Prepared by the authors.

Question 18: Indicate what you use Moodle for? Figure 4 shows that the most common use given to Moodle is to distribute materials (97%), followed by send Homework (93%) and Organize information and Resources (89%), as can be seen in Figure 4.

Question 19. Do you consider virtual classrooms to be an accurate decision in order to be incorporated as support tool in the learning process? 91% answered yes, which corroborates international trends and support in e-learning in Higher Education.

VI. DISCUSSION

The results of the investigation revealed that the inclusion of tools to support learning is just beginning. The efforts of this research are needed as real contributions to include tools such as Moodle to support on-campus teaching-learning.

The results showed the full awareness of authorities regarding the lack of using Moodle at the university; almost 50% of authorities believed that ICTs are used in fewer than 25% of the classrooms.

Awareness is the first step in solving the problem; the second step is the intention of solving the problem. 91% of the respondents supported the use of virtual classrooms as tools for on-campus work.

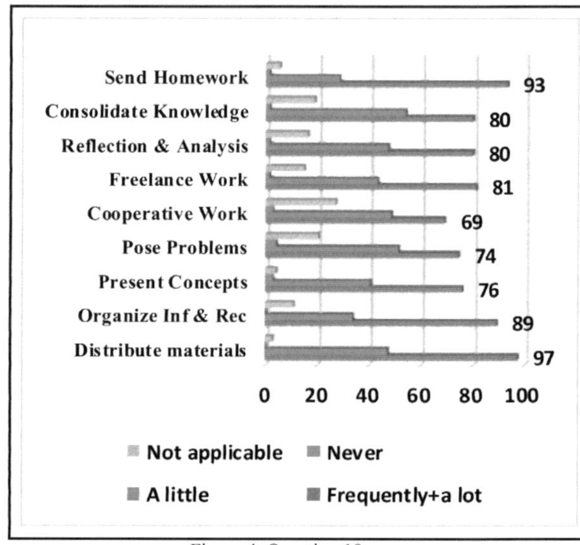

Figure 4. Question 18.

Variables that helped to confirm the research questions of this study were: optimization of professors' time and effort, ease of use, usability and b-learning as the appropriate modality for the research. Moodle reflected the optimization of time and efforts of the teachers in 74%, which will be reflected in their performance benefits [15].

The second variable considered in the study was ease of use; 70% of authorities the believed the Moodle is not easy or difficult to use.

Usability involved implicit sub-variables as effectiveness, efficiency, satisfaction with 75%. All validated variables allow us to confirm the hypothesis presented based on the confirmation of sub-variables involved. These results will encourage the authorities to include policies for the usage and implementation of virtual classrooms under Moodle.

Another important variable was that the most appropriate e-learning mode in the context of EPN is b-learning. 91% regarded it as the most appropriate mode through the use of virtual classrooms.

Another important result in the research that showed the respondents overwhelmingly considered Moodle as a means to distribute information, the respondents had a basic knowledge as to the potential of communication tools that Moodle provides us. These results confirm the underutilization of the platform, therefore it is necessary by the authorities to support training plans for teachers to solve this problem.

VII. CONCLUSION AND FUTURE WORK

We must consider that more and better ICTs do not mean more and better education; it is essential to promote digital literacy as a new skill for life [15]. One of the most important contributions of this research has been the awareness on the part of the academic authorities on the need to include ICTs in education.

However, there are still many obstacles to be overcome in order for ICTs to have the desired impact on the teaching-learning process. The main obstacle is the will of academic leaders. They have the power in economic and political topics to support these changes which will create transcendence in education as a priority, according to the development of technology in which we are immersed.

In previous research, as well as in this research, there exists information about the perception of the Institution's students, professors and academic authorities. It would be wise to carry out a comparative study with other HEIs to find similarities and differences between participants' points of views in the teaching-learning process of their respective universities in the use of Moodle. After analyzing the stake holders' opinion in the teaching-learning process under Moodle, we propose, as future work a methodological approach for the usage of virtual classrooms, as well as plans for teachers training.

ACKNOWLEDGMENT

This work has been supported by the Project PII-DICC-004-2015 from Escuela Politécnica Nacional.

REFERENCES

[1] S. Livingstone, "Critical reflections on the benefits of ICT in education, " Oxford review of education, 2012, vol. 38, no. 1, pp. 9-24, doi:10.1080/03054985.2011.577938.

[2] The World Bank, Millennium Development Goals, Available: http://data.worldbank.org/about/millennium-development-goals, [retrieved: Mar., 2016]

[3] UNESCO, Education for All 2000-2015: Achievements and Challenges; EFA Global Monitoring Report, 2015, UNESCO Publishing, Available: http://unesdoc.unesco.org/ulis/cgi-bin/ulis.pl?catno=232205&gp=1&mode=e&lin=1 Paris, [retrieved: Mar., 2016].

[4] UNESCO Institute for Statistics, Guide to measuring Information And Communication Technologies (ICT) In Education, 2009, Available: http://www.uis.unesco.org/Library/Documents/ICT_Guide_EN_v19_reprintwc.pdf, [retrieved: Mar., 2016].

[5] eLAC Comisión Económica para América Latina y el Caribe, Action Plan on the Knowledge Society of Latin America and the Caribbean. (eLAC2015), Lima, 2010, Available: http://www.cepal.org/socinfo/noticias/documentosdetrabajo/0/41770/2010-819-eLAC-Plan_de_Accion.pdf, [retrieved: Mar., 2016].

[6] UNESCO Institute for Statistics, ICT in Education in Latin America and the Caribbean: A Regional Analysis of ICT Integration and e-Readiness, Available: http://goo.gl/b03Vol, [retrieved: Mar., 2016].

[7] OREALC/UNESCO, Strategic approaches on the use of ICT in Education in Latin America and the Caribbean, 2013, Available: http://goo.gl/KaADAP, [retrieved: Mar., 2016].

[8] CES Reglamento de Régimen Académico(RRA), Available: http://www.ces.gob.ec/gaceta-oficial/reglamentos. [retrieved: Mar., 2016].

[9] CES, Categoría A, Available: http://www.ces.gob.ec/ies/universidades-y-escuelas-politecnicas/por-categoria/pregrado/categoria-a, [retrieved: Mar., 2016].

[10] E. Gutiérrez-Santiuste, M. J. Gallego-Arrufat, and A. Simone, "Barriers in computer-mediated communication: typology and evolution over time, " Journal of e-Learning and Knowledge Society, vol. 2, no. 1, 2015.

[11] V. Damnjanovic, S. Jednak, and I. Mijatovic, "Factors affecting the effectiveness and use of Moodle: students' perception," Interactive Learning Environments, vol. 23 no: 4, 2015, May. 2013, pp. 96-514, doi:10.1080/10494820.2013.789062

[12] R. Bessa Babo, A. I. Azevedo, and J. Suhonen, "Students' Perceptions about Assessment Using an e-Learning Platform, " Proc. in Advanced Learning Technologies (ICALT 15), IEEE press, Jul. 2015, pp. 244-246. doi:10.1109/ICALT.2015.73.

[13] A. K. M. N. Islam and N. Azad , "Satisfaction and continuance with a learning management system: Comparing perceptions of educators and students ," The International Journal of Information and Learning Technology, vol. 32 no: 2, 2015, pp. 109 – 123, doi: 10.1108/IJILT-09-2014-0020.

[14] M. Penafiel and S. Lujan-Mora, " Using virtual classrooms perception of students at the National Polytechnic School in Quito," in Updating New Educational Systems, vol. 1,iss: 21, ACCI, Eds. Madrid, Spain, 2014,pp. 397-419.

[15] R. Scherer, F. Siddiq and T. Teo, "Becoming more specific: Measuring and modeling teachers' perceived usefulness of ICT in the context of teaching and learning," Computers & Education, vol. 88, Oct. 2015, pp. 202-214, doi:10.1016/j.compedu.2015.05.005.

[16] H. Abdullahi, "The role of ICT in teaching science education in schools," Journal of Educational and Social Research, vol. 3, no. 9, 2013. pp. 127, doi:10.5901/jesr.2013.v3n9p127.

[17] S. Kavanoz, H. G. Yüksel, and E. Özcan, "Pre-service teachers' self-efficacy perceptions on Web Pedagogical Content Knowledge,". Computers & Education, , vol. 85, Jul. 2015, pp. 94-101, doi: 10.1016/j.compedu.2015.02.005.

[18] W. W. Goh, J. L. Hong and W. Gunawan, "Exploring students perceptions of learning management system: An empirical study based on TAM," Proc. in Teaching Assessment and Learning for Engineering (TALE 2013), IEEE press, Ago. 2013 pp. 367-372, doi:10.1109/TALE.2013.6654463.

[19] S. S. Liaw and H. M. Huang, "Perceived satisfaction, perceived usefulness and interactive learning environments as predictors to self-regulation in e-learning environments," Computers & Education, vol 60, Jan. 2013,pp. 14-24, doi:10.1016/j.compedu.2012.07.015.

[20] M. Penafiel, S. Lujan-Mora, L. M. Vintimilla, and P. Pozo Montesdeoca, "Analysis of the usage of virtual classrooms in the National Polytechnic School of Ecuador: Teachers' perception," Proc. IEEE Information Technology Based Higher Education and Training (ITHET 2015), IEEE Press, Jun. 2015, pp. 1-6, doi:10.1109/ITHET.2015.7218015.

[21] E. King, and R. Boyatt, "Exploring factors that influence adoption of e-learning within higher education, " British Journal of Educational Technology, vol. 46, no. 6, Nov. 2015, pp. 1272-1280, doi:10.1111/bjet.12195.

[22] F. R. A. Bordignon, R. A. Cicala, K. P. Cuzzani, S. I. Martinelli, and M. I. Oviedo, " School authorities and ICT: Joints and tensions. Directors and inspectors training in the UNIPE, " Ibero-American Journal of Education, vol.70, 2016, pp. 91-114.

[23] S. Farid, R. Ahmad, I. A Niaz, M. Arif, S. Shamshirband, and M. D. Khattak, "Identification and prioritization of critical issues for the promotion of e-learning in Pakistan," Computers in Human Behavior,, vol. 51, Oct. 2015, pp. 161-171, doi:10.1016/j.chb.2015.04.037.

[24] A. Assareh, and M. H. Bidokht, (2011). "Barriers to e-teaching and e-learning," Procedia computer science, vol. 3, 2011, pp. 791-795, doi:10.1016/j.procs.2010.12.129.

[25] P. K. Tulsi and M. Poonia, "Building excellence in engineering education in India," Proc. in Global Engineering Education Conference (EDUCON 2015), IEEE press, March 2015 pp.624-629, 18-20, doi:10.1109/EDUCON.2015.7096035 .

[26] L. Johnson, S. Adams Becker, V. Estrada, and A. Freeman, NMC Horizon Report: 2015 Higher Education Edition, Austin, Texas: The New Media Consortium.

[27] O. Qizhong, and Z. Qing, "Study on cultivation of teachers' ICT ability," Proc. in Computer Science & Education (ICCSE 2012), IEEE Press, pp.1564-1566, doi:10.1109/ICCSE.2012.6295361.

[28] UNESCO Institute for Statistics, Post-2015 Education Indicators Consultation, Available: http://www.uis.unesco.org/Education/Pages/post-2015-education-indicators.aspx, [retrieved: Mar., 2016].

[29] N. B. Awang and M. Y. B. Darus, "Evaluation of an open source learning management system: Claroline," Procedia-Social and Behavioral Sciences, Dec. 2012, vol.67, pp. 416-426, doi:10.1016/j.sbspro.2012.11.346.

[30] J. A., Cordero Torres, and A Caballero,. "The Moodle platform: A useful tool for training in life support. Analysis of satisfaction questionnaires from students and instructors of the semFYC advanced life support courses," Primary care, vol. 47, 2015, pp. 376-384, doi:10.1016/j.aprim.2015.02.006.

[31] O. Lee, and Y. Im, "Innovation of Higher Education in the Globalized Era," ICT in Education in Global Context, Springer Berlin Heidelberg, Jul 2014, pp. 221-247, doi:10.1007/978-3-662-43927-2_13

[32] S. Iqbal, and D. Thapa, "Initial Design Principles for an Educational, On-line Information Security Laboratory, " Advances in Web-Based Learning (ICWL 2013), Springer Berlin Heidelberg, 2013. pp.89-100, doi:10.1007/978-3-642-41175-5_10.

[33] J. Cole, and H. Foster, Using Moodle: Teaching with the popular open source course management system. O'Reilly Media, Inc. 2007.

[34] H. J. Gardner and M. A. Martin, "Analyzing Ordinal Scales in Studies of Virtual Environments: Likert or Lump It!," in Presence, vol. 16, no. 4, pp. 439-446, Aug. 1 2007. doi: 10.1162/pres.16.4.439

[35] F. Davis, R. P. Bagozzi, and P. R. Warshaw. "User acceptance of computer technology: a comparison of two theoretical models," Management Science, vol. 35, no 8, Ago. 1989, pp. 982-1003, doi.org/10.1287/mnsc.35.8.982

[36] Z. A. Shaffiei, M. Mokhsin, S. R. Hamidi, N. and M. Yusof, "A study of user's acceptance and perception towards Campus Management System (CMS) using Technology Acceptance Model (TAM), " Proc. in Engineering Education (ICEED2011), IEEE press, Dec 2011 pp.128-131, doi:10.1109/ICEED.2011.6235374.

[37] I. A Almrashdah, N. Sahari, N. A. H. Mat Zin, and M. Alsmadi, "Distance learners acceptance of learning management system". Proc. in Advanced Information Management and Service (IMS 2010), IEEE press, pp.304-309.

[38] C. Y. Dai, H. Charng-Tzer, W. F. Chen and M. T. Kao, "The study on exploring the user satisfaction of easy teaching web of Taipei by information-seeking and technology acceptance model," In Electrical and Control Engineering (ICECE, 2011), IEEE pres, pp. 7007-7011, doi:10.1109/ICECENG.2011.6056870.

[39] A. G. Money, A. Atwal, K. L. Young, Y. Day, L. Wilson and K. G. Money, "Using the Technology Acceptance Model to explore community dwelling older adults perceptions of a 3D interior design application to facilitate pre-discharge home adaptations," BMC medical informatics and decision making, vol.15, Aug 2015. pp.73, doi: 10.1186/s12911-015-0190-2.

[40] I. Akman, and A. Mishra, "Sector diversity in Green Information Technology practices: Technology Acceptance Model perspective," Computers in Human Behavior, Volume 49, 2015, pp. 477-486, doi:10.1016/j.chb.2015.03.009.

[41] C. Y. Dai, H. Charng-Tzer, W. F. Chen and M. T. Kao, "The study on exploring the user satisfaction of easy teaching web of Taipei by information-seeking and technology acceptance model," Proc. in Electrical and Control Engineering (ICECE 2011), IEEE press, 2011,pp. 7007-7011, doi:10.1109/ICECENG.2011.6056870.

[42] W. S. Lin, and C. H. Wang, "Antecedences to continued intentions of adopting e-learning system in blended learning instruction: A contingency framework based on models of information system success and task-technology fit," Jan. 2012, Computers & Education, vol. 58, pp. 88-99, doi:10.1016/j.compedu.2011.07.008.

Video Game Story Analysis Using Layered Graphs and Eye Tracking System

Iwona Grabska-Gradzińska
Department of Games Technology
Jagiellonian University
Kraków, Poland
e-mail: iwona.grabska@uj.edu.pl

***Abstract*— This paper discusses the prospects of using layered graphs and eye-tracking system for describing and analyzing player activity and his/her decisions in video game stories. Understanding how the game interface affects the user's decision is a very interesting problem, especially in the serious game field, because of real-life applications of acquired skills. Very often, the game winning strategies lead players to fall into bad habits. Reasoning based on the formal game system gives tools to game analysis and to collect information about players' behavior for further analysis. Eye-tracking information, i.e., gaze plot and heat maps give us knowledge about user perception of the game screen and helps with answering the question: what has affected the user during the decision making process? The main goal of the paper is to show usefulness of the proposed model while answering the sample questions about players' decisions.**

Keywords-game design; user decisions; narrations; eye tracking system; layered graph

I. INTRODUCTION

During the narrative game design process, especially for games with educational aim and real world dependencies and knowledge base, there are a few conditions that are extremely important. Scenarios and situations must be authentic and adequate and push the player to act. The scenarios should create the illusion of unlimited possibilities, but they should be precisely connected with the scope of knowledge and trained skills. It should be possible to replay and to explain the meaning of the winning strategies [1].

The comparison of user decisions in the game and in the real life is connected with both problems of the real life object representation in the game and the problem of the perception of the Heads-Up Display (HUD) elements. The challenge is how to prepare the "computable" model, i.e, the one which helps us compare different players' activity as well as connect user physiological reactions (eye perception) with the decisions taken.

The holistic model is based on the gameplay graph that represents the current state of the game. Different groups of elements can be identified: e.g., characters, locations, items and abstract narrative elements. These four categories reflect how players perceive games [2]. These elements could be identified in traditional narratives as well, but such formal models were not needed for their analysis. The usage of such model is connected with gameplay based on user's decision while comparing user's strategies. Our aim was to make all these elements uniform – so our model would process elements in the same way. Player actions and all other interactions in this world are denoted by connections between these elements [4].

Decision making process is correlated with elements available in the game, especially those noticed on the screen at the moment of decision making (others had to be seen prior) and player's general knowledge. Especially in narrative and serious games, it is extremely important to examine why the user picks a certain game strategy and condition of decision process. Researchers can speculate on them using two elements of a given system: typical sequences of gameplay graph states and information from the eye-tracking system.

A. *State of the art*

Eye-tracking is more and more often used in research game studies, especially as a game controlling device. Many researches were conducted ease, immersion and player satisfaction while using eye-tracker as input device, e.g. as described in [16]. Eye-tracker as an evaluation tool was also used in research studies to investigate the visual search patterns and heap maps describing the main area of interest on the screen [18]. The most popular approach is to collect heat map data and take into consideration the player activity throughout the game.

The approach presented in this paper is based on the dependence between the gaze direction immediately before decision. This approach is possible due to the graph of user strategy connected with the eye-tracker data. The gaze patterns and decision-making patterns can be associated in this approach.

B. *Research goals*

The research goal is to find a correlation between players eye-movement patterns and decision-making actions during the gameplay. During the work, the simple adventure game developed in the Department of Games Technology at Jagiellonian University was tested on a group of students and a question about their decision on choosing one of the three strategies was asked. The purpose of the research works is to show which elements of the user interface influenced the user's decision and which are useless in this context. The idea of the graph representation of the game state is presented in Section II and formal definitions are explained in Section III. Sections IV and V show the experiment and implementation details and describe user-game interactions noticed during research, especially the visual elements influence controlled by the eye-tracking system. The last two sections describe conclusions and future development.

II. GAMEPLAY GRAPH

The basis for our further considerations will be a gameplay graph, showing the game state in a specific moment. It has been developed on a layered hierarchical graph due to the expansions of the graph structure that layers and hierarchies offer. Layered graphs have been used in research models [5] and in video game design [6].

A. *Structure homogeneity*

First, as mentioned, the representation of the story with graph nodes and edges is inherently arbitrary. Our goal was to make it intuitive and homogeneous at the same time. It means that all nodes and edges are identical in their structure, so any transformation in the game world is processed in the same way, independent from its narrative meaning.

B. *Graph representation*

The key for understanding the universe of discourse is the game world with its current state. It is quite intuitive, because video game is commonly imagined as a virtual reality – simulation of the elements of the real world [3]. Two types of edges are distinguished: internal edges between nodes of the same layer and external edges between different layers. The external relational structure for the game world is represented by means of the layered graph. Figures 1 and 2 show the general structure of the used graph model and its specific subsets. Figure 1 shows the general horizontal dependences between subsets in the game word structure elements of which layers interact with each other and which can be embedded. Figure 2 shows the vertical segment of the graph (a sheaf graph), elements of all layers describing the character.

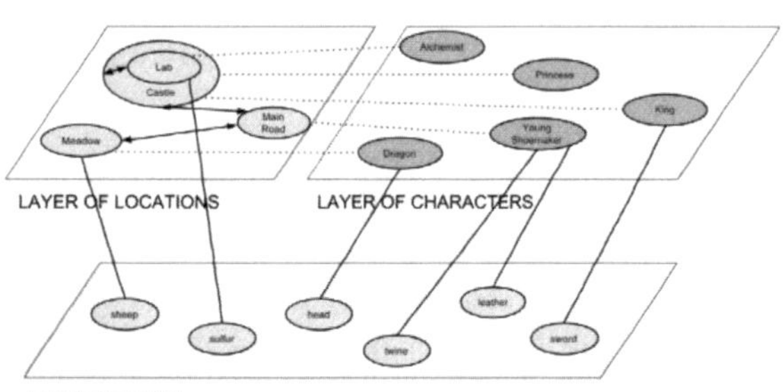

Figure 1. An example of a layered graph structure.

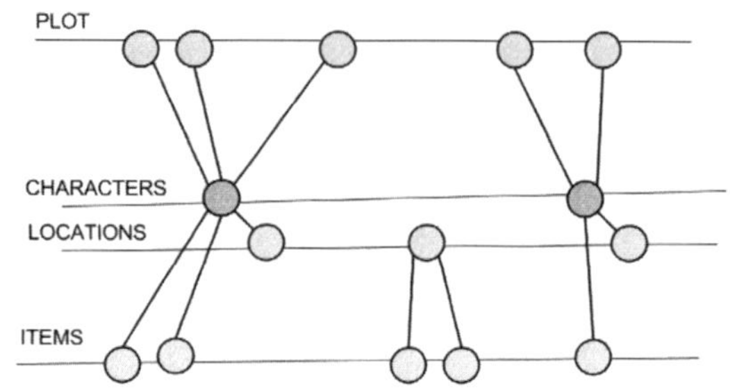

Figure 2. A sheaf graph – an arrangement of the structure

The research mode of the gameplay shows how the graph model changes after every player's decision. Researcher can investigate single players activity, creation and destruction of the edges in the graph or seek for activity patterns e. g. picking up items, changing locations, etc. it is possible to calculate time between different activities and other factors.

III. FORMAL DEFINITIONS

Graphs used for gameplay modeling were formally defined in [7][8], which in turn were inspired by [9][10]. According to them let us define the terms.

Let L be an alphabet of labels for nodes and edges. Let A be a nonempty, finite set of attributes.

Definition 1. A *hierarchical graph* is a system

$$G = (V, E, s, t, ch, lab, atr), \quad (1)$$

where:

- V and E are finite disjoint sets of *nodes* and *edges*, respectively,
- $s : E \rightarrow V$ *and* $t : E \rightarrow V$ are *edge source* and *target functions*,
- $ch : V \cup E \rightarrow 2^{V \cup E}$ is a *child nesting function*
- $lab : V \cup E \rightarrow L$ is a *labeling function*, and
- $atr : V \cup E \rightarrow 2^{A}$ is an *attributing function.*

Def. 1 determines types of attributes for nodes and edges. A graph instance needs values of attributes and is defined as follows:

Definition 2. Graph G or is *layered* if and only if:

$$\forall x \in V : lab(x) \in Y_i \Rightarrow lab(V \cap ch^{+}(x)) \in Y_i \quad (2)$$

(i.e., a node and all its descendant nodes have labels from the same layer).

IV. GAME STORY STRUCTURE AND USER DECISIONS ANALYSIS

A. *User strategy graph*

Commercial video games use high performance game engines, so graph-based models would not be used beyond design phase. The main goal of this model is to analyze player strategies through simpler graph structure – user strategy graph.

Knowledge is strong limitation for a player, whose design activity involves manipulating on the word state using elements of the language over the vocabulary [10]. As we compare the graphs created – unconsciously – by the player, we can analyze these productions.

B. Participants

Data was collected during the sessions of gameplay (students of the Jagiellonian University and the author). The used equipment was The Eye Tribe tracker (specification in [15]).

The game is based on Polish folktale, where a young shoemaker slays a dragon by feeding it sulfur-stuffed sheep (by being a shoemaker, he can easily sew the sheep back together). Apart from this, we have added a way of killing the dragon by conventional armed force. There are two versions of the game, each promotes one solution over the other. The relative difficulty between victory paths in these versions, as well as player performance are the focus of our ongoing research.

The player takes the role of the young Shoemaker and his quest is to defend the land against a Dragon. After doing it, he may marry the Princess and has the right to rule the land as a consequence.

C. Implementation

The model is currently developed in the Games Technology Department of Jagiellonian University. The game engine was built in C++ using Qt5 [18]. The communication with the eye-tracking system (The Eye Tribe tracker, 60 Hz, with latency <20 ms) was established with open Application Programming Interface relying on the standard TCP/IP protocol using open-source Node.js runtime environment.

V. Examples of user-game interactions

Thanks to the graph model, it is now possible to connect user decision moments with the specific game state and exact sequence of eye movements preceding the moment of the decision.

There were three main factors influencing players during the decision making process:

- textual scene characteristic with hints and characters dialogs,
- visualization of game scene and player condition (e.g., equipment, lives),
- players general knowledge.

In most cases, deliberated decisions were based on these factors. Of course, there are decisions made by chance, as a result of free exploration of the game world.

A. Free exploring effects

The group of players can be indicated with specific user strategy graph: many visited locations (significantly more then others), some of the locations visited repeatedly, but in unusual order (other players choose mostly one of a few sequences of locations visited). Additionally, the time of each visit was rather short.

B. General knowledge influence

In general, it is hard to prove that some players' actions arise due to general knowledge, not the game hints. An interesting result of analyzing user strategy graph was finding a fault in the story by our students. Their task was to complete the game and they had several different paths to do so. Some of them were stuck in a dead end when they fed a sheep to the dragon. The sheep was designed to be fed to the dragon, but according to the original story it should have been stuffed with sulfur before. Designers knew the story and did not try to feed the dragon with a raw sheep. However, some students did not know the story very well and fed the dragon with the sheep (as the folktale said), but they did not remember why, so they did not fill the sheep with the sulfur. As a result, the Dragon was thrived and killed the player.

C. Textual description influence

Getting information from texts or images in the gameplay is impossible to deduce from the graph, but there are sequences of eye-tracking data – gaze plot – preluding each decision made in the game.

Due to eye tracking studies taken on part of the participants, there are two main strategies of gathering information: take into consideration images, then text (an example is shown in Figure 3); take into consideration text, then images (different direction of gaze plot, as shown in Figure 4) or, surprisingly, taking into consideration only the text (as shown in Figure 5). In the figures mentioned, yellow numbers show the order of object examined before the players take action (keyboard event).

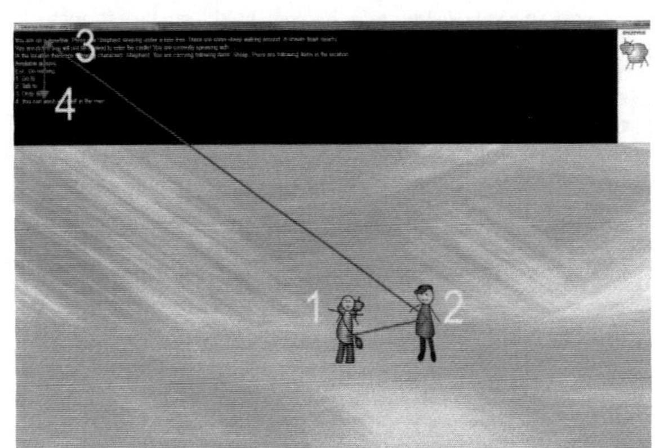

Figure 3. Most participants first stare at the screen images, then take a look at the text

Figure 4. Some participants have chosen a different order, first read the text and then look at an image

Typical behavior in the difficult moments of the game is to slow down (long time between state changes in the user strategy graph) and to follow several times different elements of the scene (textual and visual as well) with player eyes (Figure 6.)

Figure 5. Surprisingly, a few participants did not take images into consideration.

Figure 6. Typical process of looking for a solution of a difficult situation in the game

D. *Visual elements influence*

In most cases, after gathering visual information from the scene, the user has focused on the text and only then has made the decision.

There was a way to check whether the visualization bothered the reception of the gameworld or not. A scene was prepared where text gives the user advice to take a bath, but there was no visual hint to do so (Figure 7). This was the least often chosen way in the entire the game.

Figure 7. Textual hint (indicated by the yellow ring) not visualized in the image

A surprising result of eye-tracking data analysis is the fact that no one noticed the equipment backpack located in the right top corner of the screen (Figure 6: backpack with the item, Figure 7: backpack without any items). No one throws a single glance at it throughout the entire game. It is undoubtedly the fault of the user interface designer.

VI. FURTHER DEVELOPMENT

The next step of the planned research is to take into consideration educational serious games where information of the reasons of player decisions is extremely important and affects the estimate of learning efficiency.

Another problem is to prepare player strategy graphs not only in the games designed by researchers, but also for popular commercial games (in the individual cases of experiments participants, but in such way automatically).

Research field of further challenges is to find closer correlations between sequences of user decisions (currently collected in user strategies graph) and eye movement as a signal of user mental state (seeking the solvation, determined, sure or lost, etc).

VII. CONCLUSION

The proposed graph model can be considered as a tool that can be used for testing storylines, as well as analyzing user strategies. Thanks to automation and standardization, several variations of a story can be reliably compared. Players can also be surveyed for their strategies, perceived difficulty level and general satisfaction with the stories.

Furthermore the graph-based mechanisms are easily used for deduction in the assigned logic. Using this approach to the universe of discourse gives us a way to investigate designer intentions and decisions.

One of the outcomes of the eye-tracking research is the unique possibility of comparing effects of the users decisions made in the game.

ACKNOWLEDGEMENT

The project has been (partially) supported by the grant of the Polish Ministry of Science and Higher Education number 7150/E-338/M/2015).

REFERENCES

[1] C. Aldrich, Simulations and Seriuos Games, 2002.

[2] J. Juul, "What computer games can and can't do", Digital Arts and Culture conference in Bergen, 2000.

[3] J. Huizinga, Homo Ludens, 1955.

[4] I. Grabska-Gradzińska, B. Porębski, W. Palacz, and E. Grabska, "Towards a graph-based model of computer games", AITC 2012, pp. 34–39.

[5] J. Dormans and S. Bakkes, "Generating Missions and Spaces for Adaptable Play Experiences", IEEE Trans. on Computational Intelligence and AI in Games, 2011, pp. 216–228.

[6] A. Paszyńska, E. Grabska, and M. Paszyński, "A Graph Grammar Model of the hp Adaptive Three Dimensional Finite Element Method". Fundamenta Informaticae, vol. 114 no. 2, 2012, pp. 149–182.

[7] I. Grabska-Gradzińska, B. Porębski, W. Palacz, and E. Grabska, "Graph-Based Data Structures of Computer Games", Procedings of CGAT 2013, DOI: 10.5176/2251-1679_CGAT13.22

[8] W. Palacz, "Algebraic hierarchical graph transformation", JCSS, 2004, pp. 497-520.

[9] G. Rozenberg (ed.), Handbook of Graph Grammars and Computing by Graph Transformation, World Scientific, 1997.

[10] R. D. Coyne, M. A. Rosenman, A. D. Radford, M. Balachandran, and J. S. Gero, Knowledge-based Design System, Sydney, 1990.

[11] S. Staab and R. Studer, Handbook on Ontologies, Springer 2009

[12] N. H. M. Zain, F. H. A. Razak, A. Jaafar, and M. F. Zulkipli, "Eye tracking in educational games environment: evaluating user interface design through eye tracking patterns", Visual Informatics: Sustaining Research and Innovations 2011, pp. 64–73

[13] C. Conati, N. Jaques, and M. Muir, "Understanding Attention to Adaptive Hints in Educational Games: An Eye-Tracking Study", Artif Intell Educ (2013) 23, pp. 136–161

[14] A. Duchowski Eye Tracking Methodology: Theory and Practice, Springer-Verlag New York, Inc. Secaucus, NJ, USA 2003 Berlin 2003

[15] https://theeyetribe.com/ [accessed March 2016]

[16] J. D. Smith, T.C. N. Graham, "Use of eye movements for video game control". Proceedings of the 2006 ACM SIGCHI international conference on Advances in computer entertainment technology 2006.

[17] S. Almeida. Augmenting Video Game Development with Eye Movement Analysis. Universidade de Aveiro 2009

[18] http://doc.qt.io/qt-5/ [accessed March 2016]

Focus Group Study on Student Perception of Electronic Textbooks

Kimberly Anne Sheen and Yan Luximon
School of Design
The Hong Kong Polytechnic University
Hong Kong, SAR
e-mail: Kimberly.Sheen@connect.polyu.hk
sdtina@polyu.edu.hk

Abstract— **Electronic textbooks are a common topic in academic research, yet the future is not being investigated from a student perspective. This paper aims to add to the current research by outlining students' reading habits in physical and electronic textbooks and identify what students believe they need to properly study. This study utilized focus groups with design and engineering students. These disciplines were chosen due to their similar goals, yet different approaches. Findings showed that the two groups of students approach their academic readings in a different way and when looking towards future electronic textbooks require some discipline specific components. Yet, their similarities caused some of their views and ideas to be the same, such as being able to insert their own images into the textbooks and the desire for less text and more interactive components to facilitate their learning. Understanding discipline needs and including student input based on their perceived needs will assist in designing future electronic textbooks that will meet academic needs.**

Keywords - focus group; electronic textbooks; academic reading; design education; engineering education.

I. INTRODUCTION

Electronic textbooks are considered the future of textbooks in higher education. Yet, students are not as excited about this trend as many universities. While 60% of students reported using electronic textbooks during their academic studies, with half being required to by their instructors, student preference for physical textbooks has not waned [1]. In fact, many studies have shown that student preferences of some components, such as search functions and long blocks of text, negatively impacted student opinion of electronic textbooks [2].

While electronic textbooks are starting to evolve past simple .pdf representations of the physical text, they are in their infancy. It has been individual schools creating their own interactive electronic textbooks, which are shifting away from the textbook metaphor [3] and creating this evolution. This shift from the textbook metaphor will allow for additional materials and components, which will enhance and assist with the reading task [4]. Yet, creating this type of electronic textbook for individual courses is time consuming and impractical on a larger scale. On the other hand, electronic textbooks coming from major publishers tend to follow a one size fits all mentality, assuming that all components included in electronic textbooks can be used broadly across disciplines. This is already accepted as incorrect reasoning, as different disciplines are known to approach their education in different ways [5], yet is still in broad practice. Regardless of creating electronic textbooks specifically tailored for courses or broader textbooks, there is still the challenge of selecting and creating new supplemental materials and components for this new type of electronic textbook [6].

Not only would academics and publishers find creating new content difficult, advancing technology and the use of electronic textbooks may have altered the ways in which students use textbooks. Students can now easily read in cafes or while travelling [7], moving away from the desks and tables that used to confine students. Being able to study in more locations may seem positive, but without normal study aides such as highlighters and notebooks, students may find themselves slipping from the deep reading required during revision, which allows for in-depth comprehension and recall [8] to surface reading, which provides students with a more limited understanding of the materials [9]. While some components included in current electronic textbooks seem similar to the support activities students employ during reading, they are noticeably different. For example, many students take notes in the margins of their physical textbooks to support their studying. While electronic textbooks commonly offer notation software, notes are typically not displayed on the screen and require clicking on a small icon to later revisit. This could cause the students to miss their notes or interrupt their reading process leading them to become distracted. In fact, electronic annotation software is used less often than traditional note taking done with a physical textbook [10]. The lack of tangibility associated with electronic textbooks also negatively affects the reading task [11]. Past research has stated that electronic textbooks should enhance current physical active reading activities while presenting an interface that is easy to use [12].

Currently, the components being designed for future electronic textbooks are not being decided by the students [13]. This could lead to new textbooks not being able to fully support students' study habits and not only failing the student but becoming something that is looked on with derision. The purpose of the focus groups outlined in this paper was to identify, which components are important to students during their studies. Since each discipline has different approaches to studying and different needs, focus groups were separated based on the two disciplines studied: engineering and design. This allows for a better understanding of how these groups of students approach their studies. It also assists in identifying what type of supplemental content needs to be created and what tools need to be included to support academic reading in these different disciplines.

This paper also aims to bring a deeper understanding to the data from an earlier survey released at The Hong Kong Polytechnic University [14]. It also provides insights into how students complete their academic readings in physical and electronic mediums and how they envision their future electronic textbooks based on their discipline specific needs. The rest of this paper is organized the following way. Section II describes the method employed in this paper. Section III presents the results of the focus groups. Section IV discusses the results within the literature and in a more general context. Section V presents the main conclusions and presents some future areas that should be explored.

II. Method

The method chosen to uncover student needs and approaches in-depth was focus group [15]. The focus group method allows for internal validity, a better understanding of the phenomenon that would not be possible through methods that use quantitative analysis, and assists in understanding truly complex issues [15], which are necessary in this type of research.

A. *Participants*

Students were recruited from The Hong Kong Polytechnic University. There were two requirements for participation. The first, students need to be enrolled in either an undergraduate design or engineering program. The second, the students needed to have prior experience using electronic textbooks during their academic studies. Once students volunteered for participation, they were placed into three person focus groups made up of participants only from their discipline. Students were overall balanced male and female aged between 18 and 23.

B. *Session Design*

Each focus group session was designed to last approximately one hour. The sessions were made up of sixteen semi-structured interview questions, which were followed up with questions related to the answers. Students also participated in two activities during the session. The first activity asked them how they define current electronic textbooks. The second activity asked them to envision their future electronic textbooks, without considering the limitations of current technology. In this activity, students were asked to include components they wanted in their discipline specific electronic textbooks and then asked questions about how they would interact with these new textbooks. Each session was audio taped and later transcribed.

C. *Data Analysis*

Once each session was transcribed, the data was coded. The codes used in this research were grounded in the data [16] and used to organize the data into recurring topics and subtopics for easier analysis and development of theory.

III. Results

The semi-structured interview questions investigated the habits, task requirements, and preferences of students in regards to textbooks. The questions were broken up into three segments on physical textbooks, electronic textbooks, and future electronic textbooks. The same questions were used for both design and engineering focus groups, although follow up questions differed slightly based on the responses given by students. During the future electronic textbook segment, students were also asked for feedback based on ranking data gained from an earlier survey. Two activities were also completed by students, one during the electronic textbook segment and one during the future electronic textbook section. The results presented in this paper are the detailed results from one design focus group and one engineering focus group. These focus groups were a part of a larger set of focus groups conducted until homogeneity was reached [17, 18, 19].

A. *Physical Textbooks*

The questions regarding physical textbooks mostly dealt with student habits regarding physical textbook reading. Overall, design students reported to using physical textbooks around 80% of their time while doing academic readings at a desk at home for around two hours in the morning before lectures. They reported using the textbooks as the main source of learning concepts. The location preference is related to the reported issue of dizziness from reading physical textbooks on transportation. Engineering students reported to using physical textbooks less than 50% of their time while doing academic readings. How often engineering students did academic reading varied greatly from only during exam times to one hour per day in the afternoons and evenings. They agreed that it should be done in the school library due to the quiet environment away from the distractions at home. Engineering students reported that the purpose of their academic reading was to review that they had learned during the lecture.

Investigation into the task requirements of academic reading in a physical textbook was undertaken. Students were questioned about what types of supporting activities they did during physical textbook reading to help them comprehend the material. Design students reported different supporting activities such as summarizing important points from the text into lists, highlighting, and searching for more information by keywords. These students make notes in the margins of the text, or if on a separate piece of paper, they attach it to the original text. Similarly engineering students reported taking notes in the margins, highlighting, looking over drafts from class, and looking up definitions in the dictionary.

Students also reported some ergonomics issues and other considerations when deciding to use physical textbooks. Both groups of students reported that physical textbooks are very difficult to carry around and that they are much more expensive than their electronic counterparts. Yet, they believe that physical textbooks are much more convenient to take notes in.

B. *Electronic Textbooks*

1) *Definition*

Before answering questions similar to those asked during the physical textbook segment, students were asked to complete an activity in which they defined the term electronic textbook. Design students defined electronic textbooks as "a tool for learning without physical barriers. It contains lots of text, with additional elements including pictures, audio, and video." During this process, they also highlighted several components as important to their current electronic textbooks such as text, animations, images, video, dictionaries, and infographics. Text was considered especially vital to the electronic textbook as students felt that without text, the textbook loses its main purpose. They also highlighted some ways that electronic textbooks have enriched their learning experience such as facilitating communication, increased mobility, and increased interaction between the reader and the text. Engineering students defined electronic textbooks as "a portable device which includes all notes or text, video, and pictures into one appliance. It is cheap, environmentally friendly, and convenient when comparing to the physical textbook." Engineering students placed value on the electronic textbook's ability to search for keywords and additional components such as animations, video, and images that help facilitate their learning. They believe that the main purpose of electronic textbooks is to help students revise concepts they've learned in the classroom.

2) *Usage*

The questions regarding electronic textbooks mostly dealt with student habits regarding electronic textbook reading. Overall, design students reported that they spent around 20% of their time reading in electronic textbooks in the classroom at their desk during the lecture. The majority of the time they access electronic textbooks, they use laptops. They will use the phone if they need to do a short reading and they feel the convenience outweighs the limitations. Engineering students reported that they spent around 10% of their time reading in electronic textbooks at home or while travelling in the afternoon and evenings. The students access their electronic textbooks on computers most of the time.

Investigation into the task requirements of academic reading in an electronic textbook was undertaken. Students were questioned about what types of supporting activities they did during electronic textbook reading to help them comprehend the material. Design students reported using highlighting tools, music to help them focus, and Microsoft Word or the comment function to take notes. While design students reported taking notes while reading electronic textbooks, they reported taking less notes than when using physical textbooks. Engineering students reported using built in encyclopedia functions, search functions, highlighting, and screen capture functions most often.

While not explicitly asked about physical and cognitive ergonomics issues related to electronic textbooks, both engineering students and design students brought this subject up. Both groups cited eye fatigue as a major concern associated with the use of electronic textbooks, so students prefer to use them for shorter readings. Design students also discussed how they would rather print long readings instead of viewing them online to facilitate their learning, believing that the addition of too many components may destroy their creativity, and difficulties reading paragraphs in the digital form. While engineering students stressed electronic textbooks were easier to carry and allowed for more mobility.

Students also reported several technical issues and other aspects, which influence their interaction with electronic textbooks. Design students repeatedly reported the battery on their mobile devices as negatively impacting their academic reading along with the scrolling times and the size of the text. Both sets of students also discussed how the ease of sharing and downloading electronic textbooks facilitated their learning. In addition, the ability to take digital notes makes them less likely to lose said notes. Yet, students felt like typing instead of writing made it more difficult to remember and digest the concepts. Engineering students also wished for the ability to draw or write manually in their electronic textbooks, but reported that the current technology that allows these actions are buggy and slow making them unusable. These students also discussed how cost, mobility, and environmental friendliness made using electronic textbooks more desirable.

C. *Future Electronic Textbooks*

The future of electronic textbooks was investigated in many ways. Overall, design students reported that they would be more likely to use electronic textbooks if they were more interactive. They also desire more features such as accurate text to speech and improved bookmarks that used a sentence or word as the placer. Engineering students also agreed that they would be more likely to use electronic textbooks that were more interactive. They believed that this type of electronic textbook would facilitate their learning, speed up their work progress, and make them more efficient students. They wanted less text and more components such as 3D and manipulatable pictures and videos to help illuminate the concepts.

When students were presented with information regarding the answers from the previous survey, design students agreed that the top five components chosen were appropriate. They believed that text was more vital to the learning experience than students in the survey rated it, but agreed that the readings they have to read are diverse and that a lot of it seems unimportant to them, which could have influenced the ranking. Design students also reported that the findings of the undesirable components from the survey were valid. Engineering students thought survey respondents had overestimated the importance of text and underestimated components such as 3D images. They believed that this was because respondents chose components they were more familiar with and could envision. Other than that, students believed the other components chosen as desirable and undesirable were valid.

After this general information was gathered, students were asked to complete the final activity in which they were given free rein to create the perfect representation of an electronic textbook for their discipline. As this was without the constraints of current technology, many of the solutions students presented would not be fully functional at this time. Design students produced a sketch of their electronic textbook, keeping notes on functionality and features surrounding the sketch (*see Figure 1*).

Their electronic textbook took inspiration from Adobe Illustrator's interface and included the ability to add notes or photos directly inline, bullet form text instead of paragraphs, adjustable line spacing and text size, a table of contents, video, audio, adjustable images, bookmarks, the ability to synchronize across devices, translations, a dictionary, and an encyclopedia. They felt that highlighting and annotation tools would no longer be needed in their future electronic textbook because there would be much less text. Students built in the ability to hide unimportant content automatically by extending the text by clicking on the bullet point text. Many similar components appeared in the engineering future electronic textbook, yet the representation students chose to convey their textbook was a list form (see Figure 2). This electronic textbook also relied on less text, yet included some discipline specific aspects like interactive equations.

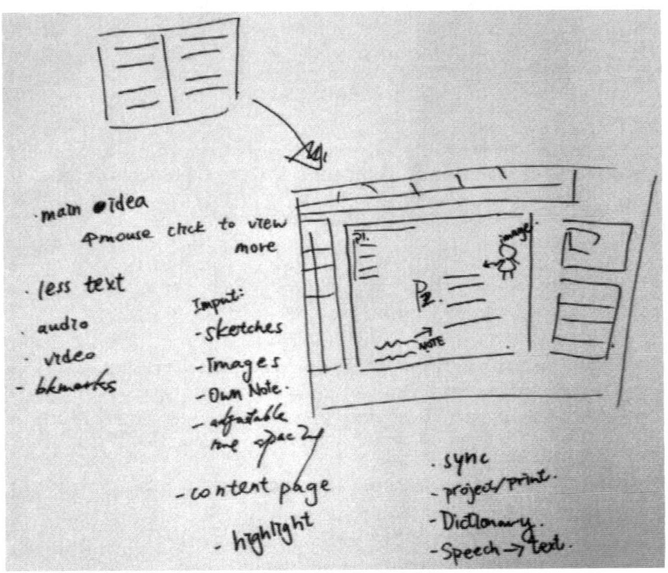

Figure 1. Future electronic textbook by Design Students.

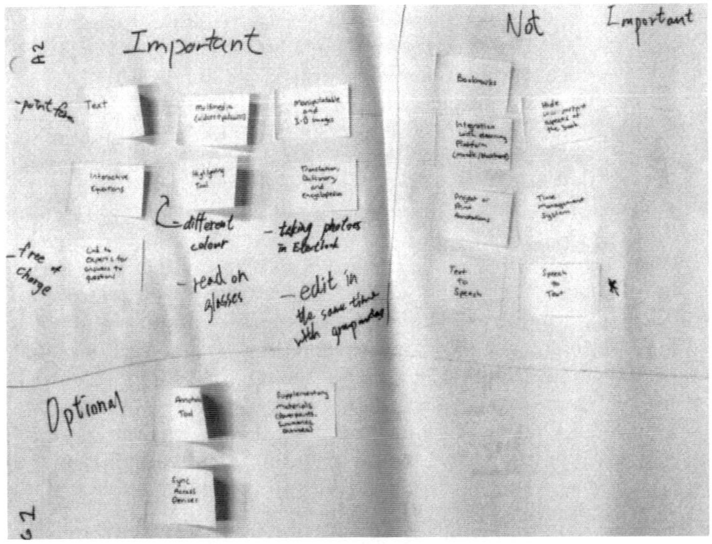

Figure 2. Future electronic textbook by Engineering Students.

IV. DISCUSSION

A. *Student Usage*

Student usage of physical and electronic textbooks differed in both disciplines in all aspects of use. The mobility offered to students by electronic textbooks change where and when they do their studies. Even with this ease of downloading and mobility, students still reported that they preferred physical textbooks [1]. Similar to what past research has uncovered, students do not want to read long blocks of text in an electronic textbook [2]. Many of the focus group participants reported that they would print out long readings, rather than printing them on the screen. Printing out pages from electronic textbooks allows for students to continue to experience the four affordances of spatial flexibility, manipulability, tangibility, and tailorability which students are nostalgic about in regard to print textbooks [11]. Supporting activities also changed for many students. They found themselves taking notes less and becoming frustrated with built in functions such as bookmarking and annotation tools [10]. Repeatedly, students reported taking notes in the physical form was easier and allowed them to see their notes with the concepts, which later assisted in revising the material. By investigating current use of both types of textbooks, the differences in usage, and understanding the reasoning behind the usage design recommendations, such as shortening blocks of text and finding opportunities to incorporate aspects reminiscent of the four affordances, such as the ability to see notes on the page instead of hidden within an icon, can be made for future electronic textbooks.

B. *Future Textbooks*

Student preference for design attributes of electronic

textbooks was similar in both fields of design and engineering, yet several components differed. Overall, all students agreed that text should be limited to the most important information presented in a bullet point form. More information could then be accessed through hovering over the text. Students also felt that creating textbooks that were more interactive would facilitate their learning and allow them to truly understand the material. Based on student responses, making this type of change would rectify the change in reading style from surface reading back to deep reading [8, 9], which is necessary for succeeding academically. While these reported changes may make electronic textbooks more appropriate for the type of reading required, reported interaction may have been influenced by current ideas of electronic textbooks like the students in the focus group found with the past survey results [14]. In addition, student enthusiasm for these components may later wane yet that should do little to the effectiveness of the components [20].

Because of the issues associated with students' dislike of long blocks of text and subsequent effect on reading quality, it is recommended that designers incorporate short blocks of text with extended information hidden. The loss of information in long form can be supplemented with components such as multimedia or other engaging components.

C. *Comparison of Disciplines*

While there are many similarities in responses from both engineering students and design students, there were some fundamental differences. One of these differences was illuminated during the second activity in which it became apparent that while similar requirements may be requested, the way students think and interact are different. Design students felt comfortable creating a visual representation of what they thought their perfect discipline specific future electronic textbook was and worked together from the start to create their ultimate proposal. This can be associated with the nature of design being undertaken as a team project. On the contrary, engineering students presented their answers in a list form and instead of compromising and discussing opinions during the creation process, waited until after their individual lists were made to try and unify their answers. This can be attributed to the often solitary nature of engineering projects.

When examining the differences in component inclusion, the discipline requirements become apparent. While both groups of students wanted to be able to add their own photos to the text inline and have text represented in bullet form, engineering students did not feel that taking their own notes were necessary in the new textbook. When asked about this, they stated that the information was now in point form and they no longer needed to take notes. On the contrary, design students still wanted to take their own notes because of the interdisciplinary and creative aspects of the design process. Engineering students also requested the component interactive equations be included in their future textbook, which is consistent with a discipline that requires equations over those that do not such as design. Based on the educational requirements of both disciplines of students, it is important to ensure that components change based on the needs of the students.

V. CONCLUSION AND FUTURE WORK

Overall, students believe that future electronic textbooks need to be improved to become more interactive to facilitate their learning and help them fully engage with the material. Although, students can agree on this, when comparing two similar disciplines that share many fundamental characteristics with differences in approaches, it becomes apparent that the one-size fits all approach to textbook design needs to be abandoned. Generally, students place high priority on making future electronic textbooks more interactive, discipline specific, and with less text. Yet, students also note discipline specific components as vital, such as interactive equations, in facilitating the understanding of their work.

While design recommendations such as these have important applications to industry and academia, more research should be conducted to truly verify the practical validity of the components suggested. The educational perspective should also be investigated to understand the use of electronic textbooks as a teaching aid. This perspective is best investigated on an individual basis because of the changing opinions of instructors.

ACKNOWLEDGMENT

The authors would like to thank The Hong Kong Polytechnic University for their support. This research was supported by the Research Grants Council for the Hong Kong PhD Fellowship Scheme (1-904Z).

REFERENCES

[1] A. Denoyelles, J. Raible, and R. Seilhamer, "Exploring students' e-textbook practices in higher education," Educause Review. [Online]. March 2016. Available from: http://er.educause.edu/articles/2015/7/exploring-students-etextbook-practices-in-higher-education

[2] M. Kropman, H. P. Schoch, and H. Y. Teoh, "An experience in e-learning: using an electronic textbook," Beyond the comfort zone: Proceedings of the 21st ASCILITE Conference, 2004, pp. 512-515.

[3] N. K. Herther, "Ebooks everywhere: the digital transformation of reading," Searcher, vol. 19(6), pp. 22-31, 2011.

[4] B. Shneiderman, Designing the user interface: Strategies for effective human computer-interaction. Boston, MA: Addison Wesley Longman, 1998.

[5] D. A. Kolb, "Learning styles and disciplinary differences," in The modern American college, A. W. Chickering Ed. London: Joseey-Bass Limited, pp. 232-255, 1981.

[6] J. Defazio, "Challenges of electronic textbook authoring: writing in the discipline," Communications in Computer and Information Science, vol. 352, pp. 8-14, 2012.

[7] G. Fairbairn and S. Fairbairn, Reading at university. Buckingham, England: Open University Press, 2001.

[8] B. J. Phillips and F. Phillips, “Sink or skim: textbook reading behaviors of introductory accounting students,” Issues in Accounting Education, vol. 22(1), pp. 21-44, 2007.

[9] J. Bowden and F. Marton, The university of learning. London: Psychology Press, 2003.

[10] K. O'Hara and A. Sellen, “A comparison of reading paper and on-line documents.” Paper presented at the Proceedings of the SIGCHI conference on Human factors in computing systems, Atlanta, GA, 1997, pp. 335-342.

[11] A. Sellen and R. Harper, The myth of the paperless office. Boston, MA: MIT Press, 2003.

[12] R. McFall, “Electronic textbooks that transform how textbooks are used.” The Electronic Library, vol. 23(1), pp. 72-81, 2005.

[13] X. Tian and B. Martin, “Value chain adjustments in educational publishing,” Publishing Research Quarterly, vol. 29(1), pp. 12-25, 2013.

[14] K. A. Sheen and Y. Luximon, “Relationship between academic discipline and user perception of the future of electronic textbooks,” Procedia Manufacturing, vol. 3, 2015, pp. 5845-5850.

[15] S. R. Vaughn, J. S. Schumm, and J. M. Sinagub, Focus group interviews in education and psychology. Thousand Oaks: Sage Publications, 1996.

[16] B. G. Glaser and A. L. Strauss, The discovery of grounded theory: strategies for qualitative research. New Brunswick, NJ: Transaction Publishers, 2009.

[17] L. Millward, “Focus groups,” in Research Methods in Psychology, G. Breakwell, S. Hammond, and C. Fife-Shaw, Eds. London: Sage Publications, pp. 274-292, 1995.

[18] R. Krueger, Focus Groups: A Practical Guide for Applied Research, 2nd ed. Thousand Oaks: Sage Publications, pp. 36-45, 1994.

[19] D. Stewart and P. Shamdasani, Focus groups Theory and Practice. Beverly Hills, CA: Sage Publications, 1990.

[20] M. Bode, M. Khorami, and D. Visscher “A Case Study of Student and Instructor Reactions to a Calculus E-Book,” PRIMUS, vol. 24(2), pp. 160-174, 2014.

A Training-assistance System using Mobile Augmented Reality for Outdoor-facility Inspection

Yoshiki Yumbe
Global Center for Social Innovation – Tokyo,
Research & Development Group, Hitachi, Ltd.
Tokyo, Japan
e-mail: yoshiki.yumbe.bc@hitachi.com

Osamu Segawa and Makoto Yamakita
Chubu Electric Power, Co., Inc.
Nagoya, Japan
e-mail: Segawa.Osamu@chuden.co.jp

Abstract— **A training-assistance system using mobile augmented reality (AR) for outdoor-facility inspection was designed, developed, and evaluated. In inspection training for pole-mounted communication facilities for electric power supply operation, the realization of efficient, effective, and autonomous learning is desired. In light of these, three AR functions supporting inspection training, namely, pole navigation, visualization for facility attributes, and facility-defect search, were proposed. To realize these functions, a hybrid tracking method for accurate AR overlaying was proposed. Moreover, a prototype system was developed and evaluated at a real training site. The evaluation results show that the proposed system supports efficient, effective, and autonomous learning. In other words, AR technology can be applied to training in outdoor-facility inspection.**

Keywords-augmented reality; facility inspection; training assistance.

I. INTRODUCTION

Recently, demand for using smart devices has been growing, such as smartphones and tablets, to access various types of information during field work. Furthermore, with improving performance of such smart devices, "augmented reality" (AR) has been increasingly becoming a strong tool for supporting field work in various industrial segments [1]-[6]. In the electric power industry, improving efficiency of facility maintenance while retaining reliability has become a significant issue. Conventionally, high reliability of pole-mounted facilities for electric-power supply operation is ensured by periodic inspection. Recently, succession of inspection skills and maintaining inspection quality have become more important. Therefore, to nurture experienced inspectors, a supporting framework for efficient, effective, and autonomous learning is desired. As for the inspection training, a training assistance system using AR technology may become an useful solution.

In this work, a training-assistance system using mobile AR technology for inspection training of outdoor facilities was proposed. The organization of the paper is as follows. In section II, the workflow of typical inspection training was surveyed. On the basis of survey results, required AR functions for supporting the training were established in section III. After the requirements were defined, an AR-based training-assistance system and an effective user interface were designed, and several technical methods for the system were proposed in section IV. In section V, a prototype system was developed. In section VI, the availability and practicability of the prototype was evaluated by active workers and trainers at a real training site. On the basis of the evaluation results, the applicability of mobile AR technology to training in outdoor-facility inspection was examined. In section VII, some related works are introduced and compared with our work. Finally, the conclusion and future works are described in section VIII.

II. ISSUES CONCERNING INSPECTION TRAINING AND RESEARCH OBJECTIVE

Electric-power companies manage their communication facilities for electric-power supply operation. The inspection-target facilities (e.g., communication lines and ancillary equipment such as hangers and closures) are mounted on utility poles. Conventionally, communication facilities are maintained by periodic inspection. During the inspection of a facility, inspectors visually check the condition of the facilities (e.g., cracks, rust, distortion, various separation distances, and botanical collision). To check a facility comprehensively, an inspector has to learn the accurate knowledge about the target facilities, namely, the type, specification, normal and abnormal conditions. Recently, succession of inspection skills and maintaining inspection quality have become more important. Therefore, to nurture experienced inspectors, an effective training framework is desired. The objectives of the inspection training are described as follows.

(1) Ensure trainees understand types, specifications, and structures of the facilities.
(2) Ensure trainees understand how to inspect the facilities. That is, trainees are taught to concretely judge whether conditions of each facility are normal or abnormal and find defects comprehensively.

In the inspection training, the trainer gives several trainees specific guidance on inspection know-how. Improving efficiency of the training and trainees' understanding are crucial issues.

In consideration of these issues, AR technology was applied to facility-inspection training with the aim of realizing efficient, effective, and autonomous learning. Furthermore, a prototype training-assistance system using mobile AR technology was designed and developed, and its availability and practicability were evaluated at a real training site.

III. Functional Requirements

First, in this section, a conventional training workflow is defined. Second, functional requirements to support the workflow and the system concepts are proposed.

A. *Training Workflow*

The inspection training is performed in a training site containing mock utility poles and pole-mounted communication facilities. Certain types of defects were preliminarily set in the mock facilities. The conventional training workflow is explained as follows. First, the trainees confirm the inspection target on a (paper) facility map. They move to the target and identify it while confirming it on the map. They confirm the target facility and its details (type, specification, structure, and so on) using paper-based manuals. After confirming the facility details, they check the condition of the target against a checklist. In other words, the trainees search for the preliminarily set facility defects. When they find a defect, they write an inspection report. These steps are performed at all facilities. Finally, the trainees receive feedback from their trainer.

B. *Functional Requirements and System Concept*

Functional requirements for the training-assistance system using mobile AR are described as follows. The system is "paper-less" and implemented on a general-purpose tablet. In view of applicability to the inspection training, the conventional training workflow should also be supported by the system. To realize efficient, effective, and autonomous learning, the three main AR functions required are summarized as follows.

(1) Pole navigation
Trainees confirm their location and surrounding facilities on a digital facility map and AR. The system assists in identifying the target facility.
(2) Visualization of facility attributes
Trainees acquire facility information (type, specification, structure, and so on) by AR, which enables the user to link the real facility to that information.
(3) Facility-defect search
The system not only provides defect information to trainees but also assists autonomous defect search utilizing AR.

IV. System Overview

This section describes technical detail of the proposed system and the concrete methods to satisfy the three above-listed AR functional requirements.

A. *Pole Navigation*

Conventionally, trainees move to a target facility while confirming the target location on a map. Therefore, a facility-navigation function for identifying the target was devised. The function informs the trainees of their relative locations in regard to surrounding facilities. The proposed pole-navigation method and user interface are shown schematically in Figure 1. The location (latitude and longitude) of each utility pole is stored in a database. A rough user location is obtained from the GPS (global positioning system). User heading is obtained from acceleration and geomagnetic sensors mounted on the tablet. First, surrounding facility's data is retrieved from the database on the basis of GPS location of the user. Location and heading of the facility in relation to the user are calculated. On the basis of the calculation results, AR tags are mapped onto the tablet's screen as shown in Figure 1. The center of the screen represents user location. Each AR tag shows the relative distance and heading of surrounding poles. Relative distance from each pole to the user is represented by the tag's color and size. These AR tags are rendered every time the GPS location and user heading are changed.

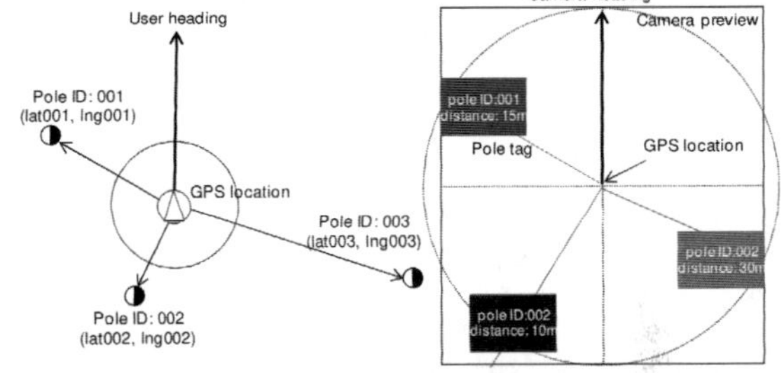

Figure 1. Pole-navigation function and user interface.

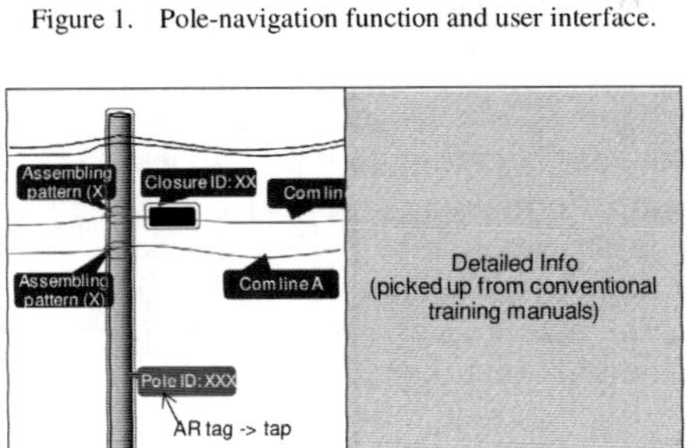

Figure 2. Visualization of facility attributes and user interface.

B. *Visualization of facility attributes*

This function enables visualization of facility information (hereafter, attributes) using AR. The function and user-interface design are summarized in Figure 2. The AR contents are defined for each type of facility. Detailed information is not suitable for visualization by AR because it is "floating" in accord with the live camera motion of the tablet. Therefore, AR is only used to point out the position of the target. Facility ID or type is displayed using AR. If the user taps an AR "balloon," detailed information appears on the right side of the screen. In this way, the user can link the real facility to related information.

To realize the function explained above, an accurate AR method is needed. In general, AR technologies are classified as vision-based or location-based methods [7][8]. Vision-based methods identify target objects by using features obtained from images. Moreover, they can be categorized as either of two approaches: marker-based [9] or marker-less [4]. In case of marker-based approaches, the target objects are identified by recognizing artificial markers. Applying marker-based approaches to pole-mounted facilities seems a distant prospect because an enormous number of markers are required. Location-based methods, on the other hand, identify target objects on the basis of GPS location, heading, and geographical locations of target objects [10][11]. While such approaches have a merit of low computational cost, their identification accuracy is low because of measurement errors. The location-based method seems to be suitable for this case because geographical locations (latitude, longitude, and ground height) of the facilities are already stored in the database.

Therefore, in our previous study, a robust identification algorithm was proposed [12]. The algorithm is an advanced approach for conventional location-based methods. It uses GPS data as well as data from acceleration and geomagnetic sensors. Concretely, the facilities are identified on the basis of not only a tablet's current location and heading obtained from these sensors but also object distance (i.e., the distance between the user and the object being inspected) by a triangulation method using acceleration and geomagnetic sensors. The facilities can be identified robustly without being influenced by measurement errors of the sensors.

A target facility is initially registered and AR objects are overlaid accurately by a robust identification method. After the target is identified, it should be continually tracked so that the AR contents can be overlaid accurately. Therefore, a hybrid tracking method is proposed. The proposed method realizes accurate tracking using a combination of tablet's attitude angles and line-detection results from camera images (see Figure 3). First, the overlaid AR objects after the robust identification keep tracking the target facility by using the tablet's attitude angles (yaw, pitch, and roll) as shown in Figure 3(a). Simultaneously, line objects are detected by using a probabilistic Hough transform and line-segment clustering (Figure 3(b)). The objectives of line detection are horizontal lines corresponding to the communication lines and vertical lines corresponding to the utility pole. In an outdoor situation, it is difficult to detect these lines only because captured images contain various background noises. Detected line objects are therefore narrowed down (Figure 3(c)). Concretely, detected line objects located near the sensor-based AR objects (Figure 3(a)) are extracted. The amount of horizontal correction is calculated by using the AR object for the pole and a couple of vertical lines (Figure 3(d)). The amount of vertical correction is calculated by using the AR object for the communication lines and the same number of horizontal lines (In Figure 3(e), the number of lines is two). The overlaid positions of the AR objects are translated by using these correction amounts. These steps are launched after the identification process is finished and repeated. In the training operation, the AR rectangles and lines shown in Figure 3(a) are hidden, and this procedure is performed in the background. The accurate tracking by the proposed hybrid tracking method realizes our training assistance functions.

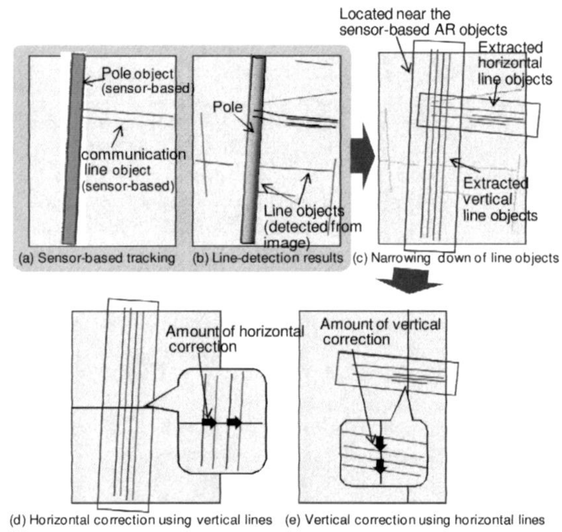

Figure 3. Summary of hybrid tracking method.

C. *Search for facility defects*

As mentioned before, the training facilities have some preliminarily set defects. The trainees learn how to inspect a facility by searching for these defects. The training-assistance system should not only provide defect information to the trainees but also assist autonomous defect search using AR. Therefore, a function for searching for autonomous defects is proposed. A summary of the proposed function is described in Figure 4. The defect locations (latitude, longitude, and ground height) are also stored in the database. AR objects for the defects are overlaid as transparent objects. The correction amounts obtained from the hybrid tracking method are used to overlay the AR objects for defects, too. First, the user searches for a facility defect. If the user finds a defect, they capture an image containing the defect the inside of the blue box shown in Figure 4(b). After capturing the image, the user selects a corresponding defect type from a check list. Once a defect type is selected, the captured image and selected defect type are linked and recorded. After the defect search is finished, the recorded results (i.e., defect type and position) are evaluated. That is, captured-image position and selected-defect type are checked by comparing them with actual defect data, and the user is informed whether or not their recorded data is correct. Finally, a hidden AR object is displayed to inform the user of the correct data.

The proposed function assists the trainees to search for facility defects autonomously while actually thinking for themselves. Moreover, learning how to inspect facilities becomes more enjoyable for the user in a similar manner to a treasure hunt.

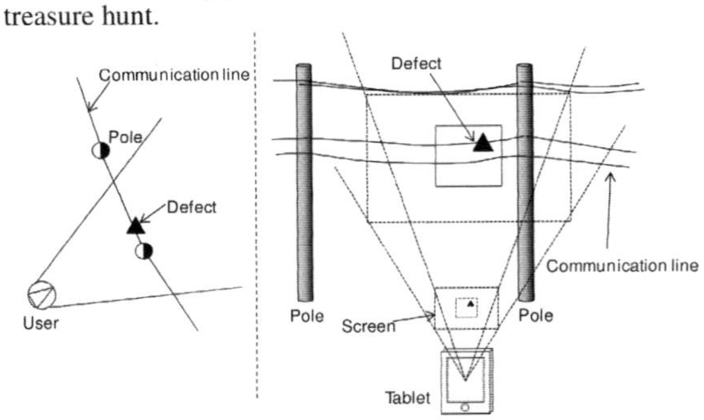

(a) Example of defect search.

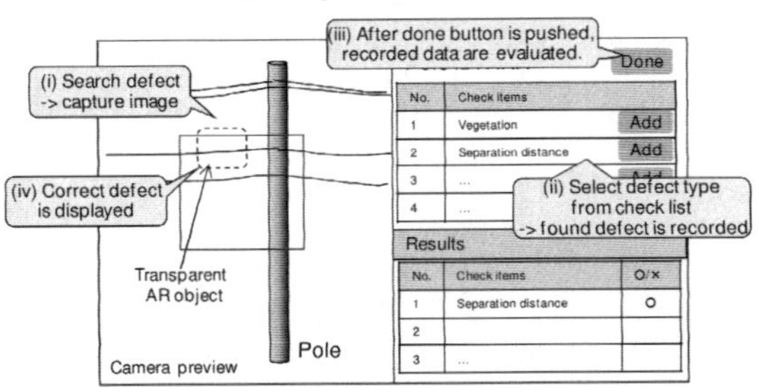

(b) Design of user interface.

Figure 4. Summary of searching for facility defects.

V. SYSTEM IMPLEMENTATION

Based on the technical methods described above, the prototype system was implemented on an Android tablet. Operation examples of each function are shown in Figures 5, 6, and 7. In Figure 5, an example of pole navigation is shown. On the left side of the screen, relative distance of each pole from the user is represented by the tag's color and size. A red tag means near the pole. On the right side of the screen, a facility map and the user's location are displayed.

Examples of the function for visualizing facility attributes are shown in Figure 6. AR is only used to point out the target position. Facility ID or type is overlaid using an AR balloon. In Figure 6(a), a pole ID is overlaid on a live camera view. If the user taps the AR balloon, detailed information about the pole is displayed on the right side of the screen. In Figure 6(b), two assembly patterns, one closure, and two communication lines are pointed out by the AR balloons. As shown in Figure 6, the AR objects are overlaid accurately by the robust identification and the hybrid tracking methods. An example of the hybrid tracking is shown in Figure 7. In normal operation, the hybrid tracking is performed in the background. Therefore, the AR rectangles and detected lines are hidden. In Figure 7, the blue rectangle and the green -lines were overlaid by sensor-based tracking. The red lines were obtained by line detection. The amounts of horizontal and vertical corrections (expressed in pixels) obtained by the hybrid tracking are displayed on the upper side of screen.

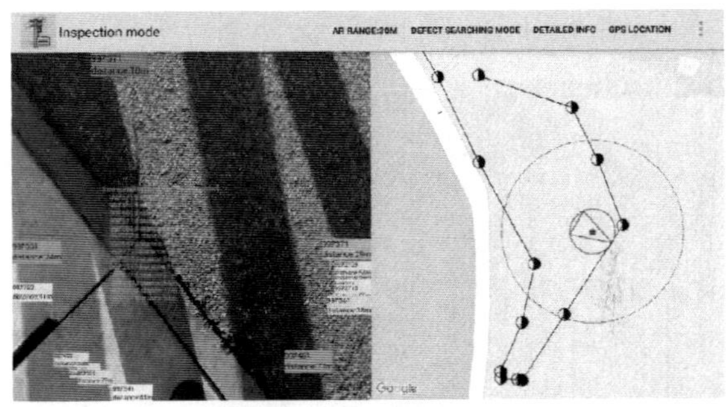

Figure 5. Pole navigation.

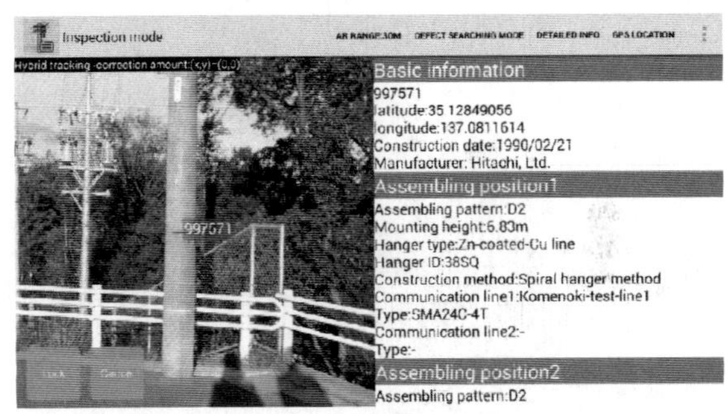

(a) Utility pole.

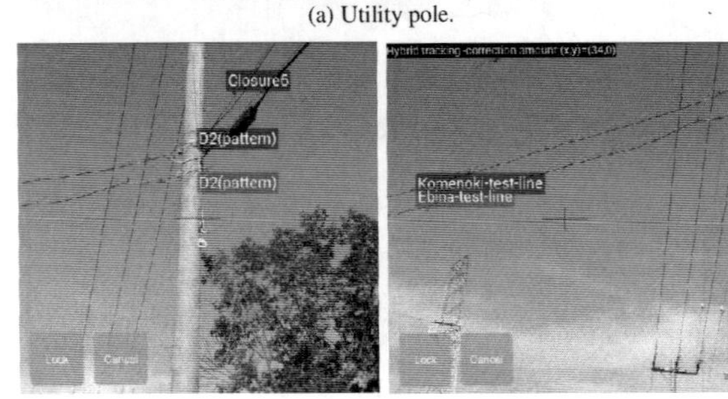

(b) Attachments (left) and communication lines (right).

Figure 6. Visualization of facility attributes.

An example of the facility-defect search function is shown in Figure 8. In this example, one facility defect was preliminarily set. The defect type is insufficient separation between two communication lines. In Figure 8(a), the user searches for the defect and captures an image containing the detected defect point inside the blue box. After capturing the image, the user selects a corresponding defect type from the check list on the right side of the screen. In Figure 8(b), the recorded data (position and type) are evaluated, and the user is informed of the evaluation result. After that, the hidden AR object is displayed to inform the user of the correct data.

As explained above, the correct operation of proposed AR functions were confirmed by prototyping.

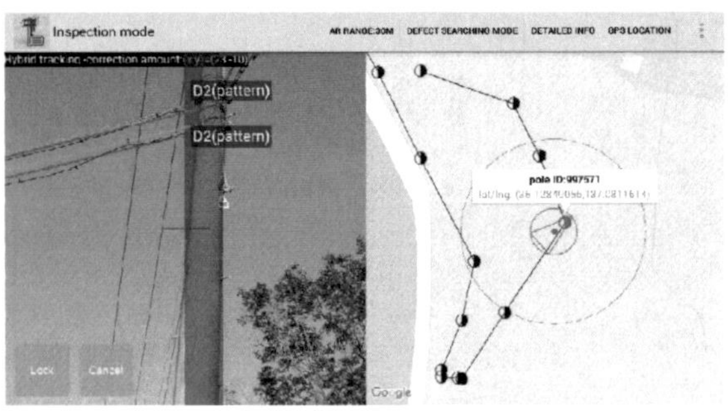

Figure 7. Hybrid tracking.

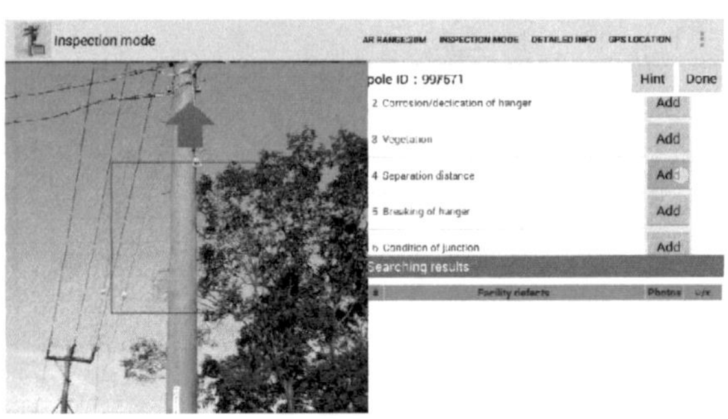

(a) Search for defect .

(b) Evaluate recorded data and inform user

Figure 8. Search for facility defect.

VI. EVALUATION

The developed AR system was evaluated as follows. On the basis of the evaluation results, the applicability of the proposed system to outdoor-facility-inspection training was examined.

A. *Evaluation Approach*

The proposed AR system was evaluated in the field (at a training center). In the evaluation, seven users were selected from active workers and trainers belonging to the power distribution department, and the communication facility department of Chubu Electric Power Co., Inc. They evaluated the system by comparing it with that used in conventional inspection training (because they already have knowledge of the training). While using the proposed system in the evaluation trial, they experience the training workflow. After finishing the trial, each user evaluated the system by questionnaire, which was based on the web-usability scale (WUS) [13], the technology-acceptance model (TAM) [14], and the AR acceptance model [15]. The questionnaire consists of 20 statements on a five-point scale (1 (disagree) to 5 (agree)) and a free-comment field. The statements were categorized into five categories: usability, autonomy, efficiency, understanding, and applicability. Autonomy, efficiency, understanding are defined in accordance with our research objective. Besides, usability is an important factor because insufficient usability may hinder the evaluation of the proposed AR functions. The statements are listed as follows.

Usability:
- The system was easy to use.
- It responded quickly to my commands.
- It was easy to understand.
- It was easy to make substantial use of the system.

Autonomy:
- The support of a trainer was unnecessary.
- Learnt to use the system was anxiety-free.
- Learning by using the system was enjoyable.

Efficiency:
- Facility information could be acquired when needed.
- Information necessary for training could be acquired.
- Learning was smooth.
- The system is more useful than paper-based manuals.

Understanding:
- It was easy to find where a facility.
- I could determine facility attributes easily.
- I could quickly learn how to inspect a facility.
- The AR contents in the left side of screen are useful.
- The detailed information appearing on the right side of screen is useful.

Applicability:
- The system is applicable to inspection work.
- The system matches the objective and workflow of inspection training.
- The system is promising for inspection training.

- I will recommend the system to new employees.

B. Evaluation Results

The evaluation results are summarized and discussed. In Figure 9, the average scores for each category were expressed as a radar chart. Average score and standard deviation for each statement are listed in Table 1. According to the figure, the average score for each category was more than 3.0, which shows the proposed AR system was given positive feedback. The category "efficiency" received the highest score among the five categories. Especially, the statements "Facility information could be acquired when needed." and "Information necessary for training could be acquired." received high scores over 4.0. For "autonomy", the statement "Learning by using the system was enjoyable." also received a high score over 4.0. The evaluation results show that the proposed AR functions and system are useful for the inspection training. As explained above, whereas the users give positive feedbacks regarding the proposed AR functions and system, the category "applicability" gets a lower score than those for the other categories. It consists of several statements for evaluating the user's intention to apply the AR system in inspection training. The low score for applicability infers that the users have some reservations in regard to applying the AR system in inspection training. To determine the reason for the slightly lower score for applicability, the free comments written by the users are reviewed as follows. Some examples of the comments are listed below.

- This system might miss facility defects that should be found.
- When the user moves in the wrong direction or chooses the wrong target, assist functions to correct these errors are required.
- The system is useful because it assists with an autonomous defect search. However, the training contents are insufficient. For example, the user should be taught not only how to identify each defect but also why it is defect and the safety risk is poses.

These comments suggest two future tasks in regard to improving the proposed AR system. First, assist functions to correct wrong operation by the user are required. It is assumed that these comments may influence the score for the statement "Learning to use the system was anxiety-free." Second, more training materials should be prepared. The AR system should cover the same training contents as those taught in the inspection training course. Moreover, the proposed AR system will be more effective if additional training materials are displayed using AR.

As described above, the evaluation results show that the proposed AR functions and system support efficient, effective, and autonomous learning. If the two above-described tasks are accomplished, the AR system will be truly applicable to training in outdoor-facility inspection.

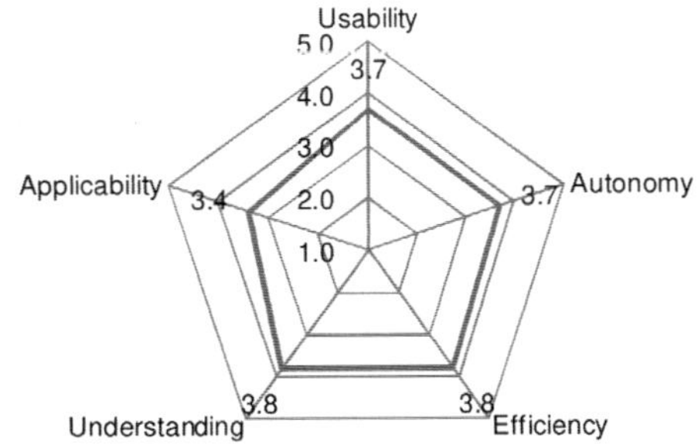

Figure 9. Summary of evaluation result.

TABLE I. AVERAGE SCORE AND STANDARD DEVIATION FOR EACH STATEMENT.

Categories	Statements	Average scores	Standard deviations
Usability	The system was easy to use.	3.6	0.7
	It responded quickly to my commands.	3.1	1.0
	It was easy to understand.	3.9	1.0
	It was easy to make substantial use of the system.	4.1	1.0
Autonomy	The support of a trainer was unnecessary.	3.6	0.9
	Learnt to use the system was anxiety-free.	3.0	1.1
	Learning by using the system was enjoyable.	4.4	0.5
Efficiency	Facility information could be acquired when needed.	4.3	1.0
	Information necessary for training could be acquired.	4.1	0.8
	Learning was smooth.	2.9	1.0
	The system is more useful than paper-based manuals.	4.0	1.1
Understanding	It was easy to find where a facility.	3.6	0.9
	I could determine facility attributes easily.	3.7	1.0
	I could quickly learn how to inspect a facility.	3.3	1.2
	The AR contents in the left side of screen are useful.	3.9	0.8
	The detailed information appearing on the right side of screen is useful.	4.4	0.5
Applicability	The system is applicable to inspection training.	3.1	1.1
	The system matches the objective and workflow of inspection training.	3.7	1.0
	The system is promising for inspection training.	3.4	1.3
	I will recommend the system to new employees.	3.1	1.0

VII. RELATED WORKS

In industrial segments, several researchers have discussed applying AR technology to industrial education and training. For example, an AR-based educational system for automotive engineering has been proposed [1][2]. Moreover, support systems for aircraft maintenance, namely, a marker-based registration method and a marker-less camera-pose estimation method, respectively, have been proposed [3][4]. An interactive AR application prototype for industrial education and training applications has also been proposed [5]. In [5], their system was applied to a simple virtual demonstration of assembling/disassembling procedures. In these works, the target facilities onto which AR information is overlaid are used indoors or located locally. Moreover, the above-described systems only present maintenance or assembly procedures by AR. From the perspective of training, these systems may not support autonomous learning sufficiently. In industrial education and training, trainees should be taught not only "how" they should work but also "why" they should work in accordance with the procedures in the manual. As described above, AR-based autonomous training systems that teach the ability to think for oneself have not been studied so much.

On the contrary, a mobile AR application for visualizing maintenance data about power-distribution facilities was proposed [6]. It was developed for facility-inspection work, not for inspection training. In detail, a conventional location-based approach was applied. However, the measurement errors of sensors mounted on a tablet were not considered. In the fields of industrial education and training area, applying AR technology to outdoor widely-scattered facilities has not been studied so much.

VIII. CONCLUSION

A training-assistance system for outdoor-facility inspection using mobile augmented reality was developed and evaluated. In early phase of the research, conventional inspection training for pole-mounted communication facilities was surveyed. On the basis of the survey results, three AR functions to realize efficient, effective, and autonomous learning, namely, a pole-navigation function, a visualization function for facility attributes, and a facility-defect search function, were proposed. A hybrid tracking method was also proposed to realize accurate AR overlaying. Moreover, the prototype system was evaluated by active workers and trainers using questionnaire at a real training site. The evaluation results show that the proposed system supports efficient, effective, and autonomous learning. In other words, AR technology can be applied to training in outdoor-facility inspection.

In future work, the proposed AR system will be improved on the basis of the feedback obtained from the evaluation. Furthermore, the effects of using the proposed system on training will be evaluated by further field evaluations by more test subjects.

After applying the proposed system to the facility inspection training, some technologies for supporting inspection work will be developed and evaluated (e. g., facility defect detection using image recognition).

ACKNOWLEDGMENT

The authors thank the staffs at Chubu Electric Power, Co., Inc., who gave us the opportunity to evaluate the prototype system and shared their knowledge of facility-inspection training.

REFERENCES

[1] I. Farkhatdinov and J.-H. Ryu., "Development of Educational System for Automotive Engineering Based on Augmented Reality", In International Conference on Engineering Education and Research, 2009.

[2] H. Regenbrecht, G. Baratoff, and W. Wilke., "Augmented Reality Project in Automotive and Aerospace Industry", IEEE Computer Graphics and Applications, Vol. 25, 6, pp. 48-56, 2005.

[3] T. Haritos and N.D. Macchiarella, "A Mobile Application of Augmented Reality for Aerospace Maintenance Training", In Proc. DASC 2005, Vol. 1, pp.5.B.3 - 5.1-9, 2005.

[4] F. De Crescenzio, M. Fantini, F. Persiani, L. Di Stefano, P. Azzari, and S. Salti., "Augmented Reality for Aircraft Mintenance Training and Operations Support", IEEE Computer Graphics and Applications, volume 31, pp. 96–101, 2011.

[5] B. Besbes, S.N. Collette, M. Tamaazousti, S. Bourgeois, and V. Gay-Bellile., "An Interactive Augmented Reality System a Prototype for Industrial Maintenance Training Applications", In Proc. IEEE/ACM International Symposium on Mixed and Augmented Reality, pp. 269-270, 2012.

[6] A. W. McMorran, S. E. Rudd, John J. Simmins, N. McCollough, and C. M. Shand., "Field Force Data Visualization: Developing an Open Mobile Platform for Integrated Data Access", In Proc. IEEE Power and Energy Society General Meeting, pp. 1-5, 2012.

[7] R. Azuma, Y. Baillot, R. Behringer, S. Feiner, S. Julier, and B. MacIntyre., "Recent advances in augmented reality", In IEEE Computer Graphics and Applications, volume 21, issue 6, pp. 34-47, 2001.

[8] D.W.F. van Krevelen and R. Poelman., "A survey of augmented reality technologies, applications and limitation", In International Journal of Virtual Reality, volume 9, number 2, pp. 1-20, 2010.

[9] M. Billinghurst, M. Hakkarainen, and C. Woodward., "Augmented assembly using a mobile phone", In Proc. 7th International Conference on Mobile and Ubiquitous Multimedia, pp. 84–87, 2008.

[10] W. Piekarski, B. Gunther, and B. Thomas., "Integrating virtual and augmented realities in an outdoor application", In Proc. 2nd IEEE and ACM International Workshop on Augmented Reality, pp. 45-54, 1999.

[11] T. Höllerer, S. Feiner, and J. Pavlik.. "Situated documentaries embedding multimedia presentations in the real world", In Proc. 3rd International Symposium on Wearable Computers, pp. 79-86, 1999.

[12] Y. Yumbe, and N. Furulawa, "A Robust Location-based Augmented-reality System for Supporting Inspection of Power-distribution Facilities", In Proc. The 76th National Convention of Information Processing Society of Japan, pp. 9-10, 2014.

[13] K. Nakagawa, T. Suda, H. Zempo, and K. Matsumoto, "The Development of Questionnaire for Evaluating Web Usability", Human Interface Society 10th Symposium, pp.421-424, 2001.

[14] F. D. Davis, R. P. Bagozzi, and P. R. Warshaw, "User acceptance of computer technology: A comparison of two theoretical models", Management Science 35: pp. 982-1003, 1989.

[15] M. Leue, D. tom-Dieck., and T. Jung, "A Theoretical Model of Augmented Reality Acceptance", e-Review of Tourism Research, pp.1-21, 2014.

Cross-Platform Web Framework for Gaze Tracking

New opportunities for mobile interaction

Nicolai Harich[1], Simon Gebauer[1]
Computer Science and Media
Stuttgart Media University
Nobelstrasse 10, 70569 Stuttgart, Germany
contact@nicolaiharich.com, mail@simon-gebauer.de

Holger Schmidt, Gottfried Zimmermann
Responsive Media Experience Research Group
Stuttgart Media University
Nobelstrasse 10, 70569 Stuttgart, Germany
schmidtho@hdm-stuttgart.de, gzimmermann@acm.org

Abstract— **Gaze tracking functionalities provide a new way of interacting with electronic devices. As things are now, they are often limited to one specific device and require proprietary hardware and software. We propose a solution for web applications to counteract those limitations. By using the latest web technologies, we ensure platform independence. Due to the design and modularity of our solution, gaze tracking solutions become interchangeable. Web applications can easily consume gaze data provided by a generic event-based web-interface. The main contribution of this work is a universal calibration and mapping functionality. The raw data of miscellaneous gaze trackers can be processed and transformed, so that the gaze points are stabilized and correctly mapped onto screen coordinates. In the present paper, we describe the three-layer-architecture we use. Our work shows how to combine recent web technologies and algorithms to supply gaze tracking functionalities in a generic way.**

Keywords-Gaze tracking; cross-platform; calibration; eye tracking; gaze events; interaction; gaze-enhanced web; e-learning; real-time; adaptivity; adaptive e-learning

I. INTRODUCTION

In the last decades, eye tracking technologies were developed and established for analyzing human eye and gaze movements. In the fields of neuroscience, psychology and marketing, but also in the field of human computer interaction it became a widely accepted tool. However, the technology has not been accessible for the consumer market for a long time. No affordable solutions existed, since most systems were based on expensive hardware components. With ongoing development of algorithms and processing units, affordable software solutions reached the consumer market.

Even mobile devices are capable of gaze tracking now, but existing solutions are still very limited. The diversity of gaze tracking hardware and software makes it hard to integrate gaze tracking functionalities into existing applications.

While trying to simplify the process of application development for desktop computers and mobile devices, a wide range of approaches emerged to handle this complexity. Applications can be written in different programming languages and even with web technologies to use them as "enriched web applications" in a browser. The latter one is advantageous for developing multi-platform applications, because a browser is available on almost every platform.

This motivates our research group to develop a gaze tracking framework based on web technologies. Previous works include a client-side web interface to connect miscellaneous gaze trackers to web applications. In this way, web applications can simply consume gaze events, without caring about the actual source.

Since gaze tracking affords high accuracy measurements and algorithms are quite sensible to various condition changes, most systems require regular re-calibrations. This makes it necessary to switch to a calibration software, which is usually supplied by the manufacturer of the eye tracker. In order to overcome this obstacle, we move the entire processing of the raw gaze data into the browser. The processing unit includes a calibration procedure and a mapping function, which transforms raw gaze data to display coordinates. This way the user can control the entire process through an arbitrary browser, without switching between applications.

The developed solution claims for general usage in web applications, but is actually part of the research project Adaptable and Adaptive Multimedia Systems (AAMS), which is an interdisciplinary research project driven by cluster 3 of the ScienceCampus Tuebingen [22]. The members of this cluster are from Tuebingen [23], Freiburg [24] [25] and Stuttgart [26]. The overall goal is to support self-regulated versus external-regulated learning from multimedia. Knowing that learning is a very individual process, future learning environments should automatically adapt to the needs of a user. In order to reach that target, advanced techniques have to be developed. Monitoring the gaze and eye movements allows to analyze the user's learning behavior and momentary emotional state, which gives the opportunity to make adaptations on the system. Furthermore gaze trackers can act as input devices to enhance the accessibility.

Before describing our concept of in-browser calibration and mapping, we will give an overview of related work in the field of eye tracking technology in section II. In particular, we focus on the use of gaze tracking together with web applications like E-Learning environments. After that, we will introduce the frameworks we used or developed that enable web applications to consume gaze data provided by miscellaneous eye trackers as part of the

[1] Authors contributed equally to the work

systems architecture in section III followed by known issues in section IV.

Next we present the results of user studies we performed with two different gaze tracking systems in section V. The first system consists of a desktop computer and a high-cost, hardware-based eye tracker for professional use and the second system is an unmodified tablet with a front camera available for the consumer market. We evaluated the accuracy of both the stationary hardware system and the tablet with a user test to be able to compare those solutions.

We describe our E-Learning environment and motivate the usage of eye tracking in future applications like e-learning, accessibility or games in section IV.

We finally discuss the project in the conclusion in section VII.

II. RELATED WORK

Since eye trackers are entering the consumer market and even have been integrated in the first mobile devices, the development of gaze tracking applications got more and more attention. Besides traditional applications for analyzing the perception of users, a broad range of different applications appeared over the years.

The idea to use gaze tracking for interactive systems as an input device is actually quite old. One of the main challenges is to find a suitable way to allow the user to select or to confirm something. The first approach to solve the so called "midas problem" was dwell time selection, which was first suggested by Ware and Mikaelian [19]. The user has to fixate a target for a specific amount of time to perform a dwell time selection. Naturally this technique introduces some latency to the process. To ensure that the user is able to keep the fixation point inside the boundaries of the target until the dwell time is reached, the target has to be of a minimum size, which depends of course on the accuracy of the tracker.

Jacob [11] discussed different gaze interactions such as object selection, object movement and scrolling for text. Drewes [8] examined different gaze selection methods on mobile devices and introduced a new technique based on gaze gestures. Dybdal [9] investigated on the feasibility of different eye control techniques performed on small smartphone displays and compared them to alternative selection methods like finger-strokes and accelerometer-based techniques. Stellmach et al. [17] examined on different modalities of gaze-supported pan and zoom. A gaze-directed panning with mouse-wheel or touch-based zooming yielded high acceptance among the study participants.

There are several options to provide gaze data for web applications. Biedert et al. [4] developed a browser plugin to transfer the data from the eye tracker into the browser. Another browser-independent approach, developed by Wassermann, Hardt and Zimmermann [20], is a generic interface via HTML5 websockets. The interface technique of Wassermann et al. was developed as early part of the AAMS project and is also used in the scenario of using an SMI native eye tracker in combination with the newly developed in-browser calibration framework.

There are several promising ideas to use gaze data within web applications. Besides using the gaze data as an input device, it is possible to improve the usability of web applications by taking additional knowledge about the user's interaction into account.

One idea is to use the user's gaze point to make a prediction on what he will do next. Rozado's, Shoghri's and Jurdak's studies [16] show that the gaze data can be used to predict which link is likely to be clicked next. With this additional information, the web content can be prefetched in order to speed up the browsing experience.

Alt et al. [2] investigated on adaptation and tailoring of web content based on gazing behavior. With a case study, they were able to prove that the adaptation induced a significant increase of the user's attention.

Similar attempts exist in the field of E-Learning environments. Several research groups investigate on the integration of eye tracking into E-Learning environments [7] [18] [15]. Copeland and Gedeon [6] investigated on the gaze-based prediction of reading comprehension. Their results have shown, that the number of fixations and total duration of fixations are suitable measures for subject familiarity and extent of answer-seeking.

E-Learning environments can make use of such measurements to offer additional assistance to the learner whenever suitable. One example is iDict, a translation aid for language courses, which displays tooltips to support the learner in case difficulties arise [10].

III. ARCHITECTURE

Gaze trackers can be classified in two main categories. Software-driven solutions have the advantage of being independent of additional devices except for a camera, thus reducing expenses. In contrast, most external modules include a dedicated capturing engine like an infrared camera with a special illumination unit, which makes the recognition of pupils more robust.

During the development of the framework, we used two different devices. On the one hand a hardware eye tracker from SensoMotoric Instruments (SMI), on the other hand an Amazon Kindle Fire tablet with a built-in front camera.

To be able to use both (or even other) devices for gaze tracking, we developed a three-layer-architecture: layer 1, which includes the gaze tracking hardware with its drivers, layer 2 including different ways to enable the communication between layer 1 and 3, and layer 3, the JavaScript-based gaze data processing unit as a web frontend which receives the gaze data from the communicator and provides functionalities for third party applications to use the gaze data.

Using this three-layer-architecture, gaze tracking functionalities can be provided on different devices and for different applications. These three layers are exchangeable if required, e.g. irrespective of the underlying hardware (layer 1), the communicator can be enabled to send the gaze data to the frontend. Moreover, the application that uses the gaze data can be exchanged, e.g. it does not matter whether it is an E-Learning-platform or a game. Fig. 1 shows the three-layer-architecture.

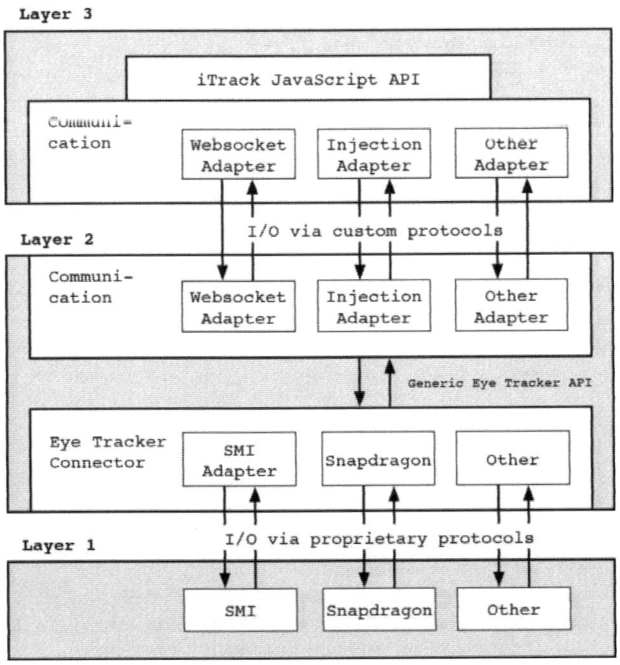

Figure 1. The three layer architecture guarantees interchangeability.

A. *Layer 1: Hardware Layer*

The base layer is the gaze tracking hardware with its proprietary drivers. Whether you use a purpose-built gaze tracking hardware, a desktop computer with a webcam or a mobile device with a built-in camera, you still need drivers to receive image data from the camera.

The SMI eye tracker is a typical, purpose-built gaze tracking solution which consists of the gaze tracking hardware and the proprietary software. The SMI eye tracker works with a video camera in combination with an infrared LED, which creates a reflection on the user's eyeball. The vector between the reflection and the centre of the pupil can be used to calculate the direction of the gaze. We use the iTrackServer as described in the following section to capture the gaze data in order to use it in the context of the three-layer-architecture.

The tablet is equipped with a front camera, which can provide a video stream of the user. By detecting the eyes in the image, it is possible to compute the gaze point of the user. We use the Snapdragon SDK [1] to do this in an efficient way. The SDK includes several facial processing algorithms which can be executed in real time. The Snapdragon SDK is compatible with Android devices equipped with appropriate Snapdragon processors.

For the gaze tracking functionality, we use the face recognition module of the Snapdragon SDK. Properties of detected faces are stored in FaceData objects, which includes the following information:

- Blink Detection - information about how wide the user's eyes are opened
- Gaze - information about the gaze point of the user
- Smile Value - probability of the user's smile
- Face Orientation - orientation of the user's head in all three axes

For our purpose we are mainly interested in the provided gaze points. They are presented in a normalized, two-dimensional camera space with values between -1 and 1. The origin is defined by the optical axis of the camera. We implemented a mapping algorithm to map this raw data onto screen coordinates, seen in Fig. 2, which is described below.

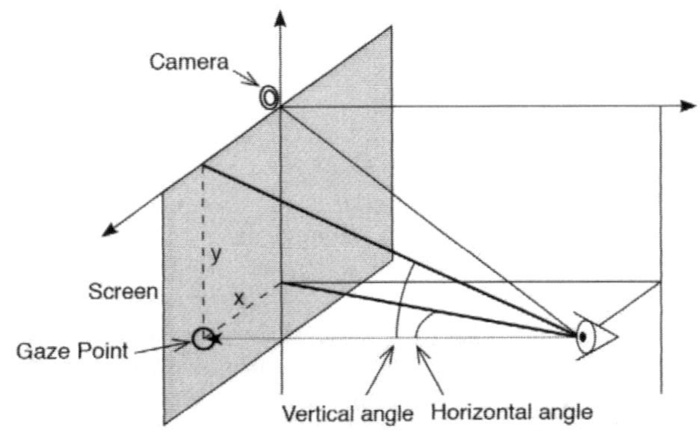

Figure 2. Visualization of gaze tracking

Since we want to use the gaze data in web applications, we embedded a webview [3] in our native application. The data is then delivered in a JSON format by injecting code into the webview. We will describe this in more detail in the next section.

B. *Layer 2: Communication Layer*

Layer 2 is a communication interface between layer 1 and layer 3, for sending the uncalibrated raw gaze data from the gaze tracker to the gaze-data processing unit. This interface is implemented in a generic and customizable way, ensuring that hardware and processing software can be exchanged.

Benjamin Wassermann and Adrian Hardt from the Stuttgart Media University developed a universal interface called iTrack [20] as part of the project AAMS. It was mainly implemented to provide an interface between data from SMI eye trackers and a browser. It consists of two parts: an iTrackServer and a JavaScript file called itrack.js. The iTrackServer is a command line tool, providing a websocket server to forward the data from the SMI software to a browser. The corresponding JavaScript is embedded into a web page to receive data from the websocket server.

Websockets offer a bidirectional communication between different hardware and software, but Android prohibits a device-local websocket communication between an Android web view and its wrapping native application for security reasons. This fact denies the use of a native webbrowser while having access to the systems front camera. In contrast, a webview does not have these limitations.

Moreover, building a client-server-architecture on a single device to establish a communication between native Android code and the contained webview is not an appropriate solution. This is why we developed a second way to let layer 1 communicate with layer 3: an injection adapter based communicator (injection communicator).

To establish a reliable connection between Android code and the contained webview, we extended the iTrack library with an injection communicator which uses JavaScript event emitting and event handlers. Depending on the availability of websockets, layer 2 provides a fallback mechanism in the form of the injection communicator, enabling the layer 1 software to send the gaze data by triggering JavaScript events.

According to the availability of the communication interface, layer 3 automatically chooses the data source to handle the raw gaze data.

C. *Layer 3: JavaScript-based processing*

Irrespective of the underlying gaze tracking hardware or communication, layer 3 is implemented in JavaScript to work in a browser. This browser can be a typical browser on a desktop computer or a webview integrated in a mobile App. Due to the usage of the extended iTrack library, layer 3 is able to automatically choose the data source through its fallback mechanism. If neither the websocket, nor the injection communication is available, layer 3 can simulate incoming data by using the mouse or touch coordinates as gaze data for testing purposes.

Like JavaScript emits mouseIn or mouseOut events when the cursor enters or leaves an object in the browser, the iTrack library emits gaze events like gazeIn or gazeOut. These events can be handled by conventional event handlers in JavaScript, providing a gaze-tracking API that is usable in different contexts.

Since the iTrack library requires previously calibrated and mapped gaze data (as provided when using a calibrated eye tracker), we extended the library to be able to handle raw gaze data.

The incoming gaze messages contain two-dimensional coordinates of a gaze point. Depending on the hardware and its drivers, this data might be normalized within distinct limits (e.g. [-1;1]), having its origin defined by the optical axis of the camera (Figure 2), but it is not implicitly the case. Therefore the calibration procedure has to be able to handle different scales and offsets of the raw data. Next we will describe our calibration procedure for mapping the (raw) gaze data to screen coordinates.

1) *Calibration*

Mapping the gaze data to screen coordinates can be done in different ways. Hardware suppliers like SMI provide their own software to calibrate and map the raw data, depending on particular hardware.

To be independent from proprietary software and to meet the requirements of different display sizes, pixel densities and camera positions, we developed a semi-automatic calibration procedure which runs in a webbrowser or webview. In the following, we give an overview of our calibration procedure.

While calibrating, the user is asked to gaze at reference points shown on the display, see **Figure 3**. These points are successively shown for a short while to collect the user's gaze data. The recording of gaze-data is shortly interrupted after the reference position moved to avoid wrong measurements due to the latency of the user's focus.

The resulting gaze data is usually noisy and contains some outliers. A simple solution to identify outliers is to look at the distances between each acquired point and the centroid of all points.

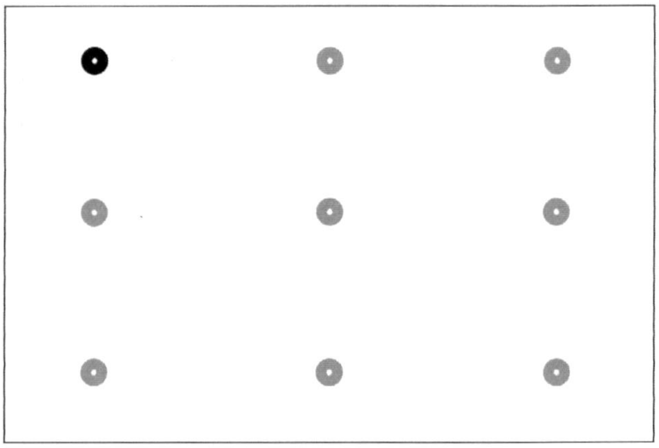

Figure 3. Screenshot of our calibration screen. We subsequently display a target point (grey targets are in fact currently invisible).

Those distances are compared to the mean of all distances among points. Points with a large relative distance are rejected from the further processing. The known screen coordinates of the reference points and the collected raw gaze data are used to approximate the transformation parameters for both horizontal and vertical direction. This is a straightforward fitting problem, called linear regression, which can be solved by a least-squares technique [27].

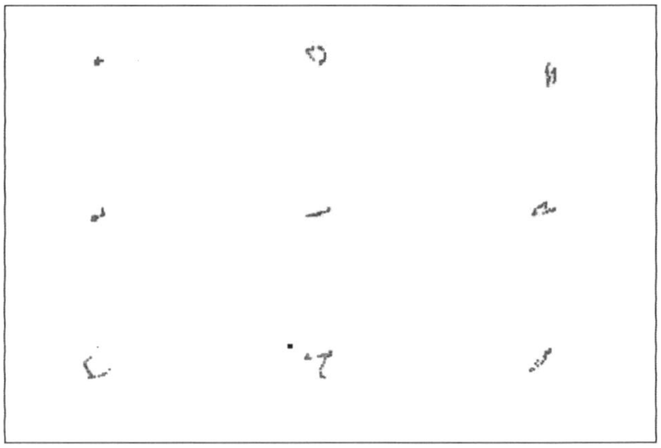

Figure 4. Acquired (noisy) data points, which build the basis to fit the mapping functions.

Since the accuracy of the calibration is influenced by conditions of attendance, such as head movement or correct gazing, a stability index is computed to check the quality of the calibration. If the index falls below a certain threshold, the user is informed about the problem and the calibration process will automatically restart.

Our described approach is quite simple and could be replaced by a more advanced technique. For example, a support vector machine (an advanced learning algorithm for classification and regression analysis) could be used to learn a mapping function from the data. During the development process we tested a so called epsilon-SVR to fit a mapping function. The epsilon-SVR has the advantage that it is more robust against outliers and therefore does not need a pre-filtering step. For our testing purpose, we used the Java implementation of libsvm [5] on the tablet. The improvements were relatively low in comparison to the loss of performance. Therefore, we kept our first approach.

2) Mapping and Filtering

The x- and y-components of the raw gaze points are mapped according to two independent, linear functions. The parameterization is provided by the previously described calibration procedure.

The signal of a gaze tracker can be relatively unstable, because it includes a certain amount of noise and also measures micro saccades of the eye. Especially, when we use the data as a pointing device, we want to smooth those small changes, as they are very disturbing for the user. Conventional smoothing algorithms, like moving averages (a series of averages of different data subsets), are unsuitable for this task, since those introduce large delays subsequent to a saccade. For this reason, we have to treat fixations and saccades separately. Furthermore, we have to ensure robustness regarding outliers. Špakov [14] compared several eye movement filters for the usage in HCI applications. The comparison was based on the introduced delay, smoothness and closeness to the idealized data. The outcome of this study was that algorithms with state detection ("fixation" and "saccade") and adapted processing generally performed better than others. The type of smoothing we use during a fixation is less important and can be quite simple. Kumar presented an algorithm [12], which uses a one-sided triangular filter to smooth the data points during fixations. For each new data point, we determine whether it is the start of a saccade, a continuation of the current fixation or a single outlier during a fixation. For further readings and instructions, we refer to the existing works [12] [13].

In addition to the smoothing effect, the algorithm indirectly generates information about the start and end of fixations. This side product can be used to generate high level gaze events as proposed by Wassermann et al. [20].

In addition, one could consider more specialized filtering solutions. For example, the stability could be enhanced for gaze pointing tasks, such as activating a button on a website, by including knowledge about the position of such gaze sensitive areas in the algorithms. Reasonable results were obtained by a "speed reduction" algorithm such as described by Xinyong, Xiangshi and Hongbin [21]. This method reduces the risk that the cursor temporarily leaves the target area due to eye jitter or noise. Especially dwell time selection benefits from this behaviour. Since our solution should be as universal as possible, we did not directly include the algorithm in our framework.

IV. Known Issues

Gaze tracking is complex, especially on mobile devices without purpose-built hardware. A reasonable use in applications demands in general high reliability and robustness. There are additional requirements depending on the purpose. Real time applications require a high-frequent data supply and applications such as gaze pointing require high precision.

A. Performance

Since the framework is based on JavaScript, its performance depends on the JavaScript performance of the device. As things are now, the performance of the Android webview [3] we used on the Kindle Fire tablet is limited: our measurements have shown, that the webview is able to process around four frames per second, irrespective of the application which uses the gaze data.

B. Latency

The latency between a user's gaze and the mapped result plays an important role. When using gaze tracking as a real-time application, the latency must be as low as possible. We developed our gaze tracking framework and the communication layer with low-latency in mind: single gaze messages can be dropped if the frontend is not able to process those. Since the performance of the webview is limited, the latency can grow up to about 250 ms, which makes real-time applications unusable.

Latency is also caused by smoothing algorithms, especially when large time windows are used. Therefore filtering algorithms should be parameterized, such that a reasonable balance between latency and smoothing is given. In addition, it is important that algorithms treat saccades and fixations differently. It is evident that fixations require stability, whereas a saccade demands an immediate response.

C. Accuracy

The accuracy of a gaze tracking solution means that the distance between the user's actual gaze point and the calculated gaze point on the screen should be as small as possible. It is influenced by many factors, which can be classified into algorithmically minimizable influences, unavoidable hardware influences and outside influences.

Lens-distortions for example can be minimized by algorithms, whereas the display size or the monocular camera position cannot be manipulated. Outside influences, like the user's position, his distance to the screen and movement or influences like light conditions, can be optimized but not avoided.

The degree of influence of these factors vary, depending on the eye tracking hard- and software.

V. Testing with Users

As described before, one of the most important parts of a gaze tracking solution is its accuracy. Within this project, we developed a gaze tracking software for a mobile device, extended the iTrack library and built an in-browser calibration algorithm. We developed an appropriate browser-based calibration checker software to be able to give a general statement about the accuracy of this solution.

Due to the fact that the framework works on both, desktop computers and mobile devices, we are now able to compare (a) the desktop solution with a hardware-based eye tracker, (b) the hardware-based eye tracker combined with the in-browser calibration, (c) the mobile solution with the software-based eye tracker and a calibration process written in native Android code and (d) the software-based eye tracker combined with the in-browser calibration.

TABLE 1. OVERVIEW OF OUR DIFFERENT TEST-SETTINGS

calibration	Desktop	Mobile
native	a	c
in-browser	b	d

We invited people to an appropriate user test to find out if the results are comparable and probably determine a factor to compare the accuracy of those solutions. We tested the four different calibration methods with 45 subjects. Most of them had never used an eye tracker before, neither a stationary one nor a mobile one.

A. *Testing a calibration*

It is at first required to calibrate the gaze tracking software to test a calibration. The calibration shows reference points on the display and meanwhile collects gaze data of the subject to determine the mapping function from raw data to gaze points. The calibration checker acts in a similar way, after collecting data it saves the reference points' coordinates with the actual gaze points' coordinates in a plain text format. Subsequent to the user test, we aggregated and evaluated the collected data.

B. *Test conditions*

Both, the stationary eye tracker and the mobile device, were placed on a table to avoid influences of movement of the hardware. The subjects sat on chairs and were told to move as little as possible. We tested in a low-distraction environment and under constant conditions concerning lighting to reduce ambient impacts on the results.

C. *Test procedure*

Every subject was asked to test both, the stationary gaze tracker as well as the mobile solution. Both devices support a native calibration and our in-browser calibration, so every subject had to calibrate and evaluate four times. We shuffled the order of calibration processes randomly between subjects to avoid systematic errors.

In every situation, the calibration procedure was started first. Afterwards, the calibration checker was started to collect data for the evaluation of the calibration.

SMI provides a proprietary calibration method built into the software shipped with the hardware. Since SMI does not disclose its calibration algorithms, we cannot provide any information on them.

When calibrating the SMI device, the software creates a plain text configuration file. This file contains calibration parameters in the form of (a) screen points from the calibration, (b) numeric RAWLEFT and RAWRIGHT values and (c) numeric COEFFLEFT and COEFFRIGHT values and is used by the SMI software to map the raw data to screen coordinates. The iTrackServer then sends the resulting data of the software to a websocket, which makes it impossible to use the SMI eye tracker raw data in an uncalibrated state. Since the in-browser calibration needs to be tested with an uncalibrated gaze tracker, we overwrote the values of (b) and (c) in the mentioned file with random numbers. The resulting calibration file was then loaded into the SMI calibration software to simulate an uncalibrated state.

D. *Evaluation*

The collected data consists of plain-text files containing the two-dimensional coordinates of the reference points and the actual gaze coordinates for each of the calibration methods. The absolute distance between the reference point and the actual gaze point describes the mean absolute error (MAE).

TABLE 2. STATISTICAL DATA OF THE EVALUATION

	Desktop		Kindle	
	Browser	Native	Browser	Native
MAE [px]	89.6	80.0	176.9	163.7
Std deviation [px]	15.7	14.9	27.2	25.0
Sample size	20,812	20,330	19,260	18,780
Outlier count	271	977	1,023	834
Outlier-ratio [%]	1.30	4.81	5.31	4.44

The aggregated data contains between 1.30 % and 5.31 % outliers, which are points with distances greater than the threshold of 500 pixels (marked grey in TABLE 3 below). This threshold is about half the display size of the mobile device, so we decided to reject those outliers from further processing. These outliers can occur (a) through distraction of the subject, followed by a gaze point outside of the calibrated area or even outside of the monitor, (b) by saccades of the eyes of the subject, which are not measureable or (c) due to measuring inaccuracy of the gaze tracking hard- or software (also due to external influences like reflections).

TABLE 3. NUMBER OF GAZE POINTS WITH A DISTANCE TO THE REFERENCE GREATER THAN GIVEN ERROR

	Desktop		Kindle	
Error [px]	Browser	Native	Browser	Native
> 0	9,196	8,712	8,160	8,160
> 1	9,196	8,711	8,160	8,160
> 10	9,195	8,532	8,096	8,136
> 100	5,749	1,852	5,351	5,610
> 500	170	401	414	475
> 1,000	63	231	155	82
> 10,000	3	205	0	0
> 100,000	3	205	0	0

Excluding those outliers, the mean distances between the reference points and the gaze points vary from about 80 pixels (desktop) up to about 180 pixels (mobile device). In Figure 5, these mean absolute errors are shown with the standard deviation (SD). Compared to the desktop eye tracking solution, the mean distance between the reference and the actual gaze point of the mobile solution is more than twice as high which gives hints to a greater inaccuracy of the webcam based gaze detection quality.

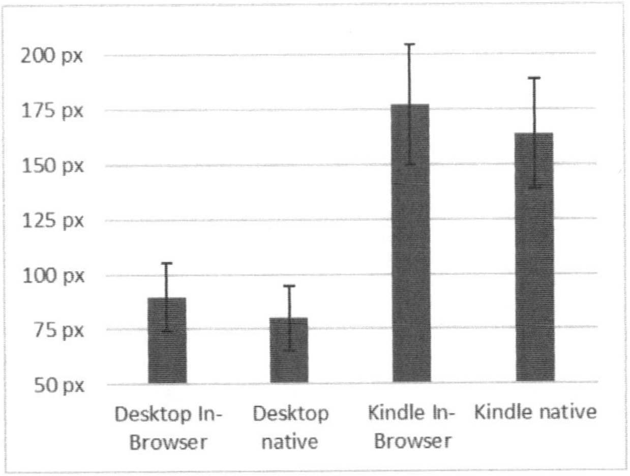

Figure 5. Mean absolute error (MAE) between the reference points and the gaze points in pixels with standard deviations

Figure 6 shows the calibration result from one of the test persons with the SMI eye tracker using the in-browser calibration. Crosses illustrates the reference points shown on the screen, the point near each of the crosses is the collected gaze data. Figure 7 shows the data from the same subject using the mobile gaze tracker with the in-browser calibration as well. Again, the cross illustrate the reference points, whereas the collected gaze data is shown as squares (upper reference), triangles (right), lines (lower) and circles (left).

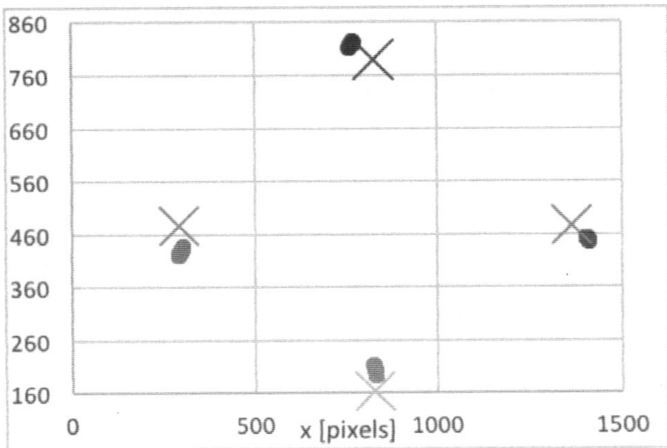

Figure 6. Calibration checker result from the SMI eye tracker, the cross show the target, the points show the actual values

As can be seen in the graph, the accuracy of the mobile gaze tracker using the same algorithm as the desktop is comparatively poor. About 26 % of the collected gaze points show an error less than 100 pixels, which is approximately one third of the amount of the desktop's native eye tracker (In-Browser calibration: 64 %, native calibration: 74 %).

The desktop eye tracker is a solution for professional use, providing binocular optics with purpose-built infrared illumination and proprietary software. In contrast, the mobile solution is built from a consumer tablet with a single front camera. Keeping these facts in mind, the mobile solution is in fact not as accurate as the desktop solution, but quite usable to get an estimate of the gaze point of the user. In the next section, we introduce possible applications for eye tracking.

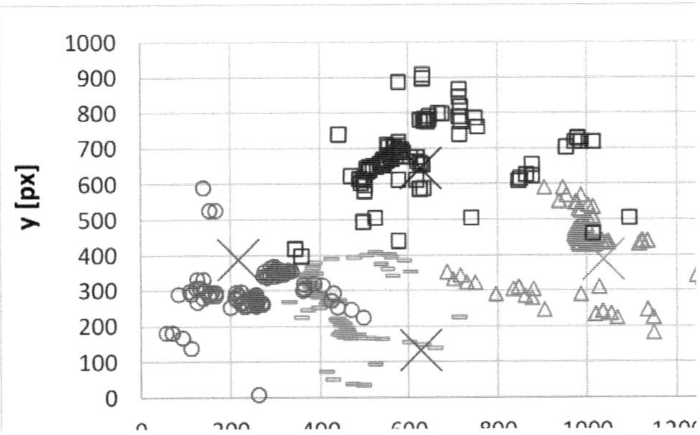

Figure 7. Calibration checker result from the Kindle tablet, the cross show the target, the other signs show the actual values

VI. POSSIBLE APPLICATIONS

Eye tracking does not necessarily require high precision gaze tracking hardware. Depending on the context of use, it might be sufficient to be able to distinguish a few screen points.

A. *E-Learning*

In the area of E-Learning, gaze tracking provides new possibilities for both, the learners and lecturers. For instance, the individual learning process could be supported by automatic adaption of content or interfaces. By deriving information about the emotional and cognitive state of a user, we can adapt the learning environment and content to their specific needs. For example, the system can provide additional information (e.g. a "Bubble Help") if it discovers that the user has problems in understanding the content. It is also possible to classify different types of learners (e.g. "visualizer", "verbalizer", "intermediate") in order to be able to present the knowledge in the most suitable form. Furthermore the accessibility can be extended by supplying an additional input device.

The lecturer can also take advantage by better understanding how people learn. He can evaluate peoples' eye movement with heat maps, determining which parts of the learning matter seem to be the most interesting parts for a particular learner.

B. *Accessibility*

Moreover, gaze tracking is an interesting field of research for accessibility. Providing hardware-independent gaze tracking can optimize functionalities on websites or in software. People with disabilities can take advantage of this technology, even if they do not own purpose-built gaze trackers.

Providing different ways to navigate through web contents improves the accessibility of a website. However, it is not standardized how to connect miscellaneous gaze trackers with web applications, which can be done using our gaze tracking framework.

C. Games

Games, especially browser-based games, can take advantage from this technology to provide a new user experience and enable attention-awareness. Using eye tracking as an input device, it is possible to replace the mouse or keyboard input with gaze data, e.g. for moving around in a virtual world.

Furthermore, gaze-supporting games can respond to the user's gaze with changing graphics, e.g. supply additional information for the gameplay when looking in one of the screen corners. An interdisciplinary field of use are serious games and e-learning games.

VII. Conclusion and Outlook

In this work we have presented a concept of providing gaze data to web applications in a generic way. The concrete implementation of the calibration functionality is kept intentionally very simple and could be substituted by more advanced algorithms. It is also thinkable, that other gaze trackers afford higher polynomial mapping functions to achieve accurate results.

User tests proved the capability of our approach for two possible systems. We looked at two extremities, a desktop computer in combination with a purpose-built eye tracker and a low-cost solution on an unmodified tablet without any external hardware.

As expected, the accuracy is highly dependent on the quality of the supplied raw data. Inaccuracies actually limit the practical use in applications. Primarily real-time usage, such as forms of user interactions, are very critical and demand high accuracy and low latency.

For the purpose of antagonizing this issue, one could deploy alternative user-interaction techniques. In some case it may be feasible to use eye or head gestures. Gestures do not require absolute precision and are therefore more robust with regard to noise and calibration inaccuracies. In spite of those advantages, gestures are not always suitable and cannot fully substitute a gaze pointer. On the other hand, we expect that the accuracy, especially of low-cost solutions, will be improved dramatically in the near future.

With this work, we made a contribution for the AAMS project towards innovative, auto-adaptive E-Learning environments of tomorrow. The very next steps will include the integration of our framework into the E-Learning system developed and used in the project AAMS called Adaptive Learning Module (ALM) and the implementation of several gaze tracking-based functionalities.

Acknowledgments

This research has been conducted within the ScienceCampus Tübingen "Informational Environments", an interdisciplinary research collaboration of the Knowledge Media Research Center and the University of Tübingen, with funding from the German state of Baden-Württemberg, Ministry of Science, Research and the Arts. This publication reflects only the authors' views and the funding agency is not liable for any use that may be made of the information contained herein.

We thank all students, who voluntarily participated in our user studies.

References

[1] Qualcomm Technologies Inc. *Snapdragon SDK for Android.* [Online] Available from: https://developer.qualcomm.com/software/snapdragon-sdk-android.

[2] F. Alt, A. Shirazi, A. Schmidt, and J. Mennenöh. "Increasing the user's attention on the web". In *the 7th Nordic Conference*, 544. DOI=10.1145/2399016.2399099.

[3] Android. *WebView.* [Online] Available from: http://developer.android.com/reference/android/webkit/WebView.html.

[4] R. Biedert, G. Buscher, S. Schwarz, M. Möller, A. Dengel, and T. Lottermann. "The text 2.0 framework". In: *the 2010 workshop*, 114–117. DOI=10.1145/2002333.2002351.

[5] C.-C. Chang and C.-J. Lin. 2011. "LIBSVM: A library for support vector machines." In: *ACM Transactions on Intelligent Systems and Technology* 2, 3, 27:1-27:27.

[6] L. Copeland and T. Gedeon. "The effect of subject familiarity on comprehension and eye movements during reading". In: *the 25th Australian Computer-Human Interaction Conference*, 285–288. DOI=10.1145/2541016.2541082.

[7] H. Drewes, R. Atterer, and A. Schmidt. 2007. "Detailed Monitoring of User's Gaze and Interaction to Improve Future e-Learning". In: *Proceedings of the 4th International Conference on Universal Access in Human-computer Interaction: Ambient Interaction.* UAHCI'07. Springer-Verlag, Berlin, Heidelberg, 802–811.

[8] H. Drewes, A. de Luca, and A. Schmidt. "Eye-gaze interaction for mobile phones". In: *the 4th international conference on mobile technology, applications, and systems and the 1st international symposium*, 364. DOI=10.1145/1378063.1378122.

[9] M. L. Dybdal, J. S. Agustin, and J. P. Hansen. "Gaze input for mobile devices by dwell and gestures". In: *the Symposium*, 225. DOI=10.1145/2168556.2168601.

[10] A. Hyrskykari, P. Majaranta, A. Aaltonen, and K.-J. Räihä. "Design issues of iDICT". In: *the symposium*, 9–14. DOI=10.1145/355017.355019.

[11] R. J. K. Jacob. "What you look at is what you get: eye movement-based interaction techniques". In: *the SIGCHI conference*, 11–18. DOI=10.1145/97243.97246.

[12] M. Kumar. 2007. "GUIDe Saccade detection and smoothing algorithm". February 2007.

[13] M. Kumar, J. Klingner, R. Puranik, T. Winograd, and A. Paepcke. 2008. "Improving the Accuracy of Gaze Input for Interaction". In: *Proceedings of the 2008 Symposium on Eye Tracking Research & Applica tions.*

[14] O. Špakov. 2012. "Comparison of eye movement filters used in HCI". In: *Proceedings of ETRA'12 Symposium on Eye Tracking Research & Applications.*

[15] M. Porta. "Implementing eye-based user-aware e-learning". In: *Proceeding of the twenty-sixth annual CHI conference extended abstracts*, 3087. DOI=10.1145/1358628.1358812.

[16] D. Rozado, A. El Shoghri, and R. Jurdak. 2015. "Gaze dependant prefetching of web content to increase speed and

comfort of web browsing". In: *International Journal of Human-Computer Studies* 78, 31–42.

[17] S. Stellmach and R. Dachselt. "Investigating gaze-supported multimodal pan and zoom". In: *the Symposium*, 357. DOI=10.1145/2168556.2168636.

[18] V. Cantoni, C. J. Perez, M. Porta, and S. Ricotti. 2012. "Exploiting eye tracking in advanced e-learning systems". In: *Proceedings of the 13th International Conference on Computer Systems and Technologies*.

[19] C. Ware and H. H. Mikaelian. 1987. "An evaluation of an eye tracker as a device for computer input". *SIGCHI Bull.* 18, 4, 183–188.

[20] B. Wassermann, A. Hardt, and G. Zimmermann. 2012. "Generic Gaze Interaction Events for Web Browsers: Using the Eye Tracker as Input Device". In: *WWW2012 Workshop: Emerging Web Technologies, Facing the Future of Education*, 6.

[21] X. Zhang, X. Ren, and H. Zha. 2008. "Improving Eye Cursor's Stability for Eye Pointing Tasks". In: *Proceedings of the SIGCHI Conference on Human Factors in Computing Systems*. CHI '08. ACM, New York, NY, USA, 525–534. DOI=10.1145/1357054.1357139.

[22] ScienceCampus Tübingen. [Online] Available from: https://www.wissenschaftscampus-tuebingen.de/www/en/index.html?ref=folder5.

[23] K. Scheiter. *Knowledge Media Research Center Tübingen*. [Online] Available from: https://www.iwm-tuebingen.de/-www/en/mitarbeiter/ma.html?uid=kscheiter.

[24] R. Plötzner. *University of Education Freiburg*. [Online] Available from: https://www.ph-freiburg.de/imb/institut/institutsleitung.html.

[25] A. Renkl. *University of Freiburg*. [Online] Available from: https://www.psychologie.uni-freiburg.de/Members/renkl.

[26] G. Zimmermann. *Stuttgart Media University*. [Online] Available from: https://www.hdm-stuttgart.de/Forschuung_transfer/forschungsschwerpunkte/responsive_media_experience/team/zimmermann.

[27] E. Weisstein. 2016. [Online] Available from: http://mathworld.wolfram.com/LeastSquaresFitting.html

CalliSmart: an Adaptive Informed Environment for Intelligent Calligraphy Training

Rémy Frenoy*, Indira Thouvenin*, Yann Soullard*, Olivier Gapenne†
*Sorbonne University, Université de technologie de Compiègne, CNRS UMR 7253 Heudiasyc
CS 60 319 - 60 203 Compiègne cedex
†Sorbonne University, Université de technologie de Compiègne, CNRS UMR 7338 Biomechanics and Bioengineering
CS 60 319 - 60 203 Compiègne cedex
Emails: {remy.frenoy — indira.thouvenin — yann.soullard — olivier.gapenne}@utc.fr

Abstract—**Gesture learning is a complex and multistep process where trainees are supposed to improve several psychomotor and cognitive skills. According to numerous studies, trainees need to be provided with various types of feedback to improve these skills. These studies also highlight that benefits of a given type of feedback depend on trainees situation. Therefore, feedback must be chosen according to an analysis of trainees activity. Sensorimotor approaches have investigated the impact of feedback on specific learning situations, but the analysis of gestural activity, which would allow the automatic selection of an appropriate type of feedback, is still a recurring issue. In this paper, we propose a new model for gestural training systems based on smart interaction. This model relies on a recognition module based on Naive Bayes classifiers, representing trainees activity by a vector describing their errors, and representing training environments by vectors describing their set of implemented types of feedback. We present a platform for calligraphy training we designed and developed based on our model. Through a user study, we emphasize the benefits of our approach on trainees development.**

Keywords–Training Systems, Interactive systems, Adaptive Systems, Gesture Recognition.

I. INTRODUCTION

Gestural training systems have been studied in various research fields, which can be divided into two families: sensorimotor approaches and modeling approaches. Sensorimotor approaches focus on the impact of providing a specific type of feedback on trainees activity. Virtual training environments belong to these approaches, and enhance training by providing real-time 3D feedback. Such systems have been used for different kinds of gestures, such as welding gestures [1], obstetric gestures [2], or pottery gestures [3]. Haptic systems are also part of sensorimotor approaches, as they investigate trainees kinesthetic memory [4] by adding proprioceptive cues during visuo-motor learning tasks [5]. These systems have proven to benefit motor skill training, including within the context of handwriting [6]. Although these fields focus on the impact of providing a specific type of feedback in a given context, they do not question the issue of modeling gestural activity, nor the issue of adapting feedback according to this model. Yet results have shown the benefits of providing diversified [7] and personalized [8] feedback on the learning experience.

Intelligent tutoring systems are part of modeling approaches. A key feature of these systems is the adaptation of learning content and difficulty level to the trainee. This adaptation requires an accurate student model [9] which allows for individualization [10]. These systems process interpretable data (results from a form, answer to a multiple-choice question). Such systems do not capture motor skills, which necessitates the use of sensors and results in huge amount of data which need to be processed to become interpretable. Furthermore, although intelligent tutoring systems model students knowledge, very few studies have tackled the issue of modeling gestural activity.

Calligraphy training is an interesting case study. When trainees learn calligraphy with a human teacher, the teacher analyzes trainees gestural and cognitive activity. The teacher also analyzes trainees drawing to identify patterns of error. From this analysis, the teacher can provide various guidance by giving verbal advice and focusing trainees attention on specific characteristics, or demonstrating the gestures. With such training, trainees build a knowledge based on their experience and the kinesthetic memory of the gestures, leading them to the acquisition of control and regularity, which are essential skills to produce calligraphy. We believe that being able to model users activity from sensor data, so that systems adapt according to this model, would enhance trainees gestural learning experience. Therefore, our goal is to model and link highly variable sensor data representing trainees performances over training time, and training environments containing their set of implemented types of feedback.

This paper proposes CalliSmart, an intelligent interactive system with gestural input, relying on a framework which makes it possible to place trainees in a representation space, from which it is possible to analyze the evolution of their performances. By placing feedback types in this representation space depending on their relevance in a given situation, the system provides appropriate types of feedback to trainees according to their activity. The paper is structured as follows: the next section present an overview of related studies. Section III introduces our interaction model. Experiments are presented in Section IV, and results are exhibited in Section V. Finally, we discuss these results and introduce future works in Section VI.

II. RELATED WORK

This section introduces several studies investigating the process of gesture learning, and the impact of feedback on this process. As these studies advocate to provide a diversity of feedback, research works on learning modeling and gesture recognition are then presented.

A. Gesture learning

Trainees learn gestures through different steps, each step involving cognitive, psychomotor or biophysical skills [4], [11]. In each of these steps, trainees build very specific gestural and kinesthetic abilities, and focus on very different parts of their activity (Figure 1).

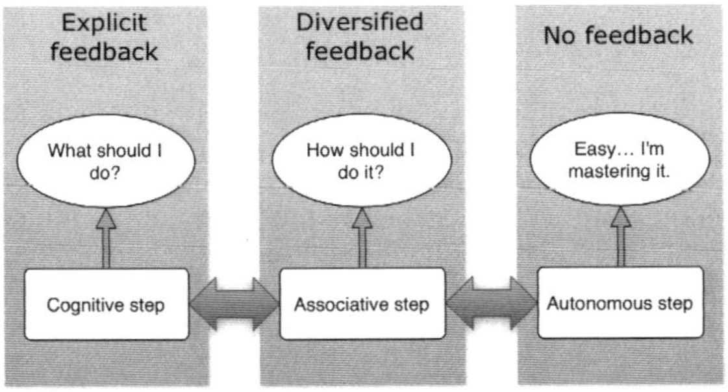

Figure 1. The three steps of motor skill learning, inspired from [11].

Although some questions still have to be answered, most learning strategies advocate to give very simple and precise information to trainees in the cognitive step, trainees in this early stage of learning being very prone to suffer from cognitive overload. In the associative step, trainees need very specific feedback to understand their errors and correct them. They can also benefit from knowledge of performance feedback (KP feedback). Finally, in the autonomous step, trainees barely need feedback, but can benefit from knowledge of results feedback (KR feedback). Hence, it is the variety of (appropriate) types of feedback which helps trainees during their learning process by enhancing their perception of their performance. This variety is also essential to avoid the syndrome of *dependence to the teacher* [12], where trainees improve their performances on a training system but are unable to transfer these improvements in a real environment.

B. Intelligent tutoring systems

Providing a variety of feedback types is a concern tackled by Intelligent tutoring systems (ITS). ITS aim at modeling the students activity by collecting knowledge about them. Knowledge represented in these models can include students skills, affect, experience, or stereotypes [13]. From these models, ITS can analyze how trainees develop over time, and use this knowledge to determine the most efficient training situation. To build and update these models, ITS use cognitive techniques (model-tracing, constraint-based), or artificial intelligence techniques (formal logic, expert-systems, planning, Bayesian belief networks). From a student representation, ITS can provide various types of feedback by following a learning strategy. The main learning strategies either follow the *behaviorist* approach, which considers learning as a set of modifications directly correlated with trainees actions within the learning environment; the *cognitive* approach, which claims that unobservable and internal constructs (perception, motivation) influence the learning process; or the *constructivist* approach, which holds that individuals construct the world in their own way, implicating that training should be focused on the student activity more than on training monolithic strategies.

ITS acquire interpretable data: a score from a test, an answer to a multiple choice quiz. Thus, ITS cannot deal with sensor data, as they are not explicit enough to be used directly. Modeling gestural activity in the same fashion ITS model students knowledge necessitates a recognition process to make gestural data acquired from sensors interpretable.

C. Recognition

Research in gesture recognition has been growing to look for the best way to make sense of sensor data. The most popular approaches [14] either rely on matching-based strategies (Dynamic Time Warping, k-Nearest Neighbors), which compute a distance between the data to label and labeled data from a training database; or on learning models (Markovian models, Support Vector Machines, Naive Bayes Classifiers), which are optimized to model or discriminate training examples from different classes. Such methods have numerous applications, from intelligent training [15], to gestural training [3], or human-robot collaboration on assembly lines [16]. A recurrent issue when dealing with the recognition of gestural or cognitive activity is the issue of multilabeling, when a data sample can be labeled not only with one label, but possibly with a set of labels [17]. The existing methods for multilabel classification can be divided into two main categories: the *problem transformation* methods, which transform a multilabel classification problem into one or more single-label classification problem, and the *algorithm adaptation* methods, which extend specific learning algorithms to directly handle multilabel data [18]. Within the context of gestural training, multilabel recognition makes it possible to detect several patterns of error at once, and hence to consider every aspects of trainees performance when determining which types of feedback to provide.

D. Feedback

Numerous research projects have investigated the impact of feedback which should, no matter whether it is delivered by a teacher or a computer, "enhance learning, performance, or both, engendering the formation of accurate, targeted conceptualizations and skills" [19]. With the possibilities brought by the emergence of tablets and haptic devices, feedback has been studied through its sensory modalities (visual, audio, visuo-haptic), certain modalities being more appropriate than others depending on the context [20]. Temporal features (static or dynamic feedback, temporal information) are also determinant, studies showing that changing feedback temporal features make trainees develop different components of their gestures [21]. If some configurations have proven to be more or less effective than others depending on the training situation, it appears that each configuration has its advantages and drawbacks, depending upon the learning situation and trainees abilities [19], [22].

III. Interaction Modeling

Providing a variety of appropriate feedback types throughout the learning enhance trainees learning [22]. A fundamental issue when creating a gesture training system is therefore to decide which type of feedback to provide in order to maximize the benefits for trainees learning. This issue can be split into four issues: 1) The recognition and modeling of gestural and cognitive activity. 2) The definition of a set of feedback types the system can provide. 3)The selection of the type of feedback to provide depending upon the situation. 4) The evaluation of trainees learning throughout the training process.

To tackle these issues, the activity first have to be captured. Then, the acquired data must be recognized and a representation model of trainees learning state must be built. Finally, various types of feedback have to be designed and implemented. Depending on the modeled learning state, a subset of feedback types is selected. This subset must be well-chosen (appropriate according to trainees learning state) to make them improve their skills (Figure 2).

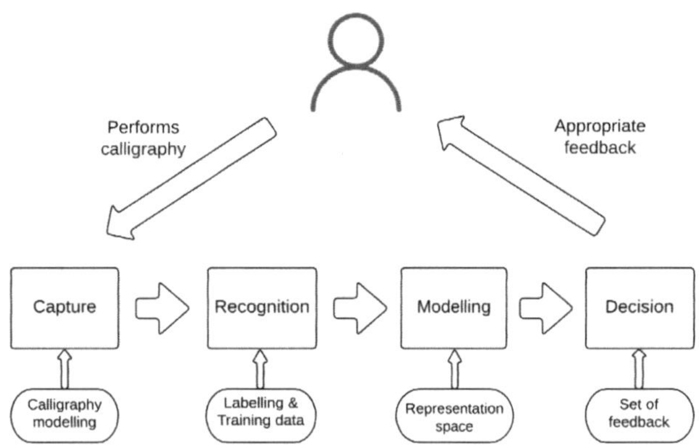

Figure 2. The CalliSmart process for smart Human-Computer gestural interaction, within the context of calligraphy training.

A. Capturing calligraphy features

Van Galen [23] defines handwriting as a "multi-component task implying cognitive, psycho-motor and biophysical processes". Handwriting is a motor gesture, where performers constantly analyze and modify their movements from their perception of their current actions, and their internal representation of the "ideal" actions. Furthermore, writers not only react to their actions, but also have a spatial and temporal representation of the shape they intend to draw. These representations imply a principle of anticipation, which means that performers have, besides modifying in real-time their movements according to their perception, to anticipate their future movements. Thus, learning handwriting necessitates having a cognitive representation of the shape to draw, and a perception of the different steps necessary in order to construct this shape (acceleration, angle, curve). It is also essential to spatially visualize the location of the current drawn shape, by comparison with locations of the previous shapes and the next ones which will be drawn (principle of anticipation, Figure 3).

In calligraphy, the goal is to analyze trainees performances according to two main criteria, which are the regularity and the visuo-spatial attention. Relying on these criteria, we propose to analyze trainees activity from identified types of errors. For each of them, we compute the probability of having the type of error given the trainee's performance. Trainees performance can be modeled by the vector $\vec{U} = \{x_1, x_2, x_3, , x_n\}$ where n is the number of patterns, and x_i corresponds to the probability of having the pattern i. Each pattern being a pattern of error, $\vec{U} = \vec{0}$ refers to an expert, and $\vec{U} = \{1, 1, 1, , 1\}$ refers to an absolute novice.

B. Interaction modeling

Three phases of interaction can be distinguished from the process illustrated in Figure 2:

- The trainee performing on the system. (A)
- The system providing feedback to the trainee. (B)
- The trainee making changes/adjustments throughout the process of interaction. (C)

We propose a space of representation S which aims at representing these processes. First, (A) is modeled by the vector $\vec{U}$ as previously explained. Each type of feedback implemented in the system is represented in S by a vector $\vec{F} = \{y_1, y_2, y_3, , y_n\}$, where n is the number of error criteria and y_i is the level of the ith error criteria for which feedback type F is the most relevant. Hence, F is considered optimal in the situation $\vec{U} = \vec{F}$ (B). Each coordinate of $\vec{F}$ is empirical and come from an expertise: the expert studies each type of feedback and decide in which situation it should be provided. Changes in trainees activity (C) can be tracked through transition vectors $\vec{Tr}_i = \vec{U}_i - \vec{U}_{i-j}, 1 \leq j \leq i \leq n$, n being the number of recorded performances for the studied trainee.

C. Decision

In our approach, $\vec{U}$ represents the performance of a trainee, and each vector $\vec{F_i}$ represents an element in the set F of implemented feedback types. According to the representation, the most appropriate feedback type is the one represented by the closest vector to the current position of the user. Let $\vec{F_a}$ be the most appropriate type of feedback in the situation $\vec{U_t}$,

$$\vec{F_a} = \underset{\vec{F_i} \in \mathcal{F}}{\text{argmin}}(||\vec{U_t} - \vec{F_i}||_p) \quad (1)$$

IV. EXPERIMENTS

By analyzing trainees performances throughout several exercises, it is possible to investigate the influence of providing various types of feedback on the evolution of their performances, and hence on their progression. Experiments should determine whether 1) providing feedback will improve the learning process, and whether 2) providing feedback will reduce the variance between performances by enforcing trainees attention on the task.

Within the process of calligraphy learning, a famous exercise is the "minimum" exercise (Figure 3). It is used to train regularity and visuo-spatial attention by asking trainees to repeat a similar pattern. On a perfectly executed exercise, white spaces between elements should have the same area, and elements should have the same shape in term of slope and size.

Figure 3. The "minimum" exercise in calligraphy.

The experiment focuses on the strait vertical lines of the minimum exercise. Participants are asked to produce a series of straight lines using a Wacom Cintiq tablet (Figure 4), with the same obligations than in the minimum exercise: spaces between lines should be regular, lines should be straight and vertical. Staves are displayed to limit the calligraphy area. This exercise exhibits the main features constituting the cognitive and psycho-motor processes surrounding calligraphy and the drawing of the "minimum" word.

Figure 4. The CalliSmart platform.

A. Recognition

A database was created to train the recognition module. 46 participants were involved in the creation of the database. They had none to very little experience using a graphic table or practicing calligraphy. Each participant was asked to perform a series of three exercises, an exercise being a sequence of 10 to 15 strokes. Experts classified and labeled these exercises by examining both the gestures (participants were video recorded) and the results (screenshots were taken at the end of each exercise). Labels identify three patterns of error: slope error, size error, and regularity errors (irregular spaces between strokes). Several errors potentially appearing on a single exercise, the recognition of an exercise is a multilabel problem. The acquired database contains 138 examples labeled by two experts. Examples are unequally distributed among error classes, as some patterns appeared more often than others. The training database has been built using a subset of the 138 acquired examples, making balanced the number of error patterns. The final training database uses 40 examples per error pattern. Recognition relies on four Naive Bayes classifiers, one per class which are trained on examples from the training database (one-vs.-rest strategy). A 5-fold cross-validation was performed on the dataset. Classifiers used the features described in Table I as a representation of an exercise. Table II shows the recognition results, using classic multilabel evaluation metrics [17]. As stated in [17], the subset accuracy metric tends to drop fast when the number of labels grow, or when the amount of data is small. In our context, finding the exact combination of label is important, but not essential. The most important feature of the recognition process is its ability to recognize correct labels (errors trainees actually made). Improving these results will be one of our challenges in the future. An increase in the amount of training data and the use of a discriminative model may lead to an improvement of the results.

B. User study

1) Participants: A total of 28 people participated in the study. Participants were people working at the university, students in computer science, design and mechanics, with no to very little expertise in calligraphy. They were randomly and evenly distributed into the two experiment conditions described below.

2) Experimental procedure: The first group *(no feedback group)* did not receive any feedback. The second group *(feedback group)* received feedback from the following set of implemented types of feedback: 1) Real-time feedback assists trainees by making them focus on a specific category. "Regularity" feedback displays where trainees should begin their next stroke (Figure 5a); "slope" feedback colors the stroke with a color from green to red depending on the slope (Figure 5b); "size" feedback highlights with a different color the limits of the drawing space (Figure 5c). Trainees can be assisted with every combination of feedback types, depending on the recognition of their activity. 2) Knowledge of results feedback (Figure 6), indicates the level of the trainee in each category ("r", "v", "l"). KR feedback is always displayed.

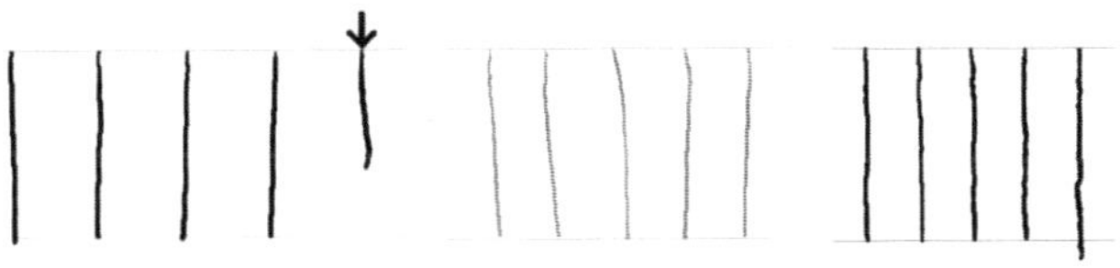

(a) (b) (c)

Figure 5. Real-time feedback aiming at assisting trainees with regularity, size, or slope error.

Figure 6. KR feedback providing trainees with explicit indications regarding their performance.

Feedback was chosen depending on trainees activity during a whole exercise. Hence, feedback depends on the previous exercise and cannot change until the end of the current exercise. Each participant was asked to perform a series of six exercises, an exercise being itself a series of 10 to 15 lines to draw. The first series was not saved and allowed trainees to familiarize with the platform. For the feedback group, the system used this first series to decide which feedback types to provide during the first recorded series. Our hypothesis are:

- **H1** Participants in the feedback group will improve better than participants in the no feedback group.
- **H2** Variance between participants will be lower in the feedback group than in the no feedback group.

At the end of the fifth series, we asked participants to perform a last series. This series was performed without any feedback from the system for the two groups, to compare their performances in the same conditions. This last experiment should test our third hypothesis:

- **H3** Participants in the feedback group will outperform participants in the no feedback group in real conditions.

V. Results

To evaluate participants performances, a dataset of expert performances was created, gathering 22 exercises performed by three different people. The same representation was used in the recognition and in the evaluation processes, participants as well as experts being represented by their feature vectors (Table I). In a similar way of a k-Nearest Neighbors algorithm,

TABLE I. Features computed from trainees activity.

Slope error	Angle of the most sloping stroke, using real stroke coordinates. Angle of the most sloping stroke, using linear regressions of strokes.
Regularity error	$\frac{\max(distance)}{\min(distance)}$, using distances between consecutive strokes. $\frac{\max(area)}{\min(area)}$, using areas between linear regressions of strokes. $\frac{(\max(area)-\min(area))}{\mu(area)}$, using areas between linear regressions of strokes.
Size error	Maximum difference between stroke vertical size and stave size

TABLE II. Validation results of the recognition process on multilabel data.

Recall	Precision	Hamming Loss	Subset Accuracy	Accuracy
0.79	0.83	0.70	0.55	0.72

we evaluate our method by computing the Euclidean distance between a trainee performance and its k-closest expert representations. Such a method reduces potential bias induced by a parametric modeling. In our experiment, the value k is empirically set to three. We carried a Shapiro-Wilk test on the result data, which showed that data were not normally distributed. Therefore, we performed the non-parametric Mann-Whitney test to confirm the efficiency of our method.

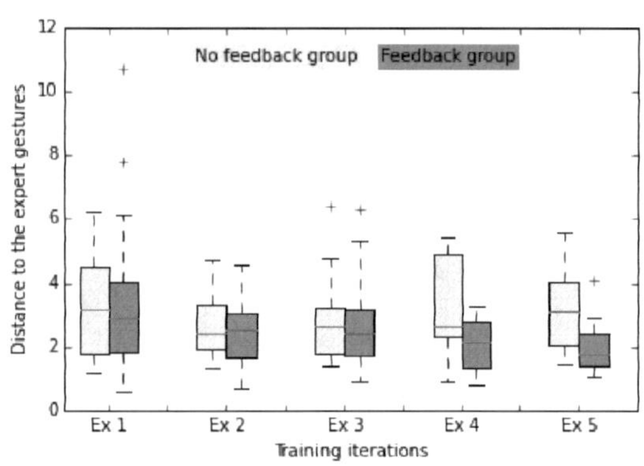

Figure 7. Distance between trainees and expert performances over the training iterations.

Figure 7 illustrates a significant improvement of performances for the feedback group, from a distance of 2.88 at the end of the first exercise, to 1.75 at the end of the fifth exercise, while the no feedback group only slightly improved, from a distance of 3.20 to 3.11. A two-tailed Mann-Whitney test was performed between the two groups for the fifth exercise, which resulted in a p-value of 0.029. We can hence confirm our first hypothesis (**H1**), which is significant at a standard 0.05 threshold. Variance between participants in the feedback group drops over the training, which implies a convergence of trainees performances (Figure 7). Variance between participants in the no feedback group stays high over the exercises. These two observations confirm our second hypothesis (**H2**). Results obtained in the no feedback group can be explained by two factors: incomprehension and weariness. The task proposed in this experiment is repetitive, and participants in the no feedback group did not see any changes in the training environment throughout the exercises. From the fourth exercise, they seem to suffer from a loss of focus as they do not see any improvement or changes that would reflect their performances. Participants often asked how well they were performing, indicating that they were seeking for information reflecting their performances. People in the feedback group could see their improvement through the KR feedback at the end of each exercise. Moreover, a real-time feedback tailored to the errors made in the previous exercise was provided, helping them understand their performance, and improve on the aspects they needed the most. Figure 8 illustrates the results of the last exercise with participants form each groups performing in real conditions, without feedback. We note that participants from the feedback group outperform participants from the no feedback group. Moreover, performances of the participants in the feedback group only decrease from a distance of 1,75 to the expert to a distance of 1,88 between the fifth exercise (with feedback) and the sixth exercise (in real conditions). This result is promising, since the *dependence to the teacher* syndrome tends to make performances drop significantly when trainees trained on aided system first perform in real conditions. However, variance between performances in the feedback group in the sixth exercise grows compared to variance measured in the fifth exercise. This grow in the variance is reflected by the Mann-Whitney test, which results for this last exercise in a p-value of 0.05486. Differences between our two groups on this last exercise is hence significant at a 0.1 threshold, but not at a 0.05 threshold. Further experiments should thus be conducted to fully confirm our third hypothesis (**H3**).

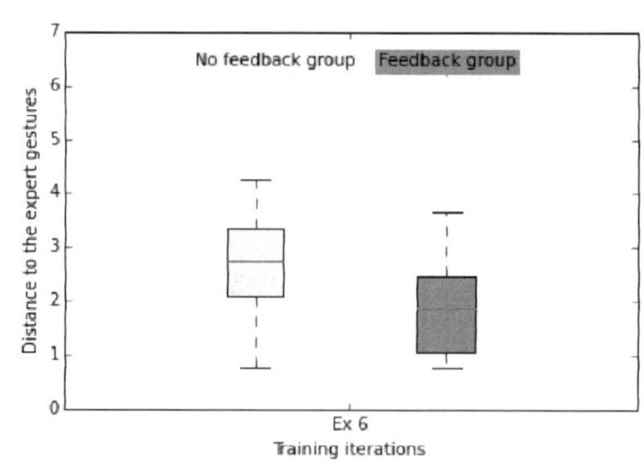

Figure 8. In real conditions (without any feedback), performances of participants trained with, and without feedback.

VI. Discussion and Conclusion

In this paper, we proposed a new model for gestural training systems based on smart interaction. In opposition to intelligent tutoring systems input data, our input data come from sensors and are not directly interpretable. Our system relies on a recognition module based on Naive Bayes classifiers, which aim at recognizing pattern of errors in trainees activity. This module provides probabilistic outputs, one per pattern of errors, that we use to build a representation of trainees activity in n dimensions, n being the number of possible errors. This representation is used to determine the types of feedback to provide to the trainee.

An experiment comparing the progression of two groups, one with feedback and one without feedback, showed that trainees perform better when provided with appropriate feedback, compared with trainees trained by practicing in real conditions. Variance between trainees performances was also reduced when they were provided with feedback. A last experiment, where participants in the feedback group had to perform in real conditions, showed that they still outperform trainees from the no feedback group, and that their performances only slightly drop from training to real conditions. These last results should be confirmed by further experiment, but seemed to highlight the benefits of our system to reduce the effects of dependence to the teacher.

In future works, we will extend our recognition system so that it should be able to detect a larger number of errors, and thus have a more precise recognition of the gestures. More types of feedback should be implemented so that the system can choose the appropriate configuration in a larger number of possible situations. An interesting issue regarding feedback is how well it is adapted to a situation, and to a trainee. In intelligent tutoring systems, the pertinence of a specific feedback type is determined empirically or from study results. One could argue that users have their own sensitivity and comprehension (cognitive and constructivist approaches, see Part II-B), and that systems should be able to reconsider, as experienced human tutors do, what they thought to be an appropriate type of feedback. We will investigate this issue, and examine the possibility of adding another degree of adaptation in our interactive gestural training system. We will also evaluate the impact of this adaptation on trainees learning experience.

Acknowledgment

This work, as part of the Descript project, is supported by the Picardy region. The authors would like to thank Patrick Doan, Morgane Rebulard and all the participants at the ESAD for their work on the creation of our training database, and Florian Baune for his work on the development of the platform.

References

[1] L. Da Dalto, F. Benus, and O. Balet, "The use and benefits of Virtual Reality tools for the welding training," in 63rd Annual Assembly & International Conference of the International Institute of Welding, Istanbul, Turkey, 2010.

[2] R. Moreau, V. Ochoa, M. Pham, P. Boulanger, T. Redarce, and O. Dupuis, "A method to evaluate skill transfer and acquisition of obstetric gestures based on the curvatures analysis of the position and the orientation," Journal of Biomedical Informatics, vol. 41, no. 6, Dec. 2008, pp. 991–1000.

[3] S. Manitsaris, A. Glushkova, F. Bevilacqua, and F. Moutarde, "Capture, modeling, and recognition of expert technical gestures in wheel-throwing art of pottery," Journal on Computing and Cultural Heritage (JOCCH), vol. 7, no. 2, 2014, p. 10.

[4] D. Feygin, M. Keehner, and F. Tendick, "Haptic guidance: Experimental evaluation of a haptic training method for a perceptual motor skill," in Haptic Interfaces for Virtual Environment and Teleoperator Systems, 2002. HAPTICS 2002. Proceedings. 10th Symposium on. IEEE, 2002, pp. 40–47.

[5] J. Bluteau, S. Coquillart, Y. Payan, and E. Gentaz, "Haptic guidance improves the visuo-manual tracking of trajectories," PLoS One, vol. 3, no. 3, 2008, p. e1775.

[6] G. Srimathveeravalli and K. Thenkurussi, "Motor skill training assistance using haptic attributes," in Eurohaptics Conference, 2005 and Symposium on Haptic Interfaces for Virtual Environment and Teleoperator Systems, 2005. World Haptics 2005. First Joint, 2005, pp. 452–457.

[7] S. R. Serge, H. A. Priest, P. J. Durlach, and C. I. Johnson, "The effects of static and adaptive performance feedback in game-based training," Computers in Human Behavior, vol. 29, no. 3, May 2013, pp. 1150–1158.

[8] S. Narciss, S. Sosnovsky, L. Schnaubert, E. Andrès, A. Eichelmann, G. Goguadze, and E. Melis, "Exploring feedback and student characteristics relevant for personalizing feedback strategies," Computers & Education, vol. 71, Feb. 2014, pp. 56–76.

[9] T. Käser, S. Klingler, A. G. Schwing, and M. Gross, "Beyond knowledge tracing: Modeling skill topologies with bayesian networks," in Intelligent Tutoring Systems. Springer, 2014, pp. 188–198.

[10] Y. Wang and N. T. Heffernan, "The Student Skill Model," in Intelligent Tutoring Systems. Springer, 2012, pp. 399–404.

[11] P.M. Fitts and M.I. Posner, Human performance. Belmont, CA: Brooks/Cole, 1967.

[12] B. Bayart, A. Pocheville, and A. Kheddar, "An adaptive haptic guidance software module for i-touch: example through a handwriting teaching simulation and a 3d maze," in Haptic Audio Visual Environments and their Applications, 2005. IEEE International Workshop on, 2005, pp. 6–pp.

[13] B. P. Woolf, Building intelligent interactive tutors student-centered strategies for revolutionizing e-learning. Amsterdam; Boston: Morgan Kaufmann Publishers/Elsevier, 2009.

[14] S. Mitra and T. Acharya, "Gesture Recognition: A Survey," IEEE Transactions on Systems, Man and Cybernetics, Part C (Applications and Reviews), vol. 37, no. 3, May 2007, pp. 311–324.

[15] L. Fricoteaux, I. Thouvenin, and D. Mestre, "GULLIVER: a decision-making system based on user observation for an adaptive training in informed virtual environments," Engineering Applications of Artificial Intelligence, vol. 33, 2014, pp. 47–57.

[16] E. Coupeté, S. Manitsaris, and F. Moutarde, "Real-time recognition of human gestures for collaborative robots on assembly-line," in 3rd International Digital Human Modeling Symposium (DHM2014), 2014, pp. 7–p.

[17] M.-L. Zhang and Z.-H. Zhou, "A review on multi-label learning algorithms," Knowledge and Data Engineering, IEEE Transactions on, vol. 26, no. 8, 2014, pp. 1819–1837.

[18] G. Tsoumakas and I. Katakis, "Multi-label classification: An overview," Dept. of Informatics, Aristotle University of Thessaloniki, Greece, 2006.

[19] V. J. Shute, "Focus on Formative Feedback," Review of Educational Research, vol. 78, no. 1, Mar. 2008, pp. 153–189.

[20] J. Danna and J. Velay, "Basic and supplementary sensory feedback in handwriting," Frontiers in psychology, vol. 6, no. 169, 2014.

[21] A. Basteris, L. Bracco, and V. Sanguineti, "Robot-assisted intermanual transfer of handwriting skills," Human Movement Science, vol. 31, no. 5, Oct. 2012, pp. 1175–1190.

[22] M. M. Nelson and C. D. Schunn, "The nature of feedback: how different types of peer feedback affect writing performance," Instructional Science, vol. 37, no. 4, Jul. 2009, pp. 375–401.

[23] G. P. van Galen, "Handwriting: Issues for a psychomotor theory," Human Movement Science, 1991, pp. 165–191.

Towards Web Accessibility Guidelines of Interaction and Interface Design for People with Autism Spectrum Disorder

Talita Cristina Pagani Britto
Department of Computer Science
Federal University of São Carlos
São Carlos, São Paulo, Brazil
talita.cpb@gmail.com

Ednaldo Brigante Pizzolato
Department of Computer Science
Federal University of São Carlos
São Carlos, São Paulo, Brazil
ednaldo@dc.ufscar.br

***Abstract*— In this paper, we describe a proposal set of Web accessibility guidelines of interaction and interface design for people with Autism Spectrum Disorder (ASD) to help Web professionals to design accessible Web interfaces for these users. The guidelines were extracted from an exploratory bibliographic survey of 17 works published between 2005 and 2015 including international recommendations, commercial or academic software and peer-reviewed papers. We identified 107 guidelines that were grouped in 10 categories using the affinity diagram technique. Then, we systematized the guidelines in each group according to similarities and duplicated statements, generating a set of 28 guidelines. As a result, we evidenced best practices to design accessible Web interfaces for people with ASD based on well succeeded solutions presented in works of different contexts. With those results, we aim to contribute to the state of the art of cognitive Web accessibility. Therefore, we intend to make the set of guidelines available in a repository on GitHub.**

Keywords- Web Accessibility; Autism; Guidelines; Universal Access; Interface Design for People with Autism.

I. Introduction

Autism Spectrum Disorder (ASD) is a syndrome which affects three developmental abilities: social, communication and interest skills [1]–[3]. People with ASD usually present difficulties regarding social interaction, verbal and non-verbal communication and imagination, as well as a restricted repertoire of interests and activities [3][4]. As a spectrum, ASD has a myriad of characteristics and severity degrees related to the level of impairment of skills, from mild (high-functional autism) to severe. As soon as it is diagnosed, ASD has effective treatments to minimize the impact of the impairment of skills and improve life quality of people with the syndrome and their families [1]–[3][5].

In the past 20 years, computer technology has been used as a support tool for parents, therapists, educators and people with ASD [5]–[8]. Previous works showed that people with ASD are interested in technology [7] and that is beneficial to a) develop their abilities [6][9]–[11]; b) facilitate their lives [12]; and c) be a helpful tool for pedagogical, therapeutic and everyday life activities [11][13][14], independent of age. Nowadays, devices exploring natural interactions and direct manipulation with touch screens, such as tablets, increase the acceptance of technology by these users [9][15]–[17].

However, even having some successful solutions available for this audience, software developers still have a limited knowledge on how to develop native or Web-based applications suitable for people with ASD. Other cognitive disabilities are also challenging for developers. This happens mainly because they still do not know how technology is used in these users' life [7]. When we analyze the Web context, Web developers and designers have a lack of experience working with accessibility [18] and, when they have it, it is usually only about people with visual disabilities.

Another bias is that we have few Human-Computer Interaction (HCI) guidelines to help Web developers design for people with ASD [6][19]. Although specific literature provides some clues [7][12][20]–[24], the state of art regarding cognitive Web accessibility contains fewer works than expected [21]. HCI guidelines provide an understandable knowledge about needs and preferences of people with ASD and can help Web developers understand how technology is used by these users [25], also allowing Web access equity [21].

Thus, researches are needed to investigate which design features are critical in providing therapeutic and pedagogical support for people with ASD in order to understand the potential impact of technology in their change of behavior [14][26] and provide a formalization of this knowledge for Web developers and designers.

In this paper, we describe a proposal set of Web accessibility guidelines for people with ASD to help Web developers to design accessible Web interfaces for these users. These guidelines systematize and formalize recommendations and best practices extracted from literature and reviewed software.

This paper is organized as follow: in Section II, we present previous works related to the development of interface and interaction design guidelines for people with ASD, including exclusive and non-exclusive guidelines. In Section III, we describe our methodological approach to identify, extract and systematize the guidelines presented in this work. Section IV presents the proposed set of guidelines and describes each category, while in Section V we discuss their potential effectiveness for people with ASD. Finally, we present our conclusions in Section VI.

II. Background

Friedman and Bryan [21] were two of the first to formally propose Web accessibility guidelines for people with cognitive or neuronal disabilities. Through an extensive literature review of 20 studies involving guidelines from experts, governments and institutions, the authors established the 22 most frequent recommendations on selected works. Similarly, Darejeh and Singh [12] investigated usability principles for people with low digital literacy, including people with cognitive disabilities and ASD. Putnam and Chong [8] conducted a survey with parents and educators of children and adolescents with autism and adults with autism through an online questionnaire to identify software solutions that cater to people with ASD. The study does not define design recommendations, but highlights aspects that can help in building technology products for people with ASD considering the objectives, interests and abilities of the public. Web Accessibility Initiative (WAI), a W3C (World Wide Web Consortium) group to delimit Web accessibility guidelines, published in 2012 a draft of principles of Web accessibility for people with cognitive or neuronal disabilities and potential barriers to this group [24]. As these recommendations were a draft, the W3C created a task force group called Cognitive and Learning Disabilities Accessibility Task Force (COGA) focusing on the area now called Cognitive Web Accessibility. In January of 2015, COGA published the results of a user research conducted to address problems and solutions concerning Web accessibility for people with cognitive, neuronal or learning disabilities [22].

In general, most of the works presented preliminary results and need further details about their proposed solutions, although they have significant contributions. An observed bias is that these works aim to focus on technology professional and tend to have more technical content. Recommendations considering the skills of a person with ASD that can be used by professionals from different areas may have a potentially greater adoption and allow multidisciplinary works to develop affordable solutions.

III. Methods

The process to identify, extract and systematize the guidelines presented in this work was conducted in three phases:

A. *Phase 1 – Studies selection*

We conducted an exploratory bibliographic survey to selected works about accessibility for people with ASD and other cognitive or neuronal disabilities published or developed between 2005 and 2015. We analyzed international recommendations, mobile and desktop applications, universal design approaches for educational purposed and peer-reviewed papers published in conferences and journals. The process of the survey involved an extensive search in databases, such as Association of Computer Machinery (ACM), IEEE, PubMed and Google Scholar. We also performed manual searches to find solutions that were not restricted to scientific papers. Table I presents the inclusion and exclusion criteria considered to select the works. Only the last inclusion criteria were mandatory to select or exclude works.

TABLE I. Inclusion and exclusion criteria to select the works to be analyzed in phase 2

Inclusion criteria	Exclusion criteria
Peer-reviewed papers published in conference proceedings or scientific journals.	Unpublished papers, blog posts and other materials that did not presented verified empirical evidences and results.
Computational solutions for people with ASD, specially children.	Computational solutions focused on parents, therapists or educators of people with ASD.
Works approaching accessibility recommendations for computing systems and/or Web acessibility for people with cognitive, neuronal or learning disabilities.	Papers that didn't described clearly the design decisions taken to develop the solution regarding the needs of people with ASD.
Works approaching mainly interaction models based on touch screens or Web interfaces.	Works focused on robotics.
Works and solutions publised or developed between 2005 and March of 2015.	Works out of the inclusion criteria.

B. *Phase 2 – Extraction*

In this phase, we performed a triage to extract recommendations from selected works, where we identified 107 potential recommendations and best practices. Subsequently, we executed a process to group them using a process similar to the affinity diagram technique, in order to arrange the extracted statements in logical sets according to the patterns we could identify in each statement. This process resulted in ten categories of guidelines.

C. *Phase 3 – Consolidation*

Upon grouping the recommendations by affinity diagram, we could perceive similarities between recommendations within a group that was not noticed during the analysis of the raw material of the 107 recommendations. Thus, we did a second grouping process to combine analogue recommendations contained in each category, refine the statements and systematize the final set of guidelines. We also wrote a detailed description of each guideline, including how to implement them and their respective importance for people with ASD, a gap we identified in the selected works.

IV. Results

Through an exploratory review of literature and available software, we selected 17 works according to the criteria of Phase 1, divided into international recommendations (3), software accessible for people with ASD (3), universal design guidelines for learning (1) and peer-reviewed papers (10). The selected works came from nine countries (United States, Brazil, Italy, England, Israel, India, Malaysia, Chile and Hong Kong), except the international recommendations, which can be considered global. Although contributions from United States correspond to 47% of works, it was still possible to bring cultural diversity from different countries.

Regarding the platform, this work is focused on Web-based interfaces, but we selected works exploring distinct platforms and applications, such as Virtual Reality, Multitouch Table and native (desktop or mobile) due to the possibility of generalizing recommendations and interaction patterns that can be platform-independent. Most of the works are technology specific or accessible for people with ASD, although all works from International Recommendations are not exclusively focused on ASD.

In Phase 2, after extracting the potential guidelines, we grouped all 107 recommendations, organizing them based on a similarity criterion. This process resulted in ten categories carefully labeled to represent common elements in Web interfaces. The categories are: (G1) Visual and Textual Vocabulary; (G2) Customization; (G3) Engagement; (G4) Redundant Representation; (G5) Multimedia; (G6) Feedback; (G7) Affordance; (G8) Navigability; (G9) System Status; (G10) Interaction with Touch Screen.

In Table II, we present a summary of recommendations extracted from the first triage, where it is observed that the most critical interface design aspects are related to *Visual and textual vocabulary*, *Customization, Engagement* and *Redundant Representation*, according to the number of extracted recommendation and number of works from which we extracted these recommendations. At first, we had a hypothesis that *Customization* guidelines would be critical due to the diversity of characteristics of people with ASD as customization allows them to be in control and to tailor the interface according to their preferences. However, one of the biggest challenges for people with ASD when using the Web are: a) to focus or comprehend lengthy sections of text [23]; and b) to understand visual/textual information due to inaccurate visual and textual communication [12][22]. It is worth mentioning that *Visual and textual vocabulary* is recommended to be the first concern for developers and should be complemented with *Redundant representation* in order to increase the potential of being understood. As people with ASD, especially children, may be uncomfortable with certain distractive elements and also present some difficulties regarding focus and attention, *Engagement* guidelines are important to work memory, attention and reading skills on the Web interface.

TABLE II. DISTRIBUTION OF EXTRACTED RECOMMENDATIONS BETWEEN CATEGORIES AND QUANTITY OF WORKS REFERENCED IN EACH CATEGORY

Category	Extracted recommendations	Referenced works
G1	26	9
G2	14	10
G3	12	9
G4	12	7
G5	10	9
G6	8	8
G7	8	6
G8	7	4
G9	6	4
G10	4	4

The final step in Phase 2 was a second arrangement process to generate unique guidelines and reduce ambiguity and redundancy, since several recommendations in each category, from different authors, presented similar statements. As a result, we would formalize a set of 28 guidelines distributed in the ten categories, as presented in Figure 1. The guidelines from *Visual and textual vocabulary*, *Customization* and *Engagement* represent about 43% of all guidelines, reinforcing their importance when designing interfaces for people with ASD.

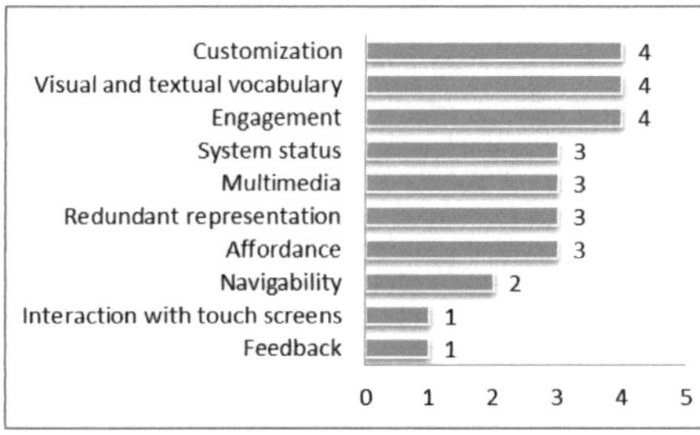

Figure 1. Number of unique guidelines generated for each category after systematization and summarization.

A. Description of the guidelines' categories

The consolidated guidelines compound a set of 28 Web accessibility recommendations to design and develop Websites and Web applications more suitable for people with ASD. As mentioned previously, the guidelines are distributed in ten categories and each one has a strategic scope regarding interface and interaction aspects of a Web interface. We describe in the following sections the scope of each category. The full set of guidelines ordered by category is presented in Table III.

1) G1 – Visual and textual vocabulary: This category presents the most important recommendations, according to the works we analyzed. They address the proper use of text and images considering particularities of people with ASD. About 50% of the works present concerns about text structure, language, verbal and pictorial communication, reading flow and color contrast. In guideline 1.2 we consolidated contributions from four works [12][22]–[24] and eight recommendations about the use of proper language. Guideline 1.4 summarizes five similar recommendations extracted from three works [15][27][28] related to real world representation of icons and interaction patterns. As people with ASD may face barriers to understand information and decode language, the guidelines of this category can improve the aspect of engaging in communication [29] and approach social and communication skills.

2) G2 – Customization: Guidelines from Customization category address recommendation to enable users to tailor interfaces according to their needs. It is the second most important category and it addresses how users with ASD can adjust the interface in a more comfortably way to them, considering that the syndrome presents a myriad of characteristics and it is often risky to identify patterns between people with ASD, such as colors preferences.

3) G3 – Engagement: The guidelines of Engagement present recommendations regarding focus, attention and strategies to help users interact with the system. These guidelines address interface design issues and intersect with recommendation of "G1- Visual and textual vocabulary" and "G6 -Feedback".

4) G4 – Redundant representation: Redundant representation, along with G5 - Multimedia, refers to guidelines reinforcing that information should not be linked exclusively to a format (text, image or audio). Multiple representations (specially graphical) work as a supplementary content [30] and contribute with enrichment of the repertory of user's vocabulary [5][9].

5) G5 – Multimedia: Complementing guidelines from Redundant Representation, Multimedia's guidelines detail the proper use of multimedia in Web interfaces to work memory, attention, visual and textual understanding and sensorial integration of people with ASD.

6) G6 – Feedback: Providing feedback for actions performed in interfaces is a common usability recommendation independent of the characteristic of users. However, incomplete feedbacks or their absence are critical for people with ASD, particularly children, due to their potential difficulties to pay attention, deal with changes and understand verbal instructions. Thus, feedbacks are important for people with ASD to guide them in performing tasks, understanding the application behavior and predicting the behavior of similar features or elements. The recommendations we extracted were very similar to each other, evidencing how this aspect is important and is consistently established in different works. As a result, we could summarize them into a single guideline.

7) G7 – Affordance: Guidelines in this category address issues to design interface elements that clearly identify how they work without a deep investigation or a high cognitive effort. Reducing cognitive workload is an important accessibility concern when designing interfaces for people with ASD. Consequently, interface designers and Web developers should pay attention to the Web page element which may not specify clearly if they are clickable, draggable, pushable, etc.

8) G8 – Navigability: The guidelines of Navigability present recommendation about the navigational structure between Web pages. A large amount of information and number of links contribute to a bad user experience for people with ASD. Therefore, it is recommended to provide to the interface: a) a simplified navigation; b) consistent location indicators; and c) sequential navigation, when applicable. Also, it is important not to prevent users to be in control of the navigation flow.

9) G9 – System status: The System status' guidelines address recommendations about progress among tasks (clearly information about errors, help instructions and information related to changes in state of elements).

10) G10 – Interaction with touch screen: The last category presents a recommendation on the use of touch screen. We consider this recommendation important since Websites and Web applications are increasingly being accessed through mobile devices with touch screens. Those devices present direct manipulation of interface elements, people with ASD tend to interact better to such devices [9][15][20] and their interaction model is considered to be more natural. Interfaces with direct manipulation require less physical efforts and present interaction patterns compatible with the real world.

V. Brief Discussion

It is possible to find some software, games and applications aimed at teaching and learning of people with ASD, both in scientific works and business solutions. However, for each of these applications, designers and developers may need to thoroughly investigate the most suitable design solution for the proposed application or may follow generic design guidelines that may not be appropriate in the context of software for people with ASD [6][27].

By proposing recommendations and guiding principles for the development of interfaces accessible to people with autism, it is possible to mitigate the lack of knowledge of developers and enable the development of more inclusive technologies. In addition to allowing the developers to know what they should consider when developing appropriate solutions for people with ASD, design recommendations can contribute to raise awareness of these professionals about the characteristics of the person with ASD and how technology can be valuable to them. Following recommended guidelines for proper software design, designers and developers can support the educational goals defined for the application.

Systematizing contributions from 17 works and selected solutions generated a consolidation of contributions that, to date, have been dispersed in different types of publications or were a tacit knowledge in the design of software solutions.

Some recommendations may not seem new regarding Web accessibility and interface design, e.g., "*provide clear error messages*" and "*provide feedback*". The difference is how the fulfillment of these factors has a different impact for people with ASD. When we suggest, for example, avoiding using metaphorical expressions in the interface content and icons, we can consider this as an important guidance for neurologically typical children in literacy age, because they often don't understand some non-literal expressions. But this recommendation is even more critical for people with ASD, considering that people with autism, in different age range, may have difficulty understanding and interpreting metaphors. The proposed guidelines can be used by interface designers, Web developers and other professionals involved in the design of applications for people with ASD as a support for decision-making to suggest information and resources more consistent with the context of children with autism and, potentially, a variety of users.

TABLE III. SET OF PROPOSED GUIDELINES

ID	Summary Description	Authors
	G1 – Visual and Textual Vocabulary	
1.1	Colors shouldn't be the only way to deliver content and the contrast between background and objects in foreground must be appropriate to distinguish items and distinct content or relate similar information	[20][21][23][30]
1.2	Use a simple visual and textual language, avoid jargons, spelling errors, metaphors, abbreviations and acronyms, using terms, expressions, names and symbols familiar to users' context	[12][22]–[24]
1.3	Be succinct, avoid writing long paragraphs and use markups that facilitate the reading flow such as lists and heading titles	[21][23]
1.4	Icons, images and label of menus and actions should be compatible to real world, representing concrete actions and everyday life activities in order to be easily recognized	[15][27][28]
	G2 – Customization	
2.1	Allow color, text size and font customization for interface elements	[12][16][21]–[23]
2.2	Provide options to customize information visualization with images, sound and text according to individual user's preferences	[6][7][16][21][31]
2.3	Provide options to customize the amount of element in the interface, their arrangement and enable features personalization	[6][9][16][17]
2.4	Enable a reading or printing mode for activities involving reading and concentration	[21][22]
	G3 – Engagement	
3.1	Avoid using elements that distract or interfere in focus and attention. In case you use it, provide options to suppress those elements on screen.	[9][23][24][31]
3.2	Design simple interfaces, with few elements and which present only the features and content need for the current task to be performed by the user	[12][15][28]
3.3	Use blank spaces between Web page elements to separate different contents or focus the user attention on a specific content	[21][23]
3.4	Provide clear instructions and orientation about tasks to ease the user understanding of the content and the content language, in order to stimulate, motivate and engage the user	[7][9][24]
	G4 – Redundant Representation	
4.1	The Website or Web application must not rely only in text to present content. Provide alternative representations through image, audio or video and ensure that they will be close to the corresponding text	[5][6][21][23][31]
4.2	Symbols, pictograms and icons should present a textual equivalent near to facilitate symbol understanding and contribute to enrich user's vocabulary	[9][21][31]
4.3	Provide audio instructions and subtitles for texts, but ensure that this is not the only alternate content representation	[21][28]
	G5 – Multimedia	
5.1	Provide information in multiple representation, such as text, video, audio and image for better content and vocabulary understand, also helping users focus on content	[5][12][16][23] [24][28][31]
5.2	Allow images magnification for better visualization and ensure they continue to be understandable when enlarged	[23]
5.3	Avoid the use of disturbing and explosive sounds, like sirens or fireworks	[20]
	G6 – Feedback	
6.1	Provide feedback confirm correct actions or alerting about potential mistakes and use audio, text and images to represent the message, avoiding icons with emotions or facial expressions	[8][9][15][17][20] [21][23][27]
	G7 – Affordance	
7.1	Similar elements and interaction must produce similar, consistent and predictable results	[12][23][24]
7.2	Use bigger icons, buttons and form controls that provide appropriate click/tap area and ensure that the elements look clickable	[9][12][21][23]
7.3	Provide immediate instructions and feedback over a interaction restriction with the system or a certain interface element	[8]
	G8 – Navigability	
8.1	Provide a simplified and consistent navigation between pages, use location and progress indicators and present global navigation buttons (Exit, Back to home page, help) on every page	[21][23][24][28]
8.2	Avoid automatic page redirects or expiration time for tasks. The user is who should control navigation and time to perform a task	[21][23]
	G9 – System status	
9.1	Present appropriate instructions to interact with interface elements, provide clear messages about errors and provide mechanisms to solve the errors	[9][23]
9.2	Allow critical actions to be reverted, cancelled, undone or confirmed	[21][23]
9.3	In interactive lessons and educational activities, it is recommended allow up to five attempts before showing the correct answer	[20]
	G10 – Interaction with touch screen	
10.1	Touch screen interactions should have the appropriate sensibility and prevent errors in selections and accidental touch in interface elements	[8][15][16][27]

VI. Conclusions and Future Work

In this work, we investigated and systematized Web accessibility recommendations and best practices to design Web interfaces suitable for people with ASD. While the works we selected usually presented the recommendations in a format of single sentence, we decided to develop an extended description for each guideline in order to help people to implement the guidelines properly and understand the rationale of the proposed approach. Some guidelines may present technical details, however, our intention is that the guidelines can be applied by multidisciplinary teams and educational professionals involved with use of digital resources for people with ASD.

Although the focus of the project is Web interfaces, we carefully propose generalized descriptions for most guidelines in order to not link them with a specific platform. The idea is to enable their application to different interaction contexts.

The full set of guidelines is available at an open-source repository on GitHub. Therefore, we hope this content may be complemented, distributed, derived and easily accessible to professionals and researches from different areas.

Finally, the proposed guidelines should provide advances in the state of the art of cognitive Web accessibility as: (1) support material to develop Websites and Web applications adapted to the needs of people with ASD, especially children; (2) a guidance documentation about best practices and potential challenges about interaction of people with ASD with interactive systems; (3) an open source repository of recommendations in constant update; (4) a complement to literature regarding the biases of Web accessibility for people with cognitive or neuronal disabilities, adding techniques related to ASD.

A. *Next steps*

In order to see if the proposed guidelines are effective in providing a better interaction for people with ASD, the next step of this work involves the development of an educational Web application using the guidelines to support the interaction design, followed by an experimental evaluation with children with ASD. The evaluation aims to observe how children react and interact with the application and collect a feedback to validate and improve the guidelines.

Alongside, we intend to: (1) interview parents and teacher of children with ASD to understand their perspective about using technology as an educational and therapeutic resource in order to contemplate their viewpoint into the guidelines; (2) perform technical evaluation of the guidelines with Web developers, accessibility experts and digital educational teachers involved with special education.

VII. ACKNOWLEDGEMENTS

Our thanks to the researchers of the Laboratory of Human Learning, Interactive Multimedia and Computerized Education (LAHMIEI) from the Federal University of São Carlos, especially Prof. PhD. Celso Goyos for contributing to this work and providing theoretical subsidy from Psychology.

References

[1] C. for D. C. and Prevention, "Prevalence of Autism Spectrum Disorders," MMRW, vol. 61, no. 3, pp. 1–19, 2012.

[2] P. T. Ozand, A. Al-odaib, H. Merza, and S. Al Harbi, "Autism : a review," J. Pediatr. Neurol., vol. 1, no. 2, pp. 55–67, 2003.

[3] A. P. Association, Diagnostic and Statistical Manual of Mental Disorders (DSM), Fifth. United States: American Psychological Association, 2013.

[4] C. A. Gadia, R. Tuchman, and N. T. Rotta, "Autism and pervasive developmental disorders," J. Pediatr., vol. 80, no. 2, pp. 83–94, 2004.

[5] H. J. Carrer, E. B. Pizzolato, and C. Goyos, "Evaluation of educational software with speech recognition in individuals with normal development and language delay," Rev. Bras. Informática na Educ., vol. 17, no. 3, pp. 67–81, 2009.

[6] L. Millen, R. Edlin-White, and S. Cobb, "The development of educational collaborative virtual environments for children with autism," Proceedings of 5th Cambridge Workshop on Universal Access and Assistive Technology (CWUAAT 2010), 2010, pp. 1–7.

[7] C. Putnam and L. Chong, "Software and technologies designed for people with autism: what do users want?," Proceedings of the 10th Int. ACM SIGACCESS Conf. Comput. Access., pp. 3–10, 2008.

[8] A. Battocchi, A. Ben-Sasson, G. Esposito, E. Gal, F. Pianesi, D. Tomasini, P. Venuti, P. Weiss, and M. Zancanaro, "Collaborative puzzle game: a tabletop interface for fostering collaborative skills in children with autism spectrum disorders," J. Assist. Technol., vol. 4, no. 1, pp. 4–13, 2010.

[9] G. F. M. Silva, L. C. de Castro Salgado, and A. B. Raposo, "Metaphors of Cultural Perspectives in the (re) definition of collaboration patterns of a multi-touch game for users with autism," Proceedings of the 12th Brazilian Symposium on Human Factors in Computing Systems, 2013, vol. 5138, pp. 112–121.

[10] L. Millen, S. V. G. Cobb, H. Patel, and T. Glover, "Collaborative virtual environment for conducting design sessions with students with autism spectrum conditions," Proceedings of the 9th Intl Conf. Disabil. Virtual Real. Assoc. Technol., pp. 10–12, 2012.

[11] M. Moore and S. Calvert, "Brief Report: Vocabulary Acquisition for Children with Autism: Teacher or Computer Instruction," J. Autism Dev. Disord., vol. 30, no. 4, pp. 359–362, 2000.

[12] A. Darejeh and D. Singh, "A review on user interface design principles to increase software usability for users with less computer literacy," J. Comput. Sci., vol. 9, no. 11, pp. 1443–1450, 2013.

[13] T. Gentry, J. Wallace, C. Kvarfordt, and K. B. Lynch, "Personal digital assistants as cognitive aids for high school students with autism: Results of a community-based trial," J. Vocat. Rehabil., vol. 32, no. 2, pp. 101–107, 2010.

[14] T. R. Goldsmith and L. a Leblanc, "Use of Technology in Interventions for Children with Autism," J. Early Intensive Behav. Interv., vol. 1, no. 2, pp. 166–178, 2004.

[15] R. Muñoz, T. Barcelos, R. Noël, and S. Kreisel, "Development of software that supports the improvement

of the empathy in children with autism spectrum disorder," Proceedings of Int. Conf. Chil. Comput. Sci. Soc. SCCC, pp. 223–228, 2013.

[16] AssistiveWare, "Proloquo2Go," 2014. [Online]. Available from: http://www.assistiveware.com/product/proloquo2go 2016.03.19

[17] PuzzlePiece, "PuzzlePiece," 2014. [Online]. Available from: https://www.getpuzzlepiece.com/ 2016.03.19

[18] J. Mankoff, G. R. Hayes, and D. Kasnitz, "Disability studies as a source of critical inquiry for the field of assistive technology," Proceedings of 12th Int. ACM SIGACCESS Conf. Comput. Access. - ASSETS '10, p. 3, 2010.

[19] D. Moore, "Computer-Based Learning Systems for People with Autism," in Disabled Students in Education: Technology, Transition, and Inclusivity, D. Moore, A. Gorra, M. Adams, J. Reaney, and H. Smith, Eds. Hershey, PA: IGI Global, pp. 84–107, 2012.

[20] K. Sitdhisanguan and N. Chotikakamthorn, "Using tangible user interfaces in computer-based training systems for low-functioning autistic children," Pers. Ubiquitous Comput., vol. 16, no. 2, pp. 143–155, 2012.

[21] M. G. Friedman and D. N. Bryen, "Web accessibility design recommendations for people with cognitive disabilities," Technol. Disabil., vol. 19, pp. 205–212, 2007.

[22] L. Seeman and M. Cooper, "Cognitive Accessibility User Research," 2015. [Online]. Available from: http://w3c.github.io/coga/user-research/ 2016.03.19

[23] WebAIM, "Evaluating Cognitive Web Accessibility with WAVE," 2014. [Online]. Available from: http://wave.Webaim.org/cognitive 2016.03.19

[24] S. Abou-Zahra, "How People with Disabilities Use the Web. Status: Draft Updated 1 August 2012," 2012. [Online]. Available from: http://www.w3.org/WAI/intro/people-use-Web/diversity 2016.03.19

[25] H. van Rijn and P. J. Stappers, "The Puzzling Life of Autistic Toddlers: Design Guidelines from the LINKX Project," Adv. Human-Computer Interact., vol. 2008, pp. 1–8, 2008.

[26] A. L. Wainer and B. R. Ingersoll, "The use of innovative computer technology for teaching social communication to individuals with autism spectrum disorders," Res. Autism Spectr. Disord., vol. 5, no. 1, pp. 96–107, 2011.

[27] P. L. T. Weiss, E. Gal, S. Eden, M. Zancanaro, and F. Telch, "Usability of a Multi-Touch Tabletop Surface to Enhance Social Competence Training for Children with Autism Spectrum Disorder," Proceedings of the Chais Conference on Instructional Technologies Research: Learning in the technological era, 2011, pp. 71–78.

[28] F. K. Lau, A. H. K. Yuen, and J. M. G. Lian, "Adapted design of multimedia-facilitated language learning program for children with autism," Psicol. Esc. e Educ., vol. 11, no. spe, pp. 13–26, 2007.

[29] C. Putnam and L. Chong, "Software and technologies designed for people with autism: what do users want?," in Proceedings of the 10th international ACM SIGACCESS conference on Computers and accessibility, 2008, pp. 3–10.

[30] D. Poulson and C. Nicolle, "Making the Internet accessible for people with cognitive and communication Impairments," Univers. Access Inf. Soc., vol. 3, no. 1, pp. 48–56, 2004.

[31] N. C. of U. D. for L. UDLCenter, "UDL Guidelines – Version 2.0," National Center of Universal Design for Learning, 2012. [Online]. Available from: http://www.udlcenter.org/aboutudl/udlguidelines 2016.03.19

Webpage Accessibility and Usability for Autistic Users: a Case Study on a Tourism Website

Antonina Dattolo
SASWEB Lab,
Dept. of Mathematics, Computer Science,
and Physics, Università di Udine, Gorizia, Italy
email: antonina.dattolo@uniud.it

Flaminia L. Luccio
DAIS
Università Ca' Foscari Venezia,
Venezia, Italy
email: luccio@unive.it

Elisa Pirone
Università Ca' Foscari Venezia,
Venezia, Italy
email: elisapirone06@gmail.com

***Abstract*—Web accessibility and usability represent an open challenge for the current research on the Web; in particular, for specific disabilities such as the Autism Spectrum Disorders (ASD), to the best of our knowledge, no experimental case study on an autistic-friendly Website on tourism is available.**
However, people with ASD are usually solitary and visual thinkers and they could take advantage by the use of the Web. This paper identifies the set of basic and general guidelines provided by the World Wide Web Consortium (W3C) to make a Website accessible and usable to this specific set of users, and extends it, integrating new specific features.
Following these new guidelines, the paper proposes a case study dedicated to a tourist, autistic-friendly, Website developed in the area of Rieti, central Italy; it has been validated through expert reviews, and several trials with users of a specialised centre for neurological and physical disabilities.

Keywords–Autistic-friendly Website; Accessibility; Usability; Tourism; Autism Spectrum Disorders.

I. INTRODUCTION

Web accessibility and usability represent an open challenge for the current research on the Web: they aim to make Web content more accessible and usable to a wider range of people with disabilities, including blindness and low vision, deafness and hearing loss, learning disabilities, cognitive limitations, limited movement, speech disabilities, photo sensitivity and combinations of these [1]. Usually, Web developers apply general standards, following the guidelines provided but the W3C [2], without considering the importance of a universal Web access. However, every country supports the application of the Web Content Accessibility Guidelines (WCAG) 2.0 [1], although adopts a different Web accessibility legislation: WCAG 2.0 are recommended, but become mandatory only in specific cases, such as, for example, in Italy, for the Web sites of public Institutions (see the so-called "Legge Stanca", literally Stanca Act [3]).

A. Autism Spectrum Disorders

In this paper, we are interested in the development of websites for people with the disabilities denominated Autism Spectrum Disorders (ASD). The American Psychiatric Association defines the ASD as neuro-developmental disorders with persistent impairments in social communication and social interaction, and restricted, repetitive patterns of behaviour, interests, or activities [4]. This general definition puts together people with a wide and different set of features and behaviours; so, it is difficult create multi-purpose environments, but some general guidelines may be followed. We have focused our attention on ASD user profiles with the following features.

Typically, the impairments in social communication are related to *language delays*, however, people with ASD often present good visual abilities. Thus, modern speech therapies are usually combined with Augmentative and Alternative Communication (AAC) techniques, i.e., powerful methods that combine different visual components in order to create syntactically and semantically correct sentences [5] [6]. Among these AAC techniques a standard approach is to use the Picture Exchange Communication System (PECS) which promotes interactions among users with the exchanging of images [7]. People with ASD are usually visual thinkers, i.e., think in pictures and express their concepts by visualising sequences of pictures of the same object [8]. They have often *limited attention*, i.e., limited time in which they might be able to concentrate on a particular task, thus defining limited, self-contained tasks is very important. They might also suffer of *Sensory Processing Disorders* (SPD), and may thus feel distressed and confused in particular situations. SPD are neurological disorders that cause difficulties with processing information from the five senses (vision, auditory, touch, olfaction, and taste), as well as from the sense of movement (vestibular system), and/or the positional sense (proprioception) [9].

B. Website usability and accessibility

Access to information and communication technologies is a basic human right as recognised in the United Nations Convention on the Rights of Persons with Disabilities (CRPD) [10].

Disabilities might be either physical (visual, auditory, etc.), or cognitive and neurological, might be temporary or boundless.

The W3C [1] [2] has proposed different guidelines to produce accessible websites, however specific features have to be considered while dealing with people with specific disabilities such as ASD. As we have previously mentioned, typical problems that people with ASD face are limited attention, sensory hypersensitiveness, different way of learning and reacting to things, problems related to limited text comprehension (e.g., not understanding figurative language, etc.). For such a reason standard usable and accessible websites might not be suitable for such users.

Web usability and accessibility are closely related: their goals, approaches, and guidelines overlap significantly [11].

Usability is all about designing an easy to use website that appeals to as many people as possible. Websites should be intuitively usable. Usability is a *quality attribute* that assesses how easy user interfaces are to use; it is is defined in [12] by five quality components:

- Learnability: How easy is it for users to accomplish basic tasks the first time they encounter the design?
- Efficiency: Once users have learned the design, how quickly can they perform tasks?
- Memorability: When users return to the design after a period of not using it, how easily can they reestablish proficiency?
- Errors: How many errors do users make, how severe are these errors, and how easily can they recover from the errors?
- Satisfaction: How pleasant is it to use the design?

For Web developers, a key aspect of usability is following a user-centred design (UCD) process to create positive and emotional user experiences [13].

Accessibility is about ensuring an equivalent user experience for people with disabilities. For the Web, accessibility means that people with disabilities can perceive, understand, navigate, and interact with websites and tools, and that they can contribute equally without barriers.

Usable accessibility combines usability and accessibility to develop positive user experiences for people with disabilities. User-centred design processes include both techniques for including users throughout design and evaluation, and using guidelines for design and evaluation. UCD helps making informed decisions about accessible design. Thus UCD is necessary to improve accessibility in websites and Web tools.

The goal of Web accessibility is to make the Web work well for people, specifically people with disabilities. While technical standards are an essential tool for meeting that goal, marking off a checklist is not the end goal. People with disabilities effectively interacting with and contributing to the Web is the end goal [11].

We note that accessibility $\neq$ usability: a website can comply with standards; pass all the automated accessibility checks, appear to be accessible. However, an accessible website is not necessarily usable; Web pages can be verified accessible by focus groups, and still be inaccessible to a third party. Individual users may have cognitive, technical, or other barriers.

In this paper, we are interested in websites which are accessible and usable by people with ASD. We thus first present the state of art of existing guidelines for the development of websites for people with ASD, and extend them with new features. We then consider the relation between autism and tourism, and show the existing solutions for proposing tours for these specific users. To the best of our knowledge, there are no existing websites that are usable and accessible for people with ASD, and let them freely navigate inside them and take independent decisions (as, e.g., the choice of a tour). We thus propose an interesting case study of a touristic website for autistic users and we show some experimental results on a set of 9 users.

The paper is organised as follows: Section II is dedicated to the state of art in autism and tourism; Section II-B presents general guidelines for accessibility and usability, specialised for users with ASD, while Section III extends them, and Section IV proposes our case study, focused on accessible and usable tourism, autistic-friendly website. Finally, Section V describes the experimentation made with a group of autistic users and the related results. Section VI ends the paper with future work.

II. Related Work

The improvement of the quality of life for autistic people is a big challenge. In this section we analyse the state of art related to two aspects:

- Autism and tourism;
- Website usability and accessibility for people with ASD.

A. *Autism and tourism*

Some issues that have to be considered are: social inclusion, e.g. in community activities, emotional well being, e.g. happiness, interpersonal relations, e.g. friendship, and physical well-being, e.g. leisure [14]. All this, may be achieved with a well planned tourism trip, being it an experience that stimulates all the above domains. However, this is not trivial since all the different activities related to a trip, i.e. transportation, accommodation, etc. have to be adjusted to meet special needs.

The first issue that has to be considered is the preparation phase since it is well known that autistic people get stressed in unknown, unexpected situations, thus everything has to be previously planned, and the user has to be prepared to tackle each of the trip steps.

In [14] [15] the authors identify some of the issues that a travel agency or whoever organises the trip should consider while planning it for an autistic user:

- *Survey phase*: A questionnaire should be provided so to identify which are the main physical, sensory, or language problems the user has, and which are his/her main interests. According to this, the agency can suggest suitable tourism destinations or trips. E.g., a person that gets stressed in very crowded, loud or noisy placed should avoid amusement parks, crowded exhibitions, etc..

- *Trip planning*: At this point a trip may be planned by taking into consideration all the provided information. The first thing is transportation, so how to move from a home place to the destination. This can be achieved in different ways, what is important is that all the steps are previously explained to the user. If the transportation is by air the airline company has to be contacted. Some airports offer some pre-planned visits of the airport [15], the airport of Dublin also offers some very interesting on-line material which visually describes the different parts of the airport, following a logical sequence of actions which a traveller is supposed to do. It also provides interesting tips on how to face all the different situations while being at the airport and also some general rules to follow during a trip [16].

- *Accommodation*: What seems to be more suitable for autistic users, are small size accommodations, such as small hotels and motels, or preferably the renting of a condo where the user can "feel at home". In the USA, there are some hotels that already provide "autism-friendly accommodations" with special rooms, staff, and meals [14].

- *Tours*: What concerns the tourism activities, is obviously based on the preference of the user. Thus, following the guidelines of the survey is a good starting point. Here, we have to distinguish between one day trips which obviously have to be planned in the surrounding area, avoiding too much stress for the trip, and longer trips of two or more days. There are obviously different options, depending on the preferences and also considering the sensory problems which autistic users might have. Possible options are sightseeing in scenic areas since autistic users often like silent places and love taking pictures, visiting historical and cultural sites, museums, aquariums etc.. Some museums are "Autism-Friendly Museums", and are prepared to host these special tourists. An example is the Royal air force museum in London which offers an autism friendly trail that can be downloaded from the site, and has won an Autism Access Award [17], or the Metropolitan museum of art in New York which offers e.g., a social narrative (PDF) about visiting the Museum with tips, and a Sensory Friendly Map of the museum with the list of quiet and less crowded areas [18].

Obviously, general considerations are that first one should prepare the autistic user to very simple day trips, then these trips might be planned for a longer time. Daily activities should not be too intense, locations should be visited in times of the day during which places are not too crowded, i.e., stressful situations should be avoided as much as possible. A good idea, is also to prepare the user for the changes of routine by illustrating the trip using brochures, photos, videos, etc. A last consideration is that, often, things might not go as expected, thus the trip should be planned with flexibility so to consider last minute changes of planes, i.e., alternative destination, activities and so on.

The site [19] encourages families with people with ASD to travel around the world; it provides interesting hints for travelling, e.g., how to let a person with ASD pack his/her luggage, interesting destinations and hotels, and so on. It also states that the benefits of travelling outweigh the problems one will face. For instance, travelling provides a hand on experience on some topics which are studied in books at school (also normal people would benefit from it). Mathematics for calculating money exchange or tips, art by visiting museum and galleries, geography by physically moving from a city to another, literature by visiting homes of famous authors, and so on. It increases flexibility not only in the daily routine but also in the dietary restrictions by encouraging the experience of tasting different food, in the interaction with other people by enhancing social and language skills, in raising family bondings, etc..

B. Website usability and accessibility for people with ASD

An interesting reading [20] is provided by Jamie Knight, autistic developer and senior accessibility specialist: he discusses on cognitive accessibility and provide some practical guidelines.

While the Web Content Accessibility Guidelines, WCAG 1.0 and WCAG 2.0 [1] represent the international standard reference model in this research domain, different practical and operative guidelines have been proposed [1] [2] [20]-[21]. Given that most of them consider similar aspects, we have analysed and summarised all of them in the following list:

a) Graphical layout: Users with ADS may easily be distracted by secondary contents, thus webpages should be very simple and should not contain information, images, frames that create distractions. The page layout should be consistent throughout the website. Images and white space should be copiously used in order to focus the user attention and to simplify the concepts absorption. Background sounds, moving text, blinking images and horizontal scrolling should be avoided.

b) Structure and Navigation: The website should have a simple and logical navigation structure, links should be easy-to-access and to find, and few options should be given in order to avoid the user confusion. The navigation inside the site should be limited by three clicks. Each page should contain the navigation information and navigation buttons at the top and the bottom of the page.

c) Fonts and colours: Words should be easily readable, thus should usually be written in plain Sans-serif fonts (e.g., Verdana) of at least 12 points. To emphasise words, bold should be used. The choice of the right color is very important, people with ASD may avoid the navigation in sites with particular predominant colours, e.g., red. Foreground and background colours should have sufficient contrast but not too much, some ASD users find e.g., that black on white, is too visually stimulating.

d) Language: The language should be simple and precise so that it does not create ambiguity, secondary and irrelevant information should be avoided. The text should be short and self-contained. The words should refer to things that "can be seen", acronyms and abbreviations, together with non-literal text, and jargon should not be used since people with ASD literally interpret the text content.

III. SPECIALISING THE GUIDELINES FOR AUTISM

The guidelines proposed in previous subsection II-B define a set of general features; in this section we specialise them, integrating new features, specific for the ASD characteristics. We list them, following the four aspects introduced above:

Graphical layout: Limit the text to very few, simple sentences, and add many images in a PECS-like style so to describe concepts and actions through sequences of images. This is the most important feature, i.e., the copious use of images throughout the site, in order to transmit all messages. Repeat concepts, and in the homepage write a sentence that let the user feel it navigates in its "own" site.

Structure and Navigation: Use simple and sketchy symbolic pictures. If the site is directed to a group of young users, add, when possible, some simple games to involve the user, and also to check his/her level of attention.

Fonts and colours: Write sentences in bold, of big size and uppercase.

Language: Use simple and minimal sentences, and illustrate concepts through images, and not though the written text.

To summarise, the main feature that we think should be added is the use of many figures to explain situations, illustrate actions, etc.. This choice is based on an Augmentative and Alternative Communication (AAC) approach that is widely used to improve standard communication. Moreover, we enforce the involvement of the user on the site navigation by adding sentences that personalise the site, and by adding games that increase his/her curiosity. As we will describe in Section V, this choice has been proved to be winning in our testing phase.

IV. SCOPRIRIETI: A TOURISM WEBSITE FOR AUTISTIC USERS

As we have mentioned in the previous Section II, there are sites that provide tourism destinations for people with ASD, or that give some tips on how to develop an autistic-friendly website, however, we could not find sites whose aim was the independent (or almost-independent) planning of a trip by a user with ASD.

In [22], we have thus proposed the Scopririeti (literally, "Discover Rieti") site [23], an autistic-friendly site, that the user may use to simply search information, or, what is more interesting, to independently choose one among different possible destinations of a one-day tourism trip in the neighbourhood of Rieti, an Italian town in the north of Rome.

A. *The website structure*

While developing the site, we made sure that it met all the accessibility and usability standards we have presented in Section II-B and Section III. We did this in collaboration with therapists and operators of the centre Nemo in Rieti, which hosts different users with neurological and physical disabilities.

Graphical layout. The page layout is essential and simple so to be enjoyable and comprehensible. The background is white and it has just some simple bars in a flexible colour (blue and orange), so to avoid too much contrast on the colour, and thus prevent visual discomfort. The header of the website contains typical standards such as the logo, the primary navigation menu and the search bar, as shown in Figure 1. We

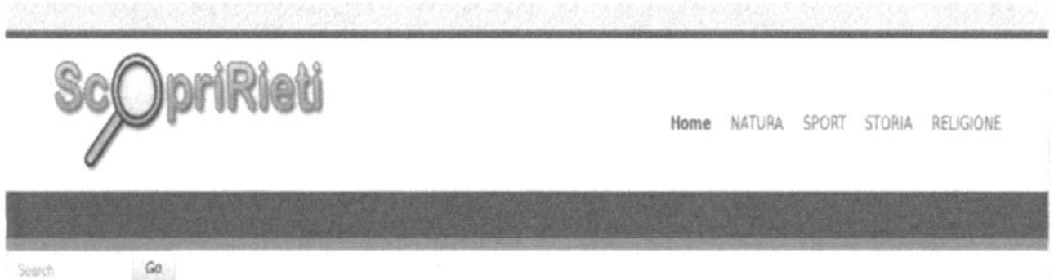

Figure 1. The header bar of our website. The menu contains four main items: nature, sport, history, and religion.

have inserted many pictures and photos in order to increase the full comprehension of the site content, which is simple, repetitive and synthetic. We have also followed the guidelines and the suggestions proposed by the therapists, and we have included travel itineraries that well suited the users. In the homepage we have written a sentence "Sei un ragazzo del Centro Nemo? Questo sito è stato realizzato proprio per te" (Translation: "Are you a guy of the Nemo center? This site has been developed for you") that would let the user feel happy to navigate inside his "own" site.

Fonts and colours. We have used simple fonts, big size and uppercase for letters in order to facilitate the reading (see Figure 2. Translation: Discover several new places of Rieti and organise a tour with your friends or your family. What do you like?).

Language. The language used is simple, sentences are minimal and do not contain acronyms or abbreviations (see, e.g., Figure 2). Note that, the site is in Italian since it had

Figure 2. The fonts.

to be accessible by Italian disabled users. We have preferred to illustrate all the tourism experience with a sequence of pictures, rather than with some text (see the entire home page in Figure 3). This prepares the user with ASD to a sequence of practical experiences and actions which he/she has already visualized and pre-processed, and thus reassures him/her.

Structure and navigation. The site is organised in at most four levels. From the logo, the user can go back to the homepage. In some pages, there is a back command. We have not included pop-ups in Javascript, background sounds, moving images so to avoid sensory annoyance.

The user may navigate from the homepage to the secondary pages by clicking (a) on the images or (b) on the green smiles below, or from the main menu in the header (see Figure 3).

Figure 3. The homepage.

We have discussed with the psychologists, and opted for the use of simple and sketchy symbolic pictures. The idea is that if a user with ASD sees a picture with a bike inside a bike trail (see Figure 4) s/he will conclude s/he can practice this sport.

In the homepage, the user faces a decision "Cosa ti piace?" ("What do you like?"), and has to choose one of the four itineraries, each of one has the same structure and contains: a simple question, an image that represents the general content of the page, links to pictures, videos, four images that link to subsections which include information on where it is located, how we can go there, what can we do there, and what to bring (see Figure 4). All these links can be used to prepare the user to the trip by visualising in advance a map of the location, the

Figure 4. A bike trail tour.

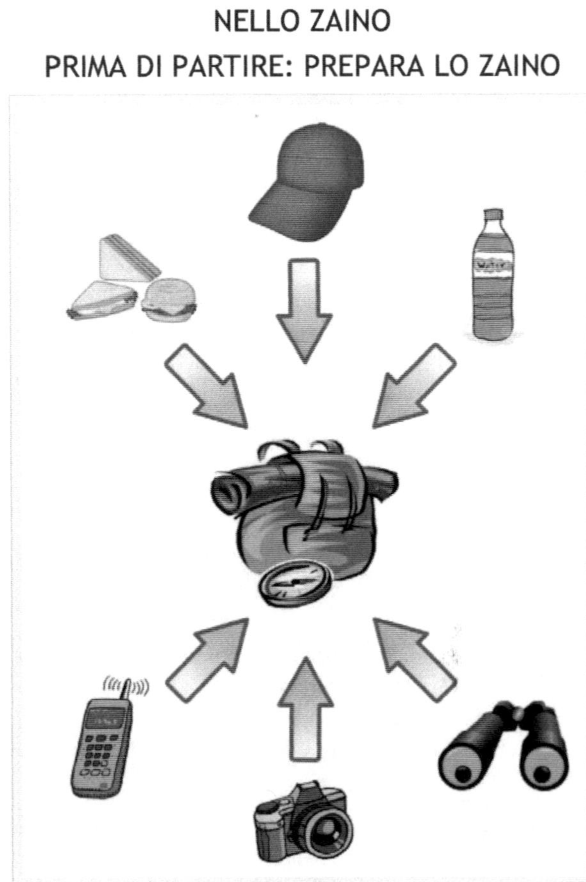

Figure 5. What to bring in the backpack.

Figure 6. A partial screenshot of the game, Sì, No (literally Yes, No).

way the trip will be done (by car, by bus, with relatives, etc), how to behave, and what to see. The last link, a backpack, contains instructions on how pack it and what to bring on that specific itinerary (see Figure 5).

Some sections contain some games, in which we can check the level of attention of the user. There are questions as: "Have you seen this image during the itinerary?" and so on (see Figure 6).

Finally, at the end of most of the pages we can find a print command ("stampa la pagina") and a back command ("torna indietro"), see Figure 7.

Itineraries. We have chosen four possible itineraries, for a one day tourism trip in the neighbourhood of Rieti and the options are: nature, sport, history, and religion. These topics, well fit these users since people with ASD like to explore quiet and relaxing places (nature and religion), love to move around (sport), are very good at memorising dates and images,

Figure 7. A print and a back command.

and often like to take pictures (history). As we will mention in Section V, all these itineraries have all been very much appreciated by the users of the experimentation.

All these itineraries can be done in one day, having as a starting position the centre Nemo, and given that some are urban tours we have pointed out known places inside town to facilitate the comprehension of the destination location.

V. EXPERIMENTAL RESULTS

We first describe the methodology we have used and we then illustrate our experimental results.

A. Methodology.

The development of the Scopririeti (literally, "Discover Rieti") site [23] has followed different steps:

Collection of medical material.

The first phase was the search for the medical material on the specific disability, and the study of the characteristics that define these specific users. This is important both to well meet the accessibility requirements, and for the choice of the appropriate content for the site.

Literature survey.

In the second phase, we have collected all the information about usable and accessible websites for users with ASD, and we have proposed some new interesting features that the site should include (e.g., pictures, games, etc.)

Interviews.

In the third phase, one of our group members (Elisa) has interviewed a group of specialised therapists and professionals of the centre Nemo of Rieti, Italy. This centre hosts people with different neurological and physical disabilities. Elisa has collected information about the different disabilities and about the limits and expectations one could meet while developing the site. She has also participated to different meetings in order to analyse the methodology used by the professionals for approaching these users. What we have realised in this phase is that the site had to be developed for users which were not "too much serious", given that it is not easy to include users with big behavioural problems in tourism activities outdoor. Thus, we have developed our site for users with non-serious or mild disabilities, that had some elementary ability with the use of a computer and with reading.

Website development.

The forth phase was the development of the website applying the four categories of guidelines (discussed in subsection II-B and in Section III), and the hints and suggestions collected in the two previous phases.

Preliminary test on a single user.

The fifth phase was a preliminary test on a single user. We wanted to ensure that the site had been appropriately developed and was comprehensible. We have collected the impressions both of the user and the therapist that was following the meeting. We have thus accordingly adjusted and improved the site.

Test on a group of 9 users.

In the sixth phase, we have then presented this new version to a wider set of users which were first instructed, and were then left free to navigate and explore the site. We have then collected their impressions.

Assessment questionnaire.

The last phase, was the collection of the impressions from the relatives of the users by an assessment questionnaire.

B. Outcomes of the tests and of the assessment questionnaire.

We have tested the site with a set of 9 users (1 female and 8 male) with non-serious or mild disabilities, with different backgrounds and general expertise, with some computer skills, and with some interest on this touring activity.

Disabilities. Our 9 users (whose names have been omitted for privacy reasons) had the following disabilities:

- U1 (19 years old), U2 (18 years old), and U3 (18 years old)
  ASD and medium mental retardation;
- U4 (19 years old)
  ASD and mild mental retardation;
- U5 (14 years old), and U6 (15 years old)
  Asperger syndrome;
- U7 (22 years old) ASD and psychosis;
- U8 (15 years old)
  medium mental retardation
- U9 (17 years old)
  mild mental retardation.

We have excluded from this group users with serious mental disabilities.

Computer skills. All the users had some basics skills on how to use the computer. Depending on the skills, we have left the users to either autonomously navigate, or we have partially helped them. Some have been able to type the name of the site, others have found it already opened. We made sure that could navigate without external distractions.

Test results. We have tested the site with one user at a time.

- User U1 has shown very good computer skills; she was able to autonomously navigate inside the site; she has chosen the historical itinerary, and has navigated inside it in a non sequential way, being intensely involved. She has spent a lot of time looking at pictures and videos.
- User U2 was able to autonomously navigate; he has shown interest for the religious itinerary, and, in general, for the preparation of the backpack in all the different itineraries.
- User U3 was almost independent in the navigation phase. He chose the historical itinerary, and got so involved by looking and photos and videos and completed the test saying "I want to go there!". He really liked the proposed games.
- User U4 has navigated inside the sport section; he has intensely observed pictures and videos, and has

autonomously discussed which places he had already explored, and which were new.

- User U5 has shown very good computer abilities. He has chosen the historical itinerary, and has explored it following the sequential sequence, observing all the pictures, and enthusiastically playing the proposed games.
- User U6 had more difficulties on the use of the computer; thus he had found the homepage open. He has chosen the naturalistic itinerary which he had already visited with the school. He has intensively observed all the pictures, and declared that he wants to go back there with his family.
- User U7 has chosen the religious itinerary; he was very curious about all the churches and saints (he did not know about), thus asking many questions during the navigation and observation of the photos.
- User U8 has chosen the naturalistic itinerary. He was not very skilled in the use of the computer, thus followed some verbal suggestions. He was enthusiastic about the pictures of lakes, plant and animals. We are not sure wether he has really understood all the information, as, e.g., the location of the lakes.
- User U9 has chosen the historical itinerary; he was enthusiastic about the pictures of the underground trail and has declared he wanted to do it soon. Even in this case he needed some verbal help, and we are not sure he has completely understood all the information collected during navigation.

To summarise, the result is that all the users were able to complete the test up to the end. All the users, except a couple of them, had previous navigational experience on the Web, and were able to follow the itineraries and to use the mouse. Figure 8 shows the percentages related to the chosen itineraries. All the users were enthusiastic, and have really

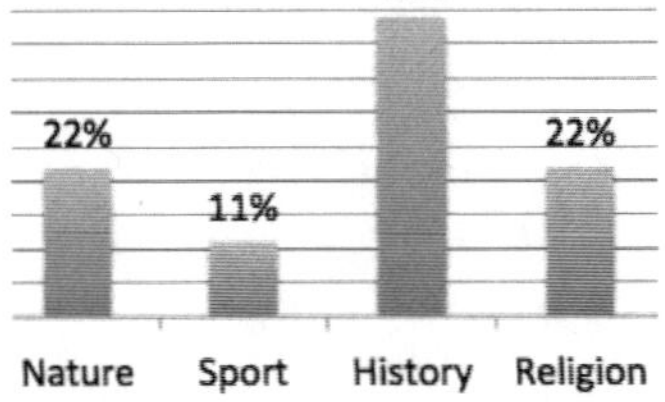

Figure 8. The typologies of chosen itineraries.

liked the site and all the itineraries. In particular, the elements they have preferred are: the pictures, an explanation on how to prepare the backpack, the proposed games. All of them have also asked questions about specific pictures, have discussed the site contents, and some of them really wanted to try the real itinerary right away. The use of the mouse facilitated the navigation. We also tried to run the tests using touch screens, but this seemed to complicate it.

As a limit, we have found that some users have shown some small difficulties on finding the location of some specific pictures, and on the sequences of some itineraries.

Assessment questionnaire. We have finally proposed an assessment questionnaire to the families. We have first met them and we have illustrated and shown the site. Some of them had already seen it previously and had given suggestions on the development of it. This project and the site have been really appreciated, since relatives were happy to have a site where their kids could "autonomously navigate". What emerged is that some of the itineraries were known, others were new. Parents really liked the section on the preparation of the backpack, and the indications on how the trip evolves in order to stimulate their kids orientation capabilities. Globally, the site has been really appreciated both for the contents and for its graphical design, and parents have claimed they will surely use it for future trips.

VI. CONCLUSION AND FUTURE WORK

In this paper, we analysed how an accessible and usable website should be developed in order to be enjoyable by a user with ASD. We have also considered, how such a user can benefit of travelling around the world, and which tips it should follow in order to be able to face in serenity the trip. We have finally presented, an interesting accessible and usable website we have developed for users with ASD. With this site, the users were able to plan and almost independently decide the trip they wanted to do. We have also shown the appreciation results it has received while experimented on a group of users with ASD. This work represented a pilot, prototypal project and the encouraging feedbacks allow us to plan future work:

- validate the usability and the accessibility of the website on a *systematic analysis of data collected on a statistically significant sample* of users. This will require: (a) the creation of new websites that will use our conceptual model; they will contain as case study other cities; (b) the definition of the features of potential user profiles, in order to generating a taxonomic analysis of the experimentation results.
- implement *a mobile app*, that will contain all the case studies and will become a concrete tool for the tourism; it should be an adaptive and ubiquitous app able to follow the users on their trips. We will collect all the information generated by the use of the app, like navigation paths, user profiles, user preferences, geo-localisations, etc.; the aim will be to analyse these data and define a reference model for an adaptive, and semantic app for the tourism of specific class of users.
- implement the *social aspects*, in such a way users could vote their preferred pages, insert a personal comment or share their trips and their experience.

ACKNOWLEDGMENT

We want to thank centro Nemo, all its therapists and operators, the families, the users, and all the people that collaborated to this project.

REFERENCES

[1] "Web content accessibility guidelines (wcag) 2.0," 2008, https://www.w3.org/TR/WCAG20 [accessed: 2016-02-01].

[2] "W3 consortium," 2016, http://www.w3.org [accessed: 2016-02-01].

[3] "Act n. 4 of 9.01.2004," 2004, http://www.normattiva.it/uri-res/N2Ls?urn:nir:stato:legge:2004-01-09;4!vig= [accessed: 2016-02-01].

[4] American Psychiatric Association, Ed., The Diagnostic and Statistical Manual of Mental Disorders: DSM 5. BookpointUS, 2013.

[5] K. Still, R. Rehfeldt, R. Whelan, R. May, and S. Dymond, "Facilitating requesting skills using high-tech augmentative and alternative communication devices with individuals with autism spectrum disorders: A systematic review," Research in Autism Spectrum Disorders, vol. 8, 2014, pp. 1184–1199.

[6] A. Dattolo and F. Luccio, "Modelling volo, an augmentative and alternative communication application," in The Eighth International Conference on Advances in Computer-Human Interactions (ACHI 2015). Lisbon, Portugal, February 22 - 27, 2015 2015.

[7] A. Bondy and L. Frost, "Mands across the water: A report on the application of the picture-exchange communication system in Peru," The Behavior Analyst, vol. 16, 1993, pp. 123–128.

[8] T. Grandin, "How does visual thinking work in the mind of a person with autism? A personal account," Philosophical Transactions of the Royal Society, vol. 364, no. 1522, May 2009, pp. 1437–1442.

[9] C. Sicile-Kira, "What is sensory processing disorder and how is it related to autism?" 2010, https://www.psychologytoday.com/blog/the-autism-advocate/201003/what-is-sensory-processing-disorder-and-how-is-it-related-autism [accessed: 2016-01-09].

[10] "Convention on the rights of persons with disabilities," 2006, http://www.un.org/disabilities/convention/conventionfull.shtml [accessed: 2016-25-01].

[11] "Web accessibility and usability working together," 2010, w3C, http://https://www.w3.org/WAI/intro/usable [accessed: 2016-01-25].

[12] J. Nielsen, "Usability 101: Introduction to usability," 2012, https://www.nngroup.com/articles/usability-101-introduction-to-usability/ [accessed: 2016-03-24].

[13] J. Nielsen and R. Budiu, Mobile Usability. New Riders, 2013.

[14] H. Hamed, "Tourism and autism: An initiative study for how travel companies can plan tourism trips for autistic people," American Journal of Tourism Management, vol. 2, 2013, pp. 1–14.

[15] A. Goehner, "Six tips for traveling with an autistic child. time special.2012." 2012, http://content.time.com/time/specials/packages/article/0,28804,1893554_1893556,00.html [accessed: 2016-20-01].

[16] "Autism asd, travelling through the airport," http://www.dublinairport.com/gns/at-the-airport/autism-asd.aspx [accessed: 2016-20-01].

[17] "Royal air force museum, london, autism friendly trail," 2016, http://www.rafmuseum.org.uk/london/things-to-see-and-do/autism.aspx [accessed: 2016-20-01].

[18] "Metropolitan museum of art in new york, resources for visitors on the autism spectrum," 2016, http://www.metmuseum.org/events/programs/met-access/visitors-with-developmental-and-learning-disabilities/for-visitors-with-autism-spectrum-disorders [accessed: 2016-20-01].

[19] "Autistic globetrotting, autism travel made easy," 2016, http://www.autisticglobetrotting.com/ [accessed: 2016-21-01].

[20] "An interview with jamie knight: autism and accessible web design," 2015, http://www.iheni.com/an-interview-with-jamie-knight-autism-and-accessible-web-design/ [accessed: 2016-25-01].

[21] "Cognitive accessibility user research," 2015, w3C, http://www.w3.org/TR/coga-user-research/ [accessed: 2016-02-01].

[22] E. Pirone, "Turismo e autismo: realizzazione di un sito web turistico per soggetti autistici," Master's thesis, Università Ca' Foscari, Venezia, 2015.

[23] ——, "Scopririeti," 2015, http://www.wordpress.scopririeti.it/ [accessed: 2016-20-02].

EYE POINTER: A Real Time Cost Effective Computer Controlling System Using Eye and Head Movement

Shahed Anzarus Sabab, Sayed Rizban Hussain, Hasan Mahmud, Md. Hasanul Kabir, Md. Kamrul Hasan
Systems and Software Lab (SSL), Department of Computer Science and Engineering
Islamic University of Technology (IUT)
Dhaka, Bangladesh
Email: {sabab05, rizban, hasan, hasanul, hasank}@iut-dhaka.edu

Abstract— **In this paper, we are introducing a low cost and real time computer interaction technique with eye and head gestures along with voice commands, based on a standard webcam. Improving the accuracy of the cursor movement was one of the main challenges while building a system like this. We have applied Kalman filtering for smoothing the mouse cursor movement. The use of voice modality, along with head and eye gestures, made the computer operation more interactive. Calculations of our own defined heuristics were used to improve the accuracy of head and eye detection rate. We obtained remarkable results in eye blink detection, voice command accuracy, and cursor movement. This new multimodal technique, named "EYE POINTER" can be a useful system for the physically impaired people, such as amputees.**

Keywords—face and eye detection; image processing; eye focus point; voice commands; kalman filter; heuristics calculation; gestures; computer navigation; eye movement synchronization.

I. Introduction

Nowadays, human computer interaction is a vital concept for researchers. The computer mouse is arguably the most fundamental element that lets us interact with our computers. As the usage of computer has increased along with the number of users, the interaction devices should provide advanced and user friendly techniques. Rather than using traditional input devices which may not fit a varieties of users, researchers are working on multimodal input, such as eye gestures, voice commands and touch based interaction.

It has been shown that the Reaction Time (RT) latency of the hand is slower than the RT latencies of the eye and head when the subject had to make a button press response with either the index or middle finger of the right hand, dependent upon whether the stimulus occurred to the right or left of the control fixation point [1]. Figure 1 shows the response time for eye and finger in ms.

The number of computer users is increasing every day. There is a large number of disabled people in the world that need to be taken into account. Among them, amputees (people who lost hands in an accident) and acheiropodia (born without hands and feet) [18] exist in great numbers and cannot have the facilities of using a computer because of the lack of having a pair of working hands. For people who do not have hands, there is no efficient solution to interact with the computer. Elderly people also face problems to use current input devices. Considering all these facts, we are introducing another technique to interact with a computer. We are only using a webcam and a microphone. The webcam is used to take the head and eye gestures and to synchronize the mouse pointer with these gestures. The microphone is used to take voice commands, which are interpreted as commands for the computer. As eye and head gestures, along with voice commands, are used to interact with computers, our system is fast and comparable with real time interaction. For the physically disabled people, this can be a way of interacting with a computer.

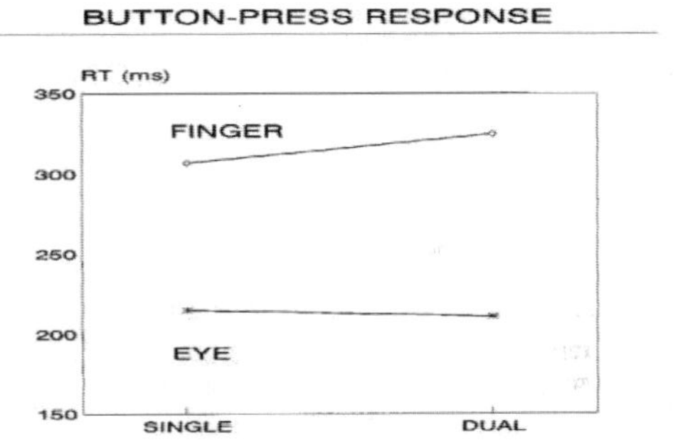

Figure 1. Mean RT latencies of eye and button in both single and dual task conditions

In our system, we have considered the standard resolution of the input image, so that the hardware cost is relatively low. The compensation of the lower resolution image is done using several filtering (median filter, Gaussian filter) and contrast stretching method. A former solution [2][3] was very expensive and did not provide all functionalities that we are providing in our system. We developed our own algorithm to detect eye and face more accurately only using a webcam. Our own developed voice commands were designed considering what human intend to perform through natural voice commands. We introduced Kalman filtering for getting better accuracy of mouse pointer movement. We developed several gestures of the head (e.g., tilting head to the left, right, up, down and movement of the head to any direction) and eye (e.g., eye blink) as navigation methods, which are new in the research area. Therefore, we believe that our interaction technique will bring a new contribution to Human Computer Interaction.

In Section II, the related works are described. Sections III contains some key terms that are defined throughout our work. In Section IV, the system overview is described. Section V has the major focus on the architecture of this system. Section VI contains evaluation and test analysis of the system.

II. Related Works

It has been found that musculoskeletal disorders due to computer work are directly related to ergonomic factors [4]. Traditional computer input devices have some difficulties. They affect the muscles in the human body in many ways. An inappropriate location of the computer can strain the shoulders. When the mouse and the keyboard are in such a place that someone needs to reach, then their shoulders extend forward and the shoulder blades rotate. Too much of these stretches of shoulder muscles causes spasm, fatigue, headaches and stiffness in the neck and shoulders. Long term effects may include severe shoulder pain and muscular imbalance [5][6]. Furthermore, any repetitive movement can result in a health problem called repetitive strain injury (RSI). Using a computer mouse for a long period of time is common cause of RSI in the wrist.

Many input techniques have been introduced as solutions of these aforementioned issues of interacting with a computer. Most of the techniques propose an external hardware. People need to wear external hardware, such as head mounted devices or extra glasses to give gaze information [3]. Tobi 1750 [2] eye tracking device takes eye gaze information using inferred camera. There are three classifications of the infrared wavelength. IR-A, IR-B and IR-C. The International Commission on Non-Ionizing Radiation Protection's (ICNIRP) statement on *Far Infrared Radiation Exposure* have concluded that mainly IR in the IR-A band in high intensities are hazardous to the skin and eye [7]. Moreover, these devices are expensive for the general people to use.

Our solution is based on a simple webcam that does not use any infrared ray. It reduces the burden of carrying external devices. The cost of a webcam minimal compared to the other aforementioned interactive devices. Some computers, such as laptop, has a webcam integrated into them, so our system reduces the cost as well. The main challenge of this system was to work with a low resolution image that we can get from standard webcam. To fetch the required information from that input image, we used image processing techniques and our own algorithm. Another challenge was to design an interactive system that can interpret human intention. We have designed our voice commands in such a way so that it can predict human intention.

III. Proposed System

Our system includes many interactive features which are very user friendly and easy to use. Our system provides whole computer navigation facility along with extensive features. We designed the system keeping in mind human cognition, intention and normal interaction techniques that a person follows while interacting in his or her daily life. Computer navigation is done by taking the movement information of the human head and eye and the commands are passed through voice input the same way a person expresses his or her intentions. The voice commands are also designed in a way such that a user need not memorize them, e.g., for moving mouse cursor the voice command is "move mouse cursor or move cursor", which is very straight forward in regards to the human intention. Again, the cursor movement is smoothened using Kalman filtering [8], so that it gives the same kind of accuracy that a traditional mouse provides. We have proposed our very own heuristics calculation for face and eye detection purpose, which allowed the system to detect face and eye with a very high accuracy rate.

To understand our system, the following keywords descriptive knowledge is necessary:

Fixation or visual fixation is the maintaining of visual gaze on a single location. Whenever someone finds something of interest, his eyes fixate in that direction.

ROI (region of interest) [9] is the selected region of information among several regions of information. Here, the facial position and the possible eye position is the region of our interest. It is used to estimate visual interest information. We have calculated the ROI using our own heuristics.

Eye and head movement refers to voluntary or involuntary movement of the eye and head, helping in acquiring, fixating and tracking visual stimuli. The path followed during the movement of eye and head is the movement path. We are using the eye and head movement calculation to synchronize the mouse cursor movement with it.

Image enhancement technique includes several image preprocessing methodologies. This is a very important step for image processing and noise removal. This enhancement technique usually varies from application to application. For image enhancement, some key processing includes, i.e., filtering (Median filter, Laplacian filter, Gaussian filter, Weighted average filter) [10]. As we worked with low resolution images, we needed several enhancement techniques to compensate for the noises.

Kalman filter [8] is a recursive process that works in real time. It works on noisy observation of data like Gaussian noise. It is largely dependable on feedback. Kalman filtering is used to improve targets tracking, robot localization etc. It takes previous data and the current actual measurement and, based on the previous data, it predicts an optimal solution. Here, prediction and correction is determined by the gain factor.

If Measurement accurate > gain high (K_k) > observation dominate the filter response.

Or if Measurement noisy > gain low (K_k) > observed position considering estimated / predicted position is considered for filter response.

Some basic equations of Kalman filter are shown in Figure2.

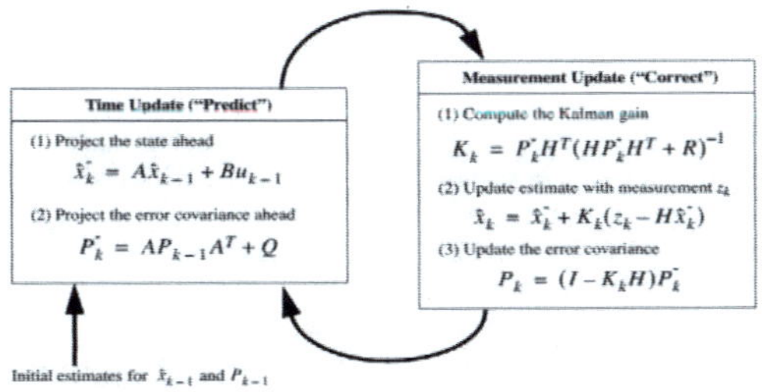

Figure 2. Equations of Kalman Filter

The time update equations can also be mentioned as predictor equations, while the measurement update equations can be mentioned as corrector equations. The final estimation algorithm resembles that of a predictor-corrector algorithm.

IV. SYSTEM OVERVIEW

The whole system is divided into two modes, i.e., "cursor control mode" (for navigation purpose) and "multi-mode" (for performing multipurpose operation).

The first mode is named the **Cursor control mode**. In this mode, the user can simply navigate throughout the computer. The user can move the cursor with eye and head gestures. Here, basic voice commands are implemented to do click options. The user can single click or double click or right click in this mode. They can perform click events with voice commands, as well as with eye blinks. Eye blink detection algorithm is used along with certain time threshold to do the click option. There is a specific voice command to activate the cursor control mode. If a user activates this mode, an activation confirmation feedback (e.g., cursor control mode is activated) will be returned from the system. In this mode, several operations can be performed, such as movement of mouse pointer, maximize or minimize windows, navigate throughout different folders, open and close programs/applications, control mouse pointer synchronization.

The second mode is named **Multi mode**. This mode is mainly introduced for multimedia purposes. After activating this mode (through voice command), voice confirmation feedback will be generated. Different voice commands are introduced here for different multimedia purpose. Here, we can watch video clips with gestures. We can fast forward the video or rewind the video using facial gestures. Other voice commands are introduced to do different tasks. There are voice commands for adjusting the volume or for watching full screen. There are commands to stop, play and pause the video. So, now, the users can enjoy and express their desire in a more flexible way. In this mode, the user can also view photo albums using head gestures. The user will be able to read document files by sliding it up and down using gestures. So, it makes the reading a more flexible and interesting technique.

V. SYSTEM FUNCTIONALITIES

Here, we describe our system functionalities and methodologies to implement them. The common functionalities are divided into 3 parts: 1) Navigation through eye and head movement, 2) Reading and multimedia control through different head and eye gestures, 3) Different operations through voice commands. Figure 3 shows the entire architecture.

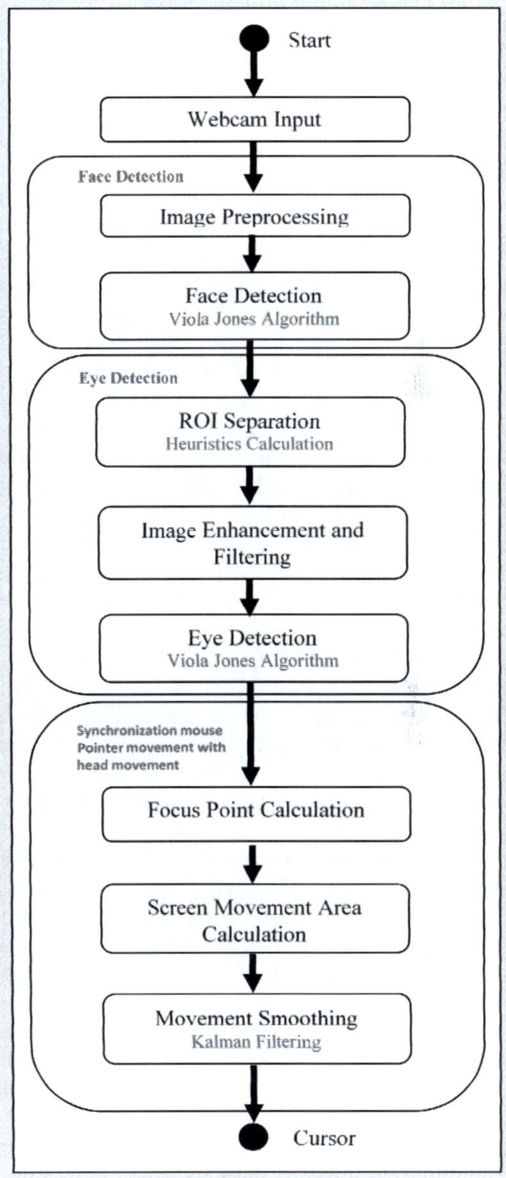

Figure 3. System Architecture

The process begins with taking an input image from an ordinary webcam. As the main challenge in this research is to work with standard resolution image, we have considered the image resolution as 800x600. The frame rate is set to the standard 30 fps. The webcam is set on top of the monitor so that the face of the user can be recorded.

1) Navigation through eye and head movement:

To implement this functionality, face detection methodology is applied by using Viola Jones algorithm [11][12]. It is a machine learning based approach. This technique employs a Haar-features (digital image features used in object recognition) based approach, which makes the rapid and accurate object detection possible. In our case, we have used a sample dataset [13] which includes thousands of negative and positive facial image information. For enhancing the poor image, input taken by the webcam is converted into gray. After that, binary thresholding is applied on the input image. Then, transformation of the image is done using image pyramid. An image pyramid is a collection of images - all arising from a single original image - that are successively down sampled until some desired stopping point is reached. There are two kinds of image pyramids. We have used Gaussian pyramid [14]. Next, contrast stretching Histogram Equalization [10] methodology is applied to enhance the contrast of the image. Face detection is done on the input image afterwards. To detect the eyes, a heuristic calculation is applied to determine the possible area of the eye within the detected face region. This area is named as Region of Interest (ROI) (orange rectangle in Figure 4).

From Figure 4, the Y coordinate of point A(X, Y) is calculated by adding top of the face rectangle (yellow box) with face rectangle height multiplied by a scale factor. Here, the scale factor is user dependent. We have found that our chosen scale factor (3/11) gives the best result for any user sitting in front of the camera. Therefore, point A(X, Y) is determined when the X coordinate is equal to the X coordinate of the face rectangle and the coordinate is previously calculated. Accordingly, the X coordinate of point B(X, Y) is the addition of X coordinate of the face rectangle (yellow box) and face rectangle width, and the Y coordinate of point B(X, Y) is previously calculated. The search area size is approximated by height: height of the face rectangle multiplied by the scale factor and width: face rectangle width. Finally, the possible ROI area (orange box) is approximated from the value of point A(X, Y) and the search area size. The calculations are as follows:

```
YCoordSearchEye = FaceRectangleTop +
(FaceRectangleHeight x 3/11)
StartingEyeSearchPoint = new Point (XCoordFaceRectangle,
YCoordSearchEye)
SearchEyeAreaSize = new Size (FaceRectangleWidth,
(FaceRectangleHeight x 3/11))
PossibleROIEyes = new Rectangle (StartingEyeSearchPoint,
SearchEyeAreaSize)
```

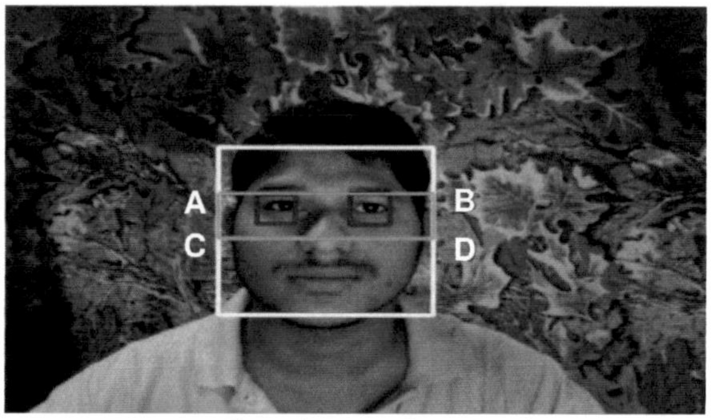

Figure 4. Face and Eye detection

For eye detection inside the ROI region (orange box), Viola Jones algorithm [11][12] is applied using a sample dataset matching of eye [15]. After completion of the detection process, synchronizing the mouse pointer movement with the head movement is needed. For that, we have considered a focus point calculation mechanism.

From Figure 5, the focus point F(X, Y) is calculated using a heuristic value. The X coordinate of F(X, Y) is the addition of the X coordinate of face rectangle (yellow box) and half of the search area size width and the Y coordinate is the addition of the Y coordinate of A(from Figure 4) and half of the search area size height.

```
FocusPoint = new Point (XCoordFaceRectangle +
SearchEyeAreaSizeWidth / 2, YCoordSearchEye +
SearchEyeAreaSizeHeight / 2)
```

The considered focus point is synchronized later as the mouse pointer. Figure 5 shows the white dot point in between the two eyes which we have considered as focus point.

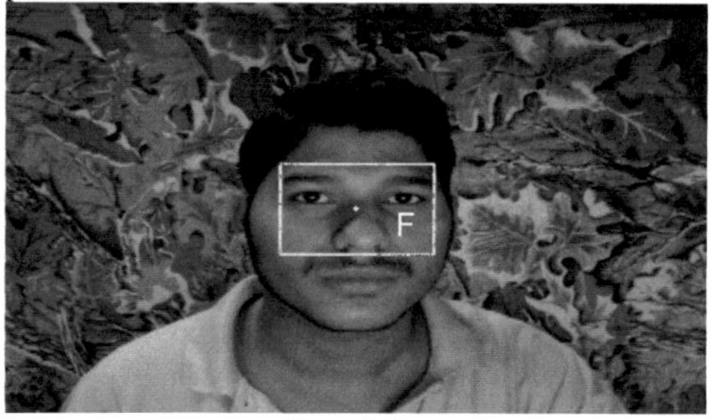

Figure 5. Focus point

Screen movement area calculation is the base region, inside where we have taken the relative focus point movement. This area is the subdivision of the total screen resolution. The movement of the focus point inside this region is multiplied by a factor to interpret that point throughout the total screen resolution. As a result, the little movement of the focus point inside the region is interpreted as the cursor movement within the monitor screen resolution. Though this rapid detection and calculation process in real time is very much effective, there were some mechanical noises which resulted in some disturbance in the movement path of the cursor. We found a blinking effect of the cursor, which is the presence and absence of the mouse cursor due to noises. Therefore, the accuracy in the navigation process was negatively affected. To compensate for this we have implemented Kalman filter [8]: a set of mathematical equations that provides an efficient computational means to estimate the state of the movement. It supports estimation of past, present and future states and it can do so even when the precise nature of the modeled system is unknown. Finally, after applying Kalman filtering we obtained a very smooth movement path resulting in greater accuracy in the navigation process.

2) Reading and multimedia control through different head and eye gestures

For reading and multimedia control, we have defined several head and eye gestures. Different operations are introduced using very effective and easy to learn head gestures. The common operations are: scrolling documents and reading documents, viewing images and switching images, forwarding and rewinding videos, switching through folders etc.

From different gestures, we have used head up, head down, head tilt left and head tilt right. Figure 6 shows the different head gestures used in "EYE POINTER".

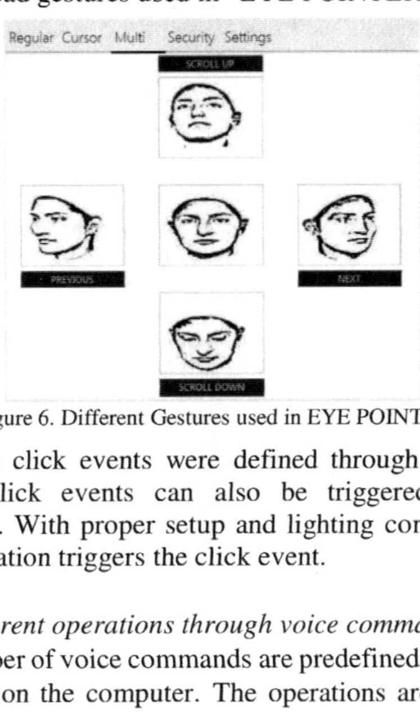

Figure 6. Different Gestures used in EYE POINTER

Mouse click events were defined through eye blinks, whereas click events can also be triggered by voice commands. With proper setup and lighting conditions, eye blink activation triggers the click event.

3) Different operations through voice commands

A number of voice commands are predefined for different operations on the computer. The operations are: maximize window, minimize window, increase /decrease volume, close any window/program, zoom in/out, play/pause video, copy/paste/cut, single click, double click, right click, show previous window, eye blink detect activation on/off, cursor movement on/off, pointer sensitivity increase/decrease, pointer speed increase/decrease, show cursor coordinate, switch through different modes, scrolling up/down, show next/previous picture, full screen on/off and many more.

VI. EVALUATION AND RESULT ANALYSIS

Evaluating a system is a continuous process. We evaluated the system on a group of twenty people of different ages. Among them, 5 were aged between 15 and 20, 9 were between 21 and 40 and the others were above 40. They were given a particular task to do using our system. Their performance was calculated based on the following parameters:

- Time to complete that task.
- Number of errors made in a particular time.
- Number of users making a particular error.
- Number of people completing the task successfully.

In real life, it was difficult to have real amputees as users to evaluate the system. So, during the experimental setup, we have chosen random people, who were restricted to use their hands for computer interaction. The task was to create a folder into a drive and copy a file from another folder which is located in another drive and paste it into that folder. In the experiment, we asked the users to do the task using the traditional mouse and then by using our system.

At the very first stage of the evaluation, we did not use the Kalman filter in our system. For that reason the evaluation results were not satisfactory although we obtained a good accuracy rate of face (100%) and eye region detection (95%).However, the pointer movement accuracy was low. The blink detection rate was moderate. Users were facing problems in performing the tasks. Our system takes voice commands with a very high accuracy rate. So, they faced no problem while providing voice commands. The main concern was the less accurate movement of the pointer. The initial accuracy was approximately 60%.

We faced an important problem while synchronizing the mouse pointer with the eye and head movements, as there was some noise in the movement path of the pointer. To compensate, we used the Kalman filter. This filter provides estimated values based on the previous values. So, this increased the accuracy of the pointer movement when some frames were still missing at the time of tracking. Issues due to missing frames were compensated by the estimated value calculation. So, the pointer movement became smoother. Accuracy increased up to 90%. Table I shows the accuracy rates of the different functionalities of our system.

TABLE I: ACCURACY RATE

Feature	Accuracy
Blink Detection	80%
Voice Commands	95%
Pointer Movement (Without Kalman)	60%
Pointer Movement (With Kalman)	90%

Previously, when the Kalman filter was not used, the average number of errors made by the users while completing the task was very high. However, after using the Kalman filter the error rate has decreased remarkably. This result is presented in Figure 7.

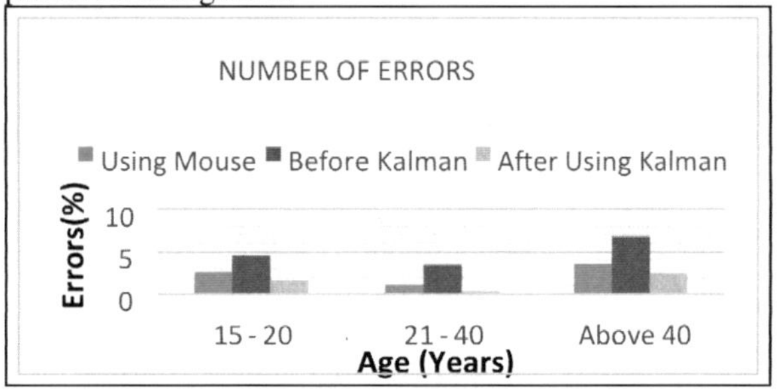

Figure 7. Average Number of errors made by the users.

Next, we repeated the experiment with the same group of people. This time the success rate was very high. Users were able to complete the task with a very high accuracy. It was found that the average time taken to complete the task was best for people aged between 21 and 40. Figure 8 shows the average time information.

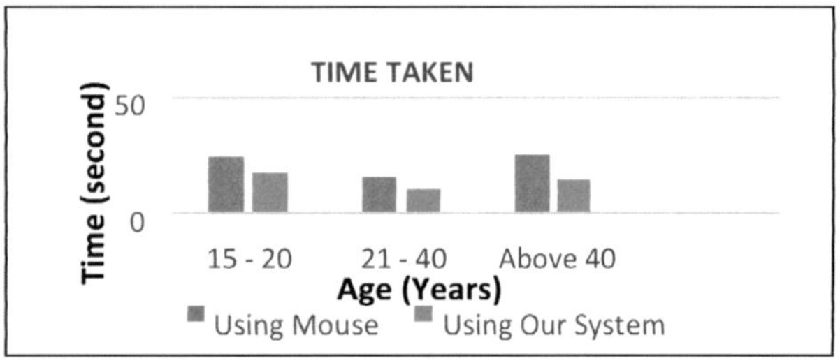

Figure 8. Average Time taken by the user

Figure 9. Success Rate.

In the final experiment, the number of people completing the task was very high. Almost everyone completed the task successfully. However, it is clear from Figure 9 that, before using Kalman, the success rate was really poor.

User overview and feedback after using our system was remarkable. People are always interested in using new technologies. Our unique system got the attention of everyone. They felt great interest in using our system.

The voice commands were preferred by the users in our experiment. The commands are so simple to learn and remember. It feels like communicating with another person. There is appropriate feedback for the commands, so the users will get a real time experience of computer interaction. There is no extra burden of using external devices to pass commands. According to the user feedback we received, we proposed this user interactive system where, there is a scope of change if needed.

VII. CONCLUSION

Trying to build a system like "Eye Pointer" is not new Researchers were trying to build this kind of system for decades [16][17]. But now, the advancement and the availability of technology gives us an advantage. The availability of the latest dataset helped us build a low-cost system that is very effective. "Eye Pointer" is an innovative approach while using these materials. This is a generic navigation system which makes the computer navigation technique a real time interactive process. The main focus point of this paper is to build a navigation system that is completely hands free with the cheapest cost possible. We have overcome many challenges in designing this interactive system such as: designing voice commands considering human cognition, increasing the mouse pointer movement accuracy rate, enhancing the detection capability of eyes and face, designing a system so that it can fit standard goals of a user. Our system is designed with the focus on disabled people. We have tried to give them a solution mechanism to interact with the computer. However, there are some limitations. Our blink detection can only work in the proper lighting condition. In case of voice input we have found that, in an environment of loud noises, our system takes wrong input. Finally, our future plan is to update our research so that our system can be an effective approach for any end user.

REFERENCES

[1] Harold Bekkering, Jos J. Adam, Herman Jingma, A. Huson and H. T. A Whiting, "Reaction time latencies of eye and hand movements in single- and dual-task conditions",in Experimental Brain Research, Springer-Verlag 1994,7 September 1993, 97(3):471-6.

[2] Young-Min Jang, Rammohan Mallipeddi, Sangil Lee, Ho-Wan Kwak and Minho Lee, "Human intention recognition based on eyeball movement pattern and pupil size vibration," School of Electrical Engineerin, Kyungpool National University, in Neurocomputing 2013 Ngip-khean Chuan and Ashok Sivaji, "Combining Eye Gaze and Hand Tracking for Pointer Control in HCI", in IEEE Colloquium on Humanities, Science & Engineering Research, 2012.

[3] Michal Kowalik, "How to build low cost eye tracking glasses for head mounted system," martin tall on gaze interaction, A blog on research and developments in eye tracking and gaze interaction, 2010.

[4] Jens Wahlström, "Ergonomics, musculoskeletal disorders and computer work," Department of Occupational and Environmental Medicine, Sundsvall Hospital, SE-851 86 Sundsvall, Sweden, 2005.

[5] Annabel Cooper and Leon Straker, "Mouse versus keyboard use: A comparison of shoulder muscle load", International Journal of Industrial Ergonomics, 1998; 22:351-357.

[6] B. M Blatter and P. M Bongers, "Duration of computer use and mouse use in relation to musculoskeletal disorders of neck or upper limb", International Journal of Industrial Ergonomics, Volume 30, Issues 4–5, October–November 2002; 295–306.

[7] Soyun Cho et al., "Effects of Infrared Radiation and Heat on Human Skin Aging ", Journal of Investigative Dermatology Symposium Proceedings (2009) 14; 15–19.

[8] Greg Welch and Gary Bishop, "An Introduction to Kalman Filter," Department of Computer Science, University of North Carolina, Technical Report ,TR 95-041, July 24, 2006.

[9] Jing Zhang, Li Zhuo, Zhenwei Li and Yingdi Zhao, "An Approach of Region of Interest Detection Based on Visual Attention and Gaze Tracking," Signal and Information Processing Laboratory, Beijing University of Technology, Communication and Computing (ICSPCC), 2012 IEEE International Conference ; 228-233.

[10] R. Gonzalez and R. Woods, Digital Image Processing, 3rd ed.: Pearson Education, Reference book, 2009.

[11] Paul Viola and Michael Jones, "Rapid Object Detection using a Boosted Cascade of Sample Features," in computer vision and pattern recognition 2001.

[12] Paul Viola and Michael J. Jones, "Robust Real-Time Face Detection," International Journal of Computer Vision, 57(2), 2004; 137–154.

[13] https://github.com/Itseez/opencv/blob/master/data/haarcascades/haarcascade_frontalface_alt_tree.xml , retrieved: October, 2015.

[14] http://docs.opencv.org/2.4/doc/tutorials/imgproc/pyramids/pyramids.html, retrieved: October, 2015

[15] https://github.com/Itseez/opencv/blob/master/data/haarcascades/haarcascade_eye.xml, retrieved: October, 2015.

[16] Mohammand Usman Ghani, Sarah Chaudhry, Maryam Sohail and Muhammad Nafees Geelani, "GazePointer: A Real Time Mouse Control Implementation Based On Eye Gaze Tracking," Department of Electrical Engineering, COMSATS Institute of Information Technology, Lahore, Pakistan , Multi Topic Conference (INMIC), 2013 16th International; 154-159.

[17] Yingbo Li, David S. Monaghan and Noel E. O'Connor, "Real-Time Gaze Estimation using Kinect and a HD Webcam," INSIGHT Centre for Data Analysis, Dublin City University, Ireland, 2014.

[18] Stefan Mundlos and Denise Horn, Limb Malfunctions: An atlas of genetic disorders of limb development, Berlin; London: Springer, 2011, P: 62.

A Process Approach to Ensuring Universally Designed Web Content

A preliminary case study of the Norwegian Broadcasting Corporation

Lars Henrik Nordli and G. Anthony Giannoumis
Department of Computer Science
Oslo and Akershus University College of Applied Sciences
Oslo, Norway
e-mail: s180492@stud.hioa.no and gagian@hioa.no

Abstract—**This work-in-progress article aims to identify and overcome procedural challenges that impede creation of universally designed content for the Norwegian Broadcasting Corporation's website. Universal design refers to the design of Web content for use by the widest possible population. This article presents initial results gathered from current policies, work practices and employee experiences. Preliminary results show that editorial employees are unfamiliar with internal and external guidelines regarding universal design of Web content, in addition to believing that they, as editors, are not responsible to ensure universally designed Web content. The lack of internal guidelines regarding universal design of Web content, and the employees' lack of knowledge about these, may act as a barrier to ensuring universal design in practice.**

Keywords-universal design; accessibility; organizational processes; Web accessibility; Web content; WCAG; ATAG.

I. Introduction

This article investigates current practices and workflows regarding universal design of Web content and explores editorial employee's experiences at the Norwegian Broadcasting Corporation. Universal design refers to the design of Web content for use by the widest possible population. The research will identify organizational issues through investigating the editorial employees' workflow, experience and concerns regarding universal design when creating Web content. The goal of the research is to contribute to extend the findings of [9] and [17]. This article asks, "How do editorial employees utilize current processes and practices regarding universal design, and how can the Norwegian Broadcast Corporation's (NRK) publication systems help editorial employees to create universally designed content?" The result of the research will provide recommendations for ensuring universal design in organizational processes, policies and workflows.

The areas of protocols, metadata standards, individual work practices and the development and use of stable and reliable workflows are not exhaustively researched and remain somewhat unanswered. Research has not yet fully examined practices and workflows regarding accessibility [13]. In addition to this, research has yet to investigate how the editorial employees experience the content management system, and how the editorial employees take universal design into consideration when creating content for the Web.

The Norwegian Broadcasting Corporation (NRK) is a non-commercial, government-owned broadcasting organization that provides TV, radio and Internet content to the population of Norway. NRK is the largest media organization in Norway with approximately 3500 employees, distributed across fourteen district offices. NRK is authorized to engage in broadcasting activities under the Broadcasting Act [11]. The Statutes for the Norwegian Broadcasting Corporation [19] provides the purpose, activities, limits and structure of NRK. Chapter two outlines NRK's social mission [15]. Most notably, that

- NRK should support and strengthen democracy [19] (§12);
- NRK should provide sufficient information so that the public can actively participate in democratic processes [19] (§12a.);
- NRK should be accessible to the public [19] (§13); and that
- NRK's services should take into consideration people with disabilities [19] (§13c.).

All these statements can be interpreted to underline the importance of universal design of NRK's products, in this case Web content on NRK's website.

NRK's website is one of Norway's most visited websites [1] and is required to comply with the national regulations [8] (§4) concerning accessibility and universal design of websites and website content. The national regulations refer to the Web Content Accessibility Guidelines (WCAG) 2.0 [20] as a measurement of compliance. Researchers argue that these guidelines may not produce accessible Web content [16].

Section 2 presents previous work on the subject in addition to acting as a frame for the research. Section 3 states the current problem and the research's importance. Section 4 describes what methods will be used in the research, and why the methods have been chosen. Section 5 presents the preliminary results from current research. Section 6 presents a conclusion that can be drawn from the results and discusses future work that exceeds the scope of this research. Finally, Section 7 describes the next steps and plans for the future of this research.

II. Previous Work

Researchers argue that there are other factors besides technical properties and usability metrics involved making the Internet accessible, e.g., political, economical and social aspects [2], and states that people, both users and workers, and processes during development or creation of a product should play a larger role in Web accessibility [6]. The research of [6] suggests the British Standard BS8878 [3] as accessibility guidelines that focuses on processes and business.

III. Statement of the Problem

NRK's website must adhere to the NRK policy [19], the Broadcasting Act and national regulations regarding universal design of ICT [8]. Norway has ratified the United Nations Convention on the Rights of Persons with Disabilities [18], which in Article 9 obligates the Norwegian government to ensure access to information and communications technology for people with disabilities.

The employees at NRK create digital print and multimedia content daily. The editorial employees are continuously revising news articles and pages on NRK's website, which makes content subject to constant change according to different work practices. In addition to this, the employees work in a fast-paced and dynamic environment. The editorial employees are likely to work on multiple tasks at once, and the cognitive effort of ensuring accessible content may not always be considered a priority for the editorial employees [12].

Content on NRK's website is created through the content management system **Polopoly** and rendering system **Panorama** as seen in Fig. 1. Most of Polopoly's functionality is developed in-house at NRK. Polopoly stores both textual content and metadata, over which the editorial employees have control. Polopoly renders Web pages based on text content and metadata. The editorial employees do not control the rendering process. However, these systems do not ensure universally designed Web content for the end-user: Polopoly does not inform about or aid the authors with creating accessible and universally designed content. There has been no investigation of the rendering tool, Panorama, and research suggests that it may have an impact on the accessibility of the content that is rendered [9]. Plug-ins for e.g., spell-check and multimedia management may play a part in the rendering process, suggested in research by [7] and [14].

Research shows that NRK's website does not comply with international accessibility guidelines WCAG 2.0 [20], their content management system does not comply with industry guidelines [21], and that consumers experience usability barriers with the Web content's structure, layout and design [17].

IV. Research Methodology

It is important to first understand what current practices, policies and workflows the editorial employees base their content creation on, so that the research can inform relevant theory. After exploring and explaining the current state of content creation at NRK, the research can further inform or extend on theory to ultimately assist editorial employees create universally designed content for nrk.no.

In order to explore and explain the current state with sufficient depth, qualitative methods will be used for data collection. Qualitative methods are in addition suitable for informing theory. This stage of the research will focus on how the editorial employees interpret their environment and tasks related to content creation. Data will be collected through field studies/on-site observations and semi-structured interviews with the editorial employees. This can be identified as (participatory) action research, which is suggested to be effective to bridge theory and practice, as well as to consider and incorporate the editorial employees' view [4]. Editorial employees will be sampled purposively because it is only relevant to investigate the employees that create content for NRK's website.

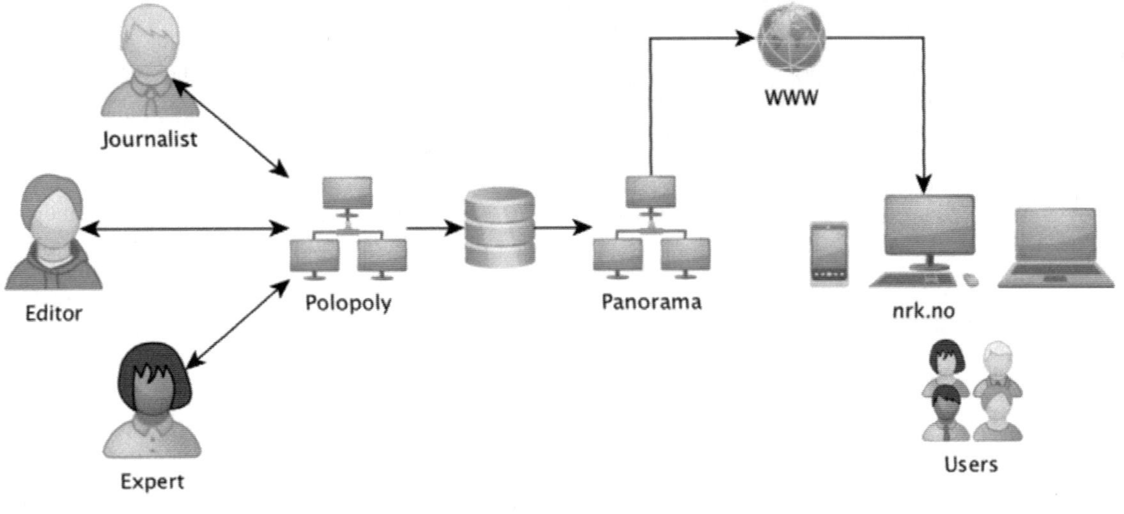

Figure 1. A simplified model of how Polopoly and Panorama create content. Editorial employees create content in Polopoly content management system.

Some themes from the interview guide are responsibility and activities; interpretation of Polopoly as a Content Management System (CMS); experiences with Polopoly as a CMS; familiarity with Universal Design (UD); utilization of UD (when creating content); the employee's knowledge of internal or external accessibility guidelines; internal processes at NRK; and plain language.

The field study has been performed with one participant. One researcher sat at the participant's desk for the duration of a whole work day while observing the participant and co-workers involved while taking notes. The participant was free to comment or elaborate at any time.

A qualitative interview has been performed with one participant. The interview was audio recorded, transcribed and analyzed for themes from the interview guide. Information that came to attention, which was not a part of the interview guide, created its own theme.

V. Preliminary Results

A. Technical Introduction of Polopoly

A technical introduction of Polopoly with the Technical Team Leader for Development was conducted in order to gain domain knowledge and to better understand terminology and situations for the field studies and semi-structured interviews. This introduction revealed that there are numerous plug-ins connected to Polopoly, including spell-check and media content management in addition to the Panorama rendering engine.

B. Field Study

One field study has been conducted. An editor was observed for five hours while creating a news article in Polypoly. Relevant points and observation was collected. The editor also made some general comments throughout the session.

The field study identified that the environment was generally hectic, but communicative and team-friendly as the employees often walked up to other employees for advice or consultation on matters. However, on few occasions one editor's workflow was being interrupted while waiting for proofreading from another colleague. This caused delays and uncertainty on a matter that had to be handled quickly. In addition to this, NRK's intranet solution was not being used as intended – or at all. This has not proven to be relevant at this time, but intranets may promote internal communication [5] and might help tackle challenges with internal communication.

Regarding universal design, an editor expressed uncertainty of what a good alternative text to an image should be. The editor was familiar with the term, and entered a description on all images in the CMS. At the same time, the editor expressed that "journalists would never enter additional text content to multimedia content when creating a news article" [22], in addition to suggesting that descriptions could be used as alternative text to images, automatically by Polopoly.

Similar to a discovery in the technical introduction, there were numerous plug-ins connected to Panorama that editors frequently used. As mentioned earlier, these systems may interfere with the universal design [7] of the content.

C. Preliminary Interview

One semi-structured interview has been conducted. The participant had no knowledge of internal NRK guidelines of policies regarding universal design or accessibility other than the NRK policy [19]. The participant also stated that "information flow and inter-department workflow was often time consuming and complicated" [22].

The qualitative interview revealed that the participant, an editor, was familiar with universal design as a term. However, it was explained exclusively as a requirement from the law, i.e., national regulations [8]. In particular, the editor did not know what WCAG 2.0 guidelines were or what the national regulations regarding universal design of ICT required [22]. Interestingly, the participant experienced universal design of Web content as "somebody else's problem" [22], referring to programmers as an example of employees that were in charge of legal compliance with universal design of content on NRK's website. Researchers argue that Web accessibility evaluation methods often require technical expertise or knowledge, which can result in unknowingness of when or how to use these evaluations [10]. This may be the case for the participant, considering the statement that other employees are responsible for universal design compliance.

VI. Conclusion and Future Work

The preliminary results suggest that there are three main barriers hindering the creation of universally designed content on NRK's website. These are social barriers, organizational barriers, and technology barriers. More specifically, the lack of awareness about UD among the editorial employees, organizational communication challenges, and the lack of policies on UD of Web content may be opportunities for change to ensure a more accessible website.

Future work may include studying similar organizations in order to identify if differences in organizational structure has an affect on how editorial employees publish content online.

VII. Next Steps

A minimum of five editorial employees will participate in the semi-structured interviews, and a minimum of two field studies/on-site observations will be conducted. Polopoly's plug-ins will be subject of evaluation regarding how they affect the universal design of Internet content. Data collection will be completed by the end of February 2016.

References

[1] Alexa Internet Incorporated. (2015). Alexa - Top Sites in Norway. Retrieved from http://www.alexa.com/topsites/countries/NO last accessed March 19, 2016

[2] D. Boos, G. Grote, and H. Guenter (2013). "A toolbox for managing organisational issues in the early stage of the

development of a ubiquitous computing application". Personal Ubiquitous Comput., 17(6), 1261-1279. doi:10.1007/s00779-012-0634-y

[3] British Standards International. (2010). BS 8878:2010 Web accessibility. Code of practice: British Standards International,.

[4] M. Brydon-Miller, D. Greenwood, and P. Maguire (2003). "Why Action Research?" Action Research, 1(1), 9-28. doi:10.1177/14767503030011002

[5] S.-c. Chiu (2015). "Can Internal Communication Drive Business? An Overview of Its Strategic Values and Practice Tips." In P. P. K. Ng & C. S. B. Ngai (Eds.), Role of Language and Corporate Communication in Greater China (pp. 203-222): Springer Berlin Heidelberg.

[6] M. Cooper, D. Sloan, B. Kelly, and S. Lewthwaite (2012). "A challenge to Web accessibility metrics and guidelines: putting people and processes first." Paper presented at the Proceedings of the International Cross-Disciplinary Conference on Web Accessibility, Lyon, France. http://dl.acm.org/citation.cfm?doid=2207016.2207028 last accessed March 19, 2016

[7] L. Eshkevari, G. Antoniol, J. R. Cordy, and M. D. Penta (2014). "Identifying and locating interference issues in PHP applications: the case of WordPress." Paper presented at the Proceedings of the 22nd International Conference on Program Comprehension, Hyderabad, India. http://dl.acm.org/citation.cfm?doid=2597008.2597153 last accessed March 19, 2016

[8] Regulations on universal design of ICT-solutions. (2013). (Forskrift om universell utforming av IKT-løsninger). "Forskrift om universell utforming av informasjons- og kommunikasjonsteknologiske (IKT)-løsninger." Retrieved from https://lovdata.no/dokument/SF/forskrift/2013-06-21-732. last accessed March 19, 2016

[9] S. Kessel, N. Sanderson, and W. Chen (2014). "Public Media on the Web for Everyone – An Evaluation of the Norwegian Broadcasting Cooperation's Website." In C. Stephanidis (Ed.), HCI International 2014 - Posters' Extended Abstracts (Vol. 435, pp. 32-36): Springer International Publishing.

[10] P. Koutsabasis, E. Vlachogiannis, and J. S. Darzentas (2010). Beyond Specifications: Towards a Practical Methodology for Evaluating Web Accessibility. J. Usability Studies, 5(4), 157-171.

[11] Broadcating Act (1992). (Lov om kringkasting og audiovisuelle bestillingstjenester (kringkastingsloven)).

[12] C. M. Law, J. S. Yi, Y. S. Choi, and J. A. Jacko (2006). "Are disability-access guidelines designed for designers?: do they need to be?" Paper presented at the Proceedings of the 18th Australia conference on Computer-Human Interaction: Design: Activities, Artefacts and Environments, Sydney, Australia. http://dl.acm.org/citation.cfm?doid=1228175.1228244 last accessed March 19, 2016

[13] P. Matthews and J. Aston (2013). Interactive multimedia ethnography: Archiving workflow, interface aesthetics and metadata. J. Comput. Cult. Herit., 5(4), 1-13. doi:10.1145/2399180.2399182

[14] H. V. Nguyen, C. Köstner, and T. N Nguyen. (2014). "Exploring variability-aware execution for testing plugin-based Web applications." Paper presented at the Proceedings of the 36th International Conference on Software Engineering, Hyderabad, India. http://dl.acm.org/citation.cfm?doid=2568225.2568300 last accessed March 19, 2016

[15] NRK Policy (2012) (NRK-plakaten). Retrieved from https://www.regjeringen.no/globalassets/upload/kud/medier/nrk/nrk-plakaten_per_18juni2012.pdf. last accessed March 19, 2016

[16] C. Power, A. Freire, H. Petrie, and D. Swallow (2012). "Guidelines are only half of the story: accessibility problems encountered by blind users on the Web". Paper presented at the Proceedings of the SIGCHI Conference on Human Factors in Computing Systems, Austin, Texas, USA. http://delivery.acm.org/10.1145/2210000/2207736/p433-power.pdf?ip=158.38.214.20&id=2207736&acc=ACTIVE SERVICE&key=CDADA77FFDD8BE08%2E4CE6010CAD F15ADE%2E4D4702B0C3E38B35%2E4D4702B0C3E38B3 5&CFID=514637104&CFTOKEN=39937494&__acm__=14 32636256_61353d95152ba292b0967360df282dc9 http://dl.acm.org/citation.cfm?doid=2207676.2207736 last accessed March 19, 2016

[17] N. Sanderson, W. Chen, and S. Kessel (2015). "The Accessibility of Web-Based Media Services – An Evaluation." In M. Antona & C. Stephanidis (Eds.), Universal Access in Human-Computer Interaction. Access to Today's Technologies (Vol. 9175, pp. 242-252): Springer International Publishing.

[18] United Nations. (2007). Convention on the Rights of Persons with Disabilities. Retrieved from http://www.un.org/disabilities/default.asp?id=150. last accessed March 19, 2016

[19] The Statutes for the Norwegian Broadcasting Corporation. (1996) (Vedtekter for Norsk rikskringkasting AS). Retrieved from https://www.regjeringen.no/globalassets/upload/kud/medier/nrk/nrks_vedtekter_per_10juni_2014.pdf. last accessed March 19, 2016

[20] World Wide Web Consortium. (2008). Web Content Accessibility Guidelines (WCAG) 2.0. Retrieved from http://www.w3.org/TR/WCAG20/ last accessed March 19, 2016

[21] World Wide Web Consortium. (2013). Authoring Tool Accessibility Guidelines (ATAG) 2.0. Retrieved from http://www.w3.org/TR/ATAG20/ last accessed March 19, 2016

[22] Participant 1 (2015). Interview. December 3, 2015

Designing and Evaluating Interfaces for the CAPTAIN MEMO Memory Prosthesis

Fatma Ghorbel[1,2], Nebrasse Ellouze[1], Elisabeth Métais[2], Faiez Gargouri[1], Fayçal Hamdi[2], Noura Herradi[2,3]
[1] Laboratoire MIRACL, Université de Sfax, Sfax, Tunisie
[2] Laboratoire CEDRIC, Conservatoire National des Arts et Métiers (CNAM), Paris, France
[3]Ecole Centrale d'Electronique (ECE), Paris, France
E-mail: fatmaghorbel6@gmail.com, nebrasse.ellouze@gmail.com, metais@cnam.fr, faiez.gargouri@isimsf.rnu.tn, faycal.hamdi@cnam.fr, noura.herradi@hotmail.com

Abstract— **This paper presents the design, development and evaluation of the interfaces of the CAPTAIN MEMO memory prosthesis that target mainly individuals who are showing early/moderate signs of Alzheimer's disease. One of the major barriers that hinder Alzheimer's disease patients using software application is its complex interface. In this paper, we present a set of design guidelines for accommodating changes which accompany the Alzheimer's disease. Based on these guidelines, we develop the interfaces of the CAPTAIN MEMO memory prosthesis that meet the special needs of Alzheimer's disease patients. The developed interfaces present the advantages that they are user-friendly, multimodal, enjoyable and configurable. The objective of this work is to promote accessibility to the target user. The evaluation of the interfaces' accessibility is carried out with 24 Alzheimer's disease patients who are living in an assisted living environment in Sfax-Tunisia. The primary results show that the majority of the users are almost satisfied with the developed interfaces.**

Keywords- alzheimer's disease; memory prosthesis; user inetrfaces; multimodalities; speech-to-text; spoken interactions; touch; adjustable interface; design for all.

I. Introduction

This paper presents user-friendly, multimodal, enjoyable and configurable interfaces that are developed for the CAPTAIN MEMO memory prosthesis [1].

In the VIVA project [2] ("Vivre à Paris avec Alzheimer en 2030 grâce aux nouvelles technologies"), we are proposing a memory aid, called CAPTAIN MEMO, to help users to palliate mnesic problems. It target mainly individuals who are showing early/moderate signs of AD (Alzheimer's Disease).This prosthesis aims to enhance the well being of AD patients' lives.

AD patients present own characteristics that differ from other user groups, parts of them are related to AD and the other parts are related to the normal effects of aging. These characteristics impair AD patients to use standard user interface. Thus, the design of the user interfaces of the CAPTAIN MEMO memory prosthesis should suit AD patients' specific needs to be accessible and easily used; becoming user-friendly interfaces. The CAPTAIN MEMO memory prosthesis tends to follow the "design-for-all" philosophy [1] that means considering not only intelligent healthy users who master technologies, but everybody of all ages and abilities, including the elderly suffering from AD.

The CAPTAIN MEMO memory prosthesis provides multimodal interfaces. Indeed, the interfaces' interactions are not restricted to traditional modalities. We add other modalities: audio, speech recognition and touch.

We add humor and fun to the interfaces in order to make it attractive and seduce more AD patients to use the CAPTAIN MEMO memory prosthesis frequently.

The interfaces are adjustable since the user can adjust text size and volume themselves. They can be adapted to the user's visual and auditory abilities.

The remainder of this paper is structured as follows: Section II gives an overview of the CAPTAIN MEMO memory prosthesis. Section III reviews the main characteristics of AD patients, including the changes related to AD and the changes related to the normal effects of aging. Section IV proposes a set of design guidelines which should be taken into account for designing interfaces dedicated to AD patients. Section V describes the implemented interfaces. In Section VI, we present the evaluation of the interfaces that it is conducted on 24 AD patients. In Section VII, we discuss some related work and describe how our work differs from the existing ones. Finally, in Section VIII, we conclude and we give some perspectives.

II. Overview of the Ongoing CAPTAIN MEMO Memory Prosthesis

This section gives an overview of the ongoing CAPTAIN MEMO memory prosthesis for persons who are showing early/moderate sign of AD.

A. *Basic Functionalities*

The CAPTAIN MEMO memory prosthesis supplies a set of services indoor and outdoor. We categorize these services into two categories: *"Life Enhancing Services"* and *"Memory Refresh/Exercising Service"*.

1) Life Enhancing Services

Life enhancing services can be categorised into the following four services: *"Family/Entourage Show", "Calendaring", "Diary" and "Event Show"*.

The first module is called *"Family/Entourage Show"*. It reminds AD patients of their family members and their surroundings. It is also devoted to "remember things about people", i.e., retrieving a person by navigation in the family/entourage tree, retrieving a person according to criteria, retrieving a person facing the camera, retrieving information about a person (name, family or conviviality relationship, age, preferences, gifts exchanged, favourite meals, recent events, shared events, etc.).

The second service is called "*Calendaring*". It reminds AD patients of all daily activities that should be performed. The events can refer to information stored in the prosthesis such as photos to help the patient recognize the person he needs to talk to or the place he needs to go to. The reminder / alarm can be set to be passive or active.

Another service is called "*Diary*". It allows AD patients to document their important events and personal details (an electronic memory). The stored data may be selectively updated, retrieved and displayed at the convenience of the user. AD patients may interrogate this electronic diary and read what they have written before to refresh memory.

The last service is called "*Event Show*". It allows AD patients to take photo and video e.g., photo and video of people, places and events. The user is then given a chance to tag the photo or video with phrases that reminds them of the subject. AD patients can go back to the stored information as frequently as needed.

2) Memory Refresh/Exercising Service

This service is called "*Biographical Quiz*". It aims to refresh the AD patients' memory by quizzing the patient about information related to their family, surrounding, event and so on, e.g., What is the favourite meal of John? What's your son's favourite animal? Is Alice black-haired? Does Robert wear clothes (Adding humor)? What does your mother work? After each question, the patient is asked to give the correct answer. The highlight of this service is that each patient has his/her own collection of questions linked to his/her private life.

B. *System Architecture and Used Technologies*

In this section, we present the system architecture and the technologies used to implement the CAPTAIN MEMO memory prosthesis.

The CAPTAIN MEMO memory prosthesis is a semantic web application based on RDF ontologies and implemented in J2EE platform. We use the Jena API [3] and the SPARQL language [4].

The CAPTAIN MEMO memory prosthesis is a distributed multitiered application, based on MVC [5] in J2EE platform. Figure 1 shows the architecture of the ongoing system.

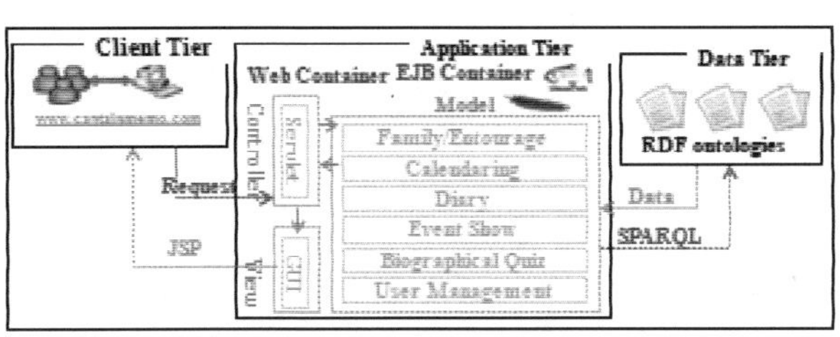

Figure 1. System architecture.

The CAPTAIN MEMO prosthesis consists of three tiers as it is distributed over three different locations: the client machines, the J2EE server machine and the data machine. We use Glassfish [6] as J2EE server and Apache [7] as HTTP server.

The CAPTAIN MEMO memory prosthesis follows the MVC design pattern. The Model components represent the business logic (EJB). The View components (JSP) represent the interface that displays the processing results of the model components. The Controller (Servlet) manages the coordination between the Model and the View.

III. CHARACTERISTICS OF ALZHEIMER'S PATIENTS

In this section, we discuss expected changes which accompany the AD. In fact, interfaces devoted to AD patients are not that common [8]. The difficulty in using interfaces is one of the reasons why AD patients are not comfortable to use computer or software [8]. The design of the interfaces should suit the user's needs [8][9] to be accessible and easily used. To adapt the interface to their needs; we first have to know their main problems. Compared to young healthy people AD patients suffer from AD-related changes and age-related changes, as shown in Figure 2.

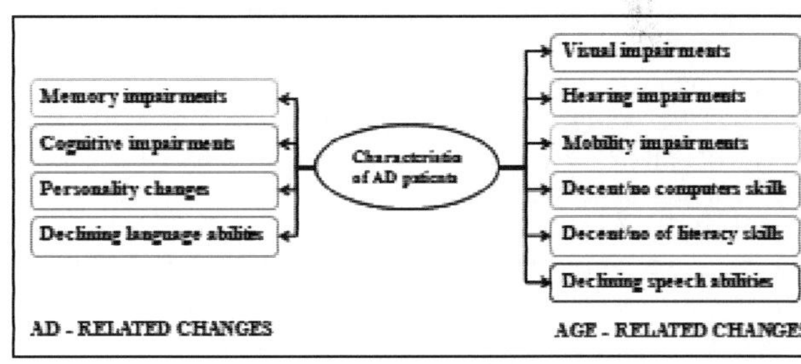

Figure 2. Characteristics of AD patients.

A. *Alzheimer's Disease-Related Changes*

Disabilities related to AD can be grouped into four groups: memory impairments, cognitive impairments, personality changes and declining language abilities.

Memory impairments - One of the most common symptoms of AD is memory loss [8][10][12][14], especially short-term memory or forgetting recently learned information. The semantic information is normally preserved in long-term memory [15], e.g., history and languages.

Cognitive impairments - The cognitive ability is one of the functions to decline due to AD [8][12]. Cognitive is the ability to generate ideas, to think, to remember and to focus on. AD causes a decrease in cognitive abilities such as the level of intelligence, speed of information processing, ability to learn, reasoning, judgment, attention ability [16], ability to solve problem and concentration ability [16].

Personality changes - AD patients experience changes in personality. The National Alzheimer's Association estimates that up to 40% of patients experience depression. They are anxious about technology [17] and may refuse to learn [18].

Declining language abilities - AD patients exhibit declining language abilities [14]. Indeed, early stage AD patients may substitute words that have similar meaning.

Moderate stage AD patients have increased difficulty in naming things.

B. *Age-Related Changes*

Most AD patients are elderly and thus have the usual limitations associated with aging [15]. Disabilities related to age can be grouped into six groups: visual impairments, hearing impairments, mobility impairments, decent/no computers skills, decent/no of literacy skills and declining speech abilities.

Visual impairments - Old people experience a decline in their vision [10][16][19]. Aging is accompanied by a loss in visual acuity [8][10][20], decline in peripheral vision [19], decrease in dark adaptation [22], impairment of near-focus [15] including a computer screen [19], and decline in color sensitivity [17][19][22]. The Alzheimer's association reports that over 60% of AD patients experience a decline in at least one visual capacity [14].

Hearing impairments - Aging is related to declines in auditory acuity [15][16][19][20][21][22]. At the age of 65 years, about 50% of men and 30% of women experience hearing loss [24]. Old people may suffer from another complaint that they can hear people talking, but they can't make out the words [15]. They may also find it hard to understand synthetic speech [22].

Mobility impairments - The mobility decline with aging [10][16][17][19][20][21][22]. Seniors with manual dexterity impairments have difficulties to operate with the mouse and keyboard. It is difficult for them to position the cursor if the target is small, and they have problems with control of fine movements. Because of the reduced motor functions, more errors occur during fine movements [16].

Decent/no computers skills - The elderly are not proficient in computer use and related technologies [17][20].

Decent/no literacy skills - The illiteracy rate of seniors aged 65 years and above are important. Besides, many seniors are literate; however they have basic literacy skills. They may not fully understand text-based information. Most seniors have difficulties with typing; they may forget how to write words.

Declining speech abilities - Speech ability declines with aging [16]. Old people have problem in pronouncing complex words. Therefore, the speech input can be limited by voice tremors.

Based on these changes, we strongly believe that AD patients will face difficulties if we adopt standard interfaces into the CAPTAIN MEMO memory prosthesis. Thus, in the next section, we propose a set of design guidelines for accommodating these changes.

IV. DESIGN GUIDELINES FOR DEVELOPING INTERFACES FOR ALZHEIMER'S PATIENT

In this section, we propose a set of design guidelines which should be taken into account for designing interfaces dedicated to AD patients. The guidelines are grouped according to changes identified in the previous section. Ten groups of accessibility guidelines are created. They are categorised into AD-related guidelines and age-related guidelines.

A. *Alzheimer's Disease-Related Design Guidelines*

This section proposes some practical design guidelines to accommodate the AD-related changes identified before.

Memory impairments - The interface should give a feedback after every action [10], use short messages [10][20], support users in their interaction e.g., through a speaking front end [20] and use consistent navigation throughout the website.

Cognitive impairments - The information should be summarised and categorised semantically into short categories. The headlines should be displayed on the top of the interface [18]. Image and icon should be simple, meaningful and easy to understand [18]. Text should be clear and avoid abbreviation [19][20]. Links should be underlined to make them identifiable. The design should be simple [15] and only main information should be displayed [21][22]. The interface's distracting elements should be avoided [18][21]. Multimodal solutions improve the accessibility and facilitate the comprehension [10][11][22].

Personality changes - It is recommended to add fun and humour to the interface [23]. The wordings should suit the adults' semantic field [13]. Error feedback messages should make it clear that the user is not the cause of the error [18].

Declining language abilities - We recommend reducing the need for keyboarding or entire text input.

B. *Age-Related Design Guidelines*

Some practical design guidelines are mentioned in this section, according to age-related changes.

Visual impairments - the interface should have an appropriate size of design elements and text [11], use at least 12-points to 14-points type size [16][21] and 16-points for headings, avoid large blocks of bold or underlined text [19], use a left aligned text [18], put the ability of zoom in the interface [15][18][22], use a sans-serif font type [19] and a medium face type [18], use soft colors [19], avoid decorative fonts [10][15], maximize the contrast between foreground and background colors [10][18][19][21] and write main body in lower cases.

Hearing impairments - It is recommended to use, by default, higher sound [18], increase the duration of sound signal [18] and place a volume control in an easy to find spot [10][18]. The auditory information should be spoken slowly [10], pause slightly after each statement [15], use male voice [18][21] and use natural speech [15][22].

Mobility impairments - The design should contain large targets for accurate selections [13], use an audio supported menu [11], avoid the use of scrolling [18][19] and pull-down menus [19] and use touch screens [16][18][21].

Decent/no computers skills - Special assistance in terms of navigation should be given [9] e.g., providing previous/next links [19], showing the current location and providing a web site map. It is important to have an easy way of inserting special characters [11] e.g., the "@" character.

Decent/no literacy skills - It is recommended to use graphical metaphors or sounding when users cannot read easily [10][22], identify buttons by icons and labels [13], minimize the use of keyboard [13] and use the speech-to-text mode for typing.

Declining speech abilities - Acoustic models specialized for elderly should be used for the speech-to-text mode [21].

Based on these design guidelines, we develop the interfaces of the CAPTAIN MEMO memory prosthesis.

V. THE DEVELOPED INTERFACES OF THE CAPTAIN MEMO MEMORY PROSTHESIS

In this section, we present the developed interfaces of CAPTAIN MEMO prosthesis for persons who are showing early/moderate sign of AD. The developed interfaces are user-friendly, multimodal, enjoyable and configurable.

We use a sans-serif font type (Arial), a medium face type and by default, 12 pt to 15 pt type size for displayed texts and 25 pt for headings. We use a black font on orange background to maximize the contrast between foreground and background. The main body is written in lower cases. We provide large buttons and images. Graphical metaphors or images are used to facilitate understanding text-based information, e.g., the use of the key metaphor associated to connection step in Figure 3.

Figure 3. Graphical metaphors to facilitate understanding text information.

We put the ability of zoom in the family tree. We provide large nodes identified by using pictures and labels, as shown in Figure 4. To ensure the simplicity of the design, we display details only on demand. We display the details of the node which is selected. Clicking on a node allows it to be bigger and distinguishable from the others.

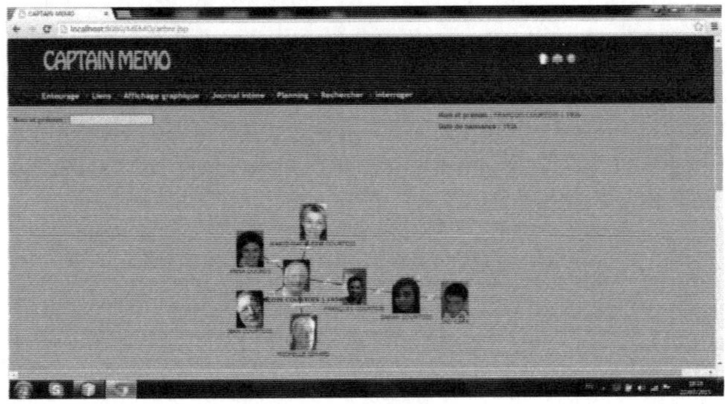

Figure 4. Identifying nodes of the family tree by using pictures and labels.

Different modalities are employed. The input modalities include speech-to-text, touch and pointing device + keyboard. The output modalities include vision and voice/audio.

We provide two modalities for typing: the traditional mode and the dictation or speech-to-text mode. We give the possibility of alternating between modalities. We reduce the need for keyboarding or entire text input. We provide choices to select from a dropdown list as possible.

We provide feedback after every action. We use two modalities of feedback: vocal and textual. The text and audio feedback have the same message. We use easy to understand and short messages. We use different tones for errors and successful entries.

We add an old parrot to the interfaces, which is known for intelligence, fun and especially for the ability to imitate human voices. We resort to funny sentence for both textual and vocal message. We use droll emoticons.

We add an auditory background to the interfaces in order to support the users in their interactions. We use a male voice and natural speech. We use, by default, higher sound for delivering the auditory information. The auditory background can turn on or off.

The interfaces are adjustable. We let the users adjust text size and the volume themselves.

The interfaces are implemented in three languages: French, English and Arabic. Figure 5 shows an interface presented in Arabic language.

Figure 5. An interface presented in Arabic language.

Finally, we have to evaluate the developed interfaces with AD patients. The next section elaborates the results.

VI. TESTS AND EVALUATION

The evaluation of the interfaces' accessibility and ease to use is carried out with 24 AD patients who are living in an assisted living environment in Sfax- Tunisia (Street Manzel Chaker km. 8). The participants have an average age of 64 years – the youngest is 55 years old and the oldest is 78. Most patients have AD in early/moderate stage. Their profiles are summarized in terms of age, stage of AD, difficulties in vision/hearing, computer skills and literacy skills.

This study was performed from July 2015 for about two months. Tasks were performed on tablet PC. A stylus pen is used to input commands to the touch-screen. The questionnaire covers five dimensions which include: "*Overall Reaction*", "*Visibility*", "*Speech-to-text*", "*Terminology*" and "*Auditory Background*". A five point scales are used: strongly disagree (1), disagree (2), neutral (3), agree (4) and strongly agree (5). Table 1 summarizes the results and the mean score for each dimension.

TABLE I. SUMMARY OF THE QUESTIONNAIRE'S RESULTS

Question	**(1)**	**(2)**	**(3)**	**(4)**	**(5)**	**Mean**
OVERALL REACTION (overall mean=4)						
Are the interfaces easy to use?		3	3	5	9	4
Is it easy to learn to use the interfaces?		7	3	10		3,15
Are the interfaces funny-to-use?			1	3	16	4,75
Are you satisfied about the interfaces?		3	3	3	11	4,1
VISIBILITY (overall mean=4,75)						
By default, can you read the main body?		4		4	12	4,2
By default, can you read headlines?				2	18	4,9
Is the ability to adjust text size useful?					20	5
Are images large enough?				2	18	4,9
SPEECH-TO-TEXT (overall mean=3,8)						
Is the speech-to-text mode helpful?	5			4	11	3,8
TERMINOLOGY (overall mean=4,72)						
Are the command names meaningful?				2	18	4,9
Icons are easy to understand?			2	3	15	4,65
Is the use of text labels improves the icon's interpretation?					20	5
Are error feedbacks helpful?		4	2	1	13	4,15
Are informative feedbacks straightforward?				2	18	4,9
AUDITORY BACKGROUND (overall mean=3,825)						
Is the voice speed reasonable?	6			10	4	3,3
Are vocal feedbacks useful?	6	2			12	3,5
Are spoken interactions helpful?	6	2			12	3,5
Is the ability to adjust volume useful?					20	5

Only 20 participants fully complete all tasks. The others just start the first test. They say that they are too old and have no motivation in learning a new technology. Those participants are the oldest with AD in moderate /late stage. They have no computer skills. We call them "patient-restricted users".

The overall mean score of the 5 dimension is between 3, 8 and 4, 74. Overall, the results indicate that the users are almost agreed that the developed interfaces are accessible and easy to use.

55% of all participants are strongly satisfied with the system. They say that they will use the CAPTAIN MEMO memory prosthesis frequently. Those participants suffer from AD in early stage, familiar with computers and have good literacy skills.

25% of all participants say that it is easier for them to type with a virtual keyboard; since their voice volume is not enough to be captured by the device's microphone. Thus, in the next iteration, we will use acoustic models specialized for elderly persons for the speech recognizer. Illiterate participants are very satisfied with the dictation modality.

30% of all participants ignore totally the speaking front end since they don't understand words. Thereafter, in the next version, we will use slower voice speed.

VII. RELATED WORK

In this section, we review some software application developed to support AD patients such as COGKNOW [25], AP@LZ [26], BACKUP MEMORY [27] and ARCUS [28]. COGKNOW and AP@LZ provide reminders to do specific activities according to a schedule. BACKUP MEMORY helps AD patients remember their families and/or surrounding. ARCUS is a virtual name directory that allows searching for names using cues. Table 2 gives a general comparison between the user interfaces of the cited applications.

TABLE II. COMPARISON BETWEEN INTERFACES OF APPLICATIONS DEDICATED TO ALZHEIMER'S PATIENTS

		COGKNOW (2007)	**AP@LZ (2010)**	**ARCUS (2012)**	**BACKUP MEMORY (2015)**	**CAPTAIN MEMO (2015)**
Visibility	Simple layout	Yes	Yes	Yes	Yes	Yes
	Maximised contrast	Yes	Yes	Yes	No	Yes
	Readable text	Yes	Yes	Yes	No	Yes
	Large buttons	Yes	No	Yes	No	Yes
	Large images	Yes	No images used	No images used	No	Yes
Modalities		Touch, vision, audio.	Vision, touch	Vision, touch.	Vision, touch.	Vision, touch, audio, speech-to-text, keyboard + mouse.
Fun		No	No	No	No	Yes
Configuration		No	No	No	No	Yes

Compared to related work, the developed interfaces of the CAPTAIN MEMO memory prosthesis provide more features than the other applications. In fact, only COGKNOW and CAPTAIN MEMO provide a good management of the screen's elements. Second, the developed interfaces provide more modalities, which can increase the chances of comprehension. Finally, only our work allow user setting the volume and the size of the font and add fun to seduce AD patient to use frequently our memory prosthesis.

VIII. CONCLUSION AND FUTURE WORK

This paper presented the developed interfaces of the ongoing CAPTAIN MEMO memory prosthesis, which is developed to assist individuals who are showing early/ moderate signs of AD to palliate mnesic problems. So, at the beginning, we discuss the expected changes related to the AD and the aging process. Based on these changes, we believe that the interface plays a big role to ensure that AD patients can use the CAPTAIN MEMO memory prosthesis easily. To accommodate those changes, we propose a set of design guidelines for interfaces dedicated to AD patients. This set of design guidelines covers the main AD-related changes and age-related changes that might affect the accessibility of the interfaces. Based on these design guidelines, we develop the interfaces of the Captain Memo memory prosthesis. The developed interfaces present the advantages that they are user-friendly, multimodal, enjoyable and configurable. Afterward, a user satisfaction evaluation of the interfaces is carried out with 24 AD patients. The results confirm that the developed interfaces are easy to use and funny to use. The majority of the participants say that they will use our prosthesis frequently. Finally, we review some related work and demonstrate how our work differs from the existing ones.

Future works will be mainly devoted:

- To integrate acoustic model specialized for elderly persons for the speech recognizer;
- To use slower voice speed for the auditory background;
- To add the haptic modality in order to offer a tactile feedback for the user ,which is a vibration that occurs when the user selects a button with his/her finger;
- To add an audio supported menu. Speech should work not only for dictation when writing a message, but also for command;
- To authenticate the users using the facial recognition modality;
- To evaluate the CAPTAIN MEMO memory prosthesis with memorizing test.

REFERENCES

[1] E. Metais et al., "Memory prosthesis," Non-pharmacological therapies in dementia, 2015, pp. 177-180.

[2] http://viva.cnam.fr/ (date of the last access: 17/03/2016)

[3] https://jena.apache.org/ (date of the last access: 17/03/2016)

[4] http://www.w3.org/TR/rdf-sparql-query/ (date of the last access: 17/03/2016)

[5] https://en.wikipedia.org/wiki/Model–view–controller (date of the last access: 14/04/2016)

[6] https://glassfish.java.net/ (date of the last access: 17/03/2016)

[7] http://www.apache.org/ (date of the last access: 17/03/2016)

[8] C. Ancient and A. Good, "Issues with designing dementia-friendly interfaces," HCI International 2013, 2013, pp. 192-196.

[9] A. Hunter, H. Sayers, and L. McDaid, "An evolvable computer interface for elderly users," HCI conference on supporting human memory with interactive systems, 2007, pp. 29-32.

[10] R. J. A. Moutinho, "A mobile phone navigator for older adults and persons with dementia," Master in informatics and computing engineering, 2011.

[11] V. Teixeira et al., "Towards elderly social integration using a multimodal human-computer interface," The 2nd International Living Usability Lab Workshop on AAL Latest Solutions, Trends and Applications, 2012, pp. 3-13.

[12] G. Gowans, R. Dye, N. Alm, and P. Vaughan, "Designing the interface between dementia patients, caregivers and computer based intervention," The design journal, 2007, pp. 12-23.

[13] A. C.de Barrosa, R. Leitãob, and J. Ribeiroa "Design and evaluation of a mobile user interface for older adults: navigation, interaction and visual design recommendations," The 5th International conference on software development and technologies for enhancing accessibility and fighting info-exclusion (DSAI 2013), 2013, pp. 369-378.

[14] B. Wang, "Designing a graphical user interface of an easy-to-use videophone for people with mild dementia," Master thesis, 2010.

[15] M. A. Farage, K. W. Miller, F. Ajayi, and D. Hutchins, "Design principles to accommodate older adults," Global journal of health science, 2012, pp. 2-25.

[16] C. Jian, "Multimodal shared-control interaction for mobile robots in AAL environments," Thesis, University of Bremen 2013.

[17] T. Phiriyapokanon, "Is a big button interface enough for elderly users? toward user interface guidelines for elderly users," Master of computer engineer, 2011.

[18] B. Loureiro and R. Rodrigues, "Design guidelines and design recommendations of multi-touch interfaces for elders," The 7th international conference on advances in computer-human interactions (ACHI 2014), 2014, pp. 568-574.

[19] A. Arch and S. Abou-Zhara, "How web accessibility guidelines apply to design for the ageing population," Proceedings of accessible design in a digital world conference, York, UK, 2008.

[20] A. Lorenz, D. Mielke, R. Oppermann, and L. Zahl, "Personalized mobile health monitoring for elderly," The 9th international conference on Human computer interaction with mobile devices and services, 2007, pp. 297-304.

[21] C. Jian et al., "Towards effective, efficient and elderly-friendly multimodal interaction," PETRA '11, 2011, pp. 45.

[22] W. IJsselsteijn, H. H.Nap, Y. de Kort, and K. Poels, "Digital game design for elderly users," The 2007 conference on future play, 2007, pp. 17-22.

[23] J. M. Carroll, "Beyond fun," Interactions, 2004, pp. 38-40.

[24] N. Caprani, N. E. O'Connor, and C. Gurrin, "Touch screens for the older user," Assistive Technologies, 2012, pp. 95-118.

[25] F. J M Meiland et al., "COGKNOW: development and evaluation of an ICT-device for people with mild dementia," Journal on information technology in healthcare, 2007, pp. 166-177.

[26] H. Imbeault et al., "Development of a personalized electronic organizer for persons with Alzheimer's disease: the AP@ lz," Gerontechnology, 2010, pp. 293.

[27] A. Pai, Samsung releases Backup Memory app for Alzheimer's patients, 2015.

[28] S. Routhier, J. Macoir, H. Pigot, and S. Giroux , "From smartphone to external semantic memory device: The use of new technologies to compensate for semantic deficits," Non-pharmacological Therapies in Dementia, 2012, pp. 81-99.

Ergonomic Criteria for the Evaluation of Context-Aware User Interface

Ines Riahi, Faouzi Moussa, Riadh Dziri
National School of Computer Sciences, Cristal Laboratory
University of Manouba, Tunisia
Emails: {ines.riahi@yahoo.fr, faouzimoussa@gmail.com, riadh.dziri@gmail.com}

***Abstract*— The need of a permanent and ubiquitous access to information is becoming increasingly apparent with the advent of new materials and the success of handheld devices. This led to the emergence of new paradigms in human-machine interaction, such as mobility and ubiquitous computing. The concept of user interfaces' adaptation has several facets. It requires a dynamic modeling approach. In this context, our paper is about designing an evaluation experiment for context-aware User Interface (UI). This evaluation is based on ergonomic rules proposed by experts. The non-contextualized ergonomics rules were adapted for the contextualized ones. In order to demonstrate context aware UI contribution, we chose to work on a critical area which is the medical field and especially on the diabetes disease.**

Keywords-Context-aware User Interface; User Interface Evaluation ; Ergonomic Rules.

I. INTRODUCTION

With increasing of devices' variety number and their use in ubiquitous environments by various types of users, user interfaces' adaptation has become a necessity rather than an option. Existing systems lack the ability to satisfy the heterogeneous needs of many users. These needs also vary according to the context, where context comprises of environmental conditions, the characteristics of device used to interact with the application, and the user characteristics. There is a need for techniques that can help the User Interface designer and developer to deal with a myriad of contextual situations. Also, the user should be provided with the facility to have an adaptive interface that adapts to changing user needs.

The final phase in the process of User Interface (UI) designing is the evaluation phase. Each created interface must be evaluated according to definite criteria. Several methods for user interface evaluation exist in the literature such as the work of Senach [1] or Grislin and Kolski [2]. However, we noted the scarcity or even the inexistence of those dedicated to contextualized interfaces.

In this paper, we propose an initial version of contextualized interfaces evaluation using some ergonomic criteria proposed specifically for non-contextualized interfaces.

We proposed in our recent works an approach for specification and generation of context-aware interfaces [3]. In this paper, we will evaluate the obtained interfaces. These interfaces are the interfaces of our application named DiaMon [3]. To test our approach, we propose DiaMon for monitoring of diabetic patients. Then, we conduct a statistical study with a medical team to evaluate our interfaces.

This paper is organized as follows: Section II discusses some literature reviews of interface evaluation approaches. In Section III, we present our approach. It is illustrated, in Section IV, with an application called DiaMon that concerns the monitoring of diabetic patients suffering from hypoglycemia in a smart hospital. In Section V, we propose the ergonomic rules for context-aware evaluation. Finally, in Section VI, we present our contextualized user interfaces used for the experimentation.

II. RELATED WORK

Several methods for evaluation UI exist in the literature. Senach [1] classified the interface evaluation methods into two types:

- Empirical evaluation methods (predictive): They are used to gather data related to user's behavior using the system. Such methods require a prototype or the real system.
- Analytical methods (experimental): they aim at evaluating the design of the system and not the usage. The use of abstract representations allows predictions of performance that cannot be performed in a purely empirical approach [1].

Grislin and Kolski [2] distinguish three main evaluation methods:

- The method centered on the opinions and/or user activities,
- The method centered on expertise. These approaches are based on the judgment of experts in Human-Computer Interaction (HCI) or on the evaluation forms or questionnaires classifying the qualities of an HCI.
- Analytical methods based on HCI modeling. These approaches are typically used to perform inspection using objective metrics from a human task model or a screen pages description.

In order to evaluate UI, some authors define some ergonomics rules. We can cite for example those proposed by Vanderdonckt [4] or Smith [5]. Ergonomics is the scientific discipline concerned with the understanding of interactions among humans and other elements of a system. Through our study, we distinguish three types of ergonomics [6]:

- Physical ergonomics: represents the characteristics of human interaction with physical activity such as work posture, manipulation of objects, repetitive movements, arrangement of the workplace, the health and safety of the user.

- Cognitive ergonomics: is interested in mental processes involved in human interaction with the system components. It aims to analyze and verify the compatibility between the interface and the user.
- Organizational ergonomics: focuses on the optimization of socio-technical systems, which are composed of the organizational structure, processes, cooperative work, communication and resource management.

In general, the ergonomic knowledge is described as ergonomic rules used for the design and evaluation of interactive software.

In the literature, there is a great variety of ergonomic rules. To facilitate the use of ergonomic rules for designers, analysts and programmers, more research has focused on their classification in categories called ergonomic criteria.

Ergonomic guides were proposed. These include, for example Vanderdonckt recommendations [4], Smith [5] and Scapin [7].

Scapin and Bastien [7] proposed eight ergonomics rules: guide, workload, explicit control, adaptability, errors management, consistency/coherence, significance of codes and names, compatibility.

All these methods were used for non-contextualized interfaces evaluation. We combined several of these techniques in order to evaluate the contextualized interfaces. Before focusing on the resulting interfaces, we present in the following section, our approach to specification and generation of these interfaces.

III. Formal Approach for Specification and Generation of Conext-Aware User Interface

The objective of our research is to develop a global approach for specification and generation of context-aware interfaces in a medical field. Our methodology is based on the use of formal tools to cover gradually and consistently all stages, from the Human-Computer System (HCS) analysis and modeling to the generation of different graphic views.

The first step in our approach, shown in Figure 1, is the detection of contextual information. Once the data are received from the sensor layer, they will be modeled and decomposed into a user model (we model here the different user's profiles), a platform model (we present here the various platforms hosted on our application and exploited by different users); and an environment model (it describes the various environment characteristics such as geographical location, schedule, etc.). This decomposition is based on the definition proposed by Calvary et al., [8]. In parallel, the analysis of the HCS is necessary.

The second step consists in the user's task analysis specifying the sequence of actions to be performed. This analysis leads to the task modeling and the user requirements' identification.

The third step ensures the context and task modeling. This will be accomplished via the Petri Nets (PN) database that contains structures and elementary compositions of PN. PN were proposed by Carl Adam Petri in 1962 and were considered as a promising tool for task modeling [9]. PN are a mathematically based formalism dedicated to the modeling of parallelism and synchronization in discrete systems. PNs are continuously expanding and are a suitable tool for HCS modeling. Initially, they were only used to describe tasks that were computerized. However, later, especially with the emergence of High Level Petri Nets, they have been used to model Human-Computer Interaction [10]. Formal modeling of the Human-Computer Interaction, with Interpreted Petri nets allows the identification of all necessary user requirements in each point of interaction [10].

The fourth step ensures the detection of the user's current situation. It aims to identify the pair of (Context, Task). After a critical review, established in our last paper [11], none of the approaches gives full consideration to the user's activity or the task to be accomplished. Thus, we have associated the user task to its context of use. All couples "context, task" are therefore, previously stored in a database. At a given time, the status of different models determines the current context of the user (Ci). The identification of the adequate task Ti requires browsing the database "context, Task".

The fifth step provides the user interface specification. In this stage, user's requirements are identified in terms of interface's objects taking into account the ergonomic rules for the presentation of a mobile interface.

The last step in this approach is dedicated to the interface's creation. More details are presented in [3].

We consider our approach as a formal one because we used formal tools (Petri Nets) for the analysis and the modeling of contextualized user interface. The use of a formal method to describe the behavior of a context-aware system allows us to deduct the properties of the system and the users' requirements in order to generate the appropriate and valid interface at a given time.

After giving an overview of the advocated approach, we will present in the next section, our application called DiaMon.

IV. DiaMon: A Contextual User Inerface Assisting Medical Teams for Monitoring Hypoglycemic Patients

The overall objective of our application is monitoring diabetic patients in a "smart hospital". Equipped with biological sensors implanted under their skin, the system periodically checks the patient's Glucose Level (GL). Thus, it regularly observes the patient's status to alert by mobile devices the medical staff in case of an intervention.

The application is continuously connected to the monitoring system. While collecting information by the server, the system can, at any time, notices an unusual value of GL. That's why; an alert is displayed on medical teams' mobile devices. The user then has access to the patient's information for better intervention.

Several problems can arise from such an application. For example, in case of urgent and immediate intervention, how to alert the medical team and how to generate valid and significant interfaces guiding the doctor/nurse to fulfill their tasks?

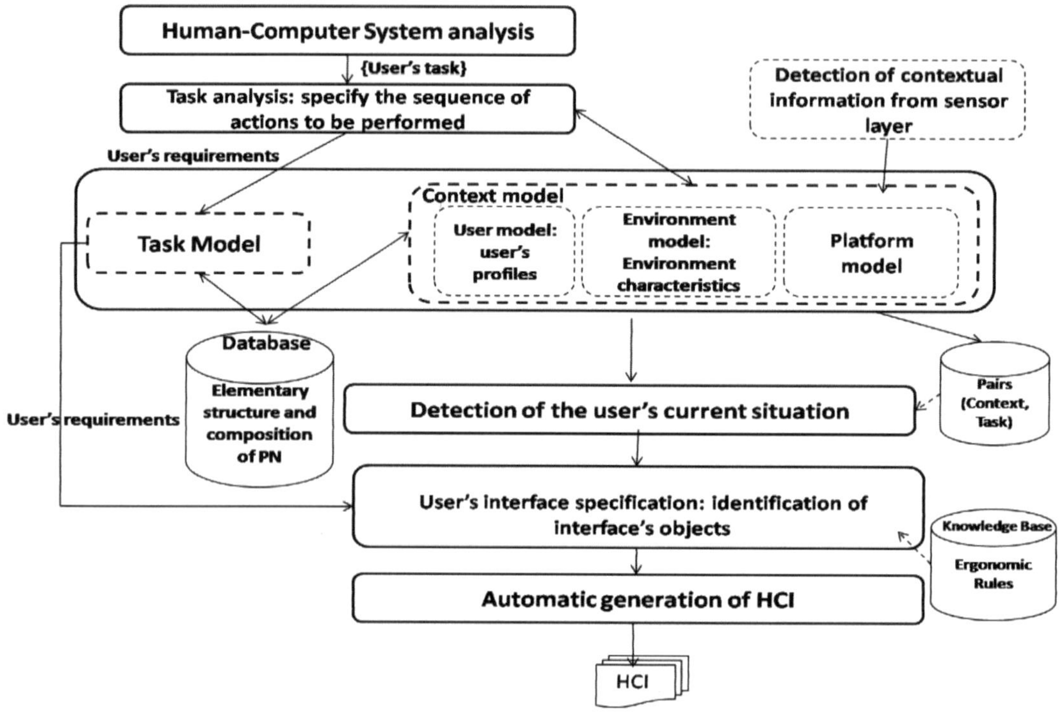

Figure 1. Proposed approach.

In case of hypoglycemic coma, how can we instantly notify those present in hospital to ensure a rapid intervention? And if the treating doctor is not present at the moment, how will the application interface adapt to the user's profile and his knowledge?

First, the application must identify the user's profile taking into account his knowledge in diabetology. Secondly, DiaMon has to detect the platform used to adjust and display the interface's graphical components. Finally, it must consider the environment in which the user evolves such as geo location and time response. Furthermore, the interface must adapt according to GL value. The graphical interface's components will change from one value to another. The originality of our application resides in the way it is designed to be used by all medical team regardless of their specialty or status (specialist, generalist, emergency physician or nurse). DiaMon fits to its context of use. It takes into account the user task, its environment, its profile and its level of knowledge. In addition, the user requirements are adapted continuously for each situation.

In this example, we are particularly interested in diabetes type 2.

For a patient with type 2 diabetes, there is a great risk of hypoglycemia. The latter represents an abnormally low sugar concentration in the blood. Hypoglycemia can result in a hypoglycemic coma that may cause the patient's death. We can recognize hypoglycemia through several signs: nausea, stomach cramps, palpitation, headache, tremor, etc.

Hypoglycemia may cause a hypoglycemic coma. This condition occurs due to a sudden onset of a state of agitation, muscle contracture, sharp reflexes and profuse sweating. Curative treatment of hypoglycemia depends on the patient's condition and his blood sugar. Two scenarios are possible: patient conscious or unconscious (Table 1) [12].

TABLE I. HYPOGLYCEMIA CURATIVE TREATMENT

Hypoglycemia with disturbance of consciousness	**Moderate hypoglycemia**
Condition : Blood glucose level between 0.3 and 0.4 g / l. Unconscious patient	**Condition :** Blood glucose level between 0.4 and 0.7 g / l conscious patient
Treatment: Slow intravenous infusion of 30 to 50 ml of 30% glucose solution, relayed by a slow infusion of serum 10% until patient wakes up. A slow intake of sugar (bread) is then recommended.	**Treatment:** Re-sugaring orally: 15g of fast sugar (3 sugar cubes diluted in water or juice) followed by a slow sugar intake (20g bread) Wait 15 minutes and repeat the Re-sugaring .

The two types of hypoglycemia treatment have a slow sugar intake (bread). In this case, we must consider the diabetics allergic to gluten (a substance into the bread). For this type of patients, it must replace the bread with gluten-free bread such as rice our, corn or buckwheat. A diabetic patient may be allergic to fructose. In this case, we must avoid the three pieces of sugar and fruit juice in case of moderate hypoglycemia. The sugar must be replaced by saccharin, aspartame, maltose or malt syrup.

Our approach resulted in a tool which produces contextualized interfaces. DiaMon provides adaptable interfaces to user profile and its current environment. The following stage is the evaluation of these interfaces. The problem with existing evaluation work is that they are primarily intended for non-contextualized interfaces. So, we have adapted those criteria to evaluate our interfaces.

The long term goal is to be able to propose new ergonomic criteria evaluation intended for contextualized interfaces.

V. ERGONOMIC RULES FOR CONTEXT-AWARE INTERFACE EVALUATION REGARDING NON-CONTEXTUALIZED INTERFACE

The evaluation of an interface is primarily intended to verify the reliability, quality, usability and usefulness of the HCI. The evaluation of the usefulness is demonstrated by answering these two questions: (i) Does the HCI meet the specifications? (ii) Can the users accomplish his task?

Concerning the usability of the HCI, it is verified by evaluating: (i) Efficiency: to achieve the expected result, (ii) User satisfaction, (iii) Ease of learning and (iv) Ease of use.

These parameters can be evaluated through an experimental evaluation (observation, data collection, interviews and questionnaires) or an analytical assessment (usage scenario and expert judgments).

In our research, experimental evaluation was conducted via questionnaire and analytical assessment was made via a scenario and expert questioning of the domain (pharmacists and doctors).

These evaluation criteria mainly concern the non-contextualized interfaces. We have noticed during this work the scarcity of ergonomic criteria for contextualized interfaces. However, some criteria proposed in the literature, have seemed interesting for the evaluation of dynamic interfaces. For example, we can mention the adaptability criterion regarding the ability of an interface to react depending on the context and the user's needs and preferences.

In order to assess the quality and the reliability of our interfaces, several measures criteria were defined. For clarity, we have broken our evaluation criteria into two sets: the observable and unobservable criteria.

A. *Observable criteria*

The observable data consist in what the subjects have been doing during the simulation such as selecting tabs, data entry or changing icons. We can also consider the simulation start or the elapsed time.

B. *Non observable criteria*

These criteria can be derived through interviews, questionnaires or other data collection techniques. For our work, we choose to use the questionnaire technique. The development of our questionnaire was governed by ergonomic rules proposed in the literature. These rules can be applied on contextualized interfaces.

We asked twelve participants to take part in the evaluation stage and go through the simulation platform then fill the survey. We have developed the interfaces of this scenario and we asked the participants to try them and answer the questionnaire.

The participants were from different backgrounds and different range of age and experience. Some of them were generalists; others were diabetologists (private and internal to Tunisian hospitals), an emergency physician and two pharmacists.

C. *Ergonomics rules for context-aware user interface*

We modified ergonomic rules for non-contextualized interface to make them relevant for contextualized interfaces. Indeed, the existing rules do not take into account the user's preferences, the environment in which he evolves and his current activity.

First, we are interested in the adaptability criterion, proposed by Scapin. The original definition of this criterion is as follows: "The adaptability of a system refers to its capacity to behave contextually and according to the users' needs and preferences. The criterion Adaptability is subdivided into two criteria: Flexibility and User Experience."

We decomposed the adaptability into four criteria:

- Adaptation to the user profile: The user interface must automatically adapt to the user's profile;
- Environment adaptation: The user interface must adapt its content according to environmental data;
- Adaptation to the user's knowledge: The user interface must identify the user's profile in terms of knowledge. It must provide the appropriate information to his level of expertise;
- User preferences: The user interface must adapt its content to the user preference.

Then, we focused on utility, ease of use, usability and the quality of UI criteria:

- Utility: The user should be able to accomplish its task using its interface. The interface must satisfy the user;
- Ease of use: The interface should be easy to use. It must be understandable and clear;
- Usability: The extent to which a UI can be used by users to achieve specified goals with effectiveness, efficiency and satisfaction;
- Quality: The information displayed in the interface must be relevant.

The criteria have been modified as follows:

- Utility of contextualized UI: The user should be able to accomplish its task using its interface and the UI should consider environment's changes. The interface must satisfy the user by automatically changing these components if the user's task evolves;
- Ease of use: The interface should be easy to use for the user. It must take into account the user profile by adopting its components;
- Usability: The extent to which a UI can be used by users to achieve specified goals with effectiveness,

efficiency and satisfaction in a specified context of use. The user's goals can change according to the current environment, so the UI must change.

- Quality: The information displayed in the interface must be relevant, valid and understandable by the user. The information must be reliable and suitable to the display area of the mobile device.

All these criteria are used in our evaluation experiment, in order to evaluate the contextualized interfaces.

VI. EVALUATION EXPERIMENT

A. *Context-aware user interface for experimentation*

By applying our approach to our application, we were able to generate contextualized interfaces. This generation is done manually for the evaluation experiment. Following the application of our approach, we got the interfaces specification. These interfaces were the subject of an experimental study. The majority of user interfaces evaluation work is based on ten to fourteen participants. We have succeeded in our work to test these interfaces on twelve doctor and pharmacist users.

During the evaluation phase, we have set up a scenario that describes an emergency physician that rescues, in the ambulance, a diabetic patient with a hypoglycemic coma.

We are inspired by the principles and general criteria for ergonomic contextualized interfaces to produce an evaluation questionnaire for DiaMon produced interfaces.

The DiaMon first interface, shown in Figure 2, displays the patient's personal information, the type of intervention that can be committed, the patient's allergies and the glucose level. The information displayed to the interface is adapted to the users profile by indicating the most suitable intervention and patient's allergies; and the patient's status by indicating the GL.

Figure 2. Initial patient status.

Once the patient glucose changes/increases, the alert message changes its position (displayed in the screen center), size and content. A message dialogue appears to alert the user to react (Figure 3). The interface's components change according to the environment's change. The alert and message dialogue adapts to this new situation (the change of Glucose Level).

Figure 3. Glucose Level change

When a hypoglycemic coma occurs, a new message appears announcing the patient's condition. The GL values change and the type of intervention is adapted (from a patient conscious to an unconscious patient (Figure 4)).

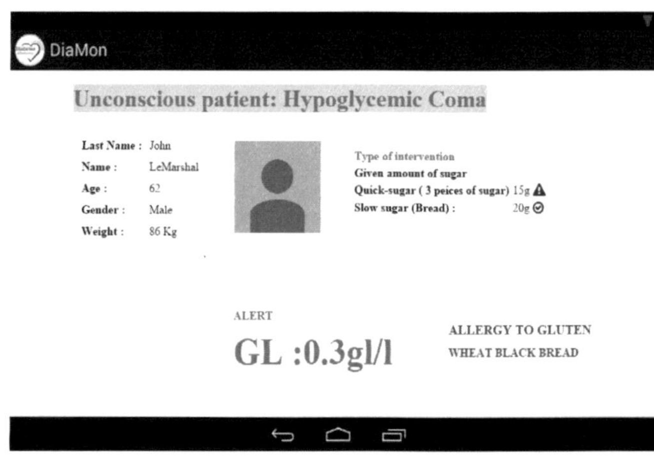

Figure 4. UI for unconscious patient

After testing our application, users answered a questionnaire. For more clarity and understanding; and in order to identify the exact view of our participants, we used the 4-point Likert scale [13]. Their responses were as follows.

B. *Results and analysis*

For the user profile adaptation, environment adaptation, adaptation to user's knowledge and user's preferences criteria, the following questions were asked:

1. Does the GL label's change help you for your intervention?
2. Is the appearance of the unconscious patient's label beneficial to you?

3. Does the appearance of gluten allergy's information help you to avoid making mistakes in your intervention?
4. Are the changes appeared in the interface beneficial for your contribution?

For the first question (Figure 5), eleven person of twelve have affirmed the usefulness of the occurrence of the label containing the glucose levels in the patient during the user's intervention.

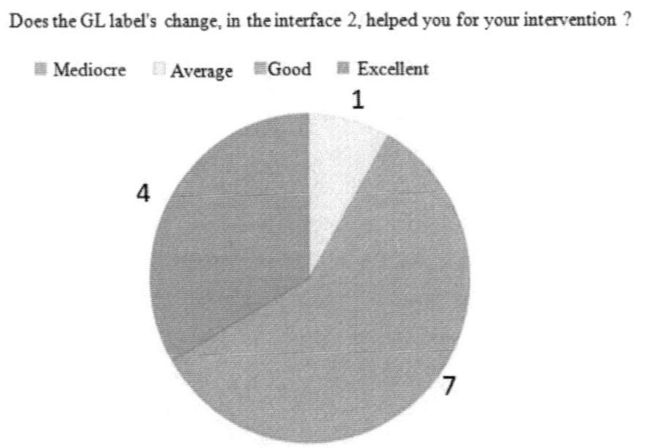

Figure 5. Appearance of GL label in the contextualized interface.

In Figure 6, over than 65% of the users found that the appearance of an alert about the fainting of the patient is excellent, while less than 25% found it good and below 5% said it was an average.

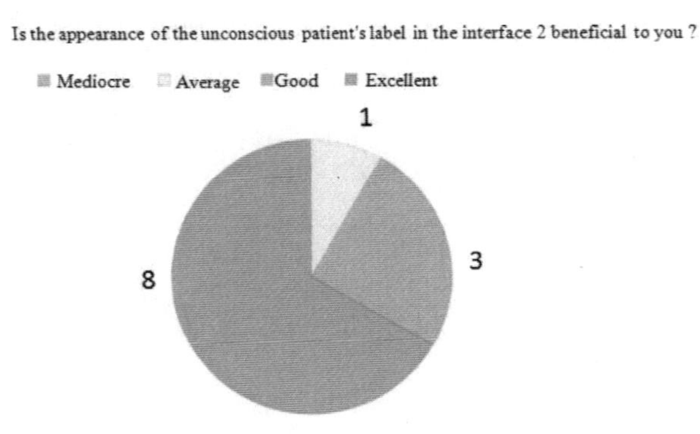

Figure 6. A question about the appearance of an alert message.

Regarding the question "what is the appearance of information "gluten allergy" was beneficial? 100% of participants affirmed that this information was necessary for the accomplishment of their tasks (Figure 7).

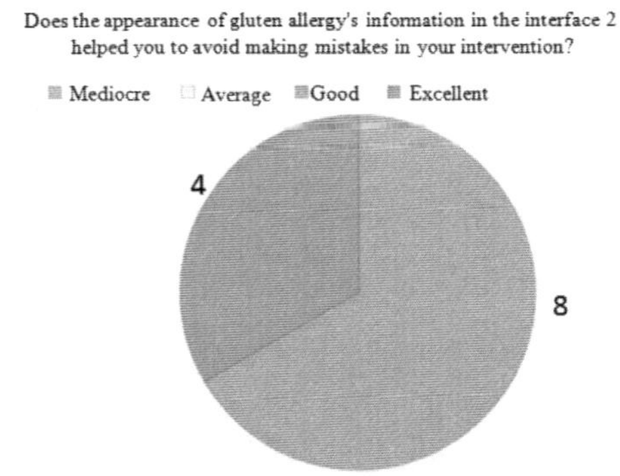

Figure 7. Appearance of information "gluten allergy".

For the last question, the majority (nine out of twelve) preferred the graphics components changes occurred in the dynamic interface. They have affirmed the advantages of the message appear on glucose levels and change of the intervention for the accomplishment of their tasks (Figure 8).

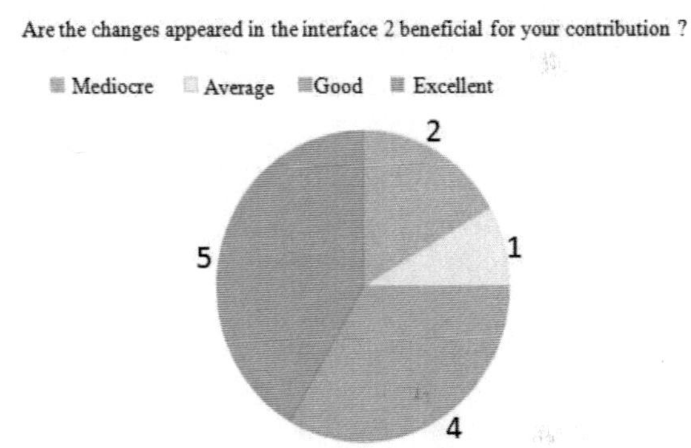

Figure 8. Graphics components changes in the dynamic UI.

For the ease of use and the quality criteria, the users' responses were as follows: the contextualized interfaces seemed to fulfill the participants' satisfaction with six out of twelve said it was good and three out of twelve said it was excellent as shown in Figure 9.

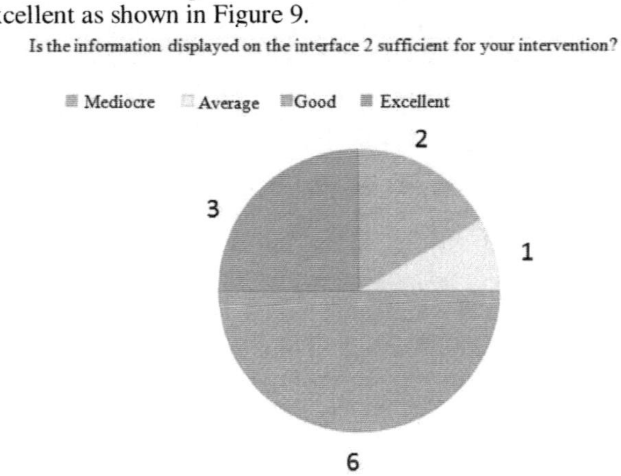

Figure 9. Information displayed in context-aware UI.

Through this study conducted with doctors and pharmacists, we confirmed that contextualized interfaces meet the ergonomic criteria listed above.

VII. CONCLUSION

In this paper, we stated some related work about existing UI evaluation methods and ergonomics rules. Then, we presented a formal and global approach for specification and generation of context-aware UI in six steps. We then presented our application named DiaMon, which is dedicating to health care staff to monitor their diabetes (type 2) patients' glucose level. This application was designed with context-aware user interfaces.

We also proposed ergonomic rules for context-aware evaluation where we modified some already existing ones and adopted them to the context-sensitive UI with respect to the HCI principles. Finally, an evaluation experiment was presented to apply our proposal to assess our Application DiaMon, and then followed by a statistical study to evaluate the contextualized interface.

In the near future, we will try to test our interfaces on more people and expand this study in order to develop clear and precise rules for the evaluation of contextualized interfaces.

REFERENCES

[1] B. Senach, " Ergonomic Evaluation of Human-Computer Interface", une revue de la littérature, Research Report, INRIA Publications, 1990.

[2] M. Grislin and C. Kolski, "Evaluation of Human-Computer Interfaces in the development of interactive systems", Technique et Science Informatiques (TSI), vol. 15, no. 3, 1996, pp. 265-296.

[3] I. Riahi and F. Moussa, "A formal approach for modeling context-aware human-computer system", Computers & Electrical Engineering, vol. 44, 2015, pp. 241-261.

[4] J. Vanderdonckt, "The presentation of an aided design ergonomic Human-Computer interface for a highly interactive management application". Thesis University of Notre-Dame de la Paix, France, 1997.

[5] J. N. Mosier and S. L. Smith, "Application of guidelines for designing user interface software", Behaviour & information technology, vol. 5, no. 1, 1986, pp.39-46.

[6] R. Baggen, J.P. Correia, K. Schill and J. Visser, "Standardized code quality benchmarking for improving software maintainability" Software Quality Journal, vol. 20, no. 2, 2012, pp. 287-307.

[7] D. L. Scapin and J. C. Bastien, "Ergonomic criteria for evaluating the ergonomic quality of interactive systems", Behaviour & information technology, vol. 16, no. 4, 1997, pp. 220-231.

[8] G. Calvary, A. Demeure, J. Coutaz, and O. Dassi, "Adaptation of human-computer interfaces in their context of use: plasticityof HCI", Revue d'Intelligence Artificielle, vol. 18, no. 4, 2004, pp. 577-606.

[9] C.A. Petri, « Kommunication mit automaten », PhD Dissertion. University of Bonn, 1962.

[10] M.Moalla, "Interpreted Petri Nets", TSI de l'AFCET, vol.4, 1985.

[11] I. Riahi and F. Moussa, "Formal Modeling For Pervasive Human-Computer Interface Design", UBICOMM, 2014, pp. 35-43.

[12] F. Chaker and N. Mchirgui, " Diabetes mellitus", Technical Report. 34, Faculty of Medecine Tunis, 2013.

[13] G. Norman, "Likert scales, levels of measurement and the "laws" of statistics", Advances in health sciences education, vol. 15, no. 5, 2010, pp. 625-632.

Designing for Sustainability: Challenges and Theoretical Considerations

Discussing theoretical considerations for framing strategic sustainable design approaches

Swati Srivastava
Design of Information Systems, Department of Informatics
University of Oslo
Oslo, Norway
swatisr@ifi.uio.no

Sumit Pandey
Design of Information Systems, Department of Informatics
University of Oslo
Oslo, Norway
sumitp@ifi.uio.no

Abstract— **Product demand and high consumption have been traditionally viewed as traits of successful business in the mass market. However, the environment is under immense strain to sustain hyper-consumption driven lifestyles fueled by conventional mass market business strategies. Sustainable services have started to emerge to disrupt such business practices and alter consumption driven processes to reduce the harmful impact on the environment. However, the adoption of such services has largely been limited to a niche environmentally conscious audience. Research has argued that for sustainable services to have a noticeable environmental impact, they need to be adopted in the mass market. In this paper, we discuss the challenges and outline the theoretical design considerations needed to frame desirable value propositions for sustainable services intended for the mass market. To do this, we review literature from the fields of strategic design, service design and Human Computer Interaction (HCI) and identify conceptual overlaps with broader discussions on sustainability and suggest that sustainability can potentially find a familiar voice in design due to their common interest in advocating an emphasis on people's needs and aspirations for a better present and future. Mutually, design and sustainability can discover new representations and opportunities for a better future beyond offerings designed to fuel incessant consumption of resources.**

Keywords-Sustainability; Strategic Design; Service Design; Mass Market; Value Propositions.

I. INTRODUCTION

Mass-market businesses have traditionally functioned with a singular focus on generating profits. Consequently, their business strategies are carefully crafted for fast product absorption and long term consumer engagement with the brand. Product demand and high consumption have been traditionally viewed as traits of successful business [1]. This conclusion largely stems from a business perspective based on general desires and needs driven consumer behavior [1] [2]. Therefore, one of the key strategies employed by conventional businesses to promote their services is based not just on fulfillment of basic consumer needs but also capitalizing on the association of social status and exclusive ownership of the newest generation of products. Businesses use marketing strategies that aim to create and encourage consumer desires and aid higher product sales and increasing consumption.

While these consumption oriented market practices offer purchase options with attractive buying experiences to improve a consumer's quality of life, they have simultaneously become a threat to the very quality of consumer life that they advertise to improve. This can be illustrated by the purchase and short disposal cycles of smart phones, which are providing users with technology to simplify their day to day activities while negatively impacting the environment through harmful electronic waste [3]. The environment is under immense strain to sustain the lifestyles supported by both production and consumption of unsustainable products and services [3][4] and has also been conclusively established through research studies studying the adverse affects of over-consumption on the environment [5].

On the other hand, there has been a rise in the efforts by a few companies to capitalize on the increasing awareness of the effects of unsustainable services on the environment and society and bringing sustainable services into the mass market. Such efforts to make existing products sustainable are focusing on extending the product life cycle and building efficient after sales services [6]. Greenphones [7], for instance, provides an after-sale service where enterprises and consumers sell and buy smartphones and tablets. Greenphones [7] benefits from the dynamics of this market, and seeks to prolong the lifetime of these devices. However, such products and services are still largely limited to the niche and/or premium market segments stemming from environmentally conscious consumers [1]. Consumers share a long relationship with certain brands and their products despite having an awareness of their environmentally damaging effects. Sustainable replacements of such products are either not easily available or lack the same ease of use or brand recognition as their mass market counterparts. The buying patterns of consumers in the mass market are still primarily driven by a product's newness, cost, quality and brand [2], leading to a vicious circle of the demand and supply of unsustainable services [8].

Therefore, it is becoming increasingly difficult to ignore unsustainable patterns of production and consumption [8] and a growing need for disruptive innovation through the introduction of sustainable products and services [9]. These disruptive practices can be used to explore new and environmentally efficient value propositions framed around sustainable products and services positioned as desirable offerings in the mass market. In this paper, we discuss the challenges and outline the theoretical design considerations needed to create sustainable products and services and frame desirable value propositions. Understanding the design considerations for the creation of sustainable products and services and how it can lead to sustainable business models is both timely and interesting. It is timely because of the the growing awareness of environmentally damaging effects of conventional products and services and efforts to introduce alternative sustainable value propositions in the mass market. Additionally, it is interesting because of the dilemma between making a sustainable solution a mass-market phenomenon and the consumption driven ethos of the mass market. We outline these design considerations and build our theoretical framework by reviewing literature from the fields of sustainability, strategic design, service design and HCI. Further, we juxtapose concepts from these fields to present a multi-disciplinary perspective on designing for sustainability.

This paper is structured as follows: Section II presents a condensed introduction to the key theoretical concepts that we use to ground our discussion followed by an overview of the different approaches to sustainable design in Section III. Section IV presents a discussion of the key design considerations needed for mass market sustainable design solutions followed by a conclusion in Section V.

II. Theoretical Framework

This section presents a condensed description of the theoretical framework that acts as a conceptual anchor for our investigation into design considerations for sustainable products and services.

Sustainability

WCED [10] has strongly stressed the need for a balanced developmental paradigm that advocates equal importance to be given to social concerns of both present and future generations. It proposes that:

"Sustainable development is development that meets the needs of the present without compromising the ability of future generations to meet their own needs." [10].

Most importantly, it can be observed that the definition of sustainability outlined by WCED shifts the focus from *"sustainability to save the environment"* to *"sustainability for the well being of human kind"*. This, as discussed in the introduction, is the perspective on sustainability that we work towards in this paper as well. This perspective views (see Figure 1) sustainability as the integration of environmental, social and economic as the three key dimensions of well being [11]. The paradigm proposed by WCED viewed environment preservation as one of the considerations for achieving well being and required the incorporation of social as well as economic considerations into sustainable solution. Further, the World Congress on Challenges of a Changing Earth proposes that:

"Common to the definitions, however, is an emphasis on the need to consolidate features from different knowledge systems into practical methods and tools that can be practically applied to promote sustainability on a worldwide scale." [12]

Kieffer et al. [11] built on the key considerations defined in the World Congress and discussed the instrumental role of the widespread deployment of sustainable developmental paradigms to generate a measurable impact and proposed sustainability science as a potential framework to achieve the desired impact of this vision. With the significance of large scale deployment and a focus on holistic socio-economic sustainable innovation to support the pro-environmental willingness of consumers, we argue that sustainable entrepreneurship and sustainable design oriented towards the mass market can act as interdependent agents for achieving the holistic vision of sustainability outlined above. Further, we suggest that sustainability can potentially find a familiar voice in design due to their common interest in advocating an emphasis on people's needs and aspirations for a better present and future. Mutually, design and sustainability can discover new representations and opportunities for a better future beyond offerings designed to fuel incessant consumption of resources.

A. Sustainable Entrepreneurship

In businesses, an increase in product consumption is traditionally viewed as a reflection of profits and market demand while environmental concerns have largely been centered on meeting environmental standards of product manufacture and responsible disposal and little to no attention to the negative consequences of increased consumption on the environment. However, studies on hyper consumption are presenting opportunities for companies to innovate and gain a competitive edge by challenging the traditional ethos of consumption led profits [1][13]. This has propelled several entrepreneurial initiatives aiming to disrupt mainstream markets by focusing on environmental and social value creation along with economic value.

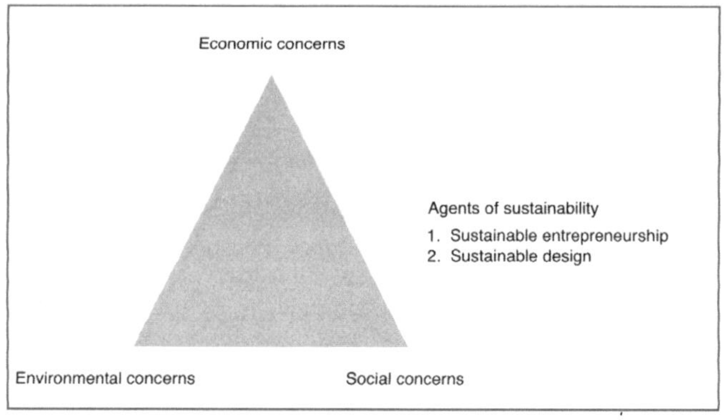

Figure 1. The three pillars of sustainable development

Building upon Schumpeter's [14] constructs of entrepreneurship as a process of creating "market disequilibria" through innovation [15], Hockerts and Wüstenhagen [13] define sustainable entrepreneurship as:

"the discovery and exploitation of economic opportunities through the generation of market disequilibria that initiate the transformation of a sector towards an environmentally and socially more sustainable state."

Sustainable entrepreneurship focuses on bridging environmental progress and market success by channeling innovative products and services [16]. Sustainable entrepreneurs operate with a profit motive as well but function with a framework of sustainability driven competitive solutions offering appealing value propositions to consumers. In contrast to having a sole orientation towards increasing the demand for products, sustainable entrepreneurship disrupts the market by shifting the paradigm from selling products to selling services and value along with manufacturing innovations for improving the eco-efficiency of tangible offerings as well. We argue that the mass market presents a powerful medium for sustainable entrepreneurs for reaching the most consumers for large scale impact. In this sense, sustainable entrepreneurship can be the realization of sustainability-centric innovations that provide benefits to a larger part of society by targeting the mass market [16].

B. *Sustainable Design*

Design as a discipline grew out of the industrial revolution in the late 19th and 20th century and has since been instrumental in creating aesthetically pleasing, useful and emotionally appealing objects. While these principles of good design remain relevant to this day, the rise of consumerism and the deteriorating effects on the environment is compelling designers to re-evaluate their offerings in terms of long term effects on the well being of consumers and communities. Campbell [17] argues that design will be fundamental to closing the gap between our behavior and our aspirations because of the particular resourcefulness that designers represent. Further, she suggests that:

"*ready to improvise and prototype, brave in the face of disorder and complexity, holistic and people-centered in their approach to defining problems, designers have a vital role to play today in making society itself more resourceful*" [17].

Sherwin writes about the designers training to be creative, challenging precedents and stereotypes and calls for greater involvement of designers given their inclination towards people centered and socio-cultural dimensions of sustainability [18].

In design processes, the exploration of sustainable outcomes is primarily conducted using one of the following three approaches:

- Designing for awareness and persuasion
- Designing for eco-efficiency at the product manufacturing level
- Designing at a systemic level

Even though eco-efficiency at product constitution level is essential, it cannot function in isolation. It requires the support of a system that enables seamless sustainable practices. Manzini and Vezzoli [19] caution that environmental risks still remain in spite of significant product improvement. They argue that:

"*the practical and operational definition of this field* (sustainable design) *is outlined by two complementary strategies by their application in stages most agreeable to companies: eco-efficient system research and the development of new solutions provide an instrument to confront, with a sustainable approach, some important problems emerging in contemporary society.*" [19]

Similarly, efforts to promote reduced resource based lifestyles through awareness and persuasion fail to address the personal concerns of the individual, often driving them against sustainability related goals [20]. Therefore, all improvements in eco-efficiency and awareness seem to be offset by the steep increase in the volume of the products sold leading to a zero or even negative net effect [21]. Therefore, designing for sustainability requires systemic innovations by incorporating holistic perspectives at a product, service and individual level, in contrast to the solutions built primarily around technology or product innovation. In the following section, we discuss the sustainable design approaches mentioned above in greater detail by reviewing literature from strategic design, service design and HCI.

III. Sustainable Design Approaches

A. *Sustainability through persuation and awareness*

Extensive studies of harmful environmental impacts of consumption-mediated processes have succeeded in evoking awareness among consumers and companies [1] [8] [22]. Several international initiatives promoting sustainability have succeeded in generating substantial awareness amongst people and companies but have failed to translate into widespread proposals and adoption of sustainable products and services. While people are more than willing to adopt pro-environment practices, several factors such as lack of economic and social support structures enabling/assisting the willingness of the people has led to the failure of to translate this willingness into action. Sustainability centric campaigns driven by persuasive sustainability [23] and lifestyle rationalization [20] based on proactive consumers making sustainable choices has cracked under the pressure of daily priorities, cultural aspirations of people going about their daily routine. The limited influence of persuasiveness in the issues of sustainability has been highlighted by Brynjarsdottir et al[23]. who frame it in terms of sustainability, human behavior, and the relationship between them. They argue that:

"*while this* (awareness for pro-active action) *may help make the problem of sustainability manageable as an engineering enterprise, it also makes designs susceptible to breakdown*" [23].

B. *Sustainability through eco-efficient market alternatives*

Recognizing the issues with awareness based solutions, consistent efforts in the past decade have been directed towards developing a sustainable market space. This intent has driven businesses to explore sustainable avenues contributing to the well being of their consumers. Additionally, it has created a new segment of environment-focused businesses such as Fairphone [24][25] and Tesla [26] that are investing efforts in sustainable yet breakthrough processes. These processes perceive attaining environmental sustainability and green consumption as one of the key performance indicators in the market. While this has initiated a positive trend towards a green consumption economy, these business models lack the appeal of unsustainable yet popular products in the mass market [1][5]. Every purchase related decision of a consumer continues to be driven primarily by easily quantifiable values that relate to fulfillment of basic needs, personal desires and buying power. Popular mass-market services present several alternatives tailored to these preferences, simplifying the decision to pick and choose. The purchase of these popular products requires minimum time and cognitive effort at the consumer's end. On the other hand, consumers willing to buy sustainable services have to evaluate the trade off in quality, cost and consistent availability leading to a more complex decision making for an activity that is a means to end and not the goal itself [1][5]. Therefore, while the general awareness about low-carbon consumption has gathered adequate appreciation among consumers and has led to the creation of a space in the economy for green products, it has been limited to a niche segment of actively environmentally conscious and premium buyer segments [1][5][27]. Csikszentmihalyi [5] in his theoretical account of consumption and its effects addresses this phenomenon by stating that:

"consumers report that they are concerned about the environmental issues but they are struggling to translate these concerns into purchases of sustainable products".

In addition to a need and desire oriented market strategy, the pace of technology also plays a significant role in the creation of unsustainable product advancements. Even though consumers are aware of the available environmentally friendly alternatives, they often choose to participate in a race to get the newest or latest product instead of replacing it with an environmentally friendly one [16]. Furthermore, the tech savvy consumers and early adopters of advanced technology wish to be at the cutting edge by buying the latest products, leading to frequent product disposal. Therefore, any effective disruption in this space to make sustainable innovation a preferred option should make environment-oriented consumers feel that they are still empowered with the newest technology.

C. *Sustainability through strategic design*

The pursuit of sustainable solutions is essential in questioning the long-established norms, processes and goals of mass market oriented businesses. As markets grow fiercely competitive, sustainability focused innovation can prove essential in reinventing and delivering new services to the consumers, driving innovation trends in the mass market landscape [27]. It is evident that even though the mass market and rapidly progressing technology are one of the primary propagators of over consumption, they also offer access to a larger consumer base and opportunities of greater involvement of consumers as equal stakeholders in the design of pro-environmental solutions utilizing new technological platforms. They could potentially offer the resources to disrupt existing unsustainable markets and value networks to innovative design and business models. Systemic design integrates persuasion and awareness with desirability and ease of access to sustainable and eco-efficient service alternatives for mass market consumers. To effectively pursue the goal of making sustainable services have a greater impact on the mass market, a comprehensive study of the consumer's desires and preferences and traits of the existing popular products is a critical necessity. Given the existing niche market for eco-friendly products, an understanding of the customer's aspirations will play a pivotal role in bridging consumers' 'attitude-behavior' [2] gap and evaluating and better positioning sustainable processes in the mass market.

Building on the systemic perspectives outlined above, Manzini and Vezzoli [19] discuss the concept of *'strategic sustainable design'*, which advocates a paradigm shift aimed at the buying and selling of a system of products and services in contrast to the traditional model of buying and disposal of products. It simultaneously addresses customer and service provider needs while promoting pro-environmental practices of production and consumption. Some of the common processes and tools under strategic sustainable design are 'product service systems' [11][19], 'peer to peer services' [28] and 'product life extension through repair and second hand ownership'. Due to the reliance of strategic sustainable design on the intangibility of products and efficiency of services in delivering value, the nature of the roles played by stakeholders also differs from traditional systems. With the dissemination of services being pivotal, the ownership of a product by the consumer no longer remains constant. In some cases, such as second hand or shared ownership, the consumer also plays the part of the service provider for new consumers. With this state of constant flux in the nature of engagement of the stakeholders, strategic sustainable design approaches transform linear provider to consumer models into a mesh of participants playing the role of provider, consumer or facilitator based on the context and requiring a more intensive inter-communication system amongst the stakeholders. Therefore, we argue that systemic design in general and strategic sustainable design in particular provides the most promising framework for positioning sustainable services in the mass market. Wolfson et al. [11] suggest that:

"The main incentive behind defining sustainability as a service enables the creation of an organized framework to facilitate the active implementation of sustainability. Such a framework should characterize the nature both of the value itself and of the roles played by the participants in the value co-creation process."

IV. IDENTIFYING DESIGN CONSIDERATIONS

Although strategic sustainability offers a highly integrated approach for sustainable offerings, it also creates fairly complex dynamics of key stakeholders and contexts for simultaneously addressing economic, social and environmental aspects of the issues requiring design interventions.

This section explores the considerations needed to effectively address the dynamics of strategic sustainable design. With respect to strategic sustainable design, these theoretical constructs can be seen as four necessary facets that would need to be explored and addressed in order to design products and services for the mass market. These facets are: Design Thinking as a holistic approach, Sustainable Entrepreneurship as a mass market motivator, Product Service Systems as a potential space for disruptive innovation and User Experience as a mass market differentiator.

A. *Approach: Design Thinking*

Skoldberg et al. [29] describe design thinking as the:

"construction of the professional designer's practice (practical skills and competence) and theoretical reflections around how to interpret and characterize this non-verbal competence of the designers."

Design thinking has found applicability in a wide variety of domains like social innovation [30], healthcare services [31], organizational strategy [32] and organizational studies [33]. It is also being used for enabling resourcefulness in user groups and actively engaging them in co-design and co-creation activities through tailored tools and methods. We argue that sustainable solutions grounded in a deep understanding of the needs and context of the participants in the stakeholder network aligns with a designer's ability to translate opportunities into offerings by closely working with users.

Buchanan's seminal work [34] describing professional designer's thought process as an approach for solving 'wicked problems' (a class of social systems problems with a fundamental indeterminacy without a single solution and where much creativity is needed to find solutions [35] and is one of the foundational references for design in general. Buchanan [34] argued against the prevalent linear design process of his time with specific steps of "problem definition" and "problem solution" and instead proposed a model where problem formulation and solution continuously feed into each other and solutions are considered as "working hypothesis for exploration". This is typically facilitated through a co-design process where all participants collaboratively cycle through the process of refining the problem formulation and narrowing down the solution-space. Further, Schön [36], in his theoretical construct of '*a reflective practitioner*' outlines a practice based construct of the design process that describes *"creation and reflection upon the creation"* as two symbiotic processes working in tandem to *"allow constantly improved competence"*. Schön [36] stresses that reflection on creation does not happen after the fact but is an integral part of the whole design work and hence a part of the practice.

We argue that strategic sustainable design solutions should have a dual focus on identifying specific opportunities for interventions and innovation along with reflective and corrective measures that guide the design of future innovations. Therefore, we suggest that an approach for designing mass market strategic sustainable solutions would be best informed by a juxtaposition of the design frameworks outlined by Buchanan [34] and Schön [36], i.e. by using co-design methods and tools for framing problem areas and solutions and using the reflexive practice as an outline to guide the definition and refinement of future innovations.

B. *Motivation: Sustainable Entrepreneurship*

Sustainable entrepreneurship represents a departure from the usual focus on large firms in earlier work on corporate sustainability. It builds upon the concept that new entrants are more likely to pursue radical change than larger firms and usually lead the charge in an industry's transformation by creating 'market disequilibria' and making larger bodies react to raising market expectations.

Further, it has been stressed [13] that disruptive innovation [37] (as opposed to incremental innovation) is an integral characteristic of sustainable entrepreneurship. *'Disruptive innovation'* describes new products or services, which are presented as simpler, more convenient and inexpensive alternatives to new or less demanding customers and eventually replace the established yet more complex competitors [37]. Hence, reach and impact play a significant role in qualifying an innovation as truly disruptive. For e.g., innovation by entrepreneurs in a social niche, without a strategy or intent to broaden its reach/impact would not qualify as disruptive innovation and hence should not be categorized as sustainable entrepreneurship. Additionally, literature points us to the fact that sustainable entrepreneurs are driven by a strong motivation for industrial transformation and hence aim for mass-market transformation beyond the eco-niche [13]. Since there is growing interest in the opportunities and the business case for sustainable innovation [38] and *'green growth'* [39] it makes a strong case for sustainable entrepreneurship being treated as a motivating strategy for an approach for designing mass market strategic sustainable solutions.

C. *Opportunity: Product Service Systems*

The first formal definition of Product Service Systems (PSS) was given by Goedkoop, et al. [40] who suggested that:

"A product service-system is a system of products, services, networks of "players" and supporting infrastructure that continuously strives to be competitive, satisfy customer needs and have a lower environmental impact than traditional business models."

It builds on the management concepts of 'servitization' [41], which highlights the shift in manufacturing towards the inclusion of a service component in products. Baines et al. [42] describe the shift in emphasis advocated by PSS as a move towards the "sale of use" as opposed to the "sale of product" and outlined its key elements as:

- Product: a tangible commodity manufactured to be sold.
- Service: an activity (work) done for others with an economic value.
- System: a collection of elements including their relations.

The relations between these elements and their impact on each other considered collectively represents a *'service ecology'* [43]. Additionally, a lot of research on PSS highlights the concept of *'dematerialization'* and sustainability and the current move to a *'dematerialized economy'* [19][44]. Tim Jackson, describes this as the 'new service economy' where profitability does not depend on greater material consumption and production but from the "provision of services" that meet the essential human needs like communication, mobility etc.

From the perspective of strategic sustainable design, the concept of sustainable product service systems and the market opportunity linked to them is especially interesting. First, Sustainable PSS pushes the concept of sustainability beyond environmental optimization of products and processes , which has been shown to be an ineffective strategy for long term sustainability . Second, sustainable PSS represents a competitive proposition that outlines a viable market opportunity for sustainable entrepreneurship and disruptive innovation by *"considering alternate socio-technical systems (and ecologies) that can provide the essential end-use function, such as warmth or mobility, that an existing product offers"* [19].

D. Differentiator: User Experience

As technology has progressed, products in general and interactive products in particular have matured in terms of their usability and effectiveness in performing tasks and hence users have started looking at them as more than just tools, but rather objects to be desired [46]. Consequently, the concept of user experience has been evolving over time in Interaction Design and HCI literature from an initial focus on user behaviors and traditional usability to more expansive notions of aesthetics, effectiveness and hedonic qualities in product and technology usage [46]. Hassenzahl & Tractinsky [46] reason that this is because focusing on products and services as mere tools is insufficient to capture the variety and engaging aspects of the actual use of technology. Building upon the focus on aesthetic, emotional and hedonic qualities required to define a user experience, Hassenzahl [47] describes user experience as the consideration of:

"the pragmatic aspects of interactive products (i.e. its fit to behavioral goals) as well as about hedonic aspect, such as stimulation (i.e. personal growth, an increase of knowledge and skills), identification (i.e. self-expression, interaction with relevant others) and evocation (i.e. self-maintenance, memories)."

Hassenzahl & Tractinsky [46] also argue that since user experience considers technology from more than a simplistic and limited instrumental needs perspective the design motivations behind it would be better informed by focusing on pleasure, positivity and empowerment than on 'the absence of pain' [46]. Hassenzahl [47] builds upon this notion by suggesting that positive experiences cannot be traditionally manufactured and acquired but rather needs to be co-created by consumers and providers together.

Moreover, from a business value standpoint, literature [48], also points to the fact that the increasing commoditization of goods and services would lead to experiences emerging as key differentiators in the 'progression of economic value'. Pine and Gilmore [49] also suggest that experiences should be considered as distinct economic offerings, just like products or services. It follows that experiences should also be explicitly considered as a tangible and marketable outcome of a design process and not just an 'amorphous goal' [48] that is built around products or services and therefore can act as a viable differentiator for strategic sustainable solutions

V. Conclusion

The paper presented the challenges and outline the theoretical design considerations needed to frame desirable value propositions for sustainable services focusing on positioning services for adoption in the mass market. Building on literature from the fields of strategic design, service design and HCI, current theoretical discussions on sustainability and entrepreneurship with its key problematics and challenges are introduced.

We argue that sustainability can potentially find a familiar voice in design due to their common interest in advocating an emphasis on people's needs and aspirations for a better present and future. Mutually, design and sustainability can discover new representations and opportunities for a better future beyond offerings designed to fuel incessant consumption of resources. From the literature discussed, three primary design approaches are highlighted and discussed in detail: designing for awareness and persuasion, designing for eco-efficiency in product manufacturing and systemic design.

We propose that systemic design in general and strategic sustainable design in particular provides the most promising framework for positioning sustainable services in the mass market. As a framework, it integrates persuasion and awareness with desirability and ease of access to sustainable and eco-efficient service alternatives for mass market consumers. Further, we have highlighted four theoretical considerations needed for framing design approaches within this framework, which are '*design thinking*' for holistic and reflective problem solving, '*sustainable entrepreneurship*' to identify disruptive value propositions, '*product service systems*' for framing value propositions and design concepts as real world sustainable services and '*user experience*' as a differentiator in the mass market.

VI. Acknowledgements

The authors are indebted to the Conserve and Consume project for and all the industry partners for their participation. In addition, we would like to acknowledge University of Oslo for their partial financial support.

References

[1] J. N. Sheth, N. K. Sethia and S. Srinivas, "Mindful consumption: a customer-centric approach to sustainability," Journal of the Academy of Marketing Science, vol. 39, no. 1, Aug. 2010, pp. 21–39.

[2] A. A. Marylyn Carrigan, "The myth of the ethical consumer – do ethics matter in purchase behaviour?," Journal of Consumer Marketing, vol. 18, no. 7, 2001, pp. 560–578.

[3] X. Li, et al., Smartphone Evolution and Reuse: Establishing a more Sustainable Model (Invited Paper). .

[4] A. K. Bhuie, O. A. Ogunseitan, J.-D. M. Saphores and A. A. Shapiro, "Environmental and Economic Trade-offs in Consumer Electronic Products Recycling: A Case Study of Cell Phones and

Computers," in Proceedings of the International Symposium on Electronics and the Environment, Washington, DC, USA, 2004, pp. 74–79.

[5] M. Csikszentmihalyi, "The Costs and Benefits of Consuming," Journal of Consumer Research, vol. 27, no. 2, Sep. 2000, pp. 267–272.

[6] C. ©. M. I. of Technology and 1977-2015 All rights reserved, "Sustainability Through Servicizing," MIT Sloan Management Review. .

[7] "GreenPhones (In Norwegian)." [Online]. Available: http://www.greenphones.no/. [Accessed: 12-Jan-2016].

[8] D. A. L. C. Esty, "The Sustainability Imperative," Harvard Business Review. [Online]. Available: https://hbr.org/2010/05/the-sustainability-imperative. [Accessed: 19-Mar-2016].

[9] D. Yu and C. C. Hang, "A Reflective Review of Disruptive Innovation Theory: A Reflective Review of Disruptive Innovation Theory," International Journal of Management Reviews, vol. 12, no. 4, Dec. 2010, pp. 435–452.

[10] Brundtland Commission, "Our common future: Report of the World Commission on Environment and Development," UN Documents Gatheringa Body of Global Agreements, 1987.

[11] A. Wolfson, S. Mark, P. M. Martin and D. Tavor, Sustainability through Service. Cham: Springer International Publishing, 2015.

[12] R. Kates, et al., "Sustainability science," 2000.

[13] K. Hockerts and R. Wüstenhagen, "Greening Goliaths versus emerging Davids — Theorizing about the role of incumbents and new entrants in sustainable entrepreneurship," Journal of Business Venturing, vol. 25, no. 5, Sep. 2010, pp. 481–492.

[14] K. Śledzik, "Schumpeter's view on innovation and entrepreneurship," Management Trends in Theory and Practice,(ed.) Stefan Hittmar, Faculty of Management Science and Informatics, University of Zilina & Institute of Management by University of Zilina, 2013.

[15] J. T. Eckhardt and S. A. Shane, "Opportunities and Entrepreneurship," Journal of Management, vol. 29, no. 3, Jun. 2003, pp. 333–349.

[16] S. Schaltegger and M. Wagner, "Sustainable entrepreneurship and sustainability innovation: categories and interactions," Business Strategy and the Environment, vol. 20, no. 4, May 2011, pp. 222–237.

[17] E. Campbell, "You know more than you think you do: design as resourcefulness & self-reliance," RSA Design & Society, 2009.

[18] C. Sherwin, "Design and sustainability," The Journal of Sustainable Product Design, vol. 4, no. 1–4, Jan. 2004, pp. 21–31.

[19] E. Manzini and C. Vezzoli, "A strategic design approach to develop sustainable product service systems: examples taken from the 'environmentally friendly innovation' Italian prize," Journal of Cleaner Production, vol. 11, no. 8, Dec. 2003, pp. 851–857.

[20] K. Hobson, "Competing Discourses of Sustainable Consumption: Does the 'Rationalisation of Lifestyles' Make Sense?," Environmental Politics, vol. 11, no. 2, Jun. 2002, pp. 95–120.

[21] Design for Environmental Sustainability. London: Springer London, 2008.

[22] W. Young, K. Hwang, S. McDonald and C. J. Oates, "Sustainable consumption: green consumer behaviour when purchasing products," Sustainable Development, vol. 18, no. 1, Jan. 2010, pp. 20–31.

[23] H. Brynjarsdottir, M. H\a akansson, J. Pierce, E. Baumer, C. DiSalvo and P. Sengers, "Sustainably Unpersuaded: How Persuasion Narrows Our Vision of Sustainability," in Proceedings of the SIGCHI Conference on Human Factors in Computing Systems, New York, NY, USA, 2012, pp. 947–956.

[24] M. van der Velden, "Re-politicising Participatory Design: What can we learn from Fairphone," presented at the Ninth International Conference on Culture and Technology and Communication (CaTaC), 2014.

[25] T. Wernink and C. Strahl, "Fairphone: Sustainability from the Inside-Out and Outside-In," in Sustainable Value Chain Management, M. D'heur, Ed. Springer International Publishing, 2015, pp. 123–139.

[26] S. Reinecke, "On the Way to Sustainable Transportation," Marketing Review St. Gallen, vol. 31, no. 5, Oct. 2014, pp. 84–88.

[27] J. Olson, P. M. Clay and P. Pinto da Silva, "Putting the seafood in sustainable food systems," Marine Policy, vol. 43, Jan. 2014, pp. 104–111.

[28] "What's Mine is Yours (Botsman & Rogers, 2010)," John A. McArthur, Ph.D. .

[29] U. Johansson-Sköldberg, J. Woodilla and M. Çetinkaya, "Design Thinking: Past, Present and Possible Futures," Creativity and Innovation Management, vol. 22, no. 2, Jun. 2013, pp. 121–146.

[30] T. Brown and J. Wyatt, "Design Thinking for Social Innovation," Stanford Social Innovation Review, 2010. [Online]. Available: http://www.ssireview.org/articles/entry/design_thinking_for_social_innovation. [Accessed: 22-Mar-2015].

[31] V. Kumar, A. K. Duncan and M. A. Breslin, "Innovating health care delivery: the design of health services," Journal of Business Strategy, vol. 30, no. 2/3, 2009, pp. 13–20.

[32] D. Dunne and R. Martin, "Design thinking and how it will change management education: An interview and discussion," Academy of Management Learning & Education, vol. 5, no. 4, 2006, pp. 512–523.

[33] A. G. L. Romme, "Making a Difference: Organization as Design," Organization Science, vol. 14, no. 5, Oct. 2003, pp. 558–573.

[34] R. Buchanan, "Wicked Problems in Design Thinking," Design Issues, vol. 8, no. 2, Apr. 1992, pp. 5–21.

[35] H. W. J. Rittel and M. M. Webber, "Dilemmas in a general theory of planning," Policy Sciences, vol. 4, no. 2, Jun. 1973, pp. 155–169.

[36] D. A. Schon, The Reflective Practitioner: How Professionals Think In Action, 1 edition. New York: Basic Books, 1984.

[37] C. M. Christensen, C. W. Johnson and M. B. Horn, Disrupting Class: How Disruptive Innovation Will Change the Way the World Learns, 1st ed. Mcgraw-Hill, 2008.

[38] M. B. M. S. L. Hart, "Global Sustainability and the Creative Destruction of Industries," Sloan Management Review, vol. 41, 1999.

[39] B. Ki-moon and A. Gore, "Green growth is essential to any stimulus," Financial Times, 16-Feb-2009.

[40] M. J. Goedkoop, "Product service systems, ecological and economic basics," Ministry of Housing, Spatial Planning and the Environment, Communications Directorate, 1999.

[41] S. Vandermerwe and J. Rada, "Servitization of business: Adding value by adding services," European Management Journal, vol. 6, no. 4, 1988, pp. 314–324.

[42] T. S. Baines, et al., "State-of-the-art in product-service systems," Proceedings of the Institution of Mechanical Engineers, Part B: Journal of Engineering Manufacture, vol. 221, no. 10, Oct. 2007, pp. 1543–1552.

[43] A. Polaine, L. Løvlie and B. Reason, Service Design: From Insight to Implementation, 1st edition. Brooklyn, NY: Rosenfeld Media, 2013.

[44] R. Roy, "Sustainable product-service systems," Futures, vol. 32, no. 3–4, Apr. 2000, pp. 289–299.

[45] P. Glavič and R. Lukman, "Review of sustainability terms and their definitions," Journal of Cleaner Production, vol. 15, no. 18, Dec. 2007, pp. 1875–1885.

[46] C. Sanne, "Are we chasing our tail in the pursuit of sustainability?," International Journal of Sustainable Development, vol. 4, no. 1, Jan. 2001, pp. 120–133.

[47] M. Hassenzahl and N. Tractinsky, "User experience - a research agenda," Behaviour & Information Technology, vol. 25, no. 2, Mar. 2006, pp. 91–97.

[48] M. Hassenzahl, "Experiences Before Things: A Primer for the (Yet) Unconvinced," in CHI '13 Extended Abstracts on Human Factors in Computing Systems, New York, NY, USA, 2013, pp. 2059–2068.

[49] B. J. P. Iij. H. Gilmore, "Welcome to the Experience Economy," Harvard Business Review. [Online]. Available: https://hbr.org/1998/07/welcome-to-the-experience-economy. [Accessed: 18-Mar-2016].

[50] W. J. Orlikowski and J. J. Baroudi, "Studying Information Technology in Organizations: Research Approaches and Assumptions," Information Systems Research, vol. 2, no. 1, Mar. 1991, pp. 1–28.

From Difficult Artifacts to Easy to Use Designs

Tone Bratteteig
Department of Informatics
University of Oslo
P.B. 1080, 0316 Oslo, Norway
tone@ifi.uio.no

Guri Verne
Department of Informatics
University of Oslo
P.B. 1080, 0316 Oslo, Norway
guribv@ifi.uio.no

Abstract—**There are many reasons why artifacts and systems become difficult to use. In this paper, we investigate difficulties as a basis for design for ease of use. Difficulties may stem from the artifact or system itself, or from the artifact or system in use in context. Technology introduces new tasks, and both learning new tasks and unlearning the old ways pose challenges. We propose that users' habits and previous knowledge are used as resources for design, and present a conceptual framework for design for coherence and simplicity from a user's perspective.**

Keywords: design; competence; ease-of-use; context.

I. INTRODUCTION

Usability is often defined as the ease of use and learnability of an artifact, sometimes narrowed down to specific users in a specified use context having specific achievement goals (e.g., ISO 9241). But what does "ease of use" mean more precisely? Nielsen [1] lists five aspects of usability: learnability, efficiency, memorability, low error rate, and satisfaction. Shneiderman and Plaisant [2] present a more elaborate list of eight aspects: consistency, universal design, feedback, closure of dialogs, reversal of action, control, error prevention, and memory load. Except for universal design, all the aspects are general and concern the design of the artifact seen as a stand-alone context-independent thing. Our research shows, however, that it is difficult to achieve a total independence of contextual design elements – it is impossible and even unwanted: "All products make some reference to either products extant during previous generations or products from different companies or product families." [3: 182]. Such references are important to build on when trying to understand how to use the product. Even well-designed stand-alone artifacts can be difficult to use for users not sharing the contextual competence pre-supposed in the design. We have seen this in our research, where we focus on elderly people and the technological support that is supposed to enable them to live independently in their homes longer [4]. In this paper we discuss how knowing how technology is difficult to use can be a basis for designing solutions that are easy to use.

The paper is structured as follows: In Section II, we give a review of literature about problems in using technology. In Section III, we present reports from two studies of use of technology: the use of public services like tax, and the use of common home artifacts like remote controls or mobile devices that need charging. Section IV discusses the competencies needed for users to use an artifact, as well as how such competencies are experienced and embodied. In Section V, we discuss how we can go from knowing about the difficulties people have in using an artifact to designing an artifact that is easy for them to use. Section VI concludes the paper.

II. PROBLEMS WHEN USING TECHNOLOGY

A close study of people using IT artifacts reveals that they often find technology difficult to use [5]. A classic study is Suchman's study of use of a Xerox copy machine [6][7] demonstrating how operating a copy machine was difficult due to the difference between the scripted "plan" in the copy machine and the users' (situated) understanding of copying. Another classic is Gasser's study of how people work around computer systems that do not fit the work they need to do, show that people carry out their jobs also with non-supporting artifacts [8]. Even when an IT system works well, it may not work well together with other systems [9][5].

A different set of studies shows that an artifact can be used in different ways, e.g., Barley's classic study [10] of a CT scanner: the same technology used differently in two radiology departments demonstrates that the same artifact can be part of very different socio-technical practices.

For designers, it is particularly interesting to study the non-users of an artifact. They are, however, very difficult to get hold of (unless they can be located in a particular place, e.g., an organization). Orlikowski [11] and Star and Ruhleder [12] describe how people are not using a computer system with good reasons, indicating that contextual matters (like reward systems) may offer good reasons for not using a system – irrespective of the usability aspects of the system itself. As a way to get access to non-users of the public service web pages of the tax authorities, Verne [13] studied people calling the authorities' call centre. She found that even if tax rules are complicated most of the questions concern relatively simple tax issues and that the callers' problems are concerned with interpreting and applying the rules to their own life.

A number of studies concerning assistive technology in the homes of elderly people have been carried out, see e.g. [14]. Noting that much of the technology is not used, Greenhalgh et al [15] focus on the subjective opinions and experiences from the elderly's own technology use. They call for a different design approach in order to develop technology that supports the elderly in achieving what matters to them and enhances the quality of their life [15]. Many of the current solutions aimed at elderly users are imported from other application areas and not designed specifically for an elderly user group, e.g., touch screens [16].

We know a great deal about systems and artifacts that are not easy to use, but what is less clear is how to get from knowing what is difficult to designing a solution that is easy to use. In this paper, we have set out to do this: we analyse a set of studies of difficult-to-use-technologies in order to arrive at design ideas for easy-to-use solutions.

III. DIFFICULT-TO-USE

Investigating people's reasons for not using an artifact is very instructive for designers: there may be a range of logical and sensible reasons for not using an artifact or using it in "wrong" ways. In this section, we report from our studies of users and non-users of computer technology.

A. *Badly designed Systems and Artifacts*

Some artifacts are difficult to use because of the design. Verne's [17] study of citizens' calls to the tax information call centre showed that many callers had tried to use the online tax self-service without succeeding. Listening in to 474 telephone calls over a period of 22 months gave a basis for understanding the callers' problems. Examples of problems ranged from not finding their PIN-code to more specific questions like a woman receiving welfare benefits and had tax deducted from her pension, but being aware that welfare pension was tax free. The call centre advisors often walk the callers through the self-service web site, commenting that the online services were not user-friendly. To callers who do not know which numbers in their tax card they need to change, reporting online makes not much difference from filling out a paper form. But online tax self-services may introduce additional complexity for the citizens.

We also include a second set of examples from a study of IT technology for independent living in a home for elderly people [14], involving sensors, alarms and a tablet connected to the Internet. We have studied their use since 2012, documenting that several of the technologies do not function well in everyday use. The tablet, for example, has a wall-mounted charger station designed to charge while showing the time (Fig. 1 upper). However, the slot for positioning the charger in the right position is narrow and difficult to see, and many users do not manage to mount it right and do not discover this until the battery is empty. Also the very common stove alarm is difficult to use for people in wheel chairs or people who find it difficult to hold the turn-off-switch while stretching and bending over the stove to turn the alarm off (Fig. 1 lower).

B. *The Artifact in Use*

Some artifacts are difficult to use because of the use context and the use situation. Verne's [17] study of callers found that many people call because they need help with matching the rules and regulations with events and circumstances in their life, not because tax regulations and rules are complicated. Her data includes several examples of simple tax rules that may represent problems when applied to a person's life situation.

* When citizens move, they are required to send a notification of address to the Population Register. A citizen called to ask if he needed to send a notification to the tax authorities when he changed his job. (The answer is no.)

*A newly retired citizen needed guidance on how her new status affected her personal economy and on which of her different types of incomes are subject to which taxes.

*A house owner who earned money from renting her house asked if renovating costs could be deducted from her tax. She rented the apartment to her son, and wondered how the rules were applied in this case.

In all three examples, the life situation or circumstances of the citizen triggered the phone call. In the first example, the caller's life situation was irrelevant to the tax regulation in question, but in the two others the life situation needed to be matched with the rules and regulation by a tax expert.

Our second set of examples is from everyday technologies used by elderly people in their homes. We found that these types of difficulties arise when people use technologies that they do not have previous experience with. One example is an active woman, approximately 85 years old, who uses a hearing aid. She is well organised, educated, and has had an active work life, and she uses e.g. her TV effortlessly. Her occupational therapist has tried to teach her how to use an amplifier for her hearing aid: a wireless microphone that amplifies sounds and submits to her hearing aid.

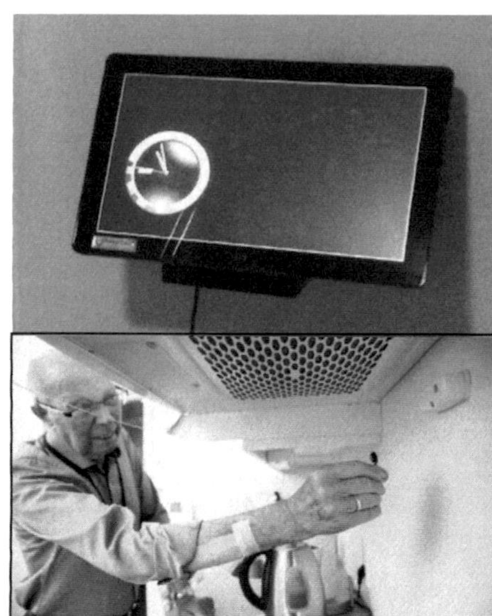

Figure 1. Welfare technology: Tablet charging (above), stove alarm (below)

The "accessory pen" is easy to use once fitted to the hearing aid: the manufacturer says that it is "zero hassle" because it is "completely simple to use, with one-click connection of receivers and fully automated settings" [18]. Using the pen involves pushing one small button in addition to charging it. However, the old woman finds the pen difficult to use. She does not remember how to use it from one therapist visit to the next. She wants to charge it before she uses it, but forgets. The occupational therapist (whose job it is to adapt support devices to individual users) has suggested that she instead charges it after she has used it, and that she keeps it in the charger until the next time she needs it. But in the "old days", keeping devices in the charger can be dangerous, and the old woman therefore does not want to do this – even if the therapist assures her that with this equipment there is no danger. The old woman often finds her hearing aid amplifier not charged when she needs it.

C. *Other's Doings*

Some technology problems are caused by factors outside the user's control, e.g., by actions or errors made by third parties. Some callers to the tax information call centre had a problem getting too little welfare support because the welfare agency "tidied up their systems" and deducted 50 % of the benefits because of a missing tax card. The tax authorities receive many calls from people who have not received a tax card in the mail, but it is often their own doing (or rather: not doing). However, in one case the street address had been changed by the municipality, without the caller being aware that she needed to send a notification of change of address – since in this case, she had not moved!

A more complicated case was a young man who had received a bill for penalty tax for underreporting income two years ago. His employer had gone bankrupt and his reported income was disputed. There was no employer who could confirm the callers' claims, and he had no documentation for his version of what had happened. In principle, he needed to document the non-event of not underreporting income. The advisor helped him by suggesting steps to take to retrieve documentation and proceed with his claims.

The smart home technologies in the apartment building for elderly people had electricity saving automation. However, the first winter everybody experienced that the apartments were very cold, and the elderly people (who normally need higher indoor temperatures because they do not move much) had to get help from the janitor service to correct the temperature. It took a long time to find out that some of the basic calculations for the electricity system were wrong resulting in faulty temperature regulation in the building [19]. We work in a smart building ourselves and have experienced similar difficulties when trying to identify the reasons for bad temperature regulation mechanisms. When using artifacts that are part of a larger complex system, the problems a user experiences may result from other people's activities or errors.

D. *What is Difficult?*

Difficulties that stem from the artifact or system itself pose different challenges than those stemming from the artifact-in-context or in-interaction. We sum up the kinds of difficulties in Table 1, and indicate what kinds of challenges they pose.

TABLE I. DIFFERENT KINDS OF DIFFICULTIES WITH ARTIFACTS AND SYSTEMS, AND THE CHALLENGES THEY POSE

What is difficult?	**Kinds of difficulties**		
	Artifact	***Context***	***Activities by others***
Examples:	Holding the turn-off switch. Positioning of the charger. Online tax self services	Personal economy when retiring. Tax deductions for renting out a house to family. Tax card when starting a new job	Bankrupcy by an employer. Welfare agency "tidies up their systems". Errors made by subcontractors.
Challenges:	Difficult to use, afraid to make errors	Matching artifact with own life situation or circumstances	Disentangling interactions and complexities

IV. COMPETENCE

Competence, as the ability to do something successfully or efficiently, is important for using technology. The examples in Section III show that competence can concern the design that makes the operation of the technology difficult (III.A) as well as the adaptation of the technology to the actual situation (III.B). In both cases, the users have to do fitting work [8] in order to use the technology

A. *What we Know*

A usability test of a video conferencing system showed that users who did not have the same technological experience as the designers: in this case: an iPhone, did not understand the interaction mechanisms and hence had problems operating the system [20]. Langdon et al [3] discuss this problem on a more general level, showing that "similarity of prior experience to the usage situation was the main determinant of performance, although there was also some evidence for a gradual, age-related capability decline." (p. 179). They conclude that in their test of driving a new car "there was ... some clear evidence that experience may be more influential than age" (p. 189). Docampo [21] has identified four technology generations: electro-mechanical period, remote control era, use of displays, and use of layered menus, basically distinguishing between before and after 1960. The generations affect learning new technology visible in a discontinuity of errors and task timings between the generations.

Previous experience is a salient feature that builds self-efficacy [22]. According to self-efficacy theory for human agency, belief in one's own competence and mastery is an important factor for succeeding. In their study of the effects of training programs in computer use for older adults, Wild et al. [23] found that after one year of consistent computer use the participants reported reduced levels of anxiety and increased self-confidence in their abilities using computers. Participants with mild cognitive impairments were less likely to demonstrate increased efficacy and competence. This is in line with our own empirical findings. We interviewed an ergo-therapist, who had the experience that elderly people with mild cognitive impairments were able to learn new practices, but with much training and follow-up from her.

Langdon et al [3] suggest that "prior experience with similar products and product features is a strong predictor of the usability of products over the wider range of capabilities. This similarity results from experience with same brand, or functionally and perceptually differing products, provided that key functional features and visual appearances are maintained." (p. 190). Hurtienne and Langdon [24] suggest a continuum of knowledge sources starting with 1) innate knowledge like reflexes and 2) sensorimotor experiences like speed, gravity (early childhood learning), 3) culture (everyday life), and 4) expertise acquired in a profession or hobby. Knowledge about tools crosses these "levels" of knowledge. They suggest that knowledge residing on the sensorimotor level of the continuum is basic to most people and is acquired early in life.

B. *How we Know*

Langdon et al found that previous experience provided guidance on how to carry out their tests [3: 182], which explained why their older test-participants were not able to use the technology, rather than they having lower cognitive capability as a result of ageing.

Using technology is also a bodily experience. Höök [25] discusses bodily ways of knowing in her study of the challenges she experienced when learning the English style of horseback riding having experience from riding Icelandic style. The horses are trained to react differently to signals (from the legs, hands, body posture) from the rider in the different riding schools. Competence in and experience from horseback riding resides in the body and becomes more or less automatic.

Höök [25] describes how she needed to practice again and again with constant feedback from the instructor to be able to learn the new movements, positioning and interactions. Even though she cognitively knew and understood how she was supposed to move and position her body, it was difficult to *do/perform* the new movements at the right moments.

C. *Learning and Un-learning*

Höök [25] describes vividly how learning new movements and ways of communication implied unlearning the old ways. Unlearning bodily ways of knowing implies consciously and deliberately practicing *not* doing the usual activity and instead practice something new. Having learnt how and when to perform a new movement is different from practicing the old habits. Unlearning bodily knowledge requires conscious cognitive work before it becomes a habitual and automated practice.

A good example is modern hearing aids, where the wearer will need to train his or her brain to filter out noise from the sound that s/he wants to hear in order to get the most out of the hearing aid. The brain needs some years to re-adjust, and middle-aged people will benefit from using the hearing aids before it is strictly necessary. The brain needs time to allow for automation that enables the activity to take place outside of the conscious brain activity [26].

Changes in rules and regulations as well as in the technology for doing taxes introduce new tasks for the citizens. In 2008 was submitting the tax return form made optional in that Norwegian citizens could just accept the figures that was already gathered by the tax authorities and presented in a pre-completed form. Accepting was done by a non-action: by *not* making changes in the pre-completed form. Hence, learning to differentiate and understand when to report changes has become a task. Many of the callers were not aware that they did not have to send in a paper form, and that they could report online [13]. In practice it can be difficult to differentiate between learning new tasks and unlearning old tasks, but we argue that analytically they create different kinds of challenges.

Wu et al [27] present a participatory design project with people with anterograde amnesia, aimed at developing a "memory aid" for and with them. They base their design on the fact that "amnestics rely heavily on external memory aids, such as a calendar or an action item list." (p. 217) providing a "tool [that] will assist amnestics when they feel lost or disoriented by providing information as to their whereabouts and their *intent* for being where they are. A person having amnesia will typically follow familiar routines in their daily life, such as the same route home, because deviating from this path will often result in disorientation. Our tool enables an amnestic to grow increasingly confident and *independent* in exploring new locations and situations – a feat that is very difficult in current practice." [27:222, original emphasis].

The tool was based on the fact that amnestics' procedural memory to a large extent remains intact; therefore it was possible to train new routines and skills for using the tool. "Interestingly, the overall similarity of products that has been experienced before does not have to be high to allow effective learning" [3: 183].

Ergo-therapists working with elderly people tell that people often install electric water heaters in the homes of their old relatives in order to avoid starting a fire when forgetting the kettle on the stove. However, if the elderly person has a "bad day" and is particularly forgetful, s/he may put the water heater on the stove as a bodily habit, and this may cause fire.

D. *What is difficult – seen from the user's perspective*

Looking closer at what is difficult suggests a distinction between learning and un-learning tasks. We found that the sources for the difficulties were the tasks to learn and the old tasks to unlearn: the two different processes are experienced in different ways both in cases where the artifact is difficult itself and when it is the fitting of the technology to the situation that appears as difficult. We came across examples of actions and errors made by third parties, such as vendors, employers, other public agencies and other technologies. In these cases, the situation was experienced as unpredictable and confusing and not possible to explain by the user unless s/he had a deep knowledge of the complexity of the technology in its social environment. We sum up our analysis of what is difficult in Table II, expanding Table I with rows from this more detailed analysis of the nature of the difficulties.

V. DESIGNING FOR EASE-OF-USE

The three different kinds of difficulties can be a basis for approaching design of easy-to-use technology solutions. In this section, we report from some design experiments with elderly people [4][14][28][29] as well as our own design suggestions based on analysis of identified user problems [17].

Designing from the users' perspective starts with investigating their subjective experiences and competencies. Elderly users need much practice and repetition to establish new habits and unlearning old habits may be the hardest part. Unlearning may require trust to let old habits go to be sure that they are not necessary, e.g., for security. As unlearning old tasks is a challenge in itself, a design that builds on old, habitual tasks will be experienced as less challenging for the user. Using everyday technologies like radios, mobile phones, water heaters or remote controls is normally easy and often automated and habituated. Many of our memories and competencies sit in our bodies as automatic movements or perception (e.g., music, smells) and can be carried out without conscious deliberation. A design that incorporates that the user can rely on his/her old habits can make the changing of old practices more likely and the design more robust. However, designing for new habits in old age is possible, as the example of the memory aid for the amnestic people above showed [27].

TABLE II. WHAT IS DIFFICULT SEEN FROM THE USER'S PERSPECTIVE

What is difficult	Kinds of difficulties		
	Artifact	*Context*	*Activities by others*
New tasks to learn	Holding the turn-off switch. Positioning of the charger. Online tax services.	Personal economy after retiring. Charge device after use. Check pre-completed form	Check and act if something unusual
Old tasks to unlearn	Handling paper forms. Putting kettle on stove.	Charge device before use. *Not* pushing the horse. Changed tax rules.	Need trust to stop doing.
Basic knowledge for the task	Understand tax and web pages. Understand a water boiler.	When does the new apply?	Understanding the ecology of humans and technology
Challenges:	Difficult to use, afraid to make errors	Matching artifact with own life situation or circumstances. Differentiating between old and new.	Disentangling interactions and complexities.

We will exemplify the first design approach with the design of a digital radio that was co-designed with in total 25 elderly people [29]. Johnsen et al aimed to design interaction mechanisms that built on old and familiar bodily skills when designing a new way of operating a digital radio [29]. Using rotary controls for operating the radio – like in the old days – enabled them to make sense of the interface with their body even if they intellectually could not understand or remember how to turn on the radio. They easily recognized the button as a device for rotary movement. Several buttons were designed and tested for a good grip for old hands and recognizable positioning with different textures and shapes [29], see Fig. 2.

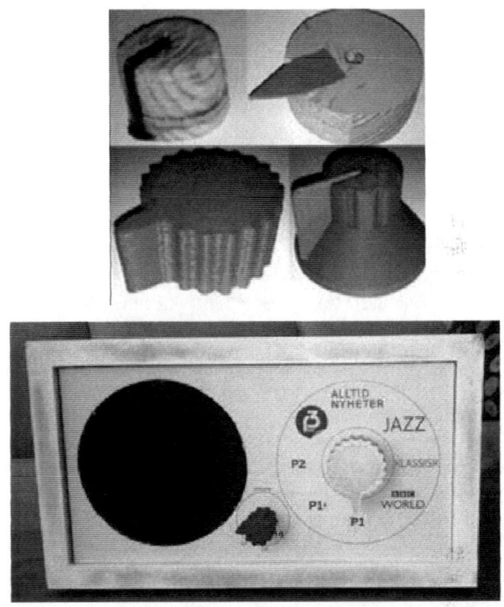

Figure 2. The prototypes for the knob (above) and the digital radio (below). Photo by Johnsen et al [29]

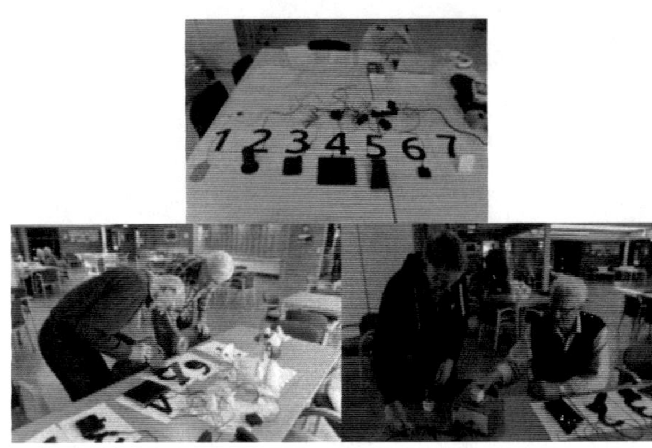

Figure 3. Testing several different induction chargers. Photo: Iversen [28]

In the second design approach, Iversen and Joshi [28][30] built on knowledge about earlier habits, e.g., the fact that in the old days telephones had wires and were usually located in a specific place, on a particular table by the entrance door. Maybe it would be easier to remember to charge the mobile phone if it was always put on a particular place like in the old days? As a way to provide easy charging of phones, Iversen and Joshi [28][30] collected seven different off-the-shelf induction chargers and had them tested by a group of elderly men (see Fig. 3). The trying out of different technologies was instructive to the elderly users as well as to us as designers.

Matching the artifact with the personal use situation and context represents a challenge [17][31], in particular if the artifact is complex (like tax). Showing ways of matching, e.g., by using several examples, can help the user in the matching of her/his situation with the technology requirements: s/he may be lucky and find an example similar to her situation. FAQs and help texts can provide such examples in the artifact itself, while human helpers like call advisors and ergo-therapists will have to assist if the matching is too difficult to carry out by the user alone. Graphical illustrations and simulations can also help explain complex systems like the tax system.

Fig. 4 illustrates our view of how technology influences the tasks done by a human user. Fig. 4a illustrates a loosely defined set of tasks for a particular purpose (like doing taxes) as seen from the human's perspective. Fig. 4b illustrates how technology takes over some of the tasks: they become obsolete. Fig. 4c shows the automated task area as seen from the human user's point of you: s/he encounters some left-over tasks that are not automated and some new tasks.

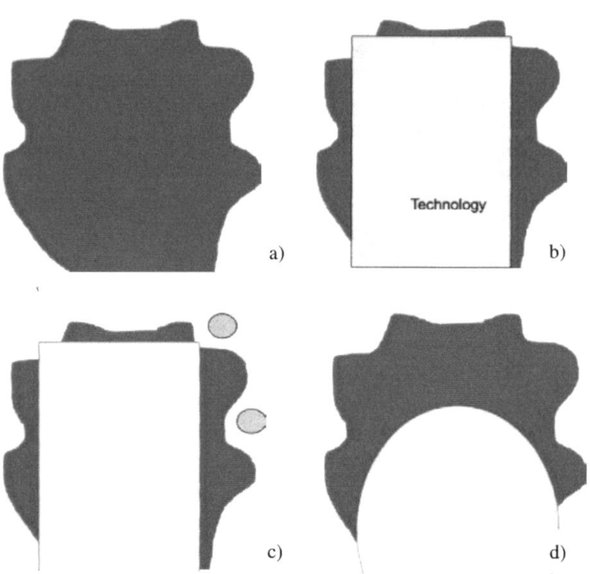

Figure 4. a) A set of tasks for a user - not clearly defined. b) Some of the tasks are made obsolete because of technology. c) Fragmented tasks left for the human user. d) A coherent set of tasks for a user.

The tasks left for the human interacting with the technology appear as fragmented and there may be no or little coherence between different subtasks. New tasks can be of a very different kind than the original set of tasks. Fig. 4d illustrates that in order to make the tasks left for the human user coherent and foreseeable, we should design a coherent set of tasks left for the user instead of let the technology decide what is automated [17][32].

Managing the boundaries between tasks made redundant by technology, tasks left for the user to do and emerging new tasks is a challenge in itself. Designing from the user's perspective aims to present the tasks for the human interacting with technology as a coherent whole and with connected subtasks. This will enable the user to disentangle the problems s/he encounters.

VI. CONCLUSIONS

Based on examples from our research on design with and for elderly people and on citizens doing taxes, we describe how artifacts and systems become difficult to use. We have reflected on how we can use knowledge about difficulties in a constructive way to suggest better designs. In the paper, we make an analytical distinction between types of difficulties according to where they appear: in the artifact / system itself or when used in its use situation / context. Our analysis also includes a discussion of the differences between learning new tasks and/or competences to benefit from the technology and un-learning old habits and practices. In addition, difficulties stemming from activities and errors made by others may occur, and in order to be able to disentangle the problem and sort out what can be done, the user needs to understand the larger ecology of the service / system.

We suggest that habits and bodily knowledge are used as resources for design where users benefit from familiarity and coherence. Building on and extending old habits instead of making them obsolete in a new design can be experienced as very simple for the user – independent of any usability assessment based on criteria that are external to and irrelevant for the particular user in the particular situation. Our aim has been to present a conceptual framework for design for the user's subjective perspective.

Our conclusion is that "easy to use" is difficult to design, and that the notion of "ease-of-use" hides the complexity that comes when artifacts are used in real life contexts. Both the identification of what makes things difficult and what turns out to be easy to use challenge a notion of "usability" that looks at the artifact as a de-contextualized object. Easy to use is a characteristic of the relation between a user, her/his activity and the technology that supports that activity. It is thus both situational and personal. This makes it even more challenging to go from what is difficult to use to designing easy to use artifacts.

ACKNOWLEDGMENTS

We would like to thank the participants in the "Autonomy and automation" and "BRIS" projects, both co-researchers – including Master students – and the elderly users. We also want to thank the staff and elderly residents at

Kampen Care+ and the advisors and managers at the Tax Information Call Centre.

REFERENCES

[1] J. Nielsen, Usability Engineering, Morgan Kaufmann Publishers, 1994, ISBN 0-12-518406-9.

[2] B. Shneiderman and C. Plaisant, Designing the User Interface: Strategies for Effective Human-Computer Interaction, Addison-Wesley Publ. Co. Reading, MA, 2010.

[3] P. Langdon, T. Lewis, and J. Clarkson, "The effects of prior experience on the use of consumer products", Univ.Access Inf.Soc., vol. 6, 2007, pp. 179-191.

[4] S. G. Joshi and T. Bratteteig, "Assembling fragments into continuous design: On participatory design with old people", Nordic Contributions in IS Research, 6th Scandinavian Conference on Information Systems, SCIS 2015, Oulu, Finland, August 9-12, 2015, Proceedings

[5] S. Bly et al., "Broken expectations in the digital home", CHI 2006, Montréal, Quebec, Canada, Apr. 22-27, pp. 568-573

[6] L. Suchman, Plans and Situated Actions. The Problem of human-machine communication. Cambridge University Press, 1987.

[7] L. Suchman, Human-Machine Reconfigurations, Cambridge University Press, New York, 2007.

[8] L. Gasser, "The Integration of Computing and Routine Work", ACM Transactions on Office Automation, vol. 4, no. 3, 1986, pp. 205-225.

[9] J. Söderström, Jävla skitsystem (in Swedish: Stupid bloody system), Karneval 2011, ISBN 9789187207525, http://www.slideshare.net/Jonas_inUse/stupid-bloody-system, retrieved 03/2016.

[10] S. R. Barley, "Technology as an occasion for structuring: Evidence from observations of CT scanners and the social order of radiology departments", Administrative science quarterly, vol. 31, no. 1, 1986, pp. 78-108.

[11] W. Orlikowski, "Learning from Notes", CSCW'92, ACM, New York, 1992, pp. 362-369.

[12] S. L. Star and K. Ruhleder, "Steps Toward an Ecology of Infrastructure: Design and access for Large Information Spaces", Information systems research, vol. 7, no. 1, 1996, pp. 111-134.

[13] G. Verne, "Two faces of autonomy. Learning from non-users of an e-service", Systems, Signs and Actions, vol. 8, no. 1, 2014, pp. 6–24

[14] S. G. Joshi, and T. Bratteteig, "Design for Prolonged Mastery. On Involving Old People in Participatory Design", Scandinavian Journal of Information Systems, vol. 28, no 1, 2016 (in press)

[15] T. Greenhalgh et al., "What is quality in assisted living technology? The ARCHIE framework for effective telehealth and telecare services", BMC Med, vol. 13, no. 91, 2015: 13: 91.

[16] A. Culén and T. Bratteteig, "Touch-Screens and Elderly users: A Perfect Match?", In Leslie Miller (ed.), ACHI 2013, IARIA, 2013, pp. 460-465.

[17] G. Verne, The winners are those who have used the old paper form. On citizens and automated public services, PhD Thesis, University of Oslo, 2015, http://urn.nb.no/URN:NBN:no-50321.

[18] http://www.phonak.com/com/b2c/en/products/wireless-accessories/products/roger.html, retrieved 03/2016.

[19] J.C. Doksrød, Understanding the complexity of error detection in smart homes, Masters thesis, Department of Informatics, University of Oslo, 2016

[20] Paulsrud, A discussion of Technological Frames applied at a Usability Test, Master thesis, Department of Informatics, University of Oslo, 2011.

[21] R. M. Docampo, Technology Generations handling complex User Interfaces, PhD dissertation, TU Eindhoven 2001, ISBN 90-386-0913-2.

[22] A. Bandura, "Self-efficacy mechanisms in human agency", American Psychologist vol. 37, no. 2, 1982, pp. 122-147.

[23] K. V. Wild et al., "Computer related self-efficacy and anxiety in older adults with and without mild cognitive impairment", Alzheimer's & dementia: the journal of the Alzheimer's Association, vol. 8, no. 6, 2012, pp. 544-552.

[24] J. Hurtienne and P. Langdon, "Prior Knowledge in Inclusive Design: The Older, the More Intuitive?", ACM Conference 2009.

[25] K. Höök, "Transferring Qualities from Horseback Riding to Design," NordiCHI, October 16-20 2010, pp. 226–235, ACM, ISBN: 978-1-60558-934-3.

[26] S. Haugland, hearing aid specialist, personal communication 2015.

[27] M. Wu, B. Richards, and R Baecker, "Participatory Design with individuals who have Amnesia", The Participatory Design Conference ,Toronto 2004, pp. 214–223, ACM, ISBN: 1-58113-851-2/04/07.

[28] T. R. Iversen, Exploring tangible interaction: Alternative interfaces for assisting elderly users, Master Thesis, Department of Informatics, University of Oslo, 2015.

[29] E. Johnsen, M. Ofstad and S. Subaschandran, Care+: Can we make the interface of the radio easier for elderly users in the digital age?, Student report, Department of Informatics, University of Oslo, 2015.

[30] T.R. Iversen, and S.G. Joshi, Exploring Spatial Interaction in Assistive Technology through prototyping, AHFE conference, Procedia Manufacturing, Elsevier Publishing Co.

[31] G. Bowker and S. L. Star, Sorting Things Out: Classification and Its Consequences. Massachussets Institute of Technology, Cambridge, Massachussets, 1999.

[32] L. Bainbridge, "Ironies of automation", Automatica vol. 19, no. 6, 1983, pp. 775-779. doi:10.1016/0005-1098(83)90046-8.

Augmented Reality as a Tutorial Tool for Construction Tasks

Wood frame wall assembly supported by smartphones

Ana Regina Mizrahy Cuperschmid, Marina Graf Grachet, Márcio Minto Fabricio
Architecture and Urbanism Institute (IAU)
University of São Paulo (USP)
São Carlos, Brazil
e-mail: fale@anacuper.com | marina.grachet@usp.br | marcio@sc.usp.br

Abstract— **Augmented Reality (AR) applications mix, by means of display devices, real world environments with virtual objects in real time. The use of AR as a support for the implementation in the construction industry is still narrowly explored. This study proposes the applicability of AR, using smartphones, to aid wood frame assembly. This research innovation proposition is the developing assembly guidance in AR, displaying a wood frame wall model in real scale through smartphones screens. An investigative approach about the possibilities of such integration is proposed and developed, including the development of a specific application. User experience evaluations were conducted. In the evaluation, the participants experienced AR in order to assemble a wood frame wall panel. After that, the participants answered a questionnaire to ascertain the profile characterization and the user experience quality. The results obtained indicated that the proposed system is a useful tutorial tool. From a technology innovation perspective, this initiative has the potential to benefit the application of AR as training and technology support for construction processes.**

Keywords - Augmented Reality; User Experience; Assembly; Civil construction.

I. Introduction

Augmented Reality (AR) applications associate through visualization devices, real environments with virtual objects in real time. Unlike Virtual Reality, that completely immerses the users in a synthetic environment, AR allows them to look at virtual models superimposed onto the physical world. By merging a range of digital and physical media, AR can be enriched by different perceptions and comprehensions offered by both physical and virtual environments.

Currently, there are few in-depth studies that assess and evaluate human factors and interaction in mobile AR systems [1], especially researches concerning Architectural, Engineering and Construction applications. There is a lack of formal studies concerning the user experience in mobile AR systems [2]. The limited understanding of human factors, which are the basis for interaction with AR systems, can be an obstacle to the diffusion of this technology beyond the laboratory prototypes [3].

As a tool to assist visualization, AR has the potential to contribute to the construction processes as it can exhibit additional information that enables better comprehension and it can also gradually guide the execution. Additional information associated with virtual models can be used if connected to the real construction elements and visualized in AR. This way, AR can provide a visualization of the assembly procedure in an interactive way at the same time it shows superimposed models onto the real world.

The wood-frame construction method combines commitment to the environment with new construction techniques. Considered as a sustainable and dry technology, around 95% of the residences in the United States of America rely on the aforementioned technology [4]; however, in Brazil its adoption is still incipient. The embracement of new construction technologies, like wood framing, depends on individuals' training to develop and execute projects that involve such technologies. Hence, it is important to highlight that new competences must be gained and applied to the work. By allowing individuals to be aided in the assembly process of wood frame edifications, the AR technology would act as a facilitator to the diffusion of this structural system.

The issue that leads this research is if and how AR could be used as a tool to assist the assembly of wood frame panels. The proposal is to convert the assembly steps and way of execution into visible and explicit images through an AR system. In this case, it is important to ensure a suitable user experience while using the AR interface. Therefore, this paper describes a User Experience (UX) evaluation of an AR application using smartphone, to assist a wood frame wall assembly.

This paper is organized as follows: section II explores the state of the art about the user evaluation of AR interfaces; section III presents the developed application; section IV describes the conducted evaluation; section V contains the results and discussion and the conclusion is presented in section VI.

II. User Evaluation of AR Interfaces

Traditional directives to evaluate the user interface cannot be exclusively used in this emerging field [1][5]–[7], since AR systems differ from desktop systems in various aspects; the most crucial is that such systems are produced for being used as a mediator or amplifier of human visualization [5]. An AR system is, in its ideal form, made to be transparent and more as part of the system of human perception than a separate entity of it [5]. In order for this to happen, the user should perceive the reality with added information and interact with the system in a natural way.

As pointed by [3], there are a number of challenges and difficulties as the hardware (e.g., display resolution, screen brightness and contrast, field of view, device weight) and the software (e.g., accuracy of the tracking algorithms, robustness, ease of calibration) that need to be overcome when evaluating user performance in AR systems. One interface of AR includes hardware, software, interface elements (e.g., menus, icons), markers, interaction techniques (e.g., mouse control, bare-hand interactions) and the content shown in AR. Depending on the device, the tracking form, the interaction technique used, the AR interface is altered. These factors may justify, in part, the lack of standard methods to evaluate AR interfaces.

According to [1], most AR user evaluations fit into one of the four categories: (i) human perception and cognition; (ii) user task performance; (iii) collaboration between users; (iv) system usability and system design evaluation. Among the research that studies user task performance, it is possible to mention a few related to this, as in [8]–[12].

Some researches aimed the consolidation of AR for assembly in the construction field [8][9], targeting the comparison between paper-based and AR manuals as guidance to the assembly; the former used as model a LEGO robot and the latter, a piping system. The results of both researches showed that the use of AR reduced significantly the operator's cognitive workload, as well as the amount of assembly errors and execution time. In [8], one can observe that the AR assembly manual lowered the learning curve of users. In [9], the use of AR proved to be suitable as guidance to trainees in the execution of highly complex tasks, in which training time is limited and errors can be either dangerous or costly. Corroborating, [9] showed that the use of AR proved productive, since it promoted savings in two-thirds of the expenses of correcting erroneous assembly.

Some researches have explored assembly with bare-hand interactions using AR [10]–[12]. In these researches, the users assemble a virtual model, which is projected through a Head Mounted Display (HMD). The virtual objects are manipulated by the movement of the thumb tip and index fingertip. Lack of realism was classified as a limitation, since the assembly is merely virtual and the models and their joints are simple. In [11], disregarding the weights of the elements contributed to the lack of naturalness and realism when handling virtual objects. Also, in [10][12], it is pointed the need to improve the level of realism through a more sophisticated algorithm for joint recognition, thus more complex models could be tested using this system.

While [8][10]–[12] dealt with the assembly of small dimension models, this research explored the assembly of a real size wood frame wall panel, hence, the assembly of a large dimension model. In [9], the assembly of a real size piping system was explored, although the visualization was provided by an external projection, while in this research it happened through the smartphone screen. Thus, this represents an innovation concerning the proposed use of AR and the way it can be used.

III. AR Application

A system that could assist the assembly of a wood frame wall structure was idealized. To support this proposal, an application was developed: given a wall and its respective virtual model, an AR application that could put in evidence the execution steps was built up. This stage was developed in three phases, described as follows:

A. *Wood frame modeling*

In the first phase, a wood frame wall structure was modeled using the Autodesk Revit® software. This structure was idealized to be assembled in laboratory and, for this reason, measures of 1.70 meters wide by 1.75 meters high were adopted. The proposed structure possesses a central opening for window, Fig. 1. Then, the model was exported to Unity 3D software, in which the AR application was developed.

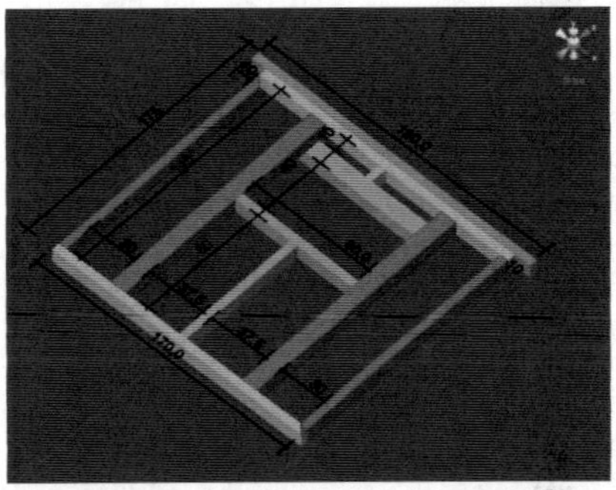

Figure 1. Unity 3D print screen: wall structure.

B. *Wood components identification*

In the second phase, the eucalyptus components, section 5 x 11 centimeters, were cut in accordance with the project. Each one was identified by color according to its length and function. Thus, the scheme shown in Table 1 was adopted.

TABLE I. LIST OF THE WOOD COMPONENTS (SECTION 5 X 11 CENTIMETERS) THAT COMPRISE THE WALL STRUCTURE

Length (cm)	Quantity	Color
190	1	Orange
170	2	Blue
145	6	Red
80	3	Pink
80	1	Green
10	1	Gray

Subsequently, the panel was physically assembled. At this moment, the components were drilled in order to offer a pre-set assemble system, Fig. 2. Letters were written to identify elements of the same color to favor its location in the panel. Corroborating, a triangle was drawn on the top of each element to the direction it should be positioned.

Figure 2. Components identification and drilling setup.

C. *Application development*

In the third phase, the application functionality, characteristics and development were determined. The "montAR" application was developed from the Metaio's Software Development Kit for Unity 3D. The application was developed to run on smartphones with Android Operating System.

Its functionality is based on the use of a marker associated with the assembly execution steps of the wood-frame panel. The marker is an image with a certain visual pattern that can be recognized by the AR system, which orientates and locates virtual objects in the scene. This marker, when seen in AR, indicates the correct location of the components that comprise the panel by the visualization of the 3D model in real scale, with highlighted indication of its position.

The "montAR" application can be accessed by its icon on the smartphone screen. When running, the application shows a menu with the options: Assemble, Verify and Acknowledgement (in Portuguese: *Montar, Verificar e Agradecimento*). In Assemble, there is a menu on the side numbered from 1 to 7 to access the panel execution steps. These steps consist of exhibition of the AR model elements and also of audio instructions that include the correct positioning, orientation (vertical/horizontal), joints and additional assembly referral, Fig. 3. In Verify, the virtual model in colors is shown, in real size, to facilitate the visual verification of the elements and their positioning on the panel.

Figure 3. "montAR" print screen: marker, virtual model and the right menu with seven steps

D. *Application testing*

Once the application was complete, the system functionality was tested. At this moment, its functionality was ascertained and issues such as the positioning and scale of the virtual elements in respect to those of the real ones were verified.

After the testing, alterations were made in order to refine the system, such as in: the execution order, the step-by-step audio instructions, the touchscreen options (drag, spin and enlarge/reduce), the maintenance of the virtual item in the scene even when it is no longer possible to visualize the marker and the insertion of a platform on the floor to favor the use of the screwdriver during the assembly.

IV. User Experience Evaluation

The purpose of this stage was to assess the quality of the experience of using the system as means of communication of the assembly steps. According to [13], for evaluations that aim to enhance the measurement, such as response time to a stimulus, objective measures are used and, for experiments designed to assess cognitive performance, subjective measures and qualitative analyzes are used. [13] and [14] suggest that evaluations designed to assess cognitive performance are the most indicative of the user experience with the interface and, therefore, subjective measures or qualitative analyzes should be adopted. In this situation, commonly, participants are asked to perform certain tasks. The major advantage of using tasks is that they tend to be more similar to the actions that users would realize with the system. Therefore, the information gained from an assessment of cognitive performance tends to be more relevant and accurate on the application utility.

The assessment process was divided in two sections. The first, being user characterization: age, gender, level of education, frequency of use of smartphone or tablet and previous knowledge of AR systems and wood framing. The second, being the evaluation of the assembly system itself.

Initially, the researcher presented the system by demonstrating its operation and, after that, the user experimented the technology for a few minutes to become familiar with it.

The next step consisted of the task of assembling the wood frame wall structure using the AR application through a Samsung Galaxy S5 smartphone. Thus, a marker was positioned over a wooden platform, which composed the assembly space. The eucalyptus components that comprise the panel, screws, an electric screwdriver and a Phillips screwdriver were disposed alongside the platform, Fig. 4.

Figure 4. Provided material for the completion of the evaluation

Following the assembly, a questionnaire was administered to the user in order to assess the quality of his/her experience, which is presented in Table 2. The method adopted was proposed by [14], in which the user experience is classified according to certain characteristics and rated in a Likert scale. To each assertion, the participant would check one of the following alternatives: Totally agree / Agree / Nothing to declare / Disagree / Totally disagree.

TABLE II. UX QUESTIONNAIRE

Q1	The step-by-step provided by the Augmented Reality system to the panel assembly was effective
Q2	I felt that the Augmented Reality system was appropriate to the proposed task
Q3	The smartphone screen size was appropriate to visualize the wood frame panel
Q4	It was comfortable to use the smartphone during the whole time
Q5	The Augmented Reality system interface seemed natural to me (menu, buttons, control and visualization)
Q6	The visualization of virtual information superimposed onto the real world did not confuse me
Q7	When using the Augmented Reality system, I felt encouraged and motived to finish the task
Q8	Guided by the Augmented Reality system, I was able to finish the assembly task at the first attempt
Q9	When I was assembling the wood frame panel, the Augmented Reality system enabled the perception and correction of errors
Q10	I felt that I accomplished the task of assembling the wood frame panel effectively
Q11	I felt satisfied with the way I performed and accomplished the task of assembling the wood frame panel using Augmented Reality
Q12	When using the Augmented Reality system, I felt the desire to continue
Q13	Using this Augmented Reality system made me feel involved in something extraordinary, something new
Q14	I enjoyed the experience of assembling the wood frame panel using Augmented Reality

a. Based on [14]

In addition to these questions, an open question was provided destined to further considerations, where the participant could comment on his/her difficulties and suggest improvements on the system.

V. RESULTS AND DISCUSSION

The evaluation involved seven participants, among Architecture and Civil Engineering students, who experimented the AR system through the smartphone screen. The assessment took place on September 2015. The data collected was analyzed aiming the quality of the UX.

Of the total number of participants, three were female and four, male, and all of them were aged between 18 and 24. When asked about the frequency of use of smartphone or tablet, all of them informed daily basis use of this kind of mobile device. None of them had previous experience in any kind of AR system neither had assembled a wood frame panel before.

Initially, the participants were given information about the research aim and explanation on the system operation. All of them took a few minutes to become familiar with the AR functioning.

All of the participants accomplished the panel assembly successfully. On average, each one took 55 minutes to complete the task. Throughout the wood frame structure assembly process, the participants' actions were recorded, Fig. 5.

Figure 5. Documentation of the assembly process

It was observed that while some participants placed the smartphone in their pockets, others laid it down on the board during the execution. It was only removed when accessing a button was necessary in order to move on to the next step, Fig. 6.

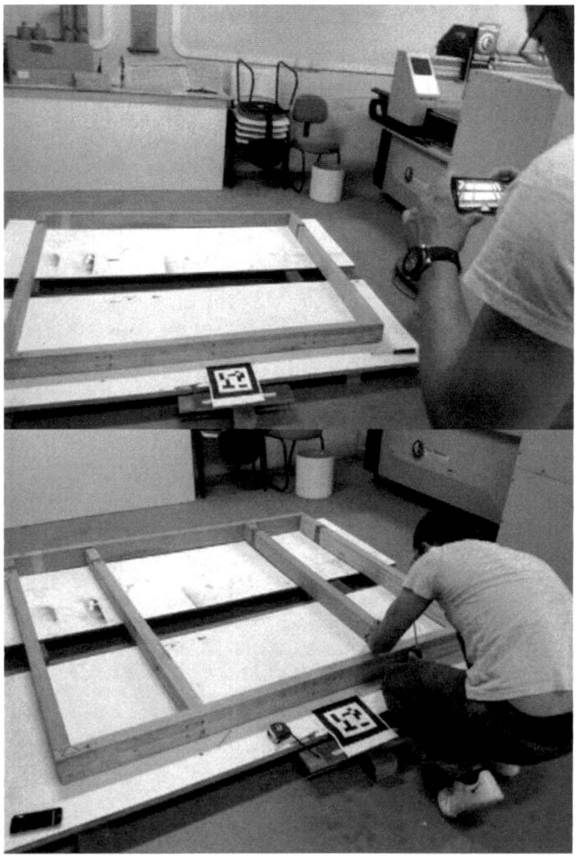

Figure 6. Participant during the assembly task

The results of the questionnaire, in general, indicate acceptance of the proposed system. All agreed that: the step-by-step provided was effective (Q1); the AR system was appropriate to the task (Q2); the screen size offered by the smartphone was appropriate to the task (Q3); the interface provided by the AR system seemed natural to the participants (Q5); they felt encouraged and motivated to finish the task (Q7); they could accomplish the task free of errors at the first attempt (Q8); they accomplished the task effectively (Q10); they felt satisfied with the way they performed and accomplished the task (Q11); they felt the desire to continue using the system (Q12); they enjoyed the experience of assembling the wood frame panel using the AR system (Q14).

On the other hand, three participants declared that the use of the smartphone did not prove comfortable during the whole assembly period (Q4). One participant stated that virtual information superimposed onto the real world caused confusion (Q6); other opted to abstain from commenting about the AR system enabling the perception and correction of errors (Q9) and another did not feel involved in something extraordinary (Q13). Fig. 7 summarizes the answers.

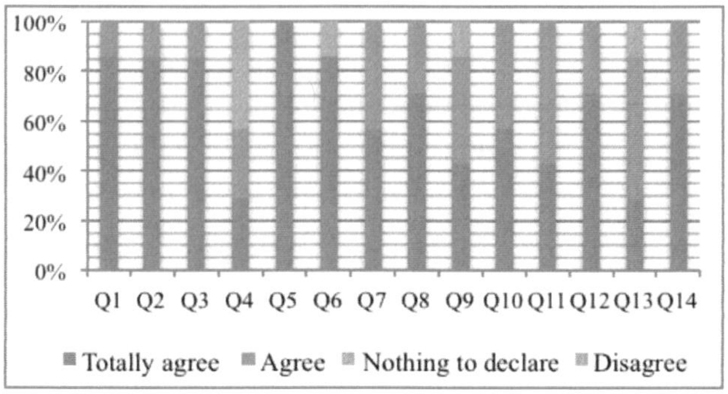

Figure 7. Results from the UX evaluation questionnaire

As warned by [15], the visual disorder may cause ambiguity or difficulty in comprehending the AR content. Corroborating, one participant complained that, at particular times, the superposition of virtual elements over the real ones wasn't accurate. In order to solve this issue, the participant suggested that the virtual elements were more transparent.

One participant suggested the inclusion of one item on the main menu, with initial instructions indicating what is necessary for the assembly, such as screws, wooden pieces, Phillips screwdriver or electric screwdriver. None of the participants, when finished with the assembly, used the "Verify" item from the application. Two participants pointed the need of visualizing the complete model before starting.

VI. CONCLUSION

In this research, an interactive guide to the assembly of a wood frame wall panel using AR is proposed. Therefore, the use of the virtual model associated with AR technologies, which provide the possibility of interaction between the user and the combination of virtual and real environments, is presented.

To that end, an AR application named "montAR" was developed for smartphones. The application exhibits the assembly process of a wood frame wall structure in an interactive way, in order to facilitate the assembly, even for beginners. The system was developed so that the users could assemble the wall without the need of paper-based manuals.

In order to better understand how "montAR" can be used, this research presents an evaluation of the UX. All of the participants were able to successfully accomplish the task of assembling the wood frame wall panel using the AR system. In general, they indicated the acceptance of the system and seemed interested in the technology.

The system needs further refinement until the application achieves a proper operation to that end. Therefore, improvements must be made in accordance with what was pointed out in the assessment, which are: more transparency to the virtual elements, inclusion of initial instructions to the menu and the option of visualization of the complete model.

The proposition of innovation of this research lies in the fact that this technology is being used here as means of offering a practical tutorial for the execution of the wood frame wall panel. Such initiative holds the potential to benefit people's training in this construction system, which is still incipient in Brazil.

Hopefully, the assembly of wood-frame edifications can be assisted by the development of an application that offers an interactive step-by-step in AR. Therefore, this application can contribute to the diffusion of the wood-framing in the Brazilian construction process, providing its adoption and propagation. The resulting artifact of this research can be used by workers in the construction site as well as Architecture and Construction professionals, teachers and students for teaching and learning.

In a wider perspective, this research indicates that the use of AR can be important for the construction process as a whole, even those which are already consolidated. For this reason, new studies in these terms are essential.

Future work will focus on developing a comparative study between the panel assembly using AR through smart glasses and smartphones. This comparative study will aim to verify which device is more likely to be accepted by the user during the assembly task.

ACKNOWLEDGMENT

The authors wish to thank the support of the Institute of Architecture and Urbanism (IAU), University of Sao Paulo (USP) and to the National Council of Scientific and Technologic Development (CNPq) for the Junior Post-doctorate scholarship (Process: 151435/2014-6) and for the Scientific Initiation scholarship (Process: 149755/2015-5).

REFERENCES

[1] A. Dünser and M. Billinghurst, "Evaluating augmented reality systems," in Handbook of Augmented Reality, Springer, 2011, pp. 289–307.

[2] M. J. Kim, "A framework for context immersion in mobile augmented reality," Autom. Constr., vol. 33, 2013, pp. 79–85.

[3] A. Y. C. Nee, S. K. Ong, G. Chryssolouris, and D. Mourtzis, "Augmented reality applications in design and manufacturing," CIRP Ann. Technol., vol. 61, no. 2, 2012, pp. 657–679.

[4] J. C. Molina and C. Calil Jr, "Sistema construtivo em 'wood frame' para casas de madeira.," Semin. Ciências Exatas e Tecnológicas, vol. 31, no. 2, 2010, pp. 143–156.

[5] S. Nilsson, "Augmentation in the wild: user centered development and evaluation of augmented reality applications," Ph.D. Dissertation, Linköping University, 2010.

[6] M. A. Schnabel, "The Immersive Virtual Environment Design Studio," in Collaborative Design in Virtual Environments, Springer, 2011, pp. 177–191.

[7] J. E. Swan and J. L. Gabbard, "Survey of user-based experimentation in augmented reality," in Proceedings of 1st International Conference on Virtual Reality, 2005, pp. 1–9.

[8] L. Hou, X. Wang, L. Bernold, and P. E. D. Love, "Using animated augmented reality to cognitively guide assembly," J. Comput. Civ. Eng., vol. 27, no. 5, 2013, pp. 439–451.

[9] L. Hou, X. Wang, and M. Truijens, "Using augmented reality to facilitate piping assembly: an experiment-based evaluation," J. Comput. Civ. Eng., vol. 29, no. 1, 2015, pp. 05014007-1 – 05014007-12.

[10] S. K. Ong and Z. B. Wang, "Augmented assembly technologies based on 3D bare-hand interaction," CIRP Ann. Technol., vol. 60, no. 1, 2011, pp. 1–4.

[11] Z. B. Wang, S. K. Ong, and A. Y. C. Nee, "Augmented reality aided interactive manual assembly design," Int. J. Adv. Manuf. Technol., vol. 69, no. 5–8, 2013, pp. 1311–1321.

[12] Z. B. Wang, L. X. Ng, S. K. Ong, and A. Y. C. Nee, "Assembly planning and evaluation in an augmented reality environment," Int. J. Prod. Res., vol. 51, no. 23–24, 2013, pp. 7388–7404.

[13] M. A. Livingston, "Issues in Human Factors Evaluations of Augmented Reality Systems," in Human Factors in Augmented Reality Environments, Springer, 2013, pp. 3–9.

[14] T. Olsson, "Concepts and subjective measures for evaluating user experience of mobile augmented reality services," in Human Factors in Augmented Reality Environments, New York: Springer, 2013, pp. 203–232.

[15] N. Li and H. B.-L. Duh, "Cognitive Issues in Mobile Augmented Reality: An Embodied Perspective," in Human Factors in Augmented Reality Environments, Springer, 2013, pp. 109–135.

A Non-commercial Approach to Experience Design Teaching

Interactive Systems Developed at Escola Superior de Desenho Industrial

Marcos André Franco Martins
ESDI (Escola Superior de Desenho Industrial)
University of the State of Rio de Janeiro
Rio de Janeiro, Brazil
e-mail: marc.a.martins@gmail.com

Abstract – **Experience design teaching faces the challenge of balancing two main pedagogical proposals: (1) commercially driven projects intended to satisfy market needs also understood as user needs; and (2) experimental projects, not primarily concerned with consuming, aimed at exploring innovative designs. In a design school, this problem is of special interest, since academic environment offers rare opportunities for experimentalism. Anxious about professionalization, both professors and students usually ignore those opportunities and tend to follow recipes provided by literature in the experience design field. In this paper, we propose, through the analysis of case studies, a pedagogical approach intended to stimulate both critical thinking and unexpected interactions. The prototypes presented here demonstrate that it is possible to teach and learn experience design through a non-commercial approach.**

Keywords – pedagogy; interactive design; experience design; non-commercial applications; experimentalism.

I. Introduction

The Interaction Design field has been marked by the term UCD (User Centered Design), since its coinage in 1986 by Don Norman [1]. His insight has created a shift in the HCI (Human Computer Interaction) field from the development of interactive systems focused on the product to the foregrounding of the user's needs. As it is known, this concept was the basis to the more recent field UXD (User Experience Design), made popular by (besides Norman himself) authors like Marc Hassenzahl [2], Bill Buxton [3] and Nathan Shedroff [4]. UXD implies that design is required to go beyond the creation of products and interfaces. It has to consider situations of use, which are now seen as "designable".

We suggest that both terms, "user centered design" and "user experience design" – in spite of their unquestionable importance in HCI history – have obscured, a simple fact: users, today, maybe more than ever, are not merely people who have "authentic" needs and everyday routines just waiting for a designer's enlightened assistance to fulfill those needs. Both needs and experiences are also *produced* by constant market demands from contemporary capitalism, named by authors such as Maurizio Lazzarato as "immaterial capitalism". To Lazzarato, contemporary "products" (which can be immaterial themselves, e.g., Facebook) are "producers of the needs, the imaginary and the tastes", creating and transforming the "ideological and cultural environment of the consumer" [5]. To Italian philosopher Giorgio Agamben "one single individual [...] can be the place of multiple processes of subjectification: the user of cellular phones, the web surfer, the writer of stories, the tango aficionado, the anti-globalization activist, and so forth." [6].

If we agree that the user is also a *product* of economical and marketing needs, it becomes difficult to view him/her as an absolute starting point for the development of design systems, as the terms UCD and UXD may imply.

Such a complex scenario brings particular challenges to teachers, schools, universities and anyone related to design teaching: In what ways can one teach experience design today? Should we just follow the widespread understanding of the user as the starting point for any design project? Should we encourage students to base and justify their projects upon supposedly infallible recipes? If we are to understand the learning environment as a rare space for lively and independent critical debate where innovative thinking can flourish, the answer is obviously no!

This paper presents the concepts *user* and *experience* beyond their immediate commercial implications. The basic proposal is to temporarily free students from market driven rules and to encourage them to design unusual interactions. While the projects they develop are playful and humorously informal, they follow rigorous methodological steps that encompass the basic knowledge related to the design of interactive systems.

In order to present our pedagogical research and results, this paper follows the following structure: Section II gives a brief historical account of interaction design teaching at ESDI (Escola Superior de Desenho Industrial). Section III provides the schematic framing in project development employed at the School and explains the approach chosen for describing the case studies. In Section IV, we will present three completed projects: (A) a radio that can broadcast news, music and soap operas from the past, (B) a real physical tightrope that uses sound and image feedback from Nintendo's computer game Super Mario Bros, and (C) an installation in which captured silhouettes and movements of participants are transformed into colorful graphics projected on a screen. Section V sums up the essential aspects demonstrated by the case studies and indicates future developments.

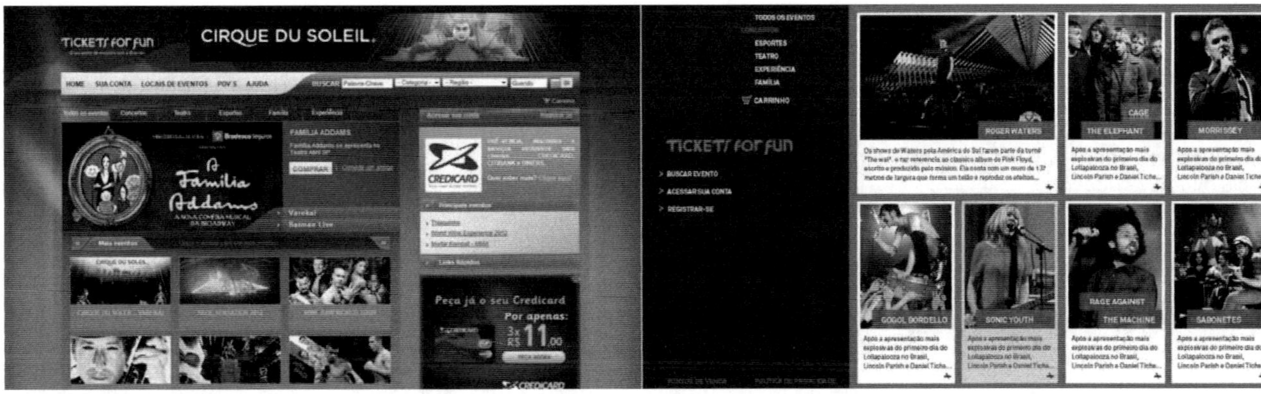

Figure 1. Before and after: Tickets for fun website re-design.

II. Experience Design Teaching at ESDI

In 2010, interaction design became part of the undergraduate curriculum at ESDI, a School traditionally devoted to Graphic and Product Design. Since then, we have been testing a variety of pedagogical approaches in order to develop students' interaction design skills, mainly focusing on practical project development.

Before describing the non-commercial applications, which are the focus of this paper, we will emphasize that, naturally, we have not abolished market driven assignments. In fact, when we started teaching interaction design, project proposals were based on existing products such as websites and tablet apps. In these cases, the focus was on the importance of visual clarity, semiotic concepts, analytical critique, usability aspects and user testing. In 2012, for instance, students were asked to search for a website they considered especially problematic. They had to analyze the site in terms of visual pleasantness and coherence, semantics, metaphor efficiency, usability and overall experience. Before and after images [7] show how their analysis have guided them in the search for better graphic and interactive solutions (Figure 1).

Projects like these were carried out exclusively through simulations, such as interactive pdfs and Adobe Flash prototypes. Gradually, we have introduced programming workshops on hardware and software platforms such as Arduino [8], Processing [9], Microsoft's Kinect [10] and MakeyMakey [11]. The benefits of teaching the logic of programming languages to design students are twofold: firstly, the logic of programming can free students from clichéd solutions (embedded in any commercial software package) and empower them with a critical awareness of design-presuppositions [12]; secondly, this very logic may be exported to projects other than interactive ones, since programming language foster the development of planning, synthesis and organizing skills.

It was this proximity with programming that has encouraged us – teachers and students – to engage in experimental projects not destined for commercial use. For design students who had never programmed before, learning was usually an arduous process. More often than not, they faced difficulties in getting their original plans executed as they had imagined, inevitably leading to frustration and discouragement. However, such "mistakes" could be (and in fact were) taken as creative "busters", once inventive solutions had to be called upon in order to adapt original plans to the constraints imposed by programming. There were, thus, two potential creative paths for the projects: an emerging acquisition of programming skills and the inclusion of random surprises.

Without abandoning the more commercial assignments mentioned above, we have welcomed an approach to teaching experience design that was experiential in itself and that encouraged project development as a nonlinear process. Besides that, it became accepted that a project's goal is not always initially clear and that innovative ideas can arise from a temporary suspension from the commitment to any existing system devised to be "used".

III. Project Stages and Guidelines for the Case Studies

Flexible and free as the following cases may seem, the employed pedagogic methods for their development have strict pre-defined traditional stages:

- Theme assignment.
- Research.
- Brainstorming.
- Project proposal.
- Low-fidelity prototyping.
- Sensorial design.
- Programming.
- User testing.
- High fidelity prototyping.
- Final demo film.

This sequence is merely a suggestion, since any one of these phases can be (and usually is) revisited and/or anticipated: for instance, a group of students in the brainstorming phase may want to jump ahead and create a quick low-fidelity prototype to fast test their ideas; another group whose design is well advanced may want to go back to research, led, say, by unexpected programming or sensorial design issues.

Given such flexibility, it would be deceiving to present the following case studies strictly under the above linear sequence. Instead, we have chosen to present all three cases according the following sequence:

- Project overall description.
- Relevant development issues and turning points specific to each project.
- Main achievements and innovative contributions.

IV. CASE STUDIES

A. Scheidemann Radio

A haunted radio that transmits music, soap operas and news from 1939 to 2012 was the proposal of a group of students for the given theme "Remix". In this assignment, students were required to search for an out-of-order object and assign to it new functionalities.

In project Scheidemann [13], an old radio was conceived as interface for a databank containing sounds from past decades. When turning a radio knob, the user could choose which category to listen to (music, soap opera or news) and combine this choice with a time selector (another knob) in order to choose a specific date. Besides this content, a mysterious character was said to "inhabit" the radio. This was Viktor Sheidemann, the device's creator, who intended his invention to predict the future. His life had ended in a tragic suicide, followed by the capturing of his soul by the radio. Since then, his voice interrupts randomly the radio transmission uttering Viktor's memories and predictions. If one listens to the radio long enough, one will be able to recompose, out of the fragmentary narrative, all relevant facts of Viktor's life.

In the project's early phases, the radio would offer little interaction. It would be standing in an ordinary busy environment, like a restaurant or a classroom, occasionally turned on by movement sensors. The project's authors imagined a situation where people would suddenly be made aware of the radio and get curious about its bizarre behavior. To better analyze the potentialities of this plan, a cardboard-made low fidelity model was used for experience prototyping. The students enacted and filmed what they imagined would happen in a real situation (Figure 2). Two of them played common passers-by who would, they presumed, be surprised by the device, while another one, using the "wizard of Oz" technique [14], would hide behind the radio and manipulate both sound transmissions and a clock pointer which should indicate a date in time.

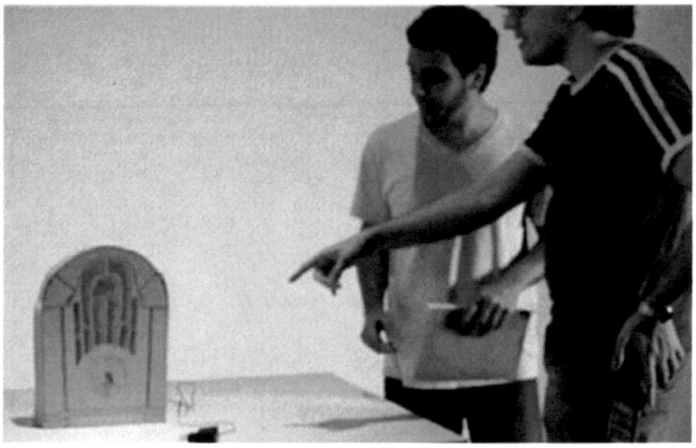

Figure 2. Radio Scheidemann's low fidelity and experience prototyping.

The film revealed little level of interaction and this poorness could potentially weaken the overall idea, as it depended too much on little sensorial appeal. They, then, resolved that the radio should have its knobs activated for interaction. Besides that, they decided to create, in the school's basement, a scenographic setting which included Viktor's diary sheets on the floor, spider webs hanging from the ceiling, a glass of water half emptied (his last one?), an open book, and finally, the radio (Figure 3).

Radio Sheidemann was a successful project, attracting the curiosity of a wide variety of users. During the project's development, students were able to understand design as an activity that needs to consider, besides the product itself, architectural, sensorial and behavioral issues, i.e., experience design typical concerns.

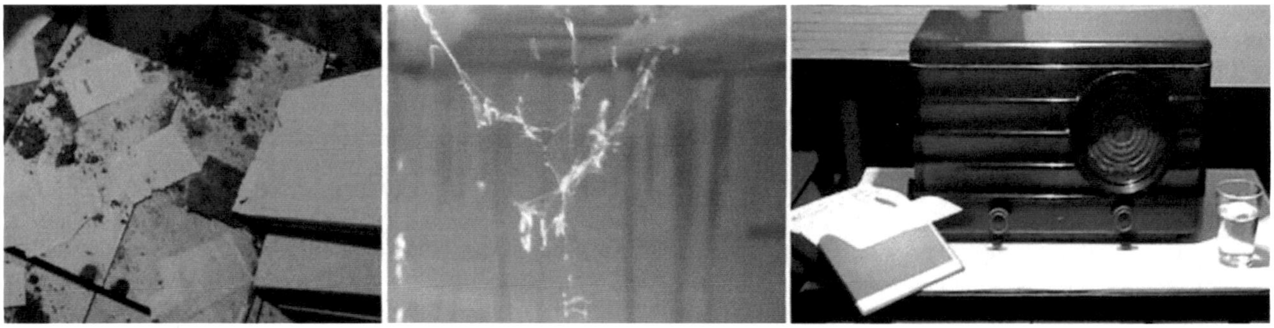

Figure 3. Ambiance and Radio Sheidemann.

Figure 4. Super Slack Bros' installation.

B. *Super Slack Bros.*

In the summer of 2014 slacklining (or tightrope equilibration) was the hit sport at Rio de Janeiro's beaches. A student came out with an original idea: an outdoor installation that would bring Nintendo's 1990's game Super Mario Bros to physical reality [15]. The piece may be described like this: interaction starts when someone jumps up a slackline stretched between two trees. He/she receives "stage accomplished", "win" and "fail" sound feedbacks imported from original Mario's soundtrack. As the user evolves on the line he/she advances on game stages, just as in a typical computer game. The "scoring" system also includes the touching of real Mario Bros' icons (printed and mounted on cardboards) that hang from another stretched line located above the user's head (Figure 4).

The basic technical setting is the assemblage of two wires (one phase and the other one signal), on the slackline, that close electrical circuit when the heel and the instep of one feet touch simultaneously the different wires. These wires are connected to MakeyMakey's input slots, which substitute for the computer's inputs (keyboard, mouse, etc.). A Processing code receives those inputs and retrieve appropriate sounds from a database. The same technique is used for the activation of the icons hanging above.

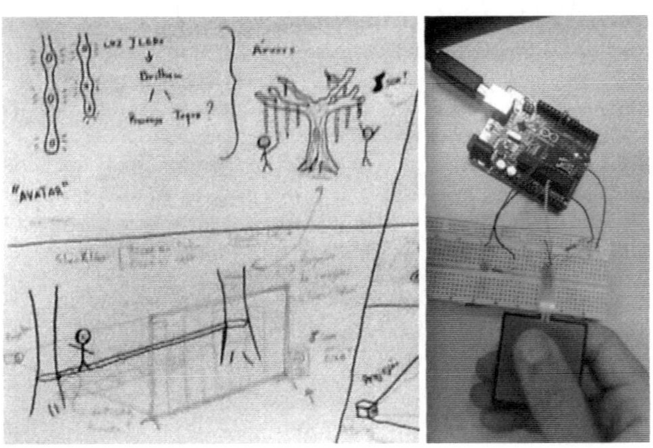

Figure 5. Super Slack Bros. First ideas and initial pressure sensor based technical solution.

In the initial plan, the input was thought of in terms of pressure sensors (Figure 5). It took many experience prototypes and intense research until the idea of a feet-closing circuit was devised. The overall experience was also refined: the student abandoned his original idea that included lights' feedback and opted to use exclusively sound, since light proved to be a distraction to a user trying to balance on a rope.

This remarkably original project attracted a lot of attention, including MakeyMakey's creator, Eric Rosenbaum's [16]. When the functional prototype was installed, a lot of people were eager to experiment with the modified game. But, besides such success, the system also provided food for thought in what concerns our intensely virtual and digitized culture. Super Slack Bros., by inverting the usual path from real to virtual, was a humorous and ironic commentary on today's widespread arrest of physical reality.

C. *Psychokinectic*

Developed in 2015, over the assigned theme "Movement and Color", this interactive system was a Microsoft Kinect-based application [17]. The system works like this: users' movements and body contours are continuously captured and sent to a computer. Through Processing Language, the contours define an area to be filled with various graphic and video elements.

This technical setting involves software and hardware knowledge usually unfamiliar to design students. During the project's developing process the authors undertook strenuous tests and research of Kinect's body recognition capabilities. They have also investigated Processing Language and Resolume Arena software in order to mix images and silhouettes in real time. The code was based on libraries Syphon and Kinect Projector Toolkit [18].

In technically complex projects like this, it is not uncommon that students get so busy researching and debugging software and hardware that they tend to neglect fundamental aspects of experience design. Almost close to

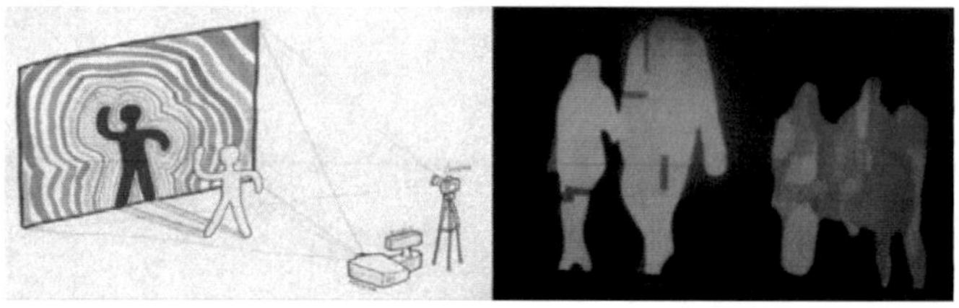

Figure 6. Psychokinectic's first draft and early imaging tests.

Figure 7. Psychokinectic's experience prototyping.

the project's final deadline, challenging conceptual problems arose. Since the very first drafts (Figure 6), there was an arrangement of actors and devices that remained unchanged: the user was expected to stand facing the projection and the Kinect's sensor and the projector would stand behind him/her. Initially the resulting shadows derived from this setting were intended as part of the project. But technical investigation had led the students do decide that images would appear inside and not outside the body's contour, thus making any shadow improper.

It was only when the main technical issues had been solved, that filmed experience prototypes were possible, revealing experiential problems. As the user interacted with the system, his/her attention was locked to the screen (Figure 7).

This disposition generated two problems. Firstly, the user's shadows, initially part of the concept, actually made it difficult for one to see what was inside the silhouette and, secondly, participants became "hypnotized" by the images, what resulted in low-level interaction amongst users themselves.

The original project's concept, framed in terms of "how to create a user experience in which the body could control images" was reformulated as "how to create a projection that interacts with user's movements without forcing his/her attention to be locked to the projection's plane". Their solution was to elevate the whole set, by hanging the screen on buildings from two sides of a street (Figure 8).

In the end, the system was finally tested and validated as a device for dance parties, such as one organized by student's themselves at the School. The final setting allowed people to interact with the system, without having to enter a specially prepared closed room. Therefore, Psychokinectic's originality was that of serving both as party decoration and interactive piece – an experience that was neither immersive nor theater-like.

V. CONCLUSION AND FUTURE WORK

This paper has demonstrated the qualities of a pedagogical method not based primarily on the user. We are hardly suggesting, though, that commercial concerns are to be forgotten in a design school, or that users are unimportant. The point addressed here is that there may be gains if we temporarily suspend those concerns. The focus on the design of the experience in itself, apart from any predefined or supposed "needs", has made it possible for students to both understand how to formulate design problems in terms of experience and to develop creative projects. In spite of not having any particular user in mind they were able to attract and enchant those who undertook the designed experiences.

Perhaps this approach points to a more flexible understanding of the user as someone who can profit emotionally and intellectually from engaging in unexpected settings, rather than solely having his/her needs quickly fulfilled. Besides that, these projects, due to their emphasis on physical collective experiences, are also critical statements against the immaterial seclusion typical of social networks. They envisage alternatives to a kind of sociability composed by lonely users, connected to one another and to the world mostly through screens.

As for future developments of the work presented here we shall pursue both external and internal endeavors. On the external level, we have been establishing connections with other design schools across the globe so as to promote collaborative initiatives following the methods described above. Internally, we plan to introduce, in our interaction design courses, a more effectively blend between commercial and non-commercial approaches, encouraging students to find inspiration in the experimental results in order to the create innovative marketable products.

Figure 8. Psychokinectic screen's final setting and party with the actual working system.

REFERENCES

[1] D. A. Norman, The Psychology of Everyday Things. New York, New York: Basic Books, 1988.

[2] M. Hassenzahl. "User experience and experience design," in Interaction Design Foundation. <http://www.interaction-design.org/printerfriendly/encyclopedia/user_experience_and_experience_design.html > [retrieved: 03, 2016].

[3] W. Buxton, Sketching User Experiences: Getting the Design Right and the Right Design. Amsterdam; Boston, Massachusetts: Elsevier/Morgan Kaufmann, 2007.

[4] N. Shedroff, Experience Design 1. Indianapolis, Indiana: New Riders, 2001.

[5] M. Lazzarato and A. Negri, Capitalismo Imaterial [Immaterial Capitalism]. Rio de Janeiro, RJ: DP&A, 2001.

[6] G. Agamben, What is an Apparatus? and Other Essays. Stanford, California: Stanford University Press, 2009.

[7] C. França, C. Ribeiro and F. Chaves, Tickets for fun Rededign, unpublished.

[8] Arduino official site. <https://www.arduino.cc/> [retrieved: 03, 2016].

[9] Processing official site. <https://processing.org/> [retrieved: 03, 2016].

[10] Kinect for windows. <https://dev.windows.com/en-us/kinect> [retrieved: 03, 2016].

[11] MakeyMakey official site. <http://www.makeymakey.com/> [retrieved: 03, 2016].

[12] M. A. F. Martins, "Prototyping in a learning environment - digital publishing projects from the Escola Superior de Desenho Industrial," in Design, User Experience, and Usability. User Experience Design for Everyday Life Applications and Services. vol. 8519, A. Marcus, Ed.: Springer International Publishing, 2014, pp. 195-206.

[13] C. Martins, F. Chaves, L. Ribeiro, Radio Scheidemann, unpublished.

[14] J. Preece, Y. Rogers, H. Sharp, Interaction Design: Beyond Human-Computer Interaction. New York, New York: J. Wiley & Sons, 2002.

[15] Y. Santos, Slack Line Bros, unpublished.

[16] Slackline Bros. <https://www.youtube.com/watch?v=J-pBbwFUXN0> [retrieved: 03, 2016].

[17] R. Bortolami, C. Menezes, N. Borba, D. Rocha, T. A. Dias, Psychokinectic, unpublished.

[18] Genekogan Library. <http://genekogan.com/> [retrieved: 03, 2016].

Eye Gaze Based Dynamic Warnings

Mini Zeng and Feng Zhu
Department of Computer Science
The University of Alabama in Huntsville
Huntsville, Alabama, USA
e-mail: mz0005@uah.edu, fz0001@uah.edu

Sandra Carpenter
Department of Psychology
The University of Alabama in Huntsville
Huntsville, Alabama, USA
e-mail: carpens@uah.edu

Abstract—**Various websites and mobile applications collect personal identity information. Personal privacy might be in danger if we exposed our identity information to a malicious third party. Warning countermeasures have been designed to mitigate identity theft. However, people often click the OK button without reading warning messages. We propose a dynamic warning system based on eye gaze information. The warning messages display just-in-time, and they fade out after users read them. To evaluate attention switch and maintenance, we developed an Eye Tracking Information Analysis tool. In addition, we built a simulated restaurant reservation app, named ReservME that integrated our dynamic warning system. We conducted a three-condition experiment with a comprehensive follow-up survey. Our experiment results show that the eye gaze based dynamic warning system helped participants reduce unnecessary identity disclosure.**

Keywords-Dynamic warning; Eye gaze interaction; Identity theft; Warning design and evaluation.

I. INTRODUCTION

People encounter many web-based security warnings in browsers and apps. People often ignore them [1] or do not even realize that a security warning is present. When individuals were asked about their concerns about the safety of their private information, they claimed that they were careful about their information when sharing [2]. This contradiction can be explained by the ineffectiveness of warnings [3].

Researchers have been studying the effectiveness of warnings for years. Frameworks such as the communication-human information processing (C-HIP) model and a sequential model of human information processing [4][5], were introduced to use as a guide to analyze the effectiveness of warnings [4]. In recent years, some web-based and mobile-based warnings have been introduced [6]–[9] to improve users' attention to warnings and risk evaluations. However, limitations exist in previous warning designs and evaluations as follows. First, surveys and interviews are widely used to analyze the effectiveness of warnings. Users' attention on warnings was not quantitatively analyzed. Second, users' attention was not used to interact with warnings. Third, attention switch and the cost of compliance are hard to evaluate. For example, active warnings with a "close" button could switch attention to a high level. However, this behavior costs time in terms of compliance, which may make users annoyed if the warnings show up too many times. Users' attention is critical to warning designs [10], but previous research has not made optimal use of it.

In this research, we propose a dynamic warning system based on eye gaze information. The dynamic warning message included a security metaphor, a message about the consequences of not complying, and a recommended safe response message, and was integrated into a restaurant table reservation app. Users' eye gaze information influenced show-up time, fade-out time, and location of the dynamic warning message. We developed an Eye Tracking Information Analysis (ETIA) tool to determine the warning's show-up time and fade-out time. ETIA is also used to evaluate the effectiveness of the dynamic warning and to record the experiment. We conducted a three-condition experiment on 128 participants. Follow-up surveys were used to evaluate the effectiveness of the dynamic warning in the presence of an identity attack.

Our study makes three main contributions. First, we provide a dynamic warning system using eye gaze information. The dynamic warning shows "at the right time and at the right place." Second, we provide a tool to analyze and visualize users' attention on warning messages. The output is used as feedback to further improve the design of future warnings. Third, the dynamic warning fades out when users do not read it.

This article is organized as follows. The next section outlines the background and related work. Then, we present an eye gaze based dynamic warning approach and its integration to a Windows 8 app. Section IV illustrates an Eye Tracking Information Analysis tool. The fifth section discusses the evaluation on the dynamic warning approach. Finally, Section VI concludes the paper.

II. BACKGROUND AND RELATED WORK

Warning countermeasures are widely used to prevent privacy attacks. Researchers have developed several frameworks [11]. Wogalter's C-HIP model [4], shown in Figure 1, is one of the most widely used frameworks in warning design. The C-HIP model is used as a guideline to warning design and identifies the reason of a warning's effectiveness or ineffectiveness. It consists of nine levels, starting with a source by using visual, tactile or auditory channel to deliver to receivers. Factors such as font size, color and audio volume in the warning stimuli have influences on behavior. The attention switch, attention maintenance, comprehension, memory, and attitudes and belief stages could also affect a receiver's behavior. Cranor

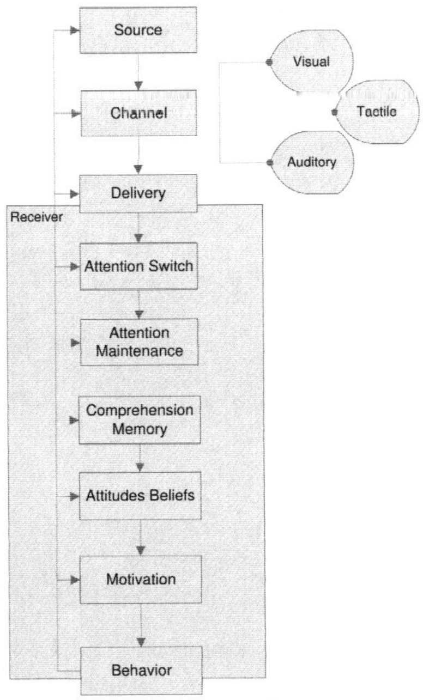

Figure 1. Diagram of the expanded C-HIP model [4]

extended C-HIP model into a human-in-the-loop security framework [12]. The human-in-the-loop security framework could be able to help design understand the behavior of humans on security-critical functions.

The typical Windows program has warnings seemingly everywhere, with warnings about things that have little significance [13]. "Over warning" makes using a program feel like a hazardous activity, and it detracts from truly significant issues [13]. The problem is, when an individual habituates to a warning, he may not have acquired all the information from the warning. Kim and Wogalter mentioned four solutions to deal with the problem of habituation [14]. First of all, incorporate features (e.g., size and color) to enhance conspicuity. Second, modify or change the warning's appearance. Third, allow warning designers to deviate from the standards. Fourth, use dynamic (changeable) warnings [14]. According to research by Racicot and Wogalter, in the workplace and in hazardous environments, warnings could be presented only during the points in time when the risk information is needed [15]. Highly sophisticated detection and warning systems could also enable personalization of the warning and varied presentation patterns that will prevent or delay habituation [16]. A warning will be more likely to attract and maintain attention when individuals are in an information-seeking mode than in other modes of thinking [17]. In other words, a person who is actively looking for hazard-related information will be more likely to see and hear a warning than a person occupied with other tasks.

Our warning design is inspired by previous research on physical security metaphor images used on security-related warnings, such as a thief sneaking away. Physical security metaphors could provide a vivid image to inform users about hazards. Raja and colleagues designed firewall warnings whose functionality is based on a physical security metaphor [8]. According to their evaluation results, their warnings facilitated the comprehension of warning information, better communicated the risk, and increased the likelihood of safe behavior. Sunshine and Egelman redesigned secure sockets layer (SSL) warnings. Their severe warning has a red background and a "Stop sign officer" security metaphor [18]. Also, research on eye movement has suggested that the pictorial-color icon produced better performance compared with those without pictorial icon or color icon [19].

According to Wogalter's suggestion [20], dynamic warnings are more noticeable than static warnings. Because dynamic aspects of warnings should be conspicuous to attract and sustain attention, they could reduce the problem of habituation. If the warning is presented distant from the hazard in terms of location and time, people may not recognize the connection or may not remember the hazard. By working with detectors or sensing devices the dynamic warning can be noticed when a warning is needed [21][22].

Our experiment is conducted to evaluate the effectiveness of dynamic warnings in the context of a mindlessness attack. A mindlessness attack is a psychological attack that attempts to access more information from users [23]. Our previous research instituted the mindlessness attacks within a web-based online shopping context and an automobile insurance quote and was shown to be effective [24][25]. Our current goal is to mitigate the effects of the mindlessness attack.

Eye tracking technology in human–computer interaction (HCI) has been highly promising for many years. Jones and Milton (1950) captured eye movements with cockpit-mounted mirrors and movie cameras to study eye movement data with painstaking frame-by-frame analysis of the pilot's face [25]. Crowe and Nrayanan emphasized that aggregating, analyzing, and visualizing eye tracking data in conjunction with other interaction data could be a powerful tool for designers and experimenters in evaluating interfaces [26]. Nielsen and Pernice use eyed tracking on web usability to discover 2503 usability guidelines for Web sites, intranets, social network postings and e-mail newsletters [27]. Takeuchi and colleagues measured participants' pupil diameter with an infrared-video-based eye-tracking device and found that pupil size increased rapidly as the learning proceeded in the early phase of training and decreased at the later phase to a level half of its maximum value [28]. In recent years, researchers started to use eye movement as an input in HCI systems. Jacob in the Naval Research Laboratory applied eye movement for object selection, moving an object with the eye controlling both scrolling text and defining a "listener" window [29]. In our research we used the eye tracking information to guide our design of the dynamic warning.

III. EYE GAZE BASED DYNAMIC WARNING SYSTEM DESIGN

We focus on four issues. What should the warning message be like? When should the warning show up? Where should the warning show up? How does the system work?

These four questions will be answered in the following subsections.

A. ReservME software

ReservME (Figure 2) is a Window 8 app running on a Microsoft Surface Pro. It is a restaurant table reservation app similar to Opentable, which is a top ten app on Windows, iOS, and Android. ReservME is using HTML5, CSS3 and JavaScript. A personal information form appears after a restaurant is chosen. First name, last name, email, phone number, address, city, state, zip code, and credit card information were requested in the app. Considering the safety of participants' privacy, we did not collect this information. Rather, we captured whether any information was entered into the data fields, represented as 0 for input, 1 for no input. Our previous research found that users are concerned about their email, phone, and zip code being exposed [25][30]. In our dynamic warning system, we use zip code as the identity element to trigger a warning. A dynamic warning appears when a user's eye gaze focuses on a field into which they can input their personal information.

B. Dynamic warning message design

The dynamic warning message includes three sentences as follows "DO NOT disclose this information!" "Someone may steal your private information here!" "TIPS: You can falsify them." We added a theft metaphor image to the right of the warning message. The pictorial theft metaphor showed a thief sneaking away with keys in one hand and a bag of stolen items in the other hand. The metaphor works with the second sentence in warning message. This provides an emotional influence on a user's risk evaluation. From the C-HIP model, an effective warning should provide instructions for avoiding consequences of a risk or indicating that effective preventive behavior cannot be guaranteed. A recommended safe response in an online table reservation context was therefore provided by the third sentence to make this warning message more effective.

From the C-HIP model and Wogalter's research [31][32] interactive warnings should be noticed, recalled and understood better than static warnings (or on-product warnings). Researchers also found that over time and exposure to environmental elements, warnings can result in habituation and become less noticeable [10]. We therefore decided to design a warning to "pop up on time" and "fade out in time." The "pop up" action of this warning should enhance the attention switch of C-HIP model, and the duration of the warning plays a role in attention maintenance. The "fade out" action could reduce habituation and the "over warning" issue by removing the warning when users do not really need the warning.

C. Dynamic warnings show up time and fade out time

The key to effective warnings is to display them the moment that users need the warning and to remove them the moment that users do not need the warning. These moments could be found by using eye information. Laughery's research on the human's eye movement on reading a warning suggested that the time people interacted with a warning

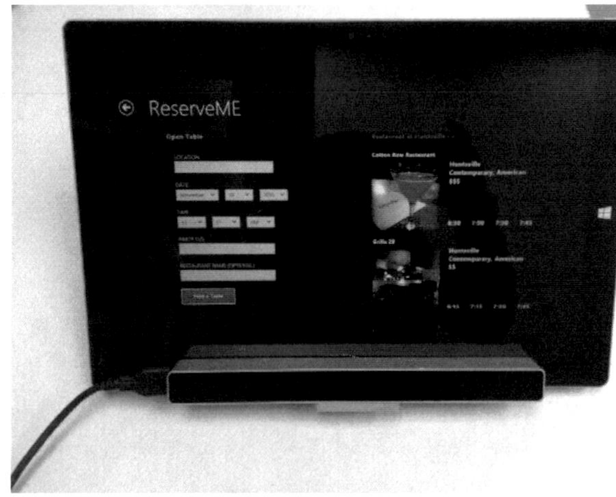

Figure 2. ReservME is running on Microsoft Surface Pro with an eye tracker

could be separated to a location time and a decision time [33].

In the pilot study, we separated the total time of eye gaze into searching time, location time, and decision time. The searching time starts from the time the identity page loaded to the time a participant's eye gaze entered the target area (the zip code data entry field in this pilot test). The location time started from when a participant's eye gaze entered the target area to when the participant's eye gaze left the area. The decision time started from when a participant's eye gaze left the target area to the time participants started to type on a key board or click on the touch screen. The mean searching time on our pilot testing was 1258ms. The mean location time was 311ms. The mean decision time was 485ms.

Based on pilot testing, we decided that the warning should show up when participant's eye gaze was maintained in the zip code data entry field for 350ms. In this way, we could make the dynamic warning pop up when a user focused on the target area (i.e., zip code data entry field) before they made a decision to input this information.

To determine the time for the fade-out of the dynamic warning, we did a second pilot study with another 12 students. This time, we added the dynamic warning that popped up on the top of the zip code data entry field but it did not fade out. We changed the target area to the warning area. By using the ETIA tool, we could ascertain searching time, location time, and decision time on this area for each participant.

In this pilot testing, searching time begins from the warning pop up to the start time of the longest duration on the dynamic warning. The location time is defined as the longest duration of eye gaze on dynamic warning. The decision time begins from the end timestamp of the longest duration of gaze on the dynamic warning to the timestamp of when a participant input something on the key board or clicked on the touch screen. The mean searching time on this pilot test is 652ms. The mean location time is 3285ms. The mean decision time is 1874ms and the max decision time is 3144ms. From these pilot testing results, we decided to design the warning message fade out if any of the following three conditions are present.

The first condition is if a participant's eye gaze leaves the warning area for 3500ms. The second condition is if the participant starts to type in something from keyboard. The third condition is if the participant clicks the touch screen. The "fade out" action relies on these three conditions because when the participants' behavior fits these conditions, they are not interested in the warning and have made decisions already. According to the location time statistic result, we decided to add a new feature to the "pop-up" action. If the participant's eye gaze duration on a warning message lasted less than 3000ms, the dynamic warning popped up again because the participants did not read the warning message carefully. We employed a red box to show the area at which participants are looking approximatly.

D. Dynamic warning location

The warning message should also be spatially optimized. Our strategy is to show the warning right next to the eye gaze spot when a user's eye gaze stays in the target area (zip code area) for 300ms. In this way, the dynamic warning could improve the attention switch indicated by the C-HIP model because the warning message shows up very close to the exact spot participants are looking. Another foundation in the eye gaze based dynamic warning interaction system is to map the two dimensional (2D) eye tracker data from EyeTribe SDK to the 2D dimensions of the ReservME App. The EyeTribe server provides a timestamp, raw gaze coordinates in pixels, average eye gaze coordinates in pixels, raw and smoothed gazed coordinates in pixels separated by left eye and right eye, pupil size, and normalized pupil coordinates.

In general, we could obtain average eye gaze coordinates $(x_{current\ avg}, y_{current\ avg})$ of left and right eyes on current time from EyeTribe SDK. Then we have the 2D eye gaze coordinates $(App.X_i, App.Y_i)$ by using (1) and (2).

$$App.X_i = (\left(\frac{x_{current\ avg}}{Width} \times \frac{Smooth}{100}\right) + App.X_{i-1} \times \left(1 - \frac{Smooth}{100}\right)) \times Width \quad (1)$$

$$App.Y_i = (\left(\frac{y_{current\ avg}}{Length} \times \frac{Smooth}{100}\right) + App.Y_{i-1} \times (1 - \frac{Smooth}{100})) \times Length \quad (2)$$

Where, *Width* and *Length* are the screen resolution. *Smooth* is a constant to smooth current eye gaze spot with the previous eye gaze spot $(App.X_{i-1}, App.Y_{i-1})$ indicates 2D eye gaze coordinate mapping on ReservME App on the previous frame $(App.X_0, App.Y_0)$ equals (0,0).

E. Design of the dynamic warning system

Our dynamic warning system interacts with the EyeTribe SDK and the ReservME App. The dynamic warning server, developed by NodeJS, has architecture as shown in Figure 3.

The EyeTribe server collected gaze coordinates from an

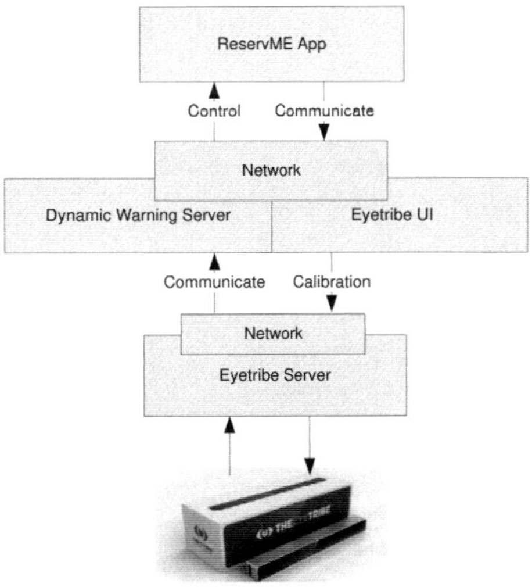

Figure 3. Eye gaze based dynamic warning system architecture

EyeTribe device attached under a Surface Pro. The EyeTribe tracker allows head movement in a 40cm*30cm box at a 65 distance on a 30Hz sampling rate [34]. The EyeTribe user interface (UI) provided by EyeTribe could help us to do calibration. The EyeTribe server provides a 0.5 to 1 degree average accuracy of visual angle. The dynamic warning server communicates with the underlying EyeTribe server to get raw eye gaze data. The communication uses Transmission Control Protocol (TCP) Sockets to exchange JSON message asynchronously [34]. The ReservME App communicates with the dynamic warning server to collect smoothed eye gaze data and times. We implemented the dynamic warning using eye control by applying constraints mentioned in previous paragraphs.

The dynamic warning server is at the center of this system. It sets up a TCP socket connection with the EyeTribe server and connects with ReservME. Figure 4 illustrates the details of communications and controls of this system. The dynamic warning server acquires eye information data from the EyeTribe server. Once the identity page in ReservME showed up, the socket between ReservME and the dynamic warning server was created. ReservME acquires the smoothed eye gaze coordinates data (App.X and App.Y calculated by (1)) and timestamps from the dynamic warning server asynchronously. The dynamic warning server checks the eye gaze coordinate and if the user's eye gaze stays in the zip code area for 350ms, the dynamic warning will pop up in ReservME and put a warning flag to an ON state. If the dynamic warning server discovers that the user's eye gaze leaves the warning for more than 3500ms or a user types on keyboard or touches the screen on a click, the dynamic warning in ReservME will fade out and the warning flag switches to an OFF state. If the dynamic warning is off, and eye gaze location time on the dynamic warning is less than 3000ms, then the dynamic warning pops up again. Step 7 to step 13 loops when the socket between the dynamic warning server and ReservME is on. The socket disconnect when the identity page is not on the browser.

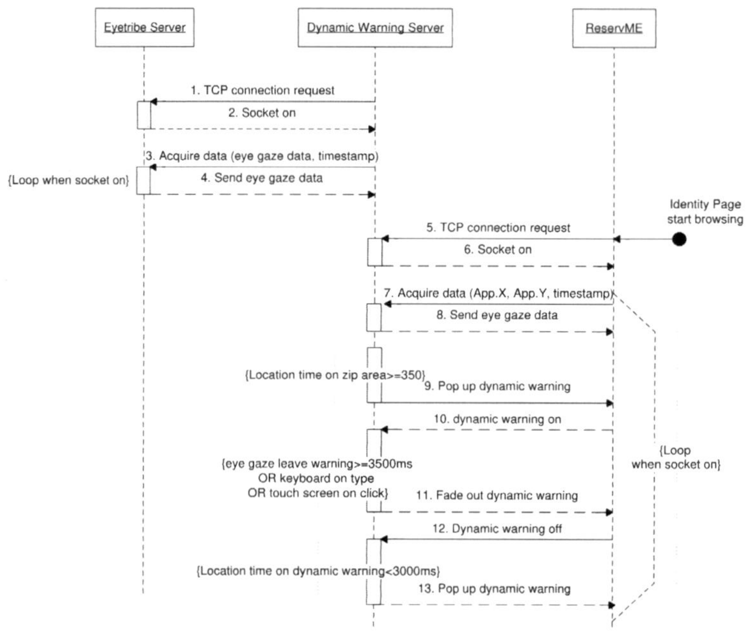

Figure 4. Dynamic warning system communications and controls

IV. EYE TRACKING INFORMATION ANALYSIS

We developed a tool named Eye Tracking Information Analysis (ETIA) as show Figure 5. It records the eye movement interaction between the dynamic warning system and ReservME. It was created using C# and Aforge.NET framework [35]. Mouse movement and eye gaze box locations are also recorded. Frames per Second (FPS) could be defined. Calibration on EyeTribe UI is required before this software is connected to the EyeTribe. Connection state, pupil size and smoothed eye gaze coordinates are captured and stored by ETIA. Smoothed eye gaze coordinates, pupil size and timestamp data are saved in a txt file. The ETIA tool was used in pilot testing and the experiment to evaluate the dynamic warning system. Another feature of the ETIA tool is EyeGaze Box (a red box show the eye focus area). The EyeGaze box indicates the eye focus area approximately.

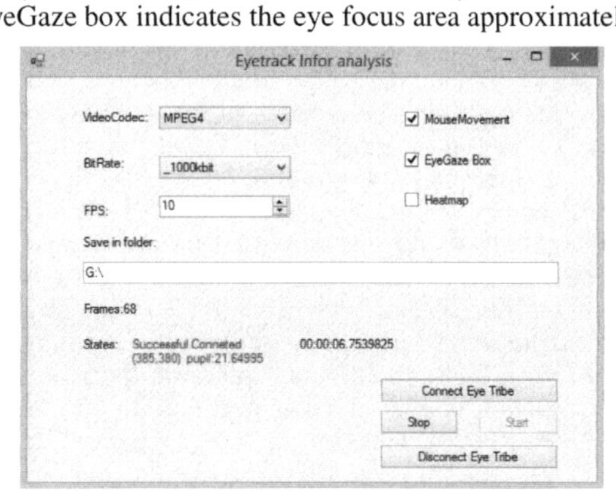

Figure 5. Eye Tracking Information Analysis Tool

V. EVALUATION

A. Participants

We recruited 128 participants to attend our experiment. They were undergraduate students across various majors. These students received partial course credit for their participation. Of the 128 participants, 77 were women, and their age ranged from 17 to 48 with a median 20 years. With respect to ethnicity, 69 participants were Caucasian, 29 had African heritage, 11 were Asian, 7 had Hispanic heritage, 2 reported Pacific Island heritage, and 10 reported other ethnicities. Seventeen additional students from the psychology and computer science department were recruited as volunteers on the pilot test. The procedures of the experiment were approved by our university's Institutional Review Board (IRB).

B. Procedures

In ReservME App, identity information was requested, and the mindlessness attack message explains the reason for requiring the identity information. For example, the reason that email is requested is "You will receive electronic coupons for the restaurant you reserved." If the participants focused on the zip code area, a dynamic warning was presented in the form of warning text and a theft metaphor image background by a yellow rectangle. The design of this experiment has three conditions: (a) *control condition* with no attack and no warning, (b) the *mindlessness attack condition* with mindlessness attack messages but no warning, and (c) the *dynamic warning condition* with the dynamic warning message showing up under mindlessness attacks.

We hypothesized that participants under the mindlessness attack would be more likely to disclose information than in control condition. We also predicted that participants in the dynamic warning condition would be less likely to disclose information than in the control condition and mindlessness condition. Additionally we explored whether participants did read the warning message carefully in dynamic warning condition.

Participants were randomly assigned to one of the three ReservME app conditions. There were 41 participants in control condition, 46 participants in mindlessness condition without a warning, and 41 participants in a dynamic warning condition under attack. They provided informed consent prior to participating. Participants were given the cover story that the app was developed by a third-party software design company, and the company was interested in feedback on its app design.

Participants were asked a variety of identity questions (including first name, last name, email address, home address, phone number, credit card information) in the context of restaurant reservation. For each type of identity information, participants could choose whether or not to provide it. Participants did not know that we were not storing any of the identity information they input before they completed a post-experimental survey. They were debriefed that their identity information was not stored or provided to a third party at the end of the experiment.

After participants completed their reservation on ReservME, they were asked follow-up survey questions about their opinion on the design of ReservME. Participants were also asked whether they had responded with truthful information when asked for identity information. We considered falsified information provided to be the same as no information provided in our analyses. The effectiveness of the dynamic warning system was evaluated by the whether or not participants disclosed their accurate identity information. We use ETIA tool to record the experiment. Our primary dependent variable was the percent of participants who disclosed truthful identity information.

C. Results

Figure 6 shows the percent of participants who provided truthful identity information under the three conditions. The percent of disclosure increased in the mindlessness condition compared with the control condition. The percent of participants who provided truthful identity information in the dynamic warning condition decreased dramatically compared with the mindlessness and control conditions. Zip code was the identity element for which the dynamic warning popped up when participants looked at the zip code textbox area. The dynamic warning successfully decreased disclosure from 89.1% to 26.8%. However, zip code is not the only element influenced by the dynamic warning. For email, the dynamic warning reduced disclosure under mindlessness attack from 93.5% to 31.7%. Similar reductions occurred for phone and address identity information.

Zip code is the identity element for which disclosure increased the most in the mindlessness condition compared with the control condition. The percentage increased from 68.3% to 89.1%. Zip code is also the element for which disclosure decreased the most in the dynamic warning condition compared with the mindlessness condition.

We used one-tailed Z-tests to compare the percentage of participants disclosing their identity information in the three conditions. The analysis showed significant differences between the control condition and the mindlessness condition for zip code ($p=0.0082$) and for credit card information ($p=0.0268$), as shown in Table I. The Z-tests between the mindlessness condition and the dynamic warning condition showed significantly differences for all identity information ($p<0.05$), as shown in Table II.

Odds ratios were also calculated. In Table I odds ratios indicate the increased likelihood that people will disclose their identity information under mindlessness attack conditions.

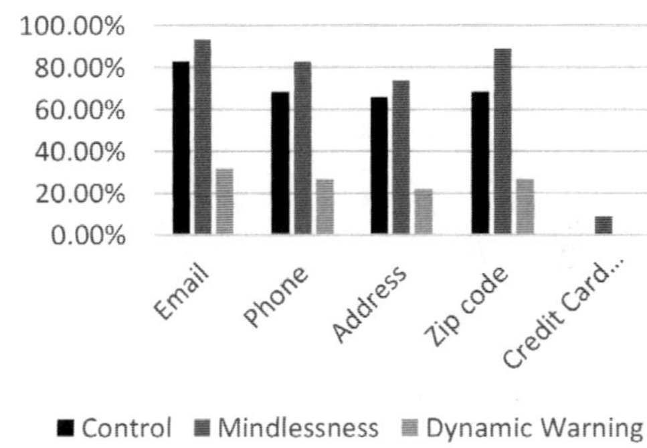

Figure 6. Percent of participants under the three conditions providing identity information

TABLE I. Z-TESTS COMPARING CONTROL AND MINDLESSNESS CONDITIONS

Identity information	Z-score	p- value	Odds ratio
Email	-1.5402	0.06178	3.48
Phone	-1.5581	0.05938	2.21
Address	-0.8198	0.20611	1.47
Zip Code	-2.3953	0.0082	3.81
Credit Card information	-1.9336	0.0268	8.79

TABLE II. Z-TESTS COMPARING MINDLESSNESS AND DYNAMIC WARNING CONDITIONS

Identity information	Z-score	p-value	Odds ratio
Email	5.7829	0.0001	30.87
Phone	5.0754	0.0001	15.11
Address	4.713	0.0001	10.07
Zip Code	5.7142	0.0001	22.36
Credit Card	1.9336	0.0268	8.79

The odds ratios in Table II refer to the decrease in people providing their information in the dynamic warning condition compared with mindlessness attack condition. The odds ratio of zip code is 22.36, which means the odds of exposing zip code in the dynamic warning condition were around 22 times less than in the mindlessness attack condition with no warning.

D. Discussion

The results of the experiment show that a dynamic warning could prevent users from disclosing identity information that they were asked to provide. The results also show that dynamic warnings can be an effective countermeasure for a mindlessness identity attack. Dynamic warnings not only impacted disclosure of the targeted identity element, but also impacted disclosure of all identity elements in the same page. ETIA video and data indicate that dynamic warnings did attract users' attention and maintained attention.

Our study has a few limitations. First, the participants in our experiment were students. Thus, the data may be biased by an age factor. We are currently conducting research using a non-student sample with a wider range of ages. Second, our experiment focuses on whether dynamic warnings changed users' behavior on identity disclosure under mindlessness attacks. The results might not be applied to other attacks that are launched to elicit private information from users.

VI. CONCLUSION

In this paper, we propose an eye gaze-based dynamic warning solution. The dynamic warning message integrated a security metaphor, a vivid consequence message, and a recommended safe response message. Eye gaze information interacted with the dynamic warning system to control the dynamic warning's pop up time, fade out time, and location. We also developed an ETIA tool to record participants' eye gaze information. ETIA was applied in pilot tests and the main experiment. Experimental results show promising impacts of the warning countermeasure to protect identity information on a web-based app. The design of dynamic warnings may reduce habituation. The eye gaze based feature is an effective way to switch and hold a user's attention at the right time in the right place. ETIA provides a virtualization and replay tool to analyze the interaction of users' eyes gaze on specific apps and warnings.

The dynamic warning system and ETIA tools can explore some of the principles of the C-HIP model and could offer guidelines for designing effective warnings to interact with the eye gaze data. We are conducting experiments to compare the effectiveness of our dynamic warning system with the traditional warnings. In addition, we are improving the effectiveness of the dynamic warning system by combining pupil size data as another interaction factor. We are also adding virtualization features to ETIA.

REFERENCES

[1] D. Akhawe and A. P. Felt, "Alice in warningland: a large-scale field study of browser security warning effectiveness," in Proceedings of the 22nd USENIX Security Symposium, 2013, pp. 257–272.

[2] D. H. Nguyen, A. Kobsa, and G. R. Hayes, "An empirical investigation of concerns of everyday tracking and recording technologies," in Proceedings of the 10th International Conference on Ubiquitous Computing, 2008, pp. 182–191.

[3] S. Kolimi, F. Zhu, and S. Carpenter, "Contexts And Sharing / Not Sharing Private Information," in Proceedings of the ACM Annual Southeast Regional Conference, 2012, pp. 1 –5.

[4] M. Wogalter, Communication-Human Information Processing (C-HIP) Model, in Handbook of Warnings, M. Wogalter, Ed. Mahwah,NJ, USA, 2006, pp. 51–62.

[5] M. S. Sanders and E. J. McCormick, Human factors in engineering and design, 7th ed. New York: McGraw-Hill, 1993.

[6] C. Bravo-Lillo, et al., "Your attention please: Designing security-decision UIs to make genuine risks harder to ignore," in SOUPS '13 Proceedings of the Ninth Symposium on Usable Privacy and Security, 2013, pp. 1–18.

[7] M. Maurer, A. D. Luca, and S. Kempe, "Using Data Type Based Security Alert Dialogs to Raise Online Security Awareness," in SOUPS '11 Proceedings of the Seventh Symposium on Usable Privacy and Security, 2011, pp. 2–14.

[8] F. Raja, K. Hawkey, S. Hsu, K. L. C. Wang, and K. Beznosov, "A brick wall, a locked door, and a bandit: a physical security metaphor for firewall warnings," in Proceedings of the 7th Symposium on Usable Privacy and Security - SOUPS '11, 2011, pp. 1–20

[9] R. Balebako, J. Jung, W. Lu, L. F. Cranor, and C. Nguyen, "'Little brothers watching you': raising awareness of data leaks on smartphones," in Proceedings of the Ninth Symposium on Usable Privacy and Security - SOUPS '13, 2013, pp. 12–24.

[10] M. S. Wogalter, Attention switch and maintenance, in Handbook of Warnings, Mahwah,NJ, USA, 2006, pp. 245–265.

[11] M. S. Wogalter, Modeling the process, in Handbook of Warnings, 1st ed., Mahwah, NJ, USA, 1999, pp. 51–107.

[12] L. F. Cranor, "A Framework for Reasoning About the Human in the Loop.," UPSEC, vol. 8, 2008.pp. 1–15

[13] Microsoft, Microsoft Warning Messages[Online]. Available from: http://msdn.microsoft.com/en-us/library/windows/desktop/dn742473%28v=vs.85%29.aspx.

[14] S. Kim and M. S. Wogalter, "Habituation, Dishabituation, and Recovery Effects in Visual Warnings," in Human Factors and Ergonomics Society Annual Meeting Proceedings, vol. 53, No. 20, 2009, pp. 1612–1616.

[15] M. S. Wogalter, B. M. Racicot, M. J. Kalsher, and S. N. Simpson, "Behavioral Compliance to Personalized Warning Signs and the Role of Perceived Relevance," Proc. Hum. Factors Ergon. Soc. Annu. Meet., 1993, pp. 950–954.

[16] M. S. Wogalter, D. DeJoy, and K. R. Laughery, Warnings and risk communication. CRC Press, 2005.

[17] M. R. Lehto, "A proposed conceptual model of human behavior and its implications for design of warnings.," Percept. Mot. Skills, vol. 73, 1991, pp. 595–611.

[18] J. Sunshine, S. Egelman, H. Almuhimedi, N. Atri, and L. F. Cranor, "Crying wolf: An empirical study of SSL warning effectiveness," in 18th USENIX Security Symposium, 2009, pp. 399–432.

[19] R. R. Duffy, M. J. Kalsher, and M. S. Wogalter, "Increased effectiveness of an interactive warning in a realistic incidental product-use situation," Int. J. Ind. Ergon., vol. 15, 1995, pp. 159–166.

[20] K. R. Laughery and M. S. Wogalter, "Designing Effective Warnings," Rev. Hum. Factors Ergon., vol. 2, No. 1999, 2006, pp. 241–271,.

[21] M. R. Lehto, "Determining Warning Label Content and Format Using Emea," in Proceedings of the Human Factors and Ergonomics Society Annual Meeting, 2000, pp. 774–777.

[22] E. Brunswick, The conceptual framework of psychology. Chicago: University of Chicago Press, 1952.

[23] F. Zhu, S. Carpenter, and S. Kolimi, "Mindlessness attacks," Procedia Manuf., vol. 3, No. Ahfe, 2015, pp. 1066–1073.

[24] S. Carpenter, F. Zhu, and S. Kolimi, "Reducing online identity disclosure using warnings," Appl. Ergon., vol. 45, No. 5, 2014, pp. 1337–1342.

[25] R. J. K. Jacob and K. S. Karn, "Eye tracking in Human–Computer interaction and usability research: Ready to deliver the promises," Mind's Eye Cogn. Appl. Asp. Eye Mov. Res., 2003, pp. 573–605.

[26] E. C. Crowe and N. H. Narayanan, "Comparing interfaces based on what users watch and do," in Proceedings of the symposium on Eye tracking research & applications - ETRA '00, 2000, pp. 29–36.

[27] J. Nielsen and K. Pernice, Eyetracking web usability. New Riders, 2010.

[28] T. Takeuchi, T. Puntous, A. Tuladhar, S. Yoshimoto, and A. Shirama, "Estimation of mental effort in learning visual search by measuring pupil response," PLoS One, vol. 6, No. 7, 2011, pp. 4–8.

[29] R. J. K. Jacob, "The use of eye movements in human-computer interaction techniques: what you look at is what you get," in ACM Transactions on Information Systems, vol. 9, No. 3, 1991, pp. 152–169.

[30] F. Zhu, S. Carpenter, A. Kulkarni, and S. Kolimi, "Reciprocity attacks," in Proceedings of the Seventh Symposium on Usable Privacy and Security - SOUPS '11, 2011, p. 1-14.

[31] M. S. Wogalter, R. R Duffy, M. J. Kalsher, "Interactive warning: An experimental examination of effectiveness," Int. J. Ind. Ergon., vol. 15, 1995, pp. 159–166.

[32] J. A. Bzostek and M. S. Wogalter, "Measuring Visual Search Time for a Product Warning Label as a Function of Icon, Color, Column and Vertical Placement," in Proceedings of the Human Factors and Ergonomics Society Annual Meeting, vol. 43, No. 1993, 1999, pp. 888–892.

[33] K. R. Laughery, S. L. Young, K. P. Vaubel, and J. J. W. Brelsford, "The Noticeability of Warnings on Alcoholic Beverage Containers," J. Public Policy Mark., vol. 12, No. 1, 1993, pp. 38–56.

[34] The EyeTribe, The EyeTribe developers guide[Online], 2014. Available from: http://dev.theeyetribe.com/dev/. [May-11-2015].

[35] Aforge.NET framework[Online]. Available from: https://aforgeffmpeg.codeplex.com/. [May-11-2015].

Tangible Technologies for the Development of Play Skills in Autistic Children

Patrizia Marti
Department of Social Political and Cognitive Science
University of Siena
Siena, Italy
Department of Industrial Design
Eindhoven University of Technology
Eindhoven, The Netherlands
e-mail: patrizia.marti@unisi.it

Luca Giacolini
Department of Industrial Design
Eindhoven University of Technology
Eindhoven, The Netherlands
e-mail: l.giacolini@student.tue.nl

Iolanda Iacono
Department of Social Political and Cognitive Science
University of Siena
Siena, Italy
e-mail: iolanda.iacono@unisi.it

Abstract— **In this paper we describe Game of Stimuli (GoS) an interactive tangible game for children and adolescents diagnosed with Autistic Spectrum Disorder. The system is designed to engage children in play scenarios addressing different stages of development from practice play to rule-based play. The objective of the game is to maintain the attention on a given task while filtering irrelevant stimuli. The study was developed adopting a research-through-design approach, a design method that uses prototypes in the real context of use to generate new knowledge and future visions. The study exploited the modularity of GoS to adapt play activities to the current level of development of autistic children, and to appreciate if the tool could support them in mastering different stages of play of increasing complexity, from practice play (initial level of child development) to rule-based play (a more advanced and skilled playful competence), in solitary and collaborative way. The paper concludes with a reflection on the knowledge gained from testing in the field. Reflection-in-action happened while prototyping solutions and it allowed us to reshape our design. Reflection-on-action occurred after the final prototype was completed. This level of reflection was achieved by reflecting back on the overall experience with therapists and parents, questioning our beliefs, decisions and obtained results.**

Playfulness, Autism, Tangible Interaction, Interactive Game, Stimuli, Requirements.

I. INTRODUCTION

Play is an essential activity to develop cognitive, social and emotional competences in childhood. Through play, children learn to create and explore a world that they are able to handle. Growing up, they will be able to transfer the knowledge gained during play to the real world, and this will help them to understand and make sense of it. In play children learn and practice new behaviours and develop social skills [1]. In fact, cognitive processes involved in play activities are very similar to those involved in learning: motivation, meaning, repetition, self-regulation and abstract thinking [2]. Also the ability to read, to speak, to count depends on the child's ability to manipulate symbols, and this ability is typically developed in play [3]. For example, during play, a piece of wood may become a doll and a stick may become a horse: these are forms of symbolic play were imaginary objects are manipulated and embedded into a meaningful context. These forms of symbolic play contribute to the acquisition of cognitive as well as social skills.

However, children who are prevented from playing, either due to cognitive, developmental or physical impairments, which affect their playing skills, experience a serious limitation in their learning potential. For this reason it is very important to develop tailored tools to encourage play in order to break down barriers for development, fostering individual development up the person's potential.

The paper addresses challenges related to play development in autistic children. Autism is a disorder spectrum characterized by a high variability of social skills and intellectual ability. Changes in symptom severity and adaptive functioning can differ significantly among children with autism spectrum disorder and this reduces the chances of designing of a unique solution that can satisfy very different needs and requirements. A further challenge is the difficulty of eliciting requirements for a so varied population with a paucity of skills necessary to engage in a meaningful way with the design team [4]. The impairments of the children may limit the degree to which they can collaborate or express themselves appropriately, and most of the communications have to be mediated by therapists or educators and therefore depend on their experience and interpretation of the problem. Successful methods for human-centred design in such a complex setting are relatively under-developed.

For this reason we applied in the study a research-through-design approach, defined by [5] as a "systematic enquiry conducted through the medium of practical action, calculated to generate or test new, or newly imported, information, ideas, forms or procedures and to generate communicable knowledge". This kind of research is knowledge-directed. It generates new knowledge through testing and must be pursued through action in the real context of application, in all its complexity.

Thus we extended the concept of user-centered design to encompass not just the designer-user direct relation, but taking in the *ecology of the environment* where we were working, in all its complexity and richness.

II. RELATED WORK

Cognitive and social development in autistic children have been investigated in different studies and a large number of technological tools have been developed to support learning and play. These technologies include computer applications, robotics, mobile applications and interactive toys [6]-[9]. Recently, digital games on tablets and smartphones have been developed to facilitate social interaction amongst children with autism. For instance, Samsung designed the app "Look at me" [10], with the aim to facilitate eye contact, which is a difficult task for autistic subjects. Beside digital applications, an alternative paradigm is emerging that focuses on tangibility and embodiment in autism therapy. Touch can successfully mediate communication, and compensate the lack of eye contact or verbal language. Reference [11] observes that the lack of verbal skills and eye contact creates the need to explore tactile interaction as a means to communicate and minimize the detrimental effect of other modalities of communication. Through tactile interaction and exploration children can discover the world in social and physical terms.

However, any intervention based on tactile interaction with autistic children has to be carefully designed. In fact, when people with Autistic Spectrum Disorders are affected in the tactile system, they may withdraw when touched and may overreact to the texture of objects, clothing or food. This may be the result of tactile misperception, which can lead to behavioural problems, irritability, withdrawal and isolation. Some sources of stimulation cause avoidance, other types of stimulation may have a calming effect. Some individuals demonstrate a preoccupation with certain tactile experiences and seek out such feedback on a frequent basis, e.g., insisting on touching smooth surfaces. Reference [12] recognized that tactile interaction, if tolerated by children with autism, might be a key vehicle of communication and interaction. They experimented with touch-based interaction with autistic children using KASPAR, a robot equipped with tactile sensors to engage the autistic child in bodily interactions. Reference [13] compared the therapeutic efficacy of a programmable toy called Topobo© in comparison with a LEGO© kit.. Playing with Topobo©, children with Autistic Spectrum Disorder increased their collaborative skills and associative play, reducing solitary play. Reference [14] evaluated Reactable, a music-based tangible system, to help autistic children in the acquisition of social interaction abilities. The results of the study show that when playing with Reactable, children improved turn-taking skills.

Our research focuses on play and development in autistic children. In the following, we briefly describe the features of the Autistic Spectrum Disorder and later we illustrate the research-through-design process leading to the development of GoS. The process includes testing intermediate prototypes in the field with six autistic adolescents and their therapists and educators.

III. Autism Spectrum Disorder

Autism Spectrum Disorder (ASD) is a lifelong disorder arising before the age of three, affecting mainly a male population. It is categorised as a pervasive developmental disorder (PDD) [15], although the scientific community agrees on defining autism as a "spectrum" [16]. The term implies a variety of skills and behaviours that might change along a continuum, from child to child and over time [15]. In fact, there is no unequivocal definition of autism related to the symptoms' analysis: every subject fluctuates on the interval in between high-functioning (or Asperger) and low-functioning, according to the level of social skills and intellectual ability. Children who fall into the low-functioning category do not possess verbal communication and they show cognitive underdevelopment together with difficulties in reading facial expressions. Children who belong to the high-functioning category do not manifest significant delays in verbal communication and cognitive development. This variance leads to the fact that criteria for diagnosis still represent a debated topic. Reference [17] first defines autism as "Triad of Impairment", stating that children with autism have problems in three different development areas: communication, cognitive and social interaction. Autistic subjects are not capable of filtering out the irrelevant interfering stimuli within the environment and therefore they process a significant amount of unnecessary information. This results in experiencing difficulties in sharing attention, adopting viewpoint of peers, taking turns in social interaction and decoding environmental stimuli.

In relation to play, children with autism spectrum disorder in most cases prefer solitary play, and rarely engage in cooperative games. Of course, the level of play that they can reach is mostly related to the level of impairment and the complexity of the game itself. Low-functioning autistic children mostly prefer practice play and their interest is directed to the physical properties of the toy. High-functioning autistic children are usually able to perform and engage in rule-based games where they can master cause and effect relations.

Objective of this study is to design a game that can sustain play activities along different types, from practice to rule-based play, that appear at different stages of the child's life. Each stage involves re-elaboration and adjustments of the competencies of the previous one. A major challenge of the study is to envision through GoS how to support different stages of play development in autistic children.

IV. Game Of Stimuli: A Research-Through-Design Process

The design process started with an extensive literature review on autism combined to an analysis of autistic children play abilities. We adopted the guidelines on play activities and disabilities as defined in the European project COST Action LUDI [18]. Four different categories of play where defined [19]:

- *practice play* (the toy can be manipulated to discover basic properties of objects and reality and how these are related to the child's own movements and the environment);
- *constructive play* (the toy can be modified in appearance and interaction capabilities by adding modules to create new games that can exploit different interaction possibilities);

- *symbolic play* (the toy can have a character, showing emotions and moods, and can participate to invented stories);
- *rule-based play* (the toy behaves in pre-defined ways activated by some specific action and stimuli initiated by the child, so that a game can be played with other children and play strategies can be developed by any player);

This play developmental model should not be regarded as a unidirectional, waterfall model. It is rather a spiral showing the progression of the play types, their coexistence and their possible contaminations and reactivation.

Following this model, we aimed at developing a game to determine the current level of development of autistic children, and to stimulate them exploring different stages of play, from practice play to rule-based play, both in solitary and collaborative mode. It must be noted that collaborative play is usually very challenging for autistic children.

In parallel with the literature review, observation in the field and the study of clinical cases and therapeutic practices, different prototypes were developed and used to brainstorm with therapists and a neuropsychiatrist. Our research-through-design approach generated a diversity of concepts that were continuously assessed by therapists and physicians. The design went through three layers of iterative cycles and layers of exploration, each one contributing to test hypotheses and to generate new research questions. The study was performed the Centre for Autism "Piccolo Principe", and the Neuropsychiatry Department of the ASL7 in Siena, Italy.

A. *First Prototype: a Chaos-generative Musical Interface*

The first step in the design process consisted in prototyping a musical instrument and exploiting the contrast between assonance and dissonance as positive or negative reinforcement feedback during the exercise. The interface (Figure 1) consisted of a 3X3 matrix where nine tokens were located. Three of them were red, three were white and three were black. At the beginning they were grouped in rows according their colour. The purpose of the game was to break the order of the tokens by moving them around the plate. When three tokens of the same colour happened to be in either the same row or same column, a disharmonic sound was generated, which we interpreted as a negative feedback. The more the order was broken, the more pleasant sounds were generated.

This first prototype was submitted to the assessment of design professionals and a clinical expert in a participatory design workshop. From a design viewpoint, the shape and material of the glasses did not afford a compelling tactile experience; from a clinical viewpoint, the system proved to be weak because the negative feedback was not properly articulated to the user. In fact, different sensorial skills might lead to different interpretations of the sound feedback, and this could impair the overall functioning of the game.

Figure 1. Chaos-generative Musical Interface.

B. *Second Prototype: a Haptic Stimuli Generator*

The focus of the second iteration was played with self-generating stimuli, in opposition to the stimuli generated by the computer of the first prototype. We also further investigated tangible interaction modalities afforded by the system, exploring the opportunity of continuous interaction as opposed to the discrete interaction enabled by the plastic glasses of the first prototype.

With the second prototype, we designed a tangible interface that mapped the pressure exerted on a simple keyboard to the visual output on a computer screen. This resulted in the building of three pressure sensors, which detected continuous input from the user. Any variation in the pressure resulted in a change in shape of the icons displayed on the screen display (Figure 2). Each sensor controlled one parameter associated to the icons (e.g. form, size, colour). The more force was applied to a sensor, the more the parameter varied the appearance of the icons creating chaotic patterns. For instance, in Figure 2, the first key (first pressure sensor) controlled the darkness of the pink circle while the second one controlled the dimension of the pink circle, and in the third one, the flickering of the entire image. When the configuration became overloading, the user could stop the animation by releasing the pressure. The user could create his own visual performance by exploring the concept of force associated to the tactile experience.

A second participatory design workshop was organized to assess the new prototype. During the workshop, which again joined design and clinical expertise, it emerged that, despite the exploratory nature of the game, the playful dimension of the activity became lost. Ultimately, the objective of the game was unclear and after few minutes the player tended to lose interest in the activity itself. On the positive side, we realised that the continuous interaction created by mapping the pressure exerted on the keyboard along with its corresponding visual animation, became a promising future option.

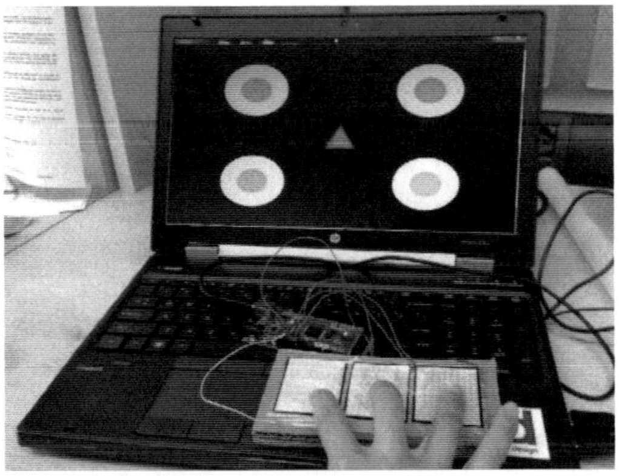

Figure 2. The Haptic Stimuli Generator.

C. *Third Prototype: a Game of Stimuli*

During the third cycle of prototyping, we built up on the outcomes of the participatory design activity of the first two iterations. On the one hand, the chaotic musical instrument informed us on the potential of the tangible interaction but on the other hand, the continuity of interaction realised in the second prototype turned out to be an opportunity for future design. The final prototype is called Game of Stimuli – GoS. It is an interactive tangible game resulting from an incremental design process where we build up on the evaluation of previous iterations. Early prototypes included a chaotic musical instrument and a haptic stimuli generator. However, none of these prototypes raised the interest of therapists and educators who collaborated to the project. Even if tangibility was considered to be a winning feature of both prototypes, none of them could cover the high variability of play skills in the autism spectrum, from low to high functioning.

For this reason we decided to develop a modular game of increasing complexity in the number of physical modules, the generated stimuli and in play scenarios ranging from practice play to rule-based play (Figure 3). The hardware consists of one core element where most of the electronic components are located. Next to it, the structure expands into a variable amount of modules, which can be attached to the main element. The materials used to build the modules varied along the prototyping process, from cardboard to plywood. The same happened for the buttons: their softness was changed many times to reach the ideal balance between malleability and robustness when pushed.

Each module consists of a block with a push button on top of it. On the one hand, the button can detect the pressure exerted, while on the other one it can emit a light by means of a RGB LED.

One additional block including a piezo speaker completes the set-up. It generates a rewarding sound as a positive reinforcement to correct actions.

The system is currently composed of five modules, but there is no limit to the amount of modules that can be added. Each module contains a pressure sensor with two foils of conductive material separated by a semi-conductor. The values detected by the sensors are continuous and managed by an Arduino. On top of each sensor, a LilyPad Tri-Colour LED is located, which is operated by the same Arduino. Eventually, a silicon-like material covers the LED with a twofold purpose: first, it can amplify the amount of light emitted, and secondly, it makes the tactile interaction more compelling. In this sense, we were interested in testing on field the relevance of viscous material in empowering the continuous tactile interaction, as opposed to rigid buttons.

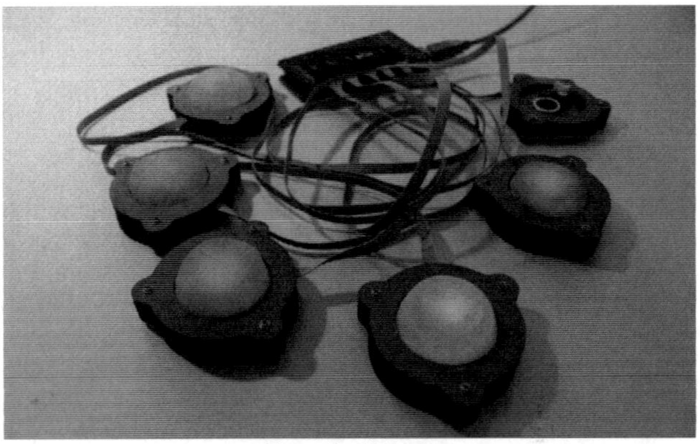

Figure 3. GoS system.

V. PLAY SCENARIOS

The play scenarios were categorised in three main groups: cause and effect, turn-taking and collaborative. Each scenario demanded a different level of engagement and interaction, from practice play, where children could explore the physical properties of the modules and their behaviour (e.g. properties of soft buttons, visual stimuli), to rule-based play, where the game was based on rules shared with the children at the beginning of the play session. The scenarios were designed in an increasing order of complexity.

A. *Scenario 1. Tactile Exploration*

The child is invited to play with four modules. At the initial stage, all the lights are turned off. The child is invited to press the buttons and see what might happen. The goal is to find where the blue light is located. The tactile interaction is used to stimulate the interest of the child to the game: the force applied to the button is mapped to the intensity of the light emitted. When the correct button is fully pressed, a rewarding sound is played. This scenario is mainly related to practice play.

B. *Scenario 2. Stimuli Recognition*

The child is invited to press only the fixed blue light, which randomly moves in between the five modules. A successful action will trigger a positive sound. The exercise is designed so to have six increasing levels of difficulty. If in the first level of difficulty there is only one light popping up at a time, the next levels introduce more disturbances. These include additional blinking red and green lights. Children are asked to maintain the focus and attention on the task, despite the irrelevant stimuli which are simultaneously presented. This scenario requires the mastering of practice play as well as rule-based play.

C. *Scenario 3. Cooperative Game*

The subject is invited to adopt a collaborative attitude with the playmate in hopes of accomplishing the game. The exercise is designed to have two levels of difficulty. In the first level, one blue light is presented simultaneously with two green lights. The subject is then asked to press a green button, and the partner is called to mimic with his own green button. When both manage to synchronise their actions, the blue light turns off and a rewarding sound is played. The lights then move randomly in between five modules. In the second level of difficulty, four green lights have to be pushed in order to turn the blue light off. This scenario is far more complex than the other two. It implies the understanding of rules and implies a social competence related to turn-taking and imitation with the playmate.

VI. TESTING IN THE FIELD

GoS was tested with six autistic children with the aim to test their stage of play development, and to engage them in play scenarios at different levels of complexity. Complexity could vary from different respects: number and type of stimuli, number of modules, play scenarios (practice or rule-based), play modality (solitary or collaborative).

As stated above, the study was conducted in the Centre for Autism "Piccolo Principe" in Siena, Italy, which accommodates children and adolescents for after-school activities. Six male children, ranging in age from ten to sixteen joined the study, together with their therapists and a neuro-psychiatrist. They were diagnosed with different levels of autism. Four children showed the typical traits of low-functioning autism, such as communication difficulties, cognitive deficits and motor skill impairments. In fact, they needed the constant presence of at least one therapist, to prevent stressful or dangerous situation. The other two subjects were twins and showed medium-functioning ASD. None of them had motor impairments. One of them had severe difficulties in social, communicative and cognitive areas. The verbalization was not always appropriate to the context, and the comprehension was only limited to simple statements. Attention level was generally low during the play activities and had to be stimulated by the therapist. Stereotyped behaviours were common. The other child had poor verbalization, but the comprehension was sufficiently developed. Furthermore, his logical and abstract thinking was underdeveloped. He showed stereotyped behaviours and socialization skills not adequate to the age.

The activity took place in a period of one month, twice per week, for a total of 8 sessions. However, not all the children managed to participate in all sessions. The four low-functioning ASD children participated in 1-2 sessions (2 children followed 2 sessions, the remaining 2 children followed only 1 session). The 2 medium-functioning ASD subjects, instead, participated in all sessions. In 4 sessions they were invited to play together.

The play sessions took place with one child at a time, because the presence of more people could be perceived as intrusive or represent an obstacle for social interaction. The same designer/experimenter conducted all sessions. If any problem occurred during the session, the therapist, who attended as non-participant observer, was allowed to intervene. Fortunately, this was not the case for any session. At the end of each session, the therapist was asked to take notes and fill in a questionnaire related to the behaviour of the child. The sessions were video-recorded. During the play sessions with children with low-functioning autism, the presence of a second therapist was necessary to support them in performing the games and in some cases contain their excitement (Figure 4).

Figure 4. A child with low-functioning autism performs the game with the support of the educational therapist.

The setting was kept simple to avoid distractions. Each play session was structured in three parts:

Welcome. The experimenter welcomed the subject, inviting him to sit. The therapist sat in a corner of the room, in a position that allowed her to observe the scene while not being visible by the child.

Playing together. The experimenter introduced the three different play scenarios described above, which were played in sequence.

Time to say Good Bye and See you next time. At the end of the session, the experimenter turned the system off and said goodbye. The therapist completed the questionnaire.

The sessions were designed to last approximately thirty minutes, but they were subject to changes, according to the attention span of the children and response behaviour.

VII. REFLECTION-IN-ACTION

The reflective practice is fundamental in research-through-design. Testing in context does not necessarily lead to a deep knowledge of the problem without a conscious look at emotions, serendipitous experiences, actions, and responses. For [20], professional knowledge in gained *within action*, at two levels. Reflection-in-action occurs during the activity as a manifestation of "theory in use". It is a mix of knowing and doing that allows the professional to act and intervene on the scene. Reflection-on-action occurs after the activity has taken place and is used to learn from a repertoire of experiences, and to generate new knowledge and visions about future activities.

In our study, reflection-in-action was conducted during the evaluation sessions, by confronting the observation of the designer, the comments of the neuropsychiatrist, and the notes of the therapists who evaluated the following items:

• *Attention*: the ability of the child to focus on the game, to swap from one stimulus to the next one and to call for attention with sharing the gaze or with gestures;

• *Mood:* child's behaviour in terms of agitation, nervousness, aggressiveness, inappropriate verbalization and sadness;

• *Autonomy*: the ability of the child to execute the activities without any prompt received by the experimenter as well as the level of proactivity during the play session;

• *Relationship with the experimenter:* the ability of the child to establish a relationship with experimenter and the level of appreciation for the given task.

Children with low-functioning autism maintained a level of attention on the game varying from 2 to 8 minutes. This testifies their difficulty with playing even the simplest scenarios. Three of them had to be physically contained by the therapist to limit their excitement. However, they were all able to engage in practice play. They enjoyed exploring the material qualities of the game, by experimenting with the soft buttons and showing interest in the visual stimuli of the changing lights. We noticed how fond they were of manipulating the objects. They were attracted by the soft material of the buttons, trying to stretch, bite and smell it. Less interest was shown towards the visual stimuli and the interactivity of the system. Even if none of them was autonomous in playing, one of them was able to fulfil the rule-based scenario through the use of verbal and physical prompt provided by the experimenter. This was a surprising achievement. The therapist knew that the child could do practice play, but she did not believe he could engage in a rule-based game. This result generated an extensive discussion about how to combine physical prompt in GoS.

Children with medium level of autism maintained a level of attention in between 15 and 22 minutes, which the therapists defined as positive (Figure 5).

Figure 5. A child with medium-functioning autism performs the game with the expert

Furthermore, one child showed a significant improvement in the area of shared attention. He started to establish eye contact with the experimenter as a means to call for attention. Regarding their mood, the therapists reported that the play activities were pleasant for both of them. Only one of them established a collaborative relationship with the experimenter, showing interest in achieving something together. The child with verbal skills showed a significant progression with the cooperative games with the experimenter. The other child improved his performance in the cognitive tasks.

Since they both were able to engage from practice to rule-based play, the complexity of the games was increased along the sessions, and they were asked to play together (Figure 6).

Figure 6. Children with medium-functioning autism playing together

In the cooperative game session the children played together, whilst the experimenter observed the activity intervening from time to time. Especially during this session we noticed that the game became extremely competitive. The peer-to-peer activity stimulated each child to score higher than the playmate and the experimenter supported their engagement with verbal support. As a result, we positively noted that their attention spanned from 10 to 12 minutes of collaborative gaming. Their performance, in terms of errors and time to complete the game, slightly improved over the four sessions.

VIII. REFLECTION-ON-ACTION

Testing GoS in the field, trying out different patterns of stimuli and play scenarios was a process of continuous learning.

The system helped us to test the play skills of the children and challenge their potential to master the evolution from one stage of play to the following. Children diagnosed with low-functioning autism can generally engage in practice play, where free exploration and manipulation of the platform are at the core. If no external help is given, they rarely can progress toward the next types of play. Both physical prompt (e.g. showing the action to be performed through physical guidance) and verbal prompt (e.g. vocal guidance) are vital during the play session and should be integrated in the interaction design of the game.

A customizable system like GoS allows for adaptability to different types of autism profiles. Quality and quantity of stimuli can be tailored to the child's play skills.

Modularity allows for tweaking the difficulty of a game. It is important that this feature is represented at hardware level (i.e., the number of modules to be used is custom) as well as software level (i.e., the various amount of stimuli that can be programmed).

The material qualities of the game are fundamental in fostering exploration and interaction. In particular, qualities like being malleable, stretchable, soft and scented. The material properties of the buttons in GoS, their softness and flexibility afforded various types of manipulation additional to pressing. The buttons were caressed, squeezed, pinched. This explorative behaviour was solitary. It stopped when the game became collaborative. Children were able to move their attention from the material qualities, which at the beginning held almost all of their attention, to the interactive features of the system.

The simplicity of the proposed games associated with the modularity of the system is definitively a winning aspect. The design of GoS enabled the generation of a wide range of interactions and a significant amount of play scenarios. A modular hardware and an easy-to-hack software allowed for tailoring the system to the different children's skills.

Furthermore, the therapist expressed the need for more independency, as until this moment it was necessary for the experimenter to manually load new lines of code every time the activity would pass on to the next one. For the future iteration we envisioned a tablet application that would allow the therapists to control the system without assistance (Figure 7). The application allows the configuration of the game by selecting the type of stimuli (e.g. colour and light patterns), play rules (e.g. turn taking) and play styles (e.g. individual vs collaborative game). Furthermore it records the progress of each subject, monitoring the development of individual play skills.

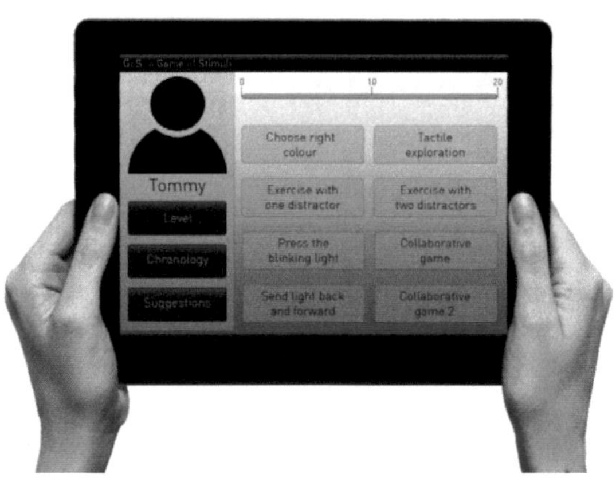

Figure 7. The screen-based interface that would allow the therapist to load and configure new play scenarios, as well as to keep track on the progress of each subject.

Testing in the field also revealed that the role of an adult supervisor is pivotal in creating a friendly, encouraging and inclusive atmosphere, and the use of a shared physical interactive toy can greatly facilitate the social exchange among them.

A major contribution of the study is the design of play scenarios that are mapped to different stages of child development as well as to different properties and functionality of the system. Since improvements of play skills in autistic child are slow and demand constant monitoring, a game like GoS can support the therapists in evaluating any improvement in play skills. Furthermore, it allows the children to practice their skills and challenge them through small, recognisable, repetitive variations of increasing complexity of the games.

ACKNOWLEDGMENT

The authors would like to thank the children who participated to the study, their families, the educational therapist of the Centre for Autism "Piccolo Principe", and the Neuropsychiatry Department of the ASL7 – Siena for their precious collaboration. We would also like to thank Michele Tittarelli and Matteo Sirizzotti for their help in the development of GoS.

REFERENCES

[1] J. Bruner, "Nature and Uses of Immaturity". American Psychologist, vol. 27, no. 8, 1972, pp. 687-708.

[2] L. E. Schulz, H. Standing, and E. B. Bonawitz, "Word, thought, and deed: The role of object labels in children's inductive inferences and exploratory play". Developmental Psychology., vol. 44, 2008, pp. 1266-1276.

[3] L. Vygotsky, "Play and its role in the Mental Development of the Child" Voprosy psikhologii (Translation by Mulholland 1966, N. 6, 1993.

[4] P. Marti and L. J. Bannon, "Exploring User-Centred Design in Practice: Some Caveats"- Knowledge, Technology & Policy". Springer Netherlands, ISSN 0897-1986 (Print) 1874-6314 (Online), vol. 22, no. 1,2009, pp 7-15.

[5] B. Archer, "The nature of research". Co-design , p 6-13, 1995.

[6] B. Robins, K. Dautenhahn, R. te Boekhorst, and A. Billard, "Effects of repeated exposure to a humanoid robot on children with autism" in Designing a more inclusive world, S. Keates, J. Clarkson, P. Langdon, P. Robinson (eds). Springer, London, pp. 225–236, 2004.

[7] H. Lehmann, I. Iacono, B. Robins, P. Marti, and K. Dautenhahn, "Make it move": playing cause and effect games with a robot companion for children with cognitive disabilities. The 30th European Conference on Cognitive Ergonomics (ECCE 2011), pp. 105–112, ISBN: 978-1-4503-1029-1.

[8] M. Coleman-Martin, K. Wolff Heller, D. Cihak, and K. Irvine, "Using computer-assisted instruction and the nonverbal reading approach to teach word identification". Focus Autism Other Dev Disabl, 20(2). 80–90, 2005.

[9] S. Parsons and P. Mitchell, "The potential of virtual reality in social skills training for people with autistic spectrum disorders". J Intellect Disabil Res, vol. 46, 2002, pp 430–443.

[10] "Look at me". https://play.google.com/store/apps/details?id=com.samsung.lookatme [Retrieved: March, 2016].

[11] P. Caldwell, "Intensive Interaction: Using Body Language to Communicate". Journal on Developmental Disabilities, vol.19, no. 1, 2013, pp. 33-39.

[12] B. Robins and K. Dautenhahn, "Tactile Interactions with a Humanoid Robot - Novel Play Scenario Implementations with Children with Autism". International Journal of Social Robotics (IJSR), vol. 6, no. 3, 2014, pp.397-415.

[13] W. Farr, N. Yuill, and H. Raffle, "Social benefits of a tangible user interface for children with Autistic Spectrum Conditions. Autism". International journal of research and practice, vol. 14, no. 3, 2010, pp 237-52.
[14] L. Villafuerte, S. Markova, and S. Jorda, "Acquisition of social abilities through musical tangible user interface: children with autism spectrum condition and the reactable". The ACM SIGCHI Conference on Human Factors in Computing Systems (*CHI '12)* Extended Abstracts on Human Factors in Computing Systems, May 05-10, Austin, Texas, USA, ISBN: 978-1-4503-1016-1.
[15] World Health Organization. The ICD-10 classification of mental and behavioural disorders: Diagnostic criteria for research, 1993.
[16] L. Wing and J. Gould, "Severe impairments of social interaction and associated abnormalities in children: Epidemiology and Classification". Journal of Autism and Developmental Disorder, vol. 9, 1979, pp. 11-29.
[17] R. Jordan, "Autistic Spectrum Disorder Pratical Strategies for Teachers and Other Professional". London and New York: Routledge, 1999.
[18] http://ludi-network.eu [Retrieved: March, 2016].
[19] S. Besio, D. Bulgarelli, and V. Stancheva Popkostadinov, "LUDI Scientific Report of Working Group no. 1". To be published as "The need of play for the sake of play", in press.
[20] D. Schön, "The Reflective Practitioner: How professionals think in action". London: Temple Smith, 1983.

Tablet Game Design and Evaluation: A Practice-based Experimentation Approach

Uttam Kokil
College of Humanities and Social Sciences
Kennesaw State University
Marietta, GA 30060, USA
E-Mail: ukokil@kennesaw.edu

Abstract—**The aim of this project is to first design, develop and evaluate an iOS adventure game for tablet devices using Practice-based Experimentation (PBE) approach. The objective of creating a digital game is to explore how usability and visual aesthetic attributes of the interfaces affect users' perception of usability and engagement. The new PBE methodology is adopted, involving two phases. First, during the practice phase, the games are designed from a user-centric approach iteratively, and modified into two visual aesthetic conditions, which serve as stimuli, to measure perception of usability and in the future to evaluate user engagement. In the second phase, the game interfaces are empirically evaluated using quantitative methods to measure users' perceptions of usability on the visual quality of the interfaces. As per extant literature, the concepts of perception of usability and visual aesthetics have been a controversial topic. Existing research on user experience have not fully explored perceived usability and visual aesthetics, in the domain of tablet gaming. This research is in its preliminary stage as data have only been collected to examine the first research question concerning users' perception of usability towards the variation of visual aesthetic quality of a tablet game user interface. The preliminary results indicate that there is no significant difference in perception of usability between the two modified visual interfaces.**

Keywords-Tablet gaming; user experience; user interface; Practice-based Experimentation.

I. INTRODUCTION

While the concepts of instrumental qualities (usability, functionality) and non-instrumental qualities (visual aesthetics, hedonics, acoustics) have been widely discussed in the field of Human Computer Interaction (HCI), they have not been applied in a coherent manner to the HCI sub-category of gaming, which is distinct from other HCI areas in that its primary aim is to entertain the user, rather than to enhance productivity or task performance. The skyrocketing use of tablets has brought the gaming experience to a new level with a new medium of interaction, the touch screen, in a mobile context. This shift in medium and context of use has only highlighted the lack of critical research on User eXperience (UX) as it relates to instrumental and non-instrumental attributes of system properties in tablets in general, and tablet-based in particular. Koutsabasis and Istikopoulou [1] explain that the methods and knowledge from a user centered design standpoint are scarce in the domain of aesthetics. In addition, UX, a relatively new field, is associated with instrumental and non-instrumental qualities [2], which still has deficiencies in terms of scope, and experiential constructs to assess the experience [3]. O'Brien & Toms [4] explain that user engagement forms part of a positive UX. The researchers further define User Engagement Scale as a multi-faceted instrument that measures experience in terms of its "appeal, novelty, focused attention, felt involvement, usability and durability." Engagement is a phenomenon determined by users' perceptions of usability and aesthetics toward product use, as well as the extent of their activities [5]. Carr [6] stipulates that the visceral property of game visual elements influences players to make choices and quick decisions during gameplay. The next section describes the design process of a new tablet game It becomes imperative to understand users' perceptions and behavior when they interact with tablet games. This will provide a deeper insight of the elements that attract and engage users to play games [7]. The study takes recourse of a novel methodology called PBE, a variant of PBR, which includes both practice and professional research. Section II provides an overview of the literature review. Section III discusses a practitioner's approach of game ideation and narrative. Section IV describes the game design process. Section V justifies the methods, including data collection procedure that is carried out using scientific inquiry. Section VI showcases the analysis portion and Section VII concludes the paper.

II. LITERATURE REVIEW

Practice-based Research (PBR) methodology concerns the generation of new knowledge contributing to understanding of the role of the artifact in that experience [8]. The role of the artifact is crucial in the generation of new knowledge but not necessarily the primary outcome. PBR begins with practice. The artifact is created first and then research questions are devised to evaluate the practical work. The artifact is modified into two conditions – a low and high visual quality prototype, for empirical evaluation by participants. PBE approach can be described as a variant of PBR, comprising of a combination of practitioner research and professional research (scientific inquiry). In this case, PBE begins with aims and pre-defined objectives, which include the creation of an artifact through a series of formal evaluations, referred to as practice. The depiction of the games (artifacts) is informed by theories. Experimental work is carried out on the artifact to create the desired conditions prior to empirical evaluation, using quantitative methods. The latter refers to scientific inquiry. PBE follows the logical sequence of theory informing practice, and the experimental evaluation process of the research questions leads to the emergence of new knowledge or theory. Arlander [9] states "sometimes artists come closer to scientists than historians since they engage in experimentation" (p 319). This implies that practitioners are already engaged in experimentation to create artifacts during their practice. The word "experimentation" in Practice-based Experimentation plays a key role in the sense that practice has always been associated with experimentation, and experimentation forms the basis of professional research. In this study, the process of PBE follows the sequence: Game Theory → Games characteristics → (Practice) Create Artifacts → Evaluate Artifacts (Empirical Evidence)→ Inform Theory. Each type of game conforms to specific requirements. For example, both Hard Fun Key and Easy Fun Key games portray distinctive characteristics to meet users' needs. Each game is devised based on Lazarro's Four Fun Keys theory [10]. In a Hard Fun Key (Action game), the user's goal is to beat his opponent, or to win against the computer. Easy Fun Key has a different goal, as the game is played for the sake of discovery, not necessarily to win. The Four Fun Keys game theory describes four different types of fun in a game: Ha*rd Fun, Easy Fun, People Factor, and Serious Fun*. For the scope of this research, an Easy Fun (adventure game) was devised. Easy Fun Key game is geared towards eliciting an appreciation for curiosity and surprise. One does not play to win but to discover or explore, as the focus is on the game activities. The game is used as a stimulus and empirically evaluated by participants to respond to the research questions, from which new knowledge or theory emerges.

Crawford [11] explains that if players find a game enjoyable, with that immersive experience, it is more probable that they will engage and deeply interact with the game. Fun is a kind of user experience triggered by various tangible (i.e., physical) and intangible qualities of products evoking certain relevant emotions in users, such as joy or amusement [12]. Admittedly, fun is related to a "sense of timelessness, similar to flow experiences [13]." Hassenzhal [14] explain that both fun and pleasure are a form of enjoyment, but there is a distinction between the two. Fun is about "distraction," implying that a user is distracted from concerns, motivations and the inner-self. Pleasure has to do with "absorption," such as being immersed in an activity, and one can still relate to one's concerns, motivations and goals. Fun is clearly an experience, not an emotion. Even though one fails 80% of the time while playing a game, the activity is still perceived to be fun [10].

III. Practitioner's Approach

Seven participants, two game developers, two designers, and three game player experts from a Midwest university volunteered to meet on two different occasions, for a three hours work session for a focus group discussion, and to shape the initial ideas for a *casual* tablet game that can be targeted towards a broader audience. A brainstorming technique, known as mind-mapping, was employed in the generation of initial ideas for the game design. Mind-mapping is a useful brainstorming tool that organically generates associations that the researcher may not otherwise have considered [15]. It relies on words and begins with a central concept or node as a focal point. Other nodes are added spontaneously to the mind map as the process unfolds. Once a mind map is completed, one needs to identify internal connections and useful adjectives and keywords that have appeared. The theme generated during the first focus group session culminated into a combination of an action and an adventure game. A game genre classifies entertainment games into action, adventure games, puzzle games, role playing games, strategy games, sports games, simulations [16]. An action and adventure game genre were created for the tablet platform. For the scope of this paper, only the adventure game was used to collect data at the time of writing. The tablet game is comprised of two phases - the narrative of first phase is an action-based game (Hard-Fun Key) referred to as a *Space Shooter* game and the second phase of the tablet game encompasses an adventure game (Easy-Fun Key), referred to as *Mars Exploration*. Phase I of the game narrative revolves around a spaceship starting its journey from Earth to planet Mars. On its way, it has to surmount multiple obstacles (storms, asteroids, aliens) to land on Mars. In Phase II, the character explores the landscape of planet Mars, grows green leaves to sustain survival, and copes with enemies (aliens), as well as sand storms on the planet. The player opens treasure chests randomly containing aliens (loses points) or gold coins (bonus points), or must avoid any abrupt sandstorms in order to earn enough points or life to sustain the green leaves. For the purpose of this study, the Easy Fun Key game was the only one used for data collection due to the shorter duration required for a participant to complete a game session.

IV. Game Design

Technology has evolved rapidly but game design has been a slow process. The goal of a game is to entertain and provide enjoyment to the user [17]. Game usability is more accentuated towards player satisfaction and learnability, whereas effectiveness and efficiency are considered secondary factors. The game design and development were devised iteratively, with the application of a user centered design approach. The structure of a digital game is composed of the following components: *game play*, *game interface*, *game mechanics*, and *game narrative* [18]. Game play is the process of encountering multiple obstacles before a player can win. Gameplay is the process during which the user overcomes a series of challenges in a simulated environment [19]. Crawford describes challenges as a mental activity aiming to develop one's skill [20]. Game interface is the mechanism through which the user interacts with the game; it includes the physical game controls as well as the game environment, assets and characters. It provides a visual representation of the game. Game mechanics form part of the physics of the game based on the programming and animation. Game mechanics are rules constructs intended to produce gameplay. It is these rules and rewards that make the activity challenging, satisfying and compelling [21]. Game narrative is the story or the plot that unfolds over time as the game is played.

The iOS game was developed using Xcode and Swift. Xcode allows the developer to build the interactive user interface elements while *Swift*-programming language responds to user events and gestures in order to express the game logic. Three participants tested the game prototype by responding to a usability survey devised by Federoff [18]. The game was refined, and underwent another round of usability testing by four other participants who played the game multiple times, under the observation of the researcher.

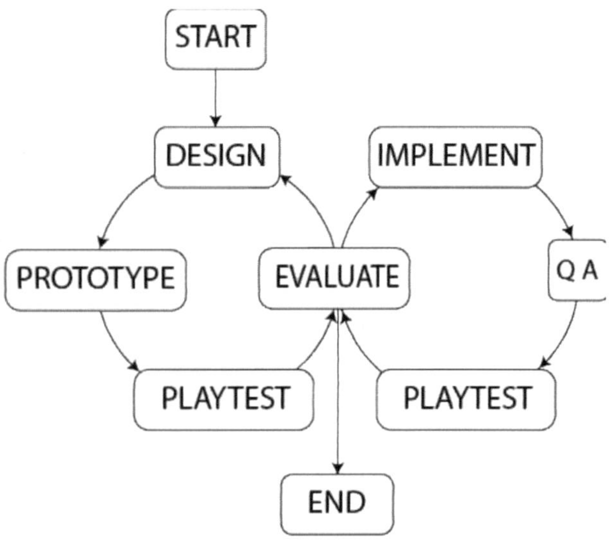

Figure 1 Rapid Iterative Testing and Evaluation (Medlock et al., 2005)

The first objective was to evaluate whether a variation of visual aesthetic quality while keeping game usability constant affects the perception of usability of players. To respond to this research question, the game interface was devised into two different levels of visual aesthetic qualities for experimentation purposes. An iterative prototyping cycle (Figure 1) session was held to showcase which visual elements could be modified while maintaining the same level of consistency, such as game play, and game mechanics between the two versions for each game category. The Easy Fun Key game was modified into a low and high visual aesthetic value. Elements and Design Principles, such as symmetry, grid system, eye flow, contrast, bitmap images quality were adopted in rendering the two versions. The low visual aesthetic quality version was designed in such a way to violate the Principles and Elements of Design [22]. For instance, to create the low visual aesthetic quality version (Figure 2b), low color contrast, low-resolution bitmaps and a monochromatic color scheme were adopted in achieving the same. This modification objectively changed the look and feel of the game user interface. To create a high visual aesthetic version (Figure 2a), the design elements were accentuated with high quality graphics rendering, high color contrast and a vivid color scheme, and low bit graphics. Seven participants rated a series of 3 different layouts, with different color schemes, graphics bits, contrast and combinations on a 27-inch iMac. After each prototype was depicted, it was evaluated using the Visual Analog Scales containing two dimensions: *Classical* and *Expressive* aesthetics [23]. The *Classical* aesthetic dimension is guided by three items: clean, pleasant, aesthetic; the *Expressive* aesthetic dimension has three items: sophisticated, creative, and fascinating. Each prototype was evaluated on a scale from *strongly disagree to strongly agree,* which was converted to a 1-7 range for analysis purposes.

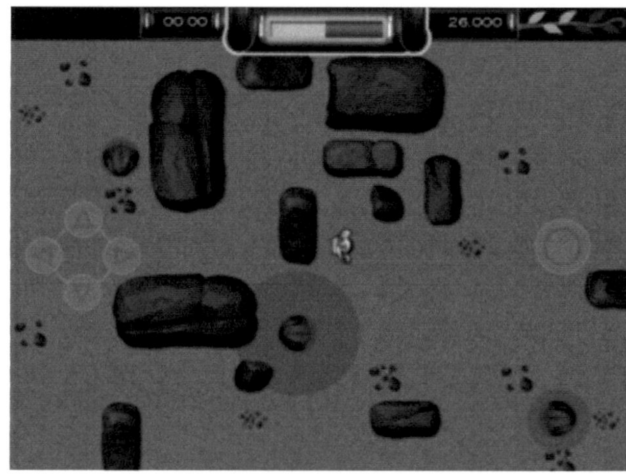

Figure 2a Easy Fun Key (Adventure) - High Visual Aesthetics

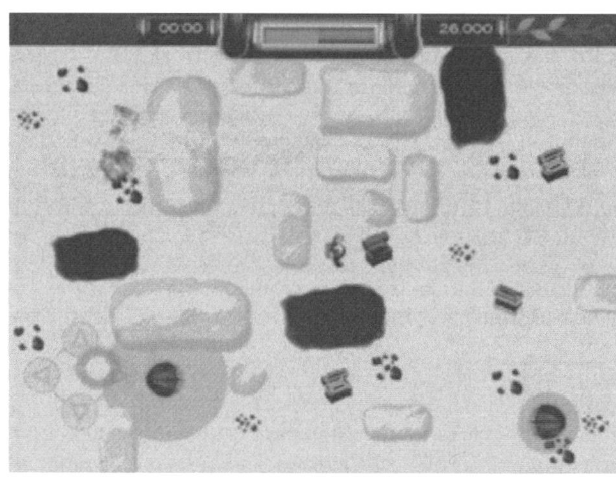

Figure 2b Easy Fun Key (Adventure) - Low Visual Aesthetics

Referring to Lim, Lee and Kim [24] concepts of user interactivity, the interaction styles most relevant to the games interaction in this study were movement speed, movement range, and response speed. The player interacts with the user interface with a navigation tool. The game begins as the character first explores. The player's goal is to successfully grow a plant on planet Mars. Every time 100 points are scored, a leaf is grown; conversely, the plant will shed a leaf every time 100 points are lost. There is no level in this game. The character explores the Red Planet, encountering aliens, falling objects and dust storms. The player must ensure that that the oxygen level is sufficient enough to carry out the mission. Destroying aliens earns points, which helps grow a leaf to sustain oxygen levels. Opening treasure chests, either accumulates bonus points or loses points, as the player randomly encounters aliens in the treasure chests.

V. METHODS

The objectives of this study were: (i) to examine if a variation of visual aesthetic level influences perceived game usability. (ii) to measure the level of game engagement of the two different game versions. In order to evaluate perceived game usability, the constructs related to pragmatic quality (PQ) of the *AttrakDiff* instrument were utilized to gather data. Similarly, the constructs related to visual aesthetics quality (VA) of the *AttrakDiff* instrument were used to gather perception of visual aesthetics data [25]. PQ is comprised of seven bi-polar items, and is related to the perceived usability assessing ease of use and whether users are attaining their goals by playing the games. Similarly, VA consists of 7 bi-polar items, aimed to measure the perceived attractiveness of the user interface. The game scores for all the participants were recorded. The procedure involved a within-subjects test whereby the same participant played both game versions. A convenience sample frame of 27 participants was chosen for this study as students 18-35 years old were recruited on a university campus. This age group represents approximately 30% of the population who plays game on their mobiles [26]. Each participant was assigned randomly to either the low or high visual aesthetic game version in order to ensure high internal validity. This also ascertains that two equivalent groups are created, as per the law of probability [27]. At the end of each 10-minute game session, participants were requested to complete the 7-items of the PQ and the 7-items of the VA section of the AttrakDiff instrument. In the future, user engagement will be measured using the *User Engagement Scale* (UES), a self-report instrument using a 31-item questionnaire to capture the six domains of experience [28]. The investigator plans to collect data using the UES tool afterwards at a later date

VI. ANALYSIS

Two results are reported from the AttrakDiff instrument using a one-way ANOVA within-subjects test. The SPSS result for the VA dependent variable shows $F(1,26)=4.056$, $p=0.054$. The mean value of the high visual aesthetic value interface was reported to be 22.26 whereas the mean value of the low aesthetic quality was 18.63; this implies that participants perceived a difference in terms of visual look and feel of the game versions, but given that $p>0.05$, the difference was not statistically significant. From the mean values reported, participants recognized and showed preference to the high visual aesthetic version.

The PQ dependent variable reveals Greenhouse-Geisser F-statistic as $F(1, 26) = 0.09$, p-value=0.925, and since $p>0.05$, this implies that the two game versions were not significantly different from each other; we fail to reject the null hypothesis. In other words, game usability of both game versions, low and high visual aesthetic qualities, was not perceived to be statistically different. Participants found both game versions to be practically usable. Therefore, a variation in visual aesthetic quality did not influence perceived usability in the Easy Fun Key game category. Furthermore, observed power was low at 0.051, which could imply the study lacked sufficient power to detect any effects. Thus, increasing the sample size of this study will certainly boost power statistics, thereby providing a robust result.

VII. CONCLUSION

The preliminary results in this study reveal that when the tablet (adventure) game interface was manipulated into low and high visual quality, game usability was not affected. One shortcoming of this study is the small sample size. Moreover, the participants' affinity to visual aesthetics in products is a confounding variable. The next stage is to screen participants using the (Centrality of Visual Products Aesthetics) CVPA instrument to understand to which degree they are sensitive to visual aesthetics in products [29]. The higher the CVPA score of the participants, the greater the level of accuracy in judging visual aesthetic quality. In future work, the level of user engagement in each game condition will be investigated to examine if the level of visual aesthetic qualities affect game engagement.

REFERENCES

[1] P. Koutsabasis and T. Istikopoulou, "Perceived Website Aesthetics by Users and Designers", International Journal of Technology and Human Interaction, vol. 9, no. 2, pp. 39-52, 2013.M. Wysocki, Ctrl-Alt-Play Essays on Control in Video Gaming. Jefferson, NC: McFarland Publisher, 2013.

[2] S. Mahlke, "User Experience of Interaction with Technical Systems", Doctoral dissertation. The Technische Universität, Berlin, Germany, 2008.

[3] E. Law, P. van Schaik, and V. Roto, "Attitudes towards user experience (UX) measurement", International Journal of Human-Computer Studies, vol. 72, no. 6, pp. 526-541, 2014.

[4] H. O'Brien and E. Toms, "Examining the generalizability of the User Engagement Scale (UES) in exploratory search", Information Processing & Management, vol. 49, no. 5, pp. 1092-1107, 2012.

[5] D. Norman and S. Draper, User centered system design. Hillsdale, N.J.: L. Erlbaum Associates, 1986.

[6] B. Carr, "Applying cultural and critical theory to video game aesthetics," Southern Mass Communication Journal, vol. 27, no. 3, pp. 1–25, 2012.

[7] A. Sutcliffe et al., "User engagement by user-centred design in e-Health", Philosophical Transactions of the Royal Society A: Mathematical, Physical and Engineering Sciences, vol. 368, no. 1926, pp. 4209-4224, 2010.

[8] L. Candy and E. Edmonds, "The role of the artifact and frameworks for practise-based research", in Routledge Companion to Art-based Research, 1st ed., M. Biggs and H. Karlsson, Eds. London: Routledge, 2011, pp. 120-138.

[9] A. Arlander, "Characteristics of Visual and performing arts", in The Routledge Companion to Research in the Arts, 1st ed., M. Biggs and H. Karlsson, Ed. NY: Routledge, 2011, pp. 315–332.

[10] N. Lazarro, "The 4 Fun Keys",Xeodesign.com, 2004. [Online].Available:http://www.xeodesign.com/whyweplaygames.html. [Accessed: 22- Jan- 2016]

[11] G. Crawford, Video gamers. London: Routledge, 2012.

[12] N. Cila, "The dimensions of users' fun experiences with consumer products", MSc Thesis, Middle East Technical University, 2008.

[13] B.R.Dubbels, "Distinguishing Games, Work, Fun, Flow and Play: A Framework for Design, Development, & Gamification." INTENSIONS ISSUE 7: Fun and Games – Playing to the Limit. York University Press, Toronto, ON: CANADA, 2014.

[14] M. Hassenzahl, "The Thing and I: Understanding the Relationship Between User and Product", in Funology: From Usability to Enjoyment, 1st ed., M. Blythe, K. Overbeeke, A. Monk and P. Wright, Ed. Dordrecht: Kluwer Academic Publishers, 2003, pp. 31-42.

[15] D. Beardslee, "Mind Mapping", Rochester Institute of Technology, NY, 2003.

[16] J. C. Herz. "Joystick nation," Little, Brown and Company. 1997.

[17] J. Lee and C.-Y. Im, "A Study on User Centered Game Evaluation Guideline Based on the MIPA Framework," Human Centered Design Lecture Notes in Computer Science, pp. 84–93, 2009.

[18] M. Federoff, "Heuristics and usability guidelines for the creation and evaluation of fun in video games", MA Thesis, Indiana University, 2002.

[19] A. Rollings and E. Adams, Andrew Rollings and Ernest Adams on game design. Indianapolis, IN: New Riders, 2003.

[20] C. Crawford, Chris Crawford on game design. Indianapolis, IN: New Riders, 2003.

[21] K. Salen and E. Zimmerman, Rules of play. Cambridge, Mass.: MIT Press, 2003.

[22] A. Tuch, J. Bargas-Avila, and K. Opwis, "Symmetry and aesthetics in website design: It's a man's business", Computers in Human Behavior, vol. 26, no. 6, pp. 1831-1837, 2010.

[23] N. Tractinsky, "Aesthetics in Information Technology: Motivation and Future Research Directions", in Human–Computer Interaction and Management Information Systems: Foundations . Advances in Management Information Systems, 1st ed., P. Zhang and D. Galletta, Ed. Armonk, NY: M.E. Sharpe, 2006, Vol 5, pp. 330–347.

[24] Y. Lim, S. Lee, and D. Kim, "Interactivity Attributes for Expression-oriented Interaction Design", International Journal of Design, vol. 5, no. 3, pp. 113–128, 2011.

[25] M. Hassenzahl and N. Tractinsky, "User experience - a research agenda", Behaviour & Information Technology, vol. 25, no. 2, pp. 91-97, 2006.

[26] "Entertainment Software Association: Game Player Data", 2015. [Online]. Available: http://www.theesa.com/wp-content/uploads/2015/04/ESA-Essential-Facts-2015.pdf. [Accessed: 22- Jan 2016] "Entertainment Software Association: Game Player Data", 2015. [Online]. Available: http://www.theesa.com/wp-content/uploads/2015/04/ESA-Essential-Facts-2015.pdf. [Accessed: 22 Jan 2016]

[27] B. Johnson and L. Christensen, Educational Research: Quantitative, Qualitative,and Mixed Approaches, 5th ed. London: Sage Publications, 2013.

[28] H. O'Brien and E. Toms, "The development and evaluation of a survey to measure user engagement", J. Am. Soc. Inf. Sci., vol. 61, no. 1, pp. 50-69, 2010. [28]

[29] P. H. Bloch, F. F. Brunel, and T. J. Arnold, "Individual Differences in the Centrality of Visual Product Aesthetics: Concept and Measurement," J Consum Res Journal of Consumer Research, vol. 29, no. 4, pp. 551–565, 2003.

A Model Driven Approach For Adaptive User Interfaces Specification: User, Task and Environment Impact

Hajer Taktak, Ines Riahi, Faouzi Moussa
CRISTAL Laboratory, National School of Computer Sciences, Manouba University, Tunisia
Email: taktakhajer@gmail.com, ines.riahi@yahoo.fr, faouzimoussa@gmail.com

Abstract— **The development of ubiquitous applications is inherently complex. The adaptation process enhances the efficiency of an application by the user interface design based on several essential steps such as: system modeling, task analysis, user profiling and interface specification. A number of different approaches have been proposed to build context-aware user interfaces. In this literature, the Human-Computer interaction, namely, the task analysis is often managed without explicitly integrating the user model. This latter is operated inside a context model and has few impacts on the interaction during its progress. In order to deal with this situation, we propose an adaptive user interface based on a model driven architecture that would transform an initial task model to an interaction model through the integration of environment information, user profile and tasks to be performed. The proposed approach takes advantages of the ontology written in Web Ontology Language (OWL) in order to define user's profile and of domain ontology for persons suffering from disabilities. The abstract task model is formalized as a Petri Net that analyzes the communication flows between users, environment and tasks.**

Keywords-Human-computer interaction; user model; task model; Petri Net; MDA; TuneIn.

I. INTRODUCTION

"Ubiquitous computing is the method of enhancing computer use by making many computers available throughout the physical environment, making them effectively invisible to the user" [1]. According to this definition, the pervasiveness is guaranteed by defining dynamic users and environmental data. The user interfaces should be able to react according to the heterogeneous environment and the different users' characteristics.

Human-computer interaction, with increasingly more complex environments and user capabilities, has become a major issue. What made this issue more challenging is the emergence of the ubiquitous computing leading to new forms of interactions. The purpose is to know which information is the most appropriate for a specific user in the current environment and to improve the interaction user-system quality in such smart environments [2] [3].

The user interfaces are commonly deduced from a task model that defines elementary actions and user's activities. Indeed, it is the best way to ensures effectiveness of the application that would allow users to reach their goals and perform their tasks [4]. However, from the user task model, it is hard to provide enough information about the user abilities, preferences, goals and activities. In addition, this model does not exhibit the impact of the environment on the user system. For example, it is impossible to specify if the user has a handicap that prohibits the standard interaction mode. Therefore, during the user interface design process, it is important to consider all relevant data involved in the interfaces personalization. In order to address this issue, the proposed approach is based on how a design method is able to explicitly specify the link between the task and the user and to generate personalized contents of the user interfaces. The aim is to achieve a Human-Computer system where the interaction would become aware of contextual variations depending on the user and/or the environment in which they perform.

This paper is organized as follows: Section 2 introduces the state of the art of interface specification researches. In Section 3, we present the user-task interaction model based on a user profile allowing the creation of applications suiting different user needs and a task model able to gather information and to deduce the user interface elements. We then demonstrate the applicability of the system referring to a case study for different persons operating in several environments.

II. RELATED WORKS

The researches on user interface specification have focused on context, user and task modeling. This section presents a description of different methods for creating context-aware architectures.

Many works have been interested in the adaptive interface design. In the table I, we present a brief review of the literature on conceptual modeling of computer applications and adaptive interfaces. Through this study, we are going to analyze the existing solutions and examine the complexity, tooling and adaptation process associated with them. We have deduced comparison criteria to determine the advantages and disadvantages of each approach in the related works. The framework CAMELEON [5] used the User Interface extended Markup Language (UsiXML), one of the most advanced Human-computer interaction (HCI) approaches. User interfaces were defined at a high abstraction level. This tool is compatible with a Model Driven Architecture (MDA) [19] and exploits user and environment ontologies. Nevertheless, it does not provide a mechanism for interface validation. This gives rise to additional efforts of the designers. Limbourg *et al.* proposed a graph transformation based approach. It did not discuss the context model and had been only interested in presentation adaptation [6]. Vanderdonckt proposed a method for developing user interfaces based on MDE. His approach has been focused on presentation, content and data adaptation [7]. Therefore, the context model is not well defined and does not use ontologies while defining the user profile. The proposed approach should be able to identify the activity of the user, so as to provide the required contextual information at run and design time. Besides, the adaptation needs to focus on user's general and specific information (preferences, abilities, physical condition, age, gender, etc.). It also requires the verification of the accuracy and the reliability through an interface validation process.

TABLE I. MEETING OF IDENTIFIED CRITERIA IN SOME RELATED WORKS

	task consideration	**Context Model**		**Tooling**	**User interface validation**	**Ontology use (explicit user representation)**	**Interface adaptation**	**Adaptation way**
		User	**Environment**					
CAMELEON[5]	Yes	User ontology	Environment ontology	UsiXML	No	Yes	Presentation and content adaptation	Automatic/Manual
TOMATO[6]	Yes	Context Model		TOMATO-L Prolog	No	No	Presentation adaptation	Semi-automatic
MDE approach[7]	Yes	Context model		UsiXML	No	No	Presentation and content	--
Hachani *et al.* [8]	Yes	Context model		EMF/ ATL	No	No	Content adaptation	Semi-automatic
COMODE[9]	No	Context model based on OWL Ontologies		EMF/ OCL2.0/ UML	No	Yes	Content Adaptation	--
Bacha *et al.* [10]	Yes	User Profile	Location Time Frame External events	BPMN/ UIML/ Ontology	No	Yes	Content adaptation	Semi-automatic
Riahi *et al.*[4]	Yes	Knowledge base		Petri Net/ PNML	Yes	No	Content adaptation	Semi-automatic

Some architectures do not consider an explicit interaction between users and task and do not concentrate enough on the information provided by users, especially their disabilities. The majority of literature works are interested in context-aware interfaces generation regardless of user's task and/or user's profile. Other works have defined ontologies for user and environment with restricted data. For example, Bacha [10] focused on the information that should be provided in each situation without considering the design elements and the user requirements. He also restricted the user's description by just identifying few criteria considered as relevant (e.g., user identification, user demographics data). Nevertheless, by linking a domain ontology to a user profile ontology, we would have dynamic interface changes considering as much user's properties (e.g., cognitive, sensorial and physical abilities, activities, etc.) as possible. Bacha based his approach on a context model to generate semi-automatic user interfaces for only two methods; automatic form filling and query enhancement. This approach lacks an interface validation process.

A complementary study has been done about context-aware approaches. The majority of literature works are interested in context-aware interfaces generation without user task and/or user profile's consideration. These applications are able to gather, manage, evaluate and disseminate context information [11][12][13]. For these platforms, none of them fully satisfies an explicit interaction between the user and task models able to dynamically generate the user interface.

While defining an adaptive user interface, the task model is useful to:

- Assess the task complexity in terms of perception, analysis, decision and motor action of users in order to reach a goal.
- Describe existing systems in order to understand the design and analyze the restrictions and the way to overcome them.
- Analyze how users think the activities should be performed.

Hierarchical Task Analysis (HTA) [14], Concur Task Trees (CTT) [15], Business Process Model and Notation (BPMN) [16] and Hamsters [17] provide a particular set of elements that would be useful especially for a specific type of systems and users.

By analyzing different related works, we have noticed that systems usually have difficulties while assisting the user in performing the task. Indeed, the user's knowledge about the domain application, the display of type of preferences, and of the tasks and willingness to interact with the system are some of the elements that can be managed in a user model. They could significantly impact the task model and thus the interface generation [18].

After a careful review of definitions referring to user and task models, a key factor has been deduced so as to conduct the software development process. In order to define the task model and the transformation rules, we propose a model driven approach. The Model Driven Architecture (MDA) of the Object Management Group (OMG) represents an example of the Model Driven Engineering (MDE) that is a software development approach family based on the use of models in the software construction [19]. MDA uses models in various steps of software development cycle. It recommends the elaboration of (i) the Computation Independent Model (CIM); (ii) Platform Independent Model (PIM) and (iii) Platform Specific Model (PSM). In fact, diverse aspects of the business process and the supporting software system are captured in models and are automatically transformed to the source code of a desired platform [20].

Using this concept of MDA, the system should transform task models formalized as CTT, BPMN or Petri Net in order to provide interaction ones. An adequate mapping should be done between the CIM, PIM and PSM levels.

Following our advanced literature review regarding the model transformations, we have decided to use Petri Net formal language [4] for task modeling as it is enforceable and has many techniques for an automatic verification of interface properties (boundedness, liveness ,etc.). We also justify the use of Petri Net by its ability to guarantee the validity of the interface. In fact, the essential reason behind this choice is that the Petri Nets-based models can reliably describe the aspects of concurrency, parallelism and dynamism which are fundamental features of ubiquitous environment. A domain ontology and a profile have also been used as elements that improve the interface personalization process.

III. USER-TASK INTERACTION MODEL

Reviewing the literature solutions, we have identified three main entities in the domain of adaptive user interfaces: *user, task* and *environment*. The major challenge is to get an interaction model according to the entities previously cited. Our interests have been focused on the user and task models impact on an adaptive user interface.

Indeed, the user affects the task model to dynamically modify the interaction model depending on his profile features such as disabilities or his environment. Let us consider an example of the radio application "TuneIn", a mobile application offering the ability to listen to streaming audio of many radio stations worldwide [21]. Basically, "TuneIn" is not aware of the environment and the user's changes. It presents an interface which is unable to modify its contents or change its behavior. In Figure 1, we present screenshots of the current application where the car mode provides a simplified user-interface to have a quick access to the application's most used features. This functionality does not sufficiently satisfy the context awareness in terms of environment, user and task's auto-detection. In fact, as shown in Figure 1, while the user is driving, the use of the car mode icon is obligatory. The vocal command requires a click on the search icon. Even if the environment conditions are not in favor to physically manipulate the interface, the user must interact with buttons. Thus, as described previously, the voice recognition is not automatic and the user should specify his context of use (driving) and his interaction mode. This leads to undesirable manipulation of an interface since the operation is potentially dangerous.

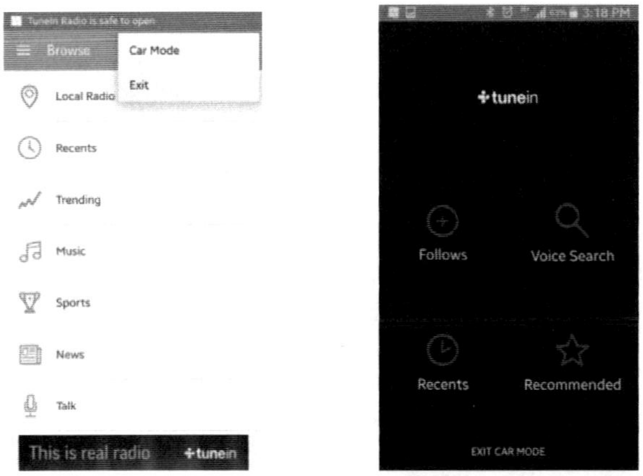

Figure 1. TuneIn Screenshots

The proposed improvements could concern user's interest and preferences (playlist, song's language, etc.) as well as user's capabilities. Therefore, based on the user profile, a blind person can interact with "TuneIn" exclusively through the voice recognition. Our research aims to make adaptive user interfaces detect the user and the environmental changes through user's profile and sensors (i.e. accelerometer).

As seen in Figure 2, the user model, combined with the environment and the task model, is able to generate a different task model (user task interaction model). To characterize this new model, we emphasize each environment parameter and the corresponding user and task.

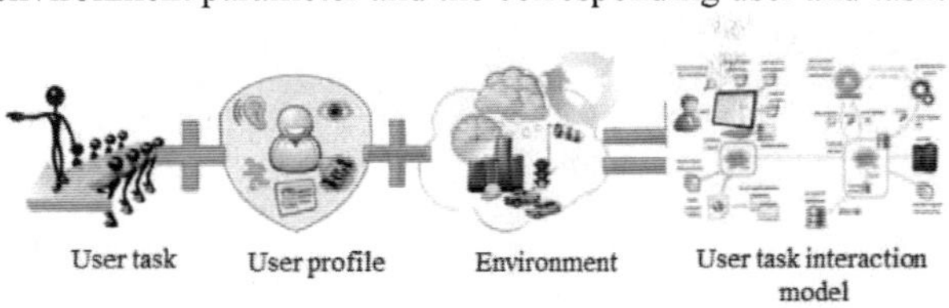

Figure 2. The user task interaction model according to the user and the environment

The user task interaction model is an alteration of elementary actions depending on users and the environment (Figure2). Indeed, any change that occurs at one of these models will impact the actions to be performed on the interfaces.

The key features of our approach are:

- Give a general and explicit representation of the user when specifying the interface.
- Get user information from a profile ontology strongly linked to domain ontology (e.g., person diseases/disabilities) for better understanding and easier interface modeling in a specific domain.
- Get generic interfaces workable by any operator. The same user interface can be exploited by a normal person and a person with disabilities. Thus,

we ensure the ability to preserve usability across multiple contexts of use [22].

- Exploit the strength and the advantages of an MDA approach to define the interaction model.
- Conceptualize the context in user interface design.
- Improve the usability and simplify the creation process.
- Reduce the complexity and ensure the validity of the interfaces.
- Provide the needed information timely and properly.
- Avoid the development of each system (or system type) in its own way with no common architecture currently available.
- Provide a set of models ensuring a dynamic interface generation depending on the user, the task and the environment in which he acts.

Thus, this work ensures the built of a standard architecture offering genericity and flexibility in smart environment. There is a need to dynamically create models that could be supported by a specific person in such environment. In order to do so, we propose an automatic model manipulation based on MDA transformation. We have been especially interested by the CIM to PIM transformation. The interaction model is deduced from the CIM representing the abstract task without showing the system structures' details. It focuses on the elementary actions to perform. The relevant information of the user and the environment is specified while defining the transformation rules. Our method should be able to automatically translate the CIM level to a PIM covering functional and environmental aspects.

Through the transformation rules, the user-task interaction model is defined at the PIM level. The interaction model is complete, generic and understandable. It includes the different information from the user, environment and task. The proposed architecture resumes our interaction model as shown in Figure 3:

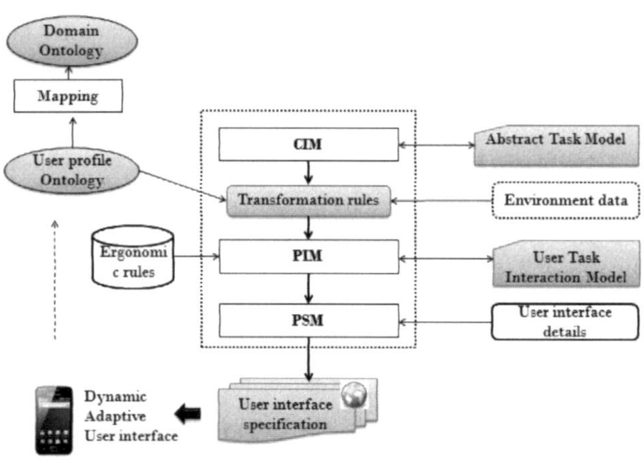

Figure 3. The proposed approach

In this architecture, we have focused on how the user actions can be influenced by the profile in a ubiquitous environment. The context is composed of static and profiled information considered as high persistence information. They are grouped in the profile ontology that communicates with domain ontology for better precision. This data is defined by the user while using his smartphone. Sensed context corresponds to information captured from sensors. In our case, this data constitutes the environment. This aspect is not addressed in this paper.

The user profile ontology is mapped to the domain ontology while the environmental data is captured through sensors. During the MDA model transformation, the PIM level holds a Petri Net Markup language (PNML) file enhanced by informational variables and user requirements. Besides, each graphic component is associated to informational and command variables.

As seen in Figure 4, the transformation consists in creating a target model from a source model by rules that describe how one or more constructs from the source model should be replaced by one or more constructs in the target model [19]. The transformation exploited in this work is an exogenous transformation meaning that the mapping of the models is written in different domain specific language [20] (as shown in Figure 4).

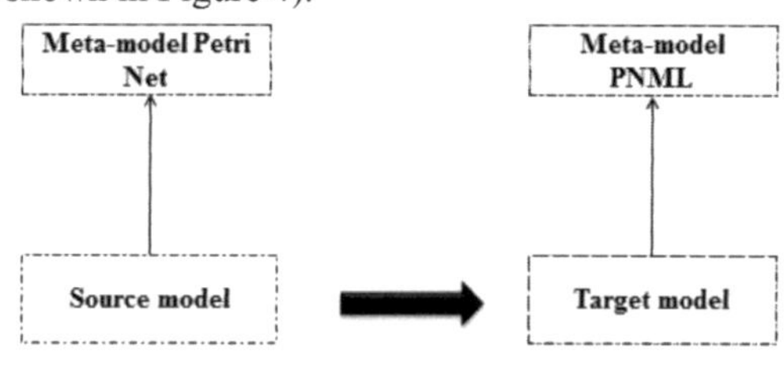

Figure 4. Exogenous transformation

To specify the source meta-model used in our approach, we have involved the meta-model proposed by our research team which consists in a process modeling based on elementary structures. This guarantees a prior validation of interfaces and saves considerable time in the development cycle of the user interface. In Figure 5, all the user's actions and components context behavior (elementary or composed) are sorted according to typical compositions: sequential, parallel, alternative, choice, iterative or of-closure. We present below, the meta-model of this process.

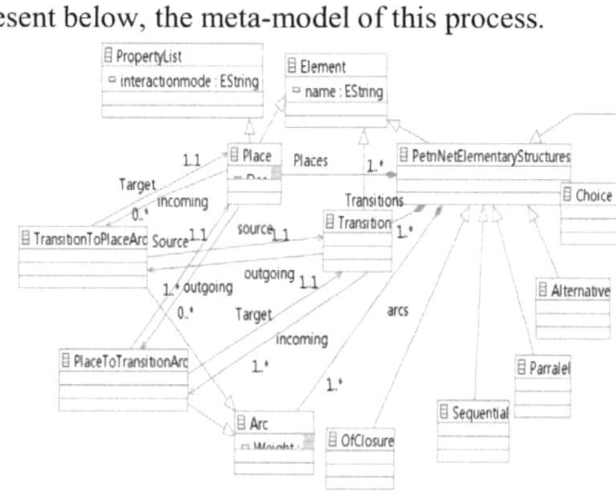

Figure 5. PetriNet Meta-Model

The target model is a PNML file aware of transformations' changes. In fact, the choice of the PNML is explained by its reliability, universality and mutuality. The main idea of PNML is that any kind of Petri net can be considered to be a labeled graph. In particular, all information that is specific to a particular kind of Petri net can be captured in labels. In the CIM to PIM transformation, Petri Net is used as an input to be transformed depending on the user profile. This step will result in a PNML file which preserves the validation features of Petri Net. Then, we use this PNML file to support the transition to a user interface markup language (UIML) to generate the interface. By this phase, we are able not only to treat context parameters affecting the user interface behavior but also to keep using the benefits of Petri Net modulation especially its validity when moving from graphical model to a markup languages. The PNML meta-model is illustrated in the Figure 6:

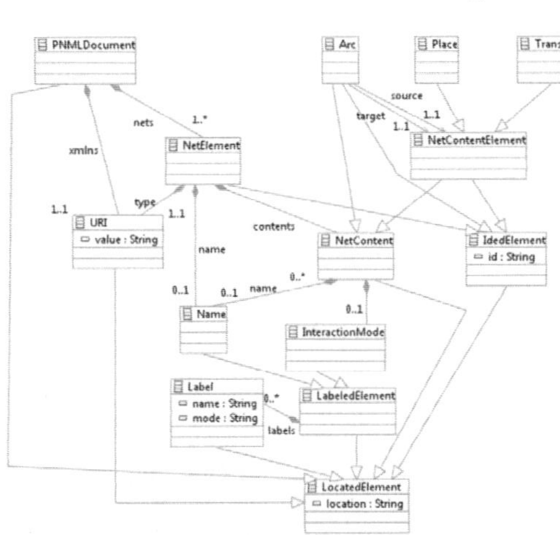

Figure 6. PNML Meta-Model

We define the transformation rules through three different levels as shown in Figure 7:

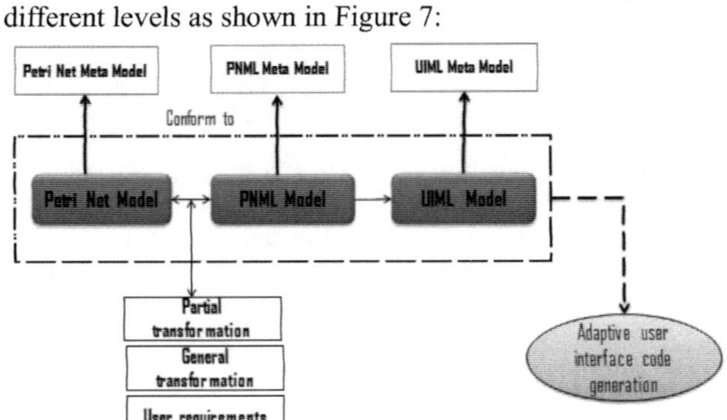

Figure 7. Transformation rules between CIM and PIM levels

The partial level concerns the transformation of some informational data of the model (e.g., the kind of music to be streamed). The general level deals with the transformation of the entire model (e.g., voice recognition). The user requirements level is based on the identification and the modification of the user's requirements according to the current situation (e.g., buttons, size, color). The user task parameters such as control and informational variables constitute the user requirements. They are mandatory while specifying an interface managing different types of context.

IV. CASE STUDY

For application and evaluation, we have conducted a case study with a view of the radio application "TuneIn" presented in Section III. The proposed model has improved the interface behavior and has allowed the combination of several entities aspects depending on the context of use (e.g., user abilities). We have modeled and defined different scenarios in order to get personalized interfaces that respond to environmental and requirements changes. The main purpose is to enable the application to adjust to its context of use and to acquire as much data. The first user is a blind person; he manipulates the interface only by voice recognition. The second person suffers from a visual impairment; he cannot see application contents properly. The third one is a normal person being attracted by rock music. If the device is used outdoor and that the user is driving, we may experience another interaction process model.

One of the problems rising from this case study is how to dynamically adapt the interface to the user profile and the environment in which he operates. The first step of our approach is the user information modeling. The architecture shows three main components. Those components are:

- The user profile (Figure 8): It describes the user information modeling. We have defined a general, yet extendable ontology able to adapt to the needs of every application, maintaining at the same time a general common structure so as to satisfy portability and communication between different applications [18]. The used ontology is mostly static and permanent. More dynamic information is captured from the environment. The figure below defines the user profile ontology upper level classes as defined in Protégé. We have used the information introduced by the user concerning his disability (blind, nearsighted, normal) and his preferences (playlist, song's language, etc.).

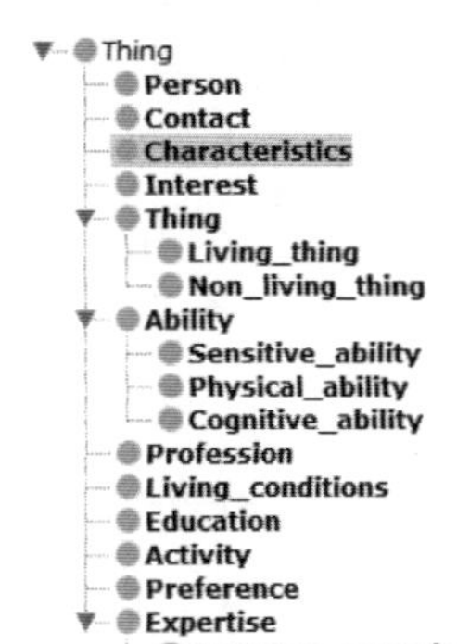

Figure 8. User Profile Ontology

- The domain ontology: It allows the retrieval of the diseases' characteristics (e.g., diseases types, symptoms, causes and treatment). We have used the Generic Human Disease Ontology (GHDO) [23] in order to deduce actions to operate. In fact, GHDO defines what the person's level of functioning is and what the needs of persons with various levels of disability, impairments, activity limitations and participation restrictions are. It defines the domain that helps us to describe changes in body function and structure, what a person with a health condition can do in a standard environment (his capacity level).
- The environment: it describes the different values captured via sensors. For our example, the environment can be geographical data (position), accelerometer, etc.

In order to change "TuneIn" interface behavior, we have specified the CIM to PIM transformation. The CIM level receives the abstract task. This latter is defined as a task with no specific type. It is useful to define a process at an abstract level as shown in Figure 9.

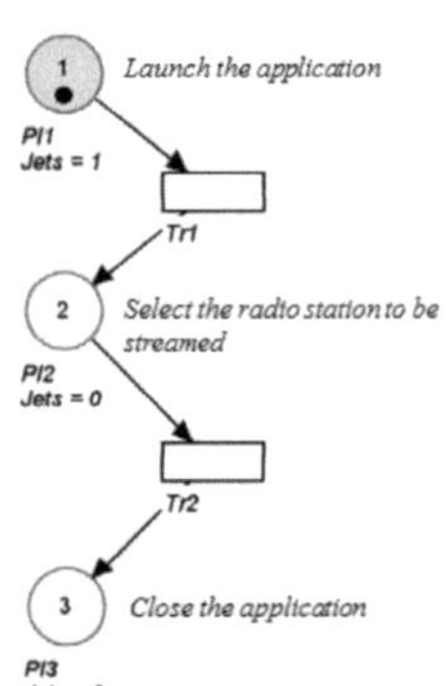

Figure 9. The abstract task Petri Net of TuneIn application

According to the abstract task and the defined rules, we deduce the new user task interaction model. By identifying the transformation rules, three new interaction models appear according to every occurred change.

Partial transformation: for a person interested by rock music, the system computes partial transformation meaning that some elementary structures are extracted from the initial Petri Net. A normal person that defines his interests (rock music) should have a restriction in the information seen in the interface. The context has the ability to change the interaction process by deleting some entities and keeping only the most significant ones. The environment information captured through sensors (accelerometer) shows that, when the user is driving, then a voice command is needed.

User requirements transformation: For a person having a binocular acuity of distant vision, the system communicates with the domain ontology and decides which are the most suitable representation and interface objects' interaction of the according users' needs. In this case, in order to generate an interface related to a nearsighted person (big characters), we should specify the size of variable information and instructions (text boxes, buttons, labels, etc.) The variable output size switches from 12 to 18 according to the user's disability.

General transformation: For a blind person, the user capabilities will influence the generation of the interaction process model. To know about these changes, it is necessary to get user capabilities information through profiles. We have used domain ontology (user abilities) from which we deduce static characteristics of a disease. For this transformation, we do not need to analyze environmental data because the only way to interact with the interface is voice command.

Atlas Transformation Language (ATL) is applied in the context of the transformations previously cited [24]. The case study of the blind person requires a transformation program that converts an initial Petri Net model to a PNML file computing data through voice recognition. Figure 10 shows some parts of the ATL transformation.

```
rule Transition {
    from
        e : PetriNet!Transition,
        user :User!UserProfile
    to
        n : PNML!Transition
        (
            name <- name,
            id <- e.name,
            userRequirements<-e.userRequirments,

        ),
        name : PNML!Name
        (
            labels <- label
        ),
        label : PNML!Label
        (
            text <- e.name
        ),
        userRequirements : PNML!userRequirements
        (
            Ability : User!Ability
        ( (
            labels <- label
        ),
        label : PNML!Label
        (
            text <- user.Ability
        ),
        ),
        )
}
```

Figure 10. An excerpt from ATL transformation rules

The "transition" rule generates tags according to the user requirements that constitute the crossing conditions from one action to another. The "place" rule generates a PNML file that contains the interaction mode according to the user disability (Blind) from the place elements. This is achieved by adding the appropriate tag (mode) inside the informational variables. The elements of the PNML file correspond to those generated by place, transition and arc rules. We do not need to specify user characteristics because they are directly extracted from the user profile (e.g., user.Ability).

The transformation rules define how the different entities have the ability of mutually affecting each other in order to generate a contextualized user interface. The proposed model allows the combination of several entities aspects (user, task and environment). Based on this combination, we have deduced the new interaction model showing the actions to be performed on the interface. From the CIM to PIM transformation described above, we can notice that the PNML file has been extended with the interaction mode tag described in Figure11. If the system detects dynamically that the user is blind, the interaction mode switches directly to voice command.

```
<contents xsi:type="Place" id="select the radio station to be streamed">
  <name>
    <labels text="select the radio station to be streamed"/>
  </name>
  <interactionmode>
  <labels mode="VoiceCommand"/>
  </interactionmode>
</contents>
```

Figure 11. An excerpt from the extended PNML file

If the extracted user profile data concerns the user requirements (binocular acuity of vision, music preferences), they are directly defined in the PNML file as shown in Figure 12.

```
<contents xsi:type="Transition" location="32:9-35:10" id="t1">
    <name>
      <labels text="t1"/>
    </name>
    <userRequirements>
      <Ability>
       <labels text=«Binocular Acuity of Vision»/>
      </Ability>
    <preferences>
       <labels text=« Rock Music »/>
    </preferences>
   </userRequirements>
</contents>
```

Figure 12. An excerpt from the extended PNML file

The model guarantees the consideration of design specification before the implementation phase. From such an interaction process, we have kept the approach at an abstract level separating application reasoning from the implementation technology. The proposed model respects the MDA architecture to generate a code corresponding to a specific model deduced from users, environment and tasks. After defining the PIM level, we would be interested in the details specifying the system behavior on each particular platform's type [19] to finally generate a contextualized interface based on the user requirements.

V. CONCLUSION

This paper presented a MDA approach that considers user profile properties and environment information in order to generate an adaptive user interface and also to satisfy an exceptional interaction need of a disabled person. Our work transforms an initial Petri Net model to a PNML based interaction one by combining tasks, users and environment. We have focused on gathering all available user abilities and preferences, since an early design stage, in order to have as generic interface adaptation as possible. Thus, we would need to enhance the re-usability of transformation rules and complete the domain ontology integration so that we would retrieve relevant description which is able to dynamically modify the interface behavior according to its matching to the symptoms of different user's disabilities. This would build a PSM model to generate the relevant code. Furthermore, we plan to develop a critical context aware application from the modeling stage until the code generation in order to investigate runtime validation techniques. We are finally working on merging our approach with contextual web services creation.

REFERENCES

[1] M. Weiser, "Some computer science issues in ubiquitous computing," Communications of the ACM, 37(7), 1993, pp. 75-83.

[2] C. Bettini, O. Brdiczka, K. Henricksen, J. Indulska, D. Nicklas, A. Ranganathan, D. Riboni, "A survey of context modeling and reasoning techniques," In Pervasive and Mobile Computing, 2010, pp. 161-180.

[3] B. Schilit, N. Adams, N.L. Want, "Context-aware computing applications," In IEEE Workshop on Mobile Computing Systems and Applications, 1994, pp.85-90.

[4] I. Riahi, F. Moussa, "A formal approach for modeling context-aware human-computer system," Computers & Electrical Engineering, 2015, pp. 241–261.

[5] G. Calvary, J. Coutaz, D. Thevenin, Q. Limbourg, L. Bouillon, J. Vanderdonckt, "A Unifying Reference Framework for multi-target user interfaces," Interacting with Computers (IWC), 2003, pp. 289-308.

[6] Q. Limbourg, J. Vanderdonckt, "Transformational Development of User Interfaces with Graph Transformations," CADUI, 2004, pp.105-118.

[7] J. Vanderdonckt, "Model-Driven Engineering of User Interfaces: Promises, Successes, Failures, and Challenges," Proceedings of Annual Romanian Conference on Human-Computer Interaction 01/2008.

[8] S. Hachani, S. Dupuy-Chessa, A. Front, "Une approche générique pour l'adaptation dynamique des IHM au contexte," In Proc. IHM ACM Press, 2009, pp. 89-96.

[9] S. Vale, S. Hammoudi, "COMODE : A Framework for the developement of Context-aware Applications in the context of MDE," Internet and Web Applications and Services, ICIW, 2009,pp 261-266.

[10] F. Bacha, K. Oliveira, M. Abed, "A Model Driven Architecture Approach for User Interface Generation Focused on Content Personalization," In Proc.IEEE RCIS, 2011, pp. 1-6.

[11] J. Hussein, A. Colman, "An architecture based approach to context-aware adaptive software systems," Tech. rep., Faculty of Information and Communication Technologies (FICT) Swinburne University of Technology, 2011, pp. 154 - 163 .

[12] F. Buttussi, "A user-adaptive and context-aware architecture for mobile and desktop training applications," In: Proceedings of the 10th international conference on human computer interaction with mobile devices and services, MobileHCI, 2008, pp. 543–543.

[13] X. Qing, X. Han, M. Li, M. Liu, "A conceptual architecutre for adaptive human computer interface of a PT operation platform based on contet-awareness," Discret Dyn Nat Soc Journal, 2014, pp 1-7.

[14] J. Annett, "Hierarchical task analysis," Handbook of cognitive task design, 2003, pp. 17-35.

[15] F. Paternò, "ConcurTaskTrees: an engineered notation for task models," The handbook of task analysis for human-computer interaction, 2004, pp. 483-503.

[16] P. Wohed, W. van der Aalst, "On the Suitability of BPMN for Business Process Modelling," 4th International Conference on Business Process Management, 2006, pp 161-176.

[17] C. Martinie, P. Palanque, M. Winckler, "Structuring and composition mechanisms to address scalability issues in task models," in Human-Computer Interaction– Article in a conference proceedings INTERACT, 2011, pp 589-609.

[18] M. Golemati ,A. Katifori ,C. Vassilakis ,G. Lepouras, C. Halatsis, "Creating an Ontology for the User Profile: Method and Applications," RCIS 2007.

[19] J. Miller, J. Mukerji, "MDA Guide Version 1.0.1.," OMG, 2003.

[20] P. Hoyer, T. Kopp, S. Abeck, "A Model-Driven Development Approach Focusing Human Interaction," Advances in Computer-Human Interactions, ACHI , 2009, pp. 90-96.

[21] https://tunein.com/get-tunein/ [accessed March 2016]

[22] V. Alvarez-Cortes, V. H. Zárate Silva, B. E. Zayas Pérez, A. R. Uresti, A. Quintero Reyes, "User and Task Models Impact on an Adaptive User Interface for the Startup of a Power Plant," Software Engineering, 2007 ICSE,.

[23] M. Hadzic, E. Chang, "Ontology-based Support for Human Disease Study," Proceedings of the 38th Hawaii International Conference on System Sciences HICSS, 2005, pp.143a.

[24] S. Cuadrado, J. Guerra, E. J. de Lara,"A Component Model for Model Transformations," Software Engineering, IEEE Transactions on ,2014, pp.1042-1060.

Body Gesture Recognition Framework for 3D Interactive Systems

Choonsung Shin, Jisoo Hong, Yougmin Kim, Sung-Hee Hong, Hoonjong Kang
Realistic Media Platform Research Center
Korea Electronics Technologies Institute
Seoul, Republic of Korea
e-mail: {cshin, jhong, rainmaker, shhong, hoonjongkang}@keti.re.kr

Abstract—**This paper proposes a body gesture recognition framework for 3D interactive systems. For this purpose, we built the gesture recognition framework via sampling, pre-processing, quantification, and building an inference model using the hidden Markov model (HMM). Using this framework, gestures are detected and classified from 3D trajectory data in real time. Evaluation proved that our recognition system successfully supports 3D interactive systems. We also tested the proposed framework using 3D virtual training systems.**

Keywords- gesture recognition; 3D interaction.

I. INTRODUCTION

With the recent advance of 3D technologies, a number of studies have been proposed to understand and recognize users' positions and gestures. In a virtual environment, such information is very important in presenting a 3D immersive environment [1]. The 3D locations and gestures of the hands and a head are especially important in allowing users to interact naturally with the 3D environment and are widely used for interactive applications.

For this purpose, we proposed a 3D gesture recognition framework for 3D interactive applications. The proposed framework consists of 3D gesture recognition and inference components. The recognition component collects and preprocesses the 3D locations of the head and hands then extracts features and builds models for inferring gestures. We applied the hidden Markov model (HMM) for modeling and inferring gestures since the gestures are made in temporal sequence [2]. The inference component then detects and selects the target gesture from the 3D trajectory of body by inferencing probability of gesture candidates in real-time. The resulting gesture and position information are delivered to 3D interactive systems.

The remaining part of this paper is organized as follows. We first define target gestures for 3D interactive systems and then introduce the gesture recognition framework in Section II. We then show how we implemented our framework in Section III. Finally we conclude with future work in Section IV.

II. RECOGNIZING BODY GESTURES

A. Target Body Gestures

First we define the body's gestures that will be used for 3D interactive systems. We are interested in interactive systems where a user is set at a fixed position in front of the system. Thus we need to detect gestures from different parts of the body. We selected upper body gestures, hand gestures, and head gestures (see Figure 1). The head gestures include left, right, up, and down movements. The hand gestures are represented as grabbing, pointing, and releasing. The upper body gestures include left, right, up, down, and directional pointing gestures.

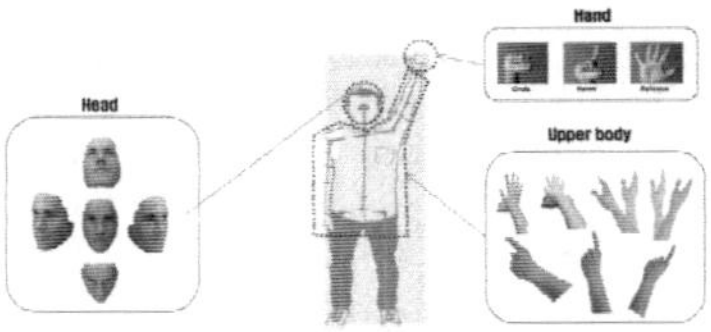

Figure 1. Target Body Gestures.

B. Body Gesture Recognition Framework

In order to recognize the gestures defined, we built a gesture recognition framework. Previous work has only focused on modeling and inferencing gestures [3]. Here we added more steps, such as gesture sampling, segmentation and labeling, pre-processing, quantification, and establishing an inference model. Figure 2 shows the overall procedure of building our gesture recognition framework.

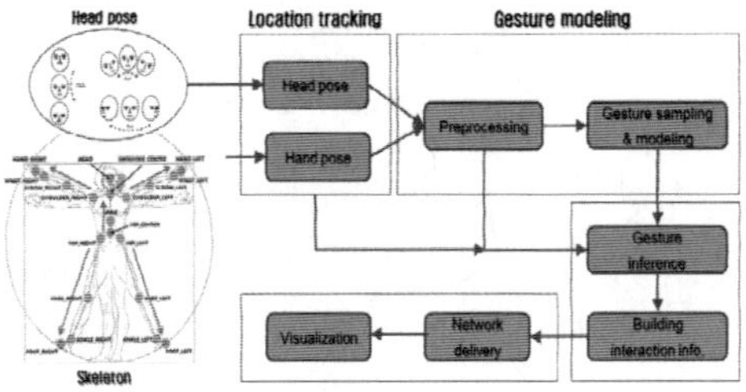

Figure 2. Overall Procedure of Body Gestures Modeling.

In the sampling, the framework collects the raw position data from a location tracking sensor. The sensor detects the body and generates the 3D position of the body parts. This sampling phase collects the raw data of all the body parts and extracts the segment of each body gesture. In the pre-processing phase, the noise is removed by filters, such as moving average, and the relative movement value is extracted for normalization. Afterward we reduce data dimension and extract features by using the k-means algorithm. Finally, we built an inference model with the features selected. As a body gesture consists of a temporal sequence, continuous machine learning algorithms are useful. We especially selected HMM since it is robust on individual differences of gestures and small numbers of samples.

C. Inferencing Body Gestures

The inference phase consists of sampling, pre-processing, detection, quantification, and inference. Thus the sampling, pre-processing, and quantification are the same as those of the modeling, but the detection and inferences are additionally required. In order to detect the existence of a gesture from 3D trajectory data, we assume that there is a small amount of 3D movement when a user is in the ready state. For this purpose, we apply a threshold to the 3D movement during a certain period of time called a window. The window ranges from 0.5 s to 2 s and is related to the length of a gesture. The amount of 3D movement is represented by the sum of the standard deviation of each axis. The threshold is less than the maximum value of the sum of the standard deviation of the gesture samples. When there is a gesture in the 3D trajectory, the quantification is applied to the trajectory data and the probability of each gesture is calculated from the inference model. Finally the gesture with the highest probability is selected as the result of the inference.

III. EVALUATION

We implemented it in a Windows 7 environment. In order to obtain fast data, we used a Microsoft Kinect version 2 sensor which provides a 1080p RGB image stream with a 640 x 480 depth map [4]. We then collected the 3D locations of the heads, hands, and upper bodies of study participants and modeled seven gestures made from hand trajectories. We selected eight upper body gestures: seven gestures (Nos. 2-8) and one ready statue (No. 1). We collected 203 gesture samples from three participants. We evaluated our framework based on a 10-fold cross validation.

As seen in Figure 3, the accuracy of the proposed framework is about 96% when three hidden nodes were used in the framework. The accuracy reached 98% when five hidden nodes were used. The accuracy was not improved even when more hidden nodes were used.

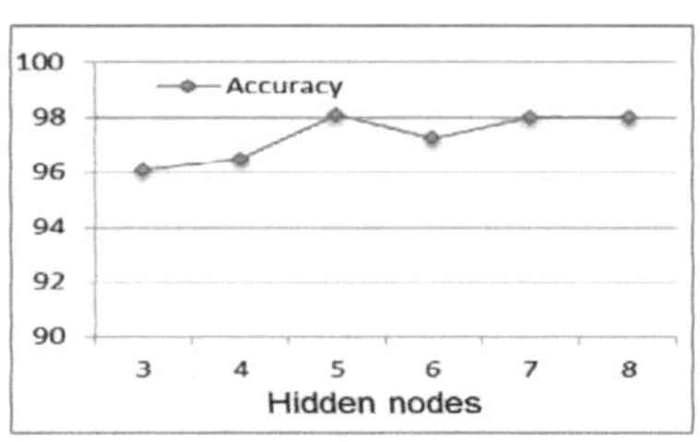

Figure 3. Accuracy of Body Gesture Recognition.

We also analyzed the quality of the individual gesture classification. We calculated the confusion matrix of the gesture recognition classification. As seen in Figure 4, the main errors were from the ready status. Three of the 25 ready status samples were misclassified as Gesture 2. Other gestures were correctly classified.

Gesture	1	2	3	4	5	6	7	8
1	**22**	**3**	0	0	0	0	0	0
2	0	**25**	0	0	0	0	0	0
3	0	0	**28**	0	0	0	0	0
4	0	0	0	**27**	0	0	0	0
5	0	0	0	0	**27**	0	0	0
6	0	0	0	0	0	**29**	0	0
7	0	0	0	0	0	0	**10**	0
8	0	0	0	0	0	0	0	**33**

Figure 4. Confusion Matrix of Body Gesture Recognition.

We also tested the proposed framework by connecting with two virtual training systems, as illustrated in Figure 5. One of the systems was a virtual train training simulator and another one was a virtual driving simulator. In order to detect a gesture from the continuous 3D trajectory of a hand, we used a 2-second window with a 0.5 second overlap. The framework then selected the gesture with the highest probability inferred from HMM in real-time. Finally the position data and resulting gesture is delivered to the systems.

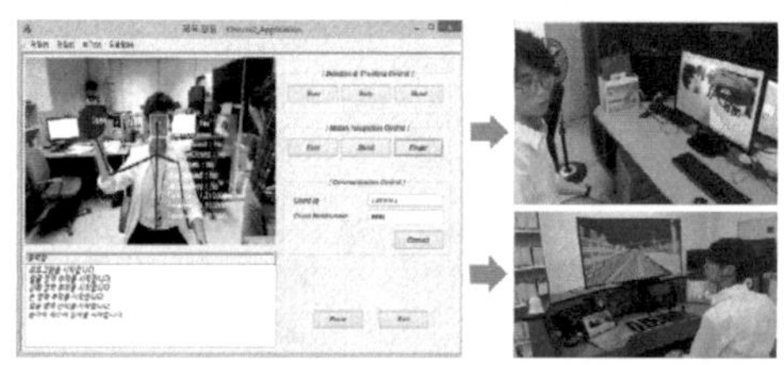

Figure 5. Testing with the Virtual Training System.

IV. CONCLUSION

This paper proposed a body gesture recognition framework for 3D interactive systems. For this purpose, the proposed framework collected, segmented, pre-processed, and quantified 3D trajectory data from a 3D tracking sensor and then built an inference model for recognizing body gestures. Later the framework detected and classified the gestures from the 3D trajectory data by inferencing their probabilities. We also evaluated the proposed framework and tested it with 3D interactive systems.

ACKNOWLEDGMENT

This paper is supported by the Ministry of Science, ICT, and Future Planning (MSIP) (Cross-Ministry Giga KOREA Project).

REFERENCES

[1] J. Weissmann and R. Salomon, "Gesture recognition for virtual reality applications using data gloves and neural networks," in Neural Networks, 1999. IJCNN '99. International Joint Conference on, Vol.3,1999, pp.2043-2046.

[2] Z. Ghahramani, "An Introduction to Hidden Markov Models and Bayesian Networks", International Journal of Pattern Recognition and Artificial Intelligence, Vol. 15, No 1, 2001, pp 9-42.

[3] C. Shin and B. Park, "3D gesture modeling and recognition for Immersive Virtual Reality", DHIP 2015, pp 59.

Evaluation of a Driver Assistant Client in the Context of Urban Logistics and Electric Vehicles

Christian Stolcis, Johan Buchholz, and Volkmar Schau

Chair of Software Technology
Friedrich Schiller University Jena, Germany
Email: {christian.stolcis, johan.buchholz, volkmar.schau}@uni-jena.de

***Abstract*—The use of Electric Vehicles (EVs) is limited. Uncertainty concerning the short range and the lack of solutions matching the users needs are factors that hinder widespread use of the technology in business and logistics contexts. In Smart City Logistik (SCL) project, a Driver Assistant Client (DAC) was developed to help to overcome fears, limited information and uncertainty in the context of urban logistics. To evaluate the users needs and intentions, an iterative and open approach was designed and consequently used. Triangulation helped to get the best possible insights out of each of three phases of development and the findings were used to improve the DAC. The beginning of the project was accompanied by a lot of uncertainty, so qualitative information was gathered to understand how the drivers work routines look like and which attitudes towards new technologies prevailed. A more quantitative approach helped to gather a broad range of opinions on specific usability topics, before the actual users will be asked about their daily experience with the system. This agile and iterative approach helped to identify important aspects while designing the DAC and to compare different solutions, e.g. regarding important functionalities, menu-structure, font, button-size, and other parameters. The implementation of these findings enabled the project partners to develop a broadly accepted user interface and system that will be used in electric vehicles in urban logistics.**

***Keywords*–Survey; Usability; Electric Vehicles.**

I. Introduction

Since the need of delivering goods increased massively in the past decade and will increase further in the next years [1], the use of Electric Vehicles (EVs) for last-mile delivery could help to reduce substantially the air and sound pollution, especially in inner cities. In fact, most researchers agree that even well beyond 2020, the capacity of batteries will not fit future range demands [2]. This restriction affects especially available EVs, that are designed for the transportation of goods. Therefore, many companies have qualms to use this new technology because of range limitations, low density of recharging stations and long charging time [3]. Nevertheless, no matter which technological restrictions appear with EVs compared to traditional vehicles, for most companies it all comes down to the ability to plan the vehicle usage, including the certainty that the planed tour can be done. In fact, many companies interviewed during the Smart City Logistik (SCL) project, have already tours within the range of an EV, or at least are able to adopt tours with little effort. The research project SCL pursues the goal to develop such a system, that provides important information on EV-specific restrictions and helps to overcome fears and to support the usage within urban logistics. As part of the German special federal research program for Information and Communication Technologies for Electric Mobility II (ICT II) [4], the SCL project supports the integration of EVs in fleets through the usage of Information and Communications Technology (ICT).

One of the most important parts in such a holistic system is the assistance of the driver. In a complex socio-technical system where EVs are used within urban logistics, the driver needs to cope with additional information (such as range, battery status, etc.) in order to fulfill his main task of delivering goods. To reduce stress and uncertainty resulting from these important additional parameters, a Driver Assistant Client (DAC) focussing on the needs of drivers was developed, evaluated and implemented as a prototype during the SCL project. Therefore, a concept for technology assessment was developed, combining existing methods from social and computer sciences for the specific project. In an agile managed project, we needed to focus on methods, that provided flexibility and direct user feedback to overcome different phases of non-knowledge, that came along with the novelty of the topic. The results help to achieve the goal, to develop and improve mockup and demonstrator along the users needs. This general concept can be applied to other projects in the field of computer-human interaction, that are confronted with similar conditions and challenges regarding uncertainty and user expectancies.

In Section II existing work regarding the DAC and the prototype evaluation will be outlined briefly, before a more detailed overview on the problem, the purpose of the DAC and its main functionality will be given (Section III). Subsequently, the research design to improve the DAC in an iterative procedure and to assess the users expectancies will be outlined. It consists of three main qualitative and quantitative surveys: In a first step, seven drivers were interviewed to get insights into their daily routines and attitudes towards supporting technology (Section IV) and the findings were used to build the prototype (Section V). Secondly, 43 participants tested two different DAC prototypes and evaluated them with a focus on usability (Section VI). The third part includes the development of the functional demonstrator and is accompanied by a beta-phase with a few drivers of EVs, followed by a qualitative interview. Additionally, a simulator-based test with a higher number of participants from logistic companies is part of the research design (Section VII). Finally, a short outlook and critical reflection of the used approach and the gathered results will conclude this paper (Section VIII).

II. State of the Art

Previous work on methods for software design show a broad range of techniques, that can be applied in different development stages. Cognitive walkthroughs, heuristic evaluation, formal usability inspections [5] offer interesting and valuable insights in a development process. More theoretical work focusses on the users needs and expectancies as relevant factors for technology acceptance. Factors that influence the use of a socio-technical system cover the perceived usefulness, the attitude towards using a technology and others [6], [7]. Other work in the field of DACs or EVs point out important factors, that are relevant in the given context [8], but focus too much on the economic decisions of private households and cannot be adapted completely to our project. Unfortunately, knowledge about important factors while using the DAC in a commercial context in EVs, is rare. When it comes to a long-term research project in a field, where user acceptance is rather unknown, a flexible methodology is needed, that provides different forms of knowledge in different project stages. Therefore, methods from social sciences were used. A qualitative research part is used to gather knowledge [9] and quantitative research helps to evaluate existing knowledge and design with a broader range of participants [10].

III. The Driver Assistance Client

In the context of urban logistics, the driver has to cope with a lot of information, which often comes along with stress and the insecurity about the actual range of an EV. Since the range depends on a lot of parameters (e.g., battery capacity, driving speed, weather conditions, weight, etc.), the consideration of all those influencing parameters would be a complex process while driving. To reduce stress and eliminate insecurity, the DAC was developed. Basically, it works as a navigation system, providing optimized routes for EV, considering different range-affecting parameters of the vehicle while focussing on the planned tour. At the start of a tour, the driver can retrieve the tour on the DAC, which is already optimized and considers all parameters for the EV he is using. During the tour, the driver will be navigated to each point, and informed about possible changes of the tour and all relevant information (e.g., traffic and weather conditions). Hereby the driver is relieved from thoughts about the range of the vehicle, because the tour is always optimized and adapted to changes, so that the driver will be able to perform his tour and drive back carefree to the starting point.

Since the DAC should assist the driver while driving and reduce the added complexity, it needs to be easy-to-use in a vehicle. To find an optimal way to support the driver we elaborated an approach for the realization of the DAC, where in each iteration the acceptance and usability has been evaluated systematically. The findings were used to improve further versions of the DAC.

IV. The Interview

In theoretical discourses on technology use, EV and driver assistance systems, different factors, that influence the attitude, expectations, and acceptability towards these technologies in general public, are described [6, p. 188] [7, p. 447]. Beside these common factors, there may be specific ones among employees in logistics who use EV, that result from their specific situation (e.g., the employer-employee relationship leads to an involuntary use of the system). In the first place, the professional drivers need to perform their work task without unwanted disruptions by technological peculiarities and EV-specific uncertainties. To overcome the theoretical debate on barriers and drivers of technology acceptance, empirical evidence was gathered in qualitative interviews. Seven drivers from different companies were interviewed, using a semi-structured guide that was developed in advance. The interviewees were asked about their individual common work tasks, their attitude towards new technologies in general and EVs in detail, their expectations towards a DAC and some demographic items as well as their employment biography. A content analysis of the interviews was conducted and the deductive-inductive creation of categories [11] shed light onto possible acceptance factors and requirements regarding a DAC in EV-based urban logistics. In theoretical debates, the general acceptance factors are described as perceived usefulness, perceived ease of use, the attitude towards using a technology [6, p. 188], and some models include the behavioural intention to use the system as well. These factors are influenced by moderators such as subjective norms, experience, the image of a technology, job relevance, output quality or the the voluntariness of use for example [7, p. 447]. We found empiric evidence in the interviews regarding these items. Using the computer-assisted qualitative data analysis software f4analyse [12], we found out, that the drivers tend to prefer a passive system, that gives them useful information on important events during their tour, while not forcing them to act in a single, specified way. Other hints pointed in the direction of up-to-date maps, estimation and inclusion of time and range restrictions, the ease of use of and favoured support while implementing the system. These important factors for technology users were considered, while developing the first versions of the DAC.

V. Building the Prototype

Taking into account the requirements that were identified in the interviews, as well as previous research, a first horizontal prototype was developed. Horizontal means in this case, that the prototype has no real functionality, and was designed as a draft for the evaluation of the user interface. Figure 1 shows the tour overview and Figure 2 shows the information overview of the prototype. Both figures offer an impression of the main design. The main menu has been arranged on the top to allow switching directly between the main views such as tour information, navigation, map, vehicle status, direct call, messages and common information. To allow the navigation through different information, the submenu is arranged on the left side in each view. Since the DAC should be used on a mobile device with touch screen, big buttons were used, enriched with understandable and clear icons. After login the user directly views the tour overview with all relevant information on stops and clients. While driving, the user will mainly use the navigation view, which represents the route guidance.

During the development of the first prototype, some details of the design were questioned. So, a second prototype was build, which offers the same basic functionality, but has a slightly different User Interface (UI) regarding the views. Figure 3 shows the tour overview for the second prototype. The main menu is also situated on the top of the screen and the submenu also on the left side, whereas the view of the

Figure 1. Tour overview of prototype 1

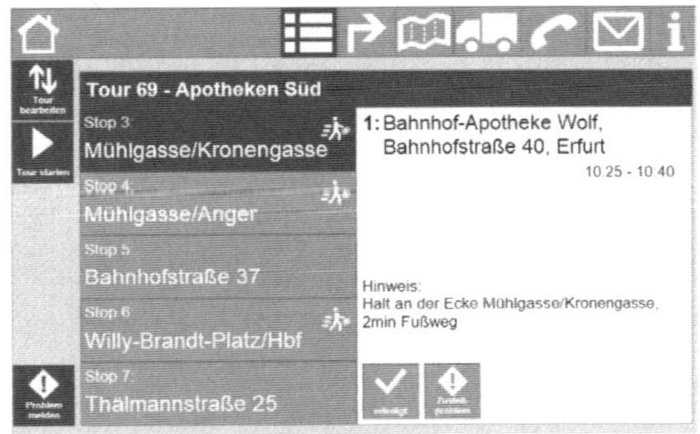

Figure 3. Tour overview of prototype 2

content is divided into two parts, the item list and the content of the selected item. In prototype 1, the list disappears when an item is selected, in prototype 2 the item list remains visual, so the user can always see which item is currently selected.

Another difference compared to prototype 1 is the overview of the main menu shown in Figure 4, which shows up directly after login. This should provide an overview about all available functionalities. Creating two prototypes allowed to evaluate more options and the advantages and disadvantages from slightly different views. The evaluation itself and the results are described in the next section.

VI. PROTOTYPE EVALUATION

After developing the first two DAC-prototypes, possible users were asked for feedback in an online survey, targeting possible difficulties that may appear while using EVs in logistics. Before the users performed some basic tasks using the two prototypes, they were asked about different aspects of usability, using a standardized questionnaire focussing on the EN ISO 9241-110 norm [13] , which was slightly adapted to the research context. For questions regarding the functions of the DAC, perceived ease of use, and intuitiveness, the user was asked to rank the specific characteristics of the prototypes on a 7-step-scale and to add qualitative information in free-text fields. Due to limitations in availability of interview partners at the partner companies who took part in the research project (and the resulting inefficiency to carry out the study on-site), an online questionnaire was developed using LimeSurvey [14], and an additional device with the DAC prototypes was brought to the partner companies. In each company, a contact person was instructed and responsible for conducting the evaluation. The access to the questionnaire was restricted by a 6-digit access code, which was handed out to the interviewees by the contact person in an envelope with some further instructions on the evaluation procedure. While the code itself was in a non-personalized envelope, it was possible to track the respondents company and the order in which both prototypes were evaluated. The evaluation order was randomized based on the access code, which also made it possible to match the answers to the proper prototype. With this step, distortions as a result of answer patterns were prevented and this procedure offered a high level of de-personalization. The online questionnaire was accessible for a period of 14 weeks and the users were able to participate independently, at their individual best point in time. When participating, the users opened the envelope, accessed the online questionnaire and answered some basic questions before the first prototype was shown on the second screen. After performing some tasks, the users were asked to answer questions and rate the usability of the prototype, before the same procedure started for the second prototype. The questionnaire concluded with free-text fields for ideas of improvement and some demographic questions.

With this approach, standardized and comparative information, as well as qualitative insights into the perceived usability of the two evaluated prototypes were gathered from 45 users. While 2 answers were excluded from the analysis due to reasonable doubt of sufficiency (e.g., when the evaluation of DAC was carried out in just a few seconds), the remaining 43 cases gave us some interesting insights on the usability

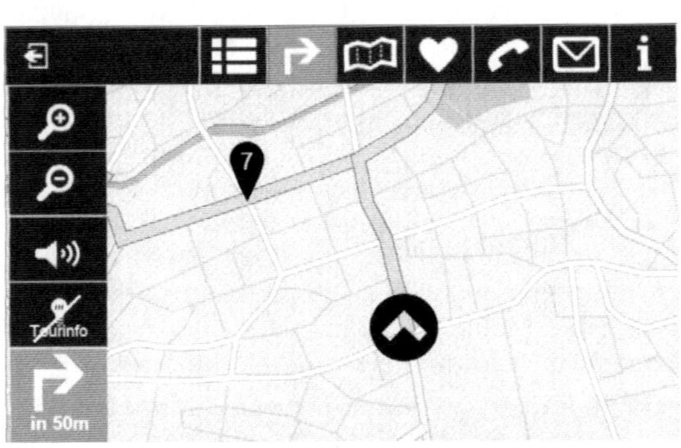

Figure 2. Navigation view of prototype 1

Figure 4. Main menu of prototype 2

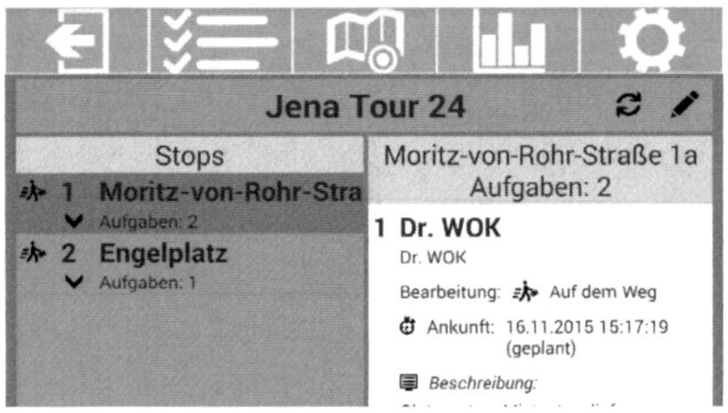

Figure 5. Tour overview of the demonstrator

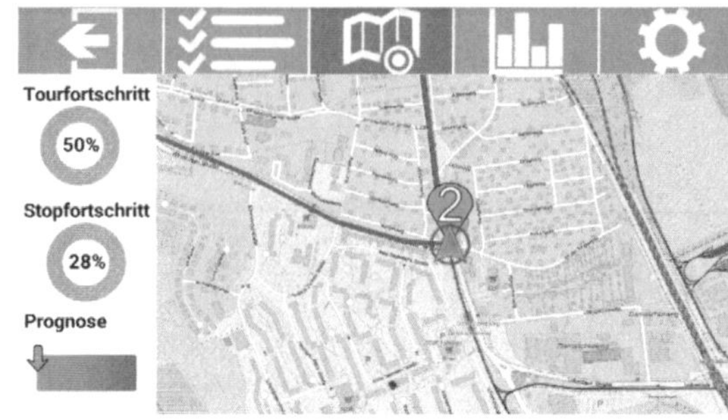

Figure 6. Navigation view of the demonstrator

of the evaluated prototypes. So it turned out that, in general, none of the two prototypes was evaluated better than the other. According to our SPSS analysis, prototype 1 showed better results regarding the usability, while prototype 2 achieved better results in clearness of the design and intuitiveness. Based on these results, a set of adaptations was elaborated. Basically, it combines the positive characteristics of both prototypes. Finally, these adaptations were used to build a functional demonstrator of the DAC, which is described in the next section.

VII. The Functional Demonstrator and Evaluation

The most important difference regarding the prototypes and the demonstrator is that the latter is fully functional. Compared to the indicated functionality of the prototypes, the demonstrator has been reduced, based on the results of the evaluation. The remaining main functionality covers the tour overview, turn by turn navigation, status overview and settings. Figure 5 shows the tour overview and on the upper border the main menu. The submenu has been removed completely, so that the available space could be used in a better way. Also, the navigation view has been improved by removing unimportant buttons, such as the zoom in and out buttons (see Figure 6). To save space and reduce complexity, the vehicle status and common information (e.g., weather, traffic, etc.) have been merged into the status overview, and the direct call and messages views have been removed.

After two iterations, the DAC has been implemented as a fully functional demonstrator based on the recommendations. To ensure a high quality and a high usefulness, another iteration step will conclude the project. In order to get further information about usability, the driver should use the DAC during his normal working day. To collect more data on possible insufficiencies, two final evaluations will be carried out. The first one will target drivers with experience in driving EVs in an EV-logistic context and will be performed as a qualitative interview. The second one will focus on drivers without specific EV-experience and is planned as a quantitative questionnaire.

For the first evaluation, drivers from the participating companies will use the DAC during their normal working day for a period of two months. Finally, they will be asked about their experiences using the DAC in a semi-structured interview, to bring to light possible deficits regarding usability. The results will be generated through a content analysis, similar to the approach described in Section IV. Due to the fact that only a few drivers at the partner companies can participate while actually using EVs and the DAC, the significance of the results is restricted as a consequence. To overcome this problem, the demonstrator will be evaluated by a higher number of professional drivers in Eltrilo [15], a simulator that was developed during the SCL project and is capable of simulating a real world environment based on map data. Specific scenarios (e.g., transportation from a hub into town with multiple stops) can be simulated and be part of the evaluation. In order to use Eltrilo, the DAC will be installed into the simulator and connected to the live-system via a mobile network connection. In a first step, the participants will get some detailed instructions on what they should do on their tour and use the DAC while performing their tasks in the simulator. During the simulation, some events affecting the tour will be triggered, in order to simulate unpredictable changes of plans. In a second step, the participants will be asked to answer some questions on their experience in the the demonstrator, as well as questions regarding usability. The approach is similar and comparable to the investigation described in Section VI but bases on the improved demonstrator.

This approach guarantees valuable insights from qualitative interview data as well as a usability evaluation by a broad range of possible users. The results can be compared to earlier research and help to improve the system in further development stages.

VIII. Conclusion and Future Work

The development of a technological solution requires multiple iteration steps, a fact that is crucial for the evaluation and that is considered in the presented research design: opening up for qualitative information in the beginning of the project, where knowledge is limited and uncertainty about important acceptance factors is high, before focussing on the gathered knowledge and comparable evaluation questions with regard to existing norms and standards, is one way to assess technology development and to gain valuable information on user expectancy and experience. Due to the agile project management, the technology evaluation has to be open at any point in time for new information and changes, and needs to combine a variety of existing qualitative and quantitative research methods. This helps to achieve the best possible results, that can be implemented in further technology development.

The first interview showed important aspects in the drivers daily work routines, that had to be considered while developing the DAC. A passive system, that gives hints and relevant, up-to-date information is preferred by the drivers. The prototype evaluation revealed the positive aspects of two slightly different mockups that were implemented in the functional demonstrator. Two iterations resulted in a fully functional prototype of the DAC, which is broadly accepted by possible users. The third iteration step will include two parts, focussing on qualitative information from a small number of real world EV-users as well as a higher number of professional drivers, using a driving simulator. Both evaluations should help to identify final enhancements regarding usability.

Finally, these results will help developers while creating DACs in the context of EVs. As a next step, the evaluation can be carried out by a higher number of participants from different contexts (e.g., private users as well) to find additional use cases for the developed technological system.

ACKNOWLEDGEMENTS

We would like to thank all members of the SCL research team here at FSU Jena – there are too many to name them all in person. We would also like to extend our gratitude to our partners within the research consortium, end users as well as research institutions and industrial developers. This project is supported by the German Federal Ministry for Economic Affairs and Energy in the IKT-II fur Elektromobilitat program under grant 01ME121(-33).

REFERENCES

[1] European Commission, A roadmap for completing the single market for parcel delivery. Brussels: European Commission, 2013.

[2] K. Young, W. Caisheng, L. Y. Wang, and K. Strunz, Electric Vehicle Battery Technologies, 1st ed. New York: Springer Science+Business Media, 2015.

[3] Nationale Platform Elektromobilität, Ladeinfrastruktur für Elektrofahrzeuge in Deutschland. Statusbericht und Handlungsempfehlung 2015 (Recharging Infrastructure for Electric Vehicles in Germany. Status Report and Recommended Action. Nationale Platform Elektromobilität, 2015.

[4] Bundesministerium für Wirtschaft und Energie, "IKT für Elektromobilität (ICT for Electromobility) II," Internet, http://www.bmwi.de/BMWi/Redaktion/PDF/Publikationen/Technologie-und-Innovation/ikt-elektromobilitaet,property=pdf,bereich=bmwi2012,sprache=de,rwb=true.pdf, 2016.03.16, 2013.

[5] J. Nielsen, "Usability inspection methods," in Conference Companion on Human Factors in Computing Systems, ser. CHI '94. New York, NY, USA: ACM, 1994, pp. 413–414. [Online]. Available: http://doi.acm.org/10.1145/259963.260531

[6] V. Venkatesh and F. D. Davis, "A theoretical extension of the technology acceptance model: Four longitudinal field studies," Management Science, vol. 46, no. 2, 2000, pp. 186–204.

[7] V. Venkatesh, M. G. Morris, G. B. Davis, and F. D. Davis, "User acceptance of information technology: Toward a unified view," MIS Quarterly, vol. 27, no. 3, 2003, pp. 425–478.

[8] S. Arndt, Evaluierung der Akzeptanz von Fahrerassistenzsystemen. Modell zum Kaufverhalten von Endkunden. VS, Verl. für Sozialwissenschaften, 2011.

[9] J. Gläser and G. Laudel, Experteninterviews und qualitative Inhaltsanalyse. Wiesbaden: VS Verlag für Sozialwissenschaften, 2009.

[10] R. Schnell, P. B. Hill, and E. Esser, Methoden der empirischen Sozialforschung. München [u.a.]: Oldenbourg, 2008.

[11] U. Kuckartz, Qualitative Inhaltsanalyse. Methoden, Praxis, Computerunterstützung (Qualitative Content Analysis. Methods, Practice, Computer-assistance). Weilheim und Basel: Beltz Juventa, 2012.

[12] Dr. dresing and Pehl GmbH, f4analyse 1.0.0-rc4- Computer Assisted Qualitative Data Analysis Software (CAQDAS), Internet, https://www.audiotranskription.de/f4-analyse, 2016.03.16, Marburg.

[13] J. Prümper, "Isonorm 9241/110-s: Evaluation of software based upon international standard iso 9241, part 110 - manuscript questionnaire," Internet, http://people.f3.htw-berlin.de/Professoren/Pruemper/instrumente/ISONORM_9241_110-S_2010.pdf, 2016.03.16, Berlin, 2010.

[14] C. Schmitz and LimeSurvey Core Development Team, "Limesurvey - free open source survey tool," Internet, https://www.limesurvey.org/en/, 2016.03.16.

[15] V. Schau, S. Apel, K. Gebhardt, J. Kretzschmar, M. Mauch, and C. Stolcis, "Evaluating ict-systems for electric vehicles within simulated environments," in Proceedings for the 19th Gulf Engineering Forum Smart Solutions, Kuwait City, in press.

Towards Model-based Usability Evaluation of Interactive Application: Detecting Unexpected Situations and Validating System Task Model

Mouna Jarraya, Faouzi Moussa
National School of Computer Sciences, Cristal Laboratory, University of Manouba
2010 Manouba, Tunisia
e-mails: {jarrayamouna, faouzimoussa}@gmail.com

***Abstract*—Usability evaluation is not fundamental only in the interactive application development process, but also at operation time. In this paper, we discuss how a task model could be used to detect any incompleteness due to poor requirements when designing an interactive application. The focus is on the comparison between user task and user activity to detect deviations in order to mend the task model. It is about detecting unexpected situations and validating the task model as it brings many benefits (e.g., it represents a user documentation; it is used for training operators, etc.). Indeed, it aims to ensure the stability and effectiveness of the system when context change of the environment system occurs.**

Keywords-Model-Based Usability Evaluation; Task Model; Petri Net; Activity Model; Human Computer Interaction; Design Validation; Unexpected Situation.

I. INTRODUCTION

The unexpected in the context of application development is defined as anytime when human operators deviate from the "linear" norm [1]. It happens when we define poor requirements throughout the design process. Literature exposes many approaches that use different techniques to detect erroneous actions and unexpected events [5].

In this work, we focus especially on how a task model enables us to evaluate and validate the effectiveness of an existing interactive application by identifying which tasks are supported by it and which ones are not. We propose a model-based approach to support usability evaluation involving users.

Task models are artifacts where we gather all the user requirements for the tasks to achieve a goal. They are usually used at the design and development process of interactive applications. However, using task models at operation time (when the interactive application has been deployed and used) brings many benefits such as users training, helps designers to evaluate their product, etc.

The remainder of the paper is structured as follows. Section II presents the state of art, gives task model and activity model definitions and it provides a quick overview of related work on how task models could be useful to improve usability of interactive applications which are already deployed and used. Section III presents some notions considered as corner stones in the development of our approach and gives an overview of it. The last section summarizes the contributions of the paper and highlights future work.

II. STATE OF THE ART

Few works addressed the issues of using task models in usability evaluation. In this section, some seminal definitions and concepts are given and we expose related work.

A. Definitions

Usability evaluation: The goal of usability evaluation is to find out possible usability problems of a system and discover ways to resolve them [10].

Likewise, the International Organization for Standardization (ISO) defined usability as the "Extent to which a product can be used by specified users to achieve specified goals with effectiveness, efficiency and satisfaction in a specified context of use" [12]. In order to measure how usable a system is, the ISO standard defines three attributes:

- Effectiveness: Accuracy and completeness with which users achieve specified goals;
- Efficiency: Resources expended in relation to the accuracy and completeness with which users achieve goals;
- Satisfaction: Freedom from discomfort, and positive attitudes towards the use of the product

Many existing models for usability are present in literature, for example, Nielsen's model [13], ISO, etc.

Usability evaluation methods can be classified as [14]:

- Model-based approaches where a significant model related to the interactive application is used to drive the evaluation. Various types of models, such as user, context and task models have proved to be useful in the design and evaluation of interactive applications;
- Inspection-based assessment, where some expert evaluates the system, or some representation of it, according to a set of criteria;
- Empirical testing where direct use of the system is considered.

Task model: Task analysis typically results in a task model, which is a description of any interactive task to be accomplished by the user of an application through the application's UI (User Interface). Individual elements in the task model represent specific actions that the user may undertake. Information regarding subtask ordering as well as conditions on task execution is also included in this model [8].

Activity model: We can characterize the activity of a human or a system who/that has to execute a task [1]. It represents actions that the user undertakes to accomplish a task. An activity model must be developed through observations and interactions with users [11]. It results from the execution of the task model. Thus, an activity model is a response to a task model.

B. *Related Work*

Several studies used task models as a tool to design interactive applications. Nevertheless, less works paid attention to their use to evaluate and validate Human-Computer interaction (HCI).

Paternò et al. [8] performs a systematic inspection-based analysis to improve both usability and safety aspects of an application. It aims to evaluate what could happen when interactions and behaviors occur differently from what the system designer assumed. It indicates a set of predefined classes of deviations that are identified by guidewords. These latter are used to analyze deviations by interdisciplinary groups. The main drawbacks are that it costs in terms of time and effort.

Another model-based approach incorporates human error analysis with task modeling [9] introducing the concept of Error Pattern. Error Patterns are prototypical deviations from abstract task models, expressed in a formal way by a model transformation. Nonetheless, task model, in this approach, is used in the design process and not at operation time.

Some authors combine different techniques including formal analysis of models, simulation and, in particular, analysis of log data in a model-based environment [7]. They extract test scenarios from the task models which will be simulated and executed to finally produce based-model logs. Thus, these logs support the assessment of the models, and allow iteration while performance of these techniques does not meet the corresponding requirements. Nevertheless, designer has to locate by himself where changes have to be made and additionally how to make them.

Martinie et al. [6] extends the previous approach and proposes a framework for connecting task models to an existing, executable, interactive application. It develops a co-execution environment that enables a systematic correspondence between the user interface elements of the interactive application and the low level tasks in the task model. It allows users to benefit from information available in the task model while interacting with the actual system such as assessing work complexity, operators' workload, identifying areas for improvement, etc.

III. OUR APPROACH/CONTRIBUTION

In the following, the HCI lifecycle is detailed to better understand how general activity model could be extracted. It is important to figure out problems and conflicts of the model and to follow up a model-based resolution as explained below [4]. This model has been used and depicted in our approach.

A. *HCI Lifecycle*

Abed et al. define the lifecycle of specification and generation of context-aware interfaces in two parts: design and implementation [2] (see Figure 1).

Human-Computer System analysis represents the identification of important subsystems in order to define their behavior. The objective is to identify the different graphics views appropriate for each subsystem.

This step will allow us to identify for each subsystem, the appropriate user's tasks. Task analysis helps to define the actions relating to the user's tasks.

Indeed, modeling the user's task has a strong impact on the design of user interface.

It allows us to deduce the user's requirements for the user's interface specification. The latter enables us to identify a set of graphic interface components for each user's task. Consequently, HCI is automatically generated.

At this stage, we define the experimental protocols for our Human-Computer System to simulate at real-time in order to detect some design errors or to identify situations not already expected by designers. For each simulation, we extract the user's cognitive activity and verify that it matches with user's task model or not. We iterate the cognitive activity analysis process until there would be no mismatch between the real activity and the designed task. We talk about validation of our HCI and we obtain the general activity model.

B. *Model-based resolution*

A task model represents a hierarchy of tasks. A task is a goal and a procedure that is a set of sub-tasks having temporal and composition relationship. Elementary tasks are only decomposable into physical actions. In the human decision theory of the operator when solving a problem in, skill-based behavior represents sensory-motor performance during acts or activities [4]. It is based on simple

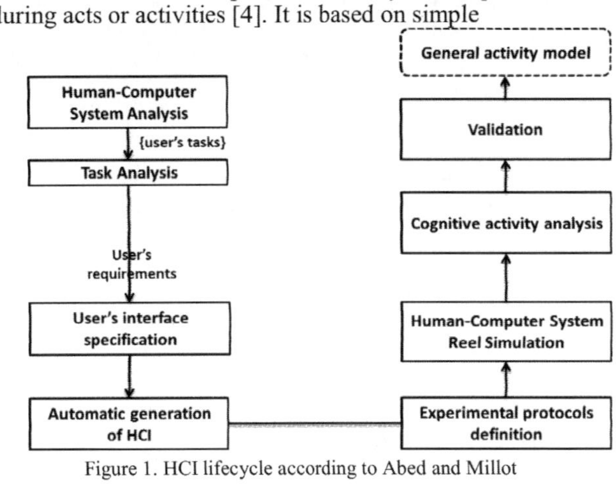

Figure 1. HCI lifecycle according to Abed and Millot

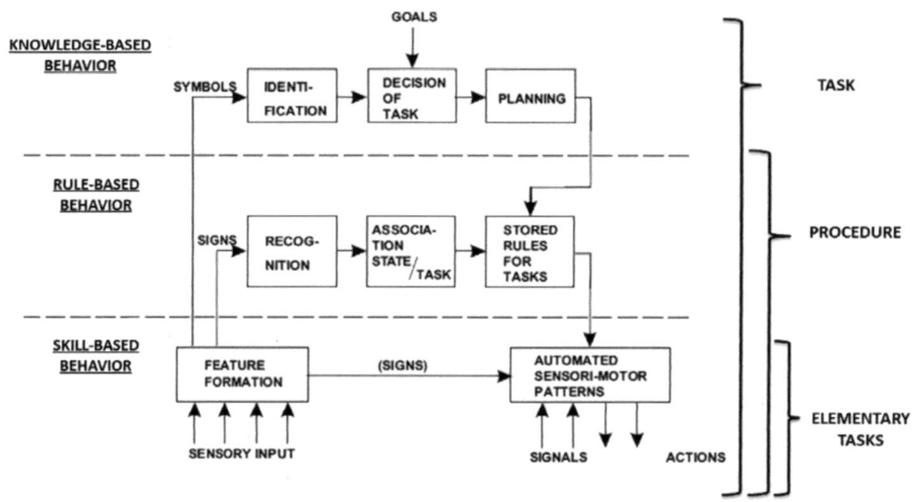

Figure 2. Simplified illustration of three level of performance of skilled human operators [4] and their correspondence with task's elements

feedback control. It corresponds to the elementary tasks level (see Figure 2).

At the next level of rule-based behavior, the composition of such sequence of subroutines in a familiar work situation is typically controlled by a stored rule or procedure. It can be related to task's procedure that is a sequence of sub-tasks controlled by a set of rules.

For unfamiliar situations with no rules for control available from previous encounters (in rule-based behavior rule), the control of performance must move to a higher conceptual level, in which activity is knowledge-based and goal-controlled. Based on model-based resolution, elementary tasks would be the starting point of the task analysis and subsequently the task model.

C. *Petri Nets modeling language for elementary tasks*

Several task modeling approaches and techniques are available. However, it is mandatory for us to choose the most suitable modeling approach. Riahi et al. [3] depict a comparative study between different models (e.g., key-value model, ontology, etc.). They find multiple proofs of the Petri Net's ability to model tasks.

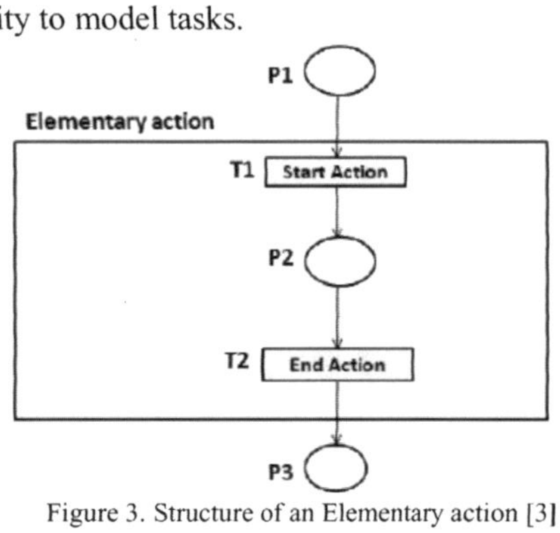

Figure 3. Structure of an Elementary action [3]

Modeling with Petri Nets (PN) enables to do formal verification and prior validation of tasks, which would save a considerable amount of time in the development cycle of the interface [3].

There is a set of criteria that convinced us to adopt Petri Nets in our work as presented in [3]. We considered that the user task is composed of sets of elementary PN structures. The modeling of an elementary structure is illustrated in Figure 3. All the users' actions (elementary or composed) are organized according to typical compositions: sequential parallel, alternative, choice, iterative or of-closure. The principles of only two compositions are described below.

Sequential composition: The composition of "n" sequential actions reflects the sequence of their execution. The sequential composition of n actions is ensured by combining the place "end" modeling the action i, with place "begin" of the action i + 1 (see Figure 4). In the example, the user performs three actions one after the other.

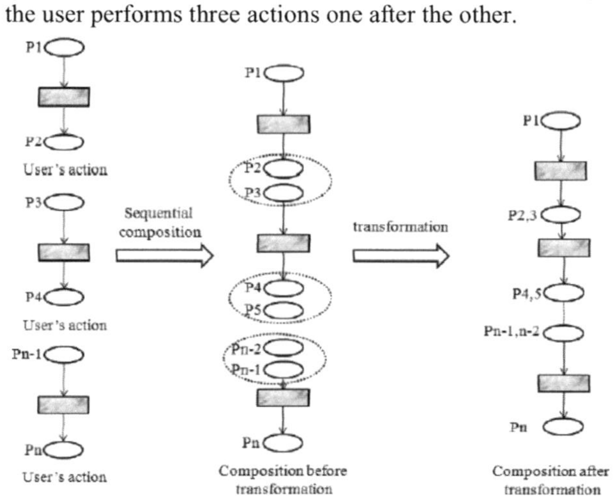

Figure 4. Sequential composition [3]

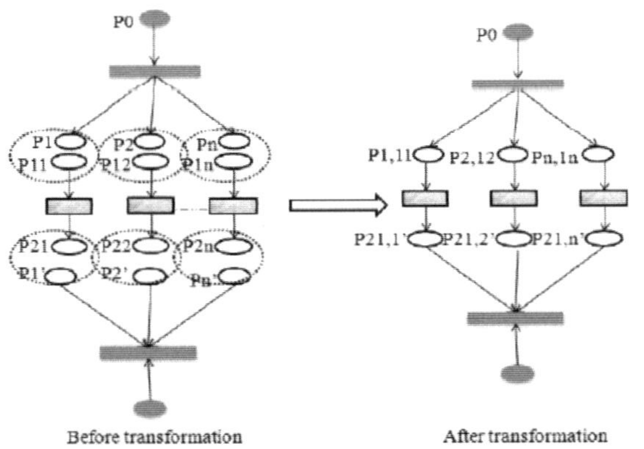

Figure 5. Parallel composition [3]

Such an interaction will be modeled by a sequential composition of three elementary structures (modeling three elementary actions).

Parallel composition: Parallel composition expresses the possibility of simultaneous execution. Parallelism is ensured thanks to an input synchronization place. This place activates at the same time all the places of initialization of the parallel actions to be executed. Ensure the parallel composition of actions; it is necessary to synchronize the places of entry and those of exit of those actions (see Figure 5).

D. *Proposed approach: an overview*

As seen above, the proposed approach aims to detect any deviation from what task model assumes comparing to interactive application's activities. For this matter, user activities would be compared to a set of elementary tasks in order to compute or to calculate a Δ. The latter would identify what, when and where dissonance or deviation occurred. If it is the case, mending the task model would be necessary (see Figure 6).

From this process, three major components are highlighted:

Computing Δ: This step requires as inputs user tasks (from task model) and user activities. For the latter, a correspondence controller traces the user actions or activities on the interface via Petri Nets mechanism mentioned above.

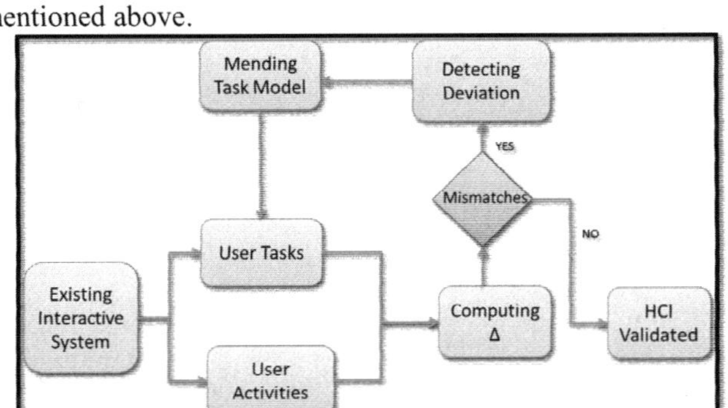

Figure 6. Usability evaluation process

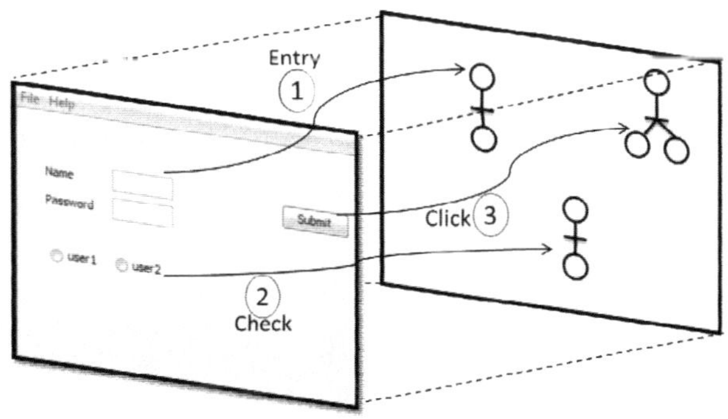

Figure 7. Correspondence Controller

In fact, for each user action, an elementary Petri Net is associated to it (see Figure 7).

After that, assembling elementary Petri Net will follow the sequence of user actions until obtaining the user activity and finally an activity model for a high-level abstraction.

Thus, user tasks and user activities are modeled in the same way as they reference to elementary actions (elementary Petri Net). They are considered now as "comparable" and the Δ can be computed by superimposing the two Petri Nets and highlighting the differences.

Detecting deviation: Differences between user task's Petri Net and user activity's Petri Net will be then automatically extracted at this stage. Indeed, activity Petri Net will indicate if there are abnormal activities (missing actions, new extra actions, abnormal sequence of actions) compared to the task Petri Net.

Mending task model: Once all deviations are detected and identified, it remains to update the user tasks and task model.

This process is iterative until validating Human Computer Interaction. It is also repetitive to ensure stability of the system when context change of the environment system occurs.

Our approach has two major purposes. First, it enables as to validate our interactive application design, especially user interfaces, through the identification of the mismatches between user tasks and user activities. Second, somehow deviations might inform us, when the design is already validated, about unexpected situation which pushes the user to act differently from what we have planned. For that matter, unexpected events could be identified by some criteria such as:

- User activity changes compared to what it used to be before (abnormal activity).
- User activity does not exist in history activity database.
- User activity does not exist in task model.

IV. Conclusion and Future Work

This paper proposed a model-based approach for usability evaluation. The main feature of this approach is that evaluation is based on models. This approach is targeted to interactive applications that are already deployed and currently used.

Such an approach can increase the use of task models that are a very costly artifact, even for already deployed applications.

More precisely, we tried to log user activities considering elementary actions by using a correspondence controller. The latter will associate for each elementary action an elementary Petri Net [3]. This enables us to build the whole activity using a Petri Net in order to compare it to the user task modeled with the same language.

The main contribution of the paper lies in computing Δ between user tasks and user activities in order to detect all possible deviations or abnormal behaviors. That aims to mend and correct the task model.

We are currently applying this research in a case study of interactive application so as to expand more every step of our approach.

References

[1] G. A. Boy, "From automation to tangible interactive objects", Annual Reviews in Control 38, April 2014, pp. 1-11, Elsevier

[2] M. Abed, H. Ezzedine, and C. Kolski, "Modelling tasks in design and evaluation of interactive systems : SADT/Petri method". In C. Kolski (Ed.), Analyse et Conception de l'IHM. Interaction Homme Machine pour les SI, vol. 1, 2001, pp. 145-174. Paris: Éditions Hermes

[3] I. Riahi and F. Moussa, "A formal approach for modeling context-aware Human-Computer System". Computers and Electrical Engineering, vol. 44, May 2015, pp. 241-261, doi:10.1016/j.compeleceng.2015.03.001

[4] J. Rassmussen, "Skills, rules and knowledge ; Signals, signs and symbols, and other distinctions in Human performance models", IEEE Transactions on systems, man and cybernetics, vol. smc 13, no. 3 May 1983, pp. 257-266

[5] F. Vanderhaegen, "Dissonance Engineering: A New Challenge to Analyse Risky", International Journal of Computers Communications and Control ISSN 1841-9836, December 2014, pp. 776-785

[6] C. Martinie, D. Navarre, P. Palanque, and C. Fayollas, "A Generic Tool-Supported Framework for Coupling Task Models and Interactive Applications", The seventh ACM SIGCHI Symposium on Engineering Interactive Computing Systems (EICS 2015), June 2015, pp. 244-253, ISBN: 978-1-4503-3646-8

[7] P. Palanque, E. Barboni, C. Martinie, D. Navarre, and M. Winckler, "A Model-based Approach for Supporting Engineering Usability Evaluation of Interaction Techniques", ACM SIGCHI Symposium on Engineering Interactive Computing Systems (EICS 2011), June 2011, pp. 21-30, ISBN: 978-1-4503-0670-6

[8] Q. Limbourg, C. Pribeanu , and J. Vanderdonckt, "Towards Uniformed Task Models in a Model-Based Approach". In: C. Johnson (ed.) DSV-IS 2001. LNCS, 2001, vol. 2220, pp. 164–182. Springer, Heidelberg

[9] R. Bastide and S. Basnyat, "Error Patterns: Systematic Investigation of Deviations in Task Models", Task Models and Diagrams for Users Interface Design, vol. 4385, October 2006, pp. 109-121, doi: 10.1007/978-3-540-70816-2_9

[10] F. Balagtas-Fernandez and H. Hussmann, "A Methodology and Framework to Simplify Usability Analysis of Mobile Applications", 24th IEEE/ACM International Conference on Automated Software Engineering, November 2009, pp. 520-524, doi: 10.1109/ASE.2009.12

[11] J. L. Crowley, P. Reignier, and R. Barranquand, "Situation Models: A Tool for Observing and Understanding Activity", Proceedings of the IEEE International Conference on Robotics and Automation ICRA 2009 Workshop on People Detection and Tracking, May 2009

[12] ISO 9241: Ergonomics Requirements for Office Work with Visual Display Terminals (VDTs) International Standards Organisation, Geneva (1997)

[13] J. Nielsen, Usability engineering, 1994, Morgan Kaufmann Pub.

[14] F. Paternò and C. Santoro, "Preventing user errors by systematic analysis of deviations from the system task model", Int. J. Human-Computer Studies, February 2002, vol. 56, issue 2, pp. 225–245 doi:10.1006/ijhc.2001.0523

Complex Emotions Expression and Recognition for Paranoid Personality Disorder

Mohamad Ab Saleh
Laboratoire de Recherche en Informatique Fondamentale et Appliquées (LaRIFA) - Lebanese University, Lebanon
Email: *mohamadabsaleh@st.ul.edu.lb*

Abstract—**This paper proposes a logical framework for the specification of some types of complex emotions related to Paranoid Personality Disorder (PPD) disease. The complex emotions we are targeting here are *despair* and *spite*. We propose a logic that allows to describe some of the psychological personality characteristics from the side view of emotion theory. It allows to express some emotions existing in Ortony, Clore and Collins theory (OCC theory) and Plutchik theories but yet formalized in logic. The logical model, that we build, can express and recognize the targeted complex emotions (i.e., *despair*, *spite*). This logical model coupled with an inference engine can help diagnosing whether a person is suffering from the emotional PPD disease.**

Keywords–Emotion; Paranoid Personality Disorder; Logic; Despair; Spite.

I. Introduction

Personality disorder diseases have gained increased importance in the society during the last years. These are common diseases to the extent that epidemiological organizations estimate that the percentage of such diseases among people living in the community is between 5% and 13%, the percentage increases to 30% and 40% for psychiatric outpatients and the percentage becomes even higher for psychiatric inpatients, with estimations between 40% to 50%. The percentage is estimated to be the highest among prisoners, between 50-78% [1].

This field is psychologically broadly covered in the literature. Peay [2] tackled the subject of the relation between law and such diseases. He submitted five key problems for the law in order to deal with people suffering from such diseases. Kemelgor *et al.* took the side of the workplace incivility and its relation with such diseases. They suggest that narcissistic traits are the modal descriptors for difficult employee, regardless of hierarchical role (boss, peer, subordinate) [3]. Wiederman *et al.* investigate the relation between such diseases and sexuality. They studied a group of people instead of individuals and tried to explain the group specifications which can be recognized by it. Their target was to shorten the treatment and understand individuals by examining their generalization [4]. Hazelden foundation published a study, related to addiction and its relation with such diseases, where people addicted to alcohol and drugs are suffering from co-occurring of the diseases [5].

Due to the lack of logic-based approaches related to Paranoid Personality Disorder (PPD), we decide to build a logical model that represents it, with emotional flavour. We propose a formalization of the psychological personality characteristics for PPD diseases where each characteristic is logically represented by its properties [6]. We focus on particular psychological states that are emotional states. We only consider the cognitive structure of emotion rather than emotion as a complex psychological phenomenon including cognitive and somatic aspects (i.e., feeling). The cognitive structure is a compound construction of noetic situations that is founded in someone mind when (he/she) is feeling some type of emotions [7].

In Section 2, we introduce the Paranoid Personality Disorder disease phenomenon, its definition and its reasons. In Section 3, a brief overview is given about emotion and how it can be classified depending on Plutchik's Theory. Complex emotions are then exposed tackling one of the most famous cognitive theory, which is the Ortony, Clore and Collins (OCC) theory. Finally, we address the subject of the facial evidences and its relation to emotions. In Section 4, we present our model to express and to recognize PPD diseases. In Section 5, we briefly discuss a possible implementation of the logical model allowing to decide whether an individual is suffering from such diseases via recognizing the two complex emotions (*despair*, *spite*). Section 6 concludes the paper.

II. Personality Disorder

Personality refers to individual differences in a collection of characteristic patterns such as thinking, feeling and behaving or characteristics that humans developed as they grow. Although individuals suffering from a Personality Disorder (PD) have problems in their relations with other people, they tend to have a narrow minded view of the world and a compound of significant problems and limitations in relationships, social encounters, work [8]. A patient suffering from the PPD disease shares some common essential features such as: hold grudges and feels easily rejected and that, except himself, other people are sickening and suspicious [9].

In this paper, we use the work of Fawzi [10] related to PPD disease. It is approximated to be the single academic article published in Iraq that concludes its results from multinational prisoners and it is considered to be one of the rare studies in the Middle East, especially that most of the studies in these countries are theoretical and/or affected by political and religious influences. An individual that suffers from the PPD disease can be resumed as a person who [10]: possesses a sense of *despair* that justifies his aggression towards others, holds *spite* against those who disagreed with him in opinion or belief, is rigid in his cognitive approach as well as in dealing with conflicts, extrapolates, from the usual events, hidden threats and insults directed against him, and finally is preoccupied with unjustified doubts about his friends.

III. Basic Materials and Motivation

In this section, we expose briefly some basic and complex types of emotion, their relation with the cognitive theories and facial evidences, then we present the motivation and the objectives of our study.

A. Emotions

As Becheiraz *et al.* [11] say "An emotion is an emotive reaction of a person to a perception". Basic emotions consist of a relatively small number of prototypes, for example: *sadness*, *fear*, etc. Basic emotions exist and can be identified easily. Complex emotions are emotions that occur as a result of a mixture or combinations of basic emotions [12]. When dealing with basic emotions, we are directed towards the idea that it happens automatically with a little cognitive processing. Complex emotions such as *despair* and *spite*, require more cognitive processing which reflects the agent's interaction and evaluation with some single event [13]. Plutchik [14] classified emotions using a wheel to illustrate some of the rules that shape the relationship among emotions. He identified eight primary emotions (*joy* vs. *sadness*, *trust* vs. *disgust*, *fear* vs. *anger*, *anticipation* vs. *surprise*). The wheel allows to blend multiple emotions to produce more complicated ones such as primary, secondary and tertiary dyads (i.e *love* is the blended emotion of *joy* and *trust*) [15].

B. Cognitive Theories

The basic notion of cognitive theories is that emotions are rational states that could be differentiated depending on cognitive analysis or suggestion components [16]. Depending on OCC Theory, emotions are triggered from the interaction of events (desirable/undesirable), actions (commendation/reproached) and objects. Each of the resulting twenty two emotions is a unique combination of these variables [17].

C. Facial Evidences

Ekman *et al.* [18] found some relationships between basic emotions such as: *happiness*, *surprise*, *fear*, *sadness* and *disgust* and evidences appearing on individuals faces affected by such emotions. The observation focused on the following face features: forehead, eyebrows, eyelids, cheeks, nose, lips and chin. Basic emotions could be blended together to produce new constructed facial evidences. However, when two emotions are blended together, not all the facial evidences of the basic emotions appear on the person's face.

D. Motivation and objectives

Based on the OCC theory and psychology literature, several studies tackle the subject of basic and complex emotions and build logical models of emotions. Guiraud *et al.* [19] propose a model that can recognize expressive speech acts, e.g., to apologize, to thank, to reproach, etc., based on emotions such as Rejoicing, Gratitude, Regret, etc. Lorini *et al.* [13] build a model for reasoning about counter-factual emotions such as regret, rejoicing, disappointment, elation. Steunebrink [17] formalize a psychological model for the twenty two types of emotions found in OCC theory such as love, hate, anger, gratitude, etc. Bonnefon *et al.* [16] build a logical framework for Trust-Related Emotions such as Joy/Distress, Hope/Fear, Satisfaction/Disappointment, Fear-confirmed/Relief and Gratitude/Anger. However, to our knowledge, none were concerned to address the logical formalization of any of the PPD diseases resulting emotions.

Moreover, we have chosen to illustrate the usefulness of our model through the implementation of a PPD disease diagnosis support system. This system is supplied with data related to the patient's knowledge such as his beliefs, goals, etc., and facial evidences of the latter. The choice of facial characteristics was guided by the richness of Ekman's work on this issue which provides a solid foundation on the relationship between basic emotions and facial evidences. We have placed this work in the context of the Plutchick's theory to express and recognize the facial evidences associated to complex emotions, if any. Thereby, our system implements the logical formalization of the two targeted complex emotions (i.e., *despair* and *spite*), gets input (patient data), and helps diagnose PPD diseases.

IV. Logical Formalisation for PPD diseases

In the model we aim to build, we suppose that an agent having a goal α or $(\neg\alpha)$ is responsible to feel some emotions towards that event (goal) [19].

Researchers used different types of logic to build models that serve their aims. We will rely on *df*STIT ("decidable and axiomatizable fragment of STIT") logic in order to overcome problems related to complex emotions representation. STIT ("Seeing to it that") logic [20] has emerged in the nineties as a tool in formal philosophy and recently was used in computer science thanks to its ease to express choices and possibilities of agents and group of agents. The language of STIT logic is built from a finite set of agents called $AGT = \{1, 2, ..., n\}$ and an infinite set of propositional variables called ATM. The well-formed formulas of STIT logic are:

$$\alpha ::= p|\neg\alpha|\alpha \wedge \alpha|[J]\alpha$$

where $p \in ATM$ and $J \subseteq AGT$. Unfortunately the version of STIT was recently proved to be undecidable and unaxiomatizable. Lorini *et al.* [13] proposed an extension to STIT, which is named *df*STIT and proved it decidable and axiomatizable. The *df*STIT was extended with knowledge modalities where modifications were operated to the syntax and semantics of STIT. This logic contains a vital chunk named STIT chunk, which deals with an agent and groups of agents. This chunk reflects the agent (group of agents) actions and concentrates on the effects of these actions. It also has the ability to express the confirmation from the viewpoint of the agent and the group of agents against an output. In Section IV-D, the STIT chunk will play an important role in constructing a cognitive structure to the *spite* emotion.

In the following, we give the syntax and semantics of our PPD logic (*PPDL*) allowing to formalize *despair* and *spite*.

A. Syntax

The ingredients of the *PPDL* syntax are: a finite non-empty set $AGT = \{a_1, a_2, ..., a_n\}$ of agents, a finite non-empty set $EVNT = \{ev_1, ev_2, ..., ev_k\}$ of atomic events, a non-empty set $ATP = \{m, n, ...\}$ of atomic propositions. The *PPDL* language is the set of formulas defined as follows:

$$Sl_{i,j} ::= p|Sl_{i,j} \wedge Sl_{i,j}|\neg Sl_{i,j}$$
$$\Omega ::= [J]Sl_{i,j}|\Omega \wedge \Omega$$
$$\alpha ::= p|Sl_{i,j}|\Omega|\neg\alpha|\alpha \wedge \alpha|Bel_i\alpha|Goal_i\alpha|Poss_iF\alpha|$$
$$Has_i\alpha| < \phi > \Omega$$

where α is an atomic event (goal), p ranges over ATP, J ranges over $2^{AGT}\backslash\{\phi\}$, (i, j) range over AGT.

The other Boolean classical constructions: $\wedge$(conjunction), $\vee$(disjunction), $\neg$(negation), $\rightarrow$(implication), $\leftrightarrow$(equivalence), $\perp$(contradiction), $\top$(tautology) are defined in a standard way.

Operators can be defined as unambiguous symbols that represent a collection of truth functions. They are as follows:

1) Operator ($\mathrm{Bel_i}\alpha$)*:* is used to represent a specific belief of agent *i* about the truthfulness of some event α. However this operator doesn't forcibly refer to the truthfulness of event in the real world. For example, "agent *i* believes that he is beautiful" but really he is not. This operator reads in the form of "agent *i* believes that α is true" [19].

2) Operator ($\mathrm{Goal_i}\alpha$)*:* is used to represent that a specific agent *i* goal is α. An agent must have a goal because of a standard compliance or it will deduce a goal from another agent goal. As an example of the standard compliance: "The hunger of agent *i* will oblige him to search for food. The hungry agent *i* forms a new goal represented by searching for food". The goal operator reads in a form "agent *i* wants α to be true" [19].

3) Operator ($\mathrm{Poss_i F}\alpha$)*:* is used to represent that a specific agent *i* thinks that α will be true in some possible world in the future. In other words, agent *i* thinks that there is at least one world, in which α will be true in all possible future worlds. Basically the $(Poss_i\alpha)$ is an abbreviation of $(\neg \mathrm{Bel_i} \neg\alpha)$ and reads in a form "agent *i* believes that there is a possibility in the future that α will be true" or "agent *i* doesn't believe that α will not be true" [16].

4) Operator ($\mathrm{Has_i}\alpha$)*:* is used to represent that a specific agent *i* has an event α. In other words, an event α is an exclusive ownership of an agent *i*. No other agent in AGT has the ownership of the event α. As an example if "agent *i* has a pen" then no other agent has the ownership of that pen. So, agent *i* has an exclusive ownership of it. Has can be defined as below:
$M, w \models Has_i\alpha$ iff $\forall v \in W, \forall i, j \in$ AGT,
$i \neq j \rightarrow M, v \models Has_i\alpha \wedge M, v \models \neg Has_j\alpha$.

5) Operator ($< \phi > \Omega$)*:* is used to represent that "an event Ω is possibly True" [13].

6) Operator ($[\phi]Sl_{i,j}$)*:* $Sl_{i,j}$ represents the same level event, which means that two agents are at the same level in: Science, Finance, Social Position, etc. This operator is used to represent that "an event $Sl_{i,j}$ is necessarily true" [13].

7) Operator($< \phi > [J]Sl_{i,j}$)*:* is a mixture of the two preceding operators, which are the possibly and necessarily operators. It represents "agent *j* sees to it that $Sl_{i,j}$ is true" or "group *J* sees to it that $Sl_{i,j}$ is true" [13]. The composition $[J]Sl_{i,j}$ is basically written in the form $\neg[J]\neg Sl_{i,j}$ and it is abbreviated to the preceding form. The $[J]$ type operator is used to express the impression of *J* to an event. The *J* symbol will refer to one agent depending on the action responsibility that is related to that agent, while it is possible for the same symbol to refer to a group of agents. An agent or group of agents can express his/their opinion to the same level event (true or false) through the chunk sees to it that($STIT$). The operator ($[J]Sl_{i,j}$) is used instead of ($< \phi > [J]Sl_{i,j}$) to refer to the expression "sees to it that". When the case to consider is related to a group of agents in $[J]Sl_{i,j}$, *J* represents a group of agents and $Sl_{i,j}$ represents an event on which the group *J* must give their opinion. In more detail, the composition $[J]\alpha$ will refer to "group *J* sees to it that α is true no matter what the other agents in the set of agents except *J* to do". If the set *J* contains only one agent such as k, then the composition $[k]\alpha$ will refer to "agent *k* sees to it that α is true no matter what the other agents in the set of agents except *k* do".

Atoms: are tagging some states that share some specifications (goodness, same level, etc.) for a specific agent [13]. In our model we need the following atoms:

8) Atom($PSTV_i\alpha$)*:* is used to represent that an event α is a good thing to an agent *i*. We can say that this atom is used for tagging a positive event to a specific agent. Basically the $(PSTV_i\alpha)$ is an abbreviation of $([\phi]Pstv_i \rightarrow \alpha)$ and reads in a form "α is positive for agent *i* if and only if α is true in all positive states" [13].

9) Atom($Sl_{i,j}$)*:* is used to represent that two agents *i, j* are at the same level. The level $(Sl_{i,j})$ is an event which indicates that *i, j* are in the same scientific, finance, social position, ... levels. This atom is read in a form "agent i and j are at the same level".

B. Semantics

M= (*W,B,G,P,H,S,V*) represent PPDL semantic where:

1) W: is a nonempty set of possible worlds or states.

2) B: $AGT \rightarrow 2^{W\times W}$ maps every agent i $\in$ AGT to serial, transitive, euclidean relation B_i over W. It represents the semantic of the agent *i* belief chunk (Bel_i), which can be expressed as a set $B_i(w) = \{v|(w,v) \in B_i\}$. This set represents the worlds that an agent *i* thinks that it is possible at world *w*. The seriality of B_i means that an agent *i* has all the time harmonic beliefs, while the transitivity and euclideanity of B_i means that good and bad beliefs of an agent are introspective bound [19].

3) G: $AGT \rightarrow 2^{W\times W}$ maps every agent i $\in$ AGT to a serial relation G_i over *W*. It represents the semantic of the agent *i* goal chunk $(Goal_i)$, which can be expressed as a set $G_i(w) = \{v|(w,v) \in G_i\}$. This set represents the worlds that an agent *i* want, i.e., working towards achieving it. The seriality of G_i means that an agent *i* must all the time have at least one state that he is working to satisfy [19].

4) P: $AGT \rightarrow 2^{W\times W}$ maps every agent i $\in$ AGT to serial, transitive, euclidean relation P_i over *W*. It represents the semantic of the agent *i* possibility chunk $(Poss_i)$, expressed as a set $P_i(w) = \{v|(w,v) \in P_i\}$. Since the chunk $(Poss_i)$ is an abbreviation of $(\neg Bel_i \neg\alpha)$, the set P_i will gain the same relations: seriality, transitivity, euclideanity as in B_i [16].

5) H: $AGT \rightarrow 2^{W\times W}$ maps every agent $i \in$ AGT to a serial relation H_i over W. It represents the semantic of the agent *i* has chunk (Has_i), which can be expressed as a set $H_i(w) = \{v|(w,v) \in H_i\}$ that represents the worlds where an agent *i* has an ownership. The seriality of H_i means that an agent *i* must all the time have at least one state that he/she has the ownership.

6) S: $2^{AGT} \rightarrow 2^{W\times W}$ maps a set of agents $J \in 2^{AGT}$ to equivalence relation S_J over *W*. It represents the semantic of the "sees to it that" chunk ($[J]$). In *S* the relation on W is a function from W to 2^W, such that for every $J \in 2^{AGT}$, the set can be expressed as $S_J(w) = \{v \in W | wS_Jv\}$. This set represents the worlds that a set of agents J seeing to them that an event is true. S_J is an equivalence relation over W such that this set must satisfy the following bonds [13]:

- $S_J \subseteq S_\phi$;
- $S_J = \cap_{j \in J} S_{\{j\}}$;
- $\forall w \in W, \forall (w_j)_{j \in AGT} \in S_\phi(w)^n, \cap_{j \in AGT} S_{\{j\}}(w_j) \neq \phi$;
- $S_{AGT} = id_W$

where S_ϕ is the relation over all possible outcomes: if $wS_\phi v$ then v is a possible outcome at the current world w.

7) V: $ATM \rightarrow 2^W$ is a valuation function. This set represents the worlds that an agent i wants/works to achieve.

C. A formalization of Disappointment Emotion: Despair

Despair is a complex emotion. This emotion type represents "total loss of hope, which may be passive or may be derive one to furious efforts" [21]. A person feeling with *despair* will not tend to have any hope. He believes that there is nothing he can do to change the situation that causes him to feel *despair* [22]. Relating to the first characteristic, Fawzi says [10] about patients who suffer from the PPD disease, that they are "Possessed by a sense of *despair*, which paid them to aggression on others". Depending on Plutchik's theory, the *despair* is a secondary dyad, which is constructed from the two basic emotions *fear* and *sadness*:

$$Despair = Fear + Sadness \quad (1)$$

Fear makes the agent displeased about the prospect of an undesirable event [17]. Depending on the preceding definition, it can be recognized that *fear* is constructed from two components, which are: agent *i* does not desire an event α to be true, and, in a specific time in the future, agent *i* believes that α may be true. The first component can be understood as, at this moment, the agent *i* does not desire an event α to be true. This understanding could be formalized by: $Goal_i \neg\alpha$. The second component can be interpreted as the agent *i* believes that, in the future, in some way or another, α will be true. Said otherwise, agent *i* believes that α will be true in some possible moment in the future: $Poss_i F\alpha$ where $F\alpha$ means that somewhere, in the future, α will be true . According to the preceding analysis, the epistemic framework for *fear* can be built as [16]:

Definition 1 (*Fear*)

$$Fear_i\alpha = Goal_i \neg\alpha \wedge Poss_i F\alpha \quad (2)$$

Sadness is one of the basic emotions, and it is the result of the person perception of the truthfulness of some event and what he aims to do. In other words, an agent *i* will feel Joy if he knows that some event α is true, agent *i* must believe that α is true and agent *i* goal is α. Relating to *sadness*, if the agent *i* realizes that α is true but his goal is $\neg\alpha$ then he feels *sad* about the fact that α is true. According to the preceding analysis, the epistemic framework for *sadness* can be built as [19]:

Definition 2 ($Sadness$)

$$Sadness_i\alpha = Goal_i \neg\alpha \wedge Bel_i\alpha \quad (3)$$

Depending on Plutchick's definition of *Despair* and definitions 1 and 2, the cognitive structure that recognizes the *despair* is:

Definition 3 ($Despair$)

$$Despair_i\alpha = [Goal_i \neg\alpha \wedge Poss_i F\alpha] \wedge [Goal_i \neg\alpha \wedge Bel_i\alpha] \quad (4)$$

The former description of *Despair* in equation (4) could be minimized to be as we can see in equation (5) since the chunck Bel_i means that $agent_i$ believes that α is always true. While the chunck $Poss_i F\alpha$ means that $agent_i$ believes that, in the future, α may or may not be true:

$$Despair_i\alpha = Goal_i \neg\alpha \wedge Bel_i\alpha \quad (5)$$

Depending on equation (5), the two emotions, which are *despair* and *sadness*, will represent the same emotion. This is a contradiction since the *despair* emotion has a different meaning and effect to the person than the *sadness* emotion. In order to differentiate between them, we searched the literature of psychology and found that Boeree [23] defined the *despair* as "*despair* is sorrow arising from the idea of a past or future object from which cause for doubting is removed. *Despair* happens when *fear* overwhelms *hope*". Johnson *et al.* [24] claimed that the *despair* is a complex emotion and defined it as "intense *sadness* and lack of *hope* as a result of inability to achieve goals". So the *despair* is hopeless while *sadness* is close to Sorrow and can be hopeful. The *despair* will be:

$$Despair = Fear + Sadness + Hopeless \quad (6)$$

Hopeless indicates that there is no possibility in the future to achieve agent *i* goal [23]. In other words, an agent *i* will feel hopeless, when some event happened and that event is the inverse of (his/her) goal and there are no possibility in the future for agent *i* goal to be achieving.

$$Despair_i\alpha = [Goal_i \neg\alpha \wedge Poss_i F\alpha] \wedge [Goal_i \neg\alpha \wedge Bel_i\alpha] \wedge [Goal_i \neg\alpha \wedge \neg Poss_i F \neg\alpha] \quad (7)$$

Depending on equation (5), the equation (7) will be:

$$Despair_i\alpha = [Goal_i \neg\alpha \wedge Bel_i\alpha] \wedge [Goal_i \neg\alpha \wedge \neg Poss_i F \neg\alpha]$$

which could be minimized to equation (8) by removing the redundancy of the chunk $Goal_i \neg\alpha$:

$$Despair_i\alpha = [Bel_i\alpha \wedge Goal_i \neg\alpha \wedge \neg Poss_i F \neg\alpha] \quad (8)$$

So equation (8) will represent the cognitive structure of the *Despair* emotion.

Example 1.
An employee named Tom works in a famous company. He knows somehow that he will be fired from the job, represented by Bel_{Tom}(fired). Tom's aim is not to be fired, represented by $Goal_{Tom}\neg$(fired). Tom realizes that there is no possibility in the future to be not fired represented by $\neg Poss_{Tom} F \neg$(fired). Tom will feel *despair* as we can see below:

$$Despair_{Tom}(\text{fired}) = [Bel_{Tom}(\text{fired}) \wedge Goal_{Tom}\neg(\text{fired}) \wedge \neg Poss_{Tom} F \neg(\text{fired})]$$

In order to improve the accuracy of complex emotion detection, we will cover some facial evidences related to such detection. Facial evidences coupled to *despair* emotion factors will be provided to the knowledge base of the system, allowing to improve the decision process to be taken by the inference engine. Equation 6 shows that *despair* is composed of three different emotions: *fear*, *sad* and *hopeless*. The first two are basic emotions and have special facial evidences for each. Unfortunately, this is not the case for the *hopeless* emotion. The facial evidences for *fear* are: Eye Brows are raised and drawn together, Upper Eye lid are raised and lower eyelid is tensed, Lips are either tensed slightly and drawn back or stretched and drawn back, Eyes are opened and tense, Mouth opens, Forehead wrinkles drawn to the center while the facial evidences for *sad* are: Inner corners of eyebrows are raised and may be drawn together, Skin below the eyebrow is triangulated with inner corner up, Upper lid inner corner is raised, Corners of the lips are drawn or lip is trembling. When the *fear* and *sad* are blended, not all the facial evidences for each are collected together, instead some evidences of each appears. The blending of *fear* and *sad* will produce the facial evidences: Inner corners of eyebrows are raised and may be drawn together, Upper lid inner corner is raised, Mouth opens by which it is regarded as facial evidences for *despair* emotion [18].

D. A formalization of Resentment Emotion: Spite

The *spite* emotion has been neglected by psychologists in their studies and research. The neglecting case of that emotion type reached the degree that there is no single article published on this topic in journals of psychology, social personality or clinical psychology. The evolutionary biologists Marcus *et al.* [25] defined *spite* as "behaviors that have negative consequences for both the actor and the recipient". *Spite* is a complex emotion and could be classified as an extreme passive type of emotion. The agent who feels it oscillates between harsh agent, sly agent, devastating agent, petty agent and seemingly unharmed agent.

According to Florey [26], *spite* is a negative, harmful feeling, which incites irrational actions. It arises when one believes that someone else exists on an even status as one's self, but has something which one does not, and because of the belief that both individuals are on the same level, one feels that they are being wronged. The two individuals, however, do not exist on the same level, and if they did, then the spiteful one would have legitimate means of achieving the desired object, and therefore, has no reason to feel spiteful". Relating to the second characteristic, Fawzi [10] said of a patient suffering from PPD disease that the patient "Holds *spite* against those who disagreed with him in opinion or belief". By using our logic, we can build a formula to recognize the *spite* emotion:

Definition 4 $(Spite)$

$$Spite_{i,j}(\alpha, Sl_{i,j}) = Bel_i \neg Has_i PSTV_i \alpha \wedge Bel_i Has_j PSTV_i \alpha \wedge Bel_i \alpha \wedge Bel_i Sl_{i,j} \wedge \neg [J] Sl_{i,j} \quad (9)$$

So equation (9) will represent the cognitive structure of *spite* emotion, where the first chunk of it represents that agent *i* will feel *spite* against agent *j* in the existence of two atomic events α and $Sl_{i,j}$. The *spite* will be achieved under the presence of several factors: agent *i* believes that he does not have a positive (good) event, which is α, agent *i* believes that agent *j* has a positive event, which is α, agent *i* believes that α is true, agent *i* believes that he and agent *j* are at the same level such as $Sl_{i,j}$ is true, and the group of agents *J* sees to it that the same level event $Sl_{i,j}$ is false.

Example 2.
Consider two neighbours Joe and Max: Joe is an employee in a small company with a simple salary while Max is a sales manager in a big company with a huge salary. Max bought an expensive new car and Joe knows it somehow, represented by $Bel_{Joe}(\text{car})$, so he believes that Max has the ownership of a positive event, which is represented by $Bel_{Joe}Has_{Max}PSTV_{Joe}(\text{car})$, but Joe did not buy an expensive new car, represented by $Bel_{Joe}\neg Has_{Joe}PSTV_{Joe}(\text{car})$. Joe believes that he and Max are at the same level, represented by $Bel_{Joe}(Sl_{Joe,Max})$. The belief of Joe came from the view point that he and Max are employees and did not take into consideration other differences. The same level event means that agents Joe and Max are of the same level in science degree, community position, financial position, etc. We assume having a group *J* of persons, which are the friends of Joe and Max, represented by the group (Tom, Tony, Ted). The composition $[J]\alpha$ can be expressed depending on a form of group (Tom, Tony, Ted) sees to it that an event Joe and Max are at the same level is true, no matter what the other agents in the set of agents except Tom, Tony, Ted do. In reality the group *J*, represented by Tom, Tony, Ted did not see that Joe and Max are at the same level. Joe will feel *spite* when the preceding events are satisfied:

$$Spite_{Joe,Max}(\text{car}, Sl_{Joe,Max}) = Bel_{Joe}Has_{Max}PSTV_{Joe}(\text{car}) \wedge Bel_{Joe}\neg Has_{Joe}PSTV_{Joe}(\text{car}) \wedge Bel_{Joe}(\text{car}) \wedge Bel_{Joe}(Sl_{Joe,Max}) \wedge \neg[\text{Tom,Tony,Ted}]\text{sees to it that}(Sl_{Joe,Max})$$

Unfortunately, there are no facial evidences relating to *spite* since this type of emotions isn't constructed from basic emotions that we can blend.

V. LOGICAL MODEL IMPLEMENTATION

The proposed system has the ability to differentiate the *despair* and *spite* emotions, which are constructed from (Input, Inference Engine, Knowledge Base and Output) as we can see in Figure 1. The Input of the system is data ranging between facial evidences and the factors of the targeted emotions of the agent. The inference engine will compare the system input to the knowledge base in order to differentiate the two targeted complex emotions. Relating to *despair* emotion, the stored data in the knowledge base are facial evidences and emotion factors while the data for *spite* are only emotion ones. The system output is to differentiate complex emotions such as *despair* and *spite*. Depending on this differentiation, we can diagnose if the agent suffers from PPD disease.

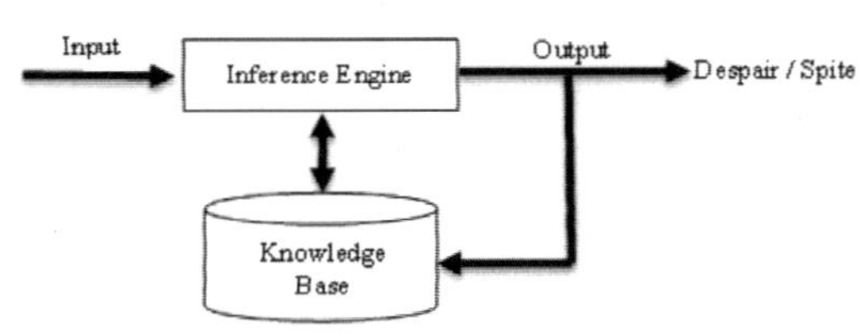

Figure 1. implementation system structure

As an example, consider two students Ed and Sam. Ed is dismissed from the university. Ed's friend Sam has a girlfriend. Let us start by analyzing the event: Ed is dismissed from the university. Ed knows somehow that he is dismissed from the university, represented by Bel_{Ed}(dismiss study). Ed's goal is not to be dismissed from his university, represented by $Goal_{Ed}\neg$(dismiss study). Ed realizes that there is no possibility in the future to be not dismissed from his university, which is represented by $\neg Poss_{Ed}F\neg$(dismiss study). The system can conclude that Ed feels *despair* when the preceding events are satisfied as we can see below:

$$Despair_{Ed}(\text{dismiss study}) = Bel_{Ed}(\text{dismiss study}) \wedge$$
$$Goal_{Ed}\neg(\text{dismiss study}) \wedge \neg Poss_{Ed}F\neg(\text{dismiss study})$$

When Ed face shows some evidences such as: inner corners of eyebrows are raised, upper lid inner corner is raised, the system cannot conclude that Ed feels *despair* since one of the facial evidences ("Mouth opens") is unavailable. Despite this problem, the system enables to diagnose that the agent feels *despair* from the existence of the emotion factors.

Now, let us consider the event: Ed's friend Sam has a girlfriend. Sam is an attractive person while Ed is not. Ed knows somehow that Sam has the ownership of a positive event (having a girlfriend), represented by $Bel_{Ed}Has_{Sam}PSTV_{Ed}$(gf) but Ed did not have a girlfriend, which is represented by $Bel_{Ed}\neg Has_{Ed}PSTV_{Ed}$(gf). Ed knows that Sam has a girlfriend, which is represented by Bel_{Ed}(gf), which means that Ed believes that an event of "have a girlfriend" is true. Ed believes that he and Sam are at the same level relating to attractiveness, which is represented by $Bel_{Ed}(Sl_{Ed,Sam})$. The belief of Ed came from the view point that he and Sam are beautiful and did not take into consideration the other differences. We assume having a group J of persons who know both Ed and Sam that is represented by the set (John, Joe, Jack). The composition $[J]\alpha$ can be expressed in a form "group (John, Joe, Jack) sees to it that an event (Ed and Sam are at the same level) is true no matter what the other agents in the set of agents except (John, Joe, Jack) do". In reality the group J did not see that Ed and Sam are at the same level, which is represented by Ed and Sam are at the same level. The system can conclude that Ed feels *spite* when the preceding events are satisfied as we can see below:

$$Spite_{Ed,Sam}(\text{gf}, Sl_{Ed,Sam}) = Bel_{Ed}Has_{Sam}PSTV_{Ed}(\text{gf}) \wedge$$
$$Bel_{Ed}\neg Has_{Ed}PSTV_{Ed}(\text{gf}) \wedge Bel_{Ed}(\text{gf}) \wedge Bel_{Ed}(Sl_{Ed,Sam})$$
$$\wedge \neg[\text{John, Joe, Jack}]seestoitthat(Sl_{Ed,Sam})$$

VI. Conclusion

In this paper, we presented a logic named PPDL that allows us to formalize and to reason about two complex emotions that are *despair* and *spite*. Unfortunately the OCC and Plutchik's Theories could not cover the emotional states of psychological personality's characteristics for the PPD disease. We overcome this problem by going deep in the psychology literatures and searching for discreet representation to reach to the unified formalization for the disease. Such formalization aims to capture the logical structure underlying a chosen psychological model of emotion; the resulting logical specification of emotions can then be used to reason about properties of emotions in a formal manner, thus gaining more insight into the workings of human emotions. By the unified formalization, we reach the goal of representing and recognizing the PPD disease by building a logical model with emotional flavour.

References

[1] DH-Pathways, "Recognizing complexity: Commissioning guidance for personality disorder services," M. Health, 2009.

[2] J. Peay, "Personality disorder and the law: Some awkward questions," Philosophy, Psychiatry, & Psychology, vol. 18, no. 3, 2011, pp. 231–244.

[3] B. Kemelgor, L. Sussman, J. Kline, and J. Zurada, "Who are the difficult employees? psychopathological attributions of their co-workers," Journal of Business & Economics Research (JBER), vol. 5, no. 10, 2007, pp. 47–62.

[4] M. W. Wiederman and R. A. Sansone, "Borderline personality disorder and sexuality," The Family Journal, vol. 17, no. 3, 2009, pp. 277–282.

[5] Hazelden-foundation, "Facts about addiction and personality disorder," http://dmh.mo.gov/docs/mentalillness/personalitydisorder.pdf, 2007.

[6] S. Lindström and K. Segerberg, "Modal logic and philosophy," Handbook of modal logic, vol. 3, 2007, pp. 1149–1214.

[7] A. Ortony, G. L. Clore, and A. Collins, The cognitive structure of emotions. Cambridge university press, 1990.

[8] Mental-Health, "Personality disorder," National Mental Health Consumer Self-Help Clearinghouse, 2015.

[9] K. P. Stoddart, "Personality disorder," Royal College of Psychiatrists, 2015.

[10] J. Fawzi, "Terrorist and personal causes of terrorism from the standpoint of academics and politicians and journalists and clerics convicted of crimes and terrorism in iraq," Ph.D. dissertation, Sulaymaniyah, Iraq, 2009.

[11] P. Becheiraz and D. Thalmann, "A behavioral animation system for autonomous actors personified by emotions," in Proceedings of the 1998 Workshop on Embodied Conversational Characters, 1998.

[12] R. Plutchik, "The nature of emotions human emotions have deep evolutionary roots, a fact that may explain their complexity and provide tools for clinical practice," American Scientist, vol. 89, no. 4, 2001, pp. 344–350.

[13] E. Lorini and F. Schwarzentruber, "A logic for reasoning about counterfactual emotions," Artificial Intelligence, vol. 175, no. 3, 2011, pp. 814–847.

[14] R. Plutchik, "Integration, differentiation, and derivatives of emotion," Evolution an Cognition, vol. 7, no. 2, 2001, pp. 114–125.

[15] S. M. Mohammad and P. D. Turney, "Crowdsourcing a word–emotion association lexicon," Computational Intelligence, vol. 29, no. 3, 2013, pp. 436–465.

[16] J.-F. Bonnefon, D. Longin, and M.-H. Nguyen, "A logical framework for trust-related emotions," Electronic Communications of the EASST, Formal Methods for Interactive Systems 2009, vol. 22, 2009, pp. 1–16.

[17] B. Steunebrink et al., "The logical structure of emotions," Ph.D. dissertation, Netherlands, 2010.

[18] P. Ekman and W. V. Friesen, Unmasking the face: A guide to recognizing emotions from facial clues. Ishk, 2003.

[19] N. Guiraud, D. Longin, E. Lorini, S. Pesty, and J. Rivière, "The face of emotions: a logical formalization of expressive speech acts," in 10th International Conference on Autonomous Agents and Multiagent Systems-Volume 3, 2011, pp. 1031–1038.

[20] F. Schwarzentruber and C. Semmling, "Stit is dangerously undecidable." in ECAI, 2014, pp. 1093–1094.

[21] R. A. Pecchenino, "The economic consequences of despair," Maynooth University, Tech. Rep., 2014.

[22] J. Panksepp, "The neuro-evolutionary cusp between emotions and cognitions: Implications for understanding consciousness and the emergence of a unified mind science," Consciousness & Emotion, vol. 1, no. 1, 2000, pp. 15–54.

[23] C. G. Boeree, "Personality theory: A biosocial approach," 2009.

[24] P. N. Johnson-Laird and K. Oatley, "The language of emotions: An analysis of a semantic field," Cognition and emotion, vol. 3, no. 2, 1989, pp. 81–123.

[25] D. K. Marcus, V. Zeigler-Hill, S. H. Mercer, and A. L. Norris, "The psychology of spite and the measurement of spitefulness," Psychological assessment, vol. 26, no. 2, 2014, p. 563.

[26] D. M. Florey, "The problem of spite," Master's thesis, Gettysburg College, 2013.

A New Scientometric Dimension for User Profile

Nedra Ibrahim, Anja Habacha Chaibi and Henda Ben Ghézala
RIADI Laboratory
ENSI, University of Manouba
2010, Manouba, Tunisia
e-mail: nedra.ibrahim@ensi-uma.tn, anja.habacha@ensi.rnu.tn and henda.benghezala@ensi.rnu.tn

Abstract— **Personalization aims to facilitate the expression of user needs and enables him/her to obtain relevant information. The data describing the user are grouped in a profile, which varies according to the application context and the type of users and their needs. By focusing on a particular type of applications (dedicated to scientific research) and a particular type of users (researchers), we note that existing personalization approaches only partially solve problems related to personalization quality (accuracy, freshness, validity period, response time, source credibility), but lacks a model involving scientific quality (content, author, container and affiliation quality). The scientific quality is assessed by a set of quantitative and qualitative measures, which are the scientometric indicators. In this paper, we propose a profile model based on scientometrics to involve the qualitative relevance of information in a retrieval system dedicated to scientific research. The proposed model will be the basis of building an ontological user profile able to store scientometric preferences.**

Keywords-user modeling; scientific quality; scientometrics; quality evaluation; user profile; profile model.

I. INTRODUCTION

Faced with a large number of heterogeneous information resources, the user is unable to express his preferences and select relevant information while referring to reliable sources of confidence.

Particularly, in the field of scientific research, the validity of scientific production and even the scientific process relies on the quality of the information. The users of information systems dedicated to scientific research are researchers. This particular kind of users is interested in the relevance of information as well as in its scientific quality. In this context, we define scientometrics, which is the set of quantitative methods that are devoted to the evaluation of scientific production (researcher, scientific paper, research group, laboratory...). Scientometrics is based on a set of quantitative metrics and measures called scientometric indicators, which include publications, citations, h-index, g-index, hi-index, hc-index, AWCR, and AW-index [1], and the qualitative measure H_X [2].

In this paper, we are interested in the personalization of user profile in the field of scientific research to meet the needs of researchers. Our user profile personalization approach comes to fill the absence of a personalization approach that involves the scientific quality of the information. This approach is based on the proposal of a profile model integrating scientific quality measured by scientometric indicators. This model is able to collect quality preferences from the user. It is based at the first level on the quality of: content, containing, author and affiliation. At the second level, going up a level of abstraction, we find the quality of: the source of document, the editor of the scientific journal, the association of the conference, the research organization and career of the authors.

This work comes as part of the proposal and the implementation of a personalized information retrieval system dedicated to scientific research and based on the scientific quality of the information processed at different stages.

This paper is organized as follows: Section II summarizes the state of the art on personalization, profile modeling, scientometrics and the works oriented to the ontological user profiles. In Section III, we present the profile models that we propose. In Section IV, we show the process of building the profile ontology and its evaluation. We finish with a conclusion in Section V.

II. RELATED WORK

The user profile is the core concept of personalization in information retrieval (IR). The user profile is defined by contextual elements directly related to the user, such as their interests, search preferences, etc. All of this information is represented in profile model. A profile model includes all the knowledge necessary for efficient query evaluation and production of relevant information tailored to each user. A profile can be defined as a personalized access to information model while a query is the expression of detailed needs that the user wishes to see in his/her profile.

The user profile is part of the user's cognitive context according to the multidimensional taxonomy presented in context [3]. Several definitions of the profile have been discussed in the literature. We distinguish the cognitive profile [4][5], the qualitative profile [6] and the multidimensional profile [7][8]. The cognitive profile exploited in several customized systems is analog to the user's cognitive context addressed in the context of the multidimensional taxonomy [3]. The qualitative profile in [6] is linked to the user's search preferences for the quality of information returned by the system (freshness, credibility of sources of information, consistency, etc.). These criteria concern the context of qualitative document processed in the context of the multidimensional taxonomy [3]. In some studies, the profile covers in addition to the interests and preferences of the user, the characteristics of the environment and the system, thus defining a multidimensional profile [8][9]. A multidimensional profile covers all possible dimensions involved in the interaction of the user with the system. P3P (Policy Languages Interest Group) [9] standard to secure the profiles, allows to define classes that distinguish between demographic attributes, professional and behavior attributes. In [8], Amato and Straccia proposed a profile model for users of a digital library consisting of five categories: personal data, collected data, delivery data, behavior data and safety data. Moreover, the authors simple profile information categories make their model extensible with difficulty. In [7], Kostadinov proposed a profile model based on Amato and Straccia profile model [8] and consisting of eight classes: centers of interest, ontologies, personal data, quality, customization, security, client feedback and divers. Based on Kostadinov's profile [7], Bouzeghoub and Kostadinov [9] enriched the profile by two other categories: delivery preferences and query history. In [11], the authors proposed a profile model combining profile content, context and preferences.

The quality was incorporated into the profile models of [9][11]. In these works, they involve the quality of personalization process and content quality:

- The quality of the query execution process and the quality of delivery data: measured by the response time. Other measures of the personalization process have been proposed by Mobasher et al. [12] as the Weighted Average Visit Percentage (WAVP), precision, coverage, F1 measure and R measure.
- The quality of content and information provider: characterized by the freshness of the information, which include the time elapsed since the establishment of the information or the time of the last update. Also the precision and accuracy of the data, which requires the opinion of an external expert.

Recent researches are oriented to design a new generation of personalization systems based on context, social networks and ontologies. In [13], the authors combined search technologies and knowledge about query and user context into a single framework. The works in [14] and [15] added the notion of context and situation. In [16], the authors proposed an ontological user profile modeling for context-aware personalization. In [17], the authors proposed an ontology-based user profile for modeling user behavior. In [11], the authors proposed an ontological user profile able to store the profile dimensions, the context and preferences. In [18], the authors used the social network annotation in user profile.

All of these techniques already mentioned are not dedicated to recognize users while remaining independent of the quality. For this, our work is oriented to design a new personalization system based on scientific quality. Our contribution aims to deliver qualitative information relevant and appropriate to the researcher needs.

The quality that has been integrated into existing personalization approaches is process oriented (independent of the information), or content oriented (decided by an expert). In this case, we confront the problems of information independency and relativity and subjectivity of experts' judgment.

We focused in this paper on the representation of an extension of existing personalization approaches.

III. MULTIDIMENSIONAL MODEL FOR REPRESENTATION OF SCIENTOMETRIC PREFERENCES

To solve the problem of absence of personalized approach involving scientific quality, we propose a new qualitative dimension to represent the expectations of researchers. Our contribution is the integration of a new dimension "scientometric preferences" to construct a multidimensional user profile concerned with the quality of scientific research.

In our approach, we study all the elements of the scientific process, which affect the scientific quality. To each element we associate the scientometric indicators, which measure its quality.

Based on works already done in the context of multidimensional profile modeling [7][9], we propose a reusable multidimensional profile that involves the scientific quality. We define a generic model, which will be instantiated to draw the profile model, which can be exploited by other user profiles.

A. *Generic model*

Figure 1 shows our representation of the generic profile model. This representation can be structured in the form of hierarchy of classes which are:

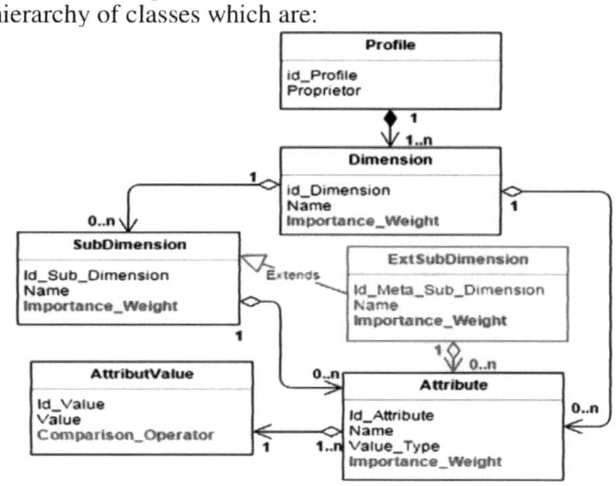

Figure 1. Generic model.

- Profile: describes the criteria that characterize a user. It contains several dimensions. For example: personal data, centers of interest, scientometric preferences, etc.
- Dimension: describes information characterizing user preferences; this information is grouped and structured in the form of a set of open dimensions. To each dimension we associate a weight describing its importance compared to other Dimensions relative to the user.
- SubDimension: information that is grouped and structured as part of a specific dimension. To each

SubDimension we assign an id, a name and an importance weight.

- ExtSubDimension: information that is grouped and structured as an extension of a specific SubDimension. This information is from a higher level of abstraction. To each ExtSubDimension we assign an id, a name and an importance weight.
- Attribute: this class represents an elementary attribute to which we assign (id, name, value type and importance weight).
- AttributeValue: describes the possible values that are associated with each attribute. To delimit the interval of the values of preference, the user has to specify a precise value accompanied by a comparison operator (<,<=,>,>=,=).

Our proposed generic model is:

- Open: it can be extended by other kinds of profiles in an easy way;
- Flexible: it is able to acquire the main categories of knowledge in the current personalization systems;
- Multifacets: it can be analyzed from different angles (dimensions, attributes, etc.);
- Evolutionary: it allows any changes or updates;
- Independent of any information system or any technology and the specialization, generalization and instantiation of this model is easy.

B. *Profile model*

Our profile model is an instantiation of the generic model described in the previous section. This model is one of the possible instances of the generic model. Because the proposed generic model is open, flexible and independent of any data, it can be instantiated with different values.

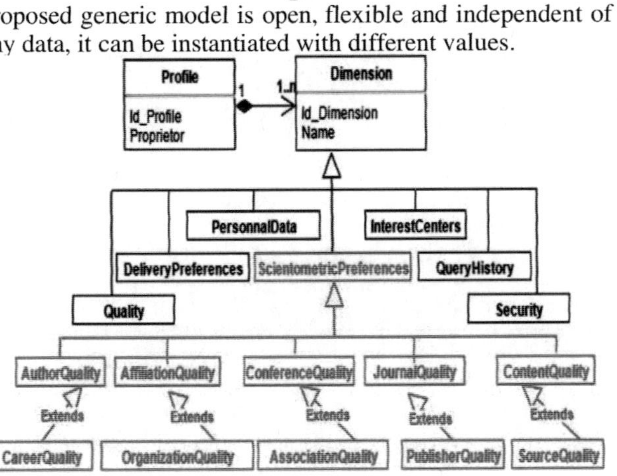

Figure 2. Profile model.

Based on the profile model of Bouzeghoub and Kostadinov [9], we propose a set of existing dimensions enriched by a new qualitative dimension which is the scientometric preferences. This proposed dimension contains the different information characterizing the scientific quality preferences introduced by the user.

In Figure 2, we present our proposed model enriched by the new scientometric dimension (scientometric preferences). Our model can be exploited in a personalization process of a scientific retrieval system.

Scientometric preferences store the necessary information describing the quality of a scientific document according to the researcher's needs. These preferences are organized into five SubDimensions which are the scientific entities affecting the scientific quality of documents. The quality of each scientific entity is measured by a set of scientometric indicators which represent the attributes of each SubDimenson. On the other hand, each SubDimesnion is extended on ExtSubDimension by moving to a higher level of abstraction. Each ExtSubDimension will be organized into attributes which represent the scientometric indicators measuring its quality.

In the following, we detail the elements of the dimension "scientometric preferences."

1) Quality of author and career

The quality of author is one of entities which affect the scientific quality of documents. Author quality is measured by the mean of four scientometric indicators (Figure 3):

- H-index (Hirsh index): is an indicator of the researcher impact. A researcher has an index of h if his/her papers are cited at least h times each [1].
- Citation number: is the number of citations received by his/her published scientific papers.
- Author position: is the position of the author in the co-authors list. He/she can be the first author, second co-author, third co-author and so on.
- Publication number: is the number of scientific papers published by the author.

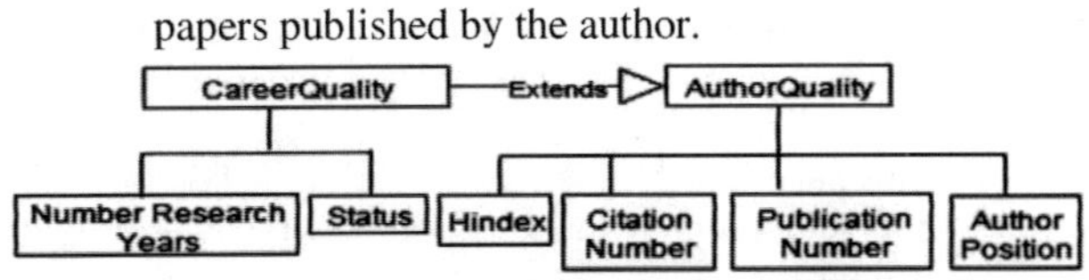

Figure 3. Quality of author and his career.

By ascending a level of abstraction, we associate the quality of career to the author quality as an extension. The quality of author career is measured by the number of years spent by the author on research in a specific discipline, and his current scientific grade (PhD student, assistant professor, professor, etc).

2) Quality of content and source

Another entity that affects the scientific quality of documents is the quality of content, to which we assign the following attributes (Figure 4):

- Citation number: the number of citations received by the published scientific document. A larger number of citations reflects a better quality of document content.
- Co-authors number: the number of authors who contributed to the realization of the scientific document.

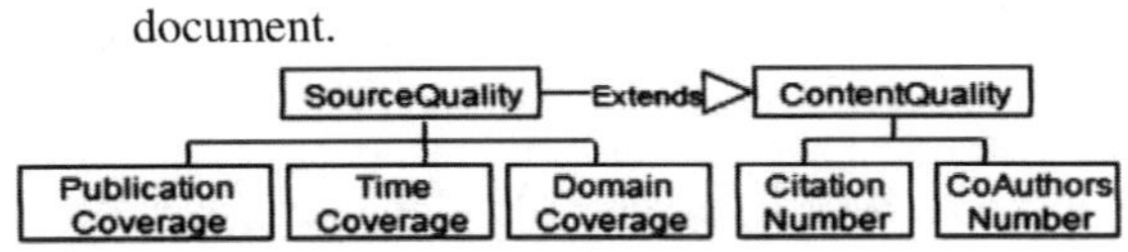

Figure 4. Quality of content and its source.

We designate by the source of scientific documents the bibliographic databases such as: Google Scholar, Scopus, dblp, MS Academic Search, etc. The quality of information source is measured by the number of publications, the interval of time and the number of domains covered by the source.

3) Quality of journal and publisher

Scientific journals are containers of scientific documents. A good quality of the journal promotes the selection of the document. As shown in Figure 5, the quality of a journal is evaluated by:

- Impact factor: is a measure of the frequency with which the average article in a journal has been cited in a particular year or period. Thus, the impact factor of a journal is calculated by dividing the number of current year citations by the source items published in that journal during the previous two years. The journal impact factor is provided by the annual Journal Citation Report (JCR) [19] of Thomson Reuters or by SCImago Journal & Country Rank (SJR) [20].
- Ranking: journal ranking is the classification of journals according to its quality. SCImago Journal & Country Rank (SJR) provides a journal ranking into four classes: Q1, Q2, Q3 and Q4. Another type of journal ranking is provided by ERA [21] into four classes: A*, A, B and C.
- Citation number: the number of citations received by all the journal publications.
- Self-citation number: when a paper published in a journal cites a previously published paper in that same journal.
- Response time: the time period taken by the publisher to provide the first response to submitted manuscript.
- Publication number: the number of publications in the journal.

Figure 5. Quality of journal and its publisher.

The quality of journal can be extended to the evaluation of publisher quality which can affect the scientific quality of documents. As examples of journals' publishers we cite: Elsevier [22], Springer [23], Emerald [24], Sage [25], ACM [26] etc. The publisher quality is measured by the number of specialties, the number of published journals and the number of published books.

4) Quality of conference and association

In the same way, we describe the SubDimension "quality of conference" and its extension "association quality". Conferences are the other type of document container. In Figure 6, we describe the different measures of the conference quality consisting on:

- Conference ranking: is the classification of conferences according to their quality. ERA provides conference ranking into four classes: A*, A, B and C.
- Citation number: the number of citations received by all the papers published in the conference.
- Self-citation number: when a paper published in a conference cites a previously published paper in that same conference.
- Publication number: the number of papers published by the conference.

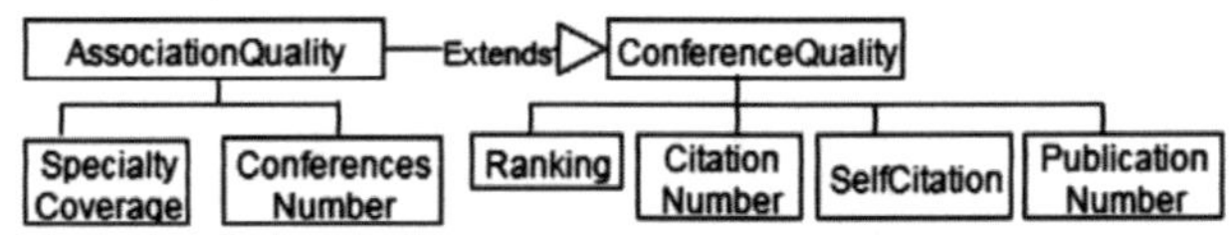

Figure 6. Quality of conference and its association.

To each conference, we join its association, such as: IEEE [27]. The quality of conference association is measured by the number of specialties and the number of conferences organized by the association.

5) Quality of affiliation and organization

In our profile model, we consider the quality of author(s) affiliation. The author affiliation is represented by the research environment or the research community such as: laboratory, research unit, university department or group of researchers working in the same discipline. Affiliation quality is measured by specific scientometric indicators represented in Figure 7:

- Group H-index: Hirsh index of a researchers group having the same affiliation is defined as the number of all the articles of the group which have been cited at least h times each.
- Citation number: the number of citations received by the papers published by the group of researchers having the same affiliation.
- Self-citation: when two members of the same affiliation site each other.
- Publication number: the number of papers published by the group of researchers having the same affiliation.

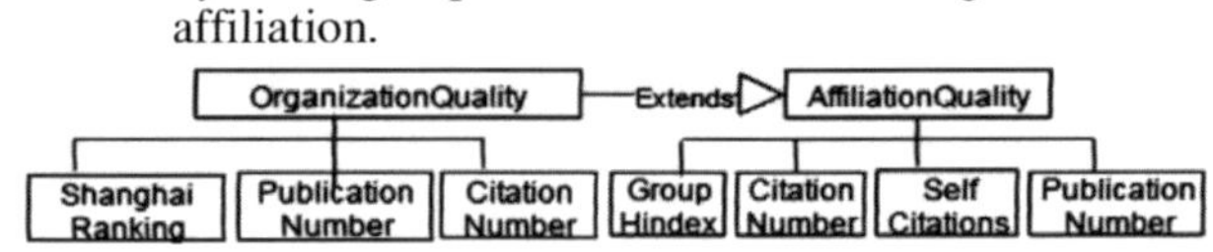

Figure 7. Quality of affiliation and its organization.

The quality of affiliation is influenced by the quality of the organization or the institution of reference, such as universities. So, we extended the affiliation quality to the organization quality measured by the Shanghai ranking [28] (in the case of academic organizations), the number of papers published by the different research entities belonging to the same organization and the number of citations received by the papers published by the different entities belonging to the same orginization.

IV. SCIENTOMETRIC ONTOLOGY

The profiles are containers of knowledge about the user. The user's preferences represent the expectations of the user.

To apply the model of the proposed profile, we opted for an ontology to represent the scientometric preferences of the user. An nntology is a good candidate for representing knowlcdgc about uscrs. It allows having a sharcd understanding between people or software agents and their relations, and a controlled vocabulary, which implies a formal definition of concepts. In addition to their contribution in terms of reusability, modularity and knowledge sharing, ontologies are used to define a precise vocabulary, which is the basis of communication between different users.

A. *From the generic model to ontology*

Ontology, such as generic models of UML (Unified Modeling Language), models the universe of discourse by means of hierarchical classes by properties association. However, an ontology has five differences compared to generic UML models [29]:

- Semantics: Ontologies are used in an Open World Assumption (OWA). In contrast, UML models are used in a Closed World Assumption (CWA).
- Goal: In ontology, the focus is generally on concepts and relations between them. In contrast, a generic model of UML emphasized the operational side of a particular computer system.
- Atomicity: In UML, each concept only makes sense in the context of the model in which it is defined. In ontology each concept is individually identified and is a basic unit of knowledge.
- Consensuality: In ontology of domain, concepts are represented as consensus of a community. Similarly, the semantic integration of all systems based on the same ontology can be easily made.
- Canonicity: Unlike generic models that use a language (UML) to describe domain information, ontologies use (OWL) formal semantics (describing logic).

The next step is to transform the classes and attributes of the profile model into concepts and slots of ontology.

B. *Implementation of the scientometric dimension*

In this section, on the basis of the generic model that we proposed in Section III, we will show the process of building our ontological user profile following the Noy's method [30].

Most ontologies were created using the OWL (Web Ontology Language) [31]. OWL is designed for use by applications that need to process the content of information instead of just presenting information to humans. OWL facilitates greater machine interpretability of Web content than that supported by XML (Extensible Markup Language), RDF (Resource Description Format), and RDF-S (RDF Schema) [31]. It provides additional vocabulary along with a formal semantic. OWL has three increasingly-expressive sublanguages: OWL Lite, OWL DL, and OWL Fulls [31]. Proposals for the design of ontologies on the theoretical and practical view can be found in [30]. Our ontological profile was implemented using OWL-DL. There are many methods for ontology engineering. In our case, we opted for Noy's method [30] proposed by Stanford University. We considered the fact that the tool with which we will build the ontology in this case PROTÉGÉ [32] which is developed by the same university.

The ontology design process can be summarized in the following steps:

- Step 1: determine the domain, scope and users of the ontology. The ontology domain is going to cover the scientometric domain (assessment tools, measures and indicators) conducted for a scientific research evaluation. The purpose of using our ontology is to describe the qualitative preferences of the user (researcher). The ontology must respond to user requests, taking into account the semantics of those requests.
- Step 2: consider reusing existing ontologies: Existing ontologies in the field of personalization systems did not satisfy our needs. So, we built our ontology fully based on our research.
- Step 3: our study of both scientometric field and user profile management, allowed us to identify a list of important terms. We can list some terms: dimension, attribute, sub-dimension, author quality, affiliation quality, source quality, citation number, journal impact factor, conference ranking etc.
- Step 4: the definition of classes and class hierarchy described in Figure 8: classes provide an abstraction mechanism for grouping resources with similar characteristics. Like RDF classes, every OWL class (OWL:class) is associated with a set of individuals called the extension of class.

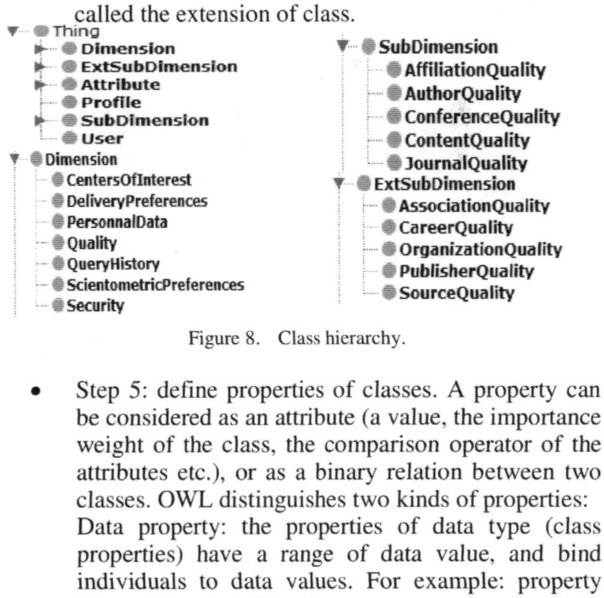

Figure 8. Class hierarchy.

- Step 5: define properties of classes. A property can be considered as an attribute (a value, the importance weight of the class, the comparison operator of the attributes etc.), or as a binary relation between two classes. OWL distinguishes two kinds of properties:
  Data property: the properties of data type (class properties) have a range of data value, and bind individuals to data values. For example: property "Name" for class "User".
  Object property: object properties (relationship) have a range of values of class individuals. For example, the property "Extends" applies to an object of class called "ExtSubDimension" and takes its values in the class called "SubDimension".

- Step 6: create instance: the instances are all objects of classes.

C. *Profile validation*

To test the profile ontology, we use the Pellet reasoner available directly from PROTÉGÉ. Pellet is a complete and capable OWL-DL reasoner with very good performance, extensive middleware, and a number of unique features [33]. Pellet is written in Java and is open source under a very liberal license. It is used in a number of projects, from pure research to industrial settings.

Pellet is the first sound and complete OWL-DL reasoner with extensive support for reasoning with individuals (including nominal support and conjunctive query). It has user defined data types, and debugging support for ontologies [33]. It implements several extensions to OWL-DL including combination formalism for OWL-DL ontologies, a non-monotonic operator, and preliminary support for OWL/Rule hybrid reasoning. It has proven to be a reliable tool for working with OWL-DL ontologies and experimenting with OWL extensions.

In this section, we describe three tests provided by Pellet: consistency checking, classification test and queries test.

Figure 9. Inferred class hierarchy.

1) *Consistency test*

Consistency checking provided by Pellet is made based on the class description, which ensures that ontology does not contain any contradictory facts. Each class must have at least one individual member. A class is considered inconsistent if it cannot have any instance. The result of this test is shown in Figure 9 representing inferred class hierarchy after invoking the reasoner. All classes are consistent.

2) *Classification test*

The classification test can check whether a class is a subclass of another class or not. It computes the subclass relations between every named class to create the complete class hierarchy. The class hierarchy can be used to answer queries such as getting all or only the direct subclasses of a class.

When this test is invoked, the consistency test is first performed for all classes of the ontology, because inconsistent classes cannot be classified correctly. Once the classification test is performed on the class hierarchy containing the logical expressions, it is possible for the classifier to infer a new hierarchy "inferred ontology class hierarchy". This is, a hierarchy where classes are classified according to the relationship superclass/ subclasses. In this case the classification test shows that no suggestion has been produced by the reasoner Pellet and that "Asserted hierarchy" and "Inferred hierarchy" are identical, indicating the validity of classification of our ontology.

3) *Test queries*

PROTÉGÉ allows querying your project and locating all instances that match the criteria you specify. You can create a simple query, or combine multiple criteria to restrict or expand your results. Queries are not part of our knowledge base, but are a way to identify the instances in your project, based on class and slot properties. We have created different queries using SPARQL tool [34].

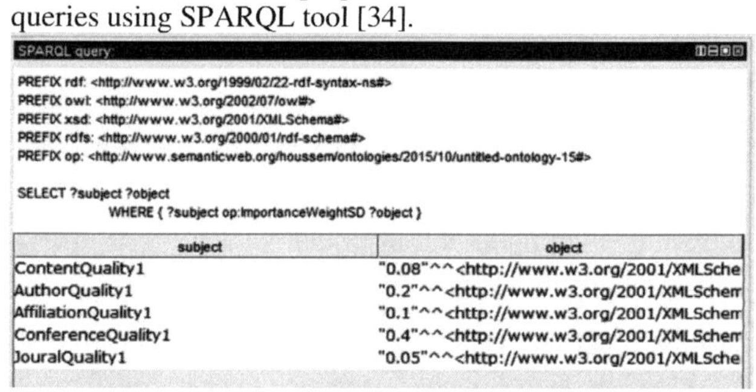

Figure 10. Query execution.

In Figure 10, we present an example of the execution of the following query: Find the importance weight preferences of all SubDimensions.

V. CONCLUSION AND FUTURE WORK

The research activity has become increasingly selective considering the importance given to the quality of scientific production and the diversity of tools and systems evaluating research activity. Researchers become selective in their choice and are more interested in the quality of information. To meet the needs of researchers, we proposed a personalization system dedicated to the researcher integrating scientific quality in the user profile.

Our contribution begins with the proposal of a generic profile model enriched by a new type of component which is the extended sub-dimension linked with an extend relationship to the sub-dimension. Our profile model was designed to be open, flexible, evolutionary, and independent of any information or technology. Its specialization, generalization and instantiation were easy. Next, we proposed a qualitative user profile which was an instantiation of our generic profile model. The novelty was the integration of a new scientometric dimension for assessing the scientific quality of the selected information. Our contribution was to improve the performance of the retrieval system in terms of information relevance and to satisfy the researcher's needs. All elements affecting the scientific quality were studied and incorporated into the user profile.

To represent user qualitative preferences, we opted for ontology. Our profile ontology is characterized by its reusability, facility of expansion, integration and instantiation. The major advantage of our ontological profile is its coherence and its consistency shown by tests on it. Thus, it is ready for future use in any personalization system that is based on user profile.

Practically, our contribution can improve the research quality and relevance. Indirectly, it can positively influence research attitudes and affect the quality of research by limiting unscientific practices, such as: considering older articles are qualitatively better; considering the number of citations as an indicator of quality; and giving equal consideration to publications at conferences and publications in journals or even publications at conferences of different classes or in journals having different impact factors.

By integrating our ontological user profile into a scientometric information retrieval system, as perspectives, we plan to apply a model for ontology evaluation based on metrics to validate our contribution.

REFERENCES

[1] Y. Okubo, "Bibliometric indicators and analysis of research systems: methods and examples," OECD Science, Technology and Industry Working Papers, Jan. 1997, OECD Publishing, Paris.

[2] N. Ibrahim, A. Habacha Chaibi, and M. Ben Ahmed, "New scientometric indicator for the qualitative evaluation of scientific production," New Library World Journal, Vol. 116, Iss. 11/12, 2015, pp. 661-676.

[3] L. Tamine, M. Boughanem, and M. Daoud, "Evaluation of contextual information retrieval : overview of issues and research," Knowl Inf Syst (Kais), Vol. 24 No.1, 2010, pp. 1-34.

[4] H. Lieberman, "Letizia : an agent that assists web browsing," Proc. International Joint Proceedings of the Fourteenth International Joint Conference on Artificial Intelligence (IJCAI 95), 1995, pp. 924–929.

[5] C. W. Leung, S. C. Chan, and F. Chung, "A collaborative filtering framework based on fuzzy association rules and multiple-level similarity," Knowledge Information System, Vol. 10 No. 3, 2006, pp. 357–381.

[6] R. Harrathi and S. Calabretto, " A model of information quality," Proc. Extraction et gestion des connaissances (EGC 2006), 2006, pp. 299–304.

[7] D. Kostadinov, "Personalization of information, definition of user profile model," Master's thesis, Université de Versailles, France, 2003.

[8] G. Amato and U. Straccia, "User Profile Modeling and Applications to Digital Libraries," Proc. 3rd European Conf. Research and Advanced Technology for Digital Libraries (ECDL 99), 1999, pp. 184-197.

[9] S. Abbar, M. Bouzeghoub, D. Kostadinov, S. Lopes, A. Aghasaryan, and S. Betge-Brezetz, "A personalized access model: concepts and services for content delivery platforms," Proc. of the 10th International Conference on Information Integration and Web-based Applications & Services, ACM, Nov. 2008, pp. 41-47.

[10] P. Vakkari, "A theory of the task-based information retrieval process : a summary and generalisation of a longitudinal study," Journal of documentation, Vol. 57 No. 1, 2001, pp. 44–60.

[11] Y. El Allioui and O. El Beqqali, "User profile Ontology for the Personalization approach," International Journal of Computer Applications, Vol. 41 No. 4, 2012, pp. 31-40.

[12] B. Mobasher, H. Dai, T. Luo, and M. Nakagawa, "Discovery and Evaluation of Aggregate Usage Profiles for Web Personalization," Data Mining and Knowledge Discovery, Vol. 6 No. 1, 2002, pp. 61-82.

[13] J. Allan et al., "Challenges in information retrieval and langage modelling," Workshop held at the center for intelligent information retrieval, Septembre, 2002, pp. 31-47.

[14] T. Saracevic, "The stratefied model of information retrieval interaction : extension and applications," Proc. the 60th annual meeting of the American Society for Information Science, Medford, NJ, 1997, pp. 313-327.

[15] M. Sutterer, O. Droegehorn, and K. David, "UPOS: User profile ontology with situation-dependent preferences support," Proc. First International Conference On Advances in Computer-Human Interaction (ACHI08), IEEE, Feb. 2008, pp. 230-235.

[16] K. L. Skillen, L. Chen, C. D. Nugent, M. P. Donnelly, W. Burns, and I. Solheim, "Ontological user profile modeling for context-aware application personalization," Proc. Springer Ubiquitous Computing and Ambient Intelligence, Berlin Heidelberg, 2012, pp. 261-268.

[17] L. Razmerita, "An ontology-based framework for modeling user behavior—A case study in knowledge management," Systems, Man and Cybernetics, Part A: Systems and Humans, IEEE Transactions, Vol. 41 No. 4, 2011, pp. 772-783.

[18] M. Mezghani, C. A. Zayani, I. Amous, and F. Gargouri, "A user profile modelling using social annotations: a survey," Proc. ACM 21st international conference companion on World Wide Web, Ap. 2012, pp. 969-976.

[19] http://scientific.thomsonreuters.com/imgblast/JCRFullCovlist-2014.pdf 2016-01-10.

[20] http://www.scimagojr.com/index.php 2016-01-10.

[21] http://portal.core.edu.au/conf-ranks/ 2016-01-10.

[22] https://www.elsevier.com/ 2016-01-10.

[23] http://www.springer.com/gp/ 2016-01-10.

[24] http://www.emeraldgrouppublishing.com/ 2016-01-10.

[25] https://uk.sagepub.com/en-gb/eur/home 2016-01-10.

[26] http://dl.acm.org/ 2016-01-10.

[27] https://www.ieee.org/index.html 2016-01-10.

[28] http ://www.shanghairanking.com/fr/index.html 2016-01-10.

[29] C. Atkinson, M. Gutheil and K. Kiko, "On the Relationship of Ontologies and Models," WoMM, Vol. 96, 2006, pp. 47-60.

[30] N. F. Noy and C. D. Hafner, "Ontological foundations for experimental science knowledge bases," Applied Artificial Intelligence, Vol. 14 No. 6, 2000, pp. 565-618.

[31] G. Antoniou, and F. Van Harmelen, "Web ontology language: Owl," In Handbook on ontologies, Springer Berlin Heidelberg 2004, pp. 67-92.

[32] http://protege.stanford.edu/ 2016-01-10.

[33] E. Sirin, B. Parsia, B. Grau, A. Kalyanpur, and Y. Katz, "Pellet: A practical OWL-DL reasoner. Web Semantics: Science, Services and Agents on the World Wide Web", Software Engineering and the Semantic Web, Vol. 5 No. 2, Jun. 2007, pp. 51-53.

[34] J. Pérez, M. Arenas, and C. Gutierrez, "Semantics and complexity of SPARQL," ACM Transactions on Database Systems (TODS), Vol. 34 No. 3, 2009, pp. 16-43.

Basic Study of an Evaluation that Uses the Center of Gravity of a Facial Thermal Image for the Estimation of Autonomic Nervous Activity

Shogo Matsuno, Shunsuke Kosuge, Shunsuke Kawazura, Naoaki Itakura, and Tota Mizuno
Dept. of Informatics, Graduate School of Informatics and Engineering
The University of Electro-Communications
Tokyo, Japan
e-mail: {m1440004, k1210058, k1430023, ita, mizuno}@edu.cc.uec.ac.jp

Hirotoshi Asano
Dept. of Electronics and Information Engineering
Faculty of Engineering
Kagawa University
Kagawa, Japan
e-mail: asano@eng.kagawa-u.ac.jp

***Abstract*—In this paper, we propose using the temperature-centroid of a facial thermal image as a new index to evaluate the Mental Work Load (MWL). The existing evaluation methods using thermal images are non-contact mental-stress–evaluation methods that measure a change in the temperature of the regions around the nose, which is caused by MWL. However, automatic evaluation of mental load is difficult because identifying a part of the nose automatically from the thermograph is difficult. In this paper, we have focused on developing a solution to this problem that combines temperature with the coordinates of the thermal image.**

Keywords-facial thermal image; nasal skin temperature; mental work load.

I. INTRODUCTION

Mental load or mental burden associated with work is called mental work load (MWL) [1]. Moderate mental load results in a positive effect on the workers; however, excessive mental load can cause negative effects such as fatigue, decreased attention span, and monotony [2][3]. Thus, if possible, MWL that leads to human errors and reduction in work efficiency should be evaluated.

In previous studies, a variety of indicators were used for the evaluation of MWL [4]-[7]; for example, behavioral assessments that use work performance, psychology evaluations using questionnaires, and physiological evaluations using electrical physiological signal indicators. In particular, the evaluation using a physiological index is an attractive option in quantitative real-time applications. The physiological indicators that are generally used are the heartbeat, respiration rate, blood pressure, electromyography (EMG), and electroencephalography (EEG). However, to measure these metrics electrically, the concerned electrodes must be attached to the skin; this calls for the development of a measurement environment such as a laboratory, for the physiological measurement of MWL. To solve this problem, we developed a technique for assessing the mental state of humans using facial thermal images. These images are obtained using non-contact infrared thermography [8]-[10]. Facial thermal images can be used to study human physiological psychology, because they vary depending on the changes in the blood-flow rate associated with human autonomic nervous activity. In addition, changes in skin temperature due to MWL are significantly different at different regions of the face. For example, the concentration of the arteriovenous anastomoses (AVA) vessels that adjust the blood flow in capillaries is higher in the periphery of the nose compared to the other sites. Furthermore, the blood-flow changes due to autonomic nervous activity and inhibition are directly reflected as skin-temperature changes because the blood vessels run through low-fat regions between the skin and the nasal bone. Thus, it is possible to quantitatively evaluate the MWL using sympathetic-activity MWL (mental arithmetic tasks) by measuring a temperature drop in the nose region for a short period. Physiological psychology assessments using facial thermal images do not use physical restraints, and hence, they are non-contact compared to assessments using other bioelectric-signal indexes. Thus, this assessment is believed to be suitable for the physiological evaluation of MWL in real work situations.

We focused on the evaluation of MWL using facial thermal images. Furthermore, we aimed for a more established, robust, and stronger measurement and evaluation system that is capable of withstanding disturbances such as changes in the subject's position, changes caused by wind, and so on. So far, we have evaluated MWL using the temperature difference between the skin at the forehead and at the nose [11]-[13]. The MWL evaluation method using thermal images has a measurement accuracy and reliability that is of the same order as those of the evaluation methods using other physiological indicators or questionnaires. However, the results of the temperature comparison between the forehead and nose regions may become less accurate because it does not use information on the position or area of the thermal images. Therefore, we consider the use of the temperature–center-of-gravity as a parameter by adding temperature information as a depth to the coordinate information. If it is possible to divide the facial thermal image into a number of regions, and evaluate the change in temperature distribution in each region, the realization of a strong physiological psychology state-estimation, in spite of disturbances such as effects of movement or shooting angle of face, can be made possible.

The method proposed in this paper was verified through experiments to determine how the temperature–center-of-gravity was affected by the number of area divisions at the time of capturing the facial thermal image. In Section II, we explain the relationship between the characteristics of the facial thermal image and MWL. This enables us to measure the change in MWL using the temperature-center-of-gravity as a first step. In Section III, we report and discuss the results of an estimation experiment. In addition, we verify the amount of change in the temperature displacement of the center-of-gravity by dividing the facial thermal image into a number of regions and examining its effectiveness.

II. CHARACTERISTICS OF THE FACIAL THERMAL IMAGE

Nasal skin temperature (NST), which refers to the difference between the forehead temperature and the nasal temperature, has been used for evaluating the MWL from the thermal image of the face. The temperature image obtained using infrared thermography captures the face; however, it is necessary to extract the forehead and nose regions from this image because the NST is the difference between the temperatures at these two locations on the face. The automatic extraction of the nose portion was previously performed using image processing [9], utilizing the local binary pattern (LBP) feature values and AdaBoost. However, to use a machine-learning algorithm such as AdaBoost, it is necessary to prepare in advance a large amount of training data to improve the identification accuracy. In addition, the efficiency of the general image-processing techniques with different detection rates tends to decrease with changes in the thermal images caused by factors such as changes in temperature, skin-temperature changes due to wind, and changes in the image caused by tilting the head. To solve these problems, we focused on the temperature differences between several regions of the image. We tried to identify areas of significant temperature changes by dividing the thermal image into multiple regions. Figure 1 shows an example of a thermal image. The temperature–center-of-gravity (*G*), which is considered as an evaluation index for the new MWL, is defined by the average of the coordinates obtained from the x and y-axes and the temperature of the thermograph obtained by adding high or low temperatures to the position information of the thermal image. This is because when the number of pixels in the image region is *n*, *G* is expressed as

$$G = \frac{1}{n}\sum_{i=1}^{n} \vec{x}_i \vec{y}_i \vec{T}_i. \quad (1)$$

where, *x* is the horizontal axis of the image, *y* is the vertical axis, and *T* denotes the temperature. Figure 2 shows an example for calculating the temperature-centroid of a complete thermal image. We hope to evaluate the effect of MWL by evaluating the temperature-centroid changes in each image region after division. Furthermore, the thermal image of the face of a person is at a higher temperature than the thermal images of the other parts of the body. Therefore, it may be possible to extract the face region easily using a temperature-centroid of the entire thermal image. This is one of the future challenges. If qualitative MWL evaluation using thermal images can be realized, it can become one of the indexes for evaluating usability in the field of human-computer interaction (HCI) such as in input user interfaces.

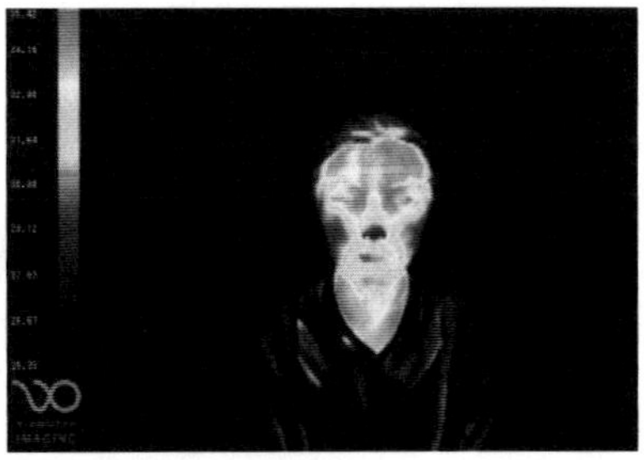

Figure 1. Example of a thermal image.

III. EXPERIMENT

We conducted an experiment to study the changes in the temperature–center-of-gravity of the facial thermal image during MWL work, using four subjects. We considered 10 divisions of 10^2 pixels each in the thermal image, for acquiring the characteristic amount of the temperature-centroid (G) by evaluating the scalar values of the center-of-gravity changes in this experiment.

A. Experimental Procedure

Figure 3 shows the outline of the experiment environment. In the experiment, an infrared thermographic camera (View Ohre IMAGING XA0350) was installed at a horizontal distance of 1 m from the nose of the subject. Specifications of the photographic image obtained from the apparatus are as follows: 320-pixel horizontal and 240-pixel vertical. The sampling frequency was 1 Hz. Figure 4 shows the measurement process. The subjects repeatedly performed simple mental arithmetic tasks with a rest time of 3 min after every 10 min. In addition, the evaluation was performed continuously, allowing the participants the resting time of 3 min even after the completion of the task. The mental arithmetic tasks involved addition of two integers between 10 and 99. The subjects were asked to enter the answers of problems displayed on the computer, using a numeric keypad. The problem was presented for 3 s. Regardless of the correctness of the input, when the problem presentation time was over, the next question was presented. Here, the importance is on the input; the correctness of the answer or feedback does not matter.

B. Experimental Result

Table 1 shows the changes in the temperature-center-of-gravity resulting from the longitudinal MWL challenges. Here, the average of the splits within the region of changes in the temperature–center-of-gravity summarizes the respective differences. Again, it shows a typical example of the change in the characteristic amount of the sum due to the region division number (scalar value) as shown in Figure 5.

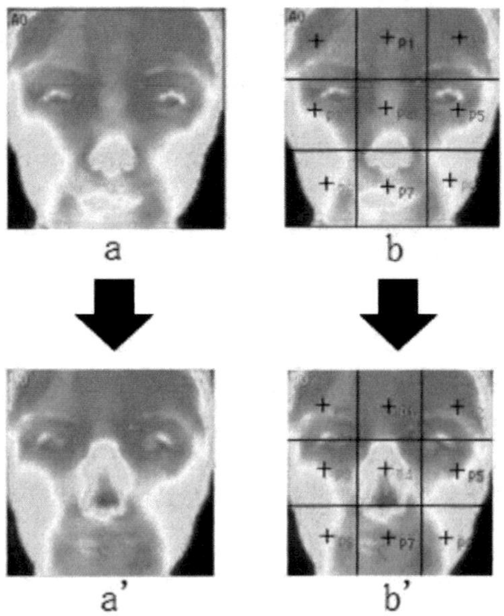

Figure 2. (a) Thermal images before and after mental arithmetic tasks. (b) Divided regions and each temperature-centroid (e.g., 3 x 3)

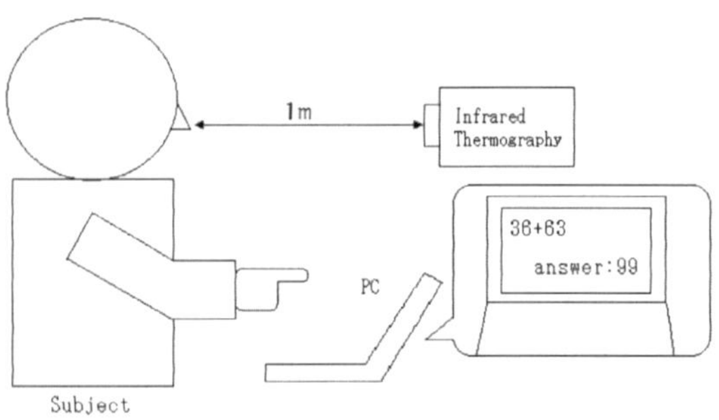

Figure 3. Experiment environment.

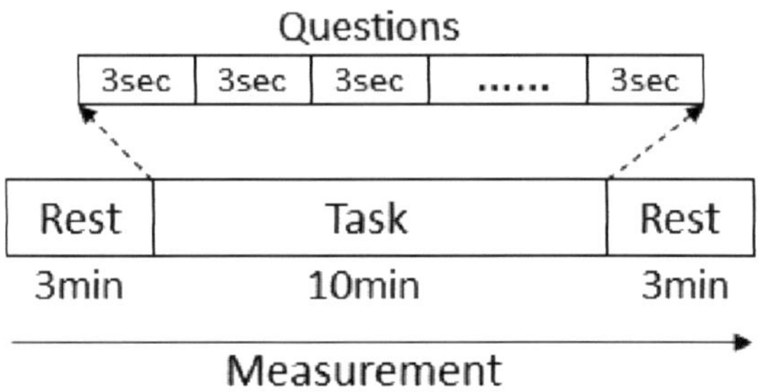

Figure 4. Experiment protocol.

TABLE I. SUM OF CHANGES IN THE TEMPERATURE-CENTROID FOR EACH NUMBER OF DIVISION [$*10^2$ PIXEL]

Division numbers	Subject A	Subject B	Subject C	Subject D
1	0	0	0	0
2	0.549	0.233	0.347	1.689
3	0.586	0.240	0.327	1.637
4	0.564	0.236	0.341	1.583
5	0.557	0.228	0.316	1.532
6	0.538	0.214	0.307	1.485
7	0.510	0210	0.295	1.437
8	0.507	0.205	0.288	1.381
9	0.483	0.201	0.283	1.327
10	0.458	0.207	0.270	1.269

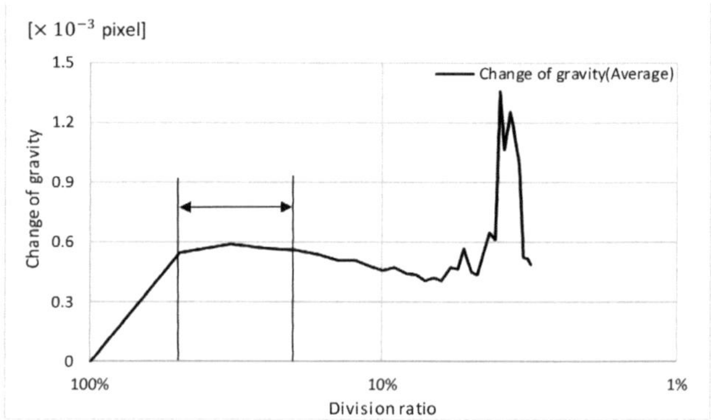

Figure 5. The sum of change in the temperature-centroid value for each division number (logarithmic graph).

C. Discussion

Figure 5 indicates that the feature amount increases monotonously, in this experiment, as the number of divided regions increases to a certain value. However, a tendency of one side of the divided area to become unstable was observed for a sum of feature values from a periphery of 1/10 or less divisions of the total number of image pixels. This is because of the availability of less amount of temperature information from the divided areas because of the influence of increased relative noise. Furthermore, the feature quantity of the sum is found to be insufficient for capturing the changes in temperature to be used for the evaluation of less mental activity in the case of reducing the number of divisions, in reverse. Therefore, it is considered that a splitting ratio of about 30%, which approaches the maximum value before the unstable evaluation sum of feature values to do the mental activity based on the temperature-centroid is suitable. In the current experiment, the most residual, even if you increase the number of divisions when using the maximum value when considering a change in temperature-centroid, was small. Therefore, it is considered stable when compared to the other two feature evaluations. In the future, we plan to estimate the autonomic nervous activity by evaluating the vector value of the temperature change using the split system that was verified in this paper.

IV. CONCLUSION

We studied analysis methods to take advantage of the temperature–center-of-gravity of the thermal image, using thermography as a non-contact and robust autonomic nervous-activity measuring method. Autonomic evaluation of the temperature changes in the facial area caused by nervous activity during MWL was carried out. We believe that it might be possible to quantitatively assess the distribution of temperature caused by the autonomic nervous activity, using the temperature-centroid (including coordinate information of the temperature change in the face area) as an index. In the first stage of the experiment in this study, the number of divisions that can be best measured was confirmed based on the changes in the temperature–center-of-gravity before and after the MWL challenges.

In future, we want to develop a more accurate verification technique by increasing the amount of data collected from the subjects. In addition, we want to establish an evaluation system for autonomic nervous activity by evaluating the change in temperature as a center-of-gravity vector. By performing these tasks, we are planning to apply and establish a usability evaluation method for user interfaces.

REFERENCES

[1] F. Nachreiner, "International standard on mental work-load – The ISO 10075 series", Industrial Health, vol. 37, no.1, 1999, pp. 125–133.

[2] H. Selye, "The Stress of Life", McGraw-Hill, 1976, p. 1956.

[3] N. Moray, "Mental Workload since 1979", International Reviews of Ergonomics, vol. 2, 1988, pp. 123–150.

[4] K. Hioki, A. Nozawa, T. Mizuno, and H. Ide, "Physiological evaluation of mental workload in time pressure", The transactions of the Institute of Electrical Engineers of Japan. C, A publication of Electronics, Information and System Society, vol. 127, no. 7, 2007, pp. 1000–1006.

[5] G. Mulder, " Mental effort and mental workload", Proc. The First International Symposium of Human Engineering for Quality of Life, 1992, pp.25–32.

[6] G. Mulder and L. J. M. Mulder, "Information processing and cardiovascular control", Psychophysiology, vol. 18, no. 4, 1981, pp. 392–402.

[7] K. J. Vincente, D. C. Thornton, and N. Moray, "Spectral analysis of sinus arrhythmia : a measure of mental effort", Human Factors, vol. 29, no. 2, 1987, pp. 171–182.

[8] T. Mizuno, S. Nomura, A. Nozawa, H. Asano, and H. Ide, "Evaluation of the effect of intermittent mental work-load by nasal skin temperture", IEICE, vol. J93-D, no. 4, 2010, pp. 535–543.

[9] S. Kawazura et al., "Estimation of the autonomic nerve activity with facial thermogram", 11th International Conf. Electrical Engineering/electronics, Computer, Telecommunications, and Information Techology, Advanced Techniques in Applications, DSP and Hardware Design, no. 1320, 2014, pp.1-6.

[10] T. Mizuno et al., "Facial Skin Temperture Fluctuation by Mental Work-Load with Thermography", Proc. the International Conf. Electronics and Software Science, 2015, pp. 212–215.

[11] H. Zenju, A. Nozawa, H. Tanaka, and H. Ide, "Estimation of unpleasant and pleasant states by nasal thermogram", IEEJ Trans. EIS, vol. 124, no. 1, 2004, pp.213–214.

[12] B. A. Rajoub and R. Zwiggelaar, "Thermal facial analysis for deception detection", IEEE Trans. Information Forensics and Security, vol. 9, no. 6, 2014, pp.1015–1023.

[13] D. Shastri, M. Papadakis, P. Tsiamyrtzis, B. Bass, and I. Pavlidis, " Perinasal imaging of physiological stress and its Affective potential", IEEE Trans. Affective Computing, vol. 3, no. 3, 2012, pp. 336–378.

Autonomic Nervous Activity Estimation Algorithm with Facial Skin Thermal Image

Tota Mizuno, Shunsuke Kawazura,
Kota Akehi, Shogo Matsuno,
Kazuyuki Mito and Naoaki Itakura
Department of Informatics Graduate
School of Informatics and Engineering
The University of Electro-Communications
Chofugaoka, Chofu, Tokyo 182-8585
Email: mizuno@uec.ac.jp, k1430023@edu.cc.uec.ac.jp,
a1540001@edu.cc.uec.ac.jp, m1440004@edu.cc.uec.ac.jp,
mito@se.uec.ac.jp and ita@se.uec.ac.jp

Hirotoshi Asano
Department of Electronics and Information
Engineering, Faculty of Engineering,
Kagawa University
Hayashi-cho 2217-20, Takamatsu,
Kagawa 761-0396, JAPAN
Email:asano@eng.kagawa-u.ac.jp

***Abstract*—The aim of this study was to achieve the absolute evaluation of mental workload (MWL) by proposing a novel algorithm for the evaluation and estimation of autonomic nervous activity with facial thermal imaging. Innovation in Information and Communication Technology(ICT) has resulted in workers experiencing an increasing mental workload, which is caused by using the computer. In our research group we have studied a method to evaluate and estimate autonomic nervous activity using facial thermal imaging as measured by infrared thermography. Previous methods extracted the forehead and nose as a method for performing the evaluation and estimation using the temperature difference. However, this approach does not consider the area. The proposed method enables parts or areas of temperature change other than the nose to be captured. This presents the possibility of accurate evaluation and estimation at levels that are more sensitive than the conventional method. In addition, there is the possibility of absolute evaluation by using one thermal image of the face. We also examined whether further high-precision evaluation and estimation would be possible. Our results showed the proposed method to be a highly accurate nasal skin temperature (NST) evaluation method compared to results obtained in previous studies.**

***Index Terms*—Facial thermal image; Nasal skin temperature; Mental work-Load.**

I. INTRODUCTION

Innovation in the area of ICT has resulted in workers experiencing a higher mental workload (MWL) [1] caused by using the computer. Although an appropriate MWL has health benefits for human beings, long-term excessive MWL can cause fatigue and lead to a drop in concentration, thereby leading to human errors and creating a health hazard. It is therefore very important for workers to evaluate their MWL, in terms of preventing and reducing human errors and the associated health hazard.

A previous study used estimation methods based on psychological, behavioral, and physiological evaluations to assess the MWL [2]–[12]. Psychological evaluations are based on the use of questionnaires or similar methods. Behavioral evaluations involve the assessment of work results and performance, for example, whereas the methods used for physiological evaluations use electrophysiological signal indices or methods such as these. In particular, the use of physiological indices for evaluation purposes enable researchers to perform assessments objectively and quantitatively and in real time. In addition, physiological indicators have excellent features that can be detected by way of the involuntary reaction of the unconscious. In general, physiological indices are often used as an indication of autonomic nerve activity derived from indicators such as the heart rate, respiration, blood pressure, myoelectric properties, and electroencephalogram (EEG) measurements.

These physiological indicators are used to evaluate autonomic nervous activity, which provides an estimation of MWL. However, when recording these bioelectric signals it is necessary to use mounted electrodes, for example, and this may cause difficulties when applied in the actual workplace.

Prompted by the need to overcome these difficulties, our research group has been studying a method based on the use of facial thermal imaging as measured by infrared thermography [12]–[24]. This method extracts the forehead and the nose from the facial thermal image to determine the temperature difference by using the nasal skin temperature (NST) to evaluate and estimate the autonomic nervous activity.

The advantage of using NST is that, unlike the measurement of electrophysiological indicators, the method obviates the need to attach sensors; hence, it is possible to measure the MWL by using low-bound and non-contact methods. However, this method uses time series data and is a relative evaluation based on the comparison of resting and task loading; thus, providing feedback of the results of the analysis is time consuming.

Therefore, we have investigated the evaluation of the physiological mental state to determine the MWL by using a heat image of the skin temperature of the whole face, as measured by infrared thermography. This method enables temperature changes of areas other than the nose to be captured. Therefore, it is possible to perform the evaluation and estimation more

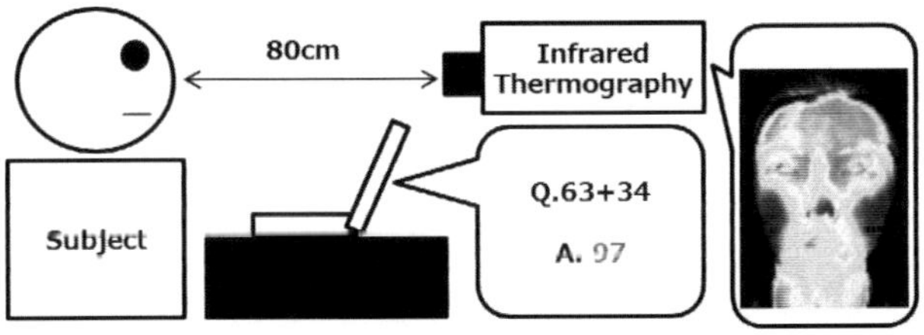

Fig. 1. Experimental system.

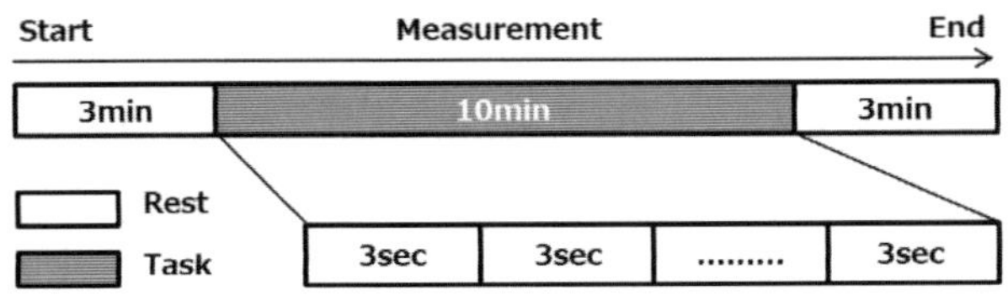

Fig. 2. Experimental protocol.

accurately and more sensitively than with the past technique. In addition, the possibility of absolute evaluation by a single thermal image of the face exists.

Previous studies of ours led to the development of a high-precision method based on the histogram of the skin temperature of the entire face. However, the MWL evaluations were not necessarily accurate, because different shooting angles could cause a reduction in the accuracy of temperature measurements. Thus, we suggest the use of a large end portion of the face by using an appropriate thermographic and photographic angle. Evaluation results that include the end portion of the face have been shown to be less accurate [25]–[27].

The objective of this study was to perform an absolute evaluation of MWL, by considering an algorithm for the evaluation and estimation of the autonomic nervous activity. Therefore, we examined the possibility of further high-precision evaluation and estimation.

II. EXPERIMENTS

Experiments were carried out to acquire facial thermal images (FTIs) of the different MWL states. We required subjects to carry out a consuming MWL task.

A. Experimental protocol

Fig.1 shows the experimental system. Thermal images were taken when a subject solved the mental arithmetic calculation. An infrared thermography device (ViewOhreIMAGING XA0350) was placed at a distance of 1 m horizontally from the nose of the subject. The thermal image size was 320 × 240 pixels, and the sampling period was 1 s. A PC display and numeric keypad were placed upon the desk. Fig.2 shows the experimental protocol.

Subjects rested for 3 min, in a sitting position. After this initial rest period, subjects began the mental arithmetic calculation task and continued this task for 10 min as MWL.

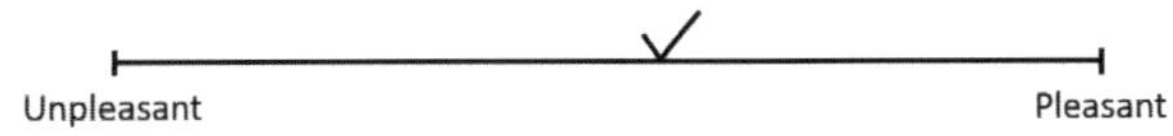

Fig. 3. Example of Visual Analogue Scale.

After completion of the task, subjects again rested for 3 min, thereby completing the experiment. The calculation involved the addition of two integers, each of which was between 10 and 99. The subject inputs the answer of the calculation displayed on the PC by using the numeric keypad. The calculation is displayed for 3 s. After 3 s, the following calculation will display on the PC, regardless of whether the subject answers the calculation within 3 s. Seven facial thermal images as physiological indices at 0, 2, 4, 6, 8, and 10 min after resting are taken during the experiment. Visual Analogue Scale (VAS) was used as psychological indices. Fig.3 shows an example of VAS. Subjective senses and feelings can be measured by marking a position on 10cm long scale characterized by a pair of opposite words or phrases at the both ends. This method is featured with little individual differences in the understanding of the description, and shorter time to perform the measurements. In this study, four pairs of words for VASs were employed. There were "Unpleasant-Pleasant", "Distracted-Concentrate", "Pleasant-Unpleasant" and "Fatigue-Vigor".

The subjects were four healthy adults from 22 to 27 years old who were well rested the night before the experiment.

B. Results and Discussion

First, we examined the estimated possible face area of the autonomic nervous activity. It shows the thermal image before and after mental arithmetic calculation task load in Fig.4.

The task takes into account that the temperature in the vicinity of the nose and lips changes significantly. In addition, according to previous studies [3], those parts of the face that require the camera to use a large shooting angle do not provide accurate temperature measurements. Therefore, as shown in 4, regions of the face that exclude the end portion of large faces and which have a suitable camera imaging angle ((a) whole face excluding the hair, (b) the eyes and the area between the eyes and downwards, only, and (c) the nose and mouth) can be used for the analysis.

Next, an analysis region is extracted from seven different thermal images of the state of the acquired MWL, and were investigated with the average of the regions (a) and (b) to determine the change. Fig.6 shows the average value and the standard deviation of the time series data of the average temperature of each subject.

Although there are differences in the average temperature of each subject, the standard deviation is within 1[Celsius]. Large variations were observed in the average temperature of the whole area due to the influence of the MWL load. As the blood flow is expected to flow to the nose and in the vicinity of the lips depending on the MWL, we considered the blood flowing to the entire face to remain unchanged. As a result, the average change in temperature was considered to be less.

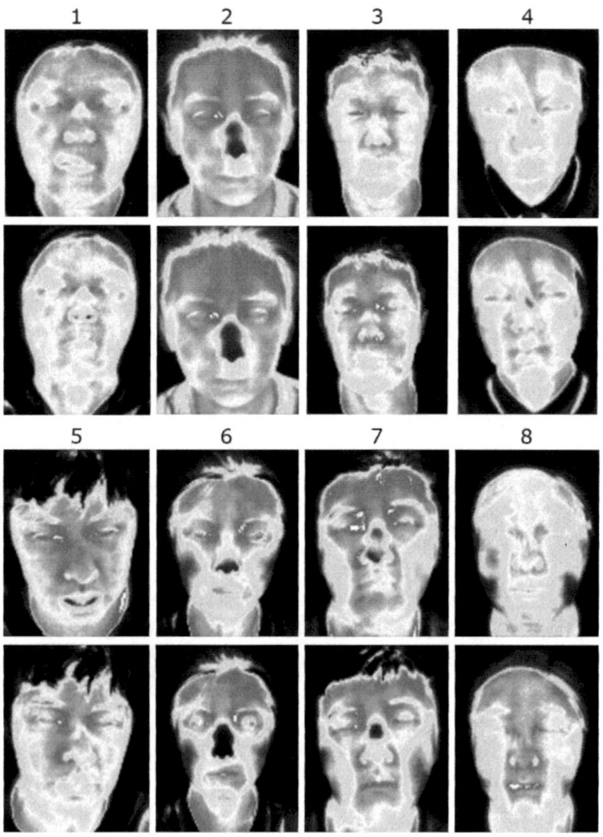

Fig. 4. Thermal image before and after mental arithmetic calculation task load.

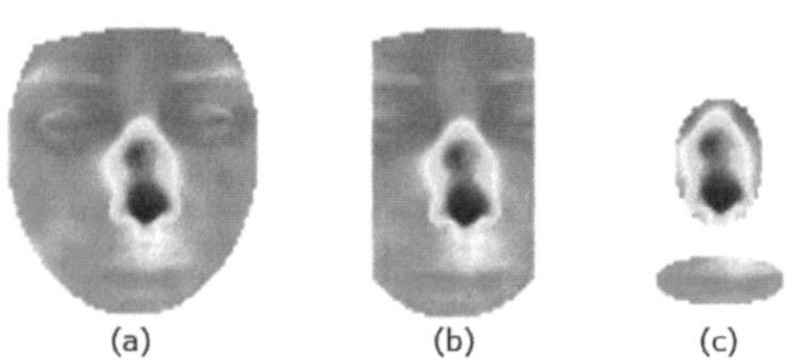

Fig. 5. Analysis region (a) whole face which does not include the hair, (b) the inside of the eyes, only (c) nose and mouth) and the analysis region.

III. PROPOSED AUTONOMIC NERVOUS ACTIVITY ESTIMATION ALGORITHM

We are aiming for absolute MWL evaluation by obtaining a single face thermal image. This study proposes an algorithm to reproduce autonomic nervous activity, with the aim of absolute MWL evaluation by using a single thermal image of the face. As our study is based on the average temperature of the entire region that undergoes little change due to the MWL, we propose an algorithm to estimate the autonomic nervous activity.

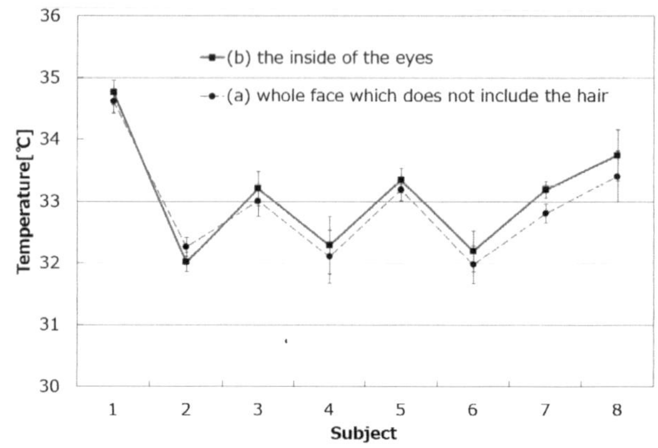

Fig. 6. The average value and the standard deviation of the time series data of the average temperature of each subject.

A. Method of calculating the estimated value

The average of the entire area was calculated by plotting the temperatures in the region, after which the sum of the difference in the region was calculated. This temperature change due to changes in the autonomic nervous activity was examined to determine whether it is a possible measurement. The calculation formula of the average temperature and the temperature difference in each area are obtained using the following equation:

$$F(x, y) = \sum_{i=0}^{n} (T - X_i)^2 \quad (1)$$

where T is the average temperature, Xi is a temperature value for each pixel in the region, and n is the number of pixels in the area. By squaring the reference and the difference of the temperature, the effect of the sign is taken into account. We evaluated the MWL using the estimates obtained for each of the three regions shown in Fig.5.

B. Evaluation method

1) General correlation between mental state and physiological indices (Evaluation method 1): We investigated the general relationship between the mental state and each proposed physiological index by comparing the psychological indicators and physiological indices that underwent change as a result of the imposed calculation problem tasks to determne the MWL. The correlations between VAS and each of the physiological indices were determined by Pearson's correlation coefficient using the mean values of all subjects.

2) (Evaluation method 2): In this case, we investigated the relationship between the mental state and each proposed physiological index within the subject by using multiple regression to determine the variations between the psychological indicators and physiological indices. We used VAS as the outcome variable, and each physiological index and the subjects as predictor variables. Subjects were treated as categorical factors using a dummy variable with eight degrees of freedom. The value from the t test for the regression slope of VAS was used

TABLE I
RESULTS OF THE ANALYSIS.

VAS	Indexes	Analysis Method 1 Coefficient of Correlation	Analysis Method 1 P Value	Analysis Method 2 Coefficient of Correlation	Analysis Method 2 P Value
Pleasure - Unpleasure	NST	0.88	0.004 **	0.41	0.008 **
	a	0.82	0.013 *	-0.38	0.014 *
	b	0.88	0.004 **	-0.47	0.002 **
	c	0.86	0.006 **	-0.47	0.002 **
Distracted - Concentrate	NST	0.35	0.400	0.03	0.876
	a	0.20	0.639	-0.05	0.733
	b	0.19	0.004	-0.12	0.447
	c	0.32	0.434	-0.13	0.425
Pleasant - Unpleasant	NST	0.75	0.031 *	0.27	0.093
	a	0.64	0.085	-0.23	0.156
	b	0.66	0.077	-0.22	0.167
	c	0.71	0.048 *	-0.40	0.010 **
Fatigue - Vigor	NST	0.75	0.030 *	0.10	0.528
	a	0.63	0.097	-0.17	0.283
	b	0.64	0.091	-0.15	0.351
	c	0.68	0.065	-0.38	0.013 *

to determine the probability of the analysis. The magnitude of correlation coefficient between VAS and each physiological index within subjects was calculated as the square root of (sum of squares for VAS)/(sum of squares for VAS + residual sum of squares). The sign of the correlation coefficient was given by that of the regression coefficient for VAS.

C. Results and Discussion

Table 1 lists the results of the analysis. Evaluation method 1 found significant correlation between some VAS and each physiological index. In particular, the correlation of Pleasure-Unpleasure was observed. These results show that the NST obtained by the proposed method, is high hedonicof the general relationship of psychology. Next, evaluation method 2, in particular, also showed a significant correlation of Pleasure-Unpleasure. Other statistically significant differences, including the Pleasant-Unpleasant correlation of VAS items was also observed. This showed that the value is lower than the NST. Thus, within subjects, the correlation that was statistically determined using the proposed method was higher than that obtained with the evaluation method using the NST of previous studies.

IV. CONCLUSION

The aim of our work was to perform the absolute MWL evaluation by using a single thermal image of the face. Thus, we proposed a novel algorithm to estimate the autonomic nervous activity. The results showed our proposed method to be highly accurate compared to the NST evaluation method proposed in previous studies.

REFERENCES

[1] S. Haga, "Theory and measurement of Mental Work-load," Japan Pabulication Service, 2001.

[2] A. Murata ,"Measurement of mental workload by heart rate variability indexes," Japan Ergonomics Society,28(2), pp.91-99, 1992.

[3] K. HIRAYANAGI, K. IWASAKI, S. KANDA and K. YAJIMA, "An experimental study on the measurement and assessment of mental workload(MWL)," Japan Ergonomics Society, pp.251-259, 1996.

[4] T. MIYAKAWA, T. YOSHIDA, R. KUBOTA, H. IKEDA," Development of the mental workload evaluation method," Human interface : proceedings of the Human Interface Symposium , Human interface : proceedings of the Human Interface Symposium

[5] R. Tokunaga, T. Hagiwara , S. Kagaya and Y. Onodera , "Effects of Talking through Cellular Telephone on Driving Behavior," Japan Society of Civil Engineers No.17 pp995-1000, 2000.

[6] H. MATSUNAGA and H.NAKAZAWA, "Relation between Mental Workload and Satisfaction Measures Evaluated from EEG," The Japan Society of Mechanical Engineers 66(648), 2884-2890, 2000.

[7] M. KARASHIMA, T. YAMAZAKI, "A study on the relationship between the time pressure by time constraints and the time estimations," Japan Ergonomics Society 39(1), 30-37, 2003.

[8] H. Zenju , A. Nozawa, H. Tanaka and H. Ide ,"The Estimation of Unpleasant and Pleasant States by Nasal Thermogram," The transactions of the Institute of Electrical Engineers of Japan. C, A publication of Electronics, Information and System Society 124(1), 213-214, 2004-01-01.

[9] H. Kaname, I. Kenichi, K. Shougo, Y. Kazuyoshi ,"An experimental study on the measurement and assessment of mental workload(MWL)," Japan Ergonomics Society, 32(5),pp.251-259, 1996.

[10] I. Hiroo Quantitative evaluation of mental work by thermography. The Society of Instrument and Control Engineers Vol.24, No.2, pp107-111, 1988.

[11] K. Mitsuhiko, Y. Tomoyuki ,"A study on the relationship between the time pressure by time constraints and the time estimations," Japan Ergonomics Society, Vol.39, No.1, pp30-37, 2003.

[12] K. Hioki, A. Nozawa, T. Mizuno and H. Ide , Physiological Evaluation of Mental Workload in Time Pressure. The transactions of the Institute of Electrical Engineers of Japan. C, A publication of Electronics, Information and System Society 127(7), 1000-1006, 2007-07-01.

[13] A. Nozawa, T. Mizuno, H. Ide, H. Asano and S. Nomura, "Evaluation of the Effect of Intermittent Mental Work-Load by Nasal Skin Temperature," The transactions of the Institute of Electrical Engineers of Japan. D, A publication of Electronics, Information and System Society Vol.J93-D, No.4, pp.535-543, 2010.

[14] A. Nozawa, S. Tomono, T. Mizuno and H.Ide ,"Detection of Fight or Flight Reaction on Facial Skin Thermogram using Spatio-Temporal Spectrum Differential Analysis," T.IEEJ Trans.FM, 126(6), pp.470-477, 2006.

[15] R. Sakamoto, A. Nozawa, H. Tanaka, T. Mizuno and H. Ide," Evaluation of the Driver's Temporary Arousal Level by Facial Skin Thermogram," Effect of Surrounding Temperature and Wind on the Thermogram. The transactions of the Institute of Electrical Engineers of Japan. C, A publication of Electronics, Information and System Society 126(7), 804-809, 2006-07-01.

[16] K. Hioki, A. Nozawa, T. Mizuno and H. Ide, "Physiological Evaluation of Mental Workload in Time Pressure," The transactions of the Institute of Electrical Engineers of Japan. C, A publication of Electronics, Information and System Society 127(7), 1000-1006, 2007-07-01.

[17] T. Mizuno, S. Nomura, A. Nozawa, H. Asano and H. Ide, "Evaluation of the Effect of Intermittent Mental Work-Load by Nasal Skin Temperature," IE-ICE, J93-D(4), pp.535-543, 2010.

[18] Advanced Industrial Science and Technology - Institute for Human Science and Biomedical Engineering," Handbook of Human measurement, Asa-kura publisher, 2003.

[19] T. Mizuno, N. Nakategawa, Y. Kume, "Color influences on human beings evaluated by nasal skin temperature," IArtificial Life and Robotics, Vol.16, Issue 4, pp 519-522, 2012.

[20] Bashar A. Rajoub, and Reyer Zwiggelaar, "Thermal Facial Analysis for Deception Detection," IEEE Transactions on Information Forensics and Security, Vol. 9, No. 6, pp.1015-1023, June 2014.

[21] Sarun Sumriddetchkajorn, Armote Somboonkaew, Tawee Sodsong, Itthipol Promduang, Niti Sumriddetchkajorn, and Thawatchai Prada-in, " Simultaneous Analysis of Far Infrared Signals From Periorbital and Nostril Areas for Nonintrusive Lie Detection: Performance From Real Case Study," Journal of Lightwave Technology, Vol. 33, No. 16, pp.3406-3412, August 2015.

[22] Dvijesh Shastri, Manos Papadakis, Panagiotis Tsiamyrtzis,Barbara Bass, and Ioannis Pavlidis, " Perinasal Imaging of Physiological Stress and Its

Affective Potential," IEEE Transactions on Affective Computing, Vol. 3, No. 3, pp.336-378, 2012.

[23] Sophie Jarlier, Didier Grandjean, Sylvain Delplanque, Karim N'Diaye, Isabelle Cayeux,Maria Ine´ s Velazco, David Sander, Patrik Vuilleumier, and Klaus R. Scherer, " Thermal Analysis of Facial Muscles Contractions," IEEE Transactions on Affective Computing, Vol. 2, No. 1, pp.2-9, 2011.

[24] Brian R. Nhan and Tom Chau, " Classifying Affective States Using Thermal Infrared Imaging of the Human Face," IEEE Transactions on Biomedical Engineering, Vol. 57, No. 4, pp.979-987, April 2010.

[25] S. Kawazura, H. Asano, A. Nozawa, M. Uchida, N. Itakura, K. Mito and T. Mizuno, "Estimation of the autonomic nerve activity with facial thermogram," 2014 11th international Conference on Electrical Engineering/Electronics, Computer, Telecommunications and Information Technology, CD-ROM Advanced Techniques in Applications, DSP and Hardware Design, No.1320, May 14-17, 2014, Thailand.

[26] T. Mizuno, S. Kawazura, H. Asano, K. Mito, Y. Kume and N. Itakura, "Evaluation of the autonomic nerve activity using facial thermal image," The Twentieth International Symposium on Artificial Life and Robotics 2015 (AROB 20th '15),PID3158279, 2015, Japan.

[27] T. Mizuno, T. Sakai, S. Kawazura, H. Asano, K. Akehi, S. Matsuno, K. Mito, Y. Kume and N. Itakura, "Facial Skin Temperature Fluctuation by Mental Work-Load with Thermography," The International Conference on Electronics and Software Science (ICESS2015) Proceedings pp. 212-215, 2015, Japan.

Minimalistic Toy Robot Encourages Verbal and Emotional Expressions in Autism

Irini Giannopulu
Pierre & Marie Curie University
Cognitive Neuroscience
Paris, France
email:igiannopulu@psycho-prat.fr

Valérie Montreynaud
Center of Medical Psychiatry
Paris, France
email:v.montreynaud@gpspv.fr

Tomio Watanabe
Okayama Prefectural University
Department of Systems Engineering
Okayama, Japan
email:watanabe@cse.oka-pu.ac.jp

***Abstract*—Language offers the possibility to transfer information between speaker and listener who both possess the ability to use it. Using a "speaker-listener" situation, we have compared the verbal and the emotional expressions of neurotypical and autistic children aged 6 to 7 years. The speaker was always a child (neurotypical or autistic); the listener was a human InterActor or an InterActor robot, i.e., a small toy robot that reacts to speech expression by nodding only. The results suggest that a robot characterized by predictable reactions facilitate autistic children in expression. When comparing to the performance of neurotypical children, the data would indicate that minimalistic artificial environments have the potential to open the way for neuronal organization and reorganization with the ability to support the embrainment of verbal and emotional information processing among autistic children.**

Keywords-brain development; neurotypical children; children with autism; minimalistic robot; language; emotion; listener-speaker.

I. Introduction

Development is the result of a complex process with at least three foci, one in the central nervous system, one in the mind and one in the child's dynamic interactions with the natural vs. artificial environment, that is, robots. The human child brain undoubtedly has its own dynamics (probably because of the extensive expression of genes in the brain) that allows neurons to interact, create their own multimodal nature, which in turn, affects the nature, development and function of the brain areas [1]. Verbal and nonverbal cognition, as well as emotion develop at the interface between neural processes. Toys have a central role. Children tend to play with toys in the first year of life. Toys are put together, sucked, kissed, piled on top of each other. The ability to play with toys becomes more and more sophisticated as development progress. The young children start to play with the toys in a symbolic manner by pretending that the toys represent something else that they love or not. They are able to move on from using themselves as an agent to using toys as (active) agents and carry out various actions [2]. Toys seem to provide an interesting account of "how" physical objects are able to act as support for the symbolic play of children. Symbolic play, like verbal development, emerges progressively as toys are the indices that assist the child to go in [3]. With development, symbolic play with action grows into language. With that in mind, we can imagine a scenery of communication between two persons: one speaking the other listening.

Neurotypically developing listeners and speakers are able to consider verbal, nonverbal (i.e., head nods) emotional (i.e., facial expressions) conventions and rules as well as each other when making referential statements. This is potentially due to the formation of a neural multimodal network, which naturally follows the evolution of the brain [4]. Using a modeling approach, recent neuroimaging studies have reported that both speech comprehension and speech expression activate a bilateral fronto-temporo-parietal network in the brain, fully characterized by the dynamic interaction among all the components [5]. Different studies emphasize the importance of multiple cortical (e.g., prefrontal cortex, temporal and parietal cortices) and subcortical areas (e.g., basal ganglia, hippocampus and cerebellum) not only for production and reception of speech but also, for cognitive nonverbal and emotional processes [1][6].

Failure of the exterior superior temporal sulcus [7], of the interior temporal lobe, amygdala included [8], of the connectivity between temporal regions [9], as well as of the inferior prefrontal cortex [10], i.e., the mirror neurone system, is accepted as an explanation for atypical neurodevelopment, such as autism [11][12]. The atypical neural architecture causes impairment in social interaction, in communication skills and interests [13][14][16] and reduces the ability of mentalizing, i.e., making representations based on the referential statements of other people [17].

Autistic children listeners and speakers perform less well than neurotypical children in conversation especially when the listener is a human, (human is essentially characterized by a high degree of variability on verbal and nonverbal emotional reactions, i.e., unpredictable reactions [18]). Adding the fact that the child is impaired in interpreting the referential statements of other people [12], the listener's verbal and nonverbal emotional contributions are not always scrutinized. There are at least two main reasons for this. The first reason is associated with the fact that autistic children have continual comprehension and language expression problems. Even if autistic children acquire language, it is often lacking any depth and is characterized by a paucity of imagination

[19]. The second reason is that autistic children experience difficulties in perception and emotion, functions which are linked to language [20] and also to social interaction and mentalising [9].

Trying to analyze child-robot interaction, different approaches have been developed. Different approaches have shown that animate robots using different stimulation encourage interaction in autistic children [20]. Quantitative metrics for autism diagnosis and treatment including robots have been developed [21]. Despite these studies, only marginal attention has been paid to the comparison of neurotypical and autistic children in human-human and human-robot interaction. Using a "speaker-listener" situation, we have compared the verbal and emotional expressions of neurotypical and autistic children aged 6 to 7 years. The speaker was always a child (neurotypical or autistic); the listener was a human or an InterActor robot, i.e., a robot, which reacts to speech expression by nodding only. Given the fact that the InterActor robot is characterized by a low degree of variability in reactions (i.e., predictable reactions) and the human by a high degree of variability in reactions (i.e., unpredictable reactions), our general hypothesis is that verbal and emotional expressions of autistic children could better be facilitated by the InterActor than by the human.

Beginning with the design of the study, we will continue with the analysis of the results in both neurotypical and autistic children. Then, we will discuss the importance of minimalistic artificial environments as support for the embrainment of cognitive verbal and emotional information processing.

II. Method

A. Participants

Two groups of children, one "neurotypical" and one "autistic" participated in the study. Twenty neurotypical children (10 boys and 10 girls) composed the "neurotypical group"; twenty children (14 boys and 6 girls) composed the "autistic group". The developmental age of typical children ranged from 6 to 7 years old (mean 6.1 years; standard deviation 7 months). The developmental age of autistic children ranged from 6 to 7 years old (mean 6 years; standard deviation 8 months). Their mean age when first words appeared was 28 months (standard deviation 7 months). The autistic children were diagnosed according to the DSM IV-TR criteria of autism [22]. The Childhood Autism Rating Scale CARS [23] has been administrated by an experienced psychiatrist. The scores varied from 31 to 35 points signifying that the autistic population was composed of mild-moderate children with autism. They were all verbal. All autistic children were attending typical school classes with typical educational arrangements. The study was approved by the local ethics committee and was in accordance with the Helsinki convention. Anonymity was guaranteed.

B. Material

- *Robot*

Figure 1. Pekoppa

An InterActor robot, i.e., a small toy robot, called "Pekoppa", was used as a listener [24]. Pekoppa is shaped like a bilobed plant and its leaves and stem make a nodding response based on speech input and support the sharing of mutual embodiment in communication (Figure 1). It uses a material called BioMetal made of a shape-memory alloy as its driving force. The timing of nodding is predicted using a hierarchy model consisting of two stages: macro and micro (Figure 2). The macro stage estimates whether a nodding response exists or not in a duration unit, which consists of a talkspurt episode $T(i)$ and the following silence episode $S(i)$ with a hangover value of 4/30 s. The estimator $Mu(i)$ is a moving-average (MA) model, expressed as the weighted sum of unit speech activity $R(i)$ in (1) and (2). When $Mu(i)$ exceeds a threshold value, nodding $M(i)$ also becomes an MA model, estimated as the weighted sum of the binary speech signal $V(i)$ in (3). Pekoppa demonstrates three degrees of movements: big and small nods and a slight twitch of the leaves by controlling the threshold values of the nodding prediction. The threshold of the leaf movement is set lower than that of the nodding prediction.

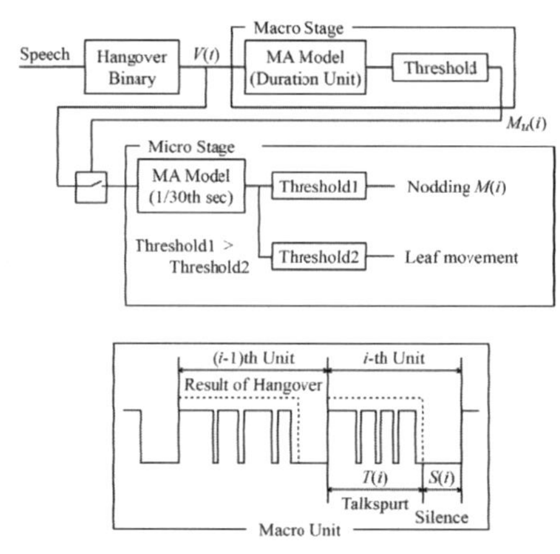

Figure 2. Listener's interaction model

$$M_u(i) = \sum_{j=1}^{J} a(j)R(i-j) + u(i) \quad (1)$$

$$R(i) = \frac{T(i)}{T(i) + S(i)} \quad (2)$$

$a(j)$: linear prediction coefficient

$T(i)$: talkspurt duration in the i-th duration unit

$S(i)$: silence duration in the i-th duration unit

$u(i)$: noise

$$M(i) = \sum_{k=1}^{K} b(j)V(i-j) + w(i) \quad (3)$$

b(j) : linear prediction coefficient

V(i) : voice

w(i) : noise

- *Procedure*

For both groups, the study took place in a room, which was familiar to the children. We defined three conditions: the first one was called "rest condition", the second was named "with human" (child-adult) and the third one was called "with robot" (child-Robot, i.e., child-Pekoppa). The second and third conditions were counterbalanced across the children. The duration of the "rest condition" was 1 minute; the second and third conditions each lasted approximately 7 minutes.

The inter-condition interval was approximately about 30 seconds. For each child, the whole experimental session lasted 15 minutes (Figure 3).

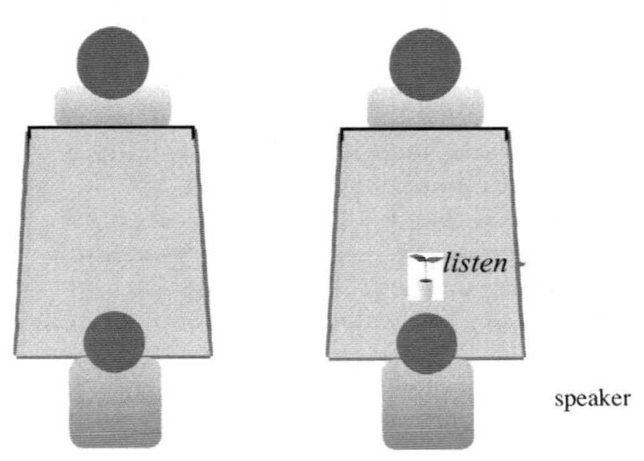

Figure 3. Listener-Speaker Situation

In order to neutralize a possible "human impact" on children's behavior, the experimenter was the same person for each child in each condition and group ("neurotypical" and "autistic"). At the beginning of each session, the experimenter presented the robot to the child explaining that the robot nods whenever the child speaks. Then, the experimenter hid the robot. The session was run as follows: during the "rest condition", the heart rate of each child was measured in silence. At the end of that condition, the child was also asked to estimate the intensity of her/his own emotion on a scale ranging from 1 (the lowest intensity) to 5 (the highest intensity) [25][26]. During the "with human" condition, the child was invited to discuss with the experimenter. The experimenter initiated discussion and after listened to the child acting as the speaker. The heart rate, as well as the frequency of words and verbs expressed by each child was measured. During the "with robot" condition, Pekoppa was set to nod movements; the experimenter gave the robot to the child inviting the child to use it. The robot was the listener, the child was the speaker and the experimenter remained silent and discreet. The heart rate and the frequency of words and verbs expressed by the child was recorded once again. At the end of the session, the child was invited to estimate the intensity of its own emotion on the same aforementioned scale. At the end of the experiment, each child was invited to respond to two questions: 1) *how did you find Pekoppa? 2) did you enjoy yourself with Pekoppa?* [see also 26].

- *Analysis*

The analysis was based on the following dependent variables a) the heart rate measured in beat per minute (bpm) b) the number of nouns and verbs expressed by each child and c) the intensity of emotional feeling (auto-estimation of emotion). The data analysis was performed with SPSS Statistics 17.0 [27].

III. RESULTS

The distributions of heart rate, words and emotional feeling reported in both age groups approximate a parametric shape. With such distributions, the mean has been chosen as a central index for comparisons. We performed statistic of comparisons using the t-student test, the ANOVA's test and the chi-square test to examine differences in heart rate, number of words and intensity of emotional feeling between the two experimental conditions ("with human" and "with Robot" i.e., Pekoppa), for neurotypical and autistic children. The obtained results were very similar. We present the results of chi-square test (χ^2 test), which can be used as a substitute for t and ANOVA tests [28].

Figure 4 represents the mean heart rate of neurotypical and autistic children both at the inter-individual and the intra-individual levels.

At the intra-individual level, the statistical analysis showed that relative to the "rest condition", the mean heart rate of neurotypical children was higher when the children were in contact with the InterActor robot (χ^2=6.68, $p<0.01$) than when they were in contact with the human (χ^2=4.09, $p<0.05$). However, the mean heart rate of neurotypical children didn't differ significantly when they interacted with the human or with the InterActor robot ($\chi^2=2.83$, $p>0.05$). Similarly, relative to the "rest condition", the mean heart rate of autistic children was higher when they interacted with the InterActor robot ($\chi^2=7.01$, $p<0.01$) than when they interacted with the human ($\chi^2=5.01$, $p<0.05$). Finally, the mean heart rate of autistic children was higher when they were with the InterActor robot than when they were with the human ($\chi^2=7.84$, $p<0.01$).

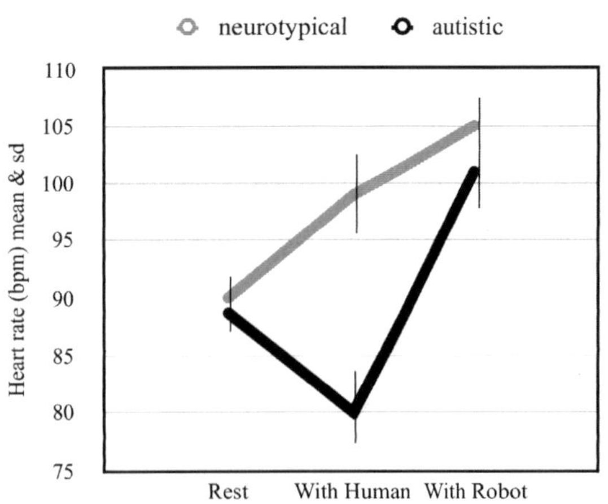

Figure 4. Mean Heart Rate

Two independent judges unfamiliar with the aim of the study completed the analysis of the number of words for each child in each experimental condition ("human InterActor" and "robot InterActor"). Both performed the analyses of audio sequences. Inter-judge reliability was assessed using intra-class coefficients to make the comparison between them. The inter-judge reliability was good (Cohen's kappa=0.82).

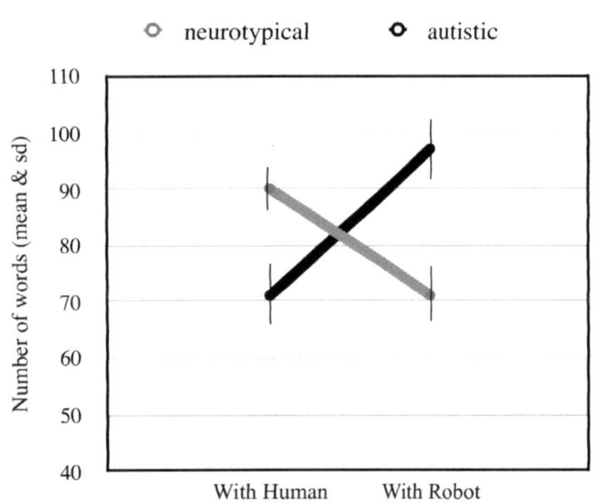

Figure 5. Number of words (nouns & verbs)

At the inter-individual level, as shown in Figure 5, the mean number of words (nouns and verbs) was low in the "with human" condition for autistic children ($\chi^2=4.86$ $p<0.05$) and in the "with robot" condition for neurotypical children ($\chi^2=5.98$, $p<0.025$). The mean number of words expressed by autistic children in the "with robot" condition didn't differ from the mean number of words expressed by neurotypical children in the "with human" condition ($\chi^2=1.34$, $p>0.10$). At the intra-individual level, the mean number of words was higher when the autistic children had the robot as interlocutor than when the interlocutor was a human ($\chi^2=5.97$, $p<0.025$). The quasi opposite configuration was observed for the neurotypical children ($\chi^2=4.78$, $p<0.05$).

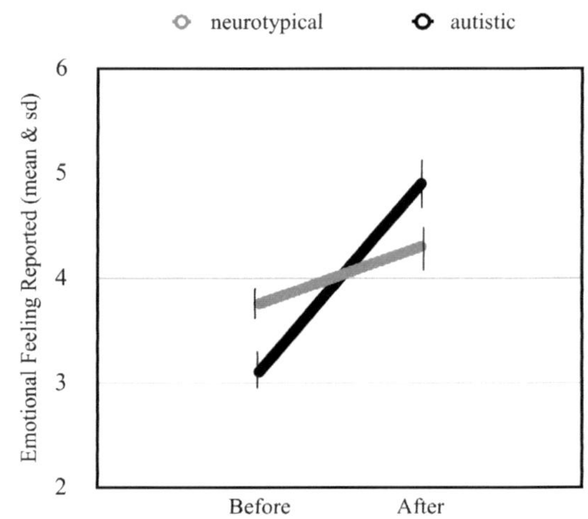

Figure 6. Emotional Feeling Reported

Figure 6 illustrates that at the inter-individual level, the intensity of emotional feeling reported didn't differ between neurotypical and autistic children within both conditions: "before robot" and "after robot" ($\chi^2=3.38$, $p>0.05$; $\chi^2=3.90$, $p>0.05$ respectively). However, intra-individually, the intensity of emotional feeling is higher "after" than "before" the interaction with the InterActor robot for autistic children ($\chi^2=6.43$, $p<0.025$) but it didn't vary for the neurotypical children ($\chi^2=2.98$, $p>0.05$).

IV. DISCUSSION

The present study aims at analyzing the embrainment of verbal and emotional expressions in neurotypical and autistic children aged 6 to 7 years. Our approach centered on investigating the effects of a human or an InterActor robot in the context of a "speaker-listener" situation: the speaker was always the child; the listener was a human or an InterActor robot, i.e., Pekoppa. To this end, physiological data (i.e., heart rate), as well as behavioral data (i.e., number of nouns and verbs in addition to the emotional feeling reported) were considered. The results showed that 1) the heart rate of autistic children is low when the listener was a human and increased nearer to levels of neurotypical children when the listener was the InterActor robot; 2) the number of words expressed by the autistic children was higher when the interlocutor was the robot; 3) the emotional feeling reported increased after the interaction with the InterActor robot.

Fundamentally, the results are consistent with our hypothesis according to which the predictability of the InterActor robot would facilitate the emotional and verbal expressions of autistic children. Our results showed significant differences of heart rate depending on whether the listener was a human or a robot. When the listener was a human, the children showed a low heart rate; when the listener was an InterActor robot, their heart rate increased. Such a result cannot be attributed to an order effect as the order of "human-human" and "human-robot" conditions have been counterbalanced. On the contrary, it could be understood as an effect of the InterActor robot on autistic children's mental state. This interpretation is supported by the fact that when the autistic children had the InterActor robot as listener, their heart rate didn't differ from the heart rate of neurotypical children in the same condition. It is also interesting to note that the heart rate of the neurotypical children didn't differ when the listener was a human or a InterActor robot. The observation reported above could reveal that an InterActor robot might improve autistic children behavior. This inference is reinforced by the fact that the physiological data we recorded reflects the modifications of orthosympathetic and parasympathetic autonomous nervous system, which is dynamically (and bidirectionally) connected to the central nervous system [29][30]. Physiologically, the lower regulation of heart rate (in "with human" condition) reflects poorer action of the myelinated vagus nerve [31], which in turn would signify poor neural activity in temporal cortex (amygdala included), in cingulate cortex and in prefrontal cortex [32] [33]. This neural architecture is hypo-activated in children with autism [14][15], causing impairment in cognitive verbal, nonverbal and emotional behavior [16][20]. Such hypo-activation would explain autistic children's behavior when the listener is the human. A restricted number of studies exist on the evaluation of heart rate in autistic children. Some of them have reported that autistic children display lower heart rate than typically developing children [34][35], some others have found the opposite [36][38]. The aforementioned studies suggest that autistic children show disruptions in autonomic responses to environmental (human) stressors. Methodological problems associated to the limited number of autistic children, to their clinical heterogeneity as well as to the various procedures and measures used are on the basis of the opposing reported data. None of the above studies have evaluated autonomic activity in a robot-child interaction vs. human-human interaction. To our knowledge, the present study is the first one having a homogeneous group of mild-moderate children with autism, which is matched on developmental age with a group of typically developing children. Contrary to the previous studies, our findings indicate that not only are there no disruptions in autonomic responses but that these responses don't exceed the physiological limits. Apparently, when the listener is the InterActor robot, the heart rate of children with autism increases likely indicating a "mobilisation" of a given mental state. Such "mobilisation" would provide support for the social engagement of autistic children. Namely, by making the autistic children available to engage emotionally (and verbally), the InterActor robot seems to modify their neural activity: the children would enjoy participating. It is noteworthy that they also verbalized such pleasurable sentiments at the end of the experiment. Such information is presented here below. Essentially, the present results are consistent with our previous assumptions following which toy robots would improve autistic children brain functioning [26][39][40].

The above considerations could account for the number of words (nouns and verbs) expressed by the children. Even if the autistic children were verbal, the present finding indicated that when the listener was an InterActor robot, the number of words expressed by the autistic children was higher than the number of words they express when the listener was a human. Interestingly, such verbal behavior doesn't differ from that of neurotypical children when these latter had a human as listener. Once again, the use of the InterActor robot seems to afford autistic children the ability to express themselves as neurotypical children do with humans. These data are consistent with previous studies, which have demonstrated that verbal expression can be facilitated by the active (but discreet) presence of a robot [20].

Although neurotypical children didn't report emotional feeling changes after their interaction with the robot, autistic children said to feel better after interaction with the robot. This is coherent not only with the physiological data we observed (heart rate) but also with parent accounts. At the end of the experiment, many parents announced: "s/he is happy", "s/he likes your robot". Autistic children also conceded that the robot was "cute", "cool" "genius", some of them even said: "if I had the robot, I would talk to it all the time". Some of them imitated the robot verbally (and emotionally).

It could be argued that the "autistic group" was made up of verbal children and that the results we observed might be due to the actual verbal capabilities of the children. However, we must underline that these children expressed themselves (both emotionally and verbally) only when the listener was the InterActor Robot. Although our results are statistically significant, we recognize that the size of our group is limited to twenty children only. We aim to study the behavior of other age groups as well. Finally, it is obvious that what we need to develop is a follow-up study to prove that the InterActor robot is the robot, which can sustainably improve the emotional and verbal behavior of autistic children.

V. CONCLUSION AND FUTURE WORK

Given the present findings, it can be concluded that an InterActor robot characterized by small-variance nonverbal behavior, (i.e., nodding when children speak), facilitates verbal and emotional expressions of autistic children. This might be related to autistic children preferences. Autistic children are rather interested in minimalist objects to which they can assign mental states of their own or of others [41]. Such a behavior might be interpreted as reflecting the children's willingness to communicate with humans using the robot: the InterActor toy robot is a miniature of a human listener, i.e., the autistic children can handle the head nods (as neurotypical children do with humans). These results (consistent with previous studies) appear to indicate that minimalistic artificial environments could probably be considered as the root of neuronal organization and reorganization with the potential to improve brain activity in order to support the embrainment of cognitive verbal and emotional information processing [41][44].

Additional studies are required with typical and autistic children. Longitudinal follow-up of the same children is necessary to examine the efficiency of minimalistic robots in improving the activity of autistic children. This is what we're developing currently in France and in Japan. In addition, with a new study we analyse the enrobotment [45] in conscious and unconscious level in neurotypical children aged 6 and 9 yeas old.

ACKNOWLEDGMENT

To all the participants and their parents, the Major, the Pedagogical Inspector, the Educational Advisor, the Director and the team of principal elementary school of the first district of Paris, and the National Department of Education and Research. The research is supported by the Franco-Japanese Foundation.

REFERENCES

1. I. Giannopulu, "Multimodal interactions in typically and atypically developing children: natural vs. artificial environments". Cognitive Processing, vol. 14, 2013, pp. 323-331.
2. A. A. Leslie, "Some implications of pretense for mechanisms underlying the child's theory of mind". In J. W. Astington, P.L. Harris, & D.R. Olson (Eds.), Developing theories of mind, 1988.
3. L. S. Vygotsky, "Play and its role in the mental development of the child". In J.S. Bruner, A. Jolly, & K. Sylva (Eds.), Play. Harmondsworth, UK: Penguin, 1976.
4. A. S. Dick, A. Solodkin, and S. L. Small, "Neural development of networks for audiovisual speech comprehension," Brain and Language, vol. 114, 2010, pp. 101–114.
5. A. Cangelosi, "Grounding language in action and perception: from cognitive agents to humanoid robots," Phys. Life Rev, vol. 7, 2010, pp. 139-151.
6. E. Fedorenko, P. J. Hsieh, A. Nieto-Castañón, S. Whitfield-Gabrieli, and N. Kanwisher, "New Method for fMRI Investigations of Language: Defining ROIs Functionally in Individual Subjects," J. Neurophysiol, vol. 104, 2010, pp. 1177–1194.
7. K. A. Pelphrey and E. J. Caster, "Charting the typical and atypical development of the social brain," Dev. Psychopathol, vol. 20, 2008, pp. 1081–1102.
8. B. A. Corbett, V. Carmean, S. Ravizza, C. Wendelken, M. L. Henry, C. Carter, and S. M. Rivera, "A functional and structural study of emotion and face processing in children with autism," Psychiatry Research, vol. 30, 2009, pp. 196-205.
9. U. Frith and C. D. Frith, "Development and neurophysiology of mentalizing," Ph. Trans. Royal Soc. B. Biol. Science, vol. 358, 2003, pp. 459-473.
10. L. Brothers, "The social brain: A project for integrating primate behaviour and neurophysiology in a new domain," Concepts Neuroscience, vol. 1, 1990, pp. 27–51.
11. M. Iacoboni and J. C. Mazziotta, "Mirror neuron system: basic findings and clinical applications," Ann. Neurol, vol. 3, 2007, pp. 213–218.
12. S. Baron-Cohen, "Mindblindness," MIT Press, Cambridge 1995.
13. R. Adolphs, A. Jansari, and D. Tranel, "Hemispheric perception of emotional valence from facial expressions," Neuropsychology, vol. 15, 2001, pp. 516–524.
14. J. P. Aggleton, "The Amygdala: A Functional Analysis," Oxford University Press, Oxford, 2000.
15. B. M. Nacewicz, K. M. Dalton, T. Johnstone, M. Long, E. M. McAuliff, T. R. Oakes et al. "Amygdala Volume and Nonverbal Social Impairment in Adolescent and Adult Males with Autism," Arch. Gen. Psy, vol. 63, 2006, pp. 1417-1428.
16. R. K. Kana, D. L. Murdaugh, L. E. Libero, M. R. Pennick, H. M. Wadsworth, R. Deshpande et al. "Probing the brain in autism using 807 fMRI and diffusion tensor imaging," J. Vis. Exp, vol. 55, 2011, pp. e3178.
17. S. Baron-Cohen, A. M. Leslie, and U. Frith, "Does the autistic child have a theory of mind?" Cognition, vol. 21, 1985, pp. 37–46.
18. A. C. Pierno, M. Mari, D. Lusher, and U. Castiello, "Robotic movement elicits visuomotor priming in children with autism," Neuropsychologia, vol. 46, 2008, pp. 448–454.
19. K. A. Pelphrey and E. J. Caster, "Charting the typical and atypical development of the social brain," Dev. Psychopathol, vol. 20, 2008, pp. 1081-1102.
20. I. Giannopulu, "Multimodal cognitive nonverbal and verbal interactions: the neurorehabilitation of autistic children via mobile toy robots," IARIA International J. Adv. Lif. Sci, vol. 5, 2013, pp. 214–222.
21. B. Scassellati, "Quantitative metrics of social response for autism Diagnosis," IEEE International Conference on Intelligence Robots and Systems, vol. 2, 2002, pp. 1134-1138.
22. DSM-IV-TR Manuel diagnostique et statistique des troubles mentaux. Paris, Editions Masson, 2003.
23. E. Schopler, R. J. Reichler, R. F. De Vellis, and K. Daly, "Toward objective classification of childhood autism: Childhood Autism Rating Scale (CARS)," JADD10, 1980, pp. 91-103.

24. T. Watanabe, "Human-entrained Embodied Interaction and Communication Technology," Emot Engineering, 2011, pp. 161-177.
25. I. Giannopulu and I. Sagot, "Positive emotion in the course of an experimental task in children," An. Médico-Psychologiques, vol. 168(10), 2010, pp. 740-745.
26. I. Giannopulu, V. Montreynaud, and T. Watanabe, "Neurotypical and Autistic Children aged 6 to 7 years in a Speaker-Listener Situation with a Human or a Minimalist InterActor Robot". In Proc IEEE RO-MAN, 2014, pp. 942-947.
27. SPSS STATISTICS 17.0, Python Software Foundation, 2008.
28. F. J Gravetter and L. B. Wallnau "Statistics for the Behavioral Sciences," 2000, 5th International edition.
29. B. A., Barres and Y. Barde, "Neuronal and glial cell biology," Curr. Opin. Neurobiol, vol. 10, 2000, pp. 642--648.
30. D. Servant, R. Logier, Y. Mouster, and M. Goudemand, "Heart rate variability. Applications in psychiatry," Encep, vol. 35, 2009, pp. 423-428.
31. S. Porges, "The polyvagal perspective" Biol. Psychology, vol. 74, 2007, pp. 116-143.
32. S. Manta, "Neurophysiological effets of vague nerve stimulation: Implication on the depression treatment and optimisation of the stimulation's parameters," Thèse de Doctorat, Université de Montréal, Canada, 2012.
33. A. Kylliäinen and J. K. Hietane, "Skin conductance responses to another person's gaze in children with autism," J. Autism Dev. Disord, vol. 36, 2006, pp. 517–525.
34. A. Vaughan Van Hecke, J. Lebow, E. Bal, D. Lamb, E. Harden, A. Kramer et al "EEG and heart rate regulation to familiar and unfamiliar people in children with autism spectrum disorders," Child Dev, vol. 80, 2009, pp. 1118-1133.
35. X. Ming, P. O. O. Julu, M. Brimacombe, S. Connor, and M. L. Daniels, "Reduced parasympthetic activity in children with autism," Brain Dev-JPN, vol. 27, 2005, pp. 509-516.
36. B. Elgiz, E. Hecke, D. Lamb, A. Vaughan Van Hecke, J. W. Denver, and S. W. Porges "Emotion Recognition in children with autism Spectrum Disorders: Relations to eye gaze and autonomic state," J. Autism Dev. Disord, vol. 40, 2010, pp. 358–370.
37. M. Toichi and Y. Kamio, "Paradoxal autonomic response to mental tasks in autism," J. Autism Dev. Disord, vol. 33, 2003, pp. 417-426.
38. V. A. van Hecke, J. Lebow, E. Bal et al.: "Electroencephalogram and heart rate regulation to familiar and unfamiliar people in children with autism spectraum disorders," Child Dev, vol. 80, 2009, pp. 1118–1133.
39. I. Giannopulu and G. Pradel, "From child-robot interaction to child-robot-therapist interaction: a case study in autism," App. Assist. Bio, vol. 9, 2012, pp. 173–179.
40. M. Puyon and I. Giannopulu, "Emergent emotional and verbal strategies in autism are based on multimodal interactions with toy robot in spontaneous game play," IEEE International Symposium on Robot and Human Interactive Communication, 2013, pp. 593–597.
41. V. Montreynaud, CMP, Private Communication, January 2014.
42. S. Kumar, N. Kuppuswamy, M. Weyland, and I. Giannopulu, "A Multimodal Mobile Toy Robot to NeuroEducate Atypical Children," ICRA Workshop, 2014.
43. I. Giannopulu and T. Watanabe, "Give children toy robots to educate and/or neuroreeeducate," MESROB Conference, EPFL: Lausanne, 2014, pp. 205-215.
44. I. Giannopulu, V., Montreynaud., and T. Watanabe, "PEKOPPA Toy Robot in a Scenery of Speaker-Listener Communication in Neurotypical and Autistic Children," Japanese Society of Child Science, Tokyo, 27-28 September, 2014, pp. 7.
45. I Giannopulu, "Enrobotment: Toy robots in the developing brain," in Springer Science, Singapore: Handbook of Digital Games and Entertainment Technologies, R. Nakatsu et al. (eds.), DOI 10.1007/978-981-4560-52-8_59-1, 2016.

User Acceptance of Social Robots

Ibrahim A. Hameed
Dept. of Automation Engineering, Faculty of Engineering and Natural Sciences
Norwegian University of Science and Technology (NTNU) in Ålesund
Larsgårdsvegen 2, 6009 Ålesund, Norway
E-mail: ibib@ntnu.no

Zheng-Hua Tan, Nicolai B. Thomsen, Xiaodong Duan
Section of Signal and Information Processing, Dept. of Electronic Systems, Aalborg University
Fredrik Bajers Vej 7, 9220 Aalborg Ø, Denmark
E-mail: {zt, nit, xd}@es.aau.dk

***Abstract*— A mismatch between the user's expectations and the actual reality of social robots may negatively impact the acceptance and use of the robot. Given that the use of personal robots may be expected to become a part of people's everyday lives, it is critical to understand and consider the factors that may increase acceptance and adoption when robots are designed and introduced. How the robot is accepted by end users may be influenced by factors, such as: 1) the role assigned to the robot (i.e., robot function), 2) the robot's social capabilities or skills such as the robot's social intelligence and emotions expressions, and 3) the robot appearance. In this paper, an experiment is conducted to investigate, understand and identify the potential impact of these factors on user's acceptance and adoption of social robots. The experiment is conducted in a culture night event where some of the attendances are voluntarily interacted with the robot and filled out a questionnaire. The questionnaire is designed to measure their expectations and impressions before and after interacting with the robot (i.e., to assess robot's social skills), their preferences regarding the robot appearance (i.e., machine-likeness or human-likeness appearance) and finally to assess the need for a secondary interactive touchscreen display on the robot chest to facilitate interface and hence improve the robot's functionality. The goal of this paper is to understand the impact of these factors on user's acceptance and adoption and giving the users a more effective role in the design of this type of technology.**

Keywords-human robot interaction (HRI); personal robots; iSocioBot;

I. Introduction

Due to the continuing technological advancements, robots have been increasingly designed for personal use to perform simple servant-like tasks (e.g., the robotic vacuum cleaner), assisting and caring for elderly people [1], providing therapy and teaching autistic children new life skills to improve their social behaviors [2]-[4], at homes and in classrooms for education [5]-[7], or to be used purely for entertainment [8], [9]. It is expected that personal robots may become a part of people's everyday lives and therefore, it is critical to understand the factors that may increase its acceptance, adoption and use when designed and presented to its end-users. Despite the ever-growing development and public interest in robotics, a theoretical model specific to robot acceptance has not developed yet [10]-[12]. Acceptance has been widely studied for other forms of technology other than robotics such as the Technology Acceptance Model (TAM) [13], the Unified Theory of Acceptance and the Use of Technology model (UTAUT) [14], and the Chain Model (TPC) [15]. These models differ in complexity and content, however, their goals are to understand, explain and predict variables that contribute to user acceptance of various types of technologies. With the advent of technology acceptance models that can provide guidance for understanding the variables that influence robot acceptance, robot developers will be able to design robots that are more likely to be adopted. The goal of this paper is to identify the impact of some potential factors that might predict user acceptance of personal and social robots. These variables have been identified in the literature as potentially impacting acceptance; robot function, robot social capabilities, and robot appearance [10], [14], [15]. Functionality of the robot includes control and interface issues, such as the appropriateness of the control method for the task, the ease of use, and suitability and easiness of user interface. Social interactive skills, social intelligence, emotion expression, and dialogue system may influence the user expectations about the robot's social capabilities. A mismatch between the user's expectations and the actual social intelligence of the robot may negatively impact the acceptance and use of the robot [10]. Robot appearance is also expected to influence acceptance. The robot physical shape, such as the human-likeness, animal-likeness, machine-likeness, and robot's gender are expected to influence perceptions of and attitudes of end-users towards robots. It has been believed that deep understanding of these factors may lead robot designers to develop personal robots that will be widely accepted and adopted. In addition to a believable appearance, the design of a social robot requires a sensory apparatus able to perceive the social and emotional world, and a control system able to generate fast and acceptable responses [16], [17].

This paper is organized as follows; an introduction to user acceptance and a review of literature is given in Section I. Section II gives a brief introduction to the build in-house robot's platform called iSocioBot which will be used in the experiment, human-robot interaction system, factors impacting robot acceptance, and finally data collection process and the questionnaire. Results and the discussion of results are given in Section III. Concluding remarks are presented in Section IV.

II. Materials and Methods

A. *Robot Platform (iSocioBot)*

The autonomous robot platform used in this experiment is a newly developed in-house intelligent social robot (iSocioBot) using off-the-shelf standard components [18]. The main goal behind building iSociobot is to attempt to make service robots socially intelligent and capable of establishing durable relationship with their end-users [19]. iSociobot is designed to work side-by-side with people and therefore its body shape is built to resemble that of the human body, as it is shown in Figure 1. The robot is 1.49m tall, which is very close to the worldwide average human female height, 1.7m. This height makes its users more comfortable in interaction with it and gives the robot cameras, on top of it, a wider field of view (FOV) for more optimal and robust face detection and recognition. The human-like body frame, round face and nick of the robot is supported by a round face and a neck built on top of a low cost TurtleBot base able to move and turn around at a speed close to human speed [20]. The face is equipped with 32×32 RGB matrix LED array to enable the robot to display different types of facial expressions, and three Pololu RGB LED strips for ears and necklace.

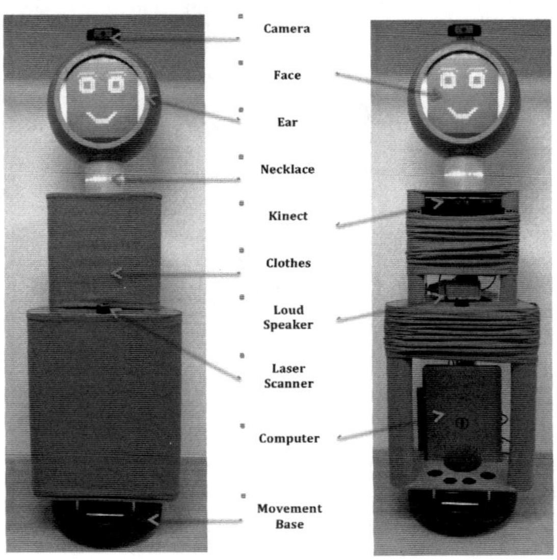

Figure 1. iSocioBot.

With the aid of the face and ears, the robot can simulate expressions such as listening, thinking and speaking. Due to the limited payload capacity of the robot base, which is maximum 5kg, it is decided to build the body frame from light materials such as plastic and wooden sticks and covering it with acoustic clothes to allow sounds to reach the acoustic devices and for the robot to look more feminine and friendly. The robot is also equipped with a range of sensors and actuators including encoders, laser range scanner, gyro, bumpers, Xbox Kinect, color camera, microphone array, loudspeaker, Wi-Fi module, two-wheel drive (2WD), etc., which can give the robot massive capabilities to sense the environment, able to localize, mapping, and navigate, avoid collision, simulate human's emotional and facial expressions, and have a dialogue system to verbally communicate with human end-users. iSocioBot software system is based on Robot Operating System (ROS) and Ubuntu. The software is a set of open source and newly written software frameworks running as a set of ROS-based processes. When all software modules are running, the robot is only limited by the capability of the onboard computer battery, which is around one hour, before the need for recharging.

B. *Human-robot interaction using speech*

In this section, we present our ongoing work in building and integrating technologies for natural and long-term human-robot interaction. The robot's ability for establishing simple and natural interaction with its users is of central importance for all kind of applications of personal robots. The system consists of spontaneous automatic speech recognition (ASR), audio-visual perceptual system, speaker localization and tracking, dialogue system, and speech synthesis. When a user speaks to the robot while they are not facing each other, the robot tends to slowly spin around until it can clearly face him/her. These components have been integrated on iSocioBot for real-time and long-term user interaction.

Although the robot has a more sophisticated artificial intelligence (AI)-based dialogue with natural language understanding system, which is able to respond to users in a more human and natural manner, in this experiment and for the sake of providing all users with the same conditions, a very primitive, flexible, and answers-independent dialogue script is used. The dialogue script consists of a set of ordered groups of sentences and questions. In the experiment, the robot randomly chose a sentence or a question from each group in order. Detecting when the user starts and stops talking timely control the transition between each script item. The dialogue starts by greeting the user using one of the welcome statements, asking about his/her name, a few sentences and questions to discuss the cultural night event, and then it ends by wishing him/her a pleasant event. The dialogue was conducted in Danish. An English translation of a part of the Danish script is shown in Table I.

C. *Data collection and questionnaire*

Data will be collected through a paper-based questionnaire [21]. The questionnaire consists of a number of questions assessing the views and impressions of participants regarding the factors that could potentially impact robot acceptance and adoptions. These factors include robot functionality, robot social capability, and robot appearance. The questionnaire will also collect some demographic data about participants such as gender, age group and previous experience in interacting with personal robotics. For children or adults with a low literacy rate, it was allowed to fill out the questionnaire verbally with the help of a staff member or parents.

TABLE I. DIALOGUE SCRIPT

No.	iSocioBot's Dialogue Script
1	Hello. Welcome to the cultural evening. I am SocioBot from Aalborg. What is your name?
2	Hello. Welcome to this glorious event. My name is SocioBot and I come from Aalborg. What is your name?
3	Hi there. Welcome to Culture Night. My name is SocioBot, and I come from Aalborg University. What is your name?
1	Great to see you.
2	Nice to meet you.
3	Om, it is nice to be with you.
1	Where are you from?
2	Where do you live?
1	It's a good place. I have heard very well about it.
2	It sounds like a nice place. I would like to visit it one day.
1	What made you decide to attend the cultural evening?
2	Why are you here tonight?
1	I am glad you are here. There is much to see. I hope to get time to look around later, but so far I have to stand here and greet people.
2	It is great that you are here. I have heard that there are many different exhibitions and stands around, so I hope to get time to try them later. For now, I greet people, when they come.
1	How many people do you think there are here tonight?
2	How many do you think there comes to culture tonight?
1	It is a great event. I guess around 3000 visitors.
2	Yes, it's a great event. My best guesses are that there will be about 3000
1	What do you think about my appearance in general?
2	What do you think of the way I look like?
1	It's good to hear. Thank you.
2	Thank you, your opinion is important to me. I would probably just consider it.
3	Thank you, it's good to hear your opinion. I way just think about it.
1	It was nice to talk to you. I hope you get a lovely evening.
2	It's been exciting to talk to you. I wish you a fun night. '

Before interacting with the robot, each participant has been given an introduction to iSocioBot, design, functions and its possible applications. They are also given a brief explanation about what kind of data the questionnaire will collect, why it is collected and how it will be used. A staff member provided explanations and guidance before and throughout the experiment to participants.

The paper questionnaire consists of four main questions with a set of standard answers, a section for demographic information, and three illustrative pictures. The first two questions are addressing the social intelligence skills of the robot by assessing the user's impressions and views before and after interacting with the robot, the third question is about the user's preferences of the robot appearance by asking whether they would prefer the human-likeness or machine-likeness of the robot and how this can affect their engagement with and acceptance of the robot, and finally the fourth question is addressing the robot functionality by assessing the need for a touchscreen display on the robot's chest to facilitate robot's control and user interface issues and how this can affect robot acceptance.

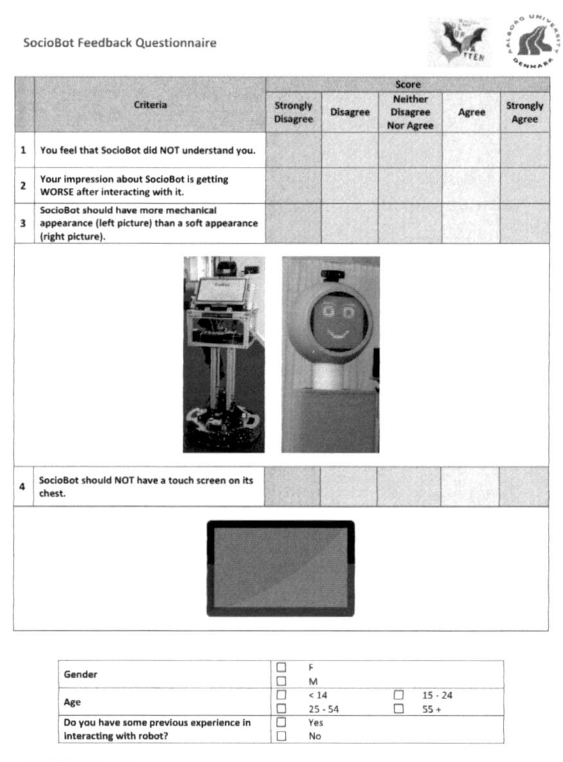

Figure 2. Paper questionnaire is designed to evaluate robot's acceptance.

For these types of questions, participants are provided with a set of categorical answers (i.e., Strongly Agree (SA), Agree (A), Neither Agree Nor Disagree (NAND), Disagree (D), Strongly Disagree (SD)) where he/she is supposed to choose only one answer for each question. Due to the fact that different age groups, genders, and educational and cultural background are expected to have different views on any given subject, and to get an idea of what kind of social, age, and gender groups are giving answers, the questionnaire asks each participant to identify his/here gender (i.e., male/female), choose an age group (less than 14, 15-24, 25-54, and above 55 years old), and answer whether he/she has previously experienced a kind of interaction with social robots. Identity of each participant he been left anonymous.

Due to the expected diversity of participants' age and educational background, questions are formulated in the most simplest way and the questionnaire is provided with a number of illustrative pictures to help respondents to get directly to the subject of each question. An English translation of the Danish questionnaire is shown in Figure 2. The experiment has been conducted during the annual culture night event organized by the Danish Ministry of Higher Education and Sciences in the city of Copenhagen. In this event, doors are opened for children and adults of all ages to experience new technology beside a massive of other cultural activities [22]. Interested attendees were asked to voluntarily take part in a dialogue with the robot and optionally fill out the questionnaire thereafter. Among hundreds of attendees, a total of 97 persons decided to participate.

III. RESULTS & DISCUSSION

97 participants in total have decided to take part in a dialogue with iSocioBot and fill out the questionnaire with a response rate above 98% (2 participants decided not to fill in the questionnaire). It has been believed that the experiment participants were a fair representative sample of the cultural night's attendees. In the following sub-sections, the collected data will be statistically analyzed.

A. *Participants' analysis*

It is believed that age, genders, and cultural background may have a certain impact on the answers of each individual participant. Therefore, we will analysis the group participants and break it down into response groups according to gender, age, and cultural background, as follows:

- *Gender*: among the 97 participants there are 40 females (around 41.24%) and 57 males (around 58.76%), as it is shown in Table II.
- *Age*: 86.60% of the participants are less than 14 years old, 1.03% from 15 to 24 years old, 9.28% from 25 to 54 years old, and 3.09% of the participants are above 55 years old, as it is shown in Table II.
- *Cultural background*: 88 participants (around 90.72%) of the sample have no previous experience in personal and social robots beforehand. Only 9 participants (around 9.28%) of the sample have experienced personal robots before. Therefore, the participant's previous experience in robotics will be considered insignificant in this study.

It is obvious, as it is shown in Table II, that the majority of the experiment participants are children under 14 years old and this indicates that young generations are more curious for testing and experiencing new and sophisticated technologies including personal and social robots. This also implies that personal and social robots are capable of attracting children and this can open the door for more applications of these robots in areas such as in education as an effective learning tool in homes and in classrooms and in useful entertainment as well [23][24].

TABLE II. AGE VS. GENDER GROUPS OF PARTICIPANTS

Age (years)	Gender		Total
	Female	Male	
<14	35	49	**84 (86.60%)**
15-24	-	1	**1 (1.03%)**
25-54	3	6	**9 (9.28%)**
>55	2	1	**3 (3.09%)**
Total	**40 (41.24%)**	**57 (58.76%)**	**97**

B. *Questionnaire analysis*

In this section, data collected through the experiment will be summarized and analyzed, as it is shown in Table III. The three factors that might affect robot acceptance and adoptions will be analyzed through the following 4 questions:

Q1: do you feel that that iSocioBot did not understand you?

Q2: your impression is getting worse after interacting with iSocioBot?

Q3: iSocioBot should have more machine-likeness than a human-likeness appearance?

Q4: iSocioBot should not have a touchscreen display on its chest?

1) Social Intelligence of the robot: Questions 1 and 2 are used to ask participants about their views and impressions about the social skills of the robot. The first question asks whether the participant has the feeling that iSocioBot can understand him/her. This question implies evaluating the ability of the employed ASR system and the dialogue system to provide appropriate and logical answers corresponding to the user's answers. The second question asks the participant whether he/she still has the same impression about social robot or it is getting worse after interacting with the robot. This question, in addition to assessing the social skills of the robots, it also assess the user's previous believes and expectations of such kind of technology and to what degree its behavior matches its humanoid appearance. Participants' answers (%) are shown in Table III.

TABLE III. STATISTICAL RESULTS OF THE QUESTIONNAIRE

Labels	Frequency of questionnaire answers			
	Q1	Q2	Q3	Q4
SA	9 (9.28%)	4 (4.12%)	7 (7.22%)	12 (12.37%)
A	23 (23.71%)	10 (10.31%)	2 (2.06%)	20 (20.62%)
NAND	13 (13.40%)	22 (22.68%)	7 (7.22%)	19 (19.59%)
D	34 (35.05%)	29 (29.90%)	27 (27.84%)	15 (15.46%)
SD	18 (18.56%)	32 (32.99%)	54 (55.67%)	31 (31.96%)

From Table III, 53.61% of the sample are disagree and strongly disagree on the hypothesis that iSocioBot cannot understand them compared to 32.99% who either agreeing or strongly agreeing that the robot cannot understand them clearly. 62.89% of the sample either disagree or strongly disagree that their impression about social robots is getting worse after interacting with iSocioBot. It could be concluded that the sample users are strongly satisfied about the current social skills of the robot and that there is a satisfactory matching between robot's humanoid appearance and its social skills. In other words, the majority of the participants strongly agree that the robot looks like human and is able to behave similarly by identifying and reacting to human communications using voice and facial expressions.

2) Robot appearance: Compared to industrial robots which are specifically designed for doing some specific tasks such as welding steel in specifically designed car factory or workshop, humanoid robots, on the other side, are designed for use by humans in daily life activities and in an unstructured and dynamic environment, therefore, these robots have to be adapted to the world in which humans are already live. However, It is not adequate that these robots would likely be designed to look like one of us, or just have a pleasing looking but it should be designed specifically for its intended function. Despite the reality that the majority of humanoid robots would have no use for their humanoid appearance and because people are naturally used to communicate and interact with other humans, people would be more accepting of these robots if they appeared and operated in a much more human manner. In this experiment, question number 3 is about user preferences regarding the robot appearance. It asks participants whether they would prefer the machine-like or human-like appearance of the robot? The majority of the participants in the interaction decided that they would prefer the human-likeness of the robot. 83.51% of the sample were either disagreeing or strongly disagreeing on the hypothesis that social robots should have a more machine-like appearance.

3) Robot functionality: To improve robots acceptance and use, question 4 is used to ask participant their views whether the robot should not have a touchscreen display on its chest. 47.42% of the participants group either disagreeing or strongly disagreeing on that hypothesis compared to 32.99% who see that it is not necessary for the robot to have a touchscreen display on its chest. Touchscreen would be used to facilitate communication with the robot and improve safety. Answers of participants are given in Table III.

IV. CONCLUSIONS

Creating robots which look, communicate and maneuver like humans has partially become a reality. These robots are now able to adequately communicate with human users using voice, identify human communications patterns and reacts accordingly, simulate human's facial expressions, and maneuvering like humans, however, it is still far to achieve the deep and complex level of human-to human communication and interaction. These robots are designed to be used by humans and in the world in which humans are actually live. In this regards, an experiment is conducted to measure the impact of some variables that are believed very effective for user acceptance and adoption of these robots. Data analysis showed that children less than 14 years old are more interested in interacting with robots. This complies with previous studies that indicated that young generations are more likely willing to experience and use new and sophisticated technologies specially robots. The success of the robot in attracting children is a signal of the usefulness of these technologies and it opens the door for employing this technology to work directly with human and operate in a variety of applications such as educating and entraining children at homes and in classrooms. If children will be major consumer of personal robots, they also should be given more effective role in designing these new technologies.

Despite the reality that the majority of robots would have no use for its humanoid appearance, results showed a strong support for the human-likeness appearance of personal robots. Because people are naturally used to communicating and interacting with other humans, it would be ideal situation for any one trying to use a personal robot. If we can design a robot which is able to react and communicate in a similar way to humans, it would no longer be thought as a machine by its user, and people would naturally be more engaged and accepting it if it appeared and operated in a much more human manner. For user acceptance and adoption, a strong matching between the humanoid appearance of the robot and its behavior must be achieved, and vice-versa. Results showed a strong support for humanoid robots to have a secondary mean of user-interface and communication rather than the natural human communication by voice. A touchscreen display on the robot's chest might give the robot's users a better feeling of safety in case the ASR system failed to work properly.

From this study, we can summarize the following concluding remarks; 1) in the area of social and humanoid robots, it is crucial to achieve a kind of matching between robot appearance and actions, if a robot's designer will go for the human-likeness appearance, a satisfying degree of robot's social intelligence and skills must be achieved, and vice versa, 2) in addition to the voice communication between the robot and its users, a secondary way, such as a touchscreen display on the robot's chest, to communicate with the robot in emergency cases or in case of ASR failure is crucial, 3) children are more interested in experiencing new technology and therefore they should be given a more effective role in the design and development of such kind of technology, and finally, 4) personal robots are very well accepted product and therefore it can be employed to work with humans in very challenging environments such as in classrooms for educating children and in nursery homes for elderly care giving.

ACKNOWLEDGMENT

Durable Interaction with Socially Intelligent Robots (iSocioBot) is a research project supported by the Danish Council for Independent Research (Technology and Production Sciences) under grant number: 1335-00162.

REFERENCES

[1] N. Roy et al., "Towards personal service robots for the elderly," Proceedings of the Workshop on Interactive Robotics and Entertainment (WIRE), 25, 184, Pittsburgh, PA, USA, 2000.

[2] J. Greczek, E. Short, C. Clabaugh, K. Swift-Spong, and M. J. Matarić, "Socially Assistive Robotics for Personalized Education for Children," AAAI Fall Symposium on Artificial Intelligence and Human-Robot Interaction (AI-HRI), Nov 2014.

[3] K. Dautenhahn, "Roles and functions of robots in human society: implications from research in autism therapy," Robotica, 21, 2003, pp 443-452.

[4] J. Greczek, E. Kaszubski, A. Atrash, and M. J. Matarić, "Graded Cueing Feedback in Robot-Mediated Imitation Practice for Children with Autism Spectrum Disorders," In 23rd IEEE Symposium on Robot and Human Interactive Communication (RO-MAN '14), Edinburgh, Scotland, UK, 2014.

[5] M. Cooper, D. Keating, W. Harwin, and K. Dautenhahn, "Robots in the classroom-tools for accessible education," Assistive technology on the threshold of the new millennium, 1999, pp. 448-452.

[6] I. R. Nourbakhsh, "Robots and Education in the classroom and in the museum: On the study of robots, and robots for study," IEEE Int. Conf. Robotic Automation, 2000.

[7] D. P. Miller, I. R. Nourbakhsh, and R. Siegwart, "Robots for education," in Springer Handbook of Robotics, B. Siciliano and O. Khatib, Eds. Springer, 2008, ch. 55.

[8] M. Fujita and K. Kageyama, "An open architecture for robot entertainment," In Proceedings of the first international conference on Autonomous agents (AGENTS '97), ACM, New York, NY, USA, 1997, pp. 435-442.

[9] M. Nakamura and H. Sawada, "Talking robot and the analysis of autonomous voice acquisition," In Proceedings of the IEEE International Conference on Intelligent Robots and Systems (2006 IEEE/RSJ), 2006, pp. 4684-4689.

[10] J. M. Beer, A. Prakash, T. L. Mitzner, and W. A. Rogers, "Understanding Robot Acceptance," Technical Report HFA-TR-1103, Georgia Institute s of Technology School of Psychology, Human Factors and Aging Laboratory, Atlanta, GA, USA, 2010.

[11] M. Heerink, B. Krose, V. Evers, and B. Wielinga, "Measuring acceptance of an assistive social robot: a suggested toolkit," In The 18th IEEE International Symposium on Robot and Human Interactive Communication, RO-MAN 2009, Toyama, Japan, 2009, pp. 528-533.

[12] K. Sääskilahti, R. Kangaskorte, S. Pieskä, J. Jauhiainen, and M. Luimula, "Needs and User Acceptance of Older Adults for Mobile Service Robot", 2012 IEEE RO-MAN: The 21st IEEE International Symposium on Robot and Human Interactive Communication. September 9-13, Paris, France, 2012, pp. 559-564.

[13] F. D. Davis, "Perceived usefulness, perceived ease of use, and user acceptance of information technology," MIS Quarterly, 13(3), 1989, pp. 319-340.

[14] V. Venkatesh, M. G. Morris, G. B. Davis, and F. D. Davis, "User acceptance of information technology: Toward a unified view," MIS Quarterly, 27(3), 2003, pp. 425-478.

[15] D. L. Goodhue and R. L. Thompson, "Task-technology fit and individual performance," MIS Quarterly, 19(2), 1995, pp. 213-236.

[16] C. Breazeal, "Socially intelligent robots," Interactions, 12(2), 2005, pp. 19–22.

[17] D. Mazzei, A. Zaraki, N. Lazzeri and D. De Rossi, "Recognition and expression of emotions by a symbiotic android head," *Humanoid Robots (Humanoids), 2014 14th IEEE-RAS International Conference on*, Madrid, 2014, pp. 134-139.

[18] Z.-H. Tan, N. B. Thomsen, and X. Duan, "Designing and Implementing an Interactive Social Robot from Off-the-shelf Components," submitted to The 3rd IFToMM Symposium on Mechanism Design for Robotics (MEDER 2015), Aalborg University, Aalborg, Denmark, 2015, pp. 1-8.

[19] Durable Interaction with Socially Intelligent Robots (iSocioBot) (retrieved from http://socialrobot.dk/ in January 2015).

[20] TurtleBot (retrieved from http://www.turtlebot.com/ in January 2015).

[21] E. Fanning, "Formatting a paper-based survey questionnaire: best practices," Practical Assessment, Research and Evaluation, 10(12), 2005, pp. 1–14.

[22] Culture Night, Copenhagen, October 10th, 2014 (retrieved from http://www.kulturnatten.dk/en/culture-night/Culture-Night-2014 in January 2015).

[23] J. M. Roschelle, R. D. Pea, C. M. Hoadley, D. N. Gordin, and B. M. Means, "Changing How and What Children Learn in School with Computer-Based Technologies," The Future of Children, Vol. 10, No. 2, Children and Computer Technology, 2000, pp. 76-101.

[24] A. Druin, "The role of children in the design of new technology," Behaviour and information technology, 21(1), 2002, pp. 1-25.

Recognition of Technical Gestures for Human-Robot Collaboration in Factories

Eva Coupeté, Fabien Moutarde, Sotiris Manitsaris and Olivier Hugues
Center of Robotics, Mines ParisTech
PSL Research University
Email: first-name.last-name@mines-paristech.fr

Abstract—**Enabling smooth Human-Robot collaboration requires enhancing perception and intelligence of robots, so that they can "understand" the actions performed by the humans with whom they are interacting. In this paper we are dealing with new industrial collaborative robots on assembly-line and supply-chain in automotive manufacturing. We are conducting research on technical gestures recognition, to allow the robot to understand which task is being executed by human worker, and react accordingly. We use two kinds of sensors: depth-camera for monitoring of human movements, and inertial sensors placed on tools. In this study, we propose and use a method for head and hands tracking using a top-view depth-map, and use HMM (Hidden Markov Models) to recognize gestures with these data. Then, we refine the results from the HMM with data from inertial sensors equipping tools. Our research shows that: i) using 3D-vision only, we can obtain already good results of gestures recognition for several workers: 80% of the gestures are correctly recognized, ii) exploiting data from tools equipped with inertial sensors significantly improve the recognition accuracy to 94% in the same multi-user evaluation. A first test of our method with a simple Human-Robot collaboration scenario is also described.**

Keywords–Human-robot collaboration; Industrial application; Assembly line; Gestures recognition; Depth camera.

I. INTRODUCTION

Robots are becoming more and more present in our everyday life. They can be used for social interaction or for medical support. In the industrial context, collaborative robots are emerging that are intrinsically "safe". These robots, devoted to tasks that are either of low added-value, or potential source of musculoskeletal disorders, are working nearby workers without barriers between them contrary to current robots in factories. Therefore, collaborative robots allow increased automation of factories, saving of space and cost while improving productivity in the industrial plants. This new configuration of collaboration between robots and humans on assembly-line and supply-chain is efficient only if human-robot collaboration can be smooth, i.e., the robot is following the human gestures in order to respond fluidly. To this end, and in order to ensure workers' safety, a collaborative robot has to be aware its environment, to be able to adapt its speed to the worker rapidity, and monitor worker's actions in order to ensure smooth cooperation.

Gesture recognition can meet these needs: by recognizing the worker's gestures, the robot can recognise which task is being executed, adapt its speed and detect when something unexpected happens. One of the difficulties of this goal is that, contrary to most Human-Computer interactions where the user can adapt to the system, the worker must be able to work "as usal" and is not supposed to make any effort for his gestures to be correctly understood by the robot.

In this paper, we are focusing on technical gestures recognition for human-robot collaboration. To enable a robust gesture recognition, we use two kinds of sensors: depth-camera and inertial sensors. Depth-camera allows us to have information on the worker's postures, and to evaluate his distance to the robot. In addition, we equip with inertial sensor some tools manipulated by human workers, in order to know when they are used. The main contribution of our paper is to show the feasibility of a robust user-independent and totally non-intrusive system for real-time recognition of typical technical gestures of human workers in a factory, for allowing natural interaction of collaborative robots. Also, one of the novelties in our work is the use, as a complement to real-time analysis of depth images, of an inertial sensor placed on a tool rather than on the operator. This increases very significantly the rate of correct gesture recognition, while keeping our system totally non-intrusive.

This paper is organized in five parts. In Section II, we present related work on human-robot interaction, gesture recognition, human pose estimation, and sensors fusion. In Section III, we present our experimental use-case. In Section IV, we detail our methodology to recognize the gestures and to fuse data from the depth-camera and the inertial sensors. In Section V, we present our results of gesture recognition and a first Human-Robot collaboration using our system. Finally in Section VI, we provide conclusions and perspectives for our future work.

II. RELATED WORK

In this Section, we present related work on the topics of human-robot collaboration and gestures recognition. In subsection II-A, we present several applications of human-robot collaboration in different fields. Then in II-B, we describe different kinds of features and frameworks for gestures recognition with depth camera only and with the addition of inertial sensors.

A. Human-Robot collaboration

With the massive arrival of robot in our everyday life the research on human-robot interaction and collaboration has been very active these last years [1].

Robots are already very present in different fields. They are used to interact with elderly people, [2], to guide visitors in a museum [3] or to assist humans during walking training [4]. To be better accepted by humans, the interaction with the robot has to be natural, using the same codes as a Human-Human collaboration. Since gestures are important factors in Human-Human conversations, non verbal interaction has already been used to enable a communication between the robot and the human, [5] and [6].

In factories, new collaborative robots are designed to be intrinsicly safe and to provide complementary skills to human co-workers like the Kuka LWR [7] and the Universal Robot UR [8]. In this context, collaborative robot and human can work together, for example carrying the same object [9]. Some studies have evaluated the worker's acceptability to work with this new kind of partner [10]. In [11], the authors present a framework enabling the robot to adapt his behaviour to a new user after a first step of joint-action demonstration.

B. Human pose estimation and gesture recognition

Human pose estimation is becoming easier since the apparition of depth-cameras, for example the Microsoft Kinect [12], [13]. This RGB-D sensor combines standard RGB images with depth information obtained by analysis of a projected infrared pattern. We can sort the methods to estimate a human pose using a depth-camera in two classes: without, [14], and with, [15] and [16], a prior posture learning. The advantage of the first class is that we do not need a previous dataset to establish the human pose but these methods can be slower to compute the human pose. Conversely, with prior learning the acquisition of a dataset and its processing can be a long first step, but the human pose estimation is performed more quickly. However, a limitation of human pose estimation using learning is that it can properly handle only postures similar to those included in the dataset used for its design and training. For example the Kinect SDK recognizes postures only when the user is facing the camera. Once these postures are extracted, they can be selected, fully or partially, to determine which ones are the most discriminant to recognize gestures. In [17], the authors use Principal Component Analysis (PCA) to select the most useful features, among skeleton joints, to recognize gestures. In [18], the authors convert the set of skeleton joints to create a more robust and less redundant pose descriptor based on joint-angles representation. They also use SVM to determine key poses which will be used to do gesture training and recognition.

Many methods to recognize gestures have been set up these past years. The 3D skeleton tracking of the subject with a depth camera is often used to recognize gesture, as in [19] and [20]. Various approaches have been proposed to handle dynamic gestures recognition. The most known are HMM [21] used, among other, in [22] and [23]. But other machine-learning algorithms have been successfully applied: Dynamic Time Wrapping (DTW), Support Vector Machines (SVM), decision forest and k-Nearest Neighbours (kNN). All gesture recognition systems have limits and constraints, for example the HMM based recognition needs a large amount of training samples to be efficient. For all systems, the number of recognizable gestures is predefined and limited. To be well distinguished, two gestures must be different enough to enable the recognition system to differentiate them.

The simultaneous utilisation of inertial sensor and depth-camera have appeared in the literature in first place to deal with calibration issue, as in [24]. Fusion of depth-map and inertial sensor for gesture recognition is done in [25]. The authors fused the data coming from the two types of sensor by re-sampling and filtering. Then, they proceed at a classification with HMM. In [26], the authors used only inertial sensor to recognize technical gestures. However, up to our knowledge no published work proposed, as we do in this paper, to improve gestures recognition by using inertial sensors placed not on monitored human, but rather on object or tool manipulated by him.

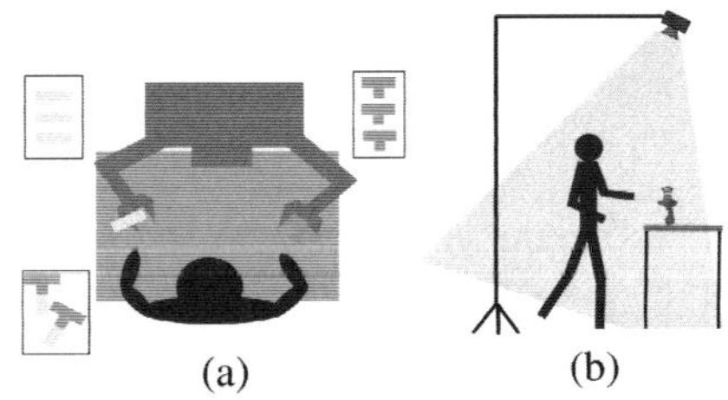

Figure 1. Description of our experimental use-case, (a): the robot gives motor parts to the worker, (b): we equipped the scene with a depth-camera and an inertial sensor fixed on a screwing-gun tool

III. PRESENTATION OF OUR EXPERIMENTAL USE-CASE

We work on a scenario where the worker and the robot share the same space and work together. The task is inspired from the assembly of motor hoses on supply chain. Presently, the assembly process of motor hoses has some drawbacks: the worker has to find the appropriate parts of the motor hoses among other motor parts, which is a lack of time and increase the cognitive load of the worker. In our set-up, the robot and the worker are facing each other, a table is separating them, see Figure 1(a).

On an assembly line, because mounting operations must be achieved quickly and efficiently, the actions to be executed by human operators are standardized as a rather strictly-defined succession of elementary sub-tasks. To ensure a natural human-robot collaboration, the robot has to perform an action accordingly to which task the operator is executing, in order to be useful at the right time and not delay the worker. In our use-case, the assembling of motor hoses requires the worker to take 2 hose parts respectively on left and right side, join them, screw them, take a third part from left, join it, screw it, and finally place the mounted motor hose in a box. The only actions performed by the robot are giving a piece with the right claw and giving a piece in the left claw. The set of human operator's gestures to be recognized by our system is therefore rather straightforwardly deduced from above-mentioned sub-tasks as:

1) to take a motor hose part in the robot right claw (G1)
2) to take a motor hose part in the robot left claw (G2)
3) to join two parts of the motor hose (G3)
4) to screw (G4)
5) to put the final motor hose in a box (G5)

These gestures will allow the robot to be synchronized with the operator by understanding when an operator is taking a piece from a claw and when the next piece is needed.

The classical sequence of gestures to assemble motor hoses is: (G1 then G2) or (G2 then G1), then G3, then G4 then G2, then G3, then G4, then G5. Some workers prefer to do the two screwings after the second execution of G3, so that we cannot suppose a strictly-defined ordering of operations, as it is essential to leave to human workers some freedom degree in their work.

We equipped the scene with a depth-camera which is filming the worker with a top-view. With this set-up, we are avoiding most of the possible occultations on a supply-chain due to workers or objects passages. We also put an inertial sensor on the screwing-gun, in order to know when it is moved by the worker, see Figure 1(b).

IV. METHODOLOGY

In this Section, we present our methodology to achieve technical gestures recognition. The global processing pipeline is illustrated on Figure 2: using segmentation and computation of geodesics on top-view depth image, we estimate a 10D feature vector characterizing operator's posture, and used for recognition of gestures. In subsection IV-A, we present our method to extract hands positions of the worker from the depth-map using geodesic distances between the top of the head and each point of the upper body of the worker. In subsection IV-B we explain how we put together information from the depth-map about the worker posture to create features to learn and recognize technical gestures. In subsection IV-C we present our learning and recognition framework, and in IV-D we show our method to merge information from the depth-map and the inertial sensors.

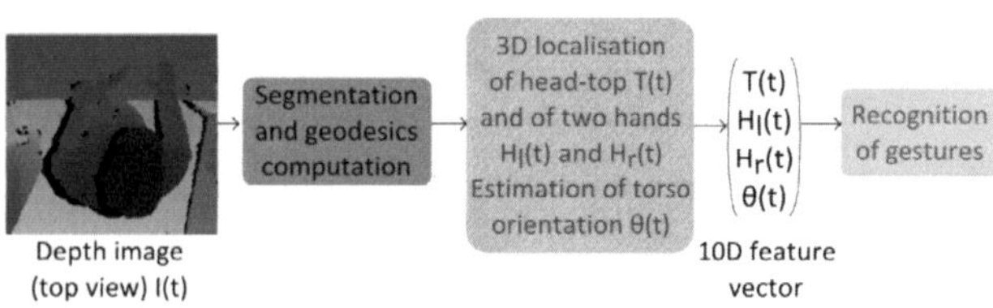

Figure 2. Pipeline from our raw depth image to gestures' recognition

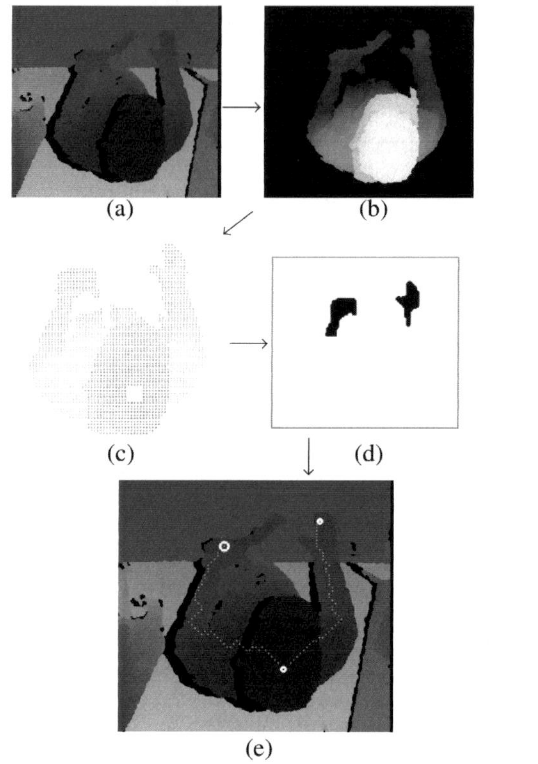

Figure 3. Our hands-tracking method. (a): initial depth map, (b): upper body of the worker, (c): geodesic distances between each point of the upper body and the head (blue to red), (d): farthest upper body parts from the head, (e): head and hands locations with the shortest paths between the hands and the head

A. *Tracking hands positions*

To localize and track hands of the worker, we have adapted and extended to top-view case the method proposed in [14]. Figure 3 illustrates our framework.

1) Upper-body and head extraction: We only need the upper-body of the operator to recognize his gestures, because the worker is staying in small area during his work and he only uses his hands for assembling the motor hoses. From the raw depth-image (see Figure 3(a)), we segment the upper-body by keeping only the depth pixels that are above the assembling table (see typical result on Figure 3(b)). Then, the top of the head is located as the biggest "blob" from the 10% highest pixels of upper-body (the 10% threshold value was determined by anatomic considerations). Finally, the center of the head top is estimated as the center of the "top-of-head blob". Additionally, using typical anatomic values of height distance from head-top to shoulders level, we locate the two shoulders on the depth-image map; this allows to estimate torso orientation as the horizontal angle of the straight line joining the two shoulders.

2) Creation of the upper-body graph: In order to locate hands, we make the assumption that they are the visible parts of the upper-body that are the farthest from the head, not in Euclidean straight line distance, but following the body surface. To find these "farthest" points, we calculate the geodesic distances between head-top and all points of the upper-body. In order to compute geodesics, we create a weighted graph with all pixels from the upper-body as nodes. The first step is to connect each pixel with its eight neighbours (only if they also belong to the upper-body). To each of these connections is associated a weight equal to the absolute value of difference between the two connected pixels (which is approximately their height difference, since the depth camera is pointing downwards and nearly vertically). In order to obtain geodesics that link only anatomically contiguous body parts (e.g. for instance, not "jumping", from an arm directly to the torso it touches), we prevent connections between depth pixels that have a too large depth difference.

3) Application of the Dijkstra algorithm for hands localization: After creation of the upper-body graph, we apply to it the Dijkstra [27] algorithm in order to find the shortest route between each point of the upper-body and the head center. A route is a succession of continuous connections from the graph and the length of the route is equal to the sum of the used connection weights. The result can be seen on Figure 3(c): pixels with colder colours (blue, green) are those that are geodesically-closest to the top of the head; conversely, pixels with warmer colours (orange, red) are geodesically-farthest from the top of the head. The hands approximate locations are then found by computing the two biggest blobs inside the part of upper-body that are farthest from the top of the head, with typical outcome shown on Figure 3(d). Finally, as can be seen on Figure 3(e), we obtain hands locations, as well as the corresponding geodesics from head-top.

B. Features

After the tracking of the hands positions, we need to define features describing the worker's posture, see Figure 4. To do learning and recognition on several persons, we need a feature that is independent from each person's morphology.

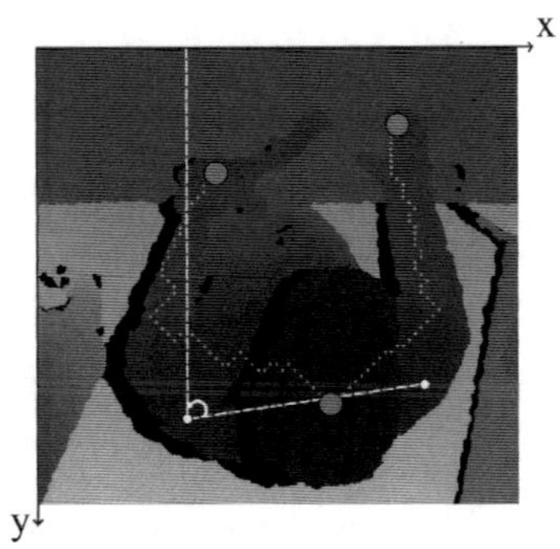

Figure 4. Representation of our features: the two hands and the head location (red dots) and the torso orientation (angle in yellow)

We chose to use the hands and head 3D locations (red dots on Figure 4) and the torso orientation (angle illustrated in yellow on 4). The third dimension of our vectors is equal to the value of the associated pixels in the depth map. These data are then concatenated in a ten-dimensions vector. For each frame, we calculate a feature which describes a posture of the worker.

C. Gestures recognition

To do the learning and the recognition we use discrete HMM, a combination of K-Means and HMM, see Figure 5. For the learning, once we have extracted the features from all the frames independently of which gesture, we use this training set to determine K clusters with the K-Means algorithm, the centroid of each cluster represents an average posture. We use this trained K-Means to quantize each series of postures, i.e., gesture. These quantized series are used as input for the HMMs for learning and recognition.

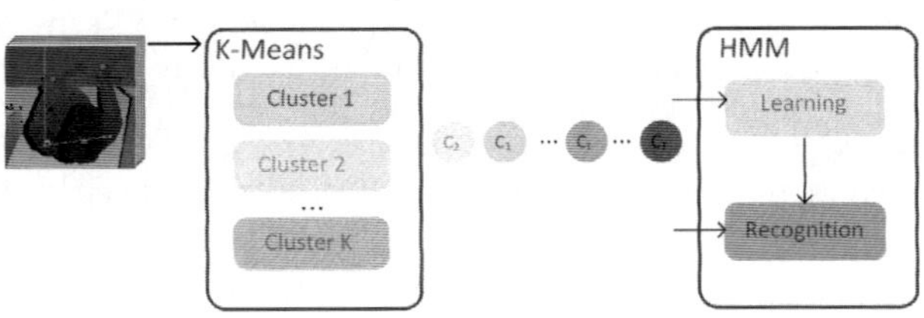

Figure 5. Pipeline of our learning and recognition method

We train one HMM for each gesture. When we want to predict which gesture is being performed, we test our quantized series of postures on each HMM. The gesture associated to the HMM with the highest likelihood to have generated this series of posture is "recognized". The Forward algorithm, described in [21], is used to establish the most likely gesture.

D. Utilisation of the inertial data

In our set-up, we also put an inertial sensor on the screwing-gun. We use this additional data source with a "late-fusion" scheme: classification by HMMs based only on features extracted from depth image is done first, and tool's inertial data is considered only afterwards to obtain the final output of our system. The screwing-gun is supposed to move only when the worker is using it to fix two parts of motor hose. We are in conflict with the result of the HMM classification in two cases:

- case 1: when the gesture G4 is recognized while the screwing gun did not move
- case 2: when a gesture which is not G4 is recognized while the screwing gun did move

For the first case, if we suppose that the inertial sensor cannot be broken, it is not possible to screw without moving the screwing-gun. Since the gesture recognized corresponds to the HMM associated with the highest likelihood to have generated the sequence of features, we look at the output likelihood of the HMM linked to gesture G4. If this likelihood is above a threshold we decide that gesture G4 has been executed, otherwise no gesture is recognized.

For the second case, it is possible that the screwing-gun moved without being used. If the worker want to move it from one side of the table to another for example. In this case we also look at the output likelihood of the HMM matching with G4. If this likelihood is above a threshold we replace the gesture previously recognized by G4, otherwise we keep the gesture associated to the HMM with the highest likelihood.

With this method, we make our system more robust by correcting wrong recognitions.

V. Results

In this Section, we will present our results of gestures recognition using either the depth-camera alone, or the combination of depth-camera with inertial sensors. We will evaluate impact of the addition of inertial sensor when we already have a depth map for our use case. We will also present a scenario of Human-Robot collaboration using our system of gesture recognition in real time. We recorded seven workers and we are using a jackknife method to evaluate our framework, i.e., we are learning HMMs with labelled gesture from six workers and testing our recognition framework on gestures of the seventh worker. We test all the seven possible combinations.

A. Using only the depth map

For our study we chose to use HMM with four hidden states and fifteen clusters for the K-Means algorithm. We obtain the results in Table I.

Table I. Gestures recognition rates with only data from the depth-camera

		Output (Maximum likelihood)					
		G1	G2	G3	G4	G5	Recall
Input Gesture	G1	**104**	15	2	3	5	81%
	G2	10	**230**	5	6	1	91%
	G3	1	7	**170**	67	10	67%
	G4	5	5	51	**180**	1	74%
	G5	2	-	2	4	**119**	94%
	Precision	85%	89%	74%	69%	88%	**80%**

We proceed at learning and recognition with all the possible combinations of six workers for the learning and one worker for the recognition. Then, we add all the results of recognition to obtain Table I.

The recall of a gesture *i* represents the rate of gestures *i* which are recognized to be a gesture of class *i*. The precision is the percentage of actual *i* gestures among all gestures that the system labels as class *i*.

The total rate of correct gesture recognition is 80% which is a good result. But we can see that gesture G1 is sometimes mistaken with gesture G2. And gestures G3 and G4 are also often mistaken. Indeed the recall and precision of G3 and G4 are low: respectively 67% and 74% for G3, and 74% and 69% for G4.

B. Using combination of depth map and inertial sensors

Table II presents results of gestures recognition after correction with data from the inertial sensor fastened to the screwing-gun, as explained in Section IV-D.

Table II. Gestures recognition rates with combined data from depth-camera and inertial sensor

		Output (Maximum likelihood)					
		G1	G2	G3	G4	G5	Recall
Input Gesture	G1	**104**	15	1	-	5	83%
	G2	10	**230**	4	-	2	93%
	G3	-	3	**191**	-	9	94%
	G4	-	-	-	**242**	-	100%
	G5	1	-	4	-	**119**	96%
	Precision	90%	93%	96%	100%	88%	**94%**

We can first observe, by comparison with Table I, that all the false recognitions of G4 that were occurring without inertial sensor data, have been corrected. The recognition rate of gesture G3 is also dramatically improved. These two gestures were previously often confused one for another. With these corrections, our system reaches a global rate of correct gestures recognition of 94%, which is an excellent result, considering that our evaluation is multi-user (7 different persons repeating several times the total assembling operation). This result also highlights the interest of equipping tools with inertial sensors and use these information as a second layer after the classification of gesture with depth data.

C. Setting up a scenario of Human-Robot collaboration

We elaborate a scenario of collaboration between the worker and the robot in our use case, see Section III. To control the claws opening, the worker originally had to press two buttons, one for each claw. We removed these buttons and now use the gesture recognition to command the claw opening. To prevent a motor piece to fall on the table without a hand to grab it underneath, we combine the gesture recognition with the detection of the hand position near the claw.

For the right claw, if we recognize gesture G1 (to take a motor hose part in the right claw) and if the right hand is near the right claw, we command the claw opening. The same principle is applied for the left claw with gesture G2. This scenario enables reduction of the cognitive load of the worker because he does not have to think about the button and remains concentrated on the motor hoses assembly.

To command the claws openings we connected our computer to the robot with a Arduino [28] board. Our algorithm is coded in C++ language and processes 12 frames per second, which allows us to enable a smooth collaboration between the worker and the robot.

VI. CONCLUSIONS AND FUTUR WORK

In this paper, we have presented our research related to Human-Robot interaction in factories of the future. The goal is to enable tight and smooth cooperations between a human worker and a collaborative safe robot. One of the pre-requisite to attain this goal is to allow the robot to monitor and "understand" the activities of its human co-worker. We therefore focus on design, implementation and test of a method for robust and non-intrusive recognition of technical gestures, as it is clearly one of the key enabling technologies for achieving smooth Human-Robot interaction in our factory context.

We chose to use a depth-camera because it is a non-intrusive sensor robust to light changes and which provides information on the worker's posture. To augment the robustness of our system, we further equipped the tools (screwing-gun in our use-case) with inertial sensors. Our system therefore does not require the workers to wear any special equipment. We focused on a scenario of "handing" over of motor parts from a collaborative robot to a worker. Our framework differs from other studies using both a depth map and inertial sensor to do gestures recognition, firstly because in our approach inertial sensor is placed on a tool rather than on the monitored human. We first presented a new method to track hands with a top-view depth map without prior knowledge: geodesic distances from head are estimated for upper-body by Dijkstra algorithm applied on a graph of depth pixels, and hands locations are determined by searching parts that are "geodesically-farthest" from the head. For gestures recognition, we proposed a simple feature based on head and hands 3D locations and torso orientation, which is discretized by K-means and fed into discrete HMMs. We have evaluated *multi-user performances* of our system on a dataset obtained by recording 7 persons repeating several times the total assembling operation. This showed that with vision-only (the top-view depth-camera), already 80% of good gesture recognition can be attained. Furthermore, when combining with data from inertial sensor attached to the screwing-gun, the recognition rate is significantly raised to an excellent 94%. We tested our method on a simple scenario to command the robot claw opening with the gestures recognition.

Two main conclusions can be drawn from our study: 1/ robust and non-intrusive *user-independant* recognition of technical gestures of workers in factory seems feasible in principle; 2/ it can be extremely valuable for improving gestures recognition in factory to instrument workers' tools with inertial sensors. From these results, we can also conclude more generally that it should be possible to develop intelligent collaborative robots that can interact and cooperate smoothly with human workers in factories.

In our future work, we will program more reactions of the collaborative robot to the worker's gestures. We shall also record gestures from a larger pool of workers to extend our results on a larger range of morphologies and gesture executions. We will also work on an user-adaptive learning to increase our correct recognition rate with the vision only.

ACKNOWLEDGMENT

This research benefited from the support of the Chair 'PSA Peugeot Citroën Robotics and Virtual Reality', led by MINES ParisTech and supported by PEUGEOT S.A. The partners of the Chair cannot be held accountable for the content of this paper, which engages the authors´ responsibility only.

REFERENCES

[1] A. Bauer, D. Wollherr, and M. Buss, "Human–robot collaboration: a survey," International Journal of Humanoid Robotics, vol. 5, 2008, pp. 47–66.

[2] M. L. Walters, K. L. Koay, D. S. Syrdal, A. Campbell, and K. Dautenhahn, "Companion robots for elderly people: Using theatre to investigate potential users' views," Proceedings - IEEE International Workshop on Robot and Human Interactive Communication, 2013, pp. 691–696.

[3] S. Thrun and M. Bennewitz, "MINERVA: A second-generation museum tour-guide robot," Proceedings of IEEE International Conference on Robotics and Automation, vol. 3, 1999.

[4] T. Sakaki, N. Ushimi, K. Aoki, K. Fujiie, R. Katamoto, A. Sugyo, and Y. Kihara, "Rehabilitation robots assisting in walking training for SCI patient," Proceedings - IEEE International Workshop on Robot and Human Interactive Communication, 2013, pp. 814–819.

[5] E. Sato, T. Yamaguchi, and F. Harashima, "Natural Interface Using Pointing Behavior for Human–Robot Gestural Interaction," IEEE Transactions on Industrial Electronics, vol. 54, 2007, pp. 1105–1112.

[6] K. Nickel and R. Stiefelhagen, "Visual recognition of pointing gestures for human–robot interaction," Image and Vision Computing, vol. 25, 2007, pp. 1875–1884.

[7] "Kuka Robotics," URL: http://www.kuka-robotics.com/fr [accessed: 2016-03-18].

[8] "Universal Robot UR," URL: http://www.universal-robots.com/fr/produits/robot-ur5/ [accessed: 2016-03-18].

[9] T. Wojtara, M. Uchihara, H. Murayama, S. Shimoda, S. Sakai, H. Fujimoto, and H. Kimura, "Human-robot collaboration in precise positioning of a three-dimensional object," Automatica, vol. 45, no. 2, 2009, pp. 333–342.

[10] V. Weistroffer, A. Paljic, P. Fuchs, O. Hugues, J.-P. Chodacki, P. Ligot, and A. Morais, "Assessing the acceptability of human-robot co-presence on assembly lines: A comparison between actual situations and their virtual reality counterparts," in The 23rd IEEE International Symposium on Robot and Human Interactive Communication. IEEE, aug 2014, pp. 377–384.

[11] S. Nikolaidis, R. Ramakrishnan, K. Gu, and J. Shah, "Efficient Model Learning from Joint-Action Demonstrations for Human-Robot Collaborative Tasks," in Proceedings of the Tenth Annual ACM/IEEE International Conference on Human-Robot Interaction, ser. HRI '15. ACM, 2015, pp. 189–196.

[12] "MicrosoftKinect," URL: https://dev.windows.com/en-us/kinect [accessed: 2016-03-18].

[13] J. Han, L. Shao, D. Xu, and J. Shotton, "Enhanced Computer Vision with Microsoft Kinect Sensor: A Review," IEEE Trans. Cybernetics, vol. 43, no. 5, 2013, pp. 1318–1334.

[14] L. A. Schwarz, A. Mkhitaryan, D. Mateus, and N. Navab, "Human skeleton tracking from depth data using geodesic distances and optical flow," Image and Vision Computing, vol. 30, no. 3, 2012, pp. 217–226.

[15] J. Shotton, A. Fitzgibbon, M. Cook, T. Sharp, M. Finocchio, R. Moore, A. Kipman, and A. Blake, "Real-time Human Pose Recognition in Parts from Single Depth Images," in Proceedings of the 2011 IEEE Conference on Computer Vision and Pattern Recognition, ser. CVPR '11. IEEE Computer Society, 2011, pp. 1297–1304.

[16] C. Migniot and F.-E. Ababsa, 3D Human Tracking in a Top View Using Depth Information Recorded by the Xtion Pro-Live Camera, ser. Lecture Notes in Computer Science. Springer Berlin Heidelberg, 2013, vol. 8034.

[17] C. Jost, P. De Loor, L. Nedelec, E. Bevacqua, and I. Stankovic, "Intelligent Technologies for Interactive Entertainment (INTETAIN), 2015 7th International Conference on," pp. 47–56, 2015.

[18] L. Miranda, T. Vieira, D. Martinez, T. Lewiner, A. W. Vieira, and M. F. M. Campos, "Real-Time Gesture Recognition from Depth Data through Key Poses Learning and Decision Forests." IEEE, aug 2012, pp. 268–275.

[19] K. Lai, J. Konrad, and P. Ishwar, "A gesture-driven computer interface using Kinect," 2012 IEEE Southwest Symposium on Image Analysis and Interpretation, 2012, pp. 185–188.

[20] A. Ramey, V. González-Pacheco, and M. A. Salichs, "Integration of a low-cost RGB-D sensor in a social robot for gesture recognition," in Proceedings of the 6th international conference on Human-robot interaction - HRI '11. New York, New York, USA: ACM Press, 2011, p. 229.

[21] L. Rabiner, "A tutorial on hidden Markov models and selected applications in speech recognition," Proceedings of the IEEE, vol. 77, no. 2, 1989, pp. 257–286.

[22] B. Lovell, P. Kootsookos, and R. Davis, "Model Structure Selection and Training Algorithms for an HMM Gesture Recognition System," Ninth International Workshop on Frontiers in Handwriting Recognition, 2004, pp. 100–105.

[23] V. Kellokumpu, M. Pietikäinen, and J. Heikkilä, "Human activity recognition using sequences of postures." MVA, 2005, pp. 570–573.

[24] J. Hol, T. Schon, F. Gustafsson, and P. Slycke, "Sensor fusion for augmented reality," in 2006 9th International Conference on Information Fusion. IEEE, 2006, pp. 1–6.

[25] K. Liu, C. Chen, R. Jafari, and N. Kehtarnavaz, "Fusion of Inertial and Depth Sensor Data for Robust Hand Gesture Recognition," IEEE Sensors Journal, vol. 14, no. 6, 2014, pp. 1898–1903.

[26] E. Coupeté, S. Manitsaris, and F. Moutarde, "Real-time recognition of human gestures for collaborative robots on assembly-line," in 3rd International Digital Human Modeling Symposium (DHM2014), 2014, pp. 7–p.

[27] E. W. Dijkstra, "A note on two problems in connexion with graphs," Numerische Mathematik, vol. 1, no. 1, 1959, pp. 269–271, ISSN:0029599X.

[28] "Arduino," URL: https://www.arduino.cc/ [accessed: 2016-03-18].

First results of Studying Human Robot Interaction in the Wild — The Hobbit Robot Tested by Older Adults at Home

Markus Vincze*, Daniel Wolf*, Markus Bajones*, Astrid Weiss*, Markus Suchi*, David Fischinger*†
and Jürgen Pripfl‡, Christoph Gisinger‡
*Automation and Control Institute, Vision for Robotics Group, Technische Universität Wien, Austria
{markus.vincze, daniel.m.wolf, markus.bajones, astrid.weiss, markus.suchi}@tuwien.ac.at
†david.fischinger@gmail.com
‡Akademie der Altersforschung am Haus der Barmherzigkeit, Austria
{juergen.pripfl, christoph.gisinger}@altersforschung.ac.at

***Abstract*—Falls are the primary cause for older adults that make it necessary to move to a care facility. One option is to wear a mobile device, with the limitation that it needs to be worn any time while a fall happens one time a year. Together with care professionals we worked on a mobile robotics solution that does not only discover falls, but is pro-active to avoid falls in the first place. Old people rapidly realized that a robot picking up objects from the floor is a great help. While tests in a laboratory setting showed the usefulness of this function, we needed to send the robot out into the user's home to learn about the real challenges when approaching a realistic use case scenario. We present results stressing Human-Robot Interaction from a study where users tested the robot in their homes in three countries. Findings indicate that the pick-up function is highly valued, even if the robot costs go up considerably as opposed to a mobile robot without arm.**

Keywords–assistive robot, mobile manipulator robots

I. Introduction

Falls are the primary cause for older adults that make it necessary to move to a care facility. Together with care professionals we worked on a mobile robotics solution that does not only discover falls but is pro-active to avoid falls in the first place. The result is the Hobbit robot, which provides a set of functions to the user with a multi-modal user interface to realize easy to use Human Robot Interaction (HRI).

While there are many service robots targeting the application of an extended video phone, there are only a few robots including an arm to interact with the environment. The top end robot with similar functionality as Hobbit is Care-o-bot [1], which was used in the SRS [2] and Accompany [3] projects to study user interaction for bringing water and other help functions in care facilities [4]. This robot is too large to operate in homes while several of the other robots such as Giraff [5] are not autonomous and need to be remotely operated.

The main novelty of of the Hobbit robot was to bring a service robot into user's homes, that can do more than as an extended video phone that is operated by a remote user including the navigational capacity. The proposed Hobbit robot provided the following functions to the user. (1) Maintaining the user's self-efficacy is addressed with exercising cognitive and physical skills without so explicitly ad-dressing the target goal of self-efficacy (social connectedness and fitness functions). (2) Increasing the perceived user's safety is addressed by managing and keeping safe at home (emergency detection, grasping from floor, transport objects, safety check, calling the robot, pa-trolling). And (3) addressing the user's well-being to maintain a positive affect (entertainment functions). A unique setting of the Hobbit study was, that users were free to select any of the functions at any time. We summarize results related to HRI and what technical realizations proved to be useful or need improvement.

The paper is structured as follows. We proceed with a closer look and comparison to other present ongoing work and then, Section II describe the Hobbit robot in more detail and in Section III the functionality that has been implemented and that it provided to the users. Section IV summarizes the user trials, how they were conducted and what was measured. And Section V summarizes and discusses the results and first findings.

A. Related Work

Ideally robot helpers for older adults should investigate the feasibility of providing robotic assistance with Activities of Daily Living (ADL) and the extended assistance functions for Instrumental ADL (IADL). Typical functions of ADL/IADL are dressing, food preparation, eating, cleaning, and rehabilitation or direct physical exercise activities. Hobbit did not set out to address these needs, since all these capabilities are yet beyond present robot capabilities. What can be achieved relates to the maintaining and safety of the home, fitness functions, and creating positive effect with socializing functions. Another aspect is where these robots are studied. There are only very few studies that go beyond trials in care facilities and study longer durations, e.g. [6] and a recent survey in [7]. In the following, we highlight recent developments.

Today most of the other service robot projects further advance the state of the art of one specific functionality. For example, in GrowMeUp [8] the user's habits, preferences, and routines are studied using multiple sensors on the robot and the environment. The robot is a reduced PAL platform without arms from Pal Robotics [9]. As we have seen in our user experiences, relying on an external sensor network may be feasible in specially designed homes but is not welcomed by users at home and requires substantial installations and the related costs.

The EU project EnrichMe [10] also studies the use of touch screen and an augmented user interface as a follow up of the Companionable project with Robosoft and their Kampai robot. Ambient Assisted Living (AAL) functions are used by introducing Radio-frequency identification (RFID) chips into objects, something long in talk but that did not yet materialize since it requires a retrofitting of items and the similar issues regarding installations at home. The research prototype Kompai is not certified for autonomous use with persons.

Another recently started project is Mario [11]. It addresses loneliness, isolation and dementia in older persons through multi-faceted interventions delivered by service robots using AAL sensor installations. The partners will use near state of the art robotic platforms based on the Robosoft robot that is "flexible, modular friendly, low cost and close to market ready in order to realize field contributions in the immediate future". A specific feature is to allow for application development for the robot to augment its functions.

The big step forward in these projects is that the robot should be at least partially autonomous in the user's home. So far robots have been operated remotely or only for very few tasks in a home during limited time of user trials, for example in projects such as SRS, Giraff++, and RobotEra. It was pointed out by coordinators of these projects that the autonomous navigation capability as developed within Hobbit will be of great use also in these projects and beyond.

In summary, user requirements as created in Hobbit already pinpoint the primary user needs. In view of this, we will in the next sections present what we would improve over the Hobbit concept. Experience has shown and our user studies have confirmed that a modular approach with customizable features would most suitably satisfy the heterogeneous group of elderly who could benefit from the use of Hobbit robot in their homes. We present next the robot itself in more detail and then enumerate the functionality that we provided for the user trials at home.

II. The Components of the Hobbit Robot

The second prototype (PT2) of the robot platform used for the home trials has differential drive kinematics, a floor-parallel depth camera, a *head* with screens as eyes and an RGB-D camera (ASUS Xtion mounted at a height of 120 cm above ground), a touch screen in front of the torso, and an arm with a gripper. The platform implements some of the lessons learned from a previous study with an older versions of the Hobbit robot [12]. The height of the Hobbit robot is now 125 cm and it has a width of maximum 56 cm at the point where the shoulder of the arm sticks slightly out beyond the robot.

The development of the system aimed to keep hardware costs as low as possible. The intention was to study if it is feasible to provide good functionality at home even with lower cost components to come closer to the target of introducing a robot into user homes. The hardware components sum up to EUR 16.000,-, Figure 1 presents the Hobbit robot and its components. Autonomous navigation was based on a virtual laser scan. The robot was operated via a Multi-Modal User Interface (MMUI) which consisted of a Graphical User Interface (GUI) with touch, Automatic Speech Recognition (ASR), Text to Speech (TTS) and Gesture Recognition Interface (GRI). It provided entertainment (radio, music, audio-books, games, fitness function), reminders, video phone service, control of a manipulator, access to an AAL environment (e.g. call buttons), and emergency call features. The robot's functionalities included automatic emergency detection (e.g. patrolling and detecting persons lying on the floor), handling emergencies (communication with relatives), and supportive fall prevention measures (transporting small items, picking up objects from the floor, searching for objects the robot had been taught by the user).

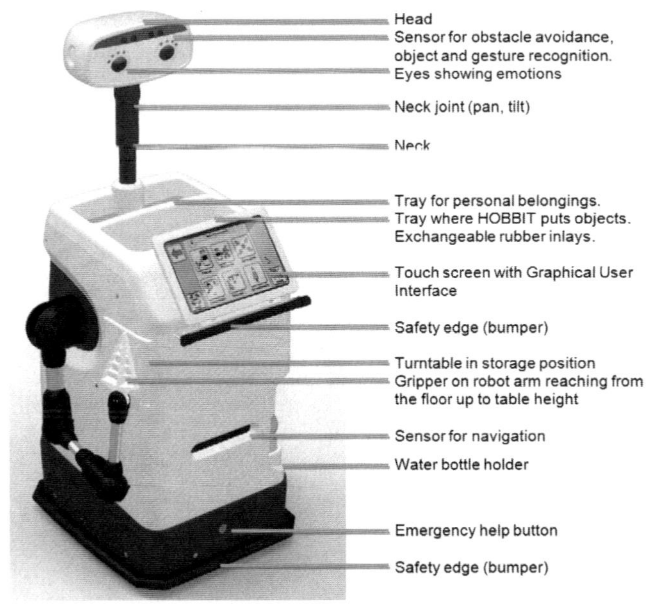

Figure 1. The Hobbit robot and its components.

III. The Functions Provided by the Hobbit Robot

In one of the first studies of its kind, a low-cost mobile social service robot with an arm that was intended to interact fully autonomously [13] over weeks was deployed in seniors' private homes, to support them with tasks and make them feel safe. Our study thus marks a major step in evaluating robotic systems under real-life conditions [14].

The selection of functions that have been implemented on the robot have been extracted from multiple interaction with users, secondary users or relatives and professional care givers. We conducted first home trials with an autonomous robot with the aim to find out what users want. Here, a lot more work is needed and recently started projects will expand our understanding. Part of this work was that we conducted two iterations of user studies and collected user requirements in [15]. These requirements give a clear picture of what older adults would want at present from a robot helper at home. Conclusions are drawn from workshops with older adults that created a longer list of requirements, which have then been ranked in studies and questionnaires, and correlated with technical feasibility given the present state of the art in service robotics. We used first user trials and lessons learned to verify the ranked requirements [16].

Before reviewing the robot system concept, let us shortly summarize the user requirements and relate them to other studies or care robots. The clear requirements formulated within the Hobbit project still hold. The main services that a home robot should provide to aid older adults target the following needs:

- Maintain the users efficacy level: this includes functions for keeping active such as

  - Social connectedness including telephone, Internet access to alternative ways of communication, such as a video call or to access weather, news and other information.
  - Physical and cognitive fitness including physical exercises that have been considered on top of the initial description of work. This includes games and playing music or video, and a function that has been surprisingly welcome by users to play the favorite radio station.
- Increase the perceived safety of user:
  - A main aspect is already the physical presence of the robot and its care functions such as seeking the user and user interaction during the patrolling function.
  - Multi-modal interaction capabilities and several ways to trigger an emergency call.
  - Pick-up of known and unknown objects from the floor which turned out be an essential aspect. The normal skepticism towards the robot went away after seeing the robot picking up an object from the floor.
  - The robot provided an additional safety check to the user, making her/him aware of hazards at home while proposing solutions or options to assist.
  - Calling the robot for help: the use of call buttons is an effective means to call the robot for any task at any time.
- Functions for the user's wellbeing: here we summarize services that are nice to have and will actually assist to accept the platform and keep it in use. In the Hobbit idea we had drawn out many of these functions as elements to make the user feel good, and possibly even create a bonding to the robot such that it is trusted and used and the previous two aspects are reached to an even better degree. Examples of these functions are:
  - A first personalization of the robot that is executed in the initialization phase. Additionally, the robot and basic guidelines for operating it are introduced.
  - Learning and finding objects is a welcome feature for the users and regarded as a great commodity.
  - An important functionality that extends the functionalities provided in Hobbit is the pick-up from high locations. Grasping objects from places high up that cannot easily be reached will be investigated in EU project Ramcip, though robot costs are expected to be considerable higher. In Hobbit we regard this functionality as a future module and a possible extension of the basic robot platform.
  - Entertainment ranging from games over music to surprising the user with the specific aim to increase user acceptance.
  - Reward functionality is a means to enhance the user binding with the hypothesis to improve the acceptance by the user.

In summary, the Hobbit robot provides a rich repertoire of functions, where several are novel and have been tested with users or at home for the first time.

IV. Design and Methods of the User Trials

We conducted user trials in Austria (seven end-users), in Greece (four end-users) and in Sweden (seven end-users). The trials with a total of 18 primary users (PU) and 16 secondary users (SU) were carried out in the homes of the users with the robot interacting autonomously for three weeks with the user. All trials took place in private homes of single-living senior adults and lasted for a total of 371 days Assessment by means of qualitative interviews and questionnaires took place at four stages of each trial: pre-trial, mid-term, end of trial, and post-trial (i.e. one week after the trial had ended). Results of the qualitative interviews as well as perceived safety measured by the Falls Efficacy Scale (FES) [17] are reported here. Out of 18 users 16 (14 female) were included for statistical analysis as two participants had to be excluded because of missing data). The mean age was 80 years, ranging from 75 to 89 years. Qualitative data was organized using NVivo (QSR International). Quantitative data was analyzed using SPSS by means of descriptive statistics and non-parametric methods (Friedman ranking-test).

A multi-method approach was applied for the evaluation of the three quality criteria usability, acceptance (including the Mutual Care concept [18]), and afford-ability. The evaluation followed a detailed evaluation plan with updates according to the inputs of the project reviewers, as well as the results of pilot user tests in their own flats. Results were gained from questionnaires, interviews, cultural probing with the participants before, during and after the trials, and continuous logging of all interaction data on the Hobbit robot.

V. Findings from the Study with Older Adults Users

As the data analysis is not yet finished we present first results and structure these into the aspects regarding the robot usage (usability, acceptance, afford-ability) and issues related to the robot hardware, software and development.

A. *Results regarding Overall Robot Usage*

The most important results of the user trials related to the three main quality criteria were:

- Usability: given there are no technical problems, Hobbit is easy to use and intuitive to handle. Different input modalities and flexibility was helpful for PUs. Utility of Hobbit's functions was however perceived to be lacking, often due to technical failures.
- Acceptance was ambivalent among users. The attitude towards a robot did not change significantly, and observed changes were of a negative kind. PT2 also failed to provide a significant feeling of safety and influence users' self-efficacy. Emotional attachment weakened over the course of the trials, possibly indicating the unfulfilled expectations of users and a sort of weariness from the trial procedure. What is more, reciprocity was not given for PUs, which shows that the Mutual Care approach needs some refinement to become effective.

- Afford-ability: From the experiences with PT2 in the trials, afford-ability (at a price of Euro 16,000.-) is not given for most users. Still, a reliably functioning version of Hobbit featuring a head, an arm, pick-up and learning functionality would be attractive for PUs.

From the qualitative data we extract how the different robot functions have been evaluated by the users. They highly appreciated the functions picking up objects from the floor, transporting things, detecting emergencies, delivering fitness and giving reminders. Concerning usability (also see above), they stated that the prototype was intuitive to handle but that errors in the actions of the robot led to frustration. The pick-up function, for example, was fully operational only for about 18% of the 371 days. And, if available, only about one out of ten attempts was successful. Furthermore, processing speed of the whole system was criticized as being too slow. Neither voice commands nor gestures worked satisfactorily, which is why the touch screen ultimately was used most. In summary, usability was negatively influenced by a lack of robustness. Quantitative data indicates that the perceived safety as measured by the FES did not change in the course of the trial ($p = 0.265$).

Furthermore, the concept of Mutual Care (MuC), developed to increase acceptance and use of Hobbit by older users, was found to have no effect. The reason for these unexpected results is, with high probability, to be found in the technical malfunctions of main features like *learn object* or *bring object*, many false positive fall detections as well as unreliability of most of the other commands. As reliability is a prerequisite for user acceptance, this result suggests that acceptance of a reliably working Hobbit would have been probably much higher and that a such a robot would also better have met the expectations of the users. Thus, a technically improved, highly reliable and cheaper version of Hobbit still has a high potential of becoming a useful and accepted tool in assisting senior adults at home.

B. Results regarding Technical Improvements towards Future Home Robots

While Hobbit already improved over other robots in terms of size - it is considerable smaller both in width and height than Care-o-bot - it is still too large. Robot height was found to be linked to the main use of the robot. Users would like the robot to be about as tall as when they are sitting. We closely reached this but a maximum height of 120 cm was found to be most appropriate. Robot width is constrained by the homes of older adults where space is typically limited. Hence, the platform should be smaller and has ideally not more than a diameter of 40 cm. At present this would cause considerable technical difficulties to integrate arms, batteries and drives but technology is getting close to this goal. And for reasons of easy navigation it is recommendable to give the robot cylindrical shape which renders rotating behaviors easier. Also in several cases doorways are as small as 65 cm and traversal will then be easier if not feasible. Finally, the robot arm should be completely inside the footprint of the platform when the arm is in home position, so it cannot collide with the environment when Hobbit is moving or rotating. A remaining issue are threshold. 25 mm have been found often and we used ramps to overcome these obstacles. It would be advantageous to find a simple wheeled solution to overcome smaller thresholds without any adaptations of the environment. Example solutions to cover thresholds are depicted in Figure 2.

Figure 2. Docking station (black) and the robot wrapped in plastic for temperature tests.

Hobbit's battery live was sufficient and lasted for more than eight hours of operation time. This is fully sufficient, since users will be tired of using the robot after a few hours and the robot can go and recharge. In terms of safety the robot should never be on a lower battery level, to make sure that a longer search for the user in their home when patrolling or in case of an emergency is supplied with sufficient power of the entire robot system. However, the battery status was not transparent for the user and ideally the robot would show the estimated remaining duration of operation.

A practical issue is a small docking station and reliable markers to assure highly robust docking. Figure 3 shows the docking station standing in front of the wall for best discernibility. However, due to space limits in homes it should merge as close as possible into the wall and it would be good to be able to place it freely. The procedure used to dock onto the charging station is designed for high fidelity 2D range finder sensor like lasers. Therefore, the shortcomings of the RGB-D (limited resolution, large stand-off distance) sensors apply negatively to docking as well. In addition to this, docking requires close-range maneuvering to the charging station, which due to the blind-spot of the depth stream of the RGB-D sensors means that the actual docking is done using dead-reckoning instead of more accurate localization methods. Again, a laser could solve this problem. Nevertheless, using imaging algorithms to visually detect the charging station or a distinct visual pattern above the charging station in the RGB stream of the sensors could also be used to make docking more robust by providing more accurate localization information when close to the docking station and would be the more cost effective solution.

Figure 3. Docking station (black) and the robot wrapped in plastic for temperature tests.

Another practical issues is a way to stop the robot at any time. In addition to the On/Off hardware button, there should also be a *cancel* hardware button/switch that would allow the user to cancel immediately whatever activity the robot is doing at any given moment remotely and without having to approach the robot. Currently, the only way the user can stop an activity is by pressing the back arrow button or kick the bumper which stops the movement, but not the running script, or turn the key of the robot which causes a complete shut-down. All of the above actions are difficult for an elderly person to perform while the robot is moving.

At night users would want Hobbit to be silent and dark, there should be no (bright) lights while Hobbit is in the charging station. The LEDs at the On/Off switches of Hobbit and the touch screen, the LEDs at the charging station and the Hobbit eyes (displays) are too bright at night when the user wants to sleep. Finally, let us investigate more closely improvements related to the active robot head, which turned out to be of great value but has scope for improvements.

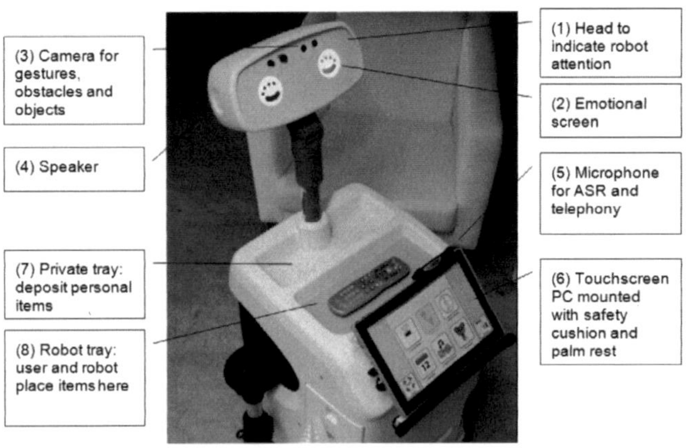

Figure 4. The upper body of Hobbit and its functionalities.

The upper body turns out to be an essential component of the robot presentation. It serves as main unit to the feeling of the presence of the robot. Figure 4 shows the upper body and head in more detail. The main functionality of the active head was to increase the field of few of the RGB-D sensor in the head and to cover with one camera functions such as obstacle detection, human detection and gesture recognition, and detecting and grasping objects from the floor. The head was designed and produced by Blue Danube Robotics [19]. It was enormously beneficial to test several head versions which lead to clear benefits of an active head. These benefits include

- Indicating robot attention to the user: the head direction naturally indicates where the robot places its attention. Users intuitively grasped that the robot is attending to them or not. This makes it extremely efficient as there is no need to present to the user in another way that the robot is busy, for example, with messages on the touch screen or spoken word.
- Extending the robot's viewing directions: the moving head allows using the camera for object search in all directions. This was used in initial search tests, where fixed robot locations and views have been used. This should be even more exploited in the future and is a powerful means to extend the operational capability of the robot without adding new hardware. One could think of it as upgrading the robot continuously with new perceptual functionalities given the same hardware.
- Obstacle detection for safe navigation: Moving the head to a looking down position allowed to reduce the blind area of the sensor and to cover a larger part of the floor. Different inclination angles were tested at the beginning in order to improve the visibility zone, also limiting obstructions caused by the tablet.

The active head has proven to be very useful in all these aspects. A limiting technical factor is the field of view of present RGB-D cameras. Typically the view is limited to $45°-60°$ horizontal field of view and a maximum of $45°$ of vertical field of view. While the pan-tilt ability of the neck enlarges this ability, the field of view for a first search is restricted.

The field of view of the Kinect or Asus sensor is $57°$ horizontally and $43°$ vertically. This limited field of view of RGBD sensors is not restricted to the Kinect but basically to all RGBD sensors available at present. Also the new Kinect, though operating on another principle, Time of Flight (TOF), has about the same field of view. Other alternatives have similar characteristics, e.g. the ARGOS 3D - P100 sensor of Bluetechnix with rather limited resolution of only 160x120, or the Sentis ToF M100 OEM plus camera that is made to fit into customer products. Another option is the Intel(R) RealSense(TM) 3D Camera (Front F200) Depth Intel RealSense F200/VF0800, yet gain with a similar field of view. The present sensor situation is even more restricted, since neither PrimeSense nor ASUS Kinect sensor are commercially available any longer.

With the tasks of viewing both the floor, obstacles, onto tables for object detection, and forward to detect persons and recognize gestures or activities, the proposed set-up is still viable, and can be improved by the addition of other sensors to increase safety. A slightly changed design with a dark face may better hide the dark holes from the camera. One way to augment the field of view is to include a wide field of view camera into the head. The human visual system covers about $180°$ horizontally. This would be of particular interest for locating the user. The head would still rotate to fixate the user, or try several fixations, until the user has been reliably detected. Again, the capability to have a gaze direction and indicate to the user where the robot attends at present comes in handy and will create the expected bonding as shown in the trials.

First work in this direction is ongoing, e.g. [20], [21]. However, there are no systems yet that would reliably and repeatedly fixate the user in an open home setting. Furthermore, only in a few works an adaptive approach to the user has been attempted and then the distance estimate was used from a laser to the single person legs in a given setting [22].

Finally, there are several practical issues that help in the design and trial phase of a home robot. It is useful to make the robot and its functionality remotely accessible via a secure Internet connection. This allows engineers to check on the platform and encountered problems without physically moving to the trial site. If issues with the hardware need to be resolved, a hull that can be easily unmounted saves a lot of effort. And there is a trade-off between simple hardware and more complex software. For example, we did not use any ultra sonic (US) sensors, which had the effect that we had to make sure that glass surfaces do not cover the full range of the height of the robot. Wooden frames typically produce sufficient signal in the RGB-D cameras to present no hazard. On the other hand, a few US sensors may improve the situation and may also aid in a simple check before driving backwards.

At the end, and mixing with experience from other projects, it is not sufficient to detect the floor alone for driving forward safely. While we did not encounter any dangerous situation when navigating with Hobbit, redundant perception of drivable floor is essential to assure robot safety in front of downward steps. Hole detectors based on infrared sensors and as a third measure a means to block access to certain areas in the navigation tool are advisable complimentary measures.

VI. Conclusion

The paper presented Hobbit - a robot developed and built to enable older people to feel safe and stay longer in their homes by using new information technology including smart environments (Ambient Assisted Living - AAL). The main goal of the robot is to provide a *feeling of safety and being supported* while maintaining or increasing the user's feeling of self-efficacy (one's own ability to complete tasks). Consequently, the functionalities focus on emergency detection (mobile vision and AAL, regular patrolling), handling emergencies (calming dialogues, communication with relatives) as well as fall prevention measures (keeping floors clutter-free, transporting items, staying active, fitness, and reminders). Moreover, high usability, user acceptance as well as a reasonable level of afford-ability are required to achieve a sustainable success of the robot.

We presented first results of a longer study of the robot in the wild, in the homes of 18 older adults. The study lasted for three weeks each, with another specific highlight of the study, that the robot was fully autonomous. Users could freely select what they wanted to do with the robot. While certain functionalities such as grasping objects from the floor and searching for objects did not provide sufficient reliability, other functions such as navigation, docking, entertainment, reminders, and the fitness function proved to be useful. Users saw the great potential of such a robot and very highly evaluated the capability to pick up something from the floor and to transport and find objects.

Regarding the effectiveness of HRI, the main finding is that an active head is a very helpful way to convey information about the robot and to facilitate human robot interaction itself. The active camera in the head does not only prove to be useful for obstacle detection and increasing the workspace, it turned out one of the most important means for HRI as it conveys in a very intuitive way the status of the robot. It was immediately obvious to users, that a robot looking down is busy while a robot looking up and then turning the head towards the user using head and torso detection is the trigger to start an interaction. In conclusion, the usage of active heads should achieve even more attention. Future work also considers to increase the head panning range to an owl, which would make it possible to also look behind the robot in case it needs to reverse. An issue of importance when space is narrow in user homes.

Acknowledgements

This research has received funding from the European Community's Seventh Framework Programme under grant agreement No. 288146 and funding from the Austrian Science Foundation under grant ALOOF. Thanks to Andreas Bley of Metralabs to show the robot docking station.

References

[1] "Care-o-bot," https://www.care-o-bot.de.

[2] "Srs project," http://srs-project.eu.

[3] "Accompany project," http://www.accompanyproject.eu.

[4] F. Amirabdollahian, S. Bedaf, R. Bormann, H. Draper, V. Evers, G. J. Gelderblom, C. Gutierrez Ruiz, D. Hewson, N. Hu, I. Iacono et al., "Accompany: Acceptable robotics companions for ageing yearsmulti-dimensional aspects of human-system interactions," in Human System Interaction (HSI), 2013 The 6th International Conference on. IEEE, 2013, pp. 570–577.

[5] "Giraff+ project," http://www.giraffplus.eu.

[6] J. Sung, H. I. Christensen, and R. E. Grinter, "Robots in the wild: understanding long-term use," in Human-Robot Interaction (HRI), 2009 4th ACM/IEEE International Conference on. IEEE, 2009, pp. 45–52.

[7] I. Leite, C. Martinho, and A. Paiva, "Social robots for long-term interaction: a survey," International Journal of Social Robotics, vol. 5, no. 2, 2013, pp. 291–308.

[8] "Growmeup project," http://www.growmeup.eu.

[9] "Pal robotics," http://pal-robotics.com.

[10] "Enrichme project," http://www.enrichme.eu.

[11] "Marios project," http://www.mario-project.eu.

[12] D. Fischinger, P. Einramhof, K. Papoutsakis, W. Wohlkinger, P. Mayer, P. Panek, S. Hofmann, T. Koertner, A. Weiss, A. Argyros et al., "Hobbit, a care robot supporting independent living at home: First prototype and lessons learned," Robotics and Autonomous Systems, vol. 75, 2016, pp. 60–78.

[13] J. M. Beer, C.-A. Smarr, T. L. Chen, A. Prakash, T. L. Mitzner, C. C. Kemp, and W. A. Rogers, "The domesticated robot: design guidelines for assisting older adults to age in place," in Proceedings of the seventh annual ACM/IEEE international conference on Human-Robot Interaction. ACM, 2012, pp. 335–342.

[14] A. Weiss, J. Beer, T. Shibata, and M. Vincze, "Socially assistive robots for the aging population: are we trapped in stereotypes?" in Proceedings of the 2014 ACM/IEEE international conference on Human-robot interaction. ACM, 2014, pp. 497–498.

[15] L. Lammer, A. Huber, A. Weiss, and M. Vincze, "Mutual care: How older adults react when they should help their care robot," in AISB2014: Proceedings of the 3rd international symposium on new frontiers in human–robot interaction, 2014, pp. 1–4.

[16] J. Pripfl, T. Körtner, D. Batko-Klein, D. Hebesberger, M. Weninger, C. Gisinger, S. Frennert, H. Eftring, M. Antona, I. Adami, A. Weiss, M. Bajones, and M. Vincze, "Results of a real world trial with a mobile social service robot for older adults," in Extended proceedings of HRI, 2016.

[17] L. Yardley, N. Beyer, K. Hauer, G. Kempen, C. Piot-Ziegler, and C. Todd, "Development and initial validation of the falls efficacy scale-international (fes-i)," Age and ageing, vol. 34, no. 6, 2005, pp. 614–619.

[18] A. Huber, L. Lammer, A. Weiss, and M. Vincze, "Designing adaptive roles for socially assistive robots: a new method to reduce technological determinism and role stereotypes," Journal of Human-Robot Interaction, vol. 3, no. 2, 2014, pp. 100–115.

[19] "Blue danube robotics," www.bluedanuberobotics.at.

[20] B. Pierce, T. Kuratate, C. Vogl, and G. Cheng, "mask-bot 2i: An active customisable robotic head with interchangeable face," in Humanoid Robots (Humanoids), 2012 12th IEEE-RAS International Conference on. IEEE, 2012, pp. 520–525.

[21] D. Das, M. Rashed, Y. Kobayashi, Y. Kuno et al., "Supporting human–robot interaction based on the level of visual focus of attention," Human-Machine Systems, IEEE Transactions on, vol. 45, no. 6, 2015, pp. 664–675.

[22] R. Mead and M. J. Mataric, "Robots have needs too: People adapt their proxemic preferences to improve autonomous robot recognition of human social signals," New Frontiers in Human-Robot Interaction, 2015, p. 100.

Evaluation of a 3D Human System Interface for Air Traffic Control

Andreas Baier
Altran AG
Zurich, Switzerland
Email: andreas.baier@altran.com

Alf Zimmer
Engineering Psychology Unit
University of Regensburg
Regensburg, Germany
Email: alf.zimmer@ur.de

Abstract - **In air traffic control, events in 3D space have to be managed with the dual goal of safety and efficiency. Due to the fact, that these events have to be constructed from a 2D airspace representation and numerical information, the resulting mental workload for air traffic controllers is very high. An experimental working model of an air traffic control workspace with a 3D airspace representation is evaluated and shown to be a possible means to reduce mental workload and to improve efficiency and learnability while maintaining the present level of safety.**

Keywords - Air Traffic Control; Situation Awareness; Mental Workload; User Centered Design; 3D; Stereoscopy.

I. INTRODUCTION

In 1943, Craik introduced the concept of mental models [1], namely that people interact with their environment not directly, but by means of simplified models of the environment, which consist of sufficiently large sets of knowledge about what is known to be true about the world and of assumptions about the dynamics of processes. This conceptualization of the interaction of individuals with their environment [2][3] has helped to understand and explain, for instance, why people are able to act successfully in a three-dimensional (3D) space while controlling the motion of objects in parallel which, in essence, is the core task in air traffic control (ATC). Mental models furthermore have strongly influenced the field of cognitive ergonomics, especially in the design of human system interfaces, e.g. the mental model is central for Endsley's model of situation awareness [4], as well as in the construction of aptitude tests for the selection and instruction of operators for human machine systems.

What is often overlooked, however, is that mental models can lead to failures because they are too domain specific, too much simplified (e.g. due to the erroneous assumption of linearity), or that they rely on erroneous analogies or over-generalizations (e.g. in the field of naïve physics). Furthermore, mental models are usually elicited by means of verbal protocols. Such protocols, however, are necessarily sequential and cannot properly represent events which happen in parallel and in a 3D space.

For the purpose of designing human system interfaces, this means that the presented information has to be congruent with the tacit knowledge of time and space, and that the mental model that is used leads to a correct understanding of the presented situations. Existing ATC workstations use a two-dimensional (2D) top-view to represent the airspace. Numerical values indicate the elevation of objects. On this basis, the air traffic controller (ATCO) needs to mentally construct an abstract 3D representation of the airspace. Such a mental construction process does not allow to grasping the ongoing events directly which results in a high mental workload and, therefore, is safety relevant. In contrast, an adequate 3D representation that contains all relevant spatial information allows what Gibson calls the direct perception of events [5], which relies on an embodied tacit knowledge of space and time. Especially the advances in 3D visual displays provide the preconditions required for such a direct event perception and therefore allow human machine interactions to go beyond traditional modes of interaction.

In Section II, the importance of situational awareness for ATC is described and it is explained, how it is linked to safety and efficiency. Section III outlines how airspace information is processed using the existing 2D human system interface. In Section IV, results are presented that demonstrate how appropriate stereoscopic 3D visualizations allow for an immediate perception of the dynamic events in the airspace, therewith making the ATCOs task easier to learn, more effective, and lead to a higher efficiency by combining the traditional mental models of ATC with tacit spatial knowledge. In Section V, the impact of stereoscopic 3D airspace visualizations on safety, efficiency, and learning is discussed. Section VI provides suggestions for applying stereoscopic 3D airspace visualizations to ATC.

II. THE AIR TRAFFIC CONTROLLERS' TASK AND THE TRADE-OFF BETWEEN SAFETY AND EFFICIENCY

The task of the ATCO is to guide aircraft safely and efficiently through the airspace. This requires a high degree of situational awareness, namely to build up and maintain an accurate understanding of the current situation and of how it is likely to develop in the near future. Especially in domains such as ATC, where the mental workload of the operator tends to be high, and poor decisions may lead to serious consequences, lacking situation awareness has been identified as a main factor for accidents that are attributed to human error [6]. Because there is a trade-off between safety and efficiency in ATC, safety, for obvious reasons, has a higher priority than efficiency. Therefore, an imminent loss of situational awareness is likely to result in less efficient decisions. Uncertainty about the development of a critical approximation between two or more aircrafts, for instance, leads ATCOs to immediately implement preventive actions rather than continuing their assessment of the situation in order to reduce the amount of uncertainty and then decide if a more resource intensive intervention is necessary [6].

III. The Existing Human System Interface for Air Traffic Control

The existing human system interface uses a 2D airspace representation combined with alpha-numerical information by means of paper-based or digital strips and verbal communications between ATCOs and pilots. It fails the above described principles for direct event perception insofar, as the aircraft positions are given in two different formats instead of one integrated format. The lateral aircraft positions are shown analogically by a top view onto the airspace on a 2D plane, whereas the vertical aircraft positions are presented numerically. The ATCOs, therefore, cannot perceive the airspace situation directly, but have to mentally construct a 3D representation. In order to understand the critical events in the airspace, additional information about the aircraft is displayed numerically, such as speed, heading, and call-signs. This information is provided within tags attached to the position signifiers of each aircraft. This means that the ATCOs need to combine information that is presented in different formats in order to understand the actual situation and how it evolves in time – a task that requires time and complex mental operations, this can cause a very high mental workload, which may lead to inefficient decisions as a result of uncertainty.

IV. Evaluation of 3D Human System Interfaces for Air Traffic Control

In the line of research presented here, two goals have been pursued; (1) the integration of the spatial information into one 3D representation and (2) the development of a cohesive interaction design tailored to what the 3D representation affords to ATCOs.

In this study three different 3D representations have been compared with a 2D representation similar to the existing 2D human system interface for ATC (see Figure 1) on the basis of safety critical situations involving two aircraft [7]; the existing 2D representation (2D), a 3D view from above (3Da), a 3D side-wise view with vertical drop-lines to the position over ground (3Ddl), and a 3D visualization that is the same as 3Ddl but without the drop-line (3D). All 3D visualizations used stereoscopy combined with a motion tracking system that allowed the adaptation of the airspace visualization to the ATCOs viewing-position in real-time.

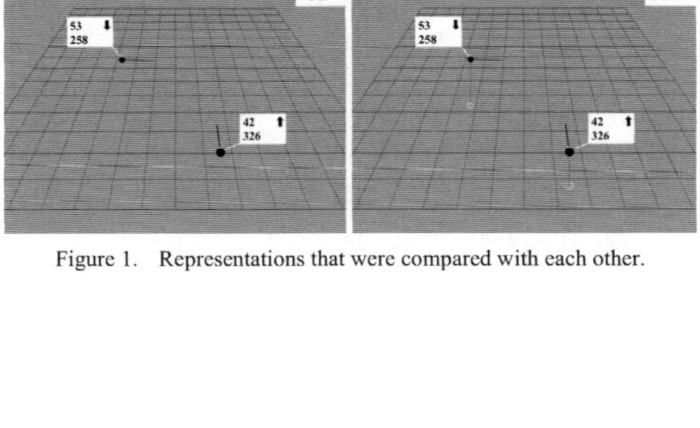

Figure 1. Representations that were compared with each other.

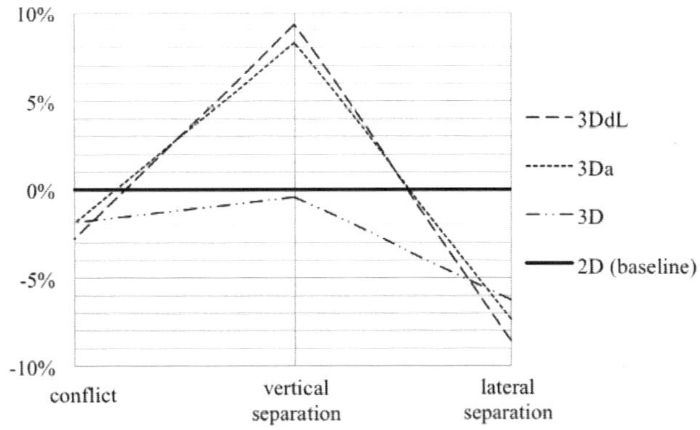

Figure 2. Judgement certainty of ATCOs under high mental workload. With values adjusted to zero 2D serves as baseline.

The situations were systematically created and presented in 50% of the times conflicts, in 25% of the times vertical separations, and in 25% lateral separations. All situations would have either resulted in a conflict or reached the closest point of approximation after 45s. However, each situation was only shown for 10s before the airspace representation was masked by a six-point rating scale that allowed the participants to indicate how certain or uncertain they were about the outcome of the situation. The rating scale ranged from 'certainly conflict' to 'certainly no conflict' with other categories in between. When the situation showed a conflict, 'certainly conflict' was interpreted as 100% certain ('hit') and 'certainly no conflict' as 0% certain ('miss') (vice versa if the situation showed a separation). Responses in between these two extremes were assigned with 80%, 60%, 40% and 20% judgment certainty. 48 participants divided into four groups with an equal number of participants (ATCOs, pilots, trained laypeople and untrained laypeople) participated in this study. The trained laypeople underwent a conflict assessment training that was based on the procedure ATCOs use with the existing 2D human system interface.

This study has demonstrated that the integration of the spatial information into one integral 3D representation can reduce the uncertainty about objects' vertical positions compared with the existing 2D representation, see Figure 2. This advantage of 3D becomes especially apparent under high mental workload conditions. However, due to the training with 2D as well as due to ambiguities along the line of sight which are implicit in all 3D representations, 2D resulted in higher judgment certainty about lateral object positions. By the selection of an appropriate elevation angle

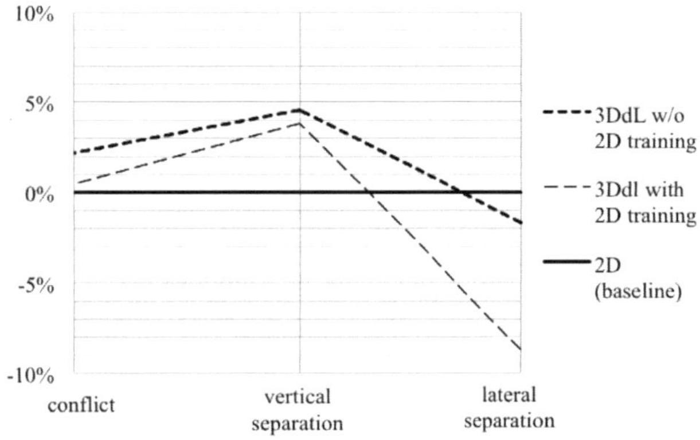

Figure 3. Judgement certainty of trained and untrained participants under high mental workload. With values adjusted to zero 2D serves as baseline.

and the provision of depth cues such as vertical drop-lines connecting the objects and the ground, grid-lines on the base area, and stereoscopy together with motion parallax effects, the disadvantage of 3D representations can be counteracted and its advantage, namely a direct event perception, further augmented.

Furthermore, the performance results show that the 3D representations allow the ATCOs' to assess such situations and discriminate with similar certainty (see Figure 2 and Figure 3) and effectiveness (see Figure 4) between separation and conflict as with 2D, because this assessment always requires processing both lateral and vertical positions. In addition to this, the training of ATCOs for assessing ATC situations with 2D apparently causes a negative effect on judgment certainty with 3D representations, as can be seen in Figure 3, that shows a comparison of the judgment certainty of trained (ATCOs and trained laypeople) and untrained (pilots and untrained laypeople) participants under high mental workload.

Because 3D resulted in an initially higher performance in the group of pilots (who are not trained in assessing ATC conflicts), it is assumed that an appropriate 3D representation allows for a direct perception of events and allows the correct use of existing mental models, see Figure 5. 3D representations such as 3Ddl or 3Da allow the ATCOs' to achieve similar performance as with the 2D representation even after little training [8], see Figure 4. Across 36 situations that were equally divided into three measuring times (MT), the ATCOs' performance rose from 71.2% in MT 1 to 87.9% in MT3 with 3DdL, and from 78.8% in MT 1 to 86.8% in MT 3 with 2D.

Overall, the higher judgment certainty concerning vertical positions promises a higher efficiency of the ATCOs' because today uncertainty about vertical positions lead more often to unnecessary preventive actions than uncertainty about lateral positions [9]. In fact, the predictions (based on the receiver operating characteristics of the ATCOs) made in this study show that with the 2D representation, 75.7% of the interventions would be unnecessary, which is in line with findings from other studies [9][10]. With 3DdL, on the other hand, 62.9% of the interventions are expected to be unnecessary [8], see Figure 6.

Because of these promising results, a cohesive interaction design tailored to what the 3D representation affords to the ATCOs was developed over three iterative development cycles [11]. First, an interactive 3D representation which was a combination of all 3D representations shown in Figure 1 was used to identify the requirements of ATCOs on a 3D Human system interface for ATC.

A total of eight ATCOs with an average of 11 years of practical experience as approach controller participated in this first development cycle in which at any one time one (active) ATCO completed a scenario using a simulator of the existing human system interface while the other (passive) ATCO observed the scenario using the interactive 3D representation. Because of the previously identified advantage of 3D representations regarding the assessment of vertical positions and distances, the ATCOs were asked to complete two different types of scenarios; a holding scenario that required to vertically stack several aircraft within a specified area and an approach scenario that required to guide several aircraft onto parallel approach routes and coordinate them tightly towards a single hand-off point (merge-point) for landing. Both types of scenarios impose particularly high requirements on processing vertical aircraft information. With an average score of 55 (where 0 indicates the lowest and 100 is the highest possible subjective

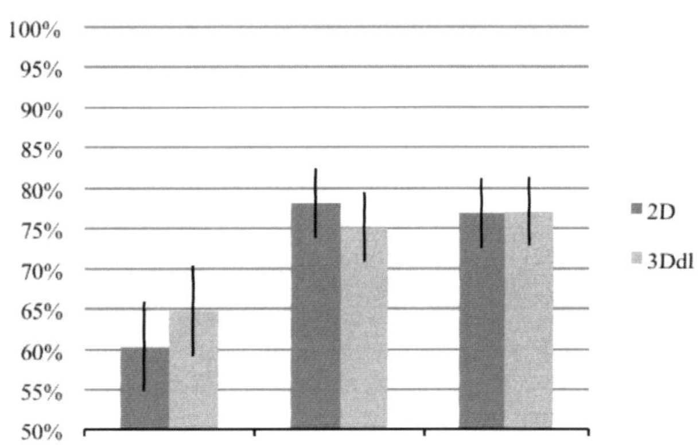

Figure 4. Performance of pilots over three measurement times (MT).

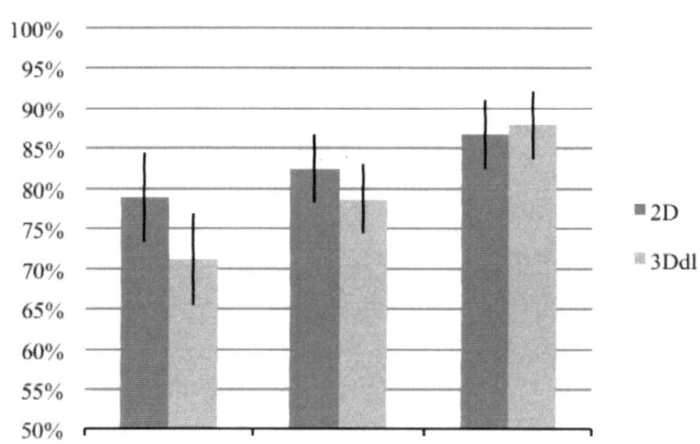

Figure 5. Performance of ATCOs over three measurement times (MT).

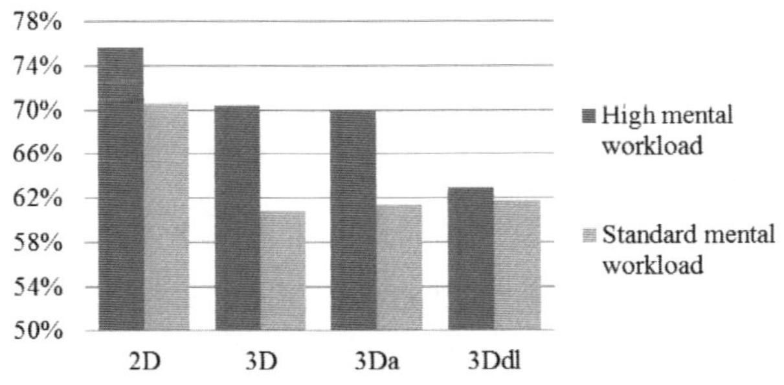

Figure 6. Predicted false alarm rates of ATCOs.

workload) on the NASA task load index [12], the holding scenario was perceived as less demanding compared with the approach scenario that received an average score of 81.

Whereas the subjective workload ratings of the active and the passive ATCOs showed no differences between the 2D and the 3D representation in the case of the holding scenario, the passive ATCOs rated the workload less high with the 3D representation (score 72) compared to the active ATCOs (score 89) who used the 2D representation. The passive ATCOs appreciated the possibility of observing the airspace depending on the situation both from the top-view as well as from the side-view.

An exaggerated representation of the vertical dimension by the factor 7 compared to the lateral dimension was the preferred option of the ATCOs and, according to them, allows obtaining an ideal representation for completing both the holding and the merge-point scenario. Regarding the lateral size of the represented airspace, 80 nautical miles was the preferred lateral airspace size with 3D. In addition to these findings, specific requirements for improving both the visualization and the interaction were derived. One of the most important of a total of 12 requirements that were gathered with respect to the visualization was to keep the font size and the size of aircraft tags constant, independently from how close or far they are represented in the 3D airspace compared to the view-point of the ATCO. Amongst the eight different requirements that were gathered with respect to the interaction with the system was the possibility for the ATCOs to individually adjust their preferred view on the 3D airspace and to save and quickly access multiple views. This function allows to use the full potential of 3D, e.g. by switching quickly from a top-view that allows for the most precise judgment of lateral distances to a side-view in order to determine the best point in time for guiding the lowest aircraft out of a holding stack. Furthermore, the ATCOs mentioned the need to access further and more detailed information on an aircraft whenever required, e.g. its heading, next waypoint on a route, and, if applicable, velocity and altitude that has been advised by the ATCO.

In the second development cycle, a cohesive visualization and interaction concept was developed as static mockups that were based on the requirements that were gathered in the first development cycle. These mock-ups were presented to four ATCOs in order to review the quality of the concept, to gather further ideas for improvement, and to prioritize the functionalities that were to be implemented in the next development cycle. Amongst the total of 11 suggestions for a further improvement the concept was, for instance, to automatically display further information of aircraft that are indicated by the automatic conflict detection system by flipping up the aircraft-tag which, in the concept, usually is manually triggered by moving the mouse-pointer onto it.

In the third development cycle that was based on the two previous development cycles, the improved visualization and interaction concept was realized as an interactive working model with a stereoscopic 3D representation of the airspace for real-time ATC. Figure 7 shows the 3D airspace representation that was used for demonstrating a merge-point approach scenario.

After the ATCOs received a brief introduction into the functionalities and logic of interaction in the 3D interactive working model, a previously recorded merge-point approach ATC scenario was shown to the ATCOs who were asked to explore the working model and to provide feedback. A structured interview procedure was applied during and after the exploration phase in order to evaluate the quality of the working model and to gather further ideas for improvement.

The ATCOs highlighted the usability of the user-interface including the head-tracking system which allows the representation to automatically and continuously adapt to the ATCO's viewing position. Therewith, the ATCOs can resolve occlusions of aircraft identifiers or tags by slight head-movements instead of using the computer mouse as with the current system. Furthermore, the orientation of the aircraft-tags is automatically adjusted to the current viewing position of the ATCO in order to ensure best legibility of their content at all times.

To further improve the interactive working model, the ATCOs suggested using a separate touch-screen instead of a standard computer keyboard to interact with the system to facilitate the selection of the most important functions. Furthermore, the following features were mentioned as desireable: 3D representations of relevant airspace borders, the current weather situation as well as the predicted weather situation, the color-coding for distinguishing in- and out-bound routes, and the display of detailed maps and specific altitude ranges. On the basis of these suggestions, the ATCOs deemed the 3D human system interface ready to be tested in real-time air traffic control.

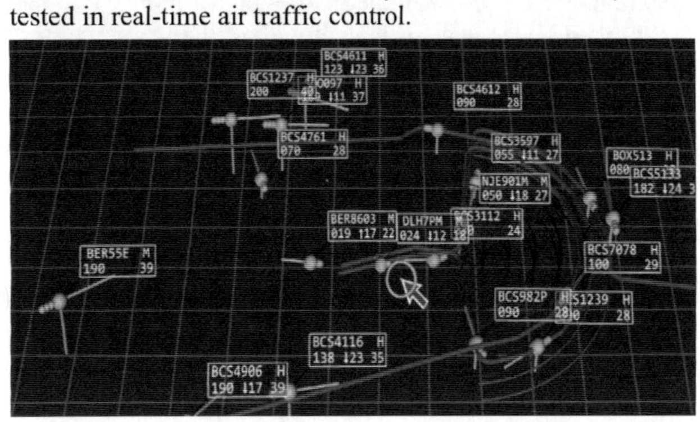

Figure 7. 3D airspace representation for demonstrating a merge-point approach scenario on the interactive working model.

V. DISCUSSION

The experimental as well as the evaluation results reveal that an adequate 3D airspace representation leads to a higher judgment certainty with less mental workload. Of special importance is that this quality of judgment can be achieved after only a short training period. It is plausible to assume that the utilization of an adequate 3D airspace representation from the very beginning of ATCO training might lead to an even more pronounced positive effect of the 3D human system interface.

The singular result that pilots immediately grasp the advantages of the 3D representation indicates the potential for establishing a better shared situation awareness of pilots and ATCOs thereby overcoming possible misunderstandings in their communication because the reference of verbal utterances can be directly linked to spatial positions. Future landing procedures, for instance, which give the pilots more responsibility would profit from this better shared ground in communication.

Immediate effects are to be expected for a better trade-off between safety and efficiency because of the marked decrease in false alarms. In comparison with published data about the given conflict detection and false alarm rates, it has been shown that an adequate 3D airspace representation results in less false alarms while achieving the same level of safety.

VI. CONCLUSION

The experimental data, the qualitative evaluation of the usability including the resulting mental workload, and the evaluation of the working model for visualization and interaction all support the conclusion that an adequate 3D airspace representation for air traffic control allows an immediate perception of danger and urgency in a given situation. Furthermore, according to the air traffic control experts the final version of the 3D human system interface has the full functionality of the existing interface while allowing a more intuitive interaction which apparently leads to a higher efficiency, a lower level of mental workload, and a better learnability. For supervisory tasks, a quick implementation of the system seems to be possible. For subsequent tests it is planned to investigate the potential functionality of the developed version of the 3D human system interface via a 'shadow mode' evaluation in real-time air traffic control.

ACKNOWLEDGMENT

This research was funded by the Bavarian State Ministry of Education and Science, Airbus Defense and Space, and DFS. The experiments and evaluations were accomplished in collaboration with C. Avenarius, C. Vernaleken, and J. Vogelmeier.

REFERENCES

[1] K. Craik, The Nature of Explanation. Cambridge: Cambridge: University Press, 1943.

[2] P.N. Johnson-Laird. Mental Models: Towards a Cognitive Science of Language, Inference, and Consciousness. Cambridge: Cambridge University Press, 1983.

[3] D. Gentner and D.R. Gentner, „Flowing waters or teeming crowds: Mental models of electricity," in Mental models, D. Gentner and A.L. Stevens, Eds. Hillsdale, NJ: Lawrence Erlbaum Associates, pp. 99-129, 1983.

[4] M.R. Endsley, "Toward a theory of situation awareness in dynamic systems," Human Factors, vol. 37, pp. 32-64, 1995.

[5] J.J. Gibson, The Ecological Approach to Visual Perception. Houghton Mifflin: Boston, USA, 1979.

[6] M.R. Endsley, "Situation Awareness and Human Error: Designing to Support Human Performance," Proceedings of the High Consequence Systems Surety Conference, Albuquerque, NM, 1999.

[7] A. Baier and A.C. Zimmer, "How 3D-Displays in ATC Permit Direct Event Perception," 17th International Conference on Human-Computer Interaction (HCI 2015), August 2015, pp. 309-316, ISBN 978-3-319-20372-0.

[8] A. Baier and A.C. Zimmer, "From Spatial Reasoning to Direct Event Perception in Air Traffic Control," 6th International Conference on Applied Human Factors and Ergonomics (AHFE 2015), July 2015, ISBN 978-1-4951-6042-4.

[9] S. Loft, S. Bolland, M.S. Humphreys and A. Neal, "A Theory and Model of Conflict Detection in Air Traffic Control: Incorporating Environmental Constraints," Journal of Experimental Psychology: Applied, vol. 15, pp. 106-124, 2009.

[10] A. Bisseret, "Application of signal detection theory to decision making in supervisory control: The effect of the operator's experience," Ergonomics, vol. 24, pp. 81–94, 1981.

[11] A. Baier, C. Vernaleken, L. Vogelmeier and A.C. Zimmer, "Machbarkeitsstudie Stereoskopische 3-D-Anzeigen für Flugsicherungsarbeitsplätze: Abschlussbericht zur ersten Projektphase 30," unpublished report about a feasibility study on stereoscopic 3D-displays for ATC workstation.

[12] S.G. Hart and L.E. Staveland, "Development of NASA-TLX (Task Load Index): Results of empirical and theoretical research," in Human Mental Workload, P.A. Hancock and N. Meshkati, Eds., Amsterdam: North Holland Press, 1988.

Study of Sign Language Expression of Medical Sign Language Words

Mina Terauchi
Polytechnic University
Kodaira–shi, Tokyo, Japan
Email: terauchi@uitec.ac.jp

Yuji Nagashima
Kogakuin University
Hachioji–shi, Tokyo, Japan
Email:nagasima@cc.kogakuin.ac.jp

Abstract—**This paper will outline the construction of a database of medical sign language words. The authors of this paper investigated the more straightforward expression of medical sign language by analyzing the problems of the existing sign language words. As a result of a number of investigations into sign language expressions, by paying attention to more straightforward sign language expressions and focusing on the consistency of movements and the unification of expressions, we have created representations for 1,324 words on the basis of the existing movements.**

Keywords–Sign Language; Medicine-Clinical Terms; Database

I. INTRODUCTION

The medical field is one of the areas in which sign language interpreting is required. Although sign language for medical use has already been investigated, the sign language expressions have not yet become widely popular. This is due to certain problems such as different expressions for words with the same meanings depending on the book, the existence of a number of sign language expressions that are not commonly used, and inconsistency in the creation of sign language words. Moreover, medical terminology includes many technical terms, and it is difficult to accurately understand the explanations of doctors and nurses and translate them into sign language [1].

This paper will examine the sign language expression of medical terminology. In Section II, for the existing medical sign language expressions, an examination will be undertaken of the problems with the existing method of creating medical sign language words. In the database of medical sign language words, an examination of the method of creating words will be undertaken by the authors of this paper. In Section III, this paper will explain the development of the Kogakuin medical sign language word database, KOSIGN V5 (hereinafter, " KOSIGN ").

II. EXISTING MEDICAL SIGN LANGUAGE EXPRESSIONS

The medical sign language expressions presented in existing books involve problems, including those listed below [2] [3].

1) Expressions that are not commonly used are included.
2) There is no consistency in the expressions, even for related words.
3) Inappropriate methods are adopted when creating words, ignoring convenience for people in terms of making movements.
4) Sign language movements are presented as still images in books, so it is difficult to understand the specific movements involved.

Moreover, in terms of the problems of medical terminology itself, there are numerous technical terms and it is sometimes difficult to correctly understand their meanings.

III. METHOD OF USING KOSIGN TO CREATE WORDS

In creating the words, we focused on the consistency of movements and the unification of sign language expressions. Moreover, while creating the words, we took into account the convenience for people in terms of making movements and a more straightforward method of expression. We created words mainly for commonly used words in a hospital setting, such as names of body parts, organs and bones, medical conditions and diseases, hospital departments, tests and equipment, and drugs. Table I shows word classification and examples.

TABLE I. Medical word classification and example words

Classification	Example words
Body parts	Head, Face, Body, Skin, Eye
Organs and Bones	Stomach, Skull, Spine, intestine, lung
Medical Conditions and Diseases	Cold, High Blood Pressure, Stomatitis, Dizziness
Hospital Departments	Surgery, Gastroenterology, Internal Medicine
tests and equipment	echocardiography, MRI, endoscopic
drugs	mouthwash, antibiotics, powdered medicine, tablets
others	doctor, receptionist, medical history, recurrence

A. Consistency of Expressions

Sign language words in KOSIGN are created in such a way that if words are related, the same expressions are used. In this paper, Japanese Sign language words are represented in $\{CAPITAL\ LETTERS\}$.

For example, for words such as $\{XXX\ \ DISEASE\}$ and $\{YYY\ \ SYNDROME\}$, the expressions are unified in all the words by placing either

$\{DISEASE\}$

or

$\{SYNDROME\} = \{VARIETY\} + \{DISEASE\}$

at the end.

Figure 1 shows an example of "Heart disease". The animation images used in Figure 1 were created using TV program Making Language (TVML), which is currently being developed by NHK Science & Technical Research Laboratories.

Moreover, for words related to $\{BONE\}$, to clarify the expression $\{BONE\}$, it has been determined that the words be expressed by including $\{BONE\}$. However, movement words that are commonly used, such as $\{SPINE\}$ and $\{CLAVICLE\}$, are expressed without including $\{BONE\}$.

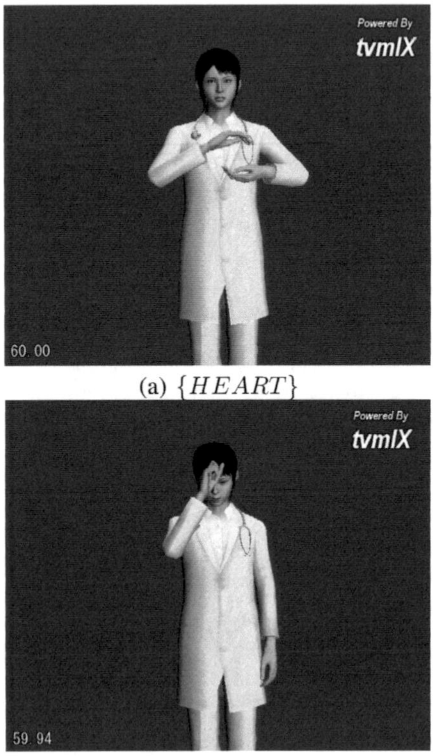

(a) $\{HEART\}$

(b) $\{DISEASE\}$

Figure 1. Sign language for the word "Heart disease"

B. Method of Creating Words

Morphological elements that are used in the expressions of sign language for medical words adopt not only the existing morphological elements, but also expressions that are similar to gestures to express medical and treatment activities. For example, in expressions related to medication, movements imitating the actions of drinking or applying are involved. Sign language sometimes expresses words by adopting movements that are similar to gestures. As a result, in the expression of medical sign language, if it is considered to be easier to understand, expressions similar to gestures are also adopted.

The signer expresses body parts that are externally visible by pointing to their own body parts. In contrast, when creating words for the names of organs that are not externally visible, the signer not only points to the position where the organ is located, but also indicates the shape of the organ.

Moreover, many explanatory sign language expressions are used to express words with difficult meanings. For example, an antacid is expressed in sign language that describes it as a medication that suppresses the rise of acid substances.

There are also expressions that use Japanese words, which are similar to explanatory sign language. This is a method of creating words to represent the expression of Japanese labels in sign language. When using Japanese words, the signer's knowledge of Japanese words is a precondition. We believe that this is not a significant problem, because the Japanese language capability of sign language native speakers has recently improved.

There are many medical terms whose meanings are explained using kanji. In such cases of expressions using kanji, the signer expresses the Chinese characters in the order in which they appear.

There are also cases when manual characters are used. In manual characters, there are cases when all the Japanese labels are expressed by manual characters, and cases when expressing some Japanese labels using manual characters plays the role of supporting the subsequent sign language expressions.

C. Database of Medical Sign Language Words: KOSIGN

The purpose of developing KOSIGN is to promote sign language by providing explanations of medical terminology and difficult terms that sign language interpreters, sign language native speakers, medical workers and other people are considered to require at the time of medical treatment. The method of creating new words is that the existing problems are analyzed and the focus is placed on the consistency of movements, the unification of expressions and a more straightforward way of making expressions.

Moreover, when using the existing sign language movements instead of creating words, investigations are also undertaken to determine whether or not the relevant movement expressions are widely used. Medical words to be created in sign language and explanatory notes were selected with the cooperation of medical workers acting as sign language interpreters, sign language interpreters, sign language native speakers and other parties. KOSIGN has determined 1,324 sign language words to date.

IV. Conclusion and Future Works

The authors of this paper have developed a database of medical sign language words. By analyzing the problems of the existing sign language, we investigated sign language expressions that are easily understood so that they will be widely used. As a result, KOSIGN has determined 1,324 words using sign language movements.

We will strive to further improve the database to achieve the popular use of the expressions of KOSIGN in the future. By examining whether or not there are other words that need to be included, we will create and add necessary words by also using the synthesis of morphological elements. In addition, we will add explanatory notes.

Acknowledgment

Part of this study was subsidized by a Grant-in-Aid for Scientific Research (A) 23240087 and (A) 26244021, a scientific research grant by the Ministry of Education, Culture, Sports, Science and Technology.

References

[1] M. Terauchi, et al., "Compilation of a sign language database for use in medical practice," Proc. of the Communications in Computer and Information Science (CCIS) series, June 2014, pp. 264–269: , HCI International 2014, ISBN: 978-3-319-07853-3.

[2] Medical Sign Language Language, Medical Sign Language Series 1-3, Publication Bureau of Japanese Federation of the Deaf, Tokyo, 2009(in Japanese).

[3] F. Nakagawa, Medical Sign Language Dictionary, Hiroshima Prefectural Sign Language Interpretation Research Association, Hiroshima, 2005(in Japanese).

Alphabet Recognition in Air Writing Using Depth Information

Robiul Islam, Hasan Mahmud, Md. Kamrul Hasan
Systems and Software Lab (SSL)
Department of Computer Science and Engineering
Islamic University of Technology (IUT)
Dhaka, Bangladesh
e-mail: r_islam@live.com, hasan@iut-dhaka.edu, hasank@iut-dhaka.edu

Husne Ara Rubaiyeat
Department of Computer Science
Natural Science Faculty
National University
Bangladesh
e-mail: rubaiyeat@yahoo.com

***Abstract*—We present a data mining approach to recognize air written English Capital Alphabets (ECAs) using depth information. The hand motion while writing the alphabet in the air was captured as depth images by a depth camera. The depth images were then processed as the hand movement time series data, which was matched with standard templates of air writing by Dynamic Time Warping (DTW) algorithm. We collected a dataset of five variations and from them standardized 20 templates for each ECA. The accuracy for ECA is 93-99% with an average of 96.3%.**

Keywords-Air Writing; Gesture Recognition; Depth Information; Time Series; Dynamic Time Warping

I. INTRODUCTION

Human gesture is an important input modality for communication with computers. In hand-based gesture recognition technology, a camera (typical stereo camera) reads the hand movement data, performs the hand tracking and then recognizes a meaningful gesture to control any device or application. For example, a person clapping his hands together in front of a camera can produce the sound of cymbals being crashed together when the gesture is fed through a computer. In hand gesture recognition research, air writing is a prominent and difficult topic. Air writing [2] means gesture based writing in the air through movement of hand fingers by which a computer system can recognize characters and other symbols in natural handwriting. Previously, air writing has been studied by using wearable hand gloves [2], an accelerometer and gyroscope augmented mobile phone [4] and a 3D gesture input device [3]. In our approach, we do not ask for any special wearable device, so that the user can write naturally without any obstruction, shown in Figure 1. Algorithmically, previous approaches studied air writing by converting them into strokes. While writing in the air, users pause unintentionally or bend abnormally and, thus, they create extra strokes into the air written characters. However, recent data mining algorithms enable us to study a gesture signal such as air written character as a time series, as shown in Figure 2, information which can be matched with standard time series character templates. In this paper, we have studied the ECAs as time series information that can be recognized by matching with templates by using a time series data mining algorithm, DTW [1][6].

Figure 1: Air writing Character A

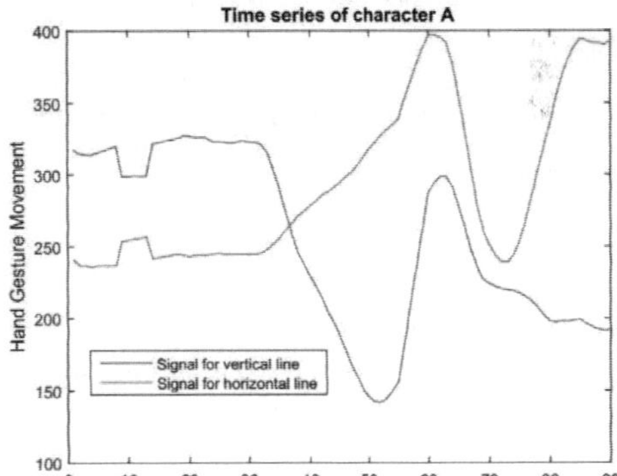

Figure 2 : Time series representation of character A

The rest of the paper has organized as follows: Section II contains the discussion on related work, Section III explains the proposed methodology, Section IV presents the result analysis, and Section V describes the conclusion and future work.

II. RELATED WORK

Agrawal et al. [4] used mobile sensors to recognize ECAs. They used gyroscope bend angles to convert the accelerometer signals into strokes. The concept of detecting strokes in air writing was first introduced in this paper. Amma et al. [2] showed how a wearable device can recognize hand gesture for air writing. A wearable hand motion tracking system captures movement signals using accelerometer and gyroscope. However converting the acceleration signal into distance covered for recognized strokes can be erroneous. Moreover, wearing a special device makes the air writing system cumbersome. Kim et al. [3] showed a way to recognize different people's handwriting on continuous images based on similarity of the different shapes of characters or digits. We studied their research and got inspired to use shape information. Lin et al. [5] showed a way to use Scale Invariance Feature Transform (SIFT) on binary images. In this approach, the motion information is not considered in SIFT descriptors.

We studied the process of generating strokes on ECAs extensively. We found that extra strokes are generated because users put some unnecessary pauses or bend their hands abnormally while writing alphabets. Those extra strokes cannot be merged together to form a regular stroke which demands complex algorithms like HMM [2] or Bayesian networks [3]. So, instead of processing strokes, we prefer to use whole ECAs written in the air as time series signals. Another motivation of using time series signals was to get the hand movement sequence of writing which are important clues to recognize air written ECAs.

III. Proposed System

Our system captures the air writing of a user using Microsoft Kinect depth camera. Each writing of an ECA generates a set of depth images. We segment the hand finger movement using depth values. The hand motion is tracked from image to image, which generates a series of points (x, y). These set of points are actually the time series information of the particular ECA. As the hand movement is noisy, the time series data is smoothed using moving average filter [7]. We did it for all 26 English capital alphabets. For example, we are showing the process of writing "A" in Figure 3.

A. Applying DTW

DTW is time series matching algorithm for which we need to match an ECA time series with standard templates of ECAs. The matching generates a distance score; the smaller the score, the better the matching. So, time series of an unknown ECA will be recognized as the best matching ECA. The calculation of the minimum distance was done using equation 1.

$$RecognizedECA = argminDTW\ (U, TECA) \tag{1}$$

Where U is a time series of unknown ECA. We define the time series U as two dimensional signals x and y; where x is the hand movement along x-axis and y is the hand movement along y-axis. TECA is the template of a particular ECA.

IV. Result Analysis

We have collected data from 5 different variances. Each user was asked to produce ECA gestures in the air five times. From those instances on, we considered as DTW template. So, for each ECA 5 templates were taken from 5 users and the rest of 20 were used to test. The dataset is available in [8]. To measure the performance. we calculated the accuracy and found maximum 100% true positive with average of 52.6% and minimum 93.75% true negative with average of 97.8% shown in Table I for our five variations. In our process, we are depending on true negative rate instance of true positive rate. We applied DTW of signal time series samples to all variation of alphabets and found best matching results for each dataset. Ideally, it gave 20 best matching and 500 are correctly rejected matching. Table I shows the total accuracy, which is calculated using (2).

$$Accuracy = \frac{\sum True\ Positive + \sum True\ Negative}{Total\ population} \tag{2}$$

TABLE I. RESULT TABLE

Alphabets	True positive rate	True positive rate	Accuracy
A	30	30	96.73076923
B	25	25	96.92307692
C	25	25	95.19230769
D	30	30	95.38461538
E	15	15	96.73076923
F	55	55	97.88461538
G	25	25	96.53846154
H	80	80	97.69230769
I	85	85	95.19230769
J	75	75	97.88461538
K	35	35	96.53846154
L	100	100	97.11538462
M	55	55	94.61538462
N	95	95	97.69230769
O	45	45	96.53846154
P	70	70	93.46153846
Q	40	40	94.42307692
R	60	60	95.38461538
S	100	100	99.80769231
T	50	50	95
U	65	65	97.69230769
V	75	75	95
W	60	60	97.88461538
X	5	5	95.19230769

Y	15	15	95.38461538
Z	75	75	99.03846154
AVG	52.6	52.6	96.31538462

V. Conclusion and Future Work

We proposed a DTW based time series matching approach to recognize air written English Capital Alphabets. Stroke detection was one of the main challenges in state-of-the-art air writing recognition algorithms, but we have converted the whole image into time series representation to detect in air gestures as ECAs. In the future, we want to collect more datasets for better results.

Acknowledgment

This work is partially supported by ICT Division, Ministry of Posts, Telecommunications and IT, Government of the People's Republic of Bangladesh.

References

[1] P. Doliotis, A. Stefan, C. Mcmurrough, D. Eckhard And V. Athitsos, "Comparing Gesture Recognition Accuracy Using Color And Depth Information," In Proceedings Of The 4th International Conference On Pervasive Technologies Related To Assistive Environments , New York, 2011.J. Clerk Maxwell, A Treatise on Electricity and Magnetism, 3rd ed., vol. 2. Oxford: Clarendon, 1892, pp.68–73.

[2] C. Amma, M. Georgi and T. Schultz, "Air writing: A wear-able handwriting recognition system," Personal and Ubiquitous Computing Volume 18, Issue 1, pp 191-203, January-2014, Springer London.

[3] D. H. Kim, H. Il Choi, J. H. Kim, "3D space handwriting recognition with ligature model," Proceedings of the Third international conference on Ubiquitous Computing Systems, October 11-13, 2006, Seoul, Korea.

[4] Sandip et al., "Using mobile phones to write in air," Proceedings of the 9th international conference on Mobile systems, applications, and services, June 28-July 01, 2011, Bethesda, Maryland, USA

[5] W. Lin, Y. Wu,W. Hung and C. Tang, "A Study of Real-Time Hand Gesture Recognition Using SIFT on Binary Images," Advances in Intelligent Systems & Applications , SIST 21, pp. 235246.Springer-Verlag Berlin Heidelberg 2013.

[6] S. Salvador and P. Chan, "FastDTW: Toward Accurate Dynamic Time Warping in Linear Time and Space," KDD Workshop on Mining Temporal and Sequential Data, pp. 70-80, 2004.

[7] J. F. Kenney and, E. S. Keeping, " Moving Averages," Section 14.2 in Mathematics of Statistics, Pt. 1, 3rd ed. Princeton, NJ: Van Nostrand, pp. 221-223, 1962.

[8] SSL ECA dataset 1: http://cse.iutoic-dhaka.edu/group/ssl/SSL_ECE_DATASET_1.rar.

(a) (b)

(c) (d)

Figure 3: Preprocessing and generating time series of an ECA: (a) RGB image with depth value (b) Hand segmentation (c) Writing of 'A' (d) 'A' after smoothing

Interacting with the Customers through New Technologies

Having a better understanding of the user's experience

Lucía Sánchez de la Guía, Marina Puyuelo Cazorla, Lola Merino Sanjuán
Escuela Técnica Superior de Ingeniería del Diseño
Universitat Politècnica de València
Camino de Vera, s/n
46022 Valencia, Spain
E-mail: lusande1@etsid.upv.es, mapuca@ega.upv.es, mamesan@ega.upv.es

Abstract— **Nowadays, new technologies and information systems are important tools to carry out many different activities in daily life. The use of these new technologies is also a means for getting information on the users' experience. This paper aims at giving a brief review of how users may participate in the development process of products and services, and how they communicate their needs and suggest their preferences through these new interactive tools. This is a preliminary study, which focuses on how companies may incorporate the concept of *Co-design* into their proposals, in order to add customer value. Our first findings show that, consciously or not, users are participating more in the development process. Thanks to the use of new technologies and tools, their involvement has increased - and so have their expectations and their perception of feeling empowered. It is argued that a direct relation exists between the interaction of users and their experience of the products or services.**

Keywords- interactivity; virtual prototypes; user experience; product development; user satisfaction.

I. Introduction

Nowadays, having information from users' experience and their interaction with products and services is an important aspect for companies and designers. The concept of user experience is becoming a key term in the world of interactive product design. The term itself lacks proper theoretical definition, and is used in many different, even contradictory, ways. Models and frameworks on user experience, as shown in Figure 1, have emerged in the last ten years [1]. In the first stage of this preliminary study, we review ideas to better understand why it is important for the user to collaborate and participate in the development of the product or service from the first stages. This paper aims at discussing the areas in which users act through usability tests and interaction tools. These new tools facilitate and increase collaboration between users and companies. Hence, companies seek to analyze the results after collaborating with users because they can provide greater knowledge on the users' needs. There are some case studies demonstrating that a lack of understanding of the users' needs results in a reduction of production. So, it is essential that the interests of users are taken into account. It is taken for granted that customer satisfaction occurs when an experience meets or exceeds the customer's needs or wants of a service [2].

Based on these premises, the new process of interaction can lead to increased user loyalty. This is possible through the new interaction tools used by companies to obtain valuable results, which they later interpret and study. Thanks to the rapid advances in new technologies and to the development of information systems, more interactive and participative innovation has taken place in recent years. User experience evaluation has become a useful tool to analyze how a firm can design and create new products, services or interfaces which respond to the characteristics and needs that users would like to see fulfilled. Furthermore, authors like Sang Lee, David Olson and Silvana Trimi [3] discuss the strategies a firm uses to focus on innovation and the use of new technologies. These authors seem to suggest that innovation is directly related to the creation of value. They justify that this has been possible because users are present in the new development process, and they take part in it.

Internet plays an important role as an interactive, multimedia technology for mass communication, which is also low cost [4, 5, 6]. It allows consumers to have a wide variety of virtual experiences with new products, and it allows interaction between producers and consumers. With more than one billion users [7], the Internet currently offers an enormous pool of knowledge, which is impossible to find elsewhere. According to von Hippel [8], users found in online communities are a promising source of innovation. Hence, the emergence of the Internet has facilitated unique and inventive opportunities to capitalize on the innovative potential and knowledge of users, resulting in what has been termed as virtual customer integration [9].

Figure 1. Network representing co-occurrence of users' keywords around innovation

Another stage of research should focus on the development and implementation of virtual interfaces. In that regard, we found that is a useful tool to have a better understanding of the future product or service. Also, users could start to take part in the design and development process.

Regarding this issue, the involvement of the user is achieved thanks to the concept of co-creation, defined by Prahalad and Ramaswamy [10] as the process of creating an experience environment in which consumers can have an active dialogue and co-construct personalized experiences. They talk about how companies interact with customers, who feel loyalty thanks to the exchange of ideas to create a new product or service.

However, an aspect to analyze is the specific point in time, or stage, during the creation process, when interaction is most interesting. Anderson and Narus [11] analyze customer collaboration during the development stage, that is, in laboratory tests and with early prototypes. This is the stage when companies need to decide between several possible applications, and it would be the most interesting stage to analyze user participation.

After analyzing these applications, obtained from the collaboration between the company and the users, the company has to analyze, using a prototype or proposed model, if there could be advantages and benefits in the near future.

Authors like Johann Füller, Hans Mühlbacher, Kurt Matzler, and Gregor Jawecki [12] research how clients take part in the virtual co-creation process and how they perceive their involvement. They state that Co-production emerges as a new form of collaboration between consumers and companies, through the use of Information Technologies (IT). This way, consumers can take on new roles throughout the New Product Development NPD process. The empirical study showed how Internet-based tools and technologies contribute to the consumers' perceived empowerment through virtual new product co-creation activities. The conclusion was that the level of empowerment experienced depends on the design of the applied virtual interaction tool. Moreover, there was an associated enjoyment of the virtual interaction, the participants' task and their product involvement, as well as their creativity and leading-user characteristics.

After researching through different scientific databases, we can say that the experience of the users is being analyzed mainly in the areas of health care and new information systems. Thanks to this previous research, we can corroborate that there is a lack of understanding of user experience in the context of product design. Therefore, this is a subject that we consider relevant and merits in-depth research in the near future.

In the sections that follow, we explain the increasing role of interaction using virtual tools. We also introduce the relationship between user participation and user satisfaction, as these are concepts which are directly related. The paper is structured in the two sections, as follows:

In Section 1, we explain some interaction tools and user participation during the design process, making reference to some authors who support its importance. We also analyze usability and user experience goals to get a wide view of the interest of these methods to get further information about them. At the same time, we introduce virtual reality as a new medium for participation.

In Section 2, we explain how the use of IT opens up a "virtual" context and an opportunity for customer integration in the design process.

Finally, in the discussion, we insist on the main idea that there is a new landscape for design based on participation in the design process.

II. Interaction Tools and User Participation

In view of the above, there is a need to establish the concept of interacting tools because, as some authors state, user interaction and participation offers advantages to the firm. Recently, some case studies have shown that the new interaction tools allow increasing the value and loyalty of users via the Internet and the new information systems. In this way, users can fulfill their goal because they are getting involved, and they meet their real needs during the process of developing a new product or service. Johann Füller and Kurt Matzler [13] show how customers can be virtually integrated into a company's innovation process. New interaction tools allow companies to gain valuable input from customers via the Internet.

Needs are present during the entire development stage of a new product or service, because they are considered as the "desires of users". In connection with this, it can be of interest to mention the KANO model [14], often used to identify customer needs in new product development. Matzler and Hinterhuber [15] help to explain why customers have difficulties expressing their needs. The model shows that it is difficult for customers to express their latent needs, as well as those which they take for granted. As a result, it is interesting to develop an adequate environment in which users can express their real needs and participate in the development process. Regarding this, we could state that new virtual interaction tools and virtual product experiences help to overcome these problems and enable customers to transfer their explicit and implicit knowledge to innovation teams.

A. *Usability and user experience goals*

The concept of usability has become important in recent years, due especially to the important role of the user in the process of development and design of products and services. The goals of usability and user experience in today's society have a great impact on new information systems and new devices. We find numerous authors, such as Pharalay and Ramasway, who have already studied this phenomenon in multimedia mobiles and what kind of involvement or interaction takes place.

Authors like Kathy Brittain White and Kwasi Amoako-Gyampah [16] examine some contingencies of user involvement and user satisfaction. User involvement has a potential impact on the success of systems, and results are obtained through a survey questionnaire to show that user perception of their level of involvement has a direct, positive and significant impact on user satisfaction. Therefore, we could say that when users take part in the development of an interaction tool, their level of satisfaction improves and they bring relevant information to develop a new product or service. However, the impact of user involvement in system development and implementation is still an issue under considerable debate.

In the same direction, research shows that there is a direct relation between user participation and information systems, and it shows that the strong participation of future users in the design of information systems (IS) leads to successful outcomes in user satisfaction.

In this respect, M. Mengoni, M. Germani, and M. Peruzzini [17] state that, during product development, usability tests allow to investigate product performance also in terms of effectiveness. For instance, Virtual Reality (VR) systems provide new modes of Human-Computer Interaction (HCI) that can support usability testing in the early design stages by adopting virtual prototypes to simulate product experience.

Usability tests generally allow assessing product performance in terms of efficiency, effectiveness and user satisfaction in order to reduce the gap between the perceived and the designed product quality. The main concern in the assessment of emotional usability is identifying product features that stimulate an affective user response and its translation into design requirements. Although usability tests can support innovation, companies seldom use them during the product development process due to the high costs connected to their implementation. In these cases, the measure of usability could be considered less relevant. But it has been shown that these tests improve the process of an enterprise and increase the value to its users.

The use of prototypes allows to include the sense of touch, which has a great importance in the emotional evaluation. It allows exploring products with the hands and collecting information about materials and shapes. Carrying out usability tests is not as easy as it seems in the beginning, but it is clear that it helps to know the needs of the user. The use of virtual prototypes allows conducting usability tests in the early design stages. However, an additional problem is that only a few usability aspects can be measured in the virtual environment, such as posture and occlusion parameters. User satisfaction in terms of pleasantness is difficult to assess, as virtual prototypes poorly support emotional and touch and feel analysis [18].

B. *Virtual reality and participation*

As a consequence of integrating customers into the creation of value, new methods are needed to allow the active involvement of customers in new product development [19]. Especially, virtual product experiences enable customers to transfer not only what they want to know, but also their unknown needs. As recently shown by Matzler and Bailom [20], companies which are able to identify customer needs and align them with their core competencies are those that champion innovation. Such companies are more profitable than others. Nowadays, new product development cannot be conceived without powerful three-dimensional (3D) modeling software to help create products better and faster.

Taking this concept a step further, manufacturers may use virtual prototypes to integrate customer ideas and needs into new product development via the Internet. Thus, customers can get their hands on innovations long before the design has been finalized, when changes to suit their opinions and wishes can be done quickly and at low cost. However, in recent decades there has been a debate about which are the correct tools for testing prototypes. In response, Dahan and Srinivasan's [21] show that virtual prototype testing online provides almost identical results as using physical prototypes, and is easier and cheaper. In connection with this, we conclude that virtual reality and virtual prototyping are fully relevant tools. Today the prototype is an interesting tool, which is possible thanks to the rapid advance of new technologies and information systems.

III. VIRTUAL CUSTOMER INTEGRATION IN CO-DESIGN

Virtual customer integration represents "one of the most promising areas of development (…) that the new virtual customer environments make possible" [22]. In a virtual environment, consumers communicate their knowledge through an electronic interface, with no direct personal contact with the product or service. They do not get immediate personal feedback. Thus, the virtual environment must be created in a way that enables and motivates consumers to play an active role in New Product Development (NPD), and to make them participate in further NPD projects. Information Technologies (IT) enable new forms of producer-consumer collaboration in NPD processes. Rooted in collaboration through the use of IT, the co-production mode has emerged as an important and growing production method. Customers can assume a number of different roles in the NPD process [23]. In the ideation phase, customers can be a resource through interactive multimedia tools, virtual brainstorming, or virtual focus groups. In the design and development phase, customers can take on the role of co-creators, and tools such as Web-based conjoint analysis, virtual user design, Internet-based design competitions, tool kits, and so forth, allow users to express their preferences and to design their own products. In the test and launch phase, IT tools such as virtual concept testing can help to provide valuable feedback on products, services or interface.

Such co-creation tools enable consumers to realistically experience virtual prototypes in real-world usage scenarios, long before they actually come into existence [24]. Displaying design and feature options, engineering constraints and price effects in real time, with easy-to-use and drag-and-drop options, support consumers in creating their ideal product.

Technologies and interaction tools enable consumers to engage virtually in meaningful and challenging NPD tasks to effectively share their knowledge with producers, making them feel like they are autonomously contributing to the collaboration. Also, if they believe that their input will be seriously considered, these tools may provide consumers with a sense of mastery. Thus, participants in virtual co-creation may feel empowered.

However, there is a lack of case studies shedding light on how to virtually integrate customers in practice. The detailed missing information is: how to identify qualified customers on the Internet; how to motivate them and how to interact with them, and under what conditions are users are willing and able to share their knowledge with producers.

Thus, it remains necessary to focus on the work of design in this field, in order to identify which are the interactions that are useful and give some guarantee of higher success both for users and for the firm. The research show that virtual customer integration provides valuable input for new product development. A number of new tools to interact virtually with customers can be found in the literature [25, 26].

Other authors suggest that, by integrating users of virtual worlds into an interactive new product development process, companies can tap into the innovative potential of customers using the latest technology [27]. They argue that the latest advances in information and communication technologies enrich the interaction process and can improve the new product development process.

DISCUSSION

This paper has sought to offer a perspective on the breadth of the concept of getting information from users by taking advantage of the new communication tools. The development of different virtual environments is promising as they give users an active role in NPD. In this article, we argue that user participation increases user satisfaction because users feel that they take part in the co-creation process.

In view of this, it is of interest to develop an adequate environment where users can express their real needs and are able to participate in new development processes. Nowadays, there are new interacting tools that allow interaction between users and companies, and generate valuable feedback. Virtual interaction and virtual product experiences help users know what their real needs are. Usability tests, play an important role in narrowing the gap with the "perceived quality" of the designed products. Therefore, usability tests increase the value that users give to products. When users take part in the development process through interactive tools, they improve their level of satisfaction and bring relevant information to the companies. As this paper shows, user involvement has a direct, positive and significant impact on user satisfaction.

As a summary, this article shows how new technologies offer a perfect setting for users, due to their variety and interactivity, and this experience provides information. For this reason, it is important to work on systems that allow greater communication with users to let them have greater participation in the design process. Some companies have seen participation in design as a new way to engage customers and achieve their loyalty.

In this sense, in future studies we will perform case studies that allow us to analyze the feasibility and effectiveness of this client-company communication.

ACKNOWLEDGMENTS

We wish to thank *Cátedra Stadler* at the School of Design Engineering for the support provided to participate in this Conference, and for the possibility of researching experiences of user participation in the field of interior design for public transport.

REFERENCES

[1] Battarbee, Katja Koskinen, Ilpo , 2008. Co- Experience: Product Experience as social interaction. Elsevier B.V, pp. 461-476.

[2] R. Oliver, "Cognitive, affective, and attribute bases of the satisfaction response". Journal of Consumer Research, 20(3), 1993, pp. 418– 430.

[3] M. Sang, O. David and Silvana, "Co-innovation: convergenomics, collaboration, and co-creation for organizational values," Management Decision, 50 (5), 2012, pp. 817-831.

[4] E. Dahan and J. R. Hauser. "The virtual customer," Journal of Product Innovation Management 19 (5), 2002, pp. 332–353.

[5] E. Dahan and J. T. Hauser, "Managing a dispersed product development process", In: Weitz, B., Wensley, R. (Eds.), Handbook of Marketing. Sage Publications Inc, Thousand Oaks, CA, 2002.

[6] G. Urban and J. R. Hauser "Listening in to find and explore new combinations of customer needs," Journal of Marketing, 68, April 2004, pp.72–87.

[7] Almanac, http://www.c-i-a.com/pr0106.htm. Accessed: August, 2006.

[8] E. Von Hippel, Democratizing Innovation. MIT Press, Cambridge, MA, 2005.

[9] T. Kohlera, K. Matzlera, and J. Füller, "Avatar-based innovation: Using virtual worlds for real-world innovation," vol. 2, June–July 2009, pp. 395–407.

[10] Prahalad, C.K. and V. Ramaswamy. "Co-creation Experiences: The Next Practice in Value Creation," Journal of Interactive Marketing, 18 (3), (2004), pp. 5–14.

[11] J. Anderson and J. A. Narus. Selectively pursuing more of your customer's business. MIT Sloan Management Review, 44(3), 2003, pp.42–49.

[12] J. Füller, H. Mühlbacher, K. Matzler, and G. Jawecki, "Consumer Empowerment through Internet-Based Co-creation," Journal of Management Information Systems, vol. 26 2009–10, pp. 71–102.

[13] J. Füller and K. Matzler, Virtual product experience and customer participation A chance for customer-centred, really new products. Technovation vol.2, 2007, pp.378-387.

[14] N. Kano, Attractive quality and must be quality. Hinshitsu (Quality) 14 (2), 1984 (in Japanese), pp. 147–156.

[15] K. Matzler and H. H. Hinterhuber, How to make product development projects more successful by integrating Kano's model of customer satisfaction into quality function deployment. Technovation vol.1, 1998, pp. 25–38.

[16] K. B. White and K. A. Gyampah,".User involvement and user satisfaction. An exploratory contigency model", Information & Management vol. 25, 1993, pp.1-10.

[17] M. Mengoni, M. Germani and M. Peruzzini, "Products experience: How can virtual prototyping improve usability testing? ", In Innovative Developments in Design and Manufacturing - Advanced Research in Virtual and Rapid Prototyping, 2010, pp. 505–514.

[18] M. Mengoni, M. Bordegoni, G. Mandorli, F. Peruzzini, "Performing Ergonomic Analysis in Virtual Environments": A Structured Protocol to Assess Humans Interaction, Proceedings of the ASME International Design Engineering Technical Conferences & Computers and Information in Engineering Conference, IDETC/CIE,New York, USA, August 2008, pp. 3–6.

[19] G. L. Lilien, P. D. Morrison, K. Searls, M. Sonnack, and E. von Hippel, "Performance assessment of the lead user idea-generation process for new product development", Management Science vol. 48 (8), 2002, pp. 1042–1059.

[20] K. Matzler and F. Bailom, "Top management innovation orientation, market orientation and competence management as antecedents of product innovation success and firm performance". In: 13th International Product Development Management Conference, Milan, 2006.

[21] E. Dahan and V. Srinivasan, "The predictive power of internet-based product concept testing using visual depiction and animation". Journal of Product Innovation Management vol.17, 2000, pp.99–109.

[22] E. Prandelli, G. Verona, and D. Raccagni, "Diffusion of Web-based product innovation", California Management Review, vol. 48, April 2006, pp-109–135.

[23] S. Nambisan, Designing virtual customer environments for new product development: Toward a theory. Academy of Management Review, vol. 27, pp. 392–413, March 2002.

[24] J. Füller and K. Matzler, Virtual product experience and customer participation—A chance for customer centered, really new products. Technovation, vol.27, July- August 2007, pp.378–387.

[25] E. Von Hippel, "Perspective: User toolkits for innovation", The Journal of Product Innovation Management vol.18 (4), 2001, pp. 247–257.

[26] E. Von Hippel, Democratizing Innovation. MIT Press, Cambridge, MA, 2005.

[27] T. Kohlera, K. Matzlera, and J. Füller, "Avatar-based innovation: Using virtual worlds for real-world innovation," vol. 2, June–July 2009, pp 395–407

A Case Study of Four IT Companies Developing Usable Public Digital Self-Service Solutions

Jane Billestrup, Jan Stage
Institute of Computer Science
Aalborg University
Aalborg, Denmark
{jane,jans}@cs.aau.dk

Marta Larusdottir
School of Computer Science
Reykjavik University
Reykjavik, Iceland
marta@ru.is

Abstract— **This paper presents a case study of implementing a user-centred approach in four software companies that, by supporting the development process, provide the municipalities with various self-service solutions for their citizens. This study outlines the process of how four companies develop their solution, including their customer involvement, end-user involvement, and product. The findings are compared to the number of usability problems identified in the four self-service applications developed by the software companies. This shows a mismatch between the usability and utility in these four solutions.**

Keywords-Case Study; Self-Service Applications; Usability; Utility; Development Process; User-Centred

I. Introduction

European countries are currently developing digital self-service solutions for their citizens. These efforts are being launched to improve citizens' services and to reduce costs [18]. Though public self-services have been on the agenda in many countries for years, getting the end-users to use these applications is not easily achieved. For citizens to accept public digital services and websites, these sites need to have a high degree of usability [11]. Wangpipatwong et al. found that public digital websites in Thailand are lacking usability due to poor design and non-employment of user-centred design methodologies [7]. Several countries like United States, United Kingdom, South Africa and Denmark have developed guidelines to ensure the development of more usable public digital applications and websites [2][3][14].

The Digital Economy and Society Index (DESI) describes the level of digitalisation of the countries in EU. This is measured in five areas, including digital public services [18]. The total degree of digitalisation varies, from Romania, Bulgaria and Greece at the bottom to Sweden, Finland, and Denmark at the top [18]. Denmark is one of the top 3 countries in regards to all other digitalisation areas in EU and is one of the leading countries in the world [18].

Denmark has a population of 5.6 million people and is divided into 98 municipalities as a single point of contact for citizens in regards to the public sector [7]. In 2012, a digitalisation process was launched with the goal that, by the end of 2015, 80% of forms completed by citizens to the municipalities are filled in and submitted digitally [1]. Until 2012, a contract based approach was used for digital public services, where the software companies competed by bidding to an offer. Since 2012, the individual municipalities have been able to choose between competing designs for each digitalisation area. Denmark has created guidelines to ensure that public digital self-service applications and websites are usable for the citizens [1].

This paper presents a case study of four competitors implementing usable digital self-service solutions for the same application area. We have focused on analysing the customer and user involvement during the software development process, and the characteristics of the 4 products developed and results of usability evaluations thereof. Section 2 presents the related work. In Section 3, the method of this case study is presented. Section 4 presents the results, and, finally, Section 5 presents the discussion and conclusion.

II. Related Work

Studies show that quality and cost are complementary, e.g. [8][9]. But from the self-service providers' point of view, focus on usability will increase the price of the product, making the developed solution harder to sell [15]. This means that, to get public self-service providers to get this focus, usability has to be made a requirement. Both Jokela et. al. [13] and Mastrangelo [21] describe the importance of usability being specified in the requirements specification document. Mastrangelo describes that public administration needs guidelines to help getting usability placed in the requirements to get the intended impact [21].

There is a disagreement in the related work in regards to what is the best approach. Jokela et. al. found that to acquire usable digital self-service solutions the specified usability requirements have to be performance-based, as only these types of requirements would be verifiable, valid and comprehensive [15]. Additionally, the usability of digital self-service solutions should be validated before the solutions are sold to the municipalities [15].

This does not correspond with what Tarkkanen et. al. found. Formal and detailed criteria for validation will cause usability workarounds by the self-service providers as they will focus only on the verification of their application in regards to the requirements, instead of focusing on getting the usability of the digital self-service solutions validated and finding and fixing usability issues [16].

III. Method

This study was conducted as a multi-case study [5][22] analysing four competitors implementing usable digital self-service solutions for the same application area. Next, the four cases are presented and the data collection and analysis are described in more detail.

A. *The Cases*

Below, the four companies are described. The organisations have developed similar solutions and are competitors in regard to the 98 municipalities in Denmark who are the potential customers. To find the differences between these companies as much as possible, we created the scale shown in Table I.

TABLE I. CATEGORISATION OF THE FOUR ORGANISATIONS AND SOLUTIONS

	Immature company	Mature organisations
New self-service solution	Case A	Case B
Optimisation of existing self-service solution	Case C Case D	

Table I shows the placement of the four cases in regards to maturity and if the digital self-service solution is new or an optimisation of an existing solution. This shows the placement of the four cases in regards to maturity and if the digital self-service solution is new or an optimisation of an existing. The organisations' maturity has been defined according to their experience developing digital self-service applications in general.

The SME scale (small and medium scale enterprise) [20] has been used in regards to number of employees and turnover, to categorise the size of the four companies involved in this case study.

This area of self-service applications was chosen as the application had a certain level of complexity. The four companies were chosen because they were the only companies developing this specific solution, and the companies and their developed self-service solutions were different in terms of maturity of the company and if the company was developing a new solution or was optimising an existing solution.

Case A is a micro/small organisation in regards to the SME scale and the turnover and number of employees. The organisation has not previously developed other public digital self-service solutions, so it is categorised as immature. They use SCRUM [27] as development method and their digital self-service solution is categorised as new for the same reason. This company is an independent consulting and software company.

Case B is a large organisation in regards to the SME scale. The organisation is categorised as mature in regards to digital self-service solutions in general as they have developed several public digital self-service solutions previously. They use SCRUM as development method and PRINCE2 [28] as project management method. This specific solution is categorised as new, though they already have an existing solution, as they redid both the analysis and design phase, before developing this solution. This company has departments all over Scandinavia and creates and sells software solutions to several different markets.

Case C is a large organisation on the SME scale. They use their own development method, mainly staged but sometimes with agile elements. The organisation is described as both immature and mature in regards to digital self-service solutions. In general, this area of application is fairly new to them. They have an existing solution in this self-service area. This company has departments all over Scandinavia and creates and sells software solutions to different markets.

Case D is a large organisation on the SME scale. They use a staged development method but have implemented some agile techniques. The organisation is described as mature in regards to digital self-service solutions and has developed digital self-service applications for years. This company is an independent consulting and software company.

B. *Data Collection and Analysis*

All data was gathered over a time period of a year. Qualitative interviews were conducted by phone with project managers from 11 of 12 identified digital self-service providers, with the objective of how self-service providers were accepting and using the user-centred materials and learn about each company and their development approach [19]. This lead to a focus on one public self-service area with four identified self-service providers with the objective of how the user-centred requirements were used, and we conducted a redesign of the existing requirements [10].

For our case study, we had one half-day meeting with each of the four companies. Present at this meeting was the product owner or project manager. The agenda for these meetings was an introduction to this study including a discussion of their gain of participating, as we offered inputs on their self-service solution and conducting a usability evaluation, which they could use to improve their self-service application.

After the introduction the company presented their organisation overall and, more specifically, how they were developing this chosen self-service application, including development process and method, collaboration with stakeholders and end-user involvement. They also gave a demonstration of the self-service application in its current state. Lastly, it was discussed which people to interview in the next part of our study to ensure we would cover all perspectives. We had before the meetings identified the roles of the people we would like to interview, as these roles were named differently in each company and some people would have more than one of these roles. We conducted a list of people with the meeting. The roles we had identified were the following; project manager, developer, interface designer, and the person responsible for the user experience and usability of the public self-service application. We interviewed 14 people distributed across the four companies. The purpose of the interviews was to determine current practice at each of the four companies in regards to customer and citizen involvement, and how the end-users were taken into consideration during the design and development process. We found that interviewing people with different roles and responsibilities would provide us with more data on different perspectives and areas of expertise inside each company.

All interviews were conducted by phone and transcribed afterwards. All as semi-structured qualitative interviews as described by Kvale [4]. After all, interviews were conducted, the data was analysed in regard to the different perspectives of each interviewee and their job function in to get an idea of what each company did during the development process.

We completed a content analysis of relevant documents from the companies. Both, interviews and documents were analysed using Dedoose [6]. The aim of these activities was to study the development process of the four companies developing the digital self-service solutions in this specific self-service area, into more detail. The cases were analysed exploratively.

IV. Results

In this section, we present our results. Our findings are divided into three subsections, focusing on costumer involvement, end-user focus and their final product. Table II shows an overview of the four companies in regards to these three focus areas.

TABLE II. MAIN CHARACTERISTICS OF THE FOUR CASES

		Company A	Company B	Company C	Company D
Customer Involvement	**Focus area**	Case workers and their needs	Case workers and their work-load	System fits needs of municipalities	If System is needed customers' willingness to pay
	Involved municipalities	One	Around five	All existing customers	Six
	Involvement type	4-5 workshops, Prototype s	Workshops, emails Prototypes	Workshop	Workshop, emails Online meetings
End-users	**Citizen representation**	Primarily Case Workers	Primarily Case Workers	Primarily Case Workers	Primarily Case Workers
	Goal	Decisions at once	Optimizing work flows	Flexibility to fit each municipality	Decisions at once
	Usability	Verified by Case Workers	Testing on citizens in pilot releases	Hired specialists	Testing on citizens Hired specialists
Product	**Perceived strengths**	Applications verified right away	Follows legislation	Part of healthcare system	Part of healthcare system Applications verified right away Follows legislation
	Perceived weaknesses	Lacking usability	One solution fit all	Lacking usability	Lacking usability

A. Customer Involvement

In this section, it is described how the four companies involve the customers in the development of digital self-service applications. The section is written from the perspective of the four companies.

1) Case A

The company collaborated with one municipality as a customer and stakeholder. The company insisted that the involved personnel should be case workers who understood their own and the citizens' needs and not necessarily people with IT skills. They use the case workers to learn about the field of application. "*We held a new workshop with the municipality every couple of weeks, here we created mock-ups that we used to design a new prototype, which was evaluated and redesigned at the next workshop, [...] until we were satisfied with the final prototype*". The company was confident that they have developed a solution that lives up to the wishes and needs of their on-site customer, but is less confident that their solution is covering the needs of other municipalities. "*We have discussed if we should have created a standardised solution covering the needs of as many municipalities as possible.*" They describe it as a problem for them that they were not aware of the fact that the interpretations of legislation are not the same in all municipalities.

1) Case B

The main focus of the digital self-service application is on the back-end of the system, and to ease the workload of the case workers. "*Our primary focus is to simplify the working procedures for the case workers, otherwise, this would never be a priority for the municipalities*". Before developing this solution the company hosted workshops with the municipalities that are already customers, with the purpose of analysing the working procedures, used for creating a specification of requirements and a business case.

"*On the first workshop we are not presenting anything, typically we say – we don't know anything, tell us about your work [...] we use these workshops to learn how we digitally can support the digital work flow.*" This information is used in the development phase, where first iteration is developed, and a prototype is created. The prototype was presented at the next workshop to the municipalities involved in the development process. The prototype shows the flow from a citizen filling out a form and until it lands with the case worker. They also described sending emails to all existing customers asking them to answer questions in regards to their work flow.

2) Case C

The focus of the company is creating a solution that all municipalities can use. "I*t makes a very big difference if you are designing something for a large or small municipality. There is a very big difference in relation to how things are done or used.*" They describe developing an application that fits all types of municipalities, by developing a blank form that the municipalities can set up as they wish to get the citizens' to provide the information that each municipality finds important. This also means that each municipality buying this solution has to write all the text going into this digital self-service application.

Municipalities are involved in the development process by a forum for the exchange of experience that the company is hosting for the municipalities that are existing customers. These workshops are hosted several times a year. "*In regards to this specific solution we already have a solution that the citizens can access to fill out other applications or to get an overview of their own records, so this new application will be developed to be part of this existing system.*" Existing customers have been involved through these previously held workshops but no customers are directly involved in the development of this digital self-service application.

3) Case D

The main focus of this company is on the back-end of the digital self-service application. The company has involved municipalities by conducting a workshop with people from municipalities who are already customers. Representatives from six municipalities participated as on-site customers. The company hosted a workshop to learn about the number of applications and generating of ideas. At the end of this workshop, a specification of requirements was generated.

The municipalities were involved several times during the development process but mainly through online meetings or email. This was chosen as a consideration for the employees. "E*very time we have to pull the employees away from doing their normal job in the municipalities [...] Online meetings still gives them the ability to provide inputs. [...] When ever we have a question we send an email asking if we are doing the right thing.*" They described that involving the customers during the development process is a fairly new procedure. They now see this as best practice as it means they can do changes during the development process as changes late in the process are expensive and complicated.

4) Summary of Customer Involvement

Companies A, B and D asked on-site customers to participate during both design and development process. Companies A and B held continuously design workshops, where company D held one at the beginning and later primarily had remote access to the involved municipalities. Company C gathered information from workshops before the design phase but had no customer involvement besides that. Companies B and D stated that they mainly focused on the back-end of the system to be used by the case workers. Companies B, C and D all stated that they were aware of that the municipalities have different needs as it depends on the size of the municipality and their interpretation of legislation. Company A described that they learned eventually that the municipalities have different needs, though learning this quite late in the process.

B. End-Users

In this section, it is described how the citizens as end-users are taken into consideration through the development of the citizens' digital self-service applications. Also, what each company does in regards to ensuring the back-end systems meet the requirements of the case workers.

1) Case A

The citizens are not involved in the development process but the company describes taking them into consideration by ensuring that the procedures for sending an application are as simple as possible. "*We have created the solution so it should be understandable for all types of people. We have a good feeling here and our self-service application has been verified several times (by case workers)*". They have built an application that in the simple cases can send a decision back to the applicant right away without a case worker having to go through the application first. The company also described that their main focus is on the customer and not the citizens. "*We have been focusing on the customers' needs and work procedures, it have been important for us to understand what they wanted the citizens to do*". This perspective was chosen because the municipalities are the paying customers and not the citizens.

2) Case B

The company does not involve citizens in the development process but they involve the municipalities and case workers as a representation of the citizens' needs. "T*he municipalities give us feedback in regards to what is not working for the citizens, e.g. parts of the application that citizens consistently fill out wrong*". Though focus is not directly on the citizens the company feels that an optimisation of the back-end also brings value to the citizens as this will give a better flow with the handling of their applications. The company finds that focusing on accessibility of the system is more important than focusing on usability for the citizens.

They did describe testing the application with users before launching the digital self-service application. "*We have some pilot municipalities [...] they are part of a test phase where we assemble data for statistics*". For the municipalities and case workers, they focus on improving the efficiency of the work flows.

3) Case C

The company does not involve citizens in the development process. They describe creating a system that the municipalities can change to fit their needs. "*We have structured it so the municipalities can make adjustments where and if they see fit, e.g. in regards to rewriting phrasings or functions that can be added or removed*". The municipalities and case workers were involved prior to the design and development phase. The design and work flow were designed at workshops held prior to the redesign of this digital self-service application. The company focuses on usability by having usability specialists hired.

4) Case D

For this digital self-service solution, the company describes focusing on the citizens' needs and their flow through the application. *"We know that this system is developed mainly for senior citizens, meaning that this system needs to be as simple as possible. This includes that all descriptions and wordings need to be easy understandable".* The company has discussed if they spent too much time on the citizen angle. *"The end-user is not the one buying our product, it is the municipalities, [...] what matters is if they think our self-service solution is good".* The digital self-service application is described as being part of a larger health care system, where citizens will have access to, e.g. former applications and the municipality will have everything in regards to one citizen in one record. For this digital self-service application, they have used senior citizens without much experience with computers, to fill out a digital self-service application. In regards to the case workers and municipalities, they described focusing on full automatic digital self-service applications when possible. "

5) Summary of End-User Involvement

Neither of the companies has citizens directly involved in the design or development process, although companies B and D described testing their developed public self-service application on citizens after the development has been completed. Companies A and D implemented automatic decisions when possible, benefiting for both citizens and case workers. Companies A, B, C and D all described that focusing on the needs of the citizens has not been made a priority, only the needs of the municipalities as customers. Company D described that they needed to focus less on the citizens and more on the municipalities as customers.

Companies A and D have mainly focused on the target user-group in regards to keeping the design simple for the citizens. Company B focused primarily on the flow of the end-users in their solution, and company C has used usability specialists to check if the design was usable for the citizens.

C. Product

This section is about the strengths and weaknesses perceived by the company about their own digital self-service solution, both in relation to the municipalities, case workers, and the citizens.

1) Case A

The company perceives it as a strength that they have developed what they describe as a "whole solution" covering both the necessities for the case workers and the citizens. *"Our solution has a good flow for the citizens with understandable screen displays. It is not heavy on wording and we only ask for information that is actually relevant for the municipalities to keep things as simple as possible."*

The company also identified some weaknesses in regards to their digital self-service application. They described that the fact that they only collaborated with one municipality might have been an issue, although they did not see it as a real option for them to have involved 3-5 municipalities in the development process. The company also recognises that there might be usability issues in the digital self-service application but argues that this is substantiated in what the municipalities are actually willing to pay for. *"Reality is just different than theory. If you want to pay for it, you can get the great solutions focused on usability, but that is not what the municipalities want to pay for".* The company describes that if the customers do not care about usability they will not focus on that either.

2) Case B

The company perceives it as a strength of their digital self-service application that they have involved different kinds of professionals in the development process. They feel that the role of the product owner creates more value as he also has to ensure that the digital self-service application follows the legislations even if it changes. They describe ensuring to develop usable and intuitive digital self-service applications.

Late changes are described as being possible because the application is built in modules making changes less expensive. A perceived weakness is creating one solution to fit all needs. This is done as updating or testing would be too expensive if municipalities wanted something changed.

3) Case C

The company perceives it as a strength of their digital self-service application that they have developed a solution where the citizens can do everything in one place. *"The citizens never leave their medical file when they need to fill out the self-service application".* They also perceive it as a strength that they have tried to cover all aspects of the needs that both citizens and case workers have.

A perceived weakness is that they feel they might not have spent enough time on usability when developing the digital self-service application for the citizens. *"The self-service application might be kind of crude, people need to have prior knowledge to be able to use it.."* A concern about if feeble citizens would be able to fill in the application was raised.

4) Case D

The company perceives it as a strength that they have integrated this application in their general healthcare record solution. "*The citizens can see the full catalogue of the services the municipality offers and, after they have applied for something once, it is possible to make a reorder without starting over with the application.*" They feel that they have simplified processes that otherwise might be difficult for feeble citizens. For the case workers they see their solution as a strength in regards to, when an application ends up with the case worker, the system has already validated that the citizens are entitled to what they have applied for.

It is perceived as both a strength and a weakness that they always make applications that follow the legislation though some municipalities might have other requests. It is perceived as a weakness that they have been bound by an existing design on the general healthcare record solution. They feel this application might lack usability and that some written information might be too small for the application.

5) Usability of Products

To evaluate if the development process had resulted in usable self-service applications for the citizens, a usability evaluation of these four self-service solutions was conducted. This was done as a think-aloud usability evaluation in a usability laboratory, with eight test persons. For the evaluations, all test persons received the same instructions explaining what they were meant to do during the evaluation, e.g. conduct a set of tasks and think aloud during the evaluation. All participants received the same tasks, and evaluated all four systems, but evaluated them in a different order.

The test persons were chosen to represent a user segment as large as possible. Our test persons ranged in age and had different educational backgrounds. The test persons had different level of experience with computers though all use the Internet on a regular basis. They had different level of experience in regards to public services. Most had experience with other public digital self-service areas but not this specific area.

An overview of the test persons can be found in Table III below.

TABLE III. FOUND USABILITY PROBLEMS FOR EACH DIGITAL SELF-SERVICE SOLUTION

Test person	Gender	Age	Education	Experience with public services
TP1	F	44	High school degree (early retirement because of health issues)	Yes, also for this application type, and done digitally
TP2	F	31	Phd-student in Social science	Yes, for other service areas, and done digitally
TP3	M	52	Accountant	Yes, for other service areas, and done digitally
TP4	F	64	Retired school teacher	Yes, for other service areas, but not digitally
TP5	F	66	Technical assistant	Yes, also for this service area, and done digitally
TP6	M	30	Msc. Engineering	Yes, for other service areas, and done digitally
TP7	M	65	Retired computer assistant	Yes, for other service areas, and done digitally
TP8	M	22	Bachelor student in computer science	No experience

All test persons received a small gift after participating in the evaluation.

After conducting the evaluations the data was analysed using the method Instant Data Analysis (IDA) [26]. The usability problems were categorised after the criteria described in Table IV. The problems were categorised in regards to levels of confusion and frustration of the participants, and whether they were able to fill out the forms correctly. These criteria and categorisations were described further by Skov and Stage [17].

TABLE IV. DEFINING THE SEVERITY OF THE USABILITY PROBLEMS IN THE DIGITAL SELF-SERVICE SOLUTIONS

	Slowed down	Understanding	Frustration or confusion	Test monitor
Critical	Hindered in solving the task	Does not understand how the information in the system can be used for solving the task	Extensive level of frustration or confusion – can lead to a full stop	Receives substantial assistance, could not have solved the task without it
Serious	Delayed in solving the task	Does not understand how a specific functionality operates or is activated	Is clearly annoyed by something that cannot be done or remembered or something illogical that one must do	Receives a hint, and are able to solve the task afterwords
Cosmetic	Delayed slightly in solving the task	Does actions without being able to explain why (you just have to do it)	Only small signs of frustration or confusion	Is asked a question that makes him come up with the solution

An overview of the usability problems is shown in Table V.

TABLE V. FOUND USABILITY PROBLEMS IN EACH DIGITAL SELF-SERVICE SOLUTION

	Company A	Company B	Company C	Company D
Critical	2	5	0	1
Serious	17	18	11	15
Cosmetic	17	14	6	13
Total	**36**	**37**	**17**	**29**

Of the identified problems, 11 were found across all four digital public self-solutions. Among these general problems was lack of understanding of the purpose and flow of the self-service solutions, problems with attaching files, test persons getting annoyed or confused by not being able to understand helping texts and the descriptions of the rules and regulations of the application area, leading to test persons filling in the wrong information in the text fields. And, misunderstanding data fields, also leads the test persons to fill in the wrong information in the text fields.

6) Summary of Products

Companies A and D highlight simplified processes as strengths in regards to their public self-service applications. B and D find the fact that they focus on developing applications that follow the legislation as a strength. C and D both describe it as a strength that the self-service application is integrated in one healthcare solution for all public healthcare applications. Companies A, C and D believe that a weakness of the citizen centred self-service applications might be lacking usability. This has not been made a priority by the companies as it was not a priority for the municipalities.

The applications from C and to some extent D, were significantly smaller and less complex than the applications developed by companies A and B.

Both applications from companies C and D were part of larger healthcare systems and therefore much less information had to be filled in by citizens themselves. Especially the application developed by company C was very plain and did not address any of the issues that companies A and B, and to some extent company D have tried to solve in their solutions, like adding features automatically generating decisions, or the possibility of attaching relevant documents to the application. The application from company C was created as a paper application in pdf-form. Although C and D showed a higher degree of usability, the utility of these solutions were significantly lower than the applications from A and B.

V. DISCUSSION AND CONCLUSION

The Danish digitalisation effort has been taken to support the development process and provide each municipality with more digital self-service solutions to choose from, and enhancing usability in these solutions. For this purpose, two sets of guidance materials were created, a user journey and a set of 24 usability criteria, respectively. The aim was that this approach would facilitate competition between the self-service providers, resulting in better and more user-centred self-service applications for the citizens. All four companies involved the municipalities in the design process both in regards to the back-end of the system meant for the case workers and in regards to the self-service applications meant for the citizens. Two of the companies described involving citizens quite late in the process for testing of the features, either by going live in a few "pilot-municipalities" or conducting a usability evaluation.

Though a user-centred approach has been taken, our results correspond with the findings of Wangpipatwong et al. who found that e-government websites are lacking usability due to poor design and non-employment of user-centred design methodologies [7]. The reason for this is that the municipalities according to the companies are only focusing on this to a small extent and are not willing to pay more than the bare minimum. This shows a mismatch between what the joint IT organisation of the municipalities, and the municipalities are trying to achieve. The public self-service providers are focusing on what the municipalities are willing to pay for and want the citizens to do and not taking the user-centred approach with a citizens' perspective, unless this is being requested by the municipalities. If the user-centred approach should be a success it is important to involve the municipalities as well. They need to understand that quality and cost are complementary [8][9] and why usability needs to be a focus area and why a usable system will be a good investment though it might be a bit more expensive to develop. Bruun and Stage have found that redesigning a digital self-service application focusing on usability, can reduce the amount of time the case worker has to spend on each application, with more than 50% [23].

Jokela et. al. [13] and Mastrangelo [21] describe the importance of usability being specified in the requirements. It is questionable whether this approach will be successful unless the municipalities learn the values of these requirements and get the understanding that usability will reduce cost over time. It seems very clear that as long as the municipalities are not demanding this focus on usability, the self-service providers will not focus on this aspect either.

To gain an understanding of the development of public self-service applications in Denmark, we have conducted a study of one application area with four self-service providers. We recognise this limitation in regards to drawing conclusions in a broad term about the entire development process. Also, we have conducted a case study involving the companies. As future work, it would be interesting to learn the perspectives of the municipalities from themselves, and not only through the self-service providers.

ACKNOWLEDGEMENT

We would like to thank the four companies who participated in this study and the joint IT organisation of the municipalities. We would also like to thank Infinit, for supporting this research.

REFERENCES

[1] Organisation of the Municipalities in Denmark, http://www.kl.dk/Administration-og-digitalisering/Lov-om-obligatorisk-digital-selvbetjening-og-digital-post-er-vedtaget-id105354/ [retrieved: March, 2016]

[2] M. Pretorius, and A. Calitz, "The South African user experience maturity status for website design in provincial governments". Proceedings of the 12th European Conference on eGovernment pp. 589-599, 2012.

[3] Kombit, For self-service providers, http://www.kombit.dk/indhold/leverand%C3%B8rer [retrieved: March, 2016]

[4] S. Kvale, "Interview", København: Hans Reitzel, (1997)

[5] B. Flyvbjerg, "Five misunderstandings about case-study research", Qualitative inquiry 12.2, 2006, pp. 219-245

[6] Dedoose, www.dedoose.com [retrieved: March, 2016]

[7] S. Wangpipatwong, W. Chutimaskul, and, B. Papastratorn, "Understanding citizen's continuance intention to use e-government website: A composite view of technology acceptance model and computer self-efficiancy". The Electronic Journal of e-Government, vol. 6, nr. 1 2008, pp. 55-64

[8] P. B. Crosby, "Quality is free". Mcgraw-Hill, New York, 1979.

[9] D. E. Harter, M. S. Krishnan, and S. A. Slaughter, "Effects of process maturity on quality, cycle time, and effort in software product development". Management Science, vol. 46 nr. 4 2000, pp. 451-466.

[10] J. Billestrup, A. Bruun, and J. Stage, "UX Requirements to Public Systems for All: Formalisation or Innovation". Workshop on Formalizing UX Requirements, 2015.

[11] T. Clemmensen and D. Katre, "Adapting e-gov usability evaluation to cultural contexts". Usability of e-government systems. Boston: Morgan Kaufmann, 2012, pp. 331-344.

[12] Z. Huang and M. Benyoucef, "Usability and credibility of e-government websites". Government Information Quarterly 2014, pp. 584-595.

[13] T. Jokela, "Determining Usability Requirements Into a Call-for-Tenders. A Case Study on the Development of a Healthcare System". Proceedings of NordiCHI 2010.

[14] B. Soufi and M. Maguire, "Achieving usability within e-government websites illustrated by a case study evaluation". Proceedings of Human Interface, Springer-Verlag, 2007 part II, pp. 777-784.

[15] T. Jokela, L. Juja, and M. Nieminen, "Usability in RFP's: The Current Practice and Outline for the Future". Proceedings of HCI International, 2013.

[16] K. Tarkkanen and V. Harkke, "From Usability Workarounds to Usability Around Work". Proceedings of INTERACT 2015.

[17] M. B. Skov and J. Stage, Supporting Problem Identification in usability Evaluations. Proceedings of OzCHI, 2005.

[18] DESI Index,https://ec.europa.eu/digital-agenda/en/scoreboard/ [retrieved: March, 2016]

[19] J. Billestrup and J. Stage, E-government and the Digital Agenda for Europe. Design, User Experience, and Usability. User Experience Design for Diverse Interaction Platforms and Environments. Springer International Publishing, 2014. pp. 71-80.

[20] SME definition. http://ec.europa.eu/enterprise/policies/sme/facts-figures-analysis/sme-definition/index_en.htm [retrieved: March, 2016]

[21] S. Mastrangelo, R. Lanzilotti, M. Boscarol, and C. Ardito, "Guidelines to Specify HCD Activities in the Call for Tender for Public Administration Websites". Proceedings of INTERACT 2015.

[22] R. Yin, R, "Case Study Research: Design and methods". CA, USA: Sage Publications, 1991.

[23] A. Bruun and J. Stage, "Supporting Diverse Users: Implementing Usability Improvements of an E-Government Data Entry Website". Unpublished, 2014.

[24] Kombit, User Journey for applying for a marriage certificate, December 2014 http://www.kl.dk/ImageVaultFiles/id_60480/cf_202/Illu.PDF [retrieved: March, 2016]

[25] The government agency for digitalisation in Denmark. Criteria for usability in self-service solutions. http://www.kl.dk/ImageVault/Images/id_56064/scope_0/ImageVault Handler.aspx [retrieved: March, 2016]

[26] J. Kjeldskov, M. B. Skov, and J. Stage, "Instant Data Analysis: Conducting Usability Ealuations in a Day". Proceedings of NordiCHI, 2004.

[27] K. Schwaber and M. Beedle. "Agilè Software Development with Scrum". Prentice Hall, 2001.

[28] Bentley, Colin. "Prince2: a Practical Handbook". Routledge, 2010.

Expertise and Behavior of Unix Command Line Users: an Exploratory Study

Mohammad Gharehyazie
Department of Computer Science
University of California, Davis
Davis, CA, USA
Email: gharehyazie@ucdavis.edu

Bo Zhou
Department of Computer Science & Engineering
University of California, Riverside
Riverside, CA, USA
Email: bzhou003@cs.ucr.edu

Iulian Neamtiu
Department of Computer Science
New Jersey Institute of Technology
Newark, NJ, USA
Email: ineamtiu@njit.edu

***Abstract*—Understanding users' behavioral patterns and quantifying users' expertise have a myriad applications, from predicting user actions and tailoring the environment to that specific user, to detecting masquerade attacks and assessing learning outcomes. Toward this end, we have conducted a study on three Unix command datasets, totaling 263 users and more than 1 million commands. We first introduce the notions of command expertise, command line expertise, and command category. Next, we use these metrics, combined with other attributes to define and quantify several user expertise metrics, e.g., category breadth, command line expertise. Our study has revealed many Unix commands characteristics, e.g., Unix command can be grouped into 25 categories; file management is the most common activity; the most commonly used commands are two-characters long. Our study has also revealed many insights into user expertise and behavior, such as: command line length is not an indicator of user expertise; users activity is highest on Monday and decreases every day through Saturday, picking up on Sunday; peak command usage hours are 11 a.m., 1 p.m. and 4 p.m.; development activities happen mostly in the afternoon.**

Keywords*–*User behavior; user expertise; Unix; empirical study.

I. Introduction

Unix, Unix-like, and Linux operating systems dominate the market in segments where human-computer interaction is centered around command-line; specifically, the market share of these operating systems, in January 2016, was 66.9% (server), 100% (supercomputer) and 100% (mainframe) [1]. Understanding Unix command usage and the behavior of Unix users has many applications: repetitive sequences of commands can be transformed into scripts for correctness and ease of use; temporal patterns can expose busy and idle periods hence allowing capacity to be scaled accordingly; and noticing that a user U's commands or temporal access patterns are markedly different compared to U's prior commands and usage patterns can indicate a masquerade attack [2] (i.e., U's account has been compromised and is being used by a malicious user M). Quantitative measures of user expertise can serve as a base for comparing users (e.g., who are the most competent or efficient users?), inferring user roles (e.g., student vs. seasoned developer vs. system administrator) or assessing how users learn.

Few studies have focused on understanding user behavior based on command line usage. Rather, prior studies' focus has been on: masquerade detection (malicious users taking control of a legitimate user's account) [3][4][5][6][7][8][9]; user session characterization [10] in terms of commands per session, errors encountered and directories explored; or predicting high-level user actions [11]. In Section II, we provide a detailed comparison with related work. However, none of these previous studies have attempted to quantify user or command expertise and study temporal patterns associated with users/expertise.

We start by describing the datasets and the approach we have used to identify commands and their arguments (Section III). Identifying individual commands is nontrivial due to several reasons, such as the myriad ways in which Unix commands can be chained or used as arguments for other commands.

In Section IV, we discuss the methodology we have used for quantifying expertise and assigning expertise values to commands and users. First, we assign an *expertise* value to each command — the higher the value, the higher the probability that the command is used by more advanced users, or requires more advanced knowledge. Next, using command expertise, we assign expertise values to entire command lines. We then group commands into categories such as file management, editor, and compiler. Based on these metrics, we introduce metrics for users expertise: *user category breadth* to quantify user expertise in terms of the number of different categories employed by that user, as well separating users into high- and low-expertise groups.

In Section V, we present our findings. We first characterize commands in each dataset; we found that file management is the principal activity, with `cd` and `ls` accounting for substantial percentages of user commands. We found that the most common command length is *two*; that command line length is not necessarily an indicator of expertise, and that commands/users permit a natural separation into high- and low-expertise commands/users.

We also analyzed temporal patterns in one of the datasets (the only dataset to contain command timestamps). We found that command activity tends to decrease from Monday until Saturday, and increase slightly on Sunday; that peak command usage hours are 11 a.m., 1 p.m. and 4 p.m.; and that development activities (use of editors and compilers) peaks in the afternoon.

II. Related Work

Schonlau et al. [3] have used various statistical methods to detect masquerade attacks by finding "bad data" (attacker's

TABLE I. FEATURE AVAILABILITY FOR EACH DATASET.

datasets	Mahajan	Greenberg	Schonlau
Users	45	168	50
Commands per user	709*	1,441*	15,000
Command timestamp	✓		
Session start/end		✓	
Command arguments	✓	✓	
Command chaining	✓	✓	
User Group		✓	

* Median number of commands per user.

commands) inside sequences of "good data" (benign commands issued by a legitimate user). Other studies have similarly used machine learning or grammars for masquerade detection [4][5][6][7][8][9]. Greenberg [10] has collected traces of 168 users via a modified `csh` shell; they partitioned the users into four non-overlapping categories (novice programmers, experienced programmers, computer scientists and non-programmers) and characterized user sessions in terms of commands per session, errors encountered and directories explored. Chinchani et al. [12] has focused on the reverse problem of generating user models so that synthetic command traces can be generated automatically. Fitchett and Cockburn [11] developed a predictor model for revisitation/reuse based on user actions (commands, window switching, URL accesses).

Note that our focus is different compared with the aforementioned efforts. Rather than finding suspicious/anomalous commands for purposes of masquerade detection, we aim to answer more general questions: how can command expertise, command line expertise, and user expertise be operationalized? How can users and commands be grouped into categories that generalize and are stable across datasets? What are the temporal patterns associated with commands, command categories, and users, e.g., when (time-of-day/day-of-week) does development happen, as opposed to editing, and when are experts active compared to novice users?

III. DATASETS

Our analysis is based upon three main datasets — collected by other researchers [9][3][10] — totaling 263 users and 1,023,993 commands. Table I provides an overview of the datasets and the features they include: each dataset consists of real commands collected from actual usage — ranging from 709 up to 15,000 commands per user. The dataset attributes vary: while Mahajan's set contains a timestamp for each command, the other sets do not; conversely, Greenberg's set has session start and end markers while the other two do not. Finally, Mahajan and Greenberg's sets contains command arguments, including the chaining of multiple commands on the same line (e.g., via the pipe operator), while Schonlau's only contains a command prefix (first 8 characters).

We now describe each dataset, its features, and the methodology we used to extract characteristics from that particular set.

1) Mahajan: The richest, most detailed data was gathered by Mahajan [9]: command traces for 45 users. Each command has a timestamp and the entire command line, e.g., including complex pipes, was captured. To parse each line, we first separate the command portion into sections of commands by pipes (the '|' character) and logical commands such as '&&'. After separating a line into sections, each section contains a command, along with zero or more parameters. For example, the following line will be separated into 3 sections:

```
ls -l | grep key | less
```

Backquotes or "backticks" are commands that are executed before the rest of a line, and their result is "pasted" at their position in the line. For example:

```
vim notes.`date +%F`
```

Hence we look for backquotes in each section and treat it as a separate section; we find the command and its parameters (as described below) and we treat the whole section as an extra parameter for the section which contained the backquotes.

To count the number of parameters for each command, we separate each section by space and redirection characters ('>', '>>', '<', and '<<'). As mentioned above, each section is split based on space or redirection characters. Redirection to/from a file is also considered a parameter. In some rare cases there are two commands per section such as `sudo apt-get install blah` which contains two commands ('`sudo`' with 0 parameters and '`apt-get`' with 2 parameters). Only two commands were found that used such a feature: '`sudo`' and '`time`'.

To conclude, in the aforementioned example, we detect 3 commands: '`ls`' with 1 parameter, '`grep`' with 1 parameter, and '`less`' with no parameter. Notice that all commands after the first pipe have one more parameter than immediately visible, and that is because the other parameter has been piped.

Finally, we proceeded to identifying *sessions*, i.e., start and end of time intervals when users started the command line interaction. While Mahajan's dataset is very rich in most aspects, it does not explicitly record session information, so to identify sessions we computed the time intervals between consecutive commands, plotted their distribution, and visually identified cut-off points hence session begin/end.

2) Greenberg: This dataset consists of 168 Unix users [10]. Like Mahajan's dataset, it contains command parameters, and complex command lines, but it does not contain timestamps like Mahajan's. It does however contain session delimiters. Another feature of this dataset is that it categorizes users into 4 categories based on their expertise. In detail, there are 52 computer scientists, 36 experienced programmers, 55 novice programmers and 25 non-programmers respectively. This makes it particularly valuable in evaluating our expertise extraction methods. Next, we show an example of the information contained in Greenberg's dataset (the dataset contains more information which is irrelevant to this study and has been removed from the example for clarity).

```
S Wed Feb 18 16:37:25 1987
E Wed Feb 18 16:56:22 1987

C date
C nroff terry.abs | enscript
C p audio.mail

S Fri Feb 20 12:41:39 1987
E Fri Feb 20 14:24:06 1987

C mail
```

```
C rlogin sun-fsa
C rlogin sun-e
C rlogin sun-b
...
```

3) Schonlau: Although this dataset is large, containing 15,000 command traces per user for 50 users, it is limited in three ways. First, the parameters for each command are omitted; this leads to missing complex pipes and chains of commands, which can be used to assign user expertise. Second, due to the method used for gathering data, system commands, e.g., commands invoked from C programs via `system()` or `exec()` were included. Finally, the command traces do not have timestamps, so processing any temporal information such as number and duration of each user session is impossible. On the flip side, parsing this dataset is trivial, since each line contains a simple command, with no parameters, no loops, no pipes, etc.

IV. EXPERTISE

We used the following approach for developing a uniform notion of expertise across the three datasets: we first assign an expertise value $E(C)$ to each command C, then for each command line L, including lines that consist of the chainings commands $C_1, \ldots, C_n$, we assign an expertise coefficient $lCoef(L)$ based on constituent command(s) expertise as well as the command chaining information.

Command Categories. We group commands into *categories*, e.g., `vim` or `emacs` are categorized as *editor* commands, while `ping` or `traceroute` are *network* commands, and so on. In total we have defined 25 categories. The number of categories varies little across datasets: 24 for Mahajan, 23 for Schonlau and 18 for Greenberg (Table II) which indicates that our category definitions are stable.

A. Command and Line Expertise

1) Assigning Expertise to Commands: Due to inherent differences among the three datasets, they could not be merged into one dataset, and thus assigning expertise was performed separately on each of them. We first measure the number of users that have used each command (U), along with the number of times each command was used ($Freq$). We also manually assign commands to categories based on type of application.

We group U into 4 bins and $Freq$ into 3 and assign an expertise value to each bin (U_{exp} and $Freq_{exp}$) as shown on the left of Figure 1. A level of expertise is assigned to each category (C_{exp}) as shown on the bottom of Figure 1, e.g., browser commands have expertise value 4, network and svn (version control) have value 10, while compiler commands have expertise value 14. Then, for each command we assign an intra-category expertise adjustment (I_{exp}), as explained next.[1] The reasoning behind the expertise assignments is:

- For user breadth U_{exp}, the more people utilizing a command, the less likely it is to require high expertise. At the same time, if a command is used only by a single person, there is a high chance that it is highly personal, e.g., scripts. We believe the expertise associated with this bin should be lowered, but not lower than the bin with highest number of users.
- For $Freq_{exp}$, a command that is used less frequently is likely associated with higher expertise.
- A category of commands C_{exp} is the highest indicator of expertise, e.g., a compiler command is much more complicated than a browser command.
- Within a category, there are certain commands that require a higher expertise to be used; these commands are given extra expertise points in intra-category expertise I_{exp}.

[1]Expertise values were assigned based on consensus among authors.

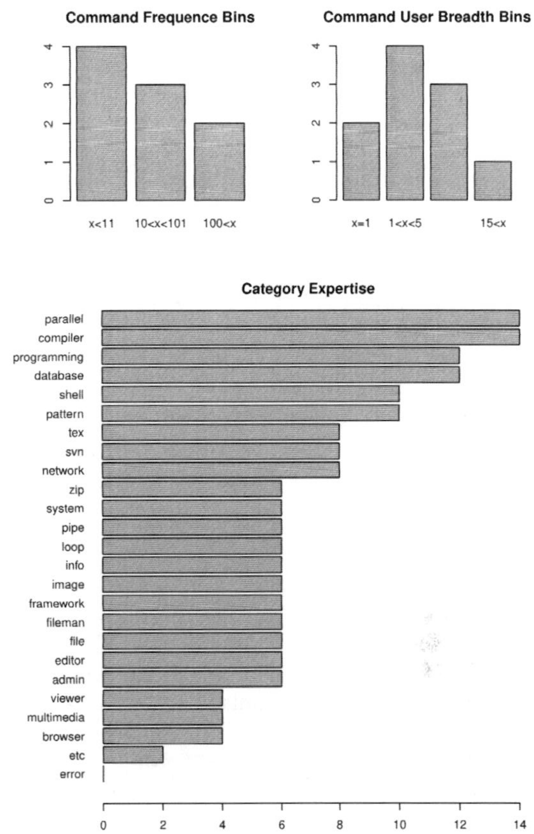

Figure 1. Expertise assigned to bins of a) command frequency (top left); b) user breadth (top right); and c) command category (bottom) for the Mahajan dataset.

Therefore, we use the following formula for assigning expertise to each command C_i:

$$Exp(C_i) = U_{exp}(C_i) + Freq_{exp}(C_i) + C_{exp}(C_i) + I_{exp}(C_i) \quad (1)$$

While the most influential element of each command's expertise is the category it belongs to, other elements can boost or hinder its expertise and thus provide a wide range of values. For example, in Schonlau's dataset, expertise values range from 6 to 22.

2) Assigning Expertise to Lines: For the dataset of Schonlau et al., each line's expertise is the same as the command in that line. But for Mahajan and Greenberg datasets, we need a measure to combine multiple commands' expertise into a single value. Adding up all the expertise is not a great idea since it can highly inflate the expertise values, and it is certainly misleading, since someone who uses 10 commands in a single line, does not necessarily possess 10x greater expertise in comparison to another person who uses the same commands on separate consecutive lines. We believe that the former's expertise is merely a fraction more than the latter's and that is due to their ability to combine multiple commands in a single line and perform complicated tasks. To this end, we have developed the following line expertise computation scheme:

$$lCoef(l_i) = \begin{cases} 1 + \frac{min(|Commands(l_i)|,4)}{10}, & \text{if } l_i \text{ contains backquotes} \\ 1 + \frac{min(|Commands(l_i)|,4)-1}{10}, & \text{otherwise} \end{cases} \quad (2)$$

$$Coef(C_j) = 1 + \frac{min(|Params(C_j)|, 4) - 1}{10} \quad (3)$$

$$Expertise(l_i) = lCoef(l_i) \times \max_{C_j \in Commands(l_i)} Exp(C_j) \times Coef(C_j) \quad (4)$$

Here, l_i is any given line, C_j is a member of the set of commands within l_i, denoted by $Commands(l_i)$ and $Params(C_j)$ gives the set of parameters for C_j. $lCoef(l_i)$ is an expertise coefficient for line l_i which gives a 10% boost to l_i's expertise for each extra command in l_i, up to 4 commands; it also gives an extra 10% boost if backquotes are used in l_i. $Coef(C_j)$ is a command coefficient which gives a 10% boost to C_j's expertise for each extra parameter provided to C_j, up to 4 parameters.

3) High- and Low-Expertise Commands: To provide a straightforward binary separation into "easy" and "advanced" commands, we use the command expertise distributions to divide all commands into low and high expertise groups. These in turn will be used to support separating users into low- and high-expertise groups. We present the results in Section V-A3.

B. User Expertise

We now provide definitions of user expertise.

1) User Category Breadth: User Category Breadth (UCB), i.e., the number of different categories they actively use, is also an indicator of expertise. To measure UCB, we identify the category of commands for each user, and apply a minimum number of commands threshold to weed out those cases where accidental or extremely infrequent use of commands would count toward category use. Specifically, we used 1.5% of the average number of commands for each user in each dataset to define the aforementioned threshold — this translates to 20 commands in Mahajan's dataset and 250 commands in Schonlau's, i.e., to count a category C toward a user U's UCB, U has to have used at least 20 and 250 commands in C, respectively.

2) High- and Low-Expertise Users: To distinguish different users, we divide them into low and high expertise groups based on high- and low- command line expertise mentioned in Equation (2). We found a clear delineation between the high- and low- expertise sets; we present the results in Section V-B2.

V. Results and Discussion

We now proceed to discuss our findings.

TABLE II. SUMMARY OF COMMAND CHARACTERISTICS.

	Mahajan	Greenberg	Schonlau
Total Commands	56,261	313,169	750,000
Unique Commands	1,218	4,117	856
Categories	24	18	23

TABLE III. TOP-20 COMMANDS FOR EACH DATASET.

Rank	Mahajan		Greenberg		Schonlau	
	Command	%	Command	%	Command	%
1	cd	15.3	ls	12.3	sh	8.7
2	ls	15.0	cd	8.8	cat	4.3
3	git	3.7	pix	6.2	netscape	4.3
4	vim	3.3	umacs	4.9	generic	4.1
5	sudo	3.1	e	4.2	ls	4.0
6	grep	2.8	rm	3.1	popper	3.3
7	vi	2.6	fg	3.1	sendmail	2.8
8	gvim	2.3	emacs	3.0	date	2.7
9	ssh	2.2	more	2.8	rm	2.3
10	mm	2.2	lpq	1.9	sed	2.1
11	rm	2.0	mail	1.8	nawk	2.0
12	java	1.9	lpr	1.8	expr	1.9
13	perl	1.6	cat	1.8	tcsh	1.8
14	javac	1.5	cp	1.4	grep	1.7
15	find	1.4	ps	1.3	tcpostio	1.4
16	clear	1.2	nroff	1.2	uname	1.4
17	mount	1.1	who	1.1	ln	1.3
18	cp	1.1	make	1.0	hostname	1.3
19	cat	0.9	fred	0.9	gcc	1.3
20	exit	0.8	u	0.8	true	1.3

A. Command Characteristics

1) Command Distribution: Table II shows the summary of each dataset. Although the Schonlau dataset has the most commands, it has the fewest *unique* commands. Note how, despite differences in datasets (e.g., provenance, year of collection, Unix system used) they have similar numbers of command categories, which indicates that our category definitions are quite stable across different Unix user populations.

Table III shows the top-20 most used commands and their percentage in each dataset. File management commands (`ls`, `cd`, `cp`, and `rm`) are the most popular by far, and they dominate the Mahajan and Greenberg datasets (more than 20% of their commands fall into this category). The Schonlau dataset is more evenly distributed, but file management is popular there as well.

Furthermore, we investigate whether commands differ between user groups. Table IV shows the top-20 most used commands and their percentage of user groups in the Greenberg dataset. For groups computer scientist, experienced programmer and non programmer, similar to the whole dataset, file management commands contribute the most, but for the novice programmer group, the compiler-related command `pix` and (Pascal interpreter and executor) and editor command `umacs` are the most used commands.

Table V shows top-5 most used categories and their percentage in each dataset. The observations are similar to the previous observations on commands: file management is prevalent, with Mahajan and Greenberg's datasets having a higher concentration of such commands compared to Schonlau's.

The Greenberg dataset comes with an assignment of users into groups: computer scientists, experienced programmers, novice programmers, and non-programmers [10]. Therefore,

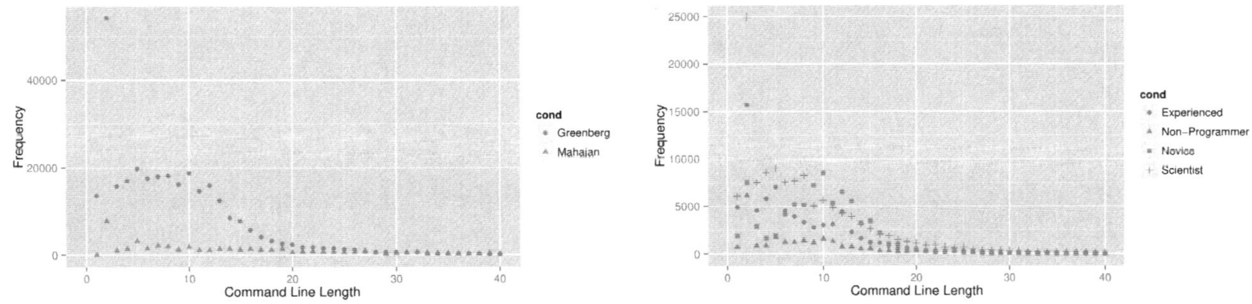

Figure 3. Distribution of command line length in Mahajan and Greenberg datasets (left) and the four user groups of the Greenberg dataset (right).

TABLE IV. TOP-20 COMMANDS OF EACH CATEGORY IN GREENBERG DATASET.

Rank	Scientist		Experienced		Novice		Non-Programmer	
	Command	%	Command	%	Command	%	Command	%
1	ls	14.6	cd	12.0	pix	24.4	ls	15.8
2	cd	10.5	ls	11.8	umacs	19.7	emacs	10.6
3	e	5.2	e	5.8	ls	7.8	nroff	9.1
4	fg	4.4	fg	4.6	rm	3.4	cd	8.5
5	rm	3.0	more	4.1	u	3.1	e	5.3
6	mail	2.8	rm	2.7	cd	2.9	rm	4.0
7	emacs	2.4	make	2.7	cat	2.7	ee	3.8
8	lpq	2.2	emacs	2.5	more	2.6	more	3.4
9	more	2.1	lpr	1.9	script	2.4	lpr	3.0
10	ps	1.8	l	1.9	lpr	2.4	hpr	2.8
11	f	1.6	cat	1.8	lpq	2.0	ptroff	2.2
12	cat	1.6	ada	1.8	cp	2.0	lpq	1.9
13	who	1.5	examples_vax	1.7	emacs	1.8	ps	1.8
14	mv	1.1	cp	1.5	pi	1.5	cp	1.4
15	lpr	1.1	a.out	1.3	p	1.2	tbl	1.4
16	man	1.1	rwho	1.3	mail	1.0	w	1.3
17	rlogin	1.0	mail	1.2	fred	1.0	col	1.2
18	cp	1.0	lpq	1.2	logout	0.8	mail	1.2
19	page	0.9	bye	1.2	pdpas	0.7	rr	1.1
20	fred	0.9	ps	1.2	man	0.6	spell	1.1

TABLE V. TOP-5 CATEGORIES FOR EACH DATASET.

Rank	Mahajan		Greenberg		Schonlau	
	Category	%	Category	%	Category	%
1	fileman	39.0	fileman	28.3	pattern	13.7
2	etc.	8.4	editor	14.7	framework	12.2
3	editor	8.2	info	13.1	etc.	12.1
4	pattern	5.8	etc.	10.7	system	11.8
5	compiler	5.1	compiler	9.2	fileman	10.1

TABLE VI. TOP-5 CATEGORIES FOR USER GROUPS OF THE GREENBERG DATASET.

Rank	Scientist		Experienced		Novice		Non-Programmer	
	Category	%	Category	%	Category	%	Category	%
1	fileman	32.3	fileman	31.7	compiler	27.4	fileman	31.2
2	info	14.4	etc.	13.2	editor	23.3	editor	21.1
3	etc.	11.8	info	12.6	fileman	17.2	info	13.1
4	editor	10.6	editor	10.7	info	11.6	Tex	11.8
5	system	9.1	system	8.4	system	7.4	etc.	11.1

for this dataset alone, we have investigated category distribution for each group. According to Table VI, we found that computer scientists and experienced programmers' groups have similar top categories, e.g., file management is the most frequent used commands. However, the novice programmer group used compiler and editor commands most often, whereas non-programmers, as expected, used file management, editor, help (info) and TeX (text processing) commands most often.

2) Command Line Expertise: We now illustrate how command line expertise differs among user groups. We classified the Mahajan dataset into 3 groups: experienced programmer, novice programmer and non programmer; we performed this classification manually by sampling each user's commands and evaluating the categories and expertise of the sampled commands. Figure 2 shows the bean-plot of average command line expertise of each group in Mahajan. The shape of the bean-plot is the entire density distribution, the short horizontal lines represent each data point, the longer thick lines are the medians, and the white diamond points are the means. While the results show that the peak density of expertise is higher for the experienced users and then for novice programmers, a *Mann-Whitney U test* shows that the differences are not statistically significant, which very well may be due to our small sample size (a total of 45 users).

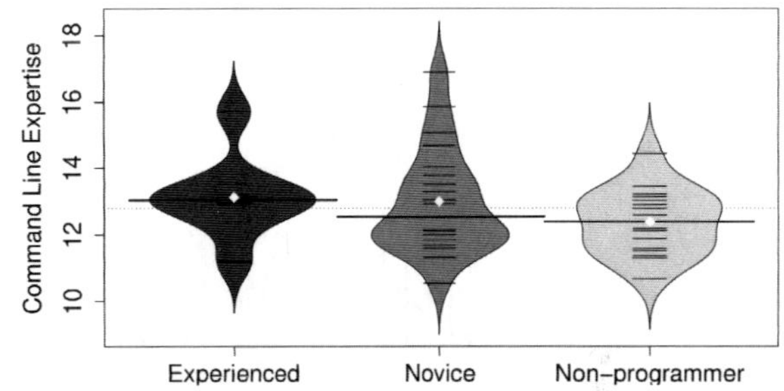

Figure 2. Beanplot of average command line expertise of each user group in Mahajan's dataset.

We use command line length as a metric to check the difference between the Mahajan and Greenberg datasets, as well as the difference between user groups in Greenberg. According to the left side of Figure 3, command line length 2 is the most frequent pattern for both Mahajan and Greenberg which is expected, as commands `ls` and `cd` have been used most often. For scientist and experienced programmers of Greenberg dataset, we found a similar pattern. But for novice programmers, command line length 10 is the most used, while command line length 9 has similar frequency with command line length 2. Upon investigation, we found that since novice programmers were learning how to program, they used commands `umacs` and `pix` (with corresponding arguments to reach line lengths 9 and 10) more often, which result in the different trend compared to scientists and experienced programmers.

3) High- and Low-Expertise Commands: Finally, we investigate the distribution of expertise for each dataset; in Figure 4, we show the result. We set the median of expertise values (which empirically is 11 across all three datasets) as the

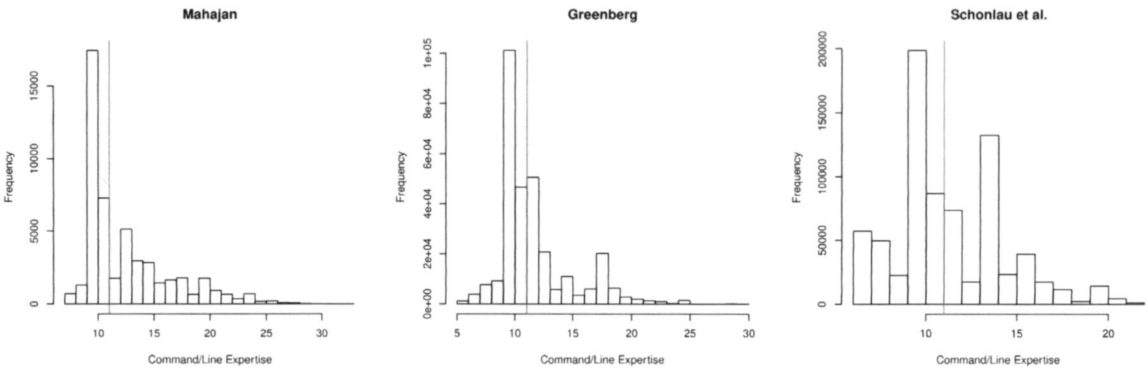

Figure 4. Distribution of expertise in commands. The red line indicates the median, which separates *low* and *high* expertise commands.

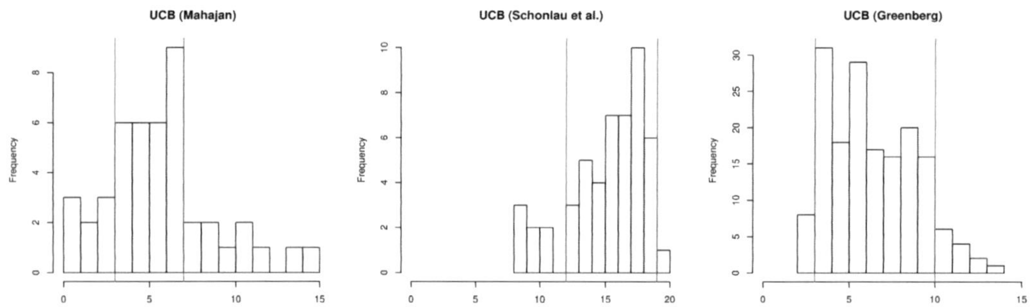

Figure 5. Histogram of number of categories of commands each user is active on. Being active in a category requires using one or more commands from that category at least 20 times.

threshold to separate *low* from *high* command line expertise. Note that, since the same value, 11, emerges as a natural threshold in all three distributions, we gain confidence in the stability of our command expertise metrics.

B. User Characteristics

1) User Category Breadth: We analyzed Mahajan's dataset as described above for UCB classes. The results are shown in Figure 5 (left). We observe 3 major patterns. First, there is a group of people who use 3 or fewer categories of commands. Second, there is a large group of people who use between 4 and 8 categories, and finally the group of people who use more than 8 categories. We name these classes *low*, *medium*, and *high* breadth classes respectively. In Mahajan's dataset, we found that 6 users are a member of low-breadth class, 10 are a member of high-breadth class, which leave the rest (29 users) in the medium-breadth class.

For Schonlau's dataset the pattern occurs again, but at different points. Here the *low* breadth class spans up to 12 categories and consists of 7 users. The *high* breadth class starts from 19 categories and consists of 1 user. This leave the *medium* group with 42 people and a range of 12 to 19 categories.

For the dataset of Greenberg, we still have similar pattern with different points. The *low* breadth class spans up to 3 categories and consists of 8 users. The *high* breadth class starts from 10 categories and consists of 29 users. Then the *medium* breadth class group with 131 users and a range between 3 to 10 categories. While the values are different, the pattern of two small classes with low and high breadth and a larger class of medium breadth is still prevalent.

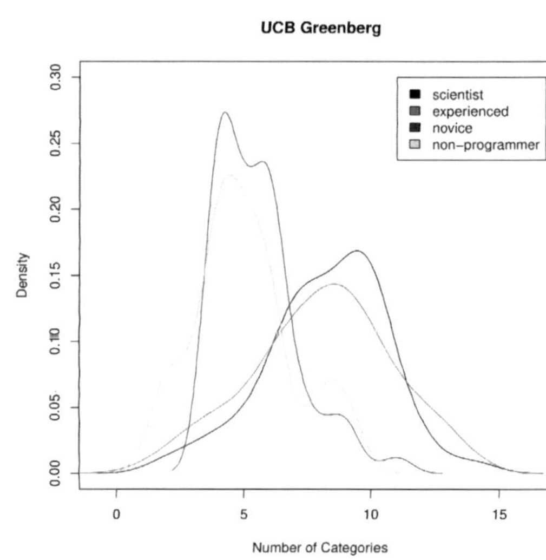

Figure 6. Kernel density function for the command category distribution of each user class in Greenberg's dataset.

We also analyzed category usage in the different user groups of Greenberg's dataset. Figure 6 shows the kernel density function for the command category distribution of each user group. We found that novice programmers and

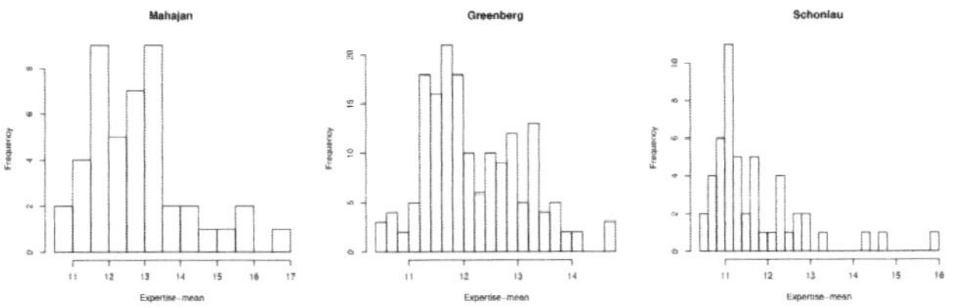

Figure 7. Histogram of mean command line expertise of each user is active on.

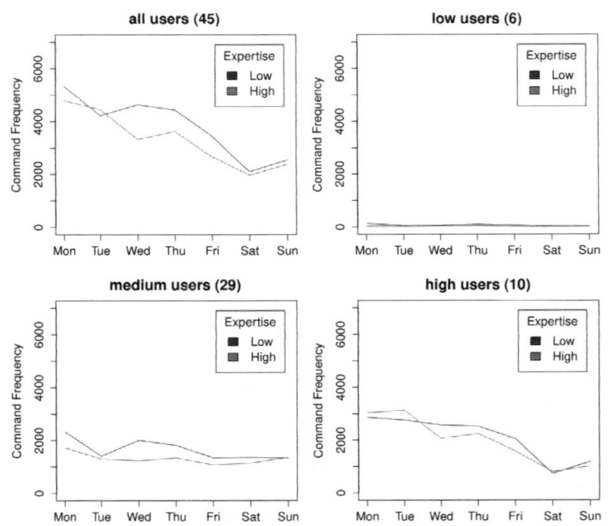

Figure 8. Frequency of low and high expertise commands used by different classes of users at different days of the week.

non programmers employ fewer command categories than scientists and experienced programmers, which is intuitive.

2) High- and Low-Expertise: We now show the results of command line expertise per user. Figure 7 shows the result. Greenberg and Schonlau datasets have similar trends, i.e., most users have only one peak value between 11 and 12; for the Mahajan dataset, we found similar trends, i.e., two peak values between 11 and 13. We believe the similarities across datasets validate our choice of expertise metrics.

C. Day-of-week Command Patterns

To understand temporal patterns for command usage, we studied Mahajan's dataset (the only dataset that come with timestamps). This process is performed for all users, and then for each breadth category separately.

Figure 8 shows the distribution of command usage over days of week. The red lines depict high expertise commands' frequency while the blue lines indicated low expertise commands' frequency. The week starts on Monday. While the frequency tends to decrease from Monday through Sunday, we need to split users into expertise levels to better understand trends. Interestingly: (a) low- and medium-expertise users show little variation (slight decrease) as the week progresses, while for high-expertise users the trend is clear and decreasing; (b) Sunday usage is higher than Saturday usage.

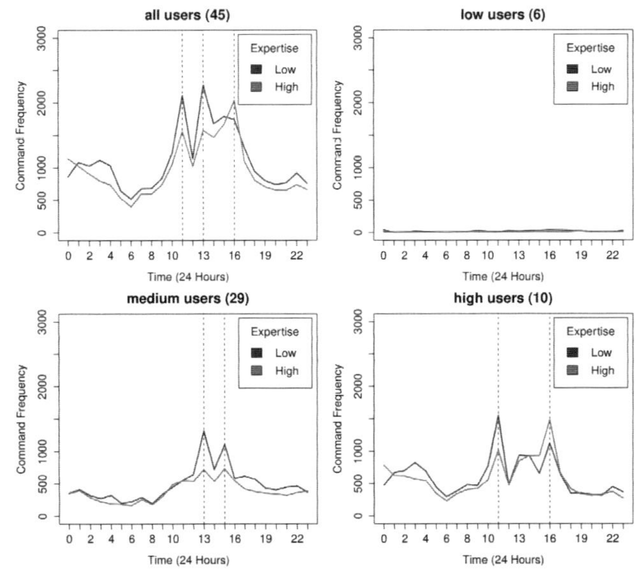

Figure 9. Frequency of low and high expertise commands used by different classes of users at different hours of the day.

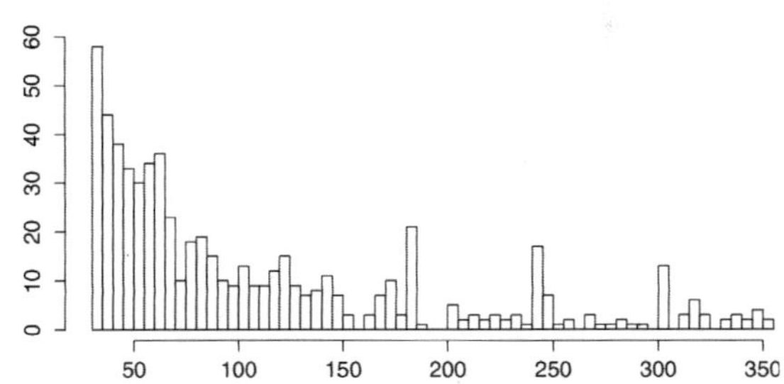

Figure 10. Histogram of temporal distance between consecutive commands for high-expertise users in the Mahajan dataset: x-axis is intercommand time in minutes, y-axis is frequency.

D. Time-of-day Command Patterns

The distribution of command usage over hours of day is shown in Figure 9. The red lines depict high expertise commands' frequency while the blue lines indicated low expertise commands' frequency. There is a clear spike in activity around 11 a.m. and a rise in activity from 1 p.m. to 4 p.m. But when we split the users based on UCB, we observe different patterns for medium and high breadth classes. The Medium breadth class shows spikes of activity around 1 p.m and 3 p.m., while the high breadth class shows a spike around 11 a.m., and a relatively high activity from 1 p.m. that peaks at 4 p.m.

E. Inter-command Time

We found that users interact with the shell in sessions, i.e., bursts of commands coming in rapid sequence, followed by long pauses. We studied inter-command time to get a sense as to how temporally close the commands are. Figure 10 illustrates this for high-expertise users in the Mahajan dataset. Note that the distribution of inter-command distances is highly skewed towards zero and has a very long tail (we trimmed both ends of the distribution — less than 30 minutes and more than 6 hours — in order to have a clearer view). As we can see in

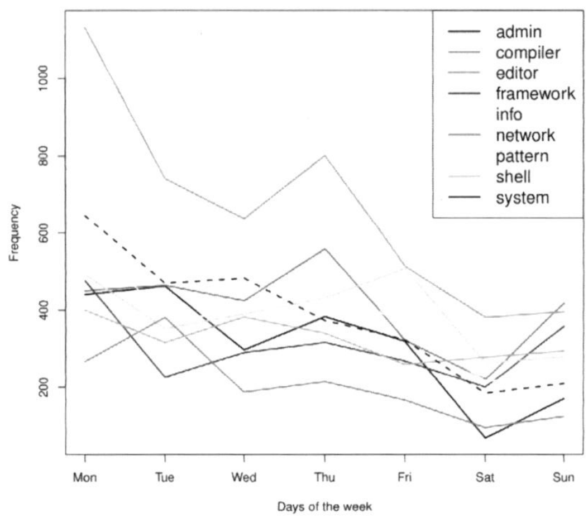

Figure 11. Frequency of several command categories used by all the users at different days of the week.

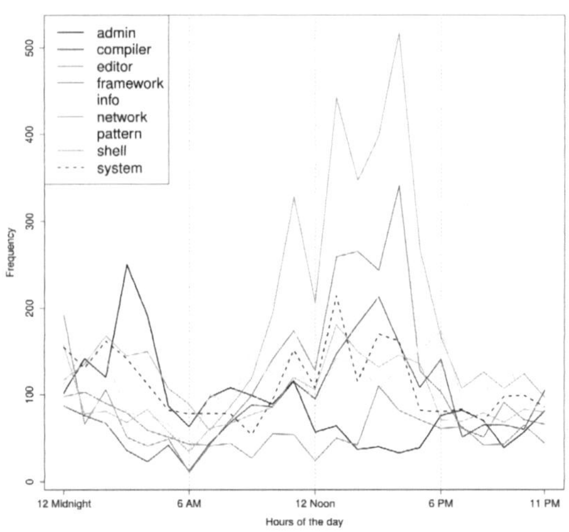

Figure 12. Frequency of several command categories used by all the users at different hours of the day.

the figure, the distribution within the defined range still looks mostly exponential.

F. Category Patterns

We also analyzed the usage pattern of categories. Figure 11 shows category frequency for each day of week: Monday and Thursday are the days with the highest activity. Moreover, "editor" is the most popular category.

Figure 12 shows the time-of-day results: 6 a.m. is the "quietest" time while there are usage spikes at 11 a.m. and 3 p.m.

VI. CONCLUSION

We have a performed a study on three sizable datasets of Unix command usage. This is the first study to operationalize command expertise and user expertise via several metrics. Based on these metrics, we found several interesting observations on both command and user characteristics that are consistent across datasets, which strengthens our belief that the metrics are stable. Finally, we performed a study on one of the datasets that reveals user behavior and command usage across time of day and day of week.

We believe that our definitions and findings can be used in various scenarios. Our command frequency analysis can be used in real-time to identify outliers, e.g., for masquerade detection. Behavioral patterns can be used to predict Unix user's behavior which helps improve Unix users' experience, from replacing long sequences of commands with scripts to reduce the potential for errors to scaling computing capacity and scheduling support staff. Being able to quantify expertise can be useful in comparing users or assessing how users learn.

ACKNOWLEDGMENTS

Research was sponsored by the Army Research Laboratory and was accomplished under Cooperative Agreement Number W911NF-13-2-0045 (ARL Cyber Security CRA). The views and conclusions contained in this document are those of the authors and should not be interpreted as representing the official policies, either expressed or implied, of the Army Research Laboratory or the U.S. Government. The U.S. Government is authorized to reproduce and distribute reprints for Government purposes notwithstanding any copyright notation here on.

REFERENCES

[1] "Usage share of operating systems," https://en.wikipedia.org/wiki/Usage_share_of_operating_systems#Market_share_by_category, Accessed: 2016-03-20.

[2] "Masquerade Attack," https://www.techopedia.com/definition/4020/masquerade-attack, Accessed: 2016-03-20.

[3] M. Schonlau, W. DuMouchel, W.-H. Ju, A. F. Karr, M. Theus, and Y. Vardi, "Computer intrusion: Detecting masquerades," Statistical science, 2001, pp. 58–74.

[4] H.-S. Kim and S.-D. Cha, "Empirical evaluation of svm-based masquerade detection using UNIX commands," Computers & Security, vol. 24, no. 2, 2005, pp. 160 – 168.

[5] R. Maxion and T. Townsend, "Masquerade detection using truncated command lines," in Dependable Systems and Networks, 2002. DSN 2002. Proceedings. International Conference on, 2002, pp. 219–228.

[6] B. Szymanski and Y. Zhang, "Recursive data mining for masquerade detection and author identification," in Information Assurance Workshop, 2004. Proceedings from the Fifth Annual IEEE SMC, June 2004, pp. 424–431.

[7] J. Seo and S. Cha, "Masquerade detection based on svm and sequence-based user commands profile," in Proceedings of the 2Nd ACM Symposium on Information, Computer and Communications Security, ser. ASIACCS '07, 2007, pp. 398–400.

[8] M. Latendresse, "Masquerade detection via customized grammars," in Detection of Intrusions and Malware, and Vulnerability Assessment, ser. Lecture Notes in Computer Science, 2005, vol. 3548, pp. 141–159.

[9] A. Mahajan, "Masquerade detection based on unix commands," master thesis, San Jose State University, 2012.

[10] S. Greenberg, "Using unix: Collected traces of 168 users," Advanced Technologies, The Alberta Research Council, 1988, pp. 1–13.

[11] S. Fitchett and A. Cockburn, "Accessrank: Predicting what users will do next," in Proceedings of the SIGCHI Conference on Human Factors in Computing Systems, ser. CHI '12. New York, NY, USA: ACM, 2012, pp. 2239–2242. [Online]. Available: http://doi.acm.org/10.1145/2207676.2208380

[12] R. Chinchani, A. Muthukrishnan, M. Chandrasekaran, and S. Upadhyaya, "Racoon: rapidly generating user command data for anomaly detection from customizable template," in Computer Security Applications Conference, 2004. 20th Annual, Dec 2004, pp. 189–202.

Towards Semantic Analysis of Training-Learning Relationships within Human-Machine Interactions

Farshad Badie
Center for Linguistics, Aalborg University,
Aalborg, Denmark. Email: badie@id.aau.dk

Abstract— **In this article First-Order Predicate Logic (FOL) is employed for analysing some relationships between human beings and machines. Based on FOL, we will be conceptually and logically concerned with semantic analysis of training-learning relationships in human-machine interaction. The central focus is on formal semantics and its role in the 'relationship' between human beings and machines. The analysed relationships between a human being and a machine will support our thoughts on and contemplations over the HowNess of establishing formal semantics within human-machine interaction.**

Keywords: **Semantics; Training-Learning Relation; Human-Machine Interaction; Predicate Logic.**

I. INTRODUCTION AND MOTIVATION

Machine Learning is a subfield of Artificial Intelligence and Computer Science. A machine learning approach attempts to develop appropriate procedures and techniques that allow machines to improve the productivity of their performances concerning a given goal, see [8]. In [2], we have focused on conceptual analysis of human-machine interactions and we have provided a conceptual and epistemological junction between human beings' minds and machines' knowledge bases. According to [6], and relying on our epistemological approach, the multilevel interactions between a human being (as a trainer) and a machine (as a metaphorical learner) could be seen as a radical constructivist account of human cognition, realisation and comprehension. Let me bring up some fundamentals in order to clarify our conception and way of thinking about the metaphorical use of 'learning'. In the expression 'machine learning', the word 'learning' has been utilised as a binary predicate with the word machine. Learning as a binary predicate has been asserted to be a role that is being performed by a machine. Thus, the act of 'learning' for a machine could be interpreted as a reflection of the [human] learning phenomenon in machines. In fact, machine learning is a metaphor that attempts to simulate the learning phenomenon with regard to the ingredients, components and concepts that are concerned with effective and successful learning processes in the real world. Let me bring the notion 'concept' into our explanation and be more specific on this research's objectives. 'Machine concept learning' approaches try to provide appropriate realisable logical descriptions for a human being's constructed concepts and their interrelationships after being transformed (from a human's mind into a machine's knowledge base) with regard to their structures and to their interrelationships to the world. Note that 'concept' is a complicated term. We see a concept as a linkage between a human's mental images of parts of reality (as things/phenomena), on the one hand, and a human's linguistic expressions and statements concerning those things/phenomena on the other hand, see [4]. In [2], we have explained that concepts are transformed in order to be represented and expressed within a machine's knowledge base. For instance, concepts can be reflected in order to be represented in the form of the entities as classes of individuals and objects. In other words, a concept is understood and is seen as an idea that can be transformed into a hypothesis in order to correspond to a distinct entity [and, respectively, to a group of entities] or to its [and their] essential attributes, features, characteristics and properties. The hypotheses can describe multiple theories based on terminologies and world descriptions. Accordingly, they support inferential and reasoning processes and satisfy multiple conditions for definitions of truth with regard to interpretation functions.

In this article, we will employ First-Order [Predicate] Logic in order to focus on relationships between human beings and machines. FOL allows us to make arbitrarily complex relationships between different objects of a system. Based on FOL we will be conceptually and logically concerned with semantic analysis of training-learning relationships in human-machine interactions. We shall stress that our main focus is on the semantics of the 'relationships' between human beings and machines. The analysed relationships between a human being and a machine will support our thoughts about the HowNess of establishing a [formal] semantics concerning human-machine interactions. According to [3], semantics is the study of the meanings, and the relation of signs to the objects to which the signs are applicable.

In the following sections you will be offered the following: (III) The Logical Specification of the Notion of Hypothesis, (IV) Preliminaries: Predicate Logic and Semantics in FOL, (V) Formal Representation and Semantic Analysis of 'Training-Learning' and (VI) Conclusions and Future Work.

II. THE LOGICAL SPECIFICATION OF THE NOTION OF HYPOTHESIS

Based on Predicate Logic and focusing on Description Logics [1], an unary predicate is supposed to be logically equivalent to a concept. For instance, we can consider the unary predicate *Set* as a concept in order to employ it in concept learning (concept expression) processes. Additionally, a concept can be logically described by a hypothesis, see [5][8]. For instance, the concept *Set* can be described as *a collection of the distinct things* in order to provide a foundation for a hypnosis. And, for instance, {a , 5, Science, ∞, Σ} and {Book, •} could be the positive (constructive) examples of the proposed hypothesis, and '{3 , T' and 'Y' could be the negative examples of the proposed hypothesis. In our opinion, (*i*) analysing the supportive inferential processes on a hypothesis, and (*ii*) focusing on world descriptions using generated hypotheses relying on defined terminologies, could collectively determine the applications of predicates, and, subsequently, the applications of terms and statements. Conceptually and logically the hypotheses focus on describing the predicates. Then they are expected to describe the same attributes, characteristics and properties. According to [8], a hypothesis as a logical description of a concept, arises during a machine learning process. Actually, it is a tentative explanation of why the objects are members (or non members) of the concept. A characteristic feature of most concept learning approaches is the use of background knowledge. In concept learning with background knowledge, a machine, with regard to the given set of training examples and background knowledge, will focus on hypothesis generation.

III. PRELIMINARIES: PREDICATE LOGIC

The Propositional Logic and its formulae (i.e., the formal and mathematical relationships or rules expressed in Propositional Logic's symbols) are constructed based on atomic objects. Note that the atomic objects, and, accordingly, the propositional formulae, could only be either true or false. First-order Predicate Logic (FOL) is constructed over propositional logic by seeing objects as the elements of sets and by applying universal and existential quantifications (restrictions). That's why some logicians and mathematicians see FOL as Quantification Theory, see [7] [9]. FOL allows us for making arbitrarily complex (specified) relationships between various objects. There are two kinds of symbols in FOL; (*i*) logical symbols and (*ii*) non logical symbols. The set of logical symbols in FOL is {Conjunction ($\wedge$), Disjunction ($\vee$), Negation ($\neg$), Implication ($\rightarrow$), Bi-conditional ($\longleftrightarrow$), Equality ($=$), Existential Restriction ($\exists$), Universal Restriction ($\forall$), Tautology ($\top$), Contradiction ($\bot$), Parentheses and brackets}. We shall stress that logical symbols always have the same meaning. It means that we are not allowed to interpret them and assign multiple values and definitions to them. The non logical symbols are represented in the following forms:

(i) *Constant Symbols.* For instance, *john*, *0* and *blue* are constant symbols.

(ii) *Unary Predicates.* In $P(x)$ and $Q(y)$, P and Q denote unary predicates. Also, x and y are variables (multiple constant symbols). These variables are the instances of P and Q. For instance, *Person*(*john*) denotes that 'John is a person'.

(iii) *Binary Predicates* (*Relations*). $R(m,n)$ is a binary predicate and makes a relation between two variables m and n. For example, *Equals*(m,n) can represent the 'equality between m and n' (i.e., m equals n).

(iv) *Function Symbols.* $f(x)$ is a function that operates the variable x. For example, *mother*(*john*) can represent the 'mother of john'.

At this point we shall draw your attention to the fact that the meanings of the non logical symbols are dependent on human being' interpretations. So, we need to interpret the non logical symbols to produce meanings and to clarify what we mean by them.

A. Semantics in FOL

In formal languages semantics is the study and analysis of the meanings of symbols and signifiers. Semantics focuses on the relationships between the signifiers of any language. In fact, the formal semantics employs the products of the human beings' interpretations in order to produce meanings. In fact, we need to consider the interpretation I that consists of (*i*) the domain of interpretation (that is a non empty set like D) and (*ii*) an interpretation function (like $\cdot^I$) that interprets the domain D in order to analyse the formal semantics of a term in FOL. For example, D = {Bob, Mary, Julian} could be interpreted (D^I) to represent the list of three PhD researchers in Metaphysics. Obviously, a meaning has been produced. Formally, the interpretation function assigns to every atomic unary predicate P (e.g., *Apple*, *Red*), a set like $P^I \subseteq D^I$. For instance, the interpretation of *Apple* ($Apple^I$) could express that "*Apple* is a Fruit and could be eaten". Also, the interpretation function assigns to every atomic binary predicate R (e.g., *Equals*) a binary predicate $R^I \subseteq D^I \times D^I$. For instance, the interpretation of *Equals* ($Equals^I$) could express that "*Equals* describes a kind of alignment between its right-hand side and its left-hand side".

Here we feel the need to describe the logical conception of equivalence relationship between two predicates. Two unary predicates (either atomic or non atomic) P and Q are equivalent ($P \equiv Q$), when for all interpretations I we have $P^I = Q^I$. On the other hand, they are not equivalent when there exists an (at least one) interpretation like J such that $P^J \neq Q^J$.

IV. TRAINING-LEARNING: FORMAL REPRESENTATION

In this section, the central focus is on conceptual and logical analysis of formal semantics within a training-learning relationship in the context of human-machine interactions. This research aims at investigating where the formal semantics come from and when it appears within a relationships between a human being and a machine. Considering the human being as the trainer and the machine as the metaphorical learner, accept the following axioms. These axioms focus on the non logical symbols of our formalism. They are the main building blocks of this research.

- The symbols h and m denote *human being* an *machine* respectively. They both represent constant symbols.

- The most significant unary predicates in our formalism are *Learner* and *Trainer.* Also, *Learner*(m) and *Trainer*(h) represent two unary predicate assertions (world descriptions over unary predicates). They demonstrate that the constant symbol m is an instance of the unary predicate *Learner* and the constant symbol h is an instance of the unary predicate *Trainer.* In other words, m is a *Learner* and h is a *Trainer.*

- Considering the unary predicates *Learner* and *Trainer*, the binary predicates *TrainerOf* and *LearnerOf* are defined. Consequently, *TrainerOf*(h,m) and *LearnerOf*(m,h) are two binary predicate assertions (or relation assertions, or world descriptions over binary predicates). The first relation describes that the human being h is the trainer of the machine m and the second one describes that the machine m is the learner of the human being h.

- Two functions *trainer*(m) and *learner*(h) are defined in order to represent the '*trainer of m*' and the '*learner of h*'.

A. Semantic Analysis

According to the proposed axioms and to the non logical symbols, we shall claim that the binary predicate *TrainerOf*(h,m) logically produces (implies) the equality *trainer*(m) = h. In fact,

$$TrainerOf(h,m) \quad \textbf{(i)}$$
$$\Rightarrow trainer(m) = h\,. \quad \textbf{(ii)}$$

The equation (*ii*) expresses the fact that the trainer of the machine m has been realised to be the person h. Note that this equality is produced with regard to our interpretation. In fact, it has been achieved based on the interpreted non logical symbols. Therefore, the equation (*i*) as a binary predicate, describes the interpreted relation between *trainer*(m) and h. We may claim that this equality is the root of the formal semantics within a training-learning relationship. The binary predicate equality describes that the meanings of its right-hand side and its left-hand side are the same. Consequently, the meaning of *trainer*(m) and h are the same. So, we shall emphasise that the achieved equality [as a binary predicate in FOL] aligns the meaning of *trainer*(m) and the meaning of h. Then we have:

$$Equals\,(trainer(m)\,,\,h). \quad \textbf{(iii)}$$

We shall maintain that the binary predicate (*iii*) has provided a supportive background for introducing the formal semantics. Considering this binary predicate, the function *trainer*(m) (as a non logical symbol) and the individual h (as a constant symbol) have been supposed to have the same meanings. Additionally, regarding the commutative laws, 'the trainer of m is h' and 'h is the trainer of m' are logically equivalent [and, thus, meaningfully, they are equal]. Consequently, 'the trainer of m implies h' and 'h implies the trainer of m'. Therefore:

$$trainer(m) = h \Rightarrow$$
$$(\,trainer(m) \rightarrow h\,) \wedge (\,h \rightarrow trainer(m)\,). \quad \textbf{(iv)}$$

The logical term (*iv*) is inherently equal to:

$$(function \rightarrow constant) \wedge (constant \rightarrow function). \quad \textbf{(v)}$$

We have already deduced that the term '*a function symbol implies a constant symbol and a constant symbol implies a function symbol*' supports the analysis of our objective. Note that the term (*iv*) has been deduced based on the binary predicate *TrainerOf*(h,m) (or (*i*)). Then, there is a bi-conditional relation between (*i*) and (*iv*). Therefore:

$$TrainerOf(h,m) \longleftrightarrow$$
$$[\,(\,trainer(m) \rightarrow h\,) \wedge (\,h \rightarrow trainer(m)\,)\,]. \quad \textbf{(vi)}$$

Equivalently:

$$TrainerOf(h,m) \rightarrow$$
$$[\,(trainer(m) \rightarrow h\,) \wedge (\,h \rightarrow trainer(m)\,)\,]$$
$$\text{AND}$$
$$[\,(\,trainer(m) \rightarrow h\,) \wedge (\,h \rightarrow trainer(m)\,)\,] \rightarrow$$
$$TrainerOf\,(h,m). \quad \textbf{(vii)}$$

The logical term (*vii*) is structurally equal to:

$$\text{Relation} \rightarrow$$
$$[\,(\text{ function} \rightarrow \text{constant}\,) \wedge (\text{ constant} \rightarrow \text{function}\,)\,]$$
$$\text{AND}$$
$$[\,(\text{ function} \rightarrow \text{constant}\,) \wedge (\text{ constant} \rightarrow \text{function}\,)\,] \rightarrow$$
$$\text{Relation}. \quad \textbf{(viii)}$$

In Figure 1, this logical conclusion has been figured out.

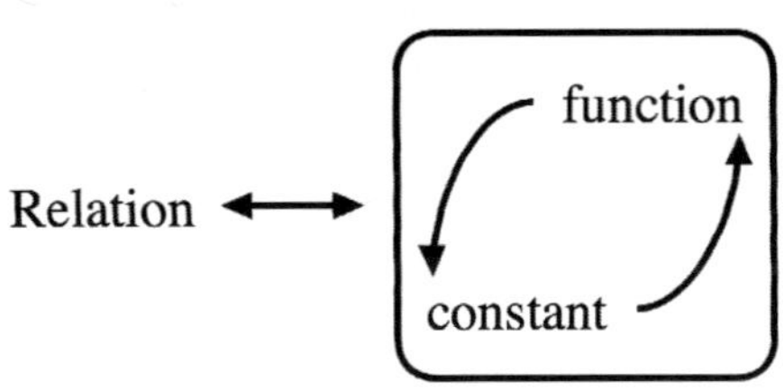

Fig.1. The General Structure of Semantics within Relationships Between Human Being & Machine

Conceptually, taking the afore-mentioned conclusions into consideration, we need to focus on four fundamental relationships: **(I)** The training relationship between human and machine (from human into machine), (**II**) The learning relationship between machine and human (from machine into human), (**III**) The iterative loops between human and machine (from human into machine and from machine into human), and (**IV**) The iterative loops between machine and human (from machine into human and from human into machine). Therefore, the formal semantics of training-learning relationship in the context of human-machine interactions is definable over four constructive implications:

I. Implying the 'iterative loops between human and machine' from the 'training relation between human and machine'. Then:

$$TrainerOf(h,m) \rightarrow [\ (\ trainer(m) \rightarrow h\ ) \land (\ h \rightarrow trainer(m)\ )\ ]. \quad \textbf{(ix)}$$

II. Implying the 'iterative loops between machine and human' from the 'learning relation between machine and human'. Then:

$$LearnerOf(m,h) \rightarrow [\ (\ learner(h) \rightarrow m\ ) \land (\ m \rightarrow learner(h)\ )\ ]. \quad \textbf{(x)}$$

III. Implying the 'training relationship between human and machine' from the 'iterative loops between human and machine'. This item is the inverse of the item (1). Then:

$$[\ (\ trainer(m) \rightarrow h\ ) \land (\ h \rightarrow trainer(m)\ )\ ] \rightarrow TrainerOf(h,m). \quad \textbf{(xi)}$$

IV. Implying the 'learning relationship between machine and human' from the 'iterative loop between machine and human'. This item is the inverse of the item (2). Then:

$$[\ (\ learner(h) \rightarrow m\ ) \land (\ m \rightarrow learner(h)\ )\ ] \rightarrow LearnerOf(m,h). \quad \textbf{(xii)}$$

Therefore:

- Fundamental **I** expresses: [(*Training Relation*) → (*Training Function* ⟷ *Learner Constant*)] .
- Fundamental **III** expresses: [(*Training Function* ⟷ *Learner Constant*) → (*Training Relation*)] .
- Fundamental **II** expresses: [(*Learning Relation*) → (*Learning Function* ⟷ *Trainer Constant*)] .
- Fundamental **IV** expresses: [(*Learning Function* ⟷ *Trainer Constant*) → (*Learning Relation*)].

According to the deduced results, we shall conclude that (**I**) the training relations (from human into machine) support the interrelationship between 'the act of training' and 'the machine', (**II**) the learning relations (from machine into human) support the interrelationships between 'machine learning' and 'human', (**III**) the interrelationship between 'the act of training' and 'the machine' support the training relation (from human into machine), and finally, (**IV**) the interrelationship between 'machine learning' and 'human' support the learning relation (from machine into human).

V. CONCLUSION AND FUTURE WORK

In this article, we have focused on First-Order formalisms in order to think of relationships between human beings and machines. The context of this research has been 'the training-learning relation between human and machine'. We have focused on logical description and logical analysis of the training-learning relations within human-machine interactions. The analysed relationships between human beings and machines have supported our thoughts about the HowNess of producing the formal semantics. This research has formed a building block of our PhD researches, which are dealing with Semantic Analysis of Constructivist Concept Leaning within Mentor-Learner-Machine Interactions. We have concluded four fundamentals that conceptualise meanings and express the structure of the formal semantics within relationships. Subsequently, we have concluded that the implications between 'relations' and 'the interrelationship of functions and constant symbols' support the formal semantics of the training-learning relationships. The conclusion of this research has prepared a strong backbone for our future research. In future research, we will focus on semantic analysis of human concept learning with regard to the semantics of her/his relationships with machines. We will also focus on the formal semantics of concept transformations from humans' minds into machine's knowledge bases with regard to our research in [10]. We will also work on semantic analysis of hypothesis generation. Human being generates a hypothesis in order to make it corresponded to a distinct entity or to its essential attributes, characteristics and properties. Semantically we will focus on an important form of HowNess: 'How do hypotheses determine the applications of the predicates?'

REFERENCES

1. F. Baader, D. Calvanese, D. McGuinness, D. Nardi, and P. Patel-Schneider, "The Description Logic Handbook: Theory, Implementation and Applications", Cambridge University Press, 2010.
2. F. Badie, "Concept Representation Analysis in The Context of Human-Machine Interactions", The 14th International Conference on e-Society Proceedings, 2016, in press.
3. S. Blackburn, "The Oxford Dictionary of Philosophy", Oxford University Press, UK, 2008.
4. H. Götzsche, "Deviational Syntactic Structures", Bloomsbury Academic: London / New Delhi / New York / Sydney, 2013.
5. J. Lehmann, "Learning OWL Class Expressions", Leipziger Beiträge zur Informatik, 2010.
6. G. McIntyre Boyd, "Conversation Theory". Handbook of Research on Educational Communications and Technology, 2004..
7. E. Mendelson, "Introduction to Mathematical Logic (3.ed.)", Chapman and Hall. 1987.
8. T. Mitchell, "Machine learning", in Machine Learning, Kluwer Academic Publishers, 1997.
9. H. J. Ohlbach, "Predicate Logic Hacker Tricks", J. Autom. Reasoning 1 (4), 1985, 435-440.
10. F. Badie, "Logical Characterisation of Concept Transformations From Human into Machine Relying on Predicate Logic", The Ninth International Conference on Advances in Computer-Human Interactions, Venice, Italy, 2016, in press.

Reduction of Dental Anxiety and Pain in Children using Robots

Mine Yasemin[1], Yelda Kasımoğlu[2], Simin Kocaaydın[2], Emine Karslı[2], Elif Bahar Tuna İnce[2], Gökhan İnce[1]
[1]Department of Computer Enginnering, Istanbul Technical University, Istanbul, Turkey
[2]Department of Pediatric Dentistry, Faculty of Dentistry, Istanbul University, Istanbul, Turkey
{yaseminm, gokhan.ince}@itu.edu.tr, {kasimogluy, kocaaydins, karslie, ebtuna}@istanbul.edu.tr

***Abstract*—In this study, we aim to use humanoid robots to implement a techno-psychological distraction technique for children between 4-10 years of age in order to reduce their anxiety and stress-related pain during their dental treatment. A multi-modal system supporting audio-based dialogues, videos, gestures and expressions based on face, head, arm, body movements have been developed for a robot. We have employed the Wizard-of-Oz technique, a popular approach in human robot interaction research. The effectiveness of the system is shown by carrying out experiments on two groups of children; one group whose treatment is conducted by the dentist's own skills alone, the other whose treatment is conducted by a dentist with the assistance of the robot. In order to evaluate the robot's effect on the anxiety and fear of children during these experiments, procedures with no anesthesia (not requiring the use of needles) have been carried out. The system has been evaluated subjectively by applying a variety of questionnaires to patients, and dentists as well as objectively by measuring patient's heart rates.**

***Keywords*—Robotics, dental treatment, WoZ experimentation, human robot interaction, multi-modal interaction, healthcare robotics.**

I. INTRODUCTION

Dental treatment-related anxiety is a common case in dentistry, especially affecting children and causing problems during their dental treatment. It is commmon that some children having oral/dental pathology do not comply to have a treatment. Some general methods preferred by healthcare workers are wearing colored and patterned clothes, and using clown doctors to encourage children, to distract their mind and to make medical procedures more fun [1]. Listening to music or watching cartoons are common procedures to relieve the pain and anxiety in children [2]. The goal of all these approach is to reduce unpleasant perceptions, to avoid negative behaviors and escaping from the treatment. In this way, completion of treatment without the need of such advanced medical techniques like sedation and general anesthesia is targeted. These systems may not always be effective enough to distract a child's attention away from pain. According to these analyses, there is obviously a need of a more comprehensive system to enable a child to engage more deeply during medical procedures. Nowadays, combining visual, auditory and tactile stimuli by making use of multi-sensory strategies is believed to provide a greater impact on pain than using a single stimulus. In this study, we aim to direct a child's attention from a painful stimulus to a more entertaining and amusing direction during their dental treatment using a humanoid robot and by making the therapy session less problematic and more comfortable in order to provide much cozier treatment environment to the dentist.

Moreover, instead of the pediatric dentists communicating with their patients by asking standard questions before treatment, the computer technologies (animation or robot), can take over these repetitive tasks. As a result, the dentist's chair time and energy loss can be minimized. It is targeted to develop positive behavior and increase treatment success.

For the past several years, robotics has been applied in the field of healthcare in various ways. Social and medical robots in this domain aim to motivate and encourage humans to keep up with the medical routine and to provide psychological therapies. The aim of this study is to provide an entertaining, and relaxing environment to the children patients with the help of robots in order to develop positive behaviors in children resulting to an increase in the success of dental treatment and to the circumvention of the high cost and risk of complications such as sedation and general anesthesia. Therefore, to the knowledge of the authors, our work is the first study in our country and in the world, which investigates the effect of child-robot interaction in reducing pain and stress during dental treatment.

II. LITERATURE REVIEW

Dental fear is an emotional reaction against the frightening stimulus during dental treatment. *Dental anxiety* is defined as unease about the fearful events that occur during dental treatment and as a feeling of loss of control accordingly. Negative expectations due to earlier experiences, negative behavior within the family, a feeling of anxiety about the pain, failed and painful experiences that occurred in earlier treatments were reported as the most important factors in feeling fear [3]. Factors associated with dental fear include age, the attitude of parents towards dental treatment, the bad experiences transmitted by those close to the child, concern about sensation of pain and past experiences of the child [3], [4], [5]. In various research works carried out on the human test subjects, the incidence of dental fear, anxiety and behavior management problems in children have been reported to range between 20-74% in several countries (74% in Brazil [6], 30.6% in Singapore [7], 27.02% in Croatia [8], 25.6% in Turkey [9], 23.1% in Sweden [10], 22.2% in Finland [11], 20.6% in Taiwan [12]).

Management of pain during dental procedures is crucial to the success of treatment. Prevention of pain is made possible by a healthy relationship between dentist and patient, establishing trust, elimination of fear and anxiety, and the creation of a positive attitude for future visits. However, the subjective nature of pain perception may alter the patients' response to treatment and prevent the correct diagnosis and treatment approaches of physicians by affecting the accurate assessment scale against painful stimuli [13].

A variety of approaches have been proposed to prevent or completely eliminate children's dental fear. The purpose of directing behaviors of the child during treatment is escaping from unpleasant and failed experiences and to ensure that the child accepts the treatment easier. The physician treating the child should be knowledgeable about the various behavior management techniques and be able to predict the child's response to treatment by properly evaluating the data regarding child's developmental level, temperament and attitude during the operation. In this sense, the behavior of dentists and accompanying dental staff plays an active role in determining children's attitudes to the treatment [14].

Several techniques have been developed to perform dental care in children with success by applying basic behavioral methods including tell-show-apply technique, self control, positive orientation and diverting attention [15]. Especially recently, unusual stimuli and technological equipments started to be utilized in the process of attracting attention to another point. In this case, the attempt is to prevent negative behavior or escaping from treatment by reducing the unpleasant perception. In this way, it is planned to complete the treatment without the need for advanced behavioral techniques such as sedation, general anesthesia.

Although there are studies indicating that listening to music and watching cartoons reduce pain and anxiety in children exposed to medical treatment [1], [2], [16], [17], such systems deprived of interactivity. Stimulating the child as just listener/viewer is not always sufficient to be effective to divert the child's attention away from the pain.

Today, it is believed that combining multisensorial strategies with visual, auditory, and tactile stimuli (e.g. using robots) provide a greater impact on pain than the effect of a single stimulus. Beran et al. have first used robots in distraction during vaccination for a study performed on 57 children between 4-9 years of age [18]. While nurses were vaccinating, it was planned that the robot interacted with the child. Compared with control group, it has been shown that children with the robots next to them during vaccination smiled more. After this experience, parents have noticed that their children remembered the robot more than the needle and they wanted the robot to be present for the next vaccinations. Robots have been found quite fun, and helpful for diversion of a child's attention and also useful for enabling children to feel less pain and anxiety during painful medical procedures [19].

In another study, in the bilateral meetings held on 21 children between 7-9 years of age, the mechanisms of communication with humans and robots were compared [20]. Talking with children has been performed by an adult in the first group and by a robot in the other group. As a result of analysis of child behavior during the bilateral talks, it has been observed that children in robot group have made eye contact more and talked for longer. Researchers have reported that robot technology can be utilized in the field of social services and healthcare applications, where robots are superior to people in contact with children.

There is also a study aimed at increasing children's health information using robots, in which children with Type-I diabetes between 8 and 12 years of age have been subjected to quizzes via robots [21]. The study has shown that children have been motivated, had fun while answering questions and their level of knowledge about diabetes was increased in this way.

Wizard-of-Oz (WoZ) is an approach whereby a human operator, unknown to the participants, operates a robot. This method, used for full teleoperation or for partial control, enables simulating and modeling the interaction and allows the collection of data and experimenting without relying on specific system components. In child-robot interaction studies which use this method, the wizard speaks with the children through the robot [22].

Based on these findings, it is observed that there is a need of more comprehensive and robust system that can make a child busy during medical procedures. Our goals in this study are, to divert child's attention to a more entertaining direction and to provide more comfortable environment to the dentist during dental treatment.

III. EXPERIMENTS

A. Participants

33 children (21 boys, 12 girls) were recruited for this study, ranging in age from 4 to 10 years old. The tests were run at a clinic in the Department of Pediatric Dentistry, Faculty of Dentistry in Istanbul University.

The inclusion criteria of the children into the experiment were the following:

- First time patients to the clinic.
- Lacking of dental treatment experience before.
- Not having pyhsical or mental disabilities.
- Not having long term bleeding or pain in teeth.
- Being given restorative or endodontic treatment plan by a dentist.
- Being accompanied by at least one parent.
- Not having any genetic syndrome or a serious systemic disease.
- Agreeing to fill out the questionnaire (both by the children or parents).

B. Hardware and Software

The robot selected for this study was IRobi, shown in Figure 1. IRobi has been developed by Yujin Robot company. It is equipped with a tablet computer, which can play videos and animations on the front panel. It can move its head, arms, and wheels, but does not change its position despite of having this ability thanks to its wheels. It has 3 DOFs (Degree of Freedom) on its head and 1 DOF on each arm. The robot has facial LEDS as a part of its own hardware system and can display five types of facial expressions: shy, disappointed, neutral, happy, and surprised. It can express various emotions with two LCD eyes and LED dot matrices on its mouth and cheeks, and react to human touch by five kinds of sensor.

Fig. 1. IRobiQ

There are many studies that IRobi helps children accelerate their learning language and speaking education [23], [24]. In this study, the robot was programmed to motivate the patient during the treatment and support the interaction with the child by performing short-time movements such as face, head and arm gestures or using audio and videos. Irobi asks children questions, gets responses and allows them to make choices on LCD screen.

The robot behaviors as well as dentistry animations and songs have been integrated to the robot by using ROCOS Studio. We have also prepared multimedia content in Adobe Flash to strengthen the interaction between the children and the robot.

C. Measures

Ethical committee approval for this study was taken from Faculty of Medicine, Istanbul University. A set of questionnaires measuring levels of pain and anxiety are applied in both pre and post session to each participant and their parents in order to assess the effects of robot assistance and basic intervention methods. Some questionnaires were administered to explore the feelings of the child during the interactions, how they perceived the robot as well as their mood during the interaction [25].

Before the procedure, it is required to fill the questionnaire to measure the child's anxiety levels. Thus, an experimenter explains the research protocol in detail to the children and their parents admitted to clinics and ask them to complete the consent forms. The consent was filled by the children and their accompanying parent in the waiting room of the clinic. After the consent was granted, parents were asked to primarily answer demographic questions, then the questions related to their children's familiarity to robots and computer technologies.

After the child entered the room, the Facial Image Scale (FIS) was administered [26]. The FIS is a measure to assess the state of children's dental anxiety and comprises a row of five faces ranging from very happy to very unhappy as given in Fig. 2. This scale is scored by giving a value of 1 to the most positive affect and 5 to the most negative affect face. The children were asked "How do you feel right now?" and were guided to show their response by pointing one of the faces. Approval studies have shown that it is a suitable measure for assessing the children's strongest expression of pain and fear sensation during the dental procedure, i.e. both in the waiting room and while sitting on the dental chair. Each child gave his/her own response independently although their parents or researchers help them in reading the instructions for children when necessary [18].

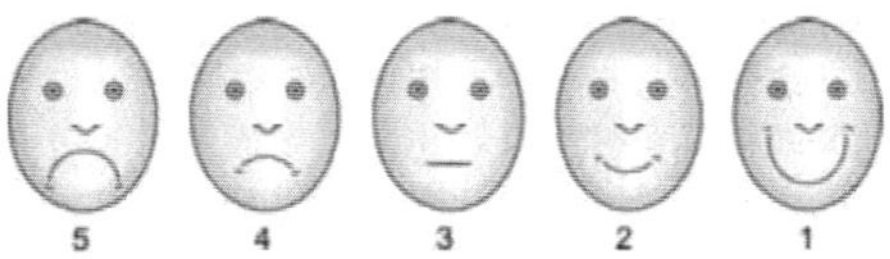

Fig. 2. Facial Image Scale (FIS) and the questionnaire used to assess dental fear and anxiety

Before beginning treatment, the dentist rated the child's behaviour on Frankl's Behaviour Rating Scale (FBRS), which is one of the more reliable and frequently used behavior rating systems in both clinical dentistry and research [27]. The FBRS categorises the child's behaviour as either one of the following: definitely positive (4), positive (3), negative (2) or definitely negative (1). This evaluation was also completed by the dentist at the end of the treatment session. Definitely negative (1) represents refusal of treatment, negative (2) means reluctance to accept treatment, positive (3) shows that the child accepted the treatment but he/she was cautious and definitely positive (4) corresponds to good rapport with dentist, the child was enjoying the dental procedure.

Anxiety level was also recorded before, during and after treatment in terms of physiological pulse rate (bpm) by using a finger type pulse measuring device (Pulse Oximeter). In the robot group, apart from measuring the children's anxiety and behaviour, we administered the question, "Would you want to have the robot in your next treatment session?", to the children. Responses were given on a 5-point scale from "not at all (1)" to "very much (5)" [18].

D. Procedure

The children's treatment plans were determined based on the first inspection carried out by specialist dentists. All children are exposed to the same dental treatment in the same clinic environment. While first patient group has been treated only by the dentist (control group, n=17), the second group has been treated by a robot accompanied by the dentist (robot group, n=16). Both groups will be subject to previously determined standard dental treatment. After clinical setting is introduced in both groups, the treatment phase starts.

Children's treatment type is divided into subgroups, according to predetermined treatment needs: 1) dental treatment of first group will be carried out without local anesthesia (restorative treatment), 2) dental treatment of second group will be applied local anesthesia (endodontic treatment). Although the prescribed average duration of treatment is 15 minutes for restorative treatment, endodontic treatment is set to 30 minutes. Treatments are planned to be completed in a single session. According to routine clinical procedures, parents were not allowed near children during treatment. In addition, all sessions will be videotaped with cameras fixed at two different locations.

Treatment of first group also called control group in the study, was performed in the routine clinical procedure. The dentist provided information about the clinic setting, equipments and processes. As a result of feedback received from the child, dentist applied the corresponding therapy using basic behavior techniques as appropriate. In the second group, or robot group, the robot was seated on a platform near the dentist at the child's eye level as in Fig. 3. The robot chatted with the child, instructed the child before and during the treatment, distracted, encouraged her/him, and played animations favoured by the children.

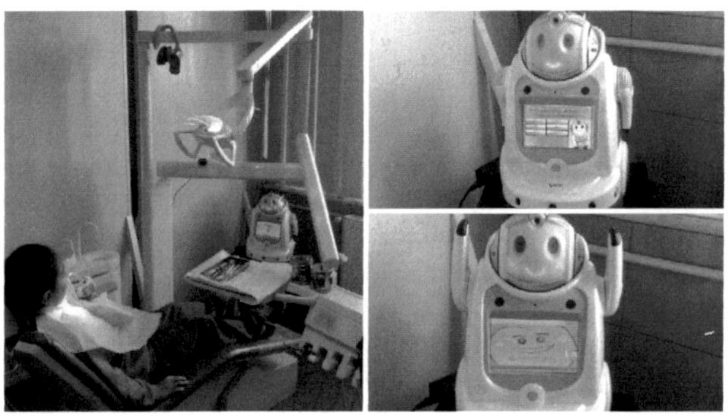

Fig. 3. IRobi performs some body movements with face expressions during a child's dental treatment.

In this context, the robot appeared acting naturally even in the lack of autonomy. For this purpose, we have used Wizard of Oz (WoZ) method, widely used in robot assisted studies to conduct our experiments. WoZ is an approach whereby a human operator, unknown to the participants, operates a robot. This method, used for full teleoperation or for partial control, enables simulating and modeling the interaction and allows the collection of data and experimenting without relying on specific system components [22].

WoZ method allows freedom in interaction and provides flexibility to make children involved in the interaction. The WoZ setup of the system is shown in Figure 4. First camera, placed in front of the child, recorded the face and body expressions and behaviors of the child. Second camera was placed in a spot with a view of the dentist, robot and child interaction. A web camera together with a microphone transmitted audio and video to the "WoZ" room. The WoZ room was away from the clinic setup. As part of the WoZ setup, an expressive verbal interaction is thought to be able to easily involve children in communication. Based on the analysis of captured videos, the majority of the children started to show more natural and expressive behavior after the wizard presented some feelings and emotions in the interaction. Because the wizard's communication skills also affect the children's behavior, we got help from a child psychiatrist about chatting with children [22].

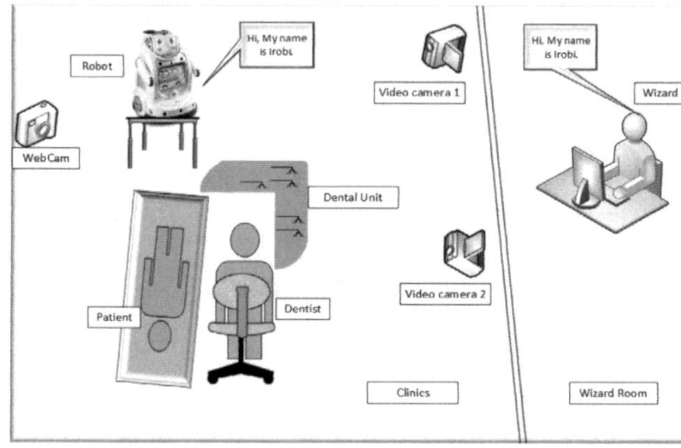

Fig. 4. WoZ setup of the system.

IRobi was programmed to help the wizard to execute the commands as distraction strategies (shaking head, swinging arms, face expressions) during the treatment. Once the WoZ system was installed, the wizard did not need to make any adjustment such as re-activate the robot for each phase. Fig. 1 shows some body movements with different face expressions performed by the robot. This way, the robot played a role as a member of both the welcoming and the treatment team.

IV. RESULTS

Fig. 5 shows the change of children's average levels of heart rate for each group. We have observed that based on the outcomes of heart rates of the children in control group as well as the video analyses, these children were more anxious and stressful during the treatment than before the treatment. As expected, after the treatment finished, they became calmer and their heart rates reached even lower than the pre-treatment levels. On the other hand, the patients in the robot group had similar pulse rates before and during the dental procedure, which indicates that the robots were effective in the reduction of the patients' anxiety. Additionally, after the treatment has been completed, these rates have returned to lower levels compared to the pre-treatment heart rates.

By investigating the quantitative heart rate changes of individual patients, we observed that 70.58% of the participants in the control group suffered from increased heart rate in the time interval between pre-treatment and during treatment, defined as *Phase 1*, whereas only 23.52% of the patients had decreased pulse rate. If the change of pulse rate stayed within a limit of $\pm 3\%$ of the original pulse rate during the phase, we defined this case as *No change*, and only 5.88% of the patients in the control group experienced this effect. The transition from the treatment time to the post-treatment is defined as *Phase 2* and 64.70% of the patients were relieved from their dental stress, while the pulse rate of the 29.41% of the patients did not

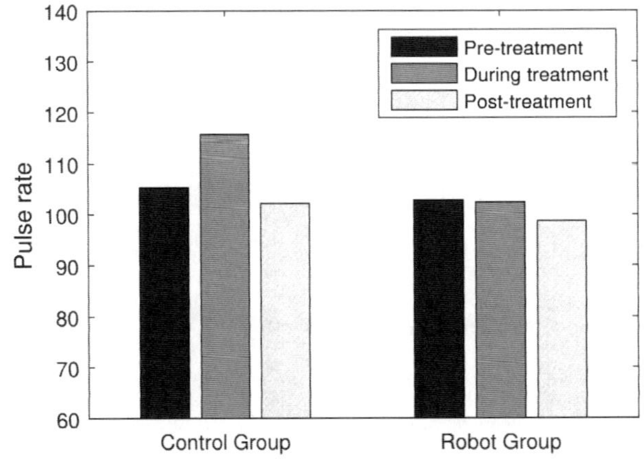

Fig. 5. Children's pulse rates before, during and after dental treatment.

change. However, the results of the robot group indicate an important trend of reduction in dental anxiety both in *Phase 1* and *Phase 2*. The total percentage of the patients having either no change or decrease in their pulse rate was 68.75% compared to 29.40% in the control group. Furthermore, the relaxation from stress after the treatment continued: a total of 87.00% of the patients had lower or equal pulse rates.

TABLE I
THE CHANGE IN THE CHILDREN'S PULSE RATE.

		Increased(%)	*Decreased(%)*	*No change(%)*
Control Group	*Phase 1*	70.58	23.52	5.88
	Phase 2	5.88	64.70	29.41
Robot Group	*Phase 1*	31.25	43.75	25.00
	Phase 2	12.5	43.75	43.75

According to the Facial Image Scale scores in Fig. 6 from pre- and post-treatment session, the percentage of children in control group having a negative or equal affect (indicating dental fear and anxiety) after the treatment (35.29%) was drastically higher than the percentage of children feeling the same way in the robot group (6.25%). %93.75 of the patients in the robot group have indicated that they felt better after the procedure. Based on these results, it is apparent that the level of anxiety of the children increased in control group, though conversely the children in robot group feel less anxiety after the procedure. Moreover, there is a remarkable difference between the levels of both groups.

Fig. 7 shows the change of the children's behavior towards dental treatment with respect to Frankl's Behavior Rating Scale. Comparing the children's treatment willingness, which was evaluated by the dentist, it can be seen that the half of the control group (50%) showed more positive attitude between the pre- and post-treatment relatively. However, the children in the robot group had more positive attitude after the treatment than they did have before the treatment (93.75%).

Tab. II shows the mean scores given by the dentists to the patients in both groups. Whereas the decrease in the average score of the patients in the control group shows a tendency of non-cooperative behavior, the increase in the willingness

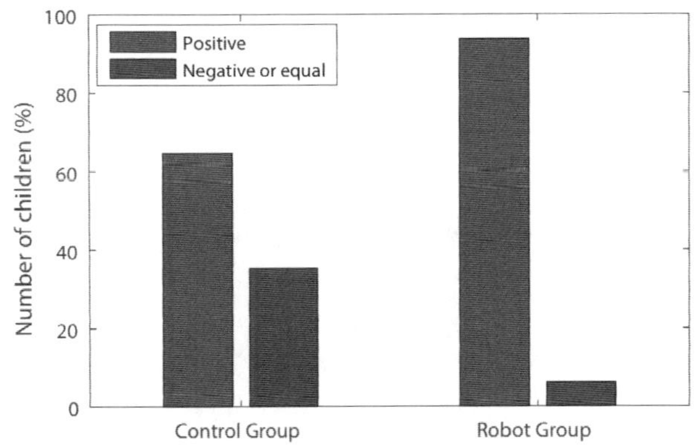

Fig. 6. The change of children's affect in Facial Image Scale.

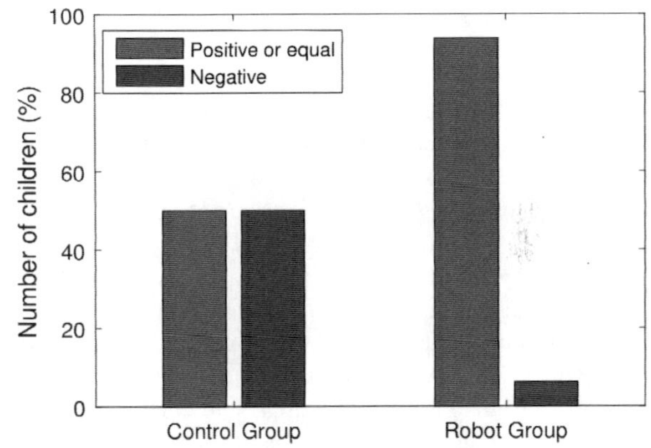

Fig. 7. The change of willingness of treatment according to Frankl's Behavior Rating Scale.

of the patients in the robot group demonstrates the promising positive effect of the usage of robots in dental treatment.

TABLE II
FRANKL BEHAVIOR RATING SCALE SCORES.

	Pre-treatment	**Post-treatment**
Control Group	*2.64*	*2.21*
Robot Group	*2.87*	*3.18*

Another assessment made using the answers from the children in robot group to the question "Would you want to have the robot in your next treatment session?" using the same terminology and notations as in the study of Beran et al. [18], show that the children liked and enjoyed the presence of the robot during their dental procedure. The distribution of the children's answers is given in Fig. 8: "very much" (%81 n = 13), "a lot" (%13, n = 2), "somewhat" (%6, n = 1).

Thus, all these improvements measured using objective and subjective evaluation criteria demonstrate the fact that the robots may have long-term positive effects on children's behavior in future treatments.

V. CONCLUSION

In this paper, we have described a preliminary study, which showed that children's pain and anxiety can be reduced in

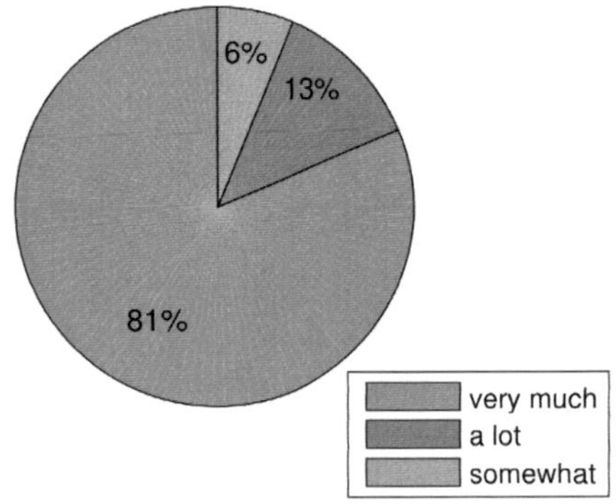

Fig. 8. Children's responses to have the robot in next treatment as well.

their dental treatment using robots. We believe that a robot can socially and emotionally aid child patients in their dental procedures to cope with stress and anxiety better than other conventional intervention methods. Furthermore, robots have advantages that they are programmable in content and level according children's age, and their usage is simple and eases the work load of health care workers [19].

In the future, we will continue to recruit more participants and present much quantitative measures relating to patient anxiety and pain. In that sense, the most urgent future work is to analyze the data obtained from all the sessions, i.e. the answers from all questionnaires, and video recordings. Furthermore, our next plan is to explore the effects of another robot Nao [28], developed by Aldebaran Robotics, to see whether there will be any differences due to the more human-like appearance and embodiment of this robot.

ACKNOWLEDGMENT

The research reported in this paper was supported by The Scientific and Technological Research Council of Turkey (TUBITAK) under the grant 214S157. We are thankful to Behiye Alyanak for her guidance and helpful comments.

REFERENCES

[1] Hoge, MA., Howard, MR., Wallace, DP., Allen, KD. 2012. "Use of video eyewear to manage distress in children during restorative dental treatment", Pediatric Dentistry, 34 (5), 378-382.

[2] Bekhuis, T. 2009. "Music therapy may reduce pain and anxiety in children undergoing medical and dental procedures", J Evid Based Dent Prac, 9 (4), 213-214.

[3] Vassend, O. 1993. "Anxiety, pain and discomfort associated with dental treatment", Behav Res Ther, 31, 659-666.

[4] Hägglin, C., Berggren, U., Hakeberg, M., Hällstrom, T., Bengtsson, C. 1999. "Variations in dental anxiety among middleaged and elderly women in Sweden: a longitudinal study between 1968 and 1996", J Dent Res, 78, 1655-1661.

[5] Locker, D., Liddell, AM. 1991. "Correlates of dental anxiety among older adults", J Dent Res, 70,198-203.

[6] Assuncão CM, Losso EM, Andreatini R, de Menezes JV. 2013. "The relationship between dental anxiety in children, adolescents and their parents at dental environment", J Indian Soc Pedod Prev Dent, 31 (3), 175-9.

[7] Chellappah, NK., Vignehsa, H., Milgrom, P., Lo, GL. 1990. "Prevalence of dental anxiety and fear in children in Singapore", Community Dent Oral Epidemiol,18, 269-71.

[8] Majstorovic, M., Veerkamp, JS., Skrinjaric, I. 2003. "Reliability and validity of measures used in assessing dental anxiety in 5- to 15-year-old Croatian children", Eur J Paediatr Dent, 4 (4), 197-202.

[9] Bayrak, Ş., Tunç, EŞ., Eğilmez, T. 2010. "Ebeveyn dental kaygısı ve sosyodemografik faktörlerin çocukların dental kaygısı üzerine etkileri", Atatürk Üniversitesi Diş Hekimliği Fakültesi Dergisi, 20 (3), 181-188.

[10] Klingberg, G., Berggren, U., Norén, JG. 1994. "Dental fear in an urban Swedish child population: Prevalence and concomitant factors" Community Dent Health, 11 (4), 208-214.

[11] Alvesalo, I., Murtomaa, H., Milgrom, P., Honkanen, A., Karjalainen, M., Tay, KM. 1993. "The Dental Fear Survey Schedule: a study with Finnish children", Int J Paediatr Dent, 3 (4), 193-198.

[12] Lee, CY., Chang, YY., Huang ST. 2007. "Prevalence of dental anxiety among 5- to 8-year-old Taiwanese children", J Public Health Dent, 67, 36-41.

[13] Köroğlu, A., Durkan, R. 2010. "Diş hekimliği uygulamalarında karşılaşılan dental anksiyete sendromunun etiyolojisinin ve tedavi yöntemlerinin değerlendirilmesi", Atatürk Üniversitesi Diş Hekimliği Fakültesi Dergisi, 20 (3), 205-212.

[14] Zhou, Y., Cameron, E., Forbes, G., Humphris, G. 2011. "Systematic review of the effect of dental staff behavior on child dental patient anxiety and behavior", Patient Education and Counselling, 85 (1), 4-13.

[15] Armfield, JM., Heaton, LJ. 2013. "Management of fear and anxiety in the dental clinic: a review", Australian Dental Journal, 58, 390-407.

[16] Klassen, JA., Liang, Y., Tjosvold, L., Klassen, TP., Hartling, L. 2008. "Music for pain and anxiety in children undergoing medical procedures: a systematic review of randomized controlled trials", Ambulatory Pediatrics, 8, 117-128.

[17] Mungara, J., Injeti, M., Joseph, E., Elangovan, A., Sakthivel, R., Selvaraju, G. 2013. "Child's dental fear: Cause related factors and the influence of audiovisual modeling", Journal of Indian Society of Pedodontics and Preventive Dentistry, 31 (4), 215-220.

[18] Beran, TN., Ramirez-Serrano, A., Vanderkooi, OG., Kuhn, S. 2013. "Reducing children's pain and distress towards flu vaccinations: A novel and effective application of humanoid robotics", Vaccine, 31, 2772-2777.

[19] Beran, TN., Ramirez-Serrano, A., Vanderkooi, OG., Kuhn, S. 2013. "Humanoid robotics in health care: An exploration of children's and parents' emotional reactions", Journal of Health Psychology, 0 (0), 1-6.

[20] Wood, LJ., Dautenhahn, K., Rainer, A., Robins, B., Lehmann, H., Syrdal, DS. 2013. "Robot-mediated interviews – how effective is a humanoid robot as a tool for interviewing young children?", PLoS ONE, 8 (3), e59448.

[21] Henkemans, OAB., Bierman, BPB, Janssen, J., Neerincx, MAN., Looije, R., van der Bosch, H., van der Giessen, JAM. 2013. "Using a robot to personalise health education for children with diabetes type 1: a pilot study", Patient Education and Counselling, 92, 174-181.

[22] Yilmazyildiz, S., Athanasopoulos, G., Patsis, G., Wang, W., Oveneke, M.C., Latacz, L., Verhelst, W., Sahli, H., Henderickx, D., Vanderborght, B., Soetens, E. and Lefeber, D. 2013. "Voice Modification for Wizard-of-Oz Experiments in Robot-Child Interaction" Workshop on Affective Social Speech Signals, WASSS.

[23] Hyun, E., Yoon, H., 2009. "Characteristics of Young Children's Utilization of a Robot during Play Time : A Case Study", Proceedings of IEEE International Symposium on Robot and Human Interactive Communication, 675-680.

[24] Hyun, E., Lee, H., Yoon, H. 2012. "Young children's perception of IrobiQ, the teacher assistive robot, with reference to speech register", Proceedings of International Conference on Computing Technology and Information Management (ICCM), 366-369.

[25] Nalin, M., Baroni, I., Kruijff-Korbayova, I., Canamero, L., Lewis, M., Beck, A., Cuayahuitl, H., Sanna, A. 2012. "Children's adaptation in multi-session interaction with a humanoid robot" The 21st IEEE International Symposium on Robot and Human Interactive Communication, IEEE RO-MAN.

[26] Buchanan, H., Niven, N. 2002. "Validation of a Facial Image Scale to assess child dental anxiety", Int J Paediatr Dent, 12, 47-52.

[27] Frankl, S.N., Shiere, F.R., and Fogels, H.R. "Should the parent remain with the child in the dental operatory?" J Dent Child 29:1,50-163, 1962

[28] "Nao Robot", 2016, URL: https://www.aldebaran.com/en/cool-robots/nao [accessed: 2016-04-15].

Recognizing Hand Gestures for Human-Robot Interaction

Zuhair Zafar and Karsten Berns

RRLAB, Department of Computer Science,
Technical University of Kaiserslautern,
Kaiserslautern, Germany
Email: {zafar,berns}@cs.uni-kl.de

Abstract—**Human-Robot Interaction is the most important aspect for the development of social service robots. Interacting with social robots via non-verbal communication makes the interaction natural and efficient for human. We present an interface that uses hand gestures to interact with humanoid robot. The major goal of this interface is to recognize gestures in dynamic environments with high accuracy and efficiency. Our proposed system enables automatic recognition of 18 different human hand gestures from RGB-D (color and depth data) device. Robot expresses different facial expressions and performs the gestures after recognizing them. We use bag-of-features approach to recognize gestures using scale invariant feature transform (SIFT) keypoints. The system is invariant to scale, slight rotation and illumination and can work in cluttered backgrounds. We use multi-class support vector machines for classification task. In order to validate our scheme, we use this interface in our humanoid robot that reports more than 94% recognition rate for 18 hand gestures.**

Keywords–Human-Robot Interaction; Nonverbal communication; Hand Gestures; Bag-of-features approach.

I. INTRODUCTION

Since last decade, many different types of human-friendly robots have been developed. Varying in the objectives, some robots are developed for helping humans in industrial environment and some are designed to function in indoor environment. As the technology gets sophisticated and more advanced, the focus has been shifted to social service robots. The goal of these robots is to communicate with human in a human-like way and perform different tasks as instructed by human. This leads us to social behavior in robots. These social robots should recognize humans, their verbal communication and gestures in order to realize natural communication. Furthermore, they should also recognize human emotions in order to predict the internal state of human for better communication.

Social behaviour in robots generally depend upon efficient human-robot interaction (HRI). The most common way of human interaction is either by vocal communication or by body gestures. Other medium includes newspapers, notes and other writing material, however, this type of communication is not applicable in face-to-face communication. According to [1], 65% of our communication consists of human gestures and only 35% consists of verbal content. This two third of our communication shows the significance of gestures. For this purpose, recognition of nonverbal content becomes essential task for HRI. Human gestures are nonverbal content, which are used with or without verbal communication in expressing the intended meaning of the speech. Gestures may include hand, arm, or body gestures and it may also include eyes, face, head etc.

Human gesture recognition has been a popular topic in computer vision field. The topic has been studied numerous times because of its important applications in surveillance systems, elderly care, in the field of medicine (e.g. gait analysis, surgical navigation), in the field of sports, augmented reality, sign language for hearing impaired people and human behavior analysis. Hand gestures are critical in face-to-face communication scenarios. Especially during discussions, hand gestures become more animated. They emphasize points and convey enthusiasm of the speaker. Hand gestures show a lot about the internal state. For example, crossing arms during face-to-face communication shows nervousness or lack of interest and clenched hands show aggressive stance of a person. They enable human to express mood state (like thumbs up) or convey some basic cardinal information (like one, two and so on). In this paper, we present a system, which enables a humanoid robot to recognize different hand gestures used in daily routine. Not only the robot recognizes them, but it expresses its emotions through its facial expressions accordingly. We also have conducted several experiments where robot is able to imitate the same gesture in real time.

This paper is organized as follows: Section 2 discusses the existing hand gesture recognition systems in context to HRI. We describe our gesture recognition approach in Section 3 and evaluate our methodology in Section 4. We conclude our paper in Section 5.

II. RELATED WORK

Numerous hand gesture recognition systems have been reported in the literature. In general, we can categorize them in two different classes: (a) data gloves based systems and (b) vision based systems. Former type of systems require use of glove sensor for storing hand and finger motion and then use this data to recognize the action. Huang et al. [2] used gloves to record the hand and fingers flex data and then use machine learning algorithms to classify 5 dimensional finger flex data. Although, this type of systems may provide a 3D representation of hand however, wearing a heavy and expensive glove is not suitable for natural human interaction. On the other side, vision based systems take the information of the hand itself as an input using a camera to collect hand movements for gesture recognition without the use of any wearable sensor. Vision based approaches can be divided into two categories, i.e., 3D hand model based method and appearance based methods. The 3D hand model can provide ample information of hand that allows to realize wide class of hand gestures but the main disadvantage lies in extraction of features in case of ambiguous poses, unclear views and high computational complexity, which makes the overall system unrealistic for real time interaction.

In appearance based approaches, images with hands are considered only for feature extraction and gesture recognition task. The simplest technique is to look for skin color regions. Marilly et al. [3] extracts hand region using skin color and foreground information. For feature extraction, they use statistical and geometric features and then classify the gestures using principle component analysis. However, this method has some serious shortcomings. The major drawback of color-based techniques is the variability of the skin color in different lighting conditions. This frequently results in undetected skin regions or falsely detected non-skin textures. The problem can be somewhat alleviated by considering only the regions of a certain size (scale filtering) or at certain spatial position (positional filtering).

Another appearance based approach presented in the literature [4], that uses Gabor filters for extraction of hand gesture features. Gabor filters can capture the most important visual properties such as spatial locality, orientation selectivity and spatial frequency. Due to the high dimensionality of features, principle component analysis is used for feature reduction. The drawback of this and other similar approaches is that these methods are not invariant to translation, rotation and scaling. Moreover, these approaches are also effected by illumination variation. In [5], cascade of classifier approach is used. Each cascade is capable of detecting hands with certain angle of rotation. The drawback of this approach is that, it can not classify the same gesture with different viewpoints and is not rotation invariant. The authors of [6] extract a distinct and unified hand contour to recognize hand gestures, and then compute the curvature of each point on the contour. Due to noise and unstable lighting in the cluttered background, it has difficulties in obtaining segmentation of integrated hand contour. The eigen space is another technique, which presents a robust representation of a huge feature set of high-dimensional points using a small set of basis vectors. However, eigen space methods are not invariant to translation, scaling, and rotation. The most common and serious shortcoming of all of these methods discussed so far is that they only work with uniform background. These approaches lack in detecting hands in cluttered and dynamic environment.

Local invariant features are used for object recognition task. In the paper [7], to perform reliable matching between different views of an object or scene, a method is presented for extracting distinctive invariant features, as known as scale invariant feature transform (SIFT) features, that can be used for object recognition. This method for image feature extraction transforms an image into a large collection of feature vectors, each of which is invariant to image translation, scaling, and rotation, partially invariant to illumination changes and robust to local geometric distortion. Hartanto et al. [8] use SIFT features along with skin detection method for background subtraction and contours for localization of hand. Their matching stage is relatively simpler and hence, reports less than 70% accuracy for Indonesian sign language database. Their approach is computationally extensive and is not applicable for real time recognition. Dardas and Georganas [9] used bag-of-features approach using SIFT features as keypoints and then used support vector machines to recognize the hand gesture. They segment the hand based on the skin color, discard the face using Viola-Jones face detector and then extract features. The shortcoming of this approach lies in segmentation of hand. It depends highly on illumination variation and the subject wearing half or full sleeves.

In order to address all of these shortcomings, we proposed to use 3D camera (e.g., ASUS Xtion Pro) to localize hands using joint information. We use depth data to locate hands using OpenNI and NiTe middleware library and their positions for hand segmentation. We describe our approach in detail in the following section.

III. Human Hand Gesture Recognition

Visual perception in complex and dynamical scenes with cluttered backgrounds is a very difficult task, which humans can solve satisfactorily. However, for a robot perception system, it performs poorly in this kind of challenging scenarios. One of the reasons of this large difference in performance is the use of context or contextual information by humans. Several studies in human perception have shown that the human visual system makes extensive use of the strong relationships between objects and their environment for facilitating the object detection and perception. Not only this, due to the notion of real time, robot has to perform its computations as fast as possible. Due to which, most of the time robot perception system is hampered with low resolution images. There is a need to develop such perception system, which can cater complex environments and work efficiently. Keeping this in mind, we propose an approach that uses depth sensor for hand segmentation using NiTe library. It uses bag-of-features approach from SIFT keypoints and classify them using support vector machines (SVMs) to recognize hand gestures. The block diagram of the approach is presented in Figure 1.

Our proposed system is highly robust and efficient. It reports 94% recognition rate for 18 different gestures when classified by multi-class support vector machines. Hand gestures are robustly recognized with dynamic and cluttered background. The system is invariant to illumination, scale and slight rotation. Figure 1 shows the schematic flow of the system. Each module of the system is described in the following sub-sections.

A. Pre-processing

Instead of using monocular camera, ASUS Xtion is used in order to use depth data. The advantage of using such devices with depth sensor lies in localization of hands. Segmenting hand on the basis of skin color can be useful in a constraint scenario but it behaves poorly when applied in dynamic environment. While using depth sensor, hands can be localized efficiently in cluttered and dynamic environments. RGB-D device delivers color and depth stream of the scene. Before extracting features directly for further processing, pre-processing is an essential step in registering images. We propose to use lower resolution 320×240 in order to reduce the computational complexity of the system.

B. Hand Detection and Segmentation

As discussed earlier, NiTe middleware library enables us to detect hands by utilizing depth and IR sensor of ASUS Xtion. Not only the algorithm detects hands but also tracks them efficiently. In our setup, ASUS Xtion sensor is used, which delivers the centroid of the hands using depth data. The

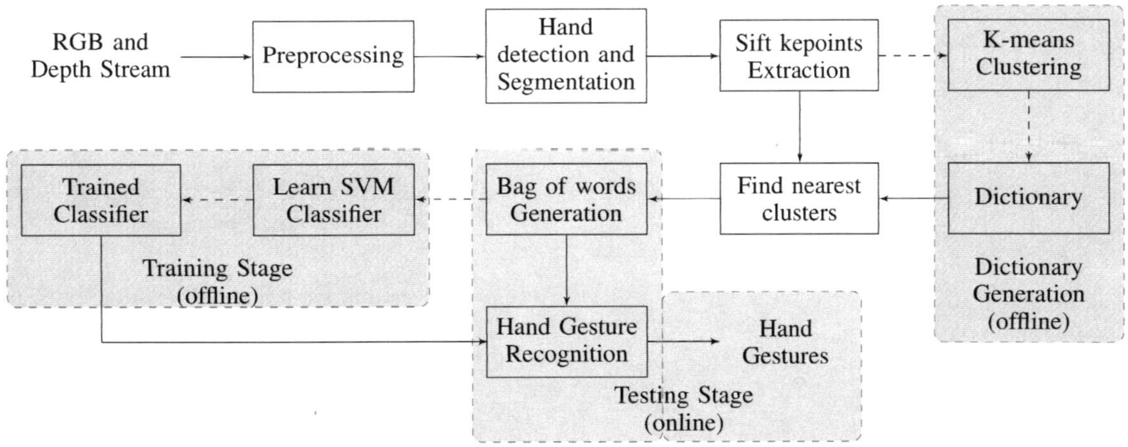

Figure 1. Working schematics of our approach. Using depth stream, hand is localized and segmented, SIFT keypoints are extracted. A dictionary is generated using k-means clustering; bag of words vectors are generated using cluster model; which are fed into SVMs for classification

algorithm can detect multiple hands if present in the scene. The most nearest hand on the basis of the depth data from the robot is selected. In order to segment the hand out of the whole image frame, firstly color and depth streams are synchronized and then a small region around the centroid of the hand is extracted from color image. This small region depends on the depth data. If a person is near the robot, this region of interest becomes bigger and if a person is far from the robot, this region of interest is small. The extracted region of interest has some irrelevant information other than the hand. In order to discard that information, pixels in the region of interest which have depth close to hand's depth are kept and everything else is discarded. Figure 2 shows the original image and hand segmented image. In order to make it scale invariant, each segmented image is registered by resizing it to 50×50 resolution.

C. Bag-of-Features Extraction

Bag-of-features (BoF) is probably the most popular technique of feature representation for videos and still images in the domain of human gesture recognition. Coming from the text mining paradigm, BoF representations allow to recognize a variety of gestures ranging from simple periodic motions (walking, running) to interactions (waiving, shaking hands). It is usually combined with other procedures in feature extraction task. The schematics include (a) keypoints extraction,

(a) (b) (c) (d)

Figure 2. (a) Hand is detected in depth stream, (b) Hand is localized in color stream based on its position (c) segmented hand after discarding background with higher depth than hand's depth and (d) SIFT keypoints extracted

(b) descriptor generation around those point, (c) dictionary generation and (d) use of clustering algorithm to create BoF vectors. In order to represent an image in BoF approach, it can be expressed as a document. Consequently, the features extracted can be expressed as words in this document. All the words or features extracted from the document or image if combined together, form a dictionary.

1) Keypoints Extraction: The initial step in BoF algorithm is to extract keypoints. These keypoints should be able to represent the whole image. For extraction of keypoints, SIFT algorithm is used. SIFT has been quite popular in object recognition and scene classification because of its robustness and efficiency. Proposed by Lowe [10], SIFT algorithm selects the features that are invariant to image scaling and rotation and to some extent illumination changes. An image is convoluted with Gaussian channels at various scales. Keypoints are taken as the maxima or minima points of the difference of Gaussian that happen at various scales. A lot of keypoints are discarded, which are not stable or have low contrast using Taylor series expansion. Figure 2 shows the extracted keypoints on a segmented image.

2) Descriptor Generation: The keypoint descriptor is computed by calculating gradient magnitude and orientation of all the keypoints around its location. The orientation histograms are relative to the keypoint location. The histogram contains 8 bins and computes array of 4×4 histogram around the keypoint. Since there are 4×4 histograms each with 8 bins, the keypoint vector is 128 dimensional. This vector is then normalized to unit length in order to boost invariance to changes in illumination. Hence, the features are illumination invariant.

3) Dictionary Generation: This is an important step in the BoF algortihm. The size of the dictionary is critical for the recognition process. If the size of the dictionary is set too small then the BoF model can not express all the keypoints and if it is set too high then it might lead to over-fitting and increasing the complexity of the system. K-means clustering algorithm is used to cluster keypoint descriptors of all the training images in k clusters, where k is the dictionary size. The centroids

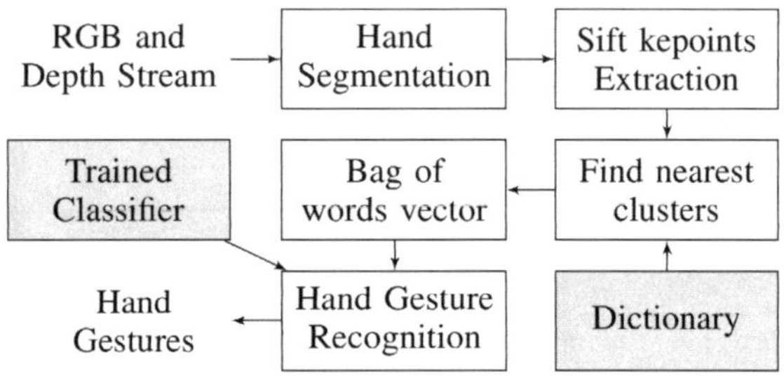

Figure 3. Block diagram of testing stage

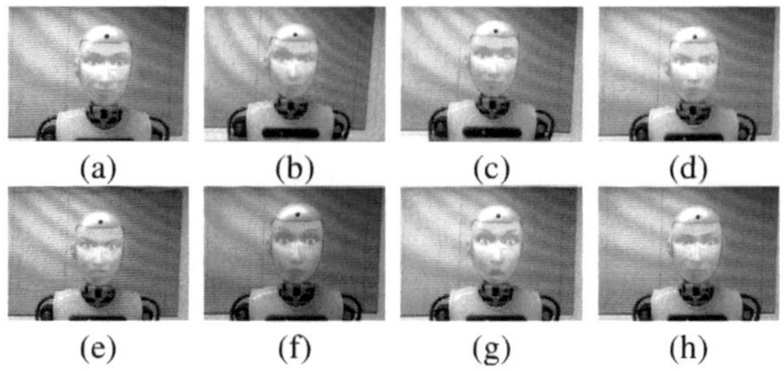

Figure 4. Robot performing facial expressions (a) Happy (b) Thinking (c) Wink (d) Frown (e) Threaten (f) Surprise (g) Astonishment (h) Disgust.

of each clusters are combined together to make a dictionary. This resulted in dictionary with $k \times 128$ size. Dictionary is generated offline and is used for making bag of words vector. In our study, $k = 400$ is used as a dictionary size.

4) Bag of Words Vector: In order to make bag of word vector, SIFT keypoints are extracted for hand segmented image. Each keypoint descriptor of the image is compared with each centroid of the cluster in the dictionary using euclidean measure. If the difference is small or keypoint is closed to a certain cluster, the count of that index is increased. Similarly other keypoints of an image are also compared and the counts of the respective indices are increased to which the keypoints are closest to. Finally, bag of words vector is generated for a single image that has size $1 \times k$ where k is the dictionary size. In our study, the size of bag of words vector becomes 1×400. One important thing to note here is the size of the feature vector. Using only SIFT keypoints, the size of feature vector is $n \times 128$ (where n is the number of keypoints) which is complex and makes the system computationally more intensive. On the other hand, BoF approach reports 400 dimensional feature vector which has the characteristics of SIFT features and considerably less complex. These bag of words vectors are computed for all the image frames for training and testing of the gestures.

D. Classification

Classification is an important step in any recognition task. There are a lot of classifiers presented and used according to the type of problem. We proposed to use SVM because of its effectiveness in high dimensional spaces [11]. SVM only uses small set of support vectors for decision making, hence it requires less memory and is used in real-time recognition tasks. With different kernel functions available, SVM can used for versatile problems. One-versus-all approach of multi-class SVM is used. Bag of words vectors for all the images are computed in training stage and labels are appended according to the class. This bag of words vectors are fed into the multi-class SVM in order to train the model that is further used in testing stage for hand gesture recognition. To validate our system, a database is generated. 600 images for each gesture are used for training. Each hand segmented image is manually selected and noisy or ambiguous images are discarded. Six different subjects have featured in the database. Each gesture is recorded at various scales and at different positions.

Figure 3 shows the working schematics of our testing phase. Color and depth frames are extracted from ASUS Xtion. Hand is localized and segmented in the same way during training stage. These segmented images are then used to extract keypoints using SIFT algorithm. The keypoints are compared with the predefined dictionary (created offline) and bag of word vectors are generated. For each testing image, the 400 dimensional feature vector is fed to SVM with already learned classifier. Hand gestures are then recognized in real-time. 18 different hand gestures have been recognized: Palm, pointing upwards, inquiring gesture, number gestures like one, two, three, four, five, thumbs up, fist, little finger, victory, etc.

IV. Experimentation and Evaluation

The goal of the system is to recognize hand gestures reliably and robustly in order to realize natural human-robot interaction. We use our humanoid robot in order to evaluate accuracy and efficiency of our system. University of Kaiserslautern is developing a social humanoid robot, Robothespian [12]. It consists of intelligent hands and arms and a backlit projected face. The whole arm has 14 degrees of freedom, where hands are able to perform nearly all type of hand gestures. The backlit projected head is able to express any facial expression using action units. Robot can also move torso and head to about ± 20 and ± 45 degrees respectively. ASUS Xtion is mounted on the chest of the robot. It has its own processor that can handle the movements of all the joints and facial expressions. It is used to evaluate our hand gesture system. In the following section, we describe the set of experiments conducted and then evaluate the performance of the system.

A. Experimental Setup

Two different experiments are conducted in our study to evaluate the hand gesture recognition system. 18 different hand gestures are used to interact with the humanoid robot. We divide them in two different categories. In the first experiment, common hand gestures that humans use during daily communication are used namely: thumbs up, fist, palm, inquire gesture, okay gesture, pointing gesture and little finger gesture. These gestures play an important role to express the inner thoughts or intentions of a human. For example, thumbs up gesture shows an approval, while fist gesture shows aggressiveness of human. In order to make HRI more natural, robot expresses facial expressions on its face according to the gesture. Table I shows different gestures and their corresponding expressions that are expressed by the robot and Figure 4 shows robot's facial expressions.

In the second experiment, basic gestures, that are used to express the fundamental information like numbers, e.g. one,

Figure 5. Subject performing different gestures in front of the robot.

two, three, four and so on, are recognized. These gestures are used to represent the numbers from one to ten using only single hand. Instead of expressing facial expressions, robot imitates the same *number* gesture as performed by human. Not only robot imitates the gesture but also verbally communicates the *number* using its built-in speaker. For natural interaction, the robot's head also focuses directly towards the hand position. In this way, wherever the hand is in the frame, robot's head move to that position as if to focus the hand. Figure 5 shows different hand gestures while Figure 7(c) shows robot's head is focusing the hand of the human in the frame.

TABLE I. DIFFERENT GESTURES AND CORRESPONDING FACE EXPRESSIONS EXPRESS BY THE ROBOT

Nr.	*Hand Gesture*	*Facial Experession*
1)	Okay gesture	Happy
2)	Pointing Up	Thinking
3)	Thumbs Up	Wink
4)	Inquiry gesture	Frown
5)	Fist	Threaten
6)	Palm	Surprise
7)	Victory	Astonishment
8)	Little finger gesture	Disgust

B. Performance Measurement

As discussed in the earlier section, the prime objective of the system is to recognize hand gestures in dynamic scenarios in context to HRI. System should recognize gestures in real time. Two set of experiments, discussed in previous section, are evaluated in order to measure the performance. For performance evaluation, the predicted gesture along with subsequent image of all the frames are stored in a separate file. In the end, we manually evaluate the results. In the first experiment, eight different gestures: thumbs up, okay gesture, pointing upwards, inquire gesture, victory, fist, palm and little finger gesture are recognized. A total of 1200 frames are stored during first experiment. Table II shows the recognition rates for each hand gesture.

As shown in the Table II, the average recognition rate in case of common hand gestures when performed in front of the robot is 93%. For Okay gesture, the recognition rate is low due to the reason that the fingers are pointing upwards

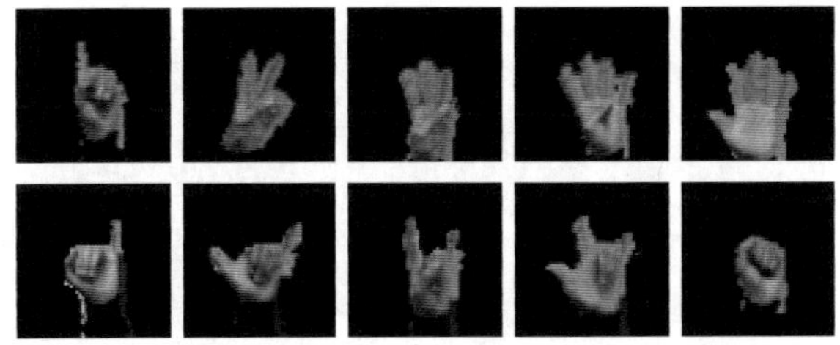

Figure 6. Hand segmented images of number gestures (1-10).

and sometimes it is confused with victory and inquire gesture. Gestures like thumbs up and little finger are occasionally confused with pointing up gesture. In all three cases, one finger is pointing upwards which results in false detection. All of the gestures are tested, when the gesture is performed dynamically or statically.

TABLE II. RECOGNITION RATES FOR COMMON HAND GESTURES.

Hand Gesture	*Number of Images*	*Correctly Classified*	Recog. Rate
Okay gesture	150	115	76.6%
Pointing Up	150	149	99.3%
Thumbs Up	150	136	90.7%
Inquiry gesture	150	141	94%
Fist	150	144	96%
Palm	150	150	100%
Victory	150	145	96.7%
Little finger gesture	150	137	91.3%
Average			**93%**

In the second experiment, *number* gestures are used for recognition task. Ten gestures are performed from a single hand to recognize numbers. Figure 6 shows ten segmented hand gestures. For this experiment, 1500 images are used to evaluate these gestures. Table III shows the number of correctly classified images along with the recognition rate of each gesture.

From Table III, it can be seen that *three* gesture has low recognition rate. According to experiments, this gesture is falsely detected as *four* gesture and occasionally, as *two* gesture. From the validation studies, we find out that performing *three* gesture perfectly is difficult for few subjects, which makes it harder to recognize. We also observe that *six* or little finger gesture is occasionally confused with *one* gesture. In both these gestures only one finger, index finger in case of *one* gesture and little finger in case of *six* gesture, is pointing up which easily confuses the gesture. The overall average recognition rate is 95.1%. Figure 7 shows our experimental

TABLE III. RECOGNITION RATES FOR NUMBER GESTURES.

Number Gesture	*Number of Images*	*Correctly Classified*	Recog. Rate
One	150	149	99.3%
Two	150	145	96.7%
Three	150	133	88.6%
Four gesture	150	134	89.3%
Five	150	150	100%
Six	150	137	91.33%
Seven	150	137	91.33%
Eight	150	148	98.7%
Nine	150	150	100%
Ten	150	144	96%
Average			**95.13%**

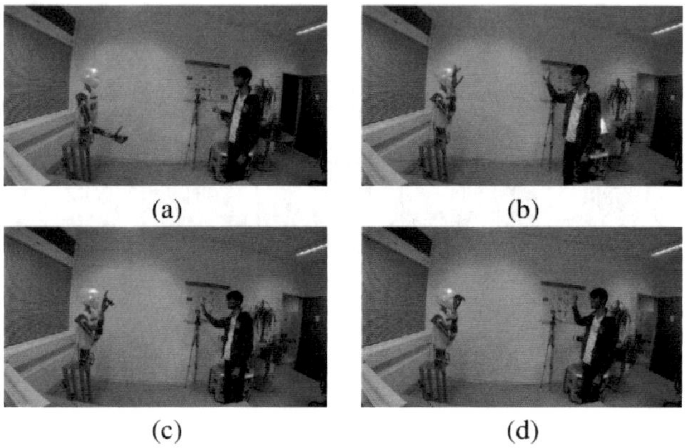

Figure 7. Robot recognizes and imitates (a) thumbs up (b) Palm (c) Point up and (d) Fist gestures. In (c) robot looks towards its left to focus hand.

setup where human is interacting with robot via hand gestures.

The most important aspect in HRI is the efficiency of the whole system. In our experimentation, the system takes $70msec$ to process each image. In other words, the system processes around 15 frames per second, which is adequate for real time processing. The size of the dictionary primarily effects the processing time. However, the size of dictionary can not be reduced immensely, otherwise it would result in poor recognition rate.

C. *Comparison with State-of-the-Art*

The system reports 94% recognition rate for 18 different hand gestures in dynamic environments. Ren et al. [13] used finger earth movers distance metric to recognize hand gesture. They used Microsoft Kinect to capture images. For 10 gestures their recognition rate is 94% on a very limited database. Their system works good for simple gestures but gestures like thumbs up, inquire gesture etc. can not recognize efficiently as fingers are closed. Yang et al. [14] used monocular camera to recognize 18 different gestures with around 97% accuracy. The main drawback of their approach is the skin detection part which is highly unstable in illumination changes. They also put a constraint on their system that human should be present on the edge of the frame. Dardas and Georganas [9] used SIFT features and bag of words model to recognize hand using monocular camera images with 94% accuracy. Their database is extremely limited with uniform background and they also use skin detection to detect the hand. Approaches using skin detection for segmenting hand report poor accuracy when dealing with dynamic environment with illumination variation.

V. CONCLUSION

Human-Robot Interaction is the most important function for the emerging social robot which is able to interact with people using natural gestures. Hand gesture based interface offers a way to enable human to interact with robots more easily and efficiently. We use ASUS Xtion for hand segmentation and use bag-of-features approach using SIFT keypoints to recognize different hand gestures. The presented approach is highly efficient and invariant to cluttered backgrounds, illumination changes, slight rotation and scale. Our hand gesture interface is used by humanoid robot that recognizes gestures in $70msec$ (real time). Robot imitates gestures and also changes its face expressions according to the gestures. Our hand gesture recognition interface reports 94% recognition rate for 18 hand gestures in dynamic environments. In future, this system can be extended for both hands and can also recognize facial expressions of a human. It would help the robot to know the emotional state of human. The same approach can be used for recognizing dynamic hand gestures for recognizing different actions, e.g., clapping, jumping, punching etc.

REFERENCES

[1] P. Noller, Nonverbal Communication in Close Relationships, 0th ed. SAGE Publications, Inc., 2006, pp. 403–421.

[2] Y. Huang, D. Monekosso, H. Wang, and J. Augusto, "A concept grounding approach for glove-based gesture recognition," in Intelligent Environments (IE), 2011 7th International Conference on, July 2011, pp. 358–361.

[3] E. Marilly, A. Gonguet, O. Martinot, and F. Pain, "Gesture interactions with video: From algorithms to user evaluation," Bell Labs Technical Journal, vol. 17, no. 4, March 2013, pp. 103–118.

[4] D.-Y. Huang, W.-C. Hu, and S.-H. Chang, "Vision-based hand gesture recognition using pca+gabor filters and svm," in Intelligent Information Hiding and Multimedia Signal Processing, 2009. IIH-MSP '09. Fifth International Conference on, September 2009, pp. 1–4.

[5] A. L. Barczak and F. Dadgostar, "Real-time hand tracking using a set of cooperative classifiers based on haar-like features," in Research Letters in the Information and Mathematical Sciences, Vol. 7. Massey University, 2005, pp. 29–42.

[6] A. A. Argyros and M. I. A. Lourakis, "Vision-based interpretation of hand gestures for remote control of a computer mouse," in In Computer Vision in Human-Computer Interaction. Springer-Verlag, 2006, pp. 40–51.

[7] I. Skrypnyk and D. Lowe, "Scene modelling, recognition and tracking with invariant image features," in Mixed and Augmented Reality, 2004. ISMAR 2004. Third IEEE and ACM International Symposium on, Nov 2004, pp. 110–119.

[8] R. Hartanto, A. Susanto, and P. Santosa, "Preliminary design of static indonesian sign language recognition system," in Information Technology and Electrical Engineering (ICITEE), 2013 International Conference on, Oct 2013, pp. 187–192.

[9] N. Dardas and N. D. Georganas, "Real-time hand gesture detection and recognition using bag-of-features and support vector machine techniques," Instrumentation and Measurement, IEEE Transactions on, vol. 60, no. 11, Nov 2011, pp. 3592–3607.

[10] D. Lowe, "Object recognition from local scale-invariant features," in Computer Vision, 1999. The Proceedings of the Seventh IEEE International Conference on, vol. 2, 1999, pp. 1150–1157.

[11] J. Weston and C. Watkins, "Multi-class support vector machines," 1998.

[12] "New Humanoid Robot tu kaiserslautern," https://agrosy.informatik.uni-kl.de/aktuelles/details/news/neuer-humanoider-roboter/, accessed: 2016-01-25.

[13] Z. Ren, J. Yuan, J. Meng, and Z. Zhang, "Robust part-based hand gesture recognition using kinect sensor," Multimedia, IEEE Transactions on, vol. 15, no. 5, Aug 2013, pp. 1110–1120.

[14] Z. Yang, Y. Li, W. Chen, and Y. Zheng, "Dynamic hand gesture recognition using hidden markov models," in Computer Science Education (ICCSE), 2012 7th International Conference on, July 2012, pp. 360–365.

Design of an Interactive System for Immersive Movie Watching Experience

Yaochi Liu, Tsai-Yen Li
Computer Science Department
National Chengchi University
Taipei, Taiwan
email: {lyc780226,li.nccu}@gmail.com

***Abstract*—As new technologies for creating digital contents are developing, more and more innovations about reading and listening are emerging. In film making, simple visual and auditory effects may not satisfy the audience any more. Besides, as home entertainment systems are becoming more popular, people see a movie not only in the theater but also at home. In this work, we present an interactive film watching system allowing a viewer to move her body in an intuitive way to change the viewing angle of the film as well as the development of the story. The system aims at using ingenious content design and immersive interaction to enhance user's viewing experience. A regular computer with a webcam is used to detect the position of the user, which is then used to control the viewing angle of the video taken through a fish-eye lens. At some specific point in the story plot, different viewing angles would automatically determine the selection of different story branches, which can greatly increase the replay value of an interactive story. We have conducted an experiment to study the effectiveness of the system. Ten users were invited to experience our system. The evaluation result shows that most users agreed with the design idea and enjoyed the new viewing experience. We believe that the system provides a new way of communication between the storyteller/director and the audience. We hope that this preliminary work can shed some lights on the future development of video-based interactive storytelling.**

Keywords- Movie Space; Immersive Experience; Human-computer Interaction.

I. INTRODUCTION

With the development of new multimedia technologies, "audience" behaviors are no longer limited by the traditional audio and video environments in the past. For example, simple visual and audial effects in a traditional theater cannot satisfy the audiences any more. Therefore, the design of wider surround screen, such as the Image MAXimum (IMAX) screen and devices to stimulate multiple senses (such as movement and smell) has emerged to bring the audience's experience to a next higher level.

On the other hand, due to the increased network bandwidth at home and the price drop of home entertainment systems, more and more people choose to watch a movie at home on a TV or on a computer [18]. Nevertheless, the watching experience at home is still not comparable with the one in a high-end theater because of the small watching screen. The dark environment in a theater helps the audience focus on the film, and the wide screen also makes people immerse into the scene more easily. Instead of changing the equipment and environment at home, in this research, we propose to design an interactive video watching system on a regular computer with contents of greater interactivity to enhance the immersion experience of an audience when she watches a movie on a small screen.

Persson thought that interaction was the main difference between movie and digital space. That is, screen can become an interactive interface instead of a simple projection surface [12]. Recently, the meaning and definition of audience started to receive new attentions [10]. The discussions about subjectivity of a film have changed the definition and behavior model of an audience. The transfer of authorship has made a passive audience become an active participant. The subjectivity of a film now includes the participation of the viewer.

Based on such a motivation, we hope to release the limitation on the traditional imaginations about film [11]. We hope to allow the audience to view the film in an intuitive and interactive way such that the whole information of the film can be acquired through active interactions. With such a system, we cannot only create a new way to watch films, but also deliver deeper meaning through user participation.

Therefore, the main objectives of this research include:

(1) Implementing a good interactive mode to provide a narrative framework allowing a user to immerse in the film-watching experience.
(2) Using computer vision techniques to see if the human-computer interaction can enhance the viewing experience and provide better enjoyment about the story.
(3) Investigating how screen and space can be used together in digital media for storytelling and learning what kind of story could be more appropriate.

The rest of the paper is organized as follows. In the next section, we will review the work pertaining to this research. In Section III, we will describe the design and implementation details of our system. In Section IV, we will present the experiment that we have conducted to evaluate our system, and in Section V, we will analyze the results obtained in the experiment. In the last two sections, we will present the possible future extensions as well as the conclusion of the paper.

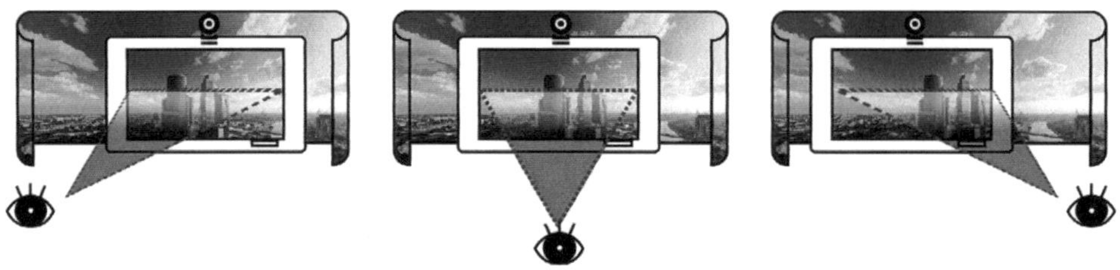

Figure 1. Illustration of the proposed interactive system. Screen is like a window, through which the world is observed.

II. Related Work

Our work pertains to previous research in immersive experience, content presentation in 'Movie Space', and Human-Computer Interactions (HCI) research on natural user interface.

A. Immersive Experience

Csikszentmihalyi was the first one to propose the theory of immersion. He regarded a person to be in an "immersion" state when he focused on the activities of a given scene by filtering out irrelevant noises [2][3]. Later researchers further remarked on the definition and considered immersion as the state when a user concentrated on the activity and enjoyed the process.

Trevino and Webster extended Csikszentmihalyi's work to consumer navigation on a digital system and proposed four properties in the state of immersion: [15]

(1) **Control:** Individuals experienced the feeling of control not only on himself but also the interactions between human and computer.
(2) **Attention Focus:** Attention was focused on an involving activity. An individual's focus can be narrowed down by filtering out irrelevant thoughts and stimuli.
(3) **Curiosity:** During the immersive state, an individual's sensory or cognitive curiosity can be aroused.
(4) **Intrinsic Interest:** Individuals were involved in an activity for the pleasure and enjoyment it provided instead of for instrumental purposes only.

Additionally, Hoffman and Novak thought that telepresence and interactivity were important because they could increase immersive experience [7].

(1) **Interactivity:** Interactivity is about the cycling process of multiple users performing listening, thinking, and speaking. Daniels regarded an Exemplary Viewer as an active participant in addition to passive viewer [4]. Webster et al. indicated that immersion emerged through interaction with the computer [15]. Johnson and Wiles also pointed out that controllability in a game brings positive affective experience [9].
(2) **Telepresence:** Presence is "the natural perception of an environment," and telepresence is "the mediated perception of an environment [5]." The more controllability on one's movement and viewpoint, the more degree of presence [19]. In addition, it was reported that the sense of presence also elicited the feelings of a user [13].

B. Movie Space

Movie space can be divided into 'on-screen space' and 'off-screen space' [1]. On-screen space can be simply defined as all you can see on the screen while off-screen space is more complicated because it allows a user to interact with the objects outside the screen and allows them to suddenly enter the screen to deliver some special meaning. The camera often represents the opinion of a narrator, and a shot is a way to deliver emotions to the audience. The techniques of shooting and camera movement, especially the composition of a shot, affect our perception of the narration in the story. Our system attempts to break the boundary between the off-screen and on-screen spaces and solves the aspect-ratio problem when a movie is displayed on a different screen.

C. Natural User Interface

The definitions between 'Natural User Interface' and 'Tangible User Interface' are often confused. A good way to distinguish the two could be on if the user is able to forget the existence of the interaction device after the user becomes familiar with it. In other words, a natural user interface becomes invisible to the user to a certain extent. An excellent interface design should allow a user to seamlessly move between the physical and virtual spaces without feeling the existence of the technologies [6][8]. For example, when a video camera is used in a system to perform image capturing and analysis, a user of such a system may often forget the existence of the camera and concentrate on the screen after some time of practice. This kind of interface can facilitate the sense of telepresence and immersion in a virtual environment.

Most of the previous interactive storytelling systems focused on the automatic generation of story contents based on user mouse selection and texts or speech inputs [14]. However, these types of interactions usually required a user to use a different modality other than simply viewing. Consequently, the switches of modality often affected the flow of viewing, which was the main modality in film watching [17]. Therefore, in this work, we hope that navigation in a digital space can be incorporated with the narrative of a film such that the enjoyment of film watching can be enhanced based on the interaction of the system.

III. System Design and Implementation

In this section, we will describe how the interactive mode for the immersive viewing experience is designed, what kinds of technologies have been used to facilitate the design, and how the movie is produced.

A. Interactive design

We hope that a user moves her body in a natural way to change her view angle interactively and to make a decision on how the story is branched. In other words, we hope that the development of the story, which was originally controlled by the director, can be partially returned to the audience with the aim of enhancing the recognition of the story by the users.

We view the computer screen as a window and the film content is what happens outside the window. From different viewing angles, one can see different parts of the world, as illustrated in Figure 1. The spaces inside and outside the window frame can then be blurred and merged. Traditional meaning of a shot through framing can be extended through interaction.

Another important factor in such a system lies on the clever design of the content such that the scene inside the window is not complete and the actors move through the boundary of the frame. The design of the layout, viewing or moving directions of the actors, and the sound effects also play an important role in enhancing the sense of suspense to trigger the curiosity and peeping desire of the user for them to move their bodies to explore the space.

Besides moving the body to change the viewing angle, at some branching point of the plot in interactive storytelling, the user can also use the viewing angle to select a specific branch, which is accomplished by attaching a separated film fragment that is deliberately designed for seamless transition. Consequently, a user may see different story plots at different runs, which increase the replay value of a film.

B. Hardware and Software

A computer with a webcam is the only required equipment in our system. We use computer vision technologies to detect the position of the viewer, and through the detected position, we interactively change the viewing angle of the film. Compared to tangible equipment and surround virtual environments, such as 3D CAVE, interacting with a web cam is not only cost effective but also intuitive. Nevertheless, the extent of the changes that can be made is somewhat limited.

In our system, we have adopted a web-based approach with HTML5 technologies to increase the accessibility of the system. The image of the user captured through the web cam is acquired from the getUserMedia API and analyzed by the open source package, called clmtrackr , released by MIT. In this package, a user's face is detected, and its position is determined to select an appropriate streaming video fragment to display on a 3D plane implemented in WebGL [16]. The plane is then moved according to the detected face position of the user, as shown in Figure 2. In order to mimic the viewing effect of a human eye, we have implemented a nonlinear mapping between the viewing direction and the field of view. When the viewing direction is farther away from the central direction, the field of view also becomes wider. In addition, we have designed a light-weight test interface at the upper right corner of the screen, as shown in Figure 3, to check the face detection and system settings, and this interface can be hidden when the experiment is conducted.

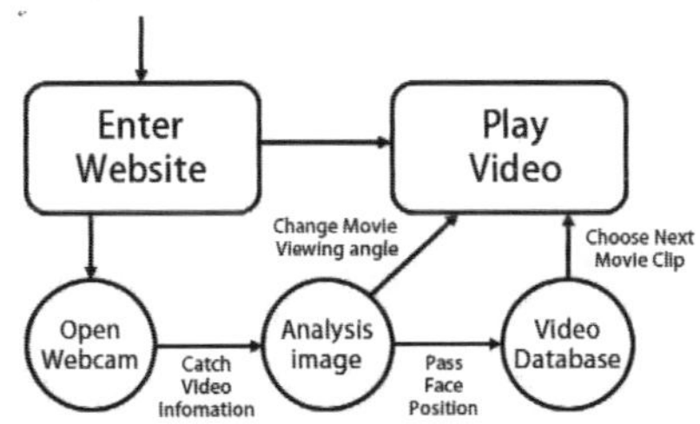

Figure 2. System flowchart

Figure 3. A screenshot with the system diagnosis tool displayed.

C. Movie Production

The video used in the main experiment is five minute long, and the style is suspense. In addition to the main plot line, there are two branches in the story that can be used as a result of user interaction. This design of interactive narratives is to increase the replay value of the film such that a user has a higher motivation to watch the film repeatedly. In most of the footages in the film, we have used long shots to allow the users to have more time to digest the contents on the screen.

Figure 4. Sample footage taken through a fisheye lens.

In the composition of the shots, we have tried to connect the on-screen and off-screen spaces to increase the possibility of communication between the film and the user. In order to facilitate the production of the film for a wider viewing angle, we have used a fish-eye lens to take the shots and adjusted distorted region of the shot through a post-production. As shown in Figure 4, the red rectangle is the initial view window and can be moved to a different position through user interaction.

IV. Evaluation

To understand the feasibility of our interactive mode design and user experience, we have designed a series of steps in our experiment as shown in Figure 5.

Figure 5. Experimental process diagram.

A. Experimental Subjects and Location

In order to understand the immersion of users during the interactive film viewing process, we have conducted experiments with ten subjects. These users were selected by a pretest survey about their film watching habits, such as the frequency of viewing a film at home and in a theater, to ensure that the subjects have a good span of user diversity.

In order to create a film watching atmosphere at home while controlling the experimental settings, we have conducted our experiments in a research laboratory as shown in Figure 6. The laboratory is decorated like a living environment such that the experiments can be conducted without disturbance and the participants can feel relaxed. In addition, the researchers can observe and analyze the behaviors of the participants through one-way mirror and a high-resolution video recording device.

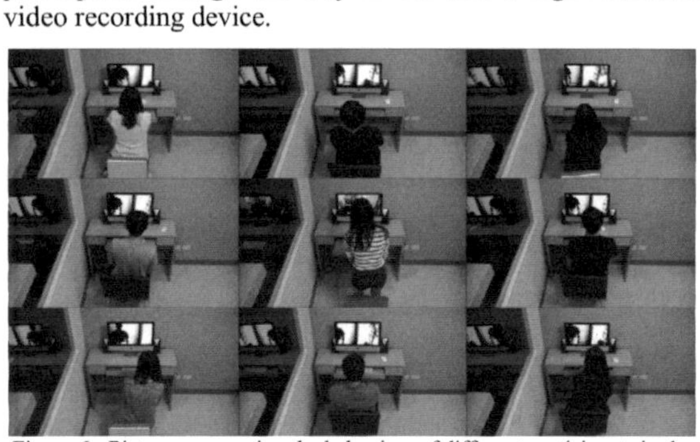

Figure 6. Pictures comparing the behaviors of different participants in the interactive film viewing experiment.

B. Experimental Process

In the first step of the process, we gave the participants an instruction describing the experimental process in order to help them understand the purpose and operational notes.

Before the formal experiments were started, we showed the participants a short film and allowed them to practice how to interact with the system by moving their bodies. When a participant felt confident about the interaction, she could initiate the formal experiment by herself. During the film viewing process, the researchers observed the participant's behavior in a control room and recorded the whole session for further analysis. When the film ended, there was a "replay" button on the screen to allow the participant to watch the film again. The participants can watch the film as many times as they want.

After the participants finished watching the film, a survey and interview session followed. The interview started with some pre-defined questions and was then followed by open discussions to understand their experience and suggestions.

C. Questionnaire Design

According to the reference and research purpose, we put together the elements related to immersive experience. We have used 'The Antecedent of Immersion' by Hoffman and Novak and 'The Features in the Immersive State' by Trevino and Webster to design the main schema of our questionnaire in the Likert 5-point scale (from 1 for "totally disagree" to 5 for "totally agree"). The means and standard deviations of the scores for these questions were then calculated for further analysis.

V. Experimental Result and Analysis

The user feedbacks are divided into two parts: content analysis and immersive experience.

A. Content Analysis

Most participants agree that the designs of actor's sight (Figure 7), actor movement (Figure 8), cropped screen (Figure 9), and scene (Figure 10) affect a viewer's behavior in watching the video.

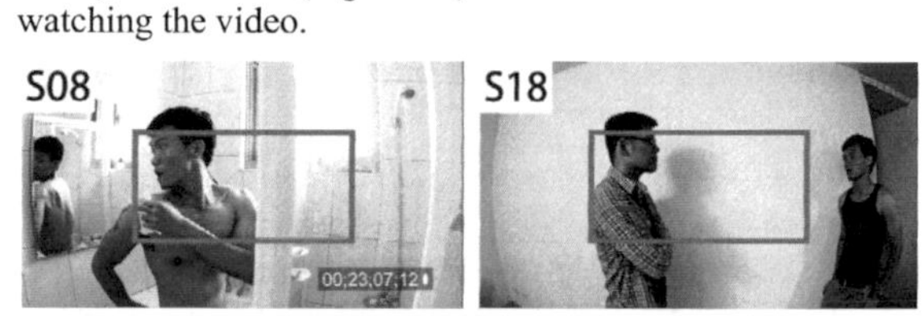

Figure 7. Character's sight may be used to catch a viewer's eyes.

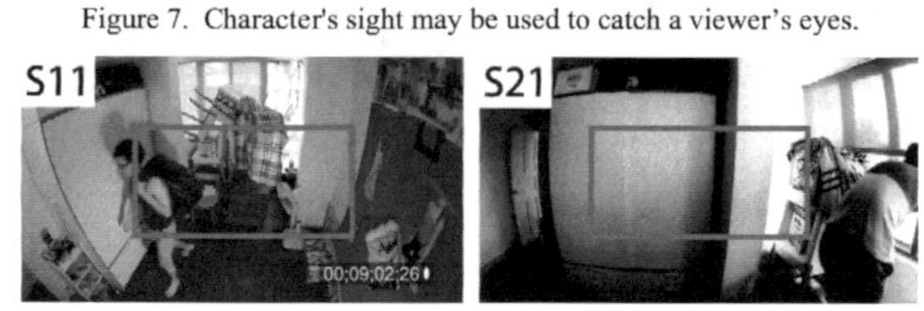

Figure 8. A character moves from the on-screen space to the off-screen space.

Figure 9. The cropped video invites the viewer to change the view angle.

As shown in Figure 10, a T-junction was used in a scene where the character tracked someone but got lost. He could turn left or right. If the user looks toward to left side, he will meet a stranger; otherwise, he will find a dumped garbage bag. In addition, the less complete a shot is, the more desire a user may have for moving her body. However, the information in a shot cannot be too diverse such that the focus of what the director would like to show is lost. Furthermore, in the shot used for branch selection, it is important to give the user a strong motivation (e.g. with life threat events) to move her body and look around.

Figure 10. Scene design for different story development

B. *Immersive Experience Analysis*

In this section, we will analyze the questionnaire in two groups: 'The Antecedent of Immersion' and 'Properties in the Immersive State.' According to the experimental data, we have also conducted in-depth interviews with the users to acquire their feedbacks behind the questionnaire.

TABLE I. THE ANTECEDENTS FOR ENTERING THE IMMERSION STATE.

	Question	avg.
Interactivity	There is no need to spend too much time to get familiar with the system.	4.5
	The interactivity of this system is interesting.	4.5
	The interactivity of this system is intuitive.	4.1
	The mode of operation of this system is smooth.	3.5
	Every shot design make me want to move my body to see the outer part.	4.8
	Every time the screen through my options is different, it makes me feel surprised.	4
Telepresence	I think that the viewport is like my eyes.	4
	Sometimes I feel myself in the scene when I watching the movie.	3.3
	Sometimes I think that I am one of the characters in the story when I watching the movie.	2.8

As shown in Table I, in the interactivity section of the antecedent conditions for immersion, most users consider our system as intuitive, interesting, and easy to understand. However, the user may get tired after some time of engagement. It is suggested that the vertical movement may be replaced by leaning forward or backward for zooming in and out.

In the section of telepresence, the scores we get are lower than the ones in the other section (especially for question #9). Some of the subjects consider that the window frame indeed may prevent them from entering the state of immersion. However, we think this may be improved by adopting more first-person shots in the cinematographic design.

TABLE II. THE FEATURE METRICS IN THE IMMERSIVE STATE.

	Question	avg.
Control	10. I feel that I can freely manipulate the system.	3.8
Attention Focus	11. My perception of the external environment will be reduced when I watching the movie.	4.2
	12. Compared with watching movie on the radetional computer, the system made me focus on more the details on the screen.	4.3
	13. Compared with watching movie on the radetional computer, the system put me in more the story.	3.8
Curiosity	14. The interaction of the system will deepen my curiosity about the movie.	4.6
	15. It satisfy my desire to watch movie by watching the outer side of the screen.	4.4
Intrinsic Interest	16. The system made me want to watch the movie again and again.	4.3
	17. Compared with watching movie on the traditional computer, the system gave me more fun.	4.3

In the section of features metrics for the immersive state as shown in Table II, we have received some unexpected interesting feedbacks. For a same shot, users of different personalities or genders may pay attention to different objects or places. For example, a female subject may pay attention to the layout of a male actor's room. This demonstrates the importance of allowing a user to have control since they may choose a different view point when interacting with the film.

However, in content design, it is still important to retain the property of storytelling and get a balance between interaction design and content creation since it is, nevertheless, a film instead of a game. In addition, sound tracks are as important as visual images since sound can attract the attention of a user on the screen. It could be even a better idea if we can implement surround sounds or better background music to enhance the audial sensation.

VI. FUTURE WORK

In this work, we have collected many suggestions and comments about the system design and film contents from the user survey. In the future, there are several directions that we can work on to improve the quality of the design and conduct more in-depth studies:

(1) **Studying the effect of film genre:** Based on the analysis of user feedbacks in this study, we will try to change the styles of the film and conduct the experiments again to compare and understand how genre may affect the immersive experience of a user.
(2) **Studying the effect of film length:** We will conduct experiments to compare the effect of film

length on the immersive experience. In this study, we have used a 5-min film to do the experiment. However, different film lengths (such as 30-sec advertisements, 10-min microfilms, 30-min short films, etc.) should also come with different interaction designs. For example, in a long film, a user may get tired easily if she needs to move her body to control the development of the story throughout the film. Instead, the interaction may be desired only in some critical sessions of the story.

(3) **Developing further applications:** In addition to applying the concept of interactive view changes to film watching, there could be many other applications that can adopt this kind of design. For example, the street view mode on Google Map can also use this method to replace mouse input in a guided tour. Other applications include on-line shopping and booking, serious games for navigation training, etc.

VII. CONCLUSION

In this work, we have used "interaction" to allow an audience to participate in a film and make the film watching experience more natural and intuitive. Consequently, richer immersive experience and better replay value have been observed in the conducted experiments.

Although the control of watching and story development have been somewhat transferred to the audience, the director still plays an important role in film making in such an interactive storytelling setting. This is because the role of director has been transformed to make the story convey more effective emotions through the use of interaction and story branching. We hope that, in the future, the design of more natural and intuitive interaction and seamless transitions between video segments can bring more and more possibility to the video-based interactive narratives.

ACKNOWLEDGMENT

The authors would like to thank the Ministry of Science and Technology in Taiwan for their financial support under project contract MOST 104-2221-E-004-006 -.

REFERENCES

[1] N. Burch, Theory Of Film Practice. Princeton: Princeton Univ Press.

[2] M. Csikszentmihalyi, Beyond Boredom and Anxiety: Experiencing Flow in Work and Play. San Francisco: Jossey-Bass, 1975.

[3] M. Csikszentmihalyi, Flow: The Psychology of Optimal Experience. New York: Harper & Row, 1990.

[4] D. Daniels, "Strategies of Interactivity," Media Art Interaction. Vienna and New York: Springer-Verlag, 2000, pp. 170-198.

[5] J. J. Gibson, The Senses Considered as Perceptual Systems. Boston: Houghton Mifflin Co, 1966.

[6] D. L. Hoffman and T. P. Novak, "Marketing in Hypermedia Compute r-Mediated Environments: Conceptual Foundations," Journal of Marketing, vol. 60, no. 3, pp.50-68, 1996.

[7] D. L. Hoffman and T. P. Novak, Measuring the Flow Experience Among Web Users. Palo Alto: Interval Research Corporation, 1997.

[8] T. Jeng, "Social and Interaction Issues in a Human-Centered Reactive Environment," Proc. of 7th CAADRIA, Cyberjaya, Malaysia: Multimedia University Malaysia, 2002, pp. 285-292.

[9] D. Johnson and J. Wiles, "Effective Affective User Interface Design in Games," Journal of Ergonomics, vol. 46, pp. 1332-1345, 2003.

[10] L. Manovich, An Archeology of a Computer Screen. Kunstforum International, 1995.

[11] D. Parkinson, 100 Ideas that Changed Film. Laurence King Publishing, 2012.

[12] P. Persson, "A Comparative Study of Digital and Cinematic Space with Special Focus on Navigational Issues," Exploring Navigation: Towards a Framework for Design and Evaluation of Navigation in Electronic Space Kista, Sweden: Swedish Institute of Computer Science, pp. 173-188, 1998.

[13] H. T. Regenbrecht and T. W. Schubert, "Measuring Presence in Virtual Environments," HCI International 1997, San Francisco, CA, 1997.

[14] U. Spierling, D. Grasbon, N. Braun, and I. Iurgel, "Setting the scene: playing digital director in interactive storytelling and creation," Computers & Graphics, vol. 26, no. 1, pp.31-44, 2002.

[15] L. K., Trevino and J. Webster, "Flow in Computer-Mediated Communication Electronic Mail and Voice Mail Evaluation and Impacts," Communication Research, vol. 19, no. 5, pp. 539-573, 1992.

[16] WebGL, https://www.khronos.org/webgl/

[17] J. Webster, K. L. Trevino, and L. Ryan, "The Dimensionality and Correlates of Flow in Human-Computer Interacitons," Computers in Human Behavior, vol. 9, no. 4, pp. 411-426, 1993.

[18] W. Williams and M. E. Shapiro, "A Study of the Effects In-Home Entertainment Alternatives Have on Film Attendance," Current Research in Film : Audiences, Economics, and Law, vol. 1, pp.93-100, 1985.

[19] B. G.Witmer and M. J. Singer, "Measuring presence in virtual environments: A presence questionnaire," Presence: Telreeoperators and Virtual Environments 7, Cambridge: The MIT Press, pp. 225-240, 1998.

Usability Analysis in the Liquid Galaxy platform

Ismael Arroyo*, Francesc Giné†, Concepció Roig‡
Distributed Computing Group, University of Lleida
Lleida, Spain
Email: *ismael.arroyo@udl.cat, †sisco@diei.udl.cat, ‡roig@diei.udl.cat

Toni Granollers§
Research Group on Human-Computer
Interaction and Data Integration, University of Lleida
Lleida, Spain
Email: §antoni.granollers@udl.cat

***Abstract*—With the falling price of the technology and the growing trend of cluster display-walls, User Experience (UX) becomes a topic to be taken into account with this new kind of systems. In this context, we present a study of a specific cluster display-wall, named Liquid Galaxy and developed by Google, that covers the three main aspects of usability: effectiveness, efficiency and satisfaction. The study was done by means of a set of tasks that users completed during UX tests, with post-task and post-tests questionnaires, while the system performance was measured. The results show positive feelings from users while using the system. In addition, we relate both system performance and user behavior to estimate whether the system will perform satisfactorily for users. According to our observations, we can see that, in general, there is an intrinsic relationship between the goodness of feelings and the quality of the performance metrics. This relationship can facilitate the inclusion of cluster display-wall systems in a broad range of scenarios with right levels of UX just by analyzing their computational characteristics.**

Keywords–Liquid Galaxy; User Experience; Cluster Display-Wall.

I. Introduction

Cluster-based solutions for creating large displays have recently generated a lot of interest [1]. Such displays have the potential to put high-performance visualization within the reach of more users. The most valuable potential of cluster display-walls is their pixel density, as the images are FullHD on every monitor, providing the system with an incredible overall resolution given the low cost of the hardware required. These systems consist of a number of commodity PCs that are interconnected over a LAN or via low-latency networks like the Myrinet [2]. Thus, visualization of the images across screens in cluster display-walls is carried out by synchronizing the data between the computers in the cluster. Nowadays, besides the fact that conventional PCs can be equipped with powerful consumer graphics cards with multiple outputs, the availability of software packages for clusters makes setting up cluster display-walls affordable. Thus, cluster-based displays are affordable, scalable in resolution, and easy to maintain. This opens a wide range of new possibilities for their use in everyday scenarios in such areas as entertainment or education.

This rising trend for cluster display-walls caught our attention and brought up some questions about how the end-user would feel when using and experiencing these new visualization systems, and how we could estimate the user experience acknowledging the system parameters. In order to answer both questions, we performed user tests to know their behavior by gathering satisfaction, effectiveness and efficiency data. Furthermore, we found a relation between them that enabled us to estimate how users would behave with a cluster display-wall with specific performance characteristics. We noted that there are some works in the literature [3][4] that deal with the desired results separately, but we want to go one step further by relating both metrics.

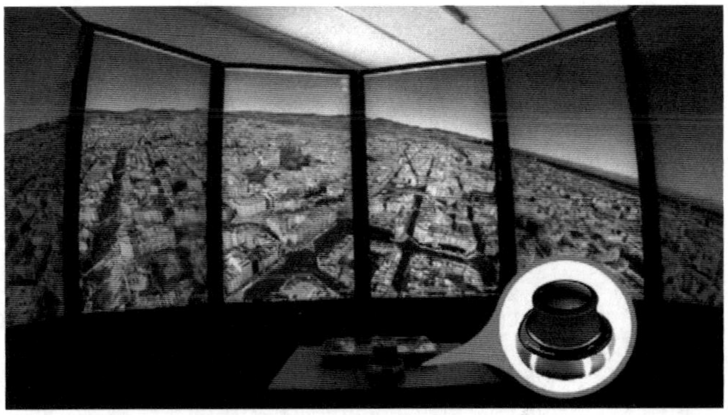

Figure 1. Liquid Galaxy.

In this work, we were interested in testing the usability related aspects of a particular cluster display-wall system, named Liquid Galaxy [5], especially on acquiring data from real users. The Liquid Galaxy technology is a cluster display-wall hemisphere infrastructure developed by Google, running the well-known Google Earth application [6], which is an example of a master-slave application. The Liquid Galaxy system is usually made up of three, five or eight displays, each connected to a computer node, and is designed to provide an immersive geographic visualization. Figure 1 shows the Google Liquid Galaxy infrastructure installed in the Technological Park in the city of Lleida (Spain) [7]. The Figure also shows the most commonly used controller, named 3D Space Navigator.

With the Liquid Galaxy infrastructure, in the present work, we carried out a pre-prepared test with 27 people. It consisted of navigating to some well-known places around the world. Additionally, everyone answered some questions about their experience while using the system. Then, we related these answers, which made up a set of qualitative performance metrics, to the quantitative performance metrics that we measured during the test. In order to measure this quantitative metrics, we have used the Visualization Rate (VR) performance parameter which has been presented in previous works [8][9]. VR is a relation between the CPU time used by the system to load all the multimedia data and the total time of the visualization.

In general, the results show that the vast majority of the participants were satisfied and had positive feelings using the system throughout the test. Additionally, we have analyzed the relationship between the user' satisfaction levels and the VR performance metric. The obtained correlation shows that the usability of the system can be roughly estimated by using only the VR in any given field test. This relationship can be determinant in facilitating an extensive use of such kind of systems, given that the knowledge of system characteristics, directly related to system performance, can give knowledge of what the UX [10] of using the system will be.

The paper is structured as following. Section II enumerates different approaches that other authors developed and describes last works that are and improvement above them. In Section III is presented the case study of Liquid Galaxy. In Section IV is described the method and results obtained for the tests. Section V summarizes and relates the obtained data from the previous tests. Finally, VI concludes the paper and discusses future directions.

II. Background and Related Work

Within the extensive literature on large displays, we focused on studies about User Experience on cluster display-walls. In general, research into this kind of system is focused on the study of the UX, such as the ones presented next.

Bi and Balakrishnan [3] focused on user behavior in large-scale displays and demonstrated that the users preferred this kind of system over single desktops. The authors made participants perform everyday work in a week-long study and compare it with single or dual-monitor desktops. The results are all about subjective opinions and observations from the users, with notes about how they used the system. This study is focused on the preferences of the users while ignoring the system performance.

Tan et al. [11] studied how their system, called Infocockpit, can make information memorable. Infocockpit is a projector-based display-wall with ambient visual and auditory displays that engage human memory for location. In their work, they made users complete semantic tasks that consist in remembering pairs of words and then recalling them. The results are both quantitative and qualitative, as they studied how many words the users could remember in Infocockpit compared with on a desktop computer. Also, participants answered a user satisfaction questionnaire after the tasks. Nevertheless, this approach does not try to relate both metrics using the system performance.

Ball and North [4] studied the effectiveness of a 3x3 large tiled display compared with two smaller displays. They concluded that display-walls that use physical navigation significantly outperform smaller displays that use pan and zoom navigation. They tested both environments with a task with quantitative results based on finding targets of different sizes. Also, they introduced observations that the users made during the test, adding a subtle qualitative study into the research. Despite this, they did not take the system performance into account.

Despite the growing literature on qualitative or quantitative views of the use of a cluster display-wall [12] [13] [14], to the best of our knowledge, there are no studies that focus on establishing a relationship between both metrics. In general, these studies are focused on the results of specific tasks, like completion time or scores, but not on system performance and how it affects user behavior and/or experience.

In previous works, we analyzed the performance of the Liquid Galaxy System in relation to different system parameters such as the scalability, heterogeneity, CPU, RAM, Network requirements, etc. However, we did not tackle neither the quality of use from the user point of view nor its relation with the system performance.

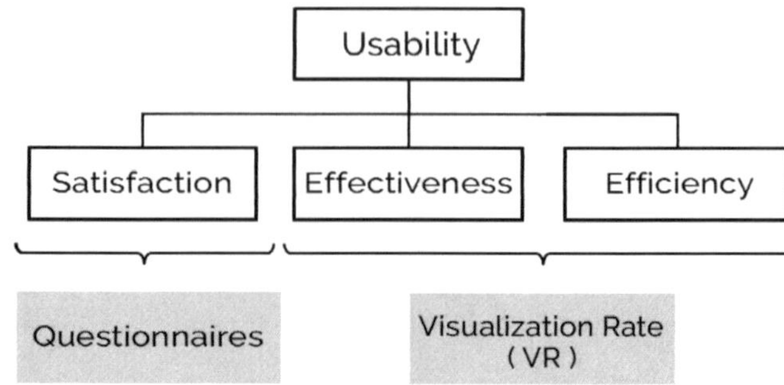

Figure 2. Measuring Usability.

In this paper, our goal is to try to relate the Usability aspects of the User Experience (satisfaction, effectiveness and efficiency [15]) of the Liquid Galaxy cluster. Thus, it will enable us to predict before-hand if a system will perform well enough from the user point of view without the need of carrying out any user test.

III. Liquid Galaxy

Liquid Galaxy [5] is a cluster display-wall that started as a Google project, made up of a custom number of computers, where every node has a single monitor. This system was originally built to run Google Earth [6] and to create an immersive experience for the user. Liquid Galaxy lets you navigate around the globe with its 6-axis controller, allowing you to instantly zoom in, zoom out, and turn in a completely fluid motion. Likewise, the immersive visualization environment of Liquid Galaxy opens up this kind of system to be used by a wide range of applications that can benefit from this feature. Some examples of applications that can be run in this system are WebGL applications like Aquarium [16] or Peruse-a-rue [17], video streaming [18] and video-games like Quake 3 Arena [19].

In the Liquid Galaxy system, every node is connected to the same network and the nodes share a distributed cache named Squid [20], included in the Liquid Galaxy repository. This is used to cache http objects for repetitive use, thus improving throughput, as Internet data requests would be reduced.

Depending on the application to be used, the interaction with the system can be carried out using devices such as a Mouse, Keyboard, Leapmotion, Myo or 3D Space Navigator (as in our case), among others.

IV. User Study

We had the necessity to study the Liquid Galaxy to know how users react to the system and how to try to predict an estimated overall satisfaction by relating it to the performance metrics. In order to achieve this, the system was tested by means of the usability attributes of satisfaction, effectiveness and efficiency [15]. To meet this aim, users had to answer some post-task questions about how they felt after completing each task and a post-test questionnaire about their feeling while using the system. At the same time, the system performance was monitored throughout the tests. This objective is depicted in Figure 2, where it can be seen how effectiveness and efficiency can be monitored using the performance parameter VR, and satisfaction is obtained by using questionnaires that users had to answer.

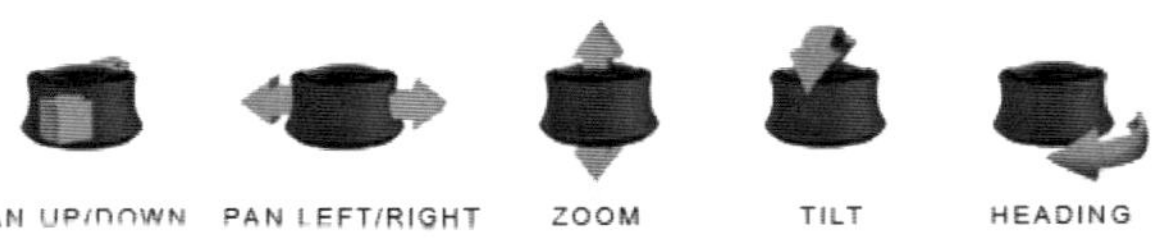

Figure 3. 3D Space Navigator Movement Options.

With these measurements, system performance and users satisfaction, we aimed to relate both metrics to be able to predict the average usability values for a specific cluster display-wall with given hardware characteristics.

The different aspects involved in the usability tests that were carried out to analyze the system performance and the users satisfaction are exposed next.

A. *Environment*

1) Cluster Display-Wall: The environment on which the tests were performed was an office equipped with a Liquid Galaxy system made up of 3 nodes. The monitors used in the cluster were a triplet of 32” monitors set vertically in a semi-hemispheric way. The interaction controller used was a 3D Space Navigator (Figure 3), which is the most widely-used controller in all Liquid Galaxy setups. This device is able to displace the view but also rotate it on all 3 axes, making it the most suitable controller for navigating through 3D scenarios.

2) Facilitator: A facilitator was running the test and guiding the participants through it. He/she attended to the participants, explained the goals of the test, the consent form and everything to make them feel comfortable. Once the test started, the facilitator could only answer specific questions or give subtle advice when the participant was struggling to complete a task for a long time.

B. *Participants*

The set of participants that carried out the tasks included a range of professional profiles, ages and skills with controllers. There were 27 participants in the test, of whom 15 were females and 12 males. Their age ranged from 12 to 68.

Table I shows some information about the participants grouped by age ranges. This corresponds to information about their occupation and the navigation skills they think to have before the test in a range from 0 to 10.

C. *Test*

Each participant was asked to do a series of four user tasks. The test used to study the User Experience of the system was a semi-guided tour, using Google Earth, around different places across the globe.

The device used to carry out the tasks of the Liquid Galaxy was the 3D Space Navigator of Figure 3. As we knew that this is a different and more complex controller than a common mouse, we dedicated some minutes helping the participants to use the device before starting the test to avoid any initial fear.

The users were also informed that all the information would be given through the monitors during the test and that they will have to answer the questions from the facilitator by voice, who wrote them down instead of the participant to avoid interference with the test.

For each participant, the test was composed of four tasks, each one corresponding to navigating to one of the following well-known places in the world:

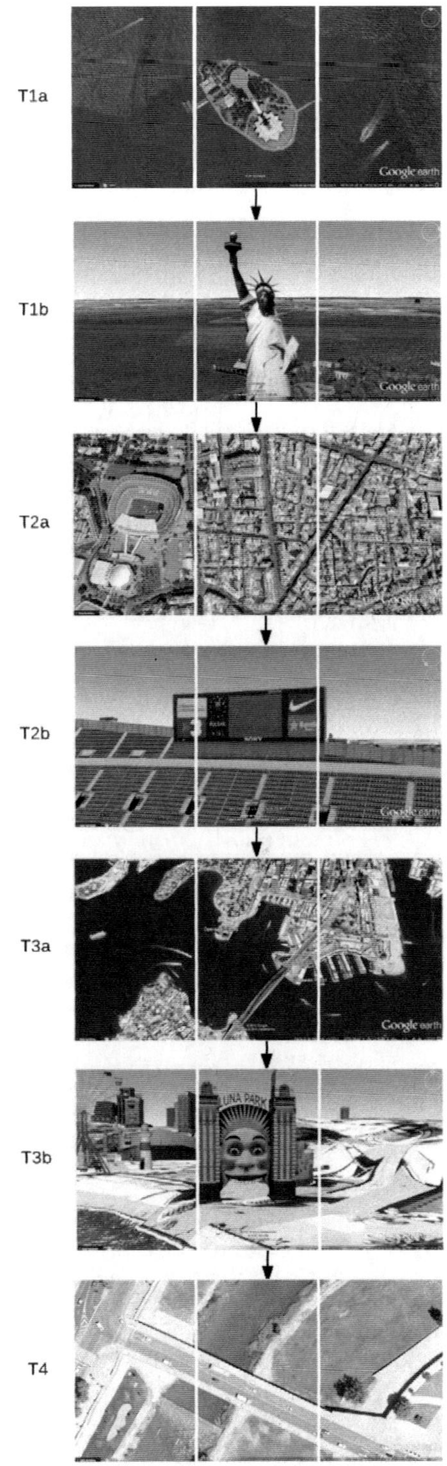

Figure 4. Tour Flowchart - T1a Statue of Liberty from above - T1b Statue of Liberty’s crown - T2a Barcelona Football Club stadium - T2b The stadium’s screen - T3a Sydney Harbour - T3b Luna Park - T4a Lleida bridge. Each picture is the composition of the 3 screens of the system.

TABLE I. BASIC PARTICIPANT INFORMATION.

Age range	*Participants*	*Avg Skill Level*	*Occupations*
12 to 16	4	7	4 Students.
16 to 21	3	9	2 Computer Science Programmers, 1 Computer Science Engineer.
22 to 35	9	6	3 Computer Science Students, 1 Pre-School Ed. Student, 1 Economics Student, 1 High School Student, 1 Restorer, 1 Industrial Engineer, 1 Computer Science Engineer.
36 to 68	11	4	5 Teachers, 4 management staff, 1 Customer Service Worker, 1 Shop Assistant.

TABLE II. DESCRIPTION OF TEST TASKS.

Task	*City*	*Sub-task*	*Positioning*	*Questions*
T1	New York	T1a	Automatic	How many vertices does the base of the Statue of Liberty have?
		T1b	Manual	How many points does the crown of the Statue of Liberty have?
T2	Barcelona	T2a	Automatic	What does it say on the Barcelona Football Club stadium stands?
		T2b	Manual	What brand is the screen in the Barcelona Football Club stadium?
T3	Sydney	T3a	Automatic	How many buildings is the Sydney Opera House made of?
		T3b	Manual	Find a structure nearby with a clown's face on it. What does it say above it?
T4	Lleida	T4	Manual	How many buses are crossing the bridge in front of the cathedral in Lleida?

TABLE III. POST-TEST QUESTIONNAIRE.

Questions	*Description*
FQ1	"From 0 to 10, mark your personal skill at using joysticks and remote control devices"
FQ2	"From 0 to 10, mark the ease of use when using the system"
FQ3	"From 0 to 10, mark how much you think that you had to learn to use the system"
FQ4	"From 0 to 10, mark how much technical help you think would be needed to use the system"
FQ5	"From 0 to 10, mark if you believe that everyone could learn the system quickly"
FQ6	"From 0 to 10, mark your personal satisfaction when using the system"
FQ7	"From 0 to 10, mark how secure you felt when interacting with Liquid Galaxy"
FQ8	"From 0 to 10, mark the degree of difficulty that you found for using this system"
FQ9	"From 0 to 10, mark your perception of system complexity"

- T1: New York (USA): Statue of Liberty.
- T2: Barcelona (Spain): Barcelona Football Club Stadium.
- T3: Sydney (Australia): Bay of the Opera House.
- T4: Lleida (Spain): City where the participants live.

Tasks T1, T2 and T3 were composed of two sub-tasks. In the first sub-task (Tia), the system positioned itself automatically

Figure 5. Emotional Choices (source LemTool).

at the first place in the city, so that participants had to answer the related question. In this way, the participants did not use the controller for the first part of each task. However, in the second sub-task (Tib), they had to use the controller to reposition the view to be able to answer the related question. Task T4 consisted of a free flight from Sydney (T3b) to a specific point of interest in Lleida city. Figure 4 shows the pictures of the 7 sub-tasks that correspond to the flow of activities in the test.

Table II shows the questions that users had to answer to complete each sub-task, thus completing each of the tasks. Even though the real answers were not so important, they were a way of forcing the user to interact with the system and show interest when doing the tasks. The tasks were designed to increase the difficulty gradually on each step and thus help the users' ability to control the 3D Space Navigator to progress.

After each task, with the aim of acquiring information to evaluate the UX with the minimum set of questions, we issued the same two questions to the participants:

TABLE IV. RESULTS OF Q1 QUESTION.

Tour	*Joy*	*Desire*	*Fascination*	*Satisfaction*	*Sadness*	*Disgust*	*Boredom*	*Dissatisfaction*
NY	7.1%	7.1%	35.7%	42.9%	7.1%	0%	0%	0%
BCN	7.1%	14.3%	21.4%	42.9%	0%	7.1%	0%	7.1%
SYD	7.1%	0%	28.6%	57.1%	0%	0%	0%	7.1%
LL	7.1%	14.3%	35.7%	42.9%	0%	0%	0%	0%

TABLE V. RESULTS OF Q2 QUESTION.

Tour	*0*	*2*	*4*	*6*	*8*	*10*
NY	0%	0%	0%	14.3%	42.9%	42.9%
BCN	7.1%	7.1%	7.1%	28.6%	42.9%	7.1%
SYD	0%	7.1%	7.1%	7.1%	50%	28.6%
LL	0%	0%	7.1%	14.3%	35.7%	42.9%

- Q1: "From the following drawings, mark which one better explains how you felt when performing the task". The drawings (Figure 5), based on the LemTool emotional tool [21], are designed to acquire the user's emotional state just after solving each task. Among others, LemTool is an auto-report tool that can be used during the interaction with the interface for its evaluation. It allows the interface to be related to the emotion evoked. The tool consists of eight figures that represent four positive and four negative emotions, combining facial expressions and body postures.
- Q2: "From 0 to 10, mark your satisfaction with the load timeout of the images". The possible answers were "0, 2, 4, 6, 8 or 10. The goal of this question is to obtain a fast and a first-hand opinion related to the satisfaction with the image loading time which is directly related to the VR parameter as will be explained in Section IV-E.

Finally, after finishing all four tasks, participants had to answer the post-test questionnaire, shown in Table III. This last questionnaire is inspired by the System Usability Scale (SUS), which has long been accepted as an industry standard [22] and adapted to fit in our tests with the Liquid Galaxy system.

D. Satisfaction Results

By processing the answers from the questions of the participants (see Tables II and III), we obtained a set of qualitative measures of the test that are presented next.

Table IV shows the level of satisfaction (question Q1) when performing the tests in New York (NY), Barcelona (BCN), Sydney (SYD) and Lleida (LL), while Table V shows the feeling of the users about the waiting time for each task (question Q2). We can see that the majority of the participants provided positive responses when using the system while doing the tests whenever everything was functioning and the waiting times were short. In general, 90% of the participants gave positive feeling responses to the tours of NY, SYD and LL, having a few cases of discomfort. However, this percentage was lower in BCN because the user had to move the Google Earth view into a view showing a significant portion of the city buildings, thus, making the application download a considerable amount of data. Because of this, some people felt that they had to wait much longer than in other tasks, especially the most demanding users, including the youngest participants or those with more technology knowledge. As a consequence, the results of BCN in Table IV shows 14.2% of participants as having negative feelings. This correlates with the waiting time shown in Table V, where in the case of BCN, 21.3% considered the waiting time unacceptable (values lower than 5). Despite some people being frustrated by the wait, they answered more positively in the question Q1 than expected. This leads us to think that they were enthusiastic about the system as it was new and fun for them. We can also say that many of them found the system challenging, but not impossible, forcing themselves to perform better and reward themselves with pride, which could affect the results by giving higher values.

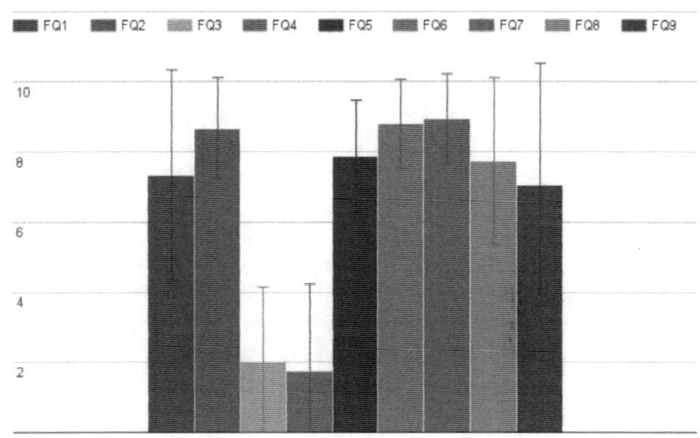

Figure 6. Mean and Error bars from Post-Test questions - Skilled Group.

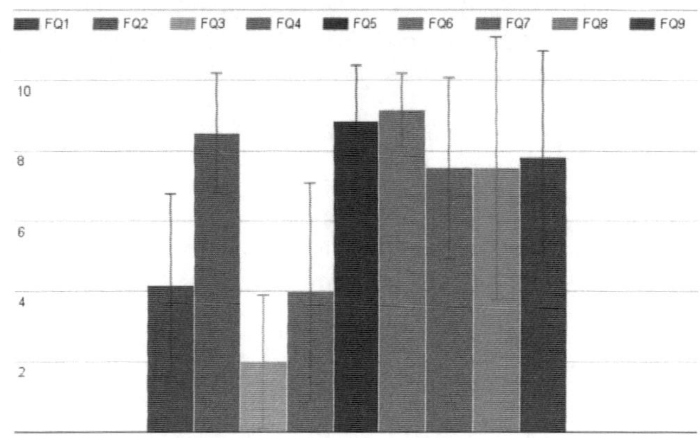

Figure 7. Mean and Error bars from Post-Test questions - Less Skilled Group.

The answers obtained for the post-test questionnaire described in Table III can be divided into two main groups: a young and more skilled profile corresponding to the 12 to 35 age range in Table I, whose answers, in average, are presented in Figure 6, and older and less skilled people, whose answers are presented in Figure 7. This skill difference can be observed with the answer to question FQ1 in both Figures. Taking the answers to FQ2 and FQ3 into account, both groups stated that they did not feel a need for prior knowledge and that the system was easy to learn and use, regardless of their experience. The main difference was about how secure they felt while using the system (FQ7), where the second group, less experienced, felt less secure as well as noting that they needed more technical help. Also, the differences between both groups in their response to the question about whether they thought technical help would be needed (FQ4) were remarkable, which is correlated with their technical skill level.

In relation to the deviation of the answers, we can see that, in general, this was higher in Figure 7 due to the differences between participants in this group, both in age and occupation. Likewise, it is worth pointing out that the question about how complex they felt the system was (FQ9) is the one with a wider range of opinions in both groups. This is because some of the participants did not know what to answer as it was a new system and it lead them to think that it would be too complex for others. Thus, some answered thinking about other people with less or similar experience than themselves. This behavior was expected as the questions were designed to take into consideration other people evaluating the system, and not how they used it.

E. Effectiveness and Efficiency Results

As stated in the introduction, one of the goals of the present work was to establish a relationship between the satisfaction (associated with the subjectivity of the participants) and the effectiveness and efficiency measures, related to the system performance (with no subjectivity associated). In our context, we understand the effectiveness as the ability of the system to load all the images while running the application, and the efficiency as the time required to load these images. In order to get the effectiveness and efficiency of the system, the Visualization Rate (VR) metric was used. This metric was used in our previous works to measure the Liquid Galaxy performance [8][9].

Taking into account that the CPU usage tells us when the system has loaded all the visual elements, VR is calculated as the average CPU idle time for a cluster of n nodes with the following equation:

$$VR = \frac{100}{n} \sum_{i=1}^{n} \frac{T\_idle_i}{T\_total}, \quad (1)$$

where T_total is the total time of the test and T_idle_i is the time when the CPU load of node n_i is below a minimum threshold. Note that a CPU load below this threshold means that the CPU is idle and the images have been fully loaded. This procedure can is illustrated in Figure 8, where the blue line near 5% CPU Usage is the threshold for this particular case. The peaks depicted in this Figure corresponds to when the CPU is processing the imagery and the values that drop below the threshold represent when the CPU becomes idle. The CPU usage information was gathered every second from the information given automatically by the system monitor. Note that when the VR is near 100%, it denotes a high visualization rate and, so, good user perception as images are fully visualized, while having a VR equal to 0% means that the data has not been fully loaded and, thus, it has been ineffective. Any value between 0% and 100% indicates how efficiently the system has performed. Given that the best feature of the system is its high pixel density visualization, if the system reports VR results near 0%, it will mean that the user does not take all the potential of the cluster.

TABLE VI. VR RANGES FOR T1a, T2a AND T3a SUB-TASKS.

Tour	*0-5%*	*5-10%*	*10-15%*	*15-30%*
NY	28.6%	42.9%	21.4%	7.1%
BCN	57.1%	35.7%	7.1%	0%
SYD	14.3%	57.1%	21.4%	7.1%

The system performance metric was monitored throughout the test, but only the tasks where comparisons could be made were recorded. Those tasks are the ones that are guided, because Google Earth follows the same path from one place to another in a guided task independently of the user, thus providing fully comparable values. This is not applicable when the user moves between locations manually, as it is almost impossible to have the same flight path for the same step, even with the same user. This means that only tasks T1a, T2a and T3a, depicted in Figure 4, were monitored to calculate the VR.

Table VI shows the VR values obtained by different users for NY, BCN and SYD for the first part of their respective tasks (Tia). For simplicity, these values are categorized in ranges which are shown as columns in the Table. For the case of NY and SYD, the highest VR values were near 25%, but for BCN, the VR achieved lower values. This is due to the fact that in BCN, in Task 2a, a lot of 3D buildings had to be rendered in order to view the desired place and, as a consequence, the loading time was higher and the users did not need to have the images fully loaded to answer the question. Another point to highlight is that all VR values were below 30%. This is because, in our test, the user only wanted to answer the questionnaire, and he/she was not interested in the specific imagery. In a free flight around points of interest by a given user, he/she would spend more time looking at a specific point, which would increase the VR metric.

V. Discussion

User tests were carried out on a Liquid Galaxy cluster in order to study the relation between the system performance and the personal satisfaction of the users when using it. In general, the results showed that there is a relation between VR values and the users' satisfaction level. From our study, we can see that SYD had the highest VR and also the highest satisfaction level, whereas BCN had the lowest VR and level of satisfaction. Despite this, people were generally satisfied and happy to use the system even though the VR values were rather low. This behavior is reflected in the results obtained from BCN. Table IV shows that the majority were satisfied and fascinated (71%), while Table VI shows that the VR of this city was the lowest, always below 15%. These data give us a hint that there might be a relation between VR and the Q1 and Q2 questions. Therefore, the possible relation between the performance and the satisfaction parameters were studied under a statistical point of view.

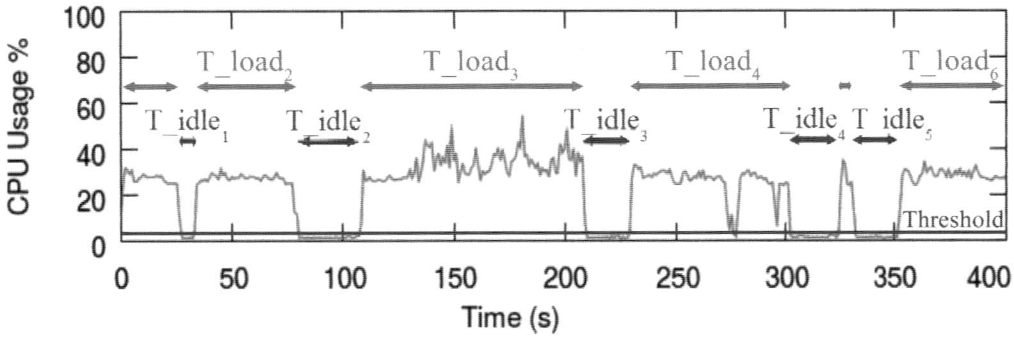

Figure 8. VR: CPU Usage.

TABLE VII. VARIANCES AND CORRELATIONS FOR Q1, Q2 AND VR.

Tour	σ^2_{Q1}	σ^2_{Q2}	σ^2_{VR}	$\sigma_{Q1,VR}$	$\sigma_{Q2,VR}$	$r_{Q1,VR}$	$r_{Q2,VR}$
NY	0,88	1,40	6,48	3,70	5,59	0,65	0,62
BCN	5,34	1,91	3,04	2,49	1,73	0,15	0,30
SYD	1,23	1,69	4,16	2,67	4,43	0,52	0,63

Table VII shows the variances (σ^2), covariances (σ) and linear correlations (r) for the answers to Q1 and Q2, and the VR performance metric. As for the correlation, values closer to 1 or -1 means that there is a strong relation between the metrics, while having values closer to 0 means that there is no relation between them. We can see that, in general, there is a positive correlation in all the cases. Likewise, as it was expected, both correlations (r_{Q1VR} and r_{Q2VR}) in NY and SYD are very strong, while correlations in BCN are the weakest. The reason of this lowest correlation in the BCN case is that in one hand it had the worst VR values due to the high number of 3D buildings to be loaded, but, on the other hand, people maintained a high interest and satisfaction when flying above Barcelona because it was the most well known tour for the spanish users. In addition, it is worth pointing out that, in general, the correlation r_{Q2VR} is slightly stronger than the r_{Q1VR}. This behavior is normal given that the Q2 question asked to the users about their feelings in relation to the loading time and the VR metric was calculated from the same loading time.

These correlation results lead us to think that the VR metric constitutes an orientative value to know the minimum required performance to guarantee a right satisfaction to the user with the system.

VI. CONCLUSION

This paper is focused on the User Experience study of a specific cluster display-wall, named Google Liquid Galaxy, by using the well-known usability standard definition which enclosures the usability as satisfaction, effectiveness and efficiency. We studied the effectiveness and efficiency using the quantitative metric VR, and the satisfaction using two post-tasks questions about satisfaction using LemTool and a post-test questionnaire based on the SUS and adapted to suit in our study. Additionally, we carried out an analysis to find the relationship between these measurements.

The satisfaction analysis was based on a series of tasks carried out with real users with different characteristics of age, occupation and skills. The results showed that the majority had positive feelings while using the system, even though they noticed a lack of speed in loading images in some parts of the test. Moreover, there was a clear difference between younger and older people. The first group are more experienced and tend to be more impatient, as they are already into this kind of technology, whereas the second group usually are less experienced and tend to be more impressed.

To acquire knowledge of system performance, we used the Visualization Rate (VR) metric that indicates the average CPU idle time of system nodes, in such a way that the time intervals when the CPU is idle (under a certain threshold) means that the images were fully loaded. A VR value equal 0% means that the system is ineffective and any value above 0% describes the percentage of efficiency of the system. During the tests, we observed that the VR was generally below 30% and above 0%. Although this could seem a low performance, it was due to the behavior of the participants when completing the tasks. Some users had only to wait to load partially the image to be able to answer the questions (usually the center screen, excluding the rest of screens) and for this reason the VR values were relatively low.

Finally, we analyzed the existing relationship that could be established between the results of the study. We were able to confirm that the VR constitutes an orientative value of what the satisfaction level will be when using a specific system infrastructure. This was confirmed by the statistical correlation between VR and the questionnaires. It shows how both satisfaction post-task questions are related to the VR values achieved in those tasks. Additionally, satisfaction levels can be higher than expected, taking the VR metric into account, whenever the tour was of high interest for the users.

Our results reveal that with the knowledge of the system performance, which can be found with objective metrics, we can estimate the suitability of a cluster display-wall to be used under certain user requirements. This is very encouraging results for us, as it can facilitate the spread of the use of the Liquid Galaxy platform to a broad number of users and fields (education, professional, research, etc.).

Future work includes mathematical modeling of the predictable system performance, specifically the VR metric, of any given hardware and configuration. Also, we plan to run a similar test in an everyday context such as a travel agency, where participants (potential clients) will use the system to extend the information of their travel plan. We think that this test context will provide us with more realistic data as the users will not perform predefined tasks and, thus, they will try to achieve their personal objectives. Thus, the VR values probably would be different in relation to the ones obtained in our test. One step further could be applying this methodology of measuring the usability in other systems by finding their own VR parameter.

ACKNOWLEDGMENT

*This work was supported by MEyC-Spain under contract TIN2012-37826-C02-02 and TIN2014-53234-C2-2-R

REFERENCES

[1] Nirnimesh, P. Harish, and P. Naraayanan, "Garuda: A scalable tiled display wall using commodity pcs." IEEE Transactions on Visualization and Computer Graphics., vol. 13, no. 5, 2007, pp. 864–877.

[2] N. J. Boden et al., "Myrinet: A gigabit-per-second local area network," IEEE micro, no. 1, 1995, pp. 29–36.

[3] X. Bi and R. Balakrishnan, "Comparing usage of a large high-resolution display to single or dual desktop displays for daily work," in Proceedings of the SIGCHI Conference on Human Factors in Computing Systems. ACM, 2009, pp. 1005–1014.

[4] R. Ball and C. North, "Effects of tiled high-resolution display on basic visualization and navigation tasks," in CHI'05 extended abstracts on Human factors in computing systems. ACM, 2005, pp. 1196–1199.

[5] Google, "Liquid Galaxy live demo at TED," 2010, lecture Notes in Computer Science, Springer.

[6] ——, "Google Earth," 2013, retrieved: March, 2016. [Online]. Available: http://www.google.com/earth/index.html

[7] Ponent 2002, "G-liquid galaxy," 2012, retrieved: March, 2016. [Online]. Available: http://www.g-liquidgalaxy.com

[8] I. Arroyo, F. Gine, C. Roig, and M. Gonzalez, "User experience on heterogenous liquid galaxy cluster display walls," in 2014 IEEE 15th International Symposium on a World of Wireless, Mobile and Multimedia Networks (WoWMoM). IEEE, 2014, pp. 1–3.

[9] I. Arroyo, F. Giné, C. Roig, and T. Granollers, "Analyzing google earth application in a heterogeneous commodity cluster display wall," Multimedia Tools and Applications, 2015, pp. 1–26. [Online]. Available: http://dx.doi.org/10.1007/s11042-015-2859-z

[10] ISO DIS, "9241-210 (2008): Ergonomics of human system interaction-part 210: Human-centered design for interactive systems," International Organization for Standardization, 2008.

[11] M. Czerwinski et al., "Toward characterizing the productivity benefits of very large displays," in Proceedings of INTERACT, vol. 3, 2003, pp. 9–16.

[12] B. Yost, Y. Haciahmetoglu, and C. North, "Beyond visual acuity: The perceptual scalability of information visualizations for large displays," in Proceedings of the SIGCHI Conference on Human Factors in Computing Systems, ser. CHI '07. New York, NY, USA: ACM, 2007, pp. 101–110. [Online]. Available: http://doi.acm.org/10.1145/1240624.1240639

[13] A. Endert, C. Andrews, Y. H. Lee, and C. North, "Visual encodings that support physical navigation on large displays," in Proceedings of Graphics Interface 2011, ser. GI '11. School of Computer Science, University of Waterloo, Waterloo, Ontario, Canada: Canadian Human-Computer Communications Society, 2011, pp. 103–110. [Online]. Available: http://dl.acm.org/citation.cfm?id=1992917.1992935

[14] C. Andrews, A. Endert, and C. North, "Space to think: Large high-resolution displays for sensemaking," in Proceedings of the SIGCHI Conference on Human Factors in Computing Systems, ser. CHI '10. New York, NY, USA: ACM, 2010, pp. 55–64. [Online]. Available: http://doi.acm.org/10.1145/1753326.1753336

[15] ISO DIS, "9241-11 (1998): Ergonomic requirements for office work with visual display terminals (vdts)-part 11-guidance on usability," International Organization for Standardization, 1998.

[16] Greggman and H. Engines, "Aquarium WebGL," 2009, retrieved at 2015-06-07. [Online]. Available: http://webglsamples.org/aquarium/aquarium.html

[17] Google, "Liquid galaxy website," 2013, retrieved: March, 2016. [Online]. Available: http://blog.endpoint.com/2013/11/liquid-galaxy-and-its-very-own-street.html

[18] "Panoramic Video Streaming," 2012, retrieved at 2015-06-07. [Online]. Available: https://code.google.com/p/liquid-galaxy/\\wiki/PanoramicVideo

[19] OpenArena Team, "OpenArena (Quake 3 Arena)," 2005, retrieved at 2014-12-01. [Online]. Available: www.openarena.ws

[20] Squid Team, "Squid web proxy cache," 2002, retrieved at 2015-06-07. [Online]. Available: http://www.squid-cache.org

[21] G. Huisman and M. Van Hout, "The development of a graphical emotion measurement instrument using caricatured expressions: the lemtool," in Emotion in HCI–Designing for People. Proceedings of the 2008 International Workshop. Citeseer, 2008, pp. 5–8.

[22] J. Brooke, "Sus: a retrospective," Journal of Usability Studies, vol. 8, no. 2, 2013, pp. 29–40.

Adaptive Smart Environments: Detecting Human Behaviour from Multimodal Observation

Rory O. Heffernan, Michael L. Walters, Neil R. Davey, Rene te Boekhorst, Kheng Lee Koay and Kerstin Dautenhahn

Adaptive Systems Research Group, School of Computer Science
University of Hertfordshire, Hatfield, Hertfordshire, UK
Email: {r.heffernan, m.l.walters, n.davey, r.teboekhorst, k.l.koay, k.dautenhahn}@herts.ac.uk

Abstract—**It is desirable to enhance the social capabilities of a smart home environment to become more aware of the context of the human occupants' activities. By taking human behavioural and contextual information into account, this will potentially improve decision making by the various smart house systems. Full mesh Wireless Sensor Networks (WSN) can be used for passive localisation and tracking of people or objects within a smart home. By monitoring changes in the propagation field of the monitored area from the link quality measurements collected from all the nodes of the network, it is feasible to infer target locations. It is planned to apply techniques from Radio Tomographic Imaging (RTI) and machine vision methods, adapted to the idiosyncrasies of RTI, which will facilitate real-time multiple target tracking in the University of Hertfordshire Robot House (UHRH). Using the Robot Operating System (ROS) framework, these data may then be fused with concurrent data acquired from other sensor systems (e.g.) 3-D video tracking and ambient audio detection in order to develop a high level contextual data model for human behaviour in a smart environment. We present experimental results which could provide support for human activity recognition in smart environments.**

Keywords–radio tomography; device-free passive localisation; wireless sensor networks; human-computer interaction; sensor fusion.

I. INTRODUCTION

There is a clear and obvious need for reliable person location sensing systems in smart environments and assisted living environments that make life more convenient and more secure for people. The convenience of automated control of lighting, heating and other electrical consumer devices is increasingly being teamed with domestic or service robots as elements within a smart home. Robots are increasingly seen as one of the main ways by which the smart home systems can interact face to face with the human occupants, as well as directly perform assistive tasks. A consequence of convergent multiple underlying technologies is the emergence of the paradigm of ubiquitous computing, also described as pervasive computing or ambient intelligence or the "Internet of Things" [1], [2]. There are also significant benefits to the wider global community derived from more efficient use of resources. In parallel with increasing global pressure on dwindling energy reserves, we are also witnessing the pressures that an ageing population places on already over-stretched health and social welfare services. Converting ordinary homes to smart living environments will require the development of unobtrusive, passive, device-free person tracking and localisation systems which are simple to install, operate and maintain. Gathering human activity information from a variety of sensor data coupled with machine learning algorithms is critical to the development of a wide variety of applications used to monitor and track the functional status of residents. The eventual aim of this current research is to enhance the social capabilities of a smart environment so enabling it to become more aware of the context of current human activities and to take this contextual information into account in order to improve the smart home systems' Artificial Intelligence (AI) assistive decision making.

The potential use of wireless sensor networks (WSN) for passive human localisation and tracking systems affords numerous desirable characteristics. In particular, people are not required to carry or wear any electronic transceiver equipment of any kind. Consequently the system performance is not affected by such human attributes as forgetting to carry or wear devices and is also able to accommodate the presence of visitors (or intruders). The convergence of advances in the key technology areas of digital microelectronics, micro-electro-mechanical systems (MEMS) and wireless communications have led to an expanding ecosystem of low cost, low-power sensor node devices which are capable of forming self-organising cooperative ad-hoc short-range radio frequency (RF) WSN [3]. WSN technology deployed within a smart environment allows unobtrusive person-tracking without the need for the person(s) being tracked to carry a transmitting device. This is also known as Device-free Passive Localisation (DfPL).

Objects moving through the space where the WSN operates result in a perturbation of the radio links. Received Signal Strength (RSS) is one of the metrics built into 802.15.4-compliant wireless nodes, another being Link Quality Indicator (LQI), both of which are discussed in the technical note at Section 2 below. Radio Tomographic Imaging (RTI) exploits these RSS fluctuations caused by multipath propagation of the radio signals as they deviate from their line of sight path due to shadowing, reflection, diffraction or scattering [4].

RTI technology is integral to the proposed sensor-based research described here. A methodology summary can be derived from the first key paper describing the work of Bocca et al. [5] in the development of RTI as a reliable DfPL technology application for multiple target tracking (see data processing steps in outline at Section 5 below). The objective is to estimate the change in the propagation field of the monitored area from the RSS/(LQI) measurements collected from all the links on the network.

Sensor fusion is also integral to this current research and a methodology summary derived from the second key paper describing the work of Brdiczka et al. [6] in the development of multimodal smart environment observation is presented at Section 3 below.

The remainder of this paper is organised as follows: Section 2 discusses related work. Section 3 discusses research challenges and goals. Section 4 describes how the WSN has been created and an analysis and discussion of initial studies are depicted. In Section 5 planned studies are outlined. Finally we identify future research and conclude this paper in Section 6.

II. Related work

The eventual aim of the work presented here is the recognition of everyday human activity, more formally referred to as Activities of Daily Living (ADL), for example, through the use of multiple sensors installed in a smart home environment. ADL include routines such as dressing/bathing, eating, ambulating (walking), toileting and hygiene [7]. Associated with each activity there will typically be at least one basic action such as opening or closing a drawer or cupboard, fetching a utensil etc.

Cook and Das [8] define a smart environment as "a small world where different kinds of smart device are continuously working to make inhabitants' lives more comfortable". Smart environments are envisioned as the by-product of inexpensive and pervasive computing, thus making Human-Computer Interaction (HCI) with the system a pleasant and intuitive experience.

A typical DfPL system currently employs a variety of sensing devices including video camera systems and physical contact sensors [9] for people and object localisation and tracking. Other DfPL systems make use of light sources and sensors [10]. Fink and Beikrich [11] usefully classify DfPL systems employing radio signals into three main categories based on measurement principles:

i. Radar-based systems which utilise trigonometry (range and angle) derived from reflected and scattered return signals [12], [13];

ii. RF-based systems which analyse attenuation of received signal strength (RSS) values on wireless links between nodes. This technique, known as RTI, while capable of monitoring large spatial volumes such as warehouses, homes and offices, is limited to line of sight (LOS) setups [4];

iii. Variance-based RTI (VRTI) systems which analyse RSS fluctuations in multipath fading environments and permit non line of sight (NLOS) localisation [14].

In a smart environment, information about human behaviour and activities can be acquired from different types of detectors, each with its own data acquisition framework or 'modality'. Brdiczka et al. [6] describe their approach to addressing learning and recognition of human behaviour models from multi-modal observations in one such smart home environment. Multi-modal observation is an innate human concept where use of combined senses is essential to the detection and discrimination of incoming signals from the environment. Consequently some multi-modal applications are based on imitating aspects of natural multi-modal sensing, with audio-visual being the most prevalent. Sensor data fusion is the combining of sensor data derived from disparate sources, such that the resulting information has less uncertainty than would be possible when these sources were used individually. Feature extraction is a key component of 3-D video tracking, but is computationally expensive as well as being context insensitive. A potential alternative to 3-D video tracking is the use of RTI in order to acquire changes in RSS and WSN link quality information (LQI) caused by moving people and objects in the monitored area [4]. RTI is a promising WSN-based imaging technique developed by Bocca, Patwari, Wilson et al. [4], [5] which is computationally less expensive than 3-D video processing and can operate in real- time. Compared to other sensing technologies applied in motion tracking, such as infrared, ultrasonic range finders [15], ultra-wideband (UWB) radios [16] and video cameras [17], WSN provides several advantages: they work in the dark and can penetrate smoke and walls; they are less invasive in domestic environments than video camera networks [18], they are significantly less expensive than UWB transceivers and their installation and maintenance time is minimal. The current work explores the possibility of using RTI for sensor fusion and machine learning as a component in a multi-modal smart environment. Bocca et al. [5] describe a state of the art RTI system which operates in real time. Our intention is to replicate or adapt aspects of their methodology, alongside the methodology of Brdiczka et al. [6] and to incorporate it into the experimental work. These data may then be fused with, or evaluated against contemporaneous data acquired from other sensor systems (e.g.) 3-D video tracking, speech and ambient audio detection, reed switches, pressure mats, etc. in order to develop a high level contextual data model for human behaviour in a smart home environment.

A. Technical note concerning RSS & LQI

1) Received Signal strength (RSS): RSS decreases with distance according to the following equation:

$$\mathrm{RSS} = -(10\mathbf{n}\log_{10}\mathbf{d} + \mathbf{A}) \quad (1)$$

Where,
n = signal propagation constant (propagation exponent)
d = distance from sender
A = received signal strength at a distance of 1 meter

RSS is a measure of how the configured transmission Power at the Transmitting device (PTx) directly affects the received signal Power at the Receiving device (PRx). In embedded RF devices, the RSS is converted to a Received Signal Strength Indicator (RSSI) which is defined as the ratio of the received Power to the ReFerence power (PRF). Typically the reference power represents an absolute value of PRF = 1mW, RSSI is typically expressed in dBm:

$$\mathrm{RSSI} = 10 * \log(\mathrm{PRX}/\mathrm{PRF}) \quad (2)$$

2) Link quality indicator (LQI): IEEE 802.15.4 radio devices provide applications with information about the incoming signal. The effect of distance and interference on RSS can be measured by the packet success rate, RSSI and LQI provided by the radio. LQI is a metric introduced in IEEE 802.15.4 that measures the error in the incoming modulation of successfully received packets (packets that pass the Cyclic Redundancy Check (CRC) criterion).

LQI measures each successfully received packet and the resulting integer ranges from 0x00 to 0xFF (0-255), indicating the lowest and highest quality signals detectable by the receiver (between -100dBm and 0dBm). The correlation value of LQI ranges between 50 and 110 where 50 indicates the minimum value and 110 represents the maximum. Software converts the correlation value to the range 0-255:

$$\text{LQI} = (\mathbf{CORR} - \mathbf{a}) * \mathbf{b} \tag{3}$$

Where,
CORR = correlation value
a and **b** are found empirically based on Packet Error Rate (PER) measurements as a function of CORR.

LQI is the preferred metric for the current work, rather than the RSSI metric used by Bocca et al. [19]. In ZigBee-compliant mesh network radios, the LQI is convenient to obtain from neighbour request packets as the instantaneous unidirectional link values are transmitted as the final byte of any message. By comparison, the RSSI value is more difficult to obtain simultaneously for all links at each sample time-point without an additional computational burden inherent in time-stamp synchronisation.

III. Research Challenges and Goals

A. Design challenges

Smart environments have enabled computerised observation of human interaction. However using this acquired information as contextual information for the purpose of adapting the behaviour of an automated environment is less well researched and is the main reason for undertaking this research. The analysis of multiple targets provides information about social context and enables computer systems to track and anticipate human interaction. The latter is a non-trivial problem because human activity is situation dependent and not necessarily planned. Smart environments need to make use of this situational information in context in order to respond appropriately to human activity. "Context is key for interaction without distraction." [6]

B. Detecting human behaviour from multimodal observation

Brdiczka et al. [6] in their 2009 paper address the problem of learning and recognition of human behaviour models from multimodal observation in a smart home environment, similar to the University of Hertfordshire Robot House (UHRH). Their approach formed part of a framework for acquiring a high-level contextual data model for human behaviour in an augmented environment. In particular, their work focused on the automatic acquisition of information about social context and activity recognition from the analysis of the interactions between small groups of two or more individuals in real-time. Their multi-modal set-up comprised audio and video information. A 3-D video tracking system was used to create and track persons. A speech analyser determined if and when participants were speaking. Background environment noise was captured with an ambient sound detector. An individual role detector derived person-specific activities such as walking or interacting with an object frame by frame from 3-D tracker data (posture, speed and interaction distance). The association of audio stream data with each individual person identified by the 3-D tracker was coded by hand prior to commencing each recording. Several set-piece social situations were learned and detected using Hidden Markov Models (HMM) based on role and audio data. The authors propose a general framework methodology for the recognition and learning of the different components comprising a human behaviour model. The learning and detection was achieved in a two-part process involving first offline analysis (learning) followed by online detection of learned behaviour models.

C. Real-time object tracking and localisation

Real-time evaluation of video and audio streams is generally costly in terms of computing power. RTI in contrast uses multiple target tracking algorithms to generate real time images (every 13.3ms) of the change in the RF propagation field. The system is capable of running on a laptop having a 2.50GHz Intel$^{(R)}$Core^{TM} i5-2450P processor and 8GB of RAM memory [5]. The application of RTI techniques for multiple person tracking as an adjunct to the methodology described in this section, may provide useful improvements both to the problem of multi-person situation recognition and to the online (real-time) detection problem. The RTI system initially developed by Wilson and Patwari [4] and later extended by Bocca et al. [5] provides a basis for the current research. Their work targeted using changes in the RSS of the links in WSN to localise and track multiple people or other targets in real time without needing them to carry or wear any electronic device. Their work represents an important step in showing that the application of methods informed by machine vision and adapted to radio tomography could be used to generate images of the changes in the propagation field as if they were frames of a video. Our current research seeks to build upon this base, and eventually to extend it to use the sensor fusion method initially developed by Brdiczka et al. [6]. Their work was targeted at learning and recognition of human behaviour models from multimodal observation in a smart home environment. This work, however, was limited in two respects. Firstly, it relied upon a computationally expensive 3-D video tracking system requiring extensive offline (and therefore non real-time) processing in order to visualise human activities and to create and to track entities (people) in a scene. Secondly, because the detection of group dynamics and group formation, which is necessary for group situation recognition in (informal) real settings, remains an open issue within 3-D video tracking technology. This requires studying the use of RTI as part of a framework for acquiring a high-level contextual model for human behaviour in an augmented environment. It is envisaged that ROS will be utilised as a framework to implement processing nodes, which can process and integrate data acquired from multiple sensor types. Additionally, if evaluation metric testing between 3-D video tracking and RTI suggests that RTI is at least as reliable as the current video sensors, it may obviate the need for video sensors in future multi-modal observation studies.

IV. Initial Studies

We constructed a minimal full mesh network comprising 5 nodes using XBee Series 2 radio modules running the ZigBee protocol firmware [20]. The individual Router nodes were labelled 'A' to 'D' respectively and the network coordinator node 'BB' Power supply is via a USB connector. Transmit power was set to minimum for all nodes. Initial simple, single person experiments were performed in a room at the University of Hertfordshire. We deployed 5 sensors spaced at approximately 2 meter intervals apart, each at a height of about 1 meter forming 3 sides of a rectangle, with the fourth side 'open'. The thick arrow indicates 'open' side walk path direction. Nodes 'A' and 'BB' not pictured but mirror positioned to 'C' and 'D' respectively. (Figure 1).

Figure 1. Experimental setup: nodes 'B', 'C' and 'D' are shown.

Evaluation was performed by walking along the length of the open side. Two walks were performed: Walk 'A' (walk away-turn-walk back) and Walk 'B' (walk away-turn then pause for 10seconds-walk back). The system collected time-series data sampled at the default rate of approximately 2 s^{-1}. Fluctuating LQI data generated from static, rotational and dynamic walk phases was captured (Figs. 2 & 3). In the Walk 'A' graph at Figure 2, the three individual phases of the motion are clearly identifiable: the pre-motion phase commences with a steady state, empty room flat line signal with no discernible noise and LQI of 255 representing the maximum value. LQI values then fall during the 'walk away' phase, bottom out during the 'turn' phase, rising again during the 'walk back' phase, finally returning to the maximum value and steady state. Data from other nodes has been omitted for visual clarity. The Walk 'B' graph at Figure 3 commences in similar fashion to the preceding graph. However the three individual phases of the motion are less clearly identifiable this time and there is less symmetry between the 'walk away' and 'walk back' phases. LQI values initially rise and return to roughly pre-motion values during the quiescent 'turn, pause' phase. During the 'walk back' phase, there is a brief dip followed by a gradual return to pre-motion values before finally returning to the maximum value and steady state. Again, data from other nodes has been omitted for visual clarity. These early results

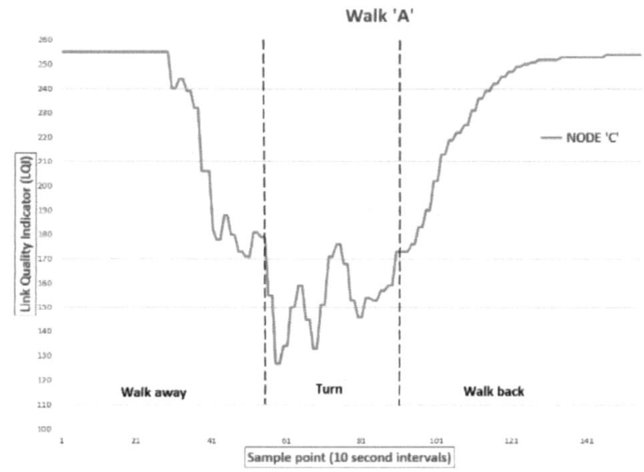

Figure 2. Walk 'A' LQI fluctuation for Node 'C'.

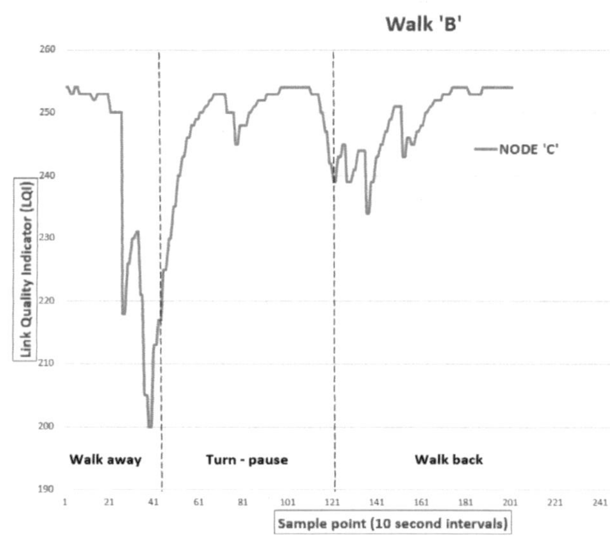

Figure 3. Walk 'B' LQI fluctuation for Node 'C'.

are promising and suggest that the use of the LQI metric is adequately responsive to differentiate characteristic phases of linear motion, rotational motion and no motion. Further, visual analysis of the graphs derived from the sensor data support the idea that specific activities produce uniquely identifiable patterns which may be classified by machine learning techniques.

V. Planned Studies

The next stage of research involves undertaking formally specified human motion studies which will be undertaken to implement basic algorithms already developed by others. The initial smart environment to develop and test the WSN for human activity detection will be deployed in the UHRH [21]. The UHRH is dedicated to Human-Robot Interaction (HRI) research in an ecologically realistic, domestic environment. It has the appearance of an ordinary British suburban, semi-detached house in a quiet residential street, with four fully-furnished bedrooms and a sizeable garden (see Figure

4). The UHRH is also inhabited by different robots designed for robot companion research. It also has a large number of embedded sensors, most connect via a WSN, allowing the recording of data from a range of different user activities.

A. Scaled WSN deployment

Initially, the number of nodes in the network will be increased from 5 to 8 and deployment will be limited to the 'living area' of the UHRH in order to collect basic data on a restricted set of activities. Later, in order to extend the sensor area coverage to include additional areas with different ADL, we intend to extend the area covered by the network to include up to 20 nodes.

Figure 4. The University of Hertfordshire Robot House showing an HRI experiment with a Care-O-Bot 3 robot.

B. Input data

The input data can be conceptualised as a sequence of vectors mainly consisting of binary sensor data from the simple sensors (reed switches, pressure mats, water flow etc.) and more complex data structures for the RTI, 3-D video and audio streams.

C. RTI data processing pipeline

Following LQI data capture, digital signal processing techniques may be applied to form radio tomographic images in real-time according to the methodology of Bocca et al. [5] in a five-stage pipeline: (i) image estimation, (ii) image denoising, (iii) cluster heads selection, (iv) tracks confirmation and deletion, (v) target tracking.

VI. CONCLUSION AND FUTURE WORK

Previous research at the UHRH has been undertaken on the design and implementation of a low-cost, resource-efficient activity recognition system that can detect ADL [22]. Following correlation with existing activity recognition collected from previously published RH studies, we intend to fuse data from existing sources/sensors in the UHRH with the RTI data based on the method developed by Brdiczka et al. [6], but using RTI data both separately and fused with 3D Tracker data. This will permit us to compare and contrast the technical performance of the two radio and optical imaging systems. We have demonstrated that we have obtained data from the ZigBee WSN, which has the potential to detect human movements. The WSN has been constructed from standard low-cost components of the type already used to connect sensors to UHRH systems etc. This raw data capture represents the essential first stage prior to implementing the RTI data processing pipeline methodology described by Bocca et al. and summarised at Section 5 above. Further, we have modified the approach taken by Bocca et al. and exploited the availability of the LQI metric in order to attempt an improvement in the reliability of the raw WSN data in an otherwise noisy 2.4 GHz environment (see Section 2 above for a technical discussion of the RSSI/LQI metrics). Graphical analysis of the initial data appears to demonstrate stable waveforms which do fluctuate appropriately in response to motion but are otherwise unperturbed (flat line, LQI value close to 255). In the next stage of research we plan to test the stability of the LQI sensor data in the noisy UHRH environment. There are several areas to which this research intends to make a contribution, namely HCI, Human-Robot Interaction (HRI) and the application of artificial intelligence (AI). The works of Patwari and Bocca have shown that RTI as a localisation and tracking technology can be used successfully to enable accurate real-time multiple target tracking with RF sensor networks. Concomitantly, the work of Brdiczka has shown that although a 3-D video tracking system is capable of creating and tracking entities (persons) in a smart environment, this is achieved not only at a substantially higher capital and computational cost than RTI, but also fails to adequately address the issue of the detection of group dynamics and group formation, which is necessary for group situation recognition. The proposed RTI methods aimed at circumventing the performance problems of 3-D video tracking systems have been shown to be successful in other tracking and localisation situations at reducing computation and memory costs.

The major unknown is to what extent RTI is capable of supplanting current optical data acquisition technologies at the machine learning level. A widely used technique for the analysis of time series data typically involves the use of feed-forward Artificial Neural Networks (ANN) employing a sliding window technique applied over the input sequence. However, before approaching the challenges of collecting time series data and subsequent processing via an appropriately selected ANN, there is a requirement to identify the optimal sample rate, embedding dimension and size of the input window [23]. In our approach to the problem of recognising activities we will consider implementing a real-time activity recognition digital signal processing (DSP) pipeline inspired by the methodology of [24]. Broadly, the pipeline architecture is envisioned in five principal stages. In the first stage raw LQI data is acquired from the WSN. Next, an aggregation step first loads the acquired live data and then initiates the downsampling, filtering and segmenting operations. Live LQI data may be written to a structured text file which may be conveniently parsed and loaded. In the third stage, windows of interest are identified from the loaded structured data by running a peak detection process. The windows of interest are slices of the LQI data corresponding to motion. Features are then extracted from the windows of interest which are then used to describe particular forms of motion (i.e. specific types of activities). In the penultimate stage, these features of interest are employed to train a recognition model for the movements detected and input. It is intended to generate a number of recognition models by exposing the data to differing classifiers in order to ascertain the optimal classifier for this time series motion data. Examples of potentially suitable classifier algorithms which are currently under consideration include Support Vector Machines, K-Nearest Neighbours, Decision Trees, Random Forest and Growing Neural Gas. In the final pipeline stage classification and validation operations will use classifiers and the dataset to perform cross-validation. Initially we intend to perform model training and classification offline by decomposing the dataset into a training set and a test set. The training set is fed into the various classifiers. The accuracy of each of the classifiers may be evaluated by comparing the classifier output predictions with the ground truth represented by the test set data.

We intend to use the Python programming language to initially implement all of the five stages of the pipeline described above. Python provides a number of excellent mature packages and libraries for DSP and machine learning including NumPy [25] and scikit-learn [26]. In the longer term, it would be desirable to develop the capability for our system to avoid the offline feature extraction and classifier training phase. In this respect the use of unsupervised learning of deep belief networks (Deep Learning) for generative pretraining of stacked Restricted Boltzmann Machines followed by supervised fine-tuning may be of interest. The Theano Python Library [27] offers tight integration with NumPy and significant performance gains through transparent use of a GPU.

REFERENCES

[1] M. Weiser, "The computer for the 21st century," Scientific American, vol. 265, no. 3, 1991, pp. 94–104.

[2] M. Weiser, R. Gold, and J. S. Brown, "The origins of ubiquitous computing research at parc in the late 1980s," IBM systems journal, vol. 38, no. 4, 1999, p. 693.

[3] I. F. Akyildiz, W. Su, Y. Sankarasubramaniam, and E. Cayirci, "Wireless sensor networks: a survey," Computer networks, vol. 38, no. 4, 2002, pp. 393–422.

[4] J. Wilson and N. Patwari, "Radio tomographic imaging with wireless networks," Mobile Computing, IEEE Transactions on, vol. 9, no. 5, 2010, pp. 621–632.

[5] M. Bocca, O. Kaltiokallio, N. Patwari, and S. Venkatasubramanian, "Multiple target tracking with RF sensor networks," Mobile Computing, IEEE Transactions on, vol. 13, no. 8, 2014, pp. 1787–1800.

[6] O. Brdiczka, M. Langet, J. Maisonnasse, and J. L. Crowley, "Detecting human behavior models from multimodal observation in a smart home," Automation Science and Engineering, IEEE Transactions on, vol. 6, no. 4, 2009, pp. 588–597.

[7] University of Ottawa. Activities of daily living (adl). [Online]. Available: www.medicine.uottawa.ca/sim/data/Disability_ADL_e.htm [retrieved: March, 2016]

[8] D. Cook and S. Das, "Smart environments: Technologies, protocols, and applications," Hoboken: John Wileyand Sons, 2005.

[9] R. J. Orr and G. D. Abowd, "The smart floor: a mechanism for natural user identification and tracking," in CHI'00 extended abstracts on Human factors in computing systems. ACM, 2000, pp. 275–276.

[10] X. Mao, S. Tang, X. Xu, X.-Y. Li, and H. Ma, "ilight: Indoor device-free passive tracking using wireless sensor networks," in INFOCOM, 2011 Proceedings IEEE. IEEE, 2011, pp. 281–285.

[11] A. Fink and H. Beikirch, "Device-free localization using redundant 2.4 ghz radio signal strength readings," in Indoor Positioning and Indoor Navigation (IPIN), 2013 International Conference on. IEEE, 2013, pp. 1–7.

[12] A. Lin and H. Ling, "Doppler and direction-of-arrival (DDOA) radar for multiple-mover sensing," Aerospace and Electronic Systems, IEEE Transactions on, vol. 43, no. 4, 2007, pp. 1496–1509.

[13] L.-P. Song, C. Yu, and Q. H. Liu, "Through-wall imaging (TWI) by radar: 2-D tomographic results and analyses," Geoscience and Remote Sensing, IEEE Transactions on, vol. 43, no. 12, 2005, pp. 2793–2798.

[14] J. Wilson and N. Patwari, "See-through walls: Motion tracking using variance-based radio tomography networks," Mobile Computing, IEEE Transactions on, vol. 10, no. 5, 2011, pp. 612–621.

[15] T. W. Hnat, E. Griffiths, R. Dawson, and K. Whitehouse, "Doorjamb: unobtrusive room-level tracking of people in homes using doorway sensors," in Proceedings of the 10th ACM Conference on Embedded Network Sensor Systems. ACM, 2012, pp. 309–322.

[16] Y. Kilic, H. Wymeersch, A. Meijerink, M. J. Bentum, and W. G. Scanlon, "Device-free person detection and ranging in UWB networks," Selected Topics in Signal Processing, IEEE Journal of, vol. 8, no. 1, 2014, pp. 43–54.

[17] F. Fleuret, J. Berclaz, R. Lengagne, and P. Fua, "Multicamera people tracking with a probabilistic occupancy map," Pattern Analysis and Machine Intelligence, IEEE Transactions on, vol. 30, no. 2, 2008, pp. 267–282.

[18] G. Okeyo, L. Chen, H. Wang, and R. Sterritt, "Dynamic sensor data segmentation for real-time knowledge-driven activity recognition," Pervasive and Mobile Computing, vol. 10, 2014, pp. 155–172.

[19] S. J. Halder, J.-G. Park, and W. Kim, Adaptive filtering for indoor localization using ZIGBEE RSSI and LQI measurement. INTECH Open Access Publisher, 2011.

[20] Digi International Inc. Digi docs: Product documentation and manuals from digi international. [Online]. Available: www.digi.com/resources/documentation/digidocs/default.htm [retrieved: March, 2016]

[21] Lehmann, H., et al., "Artists as HRI pioneers: a creative approach to developing novel interactions for living with robots," in Social robotics. Springer, 2013, pp. 402–411.

[22] I. Duque, K. Dautenhahn, K. L. Koay, L. Willcock, and B. Christianson, "Knowledge-driven user activity recognition for a smart house – development and validation of a generic and low-cost, resource-efficient system," in In Proc. Sixth International Conference on Advances in Computer-Human Interactions. Citeseer, 2013.

[23] R. J. Frank, N. Davey, and S. P. Hunt, "Time series prediction and neural networks," Journal of intelligent and robotic systems, vol. 31, no. 1-3, 2001, pp. 91–103.

[24] T. Peters, "An Assessment of Single-Channel EMG Sensing for Gestural Input." Dartmouth College, Computer Science, Hanover, NH, Tech. Rep. TR2015-767, September 2014. [Online]. Available: http://www.cs.dartmouth.edu/reports/TR2015-767.pdf [retrieved: March 2016]

[25] S. Van Der Walt, S. C. Colbert, and G. Varoquaux, "The numpy array: a structure for efficient numerical computation," Computing in Science & Engineering, vol. 13, no. 2, 2011, pp. 22–30.

[26] F. Pedregosa, G. Varoquaux, A. Gramfort, V. Michel, B. Thirion, O. Grisel, M. Blondel, P. Prettenhofer, R. Weiss, V. Dubourg, J. Vanderplas, A. Passos, D. Cournapeau, M. Brucher, M. Perrot, and E. Duchesnay, "Scikit-learn: Machine learning in Python," Journal of Machine Learning Research, vol. 12, 2011, pp. 2825–2830.

[27] F. Bastien, P. Lamblin, R. Pascanu, J. Bergstra, I. J. Goodfellow, A. Bergeron, N. Bouchard, and Y. Bengio, "Theano: new features and speed improvements," Deep Learning and Unsupervised Feature Learning NIPS 2012 Workshop, 2012.

Hand Gesture Recognition Using SIFT Features on Depth Image

Hasan Mahmud, Md. Kamrul Hasan, Abdullah-Al-Tariq, M. A. Mottalib
Systems and Software Lab (SSL), Department of Computer Science and Engineering
Islamic University of Technology (IUT)
Dhaka, Bangladesh
e-mail: {hasan, hasank, tariq93, mottalib}@iut-dhaka.edu

***Abstract*—In this paper, we present a hand gesture recognition system using Scale Invariant Feature Transform (SIFT) on depth images. Due to SIFT features and depth information, our approach is robust against rotations, scaling, illumination conditions, cluttered background, and occlusions. Previously, SIFT features were applied on binary images which do not provide enough discriminating key points to classify close gestures. We have extracted SIFT keypoints from each depth silhouette and applied k-means clustering to reduce feature dimensions. Bag-of-word features were generated using vector quantization technique, which maps keypoints from each training image into a unified dimensional histogram. These bag-of-word features were fed into multiclass Support Vector Machine (SVM) classifier for training. We have tested our results for five close symbolic gestures, compared the results for both binary and depth images and found higher accuracy for depth images. The proposed recognition scheme can be used to develop human gesture based interactive Human-Computer Interaction (HCI) applications.**

Keywords-Hand gesture recognition, SIFT features, depth image, HCI, SVM

I. INTRODUCTION

A gesture can be defined as a physical movement of the hands, arms, face and body with the intent to convey information or meaning [28]. Computer based gesture recognition technique has been an important area of research in HCI. Gesture based interaction works as a communication tool for people with cognitive or physical impairments. Hand gestures provide a complementary modality to speech for expressing one's ideas. Information associated with hand gestures in a conversation conveys information in degree, discourse structure, spatial and temporal structure.

There are two approaches to recognize human to computer interactions, one is sensor-based and the other is vision-based approach. Both of them have some advantages and disadvantages. In sensor-based approaches, the user needs to wear sensor enabled gloves, which limits the naturalness in interactions with computers. In vision-based approaches, the problem of object segmentation from the occluded background containing various illumination conditions can reduce recognition rate [32]. An ideal appearance based hand gesture recognition technique should fulfill the requirements in terms of real time performance, recognition accuracy with high degree of freedom (DoF), robustness against transformations, cluttered background, and with different hands shapes of different people. We have used SIFT features as local oriented features on depth silhouettes captured by Microsoft Kinect. Previously, SIFT feature based gesture recognition [1] was implemented using binary images captured from webcam. Binary images do not contain context information of the hand fingers and also images captured from webcams will not give better accuracy for occluded background. SIFT features are used in many other computer vision applications like robot localization and navigation, object recognition, image stitching etc. [8]. For any object in an image, interesting points or key points on the object can be extracted to provide a "feature description" of that object. This description, extracted from a training image, can then be used to identify the object when attempting to locate the object in a test image containing other objects. To perform reliable recognition, it is important that the features extracted from the training image are recognizable even under changes in image scale, noise and illumination. Such points usually lie on high-contrast regions of the image, such as object edges and are invariant to translation, rotation and scale. SIFT algorithm consider these points as key points naturally.

Object recognition based on the depth information does not have the difficulty of light variations, color distortion as they use infrared lights. Moreover, segmentation of objects from images is faster and easier using depth data captured using Kinect. Formerly, Kinect was developed for tracking full body motion. Many researchers proposed diversified applications like, interactive visual display [2], system for physical therapy [3], gesture based robot navigation [4]-[6], sign language recognition [7], etc.

In this paper, we develop a static hand gesture recognition system using SIFT features so that we can recognize gestures representing one, two, three, four and five numeric symbols. These are called symbolic gestures because they depict the numerical symbols from 1-5. These are close gestures and need to be recognized precisely. To do that, we have captured depth silhouettes after segmentation using depth data stream. We have extracted the SIFT features from those depth images for individual gestures. Individual gesture contains 100 samples and key points are extracted to generate bag-of-word features. Dimensionality of feature space has been reduced using k-means clustering because SIFT algorithm [8], produces too many local features as keypoints. Moreover, from binary images it is not possible to extract local finger context information (difference on information regarding folding of two fingers and three fingers to produce gestures for numeric symbol 3 and 2 respectively). Figure 1, shows the difference of SIFT keypoints between binary and depth images. The marked region by solid circle in the Figure 1(d) contains discriminative keypoints in depth image but those are missing in binary image, marked by dashed circle in Figure 1(b). Depth images contain discriminating keypoints, which are important to distinguish gestures precisely. In binary images, the keypoints extracted from the contours are not sufficient to get more accuracy.

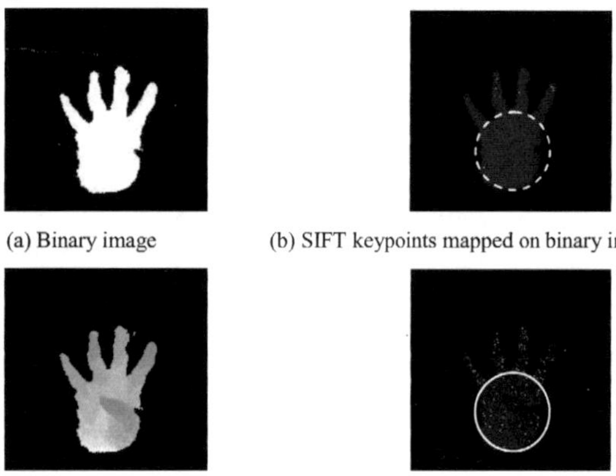

(a) Binary image (b) SIFT keypoints mapped on binary image

(c) Depth image (d) SIFT keypoints mapped on depth image

Figure 1. Comparison of discriminating keypoints mapped into binary (a) (b) and depth (c) (d) images

We tested our results and got 99% accuracy for depth images whereas binary images gave 96% correct recognition of gestures for cluster size 1600.

This paper is organized as follows: Section II briefly describes the related work. Section III explains the proposed system. Section IV shows our experimental result. Section V discusses the conclusion and future work.

II. Related Work

Appearance based hand gesture recognition using depth images captured from Microsoft Kinect device [9] does not have the difficulty of light, color distortion. Kinect sensors project an infrared pattern of 307, 200 dots in a 640×480 mesh and receive the reflected pattern through a Complementary Metal-Oxide Semiconductor (CMOS) monochrome sensor. Using the triangulation method, Kinect measures the depth value of every point presented in millimeters. This depth stream can be used to distinguish the hand region from the background image, a process called hand segmentation. Many authors have developed applications of gesture recognition using depth sensors in different fields such as interactive displays [2], physical rehabilitation [3], and robot guidance [6], [10], [11] or sign language recognition [7]. Additionally, completely different applications for Kinect have been developed such as in [12], [13]. Hand segmentation is challenging due to occlusions, different lighting conditions or appearance of skin-colored object apart from hand [14]. Some of the solutions to these problems are the assumption of some particular situations like hand being the front-most object or use of full-body tracking algorithms. There are various feature extraction techniques used for hand gesture recognition like, scale-space color feature [15], hand contour feature [16], eigenspace technique but they are not invariant to translation, rotation and scaling.

Different people have a variety of hand shapes and sizes performing the same gesture with slight variation in translation and rotation. An efficient hand gesture recognition method should be invariant to these changes. We have used SIFT algorithm that extracts local invariant features as keypoints preserving hand shape information. Previous research works have addressed local invariant features. In [17], SIFT features and Adaboost learning algorithm was applied to achieve in-plane rotation invariant property but they need to work with some other features like contrast context histogram. Haar-like features as described in [18], focus on the information of a certain area of an image rather than each important pixel or pixel containing key information. Viola and Jones [19] used learning-based object detection technique, which requires large training time, large training images and more computational power for both testing and training.

Features are interesting keypoints or salient points (corner, edges etc.) containing important local information of an image. Identifying the keypoints (detection), extracting vector feature descriptor in the neighborhood of each keypoint (description), and finding the correspondence between descriptors in multiple views are the main components of local features in order to classify images for object recognition. In computer vision, SIFT algorithm is a robust feature detection and description method for local features in images. SIFT extracts distinctive invariant features from images that are invariant to image scale, rotation and translation. SIFT has been used in different applications like image mosaic, stitching, recognition, and retrieval. Later on, other variations of SIFT were introduced like Principal Component Analysis (PCA)-SIFT [20], Gradient Location-Oriented Histogram (GLOH) [21], Speeded up Robust Features (SURF) [22], etc. SIFT is faster for lower resolution images. As the Difference of Gaussian (DOG) representation of hand gesture images are not explicitly affine invariant, we are using SIFT features instead of other variants of SIFT. Moreover, the training images from Kinect were captured in real-time under different lighting conditions so feature vector is robust in terms of scale, rotation, illumination changes, and cluttered background. The number of keypoints from each training image is different and training requires unified dimensional feature vector. Bag-of-Feature (BoF) representation was used in [23] to obtain a global information of visual data out of arrays of local point descriptors generated by SIFT algorithm.. BoF is a visual descriptor used for visual data classification. BoF was inspired by the concept of Bag of Words that is used in document classification. A bag of words is a sparse vector of occurrence counts of words; that is, a sparse histogram over the vocabulary. In computer vision, a bag of visual words of features is a sparse vector of occurrence counts of a vocabulary of local image features. BoF feature depends on dense local motion features and they do not have any relation between features on spatial domain and temporal domain. As we are recognizing static gestures, we have used BoF representations of images for training and testing. Our main contributions in this research works are: applying SIFT over depth images (extracted after segmentation using depth stream) which was not previously considered; obtaining a better accuracy by understanding the significance of BoF vector dimensions pertaining to the important keypoint descriptors found in gray scale depth image. Finally, the proposed system is robust against rotation, scaling, occlusions unlike state-of-the-art template matching approaches.

III. Proposed System

Our proposed system uses SIFT features on depth images instead of binary images. Depth images of hand gestures were captured using Microsoft Kinect following hand segmentation using depth map. The proposed system consists of (1) Hand segmentation, (2) Feature extraction using SIFT, (3) Feature dimension reduction using k-means clustering and vector quantization, (4) Gesture classification using multiclass SVM. The overall architecture is presented in Figure 2.

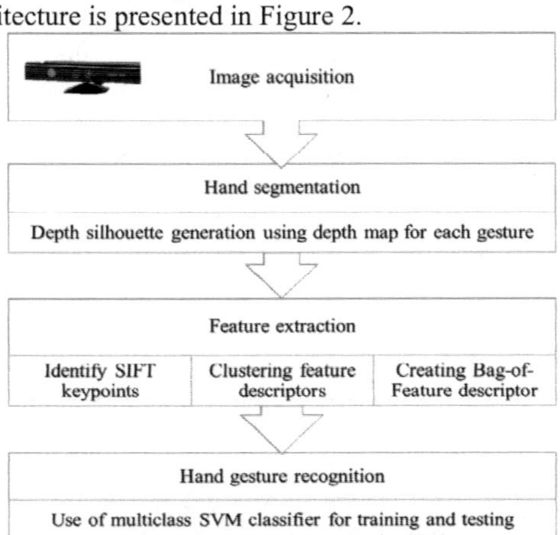

Figure 2. Hand gesture recognition architecture

A. Hand Segmentation

Segmentation is the pre-processing step in which we have used depth information to segment the hand gesture region. Traditionally, color based hand segmentation is affected by the appearance of skin color-like objects, lighting conditions and occluded scenes.

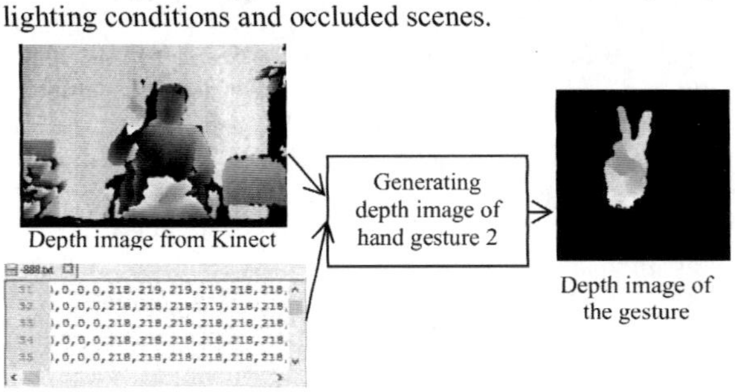

Figure 3. Hand gesture segmentation

We assume that the hand is the closest object in front of Kinect and the gesture information is contained within the 200×200 image. Using a depth threshold we eliminate all sorts of confusion related to background.

This also filters the cluttered background or overlapped images (i.e. hand overlapped with face) and illumination changes, which justifies the use of depth sensor. In the images from Kinect depth stream the hand region does not show enough contrast variations so that we can get more discriminative keypoints to differentiate close gestures. So we have assigned different contrast levels from 155-255 into 10 levels in gray scale to achieve good depth silhouettes. First, we have taken the depth map values of each gesture image of size 640×480 and extracted depth values within 200×200 region containing gesture information and generated the depth silhouette for the corresponding gesture. The segmentation process is shown in Figure 3. The binary images were generated without any gray level (i.e. just assigning 0 (background) and 255 (foreground)) values to compare our result with depth images.

B. Feature Extraction

We have extracted local discriminative features from gesture images using SIFT algorithm, which produces rotation and scale invariant 128-dimensional feature descriptors.

1) Generating SIFT feature descriptor: SIFT algorithm works in four steps.

a) Detecting scale space extrema: We calculate the Laplacian of Gaussian (LoG) for the image $I(x, y)$, with diffetent sigma (σ) values which represents the scale parameter. We convolute the image with gaussian filter to produce a blurred image, L, using "(1)".

$$L(x, y, \sigma) = G(x, y, \sigma) * I(x, y) \quad (1)$$

where, $G(x, y, \sigma) = \frac{1}{2\pi\sigma^2} e^{-(x^2+y^2/2\sigma^2)}$

SIFT algorithm uses Difference of Gaussian (DoG), using "(2)", by taking the difference of blurred images for two different σ values (σ and $k\sigma$), i.e.

$$DoG\,(x, y, \sigma) = L(x, y, k\sigma) - L(x, y, \sigma) \quad (2)$$

This process is done for different octaves of the image in Gaussian Pyramid. For our case, we got optimal values with initial $\sigma = 1.275$ and $k = \sqrt{2}$. With this process we get scale invariant representations of hand gesture features.

b) Keypoint localization and filtering: Once DoG images are found, they are searched for local extrema over scale and space. One pixel in the image is compared with its 8 neighbours as well as 9 pixels in next scale and 9 pixels in previous scale. Then, a pixel is selected if it is larger or smaller (extrema) than all 26 neighbours. This is a keypoint best representing in a scale. We remove the edge keypoints which are subject to aperture problem using Harris corner detection and reject points with low contrast using thresholding in the DoG images.

c) Orientation assignment: We have found that keypoints stable after localization and filtering. We assign orientatoin to each keypoint to get rotation invariant property. Since we already know the scale and location of the extrema, we calculate the gradient direction and magnitute of each pixel around the keyoint. Gradient magnitude and orientation are determined using "(3)" and "(4)".:

$$m(x,y)=\sqrt{(L(x+1,y)-L(x-1,y))^2+(L(x,y+1)-L(x,y-1))^2} \quad (3)$$

$$\theta(x,y)=\tan^{-1}((L(x,y+1)-L(x,y-1))/(L(x+1,y)-L(x-1,y))) \quad (4)$$

A gradient histogram (orientation histogram) is created with 36 bins covering 360 degrees for each keypoint and 80% of points represent the directions as a keypoint direction.

d) Keypoint descriptor: Each keypoint has x, y, σ, m, θ. We create the keypoint descriptor by taking a 16×16 window of neighbourhood around the keypoint. It is devided into 16 sub-blocks of 4×4 size. For each sub-block, 8 bin orientation histogram is created. So a total of 4×4×8=128 bin values are available as a vector to form the keypoint descriptor.

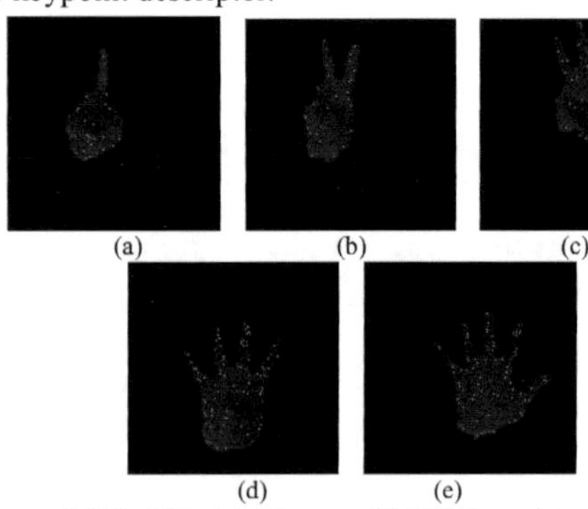

Figure 4. 200×200 training images with SIFT keypoints mapped in to depth silhouettes

We get different number of keypoints (vectors) for different hand gesture images. Figure 4 shows some training images with keypoints mapped in to them. Figures 4(a)-4(e), represent hand gestures one to five with 33, 37, 43, 75, and 87 SIFT keypoints repectively. We noticed that, as the number of fingers increases, keypoints also increases because the area of hand increases. We have used 100 images per gesture for which we extracted the keypoint descriptors, as a total we got 27389 keypoints for 500 training images. These 128 dimensional keypoints need to be distributed into suitable number of clusters so that all the gesture information produced by hand fingers is retained. So it is intuitive that, gray images will require more space to be distributed in to clusters than binary images for better accuracy.

2) Clustering feature descriptors: The number of keypoints for each gesture image is different and each keypoint is a 128 dimensional vector representing the feature descriptor. This creates difficulties because if we take a gesture image containing at least 35 keypoints the image dimension becomes 35×128 = 4480 and for 87 keypoints, 87×128 = 11136, which need to be reduced. Moreover, each training image should be represented using unified dimensional feature vector for training using a multiclass classifier such as SVM [26]. So there is a need of clustering the SIFT feature descriptors and generating unified dimensional image representation. We have used k-means clustering [24] from all the availabe state-of-the-art clustering approaches because it is faster for large datasets than hierarchical clustering. If we observe the keypoints in Figure 4, we see the keypoints are well distributed and distinctive. Morever, there were no outliers in the depth gesture images so k-means clustering should give better result with suitably chosen cluster size or codebook size. If the size of the codebook is too small, then each bag-of-words vector will not represent all the keypoints and large codebook size may increase the risk of overfitting. As the number of keypoints in the depth image is greater than the binary image, intuitively, we will get better accuracy for higher cluster size than for a binay image. We choose our cluster size 1600, the size of the codebook or visual vocabularies to build our cluster model.

K-means clustering partitions the vector space (128-dimensional feature vector) into k clusters where each feature point belongs to the cluster with nearest mean. Then the centroids (codevectors) are moved to the average location of all the keypoints assigned to them, and the assignments are redone until the assignments stop changing. The objective of k-means clustering is to minimize total intra-cluster variance or the squared error function using "(5)".

$$J=\sum_{j=1}^{k}\sum_{i=1}^{n}\left\|x_i^{(j)}-c_j\right\|^2 \quad (5)$$

where k is the number of clusters, n is number of samples, c is the centroid of clusster j.

Figure 5 shows the demonstration of k-means clustering for five keypoints: A, B, C, D, and E to form two clusters.

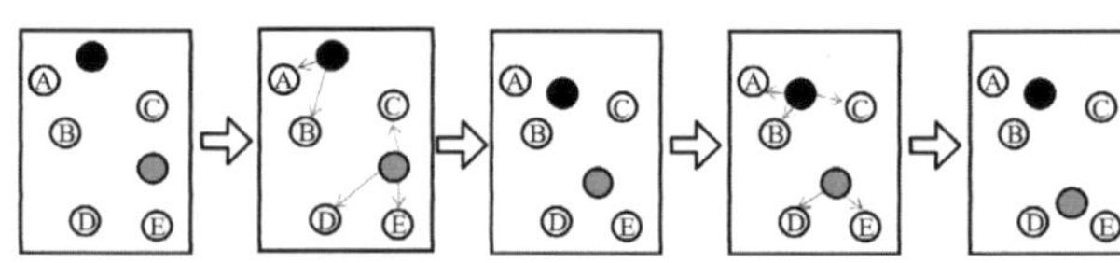

Figure 5. Demonstration of k-means clustering

The keypoint vectors for each training image are employed to build cluster model encoding each keypoint by the index of the cluster (codevector) to which it belongs. So, each feature vector (keypoint) is assigned to one cluster center which has minimum Euclidean distance in 128-dimensional feature vectors. Keypoints assigned to the same cluster center will be in the same subgroup to get k disjoint subgroups of keypoints. So, k-means clustering decreases the dimension of each training image with n keypoints ($n \times 128$) to $1 \times k$, where k is the number of clusters.

3) Generating bag-of-features: After extracting the SIFT features from depth images and building k-means clustering model, we generate bag-of-features for training. We apply vector quantization (VQ) process [25] to map keypoints of every training image into a unified dimensional histogram vector after k-means clustering.

That means, each keypoint, extracted from training image, will be represented by one component in the generated bag-of-feature vector with value equal to the index of the centroid in the cluster model with nearest Euclidean distance. Figure 6 shows the process of generating the bag-of-features.

4) Gesture recognition using SVM classifier: The generated bag-of-feature vectors with their related class label numbers are fed into the multiclass SVM training model. SVM is a supervised learning method that uses a non-linear mapping to transform original training dataset into higher dimension and searches for a linear optimal separating hyperplane. SVM finds the hyperplane using support vectors (datapoints closest to the separating hyperplane) and margins defined by the support vectors. Maximum margin hyperplane provides maximum separation between the classes.

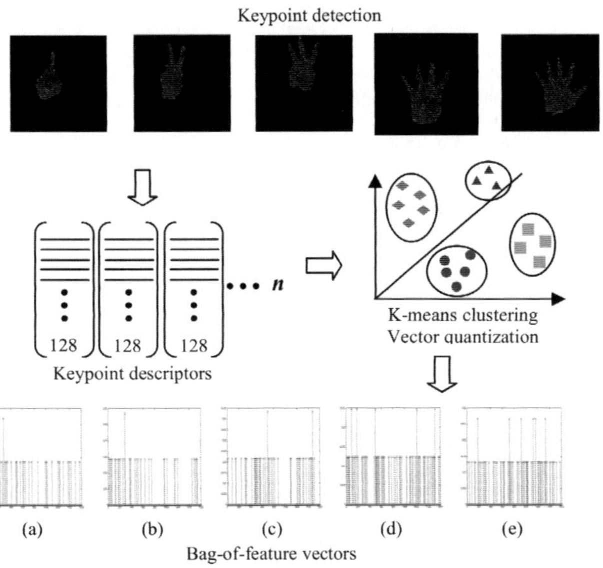

Figure 6. Generating bag-of-feature for training. (a)-(e): Bag-of-feature generated for gesture 1-5 from individual depth silhouette for 1600 clusters

There are different approaches to decompose the multiclass problem into several binary problems using SVMs as binary classifier. We have used multiclass SVM classifier that models a given training set with the corresponding group vector (representing class labels from 1 to 5) and classifies a test set using one against all approach. We have used the SVM tool found at [26]. For testing we have used 5-fold cross validation for 100 samples per gesture.

IV. Experimental Result

We have created our dataset, which contains 100 samples of size 640×480 depth images containing five gestures (representing symbolic gestures: one, two, three, four, and five). These samples are all taken in complex scenes with cluttered background. Experimental images were collected using Microsoft Kinect for Windows SDK version 1.8. The dataset can be found in [27]. Next, we cropped the 200×200 portion from the middle of every image and we took the closest 10 millimeters of each image which represent the hand of the subject. We give gray levels from 155-255 to each pixel of the hands depending on their depth and get a good contrast ratio. We collected the 128 dimensional SIFT features for each key points from each image and we divided the whole data set into 5 sections each containing 20 images. As we followed 5-fold cross validation process we used 4 of these image groups and one of them to test. We repeated the process to test each group of images. We also tested the binary images in the same process and varied the number of clusters in doing so. Then, we compiled the results for each test and took the average.

At first, we generated the confusion matrices using both binary and depth images for five gestures for different cluster size.

TABLE I. Confusion Matrix on Binary Image

	1	2	3	4	5
1	19	0	0	0	1
2	0	18	0	0	2
3	0	0	20	0	0
4	0	1	0	19	0
5	0	0	0	0	20

TABLE II. Confusion Matrix on Depth Image

	1	2	3	4	5
1	20	0	0	0	0
2	0	20	0	0	0
3	0	0	19	0	1
4	0	0	0	20	0
5	0	0	0	0	20

We took 100, 200, 400, 800, 1200 and 1600 clusters to test our proposed method and compared out results with the ones we get from binary images.

Figure 7. Overall accuracy comparison between proposed method and existing method.

According to our observation, our proposed method using depth image performs better than the binary image based approach if we increase the number of clusters. The confusion matrices generated by 5 gestures (1-5) for both binary and depth images using 1600 clusters are given in Table I and Table II. We are getting better results from our proposed method for higher number of clusters because we are using depth information and it preserves edge information more significantly than binary images.

For our given gestures, we can distinguish each position of fingers from the depth image, which is not possible for binary image. But, this can only be achieved if the cluster numbers are high enough. This is because the number of keypoints generated using the gray scale images is greater than the number of keypoints found using binary images. The overall result is shown in Figure 7.

V. CONCLUSION AND FUTURE WORK

This paper presents an effective way of exploring depth information for hand gesture recognition. We use SIFT keypoint descriptor to extract local keypoint features over depth images which is attempted for the first time in gesture recognition research. The recognition technique is inherently robust against scaling, rotation, and illumination conditions. As we have used depth images, the system is also robust against cluttered background and overlapped objects. By comparing our results with binary images, we found higher accuracy for gray-scale depth images because we get more discriminative keypoint features that preserve the hand finger shape information. Experimental results show that our system is able to achieve up to 99% accuracy over binary image based gesture recognition. We have also created our own depth gesture dataset for these gestures which are made publicly available [31]. There are three important factors that affect the system accuracy. The First factor is correctly preparing the depth images containing gestures. To produce depth silhouettes, our segmentation process is faster and effective with the help of depth map information. Secondly, the chosen number of clusters is justified because the number of keypoints in depth images is greater than binary images. These keypoints have contributed significantly to increase the recognition accuracy. We need the cluster size more than that required for binary images and our experimental results also prove that. Third, the number of training images is important and we took sufficient amount of training images to develop cluster model and later on to classify using SVM classifier. In future, we will try to analyze how the variation of clustering affects the accuracy using the PCA [20].

REFERENCES

[1] W. Lin, Y. Wu, W. Hung, and C. Tang, "A Study of Real-Time Hand Gesture Recognition Using SIFT on Binary Images," Advances in Intelligent Systems & Applications, SIST 21, Springer-Verlag Berlin Heidelberg, 2013, pp. 235–246..

[2] S. Zhang, W. He, Q. Yu, X. Zheng, "Low-Cost Interactive Whiteboard Using the Kinect," In Proceedings of the International Conference on Image Analysis and Signal Processing (IASP), Huangzhou, China, 9–11 November 2012; pp. 1–5.

[3] Y. J. Chang, S. F. Chen, J. D. Huang, "A Kinect-based system for physical rehabilitation: A pilot study for young adults with motor disabilities," Res. Dev. Disabil. 2011, 32, 2566–2570.

[4] A. Ramey, V. Gonzalez-Pacheco, M .A. Salichs, "Integration of a Low-Cost rgb-d Sensor in a Social Robot for Gesture Recognition," In Proceedings of the 6th ACM/IEEE International Conference on Human-Robot Interaction (HRI), Lausanne, Switzerland, 6–9 March 2011, pp. 229–230.

[5] M. V. D. Bergh, D. Carton, R. D. Nijs, N. Mitsou, C. Landsiedel, K. Kuehnlenz, D. Wollherr, L. Van Gool, M. Buss, "Real-time 3D hand gesture interaction with a robot for understanding directions from humans", In Proceedings of the IEEE RO-MAN, Atlanta, GA, USA, 31 July–3 August 2011, pp. 357–362.

[6] D. Xu, Y. L. Chen, C. Lin, X. Kong, X. Wu, "Real-Time Dynamic Gesture Recognition System Based on Depth Perception for Robot Navigation," In Proceedings of the IEEE International Conference on Robotics and Biomimetics, Guangzhou, China, 11–14 December 2012; pp. 689–694. Sensors 2013, 13 11860.

[7] Z. Zafrulla, H. Brashear, T. Starner, H. Hamilton, P. Presti, "American sign language recognition with the kinect," In Proceedings of the 13th International Conference on Multimodal Interfaces, Alicante, Spain, 14–18 November 2011; pp. 279–286.

[8] D. G Lowe, "Distinctive image feature from scale-invariant keypoints," Int. J. Comput. Vis., vol. 60, no. 2,pp. 91-110, Nov. 2004.

[9] Microsoft Corp. Redmond WA. Kinect for Xbox 360. 2010.

[10] A. Ramey, V. Gonzalez-Pacheco,; M. A. Salichs, "Integration of a Low-Cost rgb-d Sensor in a Social Robot for Gesture Recognition," In Proceedings of the 6th ACM/IEEE International Conference on Human-Robot Interaction (HRI), Lausanne, Switzerland, 6–9 March 2011; pp. 229–230.

[11] M. Van den Bergh, D. Carton, R. De Nijs, N. Mitsou, C. Landsiedel, K. Kuehnlenz, D. Wollherr, L. Van Gool, M. Buss, "Real-time 3D hand gesture interaction with a robot for understanding directions from humans," In Proceedings of the IEEE RO-MAN, Atlanta, GA, USA, 31 July–3 August 2011; pp. 357–362.

[12] O. M. Mozos, H. Mizutani, R. Kurazume, T. Hasegawa, "Categorization of indoor places using the Kinect sensor," Sensors 2012, 12, 6695–6711.

[13] G. Azzari, M. L. Goulden, R. B. Rusu, "Rapid characterization of vegetation structure with a Microsoft Kinect sensor," Sensors 2013, 13, 2384–2398.

[14] J. Suarez, R. R. Murphy, "Hand Gesture Recognition with Depth Images: A Review," In Proceedings of the IEEE RO-MAN, Paris, France, 9–13 September 2012, pp. 411–417.

[15] L. Bretzner, I. Laptev, and T. Lindeberg, "Hand gesture recognition using multiscale color features, hieracrchichal models and particle filtering," in Proc. Int. Conf. Autom. Face Gesture Recog., Washington, DC, May 2002.

[16] A. Argyros and M. Lourakis, "Vision-based interpretation of hand gestures for remote control of a computer mouse," in Proc. Workshop Comput. Human Interact., 2006, pp. 40–51.

[17] C. Wang and K. Wang, "Hand Gesture Recognition Using Adaboost With SIFT for Human Robot Interaction," vol. 370. Berlin, Germany: SpringerVerlag, 2008.

[18] Q. Chen, N. Georganas, and E. Petriu, "Real-time vision-based hand gesture recognition using Haar-like features," inProc. IEEE IMTC, 2007, pp. 1–6.

[19] P. Viola and M. Jones, "Robust real-time object detection," Int. J. Comput. Vis., vol. 2, no. 57, pp. 137–154, 2004.

[20] Y. Ke and R. Sukthankar, "PCA-SIFT: A more distinctive representation for local image descriptors," in Proc. IEEE Conf. Comput. Vis. Pattern Recog., 2004, pp. II-506–II-513.

[21] K. Mikolajczyk, and C. Schmid, , "A performance evaluation of local descriptors", IEEE Transactions on Pattern Analysis and Machine Intelligence, 2005, 27(10):1615–1630.

[22] H. Bay, A. Ess, T. Tuytelaars, and L. Gool, "SURF: Speeded up robust features," Comput. Vis. Image Understand. (CVIU), vol. 110, no. 3, 2008, pp. 346–359..

[23] S. Lazebnik, C. Schmid, and J. Ponce, "Beyond bags of features: Spatial pyramid matching for recognizing natural scene categories," inProc. IEEE Conf. Comput. Vis. Pattern Recog., 2006, pp. 2169–2178.

[24] D. J. C. MacKay, Information Theory, Inference, and Learning Algorithms. Cambridge, U.K.: Cambridge Univ. Press, 2003.

[25] A. Bosch, X. Munoz, and R. Marti, "Which is the best way to organize/ classify images by content?" Image Vis. Comput., vol. 25, no. 6, Jun. 2007, pp. 778–791.

[26] Multiclass Support Vector Macine Classifier, http://www.mathworks.com/matlabcentral/fileexchange/33170-multi-class-support-vector-machine/

[27] SSL hand gesture dataset 2 [http://cse.iutoic-dhaka.edu/group/ssl/SSL_HandGestureDataset_2.rar].

[28] H. Haitham, A. K. Sameem, "Human–computer interaction using vision-based hand gesture recognition systems: a survey", Journal of Neural Computing and Applications, vol. 25, issue 2, August 2014, pages 251-261.

Effects of Intervals between Roadside Columns on Speed Perception in Human Walking and Running Speed

Yohsuke Yoshioka
Division of Architecture and Urban Science,
Chiba University
Chiba, Japan
email: yoshioka.yohsuke@faculty.chiba-u.jp

Hidetoshi Watanabe
Department of Architecture and Interior,
Bunka Gakuen University
Tokyo, Japan
email: watanabe@bunka.ac.jp

Atsushi Enta
Department of Conceptual Design,
Nihon University
Chiba, Japan
email: entasan@gmail.com

Masaki Takahashi
Department of Architecture and Interior,
Bunka Gakuen University
Tokyo, Japan
email: masa-takahashi@bunka.ac.jp

Tomonori Sano
Faculty of Human Sciences,
Waseda University
Saitama, Japan
email: sano-t@waseda.jp

Abstract—**This study aimed to examine the effects of intervals between roadside columns on human speed perception. A virtual reality aided experiment was conducted, with 20 college students as participants. Each participant was asked to sit in front of a screen upon which interactive virtual space was projected. Within this space, columns emerged on the right and left of the screen at regular intervals. Participants could control the speed with which the columns moved on one side of the screen, using a mouse to move a virtual slider bar. The participants were asked to synchronize the speeds with which the controllable and uncontrollable columns moved in each experimental trial. The most important results of this study were that participants tended to increase the speed with which controllable columns moved when the intervals between them were longer relative to those between the uncontrollable columns. Results indicated that controlling the intervals between roadside columns also affected the perception of human walking and running speeds.**

Keywords*- Speed Perception; Optic Flow; Peripheral Vision; Virtual Reality; Driving Simulation*

I. INTRODUCTION

Human speed perception involves a combination of several types of environmental information received via sensory organs such as the eyes, ears, and skin. Of this sensory information, visual stimuli in the peripheral visual field provide the most important clues as to the relative speed with which objects surrounding the individual move. Gibson described the flow of visual stimuli through the peripheral visual field as "optic flow" [1].

The earliest work examining the effects of peripheral visual patterns on human speed perception was conducted by Denton [2][3]. The results of this research generally demonstrated that human speed perception was differentially influenced by the visual patterns that were presented to drivers' eyes.

Kircher [4] conducted a simulator experiment to determine how driving performance was influenced by design factors, tunnel wall color, and illumination. The results indicated that tunnel design exerted an influence on drivers' behavior, and light-colored tunnel walls were of greater importance, relative to that of strong illumination, in keeping drivers' visual attention focused forward.

Manser [5] also conducted a simulator experiment to determine the effect of visual patterns applied to transportation tunnel walls on driving performance. Results indicated that participants reduced their driving speeds gradually when exposed to decreasing visual pattern width and increased their driving speeds when exposed to increasing visual pattern width. These findings suggest that human speed perception was modified by visual patterns expressed on the tunnel wall.

Allpress [6] conducted an open-road investigation to evaluate the effects of even and decreasing roadside cone spacing at a roadwork site on traffic speed. The results showed that although both types of spacing were highly effective at reducing driving speed, uneven cone spacing led to a marked reduction in the number of speed-related accidents observed.

Godley [7] conducted an experiment using a driving simulator, in which participants drove toward intersections with peripheral transverse lines at both reducing and constant spacing. The results showed that although both types of peripheral transverse line led to a greater reduction in speed relative that of the no-line condition, speed perception was not influenced by a decrease in the spacing of the peripheral transverse lines.

Katz [8] conducted a similar experiment to investigate the effects of peripheral transverse lines. They found no significant difference between various patterns of peripheral transverse lines applied to the roadside of a simulated roadway. However, the results also indicated that the driving lane positions were significantly farther from the centerline in the design alternative involving two and four bars per second.

The objective of the present study was to examine the effects of peripheral visual stimuli presented at human walking or running speed on human speed perception. Almost all studies in this field have involved the control of driving speed, as it is one of the most effective methods for reducing the incidence of speed-related traffic accidents. This knowledge-based environmental design method for controlling human speed perception is expected to be effective in planning and designing an improved pedestrian environment, in which people undertake comfortable walking or fun running without excessive speeding.

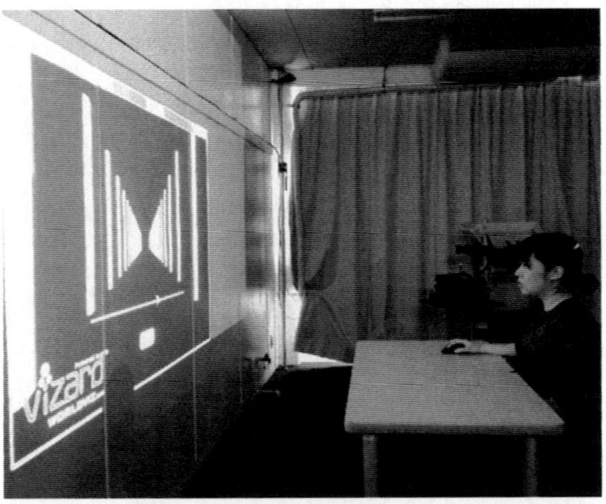

Figure 1. Experimental Setup

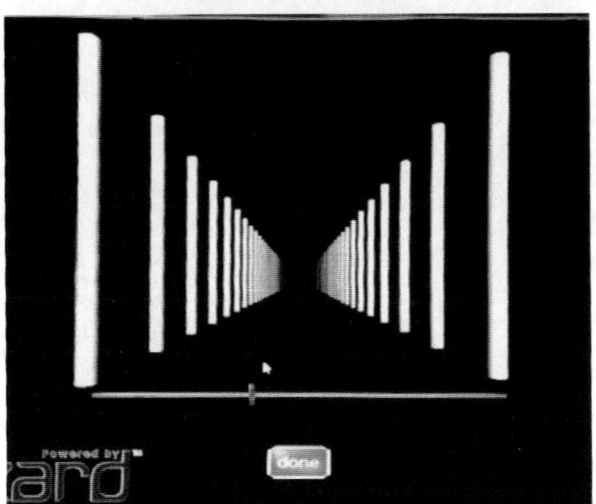

Figure 2. Projected Virtual Space

With respect to the Methods section, in Subsection A, we describe the ethical issues considered in conducting the study; in Subsection B, we describe the study design; in Subsection C, we describe details of the experimental equipment and setup; in Subsection D, we describe the features of the experimental virtual space; in Subsection E, we describe the verification of the column parameters; in Subsection F, we describe the experimental conditions.

With respect to the Results section, in Subsection A, we describe the results concerning adjusted C-column speeds with a fixed U-column speed of 1.5 m/s; in Subsection B, we describe the results concerning adjusted C-column speeds with a fixed U-Column speed of 3.0 m/s; in Subsection C, we describe the results concerning adjusted C-column speeds with a fixed U-Column speed of 6.0 m/s.

In the Discussion section, we interpret the relevance of the findings with respect to those of previous studies and describe the limitations of the study. In the Conclusion and Future Work section, we summarize the main findings of the study and suggest directions for future research.

II. Methods

A. *Ethics*

Written informed consent was obtained from all participants prior to the publication of this case report and the accompanying images. Participants were permitted to take short breaks as required, which increased the total experimental period.

B. *Design*

The participants were 20 college students (10 men and 10 women, mean age: 22.1 years). They were asked to sit on a chair in front of a wall-mounted screen, with one hand on a computer mouse placed on a desk (Figure 1).

Several types of interactive virtual movie were projected onto the screen. Two rows of columns emerged from the center of the screen and flowed to the right and left of the screen at regular intervals. Participants were able to control the speed with which one of the rows of columns moved, using the mouse to move a virtual slider bar. Participants were asked to use their own judgment to synchronize the speeds with which the controllable and uncontrollable columns moved in the experimental trials (Figure 2).

Participants were expected to be unable to adjust the speed with which the controllable columns moved to match that with which the uncontrollable columns moved when the intervals between the two types of column differed. The effects of different intervals between roadside columns on human walking speed perception were examined by comparing the adjusted speed of controllable-column movement and the fixed speed of uncontrollable-column movement.

C. Equipment and Setup

The size of the screen upon which the virtual space movie was presented was 2,200 mm wide and 1,760 mm high. Participants were asked to find a comfortable point with their eyes at a vertical distance of exactly 1,900 mm from the center of the screen, to ensure a horizontal angle of 60 degrees for the field of view on the screen.

The movie was projected using a high-contrast projector (TAXAN/KG-PH202X, Brightness: 3,500 lm, Contrast: 1/2,000) connected to a workstation (DELL/Precision M3800). The interactive virtual space was described using computer graphics software (WorldViz: Vizard5.0).

D. Virtual Space

The background to the projected virtual space was entirely black, with no earth or sky. The virtual space contained a virtual thin black fog, which gradually obscured the virtual elements within the space, with the two rows of columns hidden entirely at a depth of 100 m from the virtual viewpoint.

A horizontal angle of 60 degrees was applied to the forward field of view in the virtual space, as this corresponded to the angle of the participant's viewpoint in real space, considering the screen width and shape. The height of the viewpoint in the virtual space was set at 1,500 mm, with the vanishing point in the movie set to the vertical centerline of the screen.

E. Columns

Two rows of virtual columns emerged from the vanishing point at the center of the virtual space on the projected screen. The two rows of columns were set at a distance of 7,000 mm apart, on the right and left of the mid-horizontal ground line, toward the vanishing point on the screen (Figure 2).

The intervals between the columns were set to certain values according to experimental condition. However, in all experimental conditions, the cross-sectional shape of the columns was circular (diameter: 300 mm) and the height of the columns was 6,000 mm.

One of the two columns in each experimental condition moved at a continuous fixed speed. In this study, fixed-speed columns were known as uncontrollable columns (U columns), while columns for which the speed was controlled using the virtual slider bar were known as controllable columns (C columns).

F. Experimental Condition

There were fifty-four experimental conditions designed according to the following factors: three U-column speeds, three U-column intervals, three C-column intervals, and two right–left arrangements (one with the U columns on the right and C columns on the left, and one with the opposite right/left combination). Each participant completed fifty-four trials representing all possible combinations of these factors.

U-column speed varied according to three levels: 1.5 meters per second (m/s), 3.0 m/s, and 6.0 m/s. These three speeds represented walking, running and riding a bicycle.

U-column and C-column intervals varied according to three levels: 3.1 m, 5.9 m, and 9.7 m. These values were set at 10% of the prime numbers 31, 59, and 97, to ensure that they

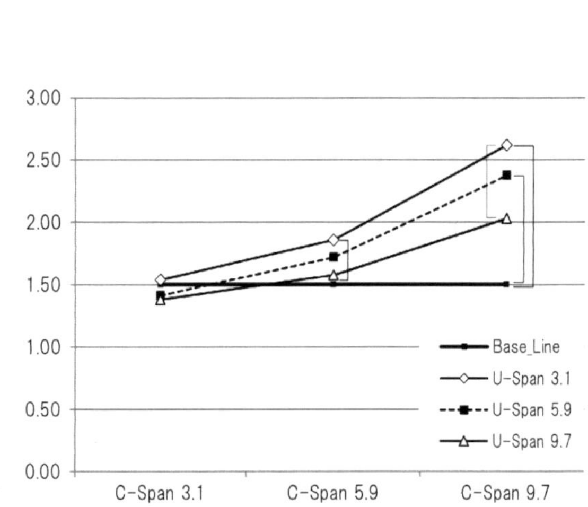

Figure 3. Transition of Mean Adjusted C-Column Speeds with Fixed U-Column Speeds of 1.5 m/s (m/s)

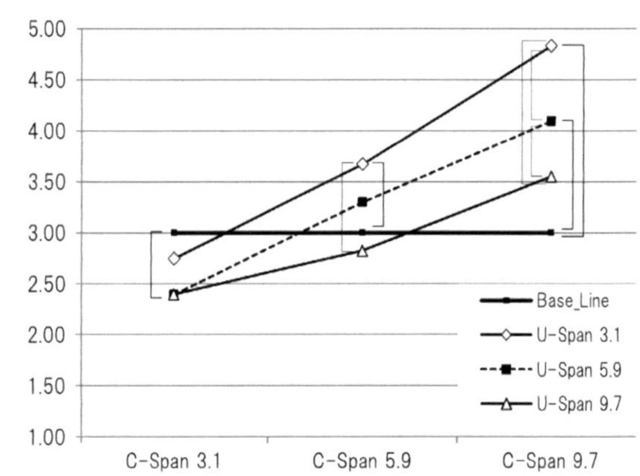

Figure 4. Transition of Mean Adjusted C-Column Speeds with Fixed U-Column Speeds of 3.0 m/s (m/s)

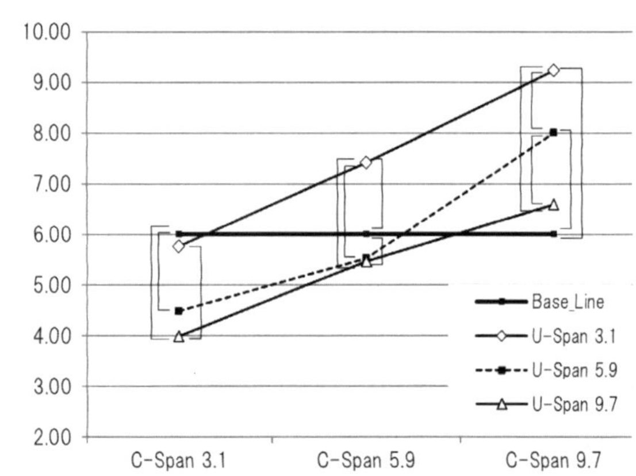

Figure 5. Transition of Mean Adjusted C-Column Speeds with Fixed U-Column Speeds of 6.0 m/s (m/s)

were similar to the numbers 3, 6, and 9, which were not used, because participants would have been able to use lower multiples of these numbers to determine common multiples of the intervals for the two rows of columns at a glance and adjust C-column speed by simply counting the number of columns flowing past on each side.

For example, if there were 3-m intervals between the right-hand columns and 6-m intervals between the left-hand columns, the third right-hand column and second left-hand column would be at the same position. Participants could adjust C-column speed by simply counting the number of columns flowing past on each side of the screen.

Participants were asked to adjust the C-column speed continuously to match the U-column speed, based on their own judgment. The virtual slider bar was placed in the lower area of the screen for ten seconds in each trial.

III. Results

Mean C-column speeds, which were adjusted by participants in each condition, are shown in Figures 3, 4, and 5. Each figure shows the aggregated data for the different fixed U-column speeds.

All main and interaction effects were analyzed using a multi-way repeated ANOVA, with significant differences in the main effects analyzed via Bonferroni post-hoc paired-comparison tests. Analyses were performed using a significance level of $p = 0.01$; significant results are shown in square brackets.

A. *Adjusted C-column Speeds with a Fixed U-column Speed of 1.5 m/s*

Figure 3 shows the transition of mean C-column speeds adjusted by participants to match the fixed U-column speed of 1.5 m/s, or walking speed.

Fixed U-column and adjusted C-column speeds did not differ significantly with the regular intervals between the C columns (C span) set at 3.1 m.

However, when the C span was 5.9 m, mean adjusted C-column and fixed U-column speeds differed significantly with the intervals between U columns (U span) set at 3.1 m and used as a baseline ($p = 0.006$). This result suggests that, with a C span of 5.9 m, C-column speed was perceived to be slower relative to that of U-Columns with a U span of 3.1 m at walking speed.

In addition, when the C span was 9.7 m, adjusted C-column and fixed U-column speeds differed significantly with U spans of 3.1 m and 5.9 m ($p < 0.001$, $p = 0.001$, respectively). This result suggests that, when the C span was 9.7 m, C-column speed was perceived to be slower relative to that of U columns with U spans of 3.1 m or 5.9 m at walking speed.

In contrast, in comparisons of pairs of adjusted C-column speeds, there were no significant differences observed between pairs of C-column speeds with C spans of 3.1 m and 5.9 m. However, with a C span of 9.7 m, however, with a C span of 97 m, in which the intervals between columns were larger relative to those with C spans of 3.1 m and 5.7 m, adjusted C-column speeds with U spans of 3.1 m and 9.7 m differed significantly ($p < 0.001$).

As there were no significant differences between pairs of adjusted C-column speeds when C spans were 3.1 m or 5.9 m, the overall picture of results shown in Figure 3 indicates that the speeds of peripheral flowing columns with intervals of 9.7 m were perceived to be slower relative to those of columns with intervals of 3.1 m at walking speed.

B. *Adjusted C-column Speeds with a Fixed U-Column Speed of 3.0 m/s*

Figure 4 shows the transition of mean adjusted C-column speeds of 3.0 m/s, with fixed U-column speed set at running speed, for all participants. In a comparison of fixed U-column and adjusted C-column speeds, significant differences between speeds were observed with C spans of 3.1 m, 5.7 m, and 9.7 m.

First, when the C span was set at 3.1 m, mean adjusted C-column and fixed U-column speeds differed significantly when U spans of 5.9 m or 9.7 m were used as a baseline ($ps < 0.001$). These results suggest that, when the C span was 3.1 m, C-column speed was perceived to be faster relative to that of U columns with U spans of 5.9 m or 9.7 m at running speed.

Second, when the C span was 5.9 m, mean adjusted C-column and fixed U-column speeds differed significantly when the U span was 3.1 m ($p = 0.005$). These results suggest that, with a C span of 5.9 m, C-column speed was perceived to be slower relative to that of U columns with a U span of 3.1 m at running speed. In contrast, in a comparison of pairs of adjusted C-column speeds, no significant differences were observed between pairs with U spans of 5.9 m and 3.1 m or 5.9 m and 9.7 m; however, pairs with U spans of 3.1 m and 9.7 m differed significantly.

Third, when the C-Span was 9.7 m, mean adjusted C-column and fixed U-column speeds differed significantly when U spans were 3.1 m and 5.9 m ($p < 0.001$ and $p = 0.003$, respectively). These results suggest that, with a C span of 9.7 m, C-column speed was perceived to be slower relative to that of U columns with U spans of 3.1 m or 5.9 m at running speed. In a comparison of pairs of adjusted C-column speeds, significant differences were observed between pairs with U spans of 3.1 m and 5.9 m, 5.9 m and 9.7 m, and 3.1 m and 9.7 m ($p < 0.001$, $p < 0.007$, and $p < 0.001$, respectively).

The overall picture of results shown in Figure 4 indicates that the speed of peripheral flowing columns with intervals of 9.7 m was perceived to be slower relative to that of those with intervals of 3.1 m or 5.9 m at running speed.

C. *Adjusted C-column Speed with a Fixed U-Column Speed of 6.0 m/s*

Figure 5 shows the transition of mean values for adjusted C-column speeds of 6.0 m/s, with fixed U-columns set at bicycle speed, for all participants. A comparison of fixed U-column and adjusted C-column speeds revealed significant differences between all comparable pairs.

With a C span of 3.1 m, mean adjusted C-column and fixed U-column speeds differed significantly when U spans were 5.9 m and 9.7 m ($ps < 0.001$). These results suggest that, when the C span was 3.1 m, C-column speed was perceived to be faster relative to that of U columns with U spans of 5.9 m or 9.7 m at bicycle speed.

With a C span of 5.9 m, mean adjusted C-column and fixed U-column speeds differed significantly when U spans were 3.1 m and 9.7 m ($p < 0.002$ and $p < 0.006$, respectively). These results suggest that, when the C span was 5.9 m, C-column speed was perceived to be faster relative to that of U columns with a U span of 3.1 m and slower relative to that of U columns with a U span of 9.7 m at bicycle speed.

With a C span of 9.7 m, mean adjusted C-column and fixed U-column speeds differed significantly when U spans were 3.1 m and 5.9 m ($p < 0.001$ and $p < 0.007$, respectively). These results suggest that, when the C span was 9.7 m, C-column speed was perceived to be slower relative to that of U columns with intervals of 3.1 m or 5.9 m at bicycle speed.

As pairs of adjusted C-column speeds with C spans of 3.1 m, 5.9 m, and 9.7 m differed significantly, the overall picture of results shown in Figure 5 indicates that the speed of peripheral flowing columns with intervals of 9.7 m was perceived to be slower relative to that of those with intervals of 3.1 m or 5.9 m; in addition, the speed of peripheral flowing columns with intervals of 5.9 m was perceived to be slower relative to that of those with intervals of 3.1 m at bicycle speed.

IV. Discussion

The results reported herein generally indicate that participants tended to adjust C-column speed (the speed of controllable columns) to be faster, relative to that of U-column speed (the speed of the fixed columns), when the C span (regular intervals between the controllable columns) was wider relative to the U span (regular intervals between the fixed columns), in all three U-column speed conditions. This finding suggests that C-column speed was perceived to be slower, relative to U-column speed, when the C span was wider relative to the U span, regardless of U-column speed condition.

In contrast, the results also indicate that the participants tended to adjust C-column speed to be slower, relative to U-column speed, when the C span was narrower relative to the U span, in all three U-column speed conditions. This finding suggests that C-column speed was perceived to be faster, relative to U-column speed, when the C span was narrower relative to the U span, regardless of U-column speed condition.

This tendency can be summarized as follows: the speed of columns with wider spans was adjusted to be faster relative to that of columns with narrower spans, and the speed of columns with narrower spans was adjusted to be slower relative to that of columns with wider spans. The results also show that this tendency increased when U-column speed was faster in the 6.0 m/s, 3.0 m/s, and 1.5 m/s U-column speed conditions.

The tendency observed in the current study was similar to that of Manser's achievements in simulator experiments in which vehicle drivers reduced their driving speeds gradually when exposed to decreasing visual pattern width and increased their driving speeds when exposed to increasing visual pattern width expressed on the peripheral walls [5]. The findings also complemented Allpress' observation in an open-road investigation, in which the uneven spacing arrangement of roadside cones at a roadwork site were highly effective at controlling driving speeds and led to a reduction in the number of speed-related accidents [6].

The findings of the current study also suggest that the speed modification method based on the nature of human speed perception, which involves controlling the design of visual stimuli expressed in the peripheral visual field, could be applicable at the slower speeds of walking or running.

However, the findings of the current study are inconsistent with Godley's [7] and Katz's [8] findings. Both studies reported that speed perception was not influenced by decreasing spacing of peripheral transverse lines on the roadside of a simulated roadway. The difference between the results of the current study and those of the earlier studies could be due to differences in the sizes of visual stimuli presented in the peripheral visual fields. In both earlier studies, the visual stimuli effects were verified via transverse bars, which were very short white lines at the side of the roadway surface. In contrast, the visual stimuli in the current study were columns of 6 m in height. Large and three-dimensional objective visual stimuli, rather than the surficial visual stimuli used in the earlier studies, could have exerted a significant effect on human speed perception.

The first limitation of the current study was that the experiment was conducted using a movie projected on a flat screen, which entailed a horizontal visual angle limited to 60 degrees. A different visual angle on the screen or an immersive experimental instrument, such as the vehicle simulator used in the earlier studies, could have yielded different results. The second limitation was that the background of the scene, which included earth and sky, was removed from the virtual space. Numerous factors could affect human speed perception, and different combinations of these factors yield different results. Other factors should be considered in future studies.

V. Conclusion and Future Work

The following results constitute the most important findings of the study:

- At 1.5 m/s, human walking speed, the speed of peripheral flowing columns with intervals of 9.7 m was perceived to be slower relative to that of those with intervals of 3.1 m.
- At 3.0 m/s, human running speed, the speed of peripheral flowing columns with intervals of 9.7 m was perceived to be slower relative to that of those with intervals of 3.1 m or 5.9 m.
- At 6.0 m/s, bicycle speed, the speed of peripheral flowing columns with intervals of 9.7 m was perceived to be slower relative to that of those with intervals of 3.1 m or 5.9 m.
- At 6.0 m/s, bicycle speed, the speed of peripheral flowing columns with intervals of 5.9 m was perceived to be slower relative to that of those with intervals of 3.1 m.

The main finding was that, as peripheral visual stimuli, intervals between roadside columns exerted a significant influence on human speed perception.

The most memorable finding was that controlling the intervals between roadside columns affected the perception of human walking and running speeds, which were slower relative to those used in early driving studies in which environmental roadside design was effective in controlling driving speeds; in other words, the findings of the present study indicated that the effects observed for higher speeds in driving studies could also be observed with slower speeds.

Future studies should examine human speed perception by varying the height and thickness of roadside columns. If future studies also find strong relationships between these parameters and human speed perception, the collective knowledge provided by their findings and those of the current study could be useful in designing an improved pedestrian environment to ensure comfortable walking and fun running.

ACKNOWLEDGMENTS

This work was supported by a JSPS KAKENHI Grant-in-Aid for Young Scientists (A), No. 22686056, and Grant-in-Aid for Scientific Research (B), No. 26289210.

REFERENCES

[1] J. J. Gibson, The Ecological Approach to Visual Perception. Lawrence Erlbaum Associates, 1986.

[2] G. G. Denton, "The Influence of Visual Pattern on Perceived Speed at Newbridge MB Midlothian," Transp. Road Res. Lab., 1973, no. LR531.

[3] G. G. Denton, "The influence of visual pattern on perceived speed.," Perception, vol. 9, no. 4, Jan. 1980, pp. 393–402.

[4] K. Kircher and C. Ahlstrom, "The impact of tunnel design and lighting on the performance of attentive and visually distracted drivers.," Accid. Anal. Prev., vol. 47, Jul. 2012, pp. 153–61.

[5] M. P. Manser and P. a Hancock, "The influence of perceptual speed regulation on speed perception, choice, and control: tunnel wall characteristics and influences.," Accid. Anal. Prev., vol. 39, no. 1, Jan. 2007, pp. 69–78.

[6] J. a Allpress and L. S. Leland, "Reducing traffic speed within roadwork sites using obtrusive perceptual countermeasures.," Accid. Anal. Prev., vol. 42, no. 2, Mar. 2010, pp. 377–83.

[7] S. T. Godley, T. J. Triggs, and B. N. Fildes, "Speed Reduction Mechanisms of Transverse Lines," Transp. Hum. Factors, vol. 2, no. 4, Dec. 2000, pp. 297–312.

[8] B. Katz, J. Molino, and H. A. Rakha, "Evaluation of Design Alternatives of Peripheral Transverse Bars to Reduce Vehicle Speeds and Center Line Encroachment in a Driving Simulator," in Transportation Research Board 87th Annual Meeting, 2008 No.08-1251.

A Software Design Tool for the Modeling of Emotions in Autonomous Agents

Xavier González-Olvera, Luis-Felipe Rodríguez, Luis A. Castro, and Ramón René Palacio
Department of Computer Science and Design,
Instituto Tecnológico de Sonora, México
Email: alternx7@gmail.com, {luis.rodriguez, luis.caztro, ramon.palacio}@itson.edu.mx

Abstract—**Cognitive agent architectures implement a series of computational models of cognitive and affective functions to enable the emergence of behaviors in autonomous agents. The design phase of these computational models is usually based on findings about the information processing in the human brain and on principles and standards established for the development of software systems. Software tools and methodologies to assist in this design process are still limited and scarce. Moreover, although available software tools cover most phases of the software development cycle, these do not take advantage of theories and models formulated in fields that study the brain information processing and architecture. In this paper, we propose a software design tool to assist in the specification and design of computational models of emotions for autonomous agents. We develop a preliminary case study in order to demonstrate the use of the proposed tool. This tool is intended to create consistent computational models of emotions that conform to theories and models that explain the process of human emotions.**

Keywords–Autonomous Agent; Computational Model of Emotion; Software Design.

I. Introduction

It has been recognized in fields such as psychology and neuroscience that human behavior is the result of the operation and interaction of brain processes such as perception, emotions, and decision-making [1]. In particular, a variety of brain structures and neural pathways have been identified as the architectural components of these cognitive and affective processes [2]. In the field of computer science, the underlying cognitive architectures (CA) of autonomous agents (AAs) are usually designed to include components that imitate the mechanisms of these cognitive and affective functions [3] [4]. The main assumption is that from the joint operation of these types of computational models of brain processes (CMB) will stem believable and human-like behavior.

Computational models included in CAs have a dual basis: 1) a theoretical support that validates the behaviors implemented, and 2) a computational basis that ensures the quality and adequacy of their development process. The design of these models is based on theories that explain human cognitive and affective functions [1] [2]. Moreover, their computational implementation has to follow principles and standards established to assist in the development cycle of software systems [5]. Although there is a considerable number of software tools and methodologies designed to assist in the development of conventional software systems (e.g., those for industry) [5], they do not seem totally appropriate to assist the construction of CMBs. These tools have been designed under the assumption that all system requirements are established by users. However, for computational models of cognitive and affective processes additional types of requirements must be considered. In this case, part of the requirements comes from user's observations of human behaviors, but the rest must be formulated from formal and well-founded evidence about the functioning of human processes. In this manner, nonsensical specifications can be prevented by considering theories and models developed in disciplines concerned with the understanding of the mechanisms and processes that underlie human behaviors. Unfortunately, few tools recognize these needs in the development of CMBs [6] [7].

In particular, the computational modeling of human emotions can lead to inconsistencies, complications, or even contradictions. This partly occurs because there is a wide variety of theories that study human emotions in very different ways. For example, the mechanisms assumed to be involved in the process of human emotions vary depending on the theory under consideration [8]. Nevertheless, despite these constraints posed by the dual nature of CMBs, several computational models of emotions (CMEs) have been proposed [9]. *EMotion and Adaptation* (EMA) is a model of emotions based on the appraisal theory and used in the development of virtual humans [10]. *A Layered Model of Affect* (ALMA) is a model that endows conversational agents with emotions, mood, and personality [11]. *Methodology for Analysis and Modeling of Individual Differences* (MAMID) is a model that associates two concepts: a generic methodology to model the influences of emotion on cognitive processing and an affective-cognitive architecture that implements such methodology.

In this paper, we propose a software design tool (CME-tool) for the construction of computational models of emotions. In particular, this CME-tool is designed to assist in the specification and design phases of the development of this type of computational model. The CME-tool acknowledges the dual nature of the computational modeling of emotions by providing a suitable framework to organize theories that explain human brain processes, which in turn guide development of CMEs. The paper is structured as follows. In Section II we present the related work. Afterwards, in Section III we introduce the proposed CME-tool and how it assists in the specification and design of integrative CMEs. Finally, we discuss future work in Section IV and provide concluding remarks in Section V.

II. Related Work

Research on understanding and facilitating the computational modeling of emotions has led to the creation of new tools and methodologies. The Emotion Markup Language (EmotionML) is a general purpose annotation language used for representing affective aspects in human-machine interactive systems [6]. It is proposed by the World Wide Web Consortium (W3C) Multimodal Interaction Working Group as an attempt to standardize the description of emotions in three main contexts: (1) manual annotation of texts, videos and anything that involves emotional data; (2) accurate representations of emotional aspects captured from user's expressions, postures, speech, etc.; and (3) for comprehensible generation of emotional responses from user interfaces. Although a specification of the syntax of EmotionML is still in progress, several elements may already be used.

Wang [12] proposed a set of denotational mathematics for the rigorous and formal description of cognitive processes and nature-inspired systems. These are expressive mathematical means that emerge in the framework of cognitive informatics, a discipline concerned with the internal information processing mechanisms of natural intelligence. Two particular instances of denotational mathematics are *concept algebra* and *real-time process algebra*. The former is appropriate to rigorously manipulate abstract concepts in a formal and coherent framework, which leads to the construction and treatment of more complex knowledge representations. The latter has been developed as a coherent notation system and formal methodology to algebraically denote and model the behaviors and architectures of systems and human cognitive and affective processes [12].

Cognitive Objects within a Graphical EnviroNmenT (COGENT) [7] is a software tool with a visual environment for the computational design and modeling of high-level cognitive processes. COGENT allows the creation and testing of cognitive models using box-arrow diagrams composed of functional components with their respective interactions. Conceptually, these components represent cognitive processes such as memory systems, knowledge networks, and decision procedures, which are embodied in computational structures such as memory buffers, knowledge bases, and connectionist networks. This tool provides an appropriate environment for executing and testing the developed models.

Although the literature presents some proposals that can be helpful in the construction of CMEs, these have primarily been designed to represent and formally describe cognitive and affective processes in general. Nevertheless, most proposals seem complementary and appropriate to assist in certain phases in the development of integrated models of emotions. In particular, the CME-tool proposed in this paper is focused on the construction of models similar to those developed in COGENT, but at a lower level. Whereas COGENT deals with high-level cognitive functions, we are concerned with modeling their structural basis supported on theories and models from fields that study the brain functioning.

III. The CME-Tool

Computational models of emotions can be included in CAs using one of the following two schemas: as stand-alone models or as integrated models. The former refer to components that are separately developed and then included as extensions of existing cognitive architectures, extending their functionality by providing affective processing. The latter have to do with emotional models that are designed and implemented as part of these cognitive frameworks. They may not be implemented as a single architectural component.

The benefits and disadvantages of each approach vary. The use of stand-alone models allows the rapid and easy integration of emotional mechanisms in CAs using pre-tested components. Architectures use these components by sending them raw data and receiving back emotionally processed information. On the other hand, models of emotions designed and implemented within integrated environments such as CAs follow a more natural design. These models are not seen as individual architectural extensions, but as processes that emerge from the joint operation of multiple mechanisms. In this case, given that multiple processes and their interactions must be understood to generate emotional data, their development becomes more complicated. However, although this approach is more error prone, many benefits can be gained. For example, because these models are built on the basis of the actual process of human emotions, they can conveniently be adapted to include other cognitive and affective processes.

TABLE I. Brain functions and structures used to create specification and design diagrams in the CME-Tool

Brain Function	Description	Related brain structures
Perception	Emotions influence perceptual processes to give a greater interpretation to novel emotional stimuli	Sensory System, Thalamus, Hippocampus, Sensory Cortex, Association Cortex
Learning	The emotional level of the perceived stimuli is used to provide a measure to learned knowledge	Amygdala, Hippocampus, Sensory Cortex, Association Cortex
Memory	Emotions influence the storing, retaining, and recalling of knowledge in AAs	Amygdala, Hippocampus, Dorsolateral Cortex, Sensory Cortex, Association Cortex, Ventromedial Cortex
Attention	Emotions facilitate AAs to concentrate on the salient elements of the environment and discard the irrelevant ones	Amygdala, Sensory Cortex, Association Cortex
Emotions	This process encodes stimuli in order to generate emotionally driven behaviors in AAs	Thalamus, Sensory Cortex, Association Cortex, Hippocampus, Amygdala
Planning	Emotions alter the creation of sequences of actions that will lead to an expected result	Orbitofrontal Cortex, Dorsolateral Cortex, Ventromedial Cortex, Sensory Cortex, Association Cortex, Amygdala, Hippocampus
Decision-Making	Emotions assist to this process to select the next action when a "rational" decision cannot be made	Orbitofrontal Cortex, Dorsolateral Cortex, Basal Ganglia, Ventromedial Cortex
Motor-Action	Fast and survival reactions are most of the time driven by emotions	Basal Ganglia, Motor Cortex, Association Cortex, Somatosensory Cortex

The proposed CME-tool is developed to assist in the specification and design of integrative CMEs as part of CAs, which are additionally restricted by findings about the functioning and architecture of human brain processes. Table I shows the brain functions and brain structures currently included as functional and architectural components in the CME-tool for the generation of specification and design diagrams. They are well documented in the literature as processes that influence or are influenced by emotions [1] [2] [13].

From a high level perspective, the design process in the CME-tool begins with the definition of users' requirements for an emotional autonomous agent (EAA). This process ends with the architectural design of a CME to be included in the CA of this EAA. Figure 1 shows the steps of this design process, which are explained in the following subsections.

A. Specification Phase

In this phase, all requirements are translated into a high-level diagram composed of functional modules and their respective interactions. Two main steps are followed to accomplish this: (1) user requirements are grouped (or decomposed) so that they can be placed in predefined modules that represent affective and cognitive brain functions such as emotions,

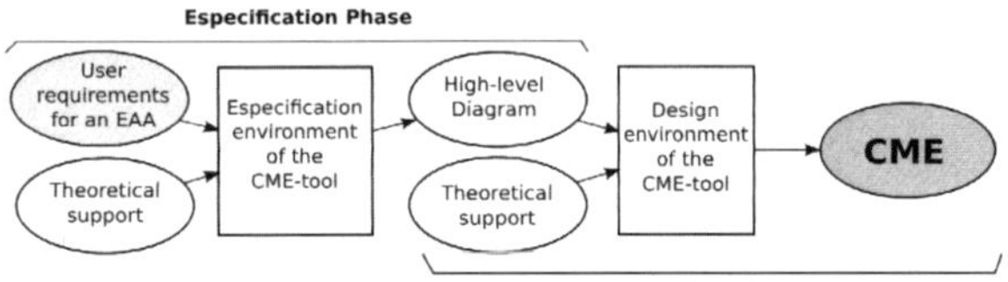

Figure 1. Design phases of the CME-tool.

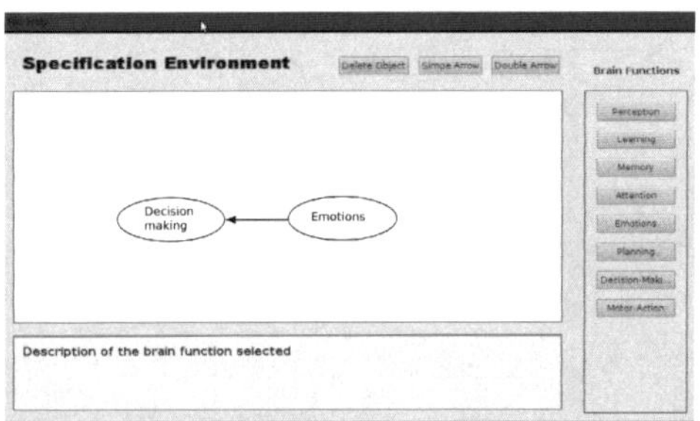

Figure 2. Specification environment of the CME-tool.

perception, and attention; (2) in order to completely meet the user's specifications, explicit operations, interactions, and other parameters should be defined for each of these modules.

The CME-tool automates this procedure by providing a series of pre-built functional modules representing specific brain functions (see Table I). These functional modules are selected by users to form a functional diagram that meets the requirements of the defined CME. The parameters of each module are configured using available information provided by theories that explain the functioning and architecture of the brain process these modules represent. Figure 2 shows the *specification environment* of the CME-tool, which includes a work space designed to organize the high-level diagram and a series of ready-for-use icons that represent brain processes.

The following list shows the information provided to define each component, which appears when a component is selected in the work space (see left part of Figure 3):

1) The role of this component: key aspects related to the functioning of the brain process it represents.
2) How emotions influence this component: roles that emotions play on the brain function it represents.
3) How this component influences emotions: how the results of this component influence emotion processing.
4) Data this component receives: information necessary for its functioning.
5) Data this component sends: information sent to communicate emotion-related aspects.
6) User parameters: open space for the user to introduce information.

At the moment the user selects one of these attributes, a window with more specific information is available. Given that there are diverse theories that formulate different hypotheses to explain the same phenomena, for each parameter the CME-tool may provide several explanations. The displayed information encourages the selection of theories that best fit the user' design goals. Thus, by following this procedure, all parameters of the entire diagram are defined.

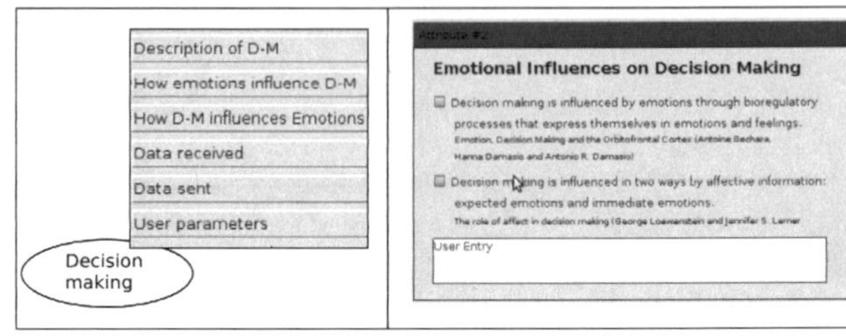

Figure 3. Left: attributes corresponding to the decision-making component. Right: Additional information about the decision-making process.

To demonstrate how this procedure works in the CME-tool, we consider a single requirement from the specification of an EAA whose decision-making should be influenced by emotions: *the EAA should be able to make decisions that meet both emotional and rational rewards, thus maintaining a general emotional balance.* From this requirement, an initial diagram with two components is drawn, see Figure 2.

In this diagram when the user selects the decision-making component, its corresponding list of attributes appears (see left part of Figure 3.) The right part of Figure 3 presents the window that appears when the second parameter is selected; it presents information to define such attribute. The format that follows the data shown in this window has two fields for each entry. One contains the explanation of the attribute and the other the information of the referred theory.

Following this procedure, as the requirements in the specification of the EAA are analyzed, new components may be incorporated, or even, only new interactions or operations between the already considered modules may be necessary to meet the whole specification. In this manner, once the attributes of all components are defined, the specification of the EAA should be totally understood from the resulting diagram.

B. Design Phase

The CME-tool generates an architectural design by refining the functional diagram resulting in the specification phase. In the design phase, all components representing brain functions in the specification diagram are decomposed into brain-inspired structures that embody mechanisms to allow the emergence of specific behaviors.

The procedure to achieve the architectural design is similar to that carried out in the specification process. Once we have the functional diagram completed, we proceed to open it in the *design environment* included in the CME-tool (see Figure 4.) This environment also provides pre-built modules that take the role of brain structures, such as the amygdala, hippocampus, and thalamus (see Table I). In this manner, when a component of the functional diagram is chosen, related pre-built modules are shown, allowing the user to select those that meet its particular design goals and according to the parameters established in the previous stage.

Each structural component should also be fully defined. The information needed to do that is provided and classified in the same manner as with the functional components of the specification phase (see the list above and Figure 3). This information is also based on theories, models, and concepts addressing aspects related to the processing of human emotions. This guides the decomposition of the modules in the functional diagram in a coherent way.

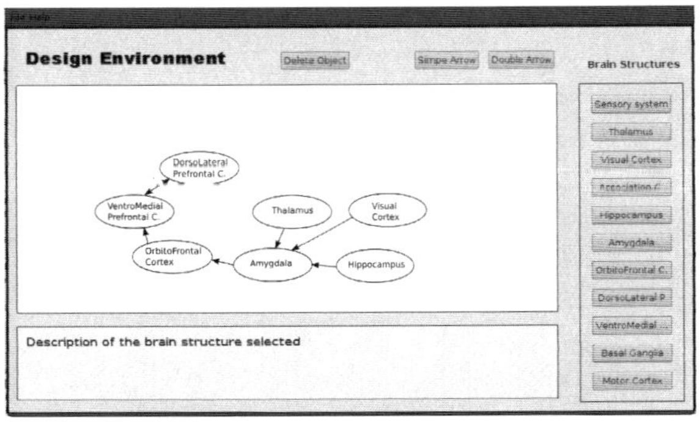

Figure 4. Design environment of the CME-tool.

To continue with the example (Figure 2), when the emotional module is selected, a number of components assuming the role of brain structures are shown. They are those supposed to be involved (directly or indirectly) in this particular process. After that, users are able to select those structures that are related to the processing of emotions in their particular design. Similarly, when we select the decision making component, structures involved with the functioning of this module appear, which allows the user to follow the same procedure (the work space in Figure 4 shows a possible architectural design for this example).

The design process implemented by the CME-tool facilitates the construction of CMEs for AAs, which are based on the brain mechanisms underlying human emotions. The first phase of the CME-tool allows users to put together desirable characteristics and functions in EAAs in a simple and organized way. The second phase assists in the translation of these abilities to an architectural design, which enables the emergence of proper emotionally-driven behaviors in EAAs. This method promotes the design of AAs by modeling brain functions, which emerge from the interaction of a number of components that embody algorithms implementing mechanisms that imitate the brain functioning and architecture. Moreover, since most of the initial user requirements for the development of CMEs are not in terms of how emotions arise or what are the components of the emotional process, but in the form of emotions as influencing certain cognitive processes, the approach of the CME-tool is adequate.

IV. Future Work

The following list presents some future work:

1. Improvements for an accurate guidance in the composition of the functional and design diagrams are being considered. The CME-tool will provide clues to prioritize users' requirements and to translate desired behaviors in AAs to brain functions, as well as to assign precedence to components constituting its functional diagram when they are being decomposed into an architectural design.

2. We are considering to design a mechanism to extend the CME-tool with information about the processes in which emotions are not playing a main role. For example, the direct operation between planning and decision making. To do that, a more robust knowledge base may be implemented, which allows users to include additional theories in the CME-tool in a consistent and meaningful way, as well as to connect the CME-tool with other available knowledge bases.

3. To consider the implementation process in the CME-tool, architectural components in the design diagram may include additional information of computational techniques to appropriately implement the process they are embodying, as well as to include user's fields to precisely indicate data structures, functions, and other data useful for the implementation phase.

4. Finally, automatic generation of complementary documentation for an easier understanding of specifications and designs is also to be implemented.

V. Conclusion

In this paper, we proposed a new software tool to assist in the specification and design of computational models of emotions as part of cognitive agent architectures. This tool was designed taking into account three basic assumptions: (1) it aims at developing integrated models, (2) it was inspired by the functioning and architecture of the mechanisms underlying human emotions, and (3) it was developed to address the specification and design phases of this type of computational models. This paper emphasizes the importance of considering the study on human mechanisms to design computational models of brain processes, as well as the significance of implementing adequate computational tools to assist in this complex task.

References

[1] E. R. Kandel, J. H. Schwartz, and T. M. Jessell, Principles of Neural Science, 4th ed., J. Butler and H. Lebowitz, Eds. New York, United States of America: McGraw-Hill, 2000.

[2] E. A. Phepls, "Emotion and cognition: Insights from studies of the human amygdala," Annual Review of Psychology, vol. 57, 2006, pp. 27–53.

[3] P. Langley, J. E. Laird, and S. Rogers, "Cognitive architectures: Research issues and challenges," Cognitive Systems Research, vol. 10, no. 2, 2009, pp. 141–160.

[4] E. Hudlicka, "Beyond cognition: Modeling emotion in cognitive architectures." in In Proceedings of the International Conference on Cognitive Modeling (ICCM)., 2004, pp. 118–123.

[5] I. Sommerville, Software Engineering, 8th ed. Addison Wesley, 2006.

[6] P. Baggia, F. Burkhardt, A. Oltramari, C. Pelachaud, C. Peter, and E. Zovato. Emotion markup language (emotionml) 1.0. [Online]. Available: http://www.w3.org/TR/emotionml/ [retrieved: December, 2015]

[7] R. Cooper and J. Fox, "Cogent: A visual design environment for cognitive modeling," Behavior Research Methods, vol. 30, no. 4, 1998, pp. 553–564.

[8] A. Moors, "Theories of emotion causation: A review," Cognition and Emotion, vol. 23, 2009, pp. 625–662.

[9] S. Marsella, J. Gratch, and P. Petta, "Computational models of emotion." in A Blueprint for Affective Computing: A Source Book, 1st ed., K. R. Scherer, T. Bänziger, and E. B. Roesch, Eds. Oxford University Press, 2010, pp. 21–46.

[10] S. C. Marsella and J. Gratch, "Ema: A process model of appraisal dynamics," Cognitive Systems Research, vol. 10, no. 1, 2009, pp. 70–90.

[11] P. Gebhard, "Alma: a layered model of affect," in Proceedings of the fourth international joint conference on Autonomous agents and multiagent systems, 2005, pp. 29–36.

[12] Y. Wang, Software Engineering Foundations: A Software Science Perspective. Auerbach Publications, 2008.

[13] J. Panksepp, Affective neuroscience: the foundations of human and animal emotions. New York: Oxford University Press, 1998.

Logical Characterisation of Concept Transformations from Human into Machine Relying on Predicate Logic

Farshad Badie
Center for Linguistics, Aalborg University,
Aalborg, Denmark. Email: badie@id.aau.dk

Abstract— **Providing more human-like concept learning in machines has always been one of the most significant goals of machine learning paradigms and of human-machine interaction techniques. This article attempts to provide a logical specification of conceptual mappings from humans' minds into machines' knowledge bases. We will focus on the representation of the mappings (transformations) relying on First-Order Predicate Logic. Additionally, the structure of concepts in the common ground between humans and machines will be analysed. It seems quite necessary to pay attention to the philosophy of constructivism and constructivist models of knowing. This research constructs a conceptual ground for expressing and analysing concepts in the common ground between humanistic and informatics sciences and in the context of human-machine interplays.**

Keywords: HCI; Concept; Concept Transformation; Predicate; Hypothesis; Predicate Logic; Machine Learning.

I. Introduction and Motivation

In an interaction between human beings (as intentional, aware and intelligent agents) and machines (as unaware and artificial agents), they exchange multiple actions and transactions concerning, e.g., identifications, descriptions, specifications and reasonings. According to [1] and based on our epistemological approach, the multilevel interactions between a trainer (a human being) and an artificial and a metaphorical learner (a machine), could be seen as a radical constructivist account of human cognition and comprehension. Also, these interactions could shape a kind of ontology. Obviously, the human-machine interactions are not agreement-oriented, because an aware agent cannot make an agreement with an unaware agent, but we suppose there is a type of agreement and convention between the human being and herself/himself to forward information about a given domain to the machine and to train the machine about some particular topics and concepts in that domain. In the next section, we will focus on the expression 'concept'. In interactions between human beings and machines, humans can develop their non-evidential and non-axiomatical conceptions of the specified underlying systematic processes in the world.

Training machines based upon personal mental images of reality in the context of human-machine interactions, could provide a proper ground for constructivist machine training. At this point, we take the philosophy of *constructivism* into consideration. Constructivism appears in a variety of guises (e.g., pedagogical, epistemological and complex combinatorial). It has been known as a philosophical theory of learning and as a model of knowing, see [2]-[5]. According to constructivism, a human being is always concerned with the active creation of personal mental representations. As for learning in the framework of constructivism, any agent generates her/his own schemata, see [13]. Relying on our approach, any schema is the product of the trainer's understanding of the world. It conceptually represents the constituents of the trainer's thought about training something. Schemata support the trainer in constructing and in developing her/his concepts (that have been constructed with regard to her/his own realisation of the world). Additionally, they provide strong backbones for the trainer's interpretations and provide proper backgrounds for describing terminologies and world descriptions. The constructivist machine training framework is heuristic, explanatory and developmental for human being's thoughts and reasoning. Actually, any constructivist machine training in the context of human-machine interaction is concerned with heuristic questions focusing on (*i*) 'What/Which is ...?', (*ii*) 'How is ...?', and (*iii*) 'Why is ...?'. The first group of questions focus on the factual, structural, existential and ontological aspects of the world, the second group focus on procedural, methodological and technical aspects of the world and the third group focus on inferential aspects of the world.

This article attempts to construct a conceptual and logical linkage between human's knowledge and machine learning. So, before getting into the details we contemplate the term 'Machine Learning'. Machine Learning is a subfield of Artificial Intelligence and Computer Science. According to [6], a machine learning approach attempts to develop strong algorithms that allow machines to improve [the productivity of] their performances on a given goal [and on an objective function]. In machine learning, the word '*learning*' has been utilised as a *predicate* for the expression '*machine*'. 'Learning' as a binary predicate describes a role that is being performed by the machine. More specifically, machines' *concept learning* approaches try to provide appropriate logical descriptions and specifications for transformed concepts and their interrelationships after having been transformed concerning their relationships with reality. A characteristic feature of most concept learning approaches is the use of background knowledge (e.g., internal knowledge base, ontological description). This feature supports more complicated and specific learning scenarios, because not only a factual (e.g., terminological) description of given examples can be used by the machine, but also structurally rich knowledge representations are taken into account, see [6][7]. In concept learning with background knowledge, with regard to the given set of training examples and background knowledge a machine focuses on hypothesis generation. In this article, we will provide a logical specification of mental mappings from humans into machines. We will focus on representations of transformations from humans' conceptions into machines' knowledge bases relying on First Order [Predicate] Logic (FOL). The results will support figuring out and analysing the most significant components of the logical characterisation of concept transformations. In the second section, we will focus on Concepts and Transforming Concepts. The third section will deal with Concept Transformation Process consisting of Logic of Transformation and the Analysis of Transformation. Section four will summarises the conclusions.

II. CONCEPTS AND TRANSFORMING CONCEPTS

First, we shall stress the fact that the notion of *concept* is a very sensitive term that must be used with caution, but we assume the use of 'concept' to be comprehensible in this context and in the logical formalisms. In our opinion, a human being's specified realisation of the world finds its real significance with regard to her/his grasp of the various concepts. Concepts support thoughts. Thoughts are also highly dependent on a human's interpretations and realisations of whether a given thing/phenomenon is an instance of a [constructed] concept or not. According to [8], and based on our conceptual approach, a concept is a linkage (relationship) between humans' mental images of reality (for instance, "an image of the *Spring*") and her/his linguistic expressions and statements (for instance, "*Spring* is one of the four conventional temperate seasons, following winter and preceding summer"). Let me represent the described linkage by —*R*—. In descriptive logical approaches, these expressions support the definitions. A *definition* is a kind of equivalence between a term referring to a thing (the thing that is going to be defined) and a description (generally built up using the inductive rules). Also, there is a strong relationship between the mental images and the mental representations of different aspects of the world. In fact, human beings need to logically apply —*R*— in their world descriptions, e.g., in assertions about real-world objects, in assertions about the empirical world, in assertional knowledge representations, in assertions about the ontologies, and in descriptions of terminologies and terminological knowledge. Therefore, human being transform —*R*— into discrete classes of things in order to see its applications. Thus, transformations play a very efficient part in the use of reasons and languages. Actually, transformations allow human to divide a continuously varying world into discrete classes of things, see [9].

At this point we focus on the concept formation process (see [10]) and acknowledge this process as the most fundamental step towards constructivist machine training. By forming concepts, a trainer (who is a human being) sorts her/his specific experiences and empirical studies into general classes [or even rules]. For instance, regarding the fact 'Drinking is a sign of thirst', s(he) represents the classes Drinking and Thirst and the rule 'Drinking → Thirst' in the machine's knowledge base. Consequently, the machine expresses the proposed classes and generates the proposed rule over the background knowledge in machine's knowledge base and with regard to other experiences of the trainer. Moreover, the machine utilises the expressed classes and the generated rules in class-based and rule-based reasoning processes. We have introduced the notion concept construction process in [11][12] and have interpreted it as the super-category of concept formation processes. A concept construction process consists of 'forming concepts' and 'reforming constructed concepts'. The trainer is highly concerned with main characteristics and features of a thing/a phenomenon in order to consider it as an instance of a class. The trainer must employ the examples that can lead her/him to discovering new classes. S(he) searches for [and itemises] the attributes and properties that can be used to distinguish exemplars from non exemplars of various classes. Additionally, s(he) identifies, specifies and relates the generalised examples and compares different examples. The following statements are derived from the above mentioned characteristics of concepts.

The descriptive logical languages and logical techniques transform the relationships between a human's mental images and her/his linguistic expressions into various ideas that are representable in the form of entities (discrete classes of things). The ideas specify the human's definitions (that are supported by linguistic expressions) by employing the logical rules that are (could be) existing between the same classes in the world. Accordingly, an idea is transformed into an hypothesis in order to correspond to a discrete class. As for the fundamental characteristics of concepts, a human being's conception within her/his interactions with a machine is equivalent to her/his act of representing various concepts and linking her/his explanations, and, respectively, definitions, with regard to her/his own mental images.

III. CONCEPT TRANSFORMATION PROCESS

"As accounted from above, a concept is a relation, and in fact, a binary predicate between humans' mental images of the world and their linguistic expressions [and, thus, definitions]". Obviously, the definitions always attempt to provide appropriate descriptions for the mental images. Subsequently, the existing interrelationships and dependencies between mental images and the provided descriptions support idea generation. At this point we focus on the analysis of idea transformation from humans' minds into machines' knowledge bases. Suppose that the trainer has considered *n* objects. For instance, the set of *n* objects is equal to $\{sofa_1, glass_2, plate_3, \ldots, brown_n\}$, and we shall draw your attention to the logical description of the transformation process.

A. Logic of Transformation

[1] The trainer assigns her/his ideas to the objects and focuses on *idea assertion*. For instance, s(he) assigns her/his first idea to the first object. So s(he) constructs $Idea_1(object_1)$. For instance, s(he) constructs *Furniture*(*sofa*) to express the fact that sofa is a furniture (or sofa is a member of the class Furniture). Similarly, s(he) assigns the second [and, respectively, the third, fourth, ... , and *n*th] ideas to the second [, third, fourth, ... , and *n*th] objects. Therefore, there are totally *n* assignments like: $Idea_1(object_1)$, $Idea_2(object_2)$, ... , $Idea_n(object_n)$. This conclusion represents a linear model. Considering $i \in [1,n]$ and relying on FOL, $Idea_i$ represents an unary predicate and $object_i$ represents a constant symbol (as an instance of the unary predicate $Idea_i$).

[2] The trainer makes a relation between her/his achievements. Employing FOL, there exists a *Relation*[$Idea_1(object_1)$, $Idea_2(object_2)$, ... , $Idea_n(object_n)$]. For instance, s(he) can relate the assertions (the world descriptions) *Furniture(sofa)* and *Colour(brown)* to each other. Then, *Relation*[*Furniture(sofa)* , *Colour(brown)*] is capable of representing different types of relationships between *sofa* and *brown* with regard to their labels in the trainer's mind. Actually, the proposed world descriptions can actively develop her/his knowledge. Also, the relationship between the world descriptions can establish various expressions in her/his mind. Let me conclude that these relationships construct more specified ideas based upon the proposed world descriptions. Relying on FOL and considering $p, q \in [1,n]$, *Relation*[$Idea_p(object_p)$, $Idea_q(object_q)$] represents a binary predicate between two unary predicates (between $Idea_p$ and $Idea_q$). This relation is also valid between $object_p$ and $object_q$ as the instances of $Idea_p$ and $Idea_q$. In this step, the trainer has produced a linear relational model, see Figure 1.

[3] The approached linear relational model is based on FOL. But it could also be represented in the form of a *j*-by-*i* matrix like *I*, where $i, j \in [1,n]$. This step represents the most significant assumption of the transformation. We shall stress the fact that we have represented the linear description *Relation*[$Idea_1(object_1)$, $Idea_2(object_2)$, ... , $Idea_n(object_n)$] in the form of a *j*-by-*i* matrix in order to allow the required linear transformation (that reflects the ideas) to be represented in a well-structured format. Additionally, a matrix can appropriately be used in establishing a transformation. Here, we have a matrix (relational model), see Figure 2.

[4] This step focuses on reflection. The idea assertion $Idea_1(object_1)$ (located in the first row and the first column of the matrix *b*) gets reflected in $Predicate_1(constant_1)$ (located in the first row and the first column of matrix *c* that is the product of the transformation) and $Idea_n(object_n)$ (located in the *j*th row and the *i*th column of the matrix *b*) gets reflected in $Predicate_n(constant_n)$ (located in the *j*th row and the *i*th column of matrix *c*). Thus, all cells in the relational model *b* collectively are reflected in an equivalent relational model (matrix), see Figure 3.

[5] The relational model *c* represents a relationship between $Predicate_1(constant_1)$, $Predicate_2(constant_2)$, ..., and $Predicate_n(constant_n)$. Therefore, we have a description like *Relation*[$Predicate_1(constant_1)$, ... , $Predicate_n(constant_n)$]. Consequently, there are *n* assignments from the [unary] $Predicate_1$ into $constant_1$, from $Predicate_2$ into $constant_2$, ..., and finally from $Predicate_n$ into $constant_n$. These assignments have been related with each other by means of *n*-ary *Relation*. Based on FOL, the effect of *n*-ary *Relation* is equivalent to *Predicate*[$Predicate_1(constant_1)$, $Predicate_2(constant_2)$, ... , $Predicate_n(constant_n)$]. Note that the outer predicate is *n*-ary and works on *n* internal unary predicates. Then, the trainer has produced a linear relational model, see Figure 4.

[6] This step focuses on generating the relational hypothesis model. Actually, the effect of the first unary predicate on the first constant symbol generates the first hypothesis (or $Hypothesis_1$), the effect of the second unary predicate on the second constant symbol generates the second hypothesis (or $Hypothesis_2$), ..., and the effect of the *n*th unary predicate on the *n*th constant symbol generates the *n*th hypothesis (or $Hypothesis_n$). Subsequently the outer *n*-ary predicate relates $Hypothesis_1$, $Hypothesis_2$, ..., $Hypothesis_n$. Therefore, there is a relationship between all generated hypotheses. Thus, we have *Predicate*[$Hypothesis_1$, $Hypothesis_2$, ... , $Hypothesis_n$]. Therefore, we have a relational hypothesis model, see Figure 5.

[7] Finally, there is a set like { $Hypothesis_1$, $Hypothesis_2$, ... , $Hypothesis_n$ } that represents the generated hypotheses for the machine.

B. Analysis of Transformation

"Suppose that (*i*) I_n denotes the *n*-component linear relational model [$Idea_1(object_1)$, $Idea_2(object_2)$, ... , $Idea_n(object_n)$], (*ii*) P_n denotes the *n*-component linear relational model [$Predicate_1(constant_1)$, $Predicate_2$ $(constant_2)$, ... , $Predicate_n(constant_n)$], and (*iii*) H_n denotes the *n*-component linear relational model [$Hypothesis_1$, $Hypothesis_2$, ... , $Hypothesis_n$]". First, we focus on the forward direction from human to machine. There are *reflection* functions like $\boldsymbol{R}_i$ from human being's ideas into predicates. Let me represent the set of $\boldsymbol{R}_i$ by $\boldsymbol{R}$. So, $\boldsymbol{R}: I_n \rightarrow P_n$. Then, $\boldsymbol{R}$ represents the transformed ideas into predicates. Semantically, the reflection functions $\boldsymbol{R}$ satisfy the *n*-component model [$Hypothesis_1$, $Hypothesis_2$, ... , $Hypothesis_n$] (i.e., provide proper models that attempt to satisfy the hypotheses). Then, there is a model like $\boldsymbol{R} \vDash H_n$. Therefore, the reflection functions $\boldsymbol{R}$ semantically satisfy the set of hypotheses in the machine (Result 1). At this point, we focus on the backward direction from machine to human. There are various *conformation* functions like $\boldsymbol{C}$ such that $H_n \vDash \boldsymbol{C}$. Semantically, any conformation function gets satisfied by a hypothesis like $Hypothesis_i$ belonging to the *n*-component relational model [$Hypothesis_1$, $Hypothesis_2$, ... , $Hypothesis_n$]. Note that $\boldsymbol{C}$ denotes the set of $\boldsymbol{C}_i$. So, $\boldsymbol{C}$ represents the transformed predicates into ideas and formally, $\boldsymbol{C}: P_n \rightarrow I_n$ (Result 2). According to the results 1 and 2 we have:

$$(\boldsymbol{R}: I_n \rightarrow P_n) \models H_n \models (\boldsymbol{C}: P_n \rightarrow I_n) .$$

$$\text{Then: } I_n \rightarrow P_n \models H_n \models P_n \rightarrow I_n .$$

In fact, the reflection transformations from ideas into predicates satisfy the hypotheses. And the hypotheses satisfy the inverse reflection transformations (or conformation transformations) from predicates into ideas.

IV. CONCLUSIONS

Training machines based upon personal mental images of the world in the context of human-machine interactions shapes the skeleton of constructivist human-machine interactions. Schemata in constructivist training frameworks could demonstrate the trainer's realisations of the world. They conceptually represent the constituents of the trainer's thoughts for training concepts. Schemata support the trainer in developing her/his constructed concepts (that have been constructed with regard to her/his own realisation of the world). In this article we have provided a logical and epistemological specification of concepts and we have seen the linkages between human's mental images and her/his linguistic expressions as the origins of manifestation of concepts. Accordingly, we have logically specified the mental mappings from human into machine and we have focused on logical representations of transformations from human beings' conceptions into machines' knowledge bases relying on First-Order Predicate Logic. We have identified the transformations from humans' mind into machines' knowledge bases by 'reflection transformations' and we have labeled the inverse cases by 'conformation transformations' in order to analyse the proposed logical descriptions. The reflection transformations from ideas into predicates satisfy the hypotheses. And the hypotheses satisfy the conformation transformations from predicates into ideas. In future research, we will employ the results in formal semantic analysis of concept transformations from minds into knowledge bases and in specifying their conceptualisations.

REFERENCES

[1] G. McIntyre Boyd, "Conversation Theory". Handbook of Research on Educational Communications and Technology, 2004.

[2] T. Husen, and T. N. Postlethwaite, "Constructivism in Education". The International Encyclopaedia of Education, Supplement Vol.1. Oxford/New York: Pergamon Press, 1989, 162–163.

[3] R. J. Spiro, P. J. Feltovich, M. J. Jacobson, and R. L. Coulson, "Cognitive Flexibility, Constructivism, and Hypertext. Random Access Instruction for Advanced Knowledge Acquisition in Ill-structured Domains", Educational Technology, 1991, 24-33.

[4] P. McGawand Peterson, "Constructivism And Learning", International Encyclopaedia of Education, Oxford: Elsevier, 2007.

[5] D. C. Phillips, "The Good, the Bad, And the Ugly: The Many Faces of Constructivism", Educational Researcher 24 - No 7, 1995, 5–12.

[6] T. Mitchell, "Machine learning", in Machine Learning, Kluwer Academic Publishers, 1997.

[7] N. Lavrac and S. Dzeroski, "Inductive Logic Programming: Techniques and Applications". Artificial Intelligence. Ellis Horwood (Simon & Schuster), 1994.

[8] H. Götzsche, "Deviational Syntactic Structures", Bloomsbury Academic: London / New Delhi / New York / Sydney, 2013.

[9] B. M. Lake, "Towards More Human-Like Concept Learning in Machines: Compositionality, Causality, and Learning-To-Learn", Massachusetts Institute of Technology, 2014.

[10] W. Parker, "Concept Formation" in http://teachinghistory.org, [accessed March 2016].

[11] F. Badie, "A Semantic Basis for Meaning Construction in Constructivist Interactions", CELDA-15 Proceedings, Ireland, 2015, 369-373.

[12] F. Badie, "Towards A Semantics-Based Framework For Meaning Construction in Constructivist Interactions:, ICERI2015 Proceedings, Spain, 2015, 7995-8002.

[13] Schema in http://plato.stanford.edu/entries/schema/, [accessed March 2016].

$Idea_1(object_1)$	...	$Idea_n(object_n)$

Fig. 1: Linear Relational Model

$Idea_1(object_1)$	...	$Idea_i(object_i)$
...		
$Idea_j(object_j)$	...	$Idea_n(object_n)$

Fig. 2: Relational Model

$Predicate_1(constant_1)$	...	$Predicate_i(constant_i)$
...		
$Predicate_j(constant_j)$	...	$Predicate_n(constant_n)$

Fig. 3: Relational Model

$Predicate_1(constant_1)$	...	$Predicate_n(constant_n)$

Fig. 4: Linear Relational Model

$Hypothesis_1$	...	$Hypothesis_n$

Fig. 5: Linear Relational Model

The Analysis of the Specific Dictionaries for Compressive Sensing of EEG Signals

Monica Fira
Institute of Computer Science
Romanian Academy
Iasi, Romania
mfira@etti.tuiasi.ro

Victor-Andrei Maiorescu[1,2], Liviu Goras[1,2]
[1]"Gheorghe Asachi" Technical University of Iaşi,
[2]Institute of Computer Science, Romanian Academy, Iasi
mandrei@etti.tuiasi.ro
lgoras@etti.tuiasi.ro

***Abstract*— In this paper the possibility of the electroencephalogram (EEG) compressed sensing based on specific dictionaries is presented. Three types of dictionaries (wavelet, temporal EEG signal specific, and channel specific) are analyzed and the results are expressed through quantitative measures (distortion) and by qualitative measures (stimulus classification rate of the Brain Computer Interface (BC)I paradigm - Spelling).**

Keywords*- *EEG; Compressed sensing; BCI; P300.

I. INTRODUCTION

In recent years, compressed sensing (CS) has attracted considerable attention in areas like applied mathematics, computer science, and electrical engineering by showing that, in certain conditions, it is possible to surpass the traditional limits of sampling theory. CS builds upon the fundamental fact that many signals can be represented using only a few non-zero coefficients in a suitable basis or dictionary. Nonlinear optimization can then be used to recover such signals from very few measurements [1].The concept of compressed sensing is an example of practical use of new mathematical results. The difficulties for using in applications of such results are related to the way such concepts are understood, in a more or less intuitive manner, in order to facilitate the fusion between theory and applications.

The literature of recent years shows an impressive number of papers in the CS field, covering both 1D and 2D medical signals. Among the 1D signals the most frequently used in CS applications are the electrocardiogram (ECG) and electroencephalogram (EEG) since they are most used in the medical world as well. In the case of EEG signals, there is often a need of records for longer periods of time (i.e., during the night) or for a large number of channels.

In this paper, we propose a compression method for EEG signals based on CS using specific dictionaries for reconstruction in the sense that the atoms of the above dictionaries are actually segments of EEG signals and compare it with a wavelet representation.

To validate the proposed method EEG recordings of the competition for Spelling, BCI Competition III - Dataset II were used, and in order to evaluate the reconstructed signal, two types of evaluation were used, namely:

- **qualitative evaluation**, by P300 detection and prediction of the watched character in the case of the spelling paradigm for data taken from the "BCI III competition Challenge 2005" on the reconstructed EEG signals and using the winner scripts (Alain Rakotomamonjy [9]).
- **quantitative evaluation,** using distortion measures such as PRDN (normalized percent of root-mean-square difference), NMSE (normalized Mean Square Error) and RMS (root mean square error) between the reconstructed and original signals.

II. COMPRESSED SENSING

Shannon's sampling theory represents, for many signal classes of interest in signal processing, a condition too strict for acquisition and representation of signals [1]. When signals are known to be compressible or sparse, only a much smaller fraction of samples may be needed to capture all the signal information, at the expense of having to use nonlinear reconstruction techniques. This area of research has evolved into the technique of "compressed sensing", also known as compressive sensing, compressive sampling and sparse sampling), perfected in the past few years by prestigious researchers such as D. Donoho [3], E. Candès [4] and M. Elad [5], and drawing the attention of many others. It consists in capturing the information from sparse or compressible signals via a set of a few linear measurements, possibly random, followed by reconstructing a signal using optimization techniques for finding sparse solutions to underdetermined linear systems. The generality of the approach coupled with the prevalence of sparsity-related signal processing for big data is considered to have an enormous potential, with multiple implications and applications, in numerous fields of exact sciences.

As already mentioned, CS studies the possibility of reconstructing a signal x from a few linear projections, also called measurements, given the a priori information that the signal is sparse or compressible in some basis Ψ . The vectors on which x is projected onto are arranged as the rows of a nxN projection matrix Φ , n < N, where N is the size of x and n is the number of measurements. Denoting the measurement vector as y, the acquisition process can be described as:

$$y = \Phi x = \Phi \Psi \gamma \qquad (1)$$

$$\hat{\gamma} = \arg\min_{\gamma} \|\gamma\|_{l_0} \quad subject\ to \quad y = \Phi\Psi\gamma \tag{2}$$

$$\hat{x} = \Psi\hat{\gamma} \tag{3}$$

The system of equations (1) is obviously undetermined. Under certain assumptions on Φ and Ψ, however, the original expansion vector γ can be reconstructed as the unique solution to the optimization problem (2); the signal is then reconstructed with (3). Note that (2) amounts to finding the sparsest decomposition of the measurement vector y in the dictionary $\Phi\Psi$. Unfortunately, (2) is combinatorial and unstable when considering noise or approximately sparse signals. Two directions have emerged to circumvent these problems: (i) pursuit and thresholding algorithms seek a sub-optimal solution of (2) and (ii) the Basis Pursuit algorithm relaxes the l_0 minimization to l_1, solving the convex optimization problem (4) instead of the original.

$$\hat{\gamma} = \arg\min_{\gamma} \|\gamma\|_{l_1} \quad subject\ to \quad y = \Phi\Psi\gamma \tag{4}$$

In the past few years, techniques inspired from the mathematic fundamentals of CS have also been applied in the field of biomedical signals, both at the level of processing methods for electrocardiographic (ECG) and electroencephalographic (EEG) signals and of practical implementation in applications such as compression, transmission and reconstruction of the ECG signal using a personal device such as a smart-phone.

III. BCI P300 SPELLER

The use of EEG signals as a vector of communication between man and machine is one of the new challenges in biomedical signal theory. The main element of this communication system known as "brain-computer interface" (BCI Brain-Computer Interface) is the proper interpretation of the EEG signals and the characteristic parameters of the brain electrical activity.

The P300 speller is based on the so-called oddball paradigm which states that rare expected stimuli produce a positive deflection in the EEG after about 300 ms.

A	B	C	D	E	F
G	H	I	J	K	L
M	N	O	P	Q	R
S	T	U	V	W	X
Y	Z	1	2	3	4
5	6	7	8	9	

Figure 1. Example of a 6 × 6 user display in P300 Speller

A P300 speller, based on this paradigm, has been introduced by Farwell and Donchin who developed a protocol whereby a subject is presented a 6 × 6 character matrix (see Figure 1) [11].

The dataset II of the BCI competition III 2005, from the competition webpage [10], has been recorded from two different subjects and 5 different spelling sessions. Each session is composed of runs, and for each run, a subject is asked to spell a word. For a given acquisition session, all EEG signals of a 64-channel scalp have been continuously collected. Before digitization at a sample rate of 240 Hz, signals have been bandpass-filtered from 0.1 to 60 Hz.

Each session is composed of runs, and for each run, a subject is asked to spell a word. Row/column intensifications were the block is randomized in blocks of 12. The sets of 12 intensifications were repeated 15 times for each character epoch (i.e., any specific row/column was intensified 15 times and thus there were 180 total intensifications for each character epoch). Each character epoch was followed by a 2.5sec period, and during this time the matrix was blank.

The training set contains 85 characters and the test set consists of 100 characters for each of the two subjects A and B. A more detailed description of the dataset can be found in the BCI competition paper [10].

The competition winners, Alain Rakotomamonjy and Vincent Guigue propose a method that copes with such variabilities through an ensemble of classifiers approach [9]. Each classifier is composed of a linear Support Vector Machine trained on a small part of the available data and for which a channel selection procedure has been performed. Their performances are a classification rate of 95.5% for the 15 sequences and 73.5% for 5 sequences [9].

IV. METHOD

The key element in the success of signal compression based on compressed sensing is the right choice of the dictionary based on which the reconstruction will be done. Generally, the ECG and EEG biomedical signals have not a very high sparsity in standard wavelet dictionaries. Therefore, in most of cases, the authors propose specific dictionaries either specific to the signal or specific for the used database.

In the following an analysis of how the results are influenced by various dictionaries is made. Three types of dictionaries have been analyzed as follows.

A. *Wavelet Dictionary*

The first choice was the Daubechies 10 type dictionary so that for all channels a single dictionary will be used [6-8].

B. *Temporal EEG signal specific dictionary*

A second choice investigated as well in [7], was to build dictionaries from segments of certain predefined EEG channels, recorded at the same time with the target EEG compressed signal channel. These dictionaries are built with EEG signals from channels that are acquired in the classical way; the dictionaries are the same for all compressed sensed channels.

To construct the necessary dictionaries for reconstruction, EEG signals from channels FPZ, F7, F8, C5, CZ, T8, PO7, PO8 and Oz were used. The rest of the channels, i.e. the 55 channels (Fig. 2) were segmented in windows with 1 second length (240 samples) and using a random matrix with size 240x24 we obtained EEG compressed signals (with size 24 and compression ratio CR = 10:1). In Figure 2 the red channels are used for dictionary construction and the signals in the white channels are compressed sensed.

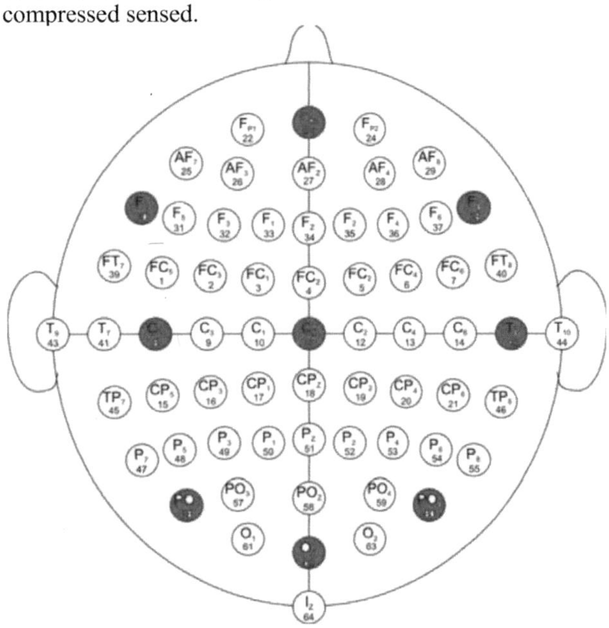

Figure 2. Electrode placement and channel name.

Thus, for each sample time we have one dictionary. Knowing the random matrix used for sensing and the dictionary with the EEG signals from the 9 channels acquired synchronously with the compressed sensed channels, the EEG signals for the CS channels could be reconstructed [7].

C. Channel specific dictionary

Third, for each EEG channel a dictionary has been built. The atoms of dictionary are actually the EEG segments of the training set. In this case, for the data acquired on 64 channels, there are 64 dictionaries. Thus, each dictionary was composed from 2x85 atoms; for every epoch from the training set, 2 segments (from 240 samples) of EEG signal were randomly selected as atoms in the dictionary.

D. Evaluation of the reconstructed signals

In order to evaluate and validate the methods, we used both quantitative measures (the reconstructed signal distortion) and signal quality measures (expressed by the classification rate of the characters tracked by a human subject, which is exactly the problem of the BCI Competition III 2005 - dataset II – Spelling).

V. Experimental Results and Discussions

For the evaluation of the analyzed methods we used the dataset II of the BCI Competition III 2005 -P300 Spelling.

Thus, for evaluation of compression we used the compression rate (CR) (5) defined as the ratio between the number of bits needed to represent the original and the compressed signal.

$$CR = \frac{b_{orig}}{b_{comp}} \quad (5)$$

For qualitative evaluation of the method based on the classification rate in spelling paradigm, we used scripts from the winners, Alain Rakotomamonjy and Vincent Guigue [9]. The used scripts implement classification based on all 64 EEG channels.

To validate the compression we evaluated the distortion between the original and the reconstructed signals by means of the PRDN (the normalized percentage root-mean-square difference):

$$PRDN\% = 100\sqrt{\sum_{n=1}^{N}(x(n)-\tilde{x}(n))^2 \Big/ \sum_{n=1}^{N}(x(n)-\bar{x})^2} \quad (6)$$

where $x(n)$ and $\tilde{x}(n)$ are the samples of the original and the reconstructed signals respectively, $\bar{x}$ is the mean value of the original signal, and N is the length of the window over which the PRDN is calculated.

For compression, the EEG signal was segmented into windows of length 1 sec, i.e. 240 samples and we used a random matrix with size 240x24 for CR = 10:1 and a random matrix with size 240x48 for CR = 5:1.

Table 1 presents the results of the three tested dictionaries. Note that in terms of reconstruction errors expressed via PDN, the smallest errors were obtained using specific in time EEG signal dictionaries, which consists of atoms regularly acquired at the same time point from the other channels. Considering the rate of classification for the spelling paradigm, the best results are obtained using channel-specific dictionaries.

TABLE I. AVERAGE RESULTS: PRDN_MEAN AND CLASSIFICATION PERFORMANCE IN % OF CORRECTLY RECOGNIZED CHARACTERS FOR THE B SUBJECTS AND FOR INCREASING NUMBER OF SEQUENCES.

	P300 Spelling - classification performance for number of sequences (classification rate %) 1 2 3 4 5 6 7 8 9 10 11 12 13 14 15	**PRDN mean**
Original data – uncompressed and classificated by Alain Rakotomamonjy and Vincent Guigue		
-	38 60 70 69 80 84 86 89 92 93 95 96 96 96 95	0
Dict_Daubechies10		
10:1	7 17 16 18 27 29 37 40 38 41 48 45 51 48 54	108.91
Dictionary=[Signal_8(i:i+239);Signal_10(i:i+239);Signal_11(i:i+239);Signal_12(i:i+239);Signal_14(i:i+239);Signal_27(i:i+239);Signal_50(i:i+239);Signal_52(i:i+239);Signal_58(i:i+239)];		
5:1	22 31 42 50 54 61 68 70 72 77 82 85 79 79 81	35.38
10:1	23 35 42 44 54 57 60 63 68 70 76 78 76 78 80	**31.42**
Dictionary = 2*85 atoms from the training set for each channel		
5:1	**29 41 50 62 68 74 73 78 82 82 86 86 86 87 90**	41.17
10:1	19 30 43 52 50 60 60 65 73 71 78 82 84 82 89	55.90

In Table II PRDN vs. channel (top figure) are presented as well as examples of original and reconstructed EEG signal (figures below). The worst results are obtained using wavelet type dictionaries. Between the classification rate in spelling paradigm and error expressed as PRDN there is a discordance, namely not always the smallest PRDN errors lead to highest classification rate (see the results in table with bold). The explanation for the discrepancy between the classification rate and average PRDN is that each channel has a certain weight in the classification rate for the spelling paradigm. The obtained results lead to the conclusion that some channels that have a higher weight in the classification rate are rebuilt better than others which have lesser meaning. Thus it can be seen that for the channel specific dictionaries, in case of both compression rates of 5:1 and 10:1, the error for the channels 22-38 is much lower compared to the rest of the channels. In fact one can speak about a group of errors in three clusters, namely, a class for the channels 1-21, the second class for the 22-40 channels, and the third class for the channels 41-64. These three groups are closely interlinked to the placement of the cranial electrodes too (see Figure 1).

TABLE II PRDN_MEAN VS. CHANNEL AND ORIGINAL VS. SIGNAL RESONSTRUCTED FOR THE THREE TESTED DICTIONARIES

Dict_Daubechies10 **CR = 10:1** **PRDN_mean = 108.91**	**Dictionary=[Signal_8(i:i+239);Signal_10(i:i+239);Signal_11(i:i+239);Signal_12(i:i+239);Signal_14(i:i+239);Signal_27(i:i+239);Signal_50(i:i+239);Signal_52(i:i+239);Signal_58(i:i+239)]** **and** **CR = 10:1 PRDN_mean = 31.42**
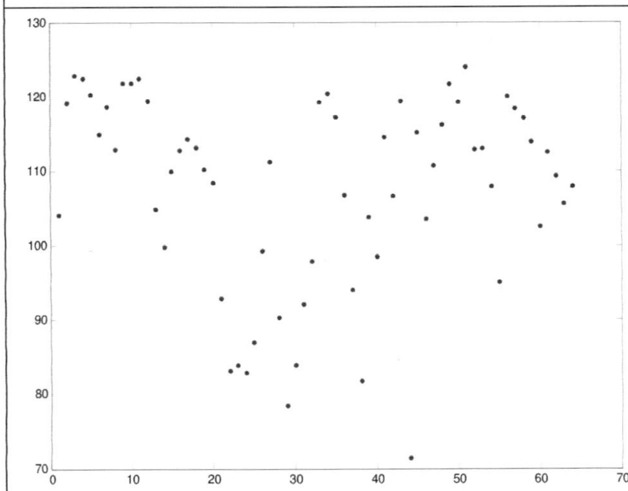	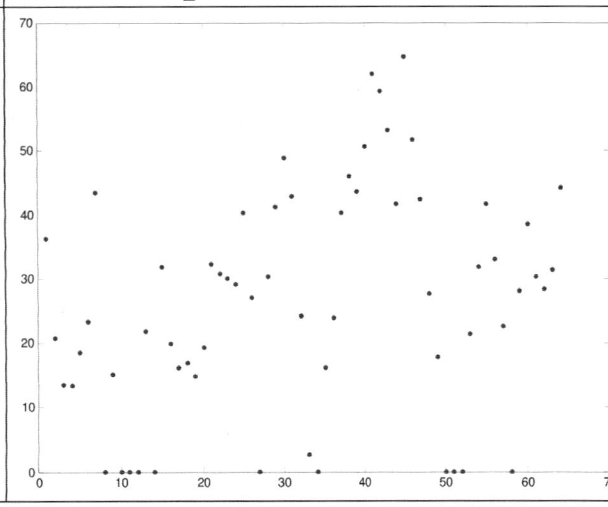

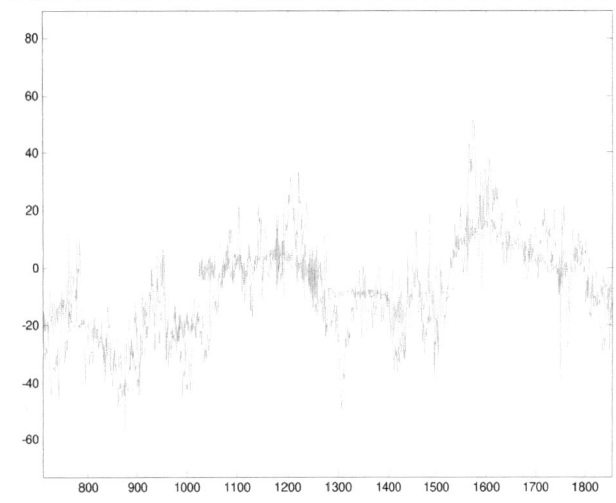

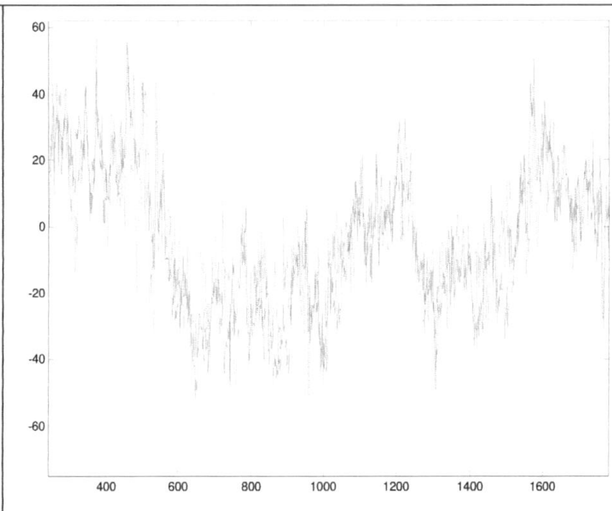

Dictionary = 2x85 atoms from the training set for each channel with
CR = 5:1 and PRDN_mean = 41.17

Dictionary = 2x85 atoms from the training set for each channel with
CR = 10:1 and PRDN_mean = 55.90

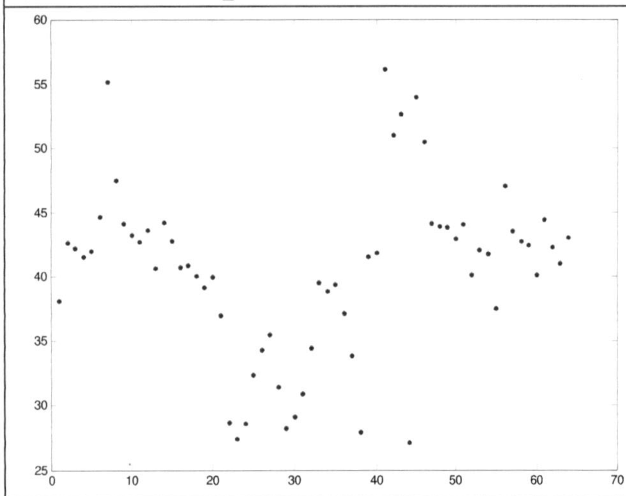

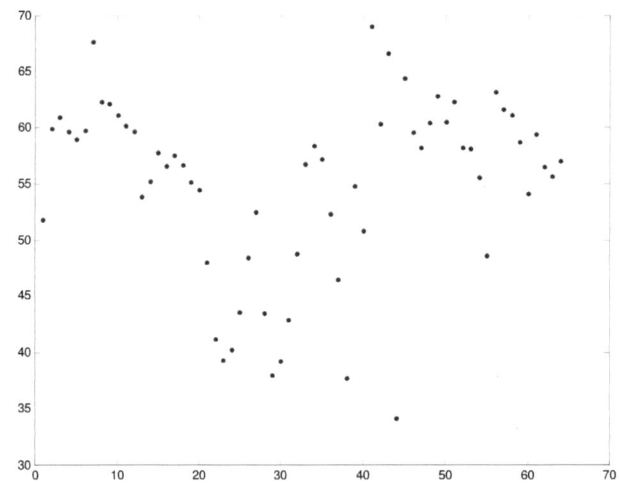

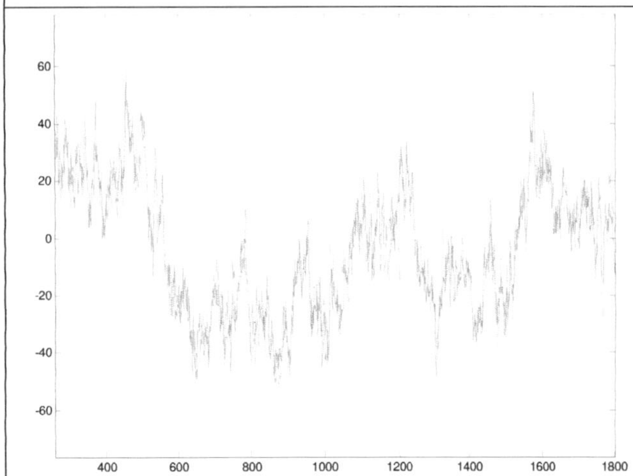

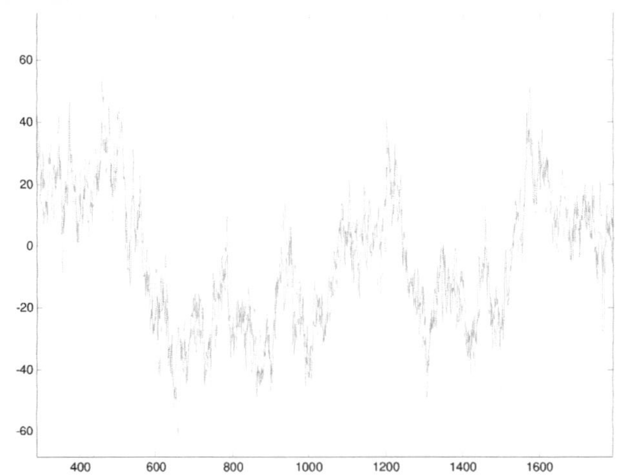

VI. CONCLUSIONS

In this paper a comparative analysis of the results obtained using three types of dictionaries for EEG signals compressed sensing is presented. The used dictionaries are: Daubechies 10 wavelet dictionary and two types of EEG signal specific dictionaries, namely, temporal EEG signal specific dictionary and channel specific dictionary. For the evaluation of the proposed method we used the dataset from the BCI Competition III 2005 - P300 Spelling. In order to evaluate the results of the EEG signal reconstruction the PRDN was used in parallel with the classification rate of the spelling paradigm assessed using the scripts from the winner of the competition (the version of classification using all 64 channels). Based on the analysis it is found that the worst results are obtained when standard wavelet dictionaries were used. The other two EEG signal specific dictionaries, lead to better results. Thus, for the channel specific dictionaries the best results in terms of classification at the spelling paradigm are obtained for CR = 5:1 and 10:1 when the achieved classification rate was 90%, respectively, 89% (for the original signals the classification rate was 95%). The temporal EEG signal specific dictionaries lead to the best results in terms of error expressed as PRDN, i.e. for a compression of 5:1 it was obtained a PRDN = 35.38 and for 10: 1 the obtained PRDN was 31.42.

The obtained results demonstrate that channel specific dictionaries and temporal EEG signal specific dictionaries provide much improved results compared to the standard wavelet dictionaries.

ACKNOWLEDGMENT

This work was supported by a grant of the Romanian National Authority for Scientific Research and Innovation, CNCS – UEFISCDI, project number PN-II-RU-TE-2014-4-0832 *"Medical signal processing methods based on compressed sensing; applications and their implementation."*

REFERENCES

[1] M. A. Davenport, M. F. Duarte, Y. C. Eldar, and G. Kutyniok, "Introduction to Compressed Sensing," in Compressed Sensing: Theory and Applications, Cambridge University Press, 2012.

[2] D. Donoho, Compressed sensing, IEEE Trans. on Information Theory, 52(4) (2006) 1289 – 1306

[3] D. Donoho, Compressed sensing, Technical Report, Stanford Univ., 2004

[4] E. Candè, M. Wakin, An introduction to compressive sampling. (IEEE Signal Processing Magazine 25(2) (2008) 21-30

[5] M. Elad, "Optimized Projections for Compressed Sensing", IEEE Transactions on Signal Processing, 2007, Vol. 52

[6] M. Fira, L. Goras, "A New Method for EEG Compressive Sensing," Advances in Electrical and Computer Engineering, vol. 12, no. 4, 2012, pp. 71-76

[7] M. Fira, L. Goras , "Biomedical Signal Compression based on Basis Pursuit", International Conference on Convergence and Hybrid Information Technology, ICHIT 2009, in Daejeon, Coreea de Sud; 2009, pag. 541-545

[8] M. Fira, L. Goras, "Biomedical Signal Compression based on Basis Pursuit", International Journal of Advanced Science and Technology, Science and Engineering Research Support Center (SERSC), Vol. 14, pag. 1-14, January 2010, ISSN: 2005-4238

[9] A. Rakotomamonjy, V. Guigue, BCI Competition III: Dataset II- Ensemble of SVMs for BCI P300 Speller, IEEE Transactions on Biomedical Engineering,Volume:55, Issue: 3, 2008, pp. 1147 – 1154

[10] B. Blankertz, "BCI competition III webpage." [Online]. Available: http://ida.first.fraunhofer.de/projects/bci/competition iii

[11] L. A. Farwellm E. Donchin, "Talking off the top of your head: toward a mental prothesis utilizing event-related brain potentials", Electroenceph clin Neurophysiol, Vol. 70, 1988, pp. 510–523

FIRMA: A Development Framework for Elderly-Friendly Interactive Multimodal Applications for Assistive Robots

Nikolaos Kazepis[1], Margherita Antona[1], Constantine Stephanidis[1,2]
[1]Foundation for Research and Technology – Hellas (FORTH), Institute of Computer Science
[2]University of Crete, Department of Computer Science
Heraklion, GR–70013, Greece
e-mail: {kazepis,antona,cs}@ics.forth.gr

***Abstract*—The continuous growth of the older population and the progressive ageing of society worldwide bring about the need for new technological solutions for improving independent living, quality of life and active ageing of older citizens. Recent research efforts have focused on incorporating assistive robotic platforms in the elderly's homes under the role of domestic care givers or social companion. Robotic platforms have been around for quite some time, and researchers have been focused on overcoming essential problems that are related to the nature of robotics and their usage in domestic environments. However, since the field of robotics has matured over the last years, a focus shift from the hardware itself to Human Robot Interaction (HRI) in domestic environments is becoming increasingly necessary. This paper focusses on interaction in the context of the collaborative co-existence of the elderly and the robot. In this context, interaction should be tailored to the end users taking into account the specific requirements of each individual, the environmental state but also the capacity of the input/output channels provided by the robotic platform. To this end, this paper proposes a generic platform targeted to support the development of multimodal, elderly friendly, interactive applications that target assistive robots for elderly users.**

Keywords-development framework; multimodal interaction; adaptation; assistive robots.

I. INTRODUCTION

Older people are increasingly becoming the dominant group of customers of a variety of technological products and services (both in terms of number and buying power). Recent advances in Information and Communication technologies (ICT) have great potential for meeting the needs of older people and help them stay healthier, live independently for longer, counteract reduced capabilities due to age, and remain active.

In particular, the field of assistive domestic robotic platforms has been drawing considerable attention in recent years. As opposed to other domestic robotic devices, such as automatic floor cleaners or pure surveillance robots, assistive robotic platforms are designed to provide services to their human users through direct interaction, like displaying information, supporting communication with other people or simply entertaining the users [1].

The primary goal of these robots is to make their older users feel safe and less lonely at home, while enabling and facilitating them in their independent or semi-independent living [2], often in the context of an Ambient Assisted Living environment [9].

Designing and developing appropriate user interfaces for assistive robots presents several challenges due to the demanding target user group and the complexity of the environment.

Multimodal interaction including a graphical user interface, speech input and output, as well as gesture input has been found in various research efforts as an adequate solution for older users to interact with robots [10]. However, at present developing such interfaces is a very demanding task mainly performed ad-hoc, due to the lack of tools and systematic approaches. An additional important need is to support the adaptation of modalities to cater for the target user diversity.

This paper proposes a framework, named FIRMA, to support the development of multimodal, elderly friendly, interactive applications for assistive robots targeted to elderly users in AAL environments. FIRMA provides developers with the necessary technologies, tools and building blocks for creating elderly-friendly multimodal applications in AAL environments, with particular focus on robotic platforms, thus increasing their level of adaptation to users' needs. Using the proposed framework makes these applications inherently friendly to the elder users and capable of adapting to their needs, the surrounding environment and the context of use. The framework facilitates the effective and efficient development of the supported user interfaces, thus simplifying to a great extent the developer's work.

The rest of this paper is organized as follows. Section II discusses the implications of designing for elderly users and overview state of the art research on elderly-friendly multimodal applications for assistive robots. Section III describes the architecture of the FIRMA framework. Section IV discusses FIRMA's implementation. Section V demonstrates a test case application built based on the FIRMA framework. Section VI discusses the evaluation of the FIRMA framework and section VII concludes the article.

II. BACKGROUND

Several user studies have shown that elderly people and their families regard social inclusion, safety and home automation as important features of future homecare environments [11]. With respect to interaction in such environments, one of the main research challenges is the design of adequate user interfaces. This is due to the fact that elderly people vary considerably in their physical and cognitive abilities, which makes it difficult to use traditional forms of interaction [3]. Focusing on single interaction strategies may not always provide appropriate solutions [4], as many older computer users are affected by multiple functional limitations.

To address this problem various authors developed intelligent user interfaces, which support users according to their individual needs. For example, [25] introduces a spatial metaphor for universal control devices to structure available services based on the elderly person's own apartment. The results of the study showed that the apartment metaphor is actually appropriate to enable elderly people to access a large number of services available in an AAL environment in an intuitive way. The metaphor showed a way for structuring and visualizing services in a universal control device.

Furthermore, [26] presented a novel general framework for multimodal dialogue processing, which is conceived following an application-independent philosophy. In fact, it is able to manage multimodal communication between people and the environment in different application scenarios. The core of the framework architecture is composed of the analysis and planning levels, which enable the processing of information derived from whatever input modalities, giving these inputs an appropriate representation and integrating these individual representations into a joint semantic interpretation.

Moreover, [27] presents a prototype for a Web 2.0–enabled ambient assisted living (AAL) device that offers easy-to-use functionality to help elderly people keep and establish new contacts, find events that match their interests and be aided in sustaining their mobility. The prototype consists of a hardware device for mobile usage which host the desired functionality while being adequate for use by elderly people. An internet tablet was selected accommodating a large touch screen.

If carefully designed, multimodal user interfaces can provide an appropriate solution to cater for the needs of elderly users [12]. The main objective is to achieve interaction as natural as human-human communication, while increasing robustness by means of redundant or complementary information. The selection, activation, deactivation and fusion of the appropriate modalities plays a significant role during human-robot interaction, as it offers the users a fully usable system to interact with as well as adapting to their needs, preferences and to the changing semantic context of the interaction.

Regarding touch based interactions targeted to elder users, several research efforts have provided valuable insights regarding the different aspects of how the respective systems should be designed. The research findings include the optimal inter-key threshold that has to be defined (100ms-150ms) [35], the minimum touch target sizes (8 mm or larger) [36], the significance of employing familiar interactions and behaviors to help in orienting older users with new applications [37], new touchscreen input methods for elderly users with tremor (e.g., swabbing) [38], appropriate touch based gestures [39][40], as well as the benefits of employing multimodal feedback to improve task performance [41].

Furthermore when designing speech recognition systems for the elderly target user group, its heterogeneity should be taken into account. Individual persons have different individual needs based on their different age related health impairments. Such impairments can affect the person's speech capabilities which results either in an increasingly limited vocabulary or fluctuations in their pronunciation clarity [42]. These limitations should be taken under consideration when designing the parameterization properties of such speech engines.

Moreover, the heterogeneity of the elderly user group implies various restrictions when designing and developing gestural interaction modalities for the elder users. Individual persons have different individual needs based on their different age related health impairments. Such impairments can affect the person's mobility capabilities and cognitive functions which results in mobility restrictions in different body parts and difficulties in remembering the specified gestures and the optimal way of performing them. These limitations should be taken under consideration when designing the parameterization properties of such gesture recognition engines [43].

Despite the fact that multimodal user interfaces have been in focus for quite some time [1], and much research has been conducted to address the main challenges of modality interpretation, coordination, parameterization and integration [13], developing multimodal user interfaces is still a difficult endeavor. Various approaches have been investigated to facilitate multimodal user interface development, such as, for example, [14][15][16]. However, these approaches are dependent on the interaction platform and mainly target conventional PCs and mobile devices.

According to [20] recently developed assistive robots, such as ALIAS [17], DOMEO [17], KSERA [18], CompanionAble [19] and HOBBIT [20], despite the differences introduced by the various robotic platforms, have multimodal user interfaces characterized by similar modality options and architectures. The basic offered modalities are touch-based interaction on some screen integrated in the robot, speech input and output, and gestures. A central module, in some cases called "Dialogue Manager", is responsible to control the output based on user input and system state and coordinating the different input and output modalities.

Despite their similarities, all the above mentioned interfaces have been developed ad hoc, as no reference framework currently exist for facilitating developers of multimodal user interfaces for assistive robots. As a consequence, the developed interfaces suffer from lack of flexibility, are difficult to customize, modify and reuse, require cumbersome solutions to communicate with both the ROS operating system [22] running on the robot and the AAL environment, and exhibit limited adaptation capabilities.

Against the above background, the proposed FIRMA framework allows the effective and efficient development of

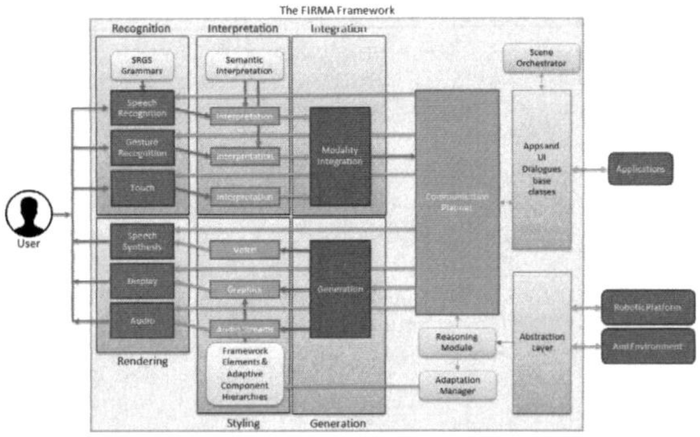

Figure 1. Orchestration of the different conceptual layers

multimodal adaptable user interfaces for assistive robot applications, relieving developers form the burden of programming ad hoc solutions.

III. ARCHITECTURE

The FIRMA framework comprises a collection of conceptual layers which can be seen in Figure 1.

A. The interaction recognition layer

The user is able to interact with the system through the interaction recognition layer. This layer consists of the different available interaction modalities that are provided. Additional interaction modalities can be added in future work such as hardware buttons and switches. The user is able to interact with the robot using touch, gestures and voice. These modalities are adapted to the profile of the user, his preferences and the context of use. They are managed, selected and fused together by the communication planner functional submodule. The touch recognition modality corresponds to the touch interactions between the user and the robotic platform's onboard touch screen.

The gesture recognition modality refers to the set of preselected gestures that the user is able to perform and the robot is able to understand and behave accordingly based on the context of the interaction. Finally, the speech recognition input modality refers to the predefined set of SRGS speech recognition grammars that describe the set of vocal commands that the robotic platform is able to understand. This set of SRGS grammars is loaded into the speech recognition engine so that the robot will be able to interpret the user's speech accordingly.

B. The input interpretation layer

The output of the interaction recognition layer is fed into the input interpretation layer. This layer consists of the processing of the user input in term of semantic interpretation based on the context of interaction. Each input modality of the input recognition layer is interpreted accordingly to the profile of the user and the interaction context. The speech recognition modality is interpreted according to the semantic speech annotations that are included in the corresponding SRGS speech grammars. The gesture recognition modality input is interpreted according to the respective application's logic that is active during the interaction, as well as the context of the interaction. For example, the same affirmative gesture may have different interpretations according to the context, and hence it could be interpreted either as a "YES" in the context of a question or as a "NEXT" in the context of an interaction process. Finally, the touch modality input is interpreted based on the dialogue that is displayed at the time that the interaction took place.

C. The modality integration layer and the low level framework architecture

The interpreted input is fed from the input interpretation layer into the modality integration layer, where the input from all the different available modalities is integrated based on high level integration scripting. For this purpose, the ACTA runtime (see Section IV.A) is used to integrate all the available modalities into a uniform input channel that can be routed to the communication planner functional component in order to take the necessary decisions regarding the orchestration of the input and output modalities. The same integrated input becomes available to the respective active applications through the low level input mechanisms that the FIRMA framework provides through the base classes that the developed applications inherit. Furthermore, the different available applications can communicate with the scene orchestrator functional component in order to gain access to the functionality it provides regarding the management of the different application screens and their display on the onboard robot screen. The input from the sensors of the robotic platform as well as the input from the environment is transformed into system readable format. The input from these sources is then routed through the reasoning module of the framework in order to infer all the necessary adaptation and communication decisions. When there is need for output from the system to the user, the communication planner decides over the selection and the fusion among the different available modalities to generate the information to be conveyed to the user.

D. The output styling layer

The information to be conveyed to the user goes from the generation layer to the output styling layer. This layer is where all the styling over the information delivery takes place. For each one of the available modalities, the appropriate styling is selected according to the user model, his preferences and the context of the interaction. The styling can refer to the output for the speech synthesis modality, the output for the UI display modality or the output for the audio modality. For the speech synthesis modality, the appropriate voice is selected according to the preferences of the user. Additionally, the appropriate rate, volume and pitch of the voice is selected and the output speech is styled using the SSML markup language. For the UI display modality, the appropriate UI selection and adaptation takes place according to the decisions of the adaptation manager functional component. The appropriate UI elements and dialogues are selected, the appropriate component hierarchies are instantiated and the output is delivered to the robot's display for the user to interact with. Furthermore, for the audio output modality, the appropriate auditory feedback is selected and the parameters of the audio output are specified. Finally, the output from the output styling layer is wired to the output rendering layer.

E. *The output rendering layer*

The final stage of the output delivery is the output rendering layer. This is the layer responsible for delivering the actual output to the users. It comprises the different available output modalities as they have been selected and fused by the communication planner functional component. For the speech synthesis output modality, the actual speech is generated based on the SSML annotations from the styling layer and the final auditory feedback is delivered to the user. For the touch display output modality, the appropriately selected framework elements, components and dialogues are instantiated and the result is presented on the robot's onboard display. Finally, for the audio output modality, the appropriate adaptation parameters are applied and the auditory feedback is delivered to the user.

IV. IMPLEMENTATION

FIRMA is a fully integrated development framework that can support the design and development of elderly friendly, multimodal interactive applications that are deployed on domestic robotic taking full advantage of the possibilities they can offer. The results of this research effort include all the necessary tools and building blocks for the creation of speech enabled, voice recognition enabled, gesture recognition enabled, and touch enabled adaptable and adaptive interactive applications.

The hardware requirements for the FIRMA framework are relatively low. The framework runs under windows 7 or later either 32 or 64 bit and requires a Core 2 Duo or better processor. The touch enabled interactions require a touch screen tablet / laptop or a touch enabled monitor. All the framework components tools and modalities run under Windows on the touch enabled computer except for the gesture recognition modality that runs under Linux on the robotic platform and communicates with the rest of the framework through the ROS middleware.

A. *ACTA: A general purpose finite state machine (FSM) description language for ACTivity Analysis*

ACTA is a general purpose finite state machine (FSM) description language [5]. ACTA's primary design goal was to facilitate the activity analysis process during smart game design by early intervention professionals who are not familiar with traditional programming languages. However, developers can use ACTA also for applications whose behavior is composed of a finite number of states, transitions between those states and actions, as well as for application based on rules driven workflows. The ACTA runtime mechanism provided the base on which the framework's reasoning and adaptation mechanisms were built. ACTA's Runtime has been adopted and adapted to fit the needs of the creation of Multimodal interactive Applications (ARMA).

B. *ARMA: Extending ACTA Runtime to support the development of Multimodal elderly friendly Applications*

ACTA's runtime is based on the Windows Workflow Foundation framework (WWF). The ACTA IDE is used to code all the application interaction logic which can then be extracted to an XML rules file for further use. The rules file can be loaded into a WWF Rule Engine which is an event driven reasoning engine that can run the provided rules and conclude to the desired actions and transitions between the different states of the application's logic.

The main workflow for creating an interactive application includes the definition and design of its different screens and then the definition of its various states. Usually, one state is then mapped to one application dialogue screen. However, states with no visual output can exist, and UI dialogue screens can map to more than one different states of the application.

C. *Loading and unloading rules at runtime*

A very useful functionality that has been added to the ACTA backend in ARMA is the option to load and unload rules at runtime. This contributes to the reduction of the rules that are loaded at any given time. Furthermore, it offers the ability to change the behavior of the developed applications based on the subset of rules that are loaded at a given point in time. This enables the use of abstract task hierarchies that can be instantiated at runtime, while the respective rules that support their functionality are loaded at runtime. Furthermore, this addition opens new paths for adaptation based on the extra subset of loaded rules. For example, the experience of the user can be taken into account when he/she is expected to fulfill specific tasks and the UI that he/she is presented with can change accordingly. Moreover, tasks that are frequently required are automatically adapted and embedded into the framework.

The dynamic loading and unloading of rules has been implemented in full compliance with the functionalities of the language for rule activation/deactivation, rule prioritization etc. The backend has been extended to support the dynamic rule loading by respecting the aforementioned properties and treating them appropriately. Since the WWF does not provide the necessary functionality for merging rulesets, the whole process of the dynamic rule loading was added. Loading and unloading extra rules as needed is more convenient than having all the rules loaded at all times and then activating or deactivating a subset of them as desired, since the latter approach can have a huge performance impact on the whole rule engine (which would have to linearly browse through the whole ruleset to find the respective active rules) and was thus avoided. During the loading of new rules, the rule engine is temporarily paused and the new rules are appended to the currently active ruleset. The old pre-existing rules are not removed or disabled because their functionality is still needed as the new rules do not substitute the old ones but merely temporarily extend the functionality of the application. After loading the new rules, the back-end ACTA data structures are augmented accordingly to support the rule addition without affecting the language's mechanisms such as the mechanism for dynamic rule activation and deactivation or the capability for rule prioritization. Upon a successful append, the rule engine is resumed to activate the functionality that is offered by the new rules. Finally, when the functionality that is offered by the new rules is no longer needed, they are unloaded and the back-end data structure changes are reverted.

When a new set of rules is loaded, it is validated against the rule engine and then run against the instance of the application. The validation is always successful because all the function calling and property manipulation of the rules is implemented through a set of auxiliary helping functions. This functionality is inherently embedded into the ACTA language so that the produced ruleset is transcribed using these functions. This approach has the advantage that most of the fatal conditions can be silently ignored with the corresponding error messages being printed on an error log file while the state of the application remains stable. This means that if the ACTA script contains instructions for calling functions or setting properties that can't be found neither in the framework base classes nor in the developer-created derived instances, the invocation of those functions can fail silently without compromising the stability of the whole system.

D. *Modality integration*

Modality integration has been realized by leveraging the different modality generated events and consolidating them at a higher level where the corresponding application can treat them appropriately. This was achieved by implementing various mechanisms in the ACTA backend and in the frameworks base classes.

The framework contains backing fields for modality events. The ACTA backend was extended accordingly to support these fields. When the user interacts with the UI using touch events and touch gestures, these interactions are interpreted into the corresponding events and transferred to a higher level inside the application. For example, when the user presses a button, it generates an event in the base class of the application which is part of the framework. The base class contains the rule engine that can run the loaded ruleset against such events. The user is then able to interact with the UI based on the functionality that has been coded into the application's ACTA script. The result of the activation of the different rules includes state changes and UI dialogues activation in the derived application classes. This way the sequence of the application's dialogues can be easily tweaked and rearranged by the developer as needed.

A very useful feature of the FIRMA framework is the functionality it provides for modality integration at two different levels. The various available modalities can be integrated in the scope of an application's dialogue screen where the developer has to cater for each of the available modalities' events and act accordingly. Another approach would be the consolidation of the modalities into a single one and then develop a corresponding modality handling script that caters for this consolidated modality. Furthermore, modality consolidation can happen either in the scope of an application's dialogues or in the higher scope of the ACTA logic. For example, if the user can issue a command by touch, voice or gesture, the different modalities could be consolidated into the button press in the scope of the application dialogue or in the scope of the ACTA scripting logic which is at a higher level. The developer then could only cater for the single touch press modality as the other two modalities would automatically get consolidated into the touch modality scope.

Taking the modality events and raising to a higher level where they can be easily handled by the ACTA script contributes to the modular nature of the proposed framework's architecture, as the framework's components are loosely coupled and completely asynchronous. Additional modalities such as hardware switches and different kinds of sensors and actuators can be incorporated into the framework with minimal effort, extending the provided functionalities and conforming to the user's needs.

E. *Interaction Modalities*

The modalities that have been developed and integrated into the proposed framework range from speech recognition and synthesis to gesture recognition and touch interaction. They all have been developed to be fully extensible and configurable both at startup and at runtime so that they can change to reflect the changing needs of the users or the dynamically changing factors of the surrounding environment e.g., ambient lighting, environment noise, active electric appliances etc. In addition, the configurable parts of the developed integrated modalities have been offered as ROS services to the system to support dynamic adaptation based on interaction logic that runs on the robotic platform.

1) *Speech Recognition Modality*

Speech is an effective and natural way for people to interact with applications, complementing or even replacing the use of mice, keyboards, controllers, and gestures. A hands-free, yet accurate way to communicate with applications, speech lets people be productive and stay informed in a variety of situations where other interfaces would be difficult to use.

The implemented speech recognition modality engine supports adaptation based on the distance between the robot and the user, the vocabulary and the variety of the individual equivalent commands that can be used by the users and understood by the system, the semantic interpretation of recognized commands and the recognition confidence threshold. Furthermore, it supports the dynamic activation of both plain text and compiled speech recognition (SRGS) grammars and is accessible through a ROS node to the rest of the system.

2) *Speech Synthesis Modality*

The speech synthesis modality of the FIRMA framework has been based on the speech engine functionality provided by the Microsoft Speech Synthesis namespace. This namespace contains classes that offer the initialization and configuration of a speech synthesis engine, the creation of prompts, the generation of speech, and the modification of the synthesized voice characteristics. Speech synthesis is often referred to as text-to-speech or TTS.

The implemented speech synthesis modality engine can be tailored to the needs and preferences of the users as well as the context of the interaction by offering adaptation parameters exposing the gender of the used voice, the speech volume, the rate as well as the pitch of the generated output.

3) Gesture Recognition Modality

Gesture recognition is the process by which gestures made by the user are made known to the intelligence system. Gesture recognition plays a significant role in Human Robot Interaction since it adds a natural dimension to the interaction process. People inherently use their hands when talking to convey their thoughts, intentions and feelings. Providing robotic platforms with a way to understand this kind of body language, opens new dimensions for intelligent household robotics that can understand their user more accurately.

The gesture recognition modality has been integrated into the proposed framework. The recognition engine that has been developed to cover the gesture modality needs of the proposed framework is able to understand a predefined set of gestures that are relatively easy to perform and be remembered by the end users of the platform. FORTH's gesture recognition module [6][7] has been used to this end. This gesture recognition module is subdivided into three submodules, a submodule capable of tracking the upper body joints, a submodule capable of tracking the person's full body, and a submodule for tracking the hands and fingers of the person.

4) Touch Modality

The touch modality refers to the interaction that takes place between the human and the touchscreen tablet pc that is onboard household robotic platforms. Touch is an important aspect of human robot interaction because it consists a natural human approach. Selecting between desired items, reaching for different types of controls and adjusting various sensors are all part of humans' daily lives. The simulation of such daily activities can be done by using a touchscreen tablet PC that can be used both for output and input form the users to the robotic platform.

The proposed framework integrates all the aforementioned modalities into a seamless set of interaction modes between the robot and its users. This results into a more natural form of interaction, since the user is free to choose how to interact with the system based both on his/her preferences and the context of interaction. The robot can display its output on the onboard touchscreen device and use sound at the same time as redundant auditory feedback just like when people interact with each other. Furthermore, the robot is able to understand touches on the touchscreen device, gestures in front of the monitoring image acquisition sensors as well as speech commands given by the users. This provides redundant feedback which has been proved to be necessary especially when designing for the elderly user group [8].

Regarding the Graphical User Interfaces that are being produced based on the proposed framework, they are tailored to the needs of the end users.

The framework's building blocks have been designed based on the user-centric design principles and based on simplicity and clarity of the individual modes that each module represents (e.g., time selection module, binary decision module, multiple selection option module, etc).

Furthermore, the used vocabulary can be easily adapted to the cognitive abilities of the users. The generated UIs are inherently translated into the user's native languages in the sense that the translation files are automatically generated by the framework and the developers are only required to provide the literal translation of the set of sentences that they are being given into the end-users' native language. In other words, the produced user interfaces are globalization and localization ready since the necessary language translation files are automatically generated by the system at runtime and can be edited offline.

Finally, the framework provides quick exit shortcuts to the main menu and access to emergency scenarios.

F. Adaptation

The different modalities that are supported by the framework can be activated or deactivated individually according to the preferences of the users and the context of interaction. The framework can decide on the optimal set of modalities to enable, fine-tune and fuse together in order to provide the end users with an interaction as seamless and as natural as possible. Furthermore, the selection of the different modalities and their fusing is transparent to the developer, as it is handled automatically by the framework.

The developer has full control over which modalities are going to be supported at any given time as well as when and how they will be activated or deactivated. However, the developer is also given the opportunity to provide the basic functionality that he wants to make available to each of the aforementioned modalities and then let the framework decide on how and when each modality gets activated. For example, the developer can explicitly specify which parts of his application can benefit from a specific modality and which parts must be contained only to specific modes of interaction. He can specify when he wants only a specific modality to be used or when any input from any of the available modalities can be considered valid. For example, he can enforce that for critical application decisions, only the touch modality will be considered a valid way of confirmation, while for all other parts, any speech or gestural input will be allowed to be interpreted and treated accordingly. Finally, the framework is able to handle tricky cases where one modality might have to be deactivated due to dynamically changing conditions, although the developer has allowed its input. For example, the speech modality might have to be deactivated in noisy environments, or the gesture recognition modality might have to be deactivated in situations where the environment light is insufficient.

FIRMA supports adaptation through both adaptive component hierarchies and adaptive style hierarchies. The former is based on the design and implementation principles of unified user interfaces [21], while the latter is based on the use of adaptive style hierarchies as they are supported by the Windows presentation framework, to either specify the desired application coloring scheme and sizing guide for the different controls and UI elements, or change completely the different framework elements' appearance.

Adaptive component hierarchies are inherently supported by the proposed framework. Tasks are described in an abstract manner at a higher level using ACTA, while general guidelines are provided according to their instantiation strategies. For example, the time selection task can be declared to comprise the consequent selection of hours, minutes and time specifiers according to the time of the day. General guidelines can be stated according to the expertise of the user encoded in his profile. These guidelines specify how the whole task of time selection can be orchestrated in order to be presented to the user who is going to be guided through the process of time selection. Furthermore, user preferences are taken into account, so that specific user control are used or omitted during the process. Finally, the entire task is realized in a transparent to the developer manner who can simply declare that he needs the time selection process at the desired place inside the applications that he builds. The initiation of the task takes place automatically, and the developer can explicitly declare the starting and ending state and consequently the starting and ending application dialogue that will be displayed to the end user.

In addition to the adaptive component hierarchies' principles and design guidelines, the approach of adaptive style hierarchies has been adopted. According to this approach, the sizes and colors of the displayed framework elements can be controlled by styles that can be applied both at design time and at runtime. A number of cascading stylesheets have been developed to be used in the context of adaptation based on this approach. A subset of the developed styles have been used during design time so that the developer can have a clear understanding of the appearance of the different user controls and dialogues that he/she is incorporating into the developed applications. The design time styles collection has been consolidated into a single higher level style file which can be included in the designed user controls and dialogues.

The adaptive style hierarchies that are used for adaptation purposes during runtime have been split into three major categories. The first contains all the styles that handle how the different framework elements will be displayed. These styles contain all the individual stylistic decisions that drive the appearance and define the visual tree of all the framework elements such as buttons, lists, dialogues, text entry controls, labels etc. The second category contains all the styles that define the coloring scheme of the application including foreground and background colors for all framework elements, border brushes of the different user controls, darker backgrounds for giving emphasis to specific UI elements, etc. Finally, the third major category contains all the styles that correspond to the sizing decisions of all the framework elements and UI dialogues, including button sizes, dialogue sizes, virtual keyboard sizes and margins, text input control sizes, etc. The appearance of the final user interface is decided at runtime by the adaptation manager through a process of "pick and match" among the different available cascading adaptive style hierarchies, by selecting one from each major category. As a result, one style for visual appearance is selected, one style that defines the coloring scheme is placed on top of that and finally one more style that defines the overall sizes of every element is superimposed on the selection for filling in the missing sizing information and restoring the dynamic bindings between all three style collections. As a result, every style can refer to any other category of styles through the use of dynamic resources declarations. This means that each style is only responsible for its own category while being allowed to contain bindings across different categories. Hence, the visual appearance styles can contain bindings to the sizing category styles which are going to be realized once the specific sizing resource dictionary that is going to be used, has been defined and linked to the runtime of the framework. This approach can create an arbitrary number of application appearances based on the selection of the activated styles and the possible combinations among them. For example, if there are three different styles defined in each of the three different major style categories, the developers can choose among any of the twenty seven combinations (i.e., 3x3x3) of the available UI instantiations. However, the selection of the developers are being superseded by the adaptation manager decisions as deemed necessary at runtime.

G. *Globalization and Localization*

The proposed framework provides inherent support for globalizing and localizing the developed applications to the native language of the users. The supported globalization functionality is provided by supporting the automatic generation of the necessary translation files. The developers are only required to edit these files to provide the literal translations of the provided phrases in the end-users' native language. The automatic translation is supported for all the framework user controls, dialogues and elements that are being used. The localization of the developed applications is realized by means of a universal translator auxiliary helper class that has been developed as part of the framework. The localization is based on localized culture and locale specific resource files that can be translated by either the developer or by expert translators to the end user's native language.

One major point of the translation module is that all translations are based on keys which can be prefixed with any desired phrase. The translation mechanism was designed having in mind that each translated string should have a corresponding key which could be prefixed by the fully qualified name of the assembly that the translated element belongs to, followed by the name of the application that contains the element. However, when a translated control belongs to a specific application dialogue, the name of the respective dialogue is used instead of the application name.

V. The Alarm Clock Application Test Case

To demonstrate the functionality and the effectiveness of the FIRMA framework, this section presents a sample multimodal application developed using FIRMA. It is an alarm clock application that can be used for managing a user's daily tasks scheduled for specific times of the day. The user can use the application to see the current time, see daily notifications, add new alarms, delete existing alarms and snooze elapsed alarms. The application supports speech recognition and synthesis, gesture recognition, touch enabled interactions and is adaptable and adaptive to fit the needs of the users.

The adaptations that have been implemented for this test case application concern the coloring scheme of the application, which changes depending on the level of the ambient lighting in the surrounding environment, and the size of the used controls, dialogues and messages with respect to the relative position of the user and the distance between the robot and the user. When the lighting level of the room increases, the coloring scheme of the application changes to darker colors that have higher contrast for the user to be able to see more clearly. Furthermore, when the level of ambient lighting is reduced, the application automatically changes into a more vibrant color scheme to compensate for the lighting changes. When the user is seating, the size of the used controls, dialogues and messages adapt according to the distance between the user and the robotic platform. The application supports three different sizes, a large sized scheme for bigger distances, a medium sized scheme for average distances and a small sized scheme for a more comfortable interaction when the robotic platform is very close to the user. Furthermore, the application supports a dark colored scheme for the night and a light colored scheme for the day. Moreover, when the robot detects that the user is not wearing his/her glasses, the application's scheme changes to a high contrast coloring scheme for convenience. Figure 2 shows the different coloring and sizing schemes that the alarm clock application supports.

According to Figure 2, on the lower bottom right corner of the dialogues, a green visual cue representing the status of the speech recognition modality can be seen.

The speech recognition modality is active, hence the green "ear" icon is visible. The Home button of the main UI Navigator window gets enabled whenever the user navigates away from the home screen of the main menu. Whenever the robot speaks, the speech recognition modality gets deactivated to prevent the robot from understanding its own speech as commands to itself. The deactivation of the speech recognition modality is represented by a red "ear" image with an accompanying strike-through diagonal line.

Furthermore, the speech synthesis modality is represented by a similar visual cue which depicts an orange robotic face figure which animates when the robot talks.

The bottom right dialogue that is shown in Figure 2 shows the alarms screen of the alarm clock application. In the middle, the user can see a list containing all the daily alarms that are active for the respective day. For each alarm, the time of the alarm and an assigned message that describes it is being displayed. Existing alarms can be deleted and new alarm can be added.

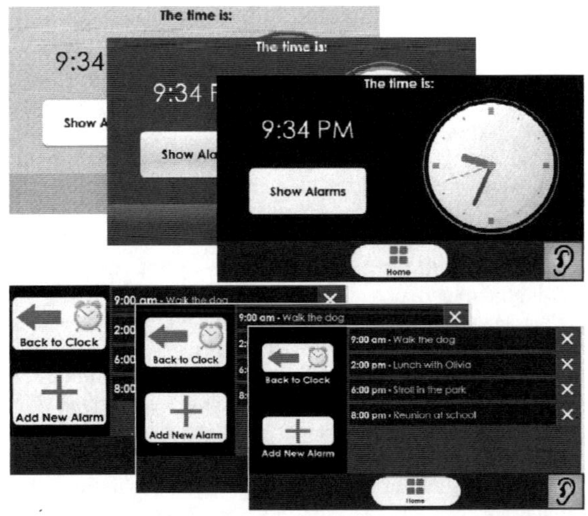

Figure 2. The different coloring and sizing schemes supported by the alarm clock application

Similarly to the alarms screen, the alarm adding screen of the application displays the current time of the system to facilitate the user when he wants to add an alarm at a relatively short time span. The time selection process is automatically tailored to the end user while the respective adaptive task hierarchy is instantiated step by step. The time selection process is adapted to the experience of the user. Different controls and additional steps can be automatically selected by the framework for average or inexperienced users. The user can select the desired time and then accept the changes or reject them to return to the previous dialogue. The user is able to cancel at any time, or press the home button to return to the main menu screen.

The user is given functionality to add a message to be assigned to the alarm. A virtual on-screen keyboard is provided to input the messages text. Finally, the application includes UI dialogues for confirming and providing feedback on the deletion of an alarm and for acknowledging or snoozing elapsed alarms.

VI. Framework Evaluation

The FIRMA framework was evaluated both in terms of being easily and effectively usable by the developers and in terms of being capable of building elderly-friendly applications by means of a heuristic evaluation. This section describes these two different kinds of evaluation. Further evaluation regarding the elderly-friendly aspect of the framework is yet to be conducted in the context of the European RAMCIP project trials as discussed below.

A. Developer based Evaluation

The FIRMA framework was evaluated by developers regarding its efficiency and its ease of use while building elderly-friendly multimodal interactive applications.

Given the target user group of the tool, i.e., developers, who are by definition expert users, it was decided to combine user satisfaction measurement with expert user interface evaluation in order to obtain detailed comments and suggestions on the FIRMA development framework as well as its interface design regarding the ready-made components and framework elements.

The IBM Usability Satisfaction Questionnaires [24] was adopted for subjective usability measurement. The FIRMA framework was evaluated by six expert users with substantial experience in application development. All users had at least a University degree in Computer Science or related subject. All of them had at least a few years' experience in the field of creating WPF applications using the C# programming language and some basic knowledge, but no extensive experience or practice concerning adaptation or localization practices or multimodality approaches. The user group consisted of four males and two females, whose age ranged from twenty-five to thirty-five years.

The group of users was briefly introduced to the main objectives of the FIRMA framework and of the evaluation experiments, and was provided with a brief introduction to the setup of the development environment, a brief description of the FIRMA framework's functionality and tools, and a brief scenario (including an accompanying tutorial) involving the creation of a new toy application that consisted of two dialogue screens, as well as the integration of different modalities, adaptive tasks, adaptation and localization, in order for the developers to be able to perform a more extensive testing of the system's features.

The developers were then requested to perform the tasks in the scenario and fill-in the user satisfaction questionnaires, as well as an expert evaluation report as detailed as possible. The scenario A included the creation of a new basic application while the Scenario B included the integration of the multiple modalities, the localization of the application and the introduction of a few navigation restrictions through the Communication Planner submodule.

The results of the user satisfaction measurement are reported in Table 1 (ASQ) and Table 2 (CSQU). Scenario A showed a variance of 0,019 which resulted into a standard deviation of σ=0.1384, while scenario B showed a variance of 0,056 and a standard deviation of σ=0.2380.

The conduct of the "Create a basic new application" scenario appears from the results to have been easier than the conduct of the "Integrate multimodality, localize it and add restrictions" scenario. This is probably due to the need of developers to acquire some experience in how the framework works, what functionality it offers and how this functionality can be achieved.

TABLE I. AFTER-SCENARIO QUESTIONNAIRE (ASQ) RESULTS (RANGE FROM 1 - HIGHEST - TO 7 – LOWEST)

	User 1	User 2	User 3	User 4	User 5	User 6	Average
Scenario A	2,3	2,5	2,1	2,2	2,3	2,1	2,25
Scenario B	3,7	3,2	3,6	4,0	3,6	3,5	3,60

The most appreciated aspects of the system were found to be its ease of use and overall effectiveness in the context of multimodality integration, automatic adaptation and localization and the reflection of the appearance of the end result during the design and development time in the context of creating elderly-friendly interactive multimodal applications. The users found the required workflow for the creation of new apps to be pleasant and intuitive and they were pleasantly surprised by the different supported automations that were supported by the system "out of the box" such as the multimodality integration, adaptation and localization processes. Concerning the included user interfaces and dialogues of the FIRMA framework, the users found that they are self-explaining, and that the dialogue screens do not contain information that is irrelevant. The users also appreciated the fact that the framework is carefully designed to prevent common problems from occurring in the first place (such as the automatic inclusion of the design time style sheets which reflect the appearance of the end product), and makes dialogues, actions, and dependencies visible. The developers particularly liked the decoupling between the application dialogues and the application logic and were enthusiastic about the fact that fine tuning of the application logic can be done at a higher level without requiring the recompilation of the entire application code. Error messages were also considered to be clear and precisely indicating the problem at hand. Furthermore the users offered helpful comments towards enhancements which are discussed later in this section.

The identified weak points of the framework mainly concerned the limited documentation provided. This was a known shortcoming of the prototype system, attributed to existing constraints at development time, leading to rather limited and focused documentation. The provided tutorial and documentation was focused on the parts of the workflow at which the developers were expected to have the least experience.

As already mentioned, the developers were also requested to provide an expert evaluation report accompanying the filled-in questionnaires. In these reports, the users offered their overall comments as well as more detailed suggestions for improvement of the FIRMA framework. The overall attitude of the users towards the system was positive. It was also pointed out that the tool presents a low cognitive load, and employs workflows and concepts familiar to application developers. However, it was also observed that that developers had to maintain and meddle with different

TABLE II. COMPUTER SYSTEM USABILITY QUESTIONNAIRE (CSUQ) RESULTS

	User 1	User 2	User 3	User 4	User 5	User 6	Average
SYSUSE	2,2	2,3	2,3	3,0	2,1	2,1	2,33
INFOQUAL	3,3	3,2	3,3	3,1	3,6	3,6	3,35
INTERQUAL	3,0	3,1	2,0	2,8	2,0	1,2	2,35
OVERALL	3,1	2,2	2,5	3,0	2,5	3,0	2,72

technologies to make an application work, something that was an expected forthcoming stemming from the nature of multimodal applications.

The developers pointed out that there are some parts of the workflow that could be made further error-proof by providing some additional tools and editors. For example, the developers found the ACTA scripting language rather enjoyable but almost all of them commented that they would like some kind of auto-completion and some code snippets that could expand to provide some skeleton code for creating an additional application state or a transition between the current state and the rest of the states of the current application. Furthermore, they pointed out that the translation of the ACTA scripts into WWF rulesets should be something that should be addressed by the framework itself automatically to avoid synchronization error between the rulesets and the source script files. This was a unanimous request. Moreover, the developers suggested that other parts of the workflow such as the creation of SRGS grammars or the creation of restriction rules in the Communication Planner required adding code in XML which was not very convenient for all of them in respect to their experience with the language. In particular, the majority of them suggested that an SRGS editor should be provided to minimize user errors during the creation or the localization of SRGS grammars. Furthermore the development of an additional editor was advised towards supporting the creation of restriction rules for the Communication Planner while taking advantage of the semantics of the ACTA language which could provide automatic listing of all the available states, dialogue names and transition triggers. In addition, the developers suggested the creation of automation projects for the required project types, class types and dialogue types in the Visual Studio IDE which was a foreseen request since the developers of the actual prototype system had already contemplated on the provision of such functionality in a subsequent version. Other comments concerned limitations and bugs of the current implementation (e.g., window resizing problems, lack of some confirmation dialogues, etc.).

In general, the developers stressed that the availability of such a framework would in their opinion be very helpful in creating elderly-friendly multimodal interactive applications easily and effectively. However, it was also noted that a certain degree of familiarity with the framework needs to be acquired before effective use in real development cases, particularly in relation to the order of the tasks that the user has to perform, which may not be clear at a first glance. Furthermore, some of the users had specific requests for additional functionality and system capabilities they would like to see supported in future versions of the framework. These mainly concerned the inclusion of additional modalities, the formalization of the communication protocol between the framework and the ROS operating system, the provision of automation class types in the Visual Studio IDE for creating ROS nodes and subscribers and expandable code snippets for adding application dialogues in code behind.

In general, the user evaluation of the FIRMA framework offered valuable insights into the functional and the interaction characteristics of the system and reinforced the belief that there is an actual need and demand for a framework providing the building-blocks and tools to support the design and development of elderly-friendly interactive multimodal applications for assistive robots.

B. *Heuristic Evaluation*

In order to get an initial insight into the elderly-friendliness of the applications created using FIRMA, a heuristic evaluation was performed in order to evaluate the various developed user controls and supported appearance styles. The results of this heuristic evaluation will be enriched with the planned user evaluation that will take place in the context of the EU funded RAMCIP project during spring 2017.

1) *Methodology followed*

In order to evaluate the UI controls of the FIRMA framework the following procedure was followed:

- A UI window was developed in order to host a demonstrator application for the evaluators
- From the UI window a list of buttons became available to the evaluators so as to select the UI control to evaluate
- By pressing one of the buttons a new window was opened displaying on the center the control to be evaluated
- A drop down menu was available to the evaluators that contained a number of pre-defined profiles. The selection of an option from the drop down menu resulted to the adaptation of the user control to the selected profile

This process was preferred mainly because it made easier for the evaluators to mark the identified usability errors by just filling in a table the name of the control, the selected profile and the error.

For performing the evaluation three usability experts used the presented application and through the application inspected all the available controls and recorded the identified usability problems. These problems were gathered per control and graded based on their severity.

2) *Discussion*

The results of the evaluation were rather positive in terms of the overall acceptance of the framework by the evaluators and all the identified usability errors were clearly defined and documented. Based on the feedback received, the controls were redesigned and fine-tuned. This preliminary evaluation should be considered as an intermediate step in the overall process of evaluating the outcomes of this research work.

The final evaluation will take place in the context of the European RAMCIP project trials that will take place during a six month period in Spain (Barcelona, Fundacio ACE,

Barcelona Alzheimer treatment and research center) and in Poland (Lublin Medical University). The end users will be healthy elderly volunteers and patients with mild cognitive impairments or early Alzheimer Disease. They will interact with the RAMCIP robotic platform in controlled environments during the time period April 2017 – October 2017. The UI of the RAMCIP platform will be based on the FIRMA framework and will be evaluated and validated in terms of ease of learning and ease of use, comfortable perception, acceptability and satisfaction.

All the applications that will be deployed on the RAMCIP robot will be based on the FIRMA framework. For example, a phone dialing application will be developed to enable the elderly user to place phone calls to their friends and relatives. This application will employ image buttons which will be mapped to pre-installed contact details so that the user will be able to place the desired phone call simply be pressing the respective image of the relative that he/she wants to call. FIRMA already provides multiple modality activated picture buttons that can be used by the developers for this purpose, leveraging the burden to integrate the activation of the buttons using all the different available modalities.

VII. Conclusion and Future Work

This paper has presented the FIRMA framework for the development of multimodal adaptable user interfaces for assistive robots. The framework supports modality selection, adaptation and integration, intercommunication with the ROS operating system and the AAL environment, and offers globalization and localization facilities.

The conducted evaluation has shown that the framework can significantly help developers in easily and efficiently creating elderly-friendly multimodal interactive applications for assistive robots. The preliminary heuristic evaluation of the framework has also suggested that the developed applications are inherently elderly-friendly because of the design of the FIRMA's ready-made controls and UI elements.

FIRMA constitutes the primary platform for the development of the user interfaces for the assistive robot under development in the context of the RAMCIP project funded by the European Commission under the HORIZON 2020 Programme. The robot is targeted to support elderly people with mild cognitive impairments. The validity and the effectiveness of the framework will be tested both in the lab and in real life scenarios in the pilot trials of the project which will take place simultaneously in two different European cities over a time span of about 6 months.

Two main directions of further work are anticipated in a path towards supporting the fruition of domestic assistive platforms for the elderly in AAL Environments. The first is the further enrichment and development of the system into a mature product and the second is the adaptation of the framework to cover the needs of different user categories and impairments as well as their families' and caregivers'.

Towards this end, a number of improvements are planned focusing on the currently available modalities as well as the overall system functioning in terms of performance, offered functionality and ease of use for software developers.

Ackwnoledgments

Part of this work has been conducted in the context of the Project ICT-RAMCIP "Robotic Assistant for MCI Patients at home", funded by the European Commission under the Horizon 2020 Framework Programme (Grant Agreement 643433).

References

[1] C. Schroeter et al., "Realization and User Evaluation of a Companion Robot for People with Mild Cognitive Impairments," in Proc. IEEE Int. Conf. on Robotics and Automation (ICRA 2013), Karlsruhe, Germany, 2013, pp. 1145-1151, IEEE 2013, Karlsruhe, Germany.

[2] M. Vincze, "HOBBIT - Towards a robot for Aging Well," Workshop on Human Robot Interaction (HRI) for Assistance Robots and Industrial Robots, May 6-10, ICRA 2013, Karlsruhe, 2013.

[3] A. Jacobs and J. Pierson, "Walking the Interface: Domestication Reconsidered," Brave New Interfaces, 2007, pp. 205-215.

[4] P. De Hert and E. Mantovani, "Intelligent User Interface". Working Document of the Project "SENIOR: Social Ethical and Privacy Needs in ICT for Older Citizens: A Dialogue Roadmap," 2008.

[5] E. Zidianakis, "Supporting Young Children in Ambient Intelligence Environments," Heraklion, 2015.

[6] D. Michel, K. Papoutsakis and A. Argyros, "Gesture recognition for the perceptual support of assistive robots," in International Symposium on Visual Computing (ISVC 2014), 2014, pp. 793-804, Las Vegas, Nevada, USA

[7] D. Kosmopoulos, K. Papoutsakis and A. Argyros, "Segmentation and classification of actions in the context of unmodeled actions," in British Machine Vision Conference (BMVC 2014), Nottingham, UK, 2014.

[8] C. Leonardi, A. Albertini, F. Pianesi and M. Zancanaro, "An exploratory study of a touch-based gestural interface for elderly," in Proceedings of the 6th Nordic Conference on Human-Computer Interaction Extending Boundaries - NordiCHI '10, 2010, pp. 845-850

[9] S. Payr, F. Werner and K. Werner, "AAL Robotics: State of the Field and Challenges," in EHealth2015–Health Informatics Meets EHealth: Innovative Health Perspectives: Personalized Health, vol. 212, 2015, p. 117.

[10] P. Mayer, C. Beck, and P. Panek, ""Examples of multimodal user interfaces for socially assistive robots in Ambient Assisted Living environments," in IEEE 3rd International Conference on Cognitive Infocommunications (CogInfoCom), 2012, pp. 401-406.

[11] C. Röcker, M. Ziefle, and A. Holzinger, "Social Inclusion in Ambient Assisted Living Environments: Home Automation and Convenience Services for Elderly User," in Proceedings of the 2011 International Conference on Artificial Intelligence, ICAI 2011, 2012, vol. 1, pp. 55-59,.

[12] A. B. Naumann, I. Wechsung, and J. Hurtienne, "Multimodal interaction: A suitable strategy for including older users," in Interacting with Computers, 22(6), 2010, pp. 465-474.

[13] B. Dumas, D. Lalanne and S. Oviatt, "Multimodal interfaces: A survey of principles, models and frameworks," in Human Machine Interaction, 2009, pp. 3-26, Springer Berlin Heidelberg.

[14] J. Bouchet, L. Nigay, and T. Ganille, "ICARE software components for rapidly developing multimodal interfaces," in Proceedings of the 6th international conference on Multimodal interfaces, pp. 251-258. ACM.

[15] M. Serrano, L. Nigay, J. Y. L. Lawson, A. Ramsay, R. Murray-Smith, and S. Denef, "The openinterface framework: a tool for multimodal interaction," in CHI'08 Extended abstracts on human factors in computing systems, pp. 3501-3506, ACM.

[16] F. Flippo, A. Krebs and I. Marsic, "A framework for rapid development of multimodal interfaces," in Proceedings of the 5th international conference on Multimodal interfaces(ICMI '03). ACM, New York, NY, USA, pp. 109-116. DOI=http://dx.doi.org/10.1145/958432.958455

[17] S. Goetze et al., "Multimodal Human-Machine Interaction for Service Robots in Home-Care Environments," in Proceedings of the 1st Workshop on Speech and Multimodal Interaction in Assistive Environments, Association for Computational Linguistics, 2012, pp. 1-7

[18] R. H. Cuijpers et al., "Human robot interactions in care applications", Gerontechnology 2012; 11(2), pp 353-354 doi: http://dx.doi.org/10.4017/gt.2012.11.02.186.00.

[19] A. Badii et al. "CompanionAble: An integrated cognitiveassistive smart home and companion robot for proactive lifestyle support", Gerontechnology 2012; 11(2), pp. 358.

[20] P. Mayer and P. Panek, "Towards a multi-modal user interface for an affordable Assistive Robot. In Universal Access in Human-Computer Interaction. Aging and Assistive Environments, 2014, pp. 680-691, Springer International Publishing.

[21] A. Savidis and C. Stephanidis, "Unified user interface design: designing universally accessible interactions," in Interacting with computers, 16(2), 2004, pp. 243-270.

[22] M. Quigley, et al., "ROS: an open-source Robot Operating System," in ICRA workshop on open source software (Vol. 3, No. 3.2, p. 5).

[23] M. Jackson, S. Crouch and R. Baxter, "Software Evaluation: Tutorial-based Assessment," software Sustainability Institute, Edimburgh, United Kingdom, 2011.

[24] R. J. Lewis, "IBM Computer Usability Satisfaction Questionaires: Psychometric Evaluation and Instructions for Use," in International Journal of Human-Computer Interaction, vol. 7, no. 1, 1995, pp. 57-78.

[25] S. Adam, K. Ssamula Mukasa, K. Breiner and M. Trapp, "An apartment-based metaphor for intuitive interaction with ambient assisted living applications," in BCS-HCI '08: Proceedings of the 22nd British HCI Group Annual Conference on People and Computers: Culture, Creativity, Interaction - Volume 1, 2008, pp. 67-75.

[26] A. D'Andrea, A. D'Ulizia, F. Ferri and P. Grifoni, "A multimodal pervasive framework for ambient assisted living," in PETRA '09: Proceedings of the 2nd International Conference on PErvasive Technologies Related to Assistive Environments, 2009.

[27] T. A. Majchrzak, A. Jakubiec, M. Lablans and F. Ückert, "Towards better social integration through mobile web 2.0 ambient assisted living devices," in SAC '11: Proceedings of the 2011 ACM Symposium on Applied Computing, 2011, pp. 821-822.

[28] E. Aarts and J. Encarnacao, "True Visions. The Emergence of Ambient Intelligence". ISBN 978-3-540-28972-2, Springer, 2008.

[29] A. Valli, "The design of natural interaction. Multimedia Tools and Applications," vol. 38, no. 3, pp. 295-305, 2008.

[30] E. Aarts and B. de Ruyter, "New research perspectives on Ambient Intelligence," Journal of Ambient Intelligence and Smart Environments., vol. 1, no. 1, pp. 5-14, 2009.

[31] F. Zhou, H. Been-Lirn Duh and M. Billinghurst, "Trends in augmented reality tracking, interaction and display: A review of ten years of ISMAR," ISMAR 2008, pp. 193-202, 2008.

[32] C. Ramos, "Ambient intelligence - a state of the art from artificial intelligence perspective," In Proceedings of the aritficial intelligence 13th Portuguese conference on Progress in artificial intelligence (EPIA'07)," Berlin, Heidelberg, 2007, pp 285-295.

[33] M. Alcañiz and B. Rey, "New Technologies For Ambient Intelligence, IOS Press," 2005. [Online]. Available: http://www.ambientintelligence.org.

[34] N. Streitz et al., "Smart artefacts as affordances for awareness in distributed teams in The disappearing computer, Norbert Streitz, Achilles Kameas, and Irene Mavrommati (Eds). Lecture Notes In Computer Science," vol. 4500, 2007, pp. 3-29.

[35] H. Nicolau and J. Jorge, "Elderly text-entry performance on touchscreens," in Proceedings of the 14th international ACM SIGACCESS conference on Computers and accessibility - ASSETS '12, 2012, pp. 127-134.

[36] M. Kobayashi, A. Hiyama and T. Miura, "Elderly user evaluation of mobile touchscreen interactions," in Human-Computer Interaction – INTERACT 2011 Lecture Notes in Computer Science, 2011, pp. 83-99.

[37] N. Hollinworth and F. Hwang, "Investigating familiar interactions to help older adults learn computer applications more easily," in BCS-HCI '11 Proceedings of the 25th BCS Conference on Human-Computer Interaction, 2011, pp. 473-478.

[38] C. Wacharamanotham, J. Hurtmanns, A. Mertens, M. Kronenbuerger, C. Schlick and J. Borchers, "Evaluating swabbing: a touchscreen input method for elderly users with tremor," in Proceedings CHI '11 Proceedings of the SIGCHI Conference on Human Factors in Computing Systems, 2011, pp. 623-626.

[39] C. Stößel and L. Blessing, "Mobile device interaction gestures for older users," in Proceedings of the 6th Nordic Conference on Human-Computer Interaction Extending Boundaries - NordiCHI '10, 2010, pp. 793-796.

[40] C. Leonardi, A. Albertini, F. Pianesi and M. Zancanaro, "An exploratory study of a touch-based gestural interface for elderly," in Proceedings of the 6th Nordic Conference on Human-Computer Interaction Extending Boundaries - NordiCHI '10, 2010, pp. 845-850.

[41] J. A. Jacko et al., "Effects of Multimodal Feedback on the Performance of Older Adults with Normal and Impaired Vision," in Universal Access Theoretical Perspectives, Practice, and Experience Lecture Notes in Computer Science, 2003, pp. 3-22.

[42] M. D. Lezak, D. B. Howieson, E. D. Bigler, and D. Tranel, "Neuropsychological Assessment, " fifth edition, Oxford University Press, New York, 2004

[43] Weiqin Chen, "Gesture-Based Applications for Elderly People," in Human-Computer Interaction. Interaction Modalities and Techniques, 15th International Conference, HCI International 2013, Las Vegas, NV, USA, July 21-26, 2013, pp 186-195

The Characteristics and Application of Anthropomorphic Interface: A Design Spectrum

Nooralisa Mohd Tuah[1], Gary B Wills[2]
Electronic and Computer Science
University of Southampton
Southampton, United Kingdom
Email: N.Mohd-Tuah@southampton.ac.uk[1], gbw@ecs.southampton.ac.uk[2]

Ashok Ranchhod
Winchester School of Arts
University of Southampton
Winchester, United Kingdom
Email:A.Ranchhod@southampton.ac.uk

***Abstract*— This study discusses several designs of anthropomorphic computing to obtain a greater understanding of the use of anthropomorphism in the design of digital interfaces. It includes the use of avatars, interface agents, hybrid characters, and robots. This extends the links between anthropomorphism and animism in computing applications. As a result, a degree of anthropomorphism is proposed to ease the process of classifying the anthropomorphism when designing human and computer interactions. The use of anthropomorphic characters enables designers to develop more significant interactions between individuals in helping to promote a long-term relationship. In order to strengthen the interactions, a set of anthropomorphic characteristics is proposed to be emphasized in the design development. In addition, the directions for anthropomorphic designs are also discussed.**

Keywords-Human Computer Interaction; Interface Design; Anthropomorphism.

I. INTRODUCTION

As the growth of more social mobile applications increases, hence, simulating a more interactive communication in a virtual environment becomes possible. In this approach, a human-like representation is used in the interface [4]-[6]. The human-like interface which is also known as anthropomorphism, helps users to get familiar with the functions, services or facilities embedded in an application. The design of human-like representation is also useful when applied to various games in areas such as health and education. Many potential applications can benefit from this type of interface design. Most studies in anthropomorphic interfaces, such as [2]-[14], focused more on usability, acceptance and users' preferences in several software or application contexts. Noticeably, anthropomorphic interfaces are preferable as compared to interfaces without anthropomorphic character [6][12]. However, the preferences are not conclusive. The experimental setting, application environment and the design itself, play an important role in shaping the users' preferences. Therefore, the diversity in anthropomorphic design and application has led to further explorations of this study. The designs range from a simple smiley face to a combination of human form with other objects or in abstract form. Different forms of anthropomorphic designs have led to a certain extent of confusion, particularly in determining the users' preferred type of anthropomorphic interfaces rather than mainly examining the differences between anthropomorphic and non-anthropomorphic interfaces. Therefore, the type of anthropomorphic interfaces indicates that human qualities and characteristics will be applied to a certain degree in anthropomorphic designs. The exertion of this study will explore the anthropomorphic form of designs and applications. At the end, an anthropomorphism spectrum is developed to indicate how different aspects of anthropomorphism can be utilised in the human-computer interaction. This study outlines the following; In Section 1, the anthropomorphic interface is briefly explained, particularly in the context of human-computer interaction. In Section 2, the type of anthropomorphism in designs is discussed. In Section 3, the characteristics of anthropomorphism are described in detail, and in Section 4, the possible applications of anthropomorphism are explained with several examples. With the characteristics of anthropomorphism in mind, the anthropomorphism spectrum will represent the fundamental guidelines for designing anthropomorphic applications for human and computer interfaces.

II. ANTHROPOMORPHIC COMPUTING INTERFACES

Over the last decade, the application of anthropomorphism has been developed in various areas such as in education [1], healthcare [2], and e-commerce [3]. The evolvement has diversified the designs in accordance to the purpose of application. Anthropomorphism is defined by the use of an object that imitates human qualities and features within an inanimate object [4]. Złotowski [5] further extended anthropomorphism as the designation of human life to a non-living object through designs. Anthropomorphism in designs allows designers to create tools that help users to comprehend the representation perspective without any difficulty [6]. For example, a human agent representation helps in online shopping, assists users in paying bills, becomes an online help desk, and acts as a personal tutor as well as other different characters and roles. The human agent is sometimes represented in different design forms such as a paperclip, any animal oriented design or even a simple car. The designs evolve according to the anthropomorphism characteristics.

In consolidating the anthropomorphic designs, anthropomorphism is also associated with the definition of animism to a certain degree of design [1][4]. Animism also gives human qualities and essences to non-human objects [7][8]. Haber [7] described animism as "the attribution of life to a non-living object". Animism refers to a design of things that make them seem alive and pleasurable to interact with. However, the previous discussions of animism normally involved a psychological perspective, for example in [7][8], where people relate the object used in their religious practices such as a cult-statue or cult tools. The design of animism can exist in the form of human, animal, insect, plant or a combination of all mentioned. The term 'animism' is minimally utilised in computing applications. A study by Schmitz [4] associated animism with as a life-likeness design concepts in designing a usable and tangible interface. Schmitz referred it to a robot or humanoid design in relation to the animism concept. Another study by Kallery and Psillos [1] referred to animism and anthropomorphism as other types of personification. They discussed the use of animism and anthropomorphic objects from a learning perspective among young students with different ages. They found that animism and anthropomorphism help in attracting the young students' attention towards cognitive development. According to Kallery and Psillos, animism and anthropomorphism have to be installed with emotion and expression. Notably, anthropomorphism and animism are rooted from the same fundamental description, however, their usage in computing interface designs is inconsistent, depending on the domain in which the user interfaces are designed. Anthropomorphic computing refers to a representation of human with a large number of human-like features, and the design varied through the use of face, part or whole body. For example, in the Simpsons, a stylised human character is used, while in Monster Inc., a different utilisation of animal character was manipulated in the story. In animism, the degree of human form is decreased but the attribution of life remains the same. The design could be a mix of human form with others. Therefore, it becomes more abstract and hybrid such as those games characters in Angry Birds, Mickey Mouse, Pac-Man and others.

TABLE 1. DESCRIPTION OF ANTHROPOMORPHISM & ANIMISM

Anthropomorphism	
J. Złotowski [5]	*Designation of human life to the non-living object through designs.*
M. Schmitz [4]	*The use of an object that imitates human qualities and features within an inanimate object.*
E. Perry and J. Donath [33]	*A description of an abstract of the humanoid depiction of a person.*
Animism	
F. Haber [7]	*The attribution of life to a non-living object.*
M. Kallery and D. Psillos [1]	*A type of personification.*
L. A. Brown and W. H. Walker [8]	*It provides a non-human object with human qualities and essences.*

The association of human-like representation within human-computer interactions evolves in many ways. One of the human or animal character personalisations is applied commonly in a virtual world or in games environment known as an avatar. It enables the mix of human or animal features. Avatar is described as a form of human representation to signify the users' character in the virtual environment [9][32]. The application of avatar can be customised based on users' preferences and specific role [9][29]. Besides, the avatar is designed to encourage a better social interaction [11][29][32]. In most studies, such as [3][10][11], the avatar was designed with real human depiction.

The human representation is also known as Embodied Agent or Embodied Conversational Agent (ECA). ECA is an interface agent that provides users with help and direction within the application [19][20][24]. It can be a smart assistant and also a companion agent. It can also be designed in various forms such as real human, animal, non-figurative character, simulation of faces, and others. Usually, ECA is coded with a scripted answer to provide a standard level of confidence within the interaction. Either avatar or ECA, both are commonly applied with specific roles and purposes. It is noticed that the Avatar and ECA design could exist in between anthropomorphism and animism at some degree of human qualities and likeliness. Table 1 summarises the description of anthropomorphism and animism.

Nonetheless, anthropomorphism and animism are also used in designing tangible interfaces [1][4] such as mechanical devices that imitate a human or a robot, as well as intangible products such as vases, and dolls. Therefore, there is a range of possible characters that can be used in computing which makes enough sense to formulate a scale ranging from almost human to inanimate in interface designs.

III. DESIGN OF ANTHROPOMORPHISM

A. *The Degree of Anthropomorphism*

At this point, to systemise the spectrum of anthropomorphism and animism, one may classify the types involved as illustrated in Table 1 and visualise the degree of anthropomorphism as shown in Figure 1. The degree of anthropomorphism is indirectly affected by animism. A recent study by Złotowski, [5] explained the dimension of anthropomorphism in human-robot interaction (HRI), particularly in categorising the level of humanness in anthropomorphism into uniquely human (UH) or human nature (HN). Złotowski looked into the elements of humanness such as curiosity, friendliness, and sociability (HN). Subsequently, if it comes with politeness, humility, and organisational elements, then it is uniquely human (UH). The degree of anthropomorphism shows a collection of human-lifelikeness at a different stage of design. This design is shaped from computer interfaces to tangible interfaces and from anthropomorphism (highly human-lifelikeness) to animism (lesser human-lifelikeness). With this scale, users' preferences can be cultivated on various application domains with different setting.

Developing a scale for anthropomorphism helps in designing a more preferable and acceptable application. At different points of the scale, the interpretation will not be the same and will influence the users' preferences. Catrambone et al. [10] and Power et al. [14] used various degrees of anthropomorphism in comparing different characters in the same application. They [10] developed three different anthropomorphic characters ranging from human, cartoons, and iconic to observe how users perceived those designs in terms of intelligence, friendliness, pleasantness, and attractiveness. Meanwhile, the study by Power et al. [14] used two different anthropomorphic characters, lifelike and iconic, to validate their framework on how these two characters could affect users' performance during the interaction. This study further expanded the defined characters in [10][14] into a scale of human-likeness and its relation towards animism and anthropomorphism. Other studies did not mention specifically or measure in particular which degree of anthropomorphism is preferred by the users.

Nevertheless, the position of human voice and text in the degree of anthropomorphism and animism is debatable. It is like listening to a radio or reading a book, the communication or message and the sense of being together may create the same context by having an anthropomorphic interface. With several tones of human voice, it offers a different perception towards anthropomorphic interface. This indicates that voice and text can be part of anthropomorphism or animism. However, the arguments are not strong because voice and text are only used to strengthen the effect of human-like presentation. Gong [21] and Lee [23] in their study showed that human voice is important in designing a preferable and trustworthy anthropomorphism. In a recent study by Schmitz [31], wave sound was used to identify which emotion, expression or effect resulted from it. The expression is projected using human faces.

Another study conducted by Murano and Holt [12], differentiated the effect of anthropomorphic interface towards users' preferences using only anthropomorphic interface on its own, anthropomorphic interface with text and anthropomorphic interface with voice. Murano & Holt found that the addition of voice significantly affected the users' preferences. Again, it shows that the voice plays an important role in deploying a credible anthropomorphic character. For text features, apart from being an experimental controlled condition [6][12], the text plays an important role in supporting a clear voice as well as conveying a clear information. It shows that the voice and text elements are not independently designed to evaluate the human characteristics at a certain degree of anthropomorphism, but it is rather important as part of the interface for better effects. Therefore, the human-likeness form is translated into a design scale ranging from anthropomorphism to animism, as shown in Figure 1.

TABLE 2. TYPES OF ANTHROPOMORPHISM

Types of Anthropomorphism	Description
1) AVATAR	*Highly human life-likeness form.*
2) INTERFACE AGENT / SOFTWARE AGENT	*An agent with various forms of design and could be at a higher, middle or lower attribution of life.*
3) HYBRID CHARACTER	*A combination of human form and abstract character at a lower attribution of life.*
4) ROBOTIC	*A mechanical device designed in a physical form.*
5) PRODUCT ANIMATE	*Any physical product that uses a human in its design.*

Table 2 explains each design scale of anthropomorphism. Hence, mapping the anthropomorphism and animism to the degree of human-likeness may strengthen the interaction designs. Looking into a better interaction and relationship with anthropomorphic characters, it is important to determine the characteristics and elements of the anthropomorphic designs. It makes the designs look more persuasive and engaging.

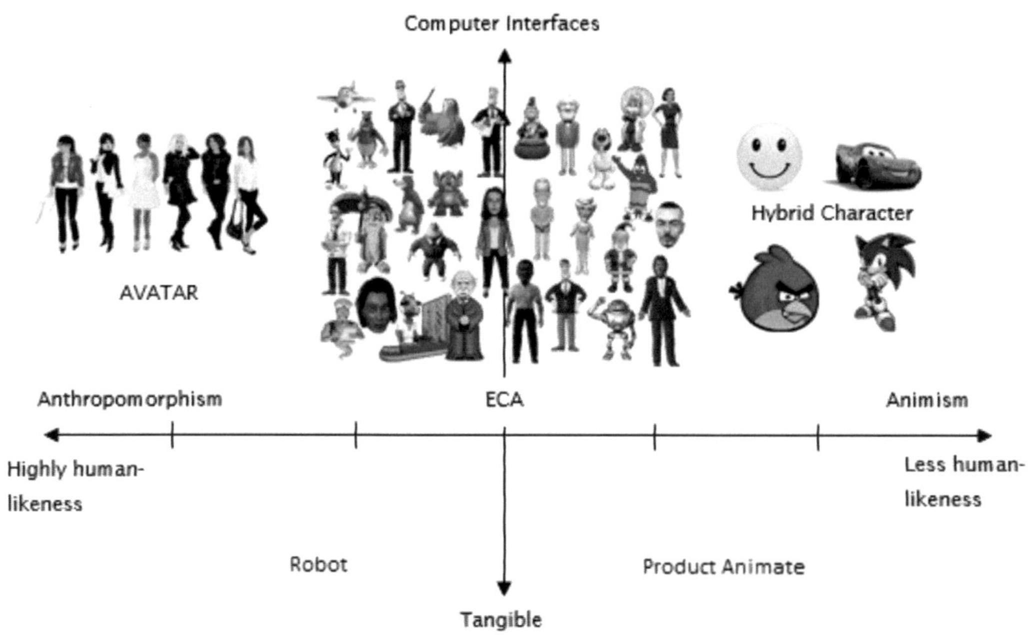

Figure 1. Degree of Anthropomorphism

B. Anthropomorphic Characteristics

The characteristics of anthropomorphism define the strength of the design. Questions have been raised about the realism of anthropomorphism and how anthropomorphism can have a better persuasive effect on human-computer interaction. The application of anthropomorphism as interface element has considerably shown a convincing social response and social presence to the users [5][16][20]. Social response elicits psychological and cognitive processes, in which the users apply and accept the social rules when interacting with the computer [16][21]. One aspect of social responses is perceived through non-verbal behaviours such as eye contact, facial expression, gesture and posture [22]. Anthropomorphism with a close-up facial shows the most affected interfaces. Facial expression [21] and flattery effect [23] could also exhibit persuasiveness through the interface. However, a better match between facial expression, voice over and flattery effect may bring a more persuasive interface. Besides, the anthropomorphic facial expression is also displayed in respond to its emotional state [5].

Power et al. [14], Prada and Paiva [20] and Forlizzi [24] indicated that an intelligence aspect also yielded a persuasive element on the anthropomorphic interface. They found that human-like interfaces were perceived to be more intelligent than other anthropomorphic interfaces. The intelligence aspect can be seen through the way anthropomorphic interface gave its feedback or responses. Meanwhile, social presence is about the users' perception and feeling in perceiving the sense of being connected with others in the virtual world [20][25]. A social presence can be interpreted by demographic (gender, ethnicity, age) and physical appearance (attractiveness). The demographic factors play an important role based on the application's purpose and functionality. Gender consideration was found to be more significantly affected by female users than male users in choosing which anthropomorphic interface types they prefer to interact more [24][26]. Female users prefer to talk to an agent that is more human-like and within the same gender. However, a different result was obtained by Qiu and Benbasat [3] and Cowell and Stanney [22], in which no significant differences were found in terms of gender preferences. Thus, gender preferences either of the same gender or the opposite are not conclusive and suggesting towards a specific domain of study that may improve its impact.

Other than gender preferences, ethnicity of anthropomorphism also showed that users prefer to interact with anthropomorphic interfaces that matches their ethnicity [3], [22][26]. Among the experimental ethnicity are Caucasian, African American, Asian and Oriental group. In Qiu and Benbasat [3], female users were significantly affected by the same ethnicity interfaces than male users. However, Angeli and Khan [26] argued that designing an interface agent with an ethnocentric approach will limit the application or interface acceptance in general. Ethnic similarity helps the users to build up their confidence because interacting with the same ethnic background provides more comfort and support during the interaction. Age and facial attractiveness of anthropomorphic interface are other preferred characteristics. Previous research showed that users prefer a young interface agent [22] with attractive interfaces [3][26] because the interface was perceived as more convincing and content. Measuring young or old is easy however, facial attractiveness is subjective and it is very challenging to be measured.

The characteristics of anthropomorphism are not conclusive. There is a need for further verification on each of the discussed characteristics. However, suggesting a set of characteristics consisting of social response and social presence may strengthen the design effects of anthropomorphism. Therefore, it will bring a more persuasive application that one may interact.

IV. Anthropomorphic Application

The degree of anthropomorphic and its characteristics can be applied in several applications. One that can be further explored is gamification – the implementation of game designs, elements, and mechanics into a non-gaming application, facility, and product [27]. There is a plausible employment of anthropomorphism in gamification and it can be seen through the utilisation of avatar [27]-[30]. Through the use of avatar, the anthropomorphism becomes the users' identification that can be personalised based on points and levels [28][29] as well as part of the application or game storyline [30]. It is foreseen that gamification can be a motivation factor towards users' engagement [27][29], and anthropomorphism is part of it. However, in gamification, other than the avatar, little consideration has been paid to other degree of anthropomorphism.

Besides, the disaggregation of anthropomorphism into a certain human-likeness scale is beneficial, if it is implemented for a specific purpose. For example, it can be applied to e-learning environment, in which different students may have different preferences on the degree of anthropomorphism that can be presented as their personal identifiers. Another example would be the health care context, in which patients may have distinctive propensities on the degree of anthropomorphism that is convincing enough for them to interact, or in the e-commerce application, on the degree of anthropomorphism that should be applied for the customer service characters and other related applications. However, the application of anthropomorphism is not limited to these areas only. It could also be extended into social media applications or in text-based communication such as Twitter, Messenger, and WhatsApp.

Therefore, the application of anthropomorphism at various scales of human-likeness may extensively enable its role in the human-computer interaction

V. Conclusions

Anthropomorphism in the human-computer interaction is not just a tool to facilitate users in completing their tasks. Anthropomorphism is beyond just an interaction, which involves designing an anthropomorphic interface varying from simple abstract character to full human body imitation. This variation leads to further classification on which anthropomorphism should be used, thus, nurturing anthropomorphism in a specific context of design. This helps the designer to understand the reasons why anthropomorphism is used. One of the reasons is for better engagement, interaction, and relationship within the application. The persuasive elements such as how anthropomorphic computing gives response physically and emotionally, and/or how the anthropomorphic interface delivers the sense of being there during the interaction were discussed to suggest a set of elements that should be implemented when designing an anthropomorphic interface. This paper indicates a way forward in the use of anthropomorphic elements in the interface design, taking into account a range of possibilities based on the scale that has been proposed. In reality, this scale would be useful, depending on the demographic of the users. For instance, younger children may prefer more animistic or object/human type interfaces, while older people may prefer avatars of some sort. Further study should focus on the design development or framework development by considering the degree and the characteristics of anthropomorphism into a specific application.

REFERENCES

[1] M. Kallery, and D. Psillos, "Anthropomorphism and Animism in Early Years Science : Why Teachers Use". Research in Science Education 34 (1991), 2004, pp. 291–311.

[2] C. Lisetti, R. Amini, U. Yasavur, and N. Rishe, "I Can Help You Change ! An Empathic Virtual Agent Delivers Behavior", Journal ACM Transactions on Management Information Systems (TMIS) - Special Issue on Informatics for Smart Health and Wellbeing, 4(4), 2013, pp. 1–28.

[3] L. Qiu, and I. Benbasat, "A study of demographic embodiments of product recommendation agents in electronic commerce". International Journal of Human-Computer Studies, 68(10), 2010, pp. 669–688.

[4] M. Schmitz, "Concepts for life-like interactive objects". Proceedings of the Fifth International Conference on Tangible, Embedded, and Embodied Interaction, ACM, New York, NY, USA, 2011, pp. 157–164.

[5] J. Złotowski, E. Strasser, and C. Bartneck, "Dimensions of anthropomorphism: from humanness to human-likeness". In Proceedings of the 2014 International Conference on Human-Robot Interaction, ACM, New York, NY, USA, 2014, pp. 66–73.

[6] N.M. Tuah, N. Jamil, D.S Ajor, "An investigation of user interface feedback in learning a photography technique". In Proceedings of the International Conference on User Science and Engineering (i-USEr), Shah Alam, Selangor, 2011, pp. 64-68.

[7] F. Haber, "Animism, Relatedness, Life: Post-Western Perspectives". Cambridge Archaeological Journal, 19(03), 2009, pp. 418.

[8] L. A. Brown, and W. H. Walker, "Prologue: Archaeology, Animism and Non-Human Agents". Journal of Archaeological Method and Theory, 15(4), 2008, pp. 297–299.

[9] W. L. Cheong, Y. Jung, and Y. Theng, "Avatar : A Virtual Face for the Elderly". In Proceedings of the 10th International Conference on Virtual Reality Continuum and Its Applications in Industry (VRCAI '11). ACM, New York, NY, USA, 2011, pp. 491–498.

[10] R. Catrambone, J. Stasko, and J. Xiao, "Anthropomorphic Agents as a User Interface Paradigm : Experimental Findings and a Framework for Research". In Proceedings of the 24th Annual Conference of the Cognitive Science Society, 2002, pp. 166–172.

[11] Y. Hsu, "Affective Interfaces of Embodied Conversational Agents". International Journal of Affective Engineering, 12(2), 2012, pp. 71–78.

[12] P. Murano, A. Gee, and P. O. Holt, "Evaluation of an anthropomorphic user interface in a travel reservation context and affordances". Journal of Computing. 3, (8). 2011.

[13] R. W. Picard, A. Wexelblat, and C. I. Nass, "Future Interfaces: Social and Emotional". In CHI'02 Extended Abstracts on Human Factors in Computing Systems, USA, 2002, pp. 698–699.

[14] G. Power, G. Wills, and W. Hall, "User Perception of Anthropomorphic Characters with Varying Levels of Interaction". People and Computers XVI - Memorable Yet Invisible, 2002, pp. 37–51.

[15] P. Murano, "Why anthropomorphic user interface feedback can be effective and preferred by users". In Proceedings of the 7th International Conference on enterprise Information Systems, Miami, USA, 2005.

[16] C. Nass, and Y. Moon, "Machines and Mindlessness: Social Responses to Computers". Journal of Social Issues, 56(1), 2000, pp. 81–103.

[17] D. Benyon, and O. Mival, "Scenarios for companions". Lecture Notes in Artificial Intelligence, Spinger Heidelberg, 7407, 2013, pp. 79–96.

[18] S. Payr, "Virtual Butlers and Real People : Styles and Practices in Long-Term Use of a Companion, Who Is Tina ?". Lecture Notes in Artificial Intelligence, Springer Heidelberg, 7407, 2013, pp. 134–178.

[19] M. Cavazza, and C. E. Vargas, "How Was Your Day ? A Companion ECA". Proceedings of 9th International Conference on Autonomous Agents and Multiagent Systems (AAMAS 2010), 1(1), 2010, pp. 1629–1630.

[20] A. Peirera, R. Prada, and A. Paiva, "Improving Social Presence in Human-Agent Interaction". Proceedings of the 32nd Annual ACM Conference on Human Factors in Computing Systems (CHI '14), ACM, Toronto, Canada, 2014, pp. 1449–1458.

[21] L. Gong, "How social is social responses to computers? The function of the degree of anthropomorphism in computer representations". Computers in Human Behavior, 24(4), 2008, pp. 1494–1509.

[22] A. J. Cowell, and K. M. Stanney, "Manipulation of non-verbal interaction style and demographic embodiment to increase anthropomorphic computer character credibility". International Journal of Human-Computer Studies, 62(2), 2005, pp. 281–306.

[23] E. J. Lee, "The more humanlike, the better? How speech type and users' cognitive style affect social responses to computers". Computers in Human Behavior, 26(4), 2010, pp. 665–672.

[24] J. Forlizzi, J. Zimmerman, V. Mancuso, and S. Kwak, "How Interface Agents Affect Interaction Between Humans and Computers". In Proceedings of the 2007 Conference on Designing Pleasurable Products and Interfaces. ACM, New York, NY, USA 2007, pp. 209–221.

[25] K. L. Nowak, and F. Biocca, "The Effect of the Agency and Anthropomorphism on Users' Sense of Telepresence, Copresence, and Social Presence in Virtual Environments". Presence: Teleoperators and Virtual Environments, 12(5), 2003, pp. 481–494.

[26] A. De Angeli, and R. Khan, "Mapping the Demographics of Virtual Humans". In Proceedings of the 21st British HCI Group Annual Conference on People and Computers: HCI...but Not as We Know It, BCS-HCI '07. British Computer Society, London, 2 September 2007, pp. 149–152.

[27] J. Hamari, J. Koivisto, and H. Sarsa, "Does Gamification Work? A Literature Review of Empirical Studies on Gamification". 47th Hawaii International Conference on System Sciences (HICSS), Waikoloa, HI, 2014, pp. 3025–3034.

[28] I. Kuramoto, T. Ishibashi, K. Yamamoto, and Y. Tsujino, "Stand up, heroes!: Gamification for standing people on crowded public transportation". Lecture Notes in Computer Science, 8013 LNCS, 2013, pp. 538–547.

[29] K. Otake, R. Sumita, M. Oka, Y. Shinozawa, T. Uetake, and A. Sakurai, "A Proposal of a Support System for Motivation Improvement Using Gamification". Lecture Notes in Computer Science, 8531 LNCS, 2014, pp. 571–580.

[30] G. Barata, S. Gama, M. J. Fonseca, D. Gonçalves, and J. Jorge, "Improving student creativity with gamification and virtual worlds". Proceedings of the First International Conference on Gameful Design, Research, and Applications - Gamification, ACM, New York, NY, USA, 2013, pp. 95–98.

[31] M. Schmitz, C. O. F. Benedict, and Mert Akbal. "Expressing Emotions With Synthetic Affect Bursts". In Proceedings of the 2015 Annual Symposium on Computer-Human Interaction in Play (CHI PLAY '15). ACM, New York, NY, USA, 2015, pp. 91-95.

[32] J. Morie, and G. Verhulsdonck, "Body/persona/action!: Emerging non-anthropomorphic communication and interaction in virtual worlds". Advances in Computer Entertainment Technology, ACM, New York, NY, USA, 2008, pp. 365–372.

[33] E. Perry and J. Donath. "Anthropomorphic visualization: a new approach for depicting participants in online spaces." In CHI '04 Extended Abstracts on Human Factors in Computing Systems (CHI EA '04). ACM, New York, NY, USA, 2004, pp.1115-1118.

Change your Perspective: Exploration of a 3D Network created from Open Data in an Immersive Virtual Reality Environment

Nico Reski and Aris Alissandrakis

Department of Media Technology
Faculty of Technology
Linnaeus University
Växjö, Sweden
Email: {nico.reski,aris.alissandrakis}@lnu.se

***Abstract*—This paper investigates an approach of how to naturally interact and explore information (based on open data) within an immersive virtual reality environment (VRE) using a head-mounted display and vision-based motion controls. We present the results of a user interaction study that investigated the acceptance of the developed prototype, estimated the workload as well as examined the participants' behavior. Additional discussions with experts provided further feedback towards the prototype's overall design and concept. The results indicate that the participants were enthusiastic regarding the novelty and intuitiveness of exploring information in a VRE, as well as were challenged (in a positive manner) with the applied interface and interaction design. The presented concept and design were well received by the experts, who valued the idea and implementation and encouraged to be even bolder, making more use of the available 3D environment.**

Keywords–human-computer interaction; virtual reality; immersive interaction; information visualization.

I. Introduction

Virtual reality (VR) is not a particularly new research area [1], however having a fully immersive VR experience required expensive equipment and elaborate maintenance in the past [2]. Touch input has introduced a natural way of interacting with digital content, because it is the most intuitive way for humans to interact with their environment [3]. Through head tracking technologies and systems like head-mounted displays (HMD), VR has the potential to achieve a similar effect regarding naturally handling digital content for human vision [2]. Putting yourself into a virtual reality environment (VRE) and thus directly inside things, dramatically changes how you feel, completely shifting your perspective in a break of tradition [3][4]. Therefore, there is a lot of potential regarding the visualization of digital content within a 3D environment suited for immersive VR [5].

Information visualizations are used by humans to gain insights and acquire an understanding of data in a more comfortable and easier way compared to, e.g., reading information in text format [6][7]. This is attributable to the human cognitive capabilities to perceive information visually, interpret the graphical representation of data, and infer meaning [7]. However, humans usually perceive digital information in a very limited way, through the small and fixed window of a computer screen while using counter-intuitive 2D tools, such as keyboard and mouse, to interact [3][8]. A combination of VR as natural user interface (NUI) for human vision, and motion controls (particularly hand tracking [2]), as NUI for the interaction with digital information, could deliver an immersive and natural user experience. This is a not a trivial task and deserves deeper investigation in terms of the interplay of these technologies, as well as the challenges of crafting interaction and interface design for presenting digital data in a VRE.

In order to address these challenges and to examine the suitability of the use of immersive VR technologies in the context of interactive information visualization (InfoVis), we have identified a number of relevant research questions:

RQ1 Is immersive virtual reality suited for exploration of open data and content retrieved from the web?

RQ2 Is the usage of head-mounted display technologies and (vision-based) motion controls suited to work together, and can they benefit from each other in order to create a natural user experience?

In this paper, we present our approach to explore open data in an immersive VRE. We designed and implemented a VR prototype using a HMD and vision-based motion controls, to visualize and enable the user to explore a network of European capital cities, based on open data obtained from DBpedia. The remaining of this paper is organized as follows: Section II describes the foundations (including the concept and design approach) and a brief overview of the technical implementation. Related work is described in Section III. Details about our applied research methodology are provided in Section IV. In Section V, we provide the results of our conducted studies. Section VII presents our conclusions and proposes possible lines of future work.

II. Foundations

Immersive VR enables its users to visually perceive computer-generated content as if it was real [2]. For VR systems, HMDs have usually a closed view in a non-see-through mode; consequently, the user is visually isolated from the real world, completely surrounded by computer-generated content. Using head- and even body-tracking, the user is able to naturally look around and explore the three-dimensional virtual scene according to the real world paradigms [9][10].

Vision-based motion controls, sometimes also referred to as vision-based gesture recognition, have the potential to be a powerful tool in order to support the user with interaction and manipulation in the 3D space without the need to hold physical sensor devices [11]. As the prefix "vision-based" indicates, technologies following this approach usually use one or multiple cameras or infrared sensors to visually recognize the user's hand or body movements, and translate these movements accordingly into the digital space [11][12][13]. As the most expressive form of human communication, gestures have the potential to be useful in HCI as their application goes directly in line with the concept of NUI [14].

The interaction between humans and computers represents the heart of modern InfoVis [7]. Especially through the growing amount of collected data, tools of different nature (from artistic to analytical to mixtures of both) have been developed in order to provide a novel perspective to our surroundings, and InfoVis is considered essential in making data more accessible to a broader audience [15]. Within the area of HCI, particularly visual analytics deal with questions regarding how to combine and integrate strengths of both humans and computers into creative and interactive mechanisms to interpret and extract knowledge [16]. In the community, the use of 3D in InfoVis is regarded with skepticism, but in certain cases, such as for spatial layouts, 3D visualizations can provide advantages over traditional 2D. However, since moving from 2D to 3D can be expensive in various ways, it needs careful justification and the benefits must outweigh the costs. If a meaningful 3D representation implicitly exists within the dataset (e.g. airflow, skeleton, location), a 3D visualization approach is easily justifiable. If the spatial model and layout is rather chosen than given, it is the visualization designer's task to carefully map values and relations of the dataset's items to appropriate variables within the 3D space [17].

A. *Concept and interaction design*

While VR using HMDs has possibilities to provide a visual NUI, approaches to create a NUI for user input in combination with VR had to be considered to create a natural user experience. Vision-based motion controls enable manipulations of virtual objects to a realistic degree [11]. This is particularly important since the user will be visually isolated of the real world surroundings when wearing a HMD [14]. The applied prototype scenario was conceptualized around these technologies.

The identification of a concrete user scenario and consequently designing towards exactly that scenario is one of the most important considerations in the process of crafting an interactive InfoVis [15]. Keeping the conducted foundational research about VR in mind, the idea to build a network of different nodes within the 3D space came up, and a user scenario with the purpose of exploring available open data about European capital cities within an immersive VRE was identified. Since VR has the potential to drastically change the user's perspective [3], the thought of putting the user "inside" the InfoVis came to mind early in the design process. In more traditional InfoVis approaches, the user is put "outside" the visualization quite often, providing an overview about the data in a role of an observer. With the HMD VR technology and the available 3D virtual space at hand, the change of the user's perspective to the inside rather than to the outside of the InfoVis seemed attractive and novel to pursue. Features to enable the user to explore the network of nodes itself as well as each individual node in more detail had to be implemented. Two options to implement the exploration of the network were considered: enabling the user to move completely free without any restrictions within the VRE, or restricting the user movement to traversing between the nodes. Since there are known cases of intensified motion-sickness when letting the user move freely around in the VR space (without physically moving in the real world) [18], the decision was made to restrict the user movement to only traverse between nodes. Wikipedia was identified to serve as the data source. A practical look at Wikipedia articles about European capital cities provided the idea to request data items within an article's "infobox" (e.g. country, geolocation, area, population, images) using DBpedia's available API and its semantic layer [19]. The concept of filtering is a common interaction technique in InfoVis [6]. Therefore options to filter all European capital cities towards their area and population were introduced to support users in their exploration of the network.

Ultimately, the conceptual interaction and interface design of our VR prototype can be summarized to contain the following key features:

- Present open data about European capital cities received from Wikipedia (through DBpedia).
- Each capital is represented by an individual node in the 3D space.
- Put the user perspective inside the network visualization rather than looking at it from the outside.
- Automatic traversal for node-to-node movement, no "free" movement in the 3D space outside the node network.
- Two view modes: *exploration* and *content* view.
  - Exploration view: present minimal information about each node, explore the entire network.
  - Content view: present detailed information about one node, explore the current node.
- Filter options to display connections to cities with higher/lower area or population.
- Scale the sizes of the nodes' 3D models to proportionally represent the cities' individual area and population in respect to all others in the network (making them visually comparable).
- Swipe gesture interaction to initiate movement to other nodes and to trigger/dismiss exploration or content view mode.
- Interactive 3D GUI to operate filter and scaling options.
- Visualization of the user's hands, and providing visual feedback for gesture interactions.

B. *Implementation of the prototype*

The developed prototype can be divided into two parts: a) a server and database and b) the VR application. Figure 1 illustrates the overall system architecture.

Server and database (see Figure 2) are based on *Node.js* and *MongoDB*, completing the following tasks:

1) Queries data items of a given European capital city from an open data source (DBpedia).
2) Persistently stores the queried data items in a structured and uniformed way.
3) Provides access to the stored data items, prepared for visualization.

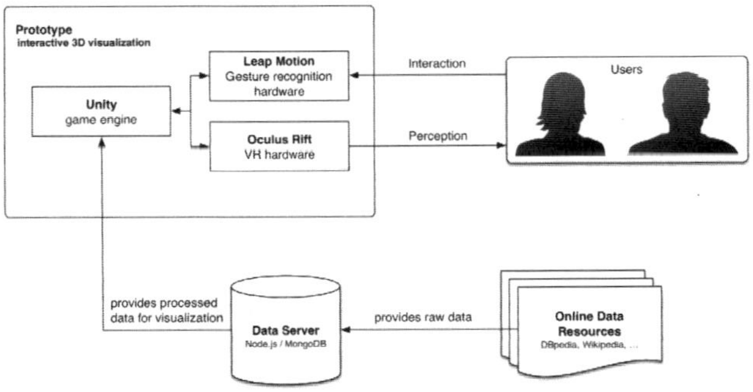

Figure 1. System architecture

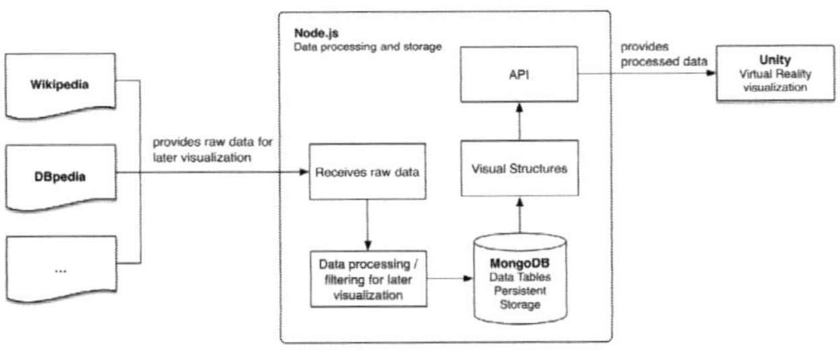

Figure 2. Server and database overview

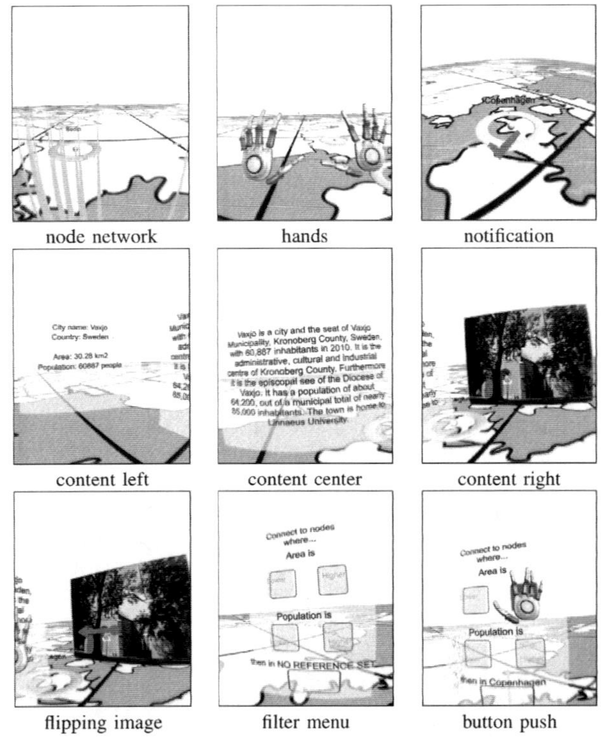

Figure 3. Multiple screenshots of the VR application

The visualization engine and thus the complete software development of the VR application is based on the cross-platform development system *Unity*. The *Oculus Rift DK2* was used as HMD, while a *Leap Motion* controller (attached in front of the HMD) served as the vision-based motion controller.

The implemented VR application can be divided into seven main GameObjects. The `NetworkVisPlayerController` GameObject handles all tasks related to the application's user, such as providing instances of the VR camera and the Leap Motion controller as well as handling the user interaction and visual feedback upon successfully recognized gesture interaction. The `NetworkCreator` GameObject is responsible for keeping track of the network's current status and is able to dynamically manipulate the nodes of the network according to the user's input. Furthermore it is able to receive information about the European capital cities from the complementary server and database and to instantiate a `VR-NetworkNode` GameObject for each city. The `NetworkVisualization` GameObject is a wrapper for holding all VR-NetworkNode GameObjects together, ultimately taking care of rendering and representing all nodes within the network. The `EuropeMapLayer` GameObject presents an underlying outline of all European countries to the user. Responsible for rendering detailed information about a network node is the `VR-NetworkNode-ContentView` GameObject, displaying description, numerical data as well as images about the city on three 2D content planes located in front of the user as well as to the left and right. The interactive 3D GUI presenting the different filter options is handled by the `VR-FilterExplorationView` GameObject. Furthermore, the VR application features a `LoggingSystem` GameObject, keeping track of every user interaction by writing detailed information in a .csv file, which can later be analyzed.

Figure 3 illustrates multiple screenshots, giving a visual impression of the created VR application. The video at [20] demonstrates the features of the developed prototype.

III. Related Work

Donalek et al. [21] recently described their initial explorations of finding optimal use practices for the application of immersive VR as a platform for interactive and collaborative data visualization and exploration. They focused on the visualization of highly dimensional data based on large digital sky surveys that can be represented as abstract feature vectors and experimented with different approaches of multidimensional data representation in VR [21]. Design challenges for a 2D gesture interface in a 3D VR environment have been explored by Lee et al. [22], who developed and evaluated an immersive VR game, concluding that cross-dimensional interfaces may significantly reduce simulator sickness. Ren and O'Neill [13] investigated 3D selection with freehand gestures and propose overall design guidelines. According to their results, designers should consider mapping 3D hand movements to 2D interaction for simpler user interfaces with few elements [13]. Abrash [4] argues that immersion can make VR interesting, but great VR requires custom software. Bayyari and Tudoreanu [5] investigated perceptual and interaction characteristics of immersive displays and conclude that they support better understanding of data and are thus superior to traditional desktop visualization.

IV. METHODOLOGY

The purpose of our investigation is to answer the questions of whether and how appropriate the application of immersive VR is in order to visualize and naturally explore content from the web. Our research approach has rather deductive characteristics [23].

We carried out a user interaction study to gain insights and real experiences about the design and operation of the developed prototype in practice. It was of particular interest to gather the user's thoughts about their ability to naturally interact with the visualized content and explore the data network. We conducted eleven one hour sessions between the researcher and each participant. The six female and five male participants, aged between 16 and 32 years, were introduced to the prototype by watching a pre-recorded video [20] that demonstrated the features of the developed prototype.

The eleven participants were given two tasks: to find a city with a population (or area) of a certain number of inhabitants (or square kilometers), using all the features of the prototype such as the filter options, the movement functionalities as well as receiving more detailed information about a visited city in network node. They were encouraged to explore the visualized network and let the researcher know once they found a city that they considered to satisfy the request of each task. Before their sessions, each participant had the chance to become familiar operating the developed prototype in order to understand the basic functionalities as well as getting used to wearing a HMD and using the vision-based motion controls. Based on the participant's prior experience with the immersive technologies, this warm-up phase took no longer than five to ten minutes. There were no time constraints regarding the completion of the tasks and the participants were asked to operate the prototype at their own speed. However, the completion of a single task should not exceed ten minutes.

A mixture of both quantitative and qualitative data collection methods were used. Self-constructed pre- and post-session questionnaires, featuring a mixture of Likert-scale and open questions, were used to examine the participants prior experiences with the presented technologies as well as examining the developed prototype in more detail. To gain focused feedback, the post-session questionnaire was structured into the following evaluation categories: *Perception of the content generated with data from the web*, *Spatial perception of my location within the 3D network*, *Interaction using the vision-based motion control interface* and *Human factors and ergonomics*. The implementation of a log-file system enabled us to evaluate all interactions of the user with the prototype, e.g., metrics such as the time needed to complete a task, the time spent on individual nodes (cities) and the amount of user interactions applied to complete a task. Each study was closely observed by the researcher, who kept written notes. After completing the tasks, each participant was asked to estimate the felt workload, based on the Task Load Index (TLX) workload estimation developed by NASA [24][25]. Receiving insights about a participant's workload helps to analyze and estimate the interaction and interface design, providing indications if the participants felt, e.g., bored, neutral or overburdened within the VRE.

Additionally, experts within the field of HCI and (interactive) InfoVis were selected from within the staff at the Faculty of Technology at Linnaeus University and invited to participate in approximately one hour long discussions between the researcher and the experts. Within these discussions, the researcher presented the concept, idea and motivation of the conducted work to the experts as well as information about the identified problem domain, scenario and research questions. The researcher conducted also a live walkthrough presenting the developed prototype to the experts, during which they were encouraged to communicate their feedback, comments and thoughts towards the project. They were furthermore encouraged to not only think about the presented scenario, but to think further, more abstract towards similar interactions or activities in similar cases.

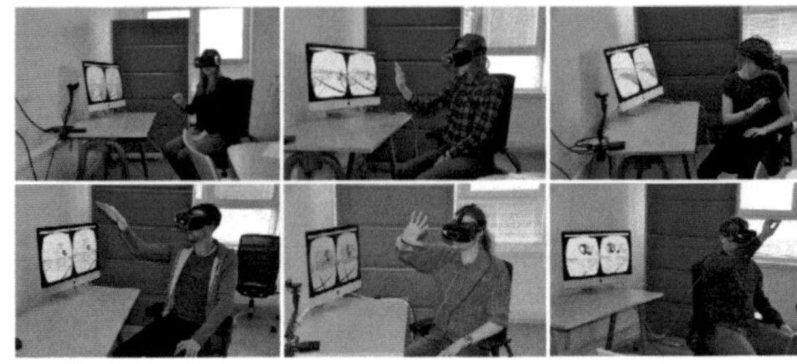

Figure 4. Participants interacting within the developed VRE

V. RESULTS AND ANALYSIS

This section presents the results of the conducted user interaction study and expert discussions as described in Section IV. Figure 4 presents some impressions of the participants during the user interaction study.

A. *User interaction study*

The participants were asked to find a European capital city close to 1.5 million inhabitants during the first task, and one featuring an area of close to 750 km^2 during the second task. Valid result sets for both tasks were identified beforehand and are illustrated in Table I. All participants had to start from the node representing Växjö (where Linnaeus University is based).

As shown in Table II, two participants did not name a solution within the set of valid results for task 1 (they chose Copenhagen and Sofia instead), but all eleven participants correctly identified a city close to the asked parameter in task 2. Additionally, it can be observed that the majority of participants were able to name a solution rather close to the asked parameter within both tasks.

Utilizing the implemented log file system, a detailed analysis of the participants' interactions was undertaken. Figure 5 gives a summary for all participants, including both average values and standard deviation for tasks 1 and 2. Comparing the two tasks, it is interesting to note that the averages of the time spent in a traveled city, as well as the amount of visited and uniquely visited cities, do not show significant differences, while it is noticeable that the overall amount of interactions increased and the overall amount of time needed for the task completion decreased within task 2. It also appears that the participants interacted more heavily with the filter related features during task 2. The task order was the same for all participants, therefore this expected outcome would indicate increasing confidence and familiarity with the interface.

TABLE I. SET OF CITIES IDENTIFYING SUCCESSFUL TASK SOLUTION

Task 1		Task 2	
City name	*Inhabitants (in million)*	*City name*	*Area (in km^2)*
Vienna	1.724	Berlin	892
Budapest	1.722	Kiev	839
Warsaw	1.717	Zagreb	641
Belgrade	1.339	Madrid	605.8
Prague	1.249		

TABLE II. PARTICIPANT TASK SOLUTIONS (CITIES ESPECIALLY CLOSE TO THE ASKED PARAMETER ARE MARKED IN BOLD)

Task 1		Task 2	
City name	*Count*	*City name*	*Count*
Vienna	1	Berlin	2
Budapest	1	**Kiev**	**3**
Warsaw	**1**	**Zagreb**	**6**
Belgrade	**5**	Madrid	0
Prague	1		
correct answer	9 / 11	correct answer	11 / 11
other / incorrect	2	other / incorrect	0

Analysis				Task 1 AVERAGE	Task 1 STDEVA	Task 2 AVERAGE	Task 2 STDEVA
Average time spent in traveled City (in sec)				32.94	12.94	31.82	10.93
Amount of unique visited cities (max. 45)				11	4	11	4
Amount of visited cities				14	5	13	5
Amount of interactions				42	15	48	19
	Movement/Travels	**SUM**		15	8	15	8
		Successful		13	5	12	5
		Unsuccessful		2	3	1	2
		Forbidden		1	3	2	2
	Content Exploration	**SUM**		14	5	13	5
		Trigger		12	4	12	5
		Dismiss		11	4	12	5
		Rotation		2	3	0	1
	Filter Menu	**SUM**		13	8	20	11
		Trigger		4	2	5	2
		Dismiss		4	2	5	2
		Connection		8	6	13	10
			Area	0	1	8	6
			Population	6	4	1	2
			Reset	2	2	4	3
		Size		1	0	2	1
			Area	0	0	1	1
			Population	1	0	0	0
			Normal	0	0	1	1
Amount of time for completion (in sec)				421.84	160.61	391.74	142.33
in minutes				7.03	2.68	6.53	2.37

Figure 5. Results - Summary of log files for both tasks

B. *NASA Task Load Index*

The estimated workload of all participants averages at 47.5 percent with a standard deviation of 17.6. Excluding the two outliers (that estimated their workload significantly lower and higher than everyone else, respectively) the workload average does not differ significantly at 48.54 percent but with a lower standard deviation of 11.2.

Looking at the participant's determined weights and ratings of the individual TLX factors *mental* and *physical demand* as well as *performance* and *effort* were rather important to the participants' experience of workload, while the factors *temporal demand* and *frustration* were of less importance during the task completion. The participants experienced comparatively higher mental and physical demands as well as the need to make efforts in order to complete the given tasks within the VRE. The average ratings also showed that the participants felt a comparatively low level of both temporal demand and frustration. Furthermore, the low performance value corresponds to a good level of performance, indicating that the participants felt rather successful and satisfied with their accomplishment by completing the tasks. It is particularly noteworthy that the participants were not given any indication about the success or failure of the task completion and their given answer.

C. *Post-session questionnaire (PTQ)*

Perception of the content generated with data from the web: The participants felt throughout rather positively about the perception of the presented content, which was ultimately generated with data received from the web. The participants valued the amount of presented information about the cities within the VRE. The textual description of a city was rated not too long nor too short. Together with providing important facts (area, population, country) in bullet point format, the designed interface enabled the participants to get a quick and pleasant rated city overview. Additionally, the participants liked that not only textual data were presented to them, but also photos about the cities, asking even to provide more images in the future. Overall, with displaying content on 2D planes in front as well as to the user's left and right (see Figure 3 middle row), the layout and the animation of the city data (`VR-NetworkNode-ContentView`) was perceived positive. Some participants commented that they felt "closer to the information (and its value)".

Spatial perception of my location within the 3D network: The participants considered to have had a solid understanding about their own location within the network at all times. Observations and answers of the open questions further indicate that the participants are in line with the prior mentioned design decision to offer node-to-node movement and no free movement within the 3D space from an interaction point of view. Furthermore, they expressed the supportive value of the underlying map, indicating the importance of such an essential cornerstone towards the visual guidance in the presented VR prototype. The visual node to node connections helped identifying potential targets to travel to, as a result of applying a filter. Most negatively mentioned within this category was the ability to change the nodes' size according to their area or population value and in relation to all other nodes within the network. Through the change of perspective and thus putting the user's perspective inside the visualization, the participants expressed their inability to properly compare the nodes' sizes, e.g., actually larger nodes in the further distance would effectively appear smaller compared to nodes closer to the users location due to the perspective.

Interaction using the vision-based motion control interface: The participants enjoyed operating the VR prototype by using gestures made through hand movements, although they had rather neutral feelings towards a precise interaction due to the inaccuracy of the gesture recognition. Some participants had to try multiple times to perform a successful gesture. The overall interaction using gestures, and thus the user's body, was received as fun, even fast and fluent, experience. The applied gesture set was easy to learn and remember. The interaction with the 3D GUI was particularly enjoyable. The implemented visual feedback, indicating the successful performance and recognition of a gesture interaction, was considered valuable, ultimately representing a crucial response from the VR prototype to the user.

Human factors and ergonomics: Providing users with a swivel chair proved to be a good idea, since the participants strongly agreed that it supported them in the 360 degree exploration of the network. Some participants expressed concern that operating the VR prototype might get physically too tiring or stressful after longer usage. This would need to be further investigated in future studies. The actual visualization of the user's hands within the 3D space and thus the visual translation of their physical hands to the virtual space was mentioned positively. Since the users are not able to see their physical hands anymore while wearing the HMD, translating these accordingly into the virtual space seemed to be an essential bridge between physical and virtual world.

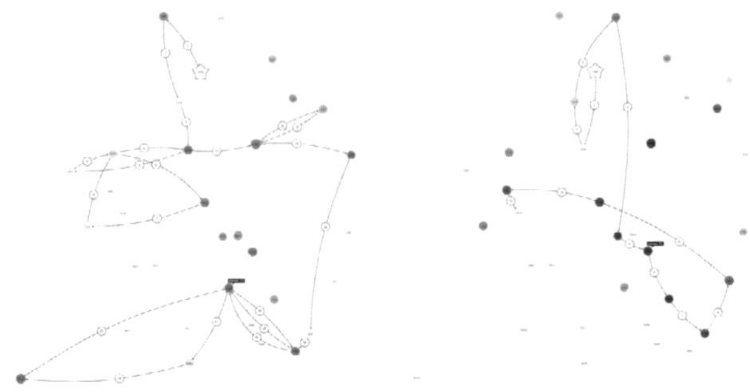

Figure 6. Explorative behavior: revisiting (left) vs. straight (right)

D. Expert discussion

As mention in Section II, the use of 3D within the InfoVis community is met with skepticism. But in case of the implemented VR prototype and considering its intention and purpose, the experts agreed that the presented scenario is one of the few where 3D interactive InfoVis works fine. Due to its focus on the exploration of data, the interactive visualization in the 3D space provides a unique perspective and thus fresh approach towards data exploration and browsing. The experts also stated that the developed VR prototype and its scenario is probably quite valuable as a learning tool, arguing that children learn from their 3D environment. Therefore being surrounded by the content instead of looking at it from above is potentially beneficial in this context. Although the implemented filter options work fine within the presented scenario, encouraging the user to play around, explore and move around as much as possible, the experts state that for "real" data exploration these are not enough and need to be assisted by the ability of putting numbers into the filters, e.g. using range sliders.

To avoid getting lost in larger networks, the experts suggested to implement features to support additional guidance or navigation, such as an isometric or aerial perspective. For future work the experts also suggested to support and implement features to select, highlight (e.g. glowing effects) and compare multiple nodes within the network. The implementation of concepts such as a radar, a minimap, or a "quest marker" (as known from computer games), could provide additional guidance and navigation depending on the given task.

Although the prototype made usage of the 3D space, the network node arrangement used 2D geometry. The experts suggested to think about the potential of the 3D environment to come up with effects and solutions to overcome some real world problems. An example they provided in the particular case of overcoming occlusion within a 2D arrangement was to investigate the implementation of a "world bending" effect, similar to the ones shown in the movie *Inception* or the *Halo* computer game series. The experts positively acknowledged the visual feedback as result of recognized gestures, reasoning it being crucial to the user. The 3D interactive GUI was received positively as well, noting that it feels very easy to operate the interface elements.

VI. Discussion

Although the participants had only minor experience with VR technologies, if any, in the past, it was particularly interesting to see their adaption to the presented setup and thus the interaction with the developed VR prototype. The participants' answers show that they were successfully able to solve the given tasks by exploring the 3D virtual network and consuming the displayed data. This furthermore confirms the proper functioning of the VR prototype, both in terms of design and implementation. Examining the log file data it appears that the participants learned and adapted quickly to the overall interaction, which is interesting given the comparatively short amount of time they spent with the prototype (approx. 20 minutes, including warm-up phase and the completion of task 1 and 2).

The implementation of a log file system for this kind of application turned out to be an essential asset for analyses as every recognized interaction between user and the prototype could be tracked (see Figure 5). Particularly interesting was the tracking of the participant's routes, visualizing their exploration while solving the given tasks. This provided some insights in their behavior and even search strategy. Two types of explorative behavior were identified, as seen in Figure 6: either featuring an increased degree of revisiting already explored network nodes, or going straight from one city to another until a suitable solution was found. At this point, it is not possible to derive concrete conclusions why sometimes each strategy was chosen. To further investigate this matter, more studies need to be conducted in the future, e.g., including the presentation of the visualized pathways to the participants after task completion and interviewing them about it.

The NASA TLX analysis revealed that the participants' estimated workload averaged at 47.5 percent. Given the participants' prior experiences with VR technologies and the novel approach of the presented VR prototype, a workload of around 50 percent can be considered ideal, indicating that the participants were neither bored nor overburdened with operating the prototype, especially considering that the majority of participants were confronted with such a setup and scenario for the first time.

The results of the post-session questionnaire, asking the participants concretely about their experience with the VR prototype, are encouraging as well. The presentation of the content was accepted positively, pointing out the overall intuitiveness, novelty and pleasantness of the designed interface. Textual content within a 3D environment can arguably be tricky, but within a VRE with no high resolution display devices, users could become faster exhausted by exclusively visually perceiving content, due to potential blurriness. Therefore, the amount and way of how to display textual content using today's broadly available HMD devices can be considered crucial to the overall user satisfaction (which was ranked satisfactory in our prototype). In general, the three element layout of putting visual content to the user's left, right and front, in combination with a HMD setup found practical acceptance. The chosen movement transition, enabling users to move exclusively from one node to another, was perceived positively as well, especially in regard to the overall physical stationary setup. While the users move in the virtual space, they do not actively translate their location in the physical space. Therefore transitional movement effects can be considered well chosen (see also "Swivel chair" experience [26]). The users were able to quickly learn and remember the functionalities of the VR prototype and make use of the complete feature set. Both the gesture and the 3D GUI interaction were perceived enjoyable and intuitive. Both interaction mechanisms have their value regarding the application within an immersive VRE. Whether to use one or the other seems highly related to the functionality or feature the interaction will embody.

Receiving the comments that the developed VR prototype and its presented scenario can be assigned to the few cases successfully demonstrating 3D interactive InfoVis was very encouraging for our proof of concept. However, at the same time the experts also argued for the importance of including more traditional features, e.g., maps or isometric perspectives, aerial respectively. Although the presented change of perspective for in this scenario feels fresh and novel, one should not forget or ignore potential limitations that it might come with it. Therefore, features to support the guidance and navigation of the user are more important than in other scenarios and should be considered when designing an application of that kind. After all, humans use even in the real world maps or other applications to assist them in their path-finding and exploration.

VII. Conclusions and Future Work

The aim of this paper was to investigate how an immersive VRE using a HMD and vision-based motion controls could be used to let the user naturally explore and interact with content and data received from open online accessible resources. We presented the design and implementation of an immersive VR prototype, ultimately enabling the user to explore a network of European capital cities based on data from Wikipedia. In order to gather insights, thoughts and recommendations of the user experience while operating the implemented VR prototype, a user interaction study and discussions with experts were conducted to explore the relevant research questions:

RQ1: Is immersive virtual reality suited for exploration of open data and content received from the web? The designed and developed VR prototype, and the gathered results, indicate that immersive VR is indeed suited for the exploration of traditional data and content from the web. Using a HMD device the users were able to perceive visually the content within the 3D space, while interacting using their hands. The results show that the participants valued the enjoyment, intuitiveness and novelty provided through the presented approach, while they learned quickly to make full use of the prototype's feature set, even solving the given tasks satisfyingly. Some participants tried to solve the given tasks very systematically, while others seemed a bit more open in their course of action. Both approaches of exploration ended in successful task completion. The fact that almost all participants were encouraged out of own will to find a particularly good solution towards the given tasks speaks for the acceptance and enjoyment of operating in the presented immersive VRE and its scenario. This is in line to the results of the NASA TLX estimation, indicating that the participants were positively challenged with the newly experienced environment and its technological components to a reasonable extent. Consequently, the developed VR prototype presents a practical approach for the overall successful design and implementation of a) translating traditional content from the web to a 3D environment and b) crafting an interaction interface enabling users to explore a 3D environment and its visualized content.

RQ2: Is the usage of head-mounted display technologies and vision-based motion controls suited to work together and can they benefit from each other in order to create a natural user experience? Although both technologies presented some minor issues (experienced blurriness, low comfortability of the HMD, inaccuracy of gesture detection), the presented VR prototype showed that HMD and vision-based motion controls can successfully work and, even more importantly, complement each other. While users are wearing a HMD, they are visually isolated from their physical environment. Designing more immersive input mechanisms is a crucial part towards supporting the user with more natural interaction possibilities. The study participants used the combination of both technologies to explore the 3D virtual environment (VE) and successfully complete their given tasks. Design approaches of the interaction through gestures and a visible 3D GUI were explored. Both found acceptance, indicating that interaction possibilities following these approaches can work in a meaningful way within a VRE. Interactive 3D GUI elements have the benefit of being visible to the user at all times, thus indicating and reminding the user on their functionalities. At the same time, interaction through gesture recognition seem to enable the user to operate fast and fluent interactions. However, these gestures need to be easy to learn and simple to remember. Overburdening the user with too complex gestures on the one hand and a set featuring too many gestures on the other, should be avoided. Furthermore, through our observations it is recognizable that the combination of both technologies requires the user to apply a higher degree of physical movements than compared to traditional HCI setups. Consequently, the intended duration of how long an application should be experienced needs to be considered within the application's design. While the combination of HMD and vision-based motion controls worked well in case of the presented prototype, the user interaction study and the dialog with the experts also revealed their curiosity towards additional (input) technologies, such as voice recognition, 3D audio and haptic interfaces, which seem promising to investigate in the future.

The presented prototype can be considered a first step and proof of concept into the direction of creating immersive VREs that feature traditional web content. Although the basic functionalities and visualization approaches throughout worked satisfactory, the experts made some valid arguments for future considerations, such as more features supporting the guidance of the user or making more use of the unique possibilities only a 3D VE can offer in order to overcome real world limitations. In conclusion, it is noticeable that which design approaches and decisions will work and which will not is highly dependent on the applied scenario and use-case and should thus be considered individually. Through its focus on exploration, the presented prototype demonstrates one of the few use cases, where immersive 3D VR InfoVis can be useful.

Still, some changes on the existing feature set of the implemented prototype can be applied. The overall color scheme could be reworked, also investigating the application of heat map filter options in order to support the ability to better compare network nodes using the newly presented perspective. Additional features to support the user's navigation and path-finding can include a minimap, the implementation of a temporary isometric or aerial perspective, or even the implementation of world-bending effects. Also, the addition of other emerging technologies such as voice-input, 3D audio or haptic interfaces needs to be in investigated in the context of immersive VREs.

Furthermore, the VR prototype should be presented to a larger audience in additional user studies in order to gain further insights. The presented results showed that participants rated the developed prototype as "enjoyable" and "intuitive". Long term studies should be performed to prove the effectiveness of VR or reveal if the participants' opinions are just an instant reaction to a new experience. Within this study, the duration of the participant interacting with the VR prototype lasted approximately 20 minutes. Longer interaction sessions and their implications could thus be investigated in the future as some participants expressed their worries particularly towards the physical exhaustion in prolonged interaction sessions.

REFERENCES

[1] I. E. Sutherland, "A head-mounted three dimensional display," in AFIPS '68 (Fall, part I) Proceedings of the December 9-11, 1968, fall joint computer conference, part I. New York, NY, USA: ACM, 1968, pp. 757–764.

[2] D. Lanman, H. Fuchs, M. Mine, I. McDowall, and M. Abrash, "Put on your 3D glasses now," in SIGGRAPH '14 ACM SIGGRAPH 2014 Courses. New York, NY, USA: ACM, Jul. 2014, pp. 12:1—12:173.

[3] J. Carmack, "The Engadget Interview: Oculus Rift's John Carmack," Video Interview, Oct. 13, 2013, URL: https://www.youtube.com/watch?v=AkasIFGpSHI [retrieved: January, 2016].

[4] M. Abrash, "What VR Could, Should, and Almost Certainly Will Be within Two Years," Presentation at the Steam Dev Days, January 15-16, 2014, URL: https://www.youtube.com/watch?v=G-2dQoeqVVo [retrieved: January, 2016].

[5] A. Bayyari and M. E. Tudoreanu, "The impact of immersive virtual reality displays on the understanding of data visualization," in Proceedings of the ACM symposium on Virtual reality software and technology - VRST '06. New York, NY, USA: ACM, 2006, pp. 368–371.

[6] M. O. Ward, G. Grinstein, and D. Keim, Interactive Data Visualization: Foundations, Techniques, and Applications. Taylor & Francis, 2010.

[7] R. Spence, Information Visualization: Design for Interaction, 2nd ed. Pearson, 2007.

[8] SpaceX, "The Future of Design," Video report, Sep. 5, 2013, URL: https://www.youtube.com/watch?v=xNqs_S-zEBY [retrieved: January, 2016].

[9] D. A. Bowman and R. P. McMahan, "Virtual Reality: How Much Immersion Is Enough?" Computer, vol. 40, no. 7, Jul. 2007, pp. 36–43.

[10] A. Sears and J. A. Jacko, The Human-Computer Interaction Handbook: Fundamentals, Evolving Technologies and Emerging Applications, 2nd ed., A. Sears and J. A. Jacko, Eds. CRC Press, 2007.

[11] G. R. S. Murthy and R. S. Jadon, "A Review of Vision Based Hand Gestures Recognition," International Journal of Information Technology and Knowledge Management, vol. 2, no. 2, 2009, pp. 405–410.

[12] D. A. Bowman et al., "3D user interfaces: new directions and perspectives." IEEE computer graphics and applications, vol. 28, no. 6, Jan. 2008, pp. 20–36.

[13] G. Ren and E. O'Neill, "3D selection with freehand gesture," Computers and Graphics, vol. 37, no. 3, 2013, pp. 101–120.

[14] J. P. Wachs, M. Kölsch, H. Stern, and Y. Edan, "Vision-based hand-gesture applications," Communications of the ACM, vol. 54, no. 2, Feb. 2011, pp. 60–71.

[15] M. Lima, Visual Complexity: Mapping Patterns of Information. Princeton Architectural Press, 2011.

[16] D. Keim et al., "Visual Analytics: Definition, Process, and Challenges," in Information Visualization: Human-Centered Issues and Perspectives, 1st ed. Springer Berlin Heidelberg, 2008, ch. 7, pp. 154–176.

[17] T. Munzner, "Process and Pitfalls in Writing Information Visualization Research Papers," in Information Visualization: Human-Centered Issues and Perspectives, 1st ed. Springer Berlin Heidelberg, 2008, ch. 6, pp. 134–153.

[18] S. Sharples, S. Cobb, A. Moody, and J. R. Wilson, "Virtual reality induced symptoms and effects (VRISE): Comparison of head mounted display (HMD), desktop and projection display systems," Displays, vol. 29, no. 2, 2008, pp. 58–69.

[19] M. Krötzsch, D. Vrandečić, M. Völkel, H. Haller, and R. Studer, "Semantic Wikipedia," Journal of Web Semantics, vol. 5, no. 4, 2007, pp. 251–261.

[20] N. Reski, "Instruction Video: Exploring data from the web in an immersive 3D virtual reality environment," 2015, URL: https://vimeo.com/126973131 [retrieved: January, 2016].

[21] C. Donalek et al., "Immersive and collaborative data visualization using virtual reality platforms," in 2014 IEEE International Conference on Big Data (Big Data). IEEE, 2014, pp. 609–614.

[22] P.-W. Lee, H.-Y. Wang, Y.-C. Tung, J.-W. Lin, and A. Valstar, "TranSection," in Proceedings of the 33rd Annual ACM Conference Extended Abstracts on Human Factors in Computing Systems - CHI EA '15. New York, New York, USA: ACM Press, apr 2015, pp. 73–76.

[23] D. E. Grey, Doing Research in the Real World, 2nd ed. SAGE Publications Ltd, 2009.

[24] NASA, "National Aeronautics and Space Administration TLX: Task Load Index," Web page, URL: http://humansystems.arc.nasa.gov/groups/TLX/ [retrieved: January, 2016].

[25] S. G. Hart, "Nasa-Task Load Index (NASA-TLX); 20 Years Later," in Proceedings of the Human Factors and Ergonomics Society Annual Meeting, vol. 50, no. 9. Santa Monica: HFES, 2006, pp. 904–908.

[26] J. Carmack, "The Dawn of Mobile VR," Talk at the Game Developers Conference (GDC), March 2 - 6, 2015, URL: http://www.gdcvault.com/play/1022304/The-Dawn-of-Mobile [retrieved: January, 2016].

User-Customizable Web Components for Building One-Page Sites

Pasquale Lisena, Jetmir Xhembulla, Giovanni Malnati
Department of Control and Computer Engineering
Politecnico di Torino
Turin, Italy
e-mail: {pasquale.lisena, jetmir.xhembulla, giovanni.malnati}@polito.it

Pasquale Morra
Research and Development Division
Seat PagineGialle S.p.a.
Turin, Italy
e-mail: morra.pasquale@seat.it

Abstract—**Most of online website builders work by combining and customizing reusable HTML modules. This approach could rise the risk of conflicts among modules. The World Wide Web Consortium (W3C) is writing the specification of Web Components. This standard provides a browser-native solution in order to realize encapsulated Document Object Model (DOM) elements, in which the Cascading Style Sheets (CSS) and JavaScript scope is locally bound and the interaction with the document is strictly designed by the component author. Upon this standard, libraries have been built, Google's Polymer being an example, which provide a declarative and easy way to realize Components. In this paper, we provide a solution to the module approach limit in website builders by using Web Components as modules that are customizable by the end user. Our approach uses standard web technologies that modern browsers are natively supporting. We describe how a customizable Web Component is designed and how to bind their options with the generator UI. Furthermore, we will show an application of this approach in a Landing Page generator. We demonstrate that the generator could import again the generated HyperText Markup Language (HTML) and edit it, without any intermediary data structure (i.e., eXtensible Markup Language, XML or JavaScript Object Notation, Json). Finally, we outline further future development of this approach.**

Keywords-Website generation, Web Components, HTML5, modularity, end-user generation, SME.

I. INTRODUCTION

The spread of smartphones in the last 5 years has deeply changed the market, forcing businesses of any kind and size to conform their online presence, in order to avoid the lack of an important market share.

Overwhelmed by contents, the constantly connected consumers use now to spend the slightest of their time on a Web site, mostly by mobile devices, becoming bothered about navigation trees and expecting to find on the first page – with no more "click and wait" – the information they need. For these and further reasons, one-page sites are nowadays very popular, often together with responsive design patterns.

This worldwide transformation is very quick and radical and produces two consequences: on one hand, businesses - which are mostly devoid of the required skills for managing and distributing contents on their own - had to delegate these tasks to service companies; on the other hand, the media agencies - in order to reduce costs and fulfill the market demand of high customized products - have left the previous artisanal production methods in favor of a modules-based approach.

Following the mission of digitalizing its wide customer portfolio of enterprises, the Italian media agency Seat PagineGialle has identified the semi-automatization of the process for creating pages as a key point in various context: we are talking about low budgets, e.g., small and medium sized enterprises (SMEs) websites [1], and time limited contents, e.g., a promotional online campaign.

The new World Wide Web Consortium (W3C) standard of Web Components represents a standard solution for modularization and reusing of HyperText Markup Language (HTML) in a web page. Isolation of scope, reusability, and freedom from server-side logic are some of the advantages of this standard. This solution is – either natively or thanks to the so called "polyfills" – built directly in the browser.

This paper will present a Web page generator that uses Web Components as modules. In our Web application, these Web Components should not be assembled on the code by the developer, but a friendly interface makes their combination, manipulation and customization available to the end-user. As corporate requirement, integration with other existing and different Seat PagineGialle products must be possible. The rest of the paper is structured as follows: Section II overviews briefly current trends in website generator, with strengths and limits and describes the standard of Web Components, that we use as modules in Section III. Section IV shows an application in a real production environment. Finally, conclusions are drawn in Section V.

II. STATE OF THE ART

A. *Trends and limits in website building*

A notable number of online website builders is available on the market, designed for the end user with no knowledge about HTML, Cascading Style Sheets (CSS and JavaScript. These tools have the most common and powerful feature in the modular design [2]: standalone parts of the page, called *modules*, could be combined – often thanks to a drag and drop interface - and customized in style, color, text content and position, so that their reuse produces each time a different look and content. In the resulting HTML document, modules are actually slices of its Document Object Model (DOM) that represent headers, footers, images gallery, text boxes and various kinds of widgets. Each module should follow the generator internal set of rules and conventions (framework) in order to avoid conflicts with its siblings: duplicated IDs, influence of CSS rules from other modules (or vice versa, overflow of their CSS outwards), not scoped scripts [3]. Each framework has his own syntax that produces a lack of interoperability between different technologies [4].

Usually, the final output of this builder is a thick tree of nested tag (mostly DIVs, the most common Document Division in HTML) that is hardly to reconvert into an editable format. These template-based solutions [1] [5] need an eXtensible Markup Language (XML) or JavaScript Object Notation (Json) structure with a list of modules and options, stored on the builder server for future editing purpose; this is an expedient, because the proper language for describing a Web page is HTML. Other applications could use modules generated on the server, like portlets: however, they need specific server environments able to deploy and serve them, hardly to integrate in custom applications as it happens in the Seat PagineGialle case.

B. The Web Components standard

In the context of the HTML5 revolution, the W3C is defining a standard for Web Components. This standard allows you to create new type of DOM elements and use them in a document as if they were DIVs, INPUTs and other standard HTML tags. Creating a component means writing its HTML template, defining its CSS rules and managing its properties, method and lifecycle with JavaScript. For a Web developer, using a Web Component is as simple as inserting a tag <my-component-name> in the HTML and dealing with it like any HTML native tag.

The family of the Web Components W3C standards includes four new specifications about:

- Custom Elements [6], that enable to define and use custom DOM elements in a document;
- HTML Imports [7], for including and reusing HTML documents as dependencies;
- Templates [8], inert DOM elements for describing HTML structures;
- Shadow DOM [9], a method for encapsulating DOM trees and bounding their interaction with the whole document.

Thanks to these technologies, we can define the structure of a component in a not-rendered <template> tag and register it as Custom Element, so that the browser becomes aware of the match between the component tag name, e.g., <descriptive-content>, and its definition. When an instance of a registered component is created in the page, the browser creates a parallel tree of DOM – called Shadow DOM – associated to the component element. This Shadow DOM contains the structure we defined in the <template>. Although not visible as a child node of the element, this structure is rendered and the user can interact with it. All that lives in the Shadow DOM has its own isolated scope and can react to events and attributes modification on its parent component. This isolation solves all problems about duplicated IDs and ingestion of external CSS; besides, it provides a bounded scope to scripts: the Shadow DOM is solidly separated from the main document [10] [11], and the only possible interactions are those explicitly allowed by the component designer. Finally, the specification introduce a standard way for importing components, with <link rel="import"> tag.

At a glance, this specification covers all the needed requirements: reusability, isolation of JS and CSS and it is a browser standard, so it is fully compatible with any other technology that runs on the server or on the client. These and other advantages of Web Components ecosystem have been investigated thoroughly in [4].

C. Polymer

In the last years, many libraries have been developed with the dual aim to extend the support to older browsers by using polyfills [12], and to further simplify the implementation of the Web Components. Recently Google released the version 1.0 of the *Polymer* library [13], which offers a declarative way for creating components. In Polymer, a component definition is an HTML page that contains imported resources (dependencies, style, template) and a call to the *Polymer* function for the configuration of properties, methods and lifecycle callbacks. We choose Polymer for the clearness of component's code and for its ease-of use.

III. Web Components as Modules

We can split the core of our approach in two complementary branches: the design of a component and its manipulation.

A. Design of a component

Polymer provides a declarative syntax for creating Web Components. We describe the general structure of a Polymer component and we provide details only in those parts that we added or that are functional to the next tasks. We refer to the example in Figure 1.

The whole component is wrapped in an inert tag `<dom-module>`. Its id attribute is the tag name of our component. All the nodes contained in `<dom-module>` will be encapsulated in the Shadow DOM of the tag. We can group these nodes in three distinct sections.

The first one is the style section, which defines the look of the component. Thanks to DOM isolation, there are no constraints about specificity of rules, because they will be applied only in the context of the component. Polymer also allows including other style-specific components for styling, like a CSS-reset or a common base style for all components. Moreover, the library includes support to the CSS Variables specification [14], currently at working draft state. For our purposes, we need to know that you can apply the same CSS variable and so the same value to different selectors and that this value could be set through Polymer Application programming interface (API).

The second part is the <template> tag, the content of which will form the internal DOM structure of our component. Double curly brackets denote the insertion point for properties value, so that "{{text}}" will be replaced with the value of the "text" property.

```
<dom-module id="descriptive-content">
 <style include="component-base"></style>
 <style>
   p { color: var(--descriptive-text-color);  }
 </style>
 <template><p>{{text}}</p></template>
 <script>
   Polymer({
     is: 'descriptive-content',
     behaviors: [ComponentBehavior],
     properties: {
        text: {
          type: String,
          logicType: 'textarea',
          value: 'Lorem ipsum....',
          label: 'Text',
          reflectToAttribute: true,
          customizable: true
        },
        textColor: {
          type: String,
          logicType: 'color',
          value: '#ffffff',
          cssVariable: '--descriptive-text-color',
          label: 'Text color',
          reflectToAttribute: true,
          customizable: true,
          observer: 'computeStyle'
        }, // other properties
     }
     //methods and lifecycle callback
});
</dom-module>
```

Figure 1. The definition of <descriptive-content> component.

```
<descriptive-content text="Lorem ipsum..." text-
color="#ffffff">
    #shadow-root //not shown
        <style> ... </style>
        <p> Lorem ipsum...</p>
</descriptive-content>
```

Figure 2. The usage of <descriptive-content> component.

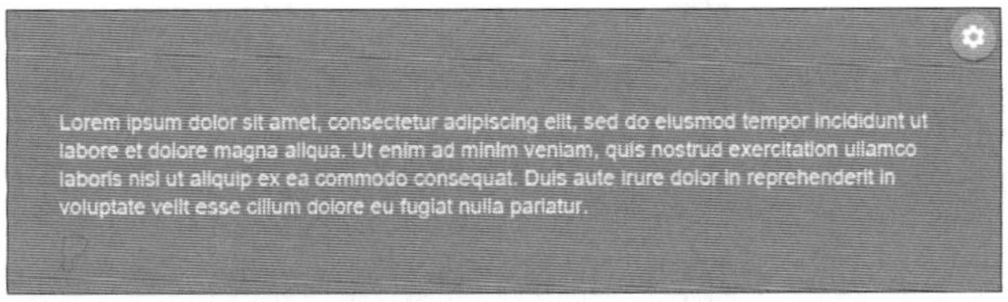

Figure 3. The <descriptive-content> component as it appears in a browser, with the button for customizing settings.

Finally, we deal the registration of the component through the Polymer function. The *properties* object contains the value that will be bound in the template. According to the library, a property has the following sub properties:

- *type*, the JavaScript type of the property,
- *value*, its default value,
- *reflectToAttribute*, if true, causes attribute to be set on the host node when the property value changes,
- *observer*, a method to call on property changes.

In addition, we added the following properties:

- *customizable*, when set to true, this property should be used as customizable option,
- *logicType*, refers to a human concept rather than a coding one; each logic type has a specific User Interface (UI) input element; we support as logic types "text", "color", "background", "textarea", "image";
- *cssVariable*, means that this property is connected to a CSS variable in the <style> tag,
- a human-readable *label* for displaying purpose.

A modification of the attributes on the component host tag (Figure 2) will reflect in a modification on the properties and consequently on the component's content or style as it is rendered by the browser (Figure 3).

We specify also a *behavior,* which is Polymer's way of making certain properties and methods inheritable. The *ComponentBehavior* is a custom behavior that manages some customization-related tasks. It shows an options button on the element that triggers, when clicked, a "settingRequested" event. Additionally, it defines the "computeStyle" method, set as observer of properties with cssVariable in order to propagate changes to the CSS variables.

B. *Component manipulation*

The generator should read the components properties and provide the user with a proper User Interface (UI) for modifying it.

Manipulation starts when our page generator interceps the "settingRequested" event from one of the components. Component customizable properties are retrieved from the source DOM element via JavaScript. For each of them, we read the *logicType* property and according to it, we choose a proper input element. For some types, the choice is an HTML input element: an <input type="text"> for a "text", a <textarea> for a "textarea". For types like "background" or "image", we have not a suitable input tag. Once again, we use Web Components specification for creating custom <background-input> and <image-input> element. For example, we implement a complex input for background, letting the user to choose between a color, an uploaded image, an image from our gallery and a transparent

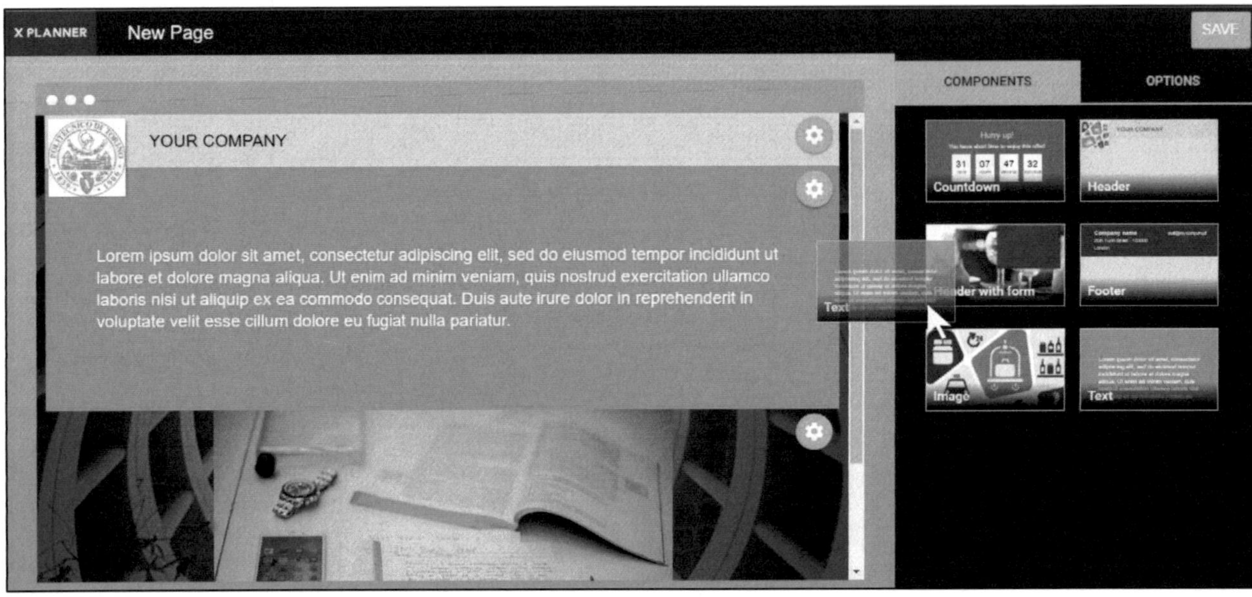

Figure 4. The GUI of the page generator.

background. This complex component – and all option components we defined – exposes a *value* property that contains the current selection, exactly like native input elements. We valorize the component with the current value of the property, and display its *label*.

The value of the *value* property of the input element changes upon user interaction. Consequently, we overwrite the corresponding property on the source element: this change propagates to the component Shadow DOM and to its attributes in the HTML, thanks to the *reflectToAttribute* feature. In this way, the HTML node always contains in its attributes the current state of the component.

Form components have a special behavior. They have been designed as containers of an array of <input-field> components, each of them exposing as customizable properties the label, the placeholder, the type (i.e., text, date, mail) and the requirement. The user can modify these options and add, move or remove the input field.

IV. THE PAGE GENERATOR

We currently use the described approach in xPlanner, a beta Web app for promotional campaign management for Seat PagineGialle. A succint demo of the landing generator is available at goo.gl/LW3WGE.

A. Application overview

We propose a classic drag and drop Graphic User Interface (GUI), visible in Figure 4. On the right column, we show a gallery of modules, which are Web Components. When the user accedes to the tool for the first time, the left side appears blank: the user can drop his\her favorite component on it in the place they prefer. Once on the drop area, the component shows the settings button on top left corner.

Pressing the button, the "settingRequested" event is dispatched and the right bar shows the available options for the active component, in the appearance of the input elements described in Section 2.B (Figure 5). Every edit on those options will reflect on source components.

User can than continue to add components and modify them until it is satisfied of the result. By clicking on the "Save" button, the components are inserted in a full HTML skeleton and the final HTML is exported and stored on the server.

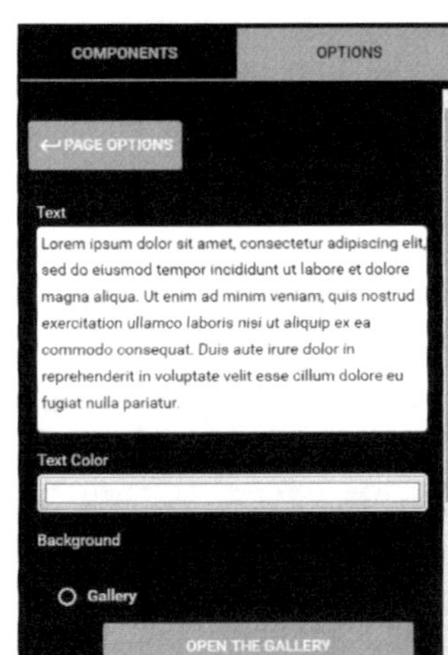

Figure 5. The right column visualize the customizable options.

```
<html>
<head><!-- dependencies loading --></head>
<body>
  <!-- other components -->
  <descriptive-content text-color="#40AAE6"
      text="Lorem ipsum dolor...">
  </descriptive-content>
  <!-- other components -->
</body>
<html>
```

Figure 6. Example of an exported page.

We reported a common result in Figure 6. As shown, the appearance of components in this HTML has not changed: the tag continues to appear without its inner template (once again hidden in the Shadow DOM) and the attributes reveal the values of properties as the user set them.

B. Application flow

Figure 7 shows the complete flow of the application. The generator is in charge of importing the components that the user can add to the page. Reading the exposed options from component description itself, the generator makes possible their manipulation, together with an eventual custom sorting. At the end of the process, it generates the HTML file. When it comes to the browser, the needed components are imported and the page is rendered.

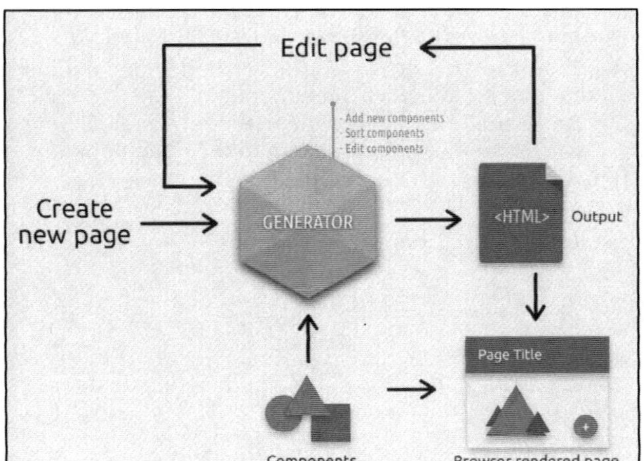

Figure 7. Scheme of the generator application.

The HTML itself is ready for further editing: when the user wants to edit again his/her page, the generator simply retrieves it from server, extracts the content from the body and insert it in the drop area of the GUI. The process continues in the same way.

The application has completely been developed using Web Components and the Polymer technology. In this case, the intrinsic isolation of each Web Component implied some implementation issue. It happens specifically when two components need to communicate each other and are not direct siblings in the DOM, i.e., the option input and the component that input refers: the isolation forced the development to propagate each information up to the nearest common parent of both, and that means to declare a data binding in the definition of multiple components. It seems useful to make an exploration about improving this approach and on the possibility of make use of alternative frameworks for Web application development on top of the components.

C. Evaluation of the usability

We introduced the complete xPlanner beta application – site generator included – to a small panel of webmasters and sales agents of SeatPG. The former have a quite good background on Web design and development, while the latter have commercial skills. The feedback has been different between the two profiles.

People with computer experience, and in particular in this type of tools, gave a good evaluation, because it fulfilled their expectation based on their own passed experience. On the other hand, the generator was considered complicated by people with low technical skills. In particular, they were lost in the large number of available options of each component. We are considering a different UI approach and the creation of a light version of the application.

V. CONCLUSION AND FUTURE WORKS

We built a Web page generator that works by combining and customizing Web Components. The feature of the standard grants native isolation to each component for CSS and Javascript, avoiding conflicts in namespace. The generated HTML is the standalone structure that can be used for viewing the page and that can be imported in the generator for further editing. Therefore, the final HTML describes the page perfectly, in a suitable way for both the browser and the generator application. No other structure needs to be stored.

For the first time, the standard of Web Components have been used in a novel way: the combination and manipulation of each component is no longer in charge to the developer through the code, but it is the final user itself to have the ability of doing this through a specific User Interface, in a context of end-user programming.

The page edit and assembly is managed client-side. Components are modular: they can be defined and edited by simply relying on the existing standard and are independent of any other client or server-side technology. The HTML generates and describe itself, following its own rules instead of backend logics. This allows components to correctly behave in complex scenarios.

In order to further improve the approach, we intend to give users with a minimum of Web development skills the possibility to add their own components. The idea is to design a collaborative platform for SeatPG webmasters, which are constantly in touch with the sales force, in order to make them autonomous in creating suitable modules that are specific to a business category. Each webmaster should be able to design a component, defining the HTML, the CSS and the customizable properties, and share it to the internal community in such a collaborative way.

Other improvements could involve the support to components with external dependencies (by using a dependency manager, e.g., npm or bower). For limiting server requests, we will add a process of concatenation of used components inside the exported HTML. This process, in the Polymer naming convention, is called Vulcanization [15]. We are also working on the definition of a color theme for the whole page, using the CSS variables.

REFERENCES

[1] Y. Jiang, and H. Dong, "TEB: A Template-Based E-commence Website Builder for SMEs," Second International Conference on Future Generation Communication and Networking Symposia, 2008 (FGCNS'08) IEEE, Vol. 1, Dec. 2008, pp. 23-28.

[2] A. K. Kalou, D. A. Koutsomitropoulos, G. D. Solomou, "CMSs, Linked Data and Semantics: A Linked Data Mashup over Drupal for Personalized Search," Metadata and Semantics Research, Springer International Publishing, 2013, pp. 48-59.

[3] M. Krug, and M. Gaedke, "SmartComposition: Enhanced Web Components for a Better Future of Web Development," Proceedings of the 24th International Conference on World Wide Web Companion (WWW'15 Companion) ACM, May 2015, pp. 207-210.

[4] T. Savage, "Componentizing the web," Communications of the ACM, vol. 58, no. 11, pp. 55-61, Nov. 2015.

[5] K. Nakano, Z. Zhenjian, M. Takeichi, "Consistent Web site updating based on bidirectional transformation," International journal on software tools for technology transfer, vol. 11, no. 6, pp. 453-468, Dec. 2009.

[6] D. Denicola, "Custom Elements," W3C Editor's Draft, Mar. 2016, [Online]. Available from: http://w3c.github.io/webcomponents/spec/custom/ 2016.03.09

[7] D. Glazkov, H. Morrita, "HTML Imports," W3C Editor's Draft, Mar. 2016. [Online]. A2016.03.09vailable from: http://w3c.github.io/webcomponents/spec/imports/ 2016.03.09

[8] S. Pieters, A. van Kesteren, et al., "HTML 5.1," W3C Editor's Draft, Mar. 2016. [Online]. Available from: https://html.spec.whatwg.org/multipage/scripting.html#the-template-element 2016.03.09

[9] D. Glazkov, H. Ito, "Shadow DOM," W3C Editor's Draft, Mar. 2016. [Online]. Available from: http://w3c.github.io/webcomponents/spec/shadow/ 2016.03.09

[10] P. De Ryck, N. Nikiforakis, L. Desmet, F. Piessens, W. Joosen, "Protected Web Components: Hiding Sensitive Information in the Shadows," IT Professional, vol. 17, no. 1, pp. 36-43, Jan.-Feb. 2015

[11] W. He, D. Akhawe, S. Jain, E. Shi, D. Song, "ShadowCrypt: Encrypted Web Applications for Everyone," Proceedings of the 2014 ACM SIGSAC Conference on Computer and Communications Security (CCS 2014) ACM, 2014, pp. 1028-1039.

[12] WebComponents.org contributors, "WebComponents Polyfills," WebComponents.org Blog, 2015. [Online]. Available from: http://webcomponents.org/polyfills/ 2016.03.09

[13] Google, "Polymer Project," Website. [Online]. Available from: https://www.polymer-project.org 2016.03.09

[14] T. Atkins Jr., "CSS Custom Properties for Cascading Variables Module Level 1," W3C Candidate Recommendation, Dec. 2015. [Online]. Available from: http://www.w3.org/TR/css-variables-1/ 2016.03.09

[15] A. Osmani, "Concatenating Web Components with Vulcanize," Polymer Website, Dec. 2013. [Online]. Available from: http://polymer-project.org/articles/concatenating-web-components.html 2016.03.09

A Natural Language Dialog System Based on Active Ontologies

Alexander Wachtel, Jonas Klamroth, Walter F. Tichy

Karlsruhe Institute of Technology
Chair for Programming Systems Prof. Walter F. Tichy
Am Fasanengarten 5, 76131 Karlsruhe, Germany
Email: alexander.wachtel@kit.edu, jonas.klamroth@student.kit.edu, walter.tichy@kit.edu

***Abstract*—Programming today requires years of training. With natural language, programming would become available to everyone and enable end users to program their devices or extend their functionality without any knowledge of programming languages. We present an assistant usable in technical domains that uses natural language understanding, programming step-by-step and an active dialog management system. It allows users to manipulate spreadsheet data by using natural language. We extend our previous system with active ontologies. By adding additional information to an ontology, such as a rule evaluation system and a fact store, it becomes an execution environment instead of just being a representation of knowledge. Sensor nodes register certain events and store them in the fact store. An evaluation mechanism tests the new facts against the existing rules and performs the associated action if one or more rules apply to the stored facts. The system also handles references to previous results and expressions, allowing the construction of complex expressions step-by-step. It also creates new formulas by using End-User Programming concepts and supports the use of repetitive tasks that involve use of conditions and negations. An evaluation shows that the active ontology-based approach resolves 90% of the input tasks which is an increase of 10% over the pattern matching approach.**

Keywords–Natural Language Processing; Natural Language Interfaces; Dialog Systems; Human Computer Interaction; End-User Programming; Spreadsheet.

I. INTRODUCTION

Since their invention, digital computers have been programmed using specialized, artificial notations, called programming languages. However, only a tiny fraction of human computer users can actually work with those notations. An alternative would be ordinary, natural language. Ordinary language would enable almost anyone to program and would thus cause a fundamental shift in the way computers are used. Rather than being a mere consumer of programs written by others, each user could write his or her own programs [3]. The idea of programming in natural language was first proposed by Sammet in 1966 [4], but enormous difficulties have resulted in disappointingly slow progress. One of the difficulties is that natural language programming requires a domain-aware counterpart that asks for clarification, thereby overcoming the chief disadvantages of natural language, namely ambiguity and imprecision. In recent years, significant advances in natural language techniques have been made, leading, for instance, to IBM's Watson [5] computer winning against the two Jeopardy! world champions, Apple's Siri routinely answering wide-ranging, spoken queries, and automated translation services such as Google's becoming usable. However, programming in natural language remains an open challenge [6][7].

Spreadsheets have been used for at least 7000 years [8]. Spreadsheet programs such as Microsoft Excel have become ubiquitous. It is estimated that each year hundreds of millions of spreadsheets are created [9]. In article [1], we presented first prototype of an assistant that uses natural language understanding and a dialog management system to allow inexperienced users to manipulate spreadsheets with natural language. Motivated by a pilot study based on the selected problems from Frey's book *Microsoft Excel 2013* [10] the system requests missing information and is able to resolve ambiguities by providing alternatives to choose from. Furthermore, the dialog system must resolve references to previous results, allowing the construction of complex expressions step-by-step.

In this paper, we extended the prototype with an active ontology. The idea of active ontology was first presented by Guzzoni in 2006 [2]. In general, an ontology is a formal representation of knowledge. By adding a rule evaluation system, a fact store and sensor nodes to an ontology it becomes an execution environment rather than just a formal representation of knowledge. Sensor nodes register certain events and save them in the fact store. An evaluation mechanism tests the new facts against the existing rules and performs the associated actions if one or more rules apply. Our paper is structured as following: section II describes the active ontology framework and the dialog system. Section III evaluates prototype in an user study, followed by performance tests. Section IV discusses both different approaches of pattern matching and active ontologies. Section V presents related work in the research areas of programming in natural language, End User Programming and natural language dialog systems. Finally, section VI presents a conclusion of our topic and future work.

II. ACTIVE ONTOLOGY-BASED DIALOG SYSTEM

The prototype is implemented as an add-in for Microsoft Excel and looks like an instant messaging system. The dialog system allows users to express spreadsheet calculations in ordinary typed English and converts the natural language input into arithmetic spreadsheet formulas. All calculations are stored as valid Excel-formulas that allows future manipulation of the spreadsheet data.

A. Active Ontology Framework

We used Guzzoni's approach [2] to develop an active ontology-based framework, further implemented a dialog system relying on this work to understand and interpret ordinary English inputs. The framework generally provides a system that enables the developer to arrange nodes and thus design an active ontology. Thus nodes can communicate directly with each other. Sensor nodes register based on regular expression evaluations whether they are affected by the given input or not. If activated each node notifies its connected nodes. This sequence recursively repeats itself. On activation, nodes that are defined as "end-nodes" advise the post-processor. This way the post-processor collects all detected events of the active ontology and the user can react accordingly. Guzzoni distinguishes between the following node types:

- Selection node: this node passes the event with the highest reliability score on to its parents, e.g., see *Instruction* node in Figure 1.
- Gather node: this node just sends an event if all children were activated, e.g., *Binary operation* node or *Unary operation*.

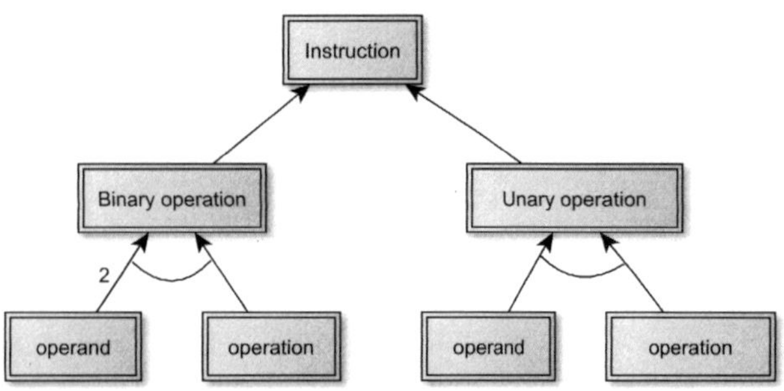

Figure 1. Example of an Active Ontology for mathematical tasks

In addition to Guzzoni, we introduced a new type of node: the generalization node. This node simply collects all incoming events and passes them on to their parent-nodes. It enables the user to combine several events and concentrate them into one single type of event. This is often useful as it enables the user to use different types of events as arguments for one and the same action. In Figure 2, the node operand is a Generalization node. Without this node the sum as well as the difference would have to have three different sum-/difference-nodes for each argument-type one.

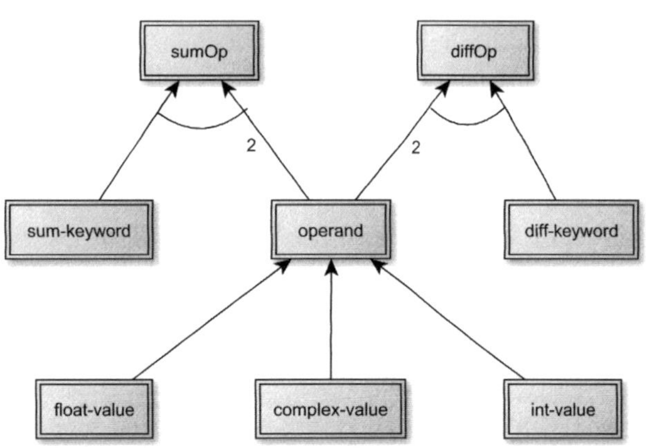

Figure 2. An example of the use of an generalization node

To further clarify how active ontology framework works we discuss the input "save 3 times 2 in A2" as an example. For *save* and *times* the respective sensor node will fire an event signaling that the keyword was found. Additionally two number-values, *3* and *2*, and cell *A2* will be found. Activated by the incoming event the multiplication-node will determine the two most fitting values and thus fire an event signaling a recognized product *(3 * 2)*. A2 is not considered as fitting operand since it is the only valid target for the save operation and thus is reserved for this argument. The product will be recognized as a new operand and thus be send to the save-action-node. Here the node triggered by the keyword *save* will find that an operand *(3 * 2)* as well as a target cell *A2* was found resulting in a new save-action-event. It represents the desired action and can now be performed by the instruction-execution-module leading to the intended outcome.

To ease the act of creating such active ontologies and ensure that there are as few design errors as possible, our framework comes with an editor. The existing active ontology can be displayed either as a graph or a tree structure. This editor not only allows the user to manipulate and create active ontologies but also validates them as far as possible to avoid typical mistakes. Any changes are checked by a validation process for errors. Duplicate names, orphaned nodes, empty regular expressions, missing end node or cycles in the ontology can be detected. Cycles can be especially problematic for recursive algorithms.

B. Dialog System

The dialog system [1] extends the active ontology framework. We use two different active ontologies: Natural Language Understanding (NLU) ontology, to interpret the user input, and Natural Language Generation (NLG) ontology, to generate answers (See Figure 3).

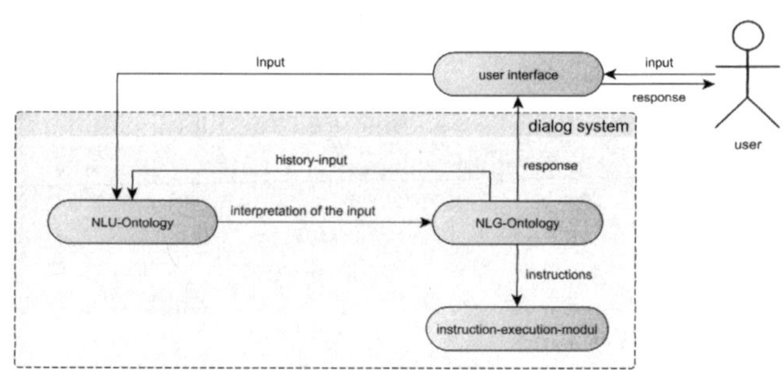

Figure 3. Overview of the active ontology-based dialog system

The active ontologies recognize several mathematical operations by searching the input, and then recursively building an entire instruction. This instruction is the input to the second active ontology that, based on the type and content of the built instructions, generates a response. When a node gets triggered it builds an answer based on patterns stored in its children. Thus the answer can be built recursively from reusable predefined patterns. The response generator carries out the process of speech generation in six basic tasks according to Reiter [11]:

- *Content determination*: the basic planning of what should be communicated in the output

- *Discourse planing*: process of imposing the order and structure over the set of messages
- *Sentence aggregation*: grouping of information that should be processed in the response sentence
- *Lexicalization*: choice of words for the sentence
- *Referring expression generation*: insertion of anaphoras to shorten the output
- *Linguistic realization*: bringing the selected words and phrases in a grammatically correct form

Our system roughly follows these steps to generate the answers. Sentence aggregation is almost irrelevant for our use case since the answers of the system are most likely just one or two sentences. The content determination is covered by the use of the input of the NLU ontology. This way the system always knows that information should be communicated in the coming answer. Discourse planning and lexicalization are implicitly stored in the structure and the content of the NLG ontology. The structure of the ontology defines the structure of the generated output and the saved words in the nodes provide this output with the necessary vocabulary. Since the content of the answer is already very specific and very short, referring expressions can be inserted in the sentence structure and do not need to be added in a separate processing step. The structure of the NLG ontology also guarantees a grammatically valid output.

The system is successful in resolving references to previously provided information, understands negations and asks questions depending on the dialog context:

User: Generate a random number between 1000 and 1500
System: Your input results in the following formula:
randbetween(1000, 1500). Where exactly do you
want me to save that in the worksheet?
User: C2
System: Ok, I did that for you
Can I do something else for you?
User: No
System: Alright

User: Calculate C5 minus D5 multiplied with C5
System: Your input may be interpreted in various ways:
a) (C5 - product(D5, C5))
b) product((C5 - D5), C5)
Which one should I use?
User: a
System: Where do you want me to save that in the
worksheet?
User: B5
System: Ok, I did that for you.

III. Evaluation

To validate our approach we conducted a user study. Furthermore, several performance tests on the active ontology framework have been done.

A. User Study

Natural language is highly dynamic and expression vary among humans. We asked 16 participants to perform several tasks in Microsoft Excel using solely our dialog system and give feedback on how well the dialog system performed. The tasks covered several complex problems such as resolving references, ambiguities, and conditionals. The study shows that the subjects were able to solve nearly 90% of the tasks and rated the system as helpful in 76% of the tasks. The participants rated the system overall as *good* and *very good* in 15 out of 16 cases. More than 80% of the participants stated they would use the system at least occasionally. Last but not least the answers of the system were appropriate in 88% of the cases according to our participants and 75% of the test persons found the answers to be natural or very natural. User experience with the system is very positive (See Figure 4). 75% of participants said they perceive the dialog system as natural or very natural. The overall quality of our prototype was ranked by 15 of the 16 participants as good or very good.

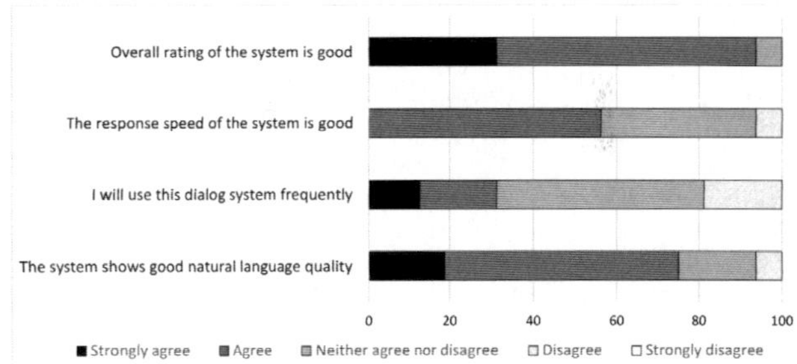

Figure 4. Overall results in %

B. Performance-Tests

One of the most important features of an interactive dialog system is the response time that is required by the dialog system to generate an appropriate answer to a given user input. The user perceives the response time of the dialog system as natural or human-like if it is less than 1s [12]. Larger response times appear as too long and unnatural. In order to evaluate the response time of the dialog system, the response time for every user input during the user study was logged. The average time was 6 ms - the standard deviation was 7.86 ms. Furthermore, our ontology with about 80 nodes and 120 edges needs 140 kB of disk space.

We also designed several automatic tests to explore response times and scaling for large ontologies. In order to avoid the manipulation of the results by choosing specific ontologies we decided to develop a tool that generates random ontologies with certain number of nodes and edges independently. We conducted three different tests measuring the response time. Each test was executed several times on different randomly generated ontologies. The average response time of the active ontology used for our dialog system was less than 6 ms while it took the previous system 150 ms to answer the same questions. It is important to note, that both systems were developed in C# and the tests were run at the same computer with the same operating system (Windows 8.1). Thus we are able to exclude the possibility that the differences are caused by programming language, operating system and/or computation power. In all tests ontologies contained over 10000 nodes and 15000 edges whereby the active ontology framework never exceeded the response time of 600 ms.

1) Length of the input: 10 ontologies all with 100 nodes and 150 edges have been created to test the scaling with length of input. Then, the response time of the system was observed for each ontology for a randomly generated entry. At the same time the length of the input was increased from 100 to 1000 characters. The experiment was repeated 100 times to obtain statistically meaningful values. Figure 5 shows the average values for each input length. While the input size increased tenfold, the response time rose far faster. The values suggest a quadratic growth. These values are negligible for our dialog system, since the input length does not reach the critical time of 1s in almost all cases.

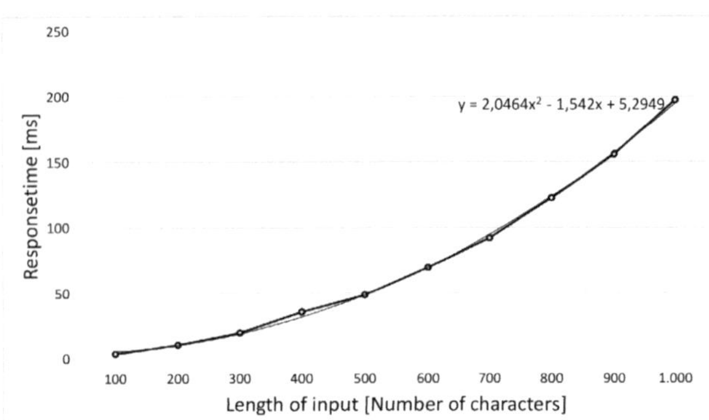

Figure 5. Performance-Test on the length of the input

2) Number of nodes: For this test, 100 ontologies with 100 nodes and 150 edges were created. During the test the number of edges was increased by 10 from 100 to 200. These values were chosen because we determined a ratio of edges to nodes of approximately 1.5 in the ontology. It turns out that in the investigated area, the response time increases linearly with a number of edges and nodes. The slope of the trend line lies below 0.3. This means that the response time increases very slow with increasing interconnectedness (See Figure 6).

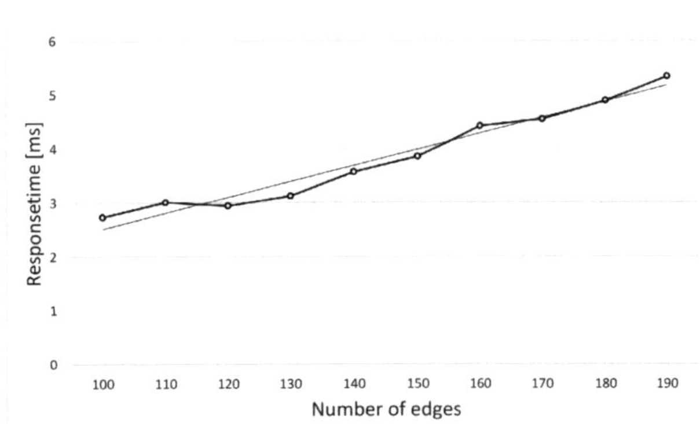

Figure 6. Performance-Test on number of nodes

This demonstrates that our approach is not only capable, but also suited to handle rather large ontologies of nearly every format.

IV. Discussion

Inspired by the Turing Test [13], we asked 17 independent spreadsheet users to formulate requests for particular calculation tasks. Each task was answered by both the prototype and a human independently. Afterwards the participants were asked to identify the computer generated response. This however turned out to be surprisingly hard to decide. With 34 decisions made in total, 47.1% falsely identified the dialog system answer as human. This result indicates that the prototype is capable of generating suitable responses for sufficiently specific requests within the language domain.

The system [1] is based on matching the user input to patterns that are stored in a database. The iterative dialog system was based on small knowledge base with 92 patterns covering all basic arithmetic operations and assists in the accomplishment of computational tasks. The approach uses a limited vocabulary and a small set of syntactic patterns organized as a grammar. As part of an example, the pattern *sum* matches the first clause, with keywords *add* and *to*, and placeholders *any* (See Figure 7). The placeholders are filled with the respective elements (*4* and *A1*). By successively matching additional patterns within the placeholder elements, more complex sentences can be transformed into a semantic representation. It builds a tree structure consisting of operators and operands which makes it easier to determine whether a valid arithmetic expression has been provided.

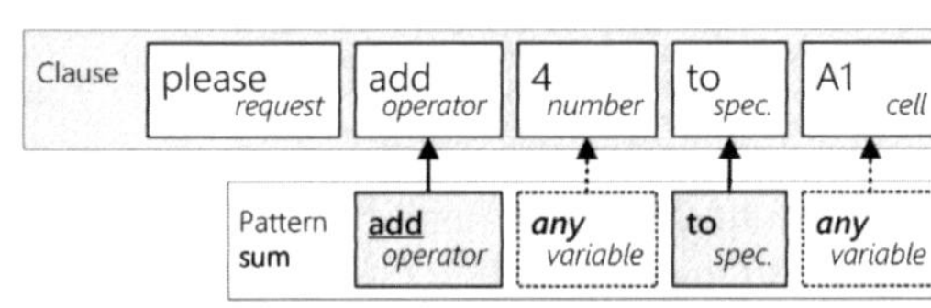

Figure 7. Examplary pattern matching

After the evaluation of an active ontology-based dialog system, we are confident that it has several advantages: it solved 10% more tasks, produces 35% more natural outputs and improves the system by 10% according to the subjects of the user study (See Figure 8).

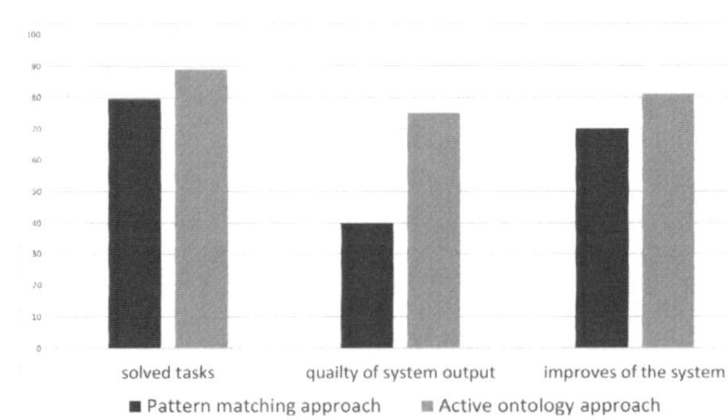

Figure 8. Comparison of pattern matching and active ontology approaches

Furthermore, the active ontology-based system is far more flexible in two ways. First, the design of the application itself is easier and more intuitive when using active ontologies as you can visually arrange the nodes. Second, using patterns the end user is far more restricted in the way talking to the rule-based system in order to be understood. If the user expresses the same action in a slightly different way the provided pattern may not match the input and the system thus fails to understand the user. Active ontologies are much more forgiving in this area as they do not expect the specific order in the input to fit a narrow pattern. This way instructions can be expressed in various ways and still result in the expected behavior.

V. Related Work

Our work combines different research on Programming in Natural Language, End User Programing and Dialog Systems.

A. *Programming in natural language*

In 1979 Ballard et al. [14][15][16] introduced their Natural Language Computer (NLC) that enables users to program simple arithmetic calculations using natural language. Our prototype extends the idea with a dialog system component for step-by-step construction of complex expression and enables users to perform tasks they otherwise would not be able to accomplish. Although NLC resolves the references as well, there is no dialog system. User feedback has been only provided by the result output. NLyze [17], an Add-In for Microsoft Excel that has been developed at the same time as our prototype, behaves in a similar manner. This approach uses a separate domain-specific language for logical interpretation of the user input. Another approach of programming in natural language is the Pegasus system [18] that creates limited executable programs from natural language using an intermediate knowledge and reference representation. Metafor introduced by Liu et al. [19] has a different orientation. Based on user stories the system tries to derive program structures to support software design. A different approach regarding software design via natural language is taken by RECAA [20]. RECAA can automatically derive UML models from the text and also keep model and specification consistent through an automatic feedback component. A limited domain end-to-end programming is introduced by Le. SmartSynth [21] allows synthesizing smartphone automation scripts from natural language description. However, there is no dialog interaction besides the results output and the output of the error messages.

B. *End User Programming*

The main question in this area of research is, how to allow users to interact with the computer more easily and allow general users, who are not software developers and have no access to the source code, to program a computer system [22]. In 2009 Myers [23] provides an overview of the research in the area of End-User Programming. Nearly 90 million people in US use computers at work, 50 million use spreadsheets at work, 12 million considered themselves programmers in a self-assessment and only 3 million people are professional programmers. As Myers summarized, many different systems for End-User Programming have already been developed - Whyline, Visual Programming or programming by example and programming by demonstration for spreadsheets. However, there are no End-User Programming systems such as our prototype that can be controlled with natural language. During a study in 2006 Ko [24] identifies six learning barriers in End-User Programming systems: Design, Selection, Coordination, Use, Understanding and Information barriers. Jones [25] encapsulates computation in spreadsheets as a function and proposes a mechanism to define functions using spreadsheet cells, formulas and references. Sestoft [26] extends it by increasing expressiveness and emphasizing execution speed of the functions thus defined by supporting recursive and higher-order functions, and fast execution by a careful choice of data representation and compiler technology. Burnett [27] shows with research language Forms/3 that graphics output, procedural and data abstraction can be supported in the spreadsheet paradigm. Cunha [28] realizes techniques for model-driven spreadsheet engineering that employs bidirectional transformations to maintain spreadsheet models and synchronized instances. Begel [29] introduces voice recognition to the software development process. His approach uses program analysis to dictate code in natural language, thereby enabling the creation of a program editor that supports voice-based programming.

C. *Natural Language Dialog Systems*

Many dialog systems have already been developed. Commercially successful systems, such as Apple's Siri, actually based on Active Ontology approach [2], and Google's Voice Search [30][31] are characterized by the cover of many domains. The reference resolution makes the systems also acts very natural. However, there is no dialog interaction besides the results output and the output of the error messages. The Mercury system [32] designed by the MIT research group is a telephone hotline for automated booking of airline tickets. Mercury guides the user through a mixed initiative dialog towards the selection of a suitable flight based on date, time and preferred airline. Furthermore, Allen [33] describes a system called PLOW developed at Stanford University. As a collaborative task agent PLOW can learn to perform certain tasks, such as extracting specific information from the internet, by demonstration, explanation, and dialog.

VI. Conclusion and Future Work

We present the implementation of an active ontology-based prototype for an assistant that uses natural language understanding and an active dialog management system. It allows inexperienced users to manipulate spreadsheet data by using the natural language. Programming languages provide loops and conditionals. Our prototype already supports conditional expressions. The implemented active ontology framework is robust with large and dense ontologies. The response time of the framework containing 1000 nodes is less than 1 ms. The entire dialog system runs faster than the previous version based on pattern matching - execution time was reduced from 150 ms to 6 ms. Furthermore, the system resolves more tasks correctly and shows better user experience. An evaluation shows that the active ontology-based approach resolves 90% of the input tasks which is an increase of 10% over the pattern matching approach.

However, plenty of work still needs to be done. The goal is to implement Excel scripts called macros from natural language input. We are exploring ways to extend the system functionality with the help of the dialog. Furthermore, the system needs to be extended for handling graphs and charts, filtering and sorting the spreadsheet data, and supporting loops. Overall, we will implement a module that uses machine learning techniques for context interpretation within spreadsheets and connects natural language to the data in the spreadsheets. That module would enable end users to search for values in the schema of the table and to address the data in spreadsheets implicitly, e.g., *what is the average age of people in group A?* Perhaps the most important insight is the following: in the past, computers were expected to follow instructions blindly, without a notion of right or wrong or what users expected. With natural language, programming would become available to everyone. We believe that systems like our prototype take first steps in the right direction and are a reasonable approach for end user software engineering, and will help to overcome the present bottleneck of professional developers.

REFERENCES

[1] Alexander Wachtel, Sebastian Weigelt, and Walter F. Tichy, "Initial implementation of natural language turn-based dialog system", International Conference on Intelligent Human Computer Interaction (IHCI), 2015.

[2] Didier Guzzoni, Charles Baur, and Adam Cheyer, "Active: A unified platform for building intelligent web interaction assistants", IEEE Web Intelligence and Intelligent Agent Technology Workshops, 2006.

[3] Walter F. Tichy, Mathias Landhäußer, Sven J. Körner. Universal Programmability - How AI Can Help. 2nd International NSF sponsored Workshop on Realizing Artificial Intelligence Synergies in Software Engineering, May 2013.

[4] Jean E. Sammet, "The Use of English as a Programming Language", Communication of the ACM, Volume 9 Issue 3, March 1966, pp. 228–230.

[5] David Ferrucci et al., "Building Watson: An Overview of the DeepQA Project", Association for the Advancement of Artificial Intelligence, Volume 31 Issue 3, 2010, pp. 59–79.

[6] Hugo Liu and Henry Liebermann. "Toward a programmatic semantics of natural language", IEEE Symposium on Visual Languages and Human Centric Computing, September 2004, pp. 281–282.

[7] Charles L. Ortiz, "The Road to Natural Conversational Speech Interfaces", IEEE Internet Computing, Volume 18, Number 2, pp. 74-78, Mar.-Apr. 2014.

[8] Matthew F. Hurst, "The interpretation of tables in texts", PhD. Thesis, University of Edinburgh, 2000.

[9] Robin Abraham, "Header and Unit Inference for Spreadsheets Through Spatial Analyses", IEEE Symposium on Visual Languages and Human Centric Computing, September 2004, pp. 165–172.

[10] Curtis D. Frye, "Microsoft Excel 2013, Step by Step", O'Reilly Media Inc., 2013.

[11] Ehud Reiter and Robert Dale, "Building applied natural language generation systems", Natural Language Engineering, Volume 3 Issue 01, March 1997, pp 57–87.

[12] Sofia Strombergsson, Anna Hjalmarsson, Jens Edlund, and David House, "Timing responses to questions in dialogue", Proceedings of INTERSPEECH 2013, pp. 2584-2588.

[13] Alan M. Turing, "Computing machinery and intelligence", 1950, pp. 433-460.

[14] Bruce W. Ballard and Alan W. Biermann, "Programming in natural language: NLC as a prototype", Association for Computing Machinery (ACM), Volume 10, 1979, pp. 228–237.

[15] Alan W. Biermann and Bruce W. Ballard, "Toward Natural Language Computation", American Journal of Computational Linguistics, Volume 6, Number 2, 1980.

[16] Alan W. Biermann, Bruce W. Ballard, and Anne H. Sigmon, "An experimental study of natural language programming", International Journal of Man-Machine Studies, January 1983, pp. 71–87.

[17] Sumit Gulwani and Mark Marron, "NLyze: Interactive programming by natural language for spreadsheet data analysis and manipulation", Proceedings of the 2014 ACM SIGMOD, 2014, pp. 803–814.

[18] Roman Knöll and Mira Mezini, "Pegasus - First Steps towards a Naturalistic Programming Language", 21st ACM SIGPLAN symposium on Object-oriented programming systems, languages, and applications, 2006, pp. 542–559.

[19] Hugo Liu and Henry Lieberman, "Metafor: Visualizing stories as code", Proceedings of the 10th international conference on Intelligent user interfaces, 2005, pp. 305–307.

[20] Sven J . Körner, Mathias Landhäußer, and Walter F. Tichy, "Transferring Research Into the Real World - How to Improve RE with AI in the Automotive Industry", First International Workshop on Artificial Intelligence for Requirements Engineering (AIRE), 2014, pp. 13-18.

[21] Vu Le, Sumit Gulwani, and Zhendong Su, "SmartSynth: Synthesizing Smartphone Automation Scripts from Natural Language", Proceeding of the 11th annual international conference on Mobile systems, applications, and services (MobiSys), 2013, pp. 193–206.

[22] Henry Liberman, Fabio Paternò, Markus Klann, and Volker Wulf, "End-User Development: An Emerging Paradigm", Springer, Human-Computer Interaction Series, Volume 9, 2006, pp. 1–8.

[23] Brad A. Myers, Andrew J. Ko, and Margaret M. Burnett, "Invited research overview: end-user programming", Extended Abstracts on Human Factors in Computing Systems, 2006, pp. 75–80.

[24] Andrew J. Ko, Brad A. Myers, and Htet Htet Aung, "Six Learning Barriers in End-User Programming Systems", Proceedings of the 2004 IEEE Symposium on Visual Languages - Human Centric Computing (VLHCC), 2004, pp. 199–206.

[25] Simon P. Jones, Alan Blackwell, and Margaret Burnett, "A user-centred approach to functions in excel", 8th ACM SIGPLAN international conference on Functional programming, 2003, pp. 165–176.

[26] Peter Sestoft and Jens Zeilund, "Sheet-defined functions: Implementation and initial evaluation", Springer, Volume 7897 of the series Lecture Notes in Computer Science, 2013, pp. 88-103.

[27] Margaret Burnett, John Atwood, Rebecca W. Djang, James Reichwein, Herkimer Gottfried, and Sherry Yang, "Forms/3: A First-Order Visual Language to Explore the Boundaries of the Spreadsheet Paradigm", Journal of Functional Programming, Volume 11 Number 2, March 2001, pp. 155–206.

[28] Jácome Cunha, João P. Fernandes, Jorge Mendes, Hugo Pacheco and João Saraiva, "Bidirectional Transformation of Model-Driven Spreadsheets. Springer Lecture Notes in Computer Science", Proceedings of the 5th International Conference on Theory and Practice of Model Transformations (ICMT), Springer, 2012, pp. 105–120.

[29] Andrew B. Begel, "Spoken Language Support for Software Development", IEEE Symposium on Visual Languages and Human Centric Computing, 2004, pp. 271 - 272.

[30] Jerome R. Bellegarda, "Spoken Language Understanding for Natural Interaction: The Siri Experience", Springer New York, Natural Interaction with Robots, Knowbots and Smartphones, 2014, pp. 3–14.

[31] Jason D. Williams, "Spoken dialogue systems: challenges and opportunities for research", IEEE Workshop on Automatic Speech Recognition & Understanding (ASRU), December 2009.

[32] Stephanie Seneff, "Response planning and generation in the MERCURY flight reservation system", Computer Speech & Language, Volume 16, Issues 34, 2002, pp. 283-312.

[33] James Allen et al., "PLOW: A Collaborative Task Learning Agent", Proceedings of the 22nd national conference on Advances in Artificial intelligence (AAAI), Volume 2, 2007, pp. 1514–1519.

Comparative Assessment of Mobile Navigation Applications using 2D Maps and Augmented Reality Interfaces

Mustafa Esengün, Gökhan İnce
Computer Engineering Department Istanbul Technical University
Istanbul, Turkey
Email: {esengun, gokhan.ince}@itu.edu.tr

***Abstract*—So far, 2D map-based navigation applications on mobile platforms have been dominating the market. However, with the rise of augmented reality technology, a new type of interface is introduced to the navigation applications. To this end, two mobile navigation applications having different interaction styles were developed for a task of navigation in Istanbul Technical University campus. The first application offers navigation within a 2D digital map view and the second application is an augmented reality browser, which provides navigation by displaying waypoints onto the phone's camera view. The aim of this study is to investigate how efficient these two different interfaces are in the tasks of navigation and exploring the campus area. In line with this purpose, a user experience test was conducted in the field and the results show that both interfaces have their own pros and cons, but they both accomplish their navigation duties with success.**

Keywords–user experience; augmented reality browser; mobile navigation.

I. Introduction

Mobile navigation applications are essential for people to figure out how to get from one point to another in any environment without getting lost. Teevan et al. [1] stated that the most common reason for performing a local search was to get directions to their target location (52%), followed by the desire to go somewhere (43%), to get a phone number of a place (28%) and to choose a specific place to visit (21%). Therefore, the main focus should not only be given to show the right path with as much clear directions as possible but also to take the elements of exploration and discovery into account. Another important factor in the development process is the type of user interaction with the application. Different interaction types may create different effects on the degree of exploration of the environment and user's satisfaction while using the application, both of which are needs to be investigated constituting the main aim of this study.

We chose to implement two different interfaces, each of which has different interaction style. The proof-of-concept system is proposed as a campus guide application to be used within the vicinity of Istanbul Technical University (ITU) [2]. The first application offers navigation functionality and features to explore the area, whose interface design was inspired from the existing Google Maps [3] application. The second application is an Augmented Reality (AR) browser application, which displays the buildings in the campus onto the live camera view of the smartphone as Points Of Interests (POI) and provides navigation by displaying arrows as waypoints directing the user to any destination. By conducting user experience tests, as well as the travel duration, the usability of these two interfaces and efficiency of these two guidance approaches were investigated.

The structure of the paper is as follows: In Section II, related researches and their differences with this study are presented. In Section III, the design and implementation details of the algorithms and applications are introduced. In Section IV, setup of the user experiments is presented, and the results are discussed. Lastly, in Section V the paper is concluded by presenting the main outcome of this study and the future work ideas.

II. Literature Review

The navigation applications allow people to find their route and explore their surroundings easily and quickly in the places they have not visited before without losing too much time [4]. Especially universities with huge campuses welcomes thousands of new students and visitors every year, and to help people find their route without getting lost, most of the universities have guidance signs located at different points around the campus. However, this kind of guidance causes extra burden for the people because they first have to spend time and energy to find those signs. To overcome this issue, different mobile solutions were developed, which are easier for the people to get access [5][6][7].

In order to get more help and benefit from the navigation applications, the interaction styles of applications plays an important role. By using advantages of recent technologies, navigation applications can provide rich contents to the users. Most of the existing mobile navigation applications use 2D map interface, which presents interactive items overlayed onto the map to provide information. This kind of interface allows user to see their surroundings from a bird's-eye view [7].

On the other hand, AR browsers offer a different kind of interactivity. The technology of AR carries the experience with the real world to a higher level by allowing to see more than what actually exists by combining the real world with the virtual data provided. AR combines the real physical world view with various media contents such as images, 3D models, animations and sounds in order to enhance the perception of the user among the environment or the objects. The media content related with real world locations and displayed onto the camera view of the phones make the users feel as if the objects really exist on those locations, which provides opportunity for the people to enhance their perception and get to know better about surroundings [8][9][10]. Another reason of usage of augmented reality in navigation applications is that AR provides a location-aware interface [9]. Since the study of Feiner et. al. [11], mobile AR applications have been one of the attractive research topics in academia and they showed that AR technology can guide the people to explore an area or a city which are not familiar to them.

In AR browser applications, as location-based AR applications, POIs are displayed onto the camera view by using information balloons or any other media content [4]. These applications use phone's camera, GPS, compass and other sensors to relate the digital content with the real world objects in order to provide much detailed information about that location[12][13]. There are couple of commercial AR applications available, such as, Wikitude [14], Layar [15] and Junaio [16], each of which enables displaying POIs on the camera view.

Comparison of user experience in using AR browser and 2D digital map applications has been discussed in some studies. Lee [13] proposed to use a 2D digital map, an AR browser and panoramic photographs interfaces to inform the tourists about the original view of the buildings which were damaged by an earthquake in Chirstchurch city. The user experience tests conducted in this study showed that 2D digital map interface was commonly used for browsing and finding the point of interests. Another application developed by Mulloni et. al. [18] provided a 2D digital map interface together with an AR browser interface within an application having a switching mode between them to offer navigation service. The results of user experience test of this study showed that AR browser interface was mostly used at crossings of the route where users tried to decide, which direction they need to turn, whereas they used 2D digital map interface mostly when they walked straight. In a similar study [17], three different applications, one with a 2D map interface developed using Google Maps Application Program Interface (API), another one with an AR browser interface and the last one with the combination of these two interfaces, were compared in terms of user experience for a navigation task. Results of this study showed that when AR browser interface was used, arriving at the destination took longer because of the obstacles on the route. The drawback of this system was that the route planning options in this interface was limited. Another outcome of this study was that using the AR browser interface user found shorter routes between two locations compared to that when using the 2D map because in the map those routes were either covered by trees or not included in the satellite images.

What distinguishes our study from the ones in the literature is the way of providing navigation service. To be more specific, AR interfaces in the literature borrowed either the 2D digital map interfaces for navigation purpose or only showed points of interests and expected the users to walk towards them. However, in our study, AR browser interface not only shows the point of interests but also it displays arrows as waypoints to guide the users their destination.

III. PROPOSED NAVIGATION APPLICATIONS

The shortest path between a selected source and target location is displayed to the users in both applications. Moreover, to help users to explore the campus, a search functionality is also implemented together with displaying buildings as groups, such as academic buildings, sport facilities, etc.

A. Finding the Shortest Path for Navigation

In both applications, the shortest path offered to the user is calculated by using Dijkstra's shortest path algorithm. For the implementation of this algorithm Liang's [19] method is used as a reference. The algorithm uses a weighted graph which includes nodes, edges and weights of each edges. The graph was created using Google Earth [20] software. To define nodes of the graph, pins are put onto the campus image for every building in the campus, and walkable areas between the buildings. Afterwards, the edges are specified and distance between each nodes are defined as the weights of the edges. A small part of the graph is shown in Figure 1, where the red lines show edges and the walkable paths for the users.

Figure 1. Representation of nodes and edges in the graph created in Google Earth program

The nodes are stored in an array with their descriptions and the edges are stored using an integer array, which has the index of the source node, followed by the index of the target node and the distance between the nodes as weights of the edges. The nodes created in Google Earth were exported and then parsed to extract and store the name, latitude and longitude information of each node to be used to construct these arrays. By using the coordinates of nodes, distance between two nodes are calculated using *Haversine Formula* [21] and then stored as weight of the edges. Haversine formula as defined in (1a)-(1f) gives us the distance between two coordinates $pos1(lat1, long1)$ and $pos2(lat2, long2)$. It presumes a spherical Earth with radius 6376.5 (1a). In order to convert $lat1, long1$ and $lat2, long2$ from degrees, minutes, and seconds to radians, each value is multiplied by $\pi/180$. It calculates the changes in latitude and longitude as in (1b) and (1c) respectively. Next, it uses (1d), (1e), (1f) to calculate the great-circle distance between two points, that is, the shortest distance over the earth's surface.

$$R = earth'sradius = 6376.5, \quad (1a)$$
$$\Delta lat = lat2.\pi/180 - lat1.\pi/180, \quad (1b)$$
$$\Delta long = long2.\pi/180 - long1.\pi/180, \quad (1c)$$
$$a = \sin^2(\Delta lat/2) + \cos(lat1). \quad (1d)$$
$$.\cos(lat2).\sin^2(\Delta long/2),$$
$$c = 2.\arcsin(\sqrt{a}), \quad (1e)$$
$$d = R.c \quad (1f)$$

where,

- lat : Latitude
- $long$: Longitude
- Δlat : change in latitude
- $\Delta long$: change in longitude
- a : the square of the half of the straight line distance between two points
- c : the great circle distance in radians
- d : distance

All the edges in this graph are bidirectional. Therefore, when an edge is defined as from A to B, another edge is also needed to be defined as from B to A. When the user wants to get to a target from his/her current position, finding the source node requires an extra calculation because user's position is defined with the corresponding GPS data and it may not be the same with any of the nodes in the graph. Therefore, when the user wants to walk or drive from his/her current position to a target destination, the source node in the algorithm is chosen by finding the closest node to the user's position. In order to find the closest node to the user's position, distance between user's position and all the nodes are again calculated using Haversine Formula.

After constructing the graph and specifying the node that is closest to the user, Dijkstra's algorithm [19] was implemented to find the shortest path from a source node to a target node. The shortest path between two nodes is defined as the path with the minimum total weights. The algorithm is known as a single-source shortest path algorithm because it finds the shortest path from the source node to all the other nodes. The pseudo code of the Dijkstra's Shortest Path Algorithm is shown in Figure 2.

function SHORTESTPATH(source)
Let V denote the set of vertices in the graph and v denotes any of the vertices in V;
Let T be a set that contains the vertices whose paths to source are known;
Initially T contains source vertex with cost[source] = 0;
while $sizeof\ T \leq n$ **do**
find v in V - T with the smallest cost[u] + w(u,v) value among all u in T;
add v to T and set cost[v] = cost[u] + w(u,v);
end while
end function

Figure 2. The pseudo code of the Dijkstra's Shortest Path Algorithm.

The algorithm returns the nodes of the path from source to destination node that were used to display route information in the applications [19]. The intermediate nodes are used to show waypoints in AR browser application and used to draw the path in the 2D digital map application.

B. Navigation Application with a 2D Digital Map Interface

This application was developed as an effort to provide navigation service and also other informative features to help the new visitors easily adapt themselves to the ITU campus. Users can search a building and get detailed information about it (Figure 3a). The 2D map interface shows the user location with a blue dot, which is updated on the map as the user moves. Moreover, on this blue dot a small arrow shows which direction the user is currently looking at. Users can also view the buildings in groups, such as academic buildings, sports facilities, dormitories etc. (Figure 3b). User can choose source and destination locations (Figure 4a) and follow the highlighted path to the destination (Figure 4b). Zoom and map orientation controls are also available in the interface.

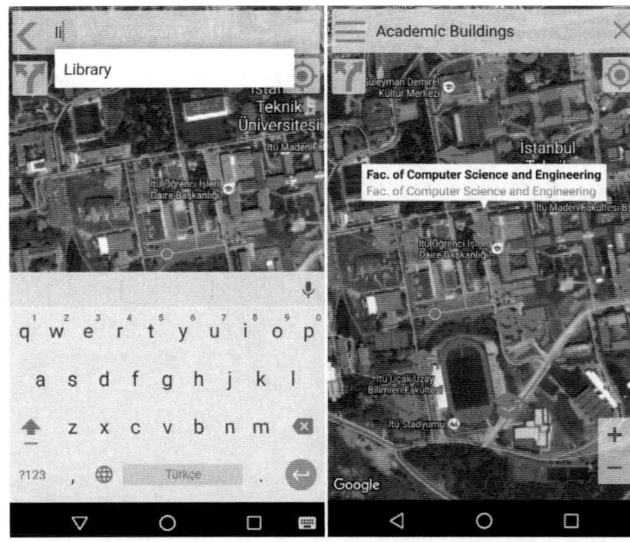

(a) **Search places** function (b) Displaying buildings in groups

Figure 3. 2D map interface

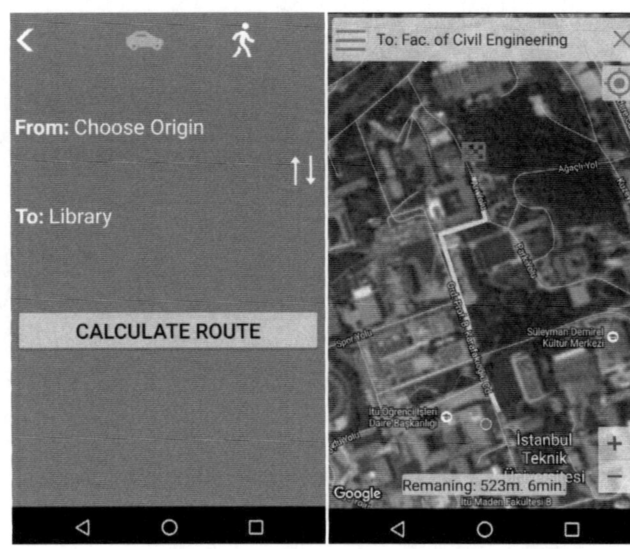

(a) Navigation menu (b) Route information

Figure 4. Shortest route to a destination

C. Navigation Application with an AR Browser Interface

POIs are presented to the user by blue boxes overlayed onto the phone's camera. POIs were defined as the buildings in the campus. The distance information between the user and the buildings are also presented. Users can also perceive their orientation to the buildings by using the radar component (Figure 5a). The features of displaying buildings in groups and searching a building from a dropdown list is also available in this application (Figure 5b). Moreover, users are free to define a range parameters to see the POIs that are located only within that range. This feature is useful if the user prefers to see only the buildings that are close to current location. A user can select any POI to see the detailed information about the building as in Figure 6a.

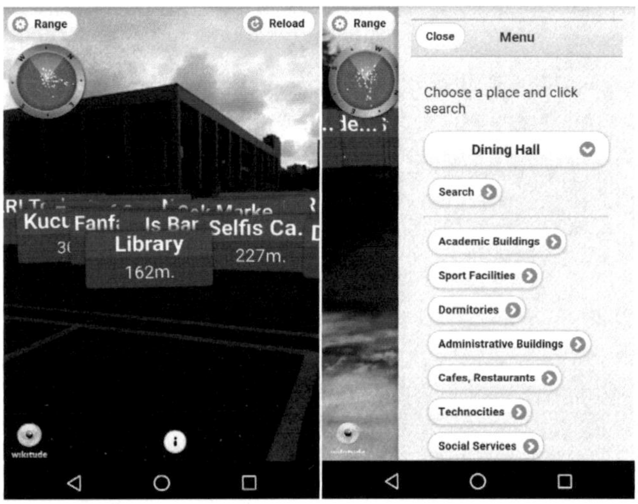

(a) POIs representation (b) Searh menu

Figure 5. AR browser application interface

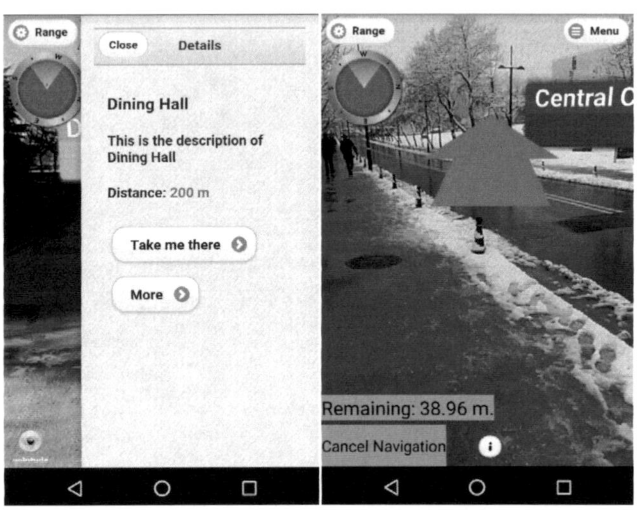

(a) Detailed builging information (b) Target and waypoint representation

Figure 6. AR browser navigation interface

Since this interface uses the camera of the phone, the route information is provided using a first-person view. The route is displayed to the user as a series of waypoints represented by red arrows (Figure 6b). Once the user gets close enough to the first waypoint, the next one appears and user is directed to the second, and so on. If the new visible waypoint is not in the field of vision of the user, s/he gets directed with a small green arrow to the new waypoint (Figure 7).

Figure 7. Arrow directing to the new waypoint

IV. EXPERIMENTS AND RESULTS

A. *Hardware and Software Settings*

Both applications were developed for Android smartphones and tested with a Nexus 5 mobile device. The application with 2D digital map interface was developed using Google Maps API [22]. By using this API, Google's map is integrated into the application and GPS sensor data was fetched. For the application with AR browser interface Wikitude Software Development Kit (SDK) [23]was used. By using this SDK, any type of information can be easily augmented onto the camera view of the smarthphones. Coordinates, names and descriptions of POIs were arranged and uploaded to a web service. The application only requests this data when it is first started and parses the data to overlay the POI's information onto the camera view as shown in (Figure 5a).

B. *Experimental Conditions*

The user experience tests were conducted with two groups of participants consisting of 5 people each (3 female, 7 male) from ages 23 to 37. They were asked to follow predefined routes unfamiliar to them. Two successive routes were defined. First group of the participants were asked to follow the first route (699 meters) with the 2D map interface and the second route (307 meters) with the AR browser interface. Conversely, second group of the participants were asked to follow the first route with the AR browser interface and the second route with the 2D map interface. By doing this, the potential effect of task familiarity on the results was intended to be eliminated. The participants were instructed to think aloud during the tests. After each route was completed, the participants were asked to fill out two questionnaires about the interface they used. The first questionnaire was called NASA TLX [24] form, which consisted of six questions with a Likert scale of 1 to 21 (1: the lowest, 21: the highest). It is applied to the participants to obtain information about how much mental, physical, temporal and psychological work load they felt for the given task. The second questionnaire was the Post Study System Usability Questionnaire (PSSUQ) [25], which had 19 questions and measured the overall user satisfaction with the applications, usefulness of the applications, information quality and interface quality of the applications.

C. Results

According to the demographic information about the users, none of them used an AR application before, whereas all of them used a 2D digital map application. Overall time spent by the two groups with the two interfaces are summarized in Table I. It is apparent that no matter which route was used, 2D digital map interface took less time to arrive to the destination than the AR browser interface.

TABLE I. MEAN ROUTE COMPLETION TIMES.

Group #	Route 1 (699 m.)	Route 2 (307 m.)
Group 1	with AR 13 min.	with 2D map 7.4 min.
Group 2	with 2D map 7.4 min.	with AR 8.2 min.

The results of NASA TLX questionnaire in Figure 8 showed that the application with the 2D map interface demanded less mental workload than the AR application. The probable reason for a difference of 2.3 points was that the participants used their intuition more with the AR interface to find the target. The application with the 2D map interface demanded less physical workload (4.8/21) than the application with the AR browser interface (12.6/21) since they needed to hold the phone always at the eye level to see the arrow and other information. Moreover, it was found out that AR browser interface caused negative feelings such as 12.9% more stress, irritation etc. because of the low stabilization of the arrow caused by hand movements and frequent GPS signal fluctuations. In terms of temporal worload, which was about how much time pressure the users felt due to the given tasks and whether the interfaces put the users in rush or not, the 2D map interface was evaluated higher by 2.2 points since some of the participants missed the route updates and then rushed to get on the previous route in order to not extend the distance towards the target. The results also show that the participants spent less effort to achieve the tasks with the 2D digital map interface (7/21) compared to the AR browser interface (9.5/21) since with the 2D application some of the participants looked the route only couple of times especially when they got close to the turning points, but with the AR application participants were always in the interaction with the application. Lastly, participants evaluated themselves more successful with the 2D digital map interface, since they arrived to the target location easier using the 2D digital map interface compared to their performance with the AR browser interface.

The results of PSSUQ is presented in Figure 9. In terms of user satisfaction, PSSUQ results showed that the 2D digital map interface (71.1% of user satisfaction) is better than AR browser interface (56.2% of user satisfaction). The reason that the users were less satisfied with the AR browser interface was due to the longer task completion times and the amount of the frustration they felt with the interface. In terms of interface quality, 2D digital map interface was considered simpler than the AR browser interface, which resulted in the 8.6% difference in the interface quality scores of the two interfaces. Moreover, 2D digital map interface was scored as 71% in terms of usefulness while AR browser interface was scored as 56% because the 2D digital map interface was easier to learn because it looked more familiar and usual than the AR browser interface, and also it was considered as more effective in the navigation tasks the participants fulfilled. Considering the information quality scores, because of the color choices (for some participants) and the low stabilization of the arrows the participants experienced with the AR browser interface, the 2D digital map interface was preferred. However, the radar feature of the AR browser interface was found useful by the participants since it helped them to stay on the right path during the navigation and also to get back on the right path when they got lost.

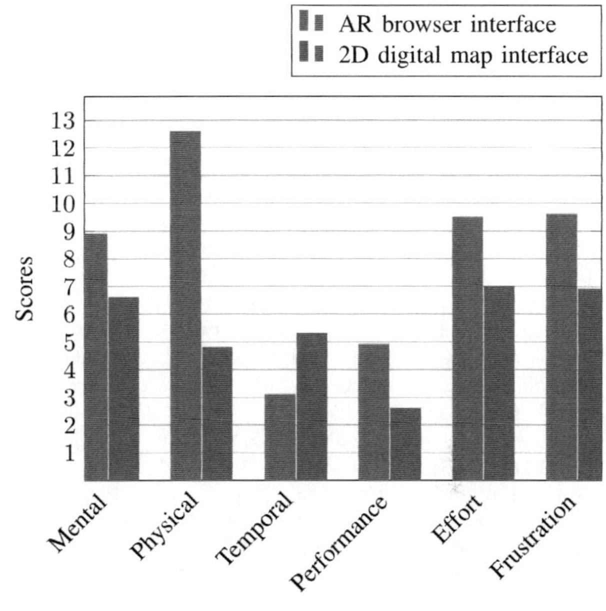

Figure 8. NASA TLX questionnaire results.

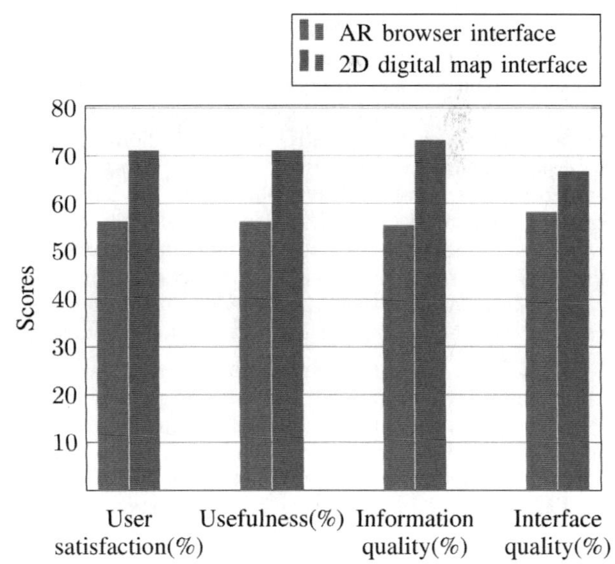

Figure 9. PSSUQ results.

Seven participants stated that they would prefer 2D digital map interface, whereas, three participants stated that the AR browser interface would be their choice. Moreover, four of the participants suggested that the combination of these two interfaces would be more useful. A seven degree scale (1: the highest, 7: the lowest) was provided to the participants to evaluate the degree of exploration they felt with the two interfaces. The answers showed that the 2D digital map interface helped them more to explore the area while walking and the average degree of exploration score given to 2D digital map interface was 4.3, whereas, average degree of exploration score of AR browser interface was 5.4 since using the AR application, users were regularly focusing on the arrow and keeping their eyes on the screen almost all the time. Moreover, the search places feature was mentioned as more useful in the AR browser interface especially when the POIs was overlapping.

Besides these questionnaires the thoughts of the participants stated during the experiments were also examined. At the beginning of the navigation task, each participant tried to orient him/herself to the map according to the direction that they are facing to. Some of the participants mentioned that radar component in the AR browser interface was helpful for finding the initial orientation. They also stated that the arrow, which shows the orientation of the user in the 2D digital map interface appeared and disappeared too much, which caused confusion about the direction to be followed. Moreover, participants stated that they had to look at the arrow all the time, which was tiring and might pose danger while walking. The blue boxes showing the target POI were mentioned as useful especially when they had difficulty to decide towards which direction they needed to walk. Most of the participants found the 2D digital map interface more helpful to get to know the environment and the route. However, when the GPS signal shows the user's location wrongly even for a moment, some of the participants got confused and felt anxious. In conclusion, all of the participants stated that the combination of these two interfaces would be more effective for a navigation task.

V. CONCLUSION AND FUTURE WORK

In this study, two different mobile navigation interfaces were compared in terms of user experience by conducting an experiment using a navigation scenario. The results of the experiment revealed the advantages and disadvantages of both interfaces. Specifically, using 2D digital map interface participants spent less time to arrive to target locations. Moreover, in terms of physical and mental workload, the 2D digital map interface was less demanding. User satisfaction was found to be higher with the 2D digital map interface since the participants found it simple and functional for the given tasks. The radar component in the AR browser interface was considered useful for orientation and locating the target point.

As a future work, the combination of these two interfaces will be implemented, which was actually suggested by some of the participants. With this new interface, displaying the point of interests according to users' preference will be also provided. It is also thought to be a useful research that an AR application similar to the one in this study can be implemented in optical head-mounted displays, such as, Google Glass or Samsung Gear VR, and tested with the users in order to observe people's behaviour and usability of these type of devices in navigation tasks.

REFERENCES

[1] J. Teevan, A. Karlson, S. Amini, A. Brush, and J. Krumm, "Understanding the Importance of Location, Time, and People in Mobile Local Search Behavior", in Proceedings of the 13th International Conference on MobileHCI 2011, Stockholm, Sweden. ACM, 2011, pp. 77-80 ISBN: 978-1-4503-0541-9, URL: http://dl.acm.org/citation.cfm?id=2037386 [accessed: 2015-11-27].

[2] "ITU Webpage", 2016, URL: http://www.itu.edu.tr [accessed: 2016-01-02].

[3] "Google Maps", 2015, URL: http://www.maps.google.com [accessed: 2015-09-05].

[4] G. Cherchi, F. Sorrentino, and R. Scateni, "AR Turn-By-Turn Navigation in Small Urban Areas and Information Browsing", in STAG - Eurographics Italian Chapter Conference 2014, Italy. The Eurographics Association, 2014, pp. 37-40, ISBN: 978-3-905674-72-9, URL: http://diglib.eg.org/ [accessed: 2015-11-20].

[5] T. J. Mehigan and I. Pitt, Harnessing Wireless Technologies for Campus Navigation by Blind Students and Visitors, Springer Berlin Heidelberg, Berlin, Heidelberg, 2012, pp. 67-74, in ICCHP 2012, Linz, Austria, July 11-13, 2012, Proceedings, Part II, ISBN: 978-3-642-31534-3.

[6] I. M. Ruffin, A. Murphy, V. Larkin, and J. E. Gilbert, "CAMPNAV: A Campus Navigation System For the Visually Impaired", Proceedings of E-Learn: World Conference on E-Learning in Corporate, Government, Healthcare, and Higher Education 2006, pp. 2944-2951. AACE, Honolulu, Hawaii, USA, 2006.

[7] T. S. Wang, D. Tjondronegoro, M. Docherty, W. Song, and J. Fuglsang, "A Recommendation for Designing Mobile Pedestrian Navigation System in University Campuses", In Proceedings of the 25th OzCHI '13, 2013, Adelaide, Australia. ACM, 2013, pp. 3-12, ISBN: 978-1-4503-2525-7, URL: http://dl.acm.org/ [accessed: 2015-11-27].

[8] J. R. Vallino, "Interactive Augmented Reality", Technical Report, University of Rochester, 1998.

[9] R. Azuma, "A Survey of Augmented Reality", Presence: Teleoperators and Virtual Environments, Vol. 6, no. 4, 1997, pp. 355-385.

[10] D. W. F. van Krevelen and R. Poelman, "A Survey of Augmented Reality Technologies, Applications and Limitations", The International Journal of Virtual Reality, Vol. 9, No. 2, 2010, pp. 1-20.

[11] S. Feiner, B. MacIntyre, T. Hollerer, and A. Webster, "A touring machine: prototyping 3D mobile augmented reality systems for exploring the urban environment", Personal Technologies, vol. 1, no. 4, 1997, pp. 208-217, ISSN: 1617-4917.

[12] T. Langlotz, J. Grubert, and R. Grasset, "Augmented Reality Browsers: Essential Products or Only Gadgets?", Communications of the ACM, vol. 56, no. 11, 2013, pp. 34-36, ISSN: 0001-0782.

[13] G. A. Lee, A. Dünser, S. Kim, and M. Billinghurst, "CityViewAR: A Mobile Outdoor AR Application for City Visualization", IEEE ISMAR-AMH Proceedings, Nov. 2012, pp. 57-64, URL: http://ieeexplore.ieee.org/ [accessed: 2015-11-22].

[14] "Wikitude", 2015, URL: http://www.wikitude.com [accessed: 2015-10-03].

[15] "Layar", 2015, URL: http://www.layar.com [accessed: 2015-10-10].

[16] "Junaio", 2015, URL: http://www.junaio.com [accessed: 2015-10-17].

[17] A. Dünser, M. Billinghurst, J. Wen, V. Lehtinen, and A. Nurminen, "Exploring the use of handheld AR for outdoor navigation", Computers & Graphics, vol. 36, Issue 8, 2012, pp. 1084-1095, ISSN: 0097-8493.

[18] A. Mulloni, H. Seichter, and D. Schmalstieg, "User Experiences with Augmented Reality Aided Navigation on Phones", in ISMAR, Oct. 2011, pp.229-230, URL: http://ieeexplore.ieee.org/ [accessed: 2015-11-22].

[19] Y. Liang, Weighted Graphs and Applications. Pearson Education, 2011, chapter 31, pp. 1094-1127, in Introduction to Java programming: Comprehensive version (8th ed., International ed.).

[20] "Google Earth", 2015, URL: http://www.earth.google.com [accessed: 2015-08-30].

[21] R. W. Sinnott, "Virtues of the Haversine", Sky and telescope 11/1984; 68(2, article 159):158.

[22] "Google Maps API", 2015, URL: http://developers.google.com/maps/ [accessed: 2015-09-06].

[23] "Wikitude SDK", 2015, URL: http://www.wikitude.com/products/wikitude-sdk/ [accessed: 2015-10-19].

[24] S. G. Hart, "NASA-Task Load Index (NASA-TLX); 20 Years Later", Proceedings of the HFES 50th Annual Meeting, vol. 50, no. 9, 2006, pp. 904-908.

[25] JR. Lewis, "Psychometric Evaluation of the Post-Study System Usability Questionnaire: The PSSUQ", Proceedings of the HFES Annual Meeting, vol. 36, no. 16, 1992, pp. 1259-1260.

Technology Concepts to Improve Knowledge Sharing During Maintenance

Susanna Aromaa, Iina Aaltonen, Antti Väätänen
Human Factors in Complex Systems
VTT Technical Research Centre of Finland Ltd
Tampere, Finland
email: susanna.aromaa@vtt.fi; iina.aaltonen@vtt.fi; antti.vaatanen@vtt.fi

Abstract—**Industrial maintenance is a complex and knowledge-intensive field. Maintenance technicians need to have special professional skills and easy access to versatile and situationally relevant knowledge. The aim of this paper is to understand the nature and needs of maintenance work and to propose new technology concepts so as to support knowledge gathering and sharing. As a result of studies in two maintenance cases, it was found that communication between different actors is a key element in maintenance. Therefore, three different technology concepts were proposed in order to support and enhance communication. These concepts include augmented reality and wearable technologies that will provide new and efficient ways to help maintenance technicians in gathering and sharing task-specific information and long-term knowledge. In the next phase of this on-going research project, these technology concepts will be tested and evaluated with maintenance technicians.**

Keywords: maintenance; knowledge; technology concept; augmented reality; wearables.

I. INTRODUCTION

The nature of maintenance work can be described as a "combination of all technical, administrative and managerial actions during the life cycle of an item intended to retain it in, or restore it to, a state in which it can perform the required function" [1]. Reason [2] defines maintenance activities as (1) unscheduled operations, including corrective maintenance, and disturbance- and failure-preventive operations (opportunity-based maintenance); (2) scheduled disturbance- and failure-preventive operations; (3) inspections; and (4) calibration and testing.

To define knowledge in a maintenance task, it is important to understand different types of knowledge: explicit and tacit. Explicit or codified knowledge refers to knowledge that is transmittable in formal, systematic language [3]. Tacit knowledge has a personal quality, which makes it hard to formalize and communicate. Tacit knowledge is deeply rooted in action, commitment, and involvement in a specific context [4]. In addition, it is essential to distinguish knowledge from information and data. For this purpose, Mertins et al. [5] use a continuum ranging from data via information to knowledge in knowledge management. Data can be facts and figures which relay something specific, but are not organized in any way. Information is a flow of messages, while knowledge is created and organized by the very flow of information, anchored in the commitment and beliefs of its holder [4]. We consider communication here as a means to share knowledge.

Several studies have compared augmented reality (AR) technologies and the more traditional ways to provide maintenance instructions [6][7][8][9][10][11][12]. By definition, AR allows the user to see the real world, with virtual objects superimposed upon or composited with the real world [13]. Results suggest that AR technologies are usable in providing instructions because they are often faster to use, errors occur less frequently, and operators approve of the use of the technology. Nee et al. [14] have summarised a few AR-assisted maintenance systems. There are only few studies about the use of AR for remote collaboration where service personnel can discuss with each other [15][16].

Baber et al. [17] have shown that wearable computing human-computer interaction can be divided into three main activities: (1) using interaction devices; (2) using display devices, and (3) domain activity. Their study also considers what kind of dialogues these activities generate. New wearable technology solutions, such as head-mounted displays (HMD) and smart watches, enable new interaction methods and online connectivity in an industrial environment. In the military domain, various HMDs and wearable solutions have been developed and tested in future soldier projects for example [18][19][20]. For industrial maintenance, however, demonstrators and concepts of wearable maintenance systems have been developed [21][22], but – to the best of our knowledge – field trial studies with HMDs and smart watches have not been conducted in the work context.

The purpose of this study was to propose new technology concepts to support knowledge gathering and sharing during maintenance. Two different industrial maintenance cases were studied, and three technology concepts to support communication were proposed. The paper is organized as follows. Section 2 describes the conducted field studies and Section 3 presents the findings. The three technology concepts are defined in Section 4 and discussed in Section 5. Conclusions are drawn in Section 6.

II. FIELD STUDIES

Maintenance work was studied in two cases. The first observation and evaluation session was related to the marine domain, and the second study was made in the crane industry. In both of these, data collection followed the same

Figure 1. Checking the condition and function of an engine's overhaul hatch.

procedure. The data were collected in two phases, by applying a semi-structured interview method and by direct observations of maintenance tasks. Two maintenance workers were observed and interviewed at both sites.

The interviews followed the principles of core-task analysis [23]. The interviews consisted of the following themes: demographics, description of the maintenance activities, safety risks, collaboration, tools and information systems, reporting, procedures and manuals, and tacit knowledge of the work community and maintenance work.

The interviews were audio-recorded and transcribed by a subcontractor. The observations ranged from a general overview of a maintenance site to a selected and detailed maintenance task. In all observation sessions, photos, videos and notes were taken during the process of maintenance tasks. The observations each lasted from one to two hours.

In the first case – solutions for the marine industry (Figure 1) – the focus was on a planned and preventive field service related to engines in a mid-sized oil tanker. The maintenance work included main and auxiliary engine overhauls. The overhaul work was done by seven maintenance workers over a period of two weeks.

The second case was related to a crane company and service activities in their customer's facilities (Figure 2). The crane company's five-membered service team was located in a large steel company's factory where the team performed planned and preventive services and on-demand corrective maintenance. Most of the equipment serviced – hoists and cranes – were from the crane company but the team also services other manufacturer's lifting equipment at the customers' facilities.

Figure 2. Inspecting and lubricating a hoist system.

III. MAINTENANCE WORK IN INDUSTRIAL CASES

Based on the field study, three things arise as core demands in the maintenance task: it is important for the maintenance technician (1) to know the object/product/item and how to repair it; (2) to keep downtime as short as possible; and (3) to have good communication skills. The first two issues are included in the maintenance terminology standard EN 13306 [1] (e.g. time related terms are defined in it), but the communication aspect is not mentioned. The importance of the social and communication related activities in maintenance work have been noted by [24], and was also supported by our findings. Three out of four maintenance technicians answered the question "What are the qualities of a good maintenance technician?" that he/she needs to have good communication skills. Maintenance technicians need to communicate with many people, such as co-workers, technical support and customers. In the marine case, communication can take place with people from the shipyard, the ship's crew, co-workers and also people from other maintenance companies. In addition, there can be several different people who represent one of these groups. In the crane case, the customer was a manufacturing company and their representatives were, for example, the factory foreman and a crane driver. From a model created for knowledge gathering and sharing in maintenance [25], it is possible to see that there are many people (and also other agents) involved in maintenance.

In the studied cases, communication took place mainly face-to-face or via mobile phones: the service technicians asked for help or other information from other co-workers or technical support. According to Orr [26], most of the communication between service technicians is related to the maintenance work they have done to the machines and other work issues such as timetables. Furthermore, service technicians often tell each other stories about past fixes and difficulties in them by a broken machine or over a cup of coffee. Franssila [27] reported that, according to the maintenance technicians, the most reasonable way to share tacit knowledge is face-to-face conversations with people working on the field.

The management of knowledge in the service industry can be challenging. Franssila [27] has listed several challenges, such as (1) the inadequacy of formal documentation; (2) unreliable networks preventing efficient knowledge management; (3) information of new products (e.g., new updates) is difficult to share in the field; and (4) tacit knowledge from the field is difficult to channel to other members in an organization. In our study, maintenance technicians reported that there is a great deal of information available, but sometimes it is difficult to find it from the information systems. It is also possible that the information is in multiple places such as in emails, manuals, notebooks or other systems. In addition, it is sometimes difficult to say whether the information in paper manuals is current and up-to-date. Most of the information gathered from the field is reported in written form. However, maintenance technicians use also their mobile phones to take pictures to add to reports.

Knowledge management in maintenance activities can contribute to the safety and reliability of industrial plants. Dhillon [28] has listed causal factors for critical incidents and reported events concerned with human maintenance errors in power plants, and many of these are directly or indirectly linked to knowledge: faulty procedures, poor unit and equipment identification, poor training and work practices. In addition, Dhillon and Liu [29] have given a comprehensive review of human error in maintenance.

Maintenance technicians need to be skilled workers. Tasks are often technically demanding and safety-critical, and there is always a time pressure. These are reasons for novice workers to work with more experienced co-workers in the beginning. Based on our interviews, most of the learning happens in a real environment from other co-workers: apprentices learn to work with their mentors through observation, imitation and practice. It can also be called on-the-job learning. The use of these approaches means that there is great deal of tacit knowledge that does not transfer just through manuals, instructions or training. In Nonaka's [4] tacit knowledge theory called "Dynamic Theory of Organizational Knowledge Creation", this process of creating tacit knowledge through a shared experience between a novice and an expert is termed "socialization". The modes of knowledge creation introduced in the theory describe the knowledge transfer in our study well.

The context of work creates challenges to the maintenance work. In these two cases, it could be observed that the working environment can be noisy, dark, greasy and hot. Work could also include working in high places (e.g., on the top of cranes) or confined spaces (e.g., inside engines). For example, during the main engine overhaul in the marine case, the maintenance worker had to get inside the engine through a small hatch on its side. In addition, the maintenance work can be performed in an environment where there is other traffic such as automatic vehicles and pedestrians. Technicians also carry different tools such as hand tools, power tools and special measuring instruments with them. In addition, the operating environment can sometimes be too challenging to use smartphones or tablet PCs or laptops, or a wireless network may not be available.

IV. PROPOSED TECHNOLOGY CONCEPTS

Based on the findings from the field studies, we selected two communication-related themes for investigation: getting help and reporting. Getting help and support from others is one key element in maintenance work. At the moment, it is mainly done by calling other people using a mobile phone. Additionally, reporting is a key element in sharing the knowledge to other people. Currently, the service companies can have several different reporting systems, including the customers' reporting systems, to be completed after the maintenance task. The documentation format is mainly in written form, although some pictures are taken with mobile phones. In addition, writing is done "back" in the office, located some distance from the maintenance site.

Three technology concepts were suggested by the research study group (researchers and company representatives) so as to improve the communication (knowledge sharing) when requesting help/information or reporting. The concepts are: (1) remote assistance; (2) instructions delivery; and (3) data collection/reporting. These technologies were selected based on the company interests and also based on an idea that maintenance technicians have an online access to up-to-date knowledge, and that knowledge can be shared in a more comprehensive and interactive way. There was interest towards many different use cases and, finally two technology concepts were selected for the marine case and one concept for the crane case.

A. *Concept 1: Augmented reality guidance*

In this concept (Figure 3), the maintenance technician receives help that is available in information systems via a tablet PC and an AR application. In planned and preventive service, the technician goes through a set of tasks. The purpose of this system is to give more comprehensive and interactive instructions to the maintenance technician. The maintenance technician will be given a list of maintenance steps and visual guidance on what to do in the following steps. The system allows the maintenance technicians to proceed at their own pace and acknowledge when a maintenance step is completed. The system therefore ensures that all necessary maintenance procedures are performed, and enables the information to be updated in the customer's system. Other technical support personnel are not needed.

B. *Concept 2: Remote assistance*

In this concept, technical help is provided to the maintenance technician via a tablet PC (Figure 4). The idea is to support communication and information sharing between different professionals. In maintenance work, technicians can face a situation in which they do not know

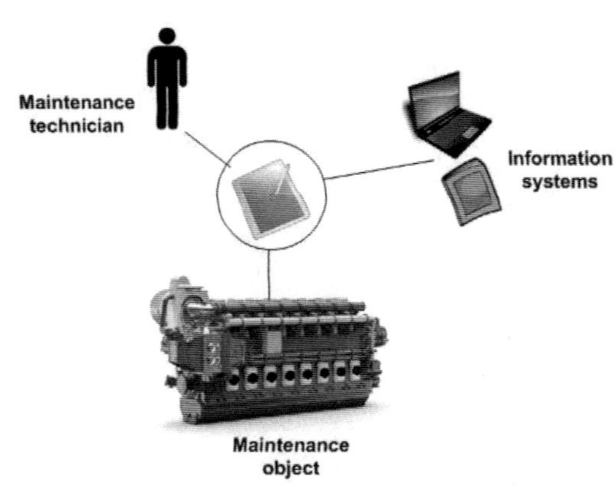

Figure 3. Augmented reality guidance concept

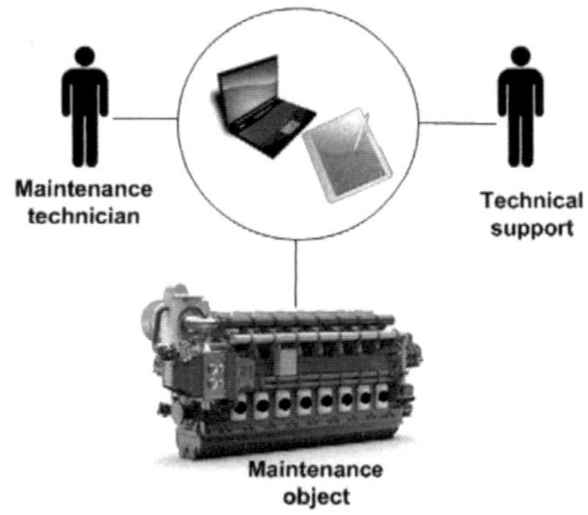

Figure 4. Remote assistance concept

how to proceed or else need support in doing so. A similar situation occurs when there is no guidance on a specific tool nor written instructions on the values of how a certain system is trimmed. In these situations, the technicians typically call their colleagues for help. The purpose of the remote assistance system is to support the maintenance technician on site. The maintenance technician will receive help and advice online from a technical support person located in a remote office. The maintenance technician will use the tablet PC and its camera as a medium to transfer images or video of the object being maintained. He/she can discuss with the technical support and be given visual indicators to the images on the tablet on how and with which components to proceed next. They are able to share the same visual image of the maintenance object. The system can also be implemented using AR technology, which – presumably – makes it easier for the technician to locate the targeted objects. The technical support will use a computer to see what the maintenance technician is doing and give instructions to him/her. The support person can also ask the technician to reposition the tablet's camera to a better viewing angle. This type of system gives the possibility for the related information to be saved to an information system for later access.

C. *Concept 3: Data collection and reporting*

In this concept (Figure 5), the communication between information systems and a maintenance technician is maintained using wearable devices. The concept utilizes a combination of three different wearable devices: a smart phone, a smart watch and smart glasses. The system facilitates checking information on the work tasks and maintenance object on-site. The maintenance procedures performed need to be reported back to the customer's information system. This concept was proposed in order to make reporting easier on site and to shorten the reporting time. With the smart watch, the maintenance technician is able to select the maintained object and component from a structured interface, and choose either picture-taking or

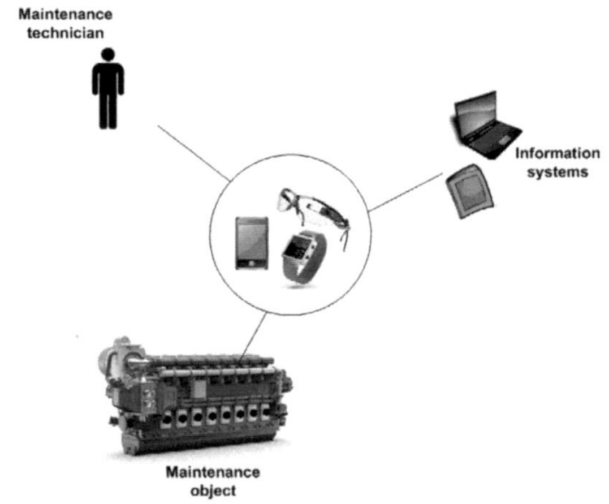

Figure 5. Data collection and reporting concept

error reporting, which are directly linked to the component selected. The smart glasses are used for checking information and taking pictures hands-free. The smart phone is used for adding text to the reports and for locating a maintenance target. This concept supports working in conditions where both hands are needed, and enables fast online reporting. It can also be used in situations when the technician needs information on earlier procedures, or numerical and statistical data on the functioning of the object maintained.

D. *Traditional and envisaged practices*

The difference between traditional and envisaged practices is illustrated in Figure 6. In addition, we hypothesize that benefits are gained from improvements in the quality of knowledge sharing and time savings in reporting.

V. Discussion

The purpose of this study was to understand the key features and requirements in maintenance work, and to propose new technology concepts to support knowledge gathering and sharing during maintenance. Based on the studies, it was found that social and communicational aspects are also important in maintenance work. Therefore, the project group focused on developing new technology concepts to support these aspects, especially the activities of getting help and reporting. Finally, three technology concepts were proposed and they are discussed here.

The augmented reality guidance concept is quite thoroughly researched as an instruction delivery tool in many studies [6][7][8][9][10][11][12][13][30][31]. Those results suggest that AR technologies are usable in providing instructions. In particular, this concept can be useful in demanding maintenance tasks that are rarely carried out or in situations where it is not possible to contact other people.

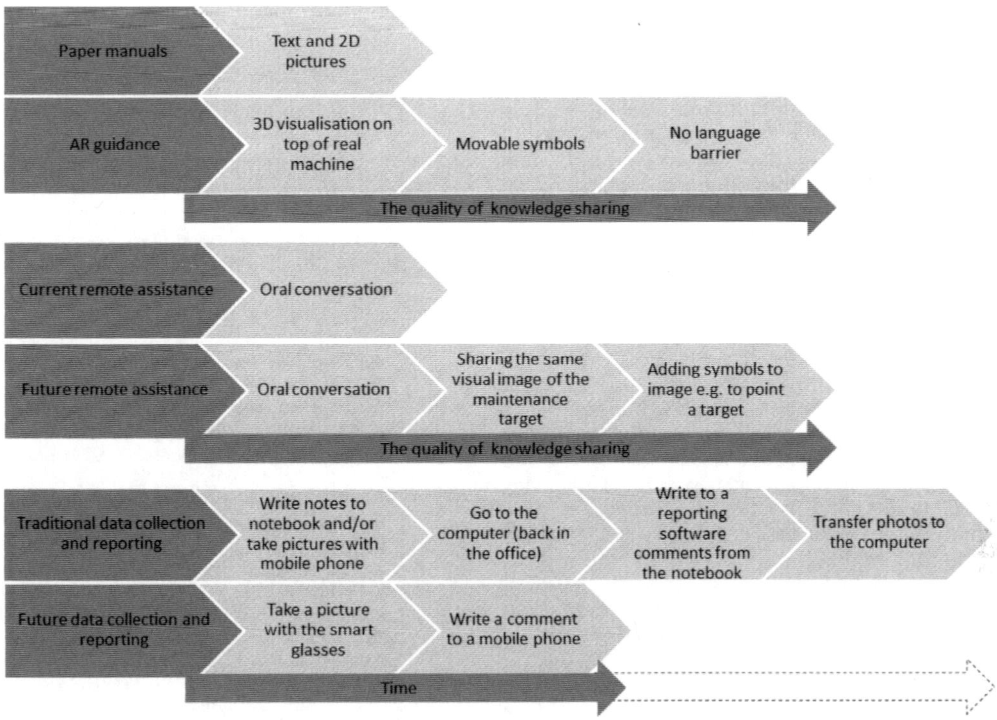

Figure 6. Comparison of current and future maintenance practices . The arrows show the expected benefits.

One of the advantages of this concept is that these instructions are easier to keep updated, and they can be more illustrative than paper manuals. It is possible, however, that this kind of technology concept is usable only in rare cases. Usually the maintenance staff is skilled and do not need instructions, or if help is needed, it is easier and faster to call a colleague. The selection of a medium for this purpose is also an issue, e.g., is the tablet-PC the best medium?. Similarly, it is also important to thoroughly consider how the information is presented in the AR solution [32].

The remote assistance concept is promising in the sense that it makes it possible to share the same visual image of the situation with others [15][16]. In addition, positive results have been reported using shared visual 3D images during the design [33][34][35]. In these studies, a virtual representation of the design object has supported knowledge sharing and provided a platform to communicate with each other in a more intuitive way. The intuitiveness is supported by the remote assistance concept by enabling a technical support person to point out some essential objects or give other interactive guidance. Compared to the currently used mobile phone calls this brings knowledge sharing closer to Nonaka's [4] "socialization" mode of creating knowledge in which tacit knowledge is created through shared experience. A possible challenge in this concept is that an online connection may not be available or it does not work reliably and uninterrupted. Furthermore, advanced remote assistance communication may take more time than using a mobile phone and increase distraction from the maintenance work.

The concept of using wearables for data collection and reporting has a chance to shorten the reporting time and improve the quality of the knowledge sharing to the customers and other people reading the reports. The expected benefit is in the automation of time-consuming secondary tasks in maintenance. Another benefit in this concept is the aim to keep maintenance both of the technicians' hands free so that they can focus on performing repair tasks. The working environment may require free hands, e.g., when using tools, climbing stairs or supporting oneself with the railings in high places. However, wearable devices have very limited screen sizes and input methods: a touch screen or gesture recognition may not be applicable in all demanding maintenance environments. Challenges can also arise from the simultaneous use of multiple devices and the selection of the best technology combination for maintenance work.

The adoption of new technologies may generate new benefits for various stakeholders such as maintenance technicians, companies and/or customers. Most of the benefits for maintenance technicians derive from the availability of up-to-date knowledge, and automated secondary tasks. Therefore, the maintenance technicians can focus on their core tasks, and allow them to work more safely, and work faster and with less mistakes and frustration. At the service company level, this will provide benefits such as improved productivity and better quality in maintenance. Customers will gain most benefits from short downtime in production, better scheduled services and enhanced communication with the maintenance company.

These concepts are the first showcases of the iterative design process. In the future, the concepts will be tested in the field so as to analyse their potential in supporting knowledge gathering and sharing during maintenance. Next, showcase generation and demonstration systems will be developed based on the results gathered from the analyses.

The field studies will be performed in real usage environments with real end users, i.e., service technicians. Two technicians will test each concept. Because of the small number of test participants, a qualitative approach for evaluation is needed, and therefore the subjective opinion of the technicians – with their knowledge and practical experience of working in the field – will be the starting point. The field study will include an experimental part with demonstrators, followed by a customized questionnaire with a subjective rating scale (a combination of Technology Acceptance Model (TAM Satisfaction Questionnaire) [36] and usability questions modified from System Usability Scale [37], and interviews. The interviews will include questions concerning the added-value to the technicians' work, and training needs, work practices and future expectations of the technicians. In the demonstrator testing phase, the qualitative evaluations are expected to give a broader set of results than could be achieved with quantitative performance metrics (e.g., time elapsed in maintenance, time spent with communicating with technical support or using the technology), which are more useful in later phases of the design process.

VI. CONCLUSIONS

Industrial maintenance is a complex and knowledge-intensive field. Maintenance technicians need to have easy access to versatile and situationally relevant knowledge. The aim of this paper was to understand key features in maintenance work and to propose new technology concepts to support knowledge gathering and sharing during maintenance.

Maintenance work was studied in marine and crane industry cases. The data were collected by interviews and direct observations of maintenance tasks were recorded. As a result of these studies, it was elicited that communication between different actors is a key element in the maintenance, in addition to more self-explanatory activities such as repairing a maintenance object. Finally, three technology concepts were suggested to support communication and knowledge sharing: (1) augmented reality guidance, (2) remote assistance, and (3) data collection and reporting with wearables.

This is an on-going research project. In the next phase, demonstrators will be developed based on the suggested concepts and tested in the field with service technicians. Findings from this study can be used to improve the understanding of the social and communication aspects in maintenance work. In addition, the technology concepts are usable in other domains, such as design and assembly, to improve knowledge gathering and sharing.

ACKNOWLEDGMENT

This study was funded by Tekes – the Finnish Funding Agency for Innovation – and was carried out as part of the S-STEP research project under FIMECC (Finnish Metals and Engineering Competence Cluster). The authors are grateful to all the researchers and company representatives who contributed to and supported the work presented in this publication.

REFERENCES

[1] EN 13306 (European Standard), Maintenance – Maintenance terminology. European Committee for Standardization, Brussels, 2010.

[2] J. Reason, Managing the Risks of Organizational Accidents. Ashgate Publishing Ltd., London, 1997.

[3] M. Polanyi, The Tacit Dimension. Anchor-Day, New York, 1966.

[4] I. Nonaka, "A Dynamic Theory of Organizational Knowledge Creation," Organization Science, vol. 5, 1994, pp. 14–37.

[5] K. Mertins, P. Heisig, and J. Vorbeck (Eds.), Knowledge management: concepts and best practices. Springer Science & Business Media, 2003.

[6] K. M. Baird and W. Barfield, "Evaluating the Effectiveness of Augmented Reality Displays for a Manual Assembly Task," Virtual Reality, vol. 4, 4, 1999, pp. 250-259.

[7] P. N. Day, G. Ferguson, P. O. B. Holt, S. Hogg, and D. Gibson, "Wearable Augmented Virtual Reality for Enhancing Information Delivery in High Precision Defence Assembly: an Engineering Case Study," Virtual Reality, vol. 8, 3, 2005, pp. 177–184.

[8] K. Kunze, F. Wagner, E. Kartal, E. M., Kluge, and P. Lukowicz, Does context matter? - a quantitative evaluation in a real world maintenance scenario, In Pervasive Computing, Springer Berlin Heidelberg, pp. 372–389, 2009.

[9] S. J. Henderson, and S. Feiner, "Evaluating The Benefits of Augmented Reality for Task Localization in Maintenance of an Armored Personnel Carrier Turret," 8th IEEE International Symposium on Mixed and Augmented Reality (ISMAR), 2009, pp. 135–144.

[10] S. Henderson and S. Feiner, "Exploring the Benefits of Augmented Reality Documentation for Maintenance and Repair," IEEE Transactions on Visualization and Computer Graphics, vol. 17, 10, 2011, pp. 1355–1368.

[11] A. Tang, C. Owen, F. Biocca, and W. Mou, "Comparative Effectiveness of Augmented Reality in Object Assembly," In Proceedings of the SIGCHI conference on Human factors in computing systems, ACM, 2003, pp. 73–80.

[12] B. Schwerdtfeger and G. Klinker, "Supporting Order Picking with Augmented Reality," In Proceedings of the 7th IEEE/ACM international Symposium on Mixed and Augmented Reality, IEEE Computer Society, Sep. 2008, pp. 91–94.

[13] R. T. Azuma, "A Survey of Augmented Reality," Presence, vol. 6, 4, 1997, pp. 355–385.

[14] A. Y. C. Nee, S. K. Ong, G. Chryssolouris, and D. Mourtzis, "Augmented Reality Applications in Design and Manufacturing," CIRP Annals-Manufacturing Technology, vol. 61, 2, 2012, pp. 657–679.

[15] G. M. Re and M. Bordegoni, An augmented reality framework for supporting and monitoring operators during maintenance tasks. In Virtual, augmented and mixed reality.

Applications of virtual and augmented reality, Springer International Publishing, pp. 443–451, 2014.

[16] F. Ferrise, G. Caruso, and M. Bordegoni, "Multimodal Training and Tele-Assistance Systems for the Maintenance of Industrial Products," Virtual and Physical Prototyping, vol. 8, 2, 2013, pp. 113–126.

[17] C. Baber, "Wearable Computers: A Human Factors Review," International Journal of Human-Computer Interaction, vol. 13, 2001, pp. 123–145.

[18] J. Laarni, et al., "Supporting Situation Awareness in Demanding Operating Environments through Wearable User Interfaces," 8th International Conference of Engineering Psychology and Cognitive Ergonomics (EPCE), Springer Berlin Heidelberg, Jul. 2009, pp. 13–21.

[19] L. R. Elliott, J. B.F. van Erp, E. S. Redden, and M. Duistermaat, Field-based validation of a tactile navigation device, "IEEE Trans Haptics", vol. 3, 2, 2010, pp.78–87

[20] R. Mynttinen, Evaluating spatially directing cues on a wearable user interface in a field setup, Masterarbeit, University of Vienna, Austria, 2010

[21] X. S. Zheng, et al., "Wearable Solution for Industrial Maintenance," In Proceedings of the 33rd Annual ACM Conference Extended Abstracts on Human Factors in Computing Systems, ACM, Apr. 2015, pp. 311–314.

[22] SAPEnterpriseMobile. SAP and Vuzix Bring you Augmented Solutions for the Enterprise. [Online]. Available from: https://youtu.be/9Wv9k_ssLcI and https://youtu.be/UlpGDrSmg38, 2016.01.05

[23] L. Norros, Acting under uncertainty: The core-task analysis in ecological study of work. VTT Publications 546, VTT Technical Research Centre of Finland, Espoo, 2004.

[24] H. Kuoppala, S. Riihiaho, P. Mannonen, and A. Salovaara, Huollon tämänhetkinen työnkuva (Present work context in maintenance). In S. Riihiaho, (ed.). Proaktiivisen tietotekniikan vaikutukset huoltotyöhön. Helsinki University of Technology, Espoo. 2003.

[25] S. Aromaa, A. Väätänen, I. Aaltonen, and T. Heimonen, "A Model for Gathering and Sharing Knowledge in Maintenance Work," Proceedings of the 33rd Annual Conference of the European Association of Cognitive Ergonomics (ECCE '15), Article 28, 2015.

[26] J. Orr, Talking about machines: an ethnography of a modern jog. ILR Press, Ithaca, N.Y., 1996.

[27] H. Franssila, Sähköisen tietämyksenhallinnan mukauttaminen ja integrointi työkäytäntöihin asennus- ja huoltotyössä (Integrating digital knowledge management in assembly and maintenance work). Hypermedia Laboratory Net Series 16, University of Tampere, 2008.

[28] B. S. Dhillon, Human Reliability, Error, and Human Factors in Power Generation. Springer Series in Reliability Engineering, Springer International Publishing, Switzerland, 2014.

[29] B. S. Dhillon and Y. Liu, "Human Error in Maintenance: a Review," Journal of Quality in Maintenance Engineering, vol. 12, 2006, pp. 21–36.

[30] S. K. Ong, M. L. Yuan, and A. Y. C. Nee, "Augmented Reality Applications in Manufacturing: a Survey," International Journal of Production Research, vol. 46, 2008, pp,. 707–2742.

[31] J. Zhu, S. K. Ong, and A. Y. C. Nee, "An Authorable Context-aware Augmented Reality System to Assist the Maintenance Technicians," The International Journal of Advanced Manufacturing Technology, 2013, vol. 66, pp. 1699–1714.

[32] K. Helin, et al., "Usability of the ARgh! Augmented Reality System for On-the-job Learning," 19th Triennial Congress of the International Ergonomics Association (IEA), Aug. 2015.

[33] D. Ma, X. Zhen, Y. Hu, D. Wu, X. Fan, and H. Zhu, (edit.), Collaborative Virtual Assembly Operation Simulation and Its Application. Virtual Reality & Augmented Reality in Industry, Shanghai Jiao Tong University Press, Shanghai and Springer-Verlag Berlin Heidelberg, 2011.

[34] S. Aromaa, S.-P. Leino, J. Viitaniemi, L. Jokinen, and S. Kiviranta, "Benefits of the Use of Virtual Environments in Product Design Review Meeting," 12th International Design Conference, University of Zagreb, May 2012, pp. 355–364.

[35] M. Bordegoni and G. Caruso, "Mixed Reality Distributed Platform for Collaborative Design Review of Automotive Interiors," Virtual and Physical Prototyping, vol.7, 2012, pp. 1–17.

[36] F. D. Davis, R. P. Bagozzi, and P. R. Warshaw, User acceptance of computer technology: a comparison of two theoretical models, "Management science", vol. 35, 8, 1989, pp. 982–1003.

[37] J. Brooke, SUS-A quick and dirty usability scale. Usability evaluation in industry. Taylor and Francis Ltd, vol. 189, pp. 4–7, 1996.

Development of A Finger Mounted Type Haptic Device Using A Plane Approximated to Tangent Plane

Makoto Yoda
Department of Information System Science
Graduate School of Engineering
Soka University, Soka Univ.
Tokyo, Japan
e-mail:e16m5223@soka-u.jp

Hiroki Imamura
Department of Information System Science
Graduate School of Engineering
Soka University, Soka Univ.
Tokyo, Japan
e-mail:imamura@soka.ac.jp

***Abstract*—In recent years, several researches of haptic devices have been conducted. By using conventional haptic devices, users can perceive touching an object, such as Computer Graphics (CG) by a force feedback. Since conventional haptic devices provide a force feedback from a single point on an object surface where users touch it, users touch an object by point contact. However, conventional haptic devices cannot provide users with a sense such as humans touching an object with a finger pad because a finger pad does not touch an object by point contact but surface contact in reality. In this paper, we propose a novel haptic device. By using this haptic device, users can perceive the slope of a CG object surface when they put fingers on it without tracing. Moreover, users can perceive grabbing a CG object with finger pads. To grab CG object, we mount the plane interface of the haptic device on each two fingers. Then, users can perceive the slope of a CG object surface where users are touching. Each plane interface provides users with the slope approximated to a tangent plane of area where they touched. In the evaluation experiments, the subjects in this experiment evaluated this haptic device. From the results, the subjects could perceive the slope of a CG object surface. In addition, they could perceive grabbing a CG object.**

Keywords-haptic device; plane interface; force feedback .

I. INTRODUCTION

In recent years, researches of human interface using Augmented Reality (AR) have been conducted. In order to touch CG objects that are drawn by AR, haptic devices have been developed. By using a haptic device, users can perceive touching CG objects by processing a force feedback. Therefore, haptic devices are expected to be used in applications such as remote control of robots and computer games.

Examples of conventional haptic devices include Falcon [1], PHANToM [2] and Dexmo [3]. Falcon and PHANToM are classified into a grounded type. This type can provide users with accurate force feedback because its fulcrum is fixed on the table. Dexmo is classified into a finger mounted type. This type can provide users with perception of grabbing CG objects easily. In addition, users can operate the device without operating range limitation. These haptic devices have been developed as a point contact haptic device. By using this type of haptic device, users can perceive touching CG objects because they are provided with a force feedback from a single point on the CG object surface where they touched. In case of perception of an objects shape, from visual information, users perceive CG objects shape of visible part. As invisible part, users must perceive CG objects shape by touching the surface. However, in a point contact type, to perceive CG objects shape, users must trace the surface because they perceive only touching CG objects. Therefore, they cannot work smoothly in that part. In order to perceive CG objects shape without tracing the surface, the direction of a force feedback must change according to a surface shape where users touched. Our laboratory focused on this characteristic. In addition, our laboratory has developed a haptic device based on an approximated plane (HaAP) [4] that is shown in Figure 1. HaAP is a grounded type. Moreover, HaAP is a surface contact type haptic device which has a plane interface that is shown in Figure 1-(a). Since as shown in Figure 1-(b), the plane interface provides users with a force feedback by being approximated to the tangent plane on a CG object surface where they touched, users can perceive the shape from the surface slope without tracing the surface. In this device, users are limited to operate HaAP in range of the HaAP vertical mechanism within 10 cm.

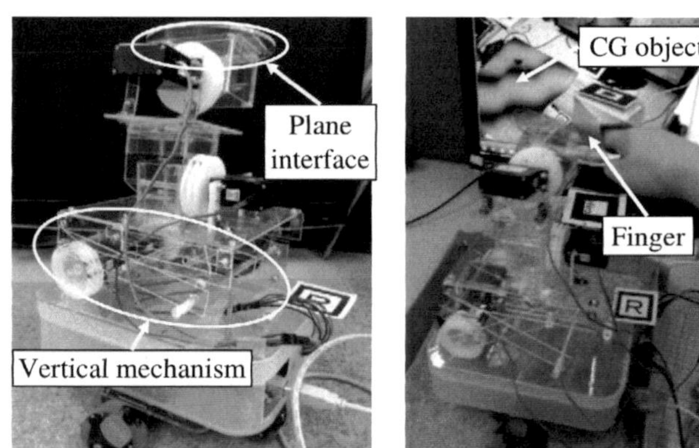

(a). Appearance of HaAP (b). Operating state

Figure 1. HaAP.

In this paper, we propose a novel haptic device. This haptic device realizes three things. First, users are provided with a force feedback by the plane interface providing the slope approximated to the tangent plane on a CG object surface. Second, users can operate this haptic device without operating range limitation. Third, by using this haptic device, users can perceive grabbing a CG object. To realize that, we develop a haptic device having characteristics of a finger mounted type and a surface contact type.

This paper is structured as follows: First, the outline of the proposed haptic device is explained in section II. In section III, the hardware construction, the system overview and the system flowchart are proposed. Evaluation experiments are carried out for the proposed haptic device in section IV. Finally, conclusions and future works end this paper.

II. Our Approach

Figure 2 shows the outline of the proposed haptic device. This device uses a plane interface having four movable points. These four movable points operate up and down separately.

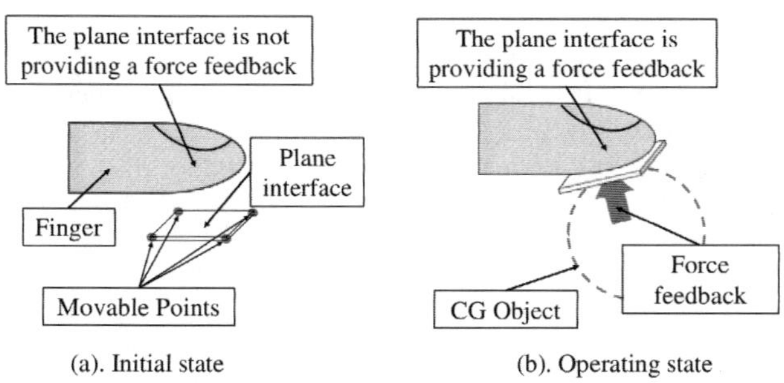

Figure 2. Outline of the proposedhaptic device.

Figure 2-(a) shows the initial state. In this state, the user is not touching a CG object. Figure 2-(b) shows the operating state. In this state, the user is touching a CG object. The plane interface provides a finger pad with a force feedback by approximating the tangent plane on the CG object.

III. The Proposed System

A. Hardware condtruction

Figure 3 shows the appearance of the proposed haptic device.

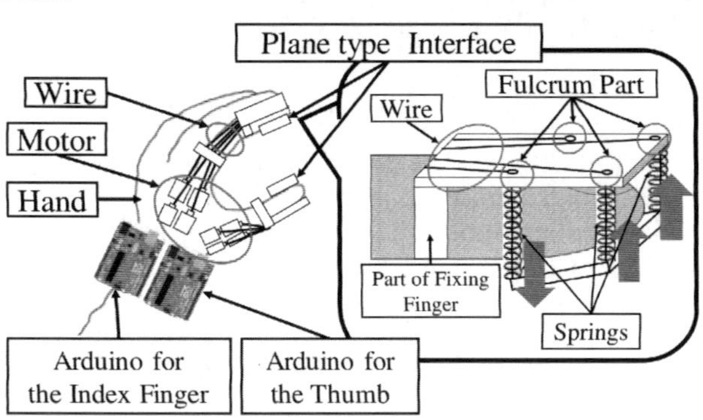

Figure 3. Appearance of the proposed haptic device.

This device is a glove type and composed of Arduino Uno, four servo motors (GWS Servo PIC+F/BB/F), four springs and a plane interface for each finger. Eight motors are mounted in the back of the hand. In addition, each motor is connected to Arduino Uno for the index finger and Arduino Uno for the thumb, respectively. Arduino Uno controls four motors in each finger. These motors pull up the movable points of the plane interface with wires. When motors pull up, wires hang at the fulcrum part. Each spring adheres to each movable point.

B. System overview

Figure 4 shows the system overview. This system consists of PC, Display, Web-Camera and the proposed haptic device. The user attaches markers on fingers and wears the proposed haptic device.

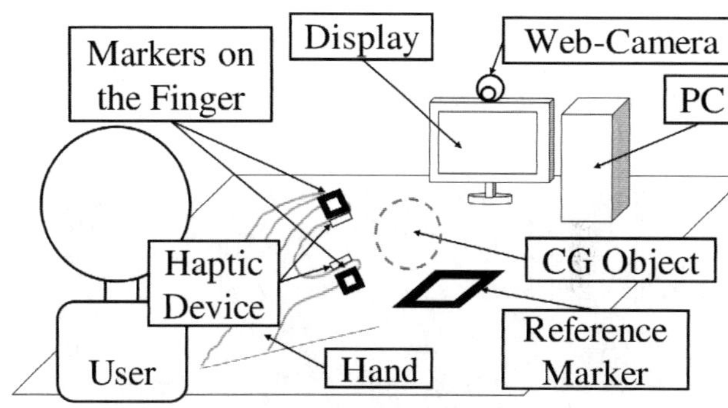

Figure 4. System overview.

C. The system flowchart

Figure 5 shows the system flowchart. The following is the explanation about processing flow in this system. In the following section, we explain each process in the flowchart.

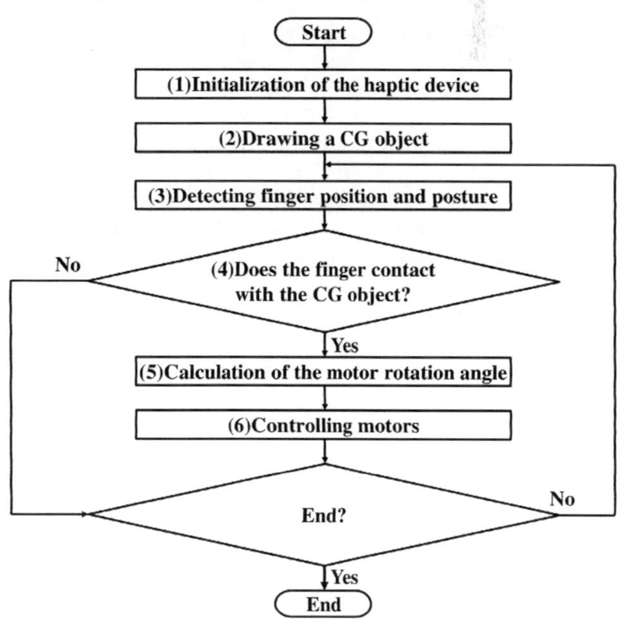

Figure 5. Flowchart.

1) Initialization of the haptic device: Arduino Uno controls motors to make springs natural length.

2) Drawing a CG object: Based on the reference marker, ARToolkit [5] draws Sphere CG object or Sin-cos curve CG object that is shown in Figures 6 and 7, respectively.

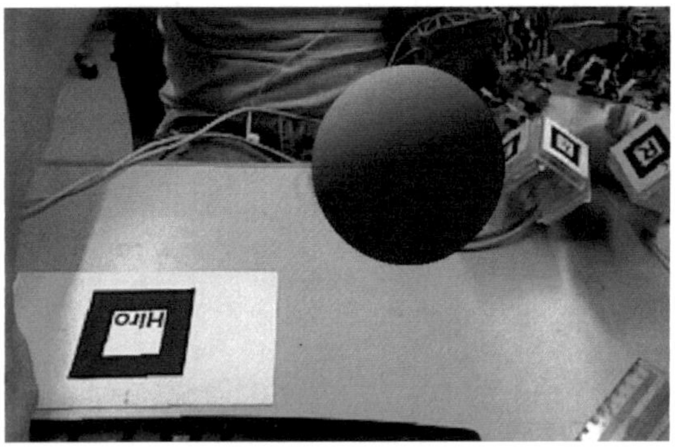

Figure 6. Sphere CG object

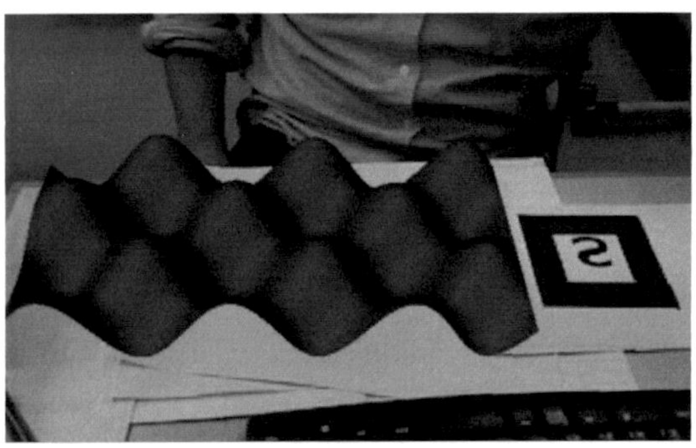

Figure 7. Sin-cos CG object

3) Detecting finger position and posture: Figure 8 shows detecting the marker on each finger position and posture. The system recognizes the reference marker and the marker on each finger from the image that is captured by the web camera. By using ARToolKit, the system obtains position (X, Y, Z) of the marker on each finger from the reference marker. In addition, by using ARToolKit, the system also calculates F_r that denotes the roll angle and F_p that denotes the pitch angle of the marker on each finger.

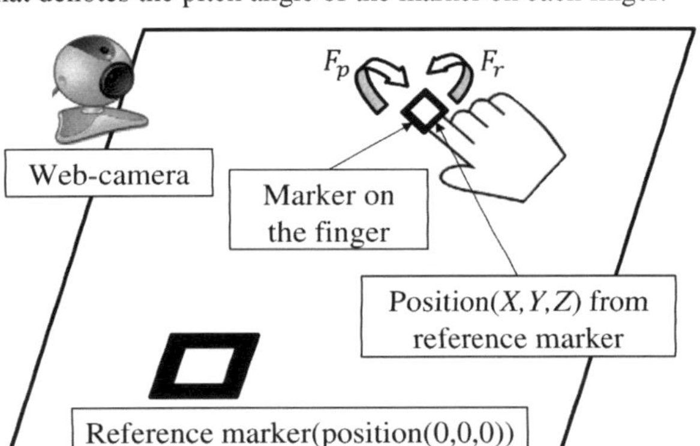

Figure 8. Detecting the finger position and posture.

4) Judgement of contact: In the case of a Sphere CG object, as shown in Figure 9, when the length between the marker on the finger position and the center of Sphere CG object is within radius of Sphere CG object, the system judges contact.

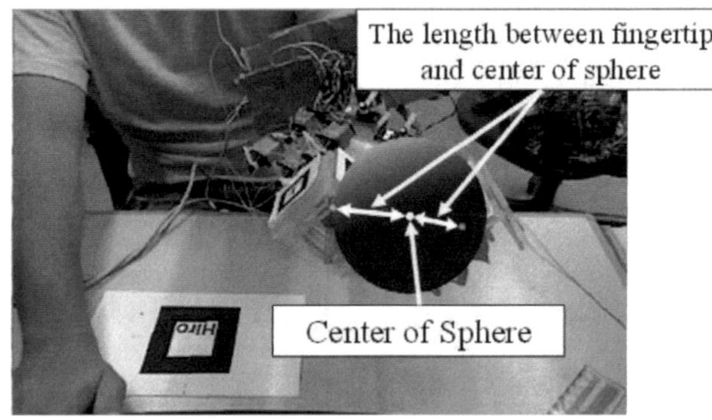

Figure 9. Touching Sphere CG object

In case of Sin-cos curve CG object, the system calculates Z-coordinate on Sin-cos curve CG object. The following is the equation of Sin-cos curve.

$$A \sin X \cos Y = Z, \tag{1}$$

where A is amplitude and X, Y and Z are X, Y and Z-coordinate on Sin-cos curve CG object. By substituting X and Y-coordinate of the marker on the finger for this equation, the system obtains Z. As shown in Figure 10, when Z-coordinate of the marker on the finger is under Z, the system judges contact.

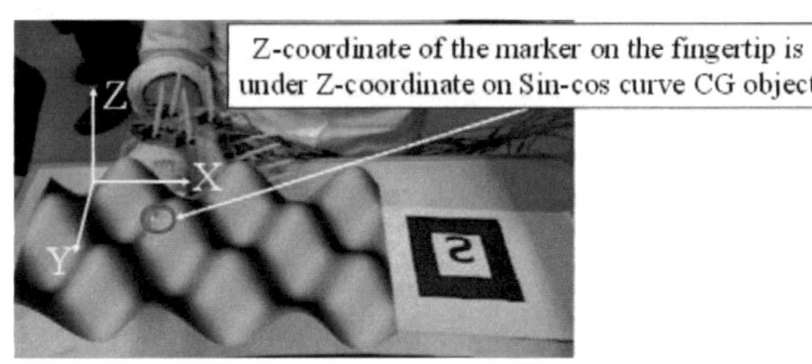

Figure 10. Touching Sin-cos curve CG object.

5) Calculation of the motor rotation angle: The system calculates the normal vector on touching point.

In case of a Sphere CG object, the vector from the center of Sphere CG object to the touching point is defined as the normal vector on the touching point.

In case of Sin-cos curve CG object, Sin-cos curve CG object is composed of many planes. Figure 11 shows calculation of the normal vector on the touching point. The system uses the equation of vector product

$$\boldsymbol{N} = \boldsymbol{A} \times \boldsymbol{B}, \tag{2}$$

where $\boldsymbol{A}$ and $\boldsymbol{B}$ are the vectors from the touching point to other points on the plane that includes the contact point. The system obtains the normal vector from right hand screw rule.

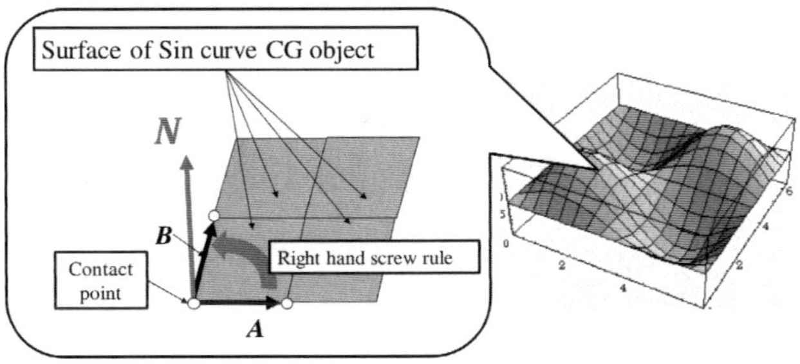

Figure 11. Calculation of the normal vector.

From the normal vector, the system calculates the roll angle and the pitch angle of the tangent plane on touching point. Figure 12 shows the calculation of the tangent plane slope on touching point in X-Z plane and Y-Z plane. The system uses

$$T_p = 90° - \theta_y, \tag{3}$$

$$T_r = 90° - \theta_x \tag{4}$$

to obtain the roll and pitch angle of the tangent plane. θ_x denotes the angle between x-axis and the normal vector and θ_y denotes the angle between y-axis and the normal vector. Using (3) and (4), the system obtains T_r that denotes the roll angle of tangent plane and T_p that denotes the pitch angle of the tangent plane.

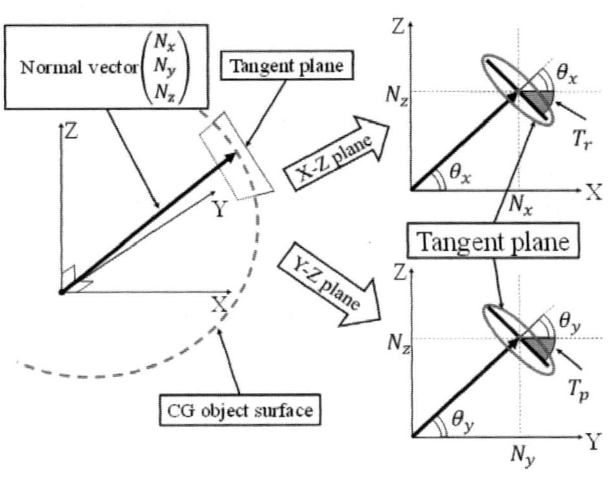

Figure 12. Calculation of the tangent plane angle.

Using equations (5) and (6), the system calculates the difference between the angle of the marker on the finger and that of the tangent plane.

$$D_p = |T_p - F_p|, \tag{5}$$

$$D_r = |T_r - F_r|. \tag{6}$$

This difference is the plane interface slope that is shown in Figure 13. F_p and F_r are shown in Figure 8. Figure 13-(a) shows D_p that denotes the difference between F_p and T_p. Figure 13-(b) shows D_r that denotes the difference between F_r and T_r.

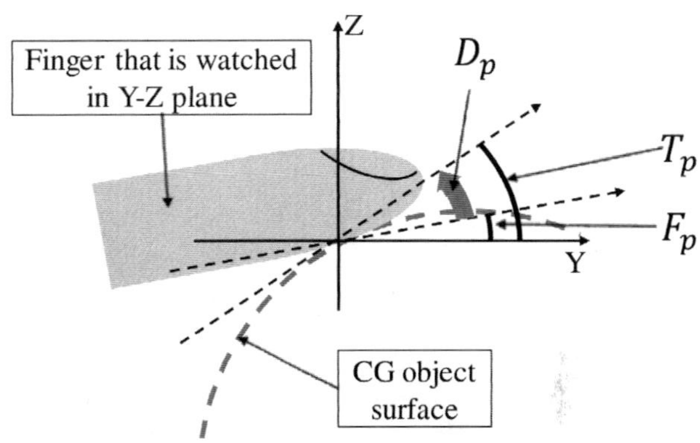

(a). Difference of the pitch angle.

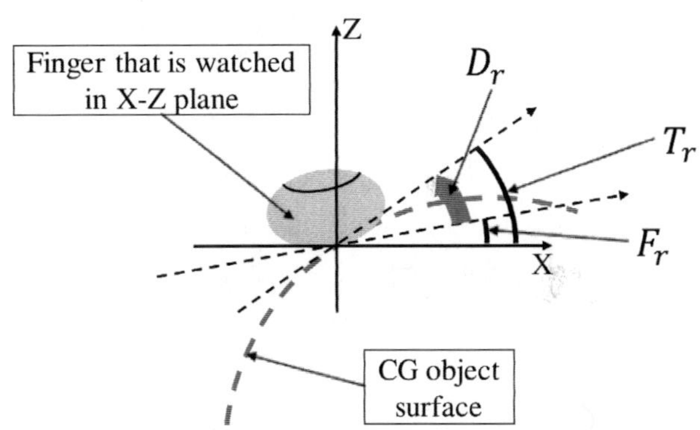

(b). Difference of the roll angle.

Figure 13. Calculation of the plane interface slope.

The system calculates the operation length of movable point from the plane interface slope. Figure 14 shows two lengths (L1 and L2). These two lengths are defined

$$\text{L1} = \frac{A}{2}\sin(|D_p|) + \frac{A}{2}\sin(|D_r|), \tag{7}$$

$$\text{L1} = \left|\frac{A}{2}\sin(|D_p|) - \frac{A}{2}\sin(|D_r|)\right| \tag{8}$$

as the operation length of movable points. Where A is the length of one side on a plane interface. Using (7) and (8), the system calculates these lengths.

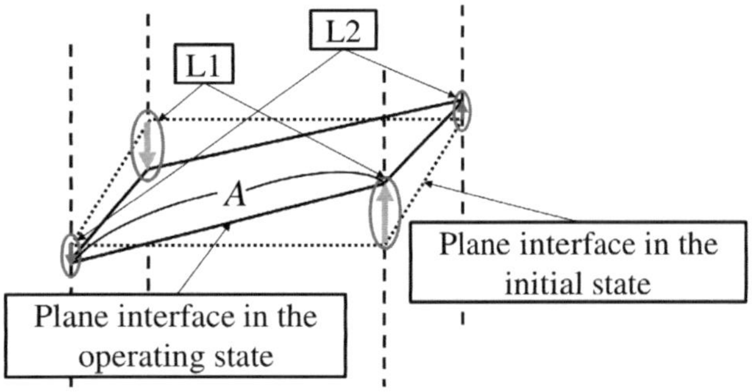

Figure 14. The operation length of movable points.

Figure 15 shows the angle of motor rotation. The system uses

$$A1 = 2\sin^{-1}\left(\frac{L1}{2\times R}\right), \quad (9)$$

$$A2 = 2\sin^{-1}\left(\frac{L2}{2\times R}\right) \quad (10)$$

to calculate the angle of motor rotation, where R denotes the length of servo horn. A1 and A2 are the amount of controlling motors. The system sends this amount to each Arduino Uno by serial communication.

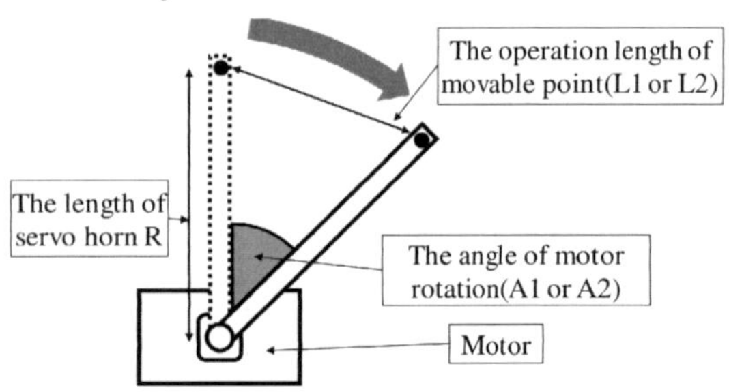

Figure 15. The angle of motor rotation.

6) Controlling the motors: Arduino Uno receives the amount of controlling motors and controls motors. Motors pull up each movable point with wires. Figure 16-(a) and (b) shows providing a finger with a force feedback when users touched Sphere CG object in Y-Z plane and X-Z plane respectively. Figure 16-(c) and (d) shows providing a finger with a force feedback when users touched Sin-cos curve CG object in Y-Z plane and X-Z plane respectively.

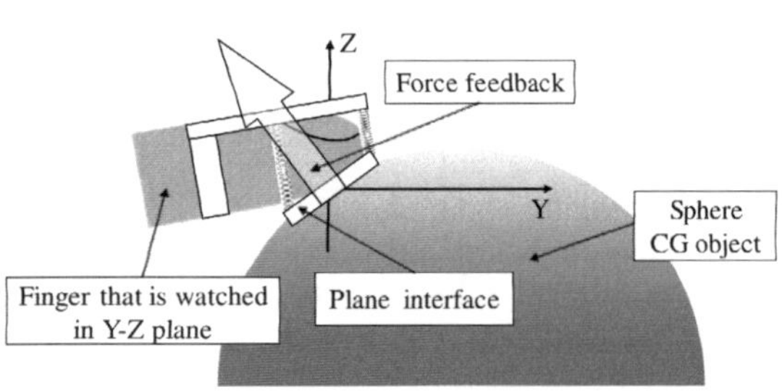

(a). Y-Z plane.

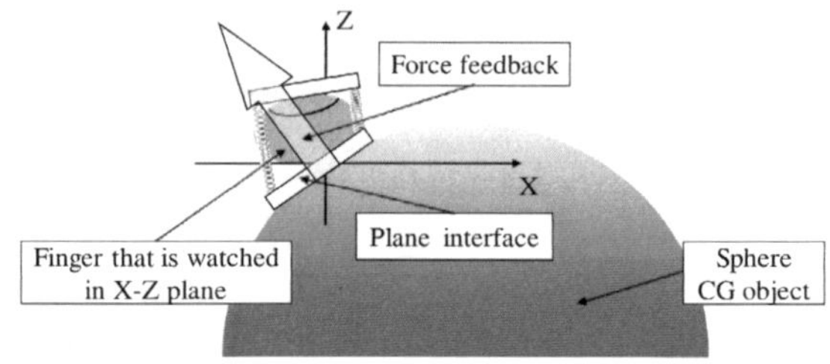

(b). X-Z plane.

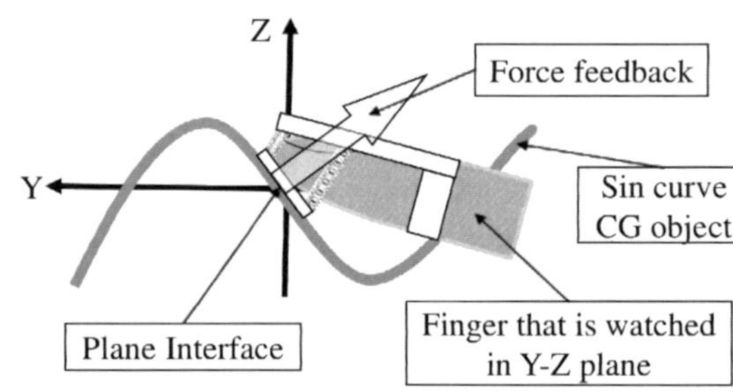

(c).Y-Z plane.

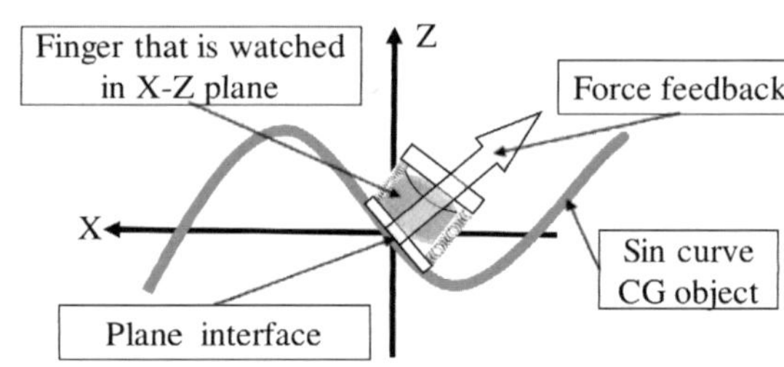

(d). X-Z plane.

Figure 16. The plane interface that provides a force feedback.

IV. EVALUATION EXPERIMENTS

A. Overview of the experiments

We had an evaluation experiment for the proposed haptic device. Sin-cos curve CG object is used in order to evaluate whether users can perceive the slope of the CG object surface or not. In addition, a Sphere CG object is used in order to evaluate whether users can perceive grabbing a CG object or not. Eleven subjects used the proposed haptic device. After that, they evaluated following items with a 5-grade score:

In case of Sin-cos CG object,

- When you touched the CG object with one finger, you perceived the slope of the CG object surface at once (Item1).
- When you touched and traced the surface of the CG object with one finger, you perceived the asperity of the CG object surface (Item2).

In case of Sphere CG object,

- When you touched the CG object with one finger, you perceived the slope of sphericity (Item1).
- When you touched and traced the surface of the CG object with one finger, you perceived the shape of sphericity (Item2).
- When you touched the CG object with two fingers, you perceived touching the CG object (Item3).
- When you touched the CG object with two fingers, you perceived grabbing the CG object (Item4).

Evaluation values are from 1 to 5 (1 : "Strongly disagree", 2 : "Disagree", 3 : "Neutral", 4 : "Agree", 5 : "Strongly agree").

B. Discussion

Table 1 shows the results of Sin-cos curve CG object. Table 2 shows the results of Sphere CG object. Each result shows the average score and the standard deviation.

TABLE I. RESULTS OF SIN-COS CURVE CG OBJECT

Item	Sin-cos curve CG object	
	Average score	*A standard deviation*
1	4.64	0.64
2	4.55	0.50

TABLE II. RESULTS OF SPHERE CG OBJECT

Item	Sphere CG object	
	Average score	*A standard deviation*
1	4.09	0.90
2	4.00	0.85
3	4.18	0.94
4	4.27	0.96

From these results, in Item1 of Tables 1 and 2, we see that users perceived the slope of CG object without tracing the surface. In Item2 of Tables 1 and 2, the results show that users perceived the asperity by tracing the surface. In addition, in Item3 and Item4 of Table 2, we see that users perceived grabbing a CG object. Therefore, we consider that the proposed haptic device can provide users with perception of the CG object surface slope. Moreover, we consider that users can perceive grabbing a CG object by using the proposed haptic device. In addition, from Tables 1 and 2, we see that the average score in Table 1 is higher than that in Table 2. Since the surface of Sin-cos curve CG object is more complex than that of Sphere CG object, the accuracy of the proposed haptic device is improved when CG object have complex surface.

V. CONCLUSIONS AND FUTURE WORKS

In this paper, we proposed a novel haptic device. The proposed haptic device has a plane interface to provide a slope approximated to the tangent plane of the CG object area where users touched. In addition, to perceive grabbing a CG object, the proposed haptic device is designed as a finger mounted type. After evaluation experiments, we see that the proposed haptic device can provide users with perception of the CG object surface slope without tracing the surface and perception of grabbing the CG object. However, we consider that users cannot grasp the sense of the distance between finger and a CG object easily. To solve the issue, we improve the proposed haptic device to grasp the sense of the distance more easily by using Head Mounted Display (HMD). In the future, we will improve the operability of the proposed haptic device by lightening the device. In addition, by using Leap Motion, we will improve the accuracy of detecting finger position and posture.

REFERENCES

[1] Novint Technologies, Inc, "http://www.novint.com/index.php/novintfalcon" (last accessed March, 2016)

[2] Geomagin, Inc, "http://www.geomagic.com/en/products/phantom-desktop/overview" (last accessed March, 2016)

[3] Dexta Robotics, Inc, "http://www.dextarobotics.com/products/dexmo"(last accessed March, 2016)

[4] A. Kawazoe, K. Ikeshiro, and H. Imamura, "A Haptic Device based on An Approximate Plane HaAP. ACM Siggraph Asia 2013 Posters", 2013, Hong Kong. CD-ROM.

[5] H. Kato, "ARToolKit:Library for Vision-based Augmented Reality" , Technical report of IEICE, PRMU, 101(625), 2002, pp.79-86.

AUTHOR INDEX

AUTHOR INDEX

International Academy, Research,
and Industry Association (IARIA)
412 Derby Way
Wilmington, DE 19810

CURRAN ASSOCIATES INC.
proceedings.com

ISBN 978-1-5108-2309-9

9 781510 823099